W9-CYS-773

The American Nation
in the 20th Century

CONTRIBUTORS AND REVIEWERS

ii

Michele Fort
Middlebury U
Middlebury, Verm

Tuls

The American Nation

▪▪ in the 20th Century

PAUL BOYER

STERLING STUCKEY

HOLT, RINEHART AND WINSTON

Harcourt Brace & Company

Austin • New York • Orlando • Atlanta • San Francisco • Boston • Dallas • Toronto • London

About the Authors

PAUL BOYER

Paul Boyer is Merle Curti Professor of History at the University of Wisconsin, Madison, and director of the university's Institute for Research in the Humanities. Dr. Boyer is the author of numerous works, including *By the Bomb's Early Light: American Thought and Culture at the Dawn of the Atomic Age.*

STERLING STUCKEY

Sterling Stuckey is Professor of History and Religious Studies and holds the President's Chair at the University of California, Riverside. Dr. Stuckey is the author of *Slave Culture: Nationalist Theory and the Foundations of Black America* and *Going Through the Storm: The Influence of African American Art in History.*

Executive Editor
Sue Miller

Managing Editor
Jim Eckel

Editorial Staff
Diana Holman Walker, *Project Editor*
Margaret Thompson, *Associate Editor*
Bob Fullilove, *Associate Editor*
Phyllis Salazar, *Administrative Assistant*

Editorial Permissions
Tamara Blanken

Design, Photo, and Production
Gene Rumann, *Production Supervisor*
Belinda Barboza, Adrian Bardin, Kim Anderson, Shirley Cantrell, *Production Team*

Christine Schueler, *Design Manager*

Peggy Cooper, *Photo Research Manager*
Bob McClellan, Sherrie Cass, Kristin Hay, Cynthia Godsey, Elinor Strot, *Photo Research Team*

PE and ATE Design and Production, *The Quarasan Group, Inc.*

Cover Photo: © Robert Landau/Westlight.

For acknowledgments, see page 837, which is an extension of the copyright page.

Printed in the United States of America

ISBN 0-03-050674-3

1 2 3 4 5 6 7 8 9 032 00 99 98 97

CONTENTS

UNIT 1

American Roots

George Washington

A 12th-century map
of the world

The Granger Collection, New York

Slaves escaping from Maryland.

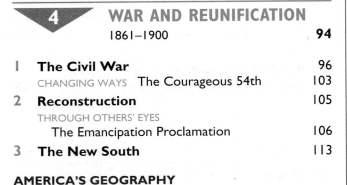

Poster
commemorating
the Emancipation
Proclamation

Sitting Bull

An immigrant mother and her
children arriving at Ellis Island

Wartime posters

World War II
victory medal

Gold coins

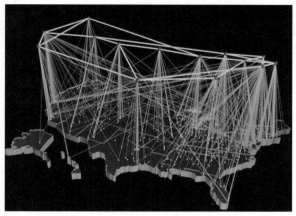

The NSFnet

Antinuclear protester Susan
Ginzberg with her son, 1961

Reference Section

Features

Sara Matthews/ Swarthmore College Peace Collection

Charts and Maps

Themes in American History

The American Nation in the Twentieth Century begins every chapter with a set of theme questions. These questions are drawn from seven broad themes central to American history: global relations, our Constitutional heritage, democratic values, technology and society, cultural diversity, geographic diversity, and economic development. They provide a context for the historical events in each chapter. This context will help you understand the connections between historical events and see how past events are relevant to today's social, political, and economic concerns.

As you begin each chapter, examine the theme questions and answer them based on your own experiences or prior knowledge. At the end of each chapter, you will be asked to answer another set of theme questions, this time using specific facts learned from studying the chapter. This process will help you develop critical thinking skills and encourage you to synthesize the information you have learned. In addition, by tracing the themes through the book, you will be able to see how each theme has developed over time.

■ GLOBAL RELATIONS

This theme asks you to explore the global context in which the United States exists. From its settlement by Asian immigrants tens of thousands of years ago to the first arrival of European, African, and later Asian immigrants to today, America has influenced and been influenced by other parts of the world. Your exploration of the Global Relations theme will help you understand how the relations the United States has maintained with other countries over time have affected our nation's political, social, and economic development. It also will help you appreciate the problems and possibilities of living in an interdependent world community.

■ CONSTITUTIONAL HERITAGE

The study of American history would not be complete without an exploration of the Constitution, the legal framework that structures our democratic government. The Constitutional Heritage theme questions ask you to think about the origin of the Constitution and the ways in which the Constitution has been interpreted and amended over time. You will explore how the laws and government institutions established in the 18th century have evolved through amendments, Supreme Court rulings, and congressional actions. Your examination of this theme will encourage you to understand the part individuals play in promoting the goals—such as justice and democratic rights—enshrined in the Constitution's preamble.

■ DEMOCRATIC VALUES

This theme concerns the continuing struggle to define and protect such democratic values as individual liberty, political representation, freedom of religion, and freedom of speech. The Democratic Values theme questions ask you to consider the impact of changing social, economic, and political conditions on these values. For example, in the years before the Civil War, enslavement of African Americans—a violation of the democratic value of individual liberty—was practiced in the South. Some slaveholders justified this practice by arguing that the democratic value of right to property should be the overriding concern. It took a bloody civil war to settle the issue. Conflicts over democratic values recur throughout American history, and this theme explores the attempts at resolution.

■ TECHNOLOGY AND SOCIETY

From computers in your homes and classrooms to communications satellites orbiting the earth, technology influences many aspects of society. The Technology and Society theme questions ask you to trace technological developments and explore their influence on the economy and our lives.

■ CULTURAL DIVERSITY

Different ethnic, racial, and religious groups have all contributed to the creation of America's rich and unique culture. The Cultural Diversity theme questions ask you to explore how the United States has dealt with diversity from the days of the first encounters between Native Americans and Spanish

and English settlers to its status today as a haven for immigrants from all over the world.

■ GEOGRAPHIC DIVERSITY

The majestic old-growth forests of the Pacific Northwest, the rich coal deposits of the Appalachian and Rocky mountains, the oil fields of Texas and Alaska, and the tropical plantations on the volcanic islands of Hawaii have enriched the U.S. economy. The Geographic Diversity theme questions ask you to consider how the development of the nation's diverse natural resources has shaped U.S. society, politics, and the economy. The questions also explore how government and public awareness of the effects of natural resource development on the environment has changed over time.

■ ECONOMIC DEVELOPMENT

The United States has developed one of the world's strongest economies. The Economic Development theme questions explore the influence of the nation's economy on domestic politics and social life and on international relations. The theme questions ask you to explore the implications of such economic issues as trade, depression and expansion, poverty, taxation, government regulation, and the status of workers.

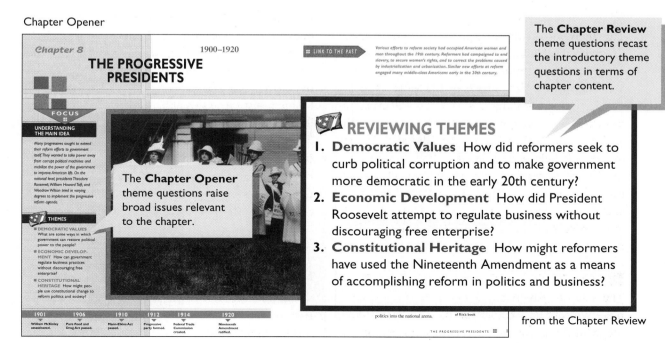

Chapter Opener

The **Chapter Review** theme questions recast the introductory theme questions in terms of chapter content.

Chapter 8 · 1900–1920 · ■■ LINK TO THE PAST

THE PROGRESSIVE PRESIDENTS

The **Chapter Opener** theme questions raise broad issues relevant to the chapter.

⚑ REVIEWING THEMES

1. **Democratic Values** How did reformers seek to curb political corruption and to make government more democratic in the early 20th century?
2. **Economic Development** How did President Roosevelt attempt to regulate business without discouraging free enterprise?
3. **Constitutional Heritage** How might reformers have used the Nineteenth Amendment as a means of accomplishing reform in politics and business?

from the Chapter Review

Critical Thinking and the Study of History

Throughout *The American Nation in the Twentieth Century,* you are asked to think critically about the events and issues that have shaped U.S. history. Critical thinking is the reasoned judgment of information and ideas. People who think critically study information to determine its accuracy. They evaluate arguments and analyze conclusions before accepting them. Critical thinkers are able to recognize and define problems and develop strategies for resolving them.

The development of critical thinking skills is essential to effective citizenship. Such skills empower you to exercise your civic rights and responsibilities. For example, critical thinking skills equip you to judge the messages of candidates for office and to evaluate news reports.

Helping you develop critical thinking skills is an important goal of *The American Nation in the Twentieth Century.* The following 14 critical thinking skills appear in the section reviews and chapter reviews. Additional skills strategies can be found in each unit's Strategies for Success and in the Skills Handbook, which begins on page 748.

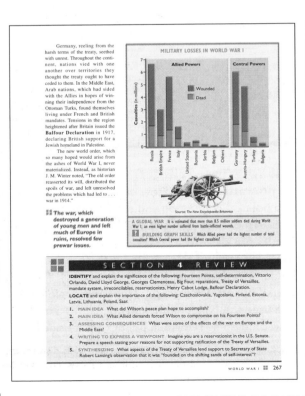

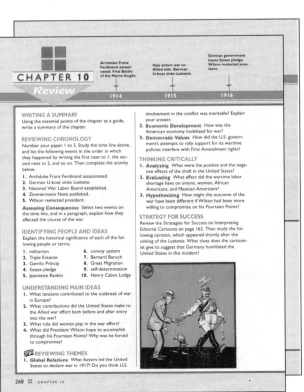

Union mortar battery

Toltec pillar

Europeans did not "discover" the Americas. They encountered a land already settled by people with complex and varied cultures.

1 **Using Historical Imagination** is mentally stepping into the past to consider an event or situation as people at the time would have considered it. In putting yourself in their place, you might note whether they lived *before* or *after* historical turning points. Ask yourself: Did these people live before or after major medical advances such as penicillin? before or after technological advances such as the automobile? before or after World War II? Keep in mind what the people of the time knew and did not know. For example, to grasp the experience of a soldier wounded in the Civil War, you need to understand that little was known then about the causes of disease and infection.

2 **Gaining an Appreciation of Diversity** means viewing historical events and situations in ways that are fair and sensitive to all cultural groups affected. Such a perspective broadens your understanding of American history while deepening your appreciation of the nation's diversity. For example, studying Native American cultures before the arrival of Columbus helps you understand that the

3 **Recognizing Point of View** means identifying the factors that color the outlook of an individual or group. Editorial cartoons, for example, present points of view about issues, events, and people. A person's point of view includes beliefs and attitudes that are shaped by factors such as age, gender, religion, race, and economic status. This thinking skill helps us

SLAVERY AS IT EXISTS IN AMERICA.

SLAVERY AS IT EXISTS IN ENGLAND.

THE ENGLISH ANTI-SLAVERY AGITATOR.

The Granger Collection, New York

This proslavery editorial cartoon from the 1850s distorts the reality of slavery by falsely suggesting that southern slaves led easier lives than English factory workers.

Struggle at Concord Bridge

examine why people see things as they do and reinforces the realization that people's views may change over time, or with a change in circumstances. When the point of view of an individual or a group is highly personal or based on unreasoned judgment, it is considered *bias*.

4 **Comparing and Contrasting** is examining events, situations, or points of view for their similarities and differences. *Comparing* focuses on both the similarities and the differences. *Contrasting* focuses on only the differences. For example, a comparison of early Irish and Chinese immigrants to the United States would point out that both groups were recruited to help build the nation's transcontinental railroad and that both groups faced discrimination and experienced difficulties in finding well-paying jobs. In

contrast, language and racial barriers generally proved more of a problem for Chinese immigrants. Other factors to compare and contrast could include reasons for immigrating to the United States.

5 **Identifying Cause and Effect** is part of interpreting the relationships between historical events. A *cause* is any action that leads to an event; the outcome of that action is an *effect*. To explain historical developments, historians may point out multiple causes and effects. For instance, the actions of the colonists as well as those of the British government brought about the American Revolution, which in turn had many far-reaching effects. (For a more detailed discussion of Identifying Cause and Effect, see page 749 in the Skills Handbook.)

6 **Analyzing** is the process of breaking something down into its parts and examining the relationships between them. Analysis enables you to better understand the whole. To analyze the outcome of the 1912 presidential election, for example, you might study a map such as the one on the next page. Analyzing the results state by state shows how Woodrow Wilson won a majority in the electoral college without winning a majority of the popular vote.

Railroad laborers

Election of 1912

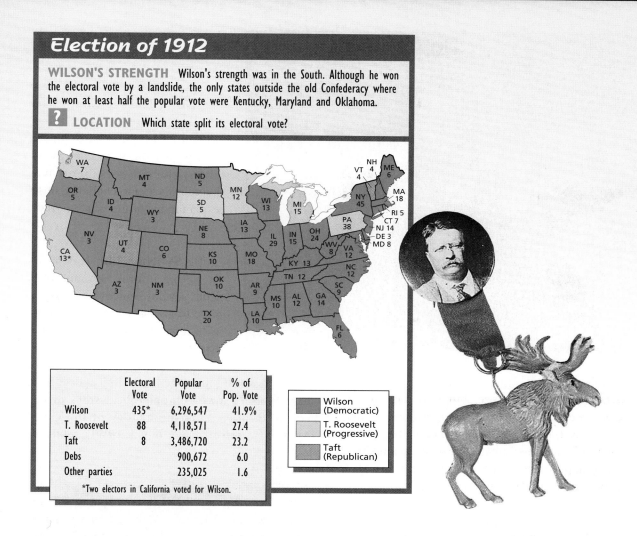

WILSON'S STRENGTH Wilson's strength was in the South. Although he won the electoral vote by a landslide, the only states outside the old Confederacy where he won at least half the popular vote were Kentucky, Maryland and Oklahoma.

? **LOCATION** Which state split its electoral vote?

	Electoral Vote	Popular Vote	% of Pop. Vote
Wilson	435*	6,296,547	41.9%
T. Roosevelt	88	4,118,571	27.4
Taft	8	3,486,720	23.2
Debs		900,672	6.0
Other parties		235,025	1.6

*Two electors in California voted for Wilson.

Wilson (Democratic)
T. Roosevelt (Progressive)
Taft (Republican)

American buffalo

7 **Assessing Consequences** means studying an action, an event, or a trend to predict its long-term effects—and to judge the desirability of those effects. *Consequences* often are effects that are indirect and unintended. They may appear long after the event that led to them. An example of assessing consequences is the federal government's weighing of the positive and negative elements of a new drug or medical procedure before permitting its use. Consequences include side effects and other possible risks, as well as benefits.

8 **Distinguishing Fact from Opinion** means separating the facts about something from what people say about it. A fact can be proved or observed; an opinion, on the other hand, is a personal belief or conclusion. We often hear facts and opinions mixed in everyday conversation on such issues as the environment—as well as

L. J. Cranstone's painting depicting a slave auction

the North and the South over control of the United States' western frontier. The historian would then organize the available evidence to support this hypothesis and to challenge other explanations of the war's causes.

11 **Synthesizing** is combining information and ideas from several sources or points in time to gain a new understanding of a topic or event. Much of the narrative writing in *The American Nation in the Twentieth Century* is a synthesis. It pulls together historical data from many sources into a chronological story of our nation. Synthesizing the history of the Great Depression, for example, might involve studying

in advertising, in political debate, and in historical sources. Although some opinions can be supported by facts, in an argument opinions do not carry as much weight as facts. (For a more detailed discussion of Distinguishing Fact from Opinion, see page 750.)

9 **Identifying Values** involves recognizing the core beliefs that a person or group holds. Values are more deeply held than opinions and are less likely to change. Values commonly concern matters of right and wrong and may be viewed as desirable in and of themselves. The values of freedom and justice, for example, motivated the struggle to abolish slavery, just as the value of equality has been a foundation of the civil rights and women's movements.

10 **Hypothesizing** is forming a possible explanation for an event, a situation, or a problem. A hypothesis is not a proven fact. Rather it is an "educated guess" based on available evidence and tested against new evidence. A historian, for instance, might hypothesize that the Civil War was primarily the result of a power struggle between the ruling classes of

Migrant Mother, photographed by Dorothea Lange during the Great Depression

economic statistics from the 1930s and photographs taken by Walker Evans, Ben Shahn, Arthur Rothstein, and Dorothea Lange for the Farm Security Administration, together with interviews of Americans who lived through the period.

12 **Problem Solving** is a process of reviewing a situation and making decisions and recommendations for improving or correcting it. Before beginning, however, the problem must be clearly identified and stated. For instance, in considering a solution to the nation's drug-abuse crisis, you might state the problem in one of the following ways:

1. in terms of the relationship of drug addiction to violent crime,

2. in terms of the economics of the drug trade,

3. in terms of the effects of drug abuse on families,

4. in terms of the economic impact on society of treatment, enforcement, and correctional institutions.

You would then propose and evaluate possible solutions or courses of action, selecting the one you think is best and giving the reasons for your choice.

Woman suffragist

Progressive reformer Robert M. La Follette

13 **Evaluating** is assessing the significance or overall importance of something, such as the success of a reform movement or the legacy of a president. You should base your judgment on standards that others will understand and are likely to share. An evaluation of the early women's movement, for example, might assess the short- and long-term effects of the focus on women's suffrage.

14 **Taking a Stand** is identifying an issue, deciding what you think about it, and persuasively expressing your position. Your stand should be based on specific information gathered from reliable sources. In taking a stand, even on controversial or emotional issues, state your position clearly and give carefully thought-out reasons to support it.

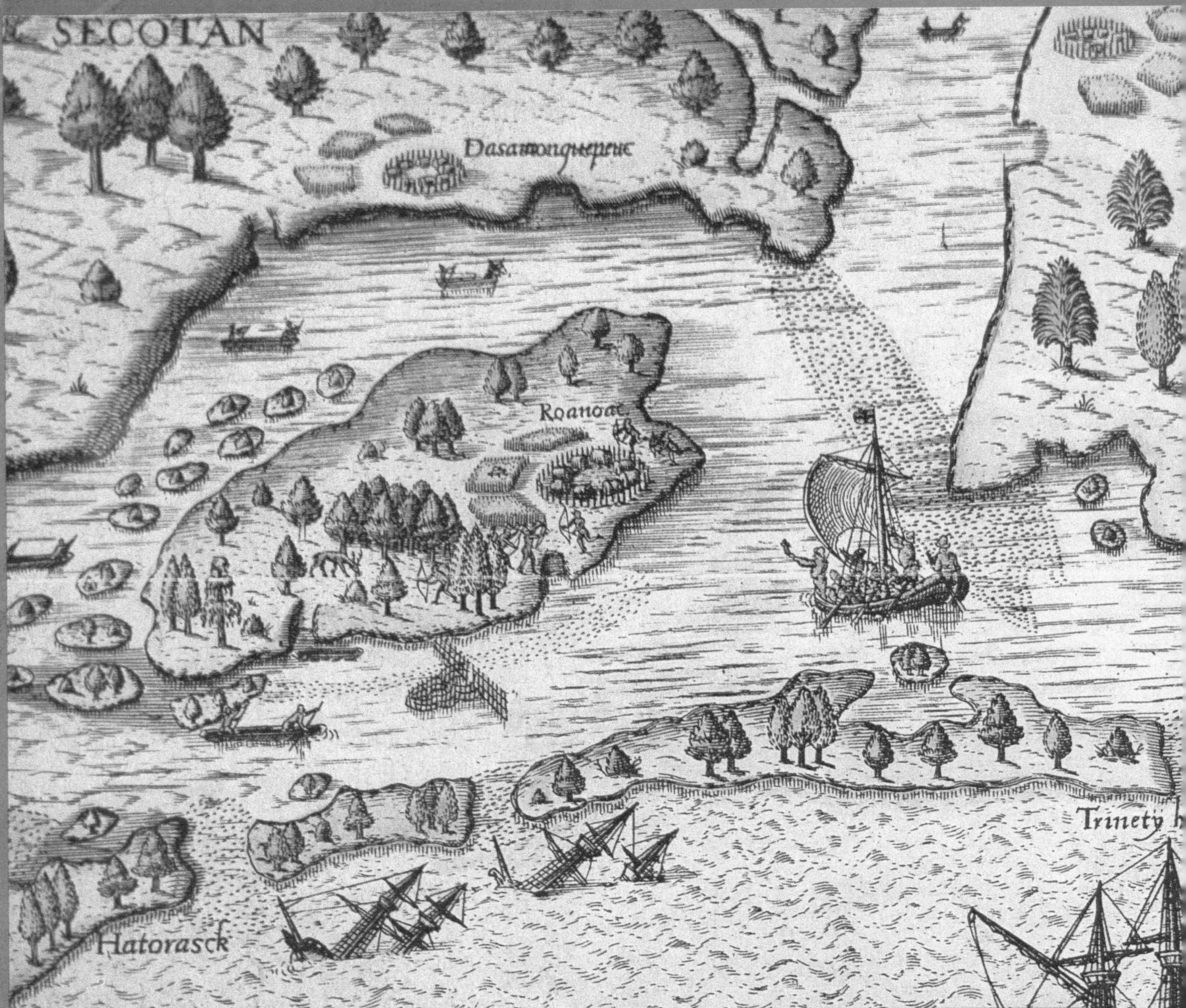
SECOTAN
Dasamonquepeuc
Roanoac
Trinety h
Hatorasck

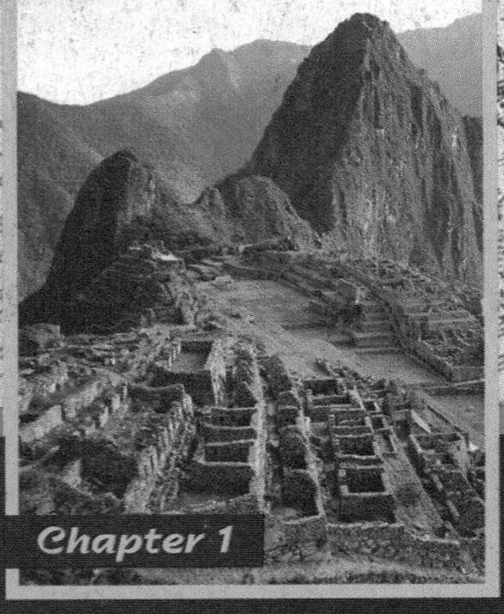

Chapter 1

BEGINNINGS TO 1763
Prehistory–1763

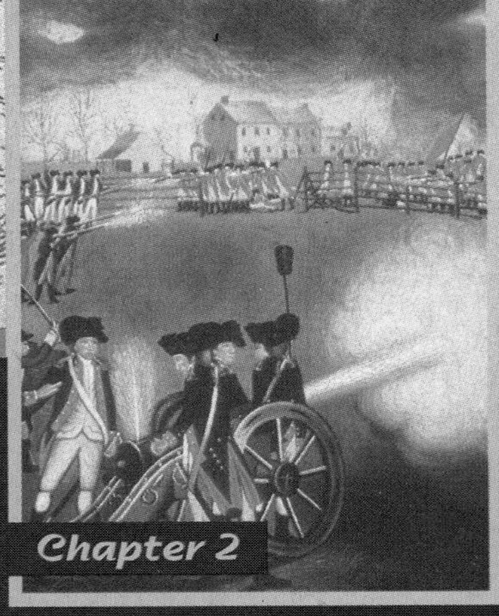

(detail) The Boatmen's National Bank, St. Louis, Missouri

Chapter 2

CREATING A NATION
1763–1815

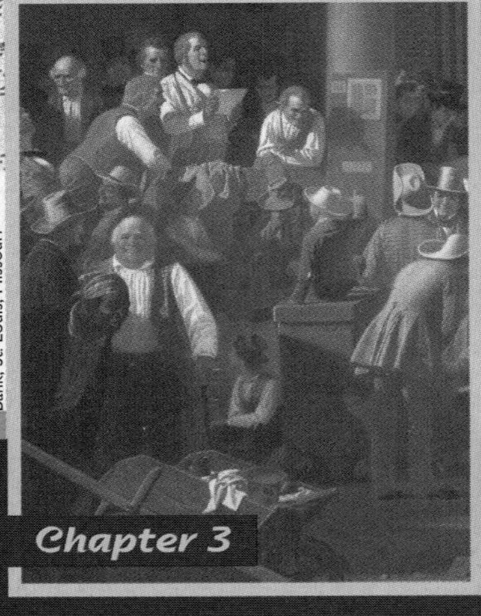

Chapter 3

GROWTH AND CHANGE
1815–1860

WEAPEME

American Roots
Beginnings – 1900

1

𝒯he first Americans migrated from Asia thousands of years ago, followed in the 16th, 17th, and 18th centuries by Europeans who established colonies throughout the Americas. During the 1700s, the United States won its independence from Great Britain. The nation's western expansion during the 1800s called attention to the institution of slavery and led to the Civil War. During the remainder of the century, settlers continued westward. By the end of the 1800s, the United States was prepared to enter the international arena.

◀ Map of Virginia, 1590

The Granger Collection, New York

Chapter 4

WAR AND REUNIFICATION 1861–1900

Chapter 5

THE WESTERN CROSSROADS 1860–1910

Chapter 6

THE NATION TRANSFORMED 1865–1910

BEGINNINGS TO 1763

FOCUS

UNDERSTANDING THE MAIN IDEA

For thousands of years great civilizations rose and fell throughout the world. Some of these civilizations had little or no contact with one another. During the Middle Ages, however, trade increasingly linked most of these cultures. By the 1400s the desire for an all-sea route to Asia propelled Europeans beyond the frontiers of their known world. As a result, in 1492 the Americas became linked with the rest of the world.

THEMES

■ **GEOGRAPHIC DIVERSITY**
How might differences in environment and land use result in diverse ways of life?

■ **GLOBAL RELATIONS**
What positive and negative effects might result from interactions between countries?

■ **CULTURAL DIVERSITY**
How might the cultural backgrounds of settlers influence the development of a region?

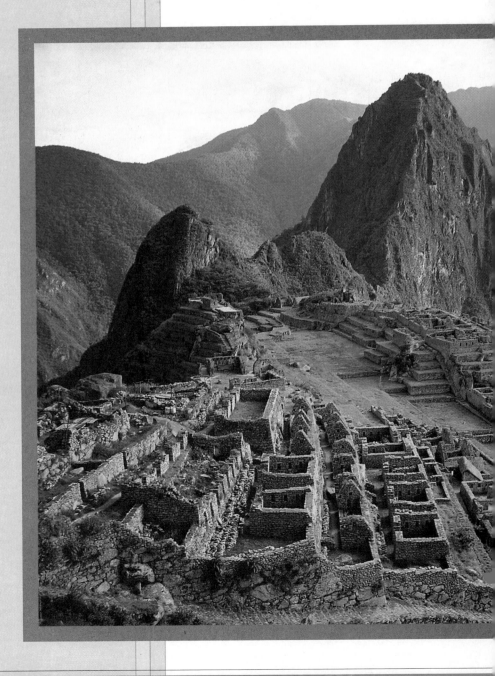

c.8000 B.C.	A.D. 610	c.700	1096	1492	1607	1763
Rise of farming in Mexico.	Muhammad founds Islam.	Rise of Mississippian culture.	Crusades begin.	Columbus lands in the Americas.	Jamestown founded.	Treaty of Paris signed.

In the 1400s, Europeans were eager to trade with Asia and Africa. Seeking a westward sea route to Asia to replace the dangerous overland routes, explorers encountered the rich and varied cultures of the Americas. The Americas soon drew thousands of European colonists who staked claims and established settlements, often in harsh environments. In the process they created new American cultures.

Incan ruins at Machu Picchu, Peru

*T*ens of thousands of years ago, a momentous migration began. Ice Age peoples, perhaps clothed in mammoth furs and carrying their few possessions, stalked herds of animals across a bridge of land linking present-day Siberia to what is now Alaska. In a series of waves, these first Americans fanned out across two continents and wove a tapestry of distinct cultures.

But many centuries would pass before the Americas were permanently linked to the rest of the world. The desire for luxury goods—from the precious silks and porcelains of China and the spices of India to the plentiful gold of Africa—launched Europeans on remarkable journeys of exploration that eventually brought them to the shores of the Americas.

In 1492, with Christopher Columbus's daring voyage, worlds apart became worlds in contact—and conflict. Columbus and the explorers and colonists who followed him carved out new lives for themselves in the Americas. Other new arrivals came unwillingly, brought from Africa to work on American plantations and mines after the devastating decline of the American Indian population. The colonies produced riches for European nations, who went to war for control of the Americas.

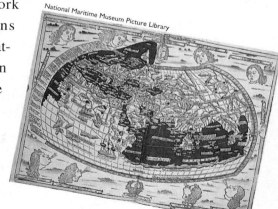

National Maritime Museum Picture Library

World map published in 1486

THE WORLD BY 1500

FOCUS

- How did the environment influence the cultures of the first Americans?
- What role did trade play in linking most of the world in the Middle Ages?
- How did the Crusades and the expansion of trade help change European society?
- How did Portugal gain control of East-West trade?

Trade played a dynamic role in linking most of the world during the Middle Ages (roughly A.D. 500–1500). Merchants traded silks, spices, and other goods between Asia, Africa, and Europe. In Europe, trade helped transform a warring group of isolated kingdoms into a continent of powerful nations. Trade eventually propelled Europeans to the Americas, where men and women originally from Asia had created diverse cultures.

Bronze figurine of a flute player from Benin, West Africa

NATIVE AMERICAN CULTURES

Most archaeologists—the scientists who study the remains of past cultures—agree that the first people to reach the vast American wilderness came from Asia during the last Ice Age. Groups of **hunter-gatherers**, peoples who stalked game and gathered edible plants, probably followed animal herds across **Beringia**, a wide land bridge between Siberia and Alaska. Scholars estimate that these first Americans, known as **Paleo-Indians**, arrived between 12,000 and 50,000 years ago.

Empires of the Americas. Groups of Paleo-Indians spread throughout the Americas, and eventually some of them shifted from hunting and gathering to agriculture. Archaeologists have found evidence that by 8000 B.C. people in Mexico were growing maize (corn), and by 2000 B.C. people in the Andes Mountains were growing potatoes. As people settled down to grow their own food, small villages formed. Over time, some villages gave way to cities and complex societies.

The earliest complex societies arose in the areas where agriculture first took hold: Mesoamerica (Central America and the southern and central regions of Mexico) and the Andes region of South America. In Mesoamerica, the Olmec civilization flourished from about 1200 to 400 B.C. The Olmecs practiced slash-and-burn agriculture, in which farmers cut down and burned sections of the forest and then planted crops in the ash-enriched soil. They also developed the beginnings of a calender and writing.

▼ **Olmec sculptors carved thousands of jade figures—often of infants and dwarfs—and buried them underneath their ceremonial courts.**

Native American Culture Areas

CULTURAL DIVERSITY By 1500 Native Americans occupied every corner of the Americas. They thrived in vastly different geographic settings: frozen tundra, mountains, dry grasslands, deserts, lush woodlands, and tropical forests.

❓ HUMAN–ENVIRONMENT INTERACTION Scholars often group Native Americans into broad culture areas based on geographic location. They do this because they believe that environment influences a people's culture. Why might environment influence culture?

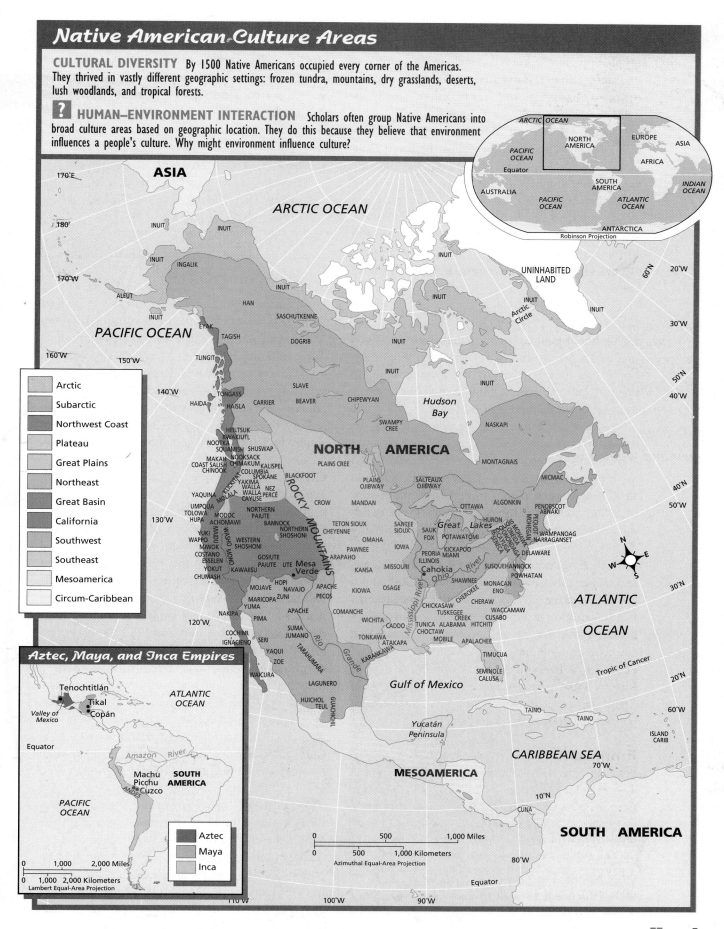

Legend:
- Arctic
- Subarctic
- Northwest Coast
- Plateau
- Great Plains
- Northeast
- Great Basin
- California
- Southwest
- Southeast
- Mesoamerica
- Circum-Caribbean

Aztec, Maya, and Inca Empires

- Aztec
- Maya
- Inca

Mayan scholars improved the Olmecs' calendar. Mayan scholars also developed a form of **glyph**, or picture writing, that included ideograms—characters that represented ideas—and phonograms—characters that represented words or syllables.

Both Olmec and Mayan societies had distinct social classes, and the people believed their kings were divine beings. Later societies, including the Aztecs, had divine kings, but a warrior class was dominant. The Aztecs conquered their neighbors, demanded tribute, and took captives to sacrifice to their gods. Like the Aztecs, the Incas of the Andes region created a militaristic empire. By the 1400s, it included some six to nine million subjects.

Cultures of North America.

By the 1400s hundreds of distinct cultural groups lived in the Americas. In North America, where the population was smaller and less dense, very few of these cultural groups created societies as large as those in Mesoamerica or the Andes.

American Indians in the Southwest developed irrigation to overcome dry conditions. Agriculture allowed the Anasazi (ahn-uh-SAHZ-ee) to settle in large villages. Between A.D. 800 and 1100 the Anasazi began to construct multistory rock and adobe dwellings. Many of these buildings nestled against cliffs and contained as many as 800 rooms.

In the woodlands of the East, the Adenas and Hopewells flourished from about 1000 B.C. to A.D. 700. Called the Mound Builders because of the distinctive earthworks they created, they based their societies on hunting, gathering, and farming. After about A.D. 700, the Mississippian culture dominated much of the Southeast and Midwest. The largest Mississippian settlement was Cahokia (kuh-HOH-kee-uh) near present-day St. Louis. Cahokia's rulers controlled trade routes that stretched from the Great Lakes into Mesoamerica.

▲ The Adenas and Hopewells built elaborate earthen mounds in the shape of animals as burial places for their dead. This aerial photograph shows the Great Serpent Mound, near present-day Hillsboro, Ohio.

■■ **As American Indians adapted to the different environments in which they lived, they developed varied cultures.**

TRADE NETWORKS

Just as many cultures of the Americas were linked through trade, trade linked the cultures of Asia, Africa, and Europe. Trade between these regions dated from at least the first century A.D., when a route, known as the Silk Road, was established between present-day Iran and China. Wars and raiding often disrupted trade, but in the seventh century, the Tang dynasty in China and the Muslim empire in Southwest Asia revitalized the trade.

China.

The Tang dynasty, which began in 618, expanded the western boundaries of China and kept the Silk Road to Central Asia clear of raiders. China's flourishing economy, which produced silk, paper, bronze artifacts, and porcelain, attracted foreign merchants. In the 1200s invaders from Mongolia overran the country. The Mongol leader Kublai Khan (KOO-bluh KAHN) made China the world's largest empire and protected the Silk Road. After Kublai Khan's death in 1294, however, the Silk Road trade declined. Later Chinese leaders emphasized sea routes, and in 1405 China launched a series of maritime expeditions. The expeditions—the most far-reaching the world had ever seen—sailed to Southeast Asia, India, the Arabian Peninsula, and East Africa. But in 1433 China officially ended foreign trade, though Asian merchants continued to trade Chinese goods.

The Islamic world.

In the seventh century the Muslim empire helped link China with the West. The empire originated with Muhammad, a merchant and prophet who began to preach the religion of Islam in about 610. Muhammad united the Arabian Peninsula, and his successors conquered surrounding empires. At its height, the

Muslim empire covered northern Africa, the Iberian Peninsula, and Southwest Asia.

Although Muslim armies helped spread the Islamic faith, many people were converted by merchants. Muslim merchants launched expeditions from Baghdad, which became the Muslim empire's capital in 762. Located on the Tigris River, Baghdad had access to the Persian Gulf and thus to India and China. Baghdad was also linked to the western end of the Silk Road, where Muslim and Jewish merchants controlled much of the trade. These merchants carried Persian rugs and textiles and African gold to eastern Asia and returned with porcelain and jewels. The Muslim merchants also carried the **Qur'an** (kuh-RAN)—the holy book of Islam—and tirelessly preached their religion.

Trade fostered other cultural exchanges. Muslims introduced Chinese technologies, such as silk and paper production, to the West. Mathematical ideas from India influenced al-Khwārizmī, a Muslim mathematician who developed algebra. Ibn Sina (IB-uhn SEE-nah), a Baghdad physician, compiled a medical encyclopedia that became a standard textbook beyond Muslim lands. Islamic maps also found their way to other lands.

Africa.
Islamic culture spread to Africa through conquest and trade. In the seventh century Arab armies captured Egypt and North Africa. In East Africa, African traders brought gold and ivory to the coast, where other traders—most of them Arabs—shipped the goods to the Arabian Peninsula and then to India and China. The most sought-after item was gold, which the Muslim empire needed to mint coins used in international trade. Over time Arabs and East Africans created a unique African culture, whose language, Swahili (swah-HEE-lee), blended Bantu and Arabic languages.

In West Africa, African merchants had early on established a trade in gold and salt across the Sahara Desert. The kingdom of Ghana flourished from this trade until the region was overrun by Muslims in the 11th century. The kingdom of Mali then rose to power, eventually controlling a huge empire that stretched from the upper Niger (NY-juhr) River westward to the Atlantic coast.

Muslim traders converted many West African rulers. Mansa Mūsā, who ruled Mali from 1307 to 1332, was a devout Muslim. After his death, Mali declined and the state of Songhay (SAWNG-hy) became the dominant power in West Africa. Songhay grew rich from the trade in gold, ivory,

◄ **Mansa Mūsā made a pilgrimage to Mecca in 1324.**

and slaves and became a center of Islamic learning. Its city of Timbuktu (tohn-book-TOO) was home to three universities and some 180 Islamic schools.

Europe.
From North Africa, Muslim armies moved into Europe. By 714 they had conquered most of present-day Spain and Portugal. Muslims introduced irrigation systems and Asian crops, such as rice. Jewish traders sold these crops, together with fine steel products and textiles, all around the Mediterranean.

▦ Through trade, the world's regions shared new technologies and religious and scientific ideas.

THE TRANSFORMATION OF EUROPE

In the 10th century, trading cities in Italy arose that traded goods from Spain and the rest of the Muslim empire throughout Europe. By the early 1100s, Venice, the most powerful of these cities, dominated the eastern Mediterranean trade. Venice, like most of Europe, was Christian under the leadership of the Roman Catholic Church. Christianity had spread to Europe after its founding in the first century A.D. in present-day Israel. Because Jesus Christ had been born there, Christians considered it to be the Holy Land. Muslims also considered the area holy. When they restricted Christians' access to the city of Jerusalem, the Europeans waged a series of wars against the Muslims. These wars, known as the **Crusades**, took place between 1096 and the late 1200s.

In the First Crusade, European soldiers captured Jerusalem and established several kingdoms in the area. (The Muslims retook the city in the late

1100s.) Though later Crusades were never as successful, the wars had important consequences for trade. Venetian merchants and bankers helped fund the Crusades in return for trading privileges.

◀ The 12th-century Arab geographer Abū al-Idrīsī developed a map of the world that consisted of many different sections. One section displaying the "Seven Climatic Zones" is shown.

This trade helped change Europe's political and social order. Increased trade created opportunities for merchants and bankers who formed a new social class—the middle class. This new class supported strong rulers who could protect trade; in return for their support, the middle class demanded greater political and economic freedom. Kings and lords reluctantly granted towns self-government. Some monarchs even organized assemblies, which were the forerunners of modern parliaments.

By the 1400s strong national monarchies existed in Portugal, France, England, and Spain. Henry VII unified England in 1485 after 30 years of fighting. Spain created a unified nation in 1492, after the kingdoms of Castile and Aragon united by marriage and Muslims and Jews were forced to leave.

The Crusades and trade also promoted a rebirth of European learning and creativity known as the **Renaissance**. Crusaders and traders brought to Europe classical Greek and Roman works and new ideas from the Byzantine Empire (the eastern half of the former Roman Empire) and from the Islamic world. These ideas spread throughout Europe after the 1450s, when Johannes Gutenberg invented a printing press that produced books quickly and cheaply. The wealth won from trade supported the work of Renaissance artists and architects.

■■ **The Crusades and trade helped broaden a new social class's political freedoms, spurred the creation of strong national monarchies, and fostered the Renaissance.**

Then and Now   THE FIVE THEMES OF GEOGRAPHY

Historical events cannot be fully understood without an understanding of the geographical settings in which they take place. History and geography, therefore, are closely linked. To organize information, geographers study the following five themes: location, place, human-environment interaction, movement, and region.

Location can be expressed in two ways. *Absolute location* is a site's exact spot on the earth. The absolute location of Chicago, for example, is 41°52' north latitude and 87°37' west longitude. *Relative location,* on the other hand, describes the position of a place in relation to other places. For instance, Chicago lies along the southwest shore of Lake Michigan.

Place refers to the physical and human characteristics of an area. Climate is an example of a physical characteristic, while population size is an example of a human characteristic.

Human-environment interaction deals with the ways in which people both adapt to and change their natural surroundings. The shelters people build to protect themselves against cold or heat are a form of adaptation. Actions that people take to change the environment include clearing forests and setting up irrigation systems.

Movement describes the way people interact as they travel, communicate, and trade goods and services. Movement includes human migration as well as the exchange of goods.

A *region* is an area defined by common physical or cultural characteristics, such as climate or religion. Geographers have divided the earth into many regions and subregions.

THE LURE OF TRADE AND EXPLORATION

By the early 1400s, goods from Africa and Asia were available in Europe, but very costly. The emerging nations of Europe wanted to share in the huge profits to be earned from this trade. But to do so, they needed to break Genoa and Venice's **monopoly**, or exclusive control, of East-West trade, by finding a new route to the East.

Portuguese exploration. Portugal, a small country with a long seafaring tradition, led the way in exploration. Prince Henry of Portugal oversaw Portuguese exploration in the 15th century. He sought to find the African "gold kingdoms" he had heard of while fighting the Muslims in Morocco.

In 1419 Prince Henry established a center for the study of navigation at Sagres (SAH-greesh), which produced accurate maps and new ships and navigation methods. Henry put the results to use by sponsoring voyages of exploration down the African coast. By the 1460s, the Portuguese had ventured nearly around the great bulge of West Africa.

The slave trade. The first Portuguese traders to land in West Africa sought gold and spices. In time, however, they turned to the sale of enslaved Africans. The Portuguese did not introduce the slave trade—slavery had long existed in Europe, Asia, and Africa. But prior to the Portuguese, Africans pressed into slavery were often criminals or captives of war. Most could marry, and their children were not slaves.

By the end of the 1500s, the slave trade had become a major economic activity. It eventually resulted in the **African diaspora** (dy-AS-pruh)—the forcible resettlement of millions of Africans to the Americas. Estimates suggest that in the four centuries the slave trade operated, more than 10 million Africans crossed the Atlantic as slaves.

The slave trade devastated African society. Warfare among West African nations increased as each sought to capture slaves. Many other slaves were captured in raids. In 1444 a Portuguese observer described the painful experience of captured Africans:

> 66 Mothers would clasp their infants in their arms and throw themselves on the ground to cover them with their bodies, disregarding any injury to their own persons, so that they could prevent their children from being separated from them. 99

But such observations did not stop the slave trade. The Portuguese continued to trade and to search for a new route to Asia. In 1488 Bartolomeu Dias rounded Africa's southern tip, and 10 years later Vasco da Gama's expedition reached India. Over the next half century, the Portuguese established trading forts in West and East Africa, India, Southeast Asia, and southern China, thereby gaining control of East-West trade. Soon other European nations sponsored voyages of exploration, this time venturing west to the Americas.

Portuguese explorers sailed around Africa and established a new East-West trade route.

SECTION 1 REVIEW

IDENTIFY and explain the significance of the following: hunter-gatherers, Beringia, Paleo-Indians, glyph, Kublai Khan, Qur'an, Crusades, Renaissance, Johannes Gutenberg, monopoly, African diaspora.

LOCATE and explain the importance of the following: Mexico, Cahokia.

1. **MAIN IDEA** Why was there great variety in American Indian cultures?

2. **MAIN IDEA** How were the world's regions linked during the Middle Ages?

3. **MAIN IDEA** In what ways did the Crusades change economic, political, and social life in Europe?

4. **WRITING TO PERSUADE** Imagine you are Vasco da Gama. Write a letter to the Portuguese monarchs explaining why it would be in their interests to fund your attempts to find a new route to Asia.

5. **SYNTHESIZING** What led to the spread of Islam and Islamic culture?

SPANISH AMERICA

- **What were some of the results of the Columbian exchange?**
- **How did the conquistadors help build a Spanish empire in the Americas? How did Native Americans respond to the conquistadors?**
- **What elements of their culture did Spanish colonists introduce to the Americas?**

ew dates in American history are as instantly recognizable as 1492. With Christopher Columbus's daring voyage, worlds apart became worlds in contact—and conflict. The explorers and colonists who came to the Americas after Columbus carved out new lives for themselves and began a new era of trade. Tragically, however, Europeans introduced diseases to the Americas that decimated Indian populations.

Flora and fauna
of the Americas

FIRST CONTACT

Christopher Columbus, a mariner from Genoa, doubted that the Portuguese route around Africa was the most direct route to Asia. He went to Lisbon, Portugal, the center of European knowledge about sea travel, and studied charts and books. Columbus concluded that the western sea could not be very large and that the great trading cities of Asia lay only about 2,400 miles west of Portugal.

In the 1480s Columbus tried to persuade various European monarchs to sponsor a westward voyage. King John II of Portugal rejected the plan because he doubted Columbus's calculation of the distance to Asia. (In fact, Columbus had underestimated the distance by about five times.) Initially, Columbus had no better luck with the Spanish monarchs, Ferdinand and Isabella. His luck changed in 1492, however, when the monarchs completed the ***Reconquista***—the reconquest of Spain from the Muslims. With that massive task accomplished, the Spanish rulers were able to back Columbus, who had persuaded them with promises of great riches and new Catholic converts.

At dawn on August 3, 1492, Columbus and his experienced crew of 90 men departed from Palos, Spain. More than two months later, Columbus's fleet—the *Santa María,* the *Niña,* and the *Pinta*—reached a tiny coral island in the central Bahamas and claimed the land for Spain.

◀ **This detail from the *Fall of Granada* by Pradilla shows Ferdinand and Isabella receiving the surrender of the Kingdom of Granada from the Moors in 1492.**

The residents of the island, the Tainos (TY-nohs), greeted the strange visitors. Columbus described their hospitality:

66 They . . . brought us parrots and balls of cotton and spears and many other things, which they exchanged for the glass beads and hawks' bells. They willingly traded everything they owned. 99

Though these were not the luxury items of the Indies Columbus sought, he saw potential profit in the situation. Noting that the Tainos—who he called "Indios," or inhabitants of the Indies, because he still believed he had reached Asia—did not have metal weapons, he concluded: "They would make fine servants. . . . With 50 men we could subjugate [conquer] them all."

Columbus expected the Tainos to lead him to gold. He sailed from island to island—naming and claiming each for Spain—in his search. Though the search yielded some gold, it produced conflict. The Spaniards' excessive demands for gold and food wore down the Tainos' generosity and led to battles between the two groups. Another source of conflict was the *encomienda* (en-koh-mee-EN-duh) system, which Columbus informally introduced and the Spanish Crown formally established in 1503. Under this system the colonists, or *encomenderos* (en-koh-muhn-DE-rohs), received the right to have a certain number of Indians work for them. The *encomenderos* used the Indians to mine gold, provide food, and build houses.

Most *encomenderos* overworked the American Indian laborers and prevented them from growing food for themselves. One prominent critic, Bartolomé de Las Casas, demanded an end to the *encomienda*. In his *Apologetic History of the Indies* (1566), Las Casas argued that American Indians should not be enslaved because their humanity and wisdom equaled that of Europeans:

66 Not only have [the Indians] shown themselves to be very wise peoples and possessed of lively and marked understanding, . . . governing and providing for their nations, . . . but they have equaled many diverse nations of the . . . past and present. 99

The end of the *encomienda* would not come through official action but through the catastrophic decline

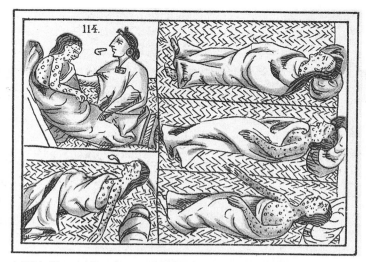

▲ This illustration from a 1500s history of New Spain written by a Spanish monk, Bernardinode Sahagun, shows the devastating effects of smallpox. Measles, malaria, and smallpox were just a few of the diseases brought by Europeans that caused epidemics among American Indian peoples.

of the American Indian population. European diseases, overwork, and malnutrition took a terrible toll. While the death rate for American Indians varied, in some areas their numbers declined by over 90 percent by the mid-16th century

COMMENTARY

The Columbian Legacy

Historians offer different interpretations of the lasting significance of Columbus's voyages to the Americas. Some applaud him for his courage and vision, for enlarging geographic knowledge; others blame him for introducing the *encomienda* system and for the drastic decline of the American Indian population.

With such conflicting interpretations of Columbus's significance, how can we judge his impact? A useful way to understand the legacy of Columbus's voyages is to see the enormous effect they had on the world. The transfer of people, ideas, plants, animals, and diseases between the Americas, Europe, Asia, and Africa that Columbus's journeys initiated has come to be called the **Columbian exchange.**

The Columbian exchange transformed the world. Gold, silver, and other resources from the Americas made many European nations wealthy and powerful. Crops from the Americas, such as corn, potatoes, and tomatoes, became staples for people everywhere. Through settlement and the slave trade, the lands of the Western Hemisphere, formerly inhabited only by American Indians, were gradually peopled with Europeans, Africans, and Asians. The introduction of European animals transformed the American landscape.

The exchange also introduced deadly diseases, such as smallpox, measles, and malaria, to North America. Because American Indians lacked resistance to these diseases, the Indian population experienced a catastrophic decline. Scholars estimate that the population of the Americas before the Europeans arrived was between 8.4 million and 112.5 million. Several centuries later, the Native American population had declined to perhaps 4 to 4.5 million.

The tragic effects of disease and military conquest on American Indians and of the introduction of African slavery understandably overshadow the positive aspects of the Columbian exchange. But when determining the significance of Columbus's voyages, we must take into account the global transformations he set in motion.

■■ **The Columbian exchange resulted in the transfer of people, precious metals, crops, and animals between the Americas and Europe, Asia, and Africa.**

THE CONQUEST OF THE MAINLAND

Columbus's voyages also fueled the rivalry between Spain and Portugal. To avoid open conflict, the two nations signed the **Treaty of Tordesillas** (tawrd-uh-SEE-uhs) in 1494. The treaty drew an imaginary line of demarcation, or separation, around the world: Territory west of the line would belong to Spain; east of the line, to Portugal.

The Spanish Crown soon sponsored new voyages. Ferdinand Magellan set out in 1519 to find a westward route to Asia. After sailing around the southern tip of South America and into the Pacific Ocean, the expedition accomplished its goal. Surviving crew members returned to Spain in 1522—the first people to **circumnavigate**, or sail completely around, the world.

Other explorers claimed lands in Central America and South America. In 1512 Vasco Nuñez de Balboa (NOON-yays day bahl-BOH-uh) explored Panama and was probably the first European to glimpse the Pacific Ocean from the Americas. Lured by stories of gold, Spanish **conquistadors** (kawng-KEES-tuh-dawrs), or conquerors, soon followed the explorers. In 1521 Hernán Cortés conquered the Aztec Empire in Mexico, and Francisco Pizarro conquered the vast Inca Empire in the 1530s.

THE SLAVE TRADE

THROUGH OTHERS' EYES

Nzinga Mbemba (en-ZING uhm-BEM-buh), "Lord of the Congo," was a central African ruler who hoped to increase contact and trade between the Congo states and the leading European powers. To aid this effort, he even adopted the Christian faith and assumed a new name: Dom Afonso. His dreams turned sour, however, as he watched Portuguese slave ships take more and more of his people by force to the Americas. In 1526 he urged King John III of Portugal to curb this practice:

❝**W**e cannot reckon how great the damage is, since the . . . [slave] merchants daily seize our subjects, sons of the land and sons of our noblemen and vassals and our relatives. . . . Thieves and men of evil conscience take them . . . and cause them to be sold: and so great, Sir, is their corruption . . . that our country is being utterly depopulated.❞

Afonso's pleas went unheeded, however. Spain and other European nations followed Portugal's lead. By 1600 several hundred thousand Africans were in bondage in the Americas.

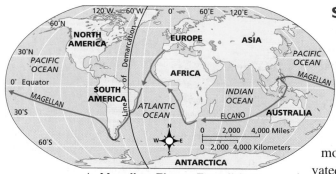

▲ **Magellan–Elcano Expedition**

The Spanish conquistadors were aided by divisions within the Indian empires and by the devastating spread of diseases. To maintain control over the conquered Indians, the Spanish tried to wipe out American Indian cultures. They tore down temples, destroyed art, and reorganized settlements. In Mexico, the Spanish leveled the Aztec capital of Tenochtitlán (tay-nawch-tee-TLAHN) and built their capital of Mexico City over its ruins.

American Indian cultures were not completely destroyed. Survival, however, usually meant the mixing of Spanish and Native American peoples and cultures. For example, many Indians developed a new religion by combining their rituals with Catholic rituals. Over time American Indian and Spanish ways blended, creating new cultures.

■■ **The conquistadors added vast territory and wealth to the Spanish American empire. Many American Indians fought the conquistadors, while others blended their culture with Spanish ways.**

SPANISH SETTLEMENT

Since North America boasted no empires as wealthy as the Aztecs or Incas, Spanish exploration and colonization there proceeded slowly. The main goals of settlement were providing ports for ships sailing up the Atlantic coast on their way back to Spain, establishing missions to convert American Indians, and preventing other countries from colonizing Spanish territory. Beginning in the mid-1500s, Spain founded settlements from coast to coast in what is now the continental United States.

Spain's northern lands. Spanish explorers first turned their attention to La Florida, the entire eastern seaboard from present-day Florida to Newfoundland. Florida's first European explorer, Juan Ponce de León (PAWN-say day lay-AWN), sought gold and perhaps the mythical "Fountain of Youth" in 1513, but established no settlements. A much more practical goal—establishing a port—motivated later explorers. In 1565, after two earlier colonizers had failed, an expedition led by Pedro Menéndez de Avilés (may-NAYN-days day ah-bee-LAYS) succeeded in planting a permanent settlement. This was St. Augustine, the oldest city founded by Europeans in what is now the United States.

In 1609, some 1,500 miles west of St. Augustine, the Spanish established Santa Fe as the capital of New Mexico. The Pueblo Indians bitterly opposed Spanish rule. In 1680 the Pueblos drove out the Spanish. After the **Pueblo Revolt**, the Pueblos attempted to return to their former way of life. However, a new governor, Diego de Vargas, reestablished Spanish rule in the 1690s.

At the same time, the Spanish began moving into Arizona. Father Eusebio Kino (ay-oo-SAYB-yoh KEE-noh) built missions near present-day Nogales (noh-GAL-uhs) in 1687 and Tucson in 1700. During the 1700s, fear of French and British expansion prompted the Spanish to speed up their colonization of this region. France's colonizing activity also spurred Spain to strengthen its hold on Texas.

▲ **The Pueblo Indians skillfully decorated pottery with beautiful symbols and designs.**

The San Francisco de los Tejas mission was established in 1690, and the San Antonio de Valero mission was built in 1718. Other settlements emerged along the Rio Grande, but the absence of gold and silver and the Apaches' and Comanches' constant raiding discouraged further settlement.

California was the last of Spain's northern territories to be colonized. Juan Rodríguez Cabrillo (kah-BREE-yoh) explored much of the California coastline as early as 1542. But not until the late 1700s did Spain, alarmed by Russian explorations in northern California, attempt to set up permanent settlements. San Diego was founded in 1769, and San Francisco in 1776. Friar Junípero Serra (hoo-NEE-pay-roh SER-rah), a scholarly missionary, also founded a string of missions along California's coast.

Colonial life. From California to Florida, colonists planted Spanish political and social institutions. The Spanish influence found today throughout the southwestern United States dates from this period. Spain's northern colonies were part of the viceroyalty, or province, of New Spain and were administered by a viceroy in Mexico City. But because transportation between the capital at Mexico City and northern New Spain was long and difficult, colonists usually exercised some independence in local government.

The Spanish founded more than 150 missions in the present-day United States to convert American Indians to the Catholic faith. At the center of the missions were the churches, whose architecture ranged from rustic to ornate. In their zeal to teach the Native Americans Spanish ways, missionaries suppressed Indian cultures and sometimes enforced a harsh labor system. Many Indians fled from the missions or died from European diseases.

Outside the missions, colonists established estates and settlements, which were usually guarded by presidios (forts). **Peons**, or workers who owned no land of their own, worked on haciendas—the biggest estates. Many peons remained tied to a hacienda by debts or by lack of other opportunities. Owners of *ranchos,* or smaller estates, usually worked alongside their laborers. The Spanish *vaqueros* (vah-KER-ohs), the horsemen who worked on cattle ranches, established many of the ranch practices that became the models for later North American cowboys.

The Granger Collection, New York

▲ **A Mexican hacienda owner, his wife, an overseer, and a *vaquero* are shown in this watercolor from the early 1830s.**

People living on haciendas, in missions, and in the bustling cities of Spanish America developed a unique social structure. *Peninsulares* (pay-nin-SOO-LAHR-uhs), Spaniards born in Spain, and *criollos* (kree-OH-yohs), Spaniards born in the colonies, held the most privileged positions in the Americas. Below the Spaniards were *mestizos* (me-STEE-zohs), men and women born of European-Indian unions. Roughly equal in status to the *mestizos* were mulattoes, people of African-European ancestry. At the bottom of the social structure were American Indians, Africans, and *zambos*, people of Indian-African ancestry.

■■ **Colonists brought Spanish government, architecture, and customs to the Americas.**

SECTION 2 REVIEW

IDENTIFY and explain the significance of the following: Christopher Columbus, *Reconquista, encomienda,* Bartolomé de Las Casas, Columbian exchange, Treaty of Tordesillas, Ferdinand Magellan, circumnavigate, conquistadors, Hernán Cortés, Francisco Pizarro, Juan Ponce de León, Pueblo Revolt, Friar Junípero Serra, peons.

1. **MAIN IDEA** What exchanges between the Americas, Europe, Asia, and Africa took place as a result of Columbus's journeys?

2. **MAIN IDEA** What roles did the conquistadors play in helping Spain build an American empire?

3. **MAIN IDEA** What elements of Spanish culture were transplanted to Spanish America?

4. **WRITING TO EXPLAIN** Write an essay explaining how American Indians kept their cultures alive in spite of the conquistadors' efforts to destroy their cultures.

5. **USING HISTORICAL IMAGINATION** Imagine you are a Taino living in the Bahamas. Draw a plan for a mural that portrays your interactions with the Spanish explorers.

THE ENGLISH COLONIES

- How did English colonization methods differ from Spanish methods?
- Why did settlers come to England's North American colonies? What kinds of societies did they establish?
- What were the main causes and results of the French and Indian War?

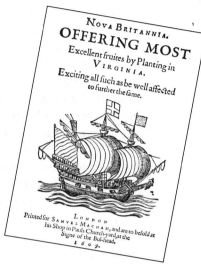

1609 English pamphlet promoting colonization

In the 1500s, as the Spanish began settling North America, other European nations—especially England and France— claimed large areas of the continent. By the end of the 17th century, English colonies flourished in North America, and the colonists, with the help of Native Americans, created distinctive societies. The 18th century, however, brought increasing conflicts with American Indians and the French over control of the land.

EARLY ENGLISH SETTLEMENT

Shortly after Columbus's first voyage, mariner John Cabot searched for a northwestern route to Asia. In 1497 and 1498 Cabot claimed Newfoundland, Nova Scotia, and New England for England. But England delayed colonizing its new territory. England was embroiled in the **Protestant Reformation**—the religious upheaval that established new churches as alternatives to Catholicism. The struggle between Protestants and Catholics became not only religious but also territorial and political. England, which became a Protestant nation in 1534, began to challenge Catholic Spain for religious and political dominance in Europe and in the Americas.

▶ The faster English ships outmaneuvered the ships of the Spanish Armada.

English pirates, known as "sea dogs," attacked Spanish galleons and seized their cargoes. To retaliate, the Spanish king, Philip, launched an attack on England in 1588. The English navy defeated Philip's force of some 130 ships, known as the **Spanish Armada**. Spain's defeat revealed Spanish military and economic weaknesses. The way was thus open for England to begin colonization.

Attempts at colonization had been made in the 1580s, but they had failed. In 1606, however, King James I issued a charter licensing two merchant groups to organize settlements in Virginia and "to dig, mine, and search for all manner of mines of gold, silver, and copper." The two groups, the Plymouth Company and the London Company, were **joint-stock companies**, which operate somewhat like corporations do today. Investors shared the cost of running the company; they also shared any profits or losses. Unlike the Spanish government, which itself organized settlements in the Americas, the English Crown left early colonization to these private companies.

▪▪ Great Britain, unlike Spain, used private companies to settle its American colonies.

Quickly following up on its charter, the London Company in 1607 sent some 100 men to Virginia, where they founded Jamestown on the Chesapeake Bay. The company insisted that the settlers search for gold. With little time to build good shelters or to plant crops, many colonists died. In 1608, to avert disaster, John Smith called off the fruitless search for gold and ordered wells dug, new shelters built, land cleared, and crops planted. The Powhatans, a confederation of some 30 small tribes, aided the settlers by giving them food and teaching them how to cultivate corn.

The colony became prosperous after the introduction of tobacco in 1612. However, tobacco required large amounts of land. Tobacco farmers soon expanded onto the Powhatans' hunting grounds. The Powhatans viewed the taking of their lands as an act of war and attacked, killing some 350 settlers. The English struck back fiercely. Thus ended peaceful relations between settlers and Indians.

𝒯HE THIRTEEN COLONIES

After Jamestown's success, English settlers flocked to the Americas. They came for varied reasons. The prospect of religious freedom drew many colonists to New England. By contrast, most settlers in the Chesapeake colonies of Virginia and Maryland came as laborers seeking a better life. Later colonies, including New York, Pennsylvania, and the Carolinas, also drew settlers from Europe. These settlers created distinctive regional societies.

New England. Not all English colonists came to the Americas to find gold or to grow tobacco. Some fled religious upheaval, which had raged since England had become a Protestant nation. Some Protestants, including the **Puritans**, wished to "purify" the Church of England of all Catholic traditions. The most radical of the Puritans—the **Separatists**, who had broken entirely with the

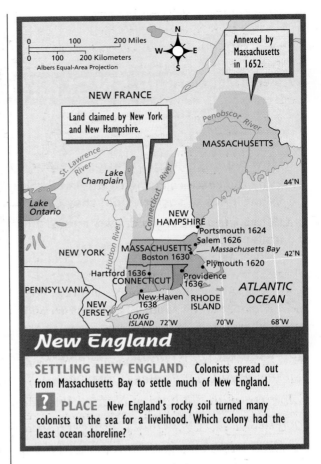

New England

SETTLING NEW ENGLAND Colonists spread out from Massachusetts Bay to settle much of New England.

❓ PLACE New England's rocky soil turned many colonists to the sea for a livelihood. Which colony had the least ocean shoreline?

church—were persecuted. They fled to the Netherlands after King James I threatened to "harry [force] them out of the land or else do worse."

In 1620 the Separatists, known as Pilgrims, left the Netherlands and established the Plymouth colony at Massachusetts' Cape Cod Bay. They adopted the **Mayflower Compact**, a document that established a self-governing colony based on the majority rule of male church members. The Mayflower Compact set a precedent for local government based on written agreements and the consent of the governed.

Growing religious persecution and economic difficulties drove other Puritans from England. Many Puritan tenant farmers were driven off their lands when landowners fenced their holdings and began to raise sheep. Then in the 1620s crop failures and an economic depression hit Puritan farmers and weavers. Beginning in 1630, in what is known as the **Great Migration**, some 60,000 Puritans left England for the Americas. Some 10,000 to 20,000 settled in Massachusetts.

In the first year of the Great Migration, some 1,000 Puritans established a colony by royal charter in Massachusetts Bay. These Puritans built a Bible **commonwealth**, in which everyone, guided by English law and the Bible, was expected to work together for the common good. All **freemen**—that is, adult male church members who owned property—could vote and participate in government. The success of the community depended on educated people who could understand the Bible. Laws thus required parents to teach their children to read and, after 1647, required towns to establish schools.

Olaudah Equiano

New England's plentiful food and healthful climate encouraged the growth of large families. New Englanders with large families had little need for servants or slaves. Fathers and sons farmed, and mothers and daughters made many of the goods their families needed.

To pay for supplies and luxury items from England, some New Englanders turned to fishing, shipping, and business. They distilled rum and built ships. They sold fish, grain, meat, naval stores (turpentine, pitch, and rosin), and lumber to England, Spain, Portugal, the West Indies, and England's other American colonies.

Chesapeake colonies. Colonists created a completely different culture in the Chesapeake—the land surrounding Chesapeake Bay. Most white colonists who came to the Chesapeake came as **indentured servants**, who were bound for a period of years to serve the person who paid for the voyage to America. Some 75 percent of indentured servants were male. Because there were so few white women in the early years, many men never married.

The vast majority of Chesapeake colonists lived on widely scattered farms and plantations. They produced tobacco for export and grew or made many of the things they needed. Since there was little need for a central market, few towns arose.

Slavery. Slavery also set the Chesapeake apart from New England. As the supply of indentured servants dwindled, the demand for slaves increased. Slave raiders began moving far into the interior of West Africa in search of Africans to enslave. Their constant attacks destroyed the African countryside and emptied villages.

Once captured, the slaves endured many horrors. In the mid-1700s, 11- or 12-year-old Olaudah Equiano (oh-LOW-duh ek-wee-AHN-oh) was kidnapped and sold into slavery. He described his ordeal during the dread **Middle Passage**—the voyage across the Atlantic—in his autobiography. Once aboard the slave ship, he was taken below deck:

> 66 There I received such a salutation in my nostrils as I had never experienced in my life; so that with the loathesomeness of the stench, and crying together, I became so sick and low that I was not able to eat. . . . I now wished for the last friend, death, to relieve me. 99

Equiano survived the voyage, but countless others did not. In the crowded and unhealthy conditions many died from suffocation, disease, or violence. Some captives killed themselves, leaping overboard, rather than face further horrors.

After Equiano arrived in the Americas, he went from slaveholder to slaveholder. By 1766 Equiano had earned enough money to buy his freedom. After working as a seaman, Equiano settled in England and began lecturing for the antislavery, or **abolition**, movement. His popular autobiography, published in 1789, convinced many people of the need to end the slave trade.

Equiano's experience was uncommon, for he did not suffer the hardships of plantation life. Laws called "slave codes" forbade slaves to leave the

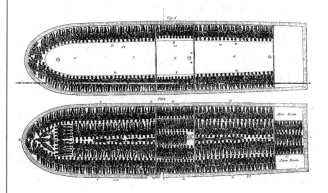

▲ When this 1786 slave ship diagram was drawn, Africans had long been in British North America. Africans first arrived in Jamestown in 1619, probably as indentured servants.

plantation, to meet together, to learn to read or write, or to own weapons. Such harsh rules did not prevent rebellion, however. There were a few uprisings, and slaves often ran away. Most slaves, however, resisted in other, less direct ways, such as by destroying property or working slowly.

Proprietary colonies. Slavery was also important in another colony—South Carolina. In 1663 Charles II granted some of his supporters a large tract of land between Virginia and Spanish Florida. The proprietors, or owners, later split the colony into North and South Carolina. Slaves from rice-growing regions in Africa transformed the swampy coastal areas of South Carolina into profitable rice plantations. By 1720 African slaves made up about 70 percent of the population of the colony. The thriving port of Charles Town attracted a diverse group of settlers, including Scots, Scotch-Irish, Germans, European Jews, West Indians, and French Huguenots (Protestants).

The king established other proprietary colonies in the 1660s. To cripple Dutch trading interests, Charles sent out a fleet to capture the Dutch colony of New Netherland. Without a shot being fired, the colony fell into English hands. Charles made his brother, James, the Duke of York, the proprietor. James renamed part of the colony New York and gave the rest—New Jersey—to two friends.

Another proprietary colony was founded in these years as a religious experiment. In 1681 William Penn, a Quaker, founded Pennsylvania as a place where people of different nationalities and religious beliefs could live peacefully together.

▼ This extract from *Colonial Office Papers* shows the earliest land grants, beginning in 1674, given to settlers in South Carolina. By 1765 more than 11,000 names appeared on this list.

▲ *The Peaceable Kingdom* was one of several paintings Edward Hicks made of animals living in harmony with nature. In this version, William Penn is shown in the background, meeting with other colonists.

Pennsylvania attracted thousands of poor immigrants from England, Denmark, and Germany. The settlers found fertile land that they could purchase cheaply and a mild climate. Farmers soon exported flour and salted meat to the West Indies.

While Pennsylvania began as a "Holy Experiment," Georgia was a social experiment. The last colony was founded in 1732 to give the English poor a fresh start. However, proprietor James Oglethorpe and his partners wanted to aid only the most "virtuous and industrious" poor. Very few debtors qualified, and the colony attracted few other settlers. By 1760 Georgia's European population numbered only some 6,000. The colony mainly served as a buffer between South Carolina's prosperous plantations and Spanish Florida.

■■ **Colonists came to the English colonies for religious and economic reasons. They built religious communities in New England, tobacco and rice plantations in the Chesapeake and in South Carolina, and small farms in Pennsylvania.**

THE FRENCH AND INDIAN WAR

Unlike Georgia, the populations of Great Britain's other colonies grew rapidly during the 18th century. Many colonists expanded into the frontier regions of New York, Massachusetts, Pennsylvania, Virginia, and North Carolina.

Conflicts arose, however, as colonists built farms on lands claimed by Indians and the French.

Both the English and the French often violated American Indian land rights. Both frequently battled American Indians to capture their lands. However, one group, the powerful **Iroquois League**—a confederation of tribes in New York and Pennsylvania formed in the 15th or 16th century—had maintained their land and independence. The league skillfully played the English and French against each other.

The French and English competition in North America stemmed from a worldwide struggle for empire. Overseas colonies were vitally important to France and England as sources of raw materials and as markets for European goods. France's North American territory, which stretched from northeastern Canada across the interior of the continent to the Gulf of Mexico, supplied precious furs. In 1749, when Virginia land speculators started to build a fort in disputed territory in the Ohio Valley, the French drove the Virginians off. The French completed the fort and named it Fort Duquesne (doo-KAYN).

The territorial conflict touched off the **French and Indian War** (1754–1763). The French won the early battles of the war. Britain's fortunes improved, however, when cabinet minister William Pitt assumed control of the war effort. His efforts paid off in July 1758, when the British captured Fort Louisbourg, effectively cutting off French supplies. Further British victories convinced the Iroquois to abandon their neutral stance and side with the British. Abandoned by their Indian allies in the Ohio Valley, French troops withdrew to Canada.

◄ **George Washington experienced his first taste of military service during the French and Indian War.**

Washington/Curtis/Lee Collection, Washington and Lee University, Lexington, Virginia

British forces followed, capturing Quebec in 1759 and Montreal the following year. With these defeats France lost the last of its Canadian holdings. Fighting dragged on for two more years in other parts of the world. In 1763 the Treaty of Paris officially ended all hostilities. The treaty granted Great Britain Canada and all French holdings east of the Mississippi except New Orleans. Spain, which had sided with the French, had earlier received France's vast Louisiana territory west of the Mississippi. By the terms of the treaty, Spain surrendered Florida to Britain.

■■ **Competition for the North American interior touched off the French and Indian War. The war cost France most of its North American holdings.**

SECTION 3 REVIEW

IDENTIFY and explain the significance of the following: Protestant Reformation, Spanish Armada, joint-stock companies, Puritans, Separatists, Mayflower Compact, Great Migration, commonwealth, freemen, indentured servants, Olaudah Equiano, Middle Passage, abolition, William Penn, Iroquois League, French and Indian War.

1. **MAIN IDEA** How did the English colonization process differ from the Spanish process?

2. **MAIN IDEA** For what reasons did settlers come to the English colonies in North America?

3. **CONTRASTING** How did the societies established by colonists in New England differ from the societies established in the Chesapeake and in South Carolina?

4. **WRITING TO DESCRIBE** Imagine you are one of the original colonists at Jamestown. Write a letter home to England, describing some of the challenges you have faced.

5. **LINKING HISTORY AND GEOGRAPHY** How did competition for land in North America cause conflicts between Britain and France? How did these conflicts end?

Rise of farming in Mexico.	Muhammad founds Islam.	Rise of Mississippian culture.	Prince Henry's navigation center established.		Bartolomeu Dias reaches Africa's southern tip.
			Crusades begin.		
c.8000 B.C.	A.D. 610	c.700	1096	1419	1488

WRITING A SUMMARY

Using the essential points of the chapter as a guide, write a summary of the chapter.

REVIEWING CHRONOLOGY

Number your paper 1 to 5. Study the time line above, and list the following events in the order in which they happened by writing the first next to 1, the second next to 2, and so on. Then complete the activity below.

1. Pueblo Revolt drives the Spanish from Santa Fe.
2. Bartolomeu Dias reaches Africa's southern tip.
3. Treaty of Paris signed.
4. Rise of Mississippian culture.
5. Jamestown established.

Linking History and Geography Pick two of the events above and explain how each illustrates one of the five themes of geography.

IDENTIFYING PEOPLE AND IDEAS

Explain the historical significance of each of the following people or terms.

1. Beringia
2. Qur'an
3. Renaissance
4. African diaspora
5. *encomienda*
6. Ferdinand Magellan
7. Friar Junípero Serra
8. Great Migration
9. Olaudah Equiano
10. Iroquois League

UNDERSTANDING MAIN IDEAS

1. Why did the Portuguese want to find a new route to Asia in the 15th century?
2. What territories in the Americas did Spain acquire following Columbus's voyages? What kinds of settlements were established in these territories?
3. How was the British government's role in colonization in the Americas less direct than the role played by the Spanish government?
4. How did American Indians respond to both Spanish and English colonization?

REVIEWING THEMES

1. **Geographic Diversity** What effects did geographical and environmental factors have on Native American cultures?
2. **Global Relations** What were the positive and negative results of the Columbian exchange?
3. **Cultural Diversity** How did the cultural backgrounds of the colonists affect the development of the English colonies in which they settled?

THINKING CRITICALLY

1. **Analyzing** How did Muslims influence cultural diffusion between Africa, Asia, and Europe?
2. **Synthesizing** Describe the various labor systems that were used by Spanish and English colonists in the Americas.
3. **Hypothesizing** How might North American territories have been divided differently in 1763 if France had won the French and Indian War?

STRATEGY FOR SUCCESS

Review the Skills Handbook entry on Identifying the Main Idea on page 748. Read the following excerpt from a 1705 study of American Indian culture. Then identify the main idea of the selection.

66 They [Native Americans] have on several accounts reason to lament [regret] the arrival of the Europeans, by whose means they seem to have lost their felicity [happiness] as well as their innocence. The English have taken away [a] great part of their country and consequently made everything less plenty amongst them. They have introduced drunkenness and luxury amongst them, which have multiplied their wants and put them up to desiring a thousand things they never dreamt of before. 99

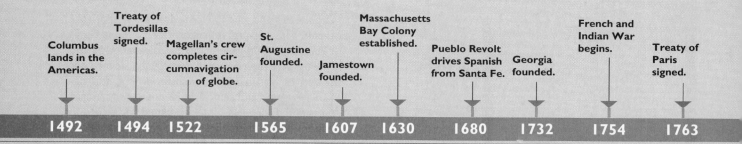

Columbus lands in the Americas.	Treaty of Tordesillas signed.	Magellan's crew completes circumnavigation of globe.	St. Augustine founded.	Jamestown founded.	Massachusetts Bay Colony established.	Pueblo Revolt drives Spanish from Santa Fe.	Georgia founded.	French and Indian War begins.	Treaty of Paris signed.
1492	1494	1522	1565	1607	1630	1680	1732	1754	1763

WRITING ABOUT HISTORY

Writing to Evaluate Write an essay about the introduction of slavery to the Americas. Be sure to include the effects of the slave trade on Africa as well as the effects of slavery on enslaved Africans.

Slaves loading tobacco barrels at a Virginia wharf

USING PRIMARY SOURCES

Read the following excerpt from a 17th-century Spanish judge's defense of Spanish treatment of Native Americans. Then write an essay summarizing the judge's arguments and evaluating how these arguments might be countered.

> *At each step they [critics] throw in our faces the fact that the Indians have been badly treated and that in many places they have completely disappeared. . . .*
>
> *In many places the Indians gave cause for their mistreatment or for war to be made against them, either because of their bestial [brutal] and savage customs or because of the excesses and treason that they attempted or committed against our people. . . .*
>
> *Moreover, it is not the Spaniards who have exterminated them, but their own vices and drunkenness or the earthquakes and repeated epidemics of smallpox and other diseases with which God in His mysterious wisdom has seen fit to reduce their numbers.* ""

LINKING HISTORY AND GEOGRAPHY

Study the map on page 5. Locate the culture area in which your community is found, and list the American Indian tribes who lived in your area in 1500. Then write down the influences of any of these tribes that still exist locally—either through place-names, artifacts, or customs.

BUILDING YOUR PORTFOLIO

Complete the following projects independently or cooperatively.

1. THE ECONOMY Imagine you are a geographer who specializes in patterns of world trade throughout history. Prepare a map that shows trade routes between Europe, Africa, Asia, and the Americas during the 1400s, 1500s, and 1600s. Draw symbols on the map to indicate major items of trade.

A trade card advertisement

2. CULTURAL DIVERSITY Imagine you are a museum researcher preparing an exhibit on cultural exchanges in the Americas. With drawings and captions, dramatic readings of first-person accounts, charts, or other suitable materials, illustrate some of the cultural exchanges that took place between American Indians, Africans, and Europeans.

EUROPEAN EXPLORATION AND SETTLEMENT

COLUMBUS'S landing introduced the Americas to the rest of the world, thus beginning a new era of exploration, trade, colonization, and cultural exchange. European explorers rushed west to search for new trade routes, seek riches, and stake out territories for the nations sponsoring them. In the 1500s the Spanish began settling North America. At the same time, other European nations—especially England and France—began claiming large areas of the continent. Nearly a century would pass, however, before the French and English successfully colonized North America. The communities the colonists founded developed in different ways, giving rise to distinctive societies.

Spain, England, and France sponsored most of the explorations of North America in the 16th and early 17th centuries. In general, the areas explored by each country were the areas that that country claimed and settled, as indicated by the maps below and at right. Spain explored and settled the southern and western parts of the continent; Britain explored and settled the eastern and northern regions; and France explored and settled the central and northeastern areas.

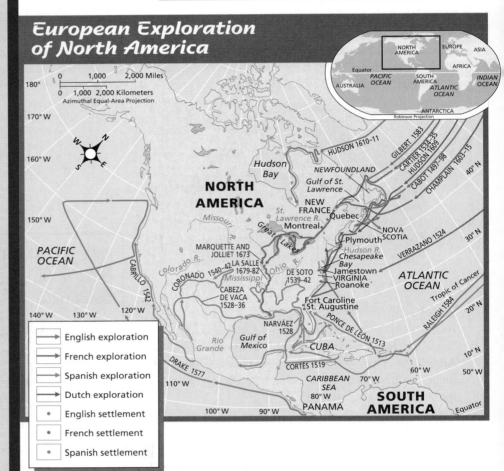

European Exploration of North America

Legend:
- English exploration
- French exploration
- Spanish exploration
- Dutch exploration
- English settlement
- French settlement
- Spanish settlement

Most of the 16th century explorers were inspired by Christopher Columbus's four round-trip voyages to the Americas between 1492 and 1504. On the final two voyages Columbus visited not only the Caribbean islands but also parts of Central and South America. Most of the lands Columbus and his crew saw became part of Spanish America.

Lands seen by Columbus and his crew

Columbus's Voyages

North America in 1754

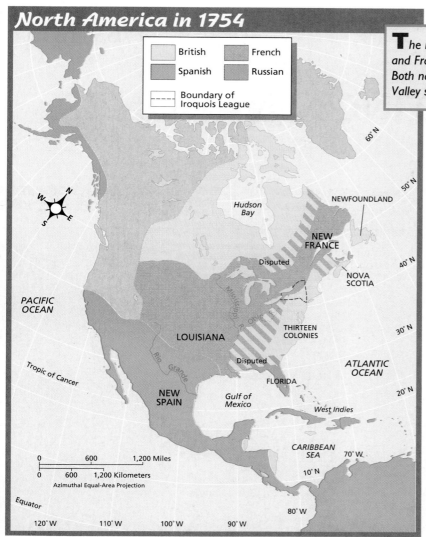

Legend:
- British
- French
- Spanish
- Russian
- – – – Boundary of Iroquois League

PACIFIC OCEAN

Hudson Bay

NEWFOUNDLAND

NEW FRANCE

Disputed

NOVA SCOTIA

60° N

50° N

40° N

30° N

20° N

10° N

Equator

LOUISIANA

THIRTEEN COLONIES

Disputed

NEW SPAIN

FLORIDA

Gulf of Mexico

West Indies

ATLANTIC OCEAN

CARIBBEAN SEA

Tropic of Cancer

Rio Grande

Mississippi R.

Ohio R.

0   600   1,200 Miles
0   600   1,200 Kilometers
Azimuthal Equal-Area Projection

120° W   110° W   100° W   90° W   80° W   70° W

The rivalry in Europe between Great Britain and France carried over to North America. Both nations' desire for the lands of the Ohio Valley sparked the French and Indian War.

The Thirteen Colonies

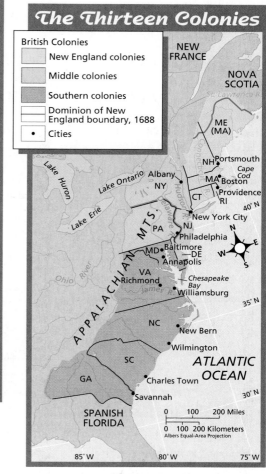

British Colonies
- New England colonies
- Middle colonies
- Southern colonies
- Dominion of New England boundary, 1688
- • Cities

NEW FRANCE

NOVA SCOTIA

St. Lawrence R.

Lake Huron

Lake Ontario

Lake Erie

Albany

ME (MA)

NH   Portsmouth

Cape Cod

MA   Boston

Providence RI

CT

NY

New York City

NJ

PA

Philadelphia

MD   Baltimore   DE

Annapolis

VA

Richmond

Chesapeake Bay

Williamsburg

James R.

APPALACHIAN MTS.

Hudson R.

Delaware R.

Ohio River

NC

New Bern

Wilmington

SC

GA

Charles Town

Savannah

ATLANTIC OCEAN

SPANISH FLORIDA

60° N
50° N
40° N
35° N
30° N

0   100   200 Miles
0   100   200 Kilometers
Albers Equal-Area Projection

85° W   80° W   75° W

Even within an area settled by a single European country, regional differences existed. For example, the diverse ethnic, economic, social, and religious backgrounds of the people in the 13 British colonies—as well as diverse geographical features—helped to create societies distinct from one another and from Great Britain.

Spanish North America in 1785

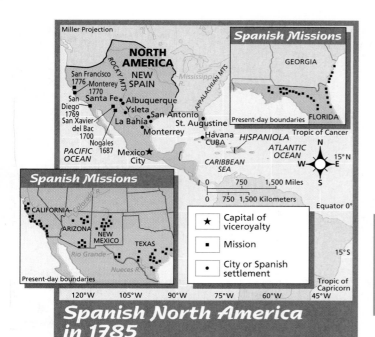

Miller Projection

NORTH AMERICA

NEW SPAIN

ROCKY MTS.

San Francisco 1776

Monterey 1770

San Diego 1769

Santa Fe

Albuquerque

Ysleta

San Xavier del Bac 1700

Nogales 1687

La Bahía

San Antonio

St. Augustine

Monterrey

Mexico City ★

Havana CUBA

HISPANIOLA

APPALACHIAN MTS.

Mississippi R.

PACIFIC OCEAN

ATLANTIC OCEAN

CARIBBEAN SEA

Tropic of Cancer

15° N

Equator 0°

15° S

Tropic of Capricorn

Spanish Missions

GEORGIA

FLORIDA

Present-day boundaries

Spanish Missions

CALIFORNIA

ARIZONA

NEW MEXICO

TEXAS

Colorado R.

Rio Grande

Nueces R.

Present-day boundaries

Legend:
- ★ Capital of viceroyalty
- ■ Mission
- • City or Spanish settlement

0   750   1,500 Miles
0   750   1,500 Kilometers

120° W   105° W   90° W   75° W   60° W   45° W

By the 1780s Spanish America was one of the largest colonial empires the world had ever known. Because of the vast size of the territory, colonists often organized their own settlements. The mission was one form of settlement established by the Spanish in the Americas.

CREATING A NATION

FOCUS

UNDERSTANDING THE MAIN IDEA

Colonial conflicts with the British erupted into a war that established American independence. A need for a strong central government to guide the new nation led to the framing of the Constitution of the United States of America. Domestic and foreign problems, however, plagued the country in its early years.

THEMES

■ **ECONOMIC DEVELOPMENT** How might the economic interests of one country conflict with those of another?

■ **CONSTITUTIONAL HERITAGE** How does the organization of government affect the way power is distributed and exercised?

■ **DEMOCRATIC VALUES** How might a democracy encourage the formation of political parties?

1775	1783	1788	1803	1812
▼	▼	▼	▼	▼
Revolutionary War begins.	**Treaty of Paris signed.**	**U.S. Constitution ratified.**	**U.S. completes Louisiana Purchase.**	**War declared against Great Britain.**

Through their victory in the French and Indian War, the British gained control of most of North America east of the Mississippi River. They now faced the tasks of governing, protecting, and financing their expanded empire.

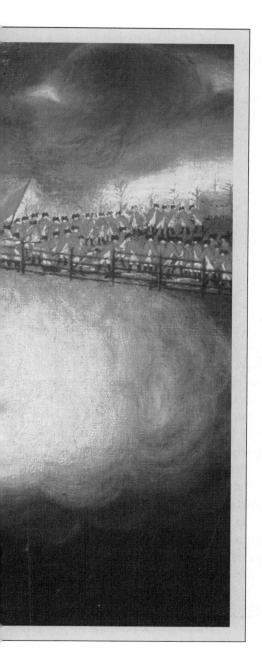

Battle of Princeton

Continental soldier

With the signing of the Treaty of Paris in 1763, Great Britain's future looked bright. Many people in Great Britain and elsewhere realized, however, that the British Empire faced new challenges. One of these observers, a French government official named Charles Gravier (grawv-yay) Comte de Vergennes (ver-ZHEN), believed that Great Britain's North American colonies would prove especially troublesome.

Mindful that France had lost its colonial claim in North America, Vergennes predicted a similar fate for Great Britain. "The American colonies stand no longer in need of England's protection," he said. "England," he continued, "will call on them to help contribute toward supporting the burden they have helped to bring on her, and they will answer by striking off all dependence."

Vergennes's prophecy would prove accurate. Thirteen years after his prediction, the British colonies along the Atlantic seaboard declared independence—and fought to win it. Although the fight was successful, the new nation faced a number of challenges. Establishing a workable form of government, easing domestic tensions, and resolving conflicts with foreign powers were among these challenges.

INDEPENDENCE!

FOCUS

- **Why did the Crown impose taxes on the colonists? How did the colonists react to these taxes?**
- **What actions did the First Continental Congress and the Second Continental Congress take?**
- **How did the Declaration of Independence justify America's break with Great Britain?**
- **How were the Americans able to defeat the British?**

Victory in the French and Indian War left Great Britain with a huge debt and more territory to govern and defend. When the British tried to make the American colonists help pay the costs of administering this expanded empire, the colonists protested. But colonial protests were unsuccessful, pushing the colonies to declare their independence, to fight for it, and, ultimately, to win it.

Colonial Williamsburg Foundation

Protests took many forms.

A RICH NEW TERRITORY

The Treaty of Paris of 1763 forced the French to give up their North American empire. With the stroke of a pen, the British gained control of Spanish Florida, Canada, and the land between the Appalachian Mountains and the Mississippi River. It was a rich land. Indian agent and trader George Croghan, who traveled through the western territory in 1765, noted in his diary that "a good hunter, without much fatigue to himself, could here daily supply one hundred men with meat."

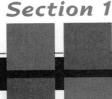

▲ **Settlers and traders to the Ohio Valley saw many colorful and unusual species of flora, such as this wild honeysuckle painted by naturalist artist Edwin Whitefield.**

Such glowing reports drew pioneer farmers and speculators to the region. Ignoring Native American claims to the land, they demanded that the territory be opened for settlement. But Native Americans, whose ways of life had already been disrupted by European trade, resented the flow of settlers into their lands.

When a series of Indian uprisings convinced British authorities that they could not effectively protect British settlers on the frontier, Great Britain issued the **Proclamation of 1763**, barring settlement west of the Appalachian Mountains. But the proclamation was difficult to enforce. Land-hungry colonists resented the measure and continued to stream into the territory.

TAXATION AND PROTEST

The royal proclamation was not the only British policy the colonists resented. They were also angered by Parliament's efforts to make them pay part of the costs of "protecting and securing" the

▲ This 1766 British cartoon celebrates the repeal of the Stamp Act. As members of the British government carry the dead act in a coffin, background ships show that trade with America is already resuming.

frontier. One of the first taxes Parliament passed to raise revenue in the colonies was the **Sugar Act** of 1764, which set an import tax on foreign sugar, molasses, and several other items. Then in 1765 Parliament passed the **Stamp Act**. Far more sweeping than the Sugar Act, the Stamp Act levied a tax on all printed matter such as newspapers, playing cards, and legal documents.

Because the colonists had no direct representation in Parliament, they felt that they were being taxed unjustly. A series of resolutions passed by the Virginia House of Burgesses in 1765 asserted that "the taxation of the people by themselves" or by their representatives was "the distinguishing characteristick of British freedom."

To protest the Stamp Act, colonial merchants resolved not to buy or import British goods. Besides this boycott, colonists also used demonstrations, petitions, public meetings, and pamphlets to rally support against the taxes. Though most protests were peaceful, some did turn violent. One of the most violent demonstrations occurred in Boston on a hot August night in 1765, when a mob wrecked a building belonging to a stamp agent and then beheaded an effigy—a crude likeness—of the agent.

The colonial protests and the boycott of British goods persuaded Parliament to repeal the Stamp Act in March 1766, but Parliament's efforts to raise revenue in the colonies continued. In 1767 Parliament passed the **Townshend Acts**, which imposed an import tax on such common items as tea, lead, glass, and dyes. The law, as well as British attempts to enforce it, aroused powerful opposition. In February 1768 the Massachusetts

legislature drafted a letter attacking taxation without representation. The British government responded by dissolving the Massachusetts assembly. This only served to fuel more protests.

In 1768 British troops were sent to Boston to quiet the protests. But tensions exploded into one violent confrontation after another. On March 5, 1770, an angry crowd gathered and began to harass a small group of British soldiers. When one soldier's gun accidentally discharged, the others opened fire on the crowd. Five colonists, including Crispus Attucks—a sailor and an escaped slave—ultimately died as a result of what colonists soon dubbed the **Boston Massacre**.

Although a partial repeal of the Townshend Acts quieted the general unrest, the calm was short-lived. Another key protest erupted in Boston in 1773, after Parliament passed an act that American merchants feared would place them at a disadvantage selling tea. On December 16, a well-organized group of colonists dressed as Mohawk Indians boarded British tea ships in Boston Harbor and dumped 90,000 pounds of tea into the water.

Many colonists cheered the **Boston Tea Party**, but British officials were furious. In 1774 Parliament passed the Coercive Acts, four laws designed to punish Massachusetts and reinforce

▶ **Crispus Attucks**

▼ **Boston silversmith Paul Revere engraved and printed** *The Boston Massacre*, **which depicts the British as the aggressors.**

British control over the colonies. The colonists referred to these laws as the **Intolerable Acts** and regarded them as part of a growing pattern of oppression by the British.

■■ **The British government taxed the colonies to finance its empire. But colonists protested "taxation without representation" through petitions, boycotts, and demonstrations.**

MOVE TOWARD INDEPENDENCE

In 1774, delegates from 12 colonies gathered at the **First Continental Congress** in Philadelphia to discuss their grievances. While expressing loyalty to the British crown, the Congress's final resolution outlined the colonists' rights as British subjects and asserted the people's right to the "exclusive power of legislation in their several provincial legislatures." To put teeth in their demands, the colonists also called for a ban on all trade with Great Britain.

For King George III, the Continental Congress was the last straw. He declared the New England governments to be "in a State of Rebellion," and Parliament ordered General Thomas Gage to reassert royal authority. On April 18, 1775, Gage began a march to Concord, Massachusetts, to seize rebel supplies. But Paul Revere and William Dawes—later joined by Samuel Prescott—galloped ahead of Gage to warn the Patriots that "the British are coming!" As a result, the colonial forces met the British in Lexington, on the way to Concord. Suddenly, someone—each side accused the other—fired the "shot heard round the world." A barrage of British gunfire followed, leaving 8 colonists dead and 10 wounded.

The British marched on to Concord, destroyed the Patriot supplies, and started back to Boston. But from behind stone

◀ **The Second Continental Congress took place in Carpenter's Hall in Philadelphia.**

walls, Patriots fired steadily at the British troops, whose traditional marching formations made them easy targets. While the Patriots suffered fewer than 100 casualties, British casualties numbered 273. A humbled British officer wrote: "Whoever looks upon them [the Patriots] as an irregular mob will find himself much mistaken."

With the news of the battles at Lexington and Concord on everyone's lips, the **Second Continental Congress** opened in Philadelphia in May. By June, the delegates had agreed to establish the Continental Army and chose George Washington of Virginia to command it.

BIOGRAPHY Born February 22, 1732, George Washington first worked as a surveyor, later assuming control of the family's large Virginia plantation, Mount Vernon. Washington acquired military experience and a reputation for bravery while fighting for the British in the French and Indian War. He also served twice as a delegate to the Continental Congress. With the colonies preparing for war, Washington devoted himself and his fortune to the "glorious cause" of American independence.

George Washington

■■ **The First Continental Congress demanded the restoration of colonists' rights; the Second established the Continental Army.**

One of the first battles the Patriots fought was the **Battle of Bunker Hill**. On June 17, 1775, New England militiamen dug in atop two hills overlooking Boston Harbor—Bunker Hill and Breed's Hill—awaiting an onslaught of British troops. To save ammunition, an American commander ordered his men: "Don't one of you fire until you see the whites of their eyes." Although the British took both hills after mounting three assaults, they suffered 1,054 casualties. Fewer than 450 Americans were killed or injured.

Even after the battle, conservatives worked to avoid a permanent break with Great Britain. They persuaded the Continental Congress to send a final plea to George III. This plea—the Olive Branch Petition—professed the colonists' loyalty and asked for the king's help in ending the conflict. The king refused the petition. Instead he ordered the Royal Navy to blockade all shipping to the colonies and sent more soldiers there as well.

INDEPENDENCE DECLARED

Although fighting had begun, most colonists insisted that they were merely resisting unjust acts of Parliament, not waging war. But to others, the time was ripe for independence. Thomas Paine's pamphlet *Common Sense,* published in January 1776, urged revolution. "The period of debate is closed," declared the pamphlet. "Every thing that is right or reasonable pleads for separation. . . . 'TIS TIME TO PART."

In June 1776 the Second Continental Congress appointed Thomas Jefferson, a Virginia lawyer and planter, and four others to draft a **Declaration of Independence**. On July 4 the Congress formally adopted the Declaration. The Declaration's immediate purpose was to win support for independence, both at home and abroad. To undermine loyalty to George III, the document listed his misdeeds. It also asserted that governments exist to secure their citizens' rights:

66 We hold these truths to be self-evident, that all men are created equal, that they are endowed by their Creator with certain unalienable Rights, that among these are Life, Liberty, and the pursuit of Happiness. 99

Furthermore, the Declaration claimed, "whenever any Form of Government becomes destructive of these ends, it is the Right of the People to alter or to abolish it." Those who signed the document knew they were now traitors in the eyes of the Crown. The price for failing to win independence might well be imprisonment or even death.

■■ **The Declaration of Independence asserted the right of people to overthrow an unjust government.**

COMMENTARY

Independence for Whom?

Thomas Jefferson's words "all men are created equal" have been a source of controversy. What exactly did he mean? Remember that 18th-century America, like Europe, was full of social, political, and economic inequalities. The delegates to the Continental Congress, as citizens of their times, would not have viewed issues of justice as we do today. Besides, they were seeking to justify a political, not a social, revolution.

Nevertheless, the Declaration and the revolution it symbolized had social consequences. Many women organized and participated in protests. During the war women took over the work of the absent men or cared for troops. As a result, some women argued for a greater voice in politics. "I desire you would remember the ladies," Abigail Adams appealed to her husband, John, a delegate to the Continental Congress. "Be more generous and favorable to them than your ancestors." John Adams, like most men of the day, did not agree.

Whether the delegates intended the words men and mankind to include women is debatable, but most certainly they did not intend the words to apply to slaves. This does not mean, however, that all of the delegates supported slavery. In Jefferson's original draft, he accused the king of violating the "sacred rights of life and liberty" of blacks "who never offended him, captivating and carrying them into slavery." But some of the southern delegates objected, and the passage was stricken from the final document. Thus America's leaders, for the first but not the last time, sidestepped the explosive issue of slavery.

▶ **Mum Bett, a Massachusetts slave, believed that the words "all men are created equal" should apply to her. In 1781 she successfully sued for her freedom. Her lawyer's daughter, Susan Sedgwick, painted this portrait of her.**

The Declaration of Independence

Thomas Jefferson wrote the first draft of the Declaration in a little more than two weeks.

In the first paragraph, the signers are justifying why they are separating from Great Britain.

impel: force

endowed: provided

Natural or "unalienable" rights (the rights to life, liberty, and the pursuit of happiness) cannot be taken away. The signers supported John Locke's view that people created governments to protect their natural rights. A government, therefore, must have the consent of the governed. If a government abuses its powers, it is the right as well as the duty of the people to do away with that government.

usurpations: wrongful seizures of power

despotism: unlimited power

tyranny: oppressive power exerted by a government
candid: fair

In Congress, July 4, 1776 The unanimous Declaration of the thirteen united States of America,

When in the Course of human events, it becomes necessary for one people to dissolve the political bands which have connected them with another, and to assume among the powers of the earth, the separate and equal station to which the Laws of Nature and of Nature's God entitle them, a decent respect to the opinions of mankind requires that they should declare the causes which impel them to the separation.

We hold these truths to be self-evident, that all men are created equal, that they are endowed by their Creator with certain unalienable Rights, that among these are Life, Liberty, and the pursuit of Happiness.

That to secure these rights, Governments are instituted among Men, deriving their just powers from the consent of the governed,

That whenever any Form of Government becomes destructive of these ends, it is the Right of the People to alter or to abolish it, and to institute new Government, laying its foundation on such principles and organizing its powers in such form, as to them shall seem most likely to effect their Safety and Happiness. Prudence, indeed, will dictate that Governments long established should not be changed for light and transient causes; and accordingly all experience hath shown, that mankind are more disposed to suffer, while evils are sufferable, than to right themselves by abolishing the forms to which they are accustomed. But when a long train of abuses and usurpations, pursuing invariably the same Object evinces a design to reduce them under absolute Despotism, it is their right, it is their duty, to throw off such Government, and to provide new Guards for their future security.

Such has been the patient sufferance of these Colonies; and such is now the necessity which constrains them to alter their former Systems of Government. The history of the present King of Great Britain is a history of repeated injuries and usurpations, all having in direct object the establishment of an absolute Tyranny over these States. To prove this, let Facts be submitted to a candid world.

He has refused his Assent to Laws, the most wholesome and necessary for the public good.

He has forbidden his Governors to pass Laws of immediate and pressing importance, unless suspended in their operation till his Assent should be obtained; and when so suspended, he has utterly neglected to attend to them.

He has refused to pass other Laws for the accommodation of large districts of people, unless those people would relinquish the right of Representation in the Legislature, a right inestimable to them and formidable to tyrants only.

He has called together legislative bodies at places unusual, uncomfortable, and distant from the depository of their public Records, for the sole purpose of fatiguing them into compliance with his measures.

He has dissolved Representative Houses repeatedly, for opposing with manly firmness his invasions on the rights of the people.

He has refused for a long time, after such dissolutions, to cause others to be elected; whereby the Legislative powers, incapable of Annihilation, have returned to the People at large for their exercise; the State remaining in the meantime exposed to all the dangers of invasion from without, and convulsions within.

He has endeavored to prevent the population of these States; for that purpose obstructing the Laws for Naturalization of Foreigners; refusing to pass others to encourage their migrations hither, and raising the conditions of new Appropriations of Lands.

He has obstructed the Administration of Justice, by refusing his Assent to Laws for establishing Judiciary powers.

He has made Judges dependent on his Will alone, for the tenure of their offices, and the amount and payment of their salaries.

He has erected a multitude of New Offices, and sent hither swarms of Officers to harass our people, and eat out their substance.

Here the Declaration lists the charges that the colonists had against King George III. How does the language of the list appeal to people's emotions?

relinquish: release, yield

inestimable: priceless

formidable: causing dread

Why do you think the king had his legislatures in the colonies meet in places that were hard to reach?

annihilation: destruction

convulsions: violent disturbances

naturalization of foreigners: the process by which foreign-born persons become citizens

appropriations of land: setting aside land for settlement

tenure: term

a multitude of: many

◀ **The Continental Congress is shown voting for independence in this painting by Robert Pine and Edward Savage.**

What wrongful acts does the
Declaration state have been committed
by the king and the British Parliament?

The "neighboring Province" that is
referred to here is Quebec.
arbitrary: not based on law
render: make

abdicated: given up

foreign mercenaries: soldiers hired
to fight for a country not their own

perfidy: violation of trust

insurrections: rebellions

petitioned for redress: asked formally
for a correction of wrongs

He has kept among us, in times of peace, Standing Armies without the Consent of our legislatures.

He has affected to render the Military independent of and superior to the Civil power.

He has combined with others to subject us to a jurisdiction foreign to our constitution, and unacknowledged by our laws; giving his Assent to their Acts of pretended Legislation:

For quartering large bodies of armed troops among us:

For protecting them, by a mock Trial, from punishment for any Murders which they should commit on the Inhabitants of these States:

For cutting off our Trade with all parts of the world:

For imposing Taxes on us without our Consent:

For depriving us in many cases, of the benefits of Trial by Jury:

For transporting us beyond Seas to be tried for pretended offences:

For abolishing the free System of English Laws in a neighboring Province, establishing therein an Arbitrary government, and enlarging its Boundaries so as to render it at once an example and fit instrument for introducing the same absolute rule into these Colonies:

For taking away our Charters, abolishing our most valuable Laws, and altering fundamentally the Forms of our Governments:

For suspending our own Legislatures, and declaring themselves invested with power to legislate for us in all cases whatsoever.

He has abdicated Government here, by declaring us out of his Protection and waging War against us.

He has plundered our seas, ravaged our Coasts, burnt our towns, and destroyed the Lives of our people.

He is at this time transporting large Armies of foreign Mercenaries to complete the works of death, desolation and tyranny, already begun with circumstances of Cruelty & perfidy scarcely paralleled in the most barbarous ages, and totally unworthy the Head of a civilized nation.

He has constrained our fellow Citizens taken Captive on the high Seas to bear Arms against their Country, to become the executioners of their friends and Brethren, or to fall themselves by their Hands.

He has excited domestic insurrections among us, and has endeavored to bring on the inhabitants of our frontiers, the merciless Indian Savages, whose known rule of warfare, is an undistinguished destruction of all ages, sexes and conditions.

In every stage of these Oppressions We have Petitioned for Redress in the most humble terms: Our repeated Petitions have been answered only by repeated injury. A Prince, whose character is thus marked by every act which may define a Tyrant, is unfit to be the ruler of a free people.

Nor have We been wanting in attentions to our British brethren. We have warned them from time to time of attempts by their legislature to extend an unwarrantable jurisdiction over us. We have reminded them of the circumstances of our emigration and settlement here. We have appealed to their native justice and magnanimity, and we have conjured them by the ties of our common kindred to disavow these usurpations, which would inevitably interrupt our connections and correspondence. They too have been deaf to the voice of justice and of consanguinity. We must, therefore, acquiesce in the necessity, which denounces our Separation, and hold them, as we hold the rest of mankind, Enemies in War, in Peace Friends.

We, therefore, the Representatives of the united States of America, in General Congress, Assembled, appealing to the Supreme Judge of the world for the rectitude of our intentions, do, in the Name, and by Authority of the good People of these Colonies, solemnly publish and declare, That these United Colonies are, and of Right ought to be Free and Independent States; that they are Absolved from all Allegiance to the British Crown, and that all political connection between them and the State of Great Britain, is and ought to be totally dissolved; and that as Free and Independent States, they have full Power to levy War, conclude Peace, contract Alliances, establish Commerce, and to do all other Acts and Things which Independent States may of right do.

And for the support of this Declaration, with a firm reliance on the protection of divine Providence, we mutually pledge to each other our Lives, our Fortunes and our sacred Honor.

unwarrantable jurisdiction: unjustified authority

magnanimity: generous spirit

conjured: called upon

consanguinity: common ancestry

acquiesce: consent to

rectitude: rightness

In this paragraph, the signers state their actual declaration of independence. What rights would the new United States of America now have as an independent nation?

Congress adopted the final draft of the Declaration of Independence on July 4, 1776. A formal copy, written on parchment paper, was signed on August 2, 1776.

John Hancock	Benjamin Harrison	Lewis Morris
Button Gwinnett	Thomas Nelson, Jr.	Richard Stockton
Lyman Hall	Francis Lightfoot Lee	John Witherspoon
George Walton	Carter Braxton	Francis Hopkinson
William Hooper	Robert Morris	John Hart
Joseph Hewes	Benjamin Rush	Abraham Clark
John Penn	Benjamin Franklin	Josiah Bartlett
Edward Rutledge	John Morton	William Whipple
Thomas Heyward, Jr.	George Clymer	Samuel Adams
Thomas Lynch, Jr.	James Smith	John Adams
Arthur Middleton	George Taylor	Robert Treat Paine
Samuel Chase	James Wilson	Elbridge Gerry
William Paca	George Ross	Stephen Hopkins
Thomas Stone	Caesar Rodney	William Ellery
Charles Carroll	George Read	Roger Sherman
of Carrollton	Thomas McKean	Samuel Huntington
George Wythe	William Floyd	William Williams
Richard Henry Lee	Philip Livingston	Oliver Wolcott
Thomas Jefferson	Francis Lewis	Matthew Thornton

THE WAR FOR INDEPENDENCE

To declare independence was one thing: to fight for it was another. The lack of a central government hindered the American war effort. The Second Continental Congress, with little real authority, could ask the states for supplies, troops, and funds, but it could not force them to comply.

Fighting the war. Without a strong government behind it, the Continental Army faced constant supply shortages. As a result, Washington's troops suffered, enduring hunger and bitter winters. In addition, unsanitary conditions led to dysentery, which caused thousands of deaths.

Washington also faced a shortage of troops. Recruiting went well only after victories, and the soldier-farmers often deserted at planting or harvesting time. And because enlistments were short-term, the training of troops was especially difficult. But despite these problems, the Patriot forces enjoyed two key advantages: they fought on familiar ground, and they were inspired by a revolutionary cause.

Among the troops were about 5,000 African Americans. Numerous black soldiers, such as Salem Poor and Peter Salem, two of many African Americans who fought at Bunker Hill, received official recognition for their courage. Hundreds more served bravely but anonymously. African Americans served the war effort in another important way as well: they provided the slave labor used in the production of tobacco. Tobacco, in turn, provided the colonies with a key source of funding for the revolution.

A few Patriot women also fought in the war, while others undertook dangerous missions as spies or messengers. Many other women accompanied the troops and worked as laundresses, nurses, and cooks. But most stayed behind and supported the war effort by distributing medical supplies, making uniforms, manufacturing bullets, and managing businesses and farms.

Both the British and the Patriots tried to recruit members of the Iroquois League. After holding a council to discuss the war in 1777, the League split over the issue. Some tribes chose to join the British; others sided with the Patriots.

The war in the North. In the summer of 1776, British general William Howe sailed into New York Harbor and easily routed Washington's troops in New York City. Thinking the war was almost won, Howe prepared to celebrate Christmas, taking few precautions against a possible Patriot attack.

But Washington and his troops ignored the customary winter halt in fighting. On Christmas night they set out to attack the foe at Trenton, New Jersey. Surprising the enemy, the Patriots quickly won a stunning victory. British plans to end the war quickly were, as one London official wrote, "blasted by the unhappy affair at Trenton."

Still in control of Canada to the north and New York City to the south, the British planned to cut off New England from the other rebel colonies. What the British did not realize—or ignored—

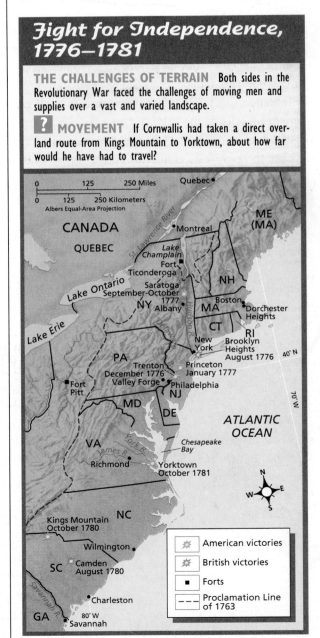

Fight for Independence, 1776–1781

THE CHALLENGES OF TERRAIN Both sides in the Revolutionary War faced the challenges of moving men and supplies over a vast and varied landscape.

? MOVEMENT If Cornwallis had taken a direct overland route from Kings Mountain to Yorktown, about how far would he have had to travel?

was that their lines of attack crossed lakes, swamps, hills, and forests teeming with Patriots. British strategy failed, and in the fall of 1777 the outfoxed and outmanned British suffered defeat at the **Battle of Saratoga**.

Saratoga was a turning point for the Americans. Encouraged by the victory, the French signed a formal alliance with the Patriots in February 1778. French aid provided Americans with money, supplies, a fleet, and troops. By 1780 Spain and the Netherlands were also aiding the Patriots.

◀ **Bernardo de Gálvez, the Spanish governor of Louisiana, defeated the British at Baton Rouge, Natchez, Mobile, and Pensacola.**

The Historic New Orleans Collection, Museum/Research Center

The war in the South.

Late in 1778 the British focused their attacks on the southern colonies, where they anticipated strong support from **Loyalists** (also known as Tories)—colonists who remained loyal to Great Britain. After crushing the Americans in the Battle of Camden in South Carolina in 1780, British and Loyalist forces under General Charles Cornwallis marched toward North Carolina.

Patriot commander Nathanael Greene stopped the British advances. Greene was a master of the tactics of **guerrilla warfare**—wearing down the enemy in surprise hit-and-run skirmishes while avoiding direct battles. The use of guerrilla tactics allowed the Patriots to make the most of their limited numbers and frustrated British hopes of winning in the South.

During the summer of 1781, Cornwallis moved his army into Yorktown, Virginia, where he had access to the British fleet and supplies. When the

French fleet moved to cut off this access, Washington's army, along with a French force, rushed south to Yorktown, completing the trap. In October, after attempts to break out failed, Cornwallis admitted defeat at the **Battle of Yorktown**. The British surrendered as their band played "The World Turned Upside Down."

■■ **Familiarity with the terrain, unconventional tactics, and European support helped the Patriots defeat the British.**

In the peace talks that followed the surrender, American negotiators won generous terms. The **Treaty of Paris**, signed on September 3, 1783, granted the United States independence. It also gave the new nation the land from the Atlantic coast westward to the Mississippi River and from the Great Lakes south to Florida.

SECTION 1 REVIEW

IDENTIFY and explain the significance of the following: Proclamation of 1763, Townshend Acts, Crispus Attucks, Boston Massacre, Boston Tea Party, Intolerable Acts, George Washington, Battle of Bunker Hill, Thomas Paine, Declaration of Independence, Battle of Saratoga, Loyalists, guerrilla warfare, Battle of Yorktown, Treaty of Paris.

LOCATE and explain the importance of the following: Trenton, New Jersey

1. **MAIN IDEA** What was the purpose of the Sugar Act and the Stamp Act? What reaction did these measures provoke?

2. **MAIN IDEA** How did the First and Second Continental Congresses respond to British actions?

3. **MAIN IDEA** What arguments did the Declaration of Independence offer in support of revolution?

4. **WRITING TO PERSUADE** Imagine you are a delegate to the Second Continental Congress. Write a letter to the government of France encouraging the French to aid the Patriots.

5. **ASSESSING CONSEQUENCES** British soldiers were well trained in traditional military procedures and tactics. How might this have been a disadvantage in the Revolutionary War?

FROM CONFEDERATION TO FEDERAL UNION

FOCUS

■ What were the weaknesses of the Articles of Confederation? What problems did these weaknesses cause?

■ What issues threatened the framing and ratification of the Constitution?

■ What are the major provisions of the Constitution?

Great Seal of the Supreme Court

*D*uring the war the colonies replaced their royal charters with republican constitutions. The Continental Congress then drafted the Articles of Confederation to guide the new nation. Soon after the Revolution, however, economic problems and political unrest led the Congress to call for revision of the Articles. In response, the Constitutional Convention drafted the Constitution of the United States of America, a blueprint for a flexible and enduring system of government.

THE ARTICLES OF CONFEDERATION

The American Revolution brought an end to monarchical rule in America, leaving a void in place of the government. To fill this void, the Second Continental Congress advised the colonies "under the authority of the people" to form new governments. Between 1776 and 1780 all of the states ratified new constitutions or revised their royal charters.

To form the new governments, the state legislatures relied on republican theory. A **republic** is a form of government in which political leaders receive from the citizens the authority to make and enforce laws. Despite differences in economy, geography, and population, all of the states adopted similar constitutions, defining executive power and voting rights.

Many states also took steps to separate church and state. Before the Revolution, some colonies had collected taxes to support official churches. But many people opposed this close relationship between the government and one particular religion. In 1779 Thomas Jefferson drafted the Virginia Statute for Religious Freedom, declaring that "No man shall be compelled to . . . support any religious worship. . . . All men shall be free to profess their . . . opinion in matters of religion." By 1833 all of the states had forbidden the establishment of official state churches supported by tax dollars.

A plan for confederation.

The state constitutions established frameworks of government for each of the former colonies, but no

◀ **Many American statesmen used the political theories of John Locke when framing state constitutions.**

such framework existed on the national level. To secure national unity, the Continental Congress knew it had to create a plan for a central government. On July 12, 1776, a committee of the Congress presented the **Articles of Confederation** to the other congressional delegates. The Articles created a confederation, or an alliance, of states while guaranteeing each state its "sovereignty, freedom, and independence."

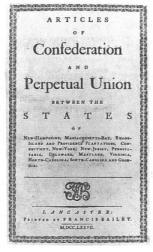

▲ **Articles of Confederation cover**

The Articles authorized Congress—in which each state had one vote—to borrow and coin money, conduct foreign affairs, and settle disputes between the states. In addition, Congress could ask, but not compel, the states to contribute money to the central government and to provide recruits for the military. Most powers, however, were retained by the states, who were willing to join in a loose union but were reluctant to give up much authority to a national government. By 1781 all of the states had agreed to enter the Confederation.

The problem of land.
The 13 states were now officially "The United States of America." But a problem remained: who would control the land between the Appalachian Mountains and the Mississippi River? To regulate disposal of the land, Congress passed the **Land Ordinance of 1785**, which marked off the land into townships. Each township was 6 miles square and divided into 36 sections of 640 acres. The ordinance permitted the cash sale of 35 of the sections but reserved one for the establishment of a school.

Then in 1787, Congress enacted the **Northwest Ordinance** to provide for governing the Northwest Territory. This area extended north of the Ohio River to the Great Lakes and west of Pennsylvania to the Mississippi River. The ordinance also outlined the steps to statehood, reflecting Congress's intent that states would be carved out of the Northwest Territory. Besides ensuring eventual self-rule in the territory, the ordinance guaranteed settlers their basic civil rights and banned slavery in the territory.

Weaknesses in the Confederation.
The land ordinances established a pattern of land settlement for the next 75 years and marked an important achievement for the Confederation. But Congress could point to few other noteworthy accomplishments. On paper the Confederation government enjoyed broad powers, but in reality it was weak. Proposed changes to the Articles needed the consent of all 13 states, and major legislation needed the approval of at least 9 states. Agreements were hard to reach because northern and southern delegates often had conflicting interests.

The government also had financial problems. Congress desperately needed cash to pay the war debt. But it could not tax the people directly; it could only ask the states for funds that some were reluctant to provide. During the war Congress had responded to the revenue shortage by printing paper money, which led to **inflation**, or an increase in prices. By 1781 people needed 100 paper dollars to purchase a product worth a dollar in gold. The

▼ **The Continental Congress had authorized states to print paper money to finance the Revolution. By 1779 more than $241 million in paper dollars, called "Continentals," had been issued. The dollars shown here were printed in Philadelphia in 1779.**

Confederation's economic worries multiplied in 1786, when the nation experienced a **depression**, a sharp drop in business activity accompanied by rising unemployment.

■■ The limitations on congressional power under the Articles of Confederation caused serious economic problems.

Shays's Rebellion. The weak Confederation also proved unable to help farmers, who had been particularly hard hit by the war and its aftermath. The depression left farmers with fewer markets in which to sell their goods and no access to credit. They also had little money to pay their debts to merchants for equipment and other goods.

In Massachusetts the merchant-controlled legislature imposed a heavy tax on land and began seizing property if the tax was not paid. Outraged farmers protested to the legislature; when the legislature did not address the issue, the farmers rebelled. Under the leadership of such men as Daniel Shays, a former Revolutionary War captain, angry farmers took up arms to defend their property rights and political representation in what became known as **Shays's Rebellion**.

▲ This 1884 painting by Howard Pyle shows Daniel Shays and his men taking possession of a courthouse.

In January 1787, Shays and some 1,200 farmers attempted to seize the federal arsenal in Springfield, Massachusetts. But when the militia killed four of the farmers, Shays's men fled. By the end of February, the militia had crushed the rebellion. Yet despite Shays's defeat, the rebellion raised doubts about the national government's ability to deal with civil unrest. As a result many people who had previously objected to a strong central government began calling for new powers for the Confederation.

DRAFTING AND RATIFYING THE CONSTITUTION

With the weaknesses of the Confederation becoming more and more apparent, congressional leaders issued a call for a **Constitutional Convention** to strengthen the government. The proceedings began in Philadelphia in May 1787.

Although charged by Congress to revise the Articles of Confederation, some delegates believed that the Articles should be replaced with a new plan of government. One such plan was James Madison's **Virginia Plan**. This plan shifted political power away from the states and toward the central government, reflecting Madison's belief that the nation's survival depended on **federalism**—the division of powers between a strong central government and the state governments. The plan gave the federal legislature vast powers, such as the rights to overturn state laws and to tax the states.

Compromise at the convention. A dispute quickly arose over the number of representatives each state could send to the legislature. States with large populations naturally favored representation based on population. But states with small populations insisted on an equal number of representatives for each state.

To balance the interests of the large and small states, a compromise was fashioned. This **Great Compromise** proposed a two-house, or bicameral, legislature. Each state, regardless of size, would have an equal voice in the upper house. In the lower house, representation would be according to population. The delegates narrowly approved this proposal, ending what Madison later described as "the most serious and threatening excitement" of the convention.

The delegates resolved one dispute only to see several others arise. Conflict between small states and large states gave way to conflict between northern and southern states as delegates debated whether slaves should be counted as part of a state's population to determine representation. In the end, delegates accepted the **Three-Fifths Compromise**, which counted three fifths of the slave population in determining state population.

Northern and southern delegates also clashed over control of commerce. Northern delegates favored giving the national government the power to regulate all of the nation's trade. But the southern economy depended on exports, and southerners feared that if the national government imposed **tariffs**, or taxes, on exports, sales would be hurt. Another compromise resolved the issue—Congress would be able to levy tariffs on imports but not on exports.

Once again, however, problems arose. Planters now worried that Congress might use its powers to tax imports to restrict or abolish the slave trade. Bowing to southern pressure, convention delegates voted to permit the slave trade until the end of 1807. They also gave slaveholders the right to pursue runaway slaves across state lines.

With these conflicts resolved, delegates began drafting the Constitution on July 26, 1787. After weeks of hammering out the details, the final document was ready for the delegates' signatures on September 17, 1787. The Constitution then went to the states for ratification.

The Federalists and the Antifederalists.

To win ratification, the Constitution required the approval of 9 of the 13 states. Most convention delegates hoped for unanimous approval as a show of national unity. But when local newspapers printed copies of the Constitution, many Americans were shocked by what they read. They

▲ This 1788 woodcut commemorates the ratification of the Constitution.

expected a revision of the Articles; what they saw was a new framework of government. Citizens soon divided over the issue of ratification.

One group, the **Federalists**, favored ratification. Wealthy merchants, planters, and lawyers generally were Federalists. They advocated a strong national government that would assure a sound currency and protect property rights. Many Americans who were not wealthy also supported the Constitution, believing that a strong national government would provide stability and security against political unrest like Shays's Rebellion. As one Massachusetts farmer explained:

> ❝ I have lived in a part of the country where I have learned the worth of good government by the lack of it. There was a black cloud of rebellion that rose in the east last winter and spread over the west. . . . Now when I saw this Constitution, I found it was a cure for these disorders. ❞

The other group, called **Antifederalists** by their opponents, opposed ratification. They believed that a powerful national government would destroy states' rights and that the concentration of power in a central government violated the principle of liberty that had guided the Revolution.

▶ The Pennsylvania Packet, and Daily Advertiser was one of several newspapers that carried the full text of the Constitution on September 19, 1787. The preamble to the Constitution is shown here.

The Pennsylvania Packet, and Daily Advertiser.

[Price Four-Pence.]   WEDNESDAY, SEPTEMBER 19, 1787.   [No. 2690.]

WE, the People of the United States, in order to form a more perfect Union, establish Justice, insure domestic Tranquility, provide for the common Defence, promote the General Welfare, and secure the Blessings of Liberty to Ourselves and our Posterity, do ordain and establish this Constitution for the United States of America.

The question of federalism versus states' rights was at the heart of the ratification struggle. Another crucial issue was individual rights. Unlike most state constitutions, the U.S. Constitution did not have a bill of rights. Some citizens, such as Amos Singletary of Massachusetts, feared that the Constitution would take away individual rights:

> 66 We contended [fought] with Great Britain . . . because they claimed a right to tax us and bind us in all cases whatever. And does not this Constitution do the same? . . . These lawyers, and men of learning, and moneyed men . . . expect to be the managers of this Constitution, and get all the power and all the money into their own hands, and then they will swallow up all us little folks. 99

■■ **Issues of representation, commerce, states' rights, and individual rights caused divisions that threatened the framing and ratification of the Constitution.**

Bitter debates took place in many of the states' ratifying conventions. By May 29, 1790, all 13 states had ratified the Constitution, some by the narrowest of margins. Americans could now hope to launch constitutional government in the United States with solid prospects for success.

THE CONSTITUTION: A LIVING DOCUMENT

Drawing on their experiences with British rule and with the Confederation, the delegates to the Constitutional Convention had worked to frame a constitution that would provide for a strong central government while protecting states' rights. Once the delegates settled on a federal system of government, they had to decide which powers would fall to the federal government and which powers the states would retain.

▶ The state seal of New York is shown here. State legislatures use seals such as this on official public documents.

They decided to give the federal government authority in matters of concern to all the people. These **delegated powers** include the rights to coin money, to regulate trade with foreign nations and among the states, and to raise and support an army and a navy. All powers not specifically granted to the federal government or denied to the states are kept, or reserved, by the states. Examples of the states' **reserved powers** include establishing local governments, overseeing schools, conducting elections, regulating businesses, and making marriage laws.

The powers that are held jointly by the federal government and the state governments are called **concurrent powers**. Examples of concurrent powers include levying and collecting taxes, borrowing money, providing for the public welfare, and establishing courts.

Recognizing that disputes might arise if the national government and the state governments passed laws that conflicted with one another, the delegates added the **supremacy clause** to Article VI of the Constitution. This clause states that the federal constitution and all federal laws override state constitutions and state laws.

To prevent the federal government from abusing its powers, the framers separated it into three branches: legislative, executive, and judicial. Each branch has specific powers the other branches cannot claim. The legislative branch makes laws, the executive branch sees that they are carried out, and the judicial branch interprets them and punishes lawbreakers. This **separation of powers** keeps any part of the federal government from becoming too powerful.

The separation of powers is upheld by a system of **checks and balances** that gives each branch of government the means to restrain the other two. Congress, for example, has the responsibility to check presidential power. The most extreme restraint on presidential authority is the legal process of **impeachment**. The House of Representatives may impeach, or charge, a president who is thought to be guilty of "treason, bribery, or other high crimes and misdemeanors." An impeached president would then be tried by the Senate and, if found guilty, removed from office.

There are other checks and balances among the three branches. The president can make treaties and appoint important officials, but only with the approval of the Senate. Congress can also check the president by refusing to spend the monies necessary to fund a presidential action. The president, in turn, can curb the powers of Congress by veto-ing, or rejecting, laws passed by Congress. Although Congress possesses the power to over-ride, or overrule, a presidential veto, the two-thirds majority necessary to do so is often difficult to obtain. The president can also check Congress's power through influence and pressure. Both the executive and legislative branches balance the judicial branch: the Senate must approve the presi-dent's appointment of federal judges, and Congress has the power to impeach judges.

The Constitution has remained effective for more than 200 years because it is a living docu-ment that can adapt to changes in our society. To allow for needed changes, the framers specified a procedure by which the Constitution may be amended. But the amendment process is difficult. Only 27 amendments have been added to the Constitution since 1789.

The Constitution's **elastic clause** has also increased the document's flexibility. To the spe-cific powers granted to Congress, this clause adds the power "to make all Laws which shall be neces-sary and proper for carrying into Execution the foregoing Powers." The elastic clause allows Congress to stretch its powers in ways not specifi-cally outlined in the Constitution.

Federalism, separation of powers, checks and balances, and the amendment process are among the Constitution's most significant provisions.

COMMENTARY

Evaluating the Constitution

The men who wrote the Constitution knew that their gathering in Philadelphia in 1787 had revolu-tionary implications far greater than the war for independence. Yet their goal was not to remake the United States but to set the new nation on more stable political, economic, and social foundations by reforming the structure of government.

In this sense many of these men were conser-vatives. Their concern was to preserve what they had created, rather than to carry out what they thought would be rash and dangerous innovations. They did not, for example, wish to grant political power to all members of society, such as women and African Americans. Nor did they squarely face the issue of slavery. Some were willing to sidestep the issue because they mistakenly believed that slavery was a dying institution. But whatever the reason, the failure to end slavery at this time—when it could have been most easily accom-plished—set the stage for more than 70 years of bitter debate and a civil war.

Yet the Constitution also had revolutionary implications. As the antislavery and women's movements would show, the promise of the Constitution was not lost on those excluded from power. In pressing for the same rights and liberties granted to free white men, all groups stood to benefit from the vision of republican government contained in the Constitution.

SECTION 2 REVIEW

IDENTIFY and explain the significance of the following: republic, Land Ordinance of 1785, Northwest Ordinance, inflation, depression, Shays's Rebellion, Constitutional Convention, James Madison, Virginia Plan, federalism, tariffs, delegated powers, reserved powers, concurrent powers, supremacy clause, separation of powers, impeachment, elastic clause.

1. **MAIN IDEA** What limits did the Articles of Confederation place on federal power? What were some of the consequences of these limits?

2. **MAIN IDEA** What were the major compromises that came out of the Constitutional Convention?

3. **MAIN IDEA** Why can the Constitution be considered a flexible, living document?

4. **WRITING TO PERSUADE** Imagine you are a Federalist or an Antifederalist delegate to a state ratifying convention. Write a speech explaining why you support or oppose ratification of the Constitution.

5. **EVALUATING** How might a system of checks and balances prevent government from being effective at times?

The Constitution of the United States of America

Preamble
The short and dignified Preamble explains the goals of the new government under the Constitution.

PREAMBLE

We the People of the United States, in Order to form a more perfect Union, establish Justice, insure domestic Tranquility, provide for the common defense, promote the general Welfare, and secure the Blessings of Liberty to ourselves and our Posterity, do ordain and establish this Constitution for the United States of America.*

Legislative Branch
Article I explains how the legislative branch, called Congress, is organized. The chief purpose of the legislative branch is to make the laws. Congress is made up of the Senate and the House of Representatives. The decision to have two bodies of government solved a difficult problem during the Constitutional Convention. The large states wanted the membership of Congress to be based entirely on population. The small states wanted every state to have an equal vote. The solution to the problem of how the states were to be represented in Congress was known as the Great Compromise.

The number of members of the House is based on the population of the individual states. Each state has at least one representative. The current size of the House is 435 members, set by Congress in 1929. If each member of the House represented only 30,000 people, the House would have more than 8,000 members.

ARTICLE I

Section 1. All legislative Powers herein granted shall be vested in a Congress of the United States, which shall consist of a Senate and House of Representatives.

Section 2. The House of Representatives shall be composed of Members chosen every second Year by the People of the several States, and the Electors in each State shall have the Qualifications requisite for Electors of the most numerous Branch of the State Legislature.

No Person shall be a Representative who shall not have attained to the Age of twenty-five Years, and been seven Years a Citizen of the United States, and who shall not, when elected, be an inhabitant of that State in which he shall be chosen.

Representatives and direct Taxes shall be apportioned among the several States which may be included within this Union, according to their respective Numbers, which shall be determined by adding to the whole Number of free Persons, including those bound to Service for a Term of Years, and excluding Indians not taxed, three fifths of all other Persons. The actual Enumeration shall be made within three Years after the first Meeting of the Congress of the United States, and within every subsequent Term of ten Years, in such Manner as they shall by Law direct. The Number of Representatives shall not exceed one for every thirty Thousand, but each State shall have at Least one Representative; and until such enumeration shall be made, the State of New Hampshire shall be entitled to choose three; Massachusetts eight; Rhode Island and Providence Plantations one; Connecticut five; New York six; New Jersey four;

* Parts of the Constitution that have been ruled through are no longer in force or no longer apply.

~~Pennsylvania eight; Delaware one; Maryland six; Virginia ten; North Carolina five; South Carolina five; and Georgia three.~~

When vacancies happen in the Representation from any State, the Executive Authority thereof shall issue Writs of Election to fill such Vacancies.

The House of Representatives shall choose their Speaker and other Officers; and shall have the sole Power of Impeachment.

Section 3. The Senate of the United States shall be composed of two Senators from each State, ~~chosen by the Legislature thereof,~~ for six Years; and each Senator shall have one Vote.

Immediately after they shall be assembled in Consequence of the first Election, they shall be divided as equally as may be into three Classes. The Seats of the Senators of the first Class shall be vacated at the Expiration of the second Year, of the second Class at the Expiration of the fourth Year, and of the third Class at the Expiration of the sixth Year, so that one third may be chosen every second Year; ~~and if Vacancies happen by Resignation, or otherwise, during the Recess of the Legislature of any State, the Executive thereof may make temporary Appointments until the next Meeting of the Legislature, which shall then fill such Vacancies.~~

No Person shall be a Senator who shall not have attained to the Age of thirty Years, and been nine Years a Citizen of the United States, and who shall not, when elected, be an Inhabitant of that State for which he shall be chosen.

The Vice President of the United States shall be President of the Senate, but shall have no Vote, unless they be equally divided.

The Senate shall choose their other Officers, and also a President pro tempore, in the Absence of the Vice President, or when he shall exercise the Office of President of the United States.

The Senate shall have the sole Power to try all Impeachments. When sitting for that Purpose, they shall be on Oath or Affirmation. When the President of the United States is tried, the Chief Justice shall preside: And no Person shall be convicted without the Concurrence of two thirds of the Members present.

Judgment in Cases of Impeachment shall not extend further than to removal from Office, and disqualification to hold and enjoy any Office of honor, Trust or Profit under the United States: but the Party convicted shall nevertheless be liable and subject to Indictment, Trial, Judgment and Punishment, according to Law.

Section 4. The Times, Places and Manner of holding Elections for Senators and Representatives, shall be prescribed in each State by the Legislature thereof; but the Congress may at any time by Law make or alter such Regulations, except as to the Places of choosing Senators.

The Congress shall assemble at least once in every Year, and such Meeting shall be on the first Monday in December, unless they shall by Law appoint a different Day.

Every state has two senators. Senators serve a six-year term, but only one third of the senators reach the end of their terms every two years. In any election, at least two thirds of the senators stay in office. This system ensures that there are experienced senators in office at all times.

The only duty that the Constitution assigns to the vice president is to preside over meetings of the Senate. Modern presidents have given their vice presidents more and varied responsibility.

The House charges a government official of wrongdoing, and the Senate acts as a court to decide if the official is guilty.

Congress has decided that elections will be held on the Tuesday following the first Monday in November of even-numbered years. The Twentieth Amendment states that Congress shall meet in regular session on January 3 of each year. The president may call a special session of Congress whenever necessary.

Congress makes most of its own rules of conduct. The Senate and the House each have a code of ethics that members must follow. It is the task of each house of Congress to discipline its own members. Each house keeps a journal, and a publication called the *Congressional Record* records what happens in congressional sessions. The general public can learn how their representatives voted on bills by reading the *Congressional Record*.

The framers of the Constitution wanted to protect members of Congress from being arrested on false charges by political enemies who did not want them to attend important meetings. The framers also wanted to protect members of Congress from being taken to court for something they said in a speech or in a debate.

The power of taxing is the responsibility of the House of Representatives. Because members of the House are elected every two years, the framers felt that representatives would listen to the public and seek its approval before passing taxes.

Section 5. Each House shall be the Judge of the Elections, Returns and Qualifications of its own Members, and a Majority of each shall constitute a Quorum to do Business; but a smaller Number may adjourn from day to day, and may be authorized to compel the Attendance of absent Members, in such Manner, and under such Penalties as each House may provide.

Each House may determine the Rules of its Proceedings, punish its Members for disorderly Behavior, and, with the Concurrence of two thirds, expel a Member.

Each House shall keep a Journal of its Proceedings, and from time to time publish the same, excepting such Parts as may in their Judgment require Secrecy; and the Yeas and Nays of the Members of either House on any question shall, at the Desire of one fifth of those Present, be entered on the Journal.

Neither House, during the Session of Congress, shall, without the Consent of the other, adjourn for more than three days, nor to any other Place than that in which the two Houses shall be sitting.

Section 6. The Senators and Representatives shall receive a Compensation for their Services, to be ascertained by Law, and paid out of the Treasury of the United States. They shall in all Cases, except Treason, Felony and Breach of the Peace, be privileged from Arrest during their Attendance at the Session of their respective Houses, and in going to and returning from the same; and for any Speech or Debate in either House, they shall not be questioned in any other Place.

No Senator or Representative shall, during the Time for which he was elected, be appointed to any civil Office under the Authority of the United States, which shall have been created, or the Emoluments whereof shall have been increased during such time; and no Person holding any Office under the United States, shall be a Member of either House during his Continuance in Office.

Section 7. All Bills for raising Revenue shall originate in the House of Representatives; but the Senate may propose or concur with Amendments as on other Bills.

Every Bill which shall have passed the House of Representatives and the Senate, shall, before it become a Law, be presented to the President of the United States; If he approve he shall sign it, but if not he shall return it, with his Objections to that House in which it shall have originated, who shall enter the Objections at large on their Journal, and proceed to reconsider it. If after such Reconsideration two thirds of that House shall agree to pass the Bill, it shall be sent, together with the Objections, to the other House, by which it shall likewise be reconsidered, and if approved by two thirds of that House, it shall become a Law. But in all such Cases the Votes of both Houses shall be determined by Yeas and Nays, and the Names of the Persons voting for and against the Bill shall be entered on the

Journal of each House respectively. If any Bill shall not be returned by the President within ten Days (Sundays excepted) after it shall have been presented to him, the Same shall be a Law, in like Manner as if he had signed it, unless the Congress by their Adjournment prevent its Return, in which Case it shall not be a Law.

Every Order, Resolution, or Vote to which the Concurrence of the Senate and House of Representatives may be necessary (except on a question of Adjournment) shall be presented to the President of the United States; and before the Same shall take Effect, shall be approved by him, or being disapproved by him, shall be repassed by two thirds of the Senate and House of Representatives, according to the Rules and Limitations prescribed in the Case of a Bill.

Section 8. The Congress shall have Power To lay and collect Taxes, Duties, Imposts and Excises, to pay the Debts and provide for the common Defense and general Welfare of the United States; but all Duties, Imposts and Excises shall be uniform throughout the United States;

To borrow Money on the credit of the United States;

To regulate Commerce with foreign Nations, and among the several States, and with the Indian Tribes;

To establish an uniform Rule of Naturalization, and uniform Laws on the subject of Bankruptcies throughout the United States;

To coin Money, regulate the Value thereof, and of foreign Coin, and fix the Standard of Weights and Measures;

To provide for the Punishment of counterfeiting the Securities and current Coin of the United States;

To establish Post Offices and post Roads;

To promote the Progress of Science and useful Arts, by securing for limited Times to Authors and Inventors the exclusive Right to their respective Writings and Discoveries;

To constitute Tribunals inferior to the supreme Court;

To define and punish Piracies and Felonies committed on the high Seas, and Offenses against the Law of Nations;

To declare War, grant Letters of Marque and Reprisal, and make Rules concerning Captures on Land and Water;

To raise and support Armies, but no Appropriation of Money to that Use shall be for a longer Term than two Years;

To provide and maintain a Navy;

To make Rules for the Government and Regulation of the land and naval Forces;

To provide for calling forth the Militia to execute the Laws of the Union, suppress Insurrections and repel Invasions;

To provide for organizing, arming, and disciplining, the Militia, and for governing such Part of them as may be employed in the Service of the United States, reserving to the States respectively, the

The veto power of the president and the ability of Congress to override a presidential veto are two of the important checks and balances in the Constitution.

The framers of the Constitution wanted a national government that was strong enough to be effective. This section lists the powers given to Congress. The last sentence in Section 8 contains the famous "elastic clause," which can be stretched (like elastic) to fit many different circumstances. The clause was first disputed when Alexander Hamilton proposed a national bank. Thomas Jefferson said that the Constitution did not give Congress the power to establish a bank. Hamilton argued that the bank was "necessary and proper" in order to carry out other powers of Congress, such as borrowing money and regulating currency. This argument was tested in the court system in 1819 in the case of *McCulloch v. Maryland,* when Chief Justice Marshall ruled in favor of the federal government. Powers given to the government by the "elastic clause" are called implied powers.

Appointment of the Officers, and the Authority of training the Militia according to the discipline prescribed by Congress.

To exercise exclusive Legislation in all Cases whatsoever, over such District (not exceeding ten Miles square) as may, by Cession of particular States, and the Acceptance of Congress, become the Seat of the Government of the United States, and to exercise like Authority over all Places purchased by the Consent of the Legislature of the State in which the Same shall be, for the Erection of Forts, Magazines, Arsenals, dock-Yards, and other needful Buildings;—And

To make all Laws which shall be necessary and proper for carrying into Execution the foregoing Powers, and all other Powers vested by this Constitution in the Government of the United States, or in any Department or Officer thereof.

Section 9. ~~The Migration or Importation of such Persons as any of the States now existing shall think proper to admit, shall not be prohibited by the Congress prior to the Year one thousand eight hundred and eight, but a Tax or duty may be imposed on such Importation, not exceeding ten dollars for each Person.~~

The Privilege of the Writ of Habeas Corpus shall not be suspended, unless when in Cases of Rebellion or Invasion the public Safety may require it.

No Bill of Attainder or ex post facto Law shall be passed.

No Capitation, or other direct, Tax shall be laid, unless in Proportion to the Census or Enumeration herein before directed to be taken.

No Tax or Duty shall be laid on Articles exported from any State.

No Preference shall be given by any Regulation of Commerce or Revenue to the Ports of one State over those of another: nor shall Vessels bound to, or from, one State, be obliged to enter, clear, or pay Duties in another.

No Money shall be drawn from the Treasury, but in Consequence of Appropriations made by Law; and a regular Statement and Account of the Receipts and Expenditures of all public Money shall be published from time to time.

No Title of Nobility shall be granted by the United States: And no Person holding any Office of Profit or Trust under them, shall, without the Consent of the Congress, accept of any present, Emolument, Office, or Title, of any kind whatever, from any King, Prince, or foreign State.

Section 10. No State shall enter into any Treaty, Alliance, or Confederation; grant Letters of Marque and Reprisal; coin Money; emit Bills of Credit; make any Thing but gold and silver Coin a Tender in Payment of Debts; pass any Bill of Attainder, ex post facto Law, or law impairing the Obligation of Contracts, or grant any Title of Nobility.

If Congress has implied powers, then there also must be limits to its powers. Section 9 lists powers that are denied to the federal government. Several of the clauses protect the people of the United States from unjust treatment. For instance, Section 9 guarantees the writ of *habeas corpus* and prohibits bills of attainder and *ex post facto* laws.

Section 10 lists the powers that are denied to the states. In our system of federalism, the state and federal governments have separate powers, share some powers, and are denied other powers. The states may not exercise any of the powers that belong to Congress.

No State shall, without the Consent of the Congress, lay any Imposts or Duties on Imports or Exports, except what may be absolutely necessary for executing its inspection Laws: and the net Produce of all Duties and Imposts, laid by any State on Imports or Exports, shall be for the Use of the Treasury of the United States; and all such Laws shall be subject to the Revision and Control of the Congress.

No State shall, without the Consent of Congress, lay any Duty of Tonnage, keep Troops, or Ships of War in time of Peace, enter into any Agreement or Compact with another State, or with a foreign Power, or engage in War, unless actually invaded, or in such imminent Danger as will not admit of delay.

ARTICLE II

Section 1. The executive Power shall be vested in a President of the United States of America. He shall hold his Office during the Term of four Years, and, together with the Vice President, chosen for the same Term, be elected, as follows.

Each State shall appoint, in such Manner as the Legislature thereof may direct, a Number of Electors, equal to the whole Number of Senators and Representatives to which the State may be entitled in the Congress: but no Senator or Representative, or Person holding an Office of Trust or Profit under the United States, shall be appointed an Elector.

The Electors shall meet in their respective States, and vote by Ballot for two Persons, of whom one at least shall not be an Inhabitant of the same State with themselves. And they shall make a List of all the Persons voted for, and of the Number of Votes for each; which List they shall sign and certify, and transmit sealed to the Seat of the Government of the United States, directed to the President of the Senate. The President of the Senate shall, in the Presence of the Senate and House of Representatives, open all the Certificates, and the Votes shall then be counted. The Person having the greatest Number of Votes shall be the President, if such Number be a Majority of the whole Number of Electors appointed; and if there be more than one who have such majority, and have an equal Number of Votes, then the House of Representatives shall immediately choose by Ballot one of them for President; and if no Person have a Majority, then from the five highest on the List the said House shall in like Manner choose the President. But in choosing the President, the Votes shall be taken by States, the Representation from each State having one Vote; A quorum for this Purpose shall consist of a Member or Members from two thirds of the States, and a Majority of all the States shall be necessary to a Choice. In every Case, after the Choice of the President, the Person having the greatest Number of Votes of the Electors shall be the Vice President. But if there should

Executive Branch
The president is the chief of the executive branch. It is the job of the president to enforce the laws. The framers wanted the president and vice president's term of office and manner of selection to be different from those of members of Congress. They decided on four-year terms, but they had a difficult time agreeing on how to select the president and vice president. The framers finally set up an electoral system, which varies greatly from our electoral process today. The Twelfth Amendment changed the process by requiring that separate ballots be cast for president and vice president. The rise of political parties has since changed the process even more.

In 1845 Congress set the first Tuesday after the first Monday in November of every fourth year as the general election date for selecting presidential electors.

The youngest elected president was John F. Kennedy; he was 43 years old when he was inaugurated. (Theodore Roosevelt was 42 when he assumed office after the assassination of McKinley.) The oldest elected president was Ronald Reagan; he was 69 years old when he was inaugurated.

Emolument means a salary, or payment. In 1969 Congress set the president's salary at $200,000 per year. The president also receives an expense account of $50,000 per year. The president must pay taxes on both.

The oath of office is administered to the president by the chief justice of the United States. Washington added "So help me, God." All succeeding presidents have followed this practice.

The framers wanted to make sure that an elected representative of the people controlled the nation's military. Today the president is in charge of the army, navy, air force, marines, and coast guard. Only Congress can decide, however, if the United States will declare war. This section also contains the basis for the formation of the president's cabinet. Every president, starting with George Washington, has appointed a cabinet.

Most of the president's appointments to office must be approved by the Senate.

~~remain two or more who have equal Votes, the Senate shall choose from them by Ballot the Vice President.~~

The Congress may determine the Time of choosing the Electors, and the Day on which they shall give their Votes; which Day shall be the same throughout the United States.

No Person except a natural born Citizen, ~~or a Citizen of the United States, at the time of the Adoption of this Constitution,~~ shall be eligible to the Office of President; neither shall any Person be eligible to that Office who shall not have attained to the Age of thirty-five Years, and been fourteen Years a Resident within the United States.

In Case of the Removal of the President from Office, or of his Death, Resignation, or Inability to discharge the Powers and Duties of the said Office, the Same shall devolve on the Vice President, and the Congress may by Law provide for the Case of Removal, Death, Resignation or Inability, both of the President and Vice President, declaring what Officer shall then act as President, and such Officer shall act accordingly, until the Disability be removed, or a President shall be elected.

The President shall, at stated Times, receive for his Services, a Compensation, which shall neither be increased nor diminished during the Period for which he shall have been elected, and he shall not receive within that Period any other Emolument from the United States, or any of them.

Before he enter on the Execution of his Office, he shall take the following Oath or Affirmation:—"I do solemnly swear (or affirm) that I will faithfully execute the Office of President of the United States, and will to the best of my Ability, preserve, protect and defend the Constitution of the United States."

Section 2. The President shall be Commander in Chief of the Army and Navy of the United States, and of the Militia of the several States, when called into the actual Service of the United States; he may require the Opinion, in writing, of the principal Officer in each of the executive Departments, upon any Subject relating to the Duties of their respective Offices, and he shall have Power to grant Reprieves and Pardons for Offenses against the United States, except in Cases of Impeachment.

He shall have Power, by and with the Advice and Consent of the Senate, to make Treaties, provided two thirds of the Senators present concur; and he shall nominate, and by and with the Advice and Consent of the Senate, shall appoint Ambassadors, other public Ministers and Consuls, Judges of the supreme Court, and all other Officers of the United States, whose Appointments are not herein otherwise provided for, and which shall be established by Law: but the Congress may by Law vest the Appointment of such inferior Officers, as they think proper, in the President alone, in the Courts of Law, or in the Heads of Departments.

The President shall have Power to fill up all Vacancies that may happen during the Recess of the Senate, by granting Commissions which shall expire at the End of their next Session.

Section 3. He shall from time to time give to the Congress Information of the State of the Union, and recommend to their Consideration such Measures as he shall judge necessary and expedient; he may, on extraordinary Occasions, convene both Houses, or either of them, and in Case of Disagreement between them, with Respect to the Time of Adjournment, he may adjourn them to such Time as he shall think proper; he shall receive Ambassadors and other public Ministers; he shall take Care that the Laws be faithfully executed, and shall Commission all the Officers of the United States.

Section 4. The President, Vice President and all civil Officers of the United States, shall be removed from Office on Impeachment for, and Conviction of, Treason, Bribery, or other high Crimes and Misdemeanors.

Every year the president presents to Congress a State of the Union message. In this message, the president explains the legislative plans for the coming year. This clause states that one of the president's duties is to enforce the laws.

ARTICLE III

Section 1. The judicial Power of the United States, shall be vested in one supreme Court, and in such inferior Courts as the Congress may from time to time ordain and establish. The Judges, both of the supreme and inferior Courts, shall hold their Offices during good Behavior, and shall, at stated Times, receive for their Services, a Compensation, which shall not be diminished during their Continuance in Office.

Section 2. The judicial Power shall extend to all Cases, in Law and Equity, arising under this Constitution, the Laws of the United States, and Treaties made, or which shall be made, under their Authority;—to all Cases affecting Ambassadors, other public Ministers and Consuls;—to all Cases of admiralty and maritime Jurisdiction;—to Controversies to which the United States shall be a Party;—to Controversies between two or more States;— between a State and Citizens of another State; —between Citizens of different States;—between Citizens of the same State claiming Lands under Grants of different States, and between a State, or the Citizens thereof, and foreign States, Citizens or Subjects.

In all Cases affecting Ambassadors, other public Ministers and Consuls, and those in which a State shall be Party, the supreme Court shall have original Jurisdiction. In all the other Cases before mentioned, the supreme Court shall have appellate Jurisdiction, both as to Law and fact, with such Exceptions, and under such Regulations as the Congress shall make.

The Trial of all Crimes, except in Cases of Impeachment, shall be by Jury; and such Trial shall be held in the State where the said Crimes shall have been committed; but when not committed within

Judicial Branch
The Articles of Confederation did not make any provisions for a federal court system. One of the first things that the framers of the Constitution agreed upon was to set up a national judiciary. With all the laws that Congress would be enacting, there would be a great need for a branch of government to interpret the laws. In the Judiciary Act of 1789, Congress provided for the establishment of lower courts, such as district courts, circuit courts of appeals, and various other federal courts. The judicial system provides a check on the legislative branch; it can declare a law unconstitutional.

Congress has the power to decide the punishment for treason, but it can punish only the guilty person. *Corruption of blood* refers to the effect of an attainder, which prohibits inheriting, keeping, or transmitting an estate. Thus punishing the family of a person who has committed treason is expressly forbidden.

The States
States must honor the laws, records, and court decisions of other states. A person cannot escape a legal obligation by moving from one state to another.

Section 3 permits Congress to admit new states to the Union. When a group of people living in an area that is not part of an existing state wishes to form a new state, it asks Congress for permission to do so. The people then write a state constitution and offer it to Congress for approval. The state constitution must set up a representative form of government and must not in any way contradict the federal Constitution. If a majority of Congress approves of the state constitution, the state is admitted as a member of the United States of America.

any State, the Trial shall be at such Place or Places as the Congress may by Law have directed.

Section 3. Treason against the United States, shall consist only in levying War against them, or in adhering to their Enemies, giving them Aid and Comfort. No Person shall be convicted of Treason unless on the Testimony of two Witnesses to the same overt Act, or on Confession in open Court.

The Congress shall have Power to declare the Punishment of Treason, but no Attainder of Treason shall work Corruption of Blood, or Forfeiture except during the Life of the Person attainted.

ARTICLE IV

Section 1. Full Faith and Credit shall be given in each State to the public Acts, Records, and judicial Proceedings of every other State. And the Congress may by general Laws prescribe the Manner in which such Acts, Records and Proceedings shall be proved, and the Effect thereof.

Section 2. The Citizens of each State shall be entitled to all Privileges and Immunities of Citizens in the several States.

A Person charged in any State with Treason, Felony, or other Crime, who shall flee from Justice, and be found in another State, shall on Demand of the executive Authority of the State from which he fled, be delivered up, to be removed to the State having Jurisdiction of the Crime.

~~No Person held to Service of Labor in one State, under the Laws thereof, escaping into another, shall, in Consequence of any Law or Regulation therein, be discharged from such Service or Labor, but shall be delivered up on Claim of the Party to whom such Service or Labor may be due.~~

Section 3. New States may be admitted by the Congress into this Union; but no new State shall be formed or erected within the Jurisdiction of any other State; nor any State be formed by the Junction of two or more States, or Parts of States, without the Consent of the Legislatures of the States concerned as well as of the Congress.

The Congress shall have Power to dispose of and make all needful Rules and Regulations respecting the Territory or other Property belonging to the United States; and nothing in this Constitution shall be so construed as to Prejudice any Claims of the United States, or of any particular State.

Section 4. The United States shall guarantee to every State in this Union a Republican Form of Government, and shall protect each of them against Invasion; and on Application of the Legislature, or of the Executive (when the Legislature cannot be convened) against domestic Violence.

ARTICLE V

The Congress, whenever two thirds of both Houses shall deem it necessary, shall propose Amendments to this Constitution, or, on the Application of the Legislatures of two thirds of the several States, shall call a Convention for proposing Amendments, which, in either Case, shall be valid to all Intents and Purposes, as Part of this Constitution, when ratified by the Legislatures of three fourths of the several States, or by Conventions in three fourths thereof, as the one or the other Mode of Ratification may be proposed by the Congress; Provided that ~~no Amendment which may be made prior to the Year One thousand eight hundred and eight shall in any Manner affect the first and fourth Clauses in the Ninth Section of the first Article; and that~~ no State, without its Consent, shall be deprived of its equal Suffrage in the Senate.

ARTICLE VI

All Debts contracted and Engagements entered into, before the Adoption of this Constitution, shall be as valid against the United States under this Constitution, as under the Confederation.

This Constitution, and the Laws of the United States which shall be made in Pursuance thereof; and all Treaties made, or which shall be made, under the Authority of the United States, shall be the supreme Law of the Land; and the Judges in every State shall be bound thereby, any Thing in the Constitution or Laws of any State to the Contrary notwithstanding.

The Senators and Representatives before mentioned, and the Members of the several State Legislatures, and all executive and judicial Officers, both of the United States and of the several States, shall be bound by Oath or Affirmation, to support this Constitution; but no religious Test shall ever be required as a Qualification to any Office or public Trust under the United States.

ARTICLE VII

The Ratification of the Conventions of nine States, shall be sufficient for the Establishment of this Constitution between the States so ratifying the Same.

DONE in Convention by the Unanimous Consent of the States present the Seventeenth Day of September in the Year of our Lord one thousand seven hundred and Eighty seven and of the Independence of the United States of America the Twelfth. IN WITNESS whereof We have hereunto subscribed our Names.

George Washington—
President and deputy from Virginia

The Amendment Process

America's founders may not have realized just how enduring the Constitution would be, but they did make provisions for changing or adding to the Constitution. They did not want to make it easy to change the Constitution. There are two different ways in which changes can be proposed to the states and two different ways in which states can approve the changes and make them part of the Constitution.

National Supremacy

One of the biggest problems facing the delegates to the Constitutional Convention was the question of what would happen if a state law and a national law conflicted. Which law would be followed? Who decided? The second clause of Article VI answers those questions. When a national and state law disagree, the national law overrides the state law. The Constitution is the supreme law of the land. This clause is often called the "supremacy clause."

Ratification

The Articles of Confederation called for all 13 states to approve any revision to the Articles. The Constitution required that the vote of 9 out of the 13 states would be needed to ratify the Constitution. The first state to ratify was Delaware, on December 7, 1787. The last state to ratify the Constitution was Rhode Island, which finally did so on May 29, 1790, almost two and a half years later.

New Hampshire
John Langdon
Nicholas Gilman

Massachusetts
Nathaniel Gorham
Rufus King

Connecticut
William Samuel Johnson
Roger Sherman

New York
Alexander Hamilton

New Jersey
William Livingston
David Brearley
William Paterson
Jonathan Dayton

Pennsylvania
Benjamin Franklin
Thomas Mifflin
Robert Morris
George Clymer
Thomas FitzSimons
Jared Ingersoll
James Wilson
Gouverneur Morris

Delaware
George Read
Gunning Bedford, Jr.
John Dickinson
Richard Bassett
Jacob Broom

Maryland
James McHenry
Daniel of St. Thomas Jenifer
Daniel Carroll

Virginia
John Blair
James Madison, Jr.

North Carolina
William Blount
Richard Dobbs Spaight
Hugh Williamson

South Carolina
John Rutledge
Charles Cotesworth Pinckney
Charles Pinckney
Pierce Buttler

Georgia
William Few
Abraham Baldwin

Attest: *William Jackson,* Secretary

Bill of Rights

One of the conditions set by several states for ratifying the Constitution was the inclusion of a Bill of Rights. Many people feared that a stronger central government might take away basic rights of the people that had been guaranteed in state constitutions. If the three words that begin the preamble—We the people—carried any meaning, then the rights of the people needed to be protected.

THE AMENDMENTS

ARTICLES in addition to, and Amendment of the Constitution of the United States of America, proposed by Congress, and ratified by the Legislatures of the several states, pursuant to the fifth Article of the original Constitution.

[The First through Tenth amendments, now known as the Bill of Rights, were proposed on September 25, 1789, and declared in force on December 15, 1791.]

First Amendment

Congress shall make no law respecting an establishment of religion, or prohibiting the free exercise thereof; or abridging the freedom of speech, or of the press; or the right of the people peaceably to assemble, and to petition the Government for a redress of grievances.

The First Amendment protects freedom of speech and thought, and forbids Congress to make any law "respecting an establishment of religion" or restraining the freedom to practice religion as one chooses.

Second Amendment

A well regulated Militia, being necessary to the security of a free State, the right of the people to keep and bear Arms, shall not be infringed.

Third Amendment

No Soldier shall, in time of peace, be quartered in any house, without the consent of the Owner, nor in time of war, but in a manner to be prescribed by law.

Fourth Amendment

The right of the people to be secure in their persons, houses, papers, and effects, against unreasonable searches and seizures, shall not be violated, and no Warrants shall issue, but upon probable cause, supported by Oath or affirmation, and particularly describing the place to be searched, and the persons or things to be seized.

A police officer or sheriff may enter a person's home with a search warrant, which allows the law officer to look for evidence that could convict someone of committing a crime.

Fifth Amendment

No person shall be held to answer for a capital, or otherwise infamous crime, unless on a presentment or indictment of a Grand Jury, except in cases arising in the land or naval forces, or in the Militia, when in actual service in time of War or public danger; nor shall any person be subject for the same offense to be twice put in jeopardy of life or limb; nor shall be compelled in any criminal case to be a witness against himself, nor be deprived of life, liberty, or property, without due process of law; nor shall private property be taken for public use, without just compensation.

The Fifth, Sixth, and Seventh amendments describe the procedures that courts must follow when trying people accused of crimes. The Fifth Amendment guarantees that no one can be put on trial for a serious crime unless a grand jury agrees that the evidence justifies doing so. It also says that a person cannot be tried twice for the same crime.

Sixth Amendment

In all criminal prosecutions, the accused shall enjoy the right to a speedy and public trial, by an impartial jury of the State and district wherein the crime shall have been committed, which district shall have been previously ascertained by law, and to be informed of the nature and cause of the accusation; to be confronted with the witnesses against him; to have compulsory process for obtaining witnesses in his favor, and to have the Assistance of Counsel for his defense.

The Sixth Amendment makes several promises, including a prompt trial and a trial by a jury chosen from the state and district in which the crime was committed. The Sixth Amendment also states that an accused person must be told why he or she is being tried and promises that an accused person has the right to be defended by a lawyer.

Seventh Amendment

In Suits at common law, where the value in controversy shall exceed twenty dollars, the right of trial by jury shall be preserved,

The Seventh Amendment guarantees a trial by jury in cases that involve more than $20, but in modern times, usually much more money is at stake before a case is heard in federal court.

and no fact tried by a jury shall be otherwise reexamined in any Court of the United States, than according to the rules of the common law.

Eighth Amendment

Excessive bail shall not be required, nor excessive fines imposed, nor cruel and unusual punishments inflicted.

Ninth Amendment

The enumeration in the Constitution, of certain rights, shall not be construed to deny or disparage others retained by the people.

The Ninth and Tenth amendments were added because not every right of the people or of the states could be listed in the Constitution.

Tenth Amendment

The powers not delegated to the United States by the Constitution, nor prohibited by it to the States, are reserved to the States respectively, or to the people.

Eleventh Amendment

[Proposed March 4, 1794; declared ratified January 8, 1798]

The Judicial power of the United States shall not be construed to extend to any suit in law or equity, commenced or prosecuted against one of the United States by Citizens of another State, or by Citizens or Subjects of any Foreign State.

The Twelfth Amendment changed the election procedure for president and vice president. This amendment became necessary because of the growth of political parties. Before this amendment, electors voted without distinguishing between president and vice president. Whoever received the most votes became president, and whoever received the next highest number of votes became vice president. A confusing election in 1800, which resulted in Thomas Jefferson's becoming president, caused this amendment to be proposed.

Twelfth Amendment

[Proposed December 9, 1803; declared ratified September 25, 1804]

The Electors shall meet in their respective states and vote by ballot for President and Vice President, one of whom, at least, shall not be an inhabitant of the same state with themselves; they shall name in their ballots the person voted for as President, and in distinct ballots the person voted for as Vice President, and they shall make distinct lists of all persons voted for as President, and of all persons voted for as Vice President, and of the number of votes for each, which lists they shall sign and certify, and transmit sealed to the seat of the government of the United States, directed to the President of the Senate;—The President of the Senate shall, in the presence of the Senate and House of Representatives, open all the certificates and the votes shall then be counted;—The person having the greatest number of votes for President, shall be the President, if such number be a majority of the whole number of Electors appointed; and if no person have such majority, then from the persons having the highest numbers not exceeding three on the list of those voted for as President, the House of Representatives shall choose immediately, by ballot, the President. But in choosing the President, the votes shall be taken by states, the representation from each state having one vote; a quorum for this purpose shall consist of a member or members from two thirds of the states, and a majority of all the states shall be necessary to a choice. ~~And if the House of Representatives shall not choose a President whenever the right of choice shall devolve upon them, before the fourth day of March next following, then the Vice President shall act as President, as in the case of the death or other constitutional disability of the President;~~ —The person having the greatest number of votes as Vice President, shall be the Vice President, if such number be a majority of the whole number of Electors appointed, and if no person have a majority, then from the two highest numbers on the list, the Senate shall choose the Vice President; a quorum for the purpose shall consist of two thirds of the whole number of Senators, and a majority of the whole number shall be necessary to a choice. But no person constitutionally ineligible to the office of President shall be eligible to that of Vice President of the United States.

Thirteenth Amendment

[Proposed January 31, 1865; declared ratified December 18, 1865]

Section 1. Neither slavery nor involuntary servitude, except as a punishment for crime whereof the party shall have been duly convicted, shall exist within the United States, or any place subject to their jurisdiction.

Section 2. Congress shall have power to enforce this article by appropriate legislation.

Fourteenth Amendment

[Proposed June 13, 1866; declared ratified July 28, 1868]

Section 1. All persons born or naturalized in the United States and subject to the jurisdiction thereof, are citizens of the United States and of the State wherein they reside. No State shall make or enforce any law which shall abridge the privileges or immunities of citizens of the United States; nor shall any State deprive any person of life, liberty, or property, without due process of law; nor deny to any person within its jurisdiction the equal protection of the laws.

Section 2. Representatives shall be apportioned among the several States according to their respective numbers, counting the whole number of persons in each State, ~~excluding Indians not taxed.~~ But when the right to vote at any election for the choice of electors for President and Vice President of the United States, Representatives in Congress, the Executive and Judicial officers of a State, or the members of the Legislature thereof, is denied to any of the ~~male~~ inhabitants of such State, being ~~twenty-one years of age, and~~ citizens of the United States, or in any way abridged, except for participation in rebellion, or other crime, the basis of representation therein shall be reduced in the proportion which the number of such ~~male~~ citizens shall bear to the whole number of ~~male~~ citizens ~~twenty-one years of age~~ in such State.

Section 3. No person shall be a Senator or Representative in

Although some slaves had been freed during the Civil War, slavery was not abolished until the Thirteenth Amendment took effect.

In 1833 Chief Justice John Marshall ruled that the Bill of Rights limited the national government but not the state governments. This ruling meant that states were able to keep African Americans from becoming state citizens. If African Americans were not citizens, they were not protected by the Bill of Rights. The Fourteenth Amendment defines citizenship and prevents states from interfering in the rights of citizens of the United States.

Congress, or elector of President and Vice President, or hold any office, civil or military, under the United States, or under any State, who, having previously taken an oath, as a member of Congress, or as an officer of the United States, or as a member of any State legislature, or as an executive or judicial officer of any State, to support the Constitution of the United States, shall have engaged in insurrection or rebellion against the same, or given aid or comfort to the enemies thereof. But Congress may by a vote of two thirds of each House, remove such disability.

Section 4. The validity of the public debt of the United States, authorized by law, including debts incurred for payment of pensions and bounties for services in suppressing insurrection or rebellion, shall not be questioned. But neither the United States nor any State shall assume or pay any debt or obligation incurred in aid of insurrection or rebellion against the United States, ~~or any claim for the loss or emancipation of any slave;~~ but all such debts, obligations and claims shall be held illegal and void.

Section 5. The Congress shall have power to enforce, by appropriate legislation, the provisions of this article.

Fifteenth Amendment

[Proposed February 26, 1869; declared ratified March 30, 1870]

The Fifteenth Amendment extended the right to vote to African American males.

Section 1. The right of citizens of the United States to vote shall not be denied or abridged by the United States or by any State on account of race, color, or previous condition of servitude.

Section 2. The Congress shall have power to enforce this article by appropriate legislation.

Sixteenth Amendment

[Proposed July 12, 1909; declared ratified February 25, 1913]

The Sixteenth Amendment made legal the income tax described in Article I.

The Congress shall have power to lay and collect taxes on incomes, from whatever source derived, without apportionment among the several States, and without regard to any census or enumeration.

Seventeenth Amendment

[Proposed May 13, 1912; declared ratified May 31, 1913]

The Seventeenth Amendment required that senators be elected directly by the people instead of by the state legislature.

The Senate of the United States shall be composed of two Senators from each State, elected by the people thereof, for six years; and each Senator shall have one vote. The electors in each State shall have the qualifications requisite for electors of the most numerous branch of the State legislatures.

When vacancies happen in the representation of any State in the Senate, the executive authority of such State shall issue writs of election to fill such vacancies: *Provided,* That the legislature of any

State may empower the executive thereof to make temporary appointments until the people fill the vacancies by election as the legislature may direct.

~~This amendment shall not be so construed as to affect the election or term of any Senator chosen before it becomes valid as part of the Constitution.~~

Eighteenth Amendment

[Proposed December 18, 1917; declared ratified January 29, 1919; repealed by the Twenty-first Amendment December 5, 1933]

~~*Section 1.* After one year from the ratification of this article the manufacture, sale, or transportation of intoxicating liquors within, the importation thereof into, or the exportation thereof from the United States and all territory subject to the jurisdiction thereof for beverage purposes is hereby prohibited.~~

~~*Section 2.* The Congress and the several States shall have concurrent power to enforce this article by appropriate legislation.~~

~~*Section 3.* This article shall be inoperative unless it shall have been ratified as an amendment to the Constitution by the legislatures of the several States, as provided in the Constitution, within seven years from the date of the submission hereof to the States by the Congress.~~

Although many people felt that Prohibition was good for the health and welfare of the American people, the amendment was repealed 14 years later.

Nineteenth Amendment

[Proposed June 4, 1919; declared ratified August 26, 1920]

The right of citizens of the United States to vote shall not be denied or abridged by the United States or by any State on account of sex.

Congress shall have power to enforce this article by appropriate legislation.

Abigail Adams was disappointed that the Declaration of Independence and the Constitution did not specifically include women. It took almost 150 years and much campaigning by women's suffrage groups for women finally to achieve voting privileges.

Twentieth Amendment

[Proposed ... declared ratified February 6, 1933]

... the President and Vice President shall ... and the terms of Senators and ... of January, of the years in ... icle had not been rati- ... e in every ... uary,

... ent elect sh... ... cho- sen before t... ... if the President elect sh... ... President

In the original Constitution, a newly elected president and Congress did not take office until March 4, which was four months after the November election. The officials who were leaving office were called "lame ducks" because they had little influence during those four months. The Twentieth Amendment changed the date that the new president and Congress take office. Members of Congress now take office on January 3, and the president takes office on January 20.

elect shall act as President until a President shall have qualified; and the Congress may by law provide for the case wherein neither a President elect nor a Vice President elect shall have qualified, declaring who shall then act as President, or the manner in which one who is to act shall be selected, and such persons shall act accordingly until a President or Vice President shall have qualified.

Section 4. The Congress may by law provide for the case of the death of any of the persons from whom the House of Representatives may choose a President whenever the right of choice shall have devolved upon them, and for the case of the death of any of the persons from whom the Senate may choose a Vice President whenever the right of choice shall have devolved upon them.

Section 5. Sections 1 and 2 shall take effect on the 15th day of October following the ratification of this article.

Section 6. This article shall be inoperative unless it shall have been ratified as an amendment to the Constitution by the legislatures of three fourths of the several States within seven years from the date of its submission.

Twenty-first Amendment

[Proposed February 20, 1933; declared ratified December 5, 1933]

Section 1. The eighteenth article of amendment to the Constitution of the United States is hereby repealed.

Section 2. The transportation or importation into any State, Territory, or possession of the United States for delivery or use therein of intoxicating liquors, in violation of the laws thereof, is hereby prohibited.

Section 3. This article shall be inoperative unless it shall have been ratified as an amendment to the Constitution by conventions in the several States, as provided in the Constitution, within seven years from the date of the submission hereof to the States by the Congress.

Twenty-second Amendment

[Proposed March 24, 1947; declared ratified March 1, 1951]

Section 1. No person shall be elected to the office of the President more than twice, and no person who has held the office of President, or acted as President, for more than two years of a term to which some other person was elected President shall be elected to the office of the President more than once. But this Article shall not apply to any person holding the office of President when this Article was proposed by the Congress, and shall not prevent any person who may be holding the office of President, or acting as President, during the term within which this Article becomes operative from holding the office of President or acting as President during the remainder of such term.

The Twenty-first Amendment is the only amendment that has been ratified by state conventions rather than by state legislatures.

From the time of President Washington's administration, it was a custom for presidents to serve no more than two terms of office. Franklin D. Roosevelt, however, was elected to four terms. The Twenty-second Amendment made into law the old custom of a two-term limit for each president, if reelected.

Section 2. ~~This Article shall be inoperative unless it shall have been ratified as an amendment to the Constitution by the legislatures of three-fourths of the several States within seven years from the date of its submission to the States by the Congress.~~

Twenty-third Amendment

[Proposed June 16, 1960; declared ratified April 3, 1961]

Section 1. The District constituting the seat of Government of the United States shall appoint in such manner as the Congress may direct:

A number of electors of President and Vice President equal to the whole number of Senators and Representatives in Congress to which the District would be entitled if it were a State, but in no event more than the least populous State; they shall be in addition to those appointed by the States, but they shall be considered, for the purposes of the election of President and Vice President, to be electors appointed by a State; and they shall meet in the District and perform such duties as provided by the twelfth article of amendment.

Section 2. The Congress shall have power to enforce this article by appropriate legislation.

Until the Twenty-third Amendment, the people of Washington, D.C., could not vote in presidential elections.

Twenty-fourth Amendment

[Proposed August 27, 1962; declared ratified February 4, 1964]

Section 1. The right of citizens of the United States to vote in any primary or other election for President or Vice President, for electors for President or Vice President, or for Senator or Representative in Congress, shall not be denied or abridged by the United States or any State by reason of failure to pay any poll tax or other tax.

Section 2. The Congress shall have power to enforce this article by appropriate legislation.

Twenty-fifth Amendment

[Proposed July 6, 1965; declared ratified February 23, 1967]

Section 1. In case of removal of the President from office or of his death or resignation, the Vice President shall become President.

Section 2. Whenever there is a vacancy in the office of the Vice President, the President shall nominate a Vice President who shall take office upon confirmation by a majority vote of both Houses of Congress.

Section 3. Whenever the President transmits to the President pro tempore of the Senate and the Speaker of the House of Representatives his written declaration that he is unable to discharge the powers and duties of his office, and until he transmits to them a written declaration to the contrary, such powers and duties shall be discharged by the Vice President as Acting President.

The illness of President Eisenhower in the 1950s and the assassination of President Kennedy in 1963 were the events behind the Twenty-fifth Amendment. The Constitution did not provide a clear-cut method for a vice president to take over for a disabled president or for the death of a president. This amendment provides for filling the office of the vice president if a vacancy occurs, and it provides a way for the vice president to take over if the president is unable to perform the duties of that office.

Section 4. Whenever the Vice President and a majority of either the principal officers of the executive departments or of such other body as Congress may by law provide, transmit to the President pro tempore of the Senate and the Speaker of the House of Representatives their written declaration that the President is unable to discharge the powers and duties of his office, the Vice President shall immediately assume the powers and duties of the office as Acting President.

Thereafter, when the President transmits to the President pro tempore of the Senate and the Speaker of the House of Representatives his written declaration that no inability exists, he shall resume the powers and duties of his office unless the Vice President and a majority of either the principal officers of the executive department or of such other body as Congress may by law provide, transmit within four days to the President pro tempore of the Senate and the Speaker of the House of Representatives their written declaration that the President is unable to discharge the powers and duties of his office. Thereupon Congress shall decide the issue, assembling within forty-eight hours for that purpose if not in session. If the Congress, within twenty-one days after receipt of the latter written declaration, or, if Congress is not in session, within twenty-one days after Congress is required to assemble, determines by two-thirds vote of both Houses that the President is unable to discharge the powers and duties of his office, the Vice President shall continue to discharge the same as Acting President; otherwise, the President shall resume the powers and duties of his office.

Twenty-sixth Amendment
[Proposed March 23, 1971; declared ratified July 5, 1971]

Section 1. The right of citizens of the United States, who are eighteen years of age or older, to vote shall not be denied or abridged by the United States or by any State on account of age.

Section 2. The Congress shall have power to enforce this article by appropriate legislation.

Twenty-seventh Amendment
[Proposed September 25, 1789; declared ratified May 7, 1992]

No law, varying the compensation for the services of the Senators and Representatives, shall take effect, until an election of Representatives shall have intervened.

The Voting Act of 1970 tried to set the voting age at 18 years old. But the Supreme Court ruled that the act set the voting age for national elections only, not state or local elections. This ruling would make necessary several different ballots at elections. The Twenty-sixth Amendment gave 18-year-old citizens the right to vote in all elections.

A STRONG START FOR THE NATION

FOCUS

■ **What steps did Congress take to strengthen the federal government?**

■ **What international and domestic issues were important to the United States between 1790 and 1800?**

■ **Why was the Louisiana Purchase important?**

■ **What were the major causes of the War of 1812?**

*D*omestic and foreign problems plagued America in its early years. The new federal government successfully addressed some of the problems at home. But relations with Europe threatened to draw the nation into war and divided Americans along political party lines. These intrigues would eventually erupt into the War of 1812.

U.S. cannon, 1815

FORGING A NATION

When Congress opened the ballots from the states on April 6, 1789, the unanimous choice for the nation's first president was George Washington. But while crowds cheered and towns celebrated Washington's inauguration, the task of shaping the new government belonged to the First Congress.

Molding the government. Congress's first order of business was to add a protection of individual liberties to the Constitution. Congress recommended twelve amendments for adoption; of these, 10 were ratified by the states in 1791 and became known as the **Bill of Rights**.

Another task of Congress was the creation of a federal court system, achieved by the **Judiciary**

▶ **This sampler celebrates Washington's inauguration.**

Museum of the City of New York

Act of 1789. Congress also created three departments to assist the president: the State Department to handle foreign affairs, the War Department to manage military affairs, and the Treasury Department to oversee the nation's finances. The president appointed the heads, or secretaries, of these departments to serve as his advisers. Over time these advisers became known as the president's cabinet.

Restoring the nation's credit. Next, Congress tackled the nation's finances, for the government had inherited serious financial problems. Not only did the Treasury lack funds to pay off war debts, it did not have enough money to run the country. Lawmakers turned to Secretary of the Treasury Alexander Hamilton for help.

Hamilton believed that America's future depended on a strong national government controlled by the rich and well born. He also believed that one of the best ways to strengthen the government, both financially and politically, was to establish economic policies that helped business and industry. If businesspeople believed the federal government had their best interests at heart, they would support it.

As a first step toward winning over the merchant class, Hamilton advised Congress to strengthen the nation's credit by paying off the national debt and by taking over the debts of the states. Hamilton knew that a nation that did not pay its debts would have trouble borrowing additional money. Despite strong resistance, particularly from the southern states, Congress eventually passed these measures. But in return for southern votes, Hamilton's supporters pledged that the nation's capital would be moved south to a site across the Potomac River from Virginia. The site was later named Washington, D.C.

In order to pay the national debt, of course, Hamilton had to raise money. Unlike today, the government did not have the power to collect an income tax. So Hamilton asked Congress to impose a tax on a few domestically produced items, most notably whiskey. The tax, to be paid by producers, hit western farmers the hardest. News of the tax infuriated them, and in the summer of 1794, farmers in western Pennsylvania rose in what became known as the **Whiskey Rebellion**. A federal force, however, quickly subdued the "Whiskey Boys."

Hamilton's bank proposal. Establishing good credit was not the only solution to the nation's financial woes. The government also lacked the means to manage the nation's money supply. Hamilton believed that the creation of a **national bank** would solve this problem, and

asked Congress to create such a bank. This proposal met with stiff opposition from many Americans who feared that the bank would be controlled by wealthy northeastern merchants.

Thomas Jefferson raised a more serious charge: nowhere in the Constitution was the federal government given the power to set up a bank. Jefferson believed that the government could only do what the Constitution specifically allows. This philosophy of constitutional interpretation is called **strict construction**. Hamilton, on the other hand, believed that the government could do anything the Constitution does not specifically forbid—the philosophy called **loose construction**.

The members of Congress debated the issue for months. In the end, President Washington sided with Hamilton, and Congress chartered the Bank of the United States in 1791. The charter granted the Bank the right to operate for 20 years, when it would again be subject to congressional approval.

■■ **To strengthen the government, Congress set up a court system, established executive departments, enhanced the nation's credit, and created a national bank.**

A DANGEROUS WORLD

Hamilton intended his financial program to enrich the American economy. In the 1790s, however, economic independence was not yet a reality. Americans still needed British money and technology to strengthen commerce and to develop manufacturing. France provided an important market for American agricultural products.

Thus, when France declared war on Great Britain, Spain, and the Netherlands in 1793, the resulting conflict disrupted American trade and threatened to draw the United States into war. Both France and Great Britain ignored the American declaration of neutrality and seized American vessels bound for enemy ports. In addition, Britain's **impressment**—or kidnapping—of U.S. sailors aroused American hostility.

The French, meanwhile, tried to stir up pro-French passions among Americans by reminding them of their 1778 military alliance treaty with France. But Washington, knowing that the United States was unprepared for war, refused to give in

The Granger Collection, New York

▲ **An excise officer is tarred and feathered by a mob in 1794.**

GEORGE WASHINGTON
1732–1799

in office 1789–1797

JOHN ADAMS
1735–1826

in office 1797–1801

THOMAS JEFFERSON
1743–1826

in office 1801–1809

JAMES MADISON
1751–1836

in office 1809–1817

to pressure. On April 22, 1793, he issued a proclamation forbidding Americans to offer support to any nation at war.

Washington managed to avoid foreign entanglements, but trouble brewed in the Northwest Territory. By the terms of the Treaty of Paris of 1783, the British granted this land to the United States. Native Americans, however, considered the territory theirs. To defend their homes, some 1,500 American Indians of various tribes joined together in a loose confederation. The confederation won several battles against American troops in 1790 and 1791, but fresh federal forces defeated the confederation in the summer of 1794. This defeat severely weakened Native American resistance and led to the surrender of additional Indian lands.

The American Indians had received weapons from British forts in the Northwest Territory. The existence of these forts violated the 1783 Treaty of Paris. This situation further strained America's shaky relations with Great Britain. Hoping to avert a war that he believed the United States could not win, President Washington sent Chief Justice John Jay to Great Britain in 1794 to negotiate a settlement. Under the terms of **Jay's Treaty** the British agreed to abandon their forts,

▶ Miami chief Little Turtle led American Indians in successful battles against American troops in the Northwest Territory during 1790–1791.

and the U.S. government agreed to pay debts owed to the British.

Fearing that an American alliance with Britain would threaten Spanish territory in North America, Spain moved to settle its disputes with the United States. The result was **Pinckney's Treaty**, negotiated in 1795 by Thomas Pinckney of South Carolina. This treaty set the southern U.S. boundary near Florida at the 31st parallel. It also guaranteed American navigation rights on the Mississippi River and use of the port at New Orleans for three years.

DOMESTIC BATTLES

By the mid-1790s heated debates over whether to side with Great Britain or France had already deepened political differences in the United States. **Sectionalism**, or loyalty to a particular part of the country, helped to create two political parties: the Federalists and the Democratic-Republicans (who soon became known as the Republicans— though the party has no historical connection to today's Republican party).

Merchants, manufacturers, and lawyers from New England and the Atlantic seaboard tended to support the Federalist party. Federalists favored a strong

▲ The Republican party believed in an agricultural America full of orderly farms, such as the one shown here.

national government and wanted to promote the development of commerce, especially with Great Britain. In contrast, the Republican party included planters, small farmers, and wage earners. The party was particularly strong on the frontier and in the South, but also found considerable support in the middle states. Republicans' main aim was to protect states' rights and individual liberties by limiting the federal government. Because they distrusted the aristocratic British, they tended to be pro-French.

The Federalists come to power. In the election of 1796 Federalists John Adams and Thomas Pinckney faced off against Republicans Thomas Jefferson and Aaron Burr. According to the Constitution, the candidate who received the most votes became president; the runner-up became vice president. When the votes were counted, however, Adams was elected president, and Jefferson—his Republican opponent—was vice president!

President Adams faced many challenges during his term. One of his goals was to improve relations with the French, who viewed Jay's Treaty as further evidence of pro-British leanings and continued to seize American ships bound for British ports. Adams's attempts to negotiate with France, however, turned into a crisis when the French made demands that seemed unreasonable to the Americans. Fortunately for Adams, a change of government in France led to an agreement.

The crisis with France increased the bad blood between the Federalists and the Republicans. In 1798 the Federalist majority in Congress added

fuel to the fire by passing the **Alien and Sedition Acts**. The Alien Act and the Alien Enemies Act authorized the president to imprison or expel "all such aliens [foreigners] as he shall judge dangerous to the peace and safety of the United States." The Sedition Act targeted American citizens, and Republicans in particular. It stated that anyone who wrote, said, or printed anything "false, scandalous, and malicious" about the government "with intent to defame" could be fined or jailed. Throughout the country, Republican newspaper editors and politicians were arrested for sedition; 25 were indicted and 10 convicted.

Many Americans saw the Sedition Act as an attempt to curb individuals' rights—rights that were guaranteed by the First Amendment. Furious Republicans voiced their protests through the **Kentucky and Virginia Resolutions**, written by Thomas Jefferson and James Madison. These resolutions declared the Alien and Sedition Acts unconstitutional. The states, they argued, had created the federal government as their agent; therefore the states had the right—and duty—to void any unconstitutional laws.

Because the Federalists controlled most state governments, the resolutions failed to win wide support. They had, however, raised an important question: Who should decide when a federal law or a government action violates the U.S. Constitution?—the states?—the Supreme Court? The resolutions came down on the side of the states. But Supreme Court chief justice John Marshall, Adams's most significant judicial appointment, took a different view a few years later in the case of *Marbury v. Madison* (1803). In this case, Marshall established the principle of **judicial review**—the right of the Supreme Court to declare an act of Congress unconstitutional. The Supreme Court thus acquired its most important role—that of final interpreter of the Constitution.

▪▪ Conflicts among European countries, disputes with American Indians, a growing sectionalism, and rivalry between political parties caused tension in the United States.

Jefferson takes office. In the election of 1800 the Republicans swept to power, gaining control of Congress. But another electoral crisis arose concerning the presidency: Jefferson and Burr, the

Abbey Aldrich Rockefeller Folk Art Center, Williamsburg, VA

two Republican candidates, had received the same number of votes! As dictated by the Constitution, the election was thrown to the House of Representatives. After a lengthy stalemate, the House selected Jefferson. To prevent future electoral crises, Congress proposed the **Twelfth Amendment** to the Constitution. Ratified in 1804, this amendment requires electors to vote for presidential and vice-presidential candidates on separate ballots.

To fulfill his promise of moderation, Jefferson left untouched some Federalist programs, including the national bank and the debt payment plan. But Jefferson had not abandoned his view that a federal government with too much power threatened individual freedoms and states' rights. Thus he led the Republican-controlled Congress in repealing taxes, cutting military funding, and reducing the size of the army and the navy.

THE NATION EXPANDS

In the election of 1800, the Republicans won every state that had a frontier on the **Trans-Appalachian West**, the area between the Appalachian Mountains and the Mississippi River. Republicans favored expansion, and Jefferson imagined "distant times, when our rapid multiplication will expand [the nation] . . . & cover the whole northern if not southern continent." This view appealed to settlers who were always seeking new land because their farming practices were hard on the soil.

Fertile land was not enough, however. Western farmers also needed access to the Mississippi River and to the port of New Orleans to get their produce to market. When Jefferson learned that Spain had secretly transferred the territory surrounding the river to France, he was alarmed. French control of the river might limit American trade and block westward expansion. To remedy the situation, Jefferson was prepared to offer Napoléon, France's ruler, as much as $10 million for New Orleans and West Florida. But to the American negotiators' surprise, Napoléon's representative asked how much the United States would pay for *all* of Louisiana—the enormous territory consisting roughly of the northern and western reaches of the Mississippi River basin. The astonished Americans quickly agreed to pay about $15 million for the land in the **Louisiana Purchase**.

President Jefferson assigned the task of mapping the huge new territory to two skilled frontiersmen, Meriwether Lewis and William Clark. The Lewis and Clark expedition, numbering about 45 men, left St. Louis in May 1804. Many Native Americans aided the expedition but none more than Sacagawea, a Shoshoni woman, who proved to be invaluable as a guide and interpreter. The expedition traveled up the Missouri River, crossed the Rocky Mountains, and canoed down the Snake

THE LOUISIANA PURCHASE

THROUGH OTHERS' EYES

Spain was unpleasantly surprised to discover in 1803 that France planned to sell Louisiana to the United States. Earlier, Spain had transferred the land to France on the condition that the French never part with it. Spain feared that if the United States acquired this vast territory, the young nation would threaten Spain's other colonies in North America, such as California and Mexico.

The Marques de Casa Irujo (eer-oo-hoh), Spain's minister to the United States, wrote a harsh letter to Secretary of State James Madison denying the United States' right to buy Louisiana: "The sale of that province to the United States is founded on the violation of a promise so absolute that it ought to be respected—a promise without which the king, my master, would not under any circumstances have let Louisiana go."

In a letter to his own government, Casa Irujo called the Louisiana Purchase "truly an evil" for the United States. He predicted the U.S. government would be unable to hold such a vast territory of diverse peoples together: "One does not need extraordinary wisdom to anticipate that the acquisition of Louisiana, far from consolidating the strength and vigor of this nation, will rather contribute to weaken it."

▲ Americans pushed westward as new territories opened. This engraving shows a family crossing the Appalachians on their way to Pittsburgh.

and Columbia rivers to the Pacific Ocean. After nearly two and a half years, the expedition returned—bringing with it detailed journals and various specimens from the explored areas.

The Louisiana Purchase added all or part of 13 future states to the nation. This increased size gave the United States greater international stature. And as Americans devoted more energy to developing the frontier, they increasingly looked west, rather than east across the Atlantic. This shift promoted a stronger sense of national identity. The purchase, however, had a negative effect on American Indians, whose claims to the land were not considered, and on many African Americans, who became slaves in the new territory.

■■ **Although the Louisiana Purchase had negative consequences for some peoples, it added to U.S. prestige and helped build national identity.**

𝒯HE WAR OF 1812

Events across the Atlantic, however, by no means went unnoticed. When Napoléon's war in Europe spilled over into the Atlantic, America was again caught in the cross fire between France and Britain. Great Britain had banned all neutral vessels from trading with France; France reacted by threatening to seize all foreign ships that cooperated with the British navy.

In the summer of 1807, events took an ugly turn when Britain stepped up the impressment of American sailors. In response, Jefferson urged Congress to pass the **Embargo Act** of 1807, which stopped shipments of food and other American products to all foreign ports. But public pressure from American merchants, farmers, and workers led Congress to repeal the embargo in 1809.

Problems abroad were compounded by events at home. Rapid westward expansion fueled tensions between settlers and Indians, who continued to look to Britain for assistance. Westerners were particularly alarmed by the activities of the Shawnee leader Tecumseh.

BIO GRAPHY Settlers had a tireless and resourceful opponent in Tecumseh (1768–1813). When whites killed his father, Tecumseh was adopted by the Shawnee chief Blackfish. As he grew older, Tecumseh became convinced that American Indians' best hope for survival rested in a military alliance among the Indian nations.

In the early 1800s Tecumseh set out to rally the Indian nations east of the Mississippi River. From the Great Lakes to the Gulf of Mexico, Tecumseh urged American

Tecumseh

Indians not to sell land to the settlers. As Tecumseh gained support, settlers pressured the government to take action. In the fall of 1811, General William Henry Harrison decided to move against Tecumseh's stronghold on the Tippecanoe River in Indiana Territory. The **Battle of Tippecanoe** ended in defeat for Native Americans, shattering Tecumseh's dream of a united confederation. Two years later, he was killed in battle.

The British had supplied Tecumseh's forces with weapons. Thus, the clamor for war against Britain again arose in Congress. James Madison, who had succeeded Jefferson as president in 1809, asked for a declaration of war. In his message to Congress on June 1, 1812, Madison cited Britain's repeated violations of neutral rights, continued impressment of American sailors, and support of American Indian uprisings on the frontier as reasons for the declaration. After some debate, Congress voted to declare war.

■■ **Frustration over violations of neutral rights, impressment of U.S. sailors, and British support of American Indians led to war.**

American war strategy focused on the conquest of Canada. With the British preoccupied by their struggle to stop Napoléon, Americans were confident of a quick victory. But repeated attempts to invade Canada failed. The United States did, however, enjoy early successes at sea. In the first eight months of the war, U.S. frigates won many victories against British warships, and American privateers disrupted British commerce. Encouraged by the naval victories, General Harrison crossed into Canada with some 4,500 troops and defeated the British and their American Indian allies. The British hold on the Northwest Territory was finally broken.

The second phase of the war took a different turn. Soon after ending its war against France early in 1814, Great Britain sent some 14,000 reinforcements to Canada. British strategists planned to invade the United States from the north through Canada and from the south through New Orleans. They would also continue to raid the Atlantic coast to disrupt American commerce.

On the night of August 24, 1814, British forces struck Washington, D.C. Within a day they had captured the city, burning the executive mansion and other public buildings before moving on. The next target for a coastal assault was the city of Baltimore, where British vessels bombarded Fort McHenry. The fort's brave stand—immortalized in Francis Scott Key's poem "The Star-Spangled Banner"—was a setback for the British.

Great Britain then assembled about 7,500 troops to strike at New Orleans. General Andrew

▲ British troops were defeated as they attacked the line of earthworks built for the defense of New Orleans. Painted by H. Charles McBarron, Andrew Jackson is shown here mounted on a horse.

Jackson, a ruthless Indian-fighter and commander of a frontier militia, led the American forces in defense. When the invasion finally came on January 8, 1815, well-protected U.S. troops easily won the **Battle of New Orleans**. Few Americans were killed, but British casualties topped 2,000.

Tragically, the fighting at New Orleans came after peace negotiations had produced the **Treaty of Ghent**, signed on Christmas Eve, 1814. The treaty consolidated American control over the Northwest Territory through the defeat of American Indians and the removal of their British allies. In addition, it resulted in a peace between the United States and Great Britain that marked the beginning of a long partnership.

SECTION 3 REVIEW

IDENTIFY and explain the significance of the following: Bill of Rights, Judiciary Act of 1789, Alexander Hamilton, Whiskey Rebellion, national bank, strict construction, loose construction, Jay's Treaty, Pinckney's Treaty, sectionalism, Alien and Sedition Acts, Kentucky and Virginia Resolutions, *Marbury* v. *Madison,* judicial review, Twelfth Amendment, Trans-Appalachian West, Embargo Act, Battle of Tippecanoe, Battle of New Orleans, Treaty of Ghent.

1. **MAIN IDEA** What actions did Congress take to establish the federal government and to strengthen the nation's finances?

2. **MAIN IDEA** How did conflicts in Europe cause political tension among Americans in the 1790s?

3. **ASSESSING CONSEQUENCES** What consequences did the Louisiana Purchase have for the United States?

4. **WRITING TO EXPLAIN** Write a paragraph explaining the causes of the War of 1812.

5. **ANALYZING** Imagine you are Tecumseh. Why do you believe American Indians should form a confederation?

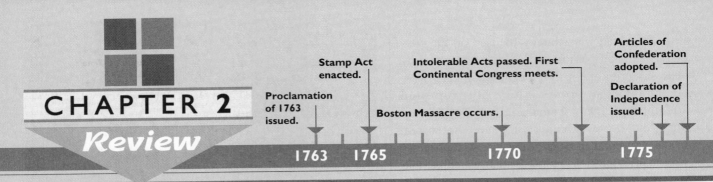

CHAPTER 2
Review

Proclamation of 1763 issued.

Stamp Act enacted.

Boston Massacre occurs.

Intolerable Acts passed. First Continental Congress meets.

Articles of Confederation adopted.

Declaration of Independence issued.

1763   1765   1770   1775

WRITING A SUMMARY

Using the essential points of the chapter as a guide, write a summary of the chapter.

REVIEWING CHRONOLOGY

Number your paper 1 to 5. Study the time line above, and list the following events in the order in which they happened by writing the first next to 1, the second next to 2, and so on. Then complete the activity below.

1. U.S. Constitution ratified.
2. Intolerable Acts passed.
3. U.S. completes Louisiana Purchase.
4. Bill of Rights ratified.
5. Declaration of Independence issued.

Evaluating Select an event on the time line, and in a paragraph, state its significance in U.S. history.

IDENTIFYING PEOPLE AND IDEAS

Explain the historical significance of each of the following people or terms.

1. Thomas Paine
2. Battle of Saratoga
3. guerrilla warfare
4. Daniel Shays
5. Three-Fifths Compromise
6. separation of powers
7. loose construction
8. Twelfth Amendment
9. Sacagawea
10. Treaty of Ghent

UNDERSTANDING MAIN IDEAS

1. What were the main reasons the colonists protested British actions?
2. Why did the Second Continental Congress issue the Declaration of Independence?
3. What were the main compromises reached during the Constitutional Convention?
4. What steps were taken by the First Congress to organize the federal government?
5. What events pushed the United States toward war with Great Britain in the early 1800s?

REVIEWING THEMES

1. **Economic Development** How did British attempts to raise revenues in the colonies conflict with colonial interests?

2. **Constitutional Heritage** How does the way the government was organized reflect concern about a powerful national government?
3. **Democratic Values** Why did two political parties form in the 1790s? How did the two parties differ?

THINKING CRITICALLY

1. **Evaluating** Some historians claim that wise leaders could have resolved the differences between Great Britain and the colonies before 1775. Do you agree? Explain.
2. **Identifying Cause and Effect** How did the experience of governing the nation under the Articles of Confederation influence the actions of the framers of the Constitution?
3. **Hypothesizing** Why did American Indians resist settlers moving west?

STRATEGY FOR SUCCESS

Review the Skills Handbook entry on Reviewing Map Basics beginning on page 752. Then number your paper 1 to 13. Study the map below, noting the numbers on it. It illustrates the states, either in full or in part, that were formed from the Louisiana Purchase. Write the name of the state next to the corresponding number.

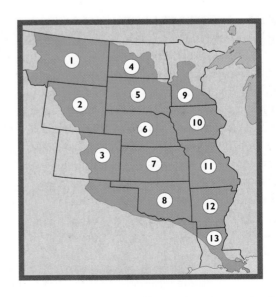

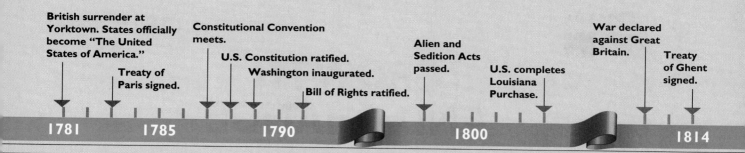

British surrender at Yorktown. States officially become "The United States of America."

Treaty of Paris signed.

Constitutional Convention meets.

U.S. Constitution ratified.

Washington inaugurated.

Bill of Rights ratified.

Alien and Sedition Acts passed.

U.S. completes Louisiana Purchase.

War declared against Great Britain.

Treaty of Ghent signed.

1781   1785   1790   1800   1814

WRITING ABOUT HISTORY

Writing to Persuade Imagine you are a business owner in New England who supports the Constitution. Write a letter to the editor of your local newspaper, explaining why you support the new plan of government over the Articles of Confederation.

USING PRIMARY SOURCES

At first some Patriot leaders opposed enlisting African Americans in the fight for freedom. However, when soldiers were needed for the southern campaign, Washington's aide, Alexander Hamilton, suggested recruiting African Americans. Read the following excerpt from a letter by Hamilton, in which he outlines his plan. Then write a summary of the points outlined in the letter.

> *Head Quarters March 14th 79*
>
> *Dear Sir:*
>
> *Colonel Laurens, who will have the honor of delivering you this letter, is on his way to South Carolina, on a project . . . to raise two, three, or four battalions of Negroes . . . by contributions from owners in proportion to the number they possess. . . .*
>
> *I have not the least doubt that the Negroes will make very excellent soldiers, with proper management. . . .*
>
> *I foresee that this project will have to combat much opposition from prejudice and self-interest. The contempt we have been taught to entertain for the blacks makes us fancy many things that are founded neither in reason nor experience. . . . An essential part of the plan is to give them their freedom with their muskets. This will secure their fidelity, animate their courage, and I believe will have a good influence upon those who remain, by opening a door to their emancipation [freedom]. . . .*
>
> *—Alexander Hamilton*

LINKING HISTORY AND GEOGRAPHY

British forces fought the Revolutionary War in physical settings that were often unfamiliar to them. Study the map on page 34. Select one of the battles or campaigns included on the map and indicate how geography might have helped or hurt British efforts.

Struggle at Concord Bridge

BUILDING YOUR PORTFOLIO

Complete the following projects independently or cooperatively.

1. CONFLICT Imagine you are a public official assigned to oversee the American war effort either in the Revolutionary War or in the War of 1812. Create a chart showing how you will recruit and train troops, coordinate and transport supplies, communicate with field commanders, and achieve whatever else might be necessary to maintain an effective military force and strategy.

2. INDIVIDUAL RIGHTS Imagine you are the editor of a colonial newspaper. Write an editorial arguing for the expansion of colonists' rights under British rule. Your editorial should list specific grievances and should explain how an expansion of rights would address these grievances.

Chapter 3

1815–1860

GROWTH AND CHANGE

FOCUS

UNDERSTANDING THE MAIN IDEA

After the War of 1812, the United States entered a period of growth. As its territory expanded and new transportation systems linked different regions of the country, the economy grew and national markets were established for the first time. Politics became more democratic in the 19th century. But growth also led to new tensions, especially over slavery.

THEMES

■ **ECONOMIC DEVELOPMENT** What are some of the factors that might influence a region's economic development? Why might regions within a large country develop different economies?

■ **DEMOCRATIC VALUES** How might people who feel left out of the democratic process bring about change in a society?

■ **GLOBAL RELATIONS** How might territorial expansion lead to international as well as domestic conflicts?

1820	1830	1836	1848	1857
▼	▼	▼	▼	▼
Missouri Compromise passed.	**Indian Removal Act passed.**	**Texas declares independence from Mexico.**	**Seneca Falls Convention held.**	***Dred Scott* case decided.**

The War of 1812, although producing no clear-cut victory for the United States, proved that the country could stand up to a major European power. Americans began to believe that the United States could become a power in its own right, free from Europe's influence and control.

Verdict of the People (1855)
by George Caleb Bingham

The Boatmen's National Bank, St. Louis, Missouri

In 1828 Frances Wright of Scotland, a travel writer, social reformer, and sometime U.S. resident, delivered a Fourth of July speech at New Harmony, Indiana. She praised the United States as the protector of "human liberty [and] the favored scene of human improvement." Soon, she predicted, "all mankind" would celebrate "the Jubilee of Independence."

The United States was far from granting liberty to all in 1828, as Native Americans and enslaved African Americans well knew. Yet the national pride and optimism expressed in Wright's speech were widespread. Indeed one British visitor noted that American national pride "blazes out everywhere and on all occasions."

The new confidence that burst forth in this era took many forms. The United States built new roads and canals, developed new industries, launched a period of economic growth, secured its borders, and warned Europe to stay out of Latin America. American optimism also fostered a renewal of religious faith and led to a variety of reform movements. The expansionist ambitions of some Americans were boundless as they envisioned a continental empire.

But growth, expansion, and reform also produced new tensions, especially between the increasingly separate societies of the North and the South. By midcentury slavery cast an ever-lengthening shadow over the future of the nation.

Frances Wright

NATIONALISM AND ECONOMIC POWER

FOCUS

- After the War of 1812 what steps did the United States take to secure its place in the world and to develop its economy?

- How were sectional tensions between the North and the South eased in the 1820s and 1830s?

- What were some of the effects of Andrew Jackson's policies?

The War of 1812 filled Americans with national pride and sparked the growth of the domestic economy. Soon, a new spirit of democracy swept the nation, as symbolized by "the man of the people," Andrew Jackson. But sectional tension and economic downturns eroded his party's strength.

Flag of the United States, 1818

The Granger Collection, New York

THE RISE OF NATIONALISM

The United States emerged from the War of 1812 with a new sense of **nationalism**, or national pride and loyalty. In addition, the war's end ushered in a period of political harmony known as the Era of Good Feelings. The newfound harmony was largely due to the collapse of the Federalist party, which had angered many Americans by opposing the war.

The young nation had successfully stood up to Great Britain, and now the new president, James Monroe, moved to secure the nation's borders. An agreement with Great Britain set much of the U.S.–Canadian border. The United States and Great Britain also agreed to occupy **Oregon Country**— the disputed area of the Pacific Northwest—jointly for 10 years, with a boundary to be set later. An agreement with Spain set the southern and western boundaries of the Louisiana Purchase and transferred Florida to the United States.

American foreign policy interests did not stop at the nation's borders. American officials were worried about reports that France was prepared to help Spain retake the newly independent countries of Latin America. In 1823, in what came to be called the **Monroe Doctrine**, the president declared that the United States would consider any European attempt to revive old colonies or establish new ones in the Western Hemisphere "as dangerous to our peace and safety."

The United States secured its borders and declared the Americas off-limits to European colonization.

PROMOTING ECONOMIC GROWTH

Americans were looking inward as well as outward after the War of 1812. While the war had given U.S. manufacturing a boost, it had also revealed weaknesses in the nation's financial system. Furthermore, the difficulty and expense of moving goods and troops during the war had underscored the nation's transportation problems. By 1815 many people were calling for national measures to improve these systems.

Henry Clay, a congressman from Kentucky, came up with a program of federal support for economic development. Clay's program, known as the **American System**, had three main features. The first was the re-creation of a national bank to provide for a sound currency and greater federal control over the nation's financial system. (The previous national bank's charter had been allowed to expire in 1811.) Congress agreed and chartered the Second Bank of the United States in 1816.

The second feature of Clay's program—a protective tariff to encourage manufacturing—also met with Congress's approval. The **Tariff Act of 1816** put a 25 percent duty on most imported factory goods, making them more expensive than their U.S.-produced counterparts.

The third feature of the American System was a national transportation system to unite northern manufacturers, western farmers, and southern planters. This feature failed to be enacted into law, and states and private companies built most roads and canals. New York, for example, began building the Erie Canal in 1817. This 363-mile-long canal linked the Hudson River with Lake Erie, reducing the cost of moving goods between Buffalo and New York City by more than 90 percent. The success of the Erie Canal spurred massive canal projects in other states. By 1840 rivers and canals combined to provide a waterway that stretched from Illinois to the Atlantic.

Technological advances also furthered the transportation revolution. The steam-powered locomotive came into commercial use in the 1830s. Between 1840 and 1850, railroads reached many isolated parts of the country as companies spent more than $200 million laying nearly 9,000 miles of track. By making it easier and cheaper to move goods long distances, new transportation systems created national markets for the first time. Regions no longer had to be relatively self-sufficient; they could import some goods and produce what was most profitable.

This creation of national markets has come to be known as the **market revolution**. The market revolution both increased profits and changed the way farmers and manufacturers did business. Before the market revolution, for example, entire families worked most northern farms. They grew

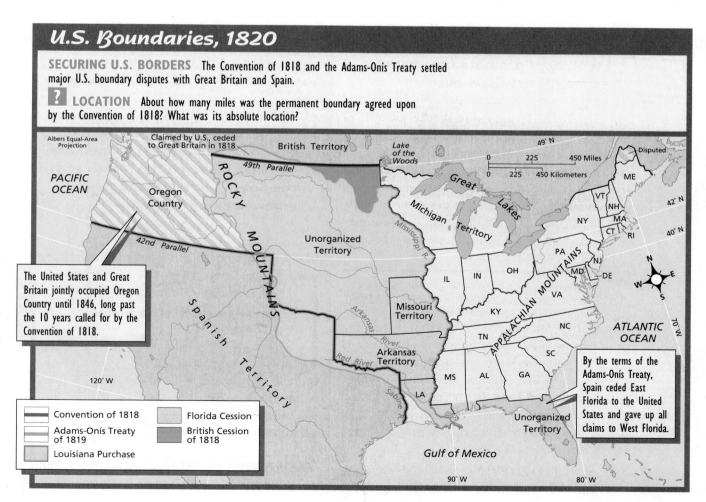

U.S. Boundaries, 1820

SECURING U.S. BORDERS The Convention of 1818 and the Adams-Onís Treaty settled major U.S. boundary disputes with Great Britain and Spain.

? LOCATION About how many miles was the permanent boundary agreed upon by the Convention of 1818? What was its absolute location?

Albers Equal-Area Projection

Claimed by U.S., ceded to Great Britain in 1818

British Territory

Lake of the Woods

49° N

Disputed

PACIFIC OCEAN

49th Parallel

ROCKY MOUNTAINS

Oregon Country

ME

Great Lakes

Michigan Territory

Mississippi R.

VT

NH

MA

CT RI

42° N

NY

40° N

42nd Parallel

Unorganized Territory

PA

NJ

MD

DE

The United States and Great Britain jointly occupied Oregon Country until 1846, long past the 10 years called for by the Convention of 1818.

Spanish Territory

IL

IN

OH

VA

KY

Missouri Territory

Arkansas River

TN

NC

APPALACHIAN MOUNTAINS

70° W

ATLANTIC OCEAN

Red River

Arkansas Territory

SC

120° W

Sabine R.

MS

AL

GA

By the terms of the Adams-Onís Treaty, Spain ceded East Florida to the United States and gave up all claims to West Florida.

LA

Unorganized Territory

Gulf of Mexico

0   225   450 Miles
0   225   450 Kilometers

Convention of 1818	Florida Cession
Adams-Onís Treaty of 1819	British Cession of 1818
Louisiana Purchase	

90° W   80° W

their own food and sold their crops locally. After the market revolution northern farmers hired laborers to help produce large cash crops to sell in national and international markets.

The market revolution was tied to a change in manufacturing. The increasing demand for goods led manufacturers to divide tasks to speed up production and to invest in new machinery that increased output. This shift from hand to machine production was part of the **Industrial Revolution**, which began in Great Britain in the mid-1700s with the invention of new spinning machines. The machines revolutionized the textile industry by allowing for mass production—the manufacture of large quantities of goods.

In the United States, inventors made their own contributions to industrialization. Eli Whitney pioneered the use of interchangeable, machine-produced parts in the manufacture of firearms. Another innovation was Francis Cabot Lowell's factory system. Lowell cut costs and increased output by using machines—housed under one roof—to accomplish every step of the manufacturing process.

■■ After the War of 1812, the transportation, market, and industrial revolutions promoted the nation's economic development.

By 1818, largely due to the growth of national markets, all sections of the country prospered. Many people borrowed money to buy land or build factories. The state banks lent more money than they could back with **specie**, or gold and silver coin. The result was the **Panic of 1819**, a chain reaction of bank failures and foreclosures.

THE RISE OF SECTIONAL TENSIONS

The United States faced more than economic problems in 1819. The nation was also plagued by political conflict caused by westward expansion. In that year the Missouri Territory, which contained some 10,000 enslaved African Americans, applied for statehood. Because the nation was equally divided between slave and free states, Missouri's entrance as a slave state would tip the congressional balance in favor of the South. An angry debate erupted.

To resolve the issue, Henry Clay led Congress in working out the **Missouri Compromise** in 1820. The agreement admitted Missouri as a slave state and Maine as a free state, thus maintaining the congressional balance. Moreover, slavery was banned in the rest of the Louisiana Purchase north of latitude 36°30'. The compromise calmed the sectional crisis, but many Americans worried that the slavery issue would reemerge.

The protective tariff was another issue dividing the nation. To protect U.S. manufacturers Congress passed a tariff in 1828 that doubled the 1816 rates for some items. Outraged southern planters, who feared that the British would retaliate by buying less southern cotton, accused Congress of favoring the industrial North. Outlining the South's position, then–Vice President John C. Calhoun argued that the states, as creators of the federal union, had the right to nullify, or refuse to obey, any act of Congress they considered unconstitutional. This view became known as the **doctrine of nullification**.

South Carolina, finding this doctrine useful, declared Congress's recent tariffs null and void and threatened to secede if the federal government tried to collect the tariffs within the state. Again Clay arranged a compromise, convincing Congress to pass a tariff in 1833 that lowered rates over a 10-year period. The crisis subsided, but sectional tensions continued to grow.

■■ The Missouri Compromise and the 1833 tariff settled immediate conflicts between the North and the South but left fundamental differences unresolved.

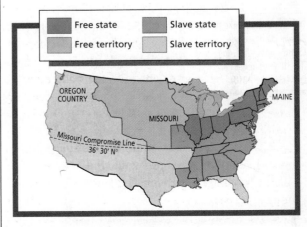

▲ The Missouri Compromise

THE JACKSONIAN ERA

Presiding over the nullification crisis was Tennessean Andrew Jackson. Known as "Old Hickory" because of his toughness, Jackson portrayed himself as a "man of the people." Defeated by John Quincy Adams in the controversial election of 1824, Jackson had won the presidency in 1828 by a wide margin.

Jackson owed his victory in part to more democratic voting laws, particularly in the frontier states. His image as a "common man" won the support of farmers, laborers, and frontier settlers. "The virtuous portion of the people have well sustained me," Jackson rejoiced. "I am filled with gratitude."

Jackson's supporters eventually became known as the Democratic party (the origin of today's party of the same name). Once in office, Jackson rewarded some of his supporters by giving them government jobs. This practice became known as the **spoils system**.

Jackson's Indian policy.

Andrew Jackson put his stamp on a decade, and his policies shaped the nation for years. Some of his most important policies involved the American Indians occupying millions of acres of fertile land in the Southeast that European American farmers and land speculators wanted. Jackson, who viewed the continued presence of American Indians in the East as a barrier to "the waves of population and civilization . . . rolling westward," agreed that the Indian lands should be opened for white settlement.

Jackson cloaked his calls for removal in humanitarian terms, claiming that Indians would be moved west for their own protection. In 1830 Congress passed the **Indian Removal Act**, providing for the relocation—by force, if need be—of tribes living east of the Mississippi to Indian Territory in present-day Oklahoma (see map on page 86). Jackson promised eastern Indians the land for "as long as the grass grows, or the water runs."

By 1840, most American Indians—among them Creeks, Chickasaws, Choctaws, Cherokees, and Seminoles—had been driven from the Southeast. Few, however, went willingly. Some appealed to Congress in the name of "liberty and justice." Others hoped the judicial system would support their cause. When Georgia seized Cherokee land to sell to white settlers, the Cherokees went to the Supreme Court. Although

▲ *The Intruders* (1966) by American Indian artist Jerome Tiger portrays the Florida home of the Seminoles.

the Court ruled in their favor, Jackson would not enforce the ruling, and Georgia kept on taking Cherokee land. Unable to hold out, the Cherokees were forced to move to Indian Territory in 1838. Some 4,000 Cherokees died on the 800-mile trek that came to be known as the **Trail of Tears**.

Other Indians, like the Seminole leader Osceola, urged outright resistance to removal:

> ❝ My Brothers! . . . the white man says I shall go, and he will send people to make me go; but I have a rifle, and I have some powder and some lead. I say, we must not leave our homes and lands. ❞

In Florida, resistance to removal led to the **Second Seminole War** (1835–1842), which was one of the most costly Indian wars in U.S. history. Although the Seminoles fought bravely, most were eventually killed or removed to Indian Territory.

■■ **In order to open land to white settlement, Jackson and the U.S. government forced most eastern Indians to move west.**

The Panic of 1837.

Indian removal remains one of the Jacksonian era's most controversial legacies. Yet for many Americans at the time, other economic issues—particularly regarding the Second Bank of the United States—seemed more important. Making the banking issue a personal crusade, Jackson attacked the Bank as a dangerous monopoly that benefited rich investors at the public's expense. To shut down the Bank, Jackson stopped depositing federal funds in it. New deposits went to state banks

JAMES MONROE
1758–1831

in office 1817–1825

JOHN QUINCY ADAMS
1767–1848

in office 1825–1829

ANDREW JACKSON
1767–1845

in office 1829–1837

MARTIN VAN BUREN
1782–1862

in office 1837–1841

WILLIAM HENRY HARRISON
1773–1841

in office 1841

JOHN TYLER
1790–1862

in office 1841–1845

chosen for their officers' loyalty to the Democratic party—**pet banks**, as Jackson's enemies called them.

Jackson won his bank war, but by weakening federal control over banking, he invited a financial crisis. His pet banks fueled inflation by issuing their own bank notes and making loans without enough specie to back them. To curb inflation, Jackson in 1836 ordered the Treasury to accept only gold and silver as payment for public land. Many people began demanding that their banks exchange bank notes for gold or silver. Unable to do this, hundreds of banks failed in the panic of 1837. Jackson left office before the inflationary bubble burst, thus leaving his successors—among them members of the new Whig party—to suffer the consequences of the country's mounting economic and sectional crises.

 Jackson's monetary policies helped cause the economic crisis of the late 1830s.

SECTION 1 REVIEW

IDENTIFY and explain the significance of the following: nationalism, American System, Tariff Act of 1816, market revolution, Industrial Revolution, specie, Missouri Compromise, doctrine of nullification, Andrew Jackson, spoils system, Indian Removal Act, Osceola, Second Seminole War, pet banks.

LOCATE and explain the significance of the following: Oregon Country, Indian Territory.

1. **MAIN IDEA** How was the U.S. economy helped by the transportation and market revolutions?

2. **MAIN IDEA** What conditions led to the Panics of 1819 and 1837?

3. **MAIN IDEA** Why did Missouri's petition for statehood and Congress's 1828 tariff cause sectional tension? How were these conflicts resolved?

4. **WRITING TO EXPLAIN** Imagine you are the editor of a European newspaper in 1823. Write an editorial explaining the significance of the Monroe Doctrine.

5. **USING HISTORICAL IMAGINATION** Imagine you are a Cherokee on the Trail of Tears. Write a poem or diary entry explaining your feelings at being forced to leave your home.

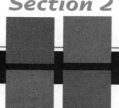

SEPARATE SOCIETIES: NORTH AND SOUTH

FOCUS

- How did the market and industrial revolutions affect life in the North?
- Why did the demand for slaves increase in the South? How did slave laborers attempt to shape their lives?
- What ideas and movements did reformers support in the first half of the 19th century?

The market and industrial revolutions changed northern and southern societies. In the North, new social divisions and new ways of working emerged. In the South, the dominance of cotton strengthened the slave-based social order. Throughout the nation, some changes in society alarmed Americans and inspired them to launch a variety of reform movements.

Carrying cotton from southern fields

NORTHERN SOCIETY

The market and industrial revolutions profoundly affected the North. New social divisions arose as a wide gap opened between the rich—merchants, bankers, and manufacturers who lived in huge, lavish homes—and the poor, who crowded into small apartments with few conveniences. And between the wealthy and the poor arose a new social class—the **middle class**. Prosperous farmers, artisans, shopkeepers, ministers, lawyers, and their families made up the new middle class. Middle-class families lived in modest but comfortable homes and had the income to buy food, clothing, and other products made available by the market revolution.

Changing working conditions. The ways people worked also changed during the early 19th century. Previously, whole families had worked together at home or in mills. But as factories needing hundreds of employees sprang up, owners found it more practical to hire individuals instead of families.

In some places, such as the textile mills of Lowell, Massachusetts, young, single women became factory workers. These women were cheaper to hire than men, since they were not seen as having to support their families. Children, too, often worked in the mills. By 1832, two out of five New England factory workers were children. Supervisors often required children to run machines late into the night.

Children were not the only ones who faced difficult working conditions, particularly as industrialization expanded. Owners—searching for larger profits—cut wages, sped up production, and increased working hours. As conditions worsened, workers organized more than 60 unions to fight for reforms, such as the 10-hour workday.

Labor unions used many methods to press for reforms. A common tactic was the **strike**—the refusal to work until employers meet union demands. During the 1830s, workers led more than 100 strikes, mostly to protest low wages or to avoid wage reductions. Workers' protests, however, had little success, as more job seekers competed for factory positions.

■■ The market and industrial revolutions created a new middle class and changed the ways people worked.

Immigration. Many of the job seekers were new immigrants. In the 1830s, more than 500,000 newcomers—eager for work, land, and equality—poured into the country. By 1860, immigrants made up about 14 percent of the U.S. population.

The largest group of immigrants—more than 1.9 million—came from Ireland. Poverty, hunger, and mistreatment by the British had driven them from their homeland. Most settled in cities, where they lived in crowded slums and often took the most dangerous and undesirable jobs. The second largest group of immigrants came from the states that make up present-day Germany. Some German immigrants sought religious freedom or refuge from political conditions. But most were displaced artisans or farmers seeking economic opportunity.

Though the Irish and Germans faced hardships in making a new life in America, they were able to forge their own communities. The Irish established hundreds of Roman Catholic churches and played an active role in local politics. Germans formed tightly knit neighborhoods, complete with European-style beer gardens where families met to socialize. Many communities also published newspapers in German.

Some native-born Americans were troubled by the immigrants' customs. They disapproved of the "clannishness" of the Germans and feared the Roman Catholicism and growing political power of the Irish. Such feelings gave rise to **nativism**—the favoring of native-born Americans over the foreign-born. Some nativists urged limiting immigrants' rights to vote and hold public office. At times nativists' fears led to violence. Anti-Catholic riots hit cities such as Boston, New York, and Philadelphia from the 1830s through the 1850s.

■■ Irish and German immigrants left economic and social hardships in Europe to seek opportunities in the United States.

⊤HE MIDDLE WEST

Not all immigrants settled in northern cities. Many, especially Germans, Swiss, Scandinavians, and Dutch, sought opportunity in the Middle West. This region was newly prosperous because growing northeastern factories and cities needed more farm products, which middle western farmers began to supply.

As the market revolution made many manufactured products less expensive, farm families began to purchase items, such as cloth, they had previously made at home. Farmers also bought machines that increased crop yields. Soon they were able to focus on growing a single crop, such as wheat or corn, for the market.

Women also began to make items to sell. For example, women earned so much money making butter and cheese that some farms began to specialize in dairy production. This work was handled by women who also performed other home and farm chores.

⠎OUTHERN SOCIETY

Like the Middle West, the South was primarily agricultural. In 1860, the South had 35 percent of the nation's population but only 15 percent of the manufacturing centers. Accordingly, most southern whites were farmers.

A slave-owning planter minority dominated southern society and politics. Below the planters on the social ladder were the hundreds of thousands of **yeoman farmers** who made up the majority of southern whites. Most of these small farmers grew their own food and raised some crop (often grain)

▲ This 1844 picture shows an anti-Catholic mob battling the state militia in Philadelphia.

The Granger Collection, New York

for cash. Below the yeoman farmers were the poorest whites who farmed the least-fertile soils and often had to depend on hunting and fishing for survival.

King Cotton and slave labor.

Despite its agricultural emphasis, the South, too, felt the effects of market and industrial changes. In particular, the invention of weaving machines that cut the cost and time of making cloth sent the demand for cotton skyrocketing. Southern

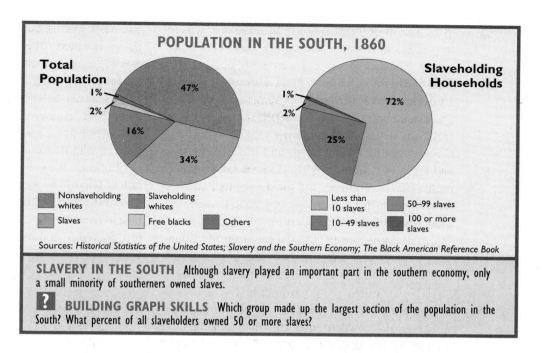

POPULATION IN THE SOUTH, 1860

Total Population

1%
2%
47%
16%
34%

Slaveholding Households

1%
2%
72%
25%

Nonslaveholding whites
Slaveholding whites
Slaves
Free blacks
Others

Less than 10 slaves
10–49 slaves
50–99 slaves
100 or more slaves

Sources: *Historical Statistics of the United States; Slavery and the Southern Economy; The Black American Reference Book*

SLAVERY IN THE SOUTH Although slavery played an important part in the southern economy, only a small minority of southerners owned slaves.

? **BUILDING GRAPH SKILLS** Which group made up the largest section of the population in the South? What percent of all slaveholders owned 50 or more slaves?

planters were able to meet the demand thanks to another new machine—the **cotton gin.** Invented by Eli Whitney in 1793, the cotton gin enabled a person to clean 50 times as much cotton as a person working by hand. The growing profitability of cotton also led to the extension of the slave system.

As cotton production expanded, the demand for slaves rose. The number of slaves grew from about 1.5 million in 1820 to some 4 million by 1860. The Upper South, with more slaves than the region needed, sold slaves to the cotton-producing states of the Lower South.

While some slaves lived in the cities and worked at skilled trades, more than 75 percent labored on southern plantations and farms. Field hands worked long hours, especially during harvest. Ex-slave Peter Clifton wrote, "The rule on the place was: Wake up the slaves at daylight, begin work when they can see, and quit work when they can't see." Some slaves—especially women—served the plantation household as maids, cooks, or nannies.

■■ **The rising demand for cotton led to an increased demand for slaves as planters sought to boost cotton production.**

On small farms slaveholders usually supervised their slaves directly. On the larger plantations **overseers**—usually planters' sons, other relatives, small farmers, or skilled workers—managed slaves. To help supervise the slaves, overseers used

drivers—assistants picked from among the slaves. Drivers had the difficult task of directing the work of their fellow slaves.

The living conditions and treatment of slaves varied from place to place. To make a profit using slave labor, planters had to make sure slaves were fed, clothed, and free from illness. However, housing was cramped and sparsely furnished. Furthermore, slaves usually had to supplement their meager rations of meat, rice, grits, and meal with food they caught or grew themselves.

While some planters used rewards to get slaves to work, others relied on the use or threat of violence. Whipping was the most common form of punishment. William Wells Brown, a former slave and the author of the first published novel by an African American, wrote that the whip was used "very frequently and freely, and a small offence on the part of a slave furnished an occasion for its use." Perhaps the worst threat held over slaves was that of being sold "down river"—away from relatives and community ties.

Resistance. African Americans resisted slavery in various ways—from running away to open rebellion. In the first half of the 19th century there were several small uprisings involving slaves in the South. Open rebellion, however, was rare. Slaves generally protested their bondage through individual actions. They might fake illness, slow their work pace, or damage tools in an effort to disrupt the plantation routine.

The most tempting form of resistance was to run away, whether for only a few days or permanently. Chances of success were slim, and punishment if caught was brutal. Some aid came from the **Underground Railroad**, a loose network of white and black abolitionists who helped slaves escape to freedom in the North or in Canada. Escaping slaves were hidden in attics and haylofts by day and taken by "conductors" to the next safe house at night. Harriet Tubman, the most famous and successful conductor and an escaped slave herself, led more than 300 slaves to safety.

Although slaves' lives were controlled during the workday, their time was mostly their own after dark and on Sundays and rare holidays. Then slaves devoted time to relatives and community, creating a unique culture. At its center were family, religion, music, folktales, and humor. Laughter helped slaves deal with painful situations and kept them from being crushed by slavery. Slaves' songs and tales often represented an indirect means of protest, one that could be made without inviting retribution. "We would sing and dance and make others laugh," former slave John Little explained. "We did it to keep down trouble, and to keep our hearts from being completely broken." Religion, too, played a vital role, and services often blended Christian and African elements. For example, the

HISTORY in the Making

BY DR. STERLING STUCKEY

Shouts Across the Ocean

When Africans were forcibly brought to North America as slaves, their traditions crossed the ocean with them. Today, African influences are visible throughout American society. American dance and music, for example, have roots in African dances and musical forms.

In much of Africa, religious and ceremonial dances are performed in a ring, with dancers slowly moving counterclockwise in a circle. The ring often symbolizes the life cycle—the cycle of birth and death. Thus, it is an important part of many burial ceremonies, used to show respect for one's ancestors.

The African ring dances were the source of the ring shout in American slave culture. Slaves sang, shouted, and clapped their hands as they moved counterclockwise in a circle. As in Africa, the dancing and singing were forms of spiritual expression directed to ancestors.

Over time the ring shout and other African dances inspired new forms of dance in America. The influence of African dance was probably most widespread in the 1920s. Few people realize that the wildly popular Charleston was based on an African religious dance.

With new forms of dance came new forms of music. Some slaves adapted songs with Christian lyrics to the ring shout. The result was the Negro spiritual, which remains an important part of many African American religious ceremonies. Several leading concert artists, such as Paul Robeson, Marian Anderson, and Roland Hayes, helped popularize spirituals.

The rhythms and emotional tones of the ring shout greatly influenced blues music

▲ Shown here are members of the Bradford Singers, a noted gospel group.

as well. And the blues, in turn, shape today's popular music. Rock musicians, such as the Rolling Stones and Eric Clapton, have drawn on the blues.

Well-known performers, such as James Brown and Aretha Franklin, trained in the musical traditions of the black church, have also influenced a new generation of artists, among them Janet Jackson. In all these ways, African dance and music, like other features of African culture, have left strong and lasting imprints on American life.

haunting religious songs called **spirituals**, or "Sorrow Songs," were modeled in part on Christian hymns and in part on African rituals and musical forms.

▪▪ In spite of harsh conditions, African Americans resisted slavery and developed a unique culture.

*R*ELIGIOUS ZEAL AND SOCIAL REFORM

Religion was an important part of life for many Americans. Beginning in the 1790s, waves of religious revivals swept the country. From the urban Northeast to the frontier areas of Kentucky, Ohio, Tennessee, and South Carolina, preachers promised that all sinners—not just a chosen few—could find salvation. Known as the **Second Great Awakening** because of an earlier wave of revivals, this renewal of faith reflected a widespread belief in the power of religion to reform people's lives.

Reforming institutions. Some Americans translated their faith in human perfection into attempts to reform society. Some men and women created **utopias**—communities that experimented with new ways of organizing family life, work, and property ownership in an attempt to create the ideal society. However, more Americans—notably those in the Northeast who were troubled by the effects of rapid industrialization—began to direct their religious zeal toward solving social problems. Middle-class women took the lead in many of these reform efforts.

In 1843 Dorothea Dix shocked the public with a report on the treatment of the mentally ill. During 18 months of visiting jails and poorhouses, Dix had found that the mentally ill were kept "in *cages, closets, cellars, stalls, pens! Chained, naked, beaten with rods, and lashed* into obedience." Dix convinced people of the need to offer the mentally ill **rehabilitation**, or treatment to restore them to a useful place in society.

▲ Dorothea Dix helped found or enlarge more than 30 mental hospitals.

Other reformers worked to rehabilitate prisoners and the poor. New systems of prison organization placed prisoners in individual cells so that they would think about their crimes and repent. Prisons also set up strict routines to teach inmates how to live disciplined lives. New poorhouses taught work skills and discipline to help the poor become self-supporting.

Some concerned people organized the **temperance movement** to persuade others to limit alcohol consumption, which was blamed for nearly all social problems including mental illness, domestic violence, poverty, and crime. In 1846 Maine became the first state to enact **prohibition**, or a ban on alcohol. A few other states followed, as did some communities. Many other states strictly licensed taverns and imposed heavy liquor taxes. By the middle of the 19th century, alcohol consumption had declined substantially.

In the 1840s and 1850s, reformers turned their attention to education. Arguing that existing schools—most of them private—were inadequate to educate citizens for participation in an expanding democracy, reformers sought to establish free public schools. In Massachusetts, Horace Mann's reforms as the state's first secretary of education established a model for free public education. Mann united local school districts into a state system, raised teachers' salaries, extended school terms, and updated the curriculum.

Not everyone supported public education. Some farming and working-class families opposed it because they depended on their children's labor. Also opposed were many Catholics who viewed public schools as a means of spreading Protestant beliefs. The public schools also failed to benefit many African American children born to free blacks; they were rarely allowed to attend public schools. And educational reform had little effect in the South. The antislavery movement made the South defensive about slavery—its "peculiar institution"—and many southerners increasingly viewed all reform with suspicion.

▪▪ Inspired to improve society, reformers supported rehabilitation, temperance, and public education.

The crusade for abolition. With the transportation, market, and industrial revolutions of the early 19th century, regional economic differences heightened the existing social and political tensions between the North and the South. As the division between the systems of slave and free labor became more pronounced, support for abolition increased among northerners.

In the 1830s black and white abolitionists began to join forces to call for an immediate end to slavery. The appearance of two important publications, David Walker's *Appeal to the Colored Citizens of the World* (1829) and William Lloyd Garrison's *Liberator* (1831), marked the start of a bold, energetic, and more organized attack on the institution of slavery. Then in 1833, abolitionists formed the first national antislavery organization devoted to immediate abolition—the **American Anti-Slavery Society**.

The society, which soon claimed more than 200 branches across the North and the Middle West, papered the country with antislavery publications and organized petition drives to protest legislation supporting slavery. Most important, the society sponsored national lecture tours of abolitionists who hoped to convince audiences that slavery was morally wrong. One of the most effective speakers was Frederick Douglass, a fugitive slave from Maryland. Douglass was also a powerful writer. His autobiography, *Narrative of the Life of Frederick Douglass* (1845), became a classic indictment of the slave system.

BIO GRAPHY Another former slave who worked tirelessly for the American Anti-Slavery Society was Sojourner Truth (c. 1797–1883). She was born Isabella Baumfree on the estate of a wealthy Dutch landowner. After escaping from her last slaveholder in 1827, she joined religious reformers who preached on the streets of New York City. In 1843 Baumfree said she had a religious vision in which God instructed her to find a new mission and a new identity. Adopting the name Sojourner (visitor) Truth, she traveled through New England preaching what she saw as the truth—abolition and women's rights.

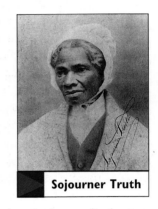

Sojourner Truth

By 1840, abolitionists had recruited some 200,000 northerners to their cause. Southern slaveholders, of course, felt threatened by the growing movement. But some northerners also opposed abolition, sometimes violently. Elijah Lovejoy, an abolitionist editor in Alton, Illinois, was killed in 1837 as he tried to prevent a mob from destroying his printing press. Much of the opposition to the antislavery cause was based on prejudice against blacks. In addition, many northern wage earners feared competing with free blacks for jobs, and northern merchants feared abolition would disrupt cotton production.

Women's rights. Women's support for African Americans' rights eventually led many women to view abolition and women's rights as parts of the same struggle. As Angelina Grimké explained, "the discussion of the rights of the slave has opened the way for the discussion of other rights."

The link between abolition and women's rights endured as the call for equal rights for women grew stronger in the 1840s. When two American abolitionists, Elizabeth Cady Stanton and Lucretia Mott, were refused the opportunity to speak at the

▲ Abolitionists used antislavery songs to protest the evils of slavery. One notable example was "The Fugitive's Song," composed in honor of Frederick Douglass's escape from slavery.

World's Anti-Slavery Convention in London in 1840, they decided to launch a movement to end the daily discrimination women faced.

Their efforts led to the first U.S. women's rights convention, held in Seneca Falls, New York, in 1848. More than 300 women and men attended the **Seneca Falls Convention**, which marked the birth of the organized women's rights movement in the United States. The convention adopted a Declaration of Sentiments modeled on the Declaration of Independence:

 We hold these truths to be self-evident: that all men and women are created equal; that they are endowed by their Creator with certain inalienable rights. . . .

Now, . . . because women do feel themselves . . . fraudulently deprived of their most sacred rights, we insist that they have immediate admission to all the rights and privileges which belong to them as citizens of the United States. 99

The Declaration of Sentiments also called for reforms to strengthen women's legal position. Most importantly—and controversially—it called for **suffrage**, or the right to vote. Stanton said attaining the right to vote was crucial to winning full equality because "the power to choose rulers and make laws, was the right by which all others could be secured."

The grievances expressed at the Seneca Falls Convention were primarily white, middle-class,

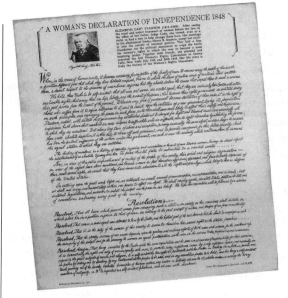

▲ **A commemorative printing of the Declaration of Sentiments is shown above. The declaration called for legal reforms such as granting women the right to vote and married women the right to be awarded custody of their children in the event of a divorce.**

married women's concerns. Most African American and white working-class women, however, had concerns different from those of middle-class women and therefore did not participate in the mainstream movement. Instead, they either joined groups that shared their concerns or formed their own organizations and found a separate path to equality.

■■ **Movements supporting abolition and women's rights gained strength in the 1830s and 1840s.**

SECTION 2 REVIEW

IDENTIFY and explain the significance of the following: middle class, strike, nativism, yeoman farmers, cotton gin, overseers, drivers, Underground Railroad, Harriet Tubman, spirituals, Second Great Awakening, utopias, Dorothea Dix, rehabilitation, temperance movement, prohibition, Horace Mann, American Anti-Slavery Society, Frederick Douglass, Sojourner Truth, Seneca Falls Convention, suffrage.

1. **MAIN IDEA** What changes did the market and industrial revolutions cause in the North and Middle West?

2. **MAIN IDEA** What factors led to an increased demand for slaves in the South?

3. **MAIN IDEA** What were some of the reforms people advocated to reduce social problems such as crime and poverty?

4. **WRITING TO DESCRIBE** You are a woman abolitionist in 1840. Write a letter to a friend describing the obstacles you face and your experiences in the movement.

5. **COMPARING AND CONTRASTING** Write an essay comparing and contrasting the lives of northern workers with the lives of southern slaves. How did each group protest or resist difficult conditions?

EXPANSION AND CONFLICT

FOCUS

■ **How did the United States gain territory in the Southwest?**

■ **Why were settlers attracted to the Far West?**

■ **Why did U.S. expansion cause conflict between the North and the South? How successfully was this conflict resolved?**

■ **What factors led to a rise in northern antislavery sentiments?**

■ **Why did the results of the 1860 presidential election cause a crisis?**

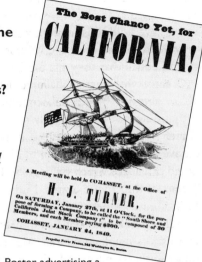

Poster advertising a voyage to California

After 1820, U.S. settlers moved west in increasing numbers, and by 1850 U.S. territory extended to the Pacific. The addition of new lands, and the accompanying argument over the extension of slavery into the West, caused the rift between the North and the South to widen. When the North elected a Republican president in 1860, the Lower South made good its threat to secede.

AMERICAN EXPANSION

As the United States gained territory, population, and economic might during the first half of the 19th century, the idea that the United States was destined to extend its territory to the Pacific Ocean became popular. This view, known as **manifest destiny**, inspired a generation of American expansionists to claim vast new territories for the country.

Texas independence. After winning its independence from Spain in 1821, Mexico encouraged U.S. immigration to its northern territory in an effort to boost Texas's non-Indian population. By 1830 non-Mexicans outnumbered Tejanos (native Mexicans living in Texas) by about two to one. Fearing that the increase in the American population might lead to a rebellion in Texas or to a U.S. invasion, the Mexican government closed the Texas border to further U.S. immigration. But immigration continued illegally, and by 1835 about

25,000 Americans, including some 3,000 slaves, lived in Texas.

When General Antonio López de Santa Anna seized control of the Mexican government in 1834 and tightened control over Texas, outraged American settlers and Tejanos rose up in revolt the next year. Isolated clashes quickly grew into a full-scale rebellion known as the **Texas Revolution**.

To put down the revolt, Santa Anna led several thousand Mexican troops in an assault on rebel-controlled San Antonio in February 1836. From the Alamo, a former Spanish mission, 187 Texas rebels fought off repeated attacks by Santa Anna's troops. On March 6, Mexican troops finally overran the fort; few of the defenders survived. The Mexicans, who suffered some 1,500 casualties, paid a heavy price for their victory.

Santa Anna won the siege of the Alamo, but six weeks later a Texas army under the command of Sam Houston surprised Santa Anna near the San Jacinto River. Shouting "Remember the Alamo!" the Texans killed about 630 Mexicans in 20 minutes and took Santa Anna prisoner. With his forces diminished and supplies low, Santa Anna agreed to grant Texas its independence.

Many Texans wanted to become part of the United States; and from 1836, when Texas won its independence, to 1845, the question of annexing the Republic of Texas never died. Supporters of annexation argued that if the United States did not admit Texas to the Union, Great Britain—which was interested in Texas as a source of cotton and a market for British goods—might increase its influence there. Opponents feared Texas's admission would upset the balance between slave and free states. These fears, coupled with Mexico's warning that it would consider U.S. annexation of Texas "equivalent to a declaration of war against the Mexican Republic," kept the U.S. Congress from acting. For nine years Texas remained an independent republic.

The Mexican War. The issue of western expansion dominated the 1844 presidential election, which was narrowly won by Democrat James K. Polk, an ardent expansionist. Once elected, Polk immediately called for Texas annexation. On March 28, 1845, in the wake of the congressional resolution annexing Texas, Mexico broke diplomatic relations with the United States.

Polk fueled the Mexican government's anger by demanding that Mexico recognize the Rio Grande as Mexico's northern border. Mexico, however, claimed all the land south of the Nueces (nooh-AY-suhs) River, about 100 miles north of the Rio Grande. To back up his demand, Polk ordered troops under General Zachary Taylor into the disputed area. Although Polk insisted that the troops were only defending U.S. territory, he hoped Mexico would commit an act that would justify war.

On May 9, 1846, Polk received the news that Mexican troops had crossed the Rio Grande and had attacked a U.S. patrol. Polk sent his war message to Congress. "Mexico," he said, has "shed American blood upon the American soil." On May 13 Congress declared war. Although some Americans, particularly Whigs and northerners, viewed the **Mexican War** as unjustified, most—eager to gain new lands—supported it.

While Taylor led American forces in fierce—and costly—fighting in northern Mexico, U.S. forces seized New Mexico and California. Then in March 1847 General Winfield Scott led some 10,000 U.S. troops on a march along the long mountainous road from Veracruz on the Gulf of Mexico to Mexico City. In spite of fierce resistance, Scott's troops captured the capital on September 14.

In February 1848 the United States dictated the terms of the **Treaty of Guadalupe Hidalgo** (GWAHD-uh-loop-ay ee-DAL-goh). Mexico gave up all claims to Texas and surrendered the territory known as the **Mexican Cession**. With this treaty, some 80,000 Spanish-speaking people became U.S. citizens. The United States acquired more Mexican territory in 1853 when U.S. diplomat James Gadsden negotiated the **Gadsden Purchase**.

■■ American expansionism led to war with Mexico and the addition of a vast new southwestern territory.

West to the Pacific. At the same time that Polk was fighting Mexico for the territories of the Mexican Cession, he was negotiating with Great Britain over Oregon Country. Since 1818, when Great Britain and the United States had agreed to occupy Oregon Country jointly, Great Britain had several times refused American requests for division of Oregon at the 49th parallel. Now Polk astounded the British by claiming all of Oregon up to the southern border of present-day Alaska.

Polk was bluffing. He hoped the threat of war would persuade the British to accept the old U.S. offer of division at the 49th parallel. In June 1846 the two sides finally agreed on the border that exists today.

Even before the boundary dispute was settled, U.S. settlers had flocked to Oregon Country. Between 1840 and 1848, thousands of settlers made the difficult journey along the **Oregon Trail** from Independence, Missouri, to Portland, Oregon. Most settlers headed for the fertile Willamette Valley, where they established farms.

White settlement of Oregon came at the expense of the region's American Indians. Increasing contact

▲ Missionary Narcissa Whitman was one of the first white women to travel along the Oregon Trail and across the Rocky Mountains.

between settlers and northwestern Indian tribes such as the Chinooks, Makahs, and Klickitats spread diseases to which the Indians had no immunity. In addition, non-Indians destroyed much of the wildlife the Indians depended on for survival.

The rush to California. Settlers also flocked to California after gold was discovered there in 1848. News of this discovery spread over the following year and drew thousands of hopeful gold seekers. Many of the U.S. **forty-niners**—so called because of the year, 1849—trekked overland to California along the California Trail, which forked off southward from the Oregon Trail. By the end of May 1849, more than 40,000 people had made this dangerous journey.

The gold rush added to the diversity of California's population, which up to this point had consisted mainly of Native Americans and Californios (the descendants of early Spanish settlers). Though nearly 80 percent of the forty-niners were Anglos or African Americans from the United States and about 8 percent were from Mexico, others came from South America, Europe, Australia, and China. This international mix of gold seekers helped swell California's non-Native American population from some 14,000 in 1848 to more than 200,000 in 1852. Anglos soon took control of the gold fields and pushed Californios, as well as Chinese and African American gold seekers, from the mines.

The gold rush also increased pressure on the Native Americans of California. Miners forced

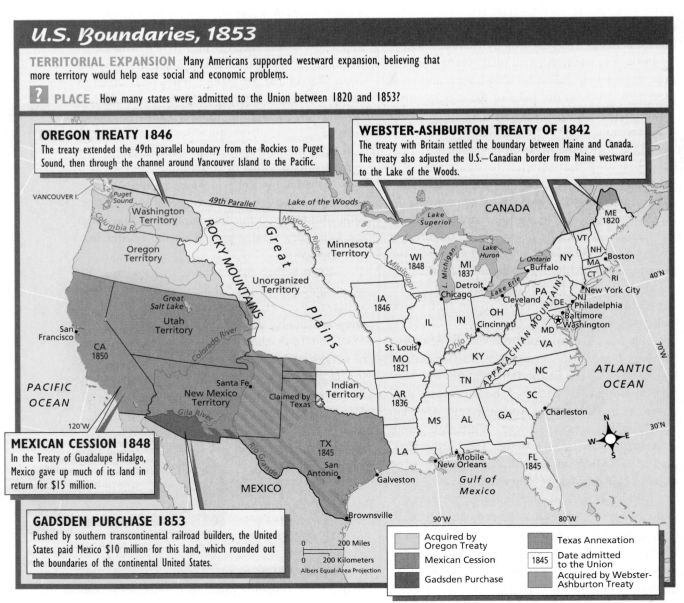

U.S. Boundaries, 1853

TERRITORIAL EXPANSION Many Americans supported westward expansion, believing that more territory would help ease social and economic problems.

? **PLACE** How many states were admitted to the Union between 1820 and 1853?

OREGON TREATY 1846
The treaty extended the 49th parallel boundary from the Rockies to Puget Sound, then through the channel around Vancouver Island to the Pacific.

WEBSTER-ASHBURTON TREATY OF 1842
The treaty with Britain settled the boundary between Maine and Canada. The treaty also adjusted the U.S.–Canadian border from Maine westward to the Lake of the Woods.

MEXICAN CESSION 1848
In the Treaty of Guadalupe Hidalgo, Mexico gave up much of its land in return for $15 million.

GADSDEN PURCHASE 1853
Pushed by southern transcontinental railroad builders, the United States paid Mexico $10 million for this land, which rounded out the boundaries of the continental United States.

0   200 Miles
0   200 Kilometers
Albers Equal-Area Projection

Acquired by Oregon Treaty
Mexican Cession
Gadsden Purchase
Texas Annexation
1845 Date admitted to the Union
Acquired by Webster-Ashburton Treaty

*I*n April 1851 Belgian Jean-Nicolas Perlot arrived in Monterey, California, with 44 other men hired by a French gold-seeking company. Upon landing, the men discovered that during their six-month voyage from Europe the company had gone bankrupt. "There we were," Perlot wrote, "thrown on the shore like castaways, without money, without resources, in an unknown land whose language we did not understand."

The group looked for work in Hornitos, a mining camp near the Yosemite Valley. "All around . . . in the creeks, in the gulches, we saw nothing but people occupied in seeking this precious metal . . . ," reported Perlot. "I estimate that there could have been at Hornitos from 250 to 300 persons, all men in the prime of life: I saw no women there, nor children, nor old people. In business, they spoke English and Spanish; in the street, still covered with brush, we heard all possible tongues spoken."

American Indians off their gold-rich lands. Many were pressed into service in the mines; others had their villages raided by the army and volunteer militia. In what became known as the **Mariposa War**, some Indians fought back. The Miwoks and the Yokuts in the Sierra Nevada and the San Joaquin Valley, whose lands had been taken over by miners, led raids on Anglo property in 1850 and in 1851. But by 1860 disease, starvation, and violence had reduced California's Indian population to about 35,000.

■■ **The fertile farmland of Oregon and the discovery of gold in California prompted migration to the Far West at mid-century.**

EXPANSION LEADS TO CONFLICT

The addition of new territories rekindled old arguments between the North and the South over slavery. When Texas was admitted to the Union as a slave state in 1845, the balance of power in Congress tipped toward the South. After the U.S. victory over Mexico, proslavery and antislavery forces in Congress quickly took sides on the issue of whether to allow slavery in territories acquired in the war.

To quiet the debate, several solutions were suggested. President Polk proposed extending the Missouri Compromise line to the Pacific Ocean.

Senators Lewis Cass of Michigan and Stephen A. Douglas of Illinois offered **popular sovereignty** as a solution: let the citizens of each new territory decide whether to permit slavery.

Neither proposal satisfied the hard-liners. Congressman David Wilmot of Pennsylvania proposed the Wilmot Proviso, an amendment banning slavery in all lands acquired from Mexico. Senator John C. Calhoun of South Carolina introduced resolutions in the Senate arguing, in part, that any ban on slavery was unconstitutional.

As the 1848 national election approached, Congress still had not settled the issue. The Democrats chose Lewis Cass, who favored popular sovereignty, as their presidential candidate. The Whigs nominated Mexican War hero General Zachary Taylor, a southerner whose political views were virtually unknown.

Angered by the reluctance of the major parties to address the slavery issue, antislavery advocates formed the **Free-Soil party** in August 1848. The Free-Soilers, who nominated former president Martin Van Buren as their candidate, demanded that Congress prohibit the expansion of slavery into the territories. Though the Free-Soil party won only about 10 percent of the vote, it tipped the election in favor of Taylor. It also demonstrated that the slavery question could no longer be ignored.

When Congress assembled in 1849, it was deeply divided over problems involving the territories newly acquired from Mexico. California wanted to join the Union as a free state, which southern members of Congress hotly opposed. In addition, Texas was claiming that its boundary extended westward into an area the federal government considered part of the New Mexico Territory. Despite opposition from southern lawmakers, the antislavery members of Congress were intent on limiting the size of Texas and on barring slavery from New Mexico.

In early 1850, a weary Henry Clay again urged northern and southern senators to compromise. Clay proposed admitting California as a free state and paying Texas $10 million to abandon its claim to the eastern part of the New Mexico Territory. To persuade southerners to accept these terms, Clay further proposed organizing the New Mexico Territory into two territories on the basis of popular sovereignty. He also advocated the passage of a tougher fugitive slave law to aid the capture of runaway slaves.

Congress angrily debated Clay's proposals for months. The most bitter attack came from the South's elder statesman, John C. Calhoun. In a speech that Calhoun was too ill to deliver himself, Calhoun argued against compromise, insisting that the nation could avoid civil war only if the North allowed slavery to exist in the territories:

> ❝ If something decisive is not now done . . . , the South will be forced to choose between abolition and secession. . . . The responsibility of saving the Union rests on the North, and not the South. ❞

Many northern members of Congress also opposed Clay's compromise. They wanted to ban slavery from the territories and were against stricter fugitive slave legislation. Many agreed with Senator William H. Seward of New York when he declared that compromise on an issue like slavery was "radically wrong and essentially vicious."

When the 73-year-old Clay became too exhausted to continue the fight for compromise, Senator Douglas assumed leadership of the cause. By September 20, 1850, Douglas had pushed all of the compromise measures through Congress. Many people considered the **Compromise of 1850** a triumph of national unity, but deep sectional divisions remained. More importantly, the basic issue—whether slavery would be allowed to expand—remained unresolved.

▪▪ The acquisition of new territories reopened the fierce debate over slavery in the West. The Compromise of 1850 kept the Union together but did not resolve the issue of slavery.

COMPROMISE COMES TO AN END

Although many people were dissatisfied with the Compromise of 1850, most Americans hoped that it had settled the slavery question. To tap into this optimistic mood, both major political parties adopted platforms supporting the compromise, vowing to avoid further debate over slavery.

The Fugitive Slave Act. The Compromise of 1850, however, soon began to crumble, largely because of the **Fugitive Slave Act**. This law made it a crime to assist runaway slaves and authorized the arrest of escaped slaves, even in states where slavery was illegal.

Harriet Beecher Stowe's 1852 novel *Uncle Tom's Cabin,* which dramatized the plight of runaway slaves, helped stir northern opposition to the law. Many northerners also reacted in horror as they came face to face with slave catchers in action. One observer wrote, "We went to bed one night old fashioned conservative Compromise Union Whigs and waked up stark mad Abolitionists." Several northern states defiantly passed "personal liberty" laws, which prevented state officials from aiding the capture and return of slaves to their owners. Some northerners took direct action. In New York and Massachusetts angry mobs freed runaway slaves who had been taken into custody and helped them on their way to freedom in Canada.

The Granger Collection, New York

▲ **Slaves escaping from Maryland are shown here.**

The Kansas-Nebraska Act. Early in 1854, Senator Douglas inflamed passions further by reigniting the debate over slavery in the West. To clear the way for construction of a railroad from his home state of Illinois to the Pacific Ocean, Douglas introduced the **Kansas-Nebraska Act**. The act organized Kansas and Nebraska into territories—a step necessary for building the railroads—on the basis of popular sovereignty. It would allow new states formed from the territories to "be received into the Union with or without slavery, as their constitution may prescribe at the time of their admission."

Passage of the act in May 1854 renewed southern hopes of expanding slavery. Antislavery northerners were outraged; many viewed the South as intent on dominating the nation. Other critics of the act feared that slavery in the territories would force out white workers and replace them with slave labor.

Within months a fierce battle erupted between proslavery and antislavery forces as they vied for control of the new territories. Groups in the North helped antislavery families move to Kansas; proslavery forces countered by urging southerners to migrate there as well. "We are playing for a mighty stake," warned Senator David Atchinson of Missouri. "If we win, we carry slavery to the Pacific Ocean."

Incidents of destruction and savagery soon plagued the new territories. In May 1856 a proslavery mob of some 700 burned the town of Lawrence, Kansas. In revenge, a group led by abolitionist John Brown attacked a proslavery settlement and brutally murdered five men. This sparked yet more violence in what newspapers began calling "Bleeding Kansas."

The *Dred Scott* decision. On July 6, 1854, a group of antislavery Whigs and Democrats, together with some Free-Soilers, founded the Republican party at a convention in Jackson, Michigan. The new political organization firmly opposed the expansion of slavery. In 1856 the Republicans nominated the popular western explorer John C. Frémont for president. Frémont finished second to the Democratic candidate, James Buchanan, but the race established the importance of the party.

A few days after Buchanan took office, the Supreme Court issued a decision that would further

▲ **A posse of proslavery men from Missouri are shown here on their way to plunder and burn Lawrence, Kansas, in 1856. Months of intense and bloody fighting followed the raid, giving rise to the nickname "Bleeding Kansas."**

divide the North and the South. The controversial case involved a Missouri slave named Dred Scott, who had accompanied his owner John Emerson to the free state of Illinois. In 1846, after Emerson's death, Scott sued for his freedom, arguing that his residence in a free state entitled him to it.

In 1857 the case reached the U.S. Supreme Court. The Court ruled against Scott, saying that he was not a citizen of the United States and thus could not bring suit. Chief Justice Roger B. Taney, one of five southerners on the Court, wrote in the majority opinion that the nation's founders had viewed blacks as "beings of an inferior order," having "no rights which the white man was bound to respect."

The Court also ruled that Scott's claim had no merit because Congress had acted unconstitutionally in passing the Missouri Compromise. The Court held that the Fifth Amendment to the Constitution, which forbids Congress to deny the right to property without "due process of law," had been violated since slaves were legally classified as property.

The ***Dred Scott*** decision outraged abolitionists and all who opposed the extension of slavery. There seemed to be no way to keep slavery from spreading into the territories.

▪▪ **The Fugitive Slave Act, violence in Kansas, and the *Dred Scott* decision all strengthened antislavery feelings in the North.**

JAMES K. POLK
1795–1849

in office 1845–1849

ZACHARY TAYLOR
1784–1850

in office 1849–1850

MILLARD FILLMORE
1800–1874

in office 1850–1853

FRANKLIN PIERCE
1804–1869

in office 1853–1857

JAMES BUCHANAN
1791–1868

in office 1857–1861

ABRAHAM LINCOLN
1809–1865

in office 1861–1865

ON THE BRINK OF WAR

The 1858 U.S. Senate race in Illinois became the forum for debate over the *Dred Scott* decision and the slavery issue. Running against incumbent Stephen Douglas was Republican Abraham Lincoln.

Born in a log cabin in 1809, Abraham Lincoln had grown up in the backwoods of Kentucky, Indiana, and Illinois. He was intelligent and ambitious. During childhood he often walked miles to borrow books.

Lincoln left home when he was 22 and settled in New Salem, Illinois, where he worked at various jobs before deciding to study law. Shortly after being admitted to the bar, Lincoln moved to Springfield, where he courted and married Mary Todd, who was from a well-to-do Kentucky family.

An able politician as well as a successful lawyer, Lincoln served in the Illinois state legislature and then in the U.S. House of Representatives. Then in 1858, largely due to his opposition to slavery, he was selected as the Republican party's candidate for the U.S. Senate seat that Douglas held. Lincoln used a quotation from the Bible as the foundation for his acceptance speech at the party's convention: "A house divided against itself cannot stand." The nation, he argued, could not remain divided into slave and free states for long.

Lincoln challenged Douglas to a series of debates between August and October 1858. In the debates, Lincoln attacked the *Dred Scott* decision and condemned slavery as "a moral, social, and political wrong." He was willing to tolerate slavery in the South, but he firmly opposed its expansion. Although Douglas narrowly defeated him in the Senate race, Lincoln had won a national reputation.

The year after the Lincoln-Douglas debates, John Brown again grabbed national attention. On October 16, 1859, John Brown and a band of some 20 men, including 5 blacks, seized the federal arsenal at Harpers Ferry, Virginia. Apparently, Brown planned to arm slaves for a rebellion. Two days later, federal troops assaulted Brown's position, killing half his men and capturing the rest. Brown was convicted of murder and other charges and was hanged. Many believed Brown got what he deserved. However, some abolitionists, among them Henry David Thoreau, saw Brown as a hero. In Congress, tension ran high.

Thus divided, the nation approached the presidential election of 1860. The election results mirrored the nation's sectional strife: votes were divided among four major candidates more or less along sectional lines. Republican candidate Abraham Lincoln won almost every northern state, as well as Oregon and California. Although Lincoln had received only about 40 percent of the popular vote and had failed to carry any of the southern states, his electoral victory was a landslide.

That a president had been elected without winning a single southern state confirmed the South's deepening sense of political powerlessness and mobilized southern leaders to action. Within days, the South Carolina legislature voted unanimously to leave the Union. Though some southern leaders urged restraint, Mississippi, Florida, Alabama, Georgia, Louisiana, and Texas soon passed similar acts of secession.

Early in 1861, delegates from six of the seven seceding states met at Montgomery, Alabama, and drafted a constitution for the Confederate States of America. The Confederate Constitution resembled the U.S. Constitution except that it guaranteed the right to own slaves and stressed that each state was "sovereign and independent." The convention chose former U.S. senator Jefferson Davis as president of the Confederacy.

▶ **Abraham Lincoln**

The southern secessionists used the doctrine of states' rights to justify their actions, asserting that since individual states had come together to form the Union, a state had the right to withdraw from the Union. The issue went beyond states' rights, however. Also at stake was southern determination to protect slavery. Southerners feared that restricting slavery in the territories would ensure that the slave states remained a minority voting bloc. Then the northern majority in Congress could not only prohibit slavery in the territories but also abolish it in the South.

Northern Republicans maintained that states did not have the right to secede and that majority rule was a fundamental principle of republican government. Abraham Lincoln, in a message to Congress, declared that the South had to accept the election results. "When ballots have fairly and constitutionally decided," he said, "there can be no successful appeal back to bullets." Many in the South thought otherwise.

■■ **Seven southern states decided to secede when Abraham Lincoln won the presidency.**

SECTION 3 REVIEW

IDENTIFY and explain the significance of the following: manifest destiny, Texas Revolution, James K. Polk, Mexican War, Treaty of Guadalupe Hidalgo, Oregon Trail, forty-niners, Mariposa War, popular sovereignty, Free-Soil party, Abraham Lincoln.

LOCATE and explain the importance of the following: Rio Grande, Mexican Cession, Gadsden Purchase.

1. **MAIN IDEA** What new territories did the United States acquire in the 1840s and 1850s, and what were the methods of acquisition?

2. **MAIN IDEA** What major issue regarding the new territories divided northerners and southerners? How did the Compromise of 1850 attempt to resolve this issue?

3. **ASSESSING CONSEQUENCES** How did northerners respond to the Fugitive Slave Act, the Kansas-Nebraska Act, and the *Dred Scott* decision?

4. **WRITING TO INFORM** Imagine you are a political commentator writing for a southern magazine. Write an article that explains to your readers the arguments the South has used to justify its actions after the election of 1860.

5. **SYNTHESIZING** Using the settlement of Oregon Country or the California gold rush as an example, explain how one group's good fortune can cause problems for other groups.

Missouri Compromise passed.

Monroe Doctrine issued.

Andrew Jackson elected president.

Indian Removal Act passed.

American Anti-Slavery Society established.

Texas declares independence from Mexico.

1820   1825   1830   1835

WRITING A SUMMARY

Using the essential points of the chapter as a guide, write a summary of the chapter.

REVIEWING CHRONOLOGY

Number your paper 1 to 5. Study the time line above, and list the following events in the order in which they happened by writing the first next to 1, the second next to 2, and so on. Then complete the activity below.

1. Seneca Falls Convention held.
2. Kansas-Nebraska Act passed.
3. Cherokees begin Trail of Tears.
4. Missouri Compromise passed.
5. Texas declares independence from Mexico.

Synthesizing In a paragraph, provide evidence that neither the Missouri Compromise nor the Kansas-Nebraska Act settled the issue of slavery in the new territories.

IDENTIFYING PEOPLE AND IDEAS

Explain the historical significance of each of the following people or terms.

1. American System
2. doctrine of nullification
3. Osceola
4. nativism
5. Harriet Tubman
6. Horace Mann
7. suffrage
8. manifest destiny
9. Mariposa War
10. popular sovereignty

UNDERSTANDING MAIN IDEAS

1. What effects did Andrew Jackson's wish to open more land for white settlement have on Native Americans? How did his bank war affect the nation as a whole?
2. How did working conditions in factories change as a result of the Industrial Revolution? What groups of people did factory owners tend to hire?
3. How did reformers work to improve the lives of poor Americans, slaves, and women?
4. Why did western expansion cause conflict? How did various members of Congress propose to deal with the issue from the 1820s through the 1850s?

5. Why did the presidential election of 1860 lead to southern secession?

REVIEWING THEMES

1. **Economic Development** How did the transportation and market revolutions lead to regional differences in economic development? How did the economies of the North, the Middle West, and the South differ?
2. **Democratic Values** How did Native Americans, slaves, and women protest discriminatory treatment in the first half of the 19th century?
3. **Global Relations** What international issues did Americans consider when debating the U.S. annexation of Texas?

THINKING CRITICALLY

1. **Synthesizing** What did the Monroe Doctrine reveal about the way the United States viewed its role in the Western Hemisphere?
2. **Hypothesizing** How might slavery have been affected if industrialization in the South had advanced as it did in the North?
3. **Contrasting** How did the reasons most people moved to California differ from the reasons most people moved to Oregon Country?
4. **Evaluating** Do you think antislavery northerners were justified in disobeying the Fugitive Slave Act or in supporting John Brown? Explain your answer.

STRATEGY FOR SUCCESS

Review the Skills Handbook entry on Studying Primary and Secondary Sources beginning on page 758. Then study the following verses from a slave spiritual. Along with its biblical and religious meaning, how might the song relate to the life of a slave in southern society? What 19th-century people and places might be represented by Moses, Israel, Egypt, and the Pharaoh?

> 66 Go down Moses,
> 'Way down in Egypt land,
> Tell ole Pharaoh,
> To let my people go.

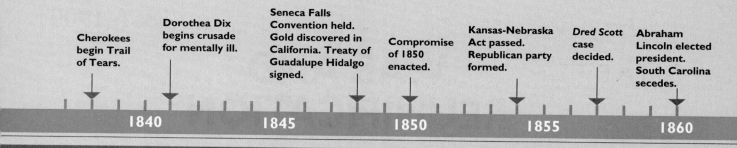

Cherokees begin Trail of Tears.

Dorothea Dix begins crusade for mentally ill.

Seneca Falls Convention held. Gold discovered in California. Treaty of Guadalupe Hidalgo signed.

Compromise of 1850 enacted.

Kansas-Nebraska Act passed. Republican party formed.

Dred Scott case decided.

Abraham Lincoln elected president. South Carolina secedes.

1840   1845   1850   1855   1860

When Israel was in Egypt land,
Let my people go,
Oppressed so hard they could not stand,
Let my people go.
Thus spoke the Lord, bold Moses said,
Let my people go,
If not I'll smite [strike] your first-born dead,
Let my people go. 99

WRITING ABOUT HISTORY

Writing to Express a Viewpoint Imagine you are a politician running for office in the 1850s. Write a short speech that explains your position on one of the following issues: rehabilitation, prohibition, public education, abolition, or women's rights.

USING PRIMARY SOURCES

When the U.S. government first began pressuring the Chickasaws to exchange their lands in the Southeast for lands in Indian Territory, the Chickasaw leaders offered the following reply. What reasons did the Chickasaws give for not wanting to move westward?

66 *We never had a thought of exchanging our land for any other, as we think that we would not find a country that would suit us as well as this we now occupy, it being the land of our forefathers, if we should exchange our lands for any other, fearing the consequences may be similar to transplanting an old tree, which would wither and die away, and we are fearful we would come to the same. . . .*

We have no lands to exchange for any other. We wish our father [the President] to extend his protection to us here, as he proposes to do on the west of the Mississippi, as we apprehend [fear] we would, in a few years, experience the same difficulties in any other section of the country that might be suitable to us west of the Mississippi. 99

LINKING HISTORY AND GEOGRAPHY

Study the maps on pages 73 and 86. How did U.S. boundaries change between 1820 and 1853? How did internal state and territorial boundaries change?

The Granger Collection, New York

"Tom Thumb" locomotive racing a horse-drawn car, 1830

BUILDING YOUR PORTFOLIO

Complete the following projects independently or cooperatively.

1.   THE ECONOMY In Chapter 1 you created a map of international trade routes. Building on that material, imagine you are a textile manufacturer in the northern United States in the 1840s. Create an illustrated chart for a new factory that shows how you will obtain cotton, what techniques you will use to produce cloth from the cotton, and how you will transport your products to markets.

2.   INDIVIDUAL RIGHTS In Chapter 2 you wrote an editorial arguing for the expansion of American colonists' rights under British rule. Building on that material, imagine you are a women's rights activist in the mid-1800s. Prepare a political poster calling for women's rights.

3.   CULTURAL DIVERSITY In Chapter 1 you created a museum exhibit showing cultural exchanges between Native Americans, Africans, and Europeans. Building on that material, imagine you are an African American slave in the South. Write a story about slave life that shows how enslaved African Americans have combined elements from different cultures to create a new, unique culture.

WAR AND REUNIFICATION

FOCUS

UNDERSTANDING THE MAIN IDEA

The Civil War dragged on far longer than anyone anticipated in 1861. Despite the South's defensive strategy and superior military leadership, the staying power of the northern forces ultimately led the Union to victory. When the war ended, the nation struggled to restore the southern states to the Union and to determine the status of the freed slaves.

THEMES

■ **GEOGRAPHIC DIVERSITY**
How might geography help or hinder a war effort?

■ **CONSTITUTIONAL HERITAGE** Why is it necessary that a plan of government be adaptable? What might happen if a government cannot adapt to changes in society?

■ **DEMOCRATIC VALUES**
Why might a nation's definition of a democratic society change over time?

1861	1863	1865	1867	1877
Fort Sumter falls.	Emancipation Proclamation goes into effect.	Lee surrenders at Appomattox.	Reconstruction Acts passed.	Reconstruction ends.

The Missouri Compromise and the Compromise of 1850 had each proved only temporary solutions to the slavery issue. The Fugitive Slave and Kansas-Nebraska acts and the Supreme Court's Dred Scott decision soon reignited tensions between the North and the South. Republican Abraham Lincoln's victory in the 1860 presidential election brought the crisis to a head.

The Battle of Chattanooga, 1863

The Granger Collection, New York

On April 15, 1861, President Abraham Lincoln declared that the nation faced an armed revolt. Mary Ashton Livermore, who would soon join the war effort as a volunteer for the United States Sanitary Commission, recorded the reaction in Boston to the president's call to arms:

> 66 Monday dawned, April 15. Who that saw that day will ever forget it! For now . . . there rang out the voice of Abraham Lincoln calling for seventy-five thousand volunteers for three months. . . . This proclamation was like the first peal of a surcharged thunder-cloud, clearing the murky air. The . . . whole North arose as one man. . . .
>
> Hastily formed companies marched to camps of rendezvous, the sunlight flashing from gun-barrel and bayonet. . . . Merchants and clerks rushed out from stores, bareheaded, saluting them as they passed. Windows were flung up; and women leaned out into the rain, waving flags and handkerchiefs. Horse-cars and omnibuses halted for the passage of the soldiers, and cheer upon cheer leaped forth from [their] thronged doors and windows. . . .
>
> I had never seen anything like this before. I had never dreamed that New England . . . could be fired with so warlike a spirit. 99

This "warlike spirit" pervaded the nation in early 1861. Amid the excitement, few Americans imagined the death and destruction that lay ahead. And perhaps even fewer imagined the difficulties they would face once the war was over—both in restoring the Union and in deciding the fate of the nearly four million newly freed slaves.

Union drum with federal eagle insignia

THE CIVIL WAR

FOCUS

- **What military advantages did each side possess at the beginning of the war?**
- **How did the military strategies of the North and the South differ?**
- **Why did some northerners oppose the war?**
- **How and why did the Union's war aims shift?**
- **What strategies did Grant and Sherman employ to win the war?**

As war became inevitable, both sides prepared for what they believed would be a short conflict. The war, however, would become a bloody struggle that lasted for years instead of months.

The *Spirit of '61* recruiting poster

THE UNION DISSOLVES!

When Abraham Lincoln took office on March 4, 1861, the nation was on the brink of collapse. South Carolina, Mississippi, Florida, Alabama, Georgia, Louisiana, and Texas had already seceded, and other southern states seemed likely to follow.

▲ **The firing on Fort Sumter on April 12, 1861, marked the beginning of four long, bloody years of war.**

The fall of Fort Sumter. The Confederacy had immediately taken over the federal forts, mints, and arsenals within its borders. However, one fort important to the South—Fort Sumter, in Charleston, South Carolina—remained in federal hands.

The North knew that losing this fort would be an admission that South Carolina had truly left the Union. But Lincoln hesitated to use force. He feared that the leaders of the eight slave states remaining in the Union would make good their threat to secede if force were used against the South.

Realizing, however, that inaction would signify weakness, Lincoln moved to send Fort Sumter desperately needed supplies. When the local Confederate commander, General P.G.T. Beauregard, learned that the supply ships were on the way, he ordered Fort Sumter evacuated. The fort's commander, Major Robert Anderson, refused.

On April 12 the Confederates opened fire. On April 14, with much of the fort ablaze, Anderson and his men formally surrendered. The next day Lincoln proclaimed the existence of a rebellion "too powerful to be suppressed by the ordinary course of judicial proceedings." He asked the governors of the loyal states to provide 75,000 militiamen to put down the rebellion.

In response to Lincoln's request, four states—Virginia, Arkansas, Tennessee, and North Carolina—decided to secede. Four other slave states—Delaware, Missouri, Kentucky, and Maryland—remained in the Union. The mountainous counties of northwestern Virginia stayed loyal to the Union as well. They set up their own government and joined the Union in 1863 as West Virginia.

The Upper South remained divided over secession, and sections of several southern states raised Union regiments. Some families split apart as members fought for different sides. Kentucky's Senator John Crittenden saw one son become a Union general; another, a Confederate general.

Comparing North and South.

On the face of it, the war that loomed after the fall of Fort Sumter seemed a mismatch. The North—with more than 22 million people—could recruit more soldiers than could the South—with a population of some 9 million, nearly 4 million of whom were slaves.

The North also enjoyed an economic advantage. It had over 85 percent of the nation's industries and almost all known supplies of iron, copper, gold, and other metals. With such resources the North could easily produce war materials; the agrarian South could not. In addition, the North had most of the nation's railroad lines and could move troops at will. The South had few connecting routes and lacked the resources to replace worn-out railroad equipment. And the North held superiority at sea—most of the U.S. Navy supported the Union.

The South, however, had two advantages. Fighting a defensive war, the South had only to protect its territory until the Union quit the fight. The South—where most of the nation's military academies were located—also had talented military leadership.

██ **The North had numerical and economic advantages in the war, but the South had the advantage of fighting on its own soil under skilled military leaders.**

RESOURCES OF THE NORTH AND SOUTH, 1861

	North	South
Total Population	22,000,000	9,000,000*
Bank Deposits	$189,000,000	$47,000,000
Railroad Mileage	20,000 miles	9,000 miles
Number of Factories	100,500	20,600

* Southern population includes slaves.

Source: *American Heritage Picture History of the Civil War, Encyclopedia of American History*

NORTH vs. SOUTH At the beginning of the Civil War, the North's abundant resources gave it a military advantage over the South.

? **EVALUATING** Which resource do you think had the greatest influence on the outcome of the Civil War? Why?

ℲIGHTING THE WAR

After the fall of Fort Sumter, Lincoln hoped to end the war quickly. In mid-July 1861 he sent General Irvin McDowell and 35,000 barely trained troops to capture Richmond, Virginia, the Confederate capital. Laughing and joking along the way, the troops were joined by sightseers and reporters who expected a quick Union victory.

But on July 21, 1861, Confederate forces—also numbering around 35,000—met the Union troops near Manassas (muh-NAS-uhs) Junction, 25 miles outside Washington. Under General Joseph E. Johnston, the Confederates dug in behind a creek called Bull Run.

At first the battle (called the **First Battle of Bull Run** in the North; the Battle of Manassas in the South) went in the Union's favor. But then southern general Thomas "Stonewall" Jackson and his men charged, filling the air with an eerie scream. Eventually known as the rebel yell, the sound struck fear in the hearts of the enemy. Union colonel Andrew Porter wrote: "Soon the slopes . . . were swarming with our retreating and disorganized forces, while riderless horses and artillery teams ran furiously through the flying crowd" of soldiers and sightseers headed for Washington.

After Bull Run, everyone realized that the war would last longer than a few months. Each side began training its forces and planning its strategy. Lincoln and his advisers chose a three-part strategy: (1) capture Richmond, (2) control the Mississippi River, and (3) institute a naval blockade of the South. The naval blockade would keep the South from importing supplies and exporting cotton.

Much of the North's plan depended on geography. The Appalachian Mountains divided most of the action in the Civil War into two arenas: the eastern theater, east of the Appalachian Mountains, and the western theater, between the mountains and the Mississippi River. Control of the Mississippi would give the North access to the Lower South and keep the Confederacy from resupplying western forces.

The South hoped to win by taking Washington, D.C., and moving north into Maryland and Pennsylvania. This offensive move, they believed, would shatter the North's morale, disrupt Union communications, and speed the war's end. The South also hoped to win European support. Because France and Great Britain depended heavily on cotton, the Confederacy expected one of those nations to respond to the North's naval blockade by aiding the South. This, however, did not happen.

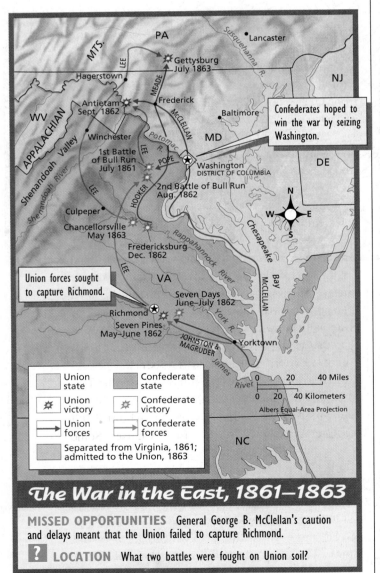

The War in the East, 1861–1863

MISSED OPPORTUNITIES General George B. McClellan's caution and delays meant that the Union failed to capture Richmond.

? LOCATION What two battles were fought on Union soil?

◼◼ The North's strategy centered on dividing the South geographically, while the South planned to capture Washington, D.C., invade the North, and win European aid.

The war in the East. The South won most of the early battles of the war, as the Union army struggled to take Richmond and the Confederacy attempted to make inroads into Union territory (see chart on page 100). The skillful military leadership provided by Joseph E. Johnston, Robert E. Lee, and Stonewall Jackson played a decisive role in the South's early victories.

Lincoln, however, had no luck finding a general during the first years of the war, and the Union's forces in the East had five different commanders in just one year. The first of them, General George B. McClellan, trained his men well, but he hesitated to commit them to battle. (Lincoln once grew so frustrated with McClellan's delays that he threatened to send a letter asking if he could borrow the army if the general had no use for it.) After McClellan allowed the defeated Confederates to escape after the Battle of Antietam in September 1862, Lincoln lost patience with McClellan and fired the overcautious general.

The revolving door for Union generals whirled on. By July 1863, General George Gordon Meade was in command. Meade led the Union to victory at Gettysburg, Pennsylvania, but at a staggering cost: Union casualties from the three days of fighting numbered more than 23,000. Furthermore, the Union army failed to end the war while it had the opportunity. A disappointed President Lincoln lamented, "Our Army held the war in the hollow of their hand and they would not close it." Nevertheless, the battle marked a turning point in the war. The Union army had proved that the Confederacy could be beaten.

In November 1863 Lincoln helped dedicate a cemetery at the Gettysburg battlefield. Lincoln's brief **Gettysburg Address** remains a classic statement of democratic ideals (see page 768).

The war in the West. From the start the war went far better for the Union army in the West. In February 1862 General Ulysses S. Grant moved into Tennessee and led his army swiftly through the state. In April he paused at Shiloh Church near the Mississippi state line. Nearby Confederates under generals Albert Sidney Johnston and P.G.T. Beauregard launched a surprise attack, but Grant forced the Confederates to retreat.

To achieve a decisive victory in the West, however, the Union had to gain control of the Mississippi River. Toward this end, David Farragut, commander of a Union naval squadron, captured New Orleans in April 1862. Despite this victory, Grant knew that gaining full control of the river meant taking Vicksburg, Mississippi. More than a year passed, however, before Grant and his men were in position to lay siege to the city and force its surrender. By July 8, 1863, the Union controlled the entire Mississippi, cutting off Arkansas, Louisiana, and Texas from the rest of the Confederacy.

The military experience. While high-level leaders were executing battle strategies, the officers under them had to train young, inexperienced recruits to fight the war. Training and field officers also had to contend with shortages of food, clothing, and even rifles—especially in the Confederate army. Eventually soldiers received their Union blue or Confederate gray uniforms, but many troops never had adequate shoes or coats. Under these difficult conditions, soldiers felt homesick, lonely, and bored. Some deserted, but most found ways to cope through activities such as card-playing and singing.

The lack of provisions, coupled with unsanitary conditions in most field camps, led to disease. Thousands died from illnesses such as typhoid, pneumonia, and influenza. And minor injuries often led to infection. In fact, disease, infection, and malnutrition were responsible for over 65 percent of troop deaths. Conditions were especially horrible in filthy, overcrowded prisoner-of-war camps.

Women and the war. Many women in both the North and the South responded to the armies' overwhelming need for medical care. The first group of women to volunteer for medical duty were Catholic nuns, who transformed convents into emergency

▶ **Sally Tompkins**

The Museum of the Confederacy, Richmond, Virginia

◀ **Elizabeth Blackwell**

hospitals throughout the North and South. These "nuns of the battlefield" treated all victims of the war, becoming the only group recognized by both Union and Confederate forces.

In the North, Elizabeth Blackwell, America's first licensed female doctor, helped run the U.S. Sanitary Commission, which worked to battle wartime diseases and infections. About 3,000 women served in the Union army as nurses. Some, like Clara Barton, ministered to the wounded on the battlefield. After the war, Barton founded the American Red Cross. In the South, Sally Louisa Tompkins founded small hospitals and clinics. Eventually

UNION STRATEGY
Control of the Mississippi would split the Confederacy and enable northern forces to reach the Lower South.

After the Union victories at Murfreesboro and Chattanooga, the Union's western armies were in position to divide the Upper and Lower South.

The War in the West, 1862–1863

JOINT OPERATIONS The Union army and navy cooperated in gaining control of the Mississippi.

? LOCATION Union victories at Fort Henry and Fort Donelson prevented the Confederates from moving into which Union state?

THE EARLY DAYS OF THE STRUGGLE: SIGNIFICANT BATTLES 1861–1863

EASTERN CAMPAIGN	
First Battle of Bull Run July 21, 1861	The Union suffered some 3,000 casualties, the South some 2,000. The battle was a tactical victory for the Confederacy and boosted southern confidence.
Battle of Seven Pines May 31–June 1, 1862	This battle was a tactical victory for the North. Confederate casualties numbered some 6,000; Union losses totaled some 5,000. Confederate general Joseph E. Johnston was severely wounded, and Robert E. Lee took command.
Seven Days' Campaign June 25–July 1, 1862	Despite some 20,000 casualties, the campaign was considered a victory for the South because McClellan retreated. (Union casualties numbered nearly 16,000.) Lincoln gave the field command to John Pope.
Second Battle of Bull Run August 29–30, 1862	A Confederate victory, this battle prepared the way for the South to invade the North. Pope's losses totaled some 16,000, and Lincoln placed McClellan back in command.
Battle of Antietam September 17, 1862	In one of the bloodiest days of the war, the South suffered more than 13,000 casualties; the North more than 12,000. While not a clear-cut Union victory, this failure of a major Confederate offensive cost the South any hope of European support. Lincoln replaced McClellan with Ambrose E. Burnside.
Battle of Fredericksburg December 13, 1862	Burnside sent his men out onto an open plain. Lee's army controlled the surrounding hillsides and easily picked off Union soldiers. The North suffered more than 12,000 casualties, the South some 5000. Lincoln put Joseph Hooker in command.
Battle of Chancellorsville May 1–4, 1863	Hooker withdrew in defeat, and morale in the North plummeted. Lee lost his most valued general, Stonewall Jackson, who was wounded by his own men. The North suffered some 17,000 casualties, the South some 13,000.
Battle of Gettysburg July 1–3, 1863	The Union's decisive victory at Gettysburg is considered the turning point of the war in the East. The battle cost the North some 23,000 casualties, the South more than 20,000.
WESTERN CAMPAIGN	
Battle of Shiloh April 6–7, 1862	Although taken by surprise, the Union forces won a costly victory. The Union suffered some 13,000 casualties, the Confederacy more than 10,000.
Vicksburg May 18–July 4, 1863	Vicksburg's surrender (which coincided with the Union victory at Gettysburg) and Port Hudson, Louisiana's fall four days later put the Union in control of the Mississippi.

MILITARY STRATEGY The South won most of the early battles but failed to make inroads into the North.

? **BUILDING CHART SKILLS** In which battle did the South fail to achieve one of its strategic goals?

commissioned as a captain, Tompkins became the Confederate army's only female officer.

Women on both sides helped in other ways. Some women, such as Loreta Janeta Velázquez (vuh-LAHS-kuhs), dressed liked men so they could fight. Others served as spies. Elizabeth Bowser, who was a maid in Confederate president Jefferson Davis's home, and Harriet Tubman both supplied information to the Union from behind enemy lines.

Women also replaced men in offices and factories. Nearly 450 women worked in the Treasury Department as clerks—the government's first female office workers. In addition, some 100,000 women worked in factories, sewing rooms, and military arsenals.

OPPOSITION TO THE WAR

While women helped meet the demand for workers at home, neither the North nor the South could fill their armies with volunteers. To raise troops the Confederate government passed a **conscription**, or draft, act in April 1862—the first draft law in American history. In March 1863 the Union also passed a draft law. Although all social classes fought, the draft laws put the burden of fighting on poor farmers and workers. In the North, wealthy men could hire substitutes to serve for them or pay the government to be exempted from service. The South exempted anyone owning 20 or more slaves.

Exemptions caused resentment in both the North and South. In the North, poor whites, especially immigrants, rioted in protest. In New York City some newspapers whipped readers into a frenzy, claiming that the draft forced white workers to fight for the freedom of African Americans who would then come north and steal their jobs. Men and women—many of them poor Irish immigrants—raged through African American neighborhoods, leaving more than 100 people dead. Draft riots did not occur in the South, but, as in the

North, many whites criticized the draft, claiming it proved the conflict was a "rich man's war and a poor man's fight."

There were others, particularly in the North, who also voiced displeasure with the war itself. Some believed that the war was too costly in terms of money and human life. Some northern Democrats, labeled **Copperheads** after a type of poisonous snake, opposed the war because they sympathized with the South. Most Copperheads limited antiwar activities to speeches and newspaper articles. But to quiet them Lincoln suspended some civil liberties. At one time or another, thousands of Copperheads and other opponents of the war were arrested and held without trial.

■■ **The draft, fear of unemployment, concern over costs, and sympathy for the South led some northerners to protest the war.**

*T*HE FINAL PHASE

Even northerners who fully supported the war began to rethink the war's aim. As more and more lives were lost, many northerners wondered whether saving the Union without ending slavery was worth such a high price. Slavery, they decided, must end. Yet Lincoln insisted: "My paramount object in the struggle *is* to save the Union, and is *not* either to save or to destroy slavery."

The Emancipation Proclamation.

Privately, however, the president had concluded that slavery was too important to the southern war effort to ignore. The Confederacy depended on slaves to raise food, haul supplies, and work in factories. Lincoln hoped that if slaves heard the North was fighting to free them, they would desert slaveholders, thereby weakening the South's economy.

Lincoln lacked the constitutional authority to abolish slavery, but he had the power to issue military measures. In September 1862 Lincoln issued the **Emancipation Proclamation**, which declared that all slaves in areas rebelling against the United States would become free on January 1, 1863. Because the proclamation applied only to areas held by the Confederacy, it did not change the status of slaves in the border states. Another three years would pass before slavery was abolished everywhere in the United States.

The Emancipation Proclamation brought a decisive change in the war. By inspiring some 500,000 slaves to leave slaveholders whenever Union troops were nearby, it struck a serious blow to the South's economy. The proclamation also encouraged African Americans to enlist as soldiers. The first official black regiments were organized in August 1862 in South Carolina. Frederick Douglass, who had been pressing for black troops, saw military service as an important step toward citizenship for African Americans:

❝ Let the black man get upon his person the brass letters, U.S.; let him get . . . a musket on his shoulder and bullets in his pocket, and there is no power on earth which can deny that he has earned the right to citizenship. ❞

▼ **Poster commemorating the Emancipation Proclamation**

By the war's end nearly 180,000 African Americans had served in the Union army. The 166 all-black regiments fought 449 engagements. More than 20 African Americans won the Congressional Medal of Honor, and over 32,000 died for the Union cause.

Although the Union army accepted African Americans, it did not offer full equality. For much of the war, black soldiers earned less than half the pay of whites. In addition, white officers commanded every black regiment. Only about 100 African Americans were commissioned as junior officers, and it was not until 1865 that Martin Delany became the first black promoted to major.

■■ **The North enlarged its war aims to include freeing the slaves in the hopes of weakening the South.**

A war of attrition. Emancipation provided Lincoln with one key to Union success. Another key was General Grant, who became commander of all Union forces. Grant's strategy was to use the North's advantages in terms of soldiers and

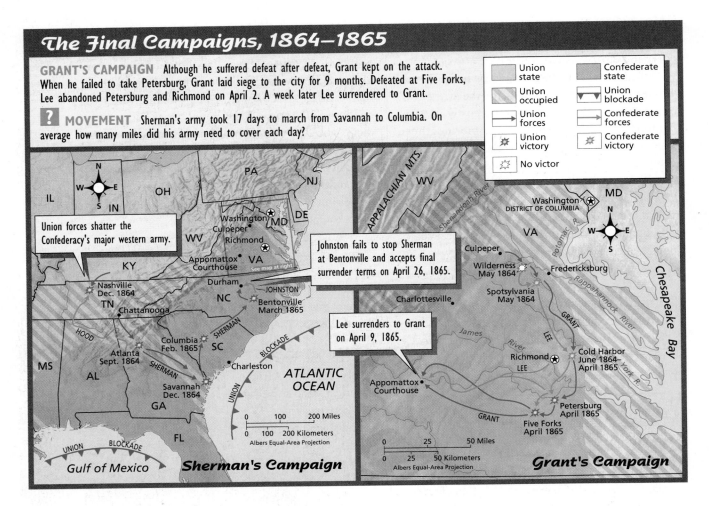

The Final Campaigns, 1864–1865

GRANT'S CAMPAIGN Although he suffered defeat after defeat, Grant kept on the attack. When he failed to take Petersburg, Grant laid siege to the city for 9 months. Defeated at Five Forks, Lee abandoned Petersburg and Richmond on April 2. A week later Lee surrendered to Grant.

? MOVEMENT Sherman's army took 17 days to march from Savannah to Columbia. On average how many miles did his army need to cover each day?

Union state	Confederate state
Union occupied	Union blockade
Union forces	Confederate forces
Union victory	Confederate victory
No victor	

Union forces shatter the Confederacy's major western army.

Johnston fails to stop Sherman at Bentonville and accepts final surrender terms on April 26, 1865.

Lee surrenders to Grant on April 9, 1865.

Sherman's Campaign

Grant's Campaign

---

supplies against an enemy reeling from shortages. Grant planned a **war of attrition**—to fight until the South ran out of men, supplies, and will. He would march on Richmond, take his losses, and press on.

In May 1864 Grant began his campaign against Lee's troops in Virginia. Although the Union suffered high casualties, Grant pushed his troops on, mile after bloody mile. His actions forced Lee to keep weary men in the field. At Spotsylvania Court House, Virginia, Union and Confederate forces clashed several times between May 10 and May 19. As before, Union losses were heavy. Shocked by the number of casualties, a southern soldier remarked of Grant: "We have met a man this time, who either does not know when he is whipped, or who cares not if he loses his whole army."

By mid-June Grant's army had suffered some 60,000 casualties. He called off the direct assault of Petersburg, Virginia, and settled down to besiege the city. Grant was achieving his goal, however. Lee's army was dwindling, with no reserves available.

Matching Grant in determination was the Union commander of the Tennessee army, General William Tecumseh Sherman. While Grant was heading to Richmond in early May, Sherman moved about 100,000 troops out of Tennessee toward Atlanta, Georgia. His troops entered the city on September 2, 1864, and cut the only Confederate railroad link across the Appalachians.

After burning much of Atlanta, Sherman marched toward Savannah, Georgia. Sherman's men, cut off from their supply line, took what they needed and destroyed what remained. They uprooted crops, burned houses, slaughtered live-stock, and tore up railroad tracks, leaving nearly stripped a swath 60 miles wide and almost 300 miles long.

Such destruction was part of Sherman's tactic of fighting a **total war**. He believed that it was not enough to fight enemy troops. To win the war, the Union had to strike at the enemy's economic resources. Sherman succeeded, but his actions left bitter scars across the South. After capturing Savannah, Sherman and his troops turned north to link up with Grant.

In 1864 Grant began wearing down the Confederates through a war of attrition, and Sherman waged total war to defeat the South economically as well as militarily.

As Sherman's army moved northward through the Carolinas, Grant's troops hammered at Richmond. On April 2, 1865, with Grant close behind, Lee withdrew. Within hours, Union troops poured into the Confederate capital. Lee tried to make a run to the west, hoping to join up with more troops. But Grant cut off Lee's escape. With his once-proud army reduced to 30,000 men, many without shoes, Lee asked for terms of surrender.

▲ Sherman's troops left a wake of destruction behind them, including torn-up railroad tracks and burned-out factories.

Grant and Lee met in the tiny village of Appomattox Courthouse on April 9, 1865. The terms of surrender were simple. Confederate

Changing Ways

THE COURAGEOUS 54TH

On July 18, 1863, the men of the 54th Massachusetts Infantry sat in camp on Morris Island in South Carolina's Charleston Harbor. Three quarters of a mile away, guarding the harbor entrance, Fort Wagner rose above the sands. More than 1,700 Confederates stood ready to defend the fort.

The Confederates held not only Fort Wagner but all the forts and batteries around Charleston, South Carolina. The Union campaign to seize control of Charleston's defenses had begun on July 10. Eight days later, despite Union bombardment, Fort Wagner was still in Confederate hands. So General Truman Seymour decided to send some 6,000 Union troops in a frontal attack against the fort—with the 54th regiment in the lead.

The 54th was no ordinary regiment. It was composed of

some of the first African American soldiers recruited for the Union army. And this battle was the first time black troops had been assigned a key role. It was up to them to break through the Confederate line, and they would surely suffer great losses. These troops also faced a danger that white Union soldiers did not. Captured blacks were shot, hanged, or sold into slavery.

As night fell, the 54th's commanding officer, Colonel Robert Gould Shaw, gave the order "Forward!" and the troops advanced. The evening exploded in a storm of gunfire. Confederate cannons all around opened fire, but somehow Colonel Shaw and his men clawed their way to the top of

▲ Charles and Lewis Douglass, sons of Frederick Douglass, both served with the 54th Massachusetts, shown here charging Fort Wagner.

Fort Wagner's walls. There, they fought hand to hand against the Confederate defenders inside. The casualties were extremely heavy.

Union troops continued the siege until September 6, when the Confederates, no longer able to hold out, evacuated the fort. Four survivors of the regiment received the Gillmore Medal for gallantry, and their courage won the 54th Regiment an honored place in U.S. military history.

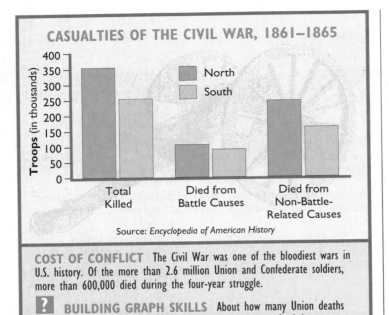

CASUALTIES OF THE CIVIL WAR, 1861–1865

Troops (in thousands)

- North
- South

Category	Values (approx.)
Total Killed	400 / 350 / 300 / 250 / 200 / 150 / 100 / 50 / 0
Died from Battle Causes	
Died from Non-Battle-Related Causes	

Source: *Encyclopedia of American History*

COST OF CONFLICT The Civil War was one of the bloodiest wars in U.S. history. Of the more than 2.6 million Union and Confederate soldiers, more than 600,000 died during the four-year struggle.

 BUILDING GRAPH SKILLS About how many Union deaths resulted from non-battle-related causes? About how many Confederate deaths resulted from non-battle-related causes?

The consequences of war. No other war on American soil has been as tragic as the Civil War in terms of human costs. Some 360,000 Union and 285,000 Confederate soldiers died. More Americans were killed in the Civil War than in all other American wars combined.

In the South the war devastated the economy and left southerners facing an uncertain future. Almost four million former slaves were without homes and ways to earn a living. Tens of thousands of Confederate veterans were also homeless and jobless.

In the North the war benefited the economy. Agriculture and industry had expanded to meet military needs, and many northern industries—steel, petroleum, food processing, manufacturing, and finance—continued to expand after the war.

The North's victory also made the Republican party the dominant political force. Moreover, it resolved the long-debated issue of slavery. Never again would the U.S. government sanction the legalized enslavement of a group of people.

officers could keep their sidearms, and all soldiers could keep their horses. Lee acknowledged that "this will do much toward conciliating [uniting] our people."

As Lee rode off, Union troops started to cheer, but Grant silenced them. "The war is over," he said; "the rebels are our countrymen again." After the surrender, Lee quietly told his men to resume their lives and "become as good citizens as you were soldiers." On April 26, 1865, General Joseph Johnston surrendered to General Sherman.

◄ **Defeated Confederates rolling up their flag**

The West Point Museum, United States Military Academy

SECTION 1 REVIEW

IDENTIFY and explain the significance of the following: First Battle of Bull Run, Robert E. Lee, Gettysburg Address, Elizabeth Blackwell, Clara Barton, conscription, Copperheads, Emancipation Proclamation, Martin Delany, war of attrition, total war.

LOCATE and explain the importance of the following: Richmond, Gettysburg, Vicksburg, Atlanta, Appomattox Courthouse.

1. **MAIN IDEA** What were the North's military strengths at the beginning of the Civil War? What were the South's strengths?

2. **MAIN IDEA** How did the North's strategy differ from the South's at the beginning of the Civil War?

3. **MAIN IDEA** How and why did the North change its war aims during the Civil War?

4. **RECOGNIZING POINTS OF VIEW** What reasons did some northern Democrats and working-class whites have for opposing the war?

5. **ASSESSING CONSEQUENCES** How did Grant's and Sherman's military strategies bring an end to the war?

RECONSTRUCTION

F O C U S

- How did the Civil War affect southern life?
- How did Lincoln, Johnson, the Moderate Republicans, and the Radicals differ in their approaches to Reconstruction?
- How did African Americans participate in rebuilding the South?
- What factors led to the end of Reconstruction?

After the Civil War, Americans faced complex problems. Politicians disagreed about how to restore the Union, and whites and blacks struggled to define the rights of former slaves.

An African American addressing Congress

THE OLD SOUTH DESTROYED

As the war ended, most of the nearly four million former slaves, or freedpeople, found themselves without money or homes. "It came so sudden on 'em," recalled former slave Parke Johnston:

> 66 Just think of whole droves of people, that had always been kept so close, and hardly ever left the plantation before, turned loose all at once, with nothing in the world, but what they had on their backs. 99

Despite the obstacles, however, most former slaves eagerly looked to the future. They hoped to get an education, to establish churches, to legalize their marriages, and especially to find family members who had been sold away.

Above all, they wanted land to support themselves and to protect their independence. In fact, many believed that it was their due. "Our wives, our children, our husbands, has been sold over and over again to purchase the lands we now locates upon," argued former slave Bayley Wyat; "we have a divine right to the land."

The planters still had land, but even they found their world "literally kicked to pieces." Mary Boykin Chesnut wrote about the despair many white southerners felt: "We are shut in here—turned with our faces to a dead wall. No mails. . . . We are cut off from the world—to eat out our own hearts."

The Union army had laid waste to parts of the South—destroying railroad lines and stripping homes, barns, and gardens. Many cities, too, lay in ruins. Disease, the grim companion of hunger and bad sanitation, swept the South—especially cities, and thousands died in the year after the war.

■■ **After the Civil War parts of the South lay in ruins and many southerners faced poverty. The former slaves, however, looked forward to shaping their own destinies.**

◀ **This family record, showing a prosperous African American family, was marketed to former slaves after the war.**

PRESIDENTIAL RECONSTRUCTION

President Lincoln had gone to war not to destroy the South but to preserve the Union. Even before war's end, he had begun to plan for **Reconstruction**—rebuilding the rebelling states and reuniting the nation. In December 1863 he had issued the Proclamation of Amnesty and Reconstruction, which offered a full pardon to almost all southerners who would swear allegiance to the U.S. Constitution and accept federal laws on slavery. The proclamation also permitted a state to rejoin the Union when 10 percent of the state's residents who had voted in 1860 swore their loyalty to the United States.

Many members of Congress objected to Lincoln's plan. They did not trust the rebels to be loyal or to protect the rights of former slaves. In 1864 Congress laid out its own Reconstruction plan in the Wade-Davis Bill. It called for former Confederate states to abolish slavery and for a *majority* of each state's white males to take a loyalty oath. Lincoln vetoed the bill because he was not ready to "be inflexibly committed to any single plan." In his Second Inaugural Address, Lincoln clarified his goal for Reconstruction:

66 With malice toward none, with charity for all, with firmness in the right as God gives us to see the right, let us strive on . . . to bind up the nation's wounds . . . to do all which may achieve and cherish a just and lasting peace. 99

▪▪ Unlike Congress, Lincoln favored a flexible, lenient policy toward the former Confederates.

What course Reconstruction might have taken under Lincoln's direction will never be known. On April 14, 1865, just days after Lee's surrender, John Wilkes Booth, a half-crazed Confederate sympathizer, shot the president.

Upon Lincoln's death the following day, Vice President Andrew Johnson—a Democrat from Tennessee and a former slaveholder—became president. Johnson was ill-suited to the challenges of Reconstruction and of defining African Americans' new rights. He suffered, one contemporary observed, from "almost unconquerable prejudices against the African race." Moreover, he lacked tact and political skill.

At first Johnson denounced southern treason, even suggesting that Jefferson Davis and other high-ranking Confederates be hanged as traitors. In May 1865, however, in a startling about-face, Johnson issued a blanket pardon to all rebels except ex-Confederate officeholders and the richest planters. These he pardoned individually. Johnson was equally lenient with the rebel states.

THE EMANCIPATION PROCLAMATION

In 1861, two years before President Lincoln issued the Emancipation Proclamation, Czar Alexander II of Russia promised more than 20 million Russian serfs freedom and land. Though the czar's own land policies eventually failed, in 1879 he criticized the proclamation for having sidestepped the issue of land. The czar charged that the decree had freed the American slaves but had left them with no means to support themselves. Alexander boasted:

66 *I did more for the Russian serf in giving him land as well as personal liberty, than America did for the Negro slave set free by the Proclamation of President Lincoln. I am at a loss to understand how you Americans could have been so blind as to leave the Negro slave without tools to work out his salvation. . . . Without property of any kind he cannot educate himself and his children. I believe the time must come when many will question the manner of American emancipation of the Negro slaves in 1863.* 99

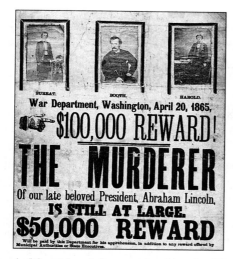

▲ After Lincoln's assassination, the War Department offered a reward for the capture of John Wilkes Booth.

For readmission to the Union, Johnson asked only that they nullify secession, abolish slavery, and refuse to pay Confederate debts.

Johnson's plan allowed former Confederate leaders—some still proudly wearing Confederate uniforms—to take charge of Reconstruction. When they complained of the "painful humiliation" caused by the presence of black soldiers, Johnson withdrew the soldiers. When Mississippi refused to ratify the **Thirteenth Amendment**—which Congress had passed in January 1865 to abolish slavery—Johnson recognized the state's new government anyway.

Johnson's actions encouraged former Confederates to adopt laws limiting the former slaves' freedom. These **black codes**, which African Americans denounced as "a disgrace to civilization," resembled prewar slave codes. Mississippi simply used its old code, substituting the word *freedman* for *slave*.

Under these laws African Americans could not hold meetings unless whites were present. They could not travel without permits or own guns. Blacks in New Orleans could not be on the streets after 10 o'clock at night, just one hour later than the previous slave curfew. The editor of the city's African American newspaper noted: "Four years of a bloody war have been fought to gain that one hour."

Above all, the codes reestablished white control over black labor. Because whites were desperate to make former slaves return to field work, some codes required freedpeople to sign labor contracts. The laws were so restrictive that one black veteran demanded: "If you call this Freedom, what do you call Slavery?"

■■ Johnson's leniency toward ex-Confederates allowed them to dominate Reconstruction and to limit the rights of African Americans.

CONGRESSIONAL RECONSTRUCTION

President Johnson's support of the former Confederates and his failure to protect African Americans' rights angered many members of Congress. Even Republicans, however, were divided over the course Reconstruction should take. The Moderates, who made up the party majority, viewed Reconstruction as a practical matter of restoring southern states to the Union. Their main concern was keeping ex-Confederates out of government. And though they favored giving African Americans civil equality, they did not think the former slaves should have voting rights.

Radical Republicans, on the other hand, insisted that African Americans be given the right to vote. They wanted Reconstruction to create a new South where all men would have equal rights. In addition, Thaddeus Stevens, the outspoken Radical from Pennsylvania, believed that land reform could change southern society. He agreed with Senator Charles Sumner of Massachusetts, who insisted that "the great plantations . . . must be broken up, and the freedmen must have the pieces." According to Stevens, economic independence for the former slaves would ensure their freedom and destroy the rebel leaders' power. But land reform never won wide support. Even many Radicals believed that the ballot, civil equality, and free labor were enough to give African Americans a chance to succeed.

Congress versus Johnson. The split between Moderates and Radicals did not last. In 1866 Congress held hearings on conditions in the South. Witness after witness recounted stories of murder and of homes, schools, and churches reduced to "ashes and cinders." These reports and others like them convinced the Moderates to join forces with the Radicals. They began work on

▲ This cartoon is a reaction to Johnson's veto of the Freedmen's Bureau Bill.

legislation to protect the rights and safety of the ex-slaves. This effort included extending the life of the Freedmen's Bureau, which Congress had established in 1865.

Originally authorized to operate for one year, the Freedmen's Bureau had been designed to aid the millions of southerners, particularly ex-slaves, left homeless by the war. The bureau distributed food, served as an employment agency, and ran hospitals and schools. While African Americans thought the Freedmen's Bureau too often encouraged blacks to remain on plantations and sign labor contracts, they acknowledged that the bureau's very presence forced white southerners to recognize emancipation.

In February 1866 Congress passed the Freedmen's Bureau Bill to keep the agency in operation. Johnson promptly vetoed the bill.

A furious Congress quickly passed the **Civil Rights Act of 1866**, which declared that everyone born in the United States was a citizen with full civil rights. Again, Johnson issued a veto, partly because he believed the bill would "operate . . . against the white race." Congress overrode the veto. Then Congress returned to the matter of the Freedmen's Bureau, passed a new bill, and overrode yet another veto.

Fearing that a future Democrat-controlled Congress might repeal the Civil Rights Act, Republicans wrote its provisions into the **Fourteenth Amendment**, passed in June 1866. The amendment required states to extend equal citizenship to all people "born or naturalized in the United States," including African Americans. The amendment's ratification in July 1868 created a national citizenship with rights—enjoyed equally by all—that were to be enforced by the federal government. The amendment did not guarantee blacks voting rights.

However, it encouraged states to grant those rights by reducing the number of representatives a state could send to Congress in proportion to the number of the state's male citizens denied the right to vote.

The Radicals come to power. In the 1866 congressional elections, Johnson appealed to voters to support candidates who opposed the Fourteenth Amendment. Few voters were receptive. Many were troubled by the ongoing violence against blacks in the South. In Memphis in May 1866, for example, white rioters killed 46 blacks and burned 12 schools and 4 churches. Fearing they might lose the fruits of their Civil War victory, northerners overwhelmingly elected Republicans in 1866.

Now firmly in command of Congress, the Republicans seized control of Reconstruction. Over Johnson's angry vetoes, Republicans passed the **Reconstruction Acts** of 1867. These acts divided the former Confederacy (except already-reconstructed Tennessee) into five military districts to be overseen by Union troops. To gain readmission to the Union, states were required to ratify the Fourteenth Amendment and to submit to Congress new constitutions giving all men the vote.

Tensions between Johnson and Congress continued to mount. In February 1868 Johnson ousted Secretary of War Edwin Stanton—an ally of the Radicals—without congressional approval. This was a violation of the Tenure of Office Act, and the House responded by voting to impeach the president. The vote in the Senate in May fell one short of the number needed to remove him from office.

▲ This 1866 poster mocks the effectiveness of the Civil Rights Act of 1866. As punishment for crimes, one freedman is being sold at auction while another is being whipped.

▼ A ticket of admission to the U.S. Senate galleries was required for people wishing to attend the impeachment trial of President Johnson.

The Granger Collection, New York

The Granger Collection, New York

The attempt to force Johnson from office cost the Radical Republicans some popular support. To retain voters in the 1868 election, they chose popular war hero General Ulysses S. Grant as their presidential candidate. Grant won the election by a slim margin.

As worried Republicans studied the election returns, they realized that new African American voters had given them their narrow win. Eager to protect their power in both the North and the South, the Republicans drew up the **Fifteenth Amendment**, which Congress passed in 1869. Short and to the point, it stated that the right "to vote shall not be denied or abridged . . . on account of race, color, or previous condition of servitude."

■■ **At first Moderate and Radical Republicans were divided over African American suffrage.**

But postwar events led them to join forces to protect African Americans' rights.

The ratification of the Fifteenth Amendment in 1870 was a triumph for African Americans. The amendment did not, however, guarantee them the right to hold office. Nor did it prevent states from limiting voting rights through discriminatory requirements, such as literacy tests.

The amendment also failed to extend the vote to women. Some women's rights leaders, believing that "this hour belongs to the negro," had urged women to wait for the more controversial women's suffrage. Elizabeth Cady Stanton replied: "My question is this: Do you believe the African race is composed entirely of males?" Stanton and others had opposed ratification until all women gained the vote. The bitter debate divided the women's suffrage movement for over 20 years and alienated many African American women from the movement.

RECONSTRUCTION IN THE SOUTH

During the debate over African American suffrage, Congress implemented its Reconstruction plan. The advent of Radical Reconstruction rekindled the former slaves' hopes for equal citizenship. Some southern blacks took dramatic actions, such as chasing overseers from plantations. But many more registered to vote and turned to political activity to press for the equality promised by the Civil Rights Act and the Fourteenth Amendment. Even the churches found that "politics got in our midst" and overtook "our revival or religious work," one freedman minister recalled.

PRESIDENTIAL LIVES

ANDREW JOHNSON
1808–1875

in office 1865–1869

UNITED STATES POSTAGE
ANDREW JOHNSON
17 CENTS 17

UNITED STATES POSTAGE
ULYSSES S. GRANT
18 CENTS 18

ULYSSES S. GRANT
1822–1885

in office 1869–1877

African Americans also joined political clubs, such as the Union League. Begun in the North as a patriotic club, the league brought the views of the Republican party to the freed slaves and to poor whites. It provided blacks in particular with a place to develop their political skills.

Most importantly, African Americans served as delegates to the 1867 conventions held to draft new state constitutions. In Louisiana and South Carolina, black delegates outnumbered whites. In other states they made up 10 to 40 percent of the delegates. Many of these delegates were ex-slaves or free-born southern blacks, but northern blacks participated, too. Many northern African American communities watched their most talented professionals go south to help with Reconstruction.

Reconstruction governments. Most convention delegates were northern Republicans or white southern Unionists. Ex-Confederates resented the northern Republicans—white or black—whom they called carpetbaggers. The newcomers, they jeered, were "needy adventurers" of "the lowest class" who could carry all their belongings in a carpetbag (cheap suitcase). Ex-Confederates heaped even more scorn on southern whites who had backed the Union and supported Reconstruction. These whites, dubbed scalawags, were considered traitors.

The alliance of groups favoring Reconstruction allowed for political change in the South. New state constitutions abolished property qualifications for jurors and for candidates for public office and guaranteed white and black men the vote. Nine states also expanded married women's property

▲ **W.L. Sheppard sketched** *Electioneering in the South* **for** *Harper's Weekly* **in 1868 to illustrate African American interest in voting.**

rights. Once Congress approved the new constitutions, state legislators raised taxes to pay for new road, bridge, and railroad construction and for increased services, such as free public education.

▪▪ Reconstruction legislatures, which included African Americans, made their state governments more democratic and increased services.

Many ex-Confederates ridiculed the new state constitutions and pointed out corruption. During Reconstruction, some southern legislators did use their offices to enrich themselves, just as they had done under slavery. But the scandals involving Reconstruction governments paled in comparison with government scandals in the North (see Chapter 6).

The Ku Klux Klan.

The Reconstruction governments' reforms and African Americans' growing political participation stirred a vicious backlash. Angry white southerners formed secret terrorist groups to keep blacks from voting. The best known group was the Ku Klux Klan. Founded in the mid-1860s, the Klan grew quickly, attracting members from all social classes.

▲ **These two members of the Ku Klux Klan, shown in their uniforms, were captured at Huntsville, Alabama, during an 1868 riot.**

The Klan did not limit its attacks to politically active white and black Republicans. Klansmen beat and killed thousands of blacks whom they regarded as "uppity" or too successful. Sarah Song, an ex-slave from Louisiana, recalled how some 20 or 30 Klansmen killed her husband:

❝ He was shot in the head while he was in bed sick. . . . They came into the room. . . . Then one . . . put the pistol to his head and shot him three times. . . . Then one of them kicked him, and another shot him again when he was down. ❞

Klansmen also burned homes and schools and stole livestock and land in an often effective effort to chase blacks and pro-Reconstruction whites from the South.

As violence mounted, African Americans demanded that Congress act to "enable us to exercise the rights of citizens." Between 1870 and 1871, Congress responded by passing three **Enforcement Acts**. The acts empowered the federal government to combat terrorism with military force and to prosecute suspects. In Mississippi alone, the federal government charged some 700 Klansmen. But most local whites resented federal intervention and seldom made convictions.

THE DEFEAT OF RECONSTRUCTION

For a time government intervention decreased Klan violence. But Republicans, and northern voters in general, began to turn their attention to economic issues and political corruption in the North. What remained of the Republicans' commitment to Reconstruction died with a severe economic downturn in 1873.

Faced with threats of strikes and hard-hit workers' and farmers' demands for relief, an Ohio Republican noted that "the overwhelming labor question has dwarfed all other questions." The partnership between northern businesspeople—the heart of the Republican party—and the former slaves had never been a stable one, and under economic pressure it dissolved altogether. "I suppose," said a former slave, "it is a fight between the poor people and the rich man now." Concerned with their own problems and weary of Reconstruction, many northerners began to accept southern whites' racist propaganda that portrayed blacks as unfit for self-government. When Jacob Cox, former secretary of the interior, suggested that the South "be governed through the part of the community that embodies the intelligency and the capital"—by which he meant its former white rulers—many northern whites nodded in agreement.

Economic discontent caused by the Panic of 1873 turned voters against the Republican-controlled Congress. In the 1874 congressional elections, Democrats gained a 60-seat majority in the House. In the South they had won white Republicans' votes with promises of lower taxes and with racist appeals to white supremacy.

▲ **This Thomas Nast engraving, entitled *To Thine Own Self Be True*, commemorates the passage of the Civil Rights Bill of 1875.**

When Congress reconvened, Republicans made one final effort to enforce Reconstruction. They pushed through the **Civil Rights Bill of 1875**, which prohibited discrimination by hotels and other businesses serving the public. Yet even white Republicans who supported the bill had begun to see Reconstruction as a political liability. They agreed with Congressman James Garfield that their recent defeats at the polls reflected "a general apathy among the people concerning . . . the negro."

Convinced that the federal government would not stop them, Democrats in the South moved to "redeem," or win back, their states from the Republicans. Beginning in 1875 the "Redeemers" used terrorism to win state elections. In contrast to the Klan, they made no effort to hide their identities or their actions. Senator Ben Tillman of South Carolina later admitted: "We took the government away. We stuffed ballot boxes. We shot them [blacks]." Whites armed with rifles—even cannons—kept blacks away from the polls. A black official called the period "the most violent time that ever we have seen."

In 1876 the Redeemers focused on the presidential election, which pitted Democrat Samuel J. Tilden of New York against Republican Rutherford B. Hayes of Ohio. Opponents of Reconstruction vowed to win the election even "if we have to wade in blood knee-deep." In the popular vote they were successful: Tilden beat Hayes by less than 250,000 votes. But challenges to the election results in four states—Florida, Louisiana, Oregon, and South Carolina—meant that the electoral vote was another story.

An electoral commission set up to rule on the validity of the returns gave Hayes the presidency by one electoral vote. The Democrats in the House protested, and a deal—the **Compromise of 1877**—was struck to end the crisis. In return for Democrats' acceptance of Hayes as president, Republicans agreed not to use the military to enforce Reconstruction legislation and to withdraw the remaining federal troops from the south.

Denied federal protection, the last of the Reconstruction governments fell. Once in power the Redeemers rewrote state constitutions and overturned many of the Reconstruction governments' reforms, trimmed spending, and cut services. Some states even closed public hospitals and did away with public education systems.

■■ By the early 1870s conditions in the North undermined Republicans' commitment to Reconstruction.

COMMENTARY

Reconstruction Perspectives

In the late 19th century, many white southerners remembered Reconstruction as a time when they were bullied by Union soldiers, lorded over by former slaves, and exploited by carpetbaggers and scalawags. Similarly, many northerners came to believe that Radical Reconstruction was a mistake.

Such views were for many years reflected in American history textbooks and in popular culture. For example, both Thomas Dixon's 1905 novel *The Clansman* and D. W. Griffith's 1915 film *Birth of a Nation,* based on Dixon's book, glorified the Klan and ridiculed Congress. Unfortunately, most white Americans accepted these views as fact, and such ideas only reinforced white southerners'

opposition to African Americans' rights.

Blacks had a different perspective. They knew that their active participation had helped shape Radical Reconstruction. Francis L. Cardozo, who had been educated in Great Britain, ably served as South Carolina's treasurer from 1872 to 1876. Hiram R. Revels, who had recruited African Americans for the Union army and had taught school, represented Mississippi in the U.S. Senate. Blanche K. Bruce, a wealthy black planter from Mississippi, served as sheriff, tax collector, superintendent of education, and U.S. senator. The Reconstruction governments, asserted John R. Lynch, a black who served as speaker of Mississippi's House and as a representative to Congress, "were the best governments those States ever had."

These men and others left behind a positive social legacy that benefited both blacks and whites. They built roads, hospitals, and established free public schools. Blacks also built up their own communities, creating churches and strong family networks that helped sustain them through the post-Reconstruction years. Later generations would draw upon these institutions in building the civil rights movement.

Reconstruction also left a legal legacy. Although practically ignored for almost a century, the Civil Rights Act of 1866 and the Fourteenth and Fifteenth amendments provided an important legal framework. They enabled later civil rights leaders to win back voting rights for African Americans and to end legal segregation.

SECTION 2 REVIEW

IDENTIFY and explain the significance of each of the following: Thirteenth Amendment, black codes, Thaddeus Stevens, Civil Rights Act of 1866, Fourteenth Amendment, Reconstruction Acts, Fifteenth Amendment, Elizabeth Cady Stanton, Enforcement Acts, Civil Rights Bill of 1875, Compromise of 1877.

1. **MAIN IDEA** How did southern life change after the Civil War?

2. **MAIN IDEA** How did Reconstruction under the Radical Republicans differ from Reconstruction under Andrew Johnson?

3. **ASSESSING CONSEQUENCES** How did the Ku Klux Klan affect Reconstruction?

4. **WRITING TO PERSUADE** Imagine you are an African American living in the South during Reconstruction. Write a speech to deliver to community members recommending a course of action to help shape Reconstruction.

5. **HYPOTHESIZING** How might the course of Reconstruction have been different if the United States had not experienced an economic downturn in 1873? Explain your answer.

THE NEW SOUTH

FOCUS

■ **What new labor arrangements appeared in the South after the emancipation of the slaves?**

■ **How did Reconstruction's end affect African Americans?**

■ **How did African Americans respond to segregation and to the loss of civil and political rights?**

The Granger Collection, New York

Grant Hamilton's *From Darkness to Light* (1895) shows a New South rising from the ashes of the Civil War.

During the 1880s white business leaders began to speak of the "New" South, urging that the region move away from its dependence on cotton toward a more varied economy. Although southerners worked to build up the region's manufacturing enterprises, many remained in rural poverty. And for blacks in the South, racial discrimination made life harsher still.

TENANT FARMING AND SHARECROPPING

After the Civil War, planters in the South faced a common problem: a shortage of labor. Few ex-slaves or whites wanted to work for the low wages planters were willing—or, in many cases, able—to pay. Many planters turned to **sharecropping** as a solution.

Under this system a sharecropper, or cropper, agreed to work a parcel of the planter's land in return for a share of the crop, a cabin, seed, tools, and a mule. Sharecropping appealed both to planters, because they got their lands worked without having to pay cash, and to the croppers—most of whom were ex-slaves—who received places to live and lands to work.

The system had a serious drawback, however. Croppers had no income until harvesttime. To obtain needed supplies, they promised their crops to local merchants who sold them goods on credit. Any debts they could not pay to the mer-

chants in a given year were added to the next year's bills.

This arrangement, known as the **crop-lien system**, made it nearly impossible for croppers—white or black—to work their way out of poverty. "Until he [the cropper] has paid the last dollar of his indebtedness, he is subject to . . . constant oversight and direction," economist Matthew Hammond noted at the time. In the judgment of former slave Thomas Hall, the system was "little better than slavery."

■ **Many southern landowners turned to sharecropping and the crop-lien system to keep cotton production up and wages down.**

The crop-lien system also kept the southern economy tied to one-crop agriculture. Merchants would only give credit to farmers who grew certain crops, most often cotton. As a result, cotton displaced other crops to such an extent that southerners had to import food and animal feed from the North.

▲ After the Civil War, the South began a slow course of industrialization. This photograph shows a worker at White Oaks Mills, a factory near Greensboro, North Carolina.

Some southerners argued that one-crop agriculture kept the South in poverty and too economically dependent on the North. They envisioned a New South that would manufacture its own goods. Supporters of the New South joined with northern and British investors to finance factories, steel mills, textile mills, improvements in railroads, and other enterprises.

Not everyone benefited equally from industrialization in the South, however. Factory owners and investors profited at the expense of workers who earned wages that were some 40 percent below what their northern counterparts earned. Most African Americans, meanwhile, could not find factory work at any wage. Many industrial workers were forced to buy goods on credit from the company store and to live in ramshackle company houses. Like sharecroppers, they soon found themselves locked in a cycle of debt.

TURNING BACK THE CLOCK

For African Americans the New South was starting to look very much like the Old South. Tied to the land through sharecropping and excluded from most factory jobs, African Americans had few economic opportunities. Moreover, Democrats, now firmly in control of the southern state legislatures, stepped up their attempts to strip blacks of their rights.

In an effort to deprive African Americans of the right to vote, southern state legislatures instituted **poll taxes**—fixed taxes imposed on every voter—and **literacy tests**—tests supposedly intended to limit the vote to those who could read. Technically, these measures did not violate the Fifteenth Amendment. However, since most black southerners were poor and had been denied an education, these laws accomplished their purpose.

To further deprive African Americans of their rights, states passed laws designed to enforce segregation, or separation, of the races. The first of these so-called **Jim Crow laws**, passed by Tennessee in 1881, required separate railway cars for blacks and whites. By the 1890s all southern states had legally segregated public transportation and schools. Segregation soon extended to parks, cemeteries, and other public places.

African Americans sued for equal treatment under the Civil Rights Act of 1875, but the Supreme Court refused to overturn the Jim Crow laws. The final blow came in 1896, when the Supreme Court's *Plessy v. Ferguson* decision ruled that "separate but equal" facilities did not violate the Fourteenth Amendment.

■■ **After Reconstruction, African Americans were deprived of their rights and had few economic opportunities.**

BLACK SOUTHERNERS ORGANIZE

Confronted by segregation and denied basic political and civil rights, some African Americans left the South for the Midwest or moved to northern cities. Most, however, stayed in the South, where their ancestors had lived for generations. To improve their lives, African Americans formed mutual aid societies, started businesses, strengthened churches, and built schools.

The key question facing African American leaders after 1877 was how to fight discrimination. Two influential leaders, Booker T. Washington, a former slave who founded Alabama's Tuskegee Institute in 1881, and Ida Wells-Barnett, a teacher and journalist, offered different answers to the discrimination question.

Washington believed that African Americans should concentrate on economic advancement. To further blacks' economic independence—which he

◄ Tuskegee Institute was founded in 1881 to teach African Americans trades and professions. A printing class is shown here.

believed was the key to political and social equality—Washington urged blacks to seek practical training in trades and professions. He also discouraged them from protesting against discrimination, arguing that such protesting merely increased whites' hostility. If economic and social progress was to be made, he claimed, blacks would need "the cooperation of the Southern whites" because "they control government and own the property." Behind the scenes, however, Washington secretly provided support to groups fighting Jim Crow laws and racial violence.

 Many African American leaders did not agree with Washington's position. They argued instead that blacks should protest unfair treatment. One such leader was Ida Wells-Barnett (born Ida Bell Wells). Born to a slave family in 1862, Ida Wells was educated in a

Ida Wells-Barnett

The Granger Collection, New York

Mississippi freedmen's school and became a teacher herself at age 14. In 1884 Wells moved to Tennessee, where she lost her teaching job when she began protesting discrimination and segregated schools.

Ida Wells then turned to journalism, becoming part owner of the *Memphis Free Speech*. In 1892, after whites lynched three of her friends, she vowed to put a stop to lynching and wrote a fiery editorial on the subject. Angry whites responded by destroying her newspaper office.

Wells then left Memphis for New York, where she continued her crusade against lynching. After moving to Chicago and marrying lawyer Ferdinand Barnett in 1895, she published *A Red Record,* the first statistical study of lynching. Though lynchings decreased only slightly in the early 1900s, Wells's tireless efforts kept the public's attention focused on the issue.

African Americans built their own institutions, and they adopted several approaches to fighting discrimination.

SECTION 3 REVIEW

IDENTIFY and explain the significance of the following: sharecropping, crop-lien system, poll taxes, literacy tests, Jim Crow laws, *Plessy* v. *Ferguson,* Booker T. Washington, Ida Wells-Barnett.

1. **MAIN IDEA** After slavery had been abolished, how did plantation owners deal with the shortage of labor?

2. **MAIN IDEA** In what ways did the New South resemble the Old South (before Reconstruction) for African Americans?

3. **MAIN IDEA** What actions did blacks take in response to their loss of rights?

4. **WRITING TO EVALUATE** Write an essay evaluating the consequences for a white sharecropper of leaving the land to seek work in a southern factory.

5. **SYNTHESIZING** How did changes in the post-Reconstruction New South harm some groups of people and benefit others?

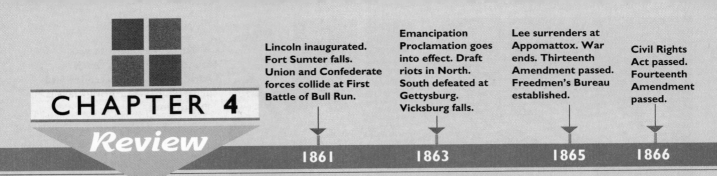

Lincoln inaugurated. Fort Sumter falls. Union and Confederate forces collide at First Battle of Bull Run.

Emancipation Proclamation goes into effect. Draft riots in North. South defeated at Gettysburg. Vicksburg falls.

Lee surrenders at Appomattox. War ends. Thirteenth Amendment passed. Freedmen's Bureau established.

Civil Rights Act passed. Fourteenth Amendment passed.

1861   **1863**   **1865**   **1866**

WRITING A SUMMARY

Using the essential points of the chapter as a guide, write a summary of the chapter.

REVIEWING CHRONOLOGY

Number your paper 1 to 5. Study the time line above, and list the following events in the order in which they happened by writing the first next to 1, the second next to 2, and so on. Then complete the activity below.

1. Lee surrenders at Appomattox.
2. First Jim Crow law passed in Tennessee.
3. Emancipation Proclamation goes into effect.
4. Reconstruction ends.
5. Reconstruction Acts passed.

Assessing Consequences Choose the two events that you think had the greatest effects on the lives of African Americans, and explain the reasons for your assessment.

IDENTIFYING PEOPLE AND IDEAS

Explain the historical significance of each of the following people or terms.

1. Robert E. Lee
2. Elizabeth Blackwell
3. Copperheads
4. Martin Delany
5. war of attrition
6. black codes
7. Civil Rights Act of 1866
8. Compromise of 1877
9. sharecropping
10. Elizabeth Cady Stanton

UNDERSTANDING MAIN IDEAS

1. How did the goals of the North change as the Civil War progressed?
2. What were the consequences of the war for the North and the South?
3. How did the Reconstruction plans of Lincoln, Johnson, and the Radical Republicans differ?
4. What political roles did African Americans play during Reconstruction?
5. How did conditions for southern farmers and laborers change from 1865 to 1900?

6. How did changes in the New South reverse the policies of the Reconstruction period?

REVIEWING THEMES

1. **Geographic Diversity** What role did geography play in helping the North win the war?
2. **Constitutional Heritage** How did the Thirteenth, Fourteenth, and Fifteenth amendments attempt to adapt the U.S. Constitution to changing conditions after the Civil War?
3. **Democratic Values** How was democratic society in the U.S. expanded during Reconstruction? How did the expansion prepare for further changes in America's definition of democracy?

THINKING CRITICALLY

1. **Hypothesizing** How might the outcome of the Civil War have been different if European powers had aided the South?
2. **Evaluating** Why did many southern whites react so strongly to gains made by African Americans during Reconstruction?
3. **Synthesizing** Compare and contrast the views of Booker T. Washington and Ida Wells-Barnett on how African Americans should deal with discrimination.

STRATEGY FOR SUCCESS

Review the Skills Handbook entry on Reading Charts and Graphs beginning on page 756. Then study the chart below. How did the value of cotton goods produced in the South change during this period? How did southern production compare with that of the New England and Middle Atlantic regions?

VALUE OF COTTON GOODS PRODUCED 1880–1900 (in millions of dollars)			
Region	**1880**	**1890**	**1900**
New England	143	181	191
Middle Atlantic	29	40	48
Southern	16	41	95

Source: *The American South*

Reconstruction
Acts passed.

Fifteenth
Amendment
passed.

Reconstruction
ends.

First Jim Crow
law passed in
Tennessee.

Ida Wells-Barnett
publishes first
statistical study
of lynching.

Supreme Court
issues ruling in
Plessy v. Ferguson.

| 1867 | 1869 | 1877 | 1881 | 1895 | 1896 |

WRITING ABOUT HISTORY

Writing to Evaluate The wisdom of Sherman's total-war tactics has been debated by historians. Write an essay evaluating whether such tactics would be practical in every war.

USING PRIMARY SOURCES

Read the following excerpt from a November 1865 letter that a group of African Americans from South Carolina wrote to the U.S. Congress. Then summarize the letter's main demands and explain the suggested basis for these demands.

66 *We would ask for no rights or privileges but such as rest upon the strong basis of justice. . . . We ask first, that the strong arm of law and order be placed alike over the entire people of this State; that life and property be secured, and the laborer free to sell his labor as the merchant his goods. . . .*

We ask that the three great agents of civilized society—the school, the pulpit, the press—be as secure in South Carolina as in Massachusetts or Vermont.

We ask that equal suffrage be conferred upon us, in common with the white men of this State.

This we ask, because "all free governments derive their just powers from the consent of the governed"; and we are largely in the majority in this State, bearing for a long period the burden of onerous taxation, without a just representation. 99

LINKING HISTORY AND GEOGRAPHY

The Civil War was commanded by generals whose knowledge of the terrain was often hampered by inaccurate maps. Read the following excerpt from T. Harry Williams's *Lincoln and His Generals* (1952). Then, in a paragraph, explain how unreliable information may have affected military campaigns in both the North and the South.

66 General Henry W. Halleck was running a campaign in the western theater in 1862 with maps he got from a book store. . . . Not until 1863 did the Army of the Potomac [the Union army] have an accurate map of northern Virginia, its theater of operations. . . . As late as 1864 there was not an office in Washington that could tell a general organizing a campaign what railroads were under military control . . . or how many men and supplies they could transport. 99

BUILDING YOUR PORTFOLIO

Complete the following projects independently or cooperatively.

1. CONFLICT In Chapter 2 you examined the logistics of organizing a war effort from a government official's point of view. Building on that experience, imagine you are a soldier drafted into a Civil War army regiment—either for the Union or for the Confederacy—in 1864. Write a journal entry expressing your reactions to the war in general and to the draft, and describing the details of your military experience.

2. INDIVIDUAL RIGHTS In chapters 2 and 3 you argued for the expansion of rights for various groups in American society prior to the Civil War. Building on that experience, imagine you are a lawyer representing a group of African Americans in Mississippi in the second half of the 19th century. Prepare a closing statement arguing that your clients' rights have been violated by the black codes, Jim Crow laws, or the actions of groups such as the Ku Klux Klan.

America's **GEOGRAPHY**

CONQUERING DISTANCE

THE late 19th century was a period of massive population shifts for the United States. Between 1860 and 1910 some 23 million immigrants crossed the Atlantic and Pacific oceans to reach America. Many of these immigrants joined the migration across country as millions of people settled the American West. This westward migration was aided by railroad lines and improved systems of communication. These means of transportation and communication linked numerous western cities together, forming the basis of a modern transcontinental economy.

Conquering Distance Overseas

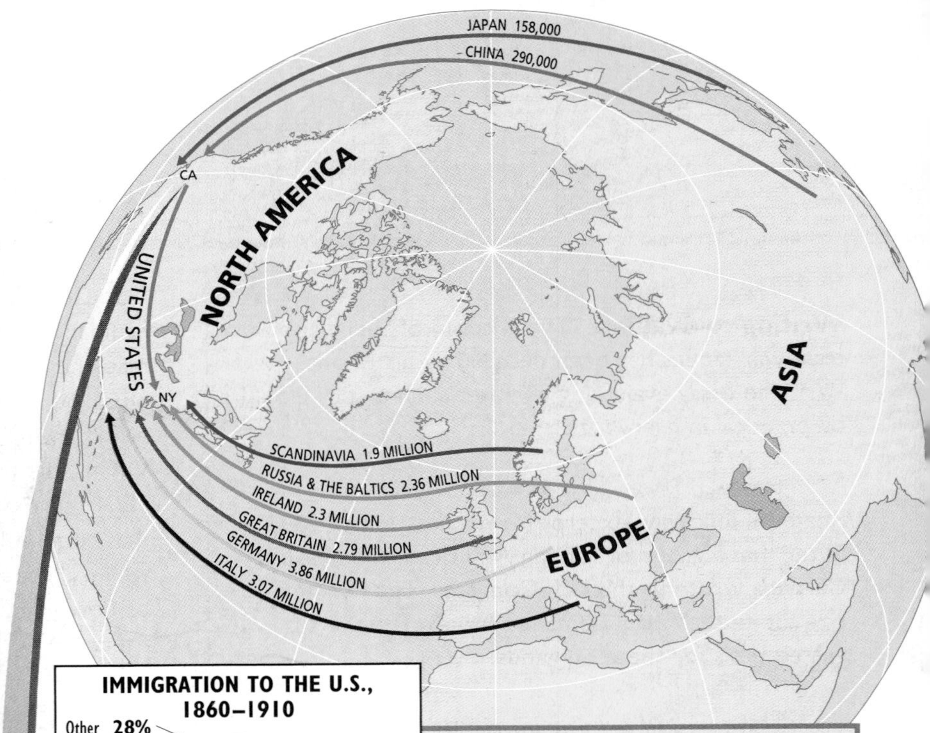

JAPAN 158,000
CHINA 290,000
CA
NORTH AMERICA
UNITED STATES
NY
ASIA
SCANDINAVIA 1.9 MILLION
RUSSIA & THE BALTICS 2.36 MILLION
IRELAND 2.3 MILLION
GREAT BRITAIN 2.79 MILLION
GERMANY 3.86 MILLION
ITALY 3.07 MILLION
EUROPE

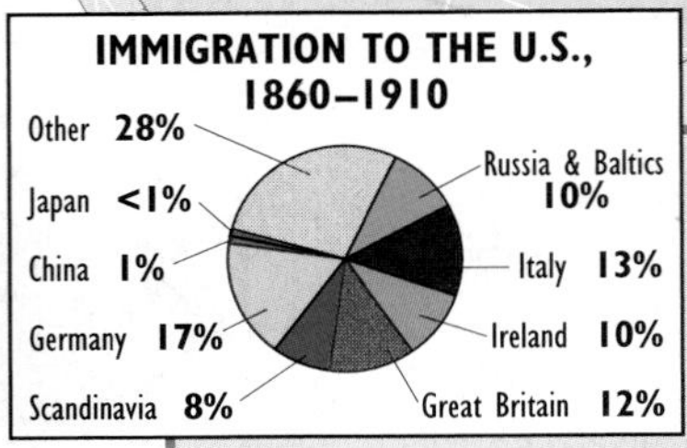

IMMIGRATION TO THE U.S., 1860–1910
Other 28%
Japan <1%
China 1%
Germany 17%
Scandinavia 8%
Russia & Baltics 10%
Italy 13%
Ireland 10%
Great Britain 12%

Compared to European immigrants, immigrants from Asia had to travel twice as far to reach the United States. The vast majority of Chinese immigrants in the late 19th century came from the province of Guangdong. Although most initially settled along the Pacific coast, particularly in the San Francisco area, some eventually journeyed across the United States. In 1870 a Massachusetts factory owner began to recruit Chinese laborers from California to take the place of striking workers. As this practice caught on, more Chinese Californians made the trek to the east coast. Today the thriving Chinatowns of Boston, New York, and San Francisco are all the results of the 19th century journeys from Guangdong.

From Across the Pacific to the Atlantic Coast

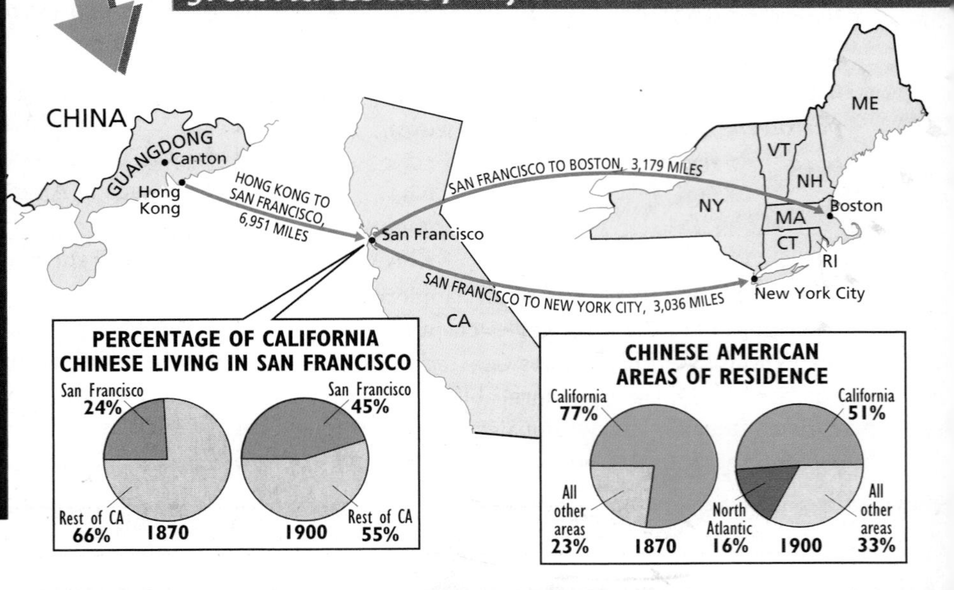

CHINA
GUANGDONG
Canton
Hong Kong
HONG KONG TO SAN FRANCISCO, 6,951 MILES
San Francisco
SAN FRANCISCO TO BOSTON, 3,179 MILES
SAN FRANCISCO TO NEW YORK CITY, 3,036 MILES
CA
NY
VT
NH
ME
MA
CT
RI
Boston
New York City
PERCENTAGE OF CALIFORNIA CHINESE LIVING IN SAN FRANCISCO
San Francisco 24%
Rest of CA 66%
1870
San Francisco 45%
Rest of CA 55%
1900
CHINESE AMERICAN AREAS OF RESIDENCE
California 77%
All other areas 23%
1870
California 51%
North Atlantic 16%
All other areas 33%
1900

Conquering Distance Across the West

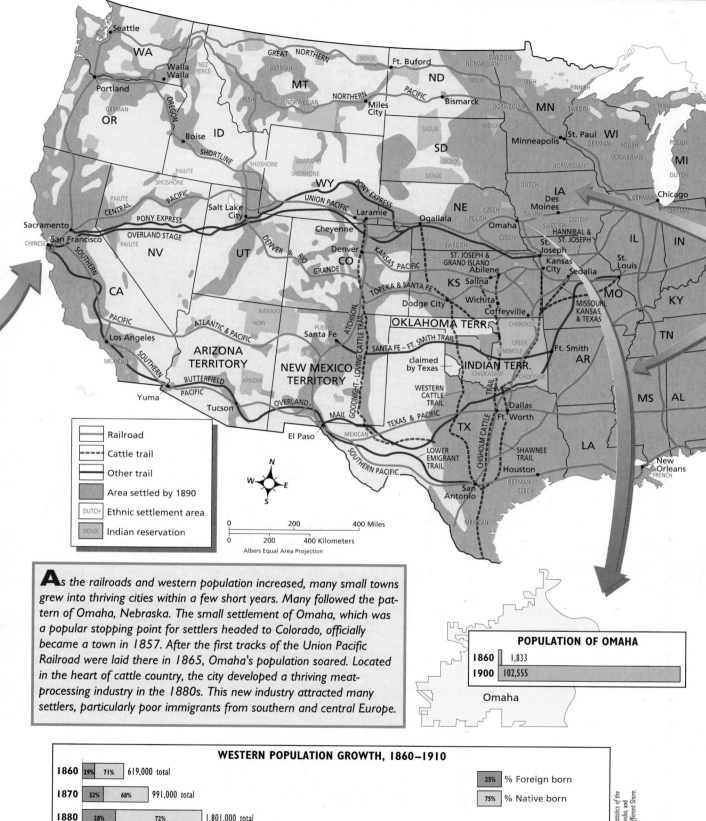

Legend

- Railroad
- Cattle trail
- Other trail
- Area settled by 1890
- DUTCH Ethnic settlement area
- SIOUX Indian reservation

0   200   400 Miles
0   200   400 Kilometers
Albers Equal Area Projection

As the railroads and western population increased, many small towns grew into thriving cities within a few short years. Many followed the pattern of Omaha, Nebraska. The small settlement of Omaha, which was a popular stopping point for settlers headed to Colorado, officially became a town in 1857. After the first tracks of the Union Pacific Railroad were laid there in 1865, Omaha's population soared. Located in the heart of cattle country, the city developed a thriving meat-processing industry in the 1880s. This new industry attracted many settlers, particularly poor immigrants from southern and central Europe.

POPULATION OF OMAHA

1860	1,833	
1900	102,555	

Omaha

WESTERN POPULATION GROWTH, 1860–1910

Year	Percentages	Total
1860	29% / 71%	619,000 total
1870	32% / 68%	991,000 total
1880	28% / 72%	1,801,000 total
1890	25% / 75%	3,134,000 total
1900	20% / 80%	4,309,000 total
1910	20% / 80%	7,082,000 total

25% % Foreign born
75% % Native born

Chart information from Historical Statistics of the United States, World Book Encyclopedia, and Ronald Takaki's Strangers from a Different Shore.

THE WESTERN CROSSROADS

FOCUS

UNDERSTANDING THE MAIN IDEA

After the Civil War the regions of the West—the Great Plains, the Southwest, and the Far West—played important roles in U.S. economic growth. People moved to the West, encouraged by the U.S. government's offers of free land and the promise of profits from ranching, farming, lumbering, and mining. In many years of conflict and treaty negotiations, the U.S. government forced Native Americans to give up much of their lands.

THEMES

- **GEOGRAPHIC DIVERSITY** What strategies might people use to survive and prosper in arid or semiarid environments?

- **CULTURAL DIVERSITY** What problems might arise when one group attempts to force another group to give up its way of life?

- **ECONOMIC DEVELOPMENT** How might a government promote economic development in a new territory?

1862	1869	1876	1879	1896
The Homestead Act passed.	First transcontinental railroad completed.	Battle of Little Bighorn occurs.	Exodusters trek west.	Gold discovered in the Klondike.

The resolution of the Oregon boundary dispute in 1846 and the Treaty of Guadalupe Hidalgo in 1848 opened up millions of acres of western land for U.S. settlement. Native Americans faced increasing pressure on their lands and resources as non-Indian settlers moved to the Far West.

Miners at Auburn Ravine, California, 1852

Ever since the Spanish planted settlements in the present-day southwestern United States, the West has been a crossroads where Native American and Asian, African, and European cultures met and influenced each other. European horses and guns, for example, changed the culture of the Plains Indians, allowing them to hunt buffalo more successfully and to move permanently from the mountains to the Plains. The Comanches—possibly the most-skilled horse raisers of the Plains—used the guns and horses to raid settlements and to dominate other Indian tribes on the southern Plains.

The Comanche way of life, however, required abundant land and buffalo. The Comanche freedom to roam the Plains was threatened after 1859, when the U.S. government stepped up its efforts to settle the Comanches on reservations in present-day Oklahoma. Ten Bears, a Comanche leader, argued against the government's plan:

66 When I was in Washington the Great Father told me that all the Comanche land was ours, and that no one should hinder us in living on it. So, why do you ask us to leave the rivers, and the sun, and the wind, and live in houses? 99

The federal government's reasons were overwhelmingly economic. As the U.S. government limited Native Americans to reservations, non-Indians rushed to the West to establish farms and ranches and to stake out mining claims. Soon the West began supplying the United States and the rest of the world with wheat, lumber, minerals, and cattle and sheep.

American Museum of Natural History

American buffalo

NATIVE AMERICAN RESISTANCE

FOCUS

- **Why did the U.S. government adopt the reservation policy?**
- **Why did so much conflict erupt between Native Americans and the federal government in the late 1800s?**
- **How did the federal government try to "Americanize" Native Americans?**

Until the 1850s most non-Indians who ventured to the West settled in California, Oregon, or Texas. By mid-century, however, non-Indians began settling on the Great Plains and in other parts of the West. To make room for the settlers, the government forced Native Americans onto reservations, provoking nearly a half century of conflict.

Sioux doll

INDIAN COUNTRY

By 1850 nearly all Native Americans—some 360,000—lived west of the Mississippi River. Indians from the old Northwest and the Southeast were confined to Indian Territory, in present-day Oklahoma. On the southern Plains, the Kiowas shared the land with the powerful Comanches. The Sioux, Blackfeet, and Crows dominated the northern Plains. In the Southwest the Apaches ranged throughout New Mexico, Arizona, and northern Mexico, while the Navajos and Hopis lived in farming or ranching communities.

Museum of the Great Plains

In the Far West, disease and conflict associated with nearly a century of contact with Hispanic and other non-Indian settlers had reduced the Indian population, including the Paiutes (PY-oots), Pimas, Miwoks, and Maidus. In California alone their numbers had dropped from an estimated 300,000 in 1769 to some 35,000 by 1860.

In the 1851 **Treaty of Fort Laramie**, the U.S. government had promised the Sioux, Cheyenne, and other tribes control of the Plains—the bulk of Indian Country. In return, each tribe had accepted a defined territory, pledged not to attack settlers moving west, and allowed the government to build roads and forts in its territories. The government, however, soon broke the promises made in the treaty.

Hearing tales (both exaggerated and accurate) about the mineral wealth and fertile land in the West, thousands of non-Indians streamed into the territory. In a series of new treaties, the government forced Native Americans to move to reservations. The treaties promised reservation land,

◄ **Driven out of Montana by the Cheyennes and Sioux, the Kiowas settled on the southern Plains, in an area stretching from Kansas to Mexico.**

money, and yearly supplies. The task of administering the reservations went to the **Bureau of Indian Affairs**, established in 1824 within the War Department. The close ties between the army and the bureau sent a clear message: Indians who resisted confinement on reservations would be dealt with by force.

Even when American Indians went quietly to reservations, the government rarely kept its side of the bargain. Bureau agents often lined their pockets by selling the supplies intended for Native Americans to non-Indians. Furthermore, the government regularly reduced the size of reservations as settlers demanded more land. As a newspaper editor noted in 1869, the government's actions showed that "when the march of our empire demands this reservation of yours, we will assign you another; . . . so long as we choose, this is your home, your prison, your playground."

> ■■ **The U.S. government attempted to restrict American Indians to reservations to make room for non-Indian settlers.**

*Y*EARS OF STRUGGLE

Angered by the government's double-dealings, several Plains tribes, including the Cheyennes, Comanches, and Sioux, fought back. To them a life without buffalo hunting was no life at all.

The Plains peoples faced strong opposition. Some 20,000 U.S. Army troops, many of them Civil War veterans, enforced Indian removal. Some 4,000 were African Americans, nicknamed "buffalo soldiers," who served in four segregated units. The army enlisted Indians as scouts or as soldiers by playing on rivalries among tribes. For example, many Pawnees, Crows, and Shoshonis helped U.S. forces battle the Sioux.

Sand Creek. One of the earliest confrontations in the West between the military and American Indians occurred in Colorado Territory. The territory's non-Indian population had been growing rapidly since the Colorado gold rush of 1858. Eager to open more land to U.S. settlers, John Evans, the territorial governor, pressured the Cheyennes and Arapahos to move to reservations. When some Cheyenne and Arapaho leaders refused to leave, Evans feared an uprising.

▲ **Some time between 1875 and 1880, Cheyenne-Arapaho artist No Horse drew this scene, entitled *Women Honoring Warriors*.**

Throughout the summer of 1864, Indian forces clashed with the local militia. By fall Black Kettle, a Cheyenne chief, was tired of fighting. He and his group made their way to Fort Lyon to surrender. When they stopped to camp along Sand Creek, most of the men left to hunt. In their absence, some 700 troops under Colonel John Chivington attacked the camp, killing some 200 Cheyennes, most of them women and children.

The **Sand Creek Massacre** horrified U.S. authorities. But Chivington was unrepentant. "Damn any man who sympathizes with Indians!" he exclaimed. "I have come to kill Indians, and believe it is right . . . to use any means under God's heaven to kill Indians."

News of the slaughter swept across the Plains, sparking raids by the Arapahos and Cheyennes. The Sioux, engaged in a long-standing war against the U.S. Army, also stepped up their efforts. But neither side emerged victorious. To end the fighting, U.S. authorities and American Indian leaders signed the **Treaty of Medicine Lodge** in 1867 and the second Treaty of Fort Laramie in 1868. In these treaties, the southern Plains Indians and the Sioux agreed to move to reservations.

The treaties did not end the fighting, however. As an editor of the *Army and Navy Journal* observed: "One of our hands holds the rifle and the other the peace-pipe, and we blaze away with both instruments at the same time. The chief consequence is a great *smoke*—and there it ends."

Sioux resistance. In 1875 the U.S. Army was again campaigning against the Sioux. Impatient to open up the Sioux's sacred Black Hills to gold prospectors, U.S. authorities ordered the Sioux to

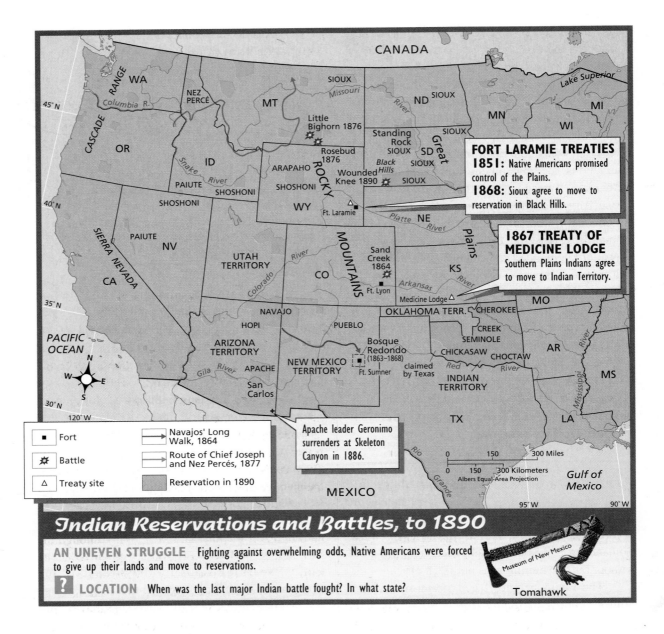

CANADA

FORT LARAMIE TREATIES
1851: Native Americans promised control of the Plains.
1868: Sioux agree to move to reservation in Black Hills.

1867 TREATY OF MEDICINE LODGE
Southern Plains Indians agree to move to Indian Territory.

Apache leader Geronimo surrenders at Skeleton Canyon in 1886.

Little Bighorn 1876
Rosebud 1876
Wounded Knee 1890
Sand Creek 1864
Ft. Lyon
Bosque Redondo (1863–1868)
Ft. Sumner
Medicine Lodge △
Ft. Laramie

- ■ Fort
- ※ Battle
- △ Treaty site
- → Navajos' Long Walk, 1864
- → Route of Chief Joseph and Nez Percés, 1877
- Reservation in 1890

150 | 300 Miles
150 | 300 Kilometers
Albers Equal-Area Projection

Indian Reservations and Battles, to 1890

AN UNEVEN STRUGGLE Fighting against overwhelming odds, Native Americans were forced to give up their lands and move to reservations.

? LOCATION When was the last major Indian battle fought? In what state?

Museum of New Mexico
Tomahawk

settle near the agencies, the local offices of the Bureau of Indian Affairs.

Among those urging resistance to the government's efforts was Tatanka Iyotake, a medicine man non-Indians called Sitting Bull. One of the principal leaders of the Sioux nation, Sitting Bull was born around 1831. He joined his first war party at 14 and soon gained a reputation for courage and military skill.

Sitting Bull mocked those who gave in to reservation life. "You are fools," he argued, "to make yourselves slaves to a piece of fat bacon, some hard-tack [biscuits], and a little sugar and coffee."

BIO GRAPHY

◄ **Sitting Bull signed his name to this 1880s photograph shortly after it was taken.**

Many Sioux and Cheyennes agreed. They joined forces under Sitting Bull and Ta-sunko-witko (Crazy Horse). By late June 1876 Sitting Bull and Crazy Horse's camp on the Little Bighorn River contained almost 2,000 men prepared to fight.

The army, misjudging the size of the Indian fighting force, decided to strike first. The Native Americans, outnumbering the army troops and led by Crazy Horse, fought off two army attacks. On June 25, General George Armstrong Custer divided his force to strike the camp from three sides. Custer led a battalion of over 200 men. After the final attack, which lasted less than an hour, Custer and all his battalion lay dead.

The **Battle of the Little Bighorn** gave the Indians only a brief triumph. Their forces broke into smaller groups to evade army troops, but group by group, they were forced to surrender and settle near the agencies. Sitting Bull fled to Canada but later returned and settled on Standing Rock Reservation, where he continued to oppose non-Indian settlement of Sioux lands.

The Ghost Dance. A tragic final chapter of the Plains Indian–U.S. Army wars unfolded on the plains of South Dakota. The seeds of this conflict were planted in 1889 when Wovoka (woh-VOH-kuh), a Paiute holy man, began the Ghost Dance religion. Wovoka proclaimed that traditional Indian ways of life would revive if Indians performed the Ghost Dance. A Sioux explained the appeal of Wovoka's message:

▲ **Some Ghost Dance performers wore Ghost Shirts similar to this one. They believed that the symbols of stars, birds, and animals on the garment protected them from harm.**

Field Museum of Natural History

❝ The rumor got about: "The dead are to return. The buffalo are to return. The Dakota [Sioux] people will get back their own way of life. The white people will soon go away, and that will mean happier times for us once more!"

That part about the dead returning . . . appealed to me. To think I should see my dear mother, grandmother, brothers and sisters again! ❞

Wovoka preached peace. The Sioux living on reservations in the Dakotas, however, added a militant tone to the religion by donning "Ghost Shirts," whose special symbols, they believed, could stop bullets. Government agents, fearing the Ghost Dance would inspire Indian resistance, moved to suppress the religious movement.

In late December 1890, about 500 soldiers of the 7th Cavalry were sent to bring in some Sioux followers of the Ghost Dance who had left their reservation. The army encountered the Sioux at Wounded Knee Creek. As the army set about disarming them, someone fired a rifle—possibly during a scuffle, possibly as a signal. Gunfire immediately erupted between U.S. soldiers and Indians. Some 300 Sioux were killed, including women and children. About 30 U.S. soldiers also died. The **Wounded Knee Massacre** marked the end of the Indian wars on the Great Plains.

CONFLICT IN THE FAR WEST

Native Americans west of the Great Plains also faced resettlement. The government tried to force the Navajos in northwestern New Mexico and northeastern Arizona to give up sheep herding and become settled farmers. To enforce the government's plan, the army waged a campaign against the Navajo in 1863, destroying homes and sheep herds. Soldiers then forced the Navajos to walk to the Bosque Redondo reservation. This came to be known as the **Long Walk**.

The government gave the Navajos seeds and farming tools, but the land proved unsuitable for farming. Living conditions were harsh, and many Navajos died from malnutrition or disease. In 1868 the government, recognizing that its plan was unworkable, granted the Navajos a reservation in New Mexico and Arizona. There the Navajos rebuilt their communities, concentrating on raising sheep, weaving, and silver-smithing.

Farther north in the Wallowa (wah-LOW-uh) River Valley of northeastern Oregon, the Nez Percés also tried to avoid relocation. Although the Nez Percés had long maintained good relations with the U.S. government and white settlers, the government ordered the Nez Percés to move to an Idaho reservation in 1877. Their leader, Chief Joseph, reluctantly agreed. Before his people could leave, however, a few Nez Percés killed some white settlers, whom they viewed as intruders. Joseph's group, fearing attack, fled.

Pursued by army troops for three months, the Nez Percés journeyed east and north through Idaho, Wyoming, and Montana, picking up additional followers along the way. They planned to escape to Canada, but as winter approached, travel became harder. The Nez Percés surrendered only 30 miles from the Canadian border. An interpreter wept as he relayed Chief Joseph's surrender statement:

❝ I am tired of fighting. Our chiefs are killed. . . . It is cold and we have no blankets. The little children are freezing to death. . . . My heart is sick and sad. From where the sun now stands, I will fight no more forever. ❞

▲ Before reaching the Canadian border, Chief Joseph surrendered to Colonel Nelson A. Miles on October 5, 1877. Shown here is *Chief Joseph Rides to Surrender* by Howard Terpning.

The Nez Percés, however, were not the last American Indians to surrender to the U.S. Army. The Apaches of the desert and canyon lands of New Mexico and Arizona mounted a long campaign against government control. The conflict began when settlers moved into Apache territory in the 1850s. Raids and attacks by both sides produced a climate of fear and hatred. In 1877 the U.S. government forced the seminomadic Apaches to settle on the San Carlos reservation in Arizona.

Most Apaches complied, but life on the reservation proved harsh. In 1881, amid rumors of an Indian uprising, army troops moved into the territory. Fearing an attack, Geronimo, an Apache chief, fled the reservation with about 75 followers. For the next five years, Geronimo's group raided settlements and evaded capture. But on September 4, 1886, with his followers outnumbered, Geronimo gave up. "Once I moved about like the wind," he told his captors. "Now I surrender to you and that is all." His words marked the end of armed resistance to the reservation system.

▪▪ The U.S. Army and American Indians clashed as the U.S. government took away Indian lands.

*R*ETHINKING INDIAN POLICY

By the 1880s American Indians had been forced to surrender more than 450 million acres to the U.S. government. The Indians had been driven off their land and onto reservations by a number of pres-sures. While the army forced Indians onto reservations, U.S. settlers, whose presence increased as railroads snaked across the West, moved onto Indian lands and killed off most of the buffalo herds. "Kill every buffalo you can," advised Colonel R. I. Dodge. "Every buffalo dead is an Indian gone." With the loss of the buffalo, American Indians had little hope of maintaining an independent existence on the Plains.

At the same time, a small but active group of reformers was voicing alarm at the mistreatment of American Indians. Helen Hunt Jackson's influential book, *A Century of Dishonor,* attacked the government for its years of broken promises and corrupt dealings with Indians. Another important reformer was Thoc-me-tony (Shell-Flower), a Paiute woman known as Sarah Winnemucca. Outraged by the Paiutes' forced removal to Yakima Reservation in Washington Territory in 1878, she began lecturing to non-Indians about the Paiutes' plight. Later she reached a wider audience with her book *Life Among the Piutes.*

▲ Sarah Winnemucca brought the plight of American Indians to the nation's attention in the 1880s.

Many government officials, as well as reformers interested in Indian welfare, viewed **assimilation**, or cultural absorption, of American Indians into "white America" as the only way to ensure Native American survival. The federal government urged them to become farmers and to move out of their dwellings and live in wooden houses. To encourage assimilation, the government passed laws to force Indians to abandon their traditional appearance and to dress like "Americans." One law ordered Indian men to cut their long hair. Another outlawed Indian religious practices.

To speed assimilation, the government set up a system of Indian schools. Some Indian children attended reservation schools, while others were forced to leave home to attend boarding schools. The Carlisle Indian School in Pennsylvania

◀ A group of Navajos from New Mexico arrived at the Carlisle Indian School in the 1880s. Six months after arrival they posed for this photograph, outfitted in school uniforms.

typified the boarding school system. Students were forced to speak only English, wear "proper" clothes, and change their names to "American" ones. The school's founder summed up his aim: to "kill the Indian and save the man."

The government's most important assimilation strategy, however, was forcing Indians to give up tribal ownership of land in favor of private ownership. Private ownership, the government argued, lay at the heart of Americanization. Western settlers and developers wanted American Indians to give up tribal ownership of land for another reason: if American Indians could be forced onto small plots, settlers and developers could then buy up surplus reservation land.

The passage of the **Dawes General Allotment Act** in 1887 established private ownership of Indian land. The act required that Indian lands be surveyed and Indian families claim an allotment of 160 acres of reservation land for farming. The remaining land would be sold.

The Dawes Act proved to be a disaster for American Indians. In less than 50 years, they lost two thirds of their land. In addition to the surplus land sold to settlers and developers, many American Indians sold or were cheated out of their allotments. By 1890 forced assimilation and warfare had reduced the U.S. Indian population to fewer than 250,000.

 By outlawing Indian customs, establishing boarding schools, and enforcing private land ownership, the U.S. government attempted to assimilate American Indians.

SECTION 1 REVIEW

IDENTIFY and explain the significance of the following: Bureau of Indian Affairs, Sand Creek Massacre, Treaty of Medicine Lodge, Sitting Bull, George Armstrong Custer, Battle of the Little Bighorn, Wovoka, Wounded Knee Massacre, Long Walk, Chief Joseph, Geronimo, Helen Hunt Jackson, Sarah Winnemucca, Dawes General Allotment Act.

LOCATE and explain the importance of the following: San Carlos Reservation.

1. **MAIN IDEA** Why did the U.S. government attempt to resettle American Indians on reservations? How did Indians respond to this attempt?

2. **MAIN IDEA** How did the government's policy toward American Indians as outlined in the Treaty of Fort Laramie differ from the government's policy in the late 1800s?

3. **MAIN IDEA** How did the U.S. government try to assimilate American Indians?

4. **WRITING TO EXPLAIN** Imagine you are a Sioux who took part in the Ghost Dance religion. Write an essay explaining the meaning of the Ghost Dance and the Ghost Shirt.

5. **ANALYZING** Why was the government's attempt to relocate Navajos unsuccessful?

WESTERN FARMERS AND CATTLE RANCHERS

Windmill on the western Great Plains

FOCUS

- **Why did many farmers move to the West in the late 1800s?**
- **What innovations helped farmers cope with the western environments?**
- **What factors led to the rise and fall of the cattle business in the 1870s and 1880s?**

*A*ttracted by the promise of free or cheap land, thousands moved to the West after the Civil War. Farmers were able to take advantage of this opportunity because new technologies enabled them to deal with the West's harsh environment. The new railroads that crossed the West provided farmers and ranchers access to eastern markets and made possible the cattle ranching boom.

ECONOMIC DEVELOPMENT OF THE WEST

After the southern states seceded from the Union, northern Republicans saw a chance to develop the West along northern lines. The Republicans wanted the new western states and territories to be free of slavery and populated by independent farmers who would develop the land. To attain these goals, Republicans passed a series of acts in 1862 to put public lands to productive use.

Land acts. Three government land acts increased non-Indian settlement of the Great Plains. The **Homestead Act** granted a 160-acre homestead, or farm, to any citizen or prospective citizen willing to live in the Great Plains and cultivate the land for five years. Some 400,000 families took advantage of this offer. The **Pacific Railway Act** gave land to railroad companies to build a transcontinental railroad linking both coasts. The **Morrill Act** granted land to the states to help finance agricultural colleges, which would train young farmers and thus help develop the West.

◀ **Daniel Freeman filed this claim in January 1863 in Brownsville, Nebraska, for 160 acres of land. He received this homestead certificate after testifying that he had built a "part log & part frame" house on his claim.**

Competition for land was fierce. In Oklahoma in 1889, for example, a flood of would-be settlers responded to a government offer of free homesteads. In March, President Benjamin Harrison announced that former Seminole and Creek lands would become available on April 22 to the first takers. By the appointed day, some 50,000 prospective homesteaders had gathered to race for the land. At exactly noon the stampede began. Settler Hamilton S. Wicks noted the result:

❝ On the morning of April 23, a city of 10,000 people, 500 houses, and innumer-able tents existed where twelve hours before was nothing but a broad expanse of prairie. ❞

Subsequent "runs" took place in other parts of Oklahoma. As a result, Native Americans lost more than 11 million acres to non-Indian settlers.

The railroads. Railroad companies also helped lure settlers to the West. Between 1869 and 1883 the companies built four transcontinental lines (see map, page 132). To pay the huge costs of laying the tracks, the companies sold settlers land

Changing Ways A TRANSCONTINENTAL RAILROAD

In the mid-1800s there was no easy way to get from the East Coast to the West Coast. Both the overland journey and the boat trip around the tip of South America could take months. To help open the West to settlers, Congress passed the Pacific Railway Act in 1862. The act awarded contracts to build a transcontinental railroad to the Central Pacific and the Union Pacific railroad companies.

The track had to cross some 1,500 miles of wilderness. The Central Pacific Railroad would lay track eastward from Sacramento, California, over the Sierra Nevada. The Union Pacific would work westward from Omaha, Nebraska, and cross the rugged Rockies.

To encourage the companies to take on the job, the federal government gave them land. The project soon became a

▲ **Laborers from different ethnic backgrounds helped build the transcontinental railroad. This 1886 photograph shows a Northern Pacific Railroad crew.**

contest to see which company would lay more track.

The railroad companies recruited thousands of workers for the often perilous work. Work crews competed against nature as well as each other as they blasted, shoveled, and pick-axed their way across the continent. During the winters snowdrifts and avalanches blocked mountain passes. Some laborers died doing the dangerous blasting work. The crews also faced attacks by Indians,

who tried to prevent "the wagons which make a noise" from invading their land.

Most of the Union Pacific's 10,000 workers were Irish immigrants. After the Civil War, veterans from both sides also signed on. The Central Pacific's work force consisted mostly of Chinese laborers. One observer called the sound of the crews' progress "a grand Anvil Chorus" that played "in triple time: three strokes to the spike; ten spikes to the rail; 400 rails to the mile." After seven years the crews met at Promontory, Utah, on May 10, 1869.

Railroad officials, politicians, and workers looked on as the last railroad tie—made of laurel wood, a symbol of victory in a contest of strength—was put into place. Leland Stanford, president of the Central Pacific and former governor of California, then drove a golden spike to complete the railroad. The telegraph built alongside the tracks flashed the news from coast to coast.

donated by federal, state, and local governments. The federal government, for example, gave the railroads more than 100 million acres of land. To attract buyers, the railroads offered free transportation and credit.

Railroads also stimulated the midwestern and western lumbering industry. Vast pine forests in Michigan, Wisconsin, Minnesota, and eventually the Pacific Northwest supplied wood for railroad ties, railroad cars, and buildings that sprang up along the railroad routes. But uncontrolled lumbering destroyed wildlife habitats, caused erosion, and had other important ecological consequences little recognized at the time.

Who moved to the West? Economic motives, the search for racial tolerance, and the promise of a better life drew three main groups to the West after the Civil War. They were (1) European Americans from the East; (2) African Americans from the South; and (3) immigrants from Europe and Asia.

Most European American newcomers came from more settled areas of the United States. As a Nebraska settler explained, "I am well satisfied that I can do better here than I can in Illinois." The high cost of transporting supplies to the West also meant that most settlers were middle-class farmers and businesspeople who could afford the move.

While African Americans moved west to obtain land, they also sought to escape violence and persecution. Kansas, where John Brown had first fought against slavery, especially appealed to African American settlers. The biggest rush of black settlers occurred during the Kansas Fever Exodus of 1879. From 20,000 to 40,000 African Americans fled the South after violence erupted during the 1878 elections. Poor and ill-equipped, these black settlers, known as **Exodusters**, were helped by established black settlers. The Exodusters eventually settled some 20,000 acres.

European immigrants also flocked to the western United States. "America Fever" infected thousands of Norwegians, Swedes, and Danes. In 1882 alone more than 100,000 came to the American West. In addition, many Irish who had helped build the railroads and a great number of Germans who had settled in the Mississippi Valley decided to move to the Plains. They were joined by Mennonites, Protestant pacifists who fled persecution in Russia. Their experience growing wheat on the Russian steppes, or grasslands, proved particularly useful on the Great Plains.

Many Chinese immigrants who had come to California during the gold rush of 1849 also turned to farming. In California in 1880 some 3,200 Chinese raised crops. Throughout the West, they worked on their own farms or as farm laborers, sharecroppers, or produce vendors.

Farmers moved onto the Great Plains for a variety of motives, but the main incentive was readily available land.

WESTERN FARMS

Environmental conditions in the West posed special problems for farmers. The cold winters and arid conditions of the Great Plains required new crops and farming techniques. The scarcity of trees meant that farmers had to find new building materials. Turning to sod, they built houses and barns out of sod chunks cut from the heavy topsoil and stacked like bricks. Sod houses were well insulated, windproof, and fireproof but also dank, dirty, full of insects, and far from rainproof.

The **U.S. Department of Agriculture,** created in 1862, helped farmers adapt to the Plains environment. Department experts sought out and publicized new varieties of wheat that would grow in the cold winters of the northern Plains.

▲ **Between 1830 and 1910 some 90 percent of all pioneers west of the Missouri River lived in sod houses. Shown here is the Scott family, photographed outside their Nebraska home in 1889.**

◄ **Bonanza farms applied the techniques of the factory system to agriculture. By 1890 some 300 farms, most of which held about 1,000 acres, covered the Red River Valley. This photograph shows one bonanza farm in the San Fernando Valley of California.**

Department of Agriculture agents also taught **dry farming** techniques, planting and harvesting methods that conserve moisture. For example, agents advised farmers to plow deep furrows to bring moisture to the surface and to break up the soil after a rainfall to prevent evaporation.

To tap water deep underground, Plains farmers adapted drilling machinery developed by petroleum companies. They also used new models of windmills—wind-powered water pumps—designed to withstand the Plains' strong winds.

Lack of water was a problem for farmers further west, too. In parts of the Southwest, Hispanic and American Indian farmers had developed irrigation systems that used canals, sloping fields, and dams to control water flow. They had also established farms that fanned out in thin strips from water sources so that all community residents had access to water. The new settlers had to adopt these methods to survive.

On the Plains new farm equipment also helped farmers. James Oliver's factory in South Bend, Indiana, produced thousands of plows with sharp, durable blades to slice through the tough prairie sod. "Self-binding" harvesters not only cut wheat but also tied it into bundles. The combine— a sort of factory on wheels—cut, threshed, and cleaned the grain all in one operation.

▪▪ Government support, innovative farming practices, and new technologies helped make farming on the Plains possible.

Efficient new farm machinery and cheap, abundant land made possible the creation of a new kind of large-scale operation, the **bonanza farm**. Most bonanza farms were owned by companies and run like factories, with professional managers.

At planting and harvesting times foremen often supervised some 500 to 1,000 extra workers.

The first bonanza farms were established in the Red River Valley in Dakota Territory and Minnesota in the mid-1870s. They were located close to the Northern Pacific Railroad, which transported their wheat to market.

Investors also organized bonanza farms farther west. In California's Central Valley one of the largest wheat farms covered more than 66,000 acres. Although California led the country in wheat production in the 1880s, by the 1890s most California farmers had turned to more-profitable fruit and vegetable crops. Farmers shipped these crops east in refrigerated railcars.

When weather and market conditions were good, bonanza farms made large profits; buying seeds and equipment in bulk meant lower production costs. But in times of drought or low wheat prices, their profits fell. Family farmers, with fewer workers to pay and less money invested in equipment, could better handle boom-and-bust cycles. Thus by the 1890s most bonanza farms had been broken up into smaller farms.

Plains farming demanded hard work from everyone in the family. Men did most of the heavy labor of building houses, fencing the land, and farming. Women, in addition to household and child-rearing tasks, also worked in the fields. One woman was her husband's "sole help in getting up and stacking at least 25 tons of hay and oats."

Children had to do their share, too. They fetched water, tended gardens, and did such routine chores as churning butter.

▪▪ Large-scale bonanza farms were profitable during boom times, but family farms were better able to keep costs down.

THE CATTLE BOOM

The factors that made bonanza farms possible—the growth of eastern markets, completion of the railroad, and access to land—also led to a boom in cattle ranching after the Civil War.

The first ranches were in Texas. There English cattle had bred with cattle first introduced by the Spanish in the 1500s. By the 1850s they had produced a new breed—the **Texas longhorn.** Although their meat was tough, the hardy longhorns could survive **long drives,** treks of hundreds of miles, to a **railhead,** a town along the railroad. There they were sold and shipped east for slaughter. In 1866 a steer that would bring about $4 in Texas could be sold for $40 to $50 in eastern markets.

On a typical long drive, a trail boss managed a crew of about 10 cowboys. Out of approximately 35,000 cowboys, about a third were African American, Mexican, or Mexican American. Some of the African American cowboys had been brought west as slaves before the Civil War; others left the South after the war. In an era when most African Americans faced segregation, black cowboys worked, bunked, and ate alongside other cowboys and received the same wages they did.

In the 1880s most Mexican and Mexican American cowboys worked on South and West Texas ranches. Although Mexican *vaqueros* had developed many ranching practices, many Anglo ranchers considered the *vaqueros* inferior to Anglo cowboys. Mexican cowboys were not allowed to supervise non-Mexicans, and they worked and lived separately from Anglo cowboys.

Cattle ranching spread west into New Mexico and Colorado and north into Kansas, Nebraska, the Dakotas, Wyoming, and Montana as the government converted Indian territory into public land. The government allowed ranchers to use it as common grazing land or **open range.** Although many families established ranches, it was mainly large companies financed by eastern

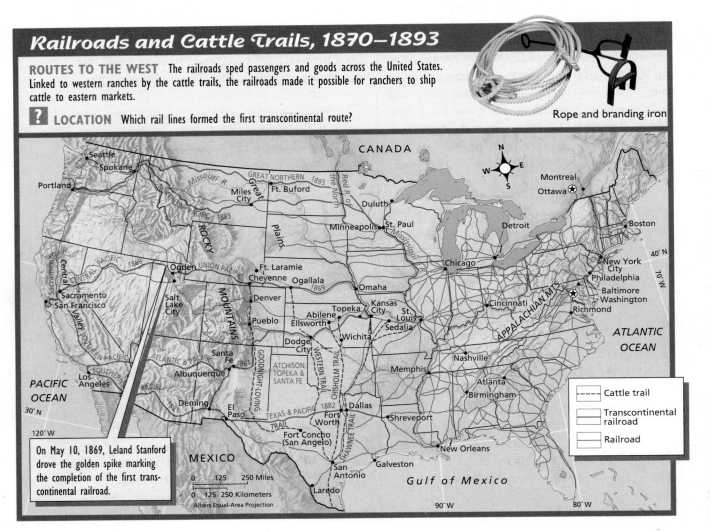

Railroads and Cattle Trails, 1870–1893

ROUTES TO THE WEST The railroads sped passengers and goods across the United States. Linked to western ranches by the cattle trails, the railroads made it possible for ranchers to ship cattle to eastern markets.

? LOCATION Which rail lines formed the first transcontinental route?

Rope and branding iron

On May 10, 1869, Leland Stanford drove the golden spike marking the completion of the first transcontinental railroad.

0 125 250 Miles
0 125 250 Kilometers
Albers Equal-Area Projection

Cattle trail
Transcontinental railroad
Railroad

and European investors that took advantage of government land. Access to this free pasture land made cattle ranching profitable. The introduction of higher-grade cattle breeds from Europe led to even bigger profits.

Sheep ranching, also introduced by the Spanish, was another important economic activity. American Indians, including the Pueblos and Navajos, raised sheep in New Mexico and Arizona. Thousands of sheep were herded west to California to feed the miners during the gold rush.

Both cattle and sheep ranches demanded hard work from everyone. As one Texan explained, the ranch owners "got right out with the boys on the trail" and "did just as much work."

This description also applied to women, who played an integral role in ranch life. On most ranches, women did housework, cooked for all the cowboys, and helped with fence-mending, herding, or other chores. Many women organized their own ranch-related businesses. For example, Ella Bird accumulated her first herd of cattle by trading hand-sewn leather gloves and vests for yearlings.

Ranch children often took on adult responsibilities at a young age. In addition to doing chores around the house, some boys and girls broke horses and herded cattle. The cowboy life offered children some interesting experiences, but the work was hard. John Norton, a young cowboy, said that he and his brother "leaped with joy" when the cattle they were herding were finally shipped for slaughter.

The cattle boom lasted only about 20 years. Several factors led to its end. First, ranchers filled the free range land with too many cattle, which led to overgrazing. The vast herds also increased the supply of beef. Prices and profits crashed in 1885, as supply far exceeded demand.

Furthermore, open-range ranching declined after the invention of barbed wire, which Joseph Glidden patented in 1874. Farmers and ranchers used this cheap fencing to control access to land and water, limiting the amount of open range land.

Bad weather dealt the final blow. On the southern Plains a severe winter in 1885–86 and a drought in 1886 diminished many herds. The following year, blizzards struck the northern Plains, killing up to 90 percent of some herds.

▲ Ex-slave Nat Love, also known as Deadwood Dick, claimed to have carried the marks of 14 bullet wounds on his body and boasted that any one of his wounds would have killed an ordinary man.

Furthermore, the end of the open range meant that ranchers had to buy their own range land. They also had to invest more in their operations. Learning from the blizzards of the mid-1880s, they began to raise hay to feed their cattle during the winters. By the 1890s the cattle boom was over.

■■ **The cattle boom began when new railroads provided access to eastern markets. The boom ended because of overgrazing, fencing of the open range, and bad weather.**

SECTION 2 REVIEW

IDENTIFY and explain the significance of the following: Homestead Act, Pacific Railway Act, Morrill Act, Exodusters, U.S. Department of Agriculture, dry farming, bonanza farm, Texas longhorn, long drives, railhead, open range, Joseph Glidden.

LOCATE and explain the importance of the following: Central Pacific Railroad, Union Pacific Railroad, Red River Valley.

1. **MAIN IDEA** What groups of people moved west in the late 1800s? Why did they move?

2. **MAIN IDEA** How were farmers able to adapt to western environments?

3. **MAIN IDEA** Why was cattle ranching so profitable in the late 1800s? Why did the cattle boom come to an end?

4. **WRITING TO DESCRIBE** Imagine you are a member of an Exoduster family in the late 1800s. Write a journal entry explaining why you left the South for Kansas.

5. **EVALUATING** How might the development of the Great Plains have been different if the government and the railroads had not been involved?

A MINING BOOM

FOCUS
- **Where did important mining discoveries take place in the late 1800s?**
- **How did early mining camps differ from more-developed mining towns?**
- **Why did mining become big business?**

*E*ver since the forty-niners had flocked to California after the discovery of gold in the Sierra Nevada, miners from all over the world had been drawn to the American West. After the richest California diggings were claimed, hundreds of forty-niners moved eastward and northward into the Rockies and beyond. A few individuals prospered from new mineral discoveries. But large mining companies reaped the greatest profits.

Chinese miner in Idaho

WESTERN MINING

The first promising mining discoveries after the California gold rush were made in Colorado. Prospectors found gold near Pikes Peak late in 1858. In 1859 another center of frantic prospecting was the Carson River Valley in present-day Nevada. In addition to gold, the area contained the famous **Comstock Lode**, one of the world's richest silver veins. Over a period of 20 years, its mines yielded more than $500 million worth of precious metals.

Some miners turned south into Arizona. Since the mid-1700s Hispanics had been mining silver there using techniques developed in Mexico and South America. These included a mill for separating gold from quartz and the *patio* process—which used mercury to extract silver from the ore. The newer arrivals used these methods to mine the Comstock Lode and in the region around Tucson. Others, trekking northward, made strikes in Idaho and Montana.

By the late 1850s others had pushed into the Fraser River Valley of British Columbia. This push into Canada had important consequences. Russia, which owned Alaska, feared a territorial dispute with the United States. To avoid this, the Russians offered to sell Alaska to the Americans. U.S. Secretary of State William H. Seward agreed to purchase Alaska in 1867 for $7,200,000—about two cents an acre. Many Americans considered Alaska worthless, calling the purchase "Seward's Folly."

But Seward's belief that Alaska "possesses treasures . . . equal to those of any other region" would prove correct. In 1896, prospectors found gold in Canada's Klondike district, which bordered Alaska. This discovery launched the **Klondike Gold Rush**. By the summer of 1897, Klondike miners had extracted gold deposits worth more than a million dollars. Gold discoveries in Alaska in 1898 and 1902 attracted settlers, who later established fish canneries, lumber companies, and coal and copper mining enterprises.

Mining booms attracted prospectors to present-day Colorado, Nevada, Arizona, Idaho, Montana, and Alaska.

LIFE IN MINING COMMUNITIES

Mining camps grew up almost overnight wherever news of possible wealth brought prospectors together. At first most mining communities were inhabited almost entirely by men. Unlike ranching or farming, prospecting generally was not a family enterprise.

Mining camps drew a wide range of settlers. In the mining zones of southern California in the 1860s, Mexicans, Californios, Peruvians, and Chileans formed separate settlements. In other regions, the prospectors included a mixture of U.S. citizens, Irish and Chinese men who had worked on the railroads, and miners from Cornwall, England. Some were seeking wealth; others were fleeing difficult circumstances.

At first, life in the mining camps was crude and comforts were few. J. Ross Browne described the first shelters of Virginia City, Nevada:

> 66 Frame shanties . . . ; tents of canvas, . . . of potato sacks . . . , with empty whisky-barrels for chimneys; smoky hovels of mud and stone; coyote holes in the mountain side forcibly seized and held by men. 99

The atmosphere in most camps was one of intense competition. Prospector William Parsons remembered a "furious race for wealth, in which men lost their identity almost, . . . and lived a . . . fearfully excited life; forgetting home and kindred; abandoning old, steady habits."

▲ The lure of gold and silver drew many men and eventually families to the mining camps of the West. This photograph of a mining family in Colorado was taken in the late 19th century.

Competition and ethnic conflicts sometimes led to violence. Miners in Colorado's Cripple Creek camp forcibly excluded Hispanics and eastern and southern Europeans. In other camps, Cornish miners fought with Irish, German, and Chinese miners. Gamblers and swindlers swarmed in, and conflicts over claims set off brawls.

But stability came to the mining camps as they grew into towns. Mining towns attracted a host of businesses eager to feed and clothe the miners. In fact, owners of saloons and stores were more apt to strike it rich than miners. Cooking and providing lodging were especially lucrative. One woman managed to earn nine hundred dollars in nine weeks by washing miners' clothes. Elizabeth Collins, later known as the "cattle queen of

---

THE WILD WEST

Fantastic stories about the untamed western lands of the United States could be heard far from America's shores in the late 1800s. Fascination with outlaw gangs, shoot-outs, and man-eating wild animals lured many European travelers to America to see for themselves. But the "Wild West" rarely lived up to its reputation. Windham T. Dunraven, a British earl, wrote about what he did *not* find in the American West:

> 66 *I never have an adventure worth a cent; nobody ever scalps me; I don't get 'jumped' by highwaymen. It never occurs to a bear to hug me, and my very appearance inspires feelings of dismay or disgust in the breast of the puma or mountain lion. It is true that I have often been horribly frightened, but generally without any adequate cause.* 99

As settlement grew in the West, so did the need for schools. Blanche Lamont posed with members of her school at Hecla, Montana, in October 1893.

Montana," was offered a job as cook for 18 men at a mining camp. "Prompted by kindness," she later wrote, and "also craving for the $75 per month—I promptly accepted the offer."

The few children in the camps hunted for gold dust and stray nuggets under sidewalks or panned and scavenged for gold dust after the miners were done for the day. Much more profitable, however, was selling fresh food to the miners. One brother and sister made $800 one summer selling butter and bacon to the miners.

As more families arrived, many camps turned into permanent communities. With prosperity came law and order as well as schools, hospitals, churches, newspapers, and singing clubs. Denver, Colorado, for example, started out as a mining camp.

▪▪ At first, mining camps were crude. With prosperity, however, came families, community life, and law and order.

MINING AS BIG BUSINESS

Individual prospectors roaming the West made the earliest mining discoveries, or strikes. But the day of the lone miner did not last. Within a few years of a strike, most of the easily accessible mineral deposits were "worked out." To get at the ore, miners had to use one of two methods: (1) **hydraulic mining**, which used water pressure to wash away mountains of gravel and expose the minerals

underneath; or (2) **hard-rock mining**, which involved sinking deep shafts to get at ore locked in veins of quartz.

Both of these methods required large sums of money—far beyond a lone prospector's resources. Thus mining became the province of large, well-financed companies. These companies relied on science rather than luck. Corps of college-educated engineers helped locate the ore and instructed the companies on how best to extract the zinc, lead, copper, and iron eastern factories demanded.

The federal government also helped develop mineral resources. It sent out several western expeditions in the 1860s. In 1879 the government organized the U.S. Geological Survey, which gathered and coordinated data about new mines.

▪▪ As mineral deposits became more expensive to extract, big business dominated mining.

Big mining companies also changed working conditions in the mines. The big companies used new machinery and hired armies of laborers who sank the shafts, built the tunnels, drilled, and processed the ore. Miners, no longer spurred on by the hope of sudden riches, grew dissatisfied with wages and working conditions.

In some communities miners formed unions. Dues paid to the unions often helped workers injured in the dangerous mines or the families of miners killed on the job. Unions also negotiated with owners who tried to cut wages. Many also fought against the hiring of Chinese miners, who received lower wages. Union resistance to wage cuts proved most effective during boom times. In the early 1880s, union miners at the Comstock

▼ New mining techniques removed ore quickly from the ground, but also eroded entire hillsides.

Lode successfully maintained their four-dollar-a-day salaries and eight-hour workdays.

When mining became big business, the land suffered. In their haste to extract ore, mining companies often ignored the environmental effects of their practices. Hydraulic mining leveled mountains and often left eroded hills in its wake. Hydraulic mining also dumped tons of earth and rocks into rivers, thus raising riverbeds and causing flooding. Flooding in some areas swept away towns and destroyed farmland. Forests disappeared as hard-rock mining companies felled acres of trees to get wood for mine shafts.

COMMENTARY

Western Myths

The solitary miner, prospecting for gold on a remote mountain stream, is a well-known character in books, movies, and television programs. So is the cowboy who rides off alone into the sunset. Almost equally familiar is the farm or ranch family in its isolated home on the vast, empty plains. All these legendary western figures represent the American ideal of rugged individuals conquering barren and uninhabited land. But these images, while powerful, are inaccurate.

Most westerners, including cowboys on ranches and prospectors in mining camps, worked for or with others. And the large companies, not the independent ranchers, farmers, or miners, generally made the biggest profits. The lands where ranchers or farmers grazed their cattle or sheep had been settled for centuries by American Indians or Hispanics. Most of the crowded, noisy mining camps were established on or near lands inhabited by Hispanics or Native Americans. And the large companies, not the independent ranchers, farmers, or miners, generally made the biggest profits. Many westerners were tied to the region by poverty, not love for the rugged landscape, as expressed in one poem:

> 66 Our neighbors are the rattlesnakes—
> They crawl up from the Badlands' breaks;
> We do not live, we only stay;
> We are too poor to get away. 99

Furthermore, Americans who settled the West could not have survived without the help of the federal government. The U.S. Army used force to open American Indian land for non-Indian settlement. The army also maintained forts to guard trails and protect settlements. The Department of the Interior, through its Bureau of Indian Affairs, resettled Native Americans and ran the reservations on which it placed them. The General Land Office disposed of public land at low rates, while Congress subsidized the railroad development that enabled farmers and ranchers as well as mine and timber interests to ship their products to market. The Department of Agriculture helped Plains farmers, and the Geological Survey aided mining interests.

Novels, songs, and traveling shows spread the myth of the "Wild West" as a region of outlaws, lone cowboys, and isolated pioneers. In reality, men and women lived and worked together in a West shaped as much by technology, big business, and the federal government as by individual effort.

SECTION 3 REVIEW

IDENTIFY and explain the significance of the following: Comstock Lode, *patio* process, William H. Seward, Klondike Gold Rush, hydraulic mining, hard-rock mining.

1. **MAIN IDEA** How did later mining camps differ from earlier mining camps?

2. **MAIN IDEA** Why did mining become the domain of large companies?

3. **GEOGRAPHY: LOCATION** Where did the most important mining discoveries take place in the late 19th century?

4. **WRITING TO EXPLAIN** Write an essay contrasting the myth of the rugged individual of the West with westerners' lives in the late 1800s.

5. **EVALUATING** How did western mining affect the environment?

Sand Creek Massacre occurs.

Treaty of Medicine Lodge signed. Seward negotiates purchase of Alaska.

The Homestead Act passed.

Second Treaty of Fort Laramie signed.

First transcontinental railroad completed.

1860   1865   1870

WRITING A SUMMARY

Using the essential points of the chapter as a guide, write a summary of the chapter.

REVIEWING CHRONOLOGY

Number your paper 1 to 5. Study the time line above, and list the following events in the order in which they happened by writing the first next to 1, the second next to 2, and so on. Then complete the activity.

1. Beef prices crash.
2. Exodusters trek west.
3. First transcontinental railroad completed.
4. Battle of Little Bighorn occurs.
5. The Homestead Act passed.

Identifying Cause and Effect Select two events on the time line, and in a paragraph, explain the cause-and-effect relationship between them.

IDENTIFYING PEOPLE AND IDEAS

Explain the historical significance of each of the following people or terms.

1. Long Walk
2. Sitting Bull
3. Sarah Winnemucca
4. Pacific Railway Act
5. Exodusters
6. long drives
7. open range
8. Comstock Lode
9. William H. Seward
10. hydraulic mining

UNDERSTANDING MAIN IDEAS

1. What caused settlers to travel to the West in the late 19th century?
2. How did farm life differ from life in the early mining camps?
3. In what areas were key mining sites and bonanza farms developed?
4. How had the businesses of cattle ranching and mining changed by the late 1890s?

REVIEWING THEMES

1. **Geographic Diversity** How did western farmers adapt to the weather and environment?
2. **Cultural Diversity** What problems arose from the federal government's attempt to assimilate Native Americans?

3. **Economic Development** How did the U.S. government promote western land development and settlement?

THINKING CRITICALLY

1. **Hypothesizing** How might Helen Hunt Jackson's *A Century of Dishonor* and Sarah Winnemucca's lectures have shaped public opinion in the late 1800s?
2. **Evaluating** What positive and negative consequences resulted from development of the West?
3. **Synthesizing** How did different cultures influence one another in the West?

STRATEGY FOR SUCCESS

Review the Skills Handbook entry on Studying Primary and Secondary Sources beginning on page 758. Then read the selections below. In the first selection, Priscilla Merriam Evans describes some of her responsibilities on a farm in Utah. In the second, author Hamlin Garland describes his mother's life. Compare and contrast their points of view.

66 We made our own cloth, which was mostly gray in color, for dresses. . . . With . . . Indigo . . . and other roots, I have colored beautiful fast colors. We were kept busy in those days carding, spinning, knitting, and doing all of our own sewing by hand. 99

66 All her toilsome, monotonous days rushed through my mind with a roar like a file of gray birds in the night . . . how tragically small her joys, and how black her sorrows, her toil, her tedium. 99

WRITING ABOUT HISTORY

Writing to Express a Viewpoint Imagine you are a prospector in a small mining camp. Write a speech expressing your views about the growth of big mining companies.

Joseph Glidden patents barbed wire.

Exodusters trek west. U.S. Geological Survey organized.

Battle of Little Bighorn occurs.

Helen Hunt Jackson publishes *A Century of Dishonor.*

Beef prices crash.

Dawes General Allotment Act passed.

Wounded Knee Massacre occurs.

Gold discovered in Canada's Klondike district.

1875   1880   1885   1890   1895

USING PRIMARY SOURCES

The following excerpt is from "Chief Joseph's Own Story," an 1879 account by the Nez Percé leader who had long been committed to peaceful relations with non-Indians. Based on the selection below, how did Chief Joseph's expectations differ from the reality of U.S. policies toward Native Americans?

" *We only ask an even chance to live as other men live. We asked to be recognized as men. We ask that the same law shall work alike on all men. . . .*

Let me be a free man—free to travel, free to stop, free to work, free to trade where I choose, free to choose my own teachers, free to follow the religion of my fathers, free to think and talk and act for myself—and I will obey every law, or submit to the penalty.

Whenever the white man treats the Indian as they treat each other, then we shall have no more wars. We shall be all alike— brothers of one father and one mother, with one sky above us and one country around us, and one government for all. Then the Great Spirit Chief who rules above will smile upon this land, and send rain to wash out the bloody spots made by brothers' hands upon the face of the earth. "

Chief Joseph

LINKING HISTORY AND GEOGRAPHY

Review the map on page 132. What areas did railroad lines open to non-Indian settlers in this period, and how did the railroads foster development of these areas?

Railroad station, c.1870s

BUILDING YOUR PORTFOLIO

Complete the following projects independently or cooperatively.

1. CONFLICT In chapters 2 and 4 you looked at conflict from the points of view of a government official and a drafted soldier. Building on that experience, imagine you are a Sioux living on a reservation in South Dakota in 1895. Compose an oral account that describes how conflict between the Sioux and farmers, ranchers, and miners has affected you and other Sioux. Be sure to work in details of the conflict.

2. THE ECONOMY In chapters 1 and 3 you explored such economic issues as trade and manufacturing. Building on that experience, imagine you are a land speculator who hopes to establish a small railhead in Nebraska. Prepare a plan for the town that shows the businesses and other public buildings—stockyard, rail station, church, school, and so on—you will include to attract residents.

Chapter 6

THE NATION TRANSFORMED

FOCUS

UNDERSTANDING THE MAIN IDEA

New technologies and new forms of business organization helped usher in a second industrial age in late-19th-century America. Millions of immigrants arrived during this period, lured by the prospect of work. By 1900 these developments had transformed the United States into an urban nation and an industrial power. The transformation, however, did not benefit everyone equally, and people formed numerous organizations to reform society or to improve their lot.

THEMES

■ **ECONOMIC DEVELOPMENT** How might technological change affect a nation's economy?

■ **CULTURAL DIVERSITY** What challenges might an influx of people with different ways of life present to a community?

■ **DEMOCRATIC VALUES** What actions might citizens take to bring about change in society?

1869	1876	1882	1889	1892
Knights of Labor founded.	Alexander Graham Bell patents telephone.	Congress passes Chinese Exclusion Act.	Jane Addams establishes Hull House.	Populist party founded.

Industrialization and immigration helped fuel the growth of the United States in the first half of the 1800s. However, the United States remained primarily a rural nation whose people continued to depend on agriculture for a living.

In the second half of the 1800s, the United States underwent another wave of industrialization. To many this process seemed almost a natural outcome of American life. "The American mechanizes as an old Greek sculptured, as the Venetian painted," the London *Times* noted in 1878. A debate quickly developed, however, over whether the negative side effects of industrialization—such as grinding poverty existing side-by-side with great wealth—were natural outcomes as well.

Critical of the new industrial order, economist Henry George condemned the growing contrast "between the House of Have and the House of Want." He argued that the poor should not have to suffer so that a few could be rich. Yale professor William Graham Sumner took the opposite view, claiming that the rich and the poor were just where nature intended and that any change would slow progress and harm society. Not all industrialists agreed with Sumner. Some proposed that they use part of their wealth to benefit all of society. But social reformer Frederic Howe argued that if industrialists really had the well-being of society at heart, they "would stop the twelve-hour day . . . increase wages and put an end to the cruel killing and maiming" of workers. Although this debate produced no solid answers about how to reconcile the existence of poverty in the midst of great wealth, it did lead to efforts to reform the worst abuses of the industrial order.

Child factory laborers

The Edison phonograph

INDUSTRY'S GOLDEN AGE

FOCUS

■ **What technological innovations contributed to the rise of the new industrial order?**

■ **How did businesses increase their profits in the late 1800s?**

■ **How did the government attempt to regulate businesses?**

From 1865 to 1910 the United States experienced a surge of industrial growth. These decades witnessed the beginnings of a "second industrial revolution." A "new industrial order" was created with the development of cheap steel, the completion of a nationwide rail network, the invention of the telephone, the introduction of new sources of energy, and the rise of big business.

First telephone, 1876

TECHNOLOGICAL INNOVATIONS

America's first industrial revolution had been driven by coal and steam. But it was steel—not steam—that spurred industrialization in the late 1800s. The heavy machinery used to mass-produce goods, the rails that enabled trains to move people and products, the bridges that spanned the rivers, and the tall buildings that dotted the cities all required steel.

In the 1850s Henry Bessemer in England and William Kelly in the United States independently developed a new method of producing steel. The Bessemer process, as the method came to be called, could produce more steel in a day than older techniques could turn out in a week. Using and improving on this technique, America's annual steel production grew from about 15 thousand tons in 1865 to over 28 million tons by 1910. As production increased, prices dropped. Steel that had sold for $100 a ton in 1873 sold for $12 by the late 1890s.

The availability of cheaper steel encouraged railroads to lay thousands of miles of new track. By the end of the century, almost a half-dozen

trunk lines, or major railroads, crossed the Great Plains to the Pacific coast. Feeder, or branch, lines connected the trunk lines to surrounding areas. This huge railroad grid joined every state and linked remote towns to urban centers.

The economic impact of the railroads was immeasurable. Not only were the railroad companies the country's major employers for much of the late 1800s, they also spurred the growth of other industries. The railroads' demands for rails, locomotives, and railcars poured money into the steel industry. Innovations like refrigerated freight cars helped develop the meat-packing industry. In addition, the network of railroad lines helped strengthen a national market. Now a Pennsylvania steel foundry could obtain iron ore from the Great Lakes region, or a Philadelphia furniture company could sell its products in small midwestern towns.

With the growth of this national market came an increased need to communicate across long distances. Samuel F. B. Morse's telegraph had attracted little attention when patented in 1837, but people now saw its business potential. Using Morse's dot-and-dash code, a telegraph operator could send a business order to a distant location in minutes. By 1866 Western Union, the leading telegraph company, had over 2,000 offices.

The "talking telegraph," or telephone, which Alexander Graham Bell patented in 1876, had an even greater impact. Big businesses quickly found the telephone indispensable. By the end of the 1800s, more than a million telephones had been installed in U.S. offices and homes.

Innovations in transportation and communications depended on abundant sources of energy. In the late 1800s inventors began to tap into two new sources of power—oil and electricity. While the existence of both had been known about for years, neither had been seen as having practical uses. Oil was seen by some as having, at best, medicinal value, while electricity was considered little more than a puzzling natural phenomenon.

In the late 1850s, American chemist Benjamin Silliman, Jr., released a report noting that oil could be refined to make kerosene, which could be burned in lamps to produce light. Prospectors hurried to sink oil wells as the demand for this inexpensive fuel rose. By the 1880s, oil wells dotted Pennsylvania, Ohio, and West Virginia, producing more than 25 million barrels of oil in 1880 alone.

Electricity's potential became clear in the mid-1800s, when European and American scientists and engineers developed the dynamo, or electric generator. Driven by steam, water, or other energy source, the dynamo produced enough electrical power to run a factory. At his workshop in Menlo Park, New Jersey, inventor Thomas Alva Edison and a team of researchers worked to find practical uses for electricity. Edison's lab produced many innovations, ranging from the incandescent

▼ **Lewis Latimer, pictured at age 70, worked to improve light bulb design.**

The Granger Collection, New York

▲ **Thomas Edison**

light bulb to the phonograph to a central electric power plant. Edison and his associates were not the only ones trying to perfect electric lighting. Lewis Latimer—who later worked for Edison—also contributed to light bulb design.

▪▪ Innovations in steel production, railroads, communications, and energy spurred industry's golden age.

THE RISE OF BIG BUSINESS

Along with these technological developments emerged new forms of business organization that added to industries' productivity—and profits. At the close of the Civil War, most businesses were **proprietorships**—small enterprises owned by individuals or families—or **partnerships**—enterprises owned by two or more people. These forms of business organization were inadequate to manage giant new industries like railroads, steel, or oil. Nor could they raise the capital needed to finance such ventures. As a result, business leaders turned to another form of business organization—the **corporation**.

In a corporation organizers raise capital by selling shares of **stock**, or certificates of ownership, in the company. Selling stock to many people allows a corporation to raise enormous sums of money. Furthermore, because a corporation is distinct from its owners, it continues to exist no matter who owns the stock. **Stockholders**—those who buy the shares—receive a percentage of the corporation's profits in the form of **dividends**, but they are not responsible for the corporation's debt or its daily operations.

Bigger is better. Some corporations responded to the fierce economic climate of the late 1800s by joining together to form an even more powerful organization—a **trust**. In a trust, a group of companies turn control of their stock over to a board of directors. The directors then run the companies as a single enterprise. A trust that gains exclusive control of an industry becomes a **monopoly**.

Andrew Carnegie, a Scot who immigrated to the United States in 1848, established some of the first monopolies. Entering the steel business in the early 1870s, Carnegie beat out his competitors by buying supplies in bulk and producing goods in large quantities. By following this principle,

THE PRICE OF INDUSTRIALIZATION

In 1871 Austrian diplomat Joseph Alexander, Graf von Hübner, visited the United States. Von Hübner was impressed by the opportunities Americans enjoyed in an industrializing society. But he also saw that fierce competition in business took its toll on working people. Von Hübner said:

> 66 *In the New World man is born to conquer. Life is a perpetual struggle, . . . a race in the open field across terrible obstacles, with the prospect of enormous rewards for reaching the goal. The American cannot keep his arms folded. He must embark on something, and once embarked he must go on and on forever; for if he stops, those who follow him would crush him under their feet. His life is one long campaign, a succession of never-ending fights, marches, and countermarches.*
>
> *In such a militant existence, what place is left for the sweetness, the repose [rest], the intimacy of home or its joys? Is he happy? Judging by his tired, sad, exhausted, anxious, and often delicate and unhealthy appearance, one would be inclined to doubt it. Such an excess of uninterrupted labor cannot be good for any man.* 99

known as **economies of scale**, Carnegie was able to lower production costs and increase profits. Carnegie also used **vertical integration** to control costs—that is, he acquired companies that provided materials and services upon which his enterprises depended. For example, Carnegie purchased iron and coal mines, which provided the raw materials for his steel mills, steamship lines, and railroads. Marveled one admirer:

> 66 From the moment these crude stuffs were dug out of the earth until they flowed in a stream of liquid steel in the ladles, there was never a price, profit, or royalty paid to an outsider. 99

◄ **Eastman Johnson completed this formal portrait of John D. Rockefeller in 1895.**

Because Carnegie controlled businesses at each stage of production, he could sell steel at a much lower price than his competitors.

Like Carnegie, oil tycoon John D. Rockefeller used vertical integration to make his company—Standard Oil—more competitive, eventually acquiring oil fields, barrel factories, pipelines, railroad tanker cars, and oil-storage facilities. But Rockefeller's main method of expansion was **horizontal integration**—one company's ownership of other companies involved in the same business, in this case, oil refining. What companies Standard Oil could not buy, it tried to control through the establishment of a trust.

Rockefeller also drove his competitors out of business by making deals with suppliers and transporters to receive cheaper supplies and freight rates. By 1899 the Standard Oil Company controlled some 90 percent of the country's petroleum refining capacity and had annual profits of some $45 million.

Mass marketing. Industrialists knew that cutting production costs and reducing competition were not the only ways to increase profits. They also developed new methods of marketing to sell their products. Some companies used brightly colored packages and distinctive logos to entice consumers. Advertising, too, became an important promotional tool. Newspapers, magazines, and roadside billboards carried advertisements urging people to buy "The Purest" soap and telephones "warranted to work *one mile,* unaffected by changes in the weather."

In cities, an unprecedented variety of goods became available at a new kind of store. Pioneered by John Wanamaker in Philadelphia, Marshall

Field in Chicago, and R. H. Macy in New York City, the department store offered shoppers shoes, clothing, hardware, and appliances—all under one roof. The department store bought products in bulk and, as a result, could offer low prices to consumers.

While department stores catered to the urban market, mail-order companies like Montgomery Ward or Sears, Roebuck, and Co. appealed to rural consumers. Customers selected goods from a catalog, then ordered, paid for, and received the merchandise by mail.

▲ Colorful advertisements such as these for processed baby food and flour flooded newspapers and magazines by the end of the 19th century.

■■ **Businesses used corporations, trusts, vertical and horizontal integration, and mass marketing to increase profits.**

BUSINESS AND GOVERNMENT

Historians refer to the late 1800s as the age of **laissez-faire capitalism**. (*Laissez faire* is French for "let it be.") The theory of laissez-faire capitalism calls for no government regulation of economic matters. Most business leaders argued that if businesses were freed from government regulation, the economy would prosper.

In reality, companies benefited from certain government policies, such as those limiting foreign competition. By placing high tariffs on imports, the federal government allowed U.S. businesses to

dominate the home market. In 1875, for example, Congress increased tariff rates to make imported steel 40 percent more expensive than domestic steel.

At the same time, however, public pressure pushed the government to take modest steps to regulate businesses. As Carnegie Steel and Standard Oil grew in power, many Americans—including some who had been driven out of their own small businesses—demanded that trusts be outlawed. Congress responded in 1890 by passing the **Sherman Antitrust Act**, which declared all monopolies and trusts in restraint of trade illegal. While its intentions appeared clear, the law failed to define what constituted a monopoly or trust. Thus the law proved difficult to enforce.

■■ **The federal government adopted the Sherman Antitrust Act in an effort to eliminate monopolies.**

SECTION 1 REVIEW

IDENTIFY and explain the significance of the following: trunk lines, Thomas Edison, proprietorships, partnerships, corporation, stock, stockholders, dividends, trust, monopoly, economies of scale, vertical integration, horizontal integration, laissez-faire capitalism, Sherman Antitrust Act.

1. **MAIN IDEA** How did steel, railroads, and innovations in communications contribute to American industry?

2. **MAIN IDEA** What organizational and selling methods did businesspeople use to increase their profits in the late 1800s?

3. **MAIN IDEA** Why did Congress pass the Sherman Antitrust Act in 1890? How did the act attempt to accomplish its purpose?

4. **WRITING TO EXPLAIN** Imagine you are the owner of a small oil company that John D. Rockefeller is trying to drive out of business. Write a letter to your congressperson explaining the need for antitrust legislation.

5. **EVALUATING** What was the effect of the new industrial order on business organization?

IMMIGRATION AND URBAN LIFE

FOCUS

- **How did the new industrial order affect society?**
- **How did immigration change in the late 1800s? How did some native-born Americans respond to the new immigrants?**
- **How did American cities change in the late 1800s?**
- **In what ways did people try to improve urban conditions?**

Chicago's Masonic Temple

Spurred by industrialization, American cities grew dramatically during the second half of the century. In 1865 only 14 American cities had populations of more than 100,000 and only 20 percent of Americans lived in urban areas. By 1900 the nation was 40 percent urban and had 29 cities with populations in excess of 100,000. With growth came other changes, and a distinct urban culture developed.

A NEW SOCIAL ORDER

In the cities the new industrial order gave rise to a new social order. The urban upper class that emerged in the late 1800s was a new breed whose wealth dwarfed that of the old upper-class merchants and bankers. These new rich had made their money in the new industries, such as railroads, iron and steel, mining, or publishing.

For some new rich, author William Dean Howells noted sarcastically, "the dollar is the measure of every value, the stamp of every success." This new class built lavish houses in the cities—some decorated like Gothic castles or Renaissance palaces. The new rich thought nothing of spending thousands of dollars to stage one night's amusement. They were often criticized for such **conspicuous consumption**, that is, spending money for the sake of showing off their wealth.

The new industrial age also created a new middle class. By the late 1800s modern corporations had swelled the ranks of the middle class with managers, engineers, accountants, clerks, and salespeople. In addition, technological innovations and the rise of big business created a new range of jobs, such as telephone operator, stenographer, salesclerk, and secretary. Business owners increasingly hired young, single middle-class women to fill these positions, paying them lower wages than men. As a result, by 1910 nearly 35 percent of the more than 1.9 million clerical workers were women.

However, most married middle-class women worked at home. Smaller families, greater reliance on purchased goods, and new household technology

▲ **During the late 19th century, many native-born middle-class women began filling clerical positions.**

such as running water, water closets, and home canning changed middle-class women's domestic work. The advent of hot and cold running water meant that doing laundry no longer required pumping, hauling, and heating the water. With more leisure time, many women joined social clubs or participated in reform movements (see Chapter 7).

Industry created a demand not only for managers and clerical workers, but also for laborers. Millions of workers were needed to staff factories, extract raw materials, and transport finished goods. Hundreds of thousands of rural Americans moved to the cities in search of jobs. Among this group were thousands of African Americans from the South who came to the North in hope of securing industrial work, from which they were often barred in the South. But industrial employment was denied to most. The best jobs still went to native-born whites or to immigrants.

By 1890 nearly 50 percent of industrial workers lived below the poverty line. As a result the ranks of women workers more than doubled between 1870 and 1890 as wives, daughters, and sisters labored to put food on the table. The number of children in the work force doubled during this period for the same reason. By 1890 close to 20 percent of American children between ages 10 and 15 worked for wages.

In the end, the great demand for labor was met, in large part, by floods of immigrants who came to the United States during the late 1800s. By 1900 one third of the country's industrial workers were foreign-born.

■■ **The new industrial order created a new wealthy class, expanded the ranks of the middle class, and increased the demand for industrial workers.**

*T*HE NEW IMMIGRANTS

Prior to 1880, most of the immigrants who had come to the United States were Protestants from northwestern Europe. In the late 1800s, however, a new wave of immigrants entered the United States. In contrast to the previous immigrants, about 70 percent of these **new immigrants** were from southern or eastern Europe, and most were Catholic, Jewish, or Greek Orthodox. French Canadians, Armenians, Arabs, Chinese, and Japanese also arrived by the thousands.

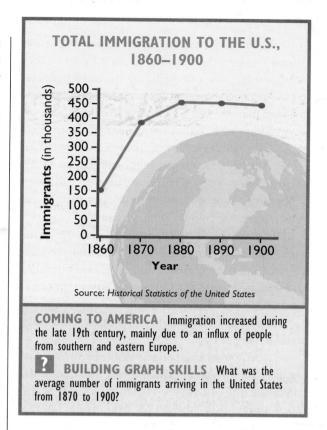

TOTAL IMMIGRATION TO THE U.S., 1860–1900

Immigrants (in thousands) — Year

Source: *Historical Statistics of the United States*

COMING TO AMERICA Immigration increased during the late 19th century, mainly due to an influx of people from southern and eastern Europe.

❓ **BUILDING GRAPH SKILLS** What was the average number of immigrants arriving in the United States from 1870 to 1900?

Many of these new immigrants came to the United States to escape poverty or persecution. Most of the southern European immigrants were Italian or Slavic males who sought economic opportunities in the United States that were scarce in their home countries. The eastern European immigrants, meanwhile, included Hungarian and Polish farmers and Jews from many countries. Most of the Jewish and Armenian families fled their homelands to escape religious or political persecution.

■■ **Most new immigrants were southern or eastern Europeans who came to America to find jobs or to escape persecution.**

▶ **This immigrant mother and her children arrived at Ellis Island, New York, around 1910.**

By the early 1900s, about 60 percent of the people living in the nation's 12 largest cities either were foreign-born or had foreign-born parents. Many big cities of the Northeast and Midwest became patchworks of ethnic neighborhoods as new immigrants settled among others from their homelands. Social reformer Jacob Riis (himself an immigrant from Denmark) suggested that an 1890s map of New York City, colored according to nationality, "would show more stripes than . . . a zebra, and more colors than any rainbow."

In these close-knit neighborhoods, residents spoke the same languages and followed the customs of the old country. Neighborhood churches and synagogues helped immigrants maintain a sense of identity and belonging. Most cities also had **benevolent societies**, or support organizations, to aid newcomers.

As with earlier immigrants, however, the vast majority of newcomers did not find paradise at the end of the difficult voyage to America. Confined to dingy slums, they worked at menial jobs for low wages. Many did the country's "dirty work"—or, as one observer put it, "the shoveling."

Furthermore, many native-born Americans viewed immigration as a threat. They agreed with Thomas Bailey Aldrich, who, in his poem "The Unguarded Gates," warned against a "wild motley throng" bringing "unknown gods and rites." Many felt that the newcomers were just too different ever to fit in. Others went further, blaming immigrants for all of society's ills.

Nativists also charged that the willingness of immigrants to work cheaply robbed native-born Americans of jobs and lowered wages for all. On the West Coast, where Chinese laborers had worked for years, the new nativist Workingmen's Party of California angrily cried "The Chinese must go" in response to mounting unemployment in the 1870s. White mobs attacked the Chinese, killing some and burning the property of others.

In some cases, nativists successfully pushed for restrictions on immigration. For example, in 1882 the U.S. Congress passed the **Chinese Exclusion Act**, which denied citizenship to people born in China and prohibited the immigration of Chinese laborers. Other attempts at limiting immigration, however, were less successful. The **Immigration Restriction League**, founded in 1894 by a group of well-to-do Bostonians, sought to make literacy a requirement for admission into the country. Congress passed such a measure, but President Grover Cleveland vetoed it in 1897, calling it "illiberal, narrow, and un-American."

Despite the efforts to impose restrictions, immigration continued. And contrary to nativists' arguments, the immigrants' varied cultures added new dimensions to American life, especially in the cities, where most immigrants settled.

■■ Prejudice and fear prompted nativists to try to restrict immigration.

URBAN LIFE

As more and more immigrants and migrants from rural areas poured into American cities, these urban areas did not just expand. Growth was accompanied by changes in the very structure and layout of cities.

The changing city. The urban areas of the mid-1800s were compact. Few buildings were taller than two or three stories. And even in the largest cities, most people lived less than a 45-minute walk from the city center, where most businesses and industries were located. But by the late 1800s, technological innovations and the great flood of people began to transform the urban landscape.

Contributing to the transformation were steel, new building techniques, and Elisha Otis's mechanized elevator, all of which allowed cities to grow upward as well as outward. No longer restricted by the number of stairs people could comfortably climb, architects designed multistory buildings, or skyscrapers.

▼ Chinese immigrants formed their own communities and businesses after arriving in the United States. This photograph is of San Francisco's Chinatown district.

▲ Trolley cars were an important part of many urban mass-transit systems. This photograph was taken in New York City around 1895.

Moreover, the development of **mass transit**—commuter trains, subways, and trolley cars—made it possible for cities to spread outward because workers no longer had to live within walking distance of their jobs. Soon, suburbs arose as some wealthier residents moved away from crowded city centers to live in "light and air."

The tenements. While some could afford to enjoy the healthy life of the suburbs, many urban Americans remained trapped by poverty in crowded, and often unhealthy, tenement houses. These dark, airless buildings sometimes housed as many as 12 families per floor. Jacob Riis described one of the apartments:

66 A room perhaps a dozen feet square, with walls and ceiling that . . . were now covered with a brown crust that, touched with the end of a club, came off in shuddering showers of crawling bugs. 99

Outside the tenements, raw sewage and piles of garbage fouled unpaved streets and alleys. Worse still, the slums usually adjoined industrial areas where factories belched pollution. "The stink is enough to knock you down," one New York resident complained. In such an environment, sickness and death were common. Diseases like tuberculosis spread rapidly through tightly packed slums.

African Americans also experienced difficulties in northern cities. Widespread discrimination

▶ Crowded tenements, such as these lining Hester Street in New York City, sprang up as urban populations swelled.

meant that most of them could get only poorly paid jobs. Moreover, African Americans had to pay outrageous rents for the most appalling apartments, and they frequently faced police harassment. Yet many preferred the North to the South. As one African American journalist explained:

66 They sleep in peace at night; what they earn is paid them, if not they can appeal to the courts. They vote without fear of the shotgun, and their children go to school. 99

■■ New technologies allowed cities to expand upward and outward. Wealthier people moved to the suburbs, but many of the poor had no choice but to live in crowded tenements.

*T*HE DRIVE FOR REFORM

As urban poverty grew and received more publicity, people debated how best to help the poor. Some saw education as the solution to the problems plaguing the cities. After 1860 more and more states passed compulsory school attendance laws and lengthened the school year from 78 to 144 days. From 1870 to 1900 the number of students in school grew from

some 7 million to more than 15 million. Many of these new students were young women.

The settlement houses.
To confront the problem of poverty more directly, some young Americans established and lived in **settlement houses**—community service centers—in poor neighborhoods. At the forefront of this effort was Jane Addams.

BIO GRAPHY

Born in 1860 to a well-to-do family in Cedarville, Illinois, Jane Addams grew up in an atmosphere of politics and charitable activity. Her Quaker father was a passionate abolitionist, and as a state senator he had worked to pass social reform legislation. The young Addams decided to dedicate her life to helping the urban poor.

In time, Addams's work included other causes. She tirelessly worked for women's suffrage and served as president of the Women's International League for Peace and Freedom from 1919 to 1935. Worldwide recognition for her work came in 1931, when she won the Nobel Peace Prize.

Addams began her settlement-house work in 1889, when she and Ellen Gates Starr established Hull House in one of Chicago's immigrant neighborhoods. The mission of Hull House, as stated in its charter, was "to provide a center for a higher civic and social life" and "to investigate and improve the conditions in the industrial districts of Chicago."

The Hull House volunteers were mostly young, college-educated women. They set up a day nursery and kindergarten for the children of working mothers and gave adult education classes. They offered recreational facilities and staffed an employment agency. And when the city failed to pick up garbage in poor neighborhoods, Addams secured an appointment as a garbage inspector to make sure the much-needed service was provided.

Hull House served as a model for others hoping to aid the poor. For example, in 1890 African American teacher Janie Porter Barrett founded one of the first African American settlement houses—the Locust Street Social Settlement—in Hampton,

Jane Addams

▲ In this early 1900s photograph, nurses from New York's Henry Street Settlement House set out to help the poor and needy.

Virginia. By 1900 almost 100 settlement houses had opened across the country.

Other reform movements.
At the same time that the settlement houses began their work, a number of Protestant religious leaders developed the idea of the **Social Gospel**, which called for people to apply Christian principles to address social problems. Many churches attempted to implement the Social Gospel by providing libraries, job training, counseling, and other social services.

Many religious groups joined the battle against urban poverty. In the 1880s the Salvation Army, an evangelical group founded in Great Britain, began offering food, clothing, shelter, and work opportunities to the poor to help put them on the path to physical and spiritual salvation.

Some people—particularly wealthy ones such as steel baron Andrew Carnegie—opposed direct aid, or handouts, to the poor. Such handouts, Carnegie argued, rewarded equally both the unworthy beggar and the worthy worker fallen on hard times. Carnegie was a firm believer in **Social Darwinism**, a theory that sought to apply the biological principles of natural selection and evolution to society. Social Darwinists thought that the "fittest" people should and would rise to positions of wealth and power, while the "unfit" would fail.

Instead of direct aid, Carnegie advocated **philanthropy**—charitable efforts to promote public welfare. The best way to benefit the lower class, he argued, was "to place within its reach the ladders upon which the aspiring can rise." Carnegie's "ladders" included universities and libraries. He gave some $350 million to such causes.

▲ Shown here is the 1866 championship game at Elysian Field, in Hoboken, New Jersey.

■■ Some people attempted to solve urban problems through settlement houses, the Social Gospel, and philanthropy.

LEISURE TIME

Philanthropic efforts often served to enrich urban cultural life for all. In addition to supporting universities and libraries, some wealthy people financed museums and art galleries and established new theater groups and symphony orchestras.

Such institutions were not the only forms of recreation urban dwellers enjoyed. Expanded education meant that by 1900 some 90 percent of Americans could read, and many did. The dramatic increase in the number of daily newspapers—from less than 600 in 1870 to some 2,600 by 1910—reflected the growth in literacy. Many people also read popular fiction—romances, mysteries, and westerns. Young boys favored Horatio Alger's success stories about hardworking street urchins who rose to middle-class respectability by courage—and luck.

Older readers enjoyed realistic books about urban life. For example, Edith Wharton's *House of Mirth* (1905) described the conflicts between the new rich and the old elite. William Dean Howells's

Rise of Silas Lapham (1885) wove a tale of greed and social ambition. Stephen Crane and Frank Norris depicted the grimmer aspects of urban life.

Sports became another popular form of recreation. In 1876, with the founding of the first professional league, baseball became a popular spectator sport—in one contemporary sportswriter's words, "the national game of the United States." But even sports could be discriminatory; widespread racism led to the exclusion of African Americans from major league baseball teams until 1947. African Americans formed their own leagues, however, which produced many outstanding players.

For children, Barnum & Bailey's Circus provided "The Greatest Show on Earth." Vaudeville shows, with roots in working-class variety acts, attracted middle-class as well as working-class audiences. Also popular, especially among immigrant and working-class families, were amusement parks with their roller coasters and Ferris wheels.

■■ An urban culture with diverse educational and leisure activities developed in the late 1800s.

SECTION 2 REVIEW

IDENTIFY and explain the significance of the following: conspicuous consumption, new immigrants, benevolent societies, Chinese Exclusion Act, Immigration Restriction League, mass transit, settlement houses, Jane Addams, Social Gospel, Social Darwinism, philanthropy.

1. **MAIN IDEA** What change occurred in immigration in the late 1800s? Why did nativists oppose the new immigrants?

2. **MAIN IDEA** In what ways did American cities change in the late 1800s?

3. **CONTRASTING** How did efforts to reform urban conditions differ from each other?

4. **WRITING TO DESCRIBE** Imagine you are visiting a New York tenement house in 1895. Write a letter to a friend describing your visit and observations about tenement life.

5. **SYNTHESIZING** How did technology and the new industrial order affect the lives of middle- and working-class women?

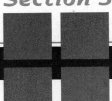

POLITICS AND PROTEST

FOCUS

- **Why did many Americans call for civil service reform?**
- **What problems led Americans to organize labor unions?**
- **What prompted farmers to organize after the Civil War?**

The abuses of power that seemed to characterize the late–19th-century political scene left many Americans deeply troubled. Some people called for political reform. Others—such as industrial workers and farmers—took matters into their own hands, organizing to protect their interests and to win their share of prosperity.

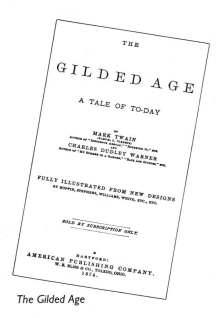

The Gilded Age

RESTORING HONEST GOVERNMENT

In their 1873 novel *The Gilded Age*, authors Mark Twain and Charles Dudley Warner suggested that, like the base material that hides beneath the glittering gold surface of a gilded picture frame, corruption and greed lurked below the polite and prosperous luster of late-19th-century American society. The image struck a chord, and the era became known as the **Gilded Age**. Corruption and greed seemed particularly evident in the politics of the time.

Graft and corruption. The rapid growth of cities in the late 19th century led to the creation of powerful **political machines**—party organizations whose primary goal was to obtain and then keep local political power. The political bosses who ran the big-city machines got their candidates elected by dispensing favors to people in return for votes. One observer described a boss's methods:

❝ To this one he lends a dollar; for another he obtains a railroad ticket without payment; he has coal distributed in the depth of winter; . . . he sometimes sends poultry at Christmas time; he buys medicine for a sick person; he helps bury the dead. ❞

Once in power, bosses used any means necessary—the rigging of elections, bribery, even violence—to stay in power. And many took advantage of their positions to plunder public treasuries.

The most notorious political machine was Tammany Hall, the Democratic party machine that controlled New York City's government. Tammany Hall's reputation for graft and corruption was launched by William Marcy Tweed, who along with his cronies—the Tweed Ring—robbed the city treasury of some $200 million between 1865 and 1871.

Politicians in Washington, D.C., played the same games, often for higher stakes. President Ulysses S. Grant's first term was marred by several financial scandals. The greatest of these surfaced in 1872 and involved Grant's vice-president, Schuyler Colfax. In 1867, the directors of the Union Pacific Railroad had formed the Crédit Mobilier Company and awarded it contracts to build part of the transcontinental railroad. Crédit Mobilier overcharged Union Pacific by more than $20 million. These "excess profits" were paid to Crédit

Mobilier's stockholders, many of whom were members of Congress, including then–Speaker of the House Colfax.

The struggle for reform.

Critics charged that corruption in national political life was in large part the result of the spoils system, in which successful political candidates rewarded their supporters with civil service jobs. Reformers proposed that appointments to government jobs be based on ability, as determined on competitive exams, rather than on party affiliation.

Political corruption and civil service reform became important issues in every presidential election between 1872 and 1888. The Republican party even split into two factions over the issue of patronage.

Because of the controversy over the issue, reform was slow to come. A spark to change, however, came on July 2, 1881, when Charles Guiteau (guh-TOH), a disappointed and mentally unstable government job seeker, shot and killed President James A. Garfield. Chester A. Arthur, who became president on Garfield's death, responded to the shooting by helping gain passage of the **Pendleton Civil Service Act** in 1883. This act established a Civil Service Commission to administer competitive examinations to those seeking government jobs.

Yet critics charged that the Pendleton act was of limited value because it covered only about 10 percent of federal jobs. And although President Grover Cleveland, a Democrat, doubled the number of jobs requiring a civil service exam after his election in 1884, many elected officials continued to make appointments based on patronage rather than on merit.

■■ **Convinced that the spoils system led to political corruption, many Americans called for civil service reform.**

THE LABOR MOVEMENT

Preoccupied with political reform, the government overlooked one of the major trends of the late 1800s—the growing gulf between the haves and the have-nots. By 1890 close to 75 percent of the nation's wealth was controlled by just 10 percent of the population, and many American industrial workers lived in poverty.

Working life.

All industrial workers labored long hours for little pay. Most white unskilled male laborers worked at least 10 hours a day, 6 days a week, for less than $10 a week. Many African American, Mexican American, and Asian American men worked the same number of hours for even lower wages. And wages for women were lower than those for men. In 1883, the average earnings of women in Boston were estimated to be less than $5 a week. Children, too, faced terrible conditions in the labor force. In some textile mills, children worked 12-hour shifts—often at night—for pennies a day.

▲ In the 1870s the Knights of Labor campaigned for legislation to protect child workers. But children continued to experience wretched working conditions throughout the next few decades.

Long hours left workers exhausted, and fatigue increased the danger in already unsafe working surroundings. In 1881 alone, some 30,000 railway workers were killed or injured on the job. Most employers felt no responsibility for work-related deaths and injuries and made little effort to improve workplace safety.

The Knights of Labor.

As conditions worsened, workers clamored for change and banded together to make employers listen. One of the earliest national unions was the **Knights of Labor**, founded in 1869. Under Terence V. Powderly, who became the leader of the Knights of Labor in 1879, the union fought for the eight-hour workday, equal pay for equal work, and an end to child labor.

Powderly—in contrast to the leaders of most other unions—opened the Knights' membership to both skilled and unskilled laborers and to women. A number of women played prominent roles in the union. Mary Harris Jones, for example, organized strikes, marches, and demonstrations. Her activities earned her the title "the most dangerous woman in America." But because she looked more motherly than radical, most people called her Mother Jones.

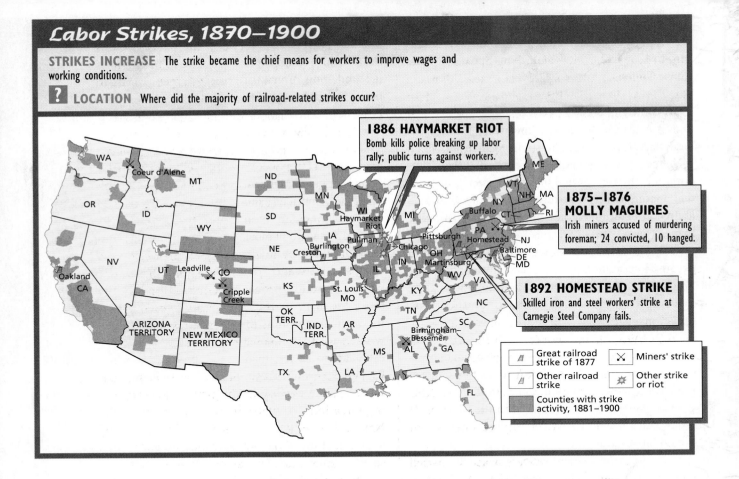

Labor Strikes, 1870–1900

STRIKES INCREASE The strike became the chief means for workers to improve wages and working conditions.

? LOCATION Where did the majority of railroad-related strikes occur?

1886 HAYMARKET RIOT
Bomb kills police breaking up labor rally; public turns against workers.

1875–1876 MOLLY MAGUIRES
Irish miners accused of murdering foreman; 24 convicted, 10 hanged.

1892 HOMESTEAD STRIKE
Skilled iron and steel workers' strike at Carnegie Steel Company fails.

Legend:
- Great railroad strike of 1877
- Other railroad strike
- Counties with strike activity, 1881–1900
- Miners' strike
- Other strike or riot

Powderly also opened the union to African Americans. By the mid-1880s the Knights claimed some 60,000 black members. The Knights were not equality-minded when it came to everyone, however. Powderly, like many working-class Americans, actively opposed Chinese workers, claiming they took jobs from white Americans. At his urging, for instance, West Coast branches of the Knights of Labor vigorously campaigned for passage of the Chinese Exclusion Act.

Industrial unrest. In 1886, the nation entered a year of intense strikes and violent labor confrontations that would become known as the **Great Upheaval**. An economic depression in the early 1880s had led to massive wage cuts. Workers needed—and demanded—relief. When negotiations with management failed, many workers took direct action. By the end of 1886, some 1,500 strikes, involving more than 400,000 workers, had swept the nation. Many of these strikes turned violent, as angry strikers clashed head-on with their employers and the police. Perhaps the best-known of these confrontations was the **Haymarket Riot**.

The seeds for the Haymarket Riot were sown when some 40,000 Chicago workers struck on May 1, 1886. On May 3 a confrontation between the police and the strikers left two strikers dead. In protest, the strikers called a meeting for the next day in Chicago's Haymarket Square. Peaceful and sparsely attended, the rally was about to break up when nearly 200 police officers appeared. Suddenly a bomb exploded in the midst of the police. The police responded with gunfire. When the smoke cleared, more than 70 people lay wounded, and seven police officers and one civilian were dead.

The police arrested eight well-known **anarchists** (people who oppose all forms of government), even though only one of them had actually attended the meeting. All eight were found guilty of incitement to murder; four went to the gallows. On the final day of the trial, one of the defendants warned:

66 I have told [Chicago Police] Captain Schaack, . . . "if you cannonade us, we shall dynamite you." . . . Let me assure you I die happy on the gallows, so confident am I that the hundreds and thousands to whom I have spoken will remember my words; . . . they will do the bomb throwing! 99

But worker activism actually decreased by the close of the year. Emboldened by the Haymarket convictions, employers struck back. They drew up **blacklists**—lists of union supporters—that they shared with one another. Blacklisted workers found it almost impossible to get jobs. Many employers also made job applicants sign agreements—called **yellow-dog contracts** by the workers—promising not to join unions. When these measures failed and workers struck anyway, many companies instituted **lockouts**, barring workers from the plant, and brought in nonunion **strikebreakers**, often African Americans or others who felt abandoned by the unions.

As labor suffered repeated defeats and the tide of public sentiment turned against workers, union membership—including the Knights'—shrank. Many of the workers who remained in unions were skilled workers who joined the newly formed **American Federation of Labor** (AFL), founded by Samuel Gompers in 1886. The AFL was a collection of independent skilled craft unions committed to advancing the interests of skilled workers.

After a few years of relative peace, industrial unrest broke out again in the 1890s. At Andrew Carnegie's Homestead steel plant in Pennsylvania, workers went on strike in 1892 after a wage cut was announced. Violence between the strikers and hired plant guards resulted in 16 deaths. The violence soon spread to other plants, and order was restored only after the state militia was called in. Then in 1894, workers at the Pullman sleeping-car factory in Chicago went on strike, again largely in response to a wage cut. The American Railway Union (ARU) supported the workers, and the strike escalated, drawing in the railroad owners and the federal government. Federal troops were ordered into Chicago, sparking violence that left scores of casualties. Within days the strike had been broken and the ARU destroyed.

■■ **Industrial workers formed unions and staged strikes and protests to try to win better wages and working conditions.**

THE RISE AND FALL OF POPULISM

The development of the new industrial order affected not only workers, but farmers as well. The rapidly growing population in the nation's cities needed to be supplied with food. The farmers responded, each year producing larger crops and more livestock. Unfortunately for the Americans, farmers in other nations did the same. Soon prices tumbled as supply exceeded demand. But railroad freight prices continued to spiral upward, as did the cost of new machinery. As farm profits plunged, farmers tried to produce more just to break even. But greater production only pushed prices even lower.

To make matters worse, almost all farm families had borrowed money to pay for their land or to buy new equipment, generally putting their farms up as security. Those who could not repay the loans lost their farms. Many ended up as tenant farmers, paying rent to the new owners. Others were forced to become farm laborers.

Early movements. In an effort to better their lot, farmers organized. The first major farmers' organization, the Patrons of Husbandry, or the **National Grange**, was founded by Oliver Hudson Kelley in 1867. The Grange began primarily as a social organization. But as membership increased and farmers' financial problems grew, the Grange began tackling economic and political issues.

To lower costs, some Grange farmers formed **cooperatives**. Cooperative members sold their products directly to big-city markets and bought farm equipment and other goods in large quantities at wholesale prices—thereby cutting costs.

The Grange's main focus, however, was on trying to get the railroads, which shipped farm products to markets, to lower freight rates. A leading granger complained that "the cost of transportation to the East eats up about one-half the value of the wheat." In response to pressure from farmers, Illinois, Iowa, Minnesota, and Wisconsin

▲ **African American farmers joined the Colored Farmers' Alliance to protect their interests against monopolies and unfair freight prices. Shown here are Virginia homesteaders during the 1890s.**

RUTHERFORD B. HAYES
1822–1893

in office 1877–1881

JAMES A. GARFIELD
1831–1881

in office 1881

CHESTER A. ARTHUR
1829–1886

in office 1881–1885

GROVER CLEVELAND
1837–1908

*in office 1885–1889
and 1893–1897*

BENJAMIN HARRISON
1833–1901

in office 1889–1893

WILLIAM McKINLEY
1843–1901

in office 1897–1901

passed laws in the early 1870s to fix maximum railroad rates. Then in 1887, Congress passed the **Interstate Commerce Act**, which stated that railroad rates had to be "reasonable and just." However, the act proved hard to enforce. The railroads almost always won when the government took them to court for violating the law.

While the Grange was fighting for railroad legislation, a more powerful farm organization—the **Farmers' Alliance**—arose. Offering a strong message of solidarity and hope, the movement had attracted some 400,000 members by 1890. Like the Grange, the Alliance organized cooperatives to buy equipment. It also offered farmers low-cost insurance and lobbied for tougher bank regulations, government ownership of the railroads, and a **graduated income tax** that taxed higher incomes at a higher rate.

The Alliance also echoed the demand that farmers had been making since the end of the Civil War: expand the money supply by printing more greenbacks, the paper money used during the war. The resulting inflation would benefit farmers by allowing them to

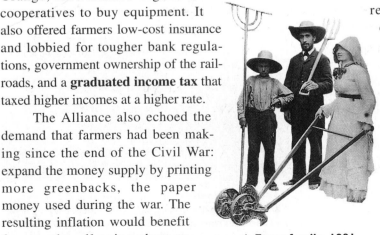

▲ **Farm family, 1881**

charge more for their products and by making it easier to repay their bank loans.

Such prospects alarmed eastern bankers who opposed increasing the amount of money in circulation. Since the money supply was backed by gold, they argued, it was limited by the amount of gold held in the U.S. Treasury. The farmers responded by demanding that the government back the money with silver (which was plentiful in the West) as well as with gold.

In the elections of 1890, Alliance members supported any candidate who accepted their pro-farmer programs. The results were remarkable. Alliance-backed candidates won 38 U.S. congressional seats, 4 southern governorships, and numerous other political offices.

■■ **Falling prices and rising costs led many farmers to join the Grange and Farmers' Alliance movements— organizations that sought economic and political change.**

The Populist party. Elated, Alliance leaders sought to build on these successes by forming a new political party. At a national convention in St. Louis in February 1892, a gathering of farmers, labor leaders, and reformers founded the People's party, which became more commonly known as the **Populist party.** Politician and author Ignatius Donnelly of Minnesota opened the convention with a thunderous address:

66 We meet in the midst of a nation brought to the verge of moral, political, and material ruin. Corruption dominates the ballot-box, the Legislatures, the Congress. . . . We seek to restore the government of the Republic to the hands of the "plain people." 99

The Populists nominated James B. Weaver to run in the 1892 presidential election. Although Democrat Grover Cleveland won the presidency, the Populist party elected 3 senators, 11 congressmen, 3 governors, and numerous state legislators. And Weaver polled a very respectable one million popular votes, carrying 4 western states and 22 electoral votes.

In the presidential election of 1896, the debate on the money supply became a central issue. The Populists threw their support to the Democratic candidate, William Jennings Bryan. Bryan, a two-term congressman from Nebraska, supported the Populists' demand for a silver-

▶ While Bryan traveled 13,000 miles and gave 600 speeches during the 1896 campaign, McKinley stayed home and received visitors on the front porch of his Ohio home. Ribbons from McKinley's campaign are shown here.

backed currency. Bryan swept the South and much of the West, but he made no headway at all in the urban industrial East or in the mixed industrial and farm states of the Midwest. When the popular votes were counted, Republican William McKinley had beaten Bryan by some 500,000 votes.

Although the power of the Populist party declined after the election, the movement stands as the first example of a large-scale effort by a disadvantaged group in the modern industrial era to use the political process to advance its interests. Furthermore, the Populist platform laid the groundwork for future reform (see Chapter 7). As Populist leader Mary Elizabeth Lease noted in 1914, "the seeds we sowed out in Kansas did not fall on barren ground."

■■ **The Populist party drew attention to problems faced by farmers and laid the groundwork for later reforms.**

SECTION 3 REVIEW

IDENTIFY and explain the significance of the following: Gilded Age, political machines, Pendleton Civil Service Act, Knights of Labor, Terence V. Powderly, Great Upheaval, Haymarket Riot, anarchists, blacklists, yellow-dog contracts, lockouts, strikebreakers, American Federation of Labor, National Grange, cooperatives, Interstate Commerce Act, Farmers' Alliance, graduated income tax.

LOCATE and explain the importance of the following: Haymarket Square, Homestead steel plant, Pullman sleeping car factory.

1. **MAIN IDEA** What obstacles did reformers face in the fight against political corruption?

2. **MAIN IDEA** What changes did the Knights of Labor want for working people?

3. **MAIN IDEA** What conditions led to the rise of the Populist party?

4. **WRITING TO EXPRESS A VIEWPOINT** Imagine you are a member of an industrial workers' union in the late 1800s. Write a proposal for changes in work rules and conditions to present to management. State why you think these changes should be made.

5. **ANALYZING** Why did expansion of the money supply appeal to farmers but not to eastern bankers?

Knights of
Labor
founded.

Mark Twain and
Charles Dudley
Warner publish
The Gilded Age.

Congress places a
40 percent tariff on
imported steel.

National Grange
founded.

Crédit Mobilier
scandal surfaces.

Alexander Graham Bell
patents telephone.

1865   1870   1875   1880

WRITING A SUMMARY

Using the essential points of the chapter as a guide, write a summary of the chapter.

REVIEWING CHRONOLOGY

Number your paper 1 to 5. Study the time line above, and list the following events in the order in which they happened by writing the first next to 1, the second next to 2, and so on. Then complete the activity below.

1. Jane Addams establishes Hull House.
2. National Grange founded.
3. Congress passes Chinese Exclusion Act.
4. Standard Oil's profits reach some $45 million.
5. Crédit Mobilier scandal surfaces.

Evaluating How did the establishment of Hull House contribute to social reform?

IDENTIFYING PEOPLE AND IDEAS

Explain the historical significance of each of the following people or terms.

1. trunk lines
2. Thomas Edison
3. monopoly
4. new immigrants
5. Social Darwinism
6. Jane Addams
7. political machines
8. Terence V. Powderly
9. lockouts
10. Farmers' Alliance

UNDERSTANDING MAIN IDEAS

1. How did the government attempt to restrict big businesses in 1890?
2. How did technological advances promote changes in American cities in the late 1800s?
3. What goals were shared by benevolent societies and by reformers involved in the settlement-house and Social Gospel movements?
4. Why did some Americans support civil service reform?
5. What problems did American industrial workers and farmers face in the late 1800s?

REVIEWING THEMES

1. **Economic Development** How did changes in technology affect the nation's economy in the late 1800s?

2. **Cultural Diversity** Why did some native-born Americans oppose immigration, and what actions did they take to prevent it?
3. **Democratic Values** What steps did reformers take to bring about social, political, and economic change in American society in the late 1800s?

THINKING CRITICALLY

1. **Evaluating** What advantages did large companies have over smaller ones in the new industrial order?
2. **Analyzing** How did the new industrial order lead to changes in the composition of the upper, middle, and working classes?
3. **Synthesizing** Was government intervention in the workers' strikes of the 1880s and 1890s in keeping with the theory of laissez-faire capitalism? Explain.

STRATEGY FOR SUCCESS

Review the Skills Handbook entry on Identifying Cause and Effect on page 749. Write a paragraph tracing the rise of big business from the development of the Bessemer process to the eventual government legislation limiting monopolies and trusts. Be sure to show the connections between causes and effects.

WRITING ABOUT HISTORY

Writing to Create
Among the best-selling books of the late 19th century were dime novels, books with paper covers that sold for 10 cents. Dime novels offered plots with lots of action and suspense. Using a 19th-century tycoon, immigrant, urban resident, reformer, or industrial worker as a main character, write an outline for a dime novel.

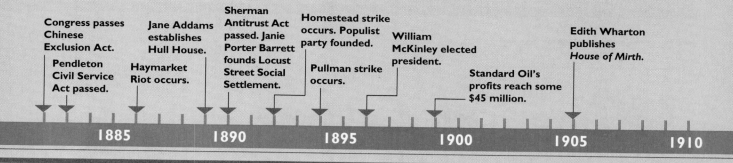

| Congress passes Chinese Exclusion Act. | Jane Addams establishes Hull House. | Sherman Antitrust Act passed. Janie Porter Barrett founds Locust Street Social Settlement. | Homestead strike occurs. Populist party founded. | William McKinley elected president. | Edith Wharton publishes *House of Mirth.* |

| Pendleton Civil Service Act passed. | Haymarket Riot occurs. | Pullman strike occurs. | Standard Oil's profits reach some $45 million. |

1885   1890   1895   1900   1905   1910

USING PRIMARY SOURCES

In the late 19th century, farmers faced a variety of problems, from unpredictable weather and pests to railroad price-fixing. Read the poem below, written by a Georgia farmer in 1890. Then explain how it reflects the problems that led to the formation of farmers' groups. What was the most severe problem?

*We worked through spring and summer,
    through winter and through fall;
But the mortgage worked the hardest
    and the steadiest of them all;
It worked on night and Sunday, it
    worked each holiday;
It settled down among us and it never
    went away.*

*Whatever we kept from it seemed
    almost as bad as theft;
It watched us every minute and ruled
    us right and left
The rust and blight was with us
    sometimes, and sometimes not;
The dark brown scowling mortgage was
    forever on the spot.*

*The weevil and the cut worm, they
    went as well they came;
The mortgage stayed forever, eating
    hearty all the same
It nailed up every window, stood
    guard at every door;
And happiness and sunshine made their
    place with us no more.*

LINKING HISTORY AND GEOGRAPHY

Review the map on page 154. In which region did most miners' strikes take place? Why do you think this was so?

BUILDING YOUR PORTFOLIO

Complete the following projects independently or cooperatively.

1. THE ECONOMY In chapters 1, 3, and 5 you explored such economic issues as trade, manufacturing, and regional development. Building on that experience, imagine you are an industrial worker and a union president in the late 1800s. Write a speech to the members of your union recommending the ways by which workers might best adapt or respond to the new industrial order.

UMW emblem, 1890

2. CULTURAL DIVERSITY In chapters 1 and 3 you examined the effects of cultural contact and exchange between various groups. Building on that experience, imagine you are an immigrant who has just arrived from southern or eastern Europe. Create a series of poems and graphics that illustrate the problems you face in your new home and your hopes for the future.

American Letters

▲ Mark Twain

Mark Twain's America

Samuel Langhorne Clemens—Mark Twain to generations of readers—remains one of America's greatest humorists and chroniclers of the American character. In the following two selections, Twain explores life in two very different settings—the Mississippi River and Washington, D.C.

From *Life on the Mississippi*

by Mark Twain

The river's earliest commerce was in great barges—keelboats, broadhorns. They floated and sailed from the upper rivers to New Orleans, changed cargoes there, and were tediously warped and poled back by hand. A voyage down and back sometimes occupied nine months. In time this commerce increased until it gave employment to hordes of rough and hardy men; rude, uneducated, brave, suffering terrific hardships with sailor-like stoicism; heavy drinkers, coarse frolickers in moral sties like the Natchez-under-the-hill of that day, heavy fighters, reckless fellows, every one, elephantinely jolly, foul-witted, profane, prodigal of their money, bankrupt at the end of the trip, fond of barbaric finery, prodigious braggarts; yet, in the main, honest, trustworthy, faithful to promises and duty, and often picturesquely magnanimous.

By and by the steamboat intruded. Then, for fifteen or twenty years, these men continued to run their keelboats downstream, and the steamers did all of the upstream business, the keelboatmen selling their boats in New Orleans, and returning home as deck-passengers in the steamers.

But after a while the steamboats so increased in number and in speed that they were able to absorb the entire commerce; and then keelboating died a permanent death. The keelboatman became a deckhand, or a mate, or a pilot on the steamer; and when steamer-berths were not open to him, he took a berth on a Pittsburgh coal-flat, or on a pine raft constructed in the forests up toward the sources of the Mississippi.

In the heyday of the steamboating prosperity, the river from end to end was flanked with coal-fleets and timber-rafts, all managed by hand, and employing hosts of the rough characters whom I have been trying to describe. . . .

By way of illustrating the keelboat talk and manners, and that now departed and hardly remembered raft life, I will throw in, in this place, a chapter from a book which I have been working at. . . . The book is a story which details some passages in the life of an ignorant village boy, Huck Finn, son of the town drunkard. . . . He has run away from his persecuting father, and from a persecuting good widow who wishes to make

▼ *Mississippi riverboat*

a nice, truth telling respectable boy of him; and with him a slave of the widow's has also escaped. They have found a fragment of a lumber-raft (it is high water and dead summer-time), and are floating down river by night, and hiding in the willows by day—bound for Cairo, [Illinois,] whence the Negro will seek freedom in the heart of the free states. But, in the fog, they have passed Cairo without knowing it. By and by they begin to suspect the truth, and Huck Finn is persuaded to end the dismal suspense by swimming down to a huge raft which they have seen in the distance ahead of them, creeping aboard under cover of the darkness, and gathering the needed information by eavesdropping: . . .

I swum down along the raft till I was most abreast the campfire in the middle, then I crawled aboard and inched along and got in among some shingles on the weather side of the fire. There was thirteen men there—they was the watch on deck of course. And a mighty rough-looking lot, too. . . .

The man they called Ed said the muddy Mississippi water was wholesomer to drink than the clear water of the Ohio; he said that if you let a pint of this yaller Mississippi water settle, you would have about a half to three-quarters of an inch of mud in the bottom, according to the stage of the river, and then it warn't no better than Ohio water—what you wanted to do was to keep it stirred up—and when the water was low, keep mud on hand to put in and thicken the water up the way it ought to be.

The Child of Calamity said that was so; he said there was nutritiousness in the mud, and a man that drunk Mississippi water could grow corn in his stomach if he wanted to. He says:

"You look at the graveyards; that tells the tale. Trees won't grow worth shucks in a Cincinnati graveyard, but in a Sent Louis graveyard they grow upwards of eight hundred foot high. It's all on account of the water the people drunk before they laid up. A Cincinnati corpse don't richen a soil any." ❖

___

From *The Gilded Age*

by Mark Twain and Charles Dudley Warner

Every individual you encounter in the City of Washington almost—and certainly every separate and distinct individual in the public employment, from the highest bureau chief, clear down to the maid who scrubs the Department halls . . . —represents Political Influence. Unless you can get the ear of a Senator, or a Congressman, or a Chief of a Bureau or Department, and persuade him to use his "influence" in your behalf, you cannot get an employment of the most trivial nature in Washington. Mere merit, fitness and capability, are useless baggage to you without "influence." The population of Washington consists pretty much entirely of government employés and the people who board them.

There are thousands of these employés, and they have gathered there from every corner of the Union and got their berths through the intercession (command is nearer the word) of the Senators and Representatives of their respective States. It would be an odd circumstance to see a girl get employment at three or four dollars a week . . . without any political grandee to back her, but merely because she was worthy, and competent, and a good citizen of a free country that "treats all persons alike." Washington would be mildly thunderstruck at such a thing as that. If you are a member of Congress, (no offence,) and one of your constituents who doesn't know anything, and does not want to go into the bother of learning something, and has no money, and no employment, and can't earn a living, comes besieging you for help, do you say, "Come, my friend, if your services were valuable you could get employment elsewhere—don't want you here?" Oh, no. You take him to a Department and say, "Here, give this person something to pass away the time at—and a salary"—and the thing is done. You throw him on his country. He is his country's child, let his country support him. There is something good and motherly about Washington, the grand old benevolent National Asylum for the Helpless. ❖

___

THINKING AND WRITING ABOUT LITERATURE

1. Toward which group does Mark Twain seem most sympathetic—the Mississippi boatmen or the public servants in Washington? Provide evidence to support your answer.

2. Twain and Charles Dudley Warner published *The Gilded Age* in 1873. What events in Washington might have influenced the tone of the book?

Strategies for Success

INTERPRETING EDITORIAL CARTOONS

Editorial cartoons are drawings that present points of view on the issues, ideas, people, and events of the day. They usually appear in the editorial sections of newspapers and newsmagazines. Although some express a positive outlook, many are critical of a person or policy.

To communicate their message, editorial cartoonists frequently use caricature and symbolism. A *caricature* is a drawing that exaggerates or distorts physical features. *Symbolism* is the use of one thing to stand for something else. For instance, cartoonists often use Uncle Sam to represent the United States, an elephant to symbolize the Republican party, and a donkey to stand for the Democrats.

Many editorial cartoons rely on labels to help identify symbols or other aspects of the picture. Most also include captions or "speech balloons," which may serve as a sort of punchline.

How to Interpret Editorial Cartoons

1. **Identify the caricatures.** Identify each figure and object. Note any distortions or exaggerations, and decide whether they cast the figure in a positive or negative light.
2. **Identify the symbols used.** Determine what each symbol stands for.
3. **Read the title and labels.** Read and determine the meaning of any title and labels.
4. **Consider the cartoonist's purpose.** Identify the points of view being expressed in the speech balloons or caption. Try to determine the cartoonist's message.

Applying the Strategy

Andrew Jackson was a popular subject for editorial cartoonists of his day. In the cartoon on this page, Jackson is shown wearing a crown and kingly robe, holding a scepter like a club and a "veto" as if it were a royal decree. Tattered papers labeled "Constitution of the United States," "Internal Improvements," and "U.S. Bank" and a book titled *Judiciary of the U. States* are strewn underfoot.

According to his critics, Jackson had abused his constitutional authority by his vetoes of bills that would have rechartered the national bank and provided for internal improvements. The cartoonist uses symbols of monarchy to accuse Jackson of acting more like a king than the president of a republic. This point is reinforced by the condition and position of the papers and by the title: "King Andrew the First."

Practicing the Strategy

Study the editorial cartoon on page xix of your textbook. Then, on a separate sheet of paper, answer the following questions.

1. Who are the central figures in the cartoon? Are they portrayed realistically, or are they caricatures?
2. What symbols does the cartoon contain?
3. How do the labels and the title help make the cartoonist's point of view and message clear?
4. What is **(a)** the cartoonist's point of view and **(b)** the cartoon's message?

▼ **Cartoon satirizing Andrew Jackson**

BUILDING YOUR PORTFOLIO

O utlined below are four projects. Independently or cooperatively, complete one and use the products to demonstrate your mastery of the historical concepts involved.

1 THE ECONOMY

The search for better trade routes first brought Europeans to the Americas, and economic factors continued to influence the United States during its early history. Using the portfolio materials you designed in chapters 1, 3, 5, and 6, create a board game tracing the nation's economic development from the time of the first European arrivals to 1900. Games should consider transportation, technology, markets, and labor.

2 CULTURAL DIVERSITY

The history of the United States is a history of the rich intermingling of a variety of cultures. Using the portfolio materials you designed in chapters 1, 3, and 6, prepare a series of one-scene plays showing experiences of and exchanges between American Indians, Africans, and Europeans in America up to 1900. Plays might describe daily life in different time periods or might focus on specific historical events and people.

3 CONFLICT

Wars and other social conflicts in early American history often affected different people or groups in different ways. Using the portfolio materials you designed in chapters 2, 4, and 5, conduct a panel discussion about the nature of conflict that showcases the views of soldiers, government planners or others responsible for organizing a war effort, and others involved in conflicts. Use specific examples.

4 INDIVIDUAL RIGHTS

American colonists protested British rule in an effort to secure individual rights, and as time passed, others also struggled to win their rights. Using the portfolio materials you designed in chapters 2, 3, and 4, prepare a presentation discussing the different ways in which individual rights can be violated and the methods by which rights can be secured.

Videodisc Review

In assigned groups, develop an outline for a video collage of America from prehistory through 1900. Choose images that best illustrate the major topics of the period. Write a script to accompany the images. Assign narrators to different parts of the script, and present your video collage to the class.

Further Reading

Foner, Eric. *A Short History of Reconstruction, 1863–1877.* HarperCollins (1990). Overview of the Reconstruction years.

Luchetti, Cathy, and Carol Olwell. *Women of the West.* Orion (1982). Firsthand accounts of women's lives in the West.

Meltzer, Milton, ed. *Voices from the Civil War.* HarperCollins (1989). Northern and southern views of the war and its effects.

Nash, Gary B. *Red, White, and Black: The Peoples of Early North America.* Prentice Hall (1992). Account of interaction between Native Americans, Africans, and whites during colonial times.

Schlereth, Thomas J. *Victorian America: Transformations in Everyday Life 1876–1915.* HarperCollins (1991). Overview of the impact of immigration, expansion, and industrialization on U.S. society.

TO MAKE THE
A DECENT PLACE
DO YOUR BUY U.S. GO

Chapter 7

THE AGE OF REFORM
1897–1920

Chapter 8

THE PROGRESSIVE
PRESIDENTS 1900–1920

Chapter 9

AMERICA AND THE
WORLD 1898–1917

A World Power

1897–1920

*B*y the turn of the century, many Americans had turned their attention to economic and social problems, which had accompanied rapid industrialization and urban growth. Some reformers fought for social change, while others worked to reform all levels of government. As the other major powers pursued policies of economic and political imperialism, the United States also sought to extend its influence abroad. The United States tried to avoid the conflict that imperialism and nationalism caused in Europe, but the nation was eventually drawn into World War I. At war's end President Wilson worked to negotiate a just peace.

◄ Liberty Loan poster, World War I

The Granger Collection, New York

Chapter 10

**WORLD WAR I
1914–1920**

THE AGE OF REFORM

FOCUS

UNDERSTANDING THE MAIN IDEA

A new reform mood swept the United States during the early 1900s. With great optimism and faith in scientific efficiency, reformers set out to conquer the negative effects of industrialization and rapid urbanization: unsafe working conditions, long hours, poor wages, and slum housing.

THEMES

■ **ECONOMIC DEVELOPMENT** How might state governments justify regulating how businesses treat workers?

■ **DEMOCRATIC VALUES** How might reform groups help extend opportunities to all citizens?

■ **CONSTITUTIONAL HERITAGE** How might reform movements lay the groundwork for constitutional change?

1900	1904	1909	1912	1919
▼	▼	▼	▼	▼
ILGWU established.	**National Child Labor Committee formed.**	**NAACP** founded.	**Massachusetts** passes minimum-wage law.	**Eighteenth Amendment ratified.**

While the Gilded Age had promoted industrial development and generated great profits for some, it had also created many problems. The Populist movement had brought to the nation's attention the plight of farmers and urban workers. Gilded Age reformers like Jane Addams and the men and women involved in the Social Gospel movement had worked to improve conditions for the urban poor.

Fifth Avenue in New York, 1913

$\mathcal{I}$n 1906 Upton Sinclair published *The Jungle,* a novel about the meat-packing industry in Chicago. In an effort to alert the public to what he saw as the consequences of capitalist greed, Sinclair described industry practices in graphic detail:

> 66 There was never the least attention paid to what was cut up for sausage. . . . There would be meat that had tumbled out on the floor, in the dirt and sawdust. . . . There would be meat stored in great piles in rooms; and the water from leaky roofs would drip over it, and thousands of rats would race about on it. . . . These rats were nuisances, and the packers would put poisoned bread out for them, they would die, and then rats, bread, and meat would go into the hoppers together. 99

Sinclair's images were so vivid that they made some readers physically sick. "I aimed at the public's heart," Sinclair remarked, "and by accident I hit it in the stomach." In response to *The Jungle,* Americans demanded federal laws prohibiting unhealthful conditions in food-processing industries.

The Jungle was part of a reform movement that swept the country in the early 20th century. Most reformers recognized the benefits of industrialism, but they were intent on correcting its abuses.

Urban child collecting firewood

THE PROGRESSIVE MOVEMENT

In spite of its name, the Progressive movement—the reform effort that swept the nation between 1900 and 1920—was not a single movement united behind a single goal. Rather it was a collection of reform-minded individuals and groups dedicated to bettering life in the United States. Building on Populist efforts and the work of 19th-century reformers, the progressives publicized the ills of industrial society and sought to remedy them.

SAMUEL GOMPERS

President
American Federation
of Labor

COURT HOUSE
Thursday, June 3
7:45 P. M.

SUBJECT:
Shorter Work Day

Announcement of an AFL meeting, 1897

THE PROGRESSIVE SPIRIT

By the early 1900s industrialization had transformed the United States. Much of the transformation was positive: economic growth, new goods and services, and an expanding middle class. However, economic growth also widened the gap between the rich and the poor and contributed to unsafe working conditions and crowded cities. These ills led to a spirit of reform known as **progressivism**.

This concern over the effects of industrialization was by no means new. In the late 1800s Populists had protested unfair or corrupt corporate practices and had pressed for government legislation to stop them. Populism, however, was mainly a rural movement. Progressivism, on the other hand, focused on urban problems, such as unsafe working conditions, bad sanitation, and corrupt political machines.

Progressives carried on the Populists' struggle to "restore government to the people" by proposing election reforms that would enable people to participate more fully in running their government (see

◄ In the early 1900s most major labor unions excluded women, even though they made up nearly one fourth of the work force. Seamstresses, such as these shown here, often formed their own unions to fight for better working conditions.

The Granger Collection, New York

◄ **The progressive spirit also influenced a new school of artists during the early 1900s. Known as the Ash Can School for the gritty and realistic subjects of their paintings, the movement included such artists as George Bellows, Robert Henri, John Sloan, George Luks, William Glackens, and Everett Shinn. Many of their paintings, such as George Bellows's *Lone Tenement* (1909), shown at left, depicted the ugly tenements and tough living conditions of poor urban neighborhoods.**

Chapter 18). Some progressives believed that the cure for democracy's ills was more democracy.

Progressives also repeated the Populists' demand for a curb on corporate power. Toward this end, they promoted legislation that prohibited monopolies and enabled smaller businesses to compete successfully in the economy.

Like Populists and the Social Gospel ministers, progressives were inspired by the spirit of social justice. To cap the skyrocketing incomes of the rich, they took up the Populists' demand for a federal graduated income tax. They also supported the Populists' cry for an eight-hour workday. In addition, they sought to institute minimum wages, assure safe working conditions, and end child labor.

The progressive spirit was deeply infused with idealism. Theodore Roosevelt, who would become a leading progressive, aptly reflected this idealism when he wrote:

> ❝ If we wish to do good work for our country, we must be unselfish, disinterested, sincerely desirous of the well-being of the commonwealth, and capable of devoted adherence to a lofty ideal. ❞

This idealism extended to a firm belief in the power of science and technology to solve social problems. The progressive philosopher John Dewey urged reformers to gather data about society's ills through observation and experimentation and then test solutions. Progressives, assisted by universities, initiated many social research projects.

▪▪ Progressives sought a more democratic government, a check on corporate power, and solutions to social problems.

Although people from all walks of life participated in reform efforts during the Progressive Era, many progressives were native born, middle or upper class, and college educated. Men and women of the urban middle class—social workers, engineers, writers, teachers, doctors, ministers, lawyers, and small-business owners were particularly attracted to progressivism. This class had grown from some 750,000 in 1870 to around 10 million by 1910. In the words of Kansas editor William Allen White, by the 1900s Populism had "shaved its whiskers, washed its shirt, put on a derby, and moved up into the middle class."

Many middle-class women were attracted to the Progressive movement for the same reason earlier generations of women had assisted reform efforts: reform work provided them with one of the

▲ **Shown here is a group of Vassar women from the 1920s.**

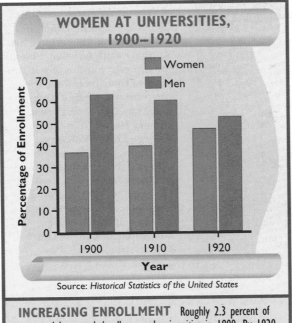

WOMEN AT UNIVERSITIES, 1900–1920

Women
Men

Percentage of Enrollment

Year

Source: *Historical Statistics of the United States*

INCREASING ENROLLMENT Roughly 2.3 percent of young adults attended colleges and universities in 1900. By 1920 the number had risen to some 4.7 percent. Over this period women made up an increasing proportion of college students.

? **BUILDING GRAPH SKILLS** In 1910, approximately what percentage of university students were women?

few acceptable avenues for influencing politics and society. Although the number of women enrolled in colleges increased during the early 1900s, women's career options were limited. Reform work provided college-educated women with a way to apply their knowledge of medicine, psychology, sociology, and other disciplines. Some women made careers of reform work; others volunteered their time through associations such as the General Federation of Women's Clubs, the Women's Trade Union League, and the National Association of Colored Women.

■■ **Not only did reform work provide women with a way to influence social change, it was one of the few career opportunities open to college-educated women.**

ℐNSPIRATION FOR REFORM

Progressive journalists helped spread the reform message. Newly founded mass-circulation magazines like *McClure's, Munsey's,* and *Cosmopolitan* filled their pages with stories that explored corruption in politics and business as well as such social problems as slums and child labor.

The progressive journalists were relentless in their assaults on social evils, leading Theodore Roosevelt to complain: "Men with a muck-rake are often indispensable to the well-being of society, but only if they know when to stop raking the muck." The vivid image stuck, and the journalists became known as **muckrakers**—a name they accepted with obvious pride.

McClure's publication of "Tweed Days in St. Louis" by journalists Lincoln Steffens and Claude Wetmore in October 1902 marked the beginning of the muckraking school of journalism. The article exposed the political machine in St. Louis, comparing corrupt city government there with New York City's government under Boss Tweed. *McClure's* went on to publish many articles on political and corporate corruption, poor working conditions, and slum life.

BIO GRAPHY In November 1902, *McClure's* ran the first installment of Ida Tarbell's "History of the Standard Oil Company." Tarbell, the daughter of an independent oil producer, was born in western Pennsylvania in 1857. She grew up admiring the independent oil man "whose ear was attuned to Fortune's call, and who had the daring and the energy to risk everything." Tarbell was deeply angered when John D. Rockefeller's Standard Oil Company began swallowing up independent oil companies. When her father went bankrupt and his partner committed suicide, 15-year-old Tarbell blamed Rockefeller.

In 1876 Tarbell entered Allegheny College, the only female in a freshman class of 40 "hostile or indifferent" males. Soon after graduation she moved to Paris and began her career

▲ *McClure's* featured the work of many prominent authors and journalists, including Rudyard Kipling and Ray Stannard Baker.

Ida Tarbell

▲ Standard Oil's practice of swallowing up independent oil companies is sharply criticized in this editorial cartoon.

as a writer. By the 1890s she was writing a popular biographical series for *McClure's*.

In 1900 the magazine's reform-minded founder, Scotch-Irish immigrant S. S. McClure, assigned her to investigate Standard Oil. "Out with you. Look, see, report," he urged. "Don't do it," warned her father, knowing too well the power of Standard Oil to punish its enemies. But she went ahead, publishing her findings in a series of 18 articles. Month after month she attacked Standard Oil's business practices:

❝ One of the most depressing features . . . is that instead of such methods arousing contempt, they are more or less openly admired. . . . There is no gaming table in the world where loaded dice are tolerated, no athletic field where men must not start fair. Yet Mr. Rockefeller has systematically played with loaded dice. . . . Business played in this way loses all its sportsmanlike qualities. It is fit only for tricksters. ❞

McClure's readers shared Tarbell's outrage, hailing her as "a modern Joan of Arc" and "the Terror of the Trusts." One reader even called her series "the *Uncle Tom's Cabin* of today." Later, Rockefeller biographer Allan Nevins would call it "the most spectacular success of the muckraking school of journalism, and its most enduring achievement."

Meanwhile, muckraking books poured off the presses. In *The Octopus* (1901) Frank Norris exposed the ways in which railroads misused their vast power. Lincoln Steffens continued to document political corruption in urban America in *The Shame of the Cities* (1904). Jack London wrote *The Iron Heel* (1907) to warn that bloody revolution might result if something was not done to curb capitalism's abuses.

Only a few progressives, however, concerned themselves with racial justice. One who did was Ray Stannard Baker. Baker traveled around the nation in 1904, examining the plight of African Americans. He found that African Americans were segregated, routinely robbed of their right to vote, and otherwise discriminated against. Worst of all, lynchings still took place. In *Following the Color Line* (1908), Baker described a lynching in Springfield, Ohio:

❝ The worst feature of all in this Springfield lynching was the apathy of the public. No one really seemed to care. A "nigger" had been hanged: what of it? But the law itself had been lynched. What of that? . . . If ever there was an example of good citizenship lying flat on its back . . . , Springfield furnished an example of that condition. ❞

■■ **Muckrakers exposed political and corporate corruption, difficult working conditions, crowded slums, and racial injustice.**

EXPLORING SOCIAL PROBLEMS

Like the muckraking journalists, novelists and intellectuals explored the darker side of the new industrial order's effect on people's behavior and values. Theodore Dreiser, in novels such as *Sister Carrie* (1900) and *The Financier* (1912),

▲ Slum life was a frequent target of muckrakers. This 1910 photograph shows a Jewish immigrant in the home he has made in a coal cellar.

◀ Jane Addams joined the settlement-house movement in order to provide college-educated women like herself an opportunity to "learn of life from life itself." Her settlement house in Chicago became a model for social reforms in child labor, health care, urban renewal, and public education.

depicted workers brutalized by low wages and business owners driven by greed.

Progressive intellectuals proposed solutions. In *The Promise of American Life* (1909), political theorist Herbert Croly praised Alexander Hamilton's call, over a century earlier, for a strong, activist central government. But instead of promoting the interests of only the business class, as Hamilton had favored, Croly held that the government should promote the welfare of all its citizens by expanding opportunities.

Social thinkers urged citizens to take responsibility as well. Jane Addams, by now well known for her settlement-house work among Chicago's immigrants, argued in *Democracy and Social Ethics* (1902) that democracy meant more than the right to vote. It demanded a society that showed concern for the well-being of everyone:

66 This is the penalty of a democracy—that we are bound to move forward or [slip backward] together. None of us can stand aside; our feet are mired in the same soil, and our lungs breathe the same air. 99

■■ **Progressive writers and intellectuals publicized social problems and offered theories on how to solve them.**

Although progressives like Addams and Croly wanted to change American society, they remained committed to democracy. Most progressives sought reforms of local government, businesses, and city life to ensure that the full promise of democracy became available to all citizens.

SECTION 1 REVIEW

IDENTIFY and explain the significance of the following: progressivism, John Dewey, muckrakers, Lincoln Steffens, Ida Tarbell, S. S. McClure, Ray Stannard Baker, Theodore Dreiser, Herbert Croly, Jane Addams.

1. **MAIN IDEA** In what ways did progressives hope to reform society?

2. **MAIN IDEA** What types of political and social evils did muckrakers expose through their writings?

3. **RECOGNIZING POINTS OF VIEW** Why were middle-class women attracted to the Progressive movement and reform activities?

4. **WRITING TO INFORM** Imagine you are a progressive writer or intellectual in the early 20th century. Write an article for *McClure's* proposing a solution to a social problem of the new industrial order.

5. **COMPARING** In what ways were the goals of Populists and progressives similar?

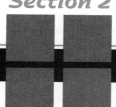

REFORMING THE NEW INDUSTRIAL ORDER

FOCUS

■ **How did progressives try to reform the workplace?**

■ **How did the Supreme Court respond to social legislation?**

■ **Which labor organizations represented workers in the Progressive Era? How did these organizations differ?**

The new industrial order changed American society in deep and disturbing ways. Many workers felt victimized by unhealthful working conditions, poor wages, and long workdays. At times progressive reformers and labor organizations joined forces, but more often they organized their own campaigns to improve conditions for workers.

IWW songbook

REFORMING THE WORKPLACE

As progressives explored working conditions first-hand, they saw men and women laboring long hours, often in dangerous jobs. In 1900 the average laborer worked nearly 10 hours a day, 6 days a

▼ **Child laborers, such as these shown in a textile mill, often worked in unsafe conditions.**

week for about $1.50 a day. Women and children workers were paid even less.

Social reformers had long argued that the conditions women and children faced in the workplace undermined home and family life. Progressives and labor-union activists campaigned for laws prohibiting or limiting child labor and improving conditions for women workers. Florence Kelley was one of the women who worked tirelessly for this cause, helping to persuade the Illinois legislature in 1893 to prohibit child labor and to limit the number of hours women could work. In 1904 she helped organize the National Child Labor Committee, which worked to persuade state legislatures to pass laws against employing young children. By 1912 the committee had helped 39 states pass child labor laws. Some states even limited older children's employment to 8 or 10 hours a day and barred them from working at night or in dangerous occupations. But enforcement of such laws was lax. Many employers, claiming that their business success depended on cheap child labor, simply refused to obey the laws and continued to hire child workers.

Progressives also campaigned for laws that would force factories to limit the long hours employers demanded of their adult workers, men

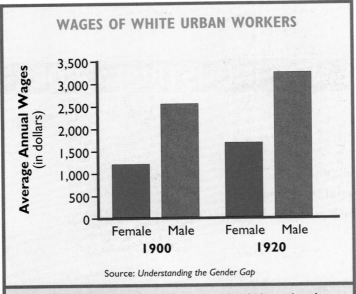

WAGES OF WHITE URBAN WORKERS

Average Annual Wages (in dollars)

Female / Male — **1900**
Female / Male — **1920**

Source: *Understanding the Gender Gap*

WOMEN IN THE WORK FORCE Even though the number of women workers increased in the early 1900s, women continued to earn less than their male counterparts.

? BUILDING GRAPH SKILLS In 1900, about how much more were white male workers earning than white female workers?

and women alike. In 1903, Florence Kelley helped lobby the Oregon legislature to pass a law limiting women laundry workers to 10 hours a day. Earlier, Utah had enacted a law that limited working days in dangerous occupations like mining and smelting to 8 hours. Other states passed similar laws.

Wages were another target for progressives. Of the some 30 million men and 8 million women employed in 1910, about one third lived in poverty. In 1912, in response to progressive agitation, Massachusetts passed the nation's first minimum-wage law—setting base wages for women and children. Gradually, other states followed suit.

But it would not be until 1938 that the nation passed a minimum-wage law for all workers.

Progressives also worked to improve workplace safety. Tragic events in March 1911 catapulted the need for such reforms onto the front pages of the nation's newspapers.

Late in the afternoon on Saturday, March 25, some 500 employees—most of them young Jewish or Italian immigrant women—were completing their six-day workweek at New York City's Triangle Shirtwaist Company. Shortly before quitting time, as they rose from their crowded worktables and started to leave, a fire erupted in a rag bin. Within moments the entire eighth floor of the 10-story building was ablaze. Escape quickly became impossible—there were only two stairways, and most of the exit doors were locked. Leaping from high windows became the last, desperate way out. Some 60 workers took it—to their death.

Through the night, weeping family members wandered among the crushed bodies on the sidewalk, looking for their loved ones. In all, more than 140 people perished in the Triangle fire, victims of a thoroughly unsafe workplace. Rose Schneiderman, a Women's Trade Union League organizer, argued that only a strong working-class movement could bring real change to the workplace. She noted:

> 66 This is not the first time girls have been burned alive in the city. Each week I must learn of the untimely death of one of my sister workers. Every year thousands of us are maimed. The life of men and women is so cheap and property is so sacred. There are so many of us for one job it matters little if 143 of us are burned to death. 99

▼ Rose Schneiderman's impassioned speech (below) after the Triangle Shirtwaist Company's fire (left) marked the beginning of sweeping reforms that improved factory safety regulations.

But it did matter. The public outcry was so great that it pressured lawmakers to pass protective legislation. The New York legislature responded by enacting the nation's strictest fire safety code.

■■ **Progressives sought laws to end child labor, limit working hours, raise wages, and improve safety.**

THE COURT'S RESPONSE

As more states passed laws regulating businesses, owners fought back through the courts—even to the Supreme Court. Owners appealed to the Fourteenth amendment to the Constitution, which prohibits states from depriving any person of "life, liberty, or property, without due process of law." They claimed that laws that limited their businesses deprived them of their "property" unfairly.

The Supreme Court sided with business owners and declared much of the early social legislation unconstitutional. The Court also ruled that some social legislation violated the constitutional "liberty" of workers by denying them **freedom of contract**. In 1905, for example, in *Lochner* v. *New York,* the Court overturned the New York law limiting bakers' workdays to 10 hours, declaring that the law robbed workers of their "liberty of contract." Workers, the Court argued, should be free to accept any conditions of employment that business owners required—including 14- or 16-hour workdays.

The Court did uphold some social legislation, however. In 1908, in *Muller* v. *Oregon,* an employer challenged the 10-hour workday law Florence Kelley had helped push through the Oregon legislature. Kelley and her co-worker, Josephine Goldmark, swung into action to convince the Court to uphold this hard-won law. Goldmark gathered data for the brief, or legal argument, to defend the law. Kelley recruited Goldmark's brother-in-law, the brilliant Boston lawyer Louis D. Brandeis, to argue the case. The "Brandeis Brief" broke new legal ground. In addition to making sound legal points, the brief included extensive evidence of the bad effects that working long hours had on women's health and well-being. This social research not only convinced the Court to uphold the Oregon law but became a model for the defense of other social legislation.

◄ **Josephine Goldmark**

The Granger Collection, New York

► **Louis Brandeis**

■■ **On the grounds of property rights and freedom of contract, the Supreme Court struck down much—but not all—progressive legislation.**

LABOR UNIONS

Progressive reformers were not the only ones fighting for workers' rights. Labor unions continued to battle for better conditions and for the

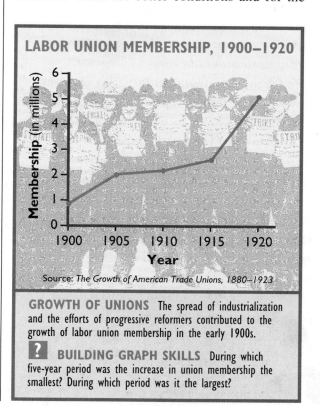

LABOR UNION MEMBERSHIP, 1900–1920

Source: *The Growth of American Trade Unions, 1880–1923*

GROWTH OF UNIONS The spread of industrialization and the efforts of progressive reformers contributed to the growth of labor union membership in the early 1900s.

❓ BUILDING GRAPH SKILLS During which five-year period was the increase in union membership the smallest? During which period was it the largest?

closed shop—a workplace where the employer hires only union members. Most union members favored "working within the system." They wanted to change how workers were treated, but they did not want to threaten capitalism's very existence. Some union members wanted to replace capitalism with an economic system that workers controlled. Many in this group favored **socialism**, the system under which the government or worker cooperatives, not private interests, own factories, utilities, and transportation and communications systems.

The AFL. The major labor organization in these years remained the American Federation of Labor (AFL). The AFL stood firmly for working within the system. Under Samuel Gompers' leadership, AFL membership grew from some 500,000 in 1900 to about 2 million in 1914. But the AFL excluded most unskilled workers—the majority of whom were Eastern European immigrants or African Americans. This left most urban workers without organized support.

THROUGH OTHERS' EYES

*P*rogressive *reformers won shorter workdays, better working conditions, and other improvements for many U.S. workers. But such changes were unknown to the immigrants who crossed the border from Mexico to work the railroads, mines, and fields of the southwestern United States. These immigrant workers experienced both poor working conditions and prejudice. In 1910 the Mexican newspaper* Diario del Hogar *wondered what drove "our workingmen, so attached to the land, to abandon the country [Mexico], even at the risk of the Yankee contempt with which they are treated on the other side of the Bravo [Rio Grande]." Indeed, some Mexican laborers were assaulted or lynched. Venustiano Carranza, Mexico's president from 1917 to 1920, claimed that 114 Mexicans had been murdered across the border.*

◄ **AFL seal, about 1890**

One AFL union that did try to assist unskilled workers was the International Ladies' Garment Workers Union (ILGWU). Established in 1900 in New York City, it sought to unionize workers—mainly Jewish and Italian immigrant women—employed in sewing shops like the Triangle Shirtwaist Company.

In order to organize workers, union leaders generally planned a strike to establish the union's power to negotiate for workers. The International Ladies' Garment Workers Union used this tactic in November 1909 when it staged the "Uprising of the Thirty Thousand." Thousands of women garment workers heeded the union's call and walked off their jobs to demand that their companies recognize the ILGWU as their union.

The strike lasted through the bitter winter. Hard-pressed strikers received generous aid from progressive groups such as the Women's Trade Union League, an organization of well-to-do women who supported the efforts of working women to form unions.

The strike's results were mixed. Most employers agreed to many of the ILGWU's demands. The employers, however, were determined to run **open shops**—or nonunion workplaces. Thus, they refused to recognize the union—the ILGWU's most important demand.

The IWW. While Gompers and his AFL trade unions negotiated with business owners for worker gains, a new union emerged with a different agenda. The Industrial Workers of the World (IWW), founded in Chicago in 1905, opposed capitalism. Its leader, "Big Bill" Haywood, proclaimed IWW's aim. Referring to the Continental Congress that had declared American independence, Haywood asserted:

❝ Fellow workers, this is the continental congress of the working class. We are here to confederate the workers of this country into a working-class movement that shall have for its purpose the emancipation of the working class from the slave bondage of capitalism. ❞

▶ Employers often used armed guards to remove picketing workers. This photograph shows local militiamen aiming their guns at strikers in Lawrence, Massachusetts.

Haywood denounced the AFL's cooperation with business owners and its failure to include unskilled workers. He vowed to organize migrant farm workers, miners, lumber workers, and textile workers to overthrow the capitalist system. In addition to enlisting African American, Hispanic American, and Asian American workers, the IWW actively recruited women workers and the wives of male workers. An IWW newspaper expressed optimism about the role of union women:

66 The advent of women side by side with men in strikes, will soon develop a fighting force that will end capitalism and its horrors in short order. . . . The industrial union movement seeks to develop the fighting quality of both sexes. 99

The Wobblies, as the members of the IWW came to be called, pursued their goals through general strikes, boycotts, and industrial sabotage. Their greatest hour came in 1912 when they led 20,000 workers in a strike against the textile mills of Lawrence, Massachusetts, to protest a 30-cent wage cut. After a bitter and much publicized two-month strike, the mill owners gave in.

Success was short-lived, however. Several later IWW-led strikes failed miserably. Most Americans grew fearful of IWW's aims, and the government cracked down on the union with increasing force. Disagreements among Wobbly leaders also weakened IWW's power. Within a few years the IWW collapsed and eventually faded from power. The AFL trade unions continued to flourish, but the majority of American industrial workers remained outside the union movement.

■■ **The AFL worked within the system and focused on skilled workers, while the IWW opposed capitalism and focused on unskilled workers.**

SECTION 2 REVIEW

IDENTIFY and explain the significance of the following: Florence Kelley, Rose Schneiderman, freedom of contract, Josephine Goldmark, Louis D. Brandeis, closed shop, socialism, Samuel Gompers, open shops, "Big Bill" Haywood.

1. **MAIN IDEA** What kinds of laws to improve the workplace did progressives seek?

2. **MAIN IDEA** What reasons did the Supreme Court use to justify striking down some progressive legislation?

3. **CONTRASTING** How did the goals of the AFL differ from those of the IWW?

4. **WRITING TO DESCRIBE** Imagine you are a worker in New York City's Triangle Shirtwaist Company in March 1911. Write a letter to a friend that describes work conditions before and after the fire.

5. **USING HISTORICAL IMAGINATION** If you were a progressive in the early 1900s, how would you balance the needs of employers with the needs of employees?

REFORMING SOCIETY

F O C U S

■ **What steps did reformers take to try to solve urban problems?**

■ **What actions did African American and Native American progressives take to address discrimination?**

■ **Why can it be said that the Progressive movement had mixed results for immigrants?**

*P*rogressive reformers were convinced that as citizens they were responsible for the well-being of their communities. While most white progressives concentrated on improving housing, public health, and personal morality, African American and Native American progressives organized to fight discrimination. Other progressives, motivated by nativist sentiments, set out to change immigrants' cultures.

Woman doing laundry, about 1910

REFORMING CITY LIFE

By 1920, for the first time in U.S. history, more than 50 percent of Americans lived in cities. As urban populations soared, the ability of cities to provide garbage collection, safe and affordable housing, health care, police and fire protection, and adequate public education was stretched to the breaking point.

Cleaning up the city. What cities needed, some reformers announced, was "municipal housekeeping," a campaign to make the cities a more healthful and livable home for all residents. "The community is one great family," explained Louise DeKoven Bowen, the president of Chicago's Woman's City Club, and "each member of it is bound to help the other." The Woman's City Club, other women's clubs, various men's clubs, and reform organizations enlisted the aid of local governments to clean up the cities. Some organizations took the cleanup campaign literally, working to rid the cities of garbage. Other reform organizations worked for better housing or to improve public education.

Progressive reformers published articles and books documenting urban problems, even assigning blame for them in some cases. For example, Lawrence Veiller (VYL-uhr), a settlement-house worker, lashed out at irresponsible tenement owners "who for the sake of a large profit on their investments sacrifice the health and welfare of countless thousands."

Veiller campaigned tirelessly for improved housing. In 1901 he succeeded in getting the New York State Tenement House bill passed. The law banned construction of dark and airless tenements. New buildings had to be constructed around an open courtyard that would let in light and air. The law also required that new buildings contain one bathroom for each apartment or for every three rooms, rather than one or two for an entire floor, as was the common practice. Housing reformers in other states used the New York law as a model for their own legislative proposals.

In another campaign to make the cities more-healthful places to live, a group of physicians and reform-minded citizens formed the National Tuberculosis Association. The association focused on education and on lobbying the government to fund special hospitals to treat victims of tuberculosis. Thanks in part to this effort, by 1915 the death rate from TB had dropped significantly.

Other reformers campaigned for more city parks and playgrounds to provide safe places for children to play. The playground developed earlier at Jane Addams's Hull House in Chicago served as the model, and by 1920, millions of dollars had been spent establishing playgrounds.

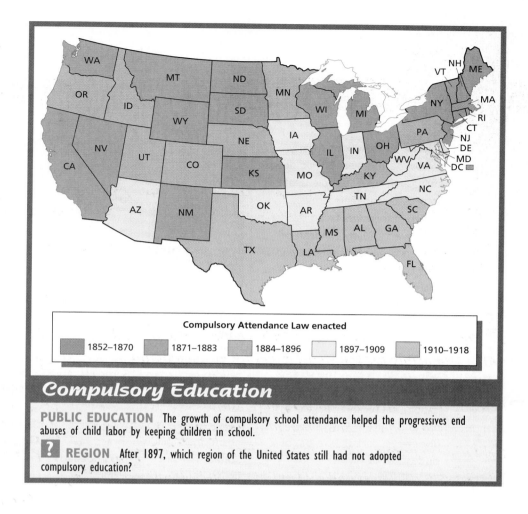

Compulsory Attendance Law enacted

1852–1870	1871–1883	1884–1896	1897–1909	1910–1918

Compulsory Education

PUBLIC EDUCATION The growth of compulsory school attendance helped the progressives end abuses of child labor by keeping children in school.

? REGION After 1897, which region of the United States still had not adopted compulsory education?

City planning. Progressives firmly believed that cleaned-up cities would produce better citizens. Out of this belief grew the city-planning movement. The first National Conference on City Planning was held in 1909. Through wise planning, its members hoped, the spread of slums could be halted and cities could be beautified. Beautiful cities and imposing public architecture, they argued, would instill patriotism among the immigrant population.

In 1909 Daniel Burnham, a leading architect and city planner, produced a magnificent plan for redesigning Chicago, the first comprehensive plan to redesign an American city. The centerpiece of Burnham's vision for Chicago was a soaring city hall that would inspire all residents to be good citizens. "Make no little plans," said Burnham. "They have no magic to stir men's blood."

City-planning commissions in Washington, D.C., Cleveland, and San Francisco also engaged Burnham to

◀ **Daniel Burnham**

◀ **Daniel Burnham's plan for Chicago included wide intersecting streets similar to the ones he saw in Paris.**

In the late 1800s and early 1900s, periodic economic down-swings left many people unable to provide for their families. Urban immigrants faced desperate poverty. Many children of broken families, or whose parents could not provide for them, roamed the streets of New York and other eastern cities.

Many of these children died; others ended up in orphanages. But most found a way to survive on the streets. They shined shoes, sold newspapers, or picked pockets by day and curled up to sleep in doorways, garbage heaps, or outhouses at night.

Progressives and other reformers pitied the abandoned children. But they also feared that without parents to teach them right from wrong, the children posed a danger to society. As the Children's Aid Society warned:

> 66 They will vote—they will have the same rights as we ourselves though they have grown up ignorant of moral principle. . . . Let society beware, when the vicious, reckless multitude of New York boys, swarming now in every foul alley and low street, come to know their power and use it! 99

The founding director of the Children's Aid Society, the minister Charles Loring Brace,

▲ Children whose parents could no longer care for them often were sent to orphanages. Some remained there until they were old enough to take care of themselves; others were placed in homes or ran away.

devised a plan to provide for abandoned children. Brace reasoned that since farmers needed laborers and street urchins needed homes, why not bring these adults and children together? By 1914 the Society had transported some 116,000 children on "orphan trains" from eastern cities to a very different life on farms in New England, the South, and the Midwest.

Photojournalist Jacob Riis, a supporter of the Society, described how "big-hearted farmers" came from miles away to meet the trains and choose from the "little troop[s]" of children. "Night falls," he wrote, "upon a joyous band returning home over the quiet country road, the little stranger snugly stowed among his new friends, one of them already, with home and life before him."

Despite this idealized picture, there were problems. Some critics justifiably charged

that the Society failed to turn away farmers who were looking for no more than cheap labor. Others condemned the lack of adequate follow-up supervision. They argued that such safeguards were necessary to protect children from being taken advantage of economically or abused physically. Still others accused the Society of "dumping" New York's juvenile delinquents. As a result, some states passed laws restricting the placement of children in foster homes across state borders.

Whatever the shortcomings of the program, it provoked a long and fruitful debate on how the nation could provide for abandoned or orphaned children. Before the first orphan train departed in 1854, child-welfare workers saw institutionalization as the only option. By 1900 "placing out"— finding homes for children—had become the preferred solution.

develop grand schemes for their cities. His plans were never fully realized, but some, such as those for Washington, D. C., were a success. Above all, his efforts helped people realize that city planning—parks, building codes, sanitation standards, and zoning—was a necessary function of municipal government.

■■ **Progressives sought to clean up the cities by enlarging the function of government to include housing standards, public health, and city planning.**

URBAN MORAL REFORM

Progressives also wanted to "clean up" what they considered to be immoral behavior. Toward this end, they pushed for prohibition—a ban on the manufacture and sale of alcoholic beverages—and for the closing of the nation's saloons. Reformers believed that prohibition and the elimination of saloons would have several benefits. These reforms would lessen social problems by removing what reformers viewed as two of the chief causes of unemployment: crime and the breakup of families. Such actions would also limit the powers of brewery and liquor interests, groups that exercised considerable influence over the government.

▲ While serving as president of the WCTU, Frances Willard also helped organize the Prohibition party in 1882.

The Anti-Saloon League (ASL) and the **Woman's Christian Temperance Union** (WCTU), an offshoot of the mid-19th-century temperance movement, led the crusade against alcohol. By 1902 the ASL had branches in 39 states with 200 paid staff members. It sent out thousands of volunteer speakers, many of them Protestant ministers, to spread the anti-saloon message in the nation's churches.

Billy Sunday, an ex-ballplayer and a Presbyterian minister, preached that the saloon was "the sum of all villainies," and "the parent of

crimes and the mother of sins." Frances Willard, who presided over the WCTU from 1879 to 1898, described the zeal she felt as she led a prayer meeting in a saloon early in her career:

❝ Kneeling on that sawdust floor, with a group of earnest hearts around me, and behind them, filling every corner and extending out into the street, a crowd of unwashed, unkempt, hard-looking drinking men, I was conscious that perhaps never in my life, save beside my sister Mary's dying bed, had I prayed as truly as I did then. ❞

A brilliant organizer and magnetic public speaker, Willard eventually made the WCTU a powerful national force for temperance, moral purity, and the rights of women.

Drawing on Americans' spirit of patriotic sacrifice, prohibitionists achieved their goal during World War I. The **Eighteenth Amendment**, which Congress passed in 1917 and the states ratified in 1919, barred the manufacture, sale, or importation of alcoholic beverages. The amendment proved unpopular and difficult to enforce, however, and was repealed in 1933 (see Chapter 12).

The growing popularity of the newly invented motion picture gave urban reformers another source of danger to worry about. The first movie to tell a story, *The Great Train Robbery,* was

No. 201
EDISON FILM
COPYRIGHTED 1903
THE GREAT TRAIN
ROBBERY

▼ Movie theaters attracted large crowds by showing action films such as *The Great Train Robbery.* Early cowboy stars gained worldwide fame from these movie westerns.

produced in 1903, and by 1910, millions of Americans were attending the movies each week. In 1916 the *New York Times* could declare that films were the fifth-largest U.S. industry.

To the urban poor a 5- to 10-cent movie ticket provided cheap, readily available entertainment. But many middle-class Americans believed that movies—especially the steamy romances—and movie houses were immoral and sources of temptation, particularly for the young. As one writer of the time reported:

> 66 The pictures thrown upon the luminous curtain of the stage have been declared extremely corrupting to the idle young people lurking in the darkness before it. The darkness itself has been held a condition of inexpressible depravity and a means of allurement to evil. 99

Declaring that moviegoing "softens the mental fibre and saps the character," reformers demanded that motion pictures be censored. Several states and cities set up censorship boards to ban movies they considered immoral. In 1909 the movie industry began to censor itself.

■■ **Reformers sought to improve American morals by working for prohibition and censorship of movies.**

THE LIMITS OF PROGRESSIVISM

For nonwhites the Progressive movement had mixed results. While most progressives were concerned about the plight of the poor, few white progressives devoted very much energy to the problems of discrimination and prejudice against African Americans and American Indians. Some progressives even expressed openly racist sentiments against these groups. Many African Americans and American Indians, however, drew on progressive ideas to develop programs appropriate to their own communities.

W.E.B. Du Bois

BIO GRAPHY

One of the most influential black leaders to emerge during this period was W.E.B. Du Bois (doo BOYS). Born in 1868 in Great Barrington, Massachusetts, Du Bois graduated from Fisk University, a black school in Nashville, Tennessee. He then studied history in Germany and at Harvard University. In 1895 he became the first African American to earn a doctorate from Harvard. Two years later he was hired as a professor of history and economics at Atlanta University, a leading African American college, where he taught until 1910.

By the early 1900s Du Bois was recognized as a brilliant thinker and strong advocate of African American civil rights and culture. He believed that the opportunity for a college education, as well as vocational training, would best ensure progress for African Americans. He also believed that African Americans should be politically active in the struggle for racial equality.

Throughout his life Du Bois maintained a passionate interest in Africa, which he regarded as the spiritual homeland of all blacks. In his influential book *The Souls of Black Folk* (1903), Du Bois eloquently expressed his dual identity as both African and American:

> 66 One feels his two-ness—an American, a Negro, two souls, two thoughts, two un-reconciled strivings, two warring ideals. . . .
> The history of the American Negro is the history of this strife. . . . He would not Africanize America. . . . He would not bleach the Negro soul in a flood of white Americanism. . . . He simply wishes to make it possible for a man to be both a Negro and an American, without being cursed and spit upon. 99

In the 1920s, in an effort to forge greater unity among blacks and to promote pride in their African heritage, Du Bois organized a series of Pan-African congresses, which attracted black leaders from around the world.

During the 1930s and 1940s, Du Bois continued his career as a scholar and political activist. By the 1950s he had embraced socialism—which attracted many prominent American intellectuals, both black and white—for its promise of social justice. In 1961, at age 93, Du Bois joined the Communist party and moved to Ghana, where he died two years later.

The fight for racial justice. In 1909, in an effort to end racial discrimination, Du Bois, along with leading white progressives such as Jane Addams, helped found the **National Association for the Advancement of Colored People** (NAACP). Through its magazine, *The Crisis,* which Du Bois edited, the NAACP publicized cases of racial inequality and called for social reforms that would ensure equal rights for African Americans.

The NAACP also worked through the courts to end restrictions on voting and on other civil rights. In 1915 it won its first major victory in *Guinn* v. *United States.* In this case the Supreme Court outlawed the "grandfather clause." Southern states used this clause to ensure that suffrage requirements designed to keep blacks from voting would not apply to whites. Two years later, NAACP lawyers won *Buchanan* v. *Warley,* which overturned

▶ **Du Bois served as editor of *The Crisis* from 1910 to 1932. This monthly magazine focused on issues important to African Americans.**

a Louisville, Kentucky, law requiring racially segregated housing. As a result, similar laws were struck down across the country. Since then the NAACP has continued to fight for blacks' legal rights.

Another important organization in the struggle for racial justice during this period was the National Urban League. Founded in 1910 by concerned blacks and whites, the League worked to improve job opportunities and housing for urban

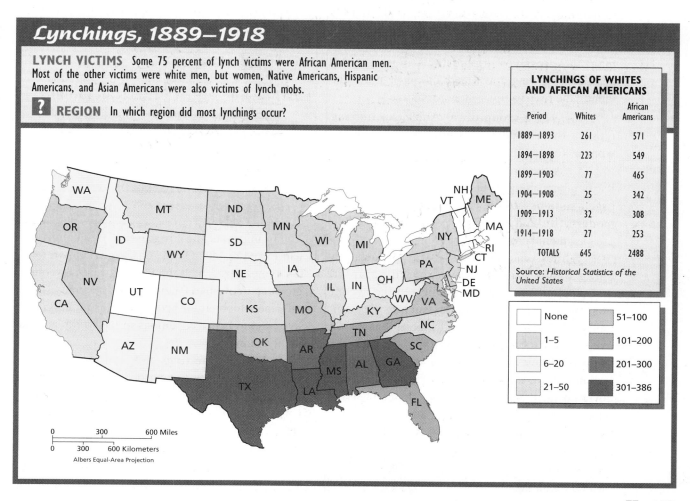

Lynchings, 1889–1918

LYNCH VICTIMS Some 75 percent of lynch victims were African American men. Most of the other victims were white men, but women, Native Americans, Hispanic Americans, and Asian Americans were also victims of lynch mobs.

? REGION In which region did most lynchings occur?

LYNCHINGS OF WHITES AND AFRICAN AMERICANS

Period	Whites	African Americans
1889–1893	261	571
1894–1898	223	549
1899–1903	77	465
1904–1908	25	342
1909–1913	32	308
1914–1918	27	253
TOTALS	645	2488

Source: *Historical Statistics of the United States*

Legend:
- None
- 1–5
- 6–20
- 21–50
- 51–100
- 101–200
- 201–300
- 301–386

0   300   600 Miles
0   300   600 Kilometers
Albers Equal-Area Projection

blacks. One of its chief goals was to help African American migrants from the South adjust to life in northern cities. Today the National Urban League carries on its efforts to end racial discrimination and to aid the disadvantaged.

The NAACP and the National Urban League made possible some important gains for black citizens. Nevertheless, most African Americans still faced discrimination and denial of equal rights. The long struggle to eliminate racism continued.

■■ Black leaders and organizations such as the NAACP and the National Urban League fought for racial justice. But racism continued to haunt American life.

American Indian progressives. Most Indian rights advocates initially supported the Dawes Act of 1887 (see Chapter 5), which encouraged American Indians to abandon reservation life and become private landowners. By the early 20th century, however, it was clear that this policy had led many Indians to lose their property to land speculators and fall deeper into poverty. Thus, many progressives argued for a more gradual approach: slowing down land allotment and maintaining the reservation system for a time.

In 1911 a group of 50 American Indians, most of them middle-class professional men and women, formed the **Society of American Indians** to address the problems facing Indians. One of its members, Seneca historian Arthur C. Parker, urged Indians "to strike out into the duties of modern life and . . . find every right that had escaped them before."

While some members supported strengthening tribal values, most favored complete assimilation. The Society publicized the accomplishments of famous Indians such as Olympic gold medalist Jim Thorpe and lobbied against the use of such derogatory terms as "buck" and "squaw." They also discussed ways to improve Indian health, education, civil rights, and local government. But the Society's moderate positions on most issues led to disputes among members, thus weakening the organization.

One member, Dr. Carlos Montezuma, a Yavapai-Apache, urged the Society to criticize the Bureau of Indian Affairs for mismanaging

▲ As a founder of the Society of American Indians, Gertrude S. Bonnin fought to protect Indians in Oklahoma from exploitation. There, land speculators used every possible tactic to secure oil leases to valuable Indian property.

reservations. Most Society members refused to take such a strong antigovernment stand, and the group's influence dwindled after 1923. While the Society did not last long, it provided a forum for Indian leaders and a basis for later attempts to improve conditions for Indians.

■■ The Society of American Indians worked to improve the image of American Indians and to solve the problems they faced.

IMMIGRANTS AND ASSIMILATION

For immigrants the Progressive movement also had mixed results. On the one hand, many reformers sympathized with the plight of the newcomers crowded into urban factories and tenements. These reformers lobbied for laws to improve immigrants' lives and to better conditions in the workplace and in city slums.

At the same time, progressives criticized immigrants, accusing them of immoral behavior— of drinking, gambling, and other vices. They also denounced immigrant support for big-city political machines. As a result, some native-born Americans with progressive ideals also favored restricting immigration. Madison Grant was a case in point. In 1916 Grant, a prominent New Yorker, published

The Passing of the Great Race. In this book he expressed racist opinions about African Americans, Jews, and immigrants from southern and eastern Europe. Yet Grant was also a progressive who supported urban planning and other reforms.

Many progressives believed immigrants should be "Americanized" as quickly as possible. Americanizing, though, often meant trying to reshape them in the mold of the native-born Protestant majority. Russian immigrant Eugene Lyons described the effects of this process in *Assignment in Utopia*:

> 66 We sensed a disrespect for the alien traditions in our homes and came unconsciously to resent and despise those traditions . . . because they seemed [impossible] barriers between ourselves and the adopted land. 99

▲ In 1890 Arnold Genthe photographed this Chinese immigrant family on an outing in San Francisco.

The Granger Collection, New York

Not all progressives viewed immigrants with suspicion, however. Some, like Jane Addams, welcomed the diverse culture that immigrant groups were helping to create. The philosopher Horace Kallen in his 1924 book on culture and democracy also envisioned a nation that would be home to a number of distinctive cultures.

In addition, the immigrant poor and the political bosses who represented them supported middle-class progressives when they fought for practical reforms such as worker protection and public-health programs. On such issues the big-city political machines sometimes played a key role. For example, a New York State legislative committee set up to investigate factory conditions after the Triangle fire won strong backing from New York City's immigrant-based democratic machine.

■■ **Immigrants supported progressive reformers on practical health and welfare issues.**

SECTION 3 REVIEW

IDENTIFY and explain the significance of the following: Lawrence Veiller, Woman's Christian Temperance Union, Frances Willard, Eighteenth Amendment, W.E.B. Du Bois, National Association for the Advancement of Colored People, Society of American Indians.

1. **MAIN IDEA** What approach did progressives use to clean up American cities?

2. **MAIN IDEA** How did reformers attempt to improve American morality?

3. **MAIN IDEA** How did African Americans and Native Americans attempt to fight racism and discrimination?

4. **WRITING TO EXPLAIN** Imagine you are an immigrant. Write a brief pamphlet for other immigrants that attempts to explain why you do or do not support the Progressive movement.

5. **ANALYZING** Why did progressives support prohibition and the elimination of saloons?

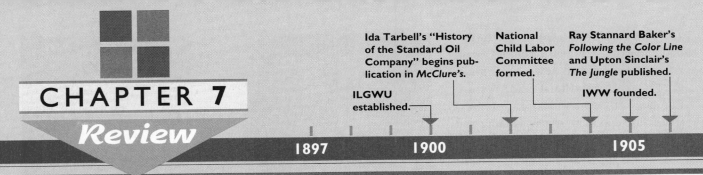

CHAPTER 7
Review

Ida Tarbell's "History of the Standard Oil Company" begins publication in *McClure's*.

National Child Labor Committee formed.

Ray Stannard Baker's *Following the Color Line* and Upton Sinclair's *The Jungle* published.

ILGWU established.

IWW founded.

1897   **1900**   **1905**

WRITING A SUMMARY

Using the essential points of the chapter as a guide, write a summary of the chapter.

REVIEWING CHRONOLOGY

Number your paper 1 to 5. Study the time line above, and list the following events in the order in which they happened by writing the first next to 1, the second next to 2, and so on. Then complete the activity below.

1. Eighteenth Amendment ratified.
2. IWW founded.
3. Massachusetts passes minimum-wage law.
4. NAACP founded.
5. National Child Labor Committee formed.

Evaluating What effect did the Triangle Shirtwaist Company fire have on improving workplace safety?

IDENTIFYING PEOPLE AND IDEAS

Explain the historical significance of each of the following people or terms.

1. progressivism
2. Josephine Goldmark
3. muckrakers
4. Florence Kelley
5. freedom of contract
6. Daniel Burnham
7. socialism
8. Lawrence Veiller
9. Frances Willard
10. Society of American Indians
11. Lincoln Steffens

UNDERSTANDING MAIN IDEAS

1. In what ways did women work for progressive goals? Why were they so active in the Progressive movement?
2. What roles did muckrakers, writers, and intellectuals play in the reform movement?
3. Which labor issues did reformers hope to remedy through legislation?
4. What actions did progressive reformers take to improve conditions in cities?
5. What steps did African American and Native American progressives take to address the problems facing their communities?

REVIEWING THEMES

1. **Economic Development** Why did states pass laws to protect workers' rights?
2. **Democratic Values** How did progressives propose to extend opportunities to all citizens? Were they successful in these efforts? Why or why not?
3. **Constitutional Heritage** How did progressives help win passage of the Eighteenth Amendment?

THINKING CRITICALLY

1. **Analyzing** How did industrialization influence progressive reform efforts?
2. **Hypothesizing** How might the course of reform have been different if the Supreme Court had supported more early social legislation?
3. **Contrasting** How did the AFL and the IWW differ in their views on the scope and nature of labor reform?

STRATEGY FOR SUCCESS

Review the Skills Handbook entry on Reading Charts and Graphs beginning on page 756. Study the two graphs below. This information was compiled as an average for all industries in the period from 1900 to 1910. What conclusions can you draw from the graph data about the impact of progressivism?

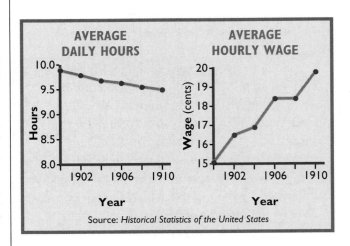

AVERAGE DAILY HOURS

AVERAGE HOURLY WAGE

Hours: 8.0, 8.5, 9.0, 9.5, 10.0

Wage (cents): 15, 16, 17, 18, 19, 20

Year: 1902, 1906, 1910

Source: *Historical Statistics of the United States*

First National Conference on City Planning held. NAACP founded.	**National Urban League founded.**	**Society of American Indians formed.**	**Massachusetts passes minimum-wage law. IWW wins textile workers' strike.**	**Supreme Court out-laws "grandfather clause" in *Guinn* v. *United States*.**	**Eighteenth Amendment ratified.**

1910　　　　　**1915**　　　　　**1920**

WRITING ABOUT HISTORY

Writing to Persuade Imagine you are the young Boston lawyer Louis D. Brandeis. Write a closing argument attempting to convince the Supreme Court to uphold laws that guarantee workers' rights. Include specific examples of working conditions to support your arguments.

USING PRIMARY SOURCES

In 1905 W.E.B. Du Bois wrote to an African American student who was discouraged about the career opportunities that would be available to her. Read the following excerpt from his letter and write a summary of his advice to her.

> ❝ *I have heard that you are a young woman of some ability but that you are neglecting your school work because you have become hopeless of trying to do anything in the world. I am very sorry for this. . . .*
>
> *There are in the U.S. today tens of thousands of colored girls who would be happy beyond measure to have the chance of educating themselves that you are neglecting. If you train yourself as you easily can, there are wonderful chances of usefulness before you: you can join the ranks of 15,000 Negro women teachers, of hundreds of nurses and physicians, of the growing number of clerks and stenographers. . . . Ignorance is a cure for nothing. Get the very best training possible & the doors of opportunity will fly open before you as they are flying before thousands of your fellows. On the other hand every time a colored person neglects an opportunity, it makes it more difficult for others of the race to get such an opportunity. Do you want to cut off the chances of the boys and girls of tomorrow?* ❞

LINKING HISTORY AND GEOGRAPHY

Review the map on compulsory education on page 179. Note that most states adopted compulsory attendance laws for school-aged children during the 19th century, but 19 states did not do so until after 1896. Where are most of these 19 states located? Drawing on what you have learned in previous chapters, what factors might help explain the link between geographic region and the timing of passage of compulsory attendance laws for school-aged children?

BUILDING YOUR PORTFOLIO

Complete the following projects independently or cooperatively.

1. **REFORM** Imagine you are a progressive reformer in the early 1900s. Write an editorial for *McClure's, Cosmopolitan,* or another progressive magazine that addresses an urban problem in government, business, the workplace, or the community. Be sure that your editorial suggests a possible solution to the problem. Editorials might examine political machines, corporate abuses, poor working conditions, or public-health concerns.

2. **DEMOCRATIC RIGHTS** Imagine you are a progressive reformer working to promote women's rights. Prepare a speech on women's rights to deliver at an Independence Day celebration. Be sure that the speech outlines the various problems and concerns faced by women in the early 1900s and indicates how progressive reformers intend to address these problems and concerns.

THE PROGRESSIVE PRESIDENTS

FOCUS

UNDERSTANDING THE MAIN IDEA

Many progressives sought to extend their reform efforts to government itself. They wanted to take power away from corrupt political machines and mobilize the power of the government to improve American life. On the national level, presidents Theodore Roosevelt, William Howard Taft, and Woodrow Wilson tried in varying degrees to implement the progressive reform agenda.

THEMES

■ **DEMOCRATIC VALUES** What are some ways in which government can restore political power to the people?

■ **ECONOMIC DEVELOP- MENT** How can government regulate business practices without discouraging free enterprise?

■ **CONSTITUTIONAL HERITAGE** How might people use constitutional change to reform politics and society?

1901	1906	1910	1912	1914	1920
William McKinley assassinated.	**Pure Food and Drug Act passed.**	**Mann-Elkins Act passed.**	**Progressive party formed.**	**Federal Trade Commission created.**	**Nineteenth Amendment ratified.**

Various efforts to reform society had occupied American women and men throughout the 19th century. Reformers had campaigned to end slavery, to secure women's rights, and to correct the problems caused by industrialization and urbanization. Similar new efforts at reform engaged many middle-class Americans early in the 20th century.

Suffrage rally, 1912

On the morning of May 6, 1895, two progressive reporters, Jacob Riis and Lincoln Steffens, waited eagerly outside New York City police headquarters. The new head of the city's four-member police commission, Theodore Roosevelt, was due to arrive any minute. The reporters eagerly wished to find out Roosevelt's plans for reforming New York's notoriously corrupt police department.

Riis and Roosevelt were already friends and political allies. Five years before, Riis had gained national attention for his book *How the Other Half Lives,* in which he documented the grim reality of slum life in New York City. Roosevelt wrote to Riis, requesting a meeting, saying, "I have read your book, and I have come to help."

Now Roosevelt would have the chance to reform the nation's largest police force. Arriving at police headquarters, he called the two reporters into his office, leaving his fellow commissioners outside. Motioning Riis and Steffens to sit down, he said, "Now then, what'll we do?" As Steffens later recalled, "It was just as if we three were the Police Board." Within days Roosevelt had fired the police chief and had begun to clean up the department. By the end of the summer, fellow commissioner Avery Andrews noted, "The whole country . . . was talking about Theodore Roosevelt."

Six years later, Roosevelt was president of the United States. He brought to the White House the same boundless energy and progressive spirit he had demonstrated as police commissioner. Under Roosevelt's leadership progressivism moved from state and local politics into the national arena.

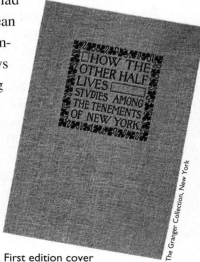

First edition cover of Riis's book

REFORMING GOVERNMENT

FOCUS

■ **What forms did government corruption take?**

■ **What election reforms did progressives support to make government more democratic?**

■ **What reforms were enacted in city and state governments during the Progressive Era?**

New York political boss Charles Murphy voting, 1916

Progressives did not limit their reform efforts to social ills. They also tackled the task of curbing the political power of the privileged few and removing the corrupt political machines that served them. Toward this end, progressives sought changes in the electoral process that would restore political power to the people.

GOVERNMENT CORRUPTION

Theodore Roosevelt and other progressive reformers found corruption at all levels of government, from city hall to Washington, D.C. As Lincoln Steffens so graphically reported in *The Shame of the Cities,* urban political machines demanded bribes from anyone wanting to do business with city government.

In Philadelphia, for instance, in order to secure jobs teachers had to pay the political machine $120 of the first $141 they earned. In Pittsburgh, public jobs went to contractors who paid bribes. Of course, they were allowed to pad their bills to make up the losses. One Pittsburgh political boss even opened his own paving firm so that he could take the lion's share of contracts himself—at inflated prices.

Government corruption did not stop at the city level. City machines were often linked to Democratic or Republican state machines. The state machines catered to "special interests," making deals with the railroads, the lumber industry, or anyone else who wanted tax breaks or other favors

from state legislatures. In return, the machines expected generous gifts, often in the form of "campaign contributions."

At the federal level some U.S. senators, who were often put in power by state machines, accepted bribes to vote the way corporations wished. In 1906 the progressive writer David Graham Phillips began

▲ **This 1926 cartoon, entitled *The National Gesture,* satirizes the widespread practice of receiving bribes among government officials.**

publishing articles that described how special interests influenced American politics. In "The Treason of the Senate," he wrote:

> 66 The greatest single hold of "the interests" is the fact that they are the "campaign contributors." ... Who pays the big election expenses of your congressman, of the men you send to the legislature to elect senators? Do you imagine those who foot those huge bills are fools? Don't you know that they make sure of getting their money back, with interest? 99

■■ Corrupt political bosses and machines accepted bribes from special interests in return for government favors.

ELECTION REFORMS

Government corruption outraged reformers. To restore honest government, they demanded, "Give the government back to the people!" Only when government heeded the public's voice, they believed, could the problems of American life be remedied.

One way progressives sought to break the powers of the bosses and the special interests was to reform the election process. First, they wanted to take the job of choosing candidates for office away from the machines. Therefore, progressives pushed for the **direct primary**—a nominating election in which voters choose the candidates who will later run in a general election. Wisconsin adopted the direct primary in 1903, and by 1916 most other states had followed suit.

Next, progressives proposed to change the method of electing U.S. senators. At the time, the U.S. Constitution mandated that state legislatures elect senators. To progressives, this law made it easy for the bosses to control government. By 1912 the progressive tide had grown strong enough to pass the **Seventeenth Amendment**, which was ratified the next year. The amendment authorized voters to elect their senators directly.

As another step toward more democratic government, the progressives sought to reform the voting process. At the time, each political party

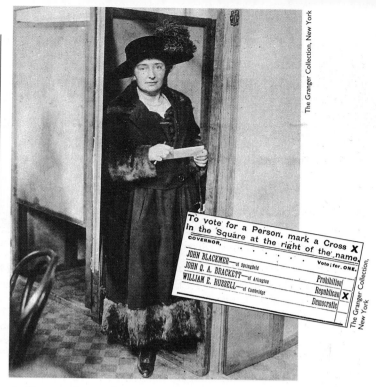

The Granger Collection, New York

The Granger Collection, New York

▲ Progressives reformed the voting process by eliminating colored ballots. With the secret ballot, people could cast their vote without revealing their party preference.

printed its own ballot in a distinctive color. On Election Day the colored ballots made it easy to see how people voted. Without secrecy, voters could be pressured to support certain candidates. To lessen this threat, progressives proposed using the secret ballot. Developed in Australia, the ballot lists all candidates on a single sheet of paper and is printed at public expense. By 1910 most states had switched to the secret ballot.

Finally, progressives urged states to adopt three other election reforms: initiative, referendum, and recall. The **initiative** gives voters the power to initiate, or introduce, legislation. If a certain percentage of voters in a state (usually 5 to 15 percent) petition their legislature to enact a measure, the legislature has to consider it. The **referendum** is a companion to the initiative. By securing a specified number of signatures on a petition, voters can compel the legislature to place a measure on the ballot. The **recall** enables voters to remove an elected official from office by calling for a new election.

■■ Progressives supported the direct primary, the direct election of U.S. senators, the secret ballot, and the initiative, referendum, and recall.

REFORMING CITY GOVERNMENT

Efforts to reform government were not motivated solely by a desire for more democracy. Businesspeople supported reform because the costs of political corruption had become too great. John Patterson of the National Cash Register Company argued that individuals "skilled in business management and social service" should run "municipal affairs on a strict business basis." Many agreed. As a result, good-government campaigns put a large number of reform mayors into office. Two of the most successful were elected in Ohio: Samuel M. Jones and Tom Johnson. Both were self-made men who had amassed their fortunes early and then in mid-life had traded business for politics.

Samuel M. "Golden Rule" Jones got his nickname from his belief in the biblical Golden Rule—"Do unto others as you would have them do unto you." Seeking to apply this principle to government, Jones successfully ran for mayor of Toledo in 1897. Over the next seven years he overhauled the police force, improved municipal services, set a minimum wage for city workers, and opened kindergartens for children.

During this same period, Tom Johnson served as Cleveland's mayor. A former streetcar magnate, he knew personally how closely business interests were tied to political bosses, and he worked to sever those ties. His success led writer Lincoln Steffens to call Johnson "the best mayor of the best governed city in the United States."

▶ Samuel M. Jones pushed through so many reforms that his party refused to renominate him for mayor in 1899. He ran as an independent, however, and defeated both of his opponents. The photograph above shows a kindergarten in Toledo, Ohio, in the early 1900s.

A few charismatic mayors alone, however, could not conquer entrenched corruption. Many reformers came to believe that only a change in the structure of city government could break the political machines. The typical city government of the time consisted of a mayor and a city council made up of aldermen. Each alderman was the elected leader of one of the wards into which a city was divided. Under this system a political machine could easily elect its own people.

Oddly enough, it was a hurricane that struck Galveston, Texas in 1900—killing some 6,000 people and destroying the city—that produced an alternative to this system. The city's government could not cope with the emergency, so the state legislature named a five-person city commission to

▶ The disastrous hurricane that struck Galveston, Texas, in 1900 led to a new structure of government.

rebuild the area. The commissioners were experts in their fields, not party loyalists, and citizens praised the commission as more honest and efficient than the previous city government. By 1913, city commissions ran more than 350 U.S. cities.

The desire for increased government efficiency also gave rise to city managers. These were expert administrators hired to run cities as they might run a business. National Cash Register's John Patterson pushed for a city-manager government in Dayton, Ohio, after a flood devastated the city in 1913.

Corporate leaders like Patterson claimed that city managers and city commissions would get politics out of city government. In fact, these reforms often increased the political clout of business leaders and reduced the power of the poor.

■■ **Many American cities elected reform mayors, formed city commissions, and hired city managers to increase government efficiency.**

REFORMING STATE GOVERNMENT

The spirit of reform also affected many state governments. In Wisconsin, Governor Robert M. "Fighting Bob" La Follette instituted reforms that turned Wisconsin into what Theodore Roosevelt would call "the laboratory of democracy."

 Born in June 1855 in Primrose, Wisconsin, La Follette worked his way through college and law school. Although a loyal Republican, he found himself at odds with

Wisconsin's Republican machine, which railroad and lumber interests dominated. After serving as a county district attorney and as a U.S. congressman in the late 1800s, he signaled his break with the party machine by refusing a bribe by a party boss.

La Follette emerged early in the progressive movement as one of its most energetic leaders. Elected governor in 1900, he vigorously backed a reform program—soon known as the **Wisconsin Idea**—that became a model for other states. First, La Follette brought the direct primary to Wisconsin. He then prodded the state legislature to increase taxes on the railroads and the public utilities—gas, electric, and streetcar companies—and to create commissions to regulate these companies in the public interest. La Follette also got laws passed to curb excessive lobbying and backed labor legislation, the conservation of Wisconsin's natural resources, and other social legislation. In 1905 the Wisconsin legislature elected La Follette to the U.S. Senate, where he battled for reform until his death in 1925.

Robert M. La Follette

■■ **La Follette's Wisconsin Idea provided a model for reforming local and state government and regulating big business.**

SECTION 1 REVIEW

IDENTIFY and explain the significance of the following: direct primary, Seventeenth Amendment, initiative, referendum, recall, Samuel M. Jones, Tom Johnson, Robert M. La Follette.

LOCATE and explain the importance of the following: Wisconsin.

1. **MAIN IDEA** What measures did progressives suggest to make government more democratic?

2. **MAIN IDEA** How did many U.S. cities try to increase government efficiency and lessen corruption?

3. **GEOGRAPHY: HUMAN-ENVIRONMENT INTERACTION** How did the Galveston hurricane help produce a new political structure for cities?

4. **WRITING TO INFORM** Imagine you are David Graham Phillips. Write an article describing political corruption at the local, state, and federal levels.

5. **ANALYZING** What reforms made up the Wisconsin Idea? Why can it be said that these reforms are examples of the progressive spirit?

ROOSEVELT AND THE SQUARE DEAL

FOCUS

■ **What was the Square Deal?**

■ **How did Theodore Roosevelt fight corruption in business?**

■ **What steps did Roosevelt take to protect the environment?**

Assassination of
President McKinley, 1901

Theodore Roosevelt brought progressivism into the White House. Taking office after the assassination of President William McKinley, Roosevelt was elected in his own right in 1904. During his two terms as president, he promoted the regulation of big business and helped preserve natural resources for future generations.

ROOSEVELT BECOMES PRESIDENT

BIO
GRAPHY

In 1900 President McKinley ran for reelection with Theodore Roosevelt as his running mate. The Democrats again nominated William Jennings Bryan and made free silver their campaign issue. But in 1900 most Americans felt prosperous, and McKinley and Roosevelt sailed to victory. Then on September 6, 1901, anarchist Leon Czolgosz shot McKinley. A week later the president died, and Roosevelt became the nation's chief executive.

Theodore Roosevelt was born in 1858 into a wealthy New York family. A sickly child, he built up his strength through rigorous exercise. From his father, he acquired a love of the outdoors, a strong sense of fair play, and concern for the less fortunate. As a student at Harvard University, he developed a taste for history and politics. After graduating, Roosevelt won election to the New York state legislature, where he served from 1882 to 1884. As a legislator he earned a reputation as a moderate but energetic reformer.

Toward the end of his third term, Roosevelt's wife, Alice Lee,

Theodore Roosevelt

died following childbirth. Deeply saddened, he did not seek reelection. Instead he headed for his ranch in the Dakota Territory. Roosevelt spent much of the next two years ranching and writing history books, including what would become the four-volume *Winning of the West*. The harsh winter of 1885–86, however, forced him out of the cattle business and back to New York. In December 1886 he married childhood friend Edith Kermit Carow.

In the 1890s Roosevelt served in a variety of local, state, and federal positions. Then, during the Spanish-American War in 1898 (see Chapter 9), he helped organize a volunteer cavalry unit—the Rough Riders—and went off to fight in Cuba. He returned a war hero that same year and was elected governor of New York.

As governor, Roosevelt worked to reform government and to regulate big business. Angered by the governor's progressive efforts, conservative Republican party leaders tried to ease Roosevelt out of state office by having him run as vice president on the McKinley ticket in 1900. Alarmed, the conservative senator Mark Hanna warned that there would be "only one life between

THEODORE ROOSEVELT
1858–1919

Theodore Roosevelt relished the limelight. As one of his children remarked, Roosevelt always wanted to be "the bride at every wedding."

This hero of the Rough Riders became a legend in his own time. Roosevelt always lived life to the hilt. "No President has ever enjoyed himself as much as I have enjoyed myself," he claimed. An old friend explained Roosevelt's great love of life: "You must

always remember that the President is about six [years old]."

His energy was legendary. For example, when the French ambassador once visited the White House, he and the president played tennis, jogged, and then worked out. Roosevelt turned to his guest and asked, "What would you like to do now?" "If it's just the same with you, Mr. President," said the ambassador, "I'd like to lie down and die."

Theodore Roosevelt

---

this madman and the Presidency." When Roosevelt moved into the White House a year later, Hanna exclaimed to a colleague, "My God, that . . . cowboy in the White House!"

Teddy, or TR, as he was now commonly called, loved hunting and sports. Only 42 years old, he brought a new style to the presidency. Journalist William Allen White described him as a "rumbling, roaring . . . tornado of a man." His no-nonsense style and toothy grin made him a favorite target of political cartoonists.

THE SQUARE DEAL

Unlike the presidents of the Gilded Age, who generally took a hands-off approach to government, Roosevelt believed that the president should use his office as a "bully pulpit" to speak out on vital issues. Roosevelt brought dynamic leadership to the progressive movement.

Soon after Roosevelt became president, a labor dispute helped define his approach to the office. In 1902 some 150,000 Pennsylvania coal miners struck for higher wages and recognition of the United Mine Workers union. But the mine owners—mostly railroad companies—would not negotiate.

Roosevelt urged the two sides to accept **arbitration**—to let a third party settle the dispute. When the mine owners refused, the president threatened to take over the mines. The mine

owners backed down. The arbitrators gave both the miners and the mine owners part of what they wanted. The compromise was a landmark: For the first time, the federal government had intervened in a strike to protect the interests of the workers and the public. Satisfied, Roosevelt pronounced the compromise a square deal.

The **Square Deal** became Roosevelt's 1904 campaign slogan. He promised to "see to it that every man has a square deal, no less and no more." This pledge summed up Roosevelt's belief in balancing the interests of labor, business, and consumers. Roosevelt's Square Deal called for limiting the power of trusts, promoting public health and safety, and improving working conditions.

The president was so popular with voters that no Republican dared challenge him for the 1904 nomination. In the election, Roosevelt easily defeated his Democratic opponent, Judge Alton Parker of New York.

■■ **Roosevelt's Square Deal pledged fair treatment for business, workers, and the public.**

REGULATING BUSINESS

One of Roosevelt's goals during both terms in office was to regulate large corporations. While he considered big business essential to the nation's growth, he also believed companies should behave responsibly.

"We don't wish to destroy corporations," he said, "but we do wish to make them subserve the public good."

Trustbusting. In 1902 the president put this philosophy into practice. He directed the attorney general to sue the Northern Securities Company, which monopolized railroad shipping in the Northwest. In 1904 the Supreme Court ruled that the monopoly violated the Sherman Antitrust Act and therefore ordered the corporation dissolved. Encouraged by this victory, Roosevelt's administration went on a "trustbusting" campaign, filing 44 suits against business combinations deemed "bad." It was not size that mattered, Roosevelt declared, but whether a trust was good or bad for the public as a whole. As he put it, "We draw the line against misconduct, not against wealth."

The Roosevelt administration also promoted railroad regulation. At the president's urging, Congress passed two laws that turned the Interstate Commerce Commission (ICC) into a significant regulatory agency. The first, the 1903 **Elkins Act,** forbade shippers from accepting rebates (money secretly given back to shippers in return for their business). The second, the 1906 **Hepburn Act,** authorized the ICC to set railroad rates and to regulate other companies engaged in interstate commerce, such as pipelines and ferries.

Protecting the consumer. Roosevelt was also concerned about the food and drug industries. By the early 1900s clear evidence existed that some drug companies, meat packers, and food processors were selling dangerous products. Some drug companies sold ineffective over-the-counter medicines that contained dangerous drugs such as cocaine or morphine. Exposing drug industry abuses, journalist Samuel Hopkins Adams wrote:

66 Gullible America will spend this year some seventy-five millions of dollars in the purchase of patent [over-the-counter]

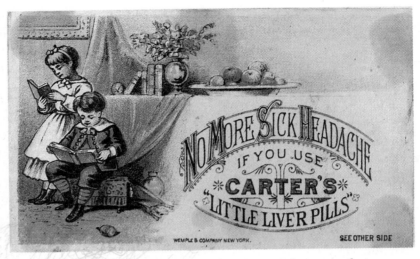

▲ **The Pure Food and Drug Act tried to prevent drug manufacturers from making false or exaggerated claims about their products. This advertisement, for example, promises the user will be spared from headaches after taking Carter's liver pills.**

medicines. . . . It will swallow huge quantities of alcohol, an appalling amount of opiates and narcotics. 99

The drug companies' claims that their "health tonics" could cure everything from baldness to cancer, Adams charged, amounted to fraud.

In response to these abuses and those of the food industry, Roosevelt and Congress enacted two consumer-protection laws in 1906. The **Meat Inspection Act** required government inspection of meat shipped from one state to another. The **Pure Food and Drug Act** forbade the manufacture, sale, or transportation of food and patent medicine containing harmful ingredients. The law also required that containers of food and medicines carry ingredient labels.

■■ **Roosevelt fought corruption in business by breaking up illegal trusts and regulating railroads and the food and drug industries.**

Protecting the environment. The president may have achieved his most enduring legacy in the field of conservation. He recognized that America's natural resources were limited and that the needs of business had always taken precedence over the environment. "In the past, we have admitted the right of the individual to injure the future of the Republic for his own present profit," he charged. "The time has come for a change."

Never content with mere talk, Roosevelt withdrew from sale millions of acres of public land and set aside some 150 million acres as forest reserves. At his urging, Congress created national parks and wildlife sanctuaries and in 1902 passed the **Newlands Reclamation Act**. The act allowed money from the sales of public land to be used for irrigation and **reclamation**—the process of making damaged land productive again. Moreover, a 1908 White House conference on conservation led to the creation of a National Conservation Commission to study natural resource issues and to the establishment of conservation agencies in 41 states.

■■ **Roosevelt saved public lands from destructive development and created wildlife sanctuaries and national parks.**

Then and Now   NATIONAL PARKS

In the late 1800s government, industry, and most Americans still believed there was no end to the nation's natural resources. Between the 1850s and the 1870s alone, millions of acres of public land were sold cheaply or even given away to mining, logging, and railroad companies for development.

However, an increasing number of Americans, including Theodore Roosevelt, believed the country's lands and wildlife were being recklessly destroyed. During his years in office, President Roosevelt fought for programs to protect public land and historic sites.

Many opposed Roosevelt's efforts, believing the economic value of the reserved land outweighed the need to conserve it. But in 1916, largely as a result of Roosevelt's efforts, Congress created the National Park Service to maintain and oversee the country's 10 national parks and 21 national monuments. Today, the National Park Service manages some 355 sites on 80 million acres of land.

Although the number and size of parks have increased tremendously since Roosevelt's day, one problem facing the Park Service remains unchanged. The agency is still caught between those who wish to preserve and expand park land and those who want to use the parks' resources.

▲ **Yellowstone National Park was established in 1872. Shown here is a detail from Thomas Moran's painting of the park, *Grand Canyon of the Yellowstone*.**

Conservationists charge that clear-cutting, strip mining, and overdevelopment are destroying wildlife habitats and old-growth forests. Logging and mining interests counter that the demand for wood and mineral products—not to mention the protection of thousands of industry jobs—requires the use of park resources. Lawmakers are caught in the middle, hoping to please voters on both sides of the issue.

Lawmakers—and Park Service officials—also face the problem of trying to maintain the parks while containing costs. More than 250 million people visit the national parks annually, and some officials argue that the visitors are literally "loving the parks to death." To counteract the strain on park resources, officials have proposed that visitation be limited in certain popular parks.

The future of the national parks is far from settled. But all sides in the debate might well consider Teddy Roosevelt's words: "A nation is obligated to manage its resources for the greatest good of the greatest number over the long run."

National Parks and Conservation

NATIONAL PARK SYSTEM The park system, which includes the national parks, national monuments, and national historic parks, protects the nation's cultural and historic sites as well as its natural wonders.

? PLACE Which state has the greatest land area set aside in national parks?

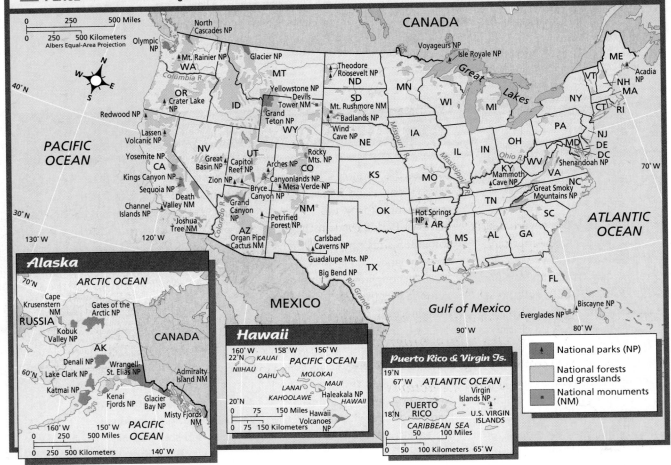

SECTION 2 REVIEW

IDENTIFY and explain the significance of the following: Theodore Roosevelt, arbitration, Square Deal, Elkins Act, Hepburn Act, Meat Inspection Act, Pure Food and Drug Act, Newlands Reclamation Act, reclamation.

1. **MAIN IDEA** What did Roosevelt pledge to accomplish through the Square Deal?

2. **MAIN IDEA** What actions did Roosevelt take against trusts and railroads?

3. **MAIN IDEA** How did the Meat Inspection Act and Pure Food and Drug Act try to protect consumers?

4. **WRITING TO EXPLAIN** Imagine you are a member of the National Conservation Commission. Write a report to the president, evaluating the impact that business has had on natural resources and offering a plan of action for protecting those resources.

5. **TAKING A STAND** Roosevelt's handling of the Pennsylvania coal miners' strike represented a new approach to labor relations. Take a stand either on the side of the miners or the mine owners and explain how that group might feel about Roosevelt's solution.

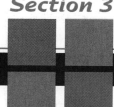

REFORM UNDER TAFT

FOCUS

- **What reforms did President Taft carry out?**
- **Why did Taft lose the progressives' support?**
- **What was the result of the 1912 election?**

*A*lthough a financial panic and sharp depression hit the nation in 1907, President Roosevelt remained popular. The Republican nomination was his for the asking, but having served almost two full terms, he chose not to run again. The Republicans then turned to William Howard Taft, who easily won the 1908 election. In some ways, Taft carried on Roosevelt's reform program. But as his term wore on, progressives became more and more unhappy with his actions.

Taft and Sherman
campaign banner, 1908

TAFT TAKES OFFICE

At the 1908 Republican convention, Roosevelt supported his secretary of war, William Howard Taft, who won the nomination on the first ballot. The Democrats again nominated William Jennings Bryan, whose prolabor platform won the backing of the American Federation of Labor. Despite labor's support, the Democrats lost the election by a wide margin.

From the start it was clear that Taft would be a different sort of president than Roosevelt. Roosevelt enjoyed being in the public eye. Taft was just the opposite. "I don't like politics," he once wrote. "I don't like the limelight."

A smart but cautious man, Taft stressed the limits on his power as president, rather than his potential for leadership. Nevertheless, he chalked up an impressive list of accomplishments. His administration filed 90 antitrust suits, more than twice the number begun under Roosevelt. At Taft's urging, Congress passed the **Mann-Elkins Act** in 1910, extending the regulatory powers of the Interstate Commerce Commission to telephone and telegraph companies.

Taft also advanced the cause of conservation. He added vast areas to the nation's forest reserves. Taft also supported reforms to aid working people. With his approval, Congress created the Department of Labor to enforce labor laws. It also passed mine-safety laws and established an eight-hour workday for employees of companies holding contracts with the federal government.

The Taft administration was partly responsible, too, for the adoption of the **Sixteenth Amendment**. Proposed in 1909 and ratified in 1913, the amendment authorizes a national tax

WILLIAM H. TAFT
1857–1930

in office
1909–1913

William Taft was an unhappy president—at heart a judge, not a politician. He seemed ill suited for public office, dozing off at official dinners or Cabinet meetings, forgetting names, procrastinating, and being tactless at the worst moments. When leaving the White House, he welcomed incoming President Woodrow Wilson by saying, "I'm glad to be going. This is the lonesomest place in the world."

What Taft really wanted was a seat on the U.S. Supreme Court. Taft had had a distinguished legal career, serving as U.S. solicitor general, as a federal judge, as a president of the American Bar Association, and as a law professor at Yale University. In 1921 Taft got his wish—he was appointed chief justice of the Supreme Court. "Presidents come and go," a happy Taft said, "but the Court goes on forever."

based on individual income. Progressives had long supported such a tax as a way to fund needed government programs in a fair manner.

■■ **Taft's administration supported the Mann-Elkins Act, conservation programs, labor reforms, and the Sixteenth Amendment.**

TAFT ANGERS THE PROGRESSIVES

Despite these reforms, Taft lost the support of progressive Republicans. The split between the president and the progressives began in April 1909 with the passage of a tariff bill.

Both Taft and the progressives favored tariff reductions to lower the prices of consumer goods. Some members of Congress, however, wanted high tariffs to protect American industry. They won out when the House sent a low-tariff bill to the Senate, and Nelson Aldrich of Rhode Island turned it into a high-tariff measure.

Taft could have vetoed the bill, now called the Payne-Aldrich Tariff, or he could have pressured Aldrich to change the rates. But Taft lacked the political skill to oppose conservative Republicans in Congress. Despite his misgivings, he signed the bill. To make matters worse, he proceeded to call it the best tariff ever passed. Outraged progressives accused Taft of betraying the reform cause.

Progressives also attacked Taft for sabotaging Roosevelt's conservation program. The dispute revolved around Taft's secretary of the interior, Richard Ballinger, who believed that the Roosevelt administration had exceeded its authority when it stopped the sale of public land. Ballinger approved the sale of a vast tract of coal-rich Alaska timberland. The head of the U.S. Forest Service, Gifford Pinchot (PIN-shoh), an ardent conservationist and Roosevelt's friend, attacked Ballinger for favoring private interests over conservation. Taft warned Pinchot to stop criticizing Ballinger. When Pinchot did not stop, Taft fired him.

For progressives the Ballinger-Pinchot affair signaled Taft's weakness on conservation.

▼ **This cartoon appeared in the *Tacoma News Tribune* in 1909 and satirizes Taft's awkward position in the Ballinger-Pinchot affair.**

Although his administration later restored the Alaska land to the federal forest reserve, the episode hurt the Republicans in the 1910 congressional elections. For the first time in 16 years, the Republicans lost control of the House of Representatives.

■■ **Taft lost progressive support when he signed the Payne-Aldrich Tariff and fired conservationist Gifford Pinchot.**

Taft made one particularly dangerous enemy—Theodore Roosevelt, who broke with Taft over the Pinchot controversy. In the congressional elections of 1910, Roosevelt campaigned for progressive Republicans who opposed Taft and the party's conservative wing. In a speech at Osawatomie (oh-suh-WAHT-uh-mee), Kansas, Roosevelt offered his **New Nationalism**—a bold program of social legislation calling for tough laws to protect workers, ensure public health, and regulate business. He declared:

66 The true friend of property, the true conservative, is he who insists that property shall be the servant and not the master of the commonwealth. . . . The citizens of the United States must effectively control the mighty commercial forces which they have themselves called into being. 99

Government, Roosevelt said, must become the "steward of the public welfare." His call for a more activist federal government represented a far more liberal position than he had taken as president. Delighted, reformers hailed the New Nationalism as a revival of the progressive spirit.

THE REPUBLICAN PARTY DIVIDES

Not long before Roosevelt's speech, a bitter dispute in Congress had further deepened the gulf between Taft and the progressives. In the spring of 1910, progressive Republicans in Congress launched a major attack on Speaker of the House Joseph ("Uncle Joe") Cannon of Illinois, a conservative Republican.

Cannon, a 73-year-old tobacco-chewing poker player, was one of Washington's most powerful politicians. As Speaker he ruled the House with an iron hand, appointing all House committees and naming their chairmen. As head of the powerful Rules Committee, which determined the order of business in the House, Cannon prevented bills he opposed from even reaching the House floor for debate.

Progressives charged that Cannon used his great power to block reform legislation. ("Not one cent for scenery," he had growled in dismissing a call for environmental protection.) In March 1910 Congressman George Norris of Nebraska, a progressive, began an effort to break Cannon's power. Norris proposed that in the future, House members elect the Rules Committee and that the Speaker be excluded from membership.

After a heated debate, Norris's motion passed. A year later, the House also stripped the Speaker of the power to appoint members of the other committees—a major progressive victory. Throughout this bitter dispute, Taft refused to take sides, further alienating progressives.

By 1912 the conservative and the progressive wings of the Republican party were deeply divided. Theodore Roosevelt, by now completely at odds with Taft, decided to run again for the presidency. Borrowing a prizefighting term, he proclaimed: "My hat is in the ring." Roosevelt won almost every Republican state primary, including the one in Taft's own state, Ohio.

At the convention the Taft forces, firmly in control of the party machinery, refused to seat many of Roosevelt's delegates. When Taft won the nomination, Roosevelt's supporters angrily walked out, and held their own convention, adopting a platform based on the New Nationalism and nominating Roosevelt as their presidential candidate. Thus was born the Progressive party, also known as the Bull Moose party after Roosevelt declared that he felt "fit as a bull moose" to run.

▲ **Part of the speech**
Theodore Roosevelt delivered on October 14, 1912, and the eyeglass case he carried are shown here. Notice the bullet holes made during the attempted assassination.

Roosevelt's candidacy, however, almost ended on October 14, 1912, when a deranged man shot him in the chest during a campaign stop. Roosevelt finished his planned speech, despite the bullet lodged in his body. This reckless display of courage reinforced his image as a larger-than-life hero.

■■ **When Roosevelt failed to win the 1912 Republican presidential nomination, he formed the Progressive party.**

A DEMOCRATIC VICTORY IN 1912

Although Roosevelt's campaign continued to pick up steam, the division in the Republican party practically assured a Democratic victory. Roosevelt and Taft were likely to split the Republican vote, while Democrats united behind one candidate. Their choice was Governor Woodrow Wilson of New Jersey, who ran on a platform calling for tariff reduction, banking reform, laws benefiting wage earners and farmers, and stronger antitrust legislation.

Wilson, a native of Virginia and a political newcomer, had long nurtured dreams of high office. In college he had made calling cards proclaiming "Thomas Woodrow Wilson, Senator from Virginia." He eventually became a professor at Princeton University in New Jersey and later served as its president. He was elected governor in 1910. In his short time as governor, he fought the state's Democratic party bosses and pushed through laws regulating business. As an outspoken reformer and eloquent speaker, Wilson was the presidential choice of progressives in the Democratic party.

In the 1912 campaign, Wilson brilliantly captured the nation's reform mood. His program, the **New Freedom**, called for a revival of small business and a return to an America where people were free from the control of big business and government. Wilson asserted:

❝ The only way that government is kept pure is by keeping . . . channels open, so that . . . there will constantly be coming new blood into the veins of the body politic. ❞

RISE OF THE SOCIALIST PARTY						
Number of Socialist Votes, 1900–1920						
Election Year	**1900**	**1904**	**1908**	**1912**	**1916**	**1920**
Presidential	87,814	402,283	420,793	900,672	585,113	919,799
Gubernatorial	0	73,914	13,694	386,828	125,907	230,907
Congressional	8,021	138,201	113,450	1,599,420	770,230	1,128,200

Sources: *Congressional Quarterly's Guide to U.S. Elections* (for gubernatorial and congressional), *Historical Statistics of the United States* (for presidential)

THE SOCIALIST CHALLENGE Dramatic social changes at the turn of the century spurred the popularity of the prolabor, reform-minded Socialist party.

? **BUILDING GRAPH SKILLS** In which year did Socialist candidates obtain the largest number of overall votes?

Although Wilson shared the progressive belief in government as an agent of reform, he believed that making government too strong could stifle individual freedom. He believed that the goal of reform should be to rid the system of corruption so that free competition could flourish, without significantly altering the system itself. In this regard he differed from Roosevelt and especially from another candidate for president, Eugene Debs of the Socialist party. The Socialist party supported radical economic reforms, including public ownership of all major industries. The party had done very well in the 1910 elections.

In Debs, Wilson, and Roosevelt, American voters had a choice of three strong reform-minded candidates. Even Taft supported some reform programs, although he appeared to represent a more conservative viewpoint.

As expected, Wilson won the election, receiving 435 electoral votes to 88 for Roosevelt and 8 for Taft. Debs won over 900,000 popular votes but no electoral votes. Out of more than 15 million votes cast, the three reform candidates received some 11 million. Some 1,200 Socialist candidates, including 79 mayors, were elected to offices across the country, reflecting the desire for new approaches to government. Although Wilson won just six million popular votes, he took office with a strong mandate for reform.

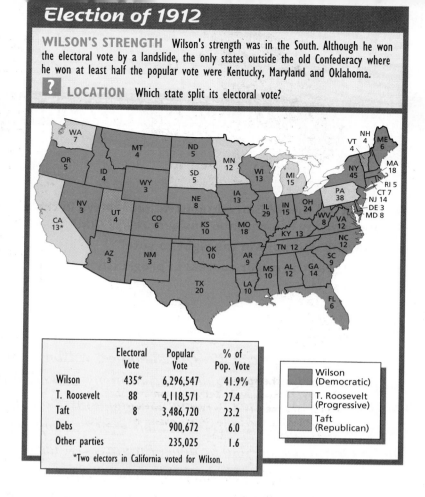

Election of 1912

WILSON'S STRENGTH Wilson's strength was in the South. Although he won the electoral vote by a landslide, the only states outside the old Confederacy where he won at least half the popular vote were Kentucky, Maryland and Oklahoma.

? LOCATION Which state split its electoral vote?

	Electoral Vote	Popular Vote	% of Pop. Vote
Wilson	435*	6,296,547	41.9%
T. Roosevelt	88	4,118,571	27.4
Taft	8	3,486,720	23.2
Debs		900,672	6.0
Other parties		235,025	1.6

*Two electors in California voted for Wilson.

Legend:
- Wilson (Democratic)
- T. Roosevelt (Progressive)
- Taft (Republican)

The split in the Republican vote and the public support for reform enabled Woodrow Wilson to win the 1912 presidential election.

SECTION 3 REVIEW

IDENTIFY and explain the significance of the following: William Howard Taft, Mann-Elkins Act, Sixteenth Amendment, Nelson Aldrich, Richard Ballinger, Gifford Pinchot, New Nationalism, Joseph Cannon, George Norris, Woodrow Wilson, New Freedom, Eugene Debs.

1. **MAIN IDEA** What contributions did the Taft administration make to reform?

2. **MAIN IDEA** What actions caused Taft to lose the support of progressives?

3. **MAIN IDEA** How did the Progressive party help determine the outcome of the 1912 presidential election?

4. **WRITING TO EXPRESS A VIEWPOINT** Imagine you are Teddy Roosevelt. Write a speech explaining your plan of action and why you formed the Progressive party.

5. **DISTINGUISHING FACT FROM OPINION** Supporters of the Progressive party believed that Taft had not lived up to the progressive ideals of the Roosevelt administration. Comparing Taft's reform record to Roosevelt's, was this a fair assessment? Why or why not?

WILSON'S "NEW FREEDOM"

FOCUS

- **What did the Wilson administration achieve in the areas of tariff and banking reforms and business regulation?**
- **How did women win the right to vote?**
- **What was the major success of progressivism?**

*D*uring the 1912 campaign, Woodrow Wilson pledged to restore opportunity in American life. Once in office, Wilson moved to lower tariffs, reform banking, regulate corporations, and aid farmers and wage earners. As Wilson began his second term in office, progressives could claim some success in their efforts to improve American life. Yet much remained to be done. Progressives had barely begun to clean up government and regulate business, women still did not have the right to vote, and the pledge of equal opportunity for all Americans remained unfulfilled.

Suffragist demonstrating in front of the White House, about 1916

REFORM ON MANY FRONTS

On March 4, 1913, President Wilson gave his first inaugural address in which he eloquently summed up the spirit of the progressive reform movement:

66 We have been proud of our industrial achievements, but we have not . . . stopped . . . to count the . . . fearful physical and spiritual cost to the men and women and children upon whom the . . . weight and burden of it all has fallen. . . . This is not a day of triumph; it is a day of dedication. Here muster, not the forces of party, but the forces of humanity. 99

A month later, Wilson presented his legislative agenda. It included tariff and banking reforms and stronger antitrust laws. Opposed by business groups and lobbyists, Wilson used all his skill to rally support for his program, both in Congress and among the American people.

Wilson's first priority was to lower tariffs, long a goal of the Democratic party's southern agrarian wing. Well aware that big business had blocked tariff reduction during Taft's presidency, Wilson mounted a public campaign to undermine the business lobby and overcome Senate opposition. His

◀ **Woodrow Wilson is shown delivering his first inaugural address on March 4, 1913.**

WOODROW WILSON
1856–1924

in office
1913–1921

Woodrow Wilson had a reputation for being very serious and often inflexible. He hated political compromise and at times would oppose legislation he originally proposed if it was amended by someone else. He once told a political associate, "I am sorry for those who disagree with me. . . . Because I know they are wrong."

Yet, despite his public image, Wilson often surprised his close associates with sudden displays of humorous behavior. Once when Wilson was riding in the country with a Secret Service agent, they passed a small boy on the road. "Did you see what that boy did?" Wilson said to the agent, very seriously "He made a face at me." Then the president asked, "Did you see what I did?" "No, Sir," said the agent. With a boyish grin, Wilson replied, "I made a face right back!"

---

strategy worked. In 1913 Congress passed the **Underwood Tariff Act**, which reduced tariffs to their lowest levels in 50 years. To make up for the lost revenue, the bill imposed a graduated income tax, taxing people with high incomes at a higher rate than those with low incomes.

Next on Wilson's agenda was banking. At the time, there was no central fund that banks could borrow from to prevent collapse during financial panics. Thus, when many people withdrew their deposits at the same time, banks commonly failed. Reform was clearly necessary, but Americans disagreed on how to change the banking system. Conservative business groups wanted to give the nation's large private banks more control. In contrast, many Democrats and progressive Republicans wanted the government to run the system.

The **Federal Reserve Act** of 1913, which Wilson helped pass, combined these two views. It created a three-level banking system. At the top was the Federal Reserve Board, a group appointed by the president and charged with running the system. At the second level were 12 Federal Reserve banks, under mixed public and private control. These "bankers' banks" served other banks rather than individuals. At the third level were private banks, which could borrow from the Federal Reserve banks at interest rates set by the Board.

■■ **Wilson worked to secure passage of the Underwood Tariff Act and the Federal Reserve Act.**

WILSON AND BIG BUSINESS

Having achieved important tariff and banking reforms, Wilson turned to business regulation. He wanted to limit the power of monopolies, which he viewed as a threat to small business. Toward this end, he backed passage of the **Clayton Antitrust Act** of 1914. This act clarified and extended the 1890 Sherman Antitrust Act by clearly stating what corporations could not do. For example, companies could not sell goods below cost to drive competitors out of business. They also could not buy competing companies' stock to create a monopoly.

The Wilson administration also backed the creation of the **Federal Trade Commission** (FTC). The FTC, which Congress established in 1914, was

◀ **This 1913 cartoon portrays Wilson's use of antitrust legislation to protect small businesses from the unfair competition of monopolies and other large corporations.**

The progressive reform spirit influenced art as well as economic policies in the early 1900s. Just as industry reformers attacked business trusts, progressive artists tackled the leading American museums' monopoly in determining which paintings and sculptures the public saw.

Resistant to change, the mainstream art community in America was hostile to the "radical" ideas and techniques of the growing modern art movement in Europe. Modernists such as Picasso, Van Gogh, Matisse, and Cézanne offered a new art style, which blurred the lines between reality and fantasy.

Resolved to introduce the American public to modern art, a small group of independent artists formed the Association of American Painters and Sculptors (AAPS) in 1912. The group planned an international exhibition, combing galleries and studios in Munich, Berlin, Paris, and the Hague for works to display. On February 17, 1913, the International Exhibition of Modern Art opened in the 69th Regiment Armory in New York City. The Armory Show presented some 1,300 works by both European and American artists.

Newspaper reporters raved about the show, calling it "an event not to be missed."

▲ The Armory Show introduced contemporary European artists and works of art, such as Marcel Duchamp's *Nude Descending a Staircase,* to a curious, but often puzzled, American public.

Art critics were not so kind. They blasted Van Gogh as "unskilled" and Cézanne as "absolutely without talent." As for Duchamp's *Nude Descending a Staircase,* they described it as "a lot of disused golf clubs and bags" and "an explosion in a shingle factory."

Ironically, the critics' remarks boosted attendance, which exceeded the organizers' wildest dreams. People came primarily to gape. "I remember one woman becoming so hysterical with laughter," an artist recalled, "that she actually rolled over on the floor—I also remember [AAPS president] Arthur B. Davies taking Teddy Roosevelt through the show—Roosevelt waved his arms and stomped through the Galleries pointing at pictures and saying 'That's not art!' 'That's not art!'"

Even if it failed to enchant Americans with modern art, the Armory Show was a huge success in terms of attendance and publicity. Before the show moved to Chicago, AAPS honored its "friends and enemies" in the press with a beefsteak dinner. Glasses were raised; speeches were made; diners sang and danced. One critic summed up the general mood: "It was a good show, but don't do it again."

authorized to investigate corporations and issue "cease and desist orders" to those engaged in unfair or fraudulent practices and to use the courts to enforce its rulings. Among the abuses the FTC targeted were mislabeled products and false claims.

■■ **Wilson backed passage of the Clayton Antitrust Act and creation of the Federal Trade Commission.**

WILSON AND WORKERS

The Wilson administration also supported legislation to aid working people. The **Federal Farm Loan Act** provided low-interest loans to farmers. The Clayton Antitrust Act included a provision that affirmed labor's right to strike so long as property was not irreparably damaged. The **Adamson Act** reduced the workday for railroad workers from 10 to 8 hours, with no cut in pay. This law not only won applause from reformers but avoided a threatened railroad strike. With Wilson's support, Congress also passed the **Federal Workmen's Compensation Act**, which provided benefits to federal workers injured on the job.

The Wilson administration was less successful in the campaign against child labor. For years progressives had wanted to get young children out of the mills, factories, and mines (see Chapter 7). As labor organizer Mother Jones later recalled:

❝ Every day little children came into Union Headquarters, some with their hands off, . . . some with their fingers off at the knuckle. They were stooped little things, round shouldered and skinny. Many were not over ten years of age. ❞

Faced with rising protests against child labor from the National Consumers' League and other groups, Congress passed the **Keating-Owen Child Labor Act** in 1916. This act, which had Wilson's backing, outlawed the interstate sale of products produced by child labor. In 1918, however, the Supreme Court declared the law unconstitutional because it restricted commerce instead of directly outlawing child labor. Another law, passed in 1919, met the same fate. Not until the 1930s would the United States outlaw child labor.

THE STRUGGLE FOR WOMEN'S SUFFRAGE

Another part of the progressive agenda—the campaign for women's suffrage—faced strong opposition. Liquor interests feared that women would vote for prohibition. Businesses feared that the vote would empower women to demand better wages and working conditions. When one state senator expressed the widely held belief that the vote would rob women of their beauty and charm, a suffragist retorted:

❝ We have women working in the foundries. . . . Women in the laundries . . . stand for 13 or 14 hours in the terrible steam and heat with their hands in hot starch. Surely these women won't lose any

WOMEN'S SUFFRAGE

THROUGH OTHERS' EYES

In 1902 the first International Woman Suffrage Conference was held in Washington, D.C. The United States was among the nations represented that had not yet granted women national suffrage. Swedish delegate Emmy Evald remarked that in her homeland women had voted on some level since 1736. She then went on to point out the contradictions in the American situation:

❝ *You can not trust the ballot into the hands of women teachers in the public schools but you give it to men who can not read or write. You can not trust the ballot to women who are controlling millions of [dollars] and helping support the country but you give it to loafers and vagabonds who know nothing, have nothing and represent nothing. You can not trust the ballot in the hands of women who are the wives and daughters of your heroes but you give it to those who are willing to sell it for a glass of beer and you trust it in the hands of anarchists.* ❞

more of their beauty and charm by putting a ballot in a ballot box once a year than they are likely to lose standing in foundries or laundries all year. 🙴

One leading force in the suffrage movement was the National American Woman Suffrage Association, or NAWSA, founded in 1890. Its first two presidents, Elizabeth Cady Stanton and Susan B. Anthony, distrusted party politics because of Republican leaders' failure after the Civil War to press for voting rights for women as well as for African Americans. As a result, they took a nonpartisan, local approach, trying to get state legislatures to grant women the vote. They achieved few successes in their first few years of lobbying, however.

In 1913 Alice Paul, a militant young Quaker suffragist, broke away from NAWSA and formed another organization, the Congressional Union for Woman Suffrage, which in 1916 became the National Woman's party. The party focused on passing an amendment to the Constitution guaranteeing women the right to vote.

Paul, who had studied in England, favored the British suffragists' more political approach. Thus when Wilson and the Democratic party failed to support woman suffrage in the 1916 election, the Woman's party campaigned against them. Wilson won, but narrowly. (See Chapter 10 for more on the election.)

Paul also favored using the attention-getting protest tactics employed by British suffragists. For example, in January 1917, with Wilson reelected, the Woman's party began round-the-clock picketing of the White House in an effort to pressure Wilson to support a suffrage amendment. They held banners asking, "Mr. President, What Will You Do for Woman Suffrage?" and "How Long Must Women Wait for Liberty?" Many were arrested. Some went on hunger strikes in prison.

Meanwhile, the NAWSA, energized by the leadership of the highly skilled organizer Carrie Chapman Catt, continued to follow traditional political means to attain voting rights. Launching what came to be called her "Winning Plan" in 1916, the NAWSA won a string of successes for suffrage at the state level. After the United States entered World War I in 1917, leaders of the movement—along with millions of American women—lent strong support to the war effort. Their patriotism helped weaken opposition to women's suffrage. By 1919 thirty states had granted women full or partial voting rights. Finally, in 1919, the U.S. Congress passed the **Nineteenth Amendment**, granting women full voting rights. It was ratified in 1920.

Carrie Chapman Catt cautioned, however, that the vote was only an "entering wedge." Women still had to

▲ Alice Paul

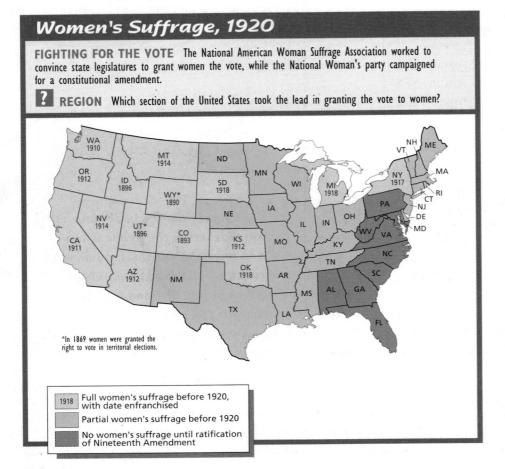

Women's Suffrage, 1920

FIGHTING FOR THE VOTE The National American Woman Suffrage Association worked to convince state legislatures to grant women the vote, while the National Woman's party campaigned for a constitutional amendment.

❓ **REGION** Which section of the United States took the lead in granting the vote to women?

WA 1910
OR 1912
ID 1896
MT 1914
ND
MN
WI
MI 1918
NY 1917
NH
VT
ME
MA
RI
CT
NJ
DE
MD
PA
NV 1914
UT* 1896
WY* 1890
SD 1918
NE
IA
IL
IN
OH
WV
VA
CA 1911
CO 1893
KS 1912
MO
KY
TN
NC
AZ 1912
NM
OK 1918
AR
MS
AL
GA
SC
TX
LA
FL

*In 1869 women were granted the right to vote in territorial elections.

1918	Full women's suffrage before 1920, with date enfranchised
	Partial women's suffrage before 1920
	No women's suffrage until ratification of Nineteenth Amendment

force their way through the "locked door" of political decision making.

■■ **In 1920, with ratification of the Nineteenth Amendment, American women won their long battle for the right to vote.**

Commentary

The Progressive Legacy

Although scholars agree that the progressive movement left a lasting legacy, they often disagree over how to define that legacy. Many scholars have noted that progressivism was primarily supported by fairly conservative, middle-class, white Americans trying to maintain some level of political and economic power. Many of the successes and shortcomings of the movement can be tied to its origins in the white middle class.

Progressivism made great strides in many areas; however, some of the economic and political reforms of the movement failed to bring about the radical changes anticipated. Such policies as the creation of the Federal Reserve System and implementation of a federal income tax did improve the government's ability to regulate the economy and pay for new programs. Yet, many regulations on businesses fell short of reforming the capitalist system; corporations were eventually able to use the regulations to their own advantage. Corporations also benefitted by being able to operate in the more orderly, predictable environment that regulation provided. On the political front, reforms such as

the initiative, referendum, and recall were primarily used on the local level and thus had little impact on broad questions of national public policy.

One of progressivism's most successful elements, the settlement-house movement, improved opportunities for women, brought great urban reform, and eased the plight of European immigrants. However, most settlement-house workers neglected to address the problems of African Americans, many of whom were new migrants from the rural South.

The progressive presidents showed little interest in racial issues. President Wilson was the least sympathetic to African American concerns. During his administration numerous bills designed to institute segregation were submitted to Congress. Although none passed, Wilson issued an executive order segregating eating and restroom facilities for federal employees. Wilson justified this policy by arguing that it prevented friction between white and black workers, but African Americans denounced it as racist.

Despite these shortcomings, however, progressives took real strides toward making the new industrial society more just and orderly. Their efforts to end child labor, to protect workers and consumers, and to promote conservation profoundly influenced the nation. Their greatest legacy, however, was in demonstrating that America's democratic system could respond and adapt to changes in American life.

■■ **Although progressivism fell short of some of its goals and failed to address racism, it made industrial society more just and humane.**

SECTION 4 REVIEW

IDENTIFY and explain the significance of the following: Underwood Tariff Act, Federal Reserve Act, Clayton Antitrust Act, Federal Trade Commission, Federal Farm Loan Act, Adamson Act, Federal Workmen's Compensation Act, Keating-Owen Child Labor Act, Alice Paul, Carrie Chapman Catt, Nineteenth Amendment.

1. **MAIN IDEA** How did Wilson hope to reduce tariffs and reform the banking system?

2. **MAIN IDEA** How did the Wilson administration attempt to regulate business?

3. **MAIN IDEA** What did the passage of the Nineteenth Amendment accomplish?

4. **WRITING TO EVALUATE** From a current perspective, write a paragraph evaluating the legacy of progressivism.

5. **ANALYZING** How successful was Wilson in enlisting the "forces of humanity" to help farmers, railroad and federal workers, and child laborers?

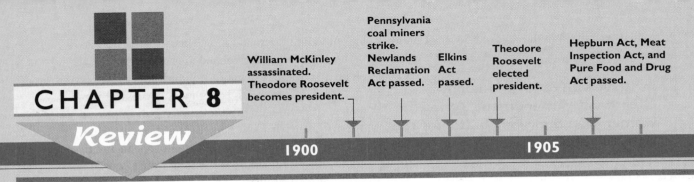

CHAPTER 8
Review

William McKinley assassinated. Theodore Roosevelt becomes president.

Pennsylvania coal miners strike. Newlands Reclamation Act passed.

Elkins Act passed.

Theodore Roosevelt elected president.

Hepburn Act, Meat Inspection Act, and Pure Food and Drug Act passed.

1900   1905

WRITING A SUMMARY

Using the essential points of the chapter as a guide, write a summary of the chapter.

REVIEWING CHRONOLOGY

Number your paper 1 to 5. Study the time line above, and list the following events in the order in which they happened by writing the first next to 1, the second next to 2, and so on. Then complete the activity below.

1. Progressive party formed.
2. Nineteenth Amendment ratified.
3. Pennsylvania coal miners strike.
4. Federal Trade Commission created.
5. William Howard Taft elected president.

Analyzing How did the Sixteenth and Seventeenth amendments promote reform?

IDENTIFYING PEOPLE AND IDEAS

Explain the historical significance of each of the following people or terms.

1. initiative
2. Samuel M. Jones
3. Hepburn Act
4. reclamation
5. Richard Ballinger
6. New Nationalism
7. Joseph Cannon
8. Federal Reserve Act
9. Adamson Act
10. Alice Paul

UNDERSTANDING MAIN IDEAS

1. Why were city commissions effective at achieving efficiency in city government?
2. How did the Wisconsin Idea lay the foundation for further reforms?
3. In what ways were Theodore Roosevelt and William Howard Taft similar in their approaches to reform?
4. Why did Roosevelt challenge Taft in 1912?
5. What were the effects of the Clayton Antitrust Act and the creation of the Federal Trade Commission on the regulation of business?
6. What was the progressive movement's greatest legacy?

REVIEWING THEMES

1. **Democratic Values** How did reformers seek to curb political corruption and to make government more democratic in the early 20th century?
2. **Economic Development** How did President Roosevelt attempt to regulate business without discouraging free enterprise?
3. **Constitutional Heritage** How might reformers have used the Nineteenth Amendment as a means of accomplishing reform in politics and business?

THINKING CRITICALLY

1. **Synthesizing** How did Roosevelt bring dynamic leadership to the progressive movement at the city, state, and national levels?
2. **Evaluating** How did the controversy over tariffs contribute to Taft's defeat in the 1912 election?
3. **Analyzing** What interests worked against the campaign for women's suffrage in the early 20th century?
4. **Hypothesizing** How might life have been different for African Americans if Wilson had pursued a different racial policy?

STRATEGY FOR SUCCESS

Review the Skills Handbook entry on Reading a Time Line on page 751. Then study the time-line entries below, which focus on the years from 1908 to 1912. What cause-and-effect relationship is suggested by the sequence of events listed? How did the events of 1910 relate to those of 1912?

1908   William Howard Taft elected president.

1909   Payne-Aldrich Tariff passed. Taft fires Gifford Pinchot.

1910   Republicans lose control of House of Representatives.

1912   Roosevelt forms Progressive party. Woodrow Wilson elected president.

WRITING ABOUT HISTORY

Writing to Evaluate Write an essay evaluating the progressives' record on racial issues.

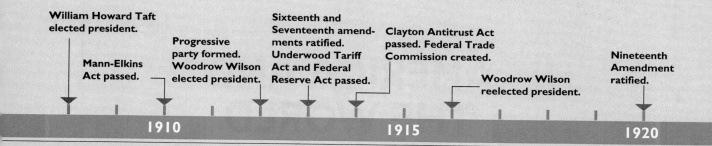

William Howard Taft elected president.

Mann-Elkins Act passed.

Progressive party formed. Woodrow Wilson elected president.

Sixteenth and Seventeenth amendments ratified. Underwood Tariff Act and Federal Reserve Act passed.

Clayton Antitrust Act passed. Federal Trade Commission created.

Woodrow Wilson reelected president.

Nineteenth Amendment ratified.

1910   1915   1920

USING PRIMARY SOURCES

In 1906 Upton Sinclair published *The Jungle,* a biting attack on the industrial practices and unsanitary conditions in the Chicago stockyards. Read the following excerpt, which describes the manufacture and processing of canned goods in "Packingtown" (Chicago). Then, in a paragraph, explain how publication of this book might have influenced the passage of the Meat Inspection Act.

66 *"Deviled ham" . . . was made out of the waste ends of smoked beef that were too small to be sliced by the machines; and also tripe, dyed with chemicals so that it would not show white, and trimmings of hams and corned beef, and potatoes, skins and all. . . . All this ingenious mixture was ground up and flavored with spices to make it taste like something. Anybody who could invent a new imitation had been sure of a fortune, . . . but it was hard to think of anything new in a place where . . . men welcomed tuberculosis in the cattle they were feeding, because it made them fatten more quickly; and where they bought up all the old rancid [stale] butter . . . rechurned it with skim milk, and sold it in bricks in the cities!* 99

Chicago stockyards, 1919

LINKING HISTORY AND GEOGRAPHY

Study the map on page 208. What might explain the link between geographic region and the granting of women's suffrage?

Sample ballot, 1892

BUILDING YOUR PORTFOLIO

Complete the following projects independently or cooperatively.

1. **REFORM** In Chapter 7 you portrayed a progressive reformer addressing a problem in your city. Building on that experience, write a platform for the Progressive party that translates the problems of political machines, women's suffrage, business regulation, and worker protection into specific reforms your party hopes to institute.

2. **DEMOCRATIC RIGHTS** In Chapter 7 you portrayed a progressive reformer preparing a speech on women's rights to deliver at an Independence Day celebration. Building on that experience, imagine you are the editor of a labor union newspaper. Write an editorial indicating why you believe that progressives are not adequately addressing the needs of working-class women.

AMERICA AND THE WORLD

FOCUS

UNDERSTANDING THE MAIN IDEA

In the waning years of the 19th century, the United States established itself as a world power by defeating Spain and acquiring Spain's last colonies in the Western Hemisphere. The progressive presidents asserted a strong foreign policy, acting to promote U.S. economic and security interests in the Pacific, the Caribbean, Asia, and Latin America.

THEMES

■ **GLOBAL RELATIONS** Why might a country acquire overseas colonies? Why might a country resist becoming a colony?

■ **ECONOMIC DEVELOPMENT** How might foreign investors influence a country's economy? What problems might arise from these investments?

■ **DEMOCRATIC VALUES** Does the acquisition of colonies conflict with democratic principles? Why or why not?

1898	1899	1904	1910	1915
▼	▼	▼	▼	▼
Spanish-American War begins.	U.S. annexes Philippines.	Russo-Japanese War begins.	The Mexican Revolution starts.	Wilson sends marines into Haiti.

Battle of Manila Bay

*D*awn was just breaking as the American fleet, its flags flying, steamed across lovely Manila Bay, in the Philippines. It was early morning, May 1, 1898—just 11 days after the United States had declared war on Spain. Commodore George Dewey stood on the bridge of his flagship, *Olympia,* his eyes trained on the Spanish guns aimed at his ships from the shore and from the small Spanish fleet anchored in the harbor.

Sighting the Americans, the Spanish opened fire. Shortly after 5:30 A.M., Commodore Dewey gave an order to his flagship captain: "You may fire when you are ready, Gridley." The boom and flash of naval guns exploded through the bay. Shells crashed into several Spanish vessels, and they erupted into flames.

The Battle of Manila Bay had begun, the first battle of the Spanish-American War. It marked America's emergence on the world stage at the end of the 19th century. Throughout most of the century, Americans had followed George Washington's advice and remained aloof from foreign entanglements. Indeed, as late as 1889, Congressman Henry Cabot Lodge of Massachusetts wrote: "Our relations with foreign nations today fill but a slight place in American politics." But this would soon change as the United States became deeply involved in events abroad, from nearby Cuba and Mexico to distant China.

U.S. soldiers question Filipino women, 1899.

WAR WITH SPAIN

FOCUS

■ **What fueled the quest for overseas territory?**

■ **Why did the United States declare war on Spain?**

■ **What was the outcome of the Spanish-American War for the United States and Spain?**

In the late 1800s the United States emerged as the world's leading industrial producer and agricultural exporter. This economic success encouraged the nation to establish overseas colonies, just as the European powers were doing. The United States hoped colonization would provide new markets for its goods and new sources of raw materials. U.S. involvement in Samoa and a short war with Spain in 1898 increased the American role in the Pacific and the Caribbean.

Recruiter, 1898

THE IMPULSE FOR IMPERIALISM

In March 1889 seven warships—one British, three German, and three American—faced off in the South Pacific harbor of Apia, in present-day Western Samoa. But before a shot could be fired, a typhoon struck, destroying all but the British ship. What brought these three powerful nations to the brink of war? **Imperialism**: the quest for colonial empires.

Between 1876 and 1915, vast areas of Africa, Asia, and Latin America fell under the control of a handful of industrialized nations locked in a race to acquire overseas colonies. Great Britain, the leading imperialist power, had colonies flung so far across the globe that the British could boast, "The sun never sets on the British Empire."

What lay behind this wave of imperialism? The desire for power and prestige played a role, but it was also a matter of economics. Industrial workers, aided by efficient machines and abundant capital, produced far more goods than could be consumed at home. In response, industrialists turned to Africa, Asia, and Latin America for new

◄ **Samoan families lived in grass-thatched huts, such as this one in Pago Pago.**

customers and new sources of raw materials. The telegraph, steamship, and railroad made even the remotest areas potential markets. To protect these new markets from competition, industrialized nations launched a campaign of colonization.

Although American enthusiasm for overseas expansion never matched that of the Europeans, support grew during the late 1800s. Some supporters, like Alfred Thayer Mahan of the U.S. Naval College, argued that overseas territories would make the United States more powerful and provide sites for naval bases and steamship fueling stations from which to conduct trade. Others claimed that the United States had a duty to spread its political system and the Christian religion to other parts of the world. This belief often went hand-in-hand with feelings of racial superiority. In his widely read book *Our Country* (1885), Josiah Strong, a Protestant minister and social reformer, proclaimed that Anglo-Saxons (people of English ancestry) had a special mission:

66 God, with infinite wisdom and skill, is training the Anglo-Saxon race for an hour sure to come in the world's future. . . .

Then this race . . . the representative, let us hope, of the largest liberty, the purest Christianity, the highest civilization . . . will spread itself over the earth. 99

▪▪ The quest for empire was fueled by strategic, economic, and cultural motives.

It was the desire for naval bases and fueling stations, rather than cultural or religious concerns, that led the United States, Great Britain, and Germany to square off in Samoa in 1889. The Samoans realized that this competition put them in grave danger. In 1898 Te'o Tuvale, a government official, warned his fellow Samoans:

66 Be kind and don't start a war in Samoa, because if you do the Three Powers [Britain, Germany, and the United States] will take over the conduct of the country and your orators and Chiefs and things that you have been accustomed to will be of no further use. 99

Te'o Tuvale's prophecy was fulfilled the next year when, in the face of overwhelming European and U.S. military might, Samoans surrendered their government. The United States won control over Eastern Samoa, and Germany was granted control over Western Samoa. Today Western Samoa is independent, while Eastern (or American) Samoa remains a U.S. territory (see map on page 220).

CONFLICT IN CUBA

The Caribbean island of Cuba, just 90 miles from the Florida Keys, provided a testing ground for U.S. imperialism. In the late 1800s Cuba simmered with unrest. Along with its Caribbean neighbor Puerto Rico, it was the last of the Spanish colonies in the Americas. Since 1868, Cubans had launched a series of unsuccessful revolts against Spanish rule. To put down the rebellion, the Spanish government exiled many leaders of the independence movement. Foremost among these exiles was the Cuban poet José Martí, who was forced out of Cuba in 1871 and again in 1879.

From his exile in New York, Martí wrote poems and newspaper articles promoting Cuban independence. He also urged Cuban exiles to mount an invasion of Cuba:

▲ José Martí

66 Let us rise up at once with a final burst of heartfelt energy. . . . Let us rise up for the true republic, those of us who, with our passion for right and our habit of hard work, will know how to preserve it. 99

When Cubans launched another revolt in February 1895, Martí and other exiles joined them. Martí became a martyr for Cuban independence when he was killed a month later in a battle with Spanish soldiers.

In 1896 Spain sent General Valeriano Weyler to put down the uprising. Within days Weyler had imprisoned thousands of farmers in concentration camps to prevent them from supplying the rebels. Over the next two years, starvation and disease claimed the lives of perhaps 200,000 Cubans.

The American press branded Weyler "the Butcher." William Randolph Hearst's *Journal* and Joseph Pulitzer's *World,* two New York City newspapers, outdid each other in publicizing Spanish atrocities. In 1897 Hearst sent artist

Frederic Remington to Cuba to send back drawings that vividly documented Spanish cruelty. Hearst hoped to sell more newspapers, but he also hoped to horrify Americans into agitating for war against Spain.

Finding nothing to draw, Remington reportedly cabled Hearst: "EVERYTHING IS QUIET. THERE IS NO TROUBLE HERE. THERE WILL BE NO WAR. WISH TO RETURN." Hearst was said to have replied: "PLEASE REMAIN. YOU FURNISH THE PICTURES AND I'LL FURNISH THE WAR."

In addition to U.S. horror at Spanish atrocities, threats to U.S. investments in Cuba convinced many that the United States should aid the Cuban rebels. In the face of mounting war fever, President William McKinley, himself a veteran of the Civil War, struggled to remain neutral and to resist committing American troops. "I have been through one war. I have seen the dead piled up, and I do not want to see another," he explained.

But early in 1898, two shattering events forced his hand. First, on February 9 Hearst's *Journal* printed a letter written by Spain's minister to the United States, Enrique Dupuy de Lôme. The letter, which had been intercepted by a Cuban spy and sold to Hearst, ridiculed President McKinley as "weak, and a bidder for the admiration of the crowd."

Americans were outraged at the Spaniard's remarks, which the *Journal* called "the worst insult to the United States in its history." Then on February 15 the American battleship *Maine*—sent to Havana, Cuba, to protect U.S. lives and property—blew up, killing 260 sailors. "DESTRUCTION OF THE WAR SHIP MAINE WAS THE WORK OF AN ENEMY!" screamed the *Journal*'s headline. Though it was later determined that a fire in a coal bin had probably caused

the explosion, many Americans blamed Spain. "Remember the *Maine!* And to hell with Spain!" became a familiar chant.

Spain tried to calm tensions by agreeing to a U.S.–proposed peace plan. But it was too late. On April 11 President McKinley bowed to public pressure and asked Congress to intervene in Cuba "in the name of humanity, in the name of civilization, and in behalf of endangered American interests."

On April 20 Congress recognized Cuban independence and voted to use U.S. military force to help Cuba attain it. Congress also adopted the **Teller Amendment**, which stated that the United States claimed no "sovereignty, jurisdiction, or control" over Cuba. Once Cuba won its independence from Spain, the amendment promised, the United States would "leave the government and control of the Island to its people."

■■ **To protect U.S. investments and to help Cuba overthrow Spanish rule, the United States declared war on Spain in April 1898.**

War with Spain

The first battles of the **Spanish-American War** were not fought in nearby Cuba, but halfway around the world, in the Spanish-held Philippine Islands. Weeks before war was declared, Assistant Secretary of the Navy Theodore Roosevelt had, without authorization, cabled Commodore George Dewey, commander of the U.S. Navy's Asiatic fleet anchored at Hong Kong. Roosevelt ordered Dewey to prepare his ships for offensive action in the Philippines.

On May 1, 1898, less than two weeks after war was declared, Dewey's fleet easily defeated the small Spanish fleet guarding the Philippine city of Manila. In order to capture the city itself, Dewey obtained the support of a rebel army of Filipino patriots led by Emilio Aguinaldo (ahg-ee-NAHL-doh). Filipinos had been fighting for independence from Spain for two years. Now, along with U.S. soldiers, they attacked and captured Manila. Cut off by Commodore Dewey's warships and surrounded by Aguinaldo's forces, Spanish forces in the Philippines surrendered on August 14, 1898.

MAINE EXPLOSION CAUSED BY BOMB OR TORPEDO?

Capt. Sigsbee and Consul-General Lee Are in Doubt---The World Has Sent a Special Tug, With Submarine Divers, to Havana to Find Out---Lee Asks for an Immediate Court of Inquiry---260 Men Dead.

IN A SUPPRESSED DESPATCH TO THE STATE DEPARTMENT, THE CAPTAIN SAYS THE ACCIDENT WAS MADE POSSIBLE BY AN ENEMY.

Dr. E. C. Pendleton, Just Arrived from Havana, Says He Overheard Talk There of a Plot to Blow Up the Ship---Capt. Zalinski, the Dynamite Expert, and Other Experts Report to The World that the Wreck Was Not Accidental---Washington Officials Ready for Vigorous Action if Spanish Responsibility Can Be Shown---Divers to Be Sent Down to Make Careful Examinations.

▲ **The United States found it difficult to maintain its neutrality in the Cuban-Spanish conflict amid the public outrage triggered by sensationalized news reports. This headline appeared in Joseph Pulitzer's *World*.**

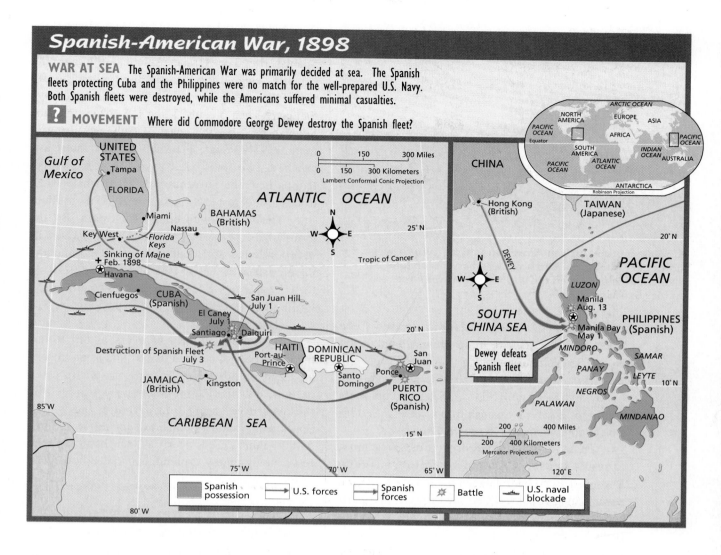

Spanish-American War, 1898

WAR AT SEA The Spanish-American War was primarily decided at sea. The Spanish fleets protecting Cuba and the Philippines were no match for the well-prepared U.S. Navy. Both Spanish fleets were destroyed, while the Americans suffered minimal casualties.

? MOVEMENT Where did Commodore George Dewey destroy the Spanish fleet?

Victory in Cuba would not come quite as easily as it had in the Philippines. With a regular army of only some 28,000 soldiers, the U.S. War Department was unprepared for land battles. Thousands of volunteers raced to enlist, but how could they be trained and equipped overnight? With little training and outfitted in heavy wool uniforms (the only ones that army storehouses could supply), U.S. troops sailed for tropical Cuba in mid-June. For rations, the men were issued canned corned beef that was supposed to keep in any weather. "Well," reported one soldier, "it commenced to explode. We had to throw it all overboard." Another soldier described life once the troops arrived in Cuba:

> 66 Heavy rains pouring down, no tents for cover, . . . standing in trenches in a foot of water and mud, day and night. . . . Ration issue consisting of a slice of sow belly, hardtack, and some grains of coffee. . . . Then came the issue of fleece-lined underwear in a 132 [degree] climate. . . . Then came on malaria. 99

▲ **Emilio Aguinaldo, shown wearing a vest, sat for this photograph with his advisers in 1896.**

▲ Soldiers of the African American 9th and 10th cavalries are shown here during the Battle of Las Guásimas on June 24, 1898. This victory paved the way for American forces to capture Santiago.

The major American land actions in Cuba began on July 1 as U.S. troops mounted an assault on the Spanish stronghold of Santiago. Their aim was to capture the heights above Santiago—El Caney and San Juan Hill—so that they could aim their guns down on Spanish troops. One U.S. division overcame Spanish forces at El Caney.

In what would become the war's most famous battle, Lieutenant Colonel Teddy Roosevelt (who had resigned his naval post) led a cavalry unit of some 1,000 men toward the garrison on San Juan Hill. Composed largely of athletes from eastern colleges, miners, cowboys, Native Americans, ranchers, and would-be adventurers, the unit was known as the Rough Riders.

Since their horses had not been shipped, the Rough Riders had to charge on foot under intense Spanish fire. The African American 9th and 10th cavalries cleared the way for the final surge. By nightfall U.S. troops controlled the ridge above Santiago. Then on July 3, the U.S. Navy sank the Spanish fleet off the coast of Cuba, resulting in more than 400 Spanish casualties. With their navy crushed, two weeks later, on July 17, Spanish troops in Cuba surrendered. Meanwhile, U.S. troops also defeated Spanish troops in Puerto Rico.

The war proved costly for Spain. By the terms of the peace treaty, Spain granted Cuba its independence and ceded Puerto Rico and the Pacific island of Guam (see map on page 220) to the United States. Spain also gave up control of the Philippines in return for a U.S. payment of $20 million.

By gaining control of overseas territories, the United States secured its position as an imperialist and world power. Expansionists expressed delight, but many Americans were troubled by the quest for empire. Furthermore, the United States paid a heavy human toll for the war. Some 5,400 soldiers died, nearly 400 in battle and the rest from dysentery, typhoid, malaria, yellow fever, or food poisoning.

■■ **The United States gained most of Spain's overseas territory through victory in the Spanish-American War.**

SECTION 1 REVIEW

IDENTIFY and explain the significance of the following: imperialism, Te'o Tuvale, José Martí, Valeriano Weyler, William Randolph Hearst, William McKinley, Enrique Dupuy de Lôme, Teller Amendment, Spanish-American War, George Dewey, Emilio Aguinaldo.

LOCATE and explain the importance of the following: American Samoa; Santiago, Cuba; Manila, Philippines; Puerto Rico; Guam.

1. **MAIN IDEA** What led the United States and other industrial powers to turn to imperialism?

2. **MAIN IDEA** What factors caused the United States to become involved in the Spanish-American War?

3. **GEOGRAPHY: PLACE** What territories did the United States gain as a result of the Spanish-American War? How did the war affect Spain?

4. **WRITING TO CREATE** Imagine you are Cuban revolutionary José Martí. Write a poem supporting Cuban independence from Spain.

5. **EVALUATING** How did publishers William Randolph Hearst and Joseph Pulitzer influence the United States to declare war on Spain in 1898?

EXPANSION IN THE PACIFIC

F O C U S

■ **How did the United States deal with Filipino calls for independence?**

■ **Why did the U.S. government annex Hawaii?**

■ **What role did the United States play in China?**

■ **What kind of relationship developed between Japan and the United States in the late 1800s and early 1900s?**

America's war with Spain began over Cuba. But, in addition to establishing a U.S. presence in the Caribbean, the war extended the U.S. presence in Asia and the Pacific. After the war, the United States established political control over the Philippines and added Hawaii to its colonial holdings. The United States also became further involved in affairs in China and took a new interest in Japan.

Hawaiian coin

UPROAR OVER THE PHILIPPINES

When Dewey's fleet steamed into Manila Bay in 1898, few Americans even knew where the Philippines were. President McKinley confessed that before he consulted a globe, he could not locate the islands "within two thousand miles." The Philippines—a group of islands—cover some 100,000 square miles in the Pacific Ocean, southeast of the Chinese coast. Now that the Philippines were "flung into [U.S.] arms by Dewey's guns," Americans faced an urgent question: Should Filipinos be forced to accept U.S. rule?

The debate over annexation. The debate over whether the United States should **annex**, or take control of, the Philippines was rooted in the larger controversy over imperialism raging across the country.

People questioned whether it was proper or wise for the United States to annex any foreign territory and rule its government and its people.

Expansionists argued forcefully in favor of annexation. In addition to making a case for annexation for commercial and naval reasons, some believed that the United States would bring democracy to the Philippines. Others held that the United States had to rule the Philippines to keep out European powers. Charles Denby, a former American

▶ **Filipino women are shown winnowing, or separating, rice on Palawan Island.**

foreign minister to China, warned opponents of annexation that times had changed:

> 66 I recognize the existence of a national sentiment in accordance with . . . Washington's Farewell Address, which is against the acquisition of foreign territory; but . . . circumstances are changed. . . . We have a great commerce to take care of. We have to compete with the commercial nations of the world in far-distant markets. Commerce, not politics, is king. 99

Opponents of American imperialism responded that, by annexing the Philippines and denying its independence, the United States would violate its own ideals expressed in the Declaration of Independence. In June 1898, opponents of U.S. imperialism formed the Anti-Imperialist League, which proclaimed:

> 66 We regret that it has become necessary in the land of Washington and Lincoln to reaffirm that all men, of whatever race or color, are entitled to life, liberty, and the pursuit of happiness. . . . We insist that the subjugation of any people is "criminal aggression" and open disloyalty to the distinctive principles of our Government. 99

After a fierce debate, the Senate narrowly approved the treaty annexing the Philippines on February 6, 1899. The vote was 57 to 27, barely reaching the two-thirds majority required.

Conquest and early rule. Filipinos, however, did not want to exchange one master for another—gaining independence from Spain only to lose it to the United States. Emilio Aguinaldo had already set up a provisional Filipino government and proclaimed himself president of the Philippine Republic. Now he warned that Filipinos would go to war if "American troops attempt to take forcible possession. Upon their heads will be all the blood which may be shed."

For the next three years, Filipino independence fighters and U.S. soldiers fought for control of the Philippines. U.S. forces captured Aguinaldo in March 1901. When Filipino resistance continued, however, U.S. forces implemented a concentration camp policy as Weyler had done in Cuba. By the time U.S. forces crushed the rebellion in 1902, the cost in Filipino lives was horrendous, estimated in the hundreds of thousands. More than 4,000 U.S. soldiers lost their lives.

In 1902 the U.S. Congress passed the **Philippine Government Act**, also known as the Organic Act. The act decreed that the Philippines would be ruled by a governor and a two-house legislature. The United States would appoint the governor and the legislature's upper house. After peace was

U.S. Territories in the Pacific

WORLD POWER The building of a modern navy and the search for overseas markets resulted in an increased interest in the Pacific and the acquisition of a number of islands.

❓ **LOCATION** Which U.S.–claimed islands lie well to the south of the equator?

▲ To suppress the Filipino uprising, the United States sent approximately 70,000 troops to the Philippines in 1899. This cartoon shows Emilio Aguinaldo's government crushed by American military might.

restored, Filipino voters would be allowed to elect the legislature's lower house.

Judge William Howard Taft became the first American governor of the Philippines. Taft authorized the construction of public schools, roads, and railroads and improved medical care and sanitation. As the United States reduced and then removed tariffs on Filipino products, U.S. trade with the Philippines flourished.

But Filipinos still lacked the independence for which they had fought so long. The **Jones Act of 1916** gave Filipinos the right to elect both houses of their legislature but stated that independence would have to wait until Congress declared that "a stable government" had been established. The wait would be a long one. The United States finally granted independence to the Philippines on July 4, 1946, nearly half a century after American and Spanish naval guns had shattered the early morning silence of Manila Bay.

■■ **Despite Filipino calls for independence, the United States annexed the Philippines and delayed independence until 1946.**

ACQUIRING HAWAII

Renewed interest in expansion after the Spanish-American War led to demands for U.S. annexation of the Hawaiian Islands, nearly 4,000 miles east of the Philippines. The United States had long been interested in Hawaii for its strategic location along trade routes to China and for its fertile lava-enriched soil. In the 1820s Protestant missionaries from New England traveled to the islands to convert Hawaiians to Christianity. The missionaries' descendants remained, becoming major landholders. By the 1870s Americans living in Hawaii controlled land and trade and exercised growing influence over the Hawaiian government.

When the Hawaiian king, Kalakaua (kah-LAH-KAH-ooh-ah), sought to restrict American influence in 1886, some 400 American businessmen, planters, and traders in Hawaii formed the secret Hawaiian League. Their aim was to overthrow the monarchy and persuade the United States to annex Hawaii.

In 1887 the League forced Kalakaua to sign a new constitution that made the Hawaiian monarch only a figurehead and limited native Hawaiians'

▼ After 1900, pineapples began to rival sugarcane as Hawaii's most important crop. Many of the laborers on Hawaiian plantations were from China, Japan, Korea, and the Philippines.

right to hold office in their own country. Hawaiians criticized what they called the "Bayonet Constitution." That same year, the United States succeeded in getting Kalakaua to grant rights to use Pearl Harbor for a U.S. naval base.

Hawaiian resentment intensified as American interests continued to lobby Washington to annex Hawaii. Then in 1891 Kalakaua died. Succeeding him was his sister, Liliuokalani (li-lee-uh-woh-kuh-LAHN-ee), champion of Hawaiian nationalism, who pledged to regain "Hawaii for Hawaiians."

Queen Liliuokalani

Liliuokalani was born into a Hawaiian ruling family in 1838. As a young girl she saw the monarchy reclaim Hawaiian independence after a brief British takeover. She would never forget the pride she felt as the Hawaiian flag was again raised over her native land.

Early in her reign, Queen Liliuokalani began working to overturn the Bayonet Constitution and replace it with one that would return power to native Hawaiians. In 1893 she announced her plans to publish a new constitution. The announcement caused the annexationists to swing into action. Forming a Committee of Safety, they forcibly occupied government buildings, declared the end of the monarchy, and set up a provisional government of their own. U.S. Marines stood by as the American foreign minister to Hawaii recognized the provisional government. A deeply saddened Queen Liliuokalani signed a paper giving up her throne:

    66 I, Liliuokalani, . . . protest against any and all acts done against myself and the constitutional government of the Hawaiian kingdom. . . . Now, to avoid any collision of armed forces and perhaps the loss of life, I do, under this protest, and impelled by said forces, yield my authority until such time as the government of the United States shall . . . undo the action of its representatives and reinstate me. **99**

▶ **Ivory vases and brightly colored fans were some of the many items sold through the lucrative China trade. The fan shows the seaport town of Huang-pu, where American ships took aboard Chinese goods.**

The U.S. government never reinstated Liliuokalani. But recognizing that native Hawaiians overwhelmingly opposed annexation, it did not annex Hawaii until 1898. Liliuokalani lived out the rest of her life in Honolulu, a proud reminder of Hawaii's past. She died in 1917 after a severe stroke and was buried in the Royal Mausoleum.

■■ **American settlers' response to Queen Liliuokalani's reforms and a renewed interest in overseas colonies led to the U.S. annexation of Hawaii.**

AMERICAN INVOLVEMENT IN CHINA

The United States had originally become interested in Hawaii because it was the gateway to the China trade. This trade had begun in 1784 when a U.S. trading ship, the *Empress of China,* sailed for the port of Guangzhou (Canton). In 1843 China officially opened five ports to trading ships from the United States and Europe.

For the next 50 years, China's rulers struggled to balance American and European interests to keep them from overrunning the country. In 1895, however, the Chinese government was overrun from another direction. Japan attacked and defeated China, winning from it the large island of Taiwan (Formosa), territory on China's Liaotung Peninsula, and control of Korea.

European powers quickly took advantage of China's weakened position. Great Britain, France, Germany, and Russia pressured the Chinese government to carve the country into separate **spheres of influence**—ports or regions where a particular country would have exclusive rights over trade, mines, and railroads.

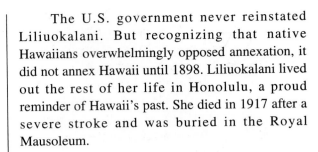

Peabody and Essex Museum, Salem, Massachusetts

The United States feared it would be squeezed out of the China trade. In 1899 Secretary of State John Hay responded by inaugurating an **Open Door policy**, which called for all nations to have equal access to trade and investment in China. Senator Henry Cabot Lodge concluded: "We ask no favors; we only ask that we shall be admitted to that great market upon the same terms with the rest of the world."

In September 1899 Hay began sending a series of Open Door notes to the European powers and Japan. The notes asked them to agree to three principles: (1) to keep all ports in their spheres open to all nations; (2) to allow Chinese officials to collect all tariffs and duties; and (3) to guarantee equal railroad, harbor, and tariff rates in their spheres to all nations trading in China. When the European nations and Japan did not reject the principles outright, Hay announced that the Open Door policy had been accepted.

Chinese resentment of foreigners continued to grow, however. It erupted in the spring of 1900, when a Chinese secret society—the "Fists of Righteous Harmony"—launched a rebellion to drive the "foreign devils" out of the country. They attacked Western missionaries and traders in northern China, killing about 300. Supported by some Chinese government officials, the "Boxers"—the name Westerners gave them because of the "Fists" in their Chinese name—laid siege to the large walled-in foreign settlement in the capital at Beijing (Peking). For eight weeks the siege continued until finally, in August, an international force rescued the foreigners.

The **Boxer Rebellion** ended, but John Hay feared that Japan and other nations would use it as an excuse to seize more Chinese territory. In a second series of Open Door notes, he pressured the foreign powers to observe open trade throughout China and to preserve China's right to rule its own territory. China retained its territory but had to pay foreign powers $333 million in damages for losses sustained during the Boxer Rebellion.

▪▪ The United States worked to maintain its trading rights in China through the Open Door policy.

⒜N EMERGING JAPAN

Japan's 1894 invasion of China marked Japan's emergence as an imperial power. A mere 41 years earlier Japan had ended its almost complete isolation from the rest of the world. From 1639 to the 1850s Japanese rulers had allowed only one Dutch trading ship a year to enter the country. However, Japan's foreign policy had suddenly changed in 1853, when Commodore Matthew Perry of the United States sailed his squadron of black-hulled warships, bristling with guns, into Edo (Tokyo) Bay. President Millard Fillmore had ordered Perry to persuade Japan to open its doors to trade with the rapidly industrializing West. The gifts Perry presented to Japan's rulers symbolized the industrial age: a telegraph transmitter and a model train.

Perry's warships and industrial wonders forced the Japanese to yield to Western demands for trade. But they also convinced Japanese rulers that they must modernize their country—build up its military might and its industry. If they did not, they reasoned, foreigners might gain control of their nation.

Japan rapidly transformed itself into an industrial power and built up its army and navy. Within four decades Japan had become a winner in the struggle for empire rather than a victim of it, as its war with China, and later with Russia, proved.

Japan and Russia were rivals for Chinese territories—especially for Korea and for the fertile soil and mineral riches of Manchuria in northern

▲ **Almost a year after Perry presented gifts to the Japanese, U.S. ships were allowed to trade in the ports of Hakodate and Shimoda.**

U.S. IMPERIALISM

	U.S. Involvement	Interim Status	Current Status
Samoa	Agreement divides islands between U.S. and Germany (1899)	German Samoa achieves independence (1962)	American Samoa under U.S. control
Philippines	Ceded to U.S. (1898)	Philippine Government Act defines government (1902)	Independent republic (1946)
		Declared a commonwealth (1935)	
Cuba	American forces occupy Cuba (1898)	Platt Amendment authorizes U.S. intervention (1902)	Independent republic (1934)
Puerto Rico	Ceded to U.S. (1898)	Foraker Act establishes government (1900)	Declared a commonwealth (1952)
		Application for statehood (1924)	
Hawaii	U.S. annexation (1898)	Application for statehood (1937)	50th state (1959)

Sources: *An Encyclopedia of World History, Webster's New Geographical Dictionary*

AMERICAN EXPANSIONISM U.S. economic and security interests extended into Asia, the Pacific, the Caribbean, and Latin America at the turn of the century.

? ASSESSING CONSEQUENCES Using one of the countries on the chart as a case study, trace U.S. involvement and its consequences for the country's current status.

By May 1905 the Japanese had won a series of crucial battles, and they asked Roosevelt to negotiate peace with Russia. Roosevelt brought representatives of the two countries together at Portsmouth, New Hampshire, where they pounded out a treaty. It granted neither side all it wanted and left both dissatisfied. But it did end the war, and it won the Nobel Peace Prize for Roosevelt.

Aware that Japan might now turn its expansionist eye toward the Pacific, including the U.S.–held Philippines, Roosevelt decided to demonstrate American military might. In late 1907 he sent a fleet of 4 destroyers and 16 battleships, painted a dazzling white, on a 46,000-mile world cruise. The "Great White Fleet" sailed into the Japanese port of Yokohama, where it underscored Roosevelt's later boast that now "the Pacific was as much our home waters as the Atlantic."

China. In February 1904, Japanese troops attacked Russian forces in Manchuria, starting the **Russo-Japanese War**. President Theodore Roosevelt watched the war closely. If Japan won, it might grow dangerously strong. If Russia won, it might cut off U.S. trade with Manchuria.

■■ **The United States came to see Japan, newly emergent as a modern world power, as a rival for influence in China and the Pacific.**

SECTION 2 REVIEW

IDENTIFY and explain the significance of the following: annex, Philippine Government Act, William Howard Taft, Jones Act of 1916, Kalakaua, Liliuokalani, spheres of influence, John Hay, Boxer Rebellion, Matthew Perry, Russo-Japanese War.

LOCATE and explain the importance of the following: Hawaii; Taiwan; Korea; Beijing, China; Yokohama, Japan.

1. **MAIN IDEA** How did the United States respond to Filipino demands for independence?

2. **MAIN IDEA** What events led to the U.S. annexation of Hawaii?

3. **MAIN IDEA** What did the Open Door policy attempt to accomplish in China?

4. **WRITING TO EXPLAIN** Imagine you are a U.S. diplomat in Japan in 1905. Write a report to President Roosevelt, explaining why the United States should reevaluate its relationship with Japan.

5. **TAKING A STAND** Do you think the United States is ever justified in annexing a foreign territory? Give reasons for your answer.

EXPANSION IN LATIN AMERICA

FOCUS

- **How did the United States deal with Cuba and Puerto Rico after the Spanish-American War?**
- **What events cleared the way for construction of the Panama Canal?**
- **How did presidents Roosevelt, Taft, and Wilson enforce the Monroe Doctrine?**

From 1898 onward, as American power grew in the Pacific, the U.S. role in Latin America expanded as well. Cuba came under U.S. control, while Puerto Rico became an out-and-out American possession. The United States built a canal across the Isthmus of Panama in these years, and the U.S. presence was felt throughout Latin America.

President Theodore Roosevelt at Panama Canal site

GOVERNING CUBA AND PUERTO RICO

Both Cuba and Puerto Rico hoped that the peace treaty ending the Spanish-American War would bring independence from Spain followed by the speedy departure of American troops. After all, the Teller Amendment had pledged to Cuba that the United States would allow Cubans to control their government. But Cubans and Puerto Ricans were disappointed. Wanting to restore order quickly in both countries and thus protect U.S. investments, President McKinley set up military governments to rule the islands.

McKinley appointed General Leonard Wood governor of Cuba in 1899. Wood authorized the construction of schools and a sanitation system. U.S. Army doctors Walter Reed and William Gorgas had called for the sanitation system to reduce the mosquito population. Carlos Finlay

▲ Carlos Finlay

(feen-LY), a Cuban doctor, had theorized that mosquitoes spread yellow fever. He was right. Once built, the system all but eliminated the disease.

Wood also presided over the writing of a new constitution that limited Cuba's independence. The U.S. Congress agreed to remove American troops only if Cuba made the **Platt Amendment** part of its constitution. The Platt Amendment (1) limited Cuba's freedom to make treaties with other countries; (2) authorized the United States to intervene in Cuban affairs as it saw necessary; and (3) required Cuba to sell or lease land to the United States for naval and fueling stations. This last clause eventually led to the establishment of the U.S. Navy base at Guantánamo Bay (see map on page 217). In effect, the Platt Amendment made Cuba an American **protectorate**: America promised to protect Cuba from other nations but reserved the right to intervene in Cuba's affairs.

In 1902, after Cuba reluctantly accepted the Platt Amendment, U.S.

troops left. But a U.S. presence remained at the naval base at Guantánamo Bay, which was leased in 1903. Over the next three decades, the United States intervened in Cuba several times. It pressured Cuba into accepting policies favorable to U.S. investors and sent in troops when it decided that the Cuban government could not keep order. The Platt Amendment remained in force until 1934, when America renounced its right to intervene in Cuba. Even then, however, U.S. influence over Cuban affairs remained great.

For Puerto Rico, U.S. policy followed a different course. No Teller Amendment guaranteed independence for Puerto Rico, so the United States ruled the island as a territory like Samoa or the Philippines in the Pacific. But just how these new territories were to be governed raised a thorny legal question for the United States. Were the people of these territories entitled to all the rights of U.S. citizens?

No, ruled the Supreme Court in 1901. The Court argued that the new territories were not fully part of the United States. Therefore, Congress could choose which rights to extend them. The Court affirmed the **Foraker Act** of 1900, which called for Puerto Rico's governor and upper house of the legislature to be appointed by the United States and a lower house to be elected by Puerto Ricans.

The **Jones Act of 1917** made Puerto Ricans American citizens and gave them the right to elect both houses of their legislature. In 1952 Puerto

▶ The Panama Canal was built by the United States between 1904 and 1914. Shown here are laborers who helped construct the canal.

Rico became a self-governing commonwealth of the United States, which retains ties of citizenship and trade with the mainland.

■■ **After the Spanish-American War, the United States retained a strong influence in Cuba, and Puerto Rico became a U.S. territory.**

THE PANAMA CANAL

With such vital interests in both the Caribbean and the Pacific, the United States looked for a way to cut the travel time between the seas. The long and hazardous voyage around Cape Horn at the southern tip of South America took several weeks. In response the United States proposed digging a canal through a narrow neck of land in Central America to allow the U.S. Navy to police both seas.

Early steps toward a canal. The idea for such a canal was not new. As far back as 1517, Vasco Núñez de Balboa had proposed that a canal be dug across the 50-mile-wide Isthmus of Panama. In 1850 the United States and Great Britain had drawn up the **Clayton-Bulwer Treaty**, proposing an equal partnership to build and run a Central American canal, but they never acted on it. In the 1880s a French company actually worked on a canal across the Isthmus. But after less than 10 years and the loss of some 20,000 lives and more than $280 million, the French abandoned the effort. Deadly tropical diseases, repeated landslides, and bankruptcy killed the project.

Finally, in 1901 President Theodore Roosevelt decided that "after four centuries of conversation" by other countries, it was time for the United States to act. He instructed Secretary of State John Hay to negotiate with Great Britain

▲ After Puerto Rico became a U.S. territory, the government built new public schools such as the one shown here.

On August 15, 1914, the SS *Ancon* completed the first passage through the Panama Canal, a 51-mile-long ribbon of waters connecting the Caribbean Sea and the Pacific Ocean. The voyage marked the completion of what Theodore Roosevelt called "the greatest task of its own kind that has ever been performed in the world at all!"

Americans began working on the canal in 1904. Roosevelt was eager "to make the dirt fly" in Panama, but harsh working conditions and shortages hampered U.S. efforts from the start. Then in late 1904 a serious outbreak of yellow fever hit. By early 1905 the project was at a near standstill.

To put the project back on track, Roosevelt appointed John F. Stevens as chief engineer and architect. Stevens tackled the technical problems, while army colonel Dr. William C. Gorgas worked on improving living conditions. Gorgas, who had helped rid Cuba of tropical diseases, had drinking water purified and buildings screened. Then, to destroy the breeding places of the mosquitoes that transmit

yellow fever and malaria, he had swamps drained and standing water coated with oil. By 1906 yellow fever had almost been eliminated. Malaria was under control by 1913.

Panama Canal Zone

STRATEGIC INTERESTS Because it took the U.S. naval vessel *Oregon* 66 days to sail from San Francisco around Cape Horn to Key West during the Spanish-American War, pressure increased to build a U.S.–controlled canal through Central America.

? LOCATION If you enter the Panama Canal from the Caribbean Sea on the Atlantic side, which direction will you travel to exit on the Pacific Ocean?

Canal construction soon resumed in force. More than 60 giant steam shovels bit into the land, digging out nearly 160 trainloads of earth each day. Workers numbered more than 43,000, many of whom were recruited from the British West Indies.

Originally, the canal was designed to be built at sea level,

but the difficulty of moving millions of tons of dirt and rock prompted a new design—an elevated waterway using locks. One group of workers dredged an approach channel and built a dam and locks on the Atlantic side. Another group dredged a passage from the Pacific through the Bay of Panama and constructed two smaller sets of locks. The hardest job fell to another group, which had to blast an eight-mile-long path through the mountainous Continental Divide. Geologic faults, heavy rains, and shifting earth caused frequent and often fatal avalanches. But finally, on October 10, 1913, President Wilson signaled crews to dynamite the protective dike at the south end of the canal. In a dramatic finale, water from the two sides rushed together—85 feet above sea level.

The human and economic costs of building the canal were staggering: some 6,000 workers died and about $366 million was spent. But the seemingly impossible had become a reality. The United States—and the rest of the world—now had a "Path Between the Seas."

to end the partnership set up by the Clayton-Bulwer Treaty. In the resulting **Hay-Pauncefote Treaty**, Britain agreed that the United States could build the canal by itself and have "exclusive management and policing of it." In return, the United States promised to keep the canal open to all the world's vessels in wartime as well as in peacetime.

Hay then began negotiations with the Republic of Colombia—of which Panama was then a part. In 1903 the **Hay-Herrán Treaty** was drafted. In return for a 99-year lease on a six-mile strip of land across the Isthmus, the United States agreed to pay Colombia $10 million and a yearly rental of $250,000. But holding out for better terms, Colombia's senate adjourned without ratifying the treaty. A furious President Roosevelt accused the Colombians of blackmail and swore that they must not be allowed "to bar one of the future highways of civilization."

▲ John Hay served as secretary of state from 1898 until his death in 1905.

Revolution in Panama. Events in Panama soon turned in Roosevelt's favor. Key Panamanian leaders who wanted the canal built began plotting revolution against the Colombian government. Helping them was Philippe Bunau-Varilla (boo-noh-vah-ree-yah), the former chief engineer for the French canal-building attempt.

Bunau-Varilla traveled to Washington to get American support for the revolution. On October 9, 1903, he met privately with President Roosevelt. Exactly what was said at the meeting remains unknown, but on November 2 the U.S. gunboat *Nashville* arrived in Panama. The following day, Panamanians began their rebellion. U.S. Marines prevented Colombian forces from reaching the rebels.

On November 4, 1903, the victorious rebels set up a new government and declared Panama an independent nation. Acting with lightning speed, the United States two days later recognized the

▲ This 1903 cartoon shows Roosevelt digging the Panama Canal and throwing dirt in the direction of Colombia, the country that had refused to ratify an earlier canal treaty.

Republic of Panama, and Hay began negotiating a new canal treaty with Panama's special envoy, Bunau-Varilla. The **Hay–Bunau-Varilla Treaty** gave the United States complete and unending sovereignty over a 10-mile-wide Canal Zone.

Did the United States engineer the Panamanian revolution? The facts remain obscure, but President Theodore Roosevelt later boasted, "I took the Canal Zone and let Congress debate." It is clear that U.S. aid to the Panamanian rebels and America's immediate recognition of Panama as an independent nation served American interests and made the Panama Canal possible. American trade and naval power grew stronger because of it, allowing the United States to extend its economic and political interests in Latin America.

▪▪ **The Panamanian revolution and a favorable treaty cleared the way for the United States to build and retain control of the Panama Canal.**

*A*PPLYING THE MONROE DOCTRINE

The American interventions in Cuba, Puerto Rico, and Panama were only three instances in a long history of U.S. involvement in Latin America. As far back as 1823, the Monroe Doctrine had cast the United States as protector of the hemisphere. But for much of the century the doctrine was little more than an idle threat. This changed following the Spanish-American War, as presidents Theodore Roosevelt, William H. Taft, and Woodrow Wilson actively enforced the Monroe Doctrine in an effort to protect U.S. interests in Latin America (see map on page 234).

The Roosevelt Corollary.

Latin America, with its wealth of raw materials and potential consumers, attracted a flood of European and American capital during the late 1800s. Much of this capital was in the form of high-interest bank loans. Although many Latin American countries welcomed the loans, difficulty in repaying them often resulted in foreign intervention. In 1902, for example, Great Britain, Germany, and Italy blockaded and attacked Venezuelan ships and ports when the nation failed to repay its loans. President Roosevelt quickly warned the three European powers not to seize any Venezuelan land and convinced them to settle the issue through arbitration.

Roosevelt's actions sent a clear signal that he intended to enforce the Monroe Doctrine. Roosevelt underscored this point in 1904 when the Dominican Republic proved unable to repay its European lenders. Fearing that the Europeans would use force to collect the loans, he issued the **Roosevelt Corollary** to the Monroe Doctrine:

> 66 If a nation . . . keeps order and pays its obligations, it need fear no interference from the United States. Chronic wrongdoing . . . in the Western Hemisphere . . . may force the United States, however reluctantly, . . . to the exercise of an international police power. 99

Without seeking approval from any Latin American nation, Roosevelt assumed the role of "international police officer" in the Western Hemisphere. He had applied in practice the West African proverb he loved to quote: "Speak softly and carry a big stick; you will go far."

Next, Roosevelt convinced the Dominican government to accept U.S. assistance. The United States pledged to use American armed forces to stop any European country from seizing Dominican territory. In exchange, the Dominican government agreed to let the United States collect all Dominican customs duties and turn half over to

foreign creditors. In 1916, when civil disturbances racked the Dominican Republic, the United States government sent in marines. They did not leave until eight years later, in 1924.

▪▪ The Roosevelt Corollary established a greater U.S. role in Latin America.

Some Latin American countries objected to Roosevelt's policy. They argued that every country should maintain control over its own affairs. Some Latin American countries issued a declaration stating that debts owed to other countries could not be collected by force. But despite Latin American protests, intervention continued.

Dollar diplomacy.

Roosevelt's successor as president, William H. Taft, further extended U.S. influence in Latin America. Taft favored "substituting dollars for bullets"—economic influence for military force—as a means of protecting U.S.

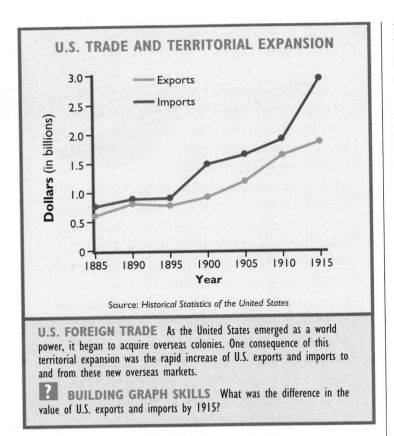

U.S. TRADE AND TERRITORIAL EXPANSION

Dollars (in billions)

— Exports
— Imports

Year

Source: *Historical Statistics of the United States*

U.S. FOREIGN TRADE As the United States emerged as a world power, it began to acquire overseas colonies. One consequence of this territorial expansion was the rapid increase of U.S. exports and imports to and from these new overseas markets.

 BUILDING GRAPH SKILLS What was the difference in the value of U.S. exports and imports by 1915?

interests in Latin America (see map on page 234). To implement this policy, which came to be called **dollar diplomacy**, Taft suggested replacing European loans with American ones. Increasing U.S. economic power, Taft argued, would reduce the chances of European intervention. By 1914 U.S. capital in Latin America had grown to over $1.6 billion, mainly invested in railroads, mines, and banana and sugar plantations.

Nicaragua was one of the places that Taft put dollar diplomacy to the test. At the invitation of the Nicaraguan president, American bankers made loans totaling $1.5 million to Nicaragua in 1911. The following year, Taft sent more than 2,000 marines to crush a revolt and to protect the U.S. investments that had poured in.

Taft's successor, President Woodrow Wilson, believed that democratic governments, not U.S. dollars, would keep European powers out of Latin America. To keep Germany from taking control of strategic Caribbean territory, Wilson sent marines to several Caribbean countries to put down rebellions and establish constitutional governments. In 1915, when revolution shook Haiti, Wilson sent in marines. Haiti was forced to accept a treaty giving the United States powers in running the Haitian government, and the marines stayed until 1934. Some 1,500 Haitians died resisting U.S. control.

■■ **Taft's dollar diplomacy and Wilson's military interventions increased U.S. political and economic influence in Latin America.**

SECTION 3 REVIEW

IDENTIFY and explain the significance of the following: Leonard Wood, Carlos Finlay, Platt Amendment, protectorate, Foraker Act, Jones Act of 1917, Clayton-Bulwer Treaty, Hay-Pauncefote Treaty, Hay-Herrán Treaty, Hay–Bunau-Varilla Treaty, Roosevelt Corollary, dollar diplomacy.

LOCATE and explain the importance of the following: Guantánamo Bay, Panama Canal, Colombia, Venezuela, Dominican Republic, Nicaragua, Haiti.

1. **MAIN IDEA** How did the U.S. relationship with Cuba and Puerto Rico change after the Spanish-American War?

2. **MAIN IDEA** Why did the United States support the Panamanian rebels and recognize the Republic of Panama?

3. **CONTRASTING** How did presidents Roosevelt, Taft, and Wilson apply the Monroe Doctrine in Latin America?

4. **WRITING TO PERSUADE** Imagine you are a political leader in a Latin American country during this period. Write a speech seeking to persuade the U.S. government not to interfere in the affairs of your country.

5. **HYPOTHESIZING** How might U.S. policy toward Puerto Rico have been different if the Teller Amendment had been extended to apply to that territory?

CONFLICT WITH MEXICO

FOCUS

- **How did the Mexican Revolution affect relations between the United States and Mexico?**
- **Why did the United States intervene in Mexico?**
- **Why did tensions between the two countries remain strong during Carranza's presidency?**

*D*ollar diplomacy played a significant role in another Latin American country: Mexico. Though many Mexicans uneasily referred to the United States as "the Colossus of the North," economic ties between the two countries increased in the late 19th century. But the Mexican Revolution of 1910 threatened these ties, bringing the two countries to the brink of war.

American artillery along the Mexican border, 1916

THE MEXICAN REVOLUTION

Dollars helped tie Mexico and the United States closer together in the late 19th century, thanks to Mexico's president, Porfirio Díaz. Díaz, who with the political support of wealthy landowners ruled Mexico for more than 30 years, offered special concessions to attract foreign investment. By 1908, U.S. companies controlled three quarters of all Mexican mining operations. Total U.S. investments amounted to almost $1 million by 1913.

Foreign investors helped develop Mexico's economy by building railroads that linked Mexico to U.S. and other foreign markets. But foreign investors and Díaz's friends profited the most from economic growth. Little trickled down to workers and peasants. Indeed, Díaz's policies helped wealthy Mexicans and foreigners take land away from peasants. As a result, most Mexicans—mainly landless peasants and struggling urban workers—lived in poverty.

In 1910 Díaz used force and fraud to defeat opposition candidate Francisco Madero. Peasants,

workers, and the middle class, angry at the lack of political democracy, rallied behind Madero in armed revolt against Díaz beginning in November. The rebels defeated Díaz's troops in key cities in northern and central Mexico, forcing Díaz into exile in Paris in 1911. In Mexico's first democratic elections in 30 years, Madero won the presidency.

Madero sought to establish a democratic government, but few agreed on the details. The revolutionary leaders who had supported Madero against

▼ **Women served in military roles during the Mexican Revolution. This 1911 photograph shows a group of female revolutionaries armed with rifles.**

Díaz thought Madero's plan did not go far enough in such areas as returning land to the peasants. Others, including conservative military officers and wealthy landowners, thought the plan went too far.

Complicating this situation was Henry Lane Wilson, the U.S. ambassador, who did not believe Madero could protect U.S. investments in Mexico. Wilson overstepped his diplomatic role by arranging for factions opposed to Madero to meet and discuss Madero's overthrow. In 1913, backed by wealthy landowners and foreign business interests, General Victoriano Huerta (WER-tah) seized control of the government and had Madero thrown into jail. Huerta's soldiers shot Madero when, they alleged, he attempted to escape.

Madero's murder outraged President Woodrow Wilson. He angrily refused to recognize Huerta, calling his regime a "government of butchers." Civil war raged in Mexico as revolutionary armies battled to drive Huerta out. President Wilson adopted a policy of "watchful waiting," hoping that the revolutionaries would be successful. He also authorized arms sales to the revolutionaries, while refusing to allow arms sales to Huerta's forces.

▲ **Pancho Villa, center, and Emiliano Zapata, right, are shown with their followers in the presidential palace in Mexico City.**

▪▪ The Mexican Revolution strained U.S.–Mexican relations as the fighting disrupted Mexico's government and society.

AMERICAN INTERVENTION

Four major revolutionary armies continued to fight Huerta. But their leaders—Venustiano Carranza (bay-noos-TYAHN-oh kahr-RAHN-sah), Francisco "Pancho" Villa, Emiliano Zapata, and Álvaro Obregón (oh-bray-GAWN)—were not united. Two of the leaders, Carranza and Villa, actually hated each other. Although the revolutionaries controlled territory throughout Mexico, Wilson worried that they would never be able to defeat Huerta.

In 1914 an incident occurred that gave Wilson an excuse to intervene directly. On April 9, Huerta's soldiers arrested several crew members from the USS *Dolphin*. The U.S. sailors had gone ashore for supplies at the Mexican port of Tampico. The Americans were released unharmed, but Wilson pursued the matter. He backed the American admiral, who demanded an apology and a public ceremony in which Mexico would "hoist the American flag in a prominent position and salute it with twenty-one guns." Huerta made the apology but refused to perform the ceremony.

On April 20 President Wilson went before Congress:

66 I . . . come to ask your approval that I should use the armed forces of the United States . . . to obtain from General Huerta and his adherents the fullest recognition of the rights and dignity of the United States, even amidst the distressing conditions now unhappily obtaining in Mexico. 99

Before Congress could act, Wilson learned that a German ship bearing arms for Huerta was heading for the Mexican port of Veracruz. He ordered the U.S. Navy to land marines at Veracruz, take the customs house, and prevent the weapons from being delivered. By the time Congress voted Wilson the authority to use force, the order had been carried out.

At this critical stage Argentina, Brazil, and Chile—sometimes called the "ABC powers"—organized a conference at Niagara Falls, Ontario, to resolve the crisis. The conference urged Huerta to resign. Since his forces were losing, he complied and fled to Spain. In August 1914 Carranza marched into Mexico City. For the next year the revolutionary generals battled each other for control of the presidency.

▪▪ The United States intervened in Mexico to help overthrow the antirevolutionary Huerta government.

CARRANZA IN POWER

In 1915 Carranza assumed the presidency, and American forces withdrew from Veracruz. The United States recognized Carranza's government in the same year, after he guaranteed that Mexico would respect foreign lives and property.

Venustiano Carranza, with his trim white goatee and his "gentlemanly bearing," hardly fit anyone's picture of a typical revolutionary. Born in 1859 in the state of Coahuila (koh-uh-WEE-luh) in

▲ **Venustiano Carranza**

northern Mexico, he was over 50 years old when he took up the rebel cause.

Carranza, who owned a large, profitable ranch, had held many government offices under Díaz. But in 1908 Díaz and Carranza clashed, and three years later, Carranza joined Madero's fight to overthrow Díaz. After Madero was deposed, Carranza helped defeat Huerta's forces. He used his experience as head of a revolutionary army and his considerable political talents to gain the presidency of Mexico.

Carranza's presidency was marked by conflict. Pancho Villa, who had hoped for U.S. support against Carranza, decided to retaliate against the Americans for recognizing Carranza as president. Villa communicated his plans to rebel leader Emiliano Zapata:

66 We have decided not to fire a bullet more against Mexicans, our brothers, and to prepare and organize ourselves to attack the Americans in their own dens and make them know that Mexico is a land for the free and a tomb for thrones, crowns, and traitors. 99

In March 1916 some 500 of Villa's men crossed the border to raid Columbus, New Mexico. Villa's men burned and looted the surprised town and the army post located there. Seventeen Americans—nine civilians and eight soldiers—were killed, while more than a hundred Mexicans died. Villa hoped the raid would provoke American intervention in Mexico that would, in turn, undermine Carranza's regime. He did not have to wait long for his expected result.

Without Carranza's approval President Wilson ordered a military expedition into Mexico to capture Villa "dead or alive." A week after Villa's raid, General John J. Pershing led a force of some 5,800 soldiers into Chihuahua, Villa's home state. Although Pershing later increased his troop size to more than 10,000 men, Villa still eluded capture. The deeper Pershing pushed into Mexican territory, the more the Mexicans resented the Americans.

A battle between Mexican and U.S. troops in June brought the United States and Mexico to the brink of war. Carranza ordered Mexican troops to prevent U.S. soldiers from advancing any farther south into Mexico. When one of Pershing's cavalry units attempted to pass through the town

▲ **In 1916 President Wilson sent U.S. soldiers into Mexico to capture revolutionary leader Pancho Villa, "dead or alive."**

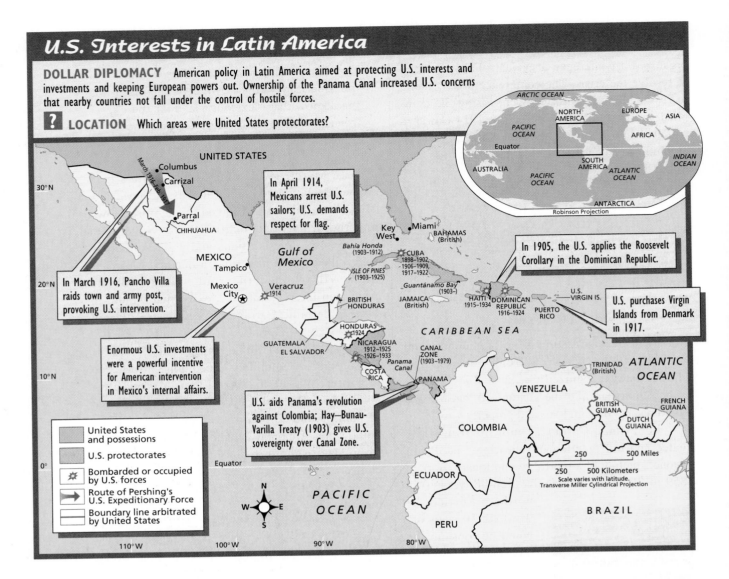

U.S. Interests in Latin America

DOLLAR DIPLOMACY American policy in Latin America aimed at protecting U.S. interests and investments and keeping European powers out. Ownership of the Panama Canal increased U.S. concerns that nearby countries not fall under the control of hostile forces.

? LOCATION Which areas were United States protectorates?

In April 1914, Mexicans arrest U.S. sailors; U.S. demands respect for flag.

In 1905, the U.S. applies the Roosevelt Corollary in the Dominican Republic.

In March 1916, Pancho Villa raids town and army post, provoking U.S. intervention.

U.S. purchases Virgin Islands from Denmark in 1917.

Enormous U.S. investments were a powerful incentive for American intervention in Mexico's internal affairs.

U.S. aids Panama's revolution against Colombia; Hay–Bunau-Varilla Treaty (1903) gives U.S. sovereignty over Canal Zone.

Legend:
- United States and possessions
- U.S. protectorates
- Bombarded or occupied by U.S. forces
- Route of Pershing's U.S. Expeditionary Force
- Boundary line arbitrated by United States

---

of Carrizal, the commander of the Mexican garrison refused passage. Instead of bypassing the town, the U.S. commander chose to enter Carrizal, and a battle ensued.

By early September 1916 nearly 150,000 U.S. National Guardsmen were stationed along the Mexican border. The prospect of armed conflict with Mexico was extremely unpopular in the United States, however, particularly in view of the events in Europe and on the high seas that threatened to pull the United States into World War I (see Chapter 10). Wilson backed down. In exchange for withdrawing U.S. troops, Wilson asked Carranza to adopt a measure that would allow the United States to intervene in Mexico to protect U.S. investments. Carranza refused to limit Mexican sovereignty in this way. Realizing that the threat of war increased with every day U.S. troops remained in Mexico, Wilson ordered U.S. troops withdrawn in January 1917.

In that same year, Carranza approved a sweeping new constitution for Mexico, but he would not have much time to put its provisions in place. In 1920 he was overthrown and killed by forces loyal to another revolutionary leader—Álvaro Obregón. Obregón and subsequent Mexican presidents gradually implemented the new constitution. This constitution would have important repercussions for U.S. oil companies operating in Mexico in the 1930s (see Chapter 15).

■■ **Villa's raid on a U.S. town and army post and Carranza's refusal to grant the United States the right to protect American investments raised tensions between the United States and Mexico to a dangerous pitch.**

COMMENTARY

Expansion in Perspective

In the years from 1890 to 1920, America's global involvement expanded enormously. In some cases this involvement meant actual military intervention and colonial rule of foreign territories. Although new territory and influence benefited the United States, many Americans believed that overseas expansion helped foreign countries as well. Many supporters of imperialism viewed Samoa, the Philippines, Puerto Rico, and other non-European countries as economically backward and uncivilized. Arguing from this point of view, American imperialists asserted that Americans had a responsibility to bring democracy, prosperity, and order to the world's nonindustrialized nations.

But did U.S. imperialism succeed in bringing all of these benefits to foreign countries? In Cuba, Puerto Rico, and the Philippines, better sanitation, education, roads, transportation, and public health followed the American flag. And in some cases, such as in Venezuela, U.S. diplomatic actions prevented European countries from colonizing Latin American territory.

U.S. economic and military interventions, however, rarely brought order or democracy to politically troubled countries. For example, U.S. dollar diplomacy in Nicaragua did not prevent a revolt, and the United States military brutally suppressed the Filipino independence movement.

Although designed to create democracy, the U.S. military governments that were established in many countries often denied citizens a basic democratic right: political representation.

U.S. attempts to spread American culture sometimes came at the expense of the other country's culture. In Puerto Rico, for example, the U.S. government ordered that English—instead of the native Spanish—be used in classrooms. English was used in order to make Puerto Ricans—in the words of Manuel Maldonado-Denis—"good North American citizens." Maldonado-Denis, a Puerto Rican who grew up under this system, recalled that "Puerto Rican students had to daily swear loyalty to the North American flag in English" and sing "songs in English composed to inspire patriotism in North American students." In this way, Maldonado-Denis concluded, the United States attempted "to rob us of every source of identification with all that is Puerto Rican."

U.S. economic expansion also created resentment against the United States around the world. The millions of dollars that U.S. banks and businesses poured into oil wells, mines, plantations, and railroad projects in poor nations gave the United States control of those nations' natural resources. The people in these nations grew angry as they watched their resources and the profits from them flow into the United States. The efforts of these countries to regain control of their own resources would provide a continuing source of tension between them and the United States.

S E C T I O N   4   R E V I E W

IDENTIFY and explain the significance of the following: Porfirio Díaz, Francisco Madero, Victoriano Huerta, Venustiano Carranza, Francisco "Pancho" Villa, Emiliano Zapata, Álvaro Obregón, John J. Pershing.

1. **MAIN IDEA** How did the Mexican Revolution impact relations between the United States and Mexico?

2. **MAIN IDEA** Why did President Wilson ask Congress for authority to use the military in Mexico?

3. **IDENTIFYING CAUSE AND EFFECT** What event during Carranza's presidency provoked U.S. intervention in Mexico? What effect did U.S. intervention have on relations between the two countries?

4. **WRITING TO EXPLAIN** Imagine you are a landless peasant in Mexico after the overthrow of Porfirio Díaz. Write a letter to a relative in the United States explaining why you took part in the revolution.

5. **SYNTHESIZING** How did U.S. intervention both help and hurt other countries?

Spanish-American War begins. U.S. gains control of Puerto Rico, Guam, and Hawaii.

U.S. annexes Philippines. Open Door policy inaugurated.

Boxer Rebellion begins in China.

U.S. recognizes Republic of Panama. Hay–Bunau-Varilla Treaty negotiated.

Philippine Government Act passed.

1898   **1900**   **1902**

WRITING A SUMMARY

Using the essential points of the chapter as a guide, write a summary of the chapter.

REVIEWING CHRONOLOGY

Number your paper 1 to 5. Study the time line above, and list the following events in the order in which they happened by writing the first next to 1, the second next to 2, and so on. Then complete the activity below.

1. Panama Canal completed.
2. U.S. recognizes Republic of Panama.
3. Venustiano Carranza assumes power in Mexico.
4. Open Door policy inaugurated.
5. Russo-Japanese War begins.

Identifying Cause and Effect Select two events from the time line, and in a paragraph, explain the cause-and-effect relationship between them.

IDENTIFYING PEOPLE AND IDEAS

Explain the historical significance of each of the following people or terms.

1. imperialism
2. José Martí
3. Emilio Aguinaldo
4. Liliuokalani
5. spheres of influence
6. John Hay
7. Carlos Finlay
8. dollar diplomacy
9. Porfirio Díaz
10. Venustiano Carranza

UNDERSTANDING MAIN IDEAS

1. What led industrialized nations to seek overseas colonies in the late 19th and early 20th centuries? What arguments did imperialists use to justify the establishment of overseas colonies?
2. What positive and negative effects did U.S. intervention in the Philippines have on that country?
3. How did U.S. relations with Hawaii and Japan eventually lead to American involvement in China?
4. How did U.S. actions in the Dominican Republic, Nicaragua, and Haiti signify Roosevelt's, Taft's, and Wilson's willingness to apply and extend the Monroe Doctrine?

5. Why were the United States, Great Britain, and Germany interested in Samoa? Who finally won control of Samoa?

REVIEWING THEMES

1. **Global Relations** Why was the United States interested in controlling Cuba? Why was Cuba surprised and angered by the position of the American government?
2. **Economic Development** How did the presence of foreign investors in Mexico affect the economy of that country? What problems resulted from these investments?
3. **Democratic Values** Why might some people argue that U.S. actions in the Philippines conflicted with democratic principles?

THINKING CRITICALLY

1. **Evaluating** How did the United States government react to revolutionaries such as Emilio Aguinaldo and Venustiano Carranza?
2. **Analyzing** Why did Japan, unlike China, not become divided into European spheres of influence?
3. **Hypothesizing** What might have been the effect on U.S. relations with Cuba, Puerto Rico, and the Philippines if the United States had adopted an Open Door policy in each of those countries?

STRATEGY FOR SUCCESS

Review the Skills Handbook entry on Writing a Paper beginning on page 761. Imagine you are a native Hawaiian in 1893 who has witnessed the overthrow of Queen Liliuokalani. What information will you need to collect if you are preparing an article for a local newspaper about this event? Suppose that you are writing a diary entry about the occupation. How will your approach to writing differ in this case?

WRITING ABOUT HISTORY

Writing to Explain Write an essay that traces the negotiations and events that helped the United States build and control the Panama Canal.

Russo-Japanese
War begins.

The Mexican
Revolution starts.

Panama Canal
completed.

Venustiano
Carranza assumes
power in Mexico.
Wilson sends
marines into Haiti.

Pancho Villa's
soldiers raid
Columbus,
New Mexico.

1904   1910   1912   1914   1916

USING PRIMARY SOURCES

A firm supporter of American expansion in the Far East, Charles Denby had been the U.S. minister to China. After the acquisition of the Philippines, he became a member of McKinley's commission to study the islands. Read the following excerpt from Denby's article "Shall We Keep the Philippines?" published in November 1898 in *Forum*. Why does Denby think the United States should keep the Philippines?

66 *The whole world sees in China a splendid market for our native products. . . . We are closer to her than any other commercial country except Japan. There is before us a boundless future which will make the Pacific more important to us than the Atlantic. San Francisco, Seattle, and Tacoma are in their infancy. They are destined to rival New Your, Chicago, and Philadelphia.*

If we give up the Philippines, we throw away the splendid opportunity to assert our influence in the Far East. We do this deliberately; and the world will laugh at us. Why did we take Manila? . . .

The Philippines are a foothold for us in the Far East. Their possession gives us standing and influence. It gives us also valuable trade both in exports and imports.

Should we surrender the Philippines, what will become of them? . . . To her [Spain] they will be valueless; and if she sells them to any continental power she will, by that act, light the torches of war. . . .

England will not stand by and see any other European power take the Philippines. They are on the line to Australia and India. . . . By holding the Philippines we postpone at least a general European war. . . . 99

LINKING HISTORY AND GEOGRAPHY

Historians have noted that the Spanish-American War was primarily decided at sea. Study the map on page 217 and the text discussion on pages 216–218. Then write a paragraph supporting this view and describing how geography might have influenced U.S. military strategy.

Teddy Roosevelt and the Rough Riders

BUILDING YOUR PORTFOLIO

Complete the following projects independently or cooperatively.

1. GLOBAL RELATIONS Imagine you are a member of the State Department in the early 1900s. Write a memorandum to the president that addresses concerns about U.S. relations with Spain, China, Japan, Latin America, or Mexico. Your memorandum should mention specific issues dealing with annexation, colonization, construction of the Panama Canal, or protection of U.S. investments, and propose courses of action.

2. WAR Imagine you are a U.S. Army recruiting officer in 1898. Create a series of recruiting posters aimed at attracting a wide range of recruits—such as college students, Native Americans, cowboys, would-be adventurers—to serve in the Spanish-American War.

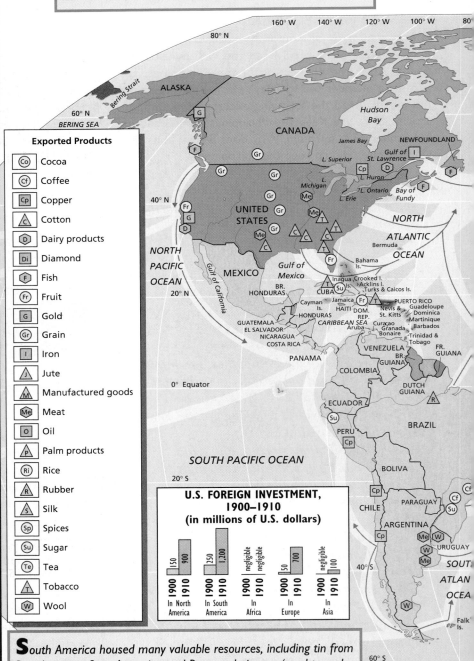

America's GEOGRAPHY

THE UNITED STATES AND THE WORLD

THE Industrial Revolution affected nations throughout the world. By 1914, the eve of World War I, many nations of the world were connected in a complex web of economic trade and investment. The vast majority of this trade and investment was controlled by European nations, particularly Great Britain, which had amassed a huge colonial empire. Japan was the only Asian nation to attempt significant foreign expansion in the early 20th century. Compared to the European empires, the United States had relatively little financial investment in other countries. Yet even the United States expanded its economic and political involvement in foreign nations during this period.

Foreign landholdings of the United States were very small compared to those of the European empires. The largest American territory, Alaska, appeared to many skeptics to be a useless, frozen wasteland. The discovery of gold, oil, and other useful minerals, however, would prove very valuable to the United States in years to come.

Exported Products

Co	Cocoa
Cf	Coffee
Cp	Copper
C	Cotton
D	Dairy products
Di	Diamond
F	Fish
Fr	Fruit
G	Gold
Gr	Grain
I	Iron
Ju	Jute
M	Manufactured goods
Me	Meat
O	Oil
P	Palm products
Ri	Rice
R	Rubber
S	Silk
Sp	Spices
Su	Sugar
Te	Tea
To	Tobacco
W	Wool

U.S. FOREIGN INVESTMENT, 1900–1910 (in millions of U.S. dollars)

	1900	1910
In North America	150	900
In South America	250	1,200
In Africa	negligible	negligible
In Europe	50	700
In Asia	negligible	100

South America housed many valuable resources, including tin from Brazil, copper from Argentina and Peru, and nitrates (used to make fertilizer and explosives) from Chile. Although the European empires did not attempt to create new colonies in South America, as they did in Africa, they invested heavily in the economic life of self-governing South American countries. The U.S. also increased investment in South America, but most of its investments were concentrated in Central America and the Panama Canal region.

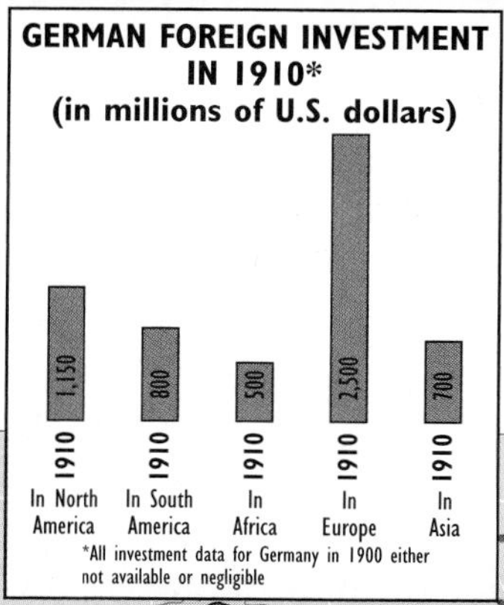

GERMAN FOREIGN INVESTMENT IN 1910*
(in millions of U.S. dollars)

1,150	800	500	2,500	700
1910	1910	1910	1910	1910
In North America	In South America	In Africa	In Europe	In Asia

*All investment data for Germany in 1900 either not available or negligible

Countries and Possessions in 1914

Great Britain	Japan
Denmark	Germany
Netherlands	France
Belgium	Spain
Italy	Portugal
Ottoman	United States
Russia	Independent

Asian empires went through dramatic changes around the turn of the century. China, which had been the largest empire in the world, suffered a series of political crises that led to a loss of many of its territories and eventually to the overthrow of the emperor in 1911. Meanwhile the tiny nation of Japan was becoming the leading Asian power as its empire expanded through military victories over China and Russia.

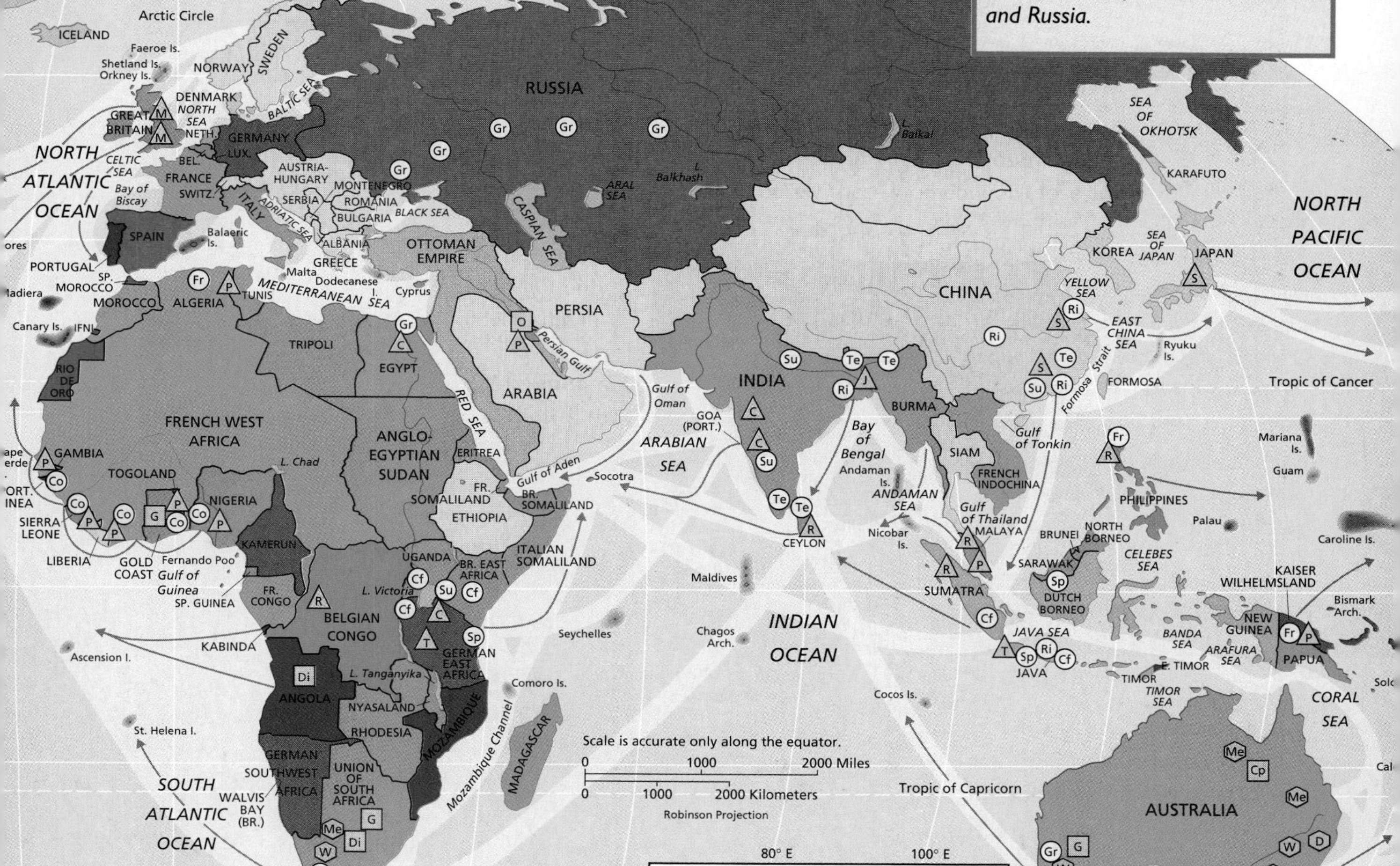

Europeans had explored and traded in Africa for many years. Except for a few small settlements, there had never been a major effort to colonize the continent. In the late 1800s, however, European countries struggled to claim African lands (and resources) for themselves. This led to a series of wars between European forces and African peoples. By 1914 Liberia, the country founded by American abolitionists in the early 1800s, and Ethiopia were the only self-governing African countries.

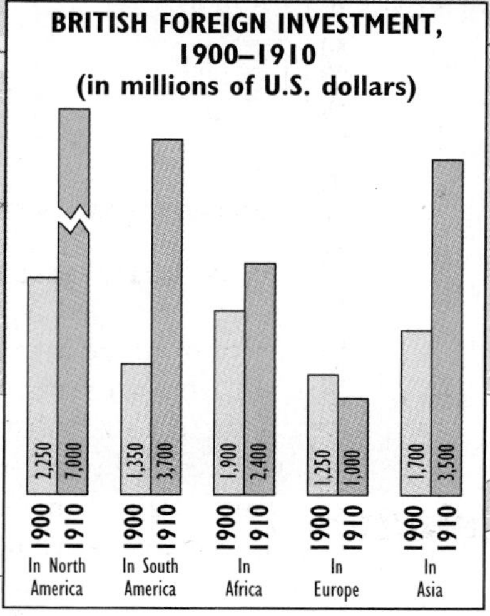

BRITISH FOREIGN INVESTMENT, 1900–1910
(in millions of U.S. dollars)

2,250	7,000	1,350	3,700	1,900	2,400	1,250	1,000	1,700	3,500
1900	1910	1900	1910	1900	1910	1900	1910	1900	1910
In North America		In South America		In Africa		In Europe		In Asia	

Chart information from *Rand McNally Atlas of World History.*

Scale is accurate only along the equator.

0   1000   2000 Miles
0   1000   2000 Kilometers

Robinson Projection

Map labels:

GREENLAND, ICELAND, Arctic Circle, Faeroe Is., Shetland Is., Orkney Is., NORWAY, SWEDEN, DENMARK, NORTH SEA, BALTIC SEA, GREAT BRITAIN, CELTIC SEA, GERMANY, NETH., BEL., LUX., FRANCE, SWITZ., Bay of Biscay, AUSTRIA-HUNGARY, ITALY, ADRIATIC SEA, MONTENEGRO, SERBIA, ROMANIA, BULGARIA, ALBANIA, BLACK SEA, GREECE, Malta, Dodecanese I., Cyprus, OTTOMAN EMPIRE, MEDITERRANEAN SEA, SPAIN, Balearic Is., PORTUGAL, SP. MOROCCO, MADEIRA, MOROCCO, ALGERIA, TUNIS, TRIPOLI, Canary Is., IFNI, RIO DE ORO, RUSSIA, ARAL SEA, CASPIAN SEA, L. Balkhash, L. Baikal, SEA OF OKHOTSK, KARAFUTO, NORTH PACIFIC OCEAN, NORTH ATLANTIC OCEAN

PERSIA, ARABIA, RED SEA, EGYPT, ANGLO-EGYPTIAN SUDAN, Persian Gulf, Gulf of Oman, Gulf of Aden, ARABIAN SEA, INDIA, GOA (PORT.), BURMA, CHINA, KOREA, SEA OF JAPAN, JAPAN, YELLOW SEA, EAST CHINA SEA, Ryuku Is., FORMOSA, Tropic of Cancer, Formosa Strait, Mariana Is., Guam

FRENCH WEST AFRICA, L. Chad, ERITREA, FR. SOMALILAND, BR. SOMALILAND, ETHIOPIA, ITALIAN SOMALILAND, Socotra, Gulf of Guinea, GAMBIA, TOGOLAND, NIGERIA, SIERRA LEONE, LIBERIA, GOLD COAST, Fernando Poo, SP. GUINEA, KAMERUN, FR. CONGO, BELGIAN CONGO, UGANDA, L. Victoria, BR. EAST AFRICA, GERMAN EAST AFRICA, KABINDA, L. Tanganyika, ANGOLA, NYASALAND, RHODESIA, MOZAMBIQUE, GERMAN SOUTHWEST AFRICA, WALVIS BAY (BR.), UNION OF SOUTH AFRICA, Mozambique Channel, MADAGASCAR, Comoro Is., Seychelles, Chagos Arch., Maldives, INDIAN OCEAN, Ascension I., St. Helena I., SOUTH ATLANTIC OCEAN, Tristan da Cunha

CEYLON, Andaman Is., ANDAMAN SEA, Nicobar Is., SIAM, FRENCH INDOCHINA, Gulf of Tonkin, Gulf of Thailand, MALAYA, SUMATRA, SARAWAK, BRUNEI, NORTH BORNEO, DUTCH BORNEO, CELEBES SEA, PHILIPPINES, Palau, Caroline Is., JAVA SEA, JAVA, TIMOR, E. TIMOR, BANDA SEA, ARAFURA SEA, TIMOR SEA, Cocos Is., Tropic of Capricorn, Bay of Bengal, Gulf of Thailand, KAISER WILHELMSLAND, NEW GUINEA, PAPUA, Bismark Arch., CORAL SEA, AUSTRALIA, Great Australian Bight, TASMAN SEA, NEW ZEALAND

Bay of Bengal

W 20° W, 0°, 20° E, 40° E, 60° E, 80° E, 100° E, 120° E, 140° E, 160° E

WORLD WAR I

FOCUS

UNDERSTANDING THE MAIN IDEA

When war enveloped Europe, the United States tried to remain neutral. In 1917, however, the United States joined the Allied cause. The government quickly moved to mobilize the economy and to build public support for the war. Then when the fighting stopped, Wilson worked to shape a just peace. He failed, however, to win congressional support for the treaty he helped write.

 THEMES

■ **GLOBAL RELATIONS** Why might a country be drawn into an international conflict in spite of efforts to remain neutral?

■ **ECONOMIC DEVELOPMENT** How might fighting a war affect a nation's economy?

■ **DEMOCRATIC VALUES** How might war affect a government's respect for its citizens' rights?

1914	1915	1917	1918	
Archduke Franz Ferdinand assassinated.	**German U-boat sinks *Lusitania*.**	**Congress declares war.**	**Wilson introduces Fourteen Points.**	**Tre Ver**

In his farewell address President Washington had warned against entangling American "peace and prosperity in the toils of European ambition." The United States had long heeded this advice and tried to remain neutral. But isolation became increasingly difficult as the nation emerged as a world power in the early 1900s.

Houplines, France, 1918

On the morning of July 29, 1914, Americans opened their newspapers to screaming headlines announcing the outbreak of war in Europe. The *New York Tribune* proclaimed: "AUSTRIA DECLARES WAR, RUSHES VAST ARMY INTO SERBIA; RUSSIA MASSES 80,000 MEN ON BORDER."

Most Americans reacted with stunned disbelief. Many were grateful that the Atlantic Ocean separated them from Europe. Urging Americans not to take sides, President Wilson attempted to steer a neutral course among the warring nations. With the passing months, however, neutrality became more difficult for the United States. Step by step, events pushed America closer to involvement. Finally, in the spring of 1917, the United States entered the fighting on the side of the Allies—one of some 30 nations on five continents formally to join the war. Before it ended, the war claimed the lives of over 8.5 million people and left some 21 million wounded or maimed.

World War I profoundly affected the American home front. It spurred government regulation of the economy, triggered a great northward migration of African Americans, and unleashed ugly forces of suspicion—even attacks—against dissenters.

President Wilson hoped that a new world order would arise from the ashes of the war. Yet, ironically, when the shooting stopped, the victors imposed a harsh peace on Germany, and the United States refused to join the League of Nations, the organization that embodied Wilson's hopes.

Red Cross unit

WORLD WAR I BREAKS OUT

F O C U S

- **What tensions helped bring about the war in Europe?**
- **What was life in the trenches like?**
- **Why did most Americans find it difficult to remain "impartial in thought" concerning the war?**
- **How did the warring nations' naval strategies challenge American neutrality?**

Soldier and horse in gas masks

*B*y the early 1900s nationalism, territorial rivalries, and militarism had turned Europe into a powder keg of hatred and petty jealousies. An assassination in a small Balkan state provided the spark that ignited this explosive mix. Within weeks, war gripped the whole continent. Everyone expected the conflict to end quickly, but it sank into a deadly stalemate. The United States declared neutrality, but the personal feelings of many Americans and the actions of the warring nations tested the country's stand.

THE ORIGINS OF THE WAR

While the Wilson administration grappled with the problems created by the Mexican Revolution, another dangerous international situation developed in Europe. On the surface Europe appeared peaceful—after all, no major conflicts had erupted since the 1870s. Furthermore, many European nations had endorsed the recommendations of two international peace conferences that arbitration be used to settle disputes among nations. But most European governments paid no more than lip service to arbitration and international cooperation. Fear, distrust, and petty jealousies often ruled their relations with other nations.

Nationalism and territorial rivalries.

At the root of the problem was the intense nationalism that engulfed Europe. Nationalism proved especially strong in northern, central, and eastern Europe. There the **Pan-German movement**, led by Germany, sought to unite all German-speaking peoples under one flag. In direct opposition, Russia supported the **Pan-Slavic movement**, which sought to bring together all the Slavic peoples of central and eastern Europe. These movements seemed destined to come into conflict, since many Slavs lived in Austria-Hungary, a part of the German world.

Another source of tension in Europe was territorial rivalry. European nations, large and small, coveted land held by their neighbors. In 1908, for example, Austria-Hungary annexed Bosnia and Herzegovina. The annexation angered Serbia, which also had designs on the small Balkan province. Other countries, too, eyed neighboring territories. Russia wanted ice-free harbors in the Baltic Sea and access for Russian warships from the Black Sea into the Mediterranean. Germany, the major Baltic power, opposed Russia's ambitions. France wanted to recover Alsace-Lorraine, a

French area the Germans had conquered in 1871, and Italy desired nearby territories belonging to Austria-Hungary.

Militarism and alliances.

This dizzying tangle of territorial claims helped generate a spirit of **militarism**, or glorification of armed strength, across the continent. Each nation built up its army and navy against the military threat posed by its neighbors. Military buildup quickly turned into an arms race as each nation tried to develop weapons more powerful than those of its neighbors.

European nations also sought to strengthen their military positions through alliances. Germany, Austria-Hungary, and Italy formed the **Triple Alliance**. Great Britain, France, and Russia joined in the **Triple Entente**. In the treaties that cemented these alliances, the members usually promised to aid any other member who came under attack from an outside power.

The spark that led to war.

These alliances helped maintain a balance of power, but they also meant that even a minor incident could provoke a war. Many observers feared that if such an incident occurred, it would be in the Balkans—a region so unstable that some called it "the powder keg of Europe." Observers also agreed that the incident would likely involve nationalist rivalries. As German general Helmuth von Moltke (MAWLT-kuh) remarked in 1912:

> 66 A European war is bound to come sooner or later, and then it will . . . be a struggle between Teuton [German] and Slav. It is the duty of all states who uphold the banner of German spiritual culture to prepare for this conflict. But the attack must come from the Slavs. 99

The attack came in 1914. In June of that year, Archduke Franz Ferdinand, the heir to the Austro-Hungarian throne, paid a goodwill visit to Sarajevo (SAHR-uh-ye-voh), the capital of Bosnia and Herzegovina. As Franz Ferdinand's open motor car proceeded along the city's streets, Serbian nationalist Gavrilo Princip (PREENT-seep) stepped out of the crowd and fired two shots, killing the archduke and his wife, Sofie.

Suspecting—correctly—that the Serbian government knew of Princip's plans, Austria-Hungary declared war on Serbia. The declaration drew each side's allies into the conflict. Russia sided with Serbia; Germany, with Austria-Hungary. Within a week France and Great Britain had declared war on Austria-Hungary and Germany. Despite membership in the Triple Alliance, Italy remained neutral until 1915, when it joined France, Great Britain, Russia, and the other **Allied Powers** against the **Central Powers** of Germany, Austria-Hungary, the Ottoman Empire (Turkey), and Bulgaria. Eventually some 30 nations would take sides in the Great War.

■■ Nationalism, territorial rivalries, militarism, and military alliances created tensions that led to war.

▼ Archduke Franz Ferdinand, his wife, and their children pose for a royal family picture.

▶ Gavrilo Princip was 19 years old when he assassinated Franz Ferdinand. He was arrested and sentenced to 20 years—the maximum prison penalty for someone under 20 years old.

THE EARLY WEEKS OF THE WAR

In 1905, accepting the inevitability of a European war, German military leaders had developed a plan for swift victory. The plan called for German forces to skirt the heavily defended Franco-German border, march through then-neutral Belgium, and invade France across the practically unguarded Belgian border before Great Britain could move its forces across the English Channel. With France and Britain knocked out of the war, Germany could focus on defeating Russia.

On August 3, 1914, the Germans launched their plan, surging into Belgium. German military leaders expected to reach the French border quickly and then sweep across northern France toward Paris. Like their kaiser (ruler), Wilhelm II, they believed that the war would end "before the leaves have fallen from the trees." But thanks to

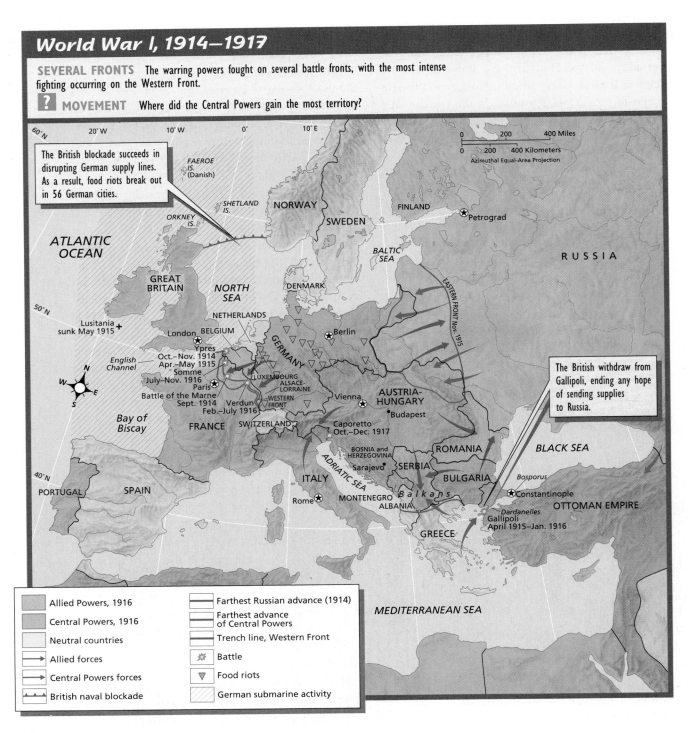

World War I, 1914–1917

SEVERAL FRONTS The warring powers fought on several battle fronts, with the most intense fighting occurring on the Western Front.

? MOVEMENT Where did the Central Powers gain the most territory?

The British blockade succeeds in disrupting German supply lines. As a result, food riots break out in 56 German cities.

The British withdraw from Gallipoli, ending any hope of sending supplies to Russia.

Lusitania sunk May 1915

Ypres Oct.–Nov. 1914 Apr.–May 1915

Somme July–Nov. 1916

Battle of the Marne Sept. 1914

Verdun Feb.–July 1916

Caporetto Oct.–Dec. 1917

Gallipoli April 1915–Jan. 1916

EASTERN FRONT Nov. 1915

WESTERN FRONT

Legend:
- Allied Powers, 1916
- Central Powers, 1916
- Neutral countries
- Allied forces
- Central Powers forces
- British naval blockade
- Farthest Russian advance (1914)
- Farthest advance of Central Powers
- Trench line, Western Front
- Battle
- Food riots
- German submarine activity

0   200   400 Miles
0   200   400 Kilometers
Azimuthal Equal-Area Projection

the small Belgian army's fierce resistance, the Germans spent nearly three weeks fighting their way across Belgium. As a result, General Joseph Joffre (zhawfruh), the French commander, had time to rush troops to the Belgian border, and the British had time to transport some 90,000 troops to northern France.

These measures managed to slow the German advance but did not stop it. The Germans' superior military might pushed the French and the British back to the Marne River in northeast France. Against heavy odds, the French and the British stopped the Germans early in September 1914 at the **First Battle of the Marne.** From roughly Ypres (eepruh) to Verdun, the German line fell back some 40 miles (see map on page 244). The French and the British launched a counteroffensive but were unable to dislodge the Germans. The Germans had no better luck advancing against the Allies. As 1914 drew to a close, leaders of both sides realized that there would be no quick victory.

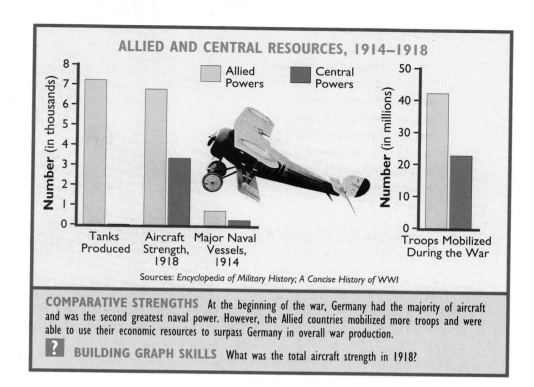

ALLIED AND CENTRAL RESOURCES, 1914–1918

Allied Powers / Central Powers

Number (in thousands): Tanks Produced, Aircraft Strength, 1918, Major Naval Vessels, 1914

Number (in millions): Troops Mobilized During the War

Sources: *Encyclopedia of Military History; A Concise History of WWI*

COMPARATIVE STRENGTHS At the beginning of the war, Germany had the majority of aircraft and was the second greatest naval power. However, the Allied countries mobilized more troops and were able to use their economic resources to surpass Germany in overall war production.

? BUILDING GRAPH SKILLS What was the total aircraft strength in 1918?

The Granger Collection, New York

▲ **This 1914 photograph shows German soldiers traveling to the western front in a train marked with the inscription "A trip to Paris—See you again on the boulevard."**

WAR REACHES A STALEMATE

By early 1915 both armies dug in along a front running some 400 miles from the North Sea to the Swiss border. Holed up in trenches and separated by a thin strip of territory called **no-man's land**, both sides struggled to advance.

Trench warfare. Even the most hardened soldier had never encountered anything like **trench warfare**. Britain's field marshal Lord Kitchener lamented, "I don't know what is to be done—this isn't war." In this war most battles began with deafening artillery fire. Then as the smoke and dust from the cannonade cleared, one army would charge the enemy trenches. Most soldiers who succeeded in getting through the barbed wire and land mines strewn across no-man's land were cut down by a hail of bullets from the enemy trenches. In the **Battle of the Somme** in 1916, for example, the British suffered some 60,000 casualties in a single day! All told, this four-month-long battle claimed more than a million dead and wounded.

Maneuvering in the trenches was nightmarish. As British soldier Charles Carrington wrote:

❝ When moving about in the trenches you turn a corner every few yards, which makes it seem like walking in a maze. It is impossible to keep your sense of direction and infinitely tiring to proceed at all. When the trenches have been fought over the confusion becomes all the greater. Instead of neat, parallel trench lines, you make the best use of existing trenches which might run in any direction. **99**

Even during lulls in the fighting, life in the trenches proved frightful. Rats and lice plagued the soldiers. Rain flooded the trenches, drenching the soldiers in mud. Artillery fire frequently prevented burial of the dead for days, and exploding shells often unearthed corpses buried earlier. Such unsanitary conditions bred disease, and sickness claimed nearly as many men as bombs and bullets did. The only way out of the trenches, a British soldier observed, was on a stretcher.

New weapons. New weapons added to the horror of trench warfare. The Germans' machine guns fired hundreds of rounds per minute, felling advancing Allied troops like a scythe cutting wheat. The Allies introduced the tank partly to counter the machine gun's deadly impact. First used at the Battle of the Somme in September 1916, the tank produced the intended effect. It

▲ **A British tank force is shown here fighting near Amiens, France, in August 1918.**

scared the Germans "out of their wits," one British soldier reported, and made them "scuttle like frightened rabbits."

But perhaps the most feared new weapon introduced during World War I was poison gas. No whistling shell announced a gas attack. The green mist silently drifted over the trenches, and the soldiers had only seconds to slip on their gas masks. Any delay meant a slow, suffocating death. After watching a comrade die of poison gas, soldier-poet Wilfred Owen wrote:

66 But someone still was yelling out
        and stumbling,
    And flound'ring like a man in fire
        or lime . . .
    Dim, through the misty panes and
        thick green light,
    As under a green sea, I saw him
        drowning. **99**

■■ **Heavy casualties, unsanitary conditions, and fearful new weapons made trench warfare a horrible experience.**

▲ **Soldiers fought much of World War I from trenches. There they struggled to protect themselves from artillery fire, exposure to all types of weather, and disease and unsanitary conditions.**

Continued stalemate. While new military technology produced horrendous casualties on both sides, it did little to break the stalemate on the western front. From 1915 to the spring of 1917, both armies launched offensives that gained them a few miles of territory, which more often than not they quickly lost.

As the months passed, many people wondered whether the fighting would ever stop. They began to suggest that only the intervention of the United States could bring the war to an end.

AMERICAN NEUTRALITY

At the outbreak of the war, most Americans had expressed surprise and horror. After the initial shock, however, Americans tended to look on the war as a faraway conflict that did not involve the United States. As one American diplomat wrote: "Again and ever I thank Heaven for the Atlantic Ocean."

Not surprisingly, then, President Wilson received strong support when he announced a policy of neutrality. All Americans, he urged, ought to be "neutral in fact as well as in name . . . impartial in thought as well as action." Wilson thought that by taking a neutral stance, the United States might help to negotiate a settlement to the conflict. He pursued this goal throughout 1915 and 1916, but without success.

As the war dragged on, most Americans remained neutral in action, but few could claim to be impartial in thought. Some 28 million Americans—almost 30 percent of the population— were immigrants or the children of immigrants. Many men and women of German, Austrian, Hungarian, or Turkish background sympathized with the Central Powers. So did many Irish Americans anxious to free Ireland from Great Britain's rule.

Most Americans, however, backed the Allies. Ties of ancestry, language, and culture bound many Americans to Britain. Strong, long-established links to France also existed. After all, the French had helped Americans win their War of Independence. The British also bolstered American support for the Allies through a skillful propaganda campaign, which painted Germans as brutal warmongers.

■■ **The U.S. government remained neutral, but most Americans— because of ancestral ties or national sympathies—favored one side or the other.**

Challenges to American neutrality.

Despite its policy of neutrality, the United States could not remain untouched by the war. When the war began, the British navy blockaded the German coast and planted explosive mines across the North Sea. The British even stopped American ships bound for ports in neutral countries and examined cargos—including the mail—for goods that might ultimately be destined for Germany. The United States protested, charging that British actions violated American neutrality.

American hostility toward Great Britain faded, however, in the face of German submarine, or U-boat, warfare. Early in 1915 the Germans established a "war zone" around Great Britain. Any ships entering this zone, even those from neutral nations, were liable to U-boat attack. In response, Wilson warned that the United States would, in accordance with international laws of neutrality, hold Germany accountable for any injury to American lives or property on the high seas.

On March 28, 1915, a U-boat sank a British liner in the Irish Sea, killing more than 100 people, including an American. While the United States debated its response, a far more serious incident occurred. On May 7, 1915, a U-boat patrolling off the Irish coast torpedoed the British passenger liner *Lusitania*. The dead included 128 Americans. The *New York Herald* accused the Germans of "piracy on the high seas," and the *New York Times* called the Germans "savages drenched with blood." Outraged Americans agreed. German leaders justified their actions, declaring that they had placed advertisements in U.S. newspapers warning Americans against sailing into the war zone. They also charged that the *Lusitania* was carrying

▶ The *Lusitania*'s 1915 voyage announcement carried a warning from the German Embassy against Atlantic sea travel.

▲ The *Lusitania* was photographed shortly before its fateful voyage from New York in 1915.

Germany's Baron von Schwarzenstein offered the following response to the outrage over the sinking of the *Lusitania*:

"**I**t was only after England declared the whole North Sea a war zone . . . that Germany with precisely the same right declared the waters around England a war zone and announced her purpose of sinking all hostile commercial vessels found therein. . . . In the case of the Lusitania the German Ambassador even further warned Americans through the great American newspapers against taking passage thereon. Does a pirate act thus? Does he take pains to save human lives? . . . Nobody regrets more sincerely than we Germans the hard necessity of sending to their deaths hundreds of men. Yet the sinking was a justifiable act of war. . . . The scene of war is no golf links, the ships of belligerent powers no pleasure places. . . . We have sympathy with the victims and their relatives, of course, but did we hear anything about sympathy . . . when England adopted her diabolical plan of starving a great nation?**"**

armaments for England—an accusation that later proved true.

Nevertheless, Wilson fired off an angry protest to the German government, demanding specific pledges against unrestricted submarine warfare. Secretary of State William Jennings Bryan, charging that the president's protest amounted to an ultimatum, resigned. Bryan argued that the United States could not issue ultimatums and remain neutral. The country, he warned, would eventually be drawn into the war.

■■ **British and German naval activities violated the rights of neutral nations and led to American protests.**

SECTION 1 REVIEW

IDENTIFY and explain the significance of the following: Pan-German movement, Pan-Slavic movement, militarism, Triple Alliance, Triple Entente, Archduke Franz Ferdinand, Gavrilo Princip, Allied Powers, Central Powers, First Battle of the Marne, no-man's land, trench warfare, Battle of the Somme.

LOCATE and explain the importance of the following: Austria-Hungary, Bosnia and Herzegovina, Alsace-Lorraine, Balkans, Belgium.

1. **MAIN IDEA** What factors contributed to the outbreak of World War I?

2. **MAIN IDEA** What effect did Britain and Germany's naval strategies have on American neutrality?

3. **RECOGNIZING POINTS OF VIEW** Did the U.S. government's policy of neutrality reflect the views of most Americans? Why or why not?

4. **WRITING TO DESCRIBE** Imagine you are a British soldier at the front during 1916. Write a diary entry that describes the conditions you experience during trench warfare.

5. **ANALYZING** How might trench warfare and new weapons have contributed to the stalemate on the western front?

Section 2

THE UNITED STATES GOES TO WAR

FOCUS

■ **Why did the United States finally enter the war?**

■ **Why did the United States institute a draft?**

■ **What part did the American military play in the Allied war effort?**

*G*ermany's continued violations of American neutrality drew the United States into World War I on the Allied side in 1917. The Americans' entry came none too soon for the Allies, who faced a desperate military situation. As U.S. forces poured into Europe the tide turned. The Germans slowly fell back, and in November 1918 the warring parties signed an armistice. The four-year nightmare had finally ended.

World War I poster

THE ROAD TO WAR

The sinking of the *Lusitania* brought the conflict in Europe closer to home for many Americans. Even so, most still hoped the United States could stay out of the war. Further challenges to American neutrality, however, were not long in coming. In August 1915 two Americans died when a German submarine sank the *Arabic,* another British liner. Then in March 1916 the French passenger vessel *Sussex* was attacked, injuring several Americans. In a sternly worded message to the German government, President Wilson threatened to sever diplomatic ties if Germany did not abandon unrestricted submarine warfare. The German government responded with the *Sussex* **pledge**, a renewal of an earlier promise not to sink liners without warning or without assuring the passengers' safety.

Wilson's actions criticized. Most Americans supported Wilson's approach. However, a number of prominent politicians, including former president Theodore Roosevelt, accused Wilson of not doing enough. Wilson, "that

infernal skunk in the White House," Roosevelt complained, had adopted a course of inaction and was little better than a "coward and weakling."

Others accused Wilson of abandoning neutrality. Former secretary of state William Jennings Bryan argued that Wilson's commercial and trade policies helped the Allies. As secretary of state, Bryan had discouraged American bankers from

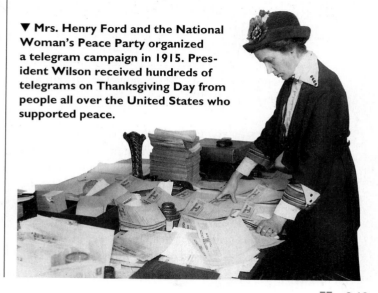

▼ **Mrs. Henry Ford and the National Woman's Peace Party organized a telegram campaign in 1915. President Wilson received hundreds of telegrams on Thanksgiving Day from people all over the United States who supported peace.**

▲ These Girl Scouts helped the war effort by collecting peach pits. The pits could be ground into a charcoal powder and placed in gas masks to help filter out the poisonous fumes during gas attacks.

making loans to either side, but this policy was soon abandoned. Bryan's successor at the State Department, Robert Lansing, encouraged trade in war materials, especially with the Allies. By 1916, arms sales to the Allies stood at some $500 million, about 80 times the amount sold in 1914.

Preparedness and peace. Bryan's fears increased when Wilson launched a military "preparedness" program. The **National Defense Act**, passed in June 1916, increased the number of soldiers in the regular army from some 90,000 to about 175,000, with an ultimate goal of about 223,000 men. It also set the size of the National Guard at some 450,000 troops and provided for their training. Another bill, passed two months later, appropriated $313 million to build up the navy.

President Wilson assured Americans that he had not abandoned neutrality. Running on the slogan "He Kept Us Out of War," Wilson won reelection in 1916, narrowly defeating the Republicans' Charles Evans Hughes.

Wilson still hoped to negotiate a settlement to the war. In a January 1917 speech, he called for "peace without victory." A lasting peace, he said, had to be one between equals, not between victor and vanquished. Once again, however, Britain and Germany rejected Wilson's effort to mediate.

Diplomatic relations broken. On February 1, 1917, Germany resumed full-scale U-boat warfare. The Germans were gambling that their U-boat fleet could defeat the Allies before the Americans joined the war. Wilson, as he had threatened, broke off diplomatic relations. He also ordered the arming of American merchant ships sailing into the war zone. Nonetheless, German torpedoes sank five American ships.

The publication on March 1, 1917, of an intercepted cable from German foreign secretary Arthur Zimmermann to the German minister in Mexico further heightened tensions. The **Zimmermann Note**, as the cable was quickly dubbed, instructed the minister that if the United States declared war on Germany, he was to propose to Mexico that it enter an alliance with Germany. With German support, the cable went on, Mexico could "reconquer the lost territory in New Mexico, Texas, and Arizona."

As the weeks passed, Wilson reluctantly concluded that the United States could not stay out of the conflict. On April 2, 1917, the president addressed Congress, asking them to vote on a declaration of war.

CONGRESS DECLARES WAR

A hushed Congress heard Wilson condemn Germany's submarine warfare for its "wanton and wholesale destruction." Wilson, however, did not rest his case solely on the evils of U-boat warfare. He summoned Americans to a crusade for a better world:

> 66 We are glad . . . to fight thus for the ultimate peace of the world and for the liberation of its peoples, . . . for the rights of nations great and small and the privilege of men everywhere to choose their way of life. . . . The world must be made safe for democracy. 99

At these words, cheers and applause rang through the Capitol. A somber Wilson later told an aide: "My message today was a message of death for our young men. How strange it seems to applaud that."

■■ **U-boat activity and the interception of the Zimmermann Note led the United States to declare war on Germany.**

BIO GRAPHY The Senate declared war on April 4; the House, two days later. The vote was not unanimous—6 senators and 50 representatives opposed the declaration. Congresswoman Jeannette Rankin of Montana was among the opposition. "I want to stand by my country," she explained, "but I cannot vote for war."

Born in Missoula, Montana, in 1880, Rankin was a committed pacifist, social worker, and leader of the women's suffrage movement. In 1916 she became the first woman elected to Congress, and in 1918 she played a key role in the passage of the Nineteenth Amendment. However, with Allied victory only days away, Rankin lost her bid for a Senate seat in the November 1918 elections.

Elected to the House again in 1940, Rankin continued to speak out against the draft and

▶ **Jeannette Rankin**

military spending, casting the only vote against the United States' entry into World War II. That vote cost her reelection in 1942. She did not give up her pacifism, however. In January 1968, at age 87, Rankin led a march on Washington, D.C., to protest the Vietnam War.

MOBILIZING AMERICAN MILITARY POWER

In his war message on April 2, President Wilson pledged all the nation's "material resources" to the Allied war effort. But what the Allies most urgently needed were fresh troops. Few Americans, however, rushed to volunteer for military service.

On May 18, 1917, Congress responded by passing the **Selective Service Act**, which required men between ages 21 and 30 to register with local draft boards. (The age range was later changed to 18–45) By the end of the war, some 24 million men had registered, and some 2.8 million had been drafted. In fact, more than half of the almost 4.8 million Americans who served in the armed forces were draftees.

Many who supported conscription argued that the draft would help build a more democratic America by bringing together soldiers from different backgrounds. In reality, Native Americans, African Americans, Mexican Americans, and many foreign-born soldiers faced discrimination.

Most foreign-born soldiers, for example, were assigned to segregated units where they were taught civics and English. Congress did, however, offer citizenship to the some 10,000 Native Americans who served during the war.

The more than 370,000 African American recruits experienced particularly harsh discrimination. They were blocked from service in the marines and limited to kitchen duties in the navy. Most African Americans in the army were confined to all-black support units commanded by white officers. And African American draftees sent to army training camps in the South often faced harassment from local whites.

Pressure from the NAACP and other African American organizations convinced the army to open up more opportunities for black soldiers. A school was established to train African American officers, and more blacks were assigned combat duty. The army, however, made no effort to integrate blacks and whites in the same units.

■■ The United States instituted the draft to bring the armed services up to full force.

▲ **Approximately 1,400 African American officers served during World War I. This officer was stationed in Saint-Dizier, France.**

OVER THERE

With mobilization well under way, American troops sailed to France as part of the American Expeditionary Force (AEF). The first U.S. troops, under the command of General John J. Pershing, reached France in late June 1917. On July 4, thousands of "Yanks," cheered on by huge crowds, marched through Paris to the tomb of the Marquis de Lafayette, the French hero of the American Revolution. "Lafayette, we are here!" proclaimed one of Pershing's aides.

Lieutenant Edward F. Graham wrote home about the sense of purpose that he—and many other soldiers—felt:

> ❝ The desperate contest between justice and empire . . . is now on. You should be proud to have me . . . participate in the

HISTORY *in the* Making

BY DR. PAUL BOYER

The Doughboy's Pack

History is much more than a study of dates, documents, or facts about influential people. Ordinary objects also leave a historical record about an event or an era. For example, common items provided to soldiers during a war tell a story about how that war was fought.

During World War I the American infantryman—or doughboy, as he was nicknamed—wearily trudged across European battlefields carrying all his necessary equipment inside a canvas "field kit" strapped to his back. Some of the items provided to American soldiers in World War I are shown on these pages. Examine the photographs carefully. What can we learn about the combat experiences of World War I soldiers by studying what they carried?

Begin with the field kit. Examine the cartridge belt attached at waist level. Notice the individual pockets. Each compartment held 10 rounds of ammunition. The around-the-

▶ Soldier equipped with gas mask and steel helmet

waist design with pockets was adopted during World War I because of automatic weapons. Rifles could now fire as many as five bullets per minute, and a soldier needed easy access to large amounts of ammunition during the heat of battle. The cartridge belt served this purpose.

Next notice the shovel strapped to the field kit, with its blade encased inside a protective flap. Until 1918 most of the war on the western front was fought from the trenches. Consequently, digging equipment was a necessity. Each squad shared a variety of tools: shovels, hand axes, pickaxes, and wire cutters. Wire cutters were particularly essential to the needs of World War I infantry. Before a soldier could

reach the enemy's trenches, he had to clear a path through coils of sharp barbed wire. Getting even a small cut from the rusty barbs could prove dangerous—infections in a minor wound often led to the amputation of an arm or a leg.

Now examine the photograph of the American soldier wearing the gas mask and steel helmet. Chlorine gas and mustard gas were greatly feared weapons introduced during World War I. The gas mask struggle as a part of the human wall against a second Dark Ages. 99

As the weeks went by, American troops arrived in France in ever-swelling numbers. To supply and maintain them, army engineers built docks and railroads and strung up networks of telephone and telegraph lines. They also constructed camps, ammunition dumps, storage sheds, and hospitals.

Some 10,000 American women worked in these hospitals. Emily Vuagniaux, an Army Medical Corps nurse, described life in a battlefield hospital:

66 We . . . have worked . . . sometimes 18 hours straight. I have the operating room and they run four tables day and night and have between 200 and 300 patients right off the field, so you may know we are quite close in. 99

filtered out poisonous fumes that could suffocate or blind a soldier. The odd-looking rubber contraption was hot and uncomfortable, but crucial to survival. The soldier's steel helmet, as you can see, extended to the top of the ear line. The helmet was designed to help prevent head wounds. A soldier was particularly vulnerable to such injuries when he first peered out from a trench—just before going "over the top."

Next look at a soldier's vital "mess" equipment. The oval "meat can" served as both a skillet and a plate. Sturdy metal containers protected two days' worth of rations from rain, rats, and insects. A doughboy carried two portions of hard biscuits called hardtack. The condiment can had separate compartments for coffee, sugar, and salt. Above the condiment can is a bacon tin. In addition to such supplies, a soldier carried emergency rations such as stringy beef, scornfully called "monkey

meat" by many soldiers. From this mess equipment and the simple nature of the rations, we can assume that a doughboy's supply lines were within a short distance of each squad. More-substantial meals were prepared by a company cook, who followed the combat units.

In addition to the items shown here, an infantryman carried a tent, tent poles, a rain poncho, a bayonet, a blanket, a sewing kit, socks, identification tags, a compass, and a flashlight. On a long march a World War I soldier might have cursed his heavy pack. But he also knew his burden could mean the difference between life and death.

▲ Field kit

◀ Bacon tin

◀ Condiment can

▲ Meat can

▲ Ambulance drivers were responsible for transporting wounded soldiers from the battlefield to hospitals behind the front lines. Many of the ambulance units included women drivers and mechanics.

Thousands more American women went to Europe as volunteers for the Red Cross, the YMCA, or other agencies.

Merchant vessels, escorted by American warships, transported troops, supplies, and volunteers through the submarine-infested North Atlantic. This **convoy system** proved quite effective. Of the more than two million American soldiers who crossed the Atlantic, not one died as the result of an enemy attack on the high seas. Other American warships patrolled the western Atlantic and laid some 70,000 mines in a lethal 240-mile necklace across the North Sea from Norway to the Orkney Islands off Great Britain. This barrier made life hazardous for German U-boats trying to return to their bases.

THE END OF THE WAR

The Americans' entry into the war came none too soon for the Allies. In an effort to break the deadlock on the western front, the Allies had launched an offensive in the summer of 1917. It failed, shattering the Allied troops' already shaky morale. That fall, mutinies broke out in French units all along the front. In October the Central Powers crashed through Italian lines at Caporetto, on the border between Italy and Austria-Hungary (see map on page 244). Only the arrival of Allied reinforcements saved Italy from collapse.

Worse news arrived from Russia. The Russian people, dissatisfied with working and living conditions, had overthrown the czar in March 1917. Political turmoil continued until November, when the **Bolsheviks**, a branch of the Russian Communist party, seized power. The Bolshevik leader, Vladimir Ilich Lenin, opposed the war. The Bolsheviks signed the **Treaty of Brest-Litovsk** with the Central Powers in March 1918, leaving the Central Powers free to mass their forces on the western front.

Germany's last bid for victory. On March 21, 1918, some one million German troops launched a do-or-die offensive against the Allies. The Germans were backed by some 6,000 heavy guns, including "Big Berthas" capable of firing 250- to 300-pound shells 74 miles. By late May the Germans had pushed the Allies back to the Marne River, only 50 miles from Paris.

General Pershing had originally insisted that American troops fight as a separate army under their own commanders. In light of the situation, however, he agreed to join a unified Allied army under the command of Marshal Ferdinand Foch of France. The introduction of American forces proved decisive. In a last-ditch defense of Paris, American troops helped the French stop the Germans at Château-Thierry on June 3–4. Nearby, a division of American marines counterattacked, recapturing Belleau Wood and two other villages. After fierce fighting, the German advance was halted, and Paris was saved.

On July 15 the Germans threw everything into a final assault around Reims. But the Allied lines held, and Foch ordered a counterattack three days later. The charge, spearheaded by American troops, pushed the Germans back. The tide had turned in favor of the Allies.

With the assistance of American troops, the Allies turned the tide against the Germans.

Allied victory. In the late summer Foch seized the initiative, ordering a major offensive along the entire western front. Over the next three months, the Allies pushed deep into German-held territory.

In this offensive the Americans fought as a separate army under Pershing's command and led the attack that pushed the Germans back at Saint-Mihiel, France, in September 1918. The Americans next drove toward Sedan, the French rail center that the Germans had held since 1914. For more than a month the Americans pushed northward along the Meuse River and through the rugged Argonne Forest, facing artillery and machine-gun fire all the way. The Americans suffered some 120,000 casualties on this drive, but by November they had reached and occupied the hills around Sedan.

Lieutenant Edward Graham was one of the casualties. By the time he died, he no longer saw the war as a noble venture. In his last letter he described it as incomprehensible:

> 66 This is a cowering war—pigmy man huddles in little holes and caves praying to escape the blows of the giant who pounds the earth with blind hammers. 99

African American troops played a major role in the Argonne offensive. Members of the 369th Infantry, an African American regiment whose men hailed from New York, so distinguished

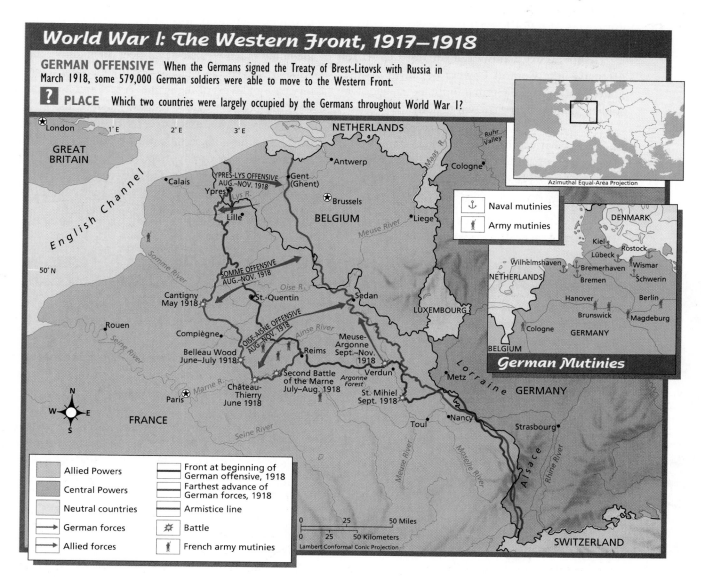

World War I: The Western Front, 1917–1918

GERMAN OFFENSIVE When the Germans signed the Treaty of Brest-Litovsk with Russia in March 1918, some 579,000 German soldiers were able to move to the Western Front.

? PLACE Which two countries were largely occupied by the Germans throughout World War I?

Azimuthal Equal-Area Projection

⚓ Naval mutinies
🪖 Army mutinies

German Mutinies

DENMARK
Kiel
Lübeck
Rostock
Wilhelmshaven
Bremerhaven
Wismar
NETHERLANDS
Bremen
Schwerin
Hanover
Berlin
Brunswick
Magdeburg
Cologne
BELGIUM
GERMANY

London
1° E
2° E
3° E
NETHERLANDS
Ruhr Valley
GREAT BRITAIN
Antwerp
Cologne
Calais
YPRES-LYS OFFENSIVE AUG.–NOV. 1918
Gent (Ghent)
Maas R.
Ypres
Lys R.
Lille
Brussels
BELGIUM
Liege
English Channel
Meuse River
Somme River
50° N
SOMME OFFENSIVE AUG.–NOV. 1918
Oise R.
Sedan
LUXEMBOURG
Cantigny May 1918
St.-Quentin
Rouen
Compiègne
OISE-AISNE OFFENSIVE AUG.–NOV. 1918
Aisne River
Meuse-Argonne Sept.–Nov. 1918
Lorraine
Seine River
Belleau Wood June–July 1918
Reims
Argonne Forest
Verdun
Metz
GERMANY
Marne R.
Château-Thierry June 1918
Second Battle of the Marne July–Aug. 1918
St. Mihiel Sept. 1918
Paris
FRANCE
N W E S
Toul
Nancy
Strasbourg
Seine River
Moselle River
Alsace
Rhine River
SWITZERLAND

Allied Powers
Central Powers
Neutral countries
→ German forces
→ Allied forces
Front at beginning of German offensive, 1918
Farthest advance of German forces, 1918
Armistice line
✪ Battle
🪖 French army mutinies

0   25   50 Miles
0   25   50 Kilometers
Lambert Conformal Conic Projection

▲ The armistice ending the war was signed in this railway passenger car on November 11, 1918.

Mutinies broke out in both the German army and navy. German civilians took to the streets demanding food, not war. Realizing that the war was lost, Wilhelm II fled to the Netherlands in early November. The following day, Germany's new government agreed to an **armistice**, or cease-fire.

On November 8, 1918, German representatives were summoned to Compiègne (kohmp-YAYN), the Allied headquarters, to hear the armistice terms. The Allies demanded that the Germans evacuate France, Belgium, Luxembourg, and Alsace-Lorraine. They also insisted that Germany surrender an enormous amount of war materials, including much of their naval fleet. In addition, the Allies reserved the right to occupy German territory east and west of the Rhine. After brief negotiations the Germans agreed to these harsh terms.

themselves that the French awarded them the *Croix de Guerre* (kwahd i GER), or "Cross of War," a French military honor.

Repeatedly hammered during the Allied offensive, the Central Powers began to disintegrate. Morale in the German military sagged. One soldier, anxious for peace, wrote home:

66 In what way have we sinned, that we should be treated worse than animals? Hunted from place to place, cold, filthy . . . we are destroyed like vermin. Will they *never* make peace? 99

Early on the morning of November 11, the warring parties signed the armistice, and at 11 A.M. the cease-fire went into effect. The constant crashing of guns was replaced, according to one American, by a "silence [that] was nearly unbearable." The Great War, at long last, had ended.

SECTION 2 REVIEW

IDENTIFY and explain the significance of the following: *Sussex* pledge, Robert Lansing, National Defense Act, Zimmermann Note, Jeannette Rankin, Selective Service Act, John J. Pershing, convoy system, Bolsheviks, Treaty of Brest-Litovsk, Ferdinand Foch, armistice.

LOCATE and explain the importance of the following: Caporetto, Château-Thierry, St. Mihiel, Sedan, Meuse River, Compiègne.

1. **MAIN IDEA** What actions provoked the United States to declare war on Germany?

2. **MAIN IDEA** Why did the United States pass the Selective Service Act?

3. **ANALYZING** What evidence suggests that conscription did not make America more democratic?

4. **WRITING TO INFORM** Imagine you are Secretary of State Robert Lansing. Write a memorandum to President Wilson that summarizes the effect the American entry into the war had on Allied efforts.

5. **HYPOTHESIZING** How might the war in Europe have been different if Germany had abandoned U-boat warfare?

THE WAR AT HOME

FOCUS

- **What steps did the federal government take to mobilize the economy for war?**
- **How did the labor force change during the war?**
- **How did the government stifle dissent and rally support for its wartime policies?**

Irving Berlin song sheet, 1918

*O*nce the United States entered the war, President Wilson quickly moved to mobilize the nation. The government set up programs to finance the war, to conserve scarce resources, and to redirect industry and labor toward wartime production. Wilson also launched a huge propaganda campaign to mobilize support for the war effort. But as the government whipped up enthusiasm for the war, intolerance of antiwar opinion spread across the land.

MOBILIZING THE ECONOMY

At the outset of the war, Wilson had noted that "there are no armies in this struggle; there are entire nations armed." To "arm" the nation, Wilson realized, the economy had to be put on a wartime footing.

The first step in this process was raising money to pay for the war, which eventually cost Americans more than $33 billion. The government raised money through four Liberty Bond issues during the war and one Victory Bond issue after the armistice. Posters, parades, and rallies promoted each bond issue. "Every person who refuses to subscribe . . . is a friend of Germany," declared William McAdoo, secretary of treasury and Wilson's son-in-law, and "is not entitled to be an American citizen." With pressure like this behind them, these promotions were a huge success, raising some $23 billion for the war.

The government also planned to raise money by increasing taxes. This proved more difficult than selling bonds. Congress debated a new tax program for months, finally reaching agreement in October 1917. The new taxes on business incomes and large personal incomes produced about $9 billion for the war—much less than expected.

Mobilizing the economy for war entailed more than raising money, however. It also involved coordinating the actions of government, business,

▲ **Movie stars Douglas Fairbanks, Mary Pickford, and Charlie Chaplin lent their support to a Liberty Bond drive in Philadelphia.**

and industry. This was done through a multitude of federal war boards. While the federal government never took complete control of the economy, it exercised sweeping economic power through these various agencies. It set the prices and production levels of hundreds of commodities and regulated businesses crucial to the war effort.

CONSERVING FOOD AND FUEL

Among the most successful of the federal war boards were the **Food Administration** and the **Fuel Administration**, which were charged with regulating the production and supply of these essential resources. To direct the Food Administration, Wilson chose Herbert Hoover, a prosperous mining engineer who had managed a food-relief campaign for war-stricken Belgium. Hoover saw his task as twofold: to encourage increased agricultural production and to conserve existing food supplies.

To stimulate wartime production, Hoover guaranteed farmers high prices. Farm production soared. For example, farmers upped wheat production, harvesting some 921 million bushels in 1919—a dramatic increase over the 1917 figure of some 637 million bushels.

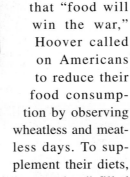
▲ **Herbert Hoover, director of the Food Administration**

Announcing that "food will win the war," Hoover called on Americans to reduce their food consumption by observing wheatless and meatless days. To supplement their diets, he suggested they plant "victory gardens" filled with vegetables. The campaign proved very effective—without, as Hoover proudly noted, forced rationing.

The Fuel Administration director, Harry Garfield, the son of the former president, took a similar course of action, encouraging people to observe heatless Mondays. Garfield was not averse to using force, however. When the nation ran short of coal in early 1918, he closed all factories east of the Mississippi for several days.

ORGANIZING INDUSTRY

Hundreds of other boards and agencies regulated industrial production and distribution. For example, the **Railroad Administration**, run by William McAdoo, reorganized the railroads, setting limits on transportation rates and workers' wages.

The work of all these boards was coordinated by the government's central war agency, the **War Industries Board** (WIB). Its director, Wall Street banker Bernard Baruch, had overall responsibility for allocating scarce materials, establishing production priorities, and setting prices. Baruch preferred to persuade business leaders to comply with his wishes. However, when steel owners refused to cut prices, the government threatened to take over their foundries and mills.

At first many business leaders were critical of Wilson's economic mobilization programs. Government intervention, they argued, would permanently damage the American free-enterprise system. As profits soared, however, they ceased to complain.

■■ **The government mobilized for war by setting up programs to raise money, conserve scarce resources, and coordinate government, business, and industry.**

MOBILIZING LABOR

Organized labor moved quickly to gain its share of wartime prosperity. With hundreds of thousands of men drafted into the army and with European immigration slowed to a trickle, industry found itself desperately short of labor as it geared up for the war effort. Taking advantage of this situation, unionized workers across the country went on strike, demanding higher wages and other benefits. Nearly 4,500 strikes involving more than one million workers occurred in 1917 alone. The tactic worked—over the war years, working conditions substantially improved.

To ensure that the voice of labor received a hearing, President Wilson established the **National War Labor Board** (NWLB) in April 1918. Composed of representatives from business and labor, the NWLB arbitrated disputes between workers and employers. In the more than 1,200

▲ Many American women helped the war effort by working in munitions factories and other industries. Here, a woman loads cartridges for rifles.

cases that it heard, the board ruled in favor of labor more often than not. In this climate of official support, union membership grew rapidly. AFL membership, for instance, rose from some 2 million in 1916 to roughly 3.2 million by 1919. By the end of the decade, some 15 percent of the nonagricultural work force was unionized.

The labor shortage that helped strengthen unions also brought about changes in the work force. The number of women working outside the home grew by about 6 percent during the war. Many of these women took traditionally male jobs. They worked as automobile mechanics, truck drivers, bricklayers, metalworkers, or railroad engineers. In all, some 1.5 million American women worked in industry during the war. Like Norma B. Kastl, an interviewer with a women's service bureau, many women considered employment their patriotic duty:

❝ The navy is taking on women as yeomen to do shore duty. . . . Every girl that becomes a yeoman can have the satisfaction of knowing that she is releasing, as from prison, some sailor who had been fuming . . . because he had to spend his days in an office instead of on the deck of a destroyer. ❞

Women also helped plan wartime mobilization. Carrie Chapman Catt, a women's suffrage leader, sat on the Women's Committee of the Council of National Defense, a civilian agency organized to support the war effort. Harriot Stanton Blatch, the daughter of Elizabeth Cady Stanton, headed the Food Administration's Speakers' Bureau.

Women's war efforts helped produce one very important political change—the passage of the Nineteenth Amendment. President Wilson, who had wavered on woman suffrage, threw his support behind the amendment in recognition of women's wartime contributions. "The greatest thing that came out of the war," Carrie Chapman Catt later noted, "was the emancipation of women, for which no man fought."

THE GREAT TREK NORTH

The labor shortage that drew women into the work force also spurred immigration from Mexico. Fleeing the Mexican Revolution and lured by southwestern employers who depended on Mexican labor, some 150,000 men and women migrated from Mexico to the United States during the war. Most took agricultural, mining, or railroad jobs in Arizona, California, Colorado, New Mexico, or Texas. But some headed northward for better-paying jobs in such industrial centers as Chicago and Cleveland.

Job opportunities and the prospect of higher wages also brought about one of the most important population shifts in American history—the **Great Migration** of African Americans from the South to northern cities between 1915 and 1930. Persuaded by recruitment agents sent by the Pennsylvania Railroad and other large employers, hundreds of thousands of African Americans moved northward during the war years (estimates range from 200,000 to 550,000). African American newspapers strongly encouraged the migration: "Get out of the South," declared an editorial in the Chicago *Defender*. "Come north . . . The *Defender* says come."

■■ **The wartime labor shortage brought large numbers of women, Mexican immigrants, and African Americans into the work force.**

▲ National guardsmen were called in to preserve the peace during the East St. Louis race riot in July 1917.

African Americans went to the North with great hope. But for many, life in the North proved harsh. Although they enjoyed a better standard of living than they had in the South, racial violence remained a serious problem. The most brutal wartime racial incident occurred in East St. Louis, Illinois, on July 2, 1917. White rioters—egged on by spectators—rampaged through black neighborhoods in an orgy of burning and shooting that left at least 39 dead. Shocked and angered, many African Americans asked themselves why they should fight for freedom in Europe when they enjoyed so little at home.

MOBILIZING ATTITUDES

Many Americans—for religious, political, or personal reasons—believed that the United States should have stayed out of the conflict. President Wilson, who wanted all Americans to support the war effort, established the **Committee on Public Information** (CPI) in the spring of 1917. Headed by George Creel, a progressive journalist, the CPI waged a vigorous propaganda campaign to sell the war to Americans.

At first much of the material that the CPI put out was based on fact but censored to present an upbeat picture of the war. Very quickly, however, the CPI began churning out raw propaganda, picturing the Germans as evil monsters. Hollywood joined in, producing movies such as *The Claws of the Hun, The Prussian Cur,* and *The Kaiser, the Beast of Berlin.* These titles vividly illustrate the message the CPI tried to convey.

CPI pamphlets warned citizens to be on the lookout for German spies. Dozens of "patriotic organizations," with names like the American Protective League and the American Defense Society, sprang up. These groups spied, tapped telephones, and opened mail in an effort to ferret out "spies and traitors."

These groups targeted almost anyone who called for peace, questioned the Allies' progress, or criticized the government's policies. They were particularly hard on German Americans, many of whom lost their jobs. Sometimes this anti-German sentiment took absurd turns. German books vanished from library shelves, schools stopped teaching German language courses, and German music disappeared from concert programs. People even renamed German-sounding items: sauerkraut became liberty cabbage, dachshunds became liberty pups, and hamburger became Salisbury steak.

Vigilantes publicly humiliated people of German heritage by forcing them to kiss the flag, recite the Pledge of Allegiance, or buy war bonds. Sometimes the vigilantes turned violent. In March 1918 John H. Wintherbotham, a midwestern representative for the government's Council of National Defense, reported:

66 All over this part of the country men are being tarred and feathered and some are being lynched. . . . These cases do not get into the newspapers nor is an effort

◀ Wartime posters inspired people to purchase savings stamps for their country.

ever made to punish the individuals concerned. In fact, as a rule, it has the complete backing of public opinion. **99**

SUPPRESSING DISSENT

Even in this hysterical atmosphere, some Americans continued to oppose the war. Quaker and Mennonite men, committed by faith to nonviolence, refused to take up arms. Considered traitors by many Americans, they faced violence and abuse.

Pacifists like Congresswoman Jeannette Rankin, Senator Robert La Follette, and settlement-house leader Jane Addams never stopped calling for peace. But such declarations held little sway with Wilson, who heaped contempt on the pacifists for their "stupidity."

The Socialist party, too, proclaimed its unalterable opposition to the war. To most party members, the war used the laboring masses as cannon fodder in a capitalist struggle for control of world markets. The Industrial Workers of the World (IWW), the radical labor union, had a similar view of the war and led strikes in a number of war-related industries.

To silence dissenters, Congress passed the **Espionage Act** in June 1917 and the **Sedition Act** a year later. These measures not only outlawed acts of treason but also made it a crime to "utter, print, write, or publish any disloyal . . . or abusive language" criticizing the government, the flag, or the military. Opposition to the draft, to war-bond drives, or to the arms industry also became a crime.

■■ **The Committee on Public Information rallied support for the war, while the Espionage and Sedition acts crushed antiwar dissent.**

More than 1,000 people—including some 200 members of the IWW—were convicted of violating these laws. Victor Berger, a Socialist congressman from Wisconsin, received a 20-year sentence for publishing antiwar articles in his newspaper, the Milwaukee *Leader*. The Socialist party leader Eugene V. Debs went to prison for 10 years for making a speech against the war.

Many Americans, even some who supported the war, believed that the Espionage and Sedition acts violated the First Amendment. The Supreme Court, however, disagreed. In the landmark case *Schenck* v. *United States* (1919), Justice Oliver Wendell Holmes wrote:

66 The question . . . is whether the words used are used in such circumstances and are of such a nature as to create a clear and present danger. . . . When a nation is at war many things that might be said in time of peace . . . will not be endured [and] no Court could regard them as protected by any constitutional right. **99**

This decision was meant to apply to extraordinary circumstances like war. Unfortunately, intolerance of unpopular ideas continued long after the war had ended.

SECTION 3 REVIEW

IDENTIFY and explain the significance of the following: William McAdoo, Food Administration, Fuel Administration, Herbert Hoover, Railroad Administration, War Industries Board, Bernard Baruch, National War Labor Board, Carrie Chapman Catt, Harriot Stanton Blatch, Great Migration, Committee on Public Information, Espionage Act, Sedition Act, Victor Berger.

1. **MAIN IDEA** How did the U.S. government mobilize the economy for war?

2. **MAIN IDEA** What effect did wartime labor shortage have on the work force?

3. **MAIN IDEA** What steps did the government take to shape and control public opinion during the war?

4. **WRITING TO EXPLAIN** Imagine you are an American opposed to the war. Write a newspaper editorial, outlining your reasons for opposing the Committee on Public Information.

5. **EVALUATING** Do you think the U.S. government was justified in taking control of the economy during the war? Why or why not?

THE LEAGUE OF NATIONS

FOCUS

- **What two major issues did Wilson's peace plan address?**
- **Why was Wilson forced to compromise on his Fourteen Points?**
- **Why did the Senate reject the Treaty of Versailles?**
- **What impact did the war have on Europe and the Middle East?**

President Wilson developed a program for a just peace even before the war ended. This program served as the focus of the Paris Peace Conference in 1919. Wilson had to compromise on many of the points, but the final treaty included the heart of his peace program—the League of Nations. The U.S. Senate, however, rejected the treaty. Without American membership, the League of Nations proved inadequate to solve the world's postwar problems.

Versailles, site of peace-treaty signing

WILSON'S FOURTEEN POINTS

News of the armistice on November 11, 1918, set off a joyful celebration in the United States. Wilson shared the people's great happiness at the Allied victory, but he knew that the task of forging a just peace lay ahead.

This challenge had long been on Wilson's mind. Late in 1917 he had invited a group of scholars to advise him on peace terms. Drawing from their work, Wilson had developed a program for world peace, which he had presented to Congress on January 8, 1918. He called his program the **Fourteen Points** because it contained 14 points, or principles.

Nine of the points dealt with the issue of **self-determination**—the right of people to govern themselves—and with the various territorial disputes created by the war. Other points focused on what Wilson considered the causes of modern war: secret diplomacy, the arms race, violations of freedom of the seas, and trade barriers. But the final point—the establishment of the League of Nations—was the heart of Wilson's program.

◀ **Jubilant Americans celebrate Armistice Day in Washington, D.C., in 1918.**

■■ In his peace plan Wilson aimed to settle territorial disputes and to end the causes of modern war.

Congress and the American public warmly received the Fourteen Points. The reaction of the Allies, however, proved lukewarm. Moreover, the German government, labeling Wilson an "American busybody," rejected the program.

However, as the war turned against them, the Germans sued for a peace settlement based on the Fourteen Points. Wilson had to push and prod the Allies, but they eventually agreed. After the armistice a peace conference was set for January 1919 in Paris. To make sure that the talks focused on his peace program, Wilson attended the conference.

THE PARIS PEACE CONFERENCE

On December 4, 1918, Wilson boarded the *George Washington* for his precedent-setting trip to Europe—he was the first president to cross the Atlantic while in office. As the ship steamed out of New York harbor, a huge crowd gave Wilson a rousing send-off. His reception at the French port of Brest some nine days later proved no less enthusiastic. And on a triumphal tour through France, Britain, and Italy, people welcomed him as a conquering hero. Elated by the cheering throngs, Wilson convinced himself that he had a mandate to shape the peace according to the Fourteen Points.

While Wilson and his fellow leaders gathered to discuss peace, the world was far from peaceful. Across central and eastern Europe, various ethnic groups, now liberated from Austro-Hungarian or Russian rule, clashed over territory. Defeated, Germany teetered on the brink of civil war. In Russia, Bolsheviks fought off the czarists' challenge. The Allied powers—including America—had become entangled in the Russian conflict, sending troops to support the czarists' effort to overthrow the Bolsheviks.

The other delegates at the conference refused to let Wilson dictate the peace terms. Italy's prime minister, Vittorio Orlando, came to Paris only to make sure his nation got the territories it had been promised on entering the war in 1915. David Lloyd George, Britain's prime minister, had just won an election with such slogans as "Hang the Kaiser." He had no intention of showing generosity

▲ Pictured here are David Lloyd George of England, Italian foreign minister Naron Sonnino, Georges Clemenceau of France, and Woodrow Wilson of the United States.

toward the Germans or of giving up Britain's naval supremacy by accepting Wilson's idea of "freedom of the seas."

The French premier, Georges Clemenceau, wanted to ensure France's security by crushing Germany. Distrustful of Wilson's idealism, Clemenceau growled: "God gave us his Ten Commandments, and we broke them. Wilson gave us his Fourteen Points—we shall see."

As the conference opened on January 18, 1919, Wilson expressed great enthusiasm for the task ahead. But the demands of the other members of the **Big Four**—as Wilson, Orlando, Lloyd George, and Clemenceau became known—soon wore Wilson down. The others insisted that Germany bear the financial cost of the war by making huge payments, called **reparations**, to the Allies. They also wanted several secret spoils-of-war treaties honored. Such demands violated practically every one of the points of President Wilson's peace plan.

Wilson had two options: he could either compromise or walk out. Indeed, at one point he ordered the *George Washington* to stand by to return him to the United States. But he realized that leaving would be an admission of failure. He also feared that without a comprehensive peace agreement, the Bolshevik Revolution might spread from Russia into the already politically unstable regions of central and eastern Europe. More than anything else, however, he wanted to see the creation of the League of Nations. The League, he believed, would remedy any injustices the treaty might contain. Wilson stayed on.

■■ Allied demands that Germany pay war damages and that secret treaties be honored forced Wilson to compromise.

THE TREATY OF VERSAILLES

After six months of debate, the delegates agreed to a peace treaty. The official signing of the **Treaty of Versailles** took place in the magnificent palace of Versailles, just outside Paris, on June 28, 1919. Publicly, the American delegation expressed satisfaction with the document. In private, however, they voiced a different opinion. Secretary of State Robert Lansing confided that he felt "disappointment, . . . regret, and . . . depression." He continued:

> 66 The terms of peace appear immeasurably harsh and humiliating. . . . Resentment and bitterness, if not desperation, are bound to be the consequences of such provisions. . . . We have a treaty of peace, but it will not bring permanent peace because it is founded on the shifting sands of self-interest. 99

According to the treaty, Germany's colonies and the Ottoman Empire (Turkey) were divided among the Allied nations, as specified in the spoils-of-war treaties. At Wilson's insistence, however, the treaty established a **mandate system** that required the new colonial rulers to report on their administration to the League of Nations. To satisfy nationalist longings in central and eastern Europe, the peace treaty also created the new nations of Czechoslovakia and Yugoslavia. (Finland, Estonia, Latvia, Lithuania, and Poland also emerged from the war as independent nations— Poland after nearly 150 years of domination by outside powers.)

The treaty proved a bitter pill for the Germans. Not only did Germany lose its colonies, but France also reclaimed Alsace-Lorraine and won 15-year control of the Saar, an industrial region of Germany rich in coal

Map legend:
- Lost by Germany
- Lost by Bulgaria
- Lost by Austria-Hungary
- Lost by Russia
- Lost by Ottoman empire
- British mandate
- French mandate
- Occupied by Allies

In 1922 the Bolsheviks were firmly in control of Russia, and they organized the Union of Soviet Socialist Republics.

Europe and the Middle East After World War I

END OF EMPIRE Four empires had collapsed by the end of the First World War—the Russian, German, Austro-Hungarian, and Ottoman.

? LOCATION How many countries were created from or received land that had belonged to Russia before the war?

and iron. In addition, Germany was disarmed, forced to admit full guilt for the war, and assessed billions of dollars in reparations.

Harsh as this treatment was, it would have been much worse but for Wilson's moderating influence. He steadfastly opposed some of the more extreme Allied demands. And, above all, the president made sure that the treaty included a covenant creating the League of Nations.

▲ The first informal meeting of the League of Nations met in Geneva in 1920.

Headquartered in Geneva, the League consisted of a permanent administrative staff; an assembly, where each member nation had one vote; and a council, or executive body. The council was intended to have five permanent members—France, Great Britain, Italy, Japan, and the United States—and four other members that were periodically elected by the assembly.

The League Covenant required member nations to try to resolve disputes peacefully. If negotiations failed, the nations were to observe a waiting period before going to war. If any member nation failed to follow this procedure, the council could apply economic pressure and even recommend the use of force against the offending nation. The heart of the League Covenant—Article 10—required each member nation to "respect and preserve" the independence and territorial integrity of all other member nations.

THE TREATY IN THE SENATE

Returning to America in July 1919, President Wilson worked to win the Senate's consent to the Treaty of Versailles. He believed that he could count on the votes of most Democratic senators, but he would need solid support from Republicans to gain the required two-thirds majority. He faced a difficult task, for most Republican senators had doubts about the treaty. Fourteen of them—called the **irreconcilables**—would have nothing to do with the League of Nations and flatly rejected the treaty. The other 35 Republican senators—the

reservationists—said they could support the treaty if the League Covenant were amended. They particularly objected to Article 10, which seemed to commit the United States to go to war in defense of any League member that came under attack. The Senate's constitutional power to declare war must be protected, they insisted.

Wilson's only hope for consent was to win over close to 20 reservationists. Gaining their support, however, meant compromising on the League, which Wilson refused to do. The more his advisers urged compromise, the more rigid Wilson became.

Henry Cabot Lodge of Massachusetts, head of the Senate Committee on Foreign Relations and Wilson's longtime enemy, led the reservationists. Lodge, too, refused to budge. Playing for time, he bottled up the treaty in the Foreign Relations Committee through the summer of 1919. Angry and frustrated, Wilson took his case to the people. Although he was not feeling well, Wilson began a grueling 9,500-mile speaking tour on September 4. In city after city he ardently defended the treaty. To Wilson's satisfaction, the crowds grew more enthusiastic as the tour went on. Lodge, however, remained unmoved. "The only people who have votes on the treaty," he declared, "are here in the Senate."

On the night of September 25, after an impassioned speech in Pueblo, Colorado, Wilson complained of a splitting headache. His worried doctor ordered him back to Washington, D.C. A few days later, Wilson collapsed from a near-fatal stroke. Wilson lived out the rest of his term in seclusion in the White House, cut off from practically everyone except his wife and his closest aides. Moody, suspicious, and increasingly out of touch with reality, Wilson refused all suggestions of compromise on the treaty.

In November, Lodge presented the treaty, with a list of 14 reservations, to the Senate. Wilson ordered Democratic senators to vote no on the document, thereby rejecting it. The treaty without the list of reservations met the same fate at the hands of the irreconcilables and reservationists. In March

1920 another vote on Lodge's version of the treaty failed, although a number of Democrats broke ranks and sided with the reservationists. A few weeks later, Wilson vetoed a congressional resolution declaring the United States at peace with the Central Powers. There would be no peace treaty, he insisted, without the League of Nations.

■■ **Wilson's refusal to compromise on the League Covenant led to U.S. rejection of the Treaty of Versailles.**

Wilson clutched at the 1920 election as his one remaining hope. He urged the nation to make the election a "great and solemn referendum" on the League Covenant. Americans, however, wanted to put the war and troublesome European problems behind them, and in November they gave the Republican party a landslide victory. By the time Wilson left office, the League of Nations had been established, but without the participation of the United States.

THE GLOBAL IMPACT OF THE WAR

While U.S. leaders debated whether or not to accept the Treaty of Versailles, the Europeans struggled to recover from the war. The destruction and human suffering were almost incomprehensible. In all, over 8.5 million died in battle, and another 21 million were wounded. Germany, with some 6 million dead and wounded, and Russia, with nearly 7 million casualties, suffered the greatest losses. (In contrast, the United States armed forces counted some 112,000 dead.) To add further misery, the influenza epidemic of 1918–1919 killed some 27 million worldwide.

The war had left the industry and agriculture of much of continental Europe in ruins. Northern France was completely destroyed. As British economist John Maynard Keynes observed:

66 For mile after mile nothing was left. No building was habitable and no field fit for the plow. . . . One devastated area was exactly like another—a heap of rubble, a morass of shell-holes, and tangle of wire. 99

Those businesses still operating could not produce enough to meet demand, and rampant inflation resulted. In Germany, food shortages were so extreme that it proved almost impossible to keep track of prices.

▼ Verdun was just one of the many cities reduced to rubble by bombing attacks during the war.

▼ American soldiers who fell in France are still remembered and honored in this cemetery.

Germany, reeling from the harsh terms of the treaty, seethed with unrest. Throughout the continent, nations vied with one another over territories they thought the treaty ought to have ceded to them. In the Middle East, Arab nations, which had sided with the Allies in hopes of winning their independence from the Ottoman Turks, found themselves living under French and British mandates. Tensions in the region heightened after Britain issued the **Balfour Declaration** in 1917, declaring British support for a Jewish homeland in Palestine.

The new world order, which so many hoped would arise from the ashes of World War I, never materialized. Instead, as historian J. M. Winter noted, "The old order reasserted its will, distributed the spoils of war, and left unresolved the problems which had led to . . . war in 1914."

 The war, which destroyed a generation of young men and left much of Europe in ruins, resolved few prewar issues.

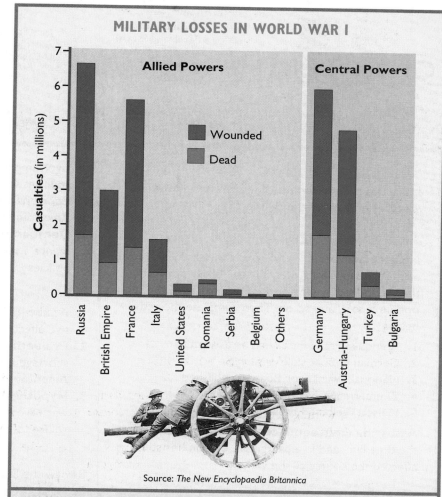

MILITARY LOSSES IN WORLD WAR I

Source: *The New Encyclopaedia Britannica*

A GLOBAL WAR It is estimated that more than 8.5 million soldiers died during World War I; an even higher number suffered from battle-inflicted wounds.

? BUILDING GRAPH SKILLS Which Allied power had the highest number of total casualties? Which Central power had the highest casualties?

SECTION 4 REVIEW

IDENTIFY and explain the significance of the following: Fourteen Points, self-determination, Vittorio Orlando, David Lloyd George, Georges Clemenceau, Big Four, reparations, Treaty of Versailles, mandate system, irreconcilables, reservationists, Henry Cabot Lodge, Balfour Declaration.

LOCATE and explain the importance of the following: Czechoslovakia, Yugoslavia, Finland, Estonia, Latvia, Lithuania, Poland, Saar.

1. **MAIN IDEA** What did Wilson's peace plan hope to accomplish?

2. **MAIN IDEA** What Allied demands forced Wilson to compromise on his Fourteen Points?

3. **ASSESSING CONSEQUENCES** What were some of the effects of the war on Europe and the Middle East?

4. **WRITING TO EXPRESS A VIEWPOINT** Imagine you are a reservationist in the U.S. Senate. Prepare a speech stating your reasons for not supporting ratification of the Treaty of Versailles.

5. **SYNTHESIZING** What aspects of the Treaty of Versailles lend support to Secretary of State Robert Lansing's observation that it was "founded on the shifting sands of self-interest"?

CHAPTER 10
Review

Archduke Franz Ferdinand assassinated. First Battle of the Marne fought.

1914

Italy enters war on Allied side. German U-boat sinks *Lusitania*.

1915

German government issues *Sussex* pledge. Wilson reelected president.

1916

WRITING A SUMMARY

Using the essential points of the chapter as a guide, write a summary of the chapter.

REVIEWING CHRONOLOGY

Number your paper 1 to 5. Study the time line above, and list the following events in the order in which they happened by writing the first next to 1, the second next to 2, and so on. Then complete the activity below.

1. Archduke Franz Ferdinand assassinated.
2. German U-boat sinks *Lusitania*.
3. National War Labor Board established.
4. Zimmermann Note published.
5. Wilson reelected president.

Assessing Consequences Select two events on the time line, and in a paragraph, explain how they affected the course of the war.

IDENTIFYING PEOPLE AND IDEAS

Explain the historical significance of each of the following people or terms.

1. militarism
2. Triple Entente
3. Gavrilo Princip
4. *Sussex* pledge
5. Jeannette Rankin
6. convoy system
7. Bernard Baruch
8. Great Migration
9. self-determination
10. Henry Cabot Lodge

UNDERSTANDING MAIN IDEAS

1. What tensions contributed to the outbreak of war in Europe?
2. What contributions did the United States make to the Allied war effort both before and after entry into the war?
3. What role did women play in the war effort?
4. What did President Wilson hope to accomplish through his Fourteen Points? Why was he forced to compromise?

REVIEWING THEMES

1. **Global Relations** What factors led the United States to declare war in 1917? Do you think U.S. involvement in the conflict was inevitable? Explain your answer.
2. **Economic Development** How was the American economy mobilized for war?
3. **Democratic Values** How did the U.S. government's attempts to rally support for its wartime policies interfere with First Amendment rights?

THINKING CRITICALLY

1. **Analyzing** What were the positive and the negative effects of the draft in the United States?
2. **Evaluating** What effect did the wartime labor shortage have on unions, women, African Americans, and Mexican Americans?
3. **Hypothesizing** How might the outcome of the war have been different if Wilson had been more willing to compromise on his Fourteen Points?

STRATEGY FOR SUCCESS

Review the Strategies for Success on Interpreting Editorial Cartoons on page 162. Then study the following cartoon, which appeared shortly after the sinking of the *Lusitania*. What clues does the cartoonist give to suggest that Germany humiliated the United States in this incident?

Zimmermann Note published. Congress declares war. Bolsheviks seize power in Russia.	Wilson introduces Fourteen Points. National War Labor Board established. Congress passes Sedition Act. Armistice signed.	Treaty of Versailles signed.	Republicans win landslide victory.
1917	**1918**	**1919**	**1920**

WRITING ABOUT HISTORY

Writing to Persuade Imagine you are an African American soldier during the war. Write your commanding officer a letter that tries to convince the army to open up more opportunities for black soldiers.

USING PRIMARY SOURCES

In his classic novel about World War I, *All Quiet on the Western Front,* Erich Maria Remarque portrayed the horrible experiences of war through the eyes of German soldiers. Read the following excerpt, which describes an encounter between German and French soldiers. What point is Remarque trying to make about trench warfare?

❝ *The moment we are about to retreat three faces rise up from the ground in front of us. Under one of the helmets [I see] a dark pointed beard and two eyes that are fastened on me. I raise my hand, but I cannot throw into those strange eyes; for one mad moment the whole slaughter whirls like a circus round me, . . . then the head rises up, . . . and my hand-grenade flies through the air and into him.*

We make for the rear, pull wire cradles into the trench and leave bombs behind us with the strings pulled, which ensures us a fiery retreat. The machine-guns are already firing from the next position.

We have become wild beasts. We do not fight, we defend ourselves against annihilation. It is not against men that we fling our bombs, what do we know of men in this moment when Death is hunting us down—now, for the first time in three days we can see his face, now for the first time in three days we can oppose him. . . . No longer do we lie helpless, . . . we can destroy and kill, to save ourselves, . . . and to be revenged. ❞

LINKING HISTORY AND GEOGRAPHY

Refer to the map on page 244. After the French and the British stopped the German advance at the Marne in 1914, the German army retreated to the Aisne River, halted, and dug themselves into trenches. Why do you think the Germans chose trench warfare rather than retreat into Germany?

Soldiers in trench

BUILDING YOUR PORTFOLIO

Complete the following projects independently or cooperatively.

1. **GLOBAL RELATIONS** In Chapter 9 you portrayed a State Department official concerned with global relations. Building on that experience, imagine you are the U.S. ambassador to Germany in 1915. Write a letter to the Kaiser, protesting German violations of neutral shipping rights.

2. **WAR** In Chapter 9 you portrayed a recruiting officer during the Spanish-American War. Building on that experience, imagine you are a senator committed to U.S. neutrality in World War I. Write a speech that states why the United States should remain neutral.

American Letters

▲ Lola Rodriguez de Tió

The Spanish–American War

As a result of the Spanish-American War, the United States won territories in the Caribbean and the Pacific. In the following selections, Cuban poet and essayist José Martí, Puerto Rican poet Lola Rodríguez de Tió, an anonymous Mexican American poet, and American writers Mark Twain and Edgar Lee Masters explore the meaning of the war for the Caribbean and the United States.

Diary Entry

by José Martí

[April 25, 1895.] Day of combat. Straight through the woods we are drawing close, already in the claws of Guantanamo. . . . The breast swells with fond reverence and overpowering affection at the sight of the vast landscape of the loved river. We cross it, near a *ceiba* tree, and after greeting a patriot family, overjoyed to see us, we enter the open wood, with sweet sun, rain-washed leaves. As over a carpet go our horses, so thick is the grass. All is garland and leaf, and through the openings, to the right, the green of the cleared fields is visible on the other bank, sheltered and compact. . . . Here as everywhere I am touched by the affection with which we are received, and the unity of soul which will not be allowed to coalesce [grow together], and which will not be recognized, and which will be overridden, harming, at least with the harm of delay, the Revolution in the impulse of its first year. The spirit I sowed, is that which has borne fruit, and that of the Island, and with it, and guiding ourselves by it, we will soon triumph, and with a better victory and for a better peace. ❖

The Song of Borinquen

by Lola Rodríguez de Tió

Awake, Borinqueños,[1]
    for they've given the signal!

Awake from your sleep
    for it's time to fight!

Come! The sound of cannon
    will be dear to us.

At that patriotic clamor
    doesn't your heart burn?

Look! The Cuban will soon be free,
    the machete will give him freedom.

The drum of war announces in its beating
    that the thicket is the place, the meeting place!

Most beautiful Borinquen, we have to follow Cuba;
    you have brave sons who want to fight!

Let us no more seem fearful!
Let us no more, timid, permit our enslavement!

We want to be free already
    and our machete is well sharpened!

Why should we, then, remain so asleep
    and deaf, asleep and deaf to that signal?

▼ *General Toral surrenders the city of Santiago to General Shaftner in 1898.*

There's no need to fear, Ricans, the sound of cannon,
for saving the homeland is the duty of the heart!

We want no more despots! Let the tyrant fall!
Women, likewise wild, will know how to fight!

We want freedom and our machete will give it to us!

Let's go, Puerto Ricans, let's go already,
for LIBERTY is waiting, ever so anxious! ❖

---

1 Borinqueños are Puerto Ricans. The word is adapted from
Borinquén, the Native American name for Puerto Rico.

The Voice of the Hispano

Anonymous

Many are the opinions
Against the Hispanic people
And they accuse them of betraying
The American government.

Making an experiment,
They will be disillusioned,
Our brave native men
Do not refuse to be soldiers.

It matters not what is said
Or how our fame is insulted,
As they will fight with pleasure
For the American eagle.

They accuse our native people
Of being rabble,
But they have not proven to be so
On the battlefield.

Like good countrymen
And faithful Americans,
We will free them from that yoke
The humble Cubans. ❖

From To the Person Sitting in Darkness

by Mark Twain

There have been lies; yes, but
they were told in a good cause.
We have been treacherous; but
that was only in order that real
good might come out of apparent
evil. True, we have crushed a
deceived and confiding people; we
have turned against the weak and the friendless who
trusted us; we have stamped out a just and intelligent
and well-ordered republic; we have stabbed an ally in
the back and slapped the face of a guest; we have
bought a Shadow from an enemy that hadn't it to sell;
we have robbed a trusting friend of his land and
liberty; . . . but each detail was for the best. ❖

"Harry Wilmans" From *Spoon River Anthology*

by Edgar Lee Masters

I was just turned twenty-one,
And Henry Phipps, the Sunday-school superintendent,
Made a speech in Bindle's Opera House.
"The honor of the flag must be upheld," he said,
"Whether it be assailed by a barbarous tribe of
     Tagalogs[1]
Or the greatest power in Europe."
And we cheered and cheered the speech and the flag
     he waved
As he spoke.
And I went to the war in spite of my father,
And followed the flag till I saw it raised
By our camp in a rice field near Manila,
And all of us cheered and cheered it.
But there were flies and poisonous things;
And there was the deadly water,
And the cruel heat,
And the sickening, putrid food. . . .
Following the flag,
Till I fell with a scream, shot through the guts.
Now there's a flag over me in Spoon River!
A flag! A flag! ❖

---

1 a people of central Luzon, Philippines

THINKING AND WRITING ABOUT LITERATURE

1. José Martí had just returned to Cuba from his exile in New York when he wrote this diary entry. Which phrases show that he missed Cuba in his absence?
2. Like Martí, Lola Rodríguez de Tió lived in New York and wrote in support of independence from Spain. Whose model does she urge Puerto Ricans to follow?
3. In the anonymous poem, what does the author believe Mexican American soldiers will prove?
4. Mark Twain's controversial essay and Edgar Lee Masters's poem use irony to express the authors' views of the war. Describe both authors' perspectives on the war.

Strategies for Success

RECOGNIZING STEREOTYPES

A stereotype is a generalization or oversimplification about a group or culture. Stereotypes deny individual differences by attributing the same characteristics to every member in a group: All poor people are lazy. All Irish drink too much. All African Americans are good athletes. All girls have difficulty with math and science. Most stereotypes are negative and often lead to discrimination and prejudice.

How to Recognize Stereotypes

1. **Examine the message.** Pay close attention to how a person or group is portrayed. Identify generalizations that lack supporting facts. Ask yourself: Are the same qualities being attributed to all individuals in a group?
2. **Note words that signal stereotyping.** Watch for clue words such as *all, always, never,* or *every* that allow no exceptions; their use may signal stereotyping.
3. **Detect bias or prejudice.** Note any bias or tone that indicates prejudice toward the subjects being described.
4. **Use your knowledge.** In evaluating general statements about people, apply what you have learned from your studies or through direct experience with individual classmates, your family members, or others.

Applying the Strategy

In the following passage, Samuel Bryan, an Anglo American sociologist, describes Mexican immigrants in the United States in 1912:

66 Socially and politically the presence of large numbers of Mexicans in this country gives rise to serious problems. . . . They . . . are slow to learn English, . . . move readily from place to place, and do not acquire or lease land to any extent. But their most unfavorable characteristic is their inclination to . . . live in a clannish manner. 99

Bryan's description is an example of the kind of stereotyping that breeds prejudice. First, he lumps together all Mexican immigrants—and, by implication, all Mexican Americans. He ignores the fact that in many areas of the United States stable, prosperous Mexican American communities existed long before Anglo settlement. Second, he blames immigrants for conditions that are a product of their immigrant status. Like members of other immigrant groups, Mexicans often found many jobs closed to them. One area in which they could find work was farm labor. Because farm labor is seasonal, Mexican farm workers were forced to move often in search of crops to harvest. This migratory existence, coupled with the low wages typical of such farm work, made it difficult for many Mexican immigrants to buy land.

Practicing the Strategy

Study the song poster below. Then, on a separate sheet of paper, answer the following questions.

1. What group is pictured in this song poster?
2. Why can this song poster be considered an example of stereotyping?

BUILDING YOUR PORTFOLIO

Outlined below are four projects. Independently or cooperatively, complete one and use the products to demonstrate your mastery of the historical concepts involved.

1 REFORM

In the late 19th century the transformation of the United States from a rural economy to an industrialized, urban society created numerous social problems. In response, the Progressive party sought reforms. Using the portfolio materials you designed in chapters 17 and 18, create a series of Progressive party campaign posters that outline the party's reform goals.

2 DEMOCRATIC RIGHTS

Historians note that progressivism was primarily a white, middle-class movement and thus did not address many of the concerns of working-class women. Using the portfolio materials you designed in chapters 17 and 18, conduct a debate between a white, middle-class progressive and a working-class woman on whether the progressive emphasis on women's suffrage best serves the needs of all women.

3 GLOBAL RELATIONS

The expansionist policies of the United States in the 19th century led to the establishment of U.S. overseas colonies, increased foreign investment, and conflicts with foreign powers. Using the portfolio materials you designed in chapters 19 and 20, create a world map showing areas of U.S. colonization, investment, and conflict through World War I.

4 WAR

The Spanish-American War and World War I brought the United States onto the world stage. Using the portfolio materials you designed in chapters 19 and 20, prepare a speech for delivery to Congress, outlining some of the costs and benefits of America's international role.

Videodisc Review

In assigned groups, develop an outline for a video collage of America in the years between 1897 and 1920. Choose images that best illustrate the major topics of the period. Write a script to accompany the images. Assign narrators to different parts of the script, and present your video collage to the class.

Further Reading

Ettinger, Albert M., and A. Churchill Ettinger. *A Doughboy with the Fighting 69th.* White Mane (1992). Reminiscence of World War I by a soldier of the 69th Rainbow Division.

Hall, Linda B., and Don M. Coerver. *Revolution on the Border: The United States and Mexico, 1910–1920.* University of New Mexico Press (1990). Examines the role that trade and investment played in U.S.–Mexico relations.

Liliuokalani. *Hawaii's Story by Hawaii's Queen.* Charles E. Tuttle (1991). Firsthand account of 19th-century Hawaii.

Schneider, Dorothy, and Carl J. Schneider. *Into the Breach.* Viking (1991). Examines the participation of American women in World War I.

Tuchman, Barbara W. *The Guns of August.* Bantam (1989). Analysis of the events of August 1914 that propelled Europe into World War I.

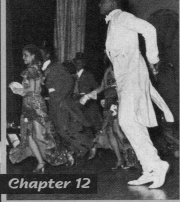

Chapter 11

A TURBULENT DECADE
1919–1929

Chapter 12

THE JAZZ AGE
1920–1930

Chapter 13

THE GREAT DEPRESSION
1929–1933

Prosperity and Crisis

1919–1945

3

The prosperity of the 1920's introduced millions of Americans to mass produced goods and mass culture and led many to question traditional values. By the end of the decade, however, the nation had plunged into the Great Depression. Facing unemployment and poverty, millions of Americans turned to President Roosevelt and his New Deal. But economic recovery remained slow until the United States entered World War II. By 1945 the United States was the world's most powerful nation.

◀ President Roosevelt, radio broadcast, 1937

Chapter 14

THE NEW DEAL
1933–1940

Chapter 15

BETWEEN THE WARS
1921–1941

Chapter 16

AMERICANS IN WORLD WAR II 1941–1945

A TURBULENT DECADE

FOCUS

UNDERSTANDING THE MAIN IDEA

The end of World War I ushered in a period of economic and social instability. Voters, eager to return to "normalcy," elected probusiness Republican presidents, and as the 1920s progressed, prosperity returned. Not all, however, shared the benefits of this economic renewal. Organized labor lost ground, and Native Americans, African Americans, and immigrants faced discrimination.

THEMES

DEMOCRATIC VALUES
How might a democratic government respond to a perceived threat of revolution?

CULTURAL DIVERSITY
In what ways might ethnic and racial groups respond to acts of discrimination?

ECONOMIC DEVELOPMENT What actions should the federal government take to promote economic prosperity?

1919	1921	1924	1927	1928
Palmer raids begin.	Congress limits immigration.	Congress grants Native Americans citizenship.	Sacco and Vanzetti executed.	Herbert Hoover elected president.

During World War I the government tried to stifle dissent, women took jobs traditionally held by men, and African Americans moved to northern cities. These and other changes in society continued to affect Americans after the war.

he end of World War I brought joyous celebration. As author Malcolm Cowley wrote, "We danced in the streets, embraced old women and pretty girls, swore blood brotherhood with soldiers in little bars, drank with our elbows locked in theirs, reeled through the streets with bottles of champagne." But this joy proved short-lived.

For many Americans life after the war did not appear promising. War veterans returned home to find few jobs available. Those who did find work soon discovered that soaring prices ate up their earnings. Economic and social problems increased. Strikes broke out across the nation, and violent race riots exploded in many American cities. Fueled by wartime fears, anti-immigrant feelings raised social tensions. Looking back on the first years after the war, author and journalist Ray Stannard Baker remarked, "I can recall no period in which life in America looked bleaker."

Aftermath of Wall Street bombing, 1920

World War I veteran with his family, 1919

POSTWAR TROUBLES

FOCUS

- **What were economic conditions like after the war?**
- **How did workers react to hard times?**
- **Why did many Americans fear that a Communist revolution was at hand?**
- **What did the Sacco and Vanzetti case reveal about America in the early 1920s?**

Children in 1916 supporting their striking relatives

The horrors of World War I shocked and disillusioned many Americans. The war, wrote novelist John Dos Passos, had been a "waste of time, waste of money, waste of lives, waste of youth." In response, many Americans tried to return to the way things had been before the war. But there was no going back. Instead of a return to the "old ways," the nation faced economic hardship and social strife.

DEMOBILIZATION

Under the best of conditions, **demobilization**, the shift from a wartime to a peacetime footing, is not an easy task for a nation. The process is made more difficult when the shift is rapid, as was the case after World War I. The war's end caught the

▲ After World War I, millions of veterans scrambled for available jobs. American Legion employment offices, such as this one in Los Angeles, tried to find work for veterans.

American government by surprise—literally. Trains carrying new recruits to boot camp were stopped en route. Within a year some four million soldiers returned to civilian life.

Women were urged to give up their jobs to make room for returning veterans. "The same patriotism which induced women to enter industry during the war should induce them to vacate their positions," declared the New York labor federation. Most of the women who did not respond to patriotic appeals were forced out of jobs traditionally held by men. As a result, the percentage of women in the work force in 1920 fell slightly below what it had been in 1910.

Adding to employment worries was a skyrocketing cost of living. With peace at hand, consumers went on a spending spree, making purchases they had put off during the war. As the demand for goods outpaced supply, prices soared until the cost of goods and services in 1920 was about twice that of 1914.

Soon, however, this trend reversed as the deep but brief recession of 1920–1921 struck and prices fell. Demobilization was one of the factors behind the recession. During the war millions of Americans worked in war industries. But at war's end the government canceled more than $2 billion in war contracts. Factories responded by cutting back production and laying off workers. By 1921 some 5 million workers—more than 10 percent of the labor force—were unemployed, and the economy was shrinking.

A farm crisis contributed to the economic problems. Farmers had benefited from wartime markets in Europe. As European farm production revived, however, these markets dried up and farm prices fell. According to the Department of Agriculture, wheat, for example, dropped from $2.16 a bushel in 1919 to less than a dollar a bushel in 1922. Burdened with debt, hundreds of thousands of American farmers lost ownership of their land during the 1920s.

■■ **After the war the cost of living soared, but prices soon fell as a recession took hold and unemployment increased.**

LABOR STRIFE

In 1919, however, Americans were still struggling with rapidly rising prices for food, clothing, and shelter. Workers watched in dismay as runaway inflation ate up their wartime financial gains. Angry and frustrated, they asked for higher wages and shorter hours. But management ignored labor's pleas. In response, many workers walked off the job. In 1919 alone, unions called more than 3,600 strikes—involving more than four million workers.

The Seattle general strike.
The first strike of 1919 occurred in January, when some 35,000 shipyard workers in Seattle, Washington, walked off the job, demanding higher wages and a shorter workday. Within two weeks 110 local unions voted to join the shipyard workers in a general strike.

The general strike began on February 6 at 10 A.M. An eerie calm fell over the city as 60,000 workers left their jobs. "It was," declared one shipyard worker, "the most beautiful thing I ever seen!"

Alarmed at such a show of unity, Seattle newspapers blamed immigrants, calling the strikers "muddle-headed foreigners" and "riffraff from Europe intent on terrorizing the community." Mayor Ole Hanson denounced the strike as the work of Bolsheviks and called in troops to prevent unrest. But no violent incidents occurred. Instead, the well-disciplined strikers took steps to preserve order and to make sure that food and essential services were available to the community. Nevertheless, the strikers came under increased public pressure to go back to work. After five days they ended the strike without winning any of their demands.

Although the strike had been peaceful, anti-labor forces tried to convince the public that Seattle had been on the brink of revolution. Mayor Hanson told the national press:

▲ **The *Seattle Union Record* published a special edition on February 6, 1919, announcing the beginning of the general strike.**

66 Revolution . . . doesn't need violence. The general strike . . . is of itself the weapon of revolution, all the more dangerous because quiet. To succeed, it must suspend everything. . . . That is to say, it puts the government out of operation. And that is all there is to revolt—no matter how achieved. 99

Many people believed these charges. In the end the Seattle strike helped turn public opinion against organized labor.

◄ **Strikes became commonplace in the years after World War I, as workers demanded better wages and conditions. Here, mounted policemen break up a group of Philadelphia strikers in 1919.**

return to work. Curtis, however, refused to reinstate them. Instead, he hired a new force made up of unemployed veterans. Union sympathizers protested. Unmoved, Coolidge backed the commissioner, proclaiming that "there is no right to strike against the public safety by anybody, anywhere, any time." Coolidge's words made him an overnight hero in conservative circles.

The Boston police strike. In September 1919 another strike, this time by the Boston police force, further inflamed antilabor sentiments. The Boston police had recently formed a union to seek better pay and working conditions. Although police in other cities had unionized without incident, Boston's police commissioner, Edwin Curtis, refused to recognize the union. Instead, he fired 19 officers for engaging in union activities. In response, some 75 percent of the police force went on strike.

Public order collapsed. Journalist William Allen White described the first night of the strike:

66 The devil was loose in Boston. . . . Little knots of boys and young men began wandering through the streets. . . . By midnight, the . . . crowds had formed one raging mob, a drunken, noisy, irresponsible mob. . . . Someone threw a loose paving stone through a store window about one o'clock. The tension snapped. . . . By two o'clock, looting had begun. 99

After two nights of violence, Governor Calvin Coolidge called in the state militia to restore order. The city's newspapers denounced the strikers as "agents of Lenin" and the strike as a "Bolshevist nightmare." The public also came out firmly against the strike. Recognizing that their cause was doomed, the police voted unanimously to

The steel strike. Two weeks after the trouble in Boston, the most important strike of 1919 began. In late September some 365,000 steelworkers—many of them immigrants—walked off the job, demanding recognition of their union and protesting low wages and long working hours. This massive walkout threatened to shut down the steel industry.

For years the major steel companies had fought efforts to unionize steelworkers. Now the companies did everything in their power to break the strike. In an effort to divide labor along ethnic lines, they portrayed foreign workers as radicals and called on "loyal" Americans to return to work.

▼ During the steel strike, Pittsburgh policemen arrested dozens of protesters. In a notice printed in several languages, the *Pittsburgh Chronicle Telegraph* declared the strike a failure and urged strikers to go back to work.

The steel bosses also brought in thousands of African Americans and Mexican Americans as replacement workers, and they hired armed thugs to attack the strikers. Strikers were jailed, beaten, or shot. Faced with such tactics, union leaders called off the strike on January 9, 1920. Labor had suffered a crushing defeat. It would be 15 years before unions again tried to organize workers in heavy industry.

■■ **Workers responded to hard times by striking for higher pay and better working conditions, but their efforts largely failed.**

▲ **This cartoon entitled** *Put Them Out & Keep Them Out* **appeared in the** *Philadelphia Inquirer* **in 1919 and expressed the fear that Bolshevism was creeping into American society.**

*T*HE RED SCARE

The 1919 strikes were prompted primarily by labor's desire for a fair deal. However, many Americans saw labor unrest as proof that Russia's Bolshevik Revolution of 1917, with its call for a worldwide revolution of workers, was spreading to American shores. This fear of communism reached fever pitch in 1919 and 1920, a period of anti-Communist hysteria known as the **Red Scare**.

Although Communists and Socialists comprised only a tiny fraction of the country's population, some Americans saw "Reds" everywhere. They even implied that Communists controlled many women's organizations. Peace groups, such as the Women's International League for Peace and Freedom, came under particularly strong attack. Antiradical fears reached such heights that several elected members of the New York State Assembly were expelled because they were members of the Socialist party. As journalist Walter Lippmann sarcastically noted:

❝ The people are shivering in their boots over Bolshevism, they are far more afraid of Lenin [the Bolshevik leader] than they ever were of the Kaiser [Wilhelm II, who ruled Germany during World War I]. We seem to be the most frightened lot of victors that the world ever saw. ❞

■■ **The Bolshevik Revolution and the strikes of 1919 led many Americans to fear that a Communist revolution was at hand.**

The Palmer raids. In 1919 a rash of bomb scares seemed to justify Americans' fears. In April, alert postal clerks discovered 36 bombs in the mail addressed to such prominent citizens as John D. Rockefeller, Supreme Court justice Oliver Wendell Holmes, and Postmaster General Albert Burleson. Then less than a month later, several bombings occurred, one of which damaged the front of Attorney General A. Mitchell Palmer's house. The assailant, an Italian anarchist, died in the blast.

Newspapers began demanding harsh action against radicals. One paper even called for "a few free treatments in the electric chair." Attorney General Palmer, hoping to further his presidential ambitions, responded by launching an anti-Red crusade. He created a special government office to

◀ **A. Mitchell Palmer**

gather information on radical activities and put J. Edgar Hoover, the future head of the FBI, in charge.

Palmer's most dramatic action was a series of raids to capture alleged radicals. The **Palmer raids** began in November 1919 and peaked on January 2, 1920, when federal officials arrested thousands of suspected radicals in 33 cities nationwide. As journalist Frederick Lewis Allen wrote:

> 66 Over six thousand men were arrested in all, . . . often without any chance to learn what was the explicit charge against them. . . . In Detroit, over a hundred men were herded into a bull-pen measuring twenty-four by thirty feet and kept there for a week. . . . In Hartford, while the suspects were in jail the authorities took the further precaution of arresting . . . all visitors who came to see them. 99

Most of those arrested were poor immigrants newly arrived in the country. In most cases, there was no real evidence against them. In fact, although the government claimed that radicals were "armed to the teeth," only three pistols were seized in the raids.

Emma Goldman. During the Red Scare hundreds of foreigners suspected of radical activities were deported to Russia. Among the deportees was Emma Goldman, a noted feminist, writer, and speaker.

Goldman was born in 1869 in Lithuania, a nation that was then part of Russia. Raised in a traditional Jewish family, Goldman was an independent, determined girl who often clashed with her authoritarian father. When she was 15, her father arranged for her to marry a man she did not love. But as she later wrote, "I would not listen to his schemes; I wanted to study, to know life, to travel. Besides, I never would marry for anything but love." So at age 16, Goldman immigrated to the United States.

The young Goldman settled in Rochester, New York, where she took a factory job. Gradually she grew disillusioned with the treatment of foreigners and workers in the United States. In 1889 at age 20, she moved to New York City and entered the world of radical politics. She soon became famous for her fiery speeches. After one such speech in 1893, she was convicted of inciting a riot and sent to prison for a year.

In 1906 Goldman started a radical monthly called *Mother Earth*. In its pages she presented articles on a wide range of topics, from birth control to modern art and literature. Above all, she used the magazine as a forum to defend freedom of speech.

In 1917 Goldman was arrested again, this time for opposing the draft. Two years later, at the height of the Red Scare, she was released from prison and deported to Russia. Like many other radicals, she was eager to see revolutionary Russia up close. "At last . . . ," she wrote, "I would behold . . . the land freed from political and economic masters." Instead of a free land, however, she found a country where freedom of expression was severely limited. Disenchanted, Goldman left Russia in 1921 and spent the rest of her life speaking and writing in Europe.

By mid-1920 public hysteria over radicalism was dying down. The fearful predictions of A. Mitchell Palmer and others that a Communist revolution was close at hand proved to be unfounded. Furthermore, many Americans had never supported the witch-hunting tactics employed by many of the anti-Communist crusaders.

SACCO AND VANZETTI

Although the Red Scare passed, hostility toward foreigners and radicals persisted. This hostility was evident during the 1921 trial of two Italian anarchists, Nicola Sacco and Bartolomeo Vanzetti. Accused of committing murder during a payroll robbery at a factory outside Boston, they were convicted and sentenced to death.

The verdict outraged defenders of civil liberties. They argued that the two men had been

Emma Goldman

◄ American poet Edna St. Vincent Millay was one of many protesters during the Sacco and Vanzetti trial.

Free Them and Save Massachusetts! American Honor Dies With Sacco and Vanzetti!

convicted not because of the evidence presented but because they were immigrants and radicals. Even the trial judge had shown bias by declaring that the men's anarchist beliefs were grounds for conviction.

The verdict and subsequent appeals drew worldwide attention. In Paris, New York City, and elsewhere, thousands of people marched in protest. Noted writers and artists rallied to the cause. Calling them "victims of race and national prejudice and class hatred," labor unions contributed to Sacco and Vanzetti's defense fund. The protesters

called for a new trial, but all these pleas failed. On August 23, 1927, Sacco and Vanzetti were executed.

Many Americans believed that radicals like Sacco and Vanzetti deserved to be punished for their views, while others saw them as heroes and martyrs. Historians still debate whether Sacco and Vanzetti were guilty or innocent. All agree, however, that the case reflected the deep divisions tearing at American society in the postwar era.

■■ **The Sacco and Vanzetti case underscored a hostility in the United States toward foreigners and radicals following the war.**

▶ In the early 1930s immigrant artist Ben Shahn created a series of paintings about the events surrounding the Sacco and Vanzetti trial.

Ben Shahn, *Bartolomeo Vanzetti and Nicola Sacco* (1931–1932)

SECTION 1 REVIEW

IDENTIFY and explain the significance of the following: demobilization, Ole Hanson, Edwin Curtis, Red Scare, A. Mitchell Palmer, Palmer raids, Emma Goldman, Nicola Sacco, Bartolomeo Vanzetti.

LOCATE and explain the importance of the following: Seattle, Washington; Boston, Massachusetts.

1. **MAIN IDEA** How did the end of World War I affect the economy?

2. **MAIN IDEA** How did workers respond to deteriorating economic conditions after the war? Were their efforts successful?

3. **IDENTIFYING CAUSE AND EFFECT** What events led to the Red Scare? What were some of the Red Scare's consequences?

4. **WRITING TO INFORM** Imagine you are a reporter covering the Sacco and Vanzetti case. Write an article exploring the public debate surrounding the anarchists' arrest and conviction.

5. **ANALYZING** Why can it be said that international events had a strong impact on American society in the postwar years?

THE REPUBLICANS IN POWER

FOCUS

■ **Why did voters elect Warren G. Harding president in 1920?**

■ **How did the economy fare under Harding?**

■ **What kind of president was Calvin Coolidge?**

■ **What were some effects of the Republicans' probusiness policies?**

*T*ired of social strife, voters in the 1920 election rejected the party of Woodrow Wilson and elected Republican Warren G. Harding president. Although the Harding years ended in scandal, Harding's Republican successor, Calvin Coolidge, restored a sense of integrity to the White House. As a result, voters elected another Republican president—Herbert Hoover—in 1928.

1924 campaign slogan favoring big business

THE ELECTION OF 1920

With the country in turmoil and Republican voters united once again, Republican leaders felt confident of victory in the 1920 presidential election. As their candidate they nominated Senator Warren G. Harding of Ohio. Harding lacked Woodrow Wilson's razor-sharp intelligence, but he was pleasant and friendly.

Harding ran on a probusiness, antilabor platform that promised tax revision, higher tariffs, limits on immigration, and some aid to farmers. What pleased war-weary voters the most, however, was Harding's call for a return to "normalcy":

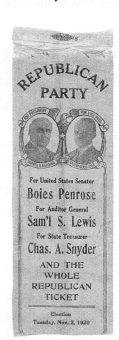

◀ With this 1920 campaign ribbon, the Republican party in Pennsylvania urged voters to support the "whole Republican ticket."

66 America's present need is not heroics but healing, not nostrums [quack cures] but normalcy, not revolution but restoration, . . . not surgery but serenity, . . . not submergence in internationality but sustainment in triumphant nationality. 99

In contrast, the Democratic candidate, Governor James M. Cox of Ohio, bowed to pressure from President Wilson and stressed support for the League of Nations.

The nation's farmers, suffering from falling farm prices, threw their support behind Harding. Many in the middle class, tired of labor strikes and high taxes, also voted Republican. Americans cast their vote for "normalcy," giving Harding some 60 percent of the popular vote.

■■ **Anxious for stability after the war and the social strife of the Wilson years, American voters elected a Republican president.**

THE HARDING ADMINISTRATION

From his first day in office, Harding set a very different tone from that of the somber Wilson. Journalist Frederick Lewis Allen commented on the change:

> 66 For four long years the gates of the White House had been locked and guarded with sentries. Harding's first official act was to throw them open, to permit . . . sightseers to roam the grounds and flatten their noses against the executive window-panes. . . . The act seemed to symbolize the return of the government to the people. 99

Focus on the economy. What the Harding administration came to symbolize, however, was—as Harding put it—"less government in business

▲ President Harding's cabinet was photographed on the White House lawn at its first meeting in 1921. Secretary of State Charles Evans Hughes is seated to Harding's right, while Vice President Calvin Coolidge is seated to his left.

WARREN G. HARDING

1865–1923

in office
1921–1923

A genial, sociable man, Warren G. Harding was fond of drinking and spending time with his friends. He was the sort "to play poker with all Saturday night," one associate recalled. Under Harding, the White House had more the atmosphere of an Elks or Moose lodge than a stately executive mansion. Liquor flowed freely at Harding's parties, despite Prohibition.

Harding, who did not like being president, compared his position to being in jail. Believing that he was unsuited for the job, he once remarked that he was "a man of limited talents from a small town."

and more business in government." His probusiness cabinet included such successful businessmen as Secretary of the Treasury Andrew W. Mellon and Secretary of Commerce Herbert Hoover.

These men believed that government should not interfere with the economy except to aid business. As a result, the administration had two main economic goals: to reduce the national debt and to promote economic growth.

Wartime spending had driven up the national debt from some $1 billion in 1914 to more than $25 billion in 1919. To eliminate the debt, the head of the newly created Bureau of the Budget, Charles Dawes, set out to slash spending. In 1922, his first year on the job, Dawes succeeded in turning the annual deficit into a surplus.

To achieve the second goal—economic growth—Secretary Mellon proposed eliminating the high wartime taxes imposed on the wealthy. If "government takes away an unreasonable share," he argued, "the incentive to work is no longer there and slackening of effort is the result." Furthermore, he claimed, if taxes were lower, the rich would have more money to invest and the economy would grow. The benefits, Mellon said, would then trickle down to the middle and lower classes in the form of jobs and higher wages. In response to Mellon's program, Congress cut taxes on wealthy Americans during the 1920s.

By 1923 Harding's economic policy appeared to be working. The postwar slump was over, unemployment was low, and most sectors of the economy had entered a period of tremendous growth. Not all sectors were flourishing, however.

The coal industry fell on hard times as oil became a popular fuel source. The producers of cotton and wool textiles suffered because of competition from new synthetic fabrics, such as rayon. These and other "sick industries" signaled that not all was well in the economy.

■■ The Harding administration's probusiness policies helped fuel an economic boom, but not all sectors of the economy benefited.

The Harding scandals. Midway through Harding's term, most Americans seemed happy with the nation's course. Yet talk of corruption had begun to haunt the Harding administration. A group of Harding's friends—known as the Ohio Gang—had followed him to Washington and were using their connections with the president to enrich themselves at the public's expense.

The first scandal came to light in the spring of 1923, when it was discovered that Charles Forbes, director of the Veterans' Bureau and Harding's close friend, had received millions of dollars as the result of corrupt schemes. Harding was deeply worried over the Forbes scandal and other signs of wrongdoing in his administration. In June 1923 he confessed to journalist William Allen White, "I have no trouble with my enemies. I can take care of my enemies all right. [It's my] friends . . . that keep me walking the floor nights." Soon after talking to White, Harding set out on an extended tour of the West. In San Francisco on August 2, he died.

After Harding's death other scandals surfaced. In 1924 Attorney General Harry Daugherty,

◀ **Teapot Dome and other scandals tarnished the reputation of the Harding administration.**

Harding's right-hand man, was forced to resign after it was discovered he had been taking bribes. Next erupted the **Teapot Dome scandal**, which took its name from a government oil reserve in Teapot Dome, Wyoming. According to a Senate investigation, Secretary of the Interior Albert Fall had received loans, cash, and cattle for leasing the oil reserve—along with another reserve in California—to private oil companies. Fall was convicted of accepting bribes and jailed in 1926—the first cabinet member to be imprisoned for crimes committed while in office.

COOLIDGE TAKES CHARGE

After Harding's death Vice President Calvin Coolidge succeeded to the presidency. Immediately he began working to limit the damage from the Harding scandals and to restore the reputation of the presidency.

Coolidge easily won the Republican presidential nomination in 1924. On the 103rd ballot the Democrats, divided between rural and urban wings and split over issues such as prohibition, chose John W. Davis, a corporate lawyer. Both parties faced strong opposition from the Progressive party's nominee, Robert La Follette. Backed by angry farmers and workers, the Progressive platform denounced federal policies favoring business and called for more aid to working people.

Despite these rumblings of discontent, Coolidge won by a landslide, receiving 15.7 million votes to Davis's 8.4 million. La Follette received about 4.8 million votes. Although the Progressive party faded from the scene when La Follette died soon after the election, its strong showing made it clear that not all Americans agreed with the Republicans' emphasis on big business.

In some ways Calvin Coolidge seemed an unlikely man to win the support of so many Americans. Stern

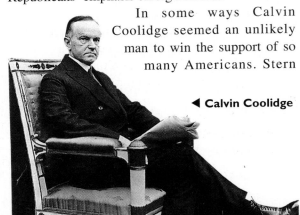

◀ **Calvin Coolidge**

CALVIN COOLIDGE
1872–1933

UNITED STATES POSTAGE

$5 CALVIN COOLIDGE 1923-1929 $5

Vermont-born Calvin Coolidge had a stern face and quiet, unemotional manner that made him seem the very picture of cold New England granite. According to his wife Grace, once at a Washington dinner party another guest told Coolidge she had bet that she could make him say at least three words to her. Tight-lipped as usual, Coolidge replied, "You lose."

"Silent Cal" could be as frugal—or even stingy—as he was quiet. Sometimes rather than buying presents, he sent out the boxes of cigars that he himself had received as gifts. Coolidge even refused to share the contents of the stream in front of his vacation home in South Dakota. One day he observed a stranger catching fish from the stream. Coolidge sent a Secret Service agent after the man to retrieve the fish, stating bluntly, "They are my fish."

and unemotional, he was known as Silent Cal. His often sour expression inspired one wit's comment that Coolidge looked as if he had been weaned on a pickle. Yet because Coolidge's no-nonsense manner and frugal habits recalled a simpler era, many Americans found him reassuring.

A staunch conservative, Coolidge was even more probusiness than Harding. "The business of America is business," he once declared. "The man who builds a factory builds a temple. The man who works there worships there." Coolidge favored legislation to aid business but generally opposed laws to help farmers or workers, arguing that such legislation stifled private initiative and harmed the economy.

Coolidge also took a tightfisted approach to government spending. In the name of economy, he vetoed a bonus bill designed to aid World War I veterans (Congress passed the bill over his veto). He also vetoed a bill designed to boost farm prices by authorizing the government to buy surplus crops and sell them abroad.

Despite these vetoes the president remained popular and almost certainly could have won reelection in 1928. Instead, to almost everyone's surprise, he announced he would not run.

▪▪ Coolidge was a conservative, probusiness president whose nononsense style won the support of most Americans.

THE ELECTION OF 1928

In 1928 the Republicans nominated Secretary of Commerce Herbert Hoover for president. Hoover had a reputation for skill and efficiency. His strongest asset, though, was the nation's apparent prosperity after eight years of Republican rule. In a campaign speech he declared:

> ❝ The poorhouse is vanishing from among us. We have not yet reached the goal, but, given a chance to go forward with the policies of the last eight years, we shall soon . . . be in sight of the day when poverty will be banished from this nation. ❞

▲ By the 1928 election Herbert Hoover was known for his integrity and humanitarian ideals.

After a bitter fight the Democrats nominated Governor Alfred E. Smith of New York, a moderate progressive. The party's choice signaled a shift in Democratic strategy—a response, in part, to the Progressive party's strength in the 1924 election. Smith's core support came from urban immigrant voters. By nominating Smith, the Democrats hoped to be seen as "the party of progress and liberal thought," as Franklin Roosevelt put it. Yet Smith had several political liabilities. He was Roman Catholic, he opposed prohibition, and he had ties to New York City's Tammany Hall. All these points stirred strong opposition to Smith's candidacy, especially in the South.

Riding on Smith's handicaps and the economy's strength, Hoover won 58 percent of the popular vote. Smith lost his own state as well as several southern states that went Republican for the first time since Reconstruction. However, Smith did well in the nation's largest cities. His appeal to these voters offered the Democrats hope for the future.

■■ **Herbert Hoover sailed to victory in 1928 on the strength of the economy and his opponent's political liabilities.**

THE EFFECTS OF REPUBLICAN POLICIES

During the 1920s the Republican administrations' probusiness policies helped promote economic growth. Yet these policies also had negative effects on the environment and on many working people.

Business growth and prosperity. One reason for the economic boom that began in 1923 was the availability of surplus capital, in part due to tax cuts. This capital allowed old industries to grow rapidly and new ones to enter the ranks of the corporate giants. The 1920s also saw more than 1,000 **mergers**—the combining of two or more companies. Business favored mergers because they brought greater efficiency and higher profits. By 1930, some 200 corporations owned nearly half the nation's corporate wealth. The government, with its favorable attitude toward business, encouraged this process of consolidation and made little effort to enforce antitrust laws.

▲ As early as 1917, the corner of 42nd St. and Madison Ave. in New York City was often congested with heavy auto traffic.

This rapid industrial growth was not without its drawbacks, however. Chemical wastes poured into the nation's rivers and lakes. Cities witnessed increased traffic congestion and air pollution. Yet few Americans saw these consequences of industrial development as problems.

Labor and farming. Workers did not share significantly in business's good fortune during the 1920s. From 1923 to 1929, business profits increased some 60 percent. Over the same period, workers' incomes grew by only about 10 percent. Many workers in "sick industries" even faced pay cuts and unemployment. Farmers were also hit hard, as the postwar slump in farm prices continued into the 1920s.

To help farmers, Congress passed the **Fordney-McCumber Tariff Act** of 1922. The act levied high duties on imported farm products in an effort to boost domestic crop prices. But it brought little relief. Farmers still faced shrinking markets, low prices, high interest rates, and crushing debts.

Organized labor also suffered during the 1920s as the government and courts sought to roll back the gains of the Progressive Era. Federal courts, for example, upheld "yellow-dog contracts," which required employees to promise not to join a union. At the same time, business leaders promoted a policy known as the **American Plan**. The plan called for open shops—factories in which workers could choose not to join unions and management did not have to negotiate with union leaders. As a result, union membership shrank from a high of more than 5 million in 1920 to some 3.6 million in 1923. Without the backing of strong unions, many people continued to work long hours for low wages under often unsafe conditions.

■■ **Republican policies contributed to business growth and general prosperity, but many workers and farmers suffered.**

THE EQUAL RIGHTS AMENDMENT

Regulating hours, working conditions, and wages for women and children had been an important part of the progressive agenda. However, in the 1920s women debated the desirability of such protective legislation. This debate came about because of the National Woman's party's efforts on behalf of the

Equal Rights Amendment, introduced into Congress in 1923. Had it passed, the amendment would have given men and women "equal rights throughout the United States." One of the amendment's effects would have been to invalidate protective legislation.

The amendment drew most of its support from middle-class and professional women. They argued that protective legislation discouraged employers from hiring women. Furthermore, they argued, limitations on working hours kept women out of many highly paid jobs.

Opponents of the amendment supported protective legislation as necessary to protect women—few of whom belonged to unions—and their families. Mary Anderson, director of the U.S. Women's Bureau, asserted:

❝ Women who are wage earners, with one job in the factory and another in the home, have little time and energy left to carry on the fight to better their economic status. They need the help of . . . labor laws. ❞

Pauline Newman of the Women's Trade Union League observed that before protective legislation women "were 'free' and 'equal' to work long hours for starvation wages, or free to leave the job and starve!"

Protective legislation did hamper women working in male-dominated occupations. However, few working-class women were employed in such occupations. Thus, they withheld their support for the amendment, which they viewed as benefiting only middle-class and upper-class women who had the training to enter the professions or skilled trades.

The debate over these issues created deep divisions in the women's movement. It would continue to divide women's organizations until the 1960s.

▪▪ The debate over the Equal Rights Amendment divided women's groups.

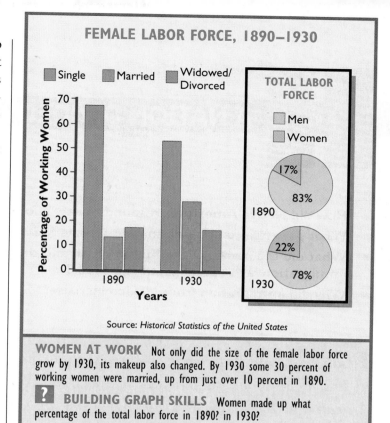

FEMALE LABOR FORCE, 1890–1930

■ Single ■ Married ■ Widowed/Divorced

Percentage of Working Women (y-axis: 0, 10, 20, 30, 40, 50, 60, 70)

Years: 1890, 1930

TOTAL LABOR FORCE
□ Men
□ Women

1890: 17% / 83%
1930: 22% / 78%

Source: *Historical Statistics of the United States*

WOMEN AT WORK Not only did the size of the female labor force grow by 1930, its makeup also changed. By 1930 some 30 percent of working women were married, up from just over 10 percent in 1890.

❓ **BUILDING GRAPH SKILLS** Women made up what percentage of the total labor force in 1890? in 1930?

SECTION 2 REVIEW

IDENTIFY and explain the significance of the following: Warren G. Harding, Andrew W. Mellon, Herbert Hoover, Charles Dawes, Teapot Dome scandal, Albert Fall, Calvin Coolidge, Alfred E. Smith, mergers, Fordney-McCumber Tariff Act, American Plan.

1. **MAIN IDEA** Why did American voters elect a Republican president in 1920?

2. **MAIN IDEA** What qualities did President Coolidge possess that won the support of most Americans in the 1920s?

3. **ASSESSING CONSEQUENCES** What effect did the probusiness policies of Harding and Coolidge have on the economy?

4. **WRITING TO PERSUADE** Imagine you are a Republican campaigning for Herbert Hoover in 1928. Write a handbill you would distribute to urge other voters to support your candidate.

5. **ANALYZING** Why were women's groups divided over support of the Equal Rights Amendment?

A NATION DIVIDED

FOCUS

■ How did Native Americans respond to new efforts to seize tribal land?

■ What gave rise to black nationalism in the 1920s?

■ What did the revival of the Ku Klux Klan and the passage of new immigration laws reveal about the 1920s?

■ Why did immigration from Mexico increase?

Although many Americans prospered during the 1920s, deep social and racial divisions still plagued American life. Native Americans, African Americans, and Mexican immigrants all struggled for a place in American society. As African Americans continued to migrate to northern cities, racial tensions increased. The Ku Klux Klan encouraged bigotry not only against African Americans but also against foreigners. Responding to the national mood, Congress passed laws limiting immigration.

Ku Klux Klansman

NATIVE AMERICAN LIFE

For Native Americans the 1920s brought some recognition of the difficulties they faced. The Dawes Act, which attempted to "Americanize"

▲ Native Americans carry water from a government well in Arizona.

Indians by dividing tribal land into individual plots (see Chapter 5) had clearly failed. The act's allotment policies—as the Board of Indian Commissioners acknowledged—had often been "a short cut to the separation of . . . Indians from their land and cash."

In the 1920s Native Americans successfully organized to fight new efforts to take tribal land. Native American leaders stopped the Harding administration's attempt to buy back all tribal land. Then in 1922 the different Pueblo tribes of the Southwest organized against the Bursum Bill, which was designed to legalize non–Native American claims to Pueblo land. Furthermore, the bill would limit the power of tribal governments. The Pueblos appealed to all Americans:

66 This bill will destroy our common life and will rob us of everything which we hold dear—our lands, our customs, our traditions. Are the American people willing to see this happen? 99

Many Americans were not. The Pueblos won the support of the General Federation of Women's Clubs and of anthropologists, as well as the support of many other influential men and women. As a result, the *New York Times* could write in January 1923 that the bill was "happily, dead."

In 1924 Congress granted citizenship to all Native Americans, partly in recognition of those who had fought in World War I. But citizenship did not soften the harsh effects of poverty that many Native Americans continued to experience.

■■ Native Americans organized to fight efforts to take their lands.

▲ **A neighborhood strewn with rubble reveals the tragic aftermath of the Chicago race riots in 1919.**

AFRICAN AMERICANS MOVE NORTH

During the 1920s some 800,000 African Americans joined the hundreds of thousands who had moved to the North during World War I. By 1930 the North's African American population had reached almost 2.5 million, more than double its size in 1910. Large African American communities sprang up in Chicago, Detroit, New York City, and other northern cities. Harlem, a section of New York City with a large black population, proudly styled itself "the capital of Black America."

The North, however, was not free of bigotry. African Americans who had risked their lives in Europe "to make the world safe for democracy" confronted lynch mobs. Others faced discrimination, and as demands for labor eased, African Americans were the first to lose their jobs.

At times, racial tensions erupted violently. One of the worst outbreaks occurred in Chicago in July 1919. The trouble began when a white man

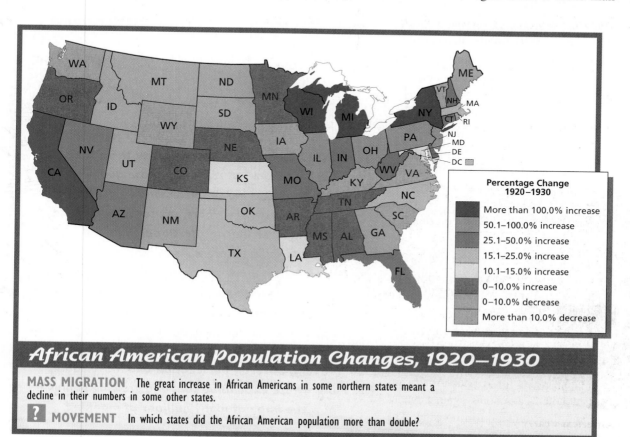

African American Population Changes, 1920–1930

Percentage Change 1920–1930
- More than 100.0% increase
- 50.1–100.0% increase
- 25.1–50.0% increase
- 15.1–25.0% increase
- 10.1–15.0% increase
- 0–10.0% increase
- 0–10.0% decrease
- More than 10.0% decrease

MASS MIGRATION The great increase in African Americans in some northern states meant a decline in their numbers in some other states.

? MOVEMENT In which states did the African American population more than double?

▲ The NAACP began as an interracial coalition fighting for African Americans' rights. James Weldon Johnson, seated behind the desk, served as executive secretary of the NAACP from 1920 to 1930. Johnson was also a noted author and songwriter.

threw rocks at an African American teenager swimming in Lake Michigan. The boy drowned. The fight that broke out between whites and blacks on shore spread to the rest of the city. The rioting continued for more than a week. White gangs fueled much of the violence as they prowled the slums, attacking African Americans and destroying property. By the time order was restored, 38 people had been killed and 537 injured.

By late 1919, some 25 race riots had erupted around the country. In June 1921, at least 30 people died during a race riot in Tulsa, Oklahoma. One resident described attacks on the black section of town:

> ❝ People were seen to flee from their burning homes, some with babes in their arms and leading crying and excited children. . . . [A] machine gun . . . was raining bullets down on our section. ❞

Faced with continued violence and discrimination, many African Americans organized to defend their rights. The National Association for the Advancement of Colored People (NAACP) stepped up its legal battle to win equal rights for African Americans and mounted campaigns against lynching and discrimination in housing. The unions' continued failure to help black

workers led labor activist A. Philip Randolph to found the Brotherhood of Sleeping Car Porters in 1925. It became a powerful voice for black workers.

BLACK NATIONALISM

Frustrated by the slow pace of change, some African Americans lost hope of ever achieving equality in the United States. What African Americans needed, they said, was a nation of their own. Foremost among these black nationalists was Marcus Garvey.

Garvey, a native of Jamaica, founded the Universal Negro Improvement Association (UNIA) in 1914. UNIA had two main goals: to foster African Americans' economic independence by establishing black-owned businesses and to create an independent black homeland in Africa. "We

THE BACK–TO–AFRICA MOVEMENT

THROUGH OTHERS' EYES

Marcus Garvey's Back-to-Africa movement drew many followers both in America and in Africa. In 1922 a representative of the king of Abyssinia (Ethiopia) read the following message to a Universal Negro Improvement Association (UNIA) convention:

> ❝ *Assure them [Garvey's followers] of the cordiality with which I invite them back to the home land, particularly those qualified to help solve our big problems and to develop our vast resources. Teachers, artisans, mechanics, writers, musicians, professional men and women—all who are able to lend a hand in the constructive work which our country so deeply feels, and greatly needs.*
>
> *Here we have abundant room and great opportunities and here destiny is working to elevate and enthrone a race which has suffered slavery, poverty, persecution and martyrdom, but whose expanding soul and growing genius is now the hope of many millions of mankind.* ❞

shall now organize," Garvey told the delegates to UNIA's first international convention, "to plant the banner of freedom on the great continent of Africa."

▲ **Marcus Garvey**

A charismatic speaker, Garvey urged African Americans to draw on their African heritage. He asserted that before Europeans were civilized:

> 66 Africa was peopled with a race of cultured black men, who were masters in art, science and literature. . . . Why, then, should we lose hope? Black men, you were once great; you shall be great again. Lose not courage, lose not faith, go forward. 99

To foster economic independence, Garvey founded the Black Star Steamship Company in 1919. He urged African Americans to invest in his company so that they "may exert the same influence on the world as the white man does today." Garvey promised investors huge returns, but the company never turned a profit. In 1925 Garvey was jailed for mail fraud in connection with his fund-raising activities. President Coolidge pardoned him in 1927 but ordered him deported. He died in 1940, still clinging to his dream.

Garvey's movement declined after he was jailed. Nevertheless, as one newspaper said in 1927, "He made black people proud. . . . He taught them that black is beautiful." Although other African American leaders, such as W.E.B. Du Bois, shared Garvey's belief in racial pride and solidarity, they opposed his Back-to-Africa movement. They insisted that African Americans should fight for justice and equality in American society.

■■ **Continued discrimination and a growing sense of black pride led to the rise of black nationalism.**

THE RETURN OF THE KU KLUX KLAN

To some degree, racism and discrimination during the 1920s reflected a broader repressive mood in American society. More and more, native-born Protestant Americans distrusted people who seemed different. One sign of this growing intolerance was the resurgence of the Ku Klux Klan.

Like the Klan of post–Civil War days, the new Klan, established in 1915 at Stone Mountain, Georgia, used kidnappings, beatings, and lynchings to terrorize African Americans in the South. However, the Klan also grew rapidly outside the South. In northern and midwestern towns and cities, the Klan targeted not only blacks but also radicals, immigrants, Catholics, and Jews, as well as such threats to traditional moral values as divorce.

The Klan grew slowly at first, but as the Red Scare took hold, membership soared. Reaching its peak in the mid-1920s, the Klan had perhaps as many as five million members. At mass rallies white-robed Klan members burned crosses and spoke out against people and ideas they considered "undesirable." Klan views also influenced politics, helping candidates win elections in such states as Louisiana, Oklahoma, Ohio, Texas—even Oregon. The Klan was particularly powerful in Indiana.

After 1925, however, the Klan declined, and by 1930 its membership had dropped to some 9,000. Rising prosperity and the end of the Red Scare diminished the Klan's appeal, but other factors also contributed. One was the conviction of an Indiana Klan leader—Grand Dragon David Stephenson—for second-degree murder. Another was the discovery that Klan promoters were getting rich from membership fees and the sale of regalia. Nevertheless, the Klan did not die out; it continues to spread its message of white supremacy.

▲ **Ku Klux Klan members taught racist attitudes to their children. Here, a baby is being enrolled into the Klan on Independence Day, 1927.**

IMMIGRATION RESTRICTIONS

During the 1920s the Klan also played on anti-immigrant feelings. Many Americans feared that the country was being overrun by immigrants—in 1920 nearly a quarter of the population was foreign-born or nonwhite. Furthermore, the number of immigrants, which had declined during the war, was once again rising, increasing from some 140,000 in 1919 to some 805,000 in 1921. This dramatic growth, coupled with the widespread belief that immigrants held radical views and took jobs from native-born Americans, led to demands for limits on immigration.

In 1921 Congress passed a law limiting the number of immigrants from each country allowed into the United States. The quota was set at 3 percent of each nationality already in the country in 1910, except for Asians, who were excluded

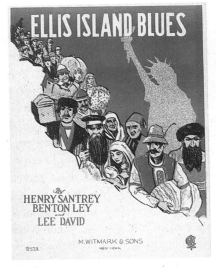

▲ "Ellis Island Blues" was one of many songs written in the 1920s about the flood of immigrants to the United States after World War I.

altogether. (Immigration from nations in the Western Hemisphere was not limited.) The **Immigration Act of 1924** reduced the quota to 2 percent of the 1890 figures for each national group. This change worked against southern and eastern Europeans because in 1890 most Americans traced their origins to England, Ireland, or northern Europe. While the 1924 law did not exclude Asians, it set the annual quota at only 100 Chinese and 100 Japanese immigrants. In 1925 the restrictions reduced the total number of new immigrants from Europe, Africa, Asia, and Australia to some 153,000.

■■ The revival of the Ku Klux Klan and new limits on immigration revealed continued hostility toward racial and ethnic groups.

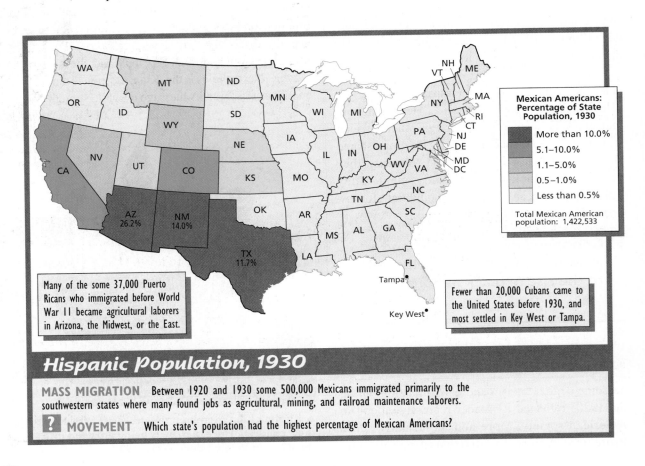

Many of the some 37,000 Puerto Ricans who immigrated before World War II became agricultural laborers in Arizona, the Midwest, or the East.

Fewer than 20,000 Cubans came to the United States before 1930, and most settled in Key West or Tampa.

Mexican Americans: Percentage of State Population, 1930

- More than 10.0%
- 5.1–10.0%
- 1.1–5.0%
- 0.5–1.0%
- Less than 0.5%

Total Mexican American population: 1,422,533

AZ 26.2%
NM 14.0%
TX 11.7%

Hispanic Population, 1930

MASS MIGRATION Between 1920 and 1930 some 500,000 Mexicans immigrated primarily to the southwestern states where many found jobs as agricultural, mining, and railroad maintenance laborers.

❓ **MOVEMENT** Which state's population had the highest percentage of Mexican Americans?

MEXICAN AMERICAN MIGRATION

In the Southwest, employers, particularly in agriculture, railroad construction, and mining, encouraged Mexican immigration, which was not affected by the restrictive legislation of the 1920s. Few people were arriving from Europe and Asia, and southwestern employers were eager to keep a steady flow of workers to fill low-wage jobs. As a result, during the 1920s some 500,000 immigrants arrived from Mexico, where wages were far lower.

Those who took agricultural jobs not only had to accept low pay but many also had to live in ramshackle labor camps. One observer noted:

66 Shelters were made of almost every conceivable thing—burlap, canvas, palm branches. . . . We found one woman carrying water in large milk pails from the irrigation ditch. . . . This is evidently all the water which they have in camp. 99

In the 1920s many Mexican immigrants also moved into urban areas. Some were drawn to well-paying factory jobs in cities such as Chicago and Detroit and established new centers of Mexican population in the Midwest. Most, however, migrated to cities in the Southwest—particularly Los Angeles, El Paso, and San Antonio (see map on page 638). Usually the men came alone, and once established, they sent for their wives and children. Many brought other relatives as well, reestablishing extended family networks. These networks helped new arrivals find jobs and housing.

Because of economic hardship, many families allowed their young, unmarried daughters to work outside the home. Many found employment in bakeries, hotels, and laundries, while others worked as maids. Their newfound independence, as one Mexican immigrant woman sadly noted, brought young women "into conflict with their parents. They learn . . . about the outside world, learn how to speak English, and then they become ashamed of their parents who brought them up here." Despite such conflicts, these new immigrants contributed to the mosaic of cultures that helps define American life.

▪▪ ▲ The promise of jobs drew Mexican immigrants, who were not subject to restrictive quotas, to cities in the Southwest and Midwest.

▲ Mexican American Victor Villaseñor wrote *Rain of Gold*, a book about his family's experiences as immigrants to California in the 1920s. Shown here is the 1929 wedding of his parents, Juan Salvador and Lupe.

SECTION 3 REVIEW

IDENTIFY and explain the significance of the following: A. Philip Randolph, Marcus Garvey, Immigration Act of 1924.

1. **MAIN IDEA** In what way did Native Americans fight government attempts to take tribal land?

2. **MAIN IDEA** What factors contributed to the rise of black nationalism?

3. **MAIN IDEA** What events in the 1920s revealed continued hostility toward racial and ethnic groups?

4. **WRITING TO EXPLAIN** Imagine you are a Mexican immigrant in the 1920s. Write a diary entry that explains why you moved to the Southwest or to the Midwest.

5. **EVALUATING** What effect did the migration of African Americans have on the North?

CHAPTER 11
Review

Palmer raids begin. Marcus Garvey founds Black Star Steamship Company.

Warren G. Harding elected president.

Race riot breaks out in Tulsa, Oklahoma. Congress limits immigration.

Pueblos organize against Bursum Bill.

1919   1921

WRITING A SUMMARY

Using the essential points of the chapter as a guide, write a summary of the chapter.

REVIEWING CHRONOLOGY

Number your paper 1 to 5. Study the time line above, and list the following events in the order in which they happened by writing the first next to 1, the second next to 2, and so on. Then complete the activity below.

1. Palmer raids begin.
2. Calvin Coolidge elected president.
3. Congress limits immigration.
4. Sacco and Vanzetti executed.
5. Equal Rights Amendment introduced into Congress.

Hypothesizing How might political events have been different during the 1920s if President Harding had not died?

IDENTIFYING PEOPLE AND IDEAS

Explain the historical significance of each of the following people or terms.

1. demobilization
2. Edwin Curtis
3. Red Scare
4. Emma Goldman
5. Andrew W. Mellon
6. Teapot Dome scandal
7. mergers
8. American Plan
9. Marcus Garvey
10. Immigration Act of 1924

UNDERSTANDING MAIN IDEAS

1. Why did the cost of living soar after the war? How did demobilization lead to recession and an increase in unemployment?
2. What were the results of the 1919 strikes in Seattle and Boston?
3. How were Warren G. Harding and Calvin Coolidge alike in their approaches to government?
4. What were the "sick industries" during the 1920s? Why did they fail to benefit from the economic boom?
5. What events and attitudes led to increased social tensions during the 1920s?

REVIEWING THEMES

1. **Democratic Values** What steps did the federal government take during the 1920s to reduce the perceived threat of revolution?
2. **Cultural Diversity** In what ways did Native Americans, African Americans, and Mexican Americans respond to discrimination?
3. **Economic Development** How did Republican probusiness policies attempt to stimulate the economy?

THINKING CRITICALLY

1. **Synthesizing** Why did many Americans vote Republican in the 1920, 1924, and 1928 presidential elections?
2. **Analyzing** Why did many farmers fail to benefit from the economic boom of the 1920s?
3. **Evaluating** Do you think women's groups that opposed the Equal Rights Amendment were justified? Why or why not?

STRATEGY FOR SUCCESS

Review the Strategies for Success on Recognizing Stereotypes on page 272. Then read the following passage from a 1926 article by Hiram Wesley Evans, the Imperial Wizard of the Ku Klux Klan. What group is the subject of this passage? Why can Evans's characterization be considered an example of stereotyping?

66 The alien . . . is unalterably fixed in his instincts, character, thought, and interests by centuries of racial selection and development. . . . He thinks first for his own people, works only with and for them, . . . considers himself always one of them, and never an American. 99

WRITING ABOUT HISTORY

Writing to Evaluate Write an essay evaluating the impact of the Sacco and Vanzetti case on public opinion.

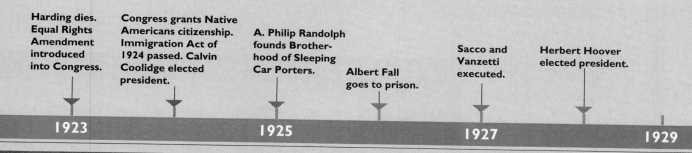

USING PRIMARY SOURCES

In 1925 more than 11,000 textile workers went on strike in Passaic, New Jersey, to demand better working conditions and higher wages. Read the following excerpt from "The War in Passaic" written by labor activist Mary Heaton Vorse. Then write a paragraph summarizing the author's views of the strike.

“ *Half the picket line is composed of young people. Mothers with children by the hand, older women and high-school boys and girls stream along, their heads thrown back, singing. . . . Passaic sprawling in its winter slush and snow watches its mill-workers make a full-hearted protest against the intolerable conditions in the mills, against the inhuman and unbearable wage cut. . . .*

The mayor of Passaic menaced the strikers with a force of three hundred mounted policemen. . . . They charged a crowd of 3,000 strikers, bludgeoned many men, women, and children, and smashed with deliberate intent the persons and cameras of the news photographers. . . . The strikers, armed with gas masks, helmets, and their unbending courage, defied the police successfully—and paraded in peace. . . .

The present Passaic strike is only a phase of the long fight of the textile workers for organization and a living wage. . . . When there is such want and suffering, when conditions of toil are so degrading, when the places that human beings live in are so indecent, it becomes the concern of the public at large to make its power felt and to see that this state of things is altered. ”

LINKING HISTORY AND GEOGRAPHY

Study the African American and Hispanic population maps on pages 291 and 294. Write a brief summary of the population trends shown on each map. Then prepare a list of possible factors that might help explain the population distributions.

Passaic strikers

BUILDING YOUR PORTFOLIO

Complete the following projects independently or cooperatively.

1. **THE ECONOMY** Imagine you are a World War I veteran in 1919. Write a letter to your senator, explaining why you feel the federal government should help you secure a job. Your letter might mention your concerns about low wages, the high cost of living, and the few employment opportunities available in the postwar economy.

2. **CULTURE AND SOCIETY** Imagine you are an immigrant artist on the staff of Emma Goldman's radical magazine *Mother Earth* in the late 1920s. Create a cover illustration for an upcoming issue that expresses your views about one of the following: the Red Scare, the Sacco and Vanzetti case, labor strikes, or the Equal Rights Amendment.

LAND USE

$\mathcal{F}$OR thousands of years Americans have used the land to grow crops. Many Native American groups cultivated crops on small plots of land long before the arrival of Europeans. In the early days of the republic, most farmers continued to grow food crops on small farms, although many large plantations in the South used the land to grow great quantities of tobacco and cotton. By the late 19th century, improved farm machinery and pesticides allowed farmers to grow larger quantities of food on smaller plots of land. Despite changes in farming techniques, some aspects of American farming have remained the same. For instance, corn is still the primary food crop grown in America—just as it was in the earliest civilizations.

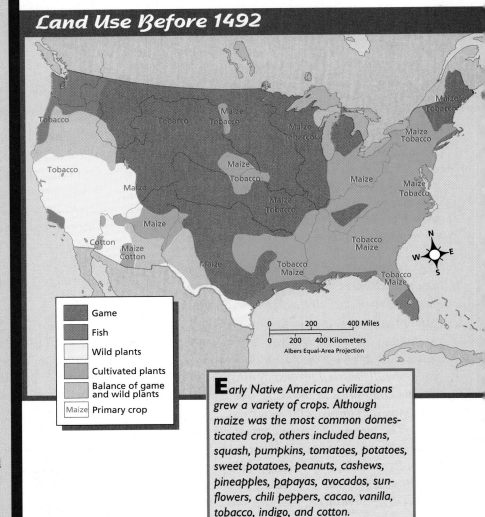

Land Use Before 1492

▨	Game
▨	Fish
▢	Wild plants
▨	Cultivated plants
▨	Balance of game and wild plants
Maize	Primary crop

Early Native American civilizations grew a variety of crops. Although maize was the most common domesticated crop, others included beans, squash, pumpkins, tomatoes, potatoes, sweet potatoes, peanuts, cashews, pineapples, papayas, avocados, sunflowers, chili peppers, cacao, vanilla, tobacco, indigo, and cotton.

The multipurpose, high-protein soybean has become the agricultural wonder of the 20th century. By 1991 it was the second most-popular crop in the United States. Soybeans are used in the processing of cattle feed, fertilizer, insect sprays, and paint, as well as in food products such as soy sauce, soy milk, baby food, cereals, processed meats, and tofu.

AGRICULTURAL PRODUCTION, 1910–1991		
	1910	1991
CORN (in bushels)	2.85 billion	7.75 billion
WHEAT (in bushels)	625 million	1.98 billion
COTTON (in bales)	11.61 million	17.5 million
TOBACCO (in pounds)	1.05 billion	1.66 billion
SOYBEANS (in bushels)	< 50,000	1.99 billion

Sources: Historical Statistics of the United States, Statistical Abstract of the United States.

Land Use, 1910

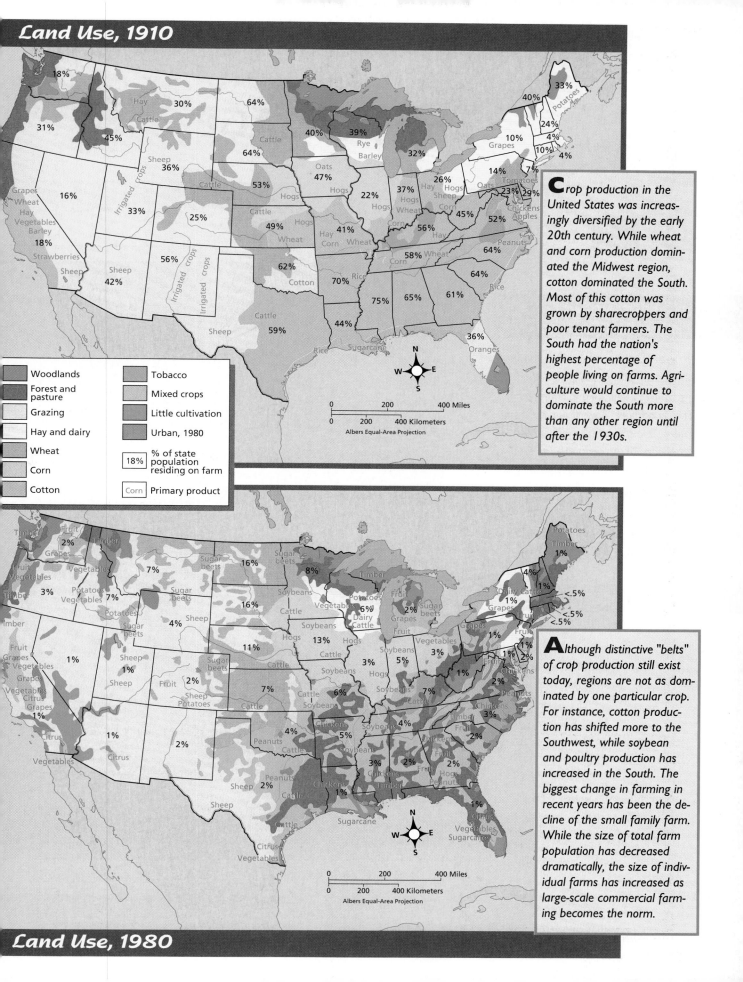

Crop production in the United States was increasingly diversified by the early 20th century. While wheat and corn production dominated the Midwest region, cotton dominated the South. Most of this cotton was grown by sharecroppers and poor tenant farmers. The South had the nation's highest percentage of people living on farms. Agriculture would continue to dominate the South more than any other region until after the 1930s.

Legend:
- Woodlands
- Forest and pasture
- Grazing
- Hay and dairy
- Wheat
- Corn
- Cotton
- Tobacco
- Mixed crops
- Little cultivation
- Urban, 1980
- 18% — % of state population residing on farm
- Corn — Primary product

Although distinctive "belts" of crop production still exist today, regions are not as dominated by one particular crop. For instance, cotton production has shifted more to the Southwest, while soybean and poultry production has increased in the South. The biggest change in farming in recent years has been the decline of the small family farm. While the size of total farm population has decreased dramatically, the size of individual farms has increased as large-scale commercial farming becomes the norm.

Land Use, 1980

Chapter 12

1920–1930

THE JAZZ AGE

FOCUS

UNDERSTANDING THE MAIN IDEA

Jazz, the upbeat musical form developed by African Americans, helped give the 1920s a unique character. The automobile, advertising, radio programs, and movies also influenced American life. Artists and writers portrayed an American society growing more urban and "modern." Many Americans found the changes of the 1920s unsettling, and the decade was marked by social conflict.

THEMES

■ **ECONOMIC DEVELOPMENT** How might increased consumer spending help improve a nation's economy?

■ **TECHNOLOGY AND SOCIETY** How might new technology transform people's lives?

■ **CULTURAL DIVERSITY** How might the cultural traditions of a particular area or group conflict with or contribute to a national culture?

1920
First radio stations go on the air.

1925
Scopes trial held in Dayton, Tennessee.

1926
Langston Hughes's *Weary Blues* published.

1927
Charles Lindbergh completes first nonstop flight from New York

1928
Amelia Earhart crosses Atlantic Ocean by plane.

Americans had cut back on purchasing goods during World War I. With the war over, men and women were eager to buy the new products that postwar American industry offered in abundance.

Jazz floor show in Chicago, 1924

An avalanche of new products transformed the lives of Americans in the 1920s—none more so than the automobile. The automobile changed the way Americans worked, socialized, and ran their households. It also helped change social roles for women. As early as 1907 a poem celebrated the growing independence of women who drove:

> 66 Like the breeze in its flight, or
> the passage of light,
> Or swift as the fall of a star.
> She comes and she goes in a nimbus
> of dust
> A goddess enthroned on a car.
> The maid of the motor, behold her
> erect
> With muscles as steady as steel.
> Her hand on the lever and always
> in front
> The girl in the automobile. 99

Life magazine cover, 1926

New forms of entertainment, including the wildly popular jazz bands, amused Americans in the generally prosperous 1920s. Radio programs, talking pictures, musical performances, and sporting events also entertained millions. But the decade was not all amusement. A small group of writers and artists revitalized American arts with their sober reflections on the war, race relations, and the nature of American society.

BOOM TIMES

FOCUS

- **What factors led to the economic boom of the 1920s?**
- **Which processes changed work habits during the twenties?**
- **How did the automobile affect American life?**
- **What developments stimulated consumerism?**

Automobile advertisement, 1920

The Granger Collection, New York

The economy prospered in the 1920s. In 1928 wages were a third higher than they had been in 1914. The gross national product climbed from $70 billion in 1922 to $100 billion just seven years later. Prosperity was accompanied by changes in the workplace and a new automobile age. Salespeople sold cars and a host of other products through aggressive campaigns that aimed to turn the United States into a nation of consumers.

PROSPERITY AND PRODUCTIVITY

Many factors led to the boom times of the 1920s. One was the Republicans' probusiness stance. Another was abundant supplies of energy—coal, oil, natural gas, and waterpower, as well as a vast network of electrical power plants. Between 1920 and 1929 fuel oil output doubled, and annual electrical production went from some 56 billion to 114 billion kilowatt-hours. By 1930 over two thirds of all U.S. homes had electricity.

The widespread availability of electricity created a demand for a dizzying array of new electrical appliances—washing machines, sewing machines, cake mixers, and food grinders. Radio and phonograph sales boomed. Chemical companies also tempted consumers, offering a variety of products made from plastic, rayon, acetate, and other new "wonder" materials. In 1930, textile mills produced more than 118 million pounds of rayon and acetate yarns—more than 13 times the 1920 production level.

A new production technique—the **assembly line**—helped factories churn out goods faster. Around 1913, after adapting techniques used in the slaughterhouses

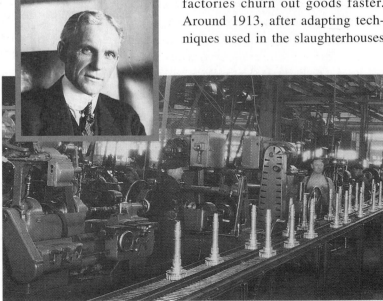

▶ **The Ford Motor Company introduced assembly-line techniques in its factories as early as 1913. This photograph of a Ford factory was taken in 1924. Henry Ford is shown in the inset.**

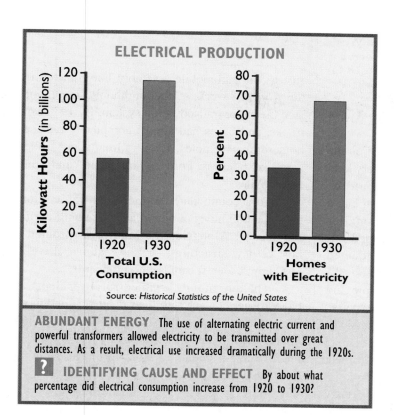

ELECTRICAL PRODUCTION

Total U.S. Consumption (Kilowatt Hours in billions)
- 1920
- 1930

Homes with Electricity (Percent)
- 1920
- 1930

Source: *Historical Statistics of the United States*

ABUNDANT ENERGY The use of alternating electric current and powerful transformers allowed electricity to be transmitted over great distances. As a result, electrical use increased dramatically during the 1920s.

? IDENTIFYING CAUSE AND EFFECT By about what percentage did electrical consumption increase from 1920 to 1930?

The assembly line allowed manufacturers to reduce the prices of cars, bringing them within reach of ordinary American families. Automobile registrations during the twenties rose from 8 million to 26 million—an average of one car for every five citizens.

In the 1920s the auto industry was the nation's biggest business. This new industrial giant consumed huge quantities of steel, glass, rubber, and other materials. Gasoline, formerly a troublesome by-product of the petroleum industry, became the industry's most-valued product. By 1929 over one million people labored in the automobile industry or a related business.

Probusiness policies, ample energy, new industries, and the assembly line fueled the economic boom of the 1920s.

of Chicago, Henry Ford introduced the assembly line in his Detroit automobile plant. Workers stood in one spot as partially assembled automobiles moved past them on a conveyor belt timed to advance precisely six feet per minute. Bit by bit, workers assembled the 5,000 parts of a Model T, or "Tin Lizzie," until the finished product could be driven out of the factory. Machinery did much of the work of producing individual parts and carrying them to workers. Boasted Ford:

> 66 Every piece of work in the shop moves; it may move on hooks, on overhead chains . . . it may travel on a moving platform, or it may go by gravity, but the point is that there is no lifting or trucking. . . . No workman has anything to do with moving or lifting anything. 99

The assembly line cut the engine assembly time for a Model T in half. Other large car manufacturers quickly followed Ford's lead and installed assembly lines. But few small companies could afford the expense of building or maintaining the new technology. Unable to compete, many were driven out of business. Soon the industry was dominated by three big corporations: Ford, General Motors, and Chrysler.

CHANGES IN WORK

Although assembly lines increased productivity, they had a human cost. Little technical skill was needed to "work the line." Thus, many higher-paid skilled laborers were thrown out of work. But even the people who found jobs on the line suffered. The work was deadening, leading many to quit within a few weeks. To counter the high turnover, Ford limited the workday to eight hours and doubled wages to an unheard-of $5 a day.

Both of these bold steps were welcomed. However, as the wife of one Ford worker noted, the pay increase did not change working conditions:

> 66 The chain system [assembly line] you have is a *slave driver! My God!* Mr. Ford. My husband has come home & thrown himself down & won't eat his supper—so done out! Can't it be remedied? . . . That $5 a day is a blessing—a bigger one than you know but *oh* they earn it. 99

The innovations of "Fordism" were more than matched by those of another movement, "Taylorism." The movement's creator, Frederick W. Taylor, called his approach **scientific management**.

◀ Frederick W. Taylor pioneered techniques used to increase workers' output.

It was based on the idea that every kind of work could be broken down into a series of smaller tasks. Trained observers conducted "time-and-motion" studies to identify these tasks and then set rates of production that people and machines had to meet. Soon "efficiency experts" were applying Taylor's methods to many areas of business.

The assembly line and scientific management changed the types of jobs available to workers. While the number of factory jobs grew only slightly during the 1920s, openings for such white-collar jobs as manager, clerical worker, and salesperson increased from slightly more than 10 million to more than 14 million. Because most of these jobs required that applicants have at least a high-school education, few newly arrived immigrants qualified. Discriminatory hiring practices also closed most of these jobs to African Americans.

Changes in technology affected domestic labor as well. Electrical appliances transformed housework for those who could afford them. Before the introduction of appliances, servants did the laundry and heavy cleaning in most middle- and upper-class homes. With the introduction of electrical appliances, many middle-class housewives took over the jobs they had previously supervised. As a result, many servants were forced to find new employment.

As more families bought cars, housewives also began taking over their families' transportation needs. Before many middle- and upper-class families had cars, their groceries and other supplies had been delivered to their homes. The automobile allowed housewives to drive to grocery stores and other shops. Thus, like household servants, delivery people often found their jobs in jeopardy.

■■ Scientific management and new technology transformed working conditions in the 1920s.

A LAND OF AUTOMOBILES

Just as the automobile assembly line transformed the world of work, so the automobile revolutionized the entire transportation system. By 1930 cars, trucks, and buses had almost completely replaced horse-drawn vehicles. Even railroads and trolley cars lost riders to Ford's "Tin Lizzie" and other automobiles.

To accommodate the increased traffic, more than 400,000 miles of new roads were built during the decade. Alongside the highways sprouted a host of new structures—filling stations, drive-in restaurants, tourist cabins, and billboards.

The automobile enabled rural residents to have greater contact with their neighbors and more access to shopping and leisure activities. Cars linked rural regions to urban areas, making it easier for rural residents to relocate to the booming cities and for city dwellers to visit the country. At the same time, however, the automobile contributed to the depopulation of America's inner

▼ With some nine million automobiles in use by 1920, more and more families explored the country in their cars. Shown here is an advertisement encouraging motorists to take the Apache Trail Motor Tour through Arizona's National Reserve.

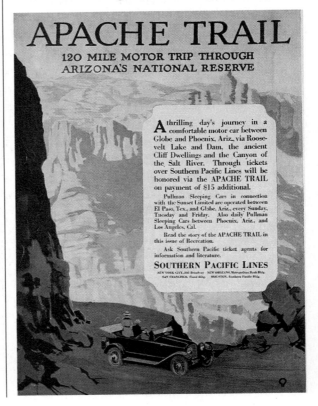

APACHE TRAIL
120 MILE MOTOR TRIP THROUGH ARIZONA'S NATIONAL RESERVE

A thrilling day's journey in a comfortable motor car between Globe and Phoenix, Ariz., via Roosevelt Lake and Dam, the ancient Cliff Dwellings and the Canyon of the Salt River. Through tickets over Southern Pacific Lines will be honored via the APACHE TRAIL on payment of $15 additional.

Pullman Sleeping Cars in connection with the Sunset Limited are operated between El Paso, Tex., and Globe, Ariz., every Sunday, Tuesday and Friday. Also daily Pullman Sleeping Cars between Phoenix, Ariz., and Los Angeles, Cal.

Read the story of the APACHE TRAIL in this issue of Recreation.

Ask Southern Pacific ticket agents for information and literature.

SOUTHERN PACIFIC LINES
NEW YORK CITY, 366 Broadway   NEW ORLEANS, Metropolitan Bank Bldg.
SAN FRANCISCO, Flood Bldg.   HOUSTON, Southern Pacific Bldg.

HITTING THE ROAD

In the 1920s, as millions of Americans purchased automobiles, a new craze swept the nation—the "autotouring" vacation. Guidebooks urged Americans to hit the road:

66 Does father crave to fish for trout and bass and pike and musky? Take him auto-touring. Does sister want to dip in the surf . . . or see the world? Take her automobile vacationing. . . . Does mother sigh for a rest from daily routines? Take her touring. . . . Does baby need fresh mountain air far from flies and heat? Take him auto-camping. 99

Freed from travel restrictions imposed by the schedules and routes of passenger trains, car owners took to the road to see America.

Most motor tourists were city dwellers who vacationed in the country to "get away from it all." But in getting away, they often took a lot of "it" with them. Camping gear for the typical autotourist included a tent, gas stove, heater, cooking utensils, pots and pans, folding table and chairs, blankets, and even beds.

Autotourists tended to camp together and had a culture all their own. They often dressed in ways that led observers to marvel and to gawk at the same time. One reporter wrote:

▲ **Families took advantage of new government autocamps while traveling on the road. This photograph shows a family camping in the 1920s.**

66 It was amazing what colorful combinations the knickered rovers [autotourists] managed to attain. They wore veils of all descriptions, flowing Egyptian veils and even gas masks [to keep out road dust]. They wore paper hats that tied under their chins, caps trimmed with the tails of squirrels, skins of rattlesnakes, and quills of porcupines. 99

At first farmers welcomed these visitors from the city. Autotourists broke the isolation of rural life and seemed likely customers for farm produce. But instead of buying fruits and vegetables, vacationers often snitched them from trees and fields. Sometimes campers even milked farmers' cows! They also dumped their garbage on farmers' land. Soon signs banning autotouring appeared in rural areas. One such sign read:

66 Trespassers will B persecuted to the full extent of 2 mongrel dogs which neve was over sochible to strangers and I doubl brl shot gun which ain't loaded with sofa pillors. 99

National and state park services, along with town governments, stepped in to keep local people and visitors from clashing. These agencies set up free autocamps to provide tourists with welcome comforts, while keeping them off private land. Electric lighting made it possible for motorists to arrive and set up camp after dark, and gas ranges eliminated the need for firewood.

The heyday of autotourism passed as the prosperity of the 1920s gave way to the depression of the 1930s. But its legacy can be seen today in the continuing appeal of sight-seeing and camping vacations and in the popularity of recreational vehicles.

cities. Suburbs, now more accessible than ever, attracted thousands of middle-class families.

The automobile also transformed family life. Cars enabled families to enjoy simple drives in the country and elaborate camping trips. The automobile created new social opportunities for teenagers as well. Sociologists Robert Lynd and Helen Lynd, whose book *Middletown* (1929) chronicled life in Muncie, Indiana, wrote:

> 66 The extensive use of this new tool [the automobile] by the young has enormously extended their mobility and the range of alternatives before them; joining a crowd motoring over to a dance . . . twenty miles away may be a matter of a moment's decision, with no one's permission asked. 99

But the automobile had negative effects as well. Critics claimed that cars reduced people's sense of neighborliness. The Lynds observed that "since the advent of the automobile and the movies" Muncie families and neighbors no longer spent "long summer evenings and Sunday afternoons on the porch or in the side yard." Also, by the twenties, cars were already causing pollution, traffic jams, and parking problems. Most serious was the steadily climbing accident rate.

■■ Cars revolutionized the nation's transportation system, eased rural isolation, aided suburban growth, and changed family and community relations.

CREATING CONSUMERS

Advertising, which became big business in the 1920s, fueled the demand for cars and other consumer goods. Before World War I, money spent on advertising had totaled some $500 million yearly. By 1929 the total had soared to more than $3 billion. Ads were everywhere. Commercial messages bombarded potential buyers not only in magazines and newspapers but also on billboards and over the new medium of radio.

Advertisements, most of which targeted women, used psychology to play on consumers' hopes and fears. Ads for Borden's milk, for instance, warned mothers that "Hardly a family— well-to-do and poor alike—escapes the menace of malnutrition. Your own child may fall victim to this insidious evil."

Companies used slogans, jingles, and testimonials by celebrities to fix product names in

▶ Advertisements often stressed the ease of operation or low maintenance of the device being offered for sale. This ad for an "unusually quiet" refrigerator appeared in 1927.

▼ Salespeople proudly display a host of new home electrical appliances that proved wildly popular in the 1920s.

customers' minds. Eleanor Roosevelt (whose husband, Franklin D. Roosevelt, was then governor of New York) praised Cream of Wheat, which their son John had eaten since babyhood. The cereal, she was quoted as saying, "has undoubtedly played its part in building his robust physique."

As the number of products expanded to meet the growing demand, new chain stores sprang up around the country. For example, the A & P grocery chain grew from some 3,000 stores in 1922 to about 14,000 by 1925. The chain grocery stores, which slowly replaced the corner markets, stocked a wide variety of new products. The chain stores could do so because cellophane, a transparent wrapping material first produced in the United States in 1924, and quick-freezing techniques preserved fresh foods longer and allowed them to be shipped over longer distances.

Effective merchandising depended above all on clever salespeople. "There are always some people that you can sell anything to if you hammer them hard enough," claimed a car dealer. Door-to-door salespeople hawked everything from cleaning supplies to encyclopedias.

People also bought more because of easy credit. Before the 1920s, consumers bought only a few expensive items, such as pianos and sewing machines, on the installment plan. By mid-decade,

▲ Chain grocery stores did not completely replace the neighborhood grocery. Immigrants continued to shop at family-run groceries such as this one, owned by Antonio and Angeline Tortolano. At such stores customers could buy ethnic foods and talk to shopkeepers in their native language.

buyers purchased about 75 percent of cars on credit. The practice soon spread to many other items. As a car dealer noted:

> ❝ To keep America growing we must keep Americans working, and to keep Americans working we must keep them wanting; wanting more than the bare necessities; wanting the luxuries and frills that make life so much more worthwhile, and installment selling makes it easier to keep Americans wanting. ❞

■■ **Advertising, merchandising, and installment buying encouraged consumerism.**

SECTION 1 REVIEW

IDENTIFY and explain the significance of the following: assembly line, Henry Ford, Frederick W. Taylor, scientific management, Robert Lynd, Helen Lynd.

1. **MAIN IDEA** What factors contributed to the economic prosperity of the 1920s?

2. **MAIN IDEA** What innovations transformed working conditions in the late 1920s?

3. **ASSESSING CONSEQUENCES** How did the invention of the automobile change the way Americans lived?

4. **WRITING TO INFORM** Imagine you are the president of a chain store. Prepare for your board of directors a brief summary of how the company plans to attract new customers.

5. **ANALYZING** Why can it be said that the technological and business innovations of the 1920s had both positive and negative consequences for American society?

LIFE IN THE TWENTIES

FOCUS

- What were the most popular forms of entertainment during the 1920s?
- In what ways did young women of the 1920s depart from traditional female behavior?
- What did the debate over Prohibition and Fundamentalism reveal about American society in the 1920s?

The decade of the 1920s has been called the gateway to modern America. For the first time a truly national mass culture emerged in the United States. Commercial radio linked Americans from coast to coast. Instant communications not only entertained people but also informed them about serious developments. The emerging mass culture also brought changes in women's roles and caused conflicts over traditional values.

Matinee idol Rudolph Valentino

POPULAR ENTERTAINMENT

Boom times in the United States meant that many—though not all—Americans had bigger paychecks and more free time than in years past. To help fill their leisure hours, many Americans turned to radio and movies.

Commercial radio arose in the twenties. The first stations, Detroit's WWJ and Pittsburgh's KDKA, went on the air in 1920. By 1929, more than 800 stations reached some 10 million homes—more than a third of the nation's households. "There is radio music in the air, every night, everywhere," gushed a San Francisco newspaper. "Anybody can hear it at home on a receiving set." Along with music, radio stations broadcast sports events, news, and comedy shows.

By the end of the decade, two networks, the National Broadcasting Company (NBC) and the Columbia Broadcasting System (CBS), aired their programs nationwide. Households across the land tuned in to the same programs.

Movies proved equally popular, having grown in both length and complexity since their beginnings in the 1890s. The earliest movie

◀ Advances in technology made radio more accessible to Americans during the 1920s. This photograph shows a young woman tuning in to a program on her radio set in 1922.

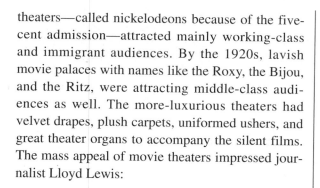

▲ Moviegoers during the 1920s stood in line to see romance films starring John Gilbert and Greta Garbo, action films with Douglas Fairbanks, or comedies featuring Charlie Chaplin.

▶ As motion pictures grew in popularity, theater owners built lavish movie palaces with elaborate balconies, box seats, and a pit for live orchestral music.

theaters—called nickelodeons because of the five-cent admission—attracted mainly working-class and immigrant audiences. By the 1920s, lavish movie palaces with names like the Roxy, the Bijou, and the Ritz, were attracting middle-class audiences as well. The more-luxurious theaters had velvet drapes, plush carpets, uniformed ushers, and great theater organs to accompany the silent films. The mass appeal of movie theaters impressed journalist Lloyd Lewis:

66 In the "de luxe" [movie] house every man is a king and every woman a queen. Most of these cinema palaces sell all their seats at the same price,—and get it; the rich man stands in line with the poor. . . . In this suave atmosphere, the differences . . . that determine our lives outside are forgotten. All men enter these portals equal, and thus the movies are perhaps a symbol of democracy. 99

In 1927 Warner Brothers released the first feature-length "talkie," *The Jazz Singer,* starring Al Jolson. Silent-screen stars with high squeaky voices soon found themselves unemployed. In their places emerged new actors with distinctive and appealing voices, among them Gary Cooper and Clara Bow. The advent of sound also led to new film forms, including musicals and newsreels,

short films summing up the news of the day. In 1929 some 80 million Americans flocked to the theaters each week.

▪▪ Americans turned to radio and movies for entertainment during the 1920s.

𝒞ELEBRITIES AND HEROES

When movie star Rudolph Valentino died in 1926 at age 31, mourners lined up for blocks to view his body. In this era of mass culture, actors became instant celebrities. So did other figures in the public eye, especially athletes and pilots.

One sports favorite was Babe Ruth. Ruth dominated baseball from 1920 to 1935, during which time he led the New York Yankees to four World Series championships. In 1927 the spindle-legged, pigeon-toed ball player astounded the sports world with a record 60 home runs. Hard-hitting tennis star Helen Wills wowed audiences

▲ During his long career, Babe Ruth hit 714 home runs—a record not broken until 1974.

THE TWENTIES

Richard Müller-Freienfels, a German professor and writer, studied industrialization and the mass culture that emerged in the early 20th century. Here is his description of American life in the 1920s:

THROUGH OTHERS' EYES

> **"*A*ll the men seem to be clothed by the same tailor, and all the women seem to have bought their hats at the same shop. . . . The most remarkable thing is that even the people impress one as having been standardized. All these clean-shaven men, all these girls, with their doll-like faces, which are generally painted, seem to have been produced somewhere in a Ford factory, not by the dozen but by the thousand. In no other country are the individuals reduced to such a dead-level as in the United States, and this appears all the more remarkable when we reflect that nowhere [else] is there such a . . . mixture of races and peoples."**

and captured more major tennis championships than any other woman in the world. Wills won the U.S. Open title seven times and Wimbledon eight times. Swimmer Gertrude Ederle broke the world record when she swam the English Channel in 1926 at age 19. She went on to set more than 20 U.S. swimming records and to win several medals in the 1924 summer Olympics.

Few athletes of the 1920s, however, enjoyed greater fame than Jim Thorpe. Born in 1888 in Oklahoma, he was of Sauk, Fox, Irish, and French ancestry. Thorpe attended the Carlisle Indian School in Pennsylvania. There he played every intercollegiate sport the school offered.

After he left Carlisle, Thorpe began training for the Olympics. At the 1912 games, held in Stockholm, Sweden, he became the first contestant to win both the pentathlon and the decathlon. "Sir, you are the greatest athlete in the world," said the Swedish king as he presented Thorpe with his gold medals. "Thanks, King," replied Thorpe with a grin.

A year later Thorpe's triumph turned to ashes. The news became public that he had played semiprofessional baseball for money. (At the time, Olympic athletes had to be amateurs.) Officials erased his name from Olympic record books and confiscated his awards. Many people felt that Thorpe had been treated unfairly; he had not realized that playing baseball for money would disqualify him from track competition.

Thorpe went on to a respectable career in major-league baseball and in the 1920s enjoyed several spectacular years playing professional football. In his later years, which were clouded by illness, he tried to become a movie actor. Not until 1982, 29 years after his death, did an Olympic committee restore his medals.

Probably the greatest celebrity of the 1920s was pilot Charles Lindbergh. In May 1927 he took off in a small single-engine plane, aiming to win a $25,000 prize that had been offered to the first pilot

BIO GRAPHY

Jim Thorpe

▶ **Charles Lindbergh's solo flight across the Atlantic Ocean in 1927 in his plane, *The Spirit of St. Louis*, made him an international celebrity.**

to fly nonstop from New York to Paris. After flying solo for 33 1/2-hours, he landed in France. Americans were delirious with joy. New Yorkers threw a ticker-tape parade for Lindbergh, and President Coolidge received the modest young man at the White House. Lindbergh's flight offered exciting glimpses of a coming era of air travel. The next year, pilot Amelia Earhart became the first woman to cross the Atlantic Ocean by plane.

THE "NEW WOMAN"

Two of the many changes in the 1920s were in women's dress and behavior. Influenced by popular actresses and by the independence of working-class women, some young women exercised new freedom in how they dressed and behaved. These women stopped wearing heavy corsets and started wearing shorter skirts and transparent silk hose. Actress Colleen Moore explained that these changes in dress represented a new independence for women:

❝ Long skirts, corsets, and flowing tresses have gone. . . . The American girl will see to this. She is independent, a thinker [who] will not follow slavishly the ordinances of those who in the past have decreed this or that for her to wear. ❞

People began to call the era's "new women" **flappers**. Flappers enjoyed defying traditional standards of womanly behavior. They wore their dresses daringly short, bobbed their hair, and wore makeup. They also drove cars, participated in sports, and smoked cigarettes.

Flappers gloried not only in their social freedom but also in their economic independence. Young women increasingly worked outside the home, which gave them more freedom to meet people and save money for themselves. If they married, however, they were expected to quit their paid employment and to fulfill their roles as wives and mothers. As Samuel Gompers, leader of the AFL, made clear in 1921 when he described the winner of the first Miss America beauty pageant, the homemaker was still the ideal of American womanhood:

❝ She represents the type of womanhood America needs—strong, red-blooded, able

to shoulder the responsibilities of home-making and motherhood. It is in her type that the hope of the country resides. ❞

■■ **The "new woman" of the twenties defied conventions in dress and behavior.**

A CRISIS OF VALUES

Many Americans found the social changes of the 1920s more troubling than exciting. For them conservative values and traditional ways of life remained important. Despite the spread of mass culture, many citizens' lives still centered on family, church, and neighborhood, and religion remained a vital part of American culture.

For these traditionalists, the flapper symbolized the unwelcome changes overtaking the country in the 1920s. With their unconventional dress and behavior, flappers rejected traditional values. To conservatives, the popularity of romantic movies and cheek-to-cheek dancing seemed signs of increasing immorality. Most critics blamed these "modern" habits on cities, noting with anxiety that radio and movies spread city ways to even the remotest rural areas. Anxiety increased when the census of 1920 revealed that for the first time, more than half of the U.S. population lived in metropolitan areas. In the face of these tremendous changes, arguments raged over such issues as alcohol and religion.

Prohibition. Progressive reformers had called for a ban on alcohol to combat such urban problems as family violence, crime, and poverty (see Chapter 7). Baptists, Methodists, and other Protestants also opposed drinking. Furthermore, during World War I, many reformers had advocated prohibition as a war measure. Playing on widespread anti-German sentiment, they had noted that German Americans owned

▲ Couples during the 1920s often held each other close in a cheek-to-cheek style while dancing to romantic music.

▲ Federal agents such as Izzy Einstein and Moe Smith often went undercover and tried to purchase alcohol in speakeasies. When the alcohol was served, the agents made their arrests.

many of the large breweries. They had also pointed out that drinking reduced the efficiency of soldiers and workers. After the Eighteenth Amendment made the manufacture, sale, and transportation of alcoholic beverages illegal in January 1919, Congress passed the **Volstead Act** in October 1919 to enforce the amendment. America entered the era of Prohibition.

In some regions Prohibition was strictly enforced, and drinking declined. But in many parts of the country, especially among immigrants, college students, and some city dwellers, Prohibition was extremely unpopular and widely ignored. Many people treated the reform as an annoyance, if not a joke. They frequented speakeasies, made their own wine or liquor, and bought bootleg (illegal) alcohol that had been smuggled from Canada or the West Indies.

Bootlegging became one of the decade's booming businesses. Criminal gangs in the large cities controlled liquor sales. Gang leaders gained the cooperation of law enforcement officials by bribing or threatening them. Al Capone, the boss of Chicago's underworld, commanded a small army of heavily armed mobsters. He and other gangsters made millions of dollars.

▼ Aimee Semple McPherson preached for nearly 20 years in a Los Angeles temple that her supporters built at a cost of $1.5 million.

Gangs branched out to seize control of gambling establishments, houses of prostitution, and dance halls. They also made money through "protection" rackets, collecting money from owners of stores and other businesses by threatening violence if their victims failed to pay.

Prohibition had some positive consequences. Alcoholism declined and so did the number of deaths from alcohol-related causes. Prohibition's negative results, however, drew more attention. Prohibition led to a widespread breakdown of law and order and turned millions of otherwise law-abiding citizens into lawbreakers. Prohibition would later be repealed with the ratification of the **Twenty-first Amendment** in 1933.

Fundamentalism. The increasing popularity of a Protestant movement called **Fundamentalism** also revealed deep cultural conflicts in 1920s America. Fundamentalists believed that every word of the Bible should be regarded as literally true. They attacked Christian "liberals" who had accepted modern scientific learning, such as the theory of evolution. This "modernism," said Fundamentalists, weakened Christianity and contributed to the moral decline of the nation.

Revivalist preachers of the "old-time religion" found an eager audience, both in rural areas and in urban areas where traditional values remained strong. Billy Sunday, who had long preached against alcohol, drew huge crowds to his tent revivals. People were spellbound by Sunday's showmanship and his rousing attacks on dancing, card playing, and drinking. When Prohibition went into effect, he held a funeral service for "John Barleycorn," who personified alcohol, and declared that "the reign of tears is over."

Another popular revivalist of the 1920s was Aimee Semple McPherson, whose practice of faith healing and message of love attracted thousands to her International Church of the Foursquare Gospel, headquartered in Los Angeles. Most of her followers were city dwellers of modest income, many of them recent migrants from the Midwest. Outfitted in her signature white dress, white shoes, and blue cape,

The Roaring Twenties was a time of short skirts, bathtub gin, gambling, jazz, and the first talking movies. It was a time when old taboos were challenged one after the other. Alarmed and outraged by what they saw as the breakdown of the nation's moral standards, many community, religious, and government groups took action.

These activists pulled from library and store shelves books and magazines that used foul language, discussed sex frankly, or supported radical political ideas. U.S. Customs officials labeled many foreign books obscene and seized them, including the novel *Ulysses* by Irish author James Joyce.

Groups also targeted the movie industry. Several states and dozens of communities formed censorship boards to ban movies deemed unsuitable for young people. To both stem the tide of censorship and

address public concerns over movie content, Hollywood set up in 1924 its own review board, a forerunner of today's movie-rating system, to screen movie content.

The American Civil Liberties Union and other groups opposed these growing

▲ Although James Joyce's *Ulysses* was initially banned, a later federal court ruling declared that it was not obscene and was a true work of literature.

restrictions on the content of movies and literature. They argued that such censorship violated the Constitution's First Amendment, which guarantees freedom of speech and freedom of the press.

Today the battle between censorship and freedom of

speech continues. The National Endowment for the Arts (NEA), for example, has come under attack for funding artists whose works some consider obscene. But while some critics judge the art as obscene and unsuitable for public funding, the artists defend their right to freedom of expression. The NEA and other agencies are caught in the middle of the battle.

Several rock and rap musicians have also come under fire for recording songs that contain violent lyrics or lyrics that degrade women. In response, the Recording Industry Association of America has begun placing warning labels on any recordings that contain lyrics that might be unsuitable for minors. But many people believe voluntary labeling is not enough. In 1992, for instance, Washington State banned the sale and distribution of certain recordings to minors.

Is such censorship a violation of free speech or a needed form of protection? American society and U.S. courts continue to struggle with this question.

McPherson addressed her followers' concerns about the new doctrines of "communism, socialism, and jazz-ism." McPherson also used radio and magazines to spread her fundamentalist message.

The Scopes trial. Fundamentalism went on trial in a famous court case in July 1925. Earlier that year the Tennessee legislature had outlawed the teaching of Charles Darwin's theory of evolution—a prime target of Fundamentalists—in the state's public schools. To test the law's constitutionality, the American Civil Liberties Union offered to defend

any Tennessee schoolteacher who would challenge the statute. John Scopes, a shy high-school biology teacher from Dayton, accepted the offer.

The trial took place in a circus atmosphere. As the trial began in Dayton, the little town was overrun by reporters, farmers in mule-drawn wagons, and big-city lawyers. Scopes's chief defense attorney was salty Clarence Darrow, a famous criminal lawyer from Chicago. The prosecution's star witness was the elderly William Jennings Bryan, the former Democratic presidential candidate and secretary of state.

► Clarence Darrow (right) devoted a large part of his legal career to defending the "underdog." This photograph shows him with John Scopes in 1925.

▼ Because the theory of evolution implied that human beings had descended from ape-like creatures, the Scopes trial became known as the "Monkey Trial."

FINAL EDITION **THE CHICAGO DAILY NEWS.** BOX SCORE
TWO CENTS—5¢ ... 50TH YEAR—173. ... TUESDAY, JULY 21, 1925. ... HOME EDITION ... 5 O'CLOCK

SCOPES "GUILTY" IN APE CASE

The Scopes trial exposed a deep division in American society between traditional religious values and new values based on scientific ways of thought. Bryan represented the many Americans who felt that the theory of evolution contradicted deeply held religious beliefs. Speaking before the trial to an audience of local admirers, Bryan declared:

66 Our purpose and our only purpose is to vindicate [uphold] the right of parents to guard the religion of their children against efforts made in the name of science to undermine faith in supernatural religion. 99

Darrow, on the other hand, expressed the views of many other Americans when he attacked the Tennessee law as a threat to free expression. In one of his courtroom speeches, he warned his listeners that "today it is the public school teachers, tomorrow the private, the next day the preachers and the lecturers, the magazines, the books, the newspapers."

Darrow's arguments failed to sway the jury. They found Scopes guilty and fined him $100. The verdict seemed a victory for Fundamentalists. But press accounts of the trial, which often portrayed Bryan and his cause as narrow-minded, colored many people's views of Fundamentalism.

■■ The debate over Prohibition and Fundamentalism revealed a crisis of values in 1920s America.

SECTION 2 REVIEW

IDENTIFY and explain the significance of the following: Babe Ruth, Helen Wills, Gertrude Ederle, Jim Thorpe, Charles Lindbergh, Amelia Earhart, flappers, Volstead Act, Twenty-first Amendment, Fundamentalism, Aimee Semple McPherson, John Scopes.

1. **MAIN IDEA** What two forms of entertainment were most popular among Americans during the 1920s?

2. **MAIN IDEA** How did the flapper represent the "new woman" of the 1920s?

3. **IDENTIFYING VALUES** In what ways did the differing views of Clarence Darrow and William Jennings Bryan in the Scopes trial reflect the clash in values of 1920s America?

4. **WRITING TO INFORM** Write an essay explaining the negative and positive consequences of Prohibition.

5. **HYPOTHESIZING** What social factors might account for the popularity of sports figures and revivalists during the 1920s?

A CREATIVE ERA

FOCUS

- **How did African Americans contribute to the arts during the Harlem Renaissance?**

- **Who were the Lost Generation writers, and how did they get their name?**

- **What factors influenced artists and designers of the 1920s?**

- **How did mass media and advertising affect American culture in the 1920s?**

Louis Armstrong

The decade of the 1920s was a period of great creative energy. African American musicians transformed popular music by introducing the nation to jazz. A new generation of writers explored the problems of postwar American life and the experience of being black. Mexican muralists brought their paintings of social protest to the United States. And new currents in art and architecture swept the nation.

MUSIC AND DANCE

The 1920s has been called the Jazz Age because this was the period when jazz, with its richly complex rhythms, first won a wide following. Jazz originated among African Americans in the South, especially in New Orleans. By the late 1800s, jazz had emerged from a blend of West African and Latin American rhythms, African American spirituals and blues, and European harmonies.

Joseph "King" Oliver, an early jazz great, helped spread jazz northward by moving from New Orleans to Chicago and founding the Creole Jazz Band. In 1922 the great jazz trumpeter Louis Armstrong joined Oliver in Chicago. Pianist and composer Ferdinand "Jelly Roll" Morton also moved north.

▶ **Ferdinand "Jelly Roll" Morton began his career playing ragtime piano in New Orleans. Later, he moved to Chicago where he formed the recording group Red Hot Peppers.**

As it became popular on a national level, jazz was adapted in various ways. White musicians—among them the cornetist and pianist Bix Beiderbecke—incorporated jazz rhythms in their music. George Gershwin's *Rhapsody in Blue,* which

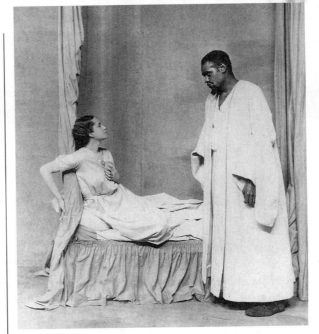

▲ In the 1920s Paul Robeson won fame as an actor in such plays as Shakespeare's *Othello*.

premiered in 1924, "translated" jazz into symphonic form. Jazz also influenced many classical musicians, including such noted composers as Igor Stravinsky and Aaron Copland.

The big bands, both black (Fletcher Henderson's and Duke Ellington's, for instance) and white (such as Paul Whiteman's), popularized jazz for dancing, creating faster and bouncier dances set to jazz rhythms. This new kind of jazz swept the nation via phonograph records, radio, and the movies. Young men and their flapper partners shocked their elders by dancing cheek-to-cheek fox-trots. The Charleston, originally an African dance performed by slaves, became *the* dance of the twenties.

While jazz became universal in the 1920s, it continued to express the particular sadness, pain, and joy of black America. African American poet Langston Hughes noted that through jazz, African Americans were saying "Why should I want to be white? I am a Negro—and beautiful!"

▲ During the 1920s jazz music such as "Tin Roof Blues" and "If You Knew Susie Like I Know Susie" became popular hits.

■■ Jazz became widely popular during the 1920s, influencing many other forms of music.

A BLACK RENAISSANCE

African American writers, artists, actors, and musicians in the 1920s expressed a growing black pride. Nowhere was this pride more evident than in the New York City neighborhood of Harlem, the nation's leading African American community. So many important African American writers, musicians, and artists lived in Harlem that this period of artistic development is known as the **Harlem Renaissance**.

The 1920s was a decade of achievement for African American musicians. They popularized not only jazz but also blues and religious songs known as spirituals. In 1920 Mamie Smith's recording of "Crazy Blues" made popular the moody melodies of blues for white audiences. Bessie Smith, "the Empress of the Blues," toured widely and made many blues recordings. Marian Anderson, a gifted singer who began her operatic career in the 1920s, and Paul Robeson, singer and actor, incorporated spirituals in their repertoires.

In an era when African Americans were limited in the theatrical roles they were allowed to play, blacks produced and staged several enormously successful Broadway musicals, including Eubie Blake's *Shuffle Along* (1921). African American actors also achieved fame. Charles Gilpin played the title role in Eugene O'Neill's drama *Emperor Jones* in 1920. Paul Robeson made history in 1924 by becoming the first black actor to play a leading role opposite a white actress.

 A leading African American actress of the 1920s was Rose McClendon. Born in 1884 in South Carolina, McClendon moved to New York City as a child. She took part in church

Rose McClendon

plays but did not become a professional actress until her thirties, after winning a scholarship to the American Academy of Dramatic Art.

McClendon first won fame in *Deep River*, a "native opera with jazz" staged in 1926. Even the simple act of descending a staircase won her praise from critics and fellow actors alike. In later years she played in the Pulitzer Prize–winning tragedy *In Abraham's Bosom*, about a would-be reformer; the first production of *Porgy*, set in Charleston, South Carolina; and *Never No More*, the story of a lynching. Her last role was in Langston Hughes's *Mulatto*.

In addition to directing plays at the Harlem Experimental Theatre, Rose McClendon helped found the Negro People's Theatre in Harlem in 1935. The organization increased opportunities for black actors and playwrights.

As important and impressive as African American contributions to movie and stage were during the Harlem Renaissance, it was above all a literary movement. Black novelists and poets produced work marked by bitterness and defiance but also by joy and hope. In his novel *Home to Harlem* (1928), Jamaica-born Claude McKay explored the excitement and stresses of Harlem life for a returned black soldier. Nella Larsen, born in Chicago of West Indian and Danish ancestry, described the quest for racial identity in her novel *Quicksand* (1928).

Among the most-famous Harlem poets were Langston Hughes and Countee Cullen. Hughes's *Weary Blues* (1926) and Cullen's *Color* (1925) viewed African American life and the African cultural heritage with sensitivity. In the poem "I, Too," Hughes sums up black pride in a few powerful lines:

> 66 I, too, sing America.
>
> I am the darker brother.
> They send me to eat in the kitchen
> When company comes,
> But I laugh,
> And eat well,
> And grow strong.

Harlem Renaissance, 1920s

HARLEM'S EXPANSION Migrants came to New York City from the South and the islands of the West Indies. During the 1920s, some 25 percent of Harlem's black population was foreign born.

? PLACE What was the extent of African American settlement in Harlem in 1920?

Famous club where Duke Ellington and other black entertainers perform for whites-only audiences.

This branch library features exhibits by African American artists and poetry readings by Countee Cullen.

Site of Marcus Garvey's UNIA rallies

W.E.B. Du Bois sometimes lectures here, and the Krigwa Players stage plays by African Americans.

Countee Cullen's column, "The Dark Tower," provides the name for this Harlem literary salon.

Johnson's 1922 anthology, *The Book of Negro Poetry*, helps launch the Harlem Renaissance. His parties draw noted intellectuals, such as Paul Robeson and Clarence Darrow.

Black settlement in Harlem, 1920
Black settlement in Harlem, 1930
Areas predominately African American
Point of interest

▲ Langston Hughes

> Tomorrow,
> I'll be at the table
> When company comes.
> Nobody'll dare
> Say to me,
> "Eat in the kitchen,"
> Then.
>
> Besides,
> They'll see how beautiful I am
> And be ashamed—
>
> I, too, am America. 99

■■ **African American musicians, actors, and writers in the 1920s flourished, creating a cultural movement known as the Harlem Renaissance.**

*T*HE LOST GENERATION

The creative spirit of the 1920s expressed itself not only in jazz, but also in the literature of the decade. Many younger writers of the time were haunted by the death and destruction of World War I and scornful of middle-class consumerism and the superficiality of the postwar years. "You are all a lost generation," said poet Gertrude Stein to one such writer, Ernest Hemingway. The label stuck, and scholars refer to writers of the era as the **Lost Generation**.

Ernest Hemingway spent much of his life in France, Spain, and Cuba. During World War I, he and several other young writers became ambulance drivers as a way to experience and develop an understanding of war. Hemingway was seriously wounded while serving at the Italian front. Later, he expressed his anger at war's futility in such novels as *The Sun Also Rises* (1926) and *A Farewell to Arms* (1929). In a famous passage from the latter book, a war veteran explains what the war means to him:

> 66 I was always embarrassed by the words sacred, glorious, and sacrifice and the expression in vain. We had heard them . . . and had read them . . . now for a long time, and I had seen nothing sacred, and the things that were glorious had no glory and the sacrifices were like the stockyards at Chicago if nothing was done with the meat except to bury it. 99

Disillusionment with World War I echoed in the works of other Lost Generation writers, including John Dos Passos's *Three Soldiers* (1919) and *Manhattan Transfer* (1925).

Another Lost Generation writer, F. Scott Fitzgerald, was the foremost chronicler of the youthful Jazz Age. In his first novel, *This Side of Paradise* (1920), Fitzgerald described the life of rich college students bored by fast living and hard liquor. In *The Great Gatsby* (1925), Fitzgerald portrayed the emptiness of life devoted to a frenzied struggle to make money and win social status in Prohibition-era America. Sinclair Lewis, another writer who criticized American society, satirized middle-class life in *Main Street* (1920) and *Babbitt* (1922).

The journalist and critic Henry L. Mencken championed the new writers. In his magazine *The American Mercury,* Mencken publicized novelists who satirized middle-class Americans, whom he ridiculed as "the booboisie." Mencken made fun of Republican politicians, fundamentalist Christians, rural southerners, residents of small towns, and many other groups.

■■ **Gertrude Stein called Ernest Hemingway and other postwar writers "a lost generation" because of their anger and sense of loss.**

▲ Diego Rivera painted many murals that focused on workers and their relationship to industrial production. Shown here is *Entry to the Mine.*

OTHER CURRENTS IN ART AND DESIGN

The artistic vitality of the 1920s can also be seen in the work of U.S. artists and designers as they confronted the machine age and reflected its influence on American society. They chronicled factories, new technology, workers, and urban landscapes.

Painting and photography. Many American painters of the 1920s depicted urban, industrial settings. Edward Hopper's New York City scenes convey a sense of loneliness. *Early Sunday Morning* (1930) shows a row of darkened stores and a street empty of people. New York City intrigued Georgia O'Keeffe, too. In the 1920s she painted pictures of its factories and tenements. Later she would move to New Mexico, paint dramatic pictures of flowers, and capture the stark beauty of the Southwest.

Photography came into its own as an art form in the early 1900s. Alfred Stieglitz (STEEG-luhts), more than anyone else, gave it new status. Stieglitz's New York gallery influenced many other American artists. In addition to striking portraits of people, his own subjects included airplanes, skyscrapers, and crowded city streets. Charles Sheeler, a photographer and painter, won fame for the "portraits of machinery" he produced for the Ford Motor Company, which commissioned him to photograph its plant near Detroit, Michigan, in 1927.

Another renaissance of the 1920s took place in Mexico and was later brought to the United States by its major artists. This artistic movement stressed American Indian traditions and the ideals of the Mexican Revolution of 1910. The artists emphasized the nobility of ordinary people—peasants and other workers—and the tyranny of wealthy capitalists. Their favorite medium was the monumental public mural because, in the words of artist José Clemente Orozco (oh-ROHS-koh), "it cannot be hidden away for the benefit of a certain privileged few. It is for the people. It is for *ALL.*"

The movement's three major artists—known in Mexico as *los tres grandes,* or "the big three"—were Orozco, David Alfaro Siqueiros (see-KAY-rohs), and Diego Rivera. Each first became known in Mexico in the 1920s and painted murals in the United States in the early 1930s. Orozco

Addison Gallery of American Art, Phillips Academy, Andover, MA

▲ This 1928 painting by Edward Hopper is called *Manhattan Bridge Loop.*

created several murals for American universities, many featuring heroic figures who helped humanity. In Los Angeles, Siqueiros painted large-scale murals outdoors, "in the free air," as he put it. Diego Rivera focused on workers' problems and industrial development in his U.S. murals. In a mural at the Detroit Institute of Art, which Rivera painted in 1932, his subject was, fittingly, assembly-line workers in automobile factories.

Industrial design. The machine age that inspired artists also gave rise to a new professional field: industrial design. Spreading from Germany to the United States in the 1920s, industrial design aimed to create objects that were pleasing to look at as well as functional.

Industrial designers, working with such new materials as stainless steel and plastics, developed a wide range of products with a "modern" look. The designers developed streamlining—contours that reduced resistance—for trains, planes, ships, and cars. They also applied streamlining to objects that did not even move, such as radios, clocks, and appliances.

Manufacturers quickly learned that a new design for what was essentially the same product boosted sales. They had discovered what came to be called **planned obsolescence**—making products specifically designed to go out of style and to be replaced by the purchase of an up-to-date model. Auto manufacturers were among the first to take advantage of planned obsolescence. In the early 1920s General Motors introduced the ideas of the yearly model change and the trade-in. Thereafter, many American families routinely traded in their "old" models and bought new cars every year.

Architecture. Industrial design, which combined function and visual appeal, had its counterpart in the world of architecture. Louis Sullivan and Frank Lloyd Wright inspired many other architects to embrace the idea that a building ought to use the materials and follow the forms most suitable to the building's purpose. The structure that most clearly illustrated this principle was the skyscraper, with its clean-cut vertical lines, its use of steel and concrete, its many glass windows, and its relative freedom from ornamentation.

New York City, whose population density and expensive real estate made it more cost effi-

▲ **Georgia O'Keeffe (inset) painted this scene, entitled *Radiator Building, Night, New York*, in 1927.**

cient to build upward than outward, witnessed a boom in skyscraper construction during the 1920s. Builders began construction of two landmarks—the Chrysler Building and the Empire State Building.

Civic boosters loved the skyscrapers, but critics voiced their doubts. For example, a verse of the time protested:

> ❝ THE
> SKY-
> SCRAPER
> TALL
> IS A
> WONDER
> TO ALL
> A THING
> TOADMIRE
> BEYOND
> QUESTION
> Butoh!downbelowwherepedestriansgo
> itcertainlyaddstocongestion ❞

COMMENTARY

A Standardized Culture?

What were the social effects of the new mass media and mass marketing of the 1920s? Most historians agree that mass media and mass marketing helped produce a standardized middle-class culture. Movies, radio, advertising, and magazines such as *The Saturday Evening Post* and *Time* reached every corner of the nation. These new forms of media promoted middle-class ways by presenting an ideal world of middle-class families very similar in behavior and values. Mass marketing promoted standardization by offering customers a limited range of choices among soap and appliance brands, car models, and food products. Rather than relying on local or regional goods, people all over the country used largely the same products.

Historians recognize, however, that mass media and mass marketing also changed life for Americans by acquainting them with the cultures of other groups of Americans. For example, many people—rich and poor, urban and rural—listened and danced to African American–influenced music and dance, and some white Americans enjoyed reading the works of Harlem Renaissance writers. Many middle-class women adopted forms of behavior previously associated with working-class women, such as wearing makeup and smoking.

The mass media also helped strengthen working-class, immigrant, and African American cultures. Musical recordings by African Americans, Mexican Americans, and others preserved traditional musical forms. Immigrant and working-class neighborhood movie theaters served as community meeting places. Some local radio stations devoted their programs exclusively to ethnic audiences, offering ethnic music and local news as well as news about the immigrants'

homelands. Ethnic newspapers continued to fulfill their role of helping to preserve the immigrants' languages and ethnic identities.

While most middle-class families bought the same brands at chain stores, most working-class and immigrant families continued to buy from their local corner groceries. These local grocers, who usually shared the ethnicity of their patrons, extended credit to their customers. The grocers sold traditional ethnic ingredients such as Italian macaroni, Jewish kosher meats, or Asian delicacies, which the chain stores rarely carried. These corner groceries thus allowed ethnic Americans to maintain traditional diets. Furthermore, these corner stores served as places where people could meet, swap news, and gossip.

The mass media thus helped maintain ethnic cultures while they promoted middle-class values. And when middle-class Americans all over the country copied the style of life presented by the movies, network radio, and mass magazines, they were adopting ways influenced by different cultural perspectives. In short, the mass media and mass marketing not only supported traditional ways but also helped to spread new ways of thinking and acting throughout the nation.

Mass media and mass marketing promoted both new and standardized modes of behavior. At the same time, the mass media also helped sustain traditional cultures.

SECTION 3 REVIEW

IDENTIFY and explain the significance of the following: Joseph "King" Oliver, Langston Hughes, Harlem Renaissance, Marian Anderson, Paul Robeson, Rose McClendon, Ernest Hemingway, Lost Generation, Diego Rivera, Alfred Stieglitz, planned obsolescence.

LOCATE and explain the importance of the following: Harlem.

1. **MAIN IDEA** In what ways did the artists of the Harlem Renaissance contribute to American culture?

2. **MAIN IDEA** Why were Ernest Hemingway and other young writers of the 1920s called "a lost generation"? Who coined this phrase?

3. **MAIN IDEA** What characteristics did the work of artists and photographers of the 1920s have in common?

4. **WRITING TO EVALUATE** How did radio help people maintain long-held customs?

5. **ANALYZING** Why might black artists, writers of the Lost Generation, and other painters and photographers of the 1920s be considered social critics?

First radio stations go on the air.

Eubie Blake's *Shuffle Along* opens.

George Gershwin composes *Rhapsody in Blue.*

1920   1922   1924

WRITING A SUMMARY
Using the essential points of the chapter as a guide, write a summary of the chapter.

REVIEWING CHRONOLOGY
Number your paper 1 to 5. Study the time line above, and list the following events in the order in which they happened by writing the first next to 1, the second next to 2, and so on. Then complete the activity below.

1. Scopes trial held in Dayton, Tennessee.
2. Eubie Blake's *Shuffle Along* opens.
3. *The Jazz Singer* released.
4. Robert Lynd and Helen Lynd's *Middletown* issued.
5. George Gershwin composes *Rhapsody in Blue.*

Assessing Consequences How did *The Jazz Singer* influence the development of American entertainment?

IDENTIFYING PEOPLE AND IDEAS
Explain the historical significance of each of the following people or terms.

1. assembly line
2. scientific management
3. Helen Lynd
4. Jim Thorpe
5. Charles Lindbergh
6. Fundamentalism
7. Harlem Renaissance
8. Rose McClendon
9. Diego Rivera
10. planned obsolescence

UNDERSTANDING MAIN IDEAS
1. How was middle-class life in the 1920s changed by mass media and advertising?
2. What postwar problems did the Lost Generation deal with in their literature?
3. What influences led women to exercise new freedom in dress and behavior?
4. How did the prosperity of the 1920s influence American entertainment?
5. What contributions did African Americans make to the changing American culture of the 1920s?

REVIEWING THEMES
1. **Economic Development** How did advertising, merchandising, and installment buying help the nation's economy in the 1920s?

2. **Technology and Society** How did new technology affect Americans' lives at work and at home?
3. **Cultural Diversity** How did the mass media help preserve ethnic cultures?

THINKING CRITICALLY
1. **Analyzing** How did increased productivity and consumerism pave the way for future environmental problems?
2. **Synthesizing** Why might the Model T be an appropriate symbol for the 1920s?
3. **Evaluating** How did social changes contribute to the popularity of religious revivals?

STRATEGY FOR SUCCESS
Review the Skills Handbook entry on Taking a Test on page 762. Below is a sample multiple-choice question that might be asked about Chapter 12. Write a paragraph summarizing how you would arrive at the correct answer.

The aspect of industrial design that most increased sales was
   a. scientific management.
   b. advertising.
   c. planned obsolescence.
   d. streamlining.

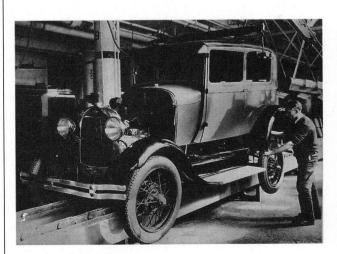

Ford automobile plant, 1921

Scopes trial held in Dayton, Tennessee.

Gertrude Ederle breaks world record for swimming English Channel. Langston Hughes's *Weary Blues* published.

The Jazz Singer released. Charles Lindbergh completes first nonstop flight from New York to Paris.

Amelia Earhart crosses Atlantic Ocean by plane.

Ernest Hemingway's *A Farewell to Arms* published. Robert Lynd and Helen Lynd's *Middletown* issued.

1926   1928   1930

WRITING ABOUT HISTORY

Writing to Explain Imagine you are a high school principal at the time of the Scopes trial. Write a letter to parents, outlining the issues involved in the trial and explaining how the verdict will affect next year's science curriculum.

USING PRIMARY SOURCES

Harlem was the social, cultural, and entertainment capital for many African Americans during the 1920s. In the following excerpt, Howard "Stretch" Johnson talks about the black basketball teams popular in the 1920s and about the influence of Paul Robeson, one of the Harlem Renaissance's major figures. Write a paragraph explaining how Robeson influenced African Americans in the 1920s.

66 *The Renaissance Big Five basketball team was a part of [the Harlem Renaissance]. . . .*

My father was a very fine professional basketball player. He played with a group called the Puritans, which later became the Renaissance Big Five. . . .

Paul Robeson played with Alpha fraternity against my father when my father was playing with St. Christopher's, another semipro team that was popular in the '20s. Paul was a great figure. People used to swarm around him when he walked out on the street. He was the inspiration in every walk of life. Those blacks who went in for law had respect for his being a Phi Beta Kappa at Columbia University. Those who aspired to be successful in the athletic field had him as an exemplar [model] with his record at Rutgers, where he got fifteen varsity letters—more varsity A's than any individual who ever went to Rutgers—in football, basketball, track, and baseball. 99

LINKING HISTORY AND GEOGRAPHY

Refer to the map on page 317. What factors might explain the birth of the Harlem Renaissance during the 1920s?

Young women in Harlem

BUILDING YOUR PORTFOLIO

Complete the following projects independently or cooperatively.

1. THE ECONOMY In Chapter 11 you portrayed an unemployed veteran. Building on that experience, imagine you are a prosperous business owner in the 1920s. Create an advertisement for a new household product aimed at the expanding consumer market. Your ad might use psychology, slogans, jingles, or celebrity testimonials to sell your product.

2. CULTURE AND SOCIETY In Chapter 11 you portrayed an immigrant artist. Building on that experience, imagine you are an African American artist during the Harlem Renaissance. Create a dance, jazz poem, or painting that expresses cultural pride in your African American heritage.

THE GREAT DEPRESSION

FOCUS

UNDERSTANDING THE MAIN IDEA

In 1929 the stock market crashed, causing financial ruin for millions of Americans. The collapse of the stock market was one of several factors that gave rise to the Great Depression. When President Hoover's efforts to revive the economy failed, Americans elected a Democratic president, Franklin D. Roosevelt, to reverse the country's economic decline.

THEMES

- **ECONOMIC DEVELOPMENT** What factors might cause an economic depression?

- **GEOGRAPHIC DIVERSITY** How might an economic crisis affect people's choices of where to live?

- **CULTURAL DIVERSITY** How and why might various ethnic groups be affected differently by an economic depression?

1929	1930	1931	1932
Stock market crashes.	Smoot-Hawley Tariff passed.	Scottsboro Boys case begins.	Franklin Roosevelt elected president.

The economic boom of the 1920s gave most Americans tremendous faith in the future. For many Americans, prosperity seemed limitless; however, the prosperity was unevenly distributed. The life-style of the Jazz Age also led to enormous debt.

Mexican American women bound for picket line in the San Joaquin Valley, California, cotton strike, 1933

*T*hursday, October 24, 1929, dawned windy and cool in New York City. Employees of the New York Stock Exchange buttoned their overcoats as they hurried down Wall Street to work. In the first few hours of stock trading, share prices fell sharply. At first, investors remained calm. The market had been shaky in recent weeks but had always resumed its upward trend. Today was different, though. As prices continued to fall, panic struck. Frantic orders to sell stock came pouring in.

All across America, grim-faced investors watched as stock tickers reported the alarming news. The plunge in prices was wiping out the life savings of millions of Americans who had invested in stocks. "One saw men looking defeat in the face," said an eyewitness. "[It was] the smash-up of the hopes of years."

The economic prosperity of the 1920s was over, and the worst economic depression in U.S. history had begun. Over the next several years the American people faced widespread unemployment and poverty. By the time of the 1932 election, they were desperate for a change.

Ticker tape machine

PROSPERITY SHATTERED

FOCUS

- **Why did many Americans invest in the stock market in the 1920s?**
- **What caused the stock market crash of 1929?**
- **What factors gave rise to the Great Depression?**

Throughout the generally prosperous 1920s, isolated voices warned of problems with the American economy. Some people pointed to the farm crisis and to "sick" industries as problems in need of attention. Yet despite these warnings, most Americans believed that the economy would continue to thrive. Then came the stock market crash of 1929. Stock prices plunged, and investors lost billions of dollars. U.S. industries, already showing signs of weakness, almost ground to a halt.

Newspaper headline, October 1929

"GET RICH QUICK"

Few Americans other than farmers and the poor worried about the nation's economic health in the late 1920s. Many Americans agreed with Herbert Hoover that the nation was "nearer to the final triumph over poverty than ever before in the history of any land."

This sense of confidence was reflected in the stock market. Stock sales had risen steadily for several years. As demand rose, so did stock prices. Many experts saw no end to the **bull market**—the upward trend in stock prices (as opposed to a **bear market**, or downward trend). Business leaders, such as General Motors executive John J. Raskob, urged Americans to invest, claiming that anyone who put $15 a month in the stock market for 20 years would end up with $80,000—a fortune at the time.

By the late 1920s, stock speculation—"playing" the market by buying and selling to make a quick profit—was widespread. Although speculation fueled economic growth, it also created problems. Rapid buying and selling inflated the prices of stocks to the point that many stocks were selling for more than they were really worth. This speculative buying was fine as long as demand was high, but if investor confidence weakened, prices would tumble.

The situation was made shakier still by **margin buying**—purchasing stocks with borrowed money. Many speculators put up as little as 10 percent of the price of a stock, borrowing the rest. Margin buying worked as long as the bull market continued. If prices fell, though, investors would find themselves deep in debt with no way to pay off their loans. It was a very risky venture.

Although consumer confidence in the market remained high throughout the summer of 1929, a few gloomy voices were heard. In early September, stock analyst Roger Babson wrote: "Sooner or later a crash is coming, and it may be terrific." Some shrewd investors saw the writing on the wall and began to sell their stocks, but most people remained confident in the market. As one eyewitness wrote: "Money is king—but there is something else. It is a high, wild time, a time of riotous spirits and belief in magic rather than cold calculation."

■■ **Hoping to earn enormous profits from rising stock prices, many Americans invested in the stock market.**

THE STOCK MARKET CRASHES

The magic faltered on October 24, 1929—**Black Thursday**. Large investors, made nervous by various factors, including rising interest rates, suddenly began to sell their shares. The dumping of so much stock on the market jolted investor confidence and caused prices to plunge. Panic gripped Wall Street. A *New York Times* reporter described the crash:

> 66 It came with a speed and ferocity that left men dazed. The bottom simply fell out of the market. . . . The streets were crammed with a mixed crowd—agonized little speculators, . . . sold-out traders, . . . inquisitive individuals and tourists seeking . . . a closer view of the national catastrophe. . . . Where was it going to end? 99

Black Thursday was only the opening stage of a long downward spiral. Prices dropped still lower the following week, as more investors sold their stocks. On October 29—**Black Tuesday**—prices sank to a shocking new low as investors dumped over 16 million shares of stock on the market.

As prices plunged, brokers fired off frantic telegrams to the customers who owed them money. The brokers demanded cash to cover their loans. Unable to raise the funds, thousands of people were forced to sell their stocks at huge losses. Many investors were wiped out. By mid-November the average value of leading stocks had been cut in half, and stockholders had lost some $30 billion. By year's end stock losses exceeded the total cost of U.S. involvement in World War I.

■■ **Speculative buying drove stock prices above their real value. When large-scale selling occurred in October 1929, the market crashed.**

THE DEPRESSION BEGINS

In the first months after the stock market crash, business leaders and public officials insisted that the setback was minor and temporary. President Hoover declared: "We have now passed the worst and . . . shall rapidly recover." But optimistic statements could not conceal the grim truth. By late 1930 it was clear that a major economic depression was under way in the United States and throughout the rest of the world.

From late 1929 to 1933 the U.S. economy sank steadily. In 1929, the last boom year of the period, America's **gross national product**—the total value of all goods and services produced in a given year—reached $103 billion. In 1933, at the depth of the depression, it fell below $56 billion. Over that same period, average income for Americans fell by half. By 1932 the auto and steel industries were producing at just a small fraction of their capacity. Factories and mines stood idle. Railroad cars sat silent and empty. Many companies shut down, and millions of workers lost their jobs.

The banking industry was also hard hit by the

THE CRASH

Company	High Price Sept. 3, 1929	Low Price Nov. 13, 1929
American Telephone and Telegraph	304	197¼
General Electric	396¼	168⅛
General Motors	72¾	36
Montgomery Ward	137⅞	49¼
United States Steel	261¾	150
Woolworth	100⅜	52¼

Source: *Only Yesterday*

FROM RICHES TO RAGS In the days following the stock market crash on October 29, 1929, stock prices continued to fall. Average stock prices reached their lowest point for the year on November 13, 1929, slightly two months after they had reached the high point for the year on September 3.

? **BUILDING GRAPH SKILLS** Which company's stock lost the greatest number of points between September 3 and November 13, 1929?

▲ Panicked by the 1929 stock market crash, many bank depositors stood in long lines to withdraw their money. This photograph was taken in New York City.

depression. After the stock market crash, many debt-ridden investors and businesses could not repay their loans, leaving banks with no incoming funds. Fearing bank failures, many depositors panicked and withdrew their savings. Under the combined weight of these factors, the banking system collapsed.

Between 1930 and 1932 more than 5,000 U.S. banks failed. Customers who went to their banks to withdraw savings often found the doors barred and their money gone. Because bank deposits were not insured, many people lost their life savings. The collapse of one big New York City bank in 1930 wiped out roughly $180 million in savings by some 400,000 depositors, including many poor immigrants.

WHAT CAUSED THE DEPRESSION?

The stock market crash of 1929 jolted the American economy and destroyed individual fortunes, but it alone did not cause the **Great Depression**, the deep economic downturn that gripped the United States between 1929 and the beginning of World War II. At the time, many observers, including President Hoover, blamed the depression on the state of the world economy following World War I. The global economy had suffered enormous setbacks because of the massive war debts incurred by European countries. But this, like the stock market crash, was only a contributing factor. Today economists and historians agree that the root causes of the Great Depression lay in numerous factors, including the American economic system itself.

The troubling twenties. Although the 1920s appeared to be a decade of unlimited

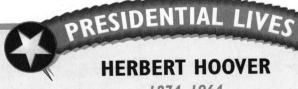

PRESIDENTIAL LIVES

HERBERT HOOVER
1874–1964

in office
1929–1933

As a young man Herbert Hoover was shy and awkward, but very hardworking. Born into a Quaker family in Iowa, he was left an orphan at age nine. He had few friends in college and would wander around with his eyes glued to the ground as if to avoid people. As one of his few friends noted, he had a habit of standing "with one foot thrust forward, jingling the keys in his trouser pocket," chuckling sometimes, but rarely laughing out loud. Even in the White House he remained self-conscious and shy.

After college Hoover rapidly built a career as a successful mining engineer and business consultant. By the age of 40 he was a millionaire. His role as coordinator of food relief during World War I also gave him a reputation as a kind and humanitarian leader. After his presidency he continued to work in public service and wrote many books and articles.

"There is little importance to men's lives," he wrote, "except the accomplishments they leave to posterity."

Herbert Hoover

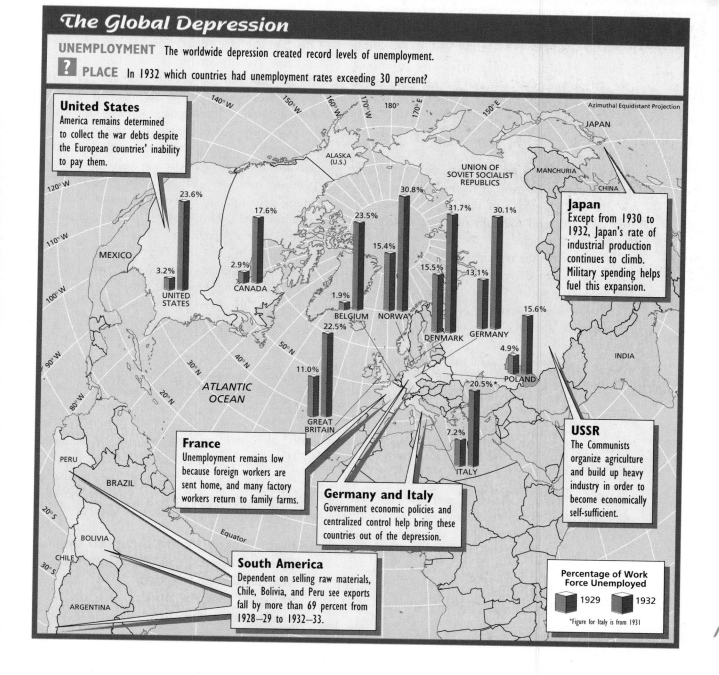

The Global Depression

UNEMPLOYMENT The worldwide depression created record levels of unemployment.

? PLACE In 1932 which countries had unemployment rates exceeding 30 percent?

United States
America remains determined to collect the war debts despite the European countries' inability to pay them.

Japan
Except from 1930 to 1932, Japan's rate of industrial production continues to climb. Military spending helps fuel this expansion.

France
Unemployment remains low because foreign workers are sent home, and many factory workers return to family farms.

Germany and Italy
Government economic policies and centralized control help bring these countries out of the depression.

USSR
The Communists organize agriculture and build up heavy industry in order to become economically self-sufficient.

South America
Dependent on selling raw materials, Chile, Bolivia, and Peru see exports fall by more than 69 percent from 1928–29 to 1932–33.

Azimuthal Equidistant Projection

UNITED STATES 3.2% 23.6%
CANADA 2.9% 17.6%
BELGIUM 1.9% 23.5%
NORWAY 15.4% 30.8%
DENMARK 15.5% 31.7%
GERMANY 13.1% 30.1%
POLAND 4.9% 15.6%
GREAT BRITAIN 11.0% 22.5%
ITALY 7.2% 20.5%*

Percentage of Work Force Unemployed
1929   1932

*Figure for Italy is from 1931

economic prosperity, many analysts place primary blame for the Great Depression on economic practices in the 1920s. These practices produced quick profits for some but in the long run contributed to economic chaos. Farm prices, for example, dropped in the 1920s. By the end of the decade, mining, textiles, construction, and other industries were also beginning to suffer.

Another disturbing trend was the widespread dependence on credit. In the late 1920s, the federal government encouraged borrowing by keeping interest rates low. The Republican administrations of the time reasoned that an easy-credit policy would promote business. Easy credit enabled consumers to buy goods when they did not actually have the money to pay for them. This was not a problem when the economy was booming. Once the economy began to slow and the government raised interest rates, however, many consumers could not pay their debts. After the crash many businesses stopped extending credit altogether.

In 1931 one department store even tried to turn the "credit crunch" to its advantage. While inviting customers to shop and spend as much as they wanted to, it advertised that it would accept only cash. The store claimed to be protecting its patrons from falling into debt. This approach depended on the hope that consumers would keep spending in the face of a depression.

Unfortunately, by 1931 few debt-ridden consumers had the cash to make any purchases. The illusion of prosperity had prevented many from realizing that the benefits of the economic policies of the 1920s had been unevenly distributed.

A mismanaged economy. Economists cite the unequal distribution of income in America as another central cause of the Great Depression. Between 1923 and 1929 the disposable income of the wealthiest 1 percent of the nation increased by 63 percent while the income of the poorest 93 percent of the nation decreased by 4 percent. As writer Upton Sinclair noted: "The . . . depression is one of abundance, not of scarcity. . . . The cause of the trouble is that a small class has the wealth, while the rest have the debts."

This income gap meant that a large portion of the population did not have the buying power needed to boost the economy. According to many economists, if workers had received better wages for their labor and farmers better prices for their crops, the depression would have been less severe or perhaps could have been avoided.

Even the global factors that Hoover blamed for the depression could have been eased by more-farsighted U.S. policies. Economists point out that the United States contributed to the worldwide economic downturn by slapping high tariffs on imported goods. Even after the crash, Congress continued to pass high tariffs, including the highest in U.S. history, the **Smoot-Hawley Tariff** of 1930.

The business cycle. Some economists argue that better fiscal planning in the 1920s could not have prevented the onset of the Great Depression. These economists view depressions as an inevitable part of the **business cycle**—the regular ups and downs of business in a free-enterprise economy. According to business-cycle theory, industries increase production and hire more workers during prosperous times so that eventually surpluses pile up. Industries then cut back on production and lay off workers, causing the start of a recession or a depression.

Events in the Great Depression support the business-cycle theory in part. While a wave of new products fueled the economic growth of the 1920s, by the end of the decade fewer Americans were buying expensive goods. Most people who wanted such products, and could afford them, had already bought them. The inability to sell their goods caused many businesses to fail and contributed to the depression.

According to this theory, however, once the surplus goods are sold, industries again gear up for production and the depression comes to an end. But the *length* and *severity* of the Great Depression went far beyond the normal rhythms of the business cycle. Thus it seems incorrect to blame the business cycle—or any one factor—for causing the most severe economic depression in U.S. history.

Many factors contributed to the Great Depression: the global economic downturn, debt, the unequal distribution of wealth, and overproduction.

SECTION 1 REVIEW

IDENTIFY and explain the significance of the following: bull market, bear market, margin buying, Black Thursday, Black Tuesday, gross national product, Great Depression, Smoot-Hawley Tariff, business cycle.

1. **MAIN IDEA** What factors encouraged many Americans to participate in the bull market of the 1920s?

2. **MAIN IDEA** How did speculation affect stock prices?

3. **IDENTIFYING CAUSE AND EFFECT** What caused the large-scale selling of stocks in October 1929? What effect did this have on the stock market?

4. **WRITING TO EXPLAIN** Write an essay outlining the factors that contributed to the Great Depression.

5. **ANALYZING** Considering the economic developments of the 1920s, how accurate was Upton Sinclair's statement that the depression was "one of abundance, not of scarcity"?

HARD TIMES

FOCUS

- **How did unemployment affect Americans in the 1930s?**
- **What were urban and rural living conditions like during the Great Depression?**
- **What did Americans do for entertainment during the period?**

The Great Depression of the 1930s was not the first depression in American history, but it was by far the worst. It lasted for most of the decade, and during that time millions of Americans lost their jobs and sank into poverty. In cities and in rural areas, many people suffered from hunger, homelessness, and despair. Life was not all bleak during the depression, though. Movies, radio, and popular fiction helped lift American spirits.

Unemployed worker, 1930

"WORK IS WHAT I WANT"

Perhaps the clearest sign of the deepening depression was a sharp rise in unemployment. In 1929 some 1.5 million Americans were unemployed; three years later that figure had risen to some 12 million, as ailing and failed businesses laid off their employees. To poet Langston Hughes, it seemed "everybody in America was looking for work."

By 1932, industrial output had fallen to about half that of 1929, resulting in massive layoffs. Even for those who managed to keep their jobs, wages fell dramatically—in some cases to as low as 10 cents an hour. Factory workers' average annual income fell by nearly one third between 1929 and 1933. For the first time in years, immigration to the United States greatly decreased. One despondent Slavic immigrant told a reporter in 1932: "If you had told me, when I come to this country that now I live like this, I shot you dead."

African Americans faced especially difficult times, as economic troubles added to the problem of racial discrimination they already faced. When factories laid off employees, black workers were often the first to go. In several cities as much as 25 to 40 percent of African Americans were out of work by 1933. One study of Chicago unemployment patterns noted the general view among whites that blacks "should not be hired as long as there are white men without work."

African American women, who made up the vast majority of domestic servants, also suffered

◄ **Thousands of unemployed workers gathered before the White House on March 6, 1930, to protest for better unemployment policies.**

Unemployment Relief

DOUBLE TROUBLE In the early 1930s a disastrous drought struck the agricultural states of the Great Plains, adding to the difficulties caused by the depression.

? PLACE Which state had the highest percentage of its people receiving unemployment?

WA
MT
ND 29%
MN
VT ME
NH
MA
OR
ID
SD 41%
WI
MI
NY
RI
CT
WY
PA
NJ
DE
MD
DC
NV
NE
IA
IL
IN
OH
WV
VA
CA
UT
CO
KS
MO
KY
TN
NC
AZ
NM 31%
OK 28%
AR
SC
MS
AL
GA
TX
LA
FL

Percentage of Total State Population Receiving Unemployment Relief

More than 25 percent
21-25 percent
16-20 percent
11-15 percent
Less than 11 percent

American women actually fell because of increased competition in domestic and agricultural work.

Some unemployed workers took to selling apples on the street, where on a good day a seller might earn $1.15, causing President Hoover to claim, "Many people have left their jobs for the more profitable one of selling apples." But few people in the depression had any choice over how or where they worked. Some even hitchhiked or hopped freight trains across the country to find jobs.

■■ During the depression one fourth of the work force lost their jobs. Many had to seek work wherever they could find it.

massive unemployment. Without regular work, many would stand on street corners and try to obtain work as maids. Two black women, Ella Baker and Marvel Cooke, referred to this method of hiring as the "Bronx Slave Market." In an investigative article they wrote for *The Crisis,* they described a typical scene:

> ❝ Rain or shine, cold or hot, you will find them there—Negro women, old and young—sometimes bedraggled, sometimes neatly dressed . . . waiting expectantly for Bronx housewives to buy their strength and energy. ❞

Since many employers could hire women more cheaply than men, the percentage of women in the work force actually increased in the 1930s. Most were employed as office workers or domestic servants. But as the percentage of women in the work force rose overall, the percentage of employed African

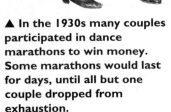

▲ **In the 1930s many couples participated in dance marathons to win money. Some marathons would last for days, until all but one couple dropped from exhaustion.**

LIFE IN THE CITY

The impact of the depression spread all across America, hitting people in cities and on farms and disrupting family life. Some of the most-lasting images of the period came from urban America, as the depression hit many cities hard. During the early 1930s the federal government did little to aid local communities.

City governments, religious groups like the Salvation Army, and charitable organizations such as the Red Cross tried to take on the burden of providing direct relief to the needy. Neighbors also helped one another. One African American woman told a visitor: "My neighbors helps me, by bringin' me a little to eat, when they knows I ain't got nothin' in the house to cook."

Mexican American communities formed *mutualistas,* or mutual-aid societies, to help local residents. Some Chinese American

▲ Shantytowns appeared outside many towns and cities during the early 1930s. Shown here is a Hooverville in New York City.

communities set out open barrels of rice so that people could draw from them privately, without asking for handouts. Harlem residents organized "rent parties"—large social gatherings that charged a small admission to help pay someone's monthly rent.

Across the country, people engaged in a daily struggle to feed themselves and their children. Haggard men and women waited in **breadlines** for bowls of soup and pieces of bread. When one hungry schoolchild was told to go home for lunch, she replied: "It won't do any good. . . . This is my sister's day to eat." Hunger was so widespread that by 1932 one out of every five children in New York City suffered from malnutrition. Meager diets caused some Americans to suffer long-term health effects in the form of stunted growth, weak bones, and dental problems.

In addition to hunger, homelessness was a serious urban problem during the depression. **Shantytowns**—collections of makeshift shelters built out of packing boxes, scrap lumber, corrugated iron, and other thrown-away items—rose up outside most cities. Blaming an unresponsive president for their plight, the homeless mockingly referred to these shantytowns as Hoovervilles and the newspapers they often slept under as Hoover blankets.

■■ **With little help from the federal government, urban communities struggled to provide for the hungry and homeless.**

LIFE ON THE FARM

The depression also struck hard at rural America, as the farm crisis of the 1920s turned into a disaster in the 1930s. People in the cities needed food but could not pay for it. As demand for farm products shrank, prices plummeted, and farmers found themselves with more goods than they could sell. While people went hungry in the cities, farmers in some areas were forced to let crops rot in the fields and to slaughter excess livestock they could not afford to feed.

As their incomes fell, many farmers were unable to keep up their mortgage payments. While banks foreclosed on farms all across America, some communities banded together to fight back. Often when a bank held a foreclosure auction to sell off a family's possessions, neighbors would

DEPRESSION WORLDWIDE

THROUGH OTHERS' EYES

The depression of the 1930s knew no borders. In a radio talk in 1931, British economist John Maynard Keynes discussed its worldwide reach:

❝*The slump in trade and employment and the business losses . . . are as bad as the worst which have ever occurred in the modern history of the world. No country is exempt. The privation [hardship] and—what is sometimes worse—the anxiety which exist today in millions of homes all over the world is extreme. In the three chief industrial countries of the world, Great Britain, Germany, and the United States, I estimate that probably 12 million industrial workers stand idle. But I am not sure that there is not even more human misery today in the great agricultural countries of the world—Canada, Australia, and South America, where millions of small farmers see themselves ruined by the fall in the prices of their products, so that their receipts after harvest bring them in much less than the crops have cost them to produce.* ❞

arrive and bid absurdly low prices, such as 25 cents for a plow. In a particularly noteworthy example, a farm with an $800 mortgage was sold for $1.90. After the auction they would then give the goods back to the farm family. Furthermore, farmers quickly warned off anyone who made serious bids. This tactic was so successful that several farm states, beginning with Iowa in 1933, passed foreclosure moratorium laws.

Conditions were especially bleak for tenant farmers in the South, where most rural residents already faced crippling poverty. As cotton prices fell from 16 cents per pound in 1929 to below 6 cents in 1931, many tenant farmers, mostly African Americans, were virtually ruined. Some were even forced off the land they had lived on all their lives. While farmers in the Midwest faced an overabundance of food, southern cotton farmers faced scarcity due to poor soil and lack of money to buy food. Gracie Turner, a sharecropper's wife, testified to the hardships of tenant life in the 1930s:

▲ Shown here is a meeting in Los Angeles, around 1940, of the group known as El Congreso, which helped organize Hispanic migrants to fight for better conditions.

66 That's all there is to expect—work hard and go hungry part time. . . . This year's been so hard we had to drop our burial insurance. . . . All it costs is twenty-five cents . . . but they don't come many twenty-five cents in this house. 99

Migrant farm workers in the Southwest, most of them recent immigrants, also encountered difficulties. As relief costs soared, local authorities chose the cheaper policy of paying Mexican migrants to return to their native land. During the 1930s some 500,000 people of Mexican descent—some of them U.S. citizens—were pressured into leaving the states. Those who remained often faced discrimination and poor working conditions.

▶ Josefina Fierro de Bright

BIO GRAPHY Some of the Mexican American families who stayed during the depression helped organize resistance to discrimination in the Southwest. One such organizer was Josefina Fierro de Bright, the daughter of migrants who had fled revolution in Mexico to settle in California. The experience of growing up during the depression in the midst of poverty and ethnic discrimination had a profound effect on her. As with many children of the depression, Fierro's life was very unstable. Her family had to move often, causing Fierro to change schools eight times. But throughout the hard times her mother always encouraged her to strive for success. "Rely on yourself, be independent," Mrs. Fierro advised. She also emphasized the importance of getting an education.

In 1938, at age 18, Josefina Fierro entered the University of California at Los Angeles. She planned to study medicine, but activism on behalf of the Mexican American community soon took up most of her time. With the aid of her husband, activist Hollywood screenwriter John Bright, she began to lead boycotts of companies that did business in Mexican American communities but did not hire Mexican American workers. Enlisting financial support from a few well-known movie stars, Fierro de Bright also started a radio program for Spanish-speaking audiences.

These activities brought her to the attention of a Mexican American group called El Congreso, which was organizing Hispanic migrants to resist oppressive conditions. In 1939 El Congreso leaders asked Fierro de Bright to help them establish a branch in Los Angeles. Over the next few years, she worked tirelessly, leading marches and hunger strikes, lobbying for expanded relief programs for Hispanic Americans, and encouraging bilingual education for migrant children. "I used to work so hard it used to kill me," she recalled. But throughout her life she never forgot the lessons her mother instilled in her during those early years of the depression. Those memories spurred her efforts to improve the lives of all working people.

■■ **Rural farm workers faced increased hardship during the depression. Some were forced to leave their land.**

Family LIFE IN THE 1930s

On farms and in cities, family members often pulled together and helped one another cope with their difficulties. They shared food and money and provided the support and encouragement their relatives needed to get through hard times. In many cases, relatives doubled up in small houses, and young adults moved back in with their parents.

▼ **Life was difficult for many families during the depression as they struggled to make ends meet. The strain is clearly evident in the faces of these migrant children and their mother.**

Economic hardship took its toll on families, however. Some eventually broke apart under the strain. The divorce rate rose during the depression. Many young people put off getting married and starting their own families, which caused marriage and birthrates to decline, especially during the early years of the depression. Looking back on those years, a Chicago schoolteacher remarked:

❝ Do you realize how many people in my generation are not married? . . . It wasn't that we didn't have a chance. I was going with someone when the Depression hit. We probably would have gotten married. . . . Suddenly he was laid off. It hit him like a ton of bricks. And he just disappeared. ❞

Life was certainly not easy for women during the depression. In the face of economic hardship, the mothers of hard-hit depression families often played roles of quiet heroism. Such daily challenges as putting food on the table and making clothes and shoes last for one more year brought constant worry. As one woman remarked: "I figured every which way I could to make ends meet . . . but some of [those] ends just wouldn't meet. They just couldn't be stretched far enough to meet." In rural and small-town households, women revived old crafts such as soap making and bread making. Others took jobs outside the home to help support their families.

Commentary

The Psychological Impact of the Depression

The Great Depression affected Americans in countless ways. Some of these effects—such as hunger and homelessness—were temporary for most people. When the depression ended, most Americans got back on their feet. Other effects, though, were longer lasting. In fact, the depression had a major long-term impact on the behavior and the outlook of the millions of Americans who struggled through hard times.

The term *depression* could just as easily describe the mood of the country as well as the economy in the 1930s. More than 20,000 Americans committed suicide in 1932, a 28 percent increase over 1929. For middle-class and well-to-do Americans, many of whom had never known poverty, the depression was a cruel blow. Many would never forget the shame they felt at being unemployed, losing their businesses or homes, and being unable to provide for their families. The attitude of an unemployed teacher in New Orleans was typical: "If with all the advantages I've had, I can't make a living, I'm just no good, I guess. I've given up ever amounting to anything. It's no use."

The depression had a devastating effect on the unemployed. Many men whose lives had been dominated by work did not know what to do without a job. They often spent their days just dawdling around the house or roaming the streets. The depression proved equally severe on working women who lost their jobs, especially those who were single or whose families depended on two incomes to survive. Many parents who could not support their families were consumed by guilt and self-doubt.

Even after the depression, the memories of those lean years remained vivid. Habits of scrimping and saving, of making every penny count, would stay with members of this generation for the rest of their lives. A strong desire for financial stability and material comforts shaped the outlook of many Americans who came of age during the depression.

POPULAR CULTURE IN THE THIRTIES

Even during hard times, Americans found ways to enjoy themselves. Many people took up inexpensive pastimes, such as reading and playing games at home. Movies and radio also offered a temporary release from economic worries.

The sound explosion. Movies were a big hit during the depression. Talking pictures, which had begun to replace silent films in the late 1920s, enthralled audiences, who flocked to the new movie theaters cropping up in nearly every town. Among the most popular movies of the early 1930s were gangster films, which portrayed tough guys fighting their way to the top against all odds. Likewise, strong women, such as Bette Davis, Greta Garbo, Mae West, and Marlene Dietrich, lit up the screen, reinforcing the theme of survival in a difficult world.

▲ Hollywood musicals flourished during the depression. In order to take their minds off their troubles, audiences flocked to see upbeat films such as *Gold Diggers of 1933.*

Meanwhile, upbeat musicals like *Gold Diggers of 1933,* featuring the song "We're in the Money," and comedies portraying the hilarious antics of comedians like the Marx Brothers proved very popular. Movie cartoons also brightened the 1930s, thanks to Walt Disney's Mickey Mouse and Donald Duck characters. Often, Disney cartoons were as popular with movie audiences as the feature films they preceded.

As the movie business flourished, radio also enjoyed its golden age. Radio was immensely popular because it offered free entertainment at home.

▲ This couple, seated beside their radio, entertained themselves by listening to their favorite radio programs.

By the 1930s baseball was the country's favorite sport and a symbol of American culture, just as it is today. But baseball in the 1930s was in some ways much different from the game we know now.

To be a baseball fan in the 1930s meant taking trips out to the ballpark. Without television to bring the game into people's homes, fans either listened to games on the radio or headed for their local baseball stadium to root for the home team. Games were held only in the daytime until 1930—the year the first night game was held in a major-league park.

Depression-era fans watched such players as home-run king Babe Ruth and pitcher Walter "Boom Boom" Beck. They cheered players who had higher batting averages and hit more home runs than today's players. The ballparks were often smaller than today's stadiums. And the day games favored batters because they could see the ball more clearly during the day than today's players can at night.

However, the biggest difference between baseball then and now was who could play the game. Professional baseball was still racially segregated in the 1930s. White owners maintained a so-called gentleman's agreement not to sign black players. So African Americans formed clubs and leagues of their own.

The Negro National League (NNL) fielded teams in the East such as the Newark Eagles and the New York Black

Yankees. The Negro American League (NAL) covered the South and Midwest with clubs like the Kansas City Monarchs and the Chicago American Giants. Players included Hall of Fame pitcher Satchel Paige and William "Judy" Johnson. Turnouts at Paige's games could be as large as any in the majors.

Although they would not sign black players, white club owners rented their ballparks to black teams when white teams were on the road. In fact, it was under just such an arrangement that the Kansas City Monarchs pioneered a portable lighting system and held the first night games in a major-league park. The Monarchs' night games drew such good crowds that within a few years scores of other ballparks also installed lighting.

In the off-season, Satchel Paige and many other baseball players—both black and white—played in Mexico, Cuba, and other countries. Like most Americans in the 1930s, baseball players needed all the money they could earn—their salaries, especially in the black leagues, provided just enough to get by. Today's off-season training camps and million-dollar contracts were unheard of during the depression. Salaries, team rosters, ballparks, and media coverage are all very different today. But the most important element—the enjoyment the game brings—remains the same.

▲ Baseball increased in popularity during the 1930s thanks to the skills of players such as Babe Ruth and Lou Gehrig. This painting by Morris Kantor, *Baseball at Night,* depicts a game from 1934.

During the 1930s the number of radio sets in the United States rose from some 12 million to about 28 million. The most popular programs allowed listeners to forget the hardships of reality. Like the voice of a comforting friend, the opening of a favorite program captured listeners:

66 Return with us now to those thrilling days of yesteryear . . . [sound of hoofbeats] . . . From out of the West comes a fiery horse with the speed of light, a cloud of dust, and a hearty 'Hi-yo Silver'—The Lone Ranger rides again! 99

Heroes such as the Lone Ranger, Little Orphan Annie, and the Shadow always triumphed over evil, offering a hopeful message to listeners.

Literature in the early 1930s. The public's desire for entertainment also gave rise to new forms of popular literature. Magazines and comic books offered cheap and accessible forms of entertainment, presenting fantastic heroes such as Superman and Tarzan. One of the best-selling magazines of the time, *Reader's Digest,* presented a selection of condensed articles from various magazines. For families on a limited budget, this "all-purpose" magazine seemed ideal.

Many of the most popular novels of the era also offered escapism. In James Hilton's *Lost Horizon* (1933), a weary traveler stumbles upon a peaceful, prosperous utopia hidden in the mountains of Tibet. The idea of discovering a perfect world appealed to many readers.

Not all fiction of the 1930s was escapist, however. James T. Farrell portrayed the grim

◀ **William Faulkner used his experiences growing up in Oxford, Mississippi, to create the mythical Yoknapatawpha County—a setting that appeared frequently in his novels.**

▶ **Book cover of *The Sound and the Fury***

life of Chicago's Irish immigrants in his *Studs Lonigan* trilogy (1932–1935), while Nathanael West presented the American dream as a nightmare in *Miss Lonelyhearts* (1933). William Faulkner, in novels such as *The Sound and the Fury* (1929) and *As I Lay Dying* (1930), tragically portrayed small-town life in fictional Yoknapatawpha County, Mississippi. Faulkner's novels later earned him the Nobel Prize for literature in 1949 and two Pulitzer prizes—one in 1955 and another in 1963.

■■ **During the 1930s Americans enjoyed many forms of popular culture, including movies, radio programs, and literature.**

SECTION 2 REVIEW

IDENTIFY and explain the significance of the following: *mutualistas,* breadlines, shantytowns, Josefina Fierro de Bright, James Hilton, James T. Farrell, Nathanael West, William Faulkner.

1. **MAIN IDEA** How did the depression affect the work force?

2. **MAIN IDEA** What impact did the Great Depression have on living conditions in rural areas?

3. **MAIN IDEA** How were urban communities affected by the Great Depression? In what ways did individuals and communities try to cope?

4. **WRITING TO DESCRIBE** Imagine you are a magazine editor researching a story on popular culture during the 1930s. Write an outline for an article that describes popular forms of entertainment during this period.

5. **EVALUATING** How did economic hardship alter family life in the 1930s?

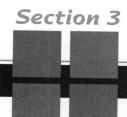

HOOVER FAILS

FOCUS

- **What beliefs shaped President Hoover's response to the depression?**
- **What effect did the Hoover administration's economic policies have on the depression?**
- **Why did Hoover lose the election of 1932?**

*W*hen the depression began, many Americans had great faith in Herbert Hoover. His skills as a businessman and as an administrator inspired confidence. Under his direction the government undertook some important measures to fight the depression. But they were not enough to end the crisis. As a result, voters in the election of 1932 rejected Hoover in favor of his Democratic opponent, Franklin D. Roosevelt.

Republican campaign button, 1932

HOOVER'S PHILOSOPHY

The most urgent task confronting President Hoover was to ease the human suffering caused by the depression. Prior to the crash most Americans believed that the government should not interfere in the free-enterprise system. Immediately after the crash, the *New York Times* advised that "the fundamental prescriptions for recovery [are] such homely things as savings . . . and hopeful waiting for the turn." Within a few months, however, the worsening crisis led to calls for the federal government to provide direct relief—food, clothing, shelter, and money—to the needy. Hoover rejected the idea of such government aid, stating:

> ❝ I do not believe that the power and duty of the [federal] Government ought to be extended to the relief of individual suffering. . . . The lesson should be constantly enforced that though the people support the Government the Government should not support the people. ❞

Direct federal relief, Hoover argued, would create a vast bureaucracy, inflate the federal budget, and undermine the self-respect of people receiving the aid. Instead, Hoover urged Americans to lift themselves up through hard work and strength of character.

Hoover's political beliefs stemmed from the notion of **rugged individualism**—the idea that

▼ **Unemployed workers protested in New York's Times Square in 1933. Demonstrators carried signs indicating they were willing to work for $1 a week.**

▲ Private charities and organizations such as the Salvation Army helped families in need of assistance by bringing them food and clothing.

▼ Nurses, such as this one in Maryland, often went door-to-door offering people free medical assistance.

success comes through individual effort and private enterprise. He believed that private charities and local communities, not the federal government, could best provide for those in need. "A voluntary deed," said Hoover, "is infinitely more precious to our national ideas and spirit than a thousandfold poured from the Treasury."

Hoover was not alone in his beliefs. Millions of Americans agreed that voluntary efforts were preferable to government intervention. It soon became clear, however, that voluntary efforts alone could not deal with the scale of the depression. Communities and private charities lacked the resources to cope with the ever-rising tide of human misery. Local governments were forced to stretch already inadequate funds to cover growing numbers of needy families. By 1933, for example, families on public welfare in New York City were paid just $23 a month.

In 1930 Hoover appointed the Committee for Unemployment Relief to assist state and local relief efforts. The committee, however, did little beyond urging Americans to contribute more to charity. The human misery of the depression continued practically unchecked.

▪▪ **Hoover's belief in rugged individualism led him to oppose direct federal relief for those in need.**

BOOSTING THE ECONOMY

Although critics would later charge that Hoover's relief plans failed because he did not get the government involved, Hoover was not totally opposed to the government intervening in the economy. In fact, despite his opposition to direct public relief, Hoover's administration played a

▲ President Hoover addressed 250 leaders of finance, industry, and commerce in August 1932. In his speech, Hoover asked business leaders to assume more responsibility for improving the economy.

more active role in attempting to shape the economy than any previous administration had.

Stimulating the economy.
Within weeks of the stock market crash, Hoover called a White House conference of top business, labor, and political leaders. The *New York Times* hailed the meeting as a step in the right direction, noting:

> 66 [It is] the largest gathering of noted heads of industrial and other corporations in Washington since the resources of the nation were marshalled for participation in the World War! 99

Hoover urged these leaders to maintain employment and wages voluntarily as a step toward reviving business activity and promoting recovery. At the same time, he issued cheerful public statements designed to boost confidence and get the economy going again.

Unfortunately, most people did not share Hoover's optimism. Many became very cynical toward the administration as trust in government and in business declined. Moaned the chairman of the Republican National Committee: "Every time an administration official gives out an optimistic statement about business conditions, the market immediately drops."

At Hoover's request, Congress funded several public-works programs, among them the giant Hoover Dam on the Colorado River. Hoover expected these projects to achieve two goals: (1) to stimulate business by providing contracts for construction and materials and (2) to provide relief by employing jobless workers. Overall, he approved some $800 million in public-works funding. Yet the crisis was so great that even this large amount had little impact on the depression.

Coping with the farm crisis.
Hoover also took some steps to ease the plight of farmers. As crop prices fell, Hoover instructed the Federal Farm Board—created through the **Agricultural Marketing Act** of 1929—to buy up surplus wheat, corn, cotton, and other farm products. Officials believed that reducing crop supplies would cause prices to rise. The government could store these commodities and then sell them when prices were higher. The scheme did not work. Farmers at first refused to limit production. Instead, they reacted to low prices by growing more crops. In 1931 the Farm Board stopped buying surplus crops, having already spent some $180 million.

Just as he opposed direct relief for jobless factory workers, Hoover resisted giving direct aid to desperate farmers. He did try to aid farmers indirectly, though, by recommending passage of the **Home Loan Bank Act** in 1932. The act provided money to savings banks, building and loan associations, and insurance companies for low-interest mortgages. Hoover believed that the act would reduce foreclosures on homes and farms and thus allow more farmers to keep their land. He also believed that the act would encourage home construction, boosting employment and increasing the flow of money through the economy.

The Reconstruction Finance Corporation.
Hoover also tried to stimulate the economy through the **Reconstruction Finance Corporation** (RFC), created by Congress in February 1932. The RFC lent large sums to railroads, insurance companies, banks, and other financial institutions. By strengthening these key businesses through federal loans, Hoover hoped to reduce bank failures and create more jobs.

By the end of Hoover's term, RFC loans had helped a number of large corporations avoid collapse. Yet the economy continued to decline, in part because the RFC offered too little, too late. It was created while the depression was in full swing, and it provided no direct aid to industries or

◀ **Hoover Dam on the Colorado River was completed in 1936. It is the main source of hydroelectric power in the Southwest.**

to small businesses, which continued to fail at an alarming rate.

Critics attacked the RFC's trickle-down approach to economic recovery. They argued that money lent to big business would not filter down quickly enough to help the real victims of the depression—ordinary citizens. As one economist put it, this was like putting fertilizer on the branches of a tree—rather than on the roots—to help the tree grow. A more effective approach, said critics, would be to funnel money directly to those in need. This would increase consumers' buying power and thereby stimulate business. Newspaper columnist Walter Lippmann reflected popular sentiments when he wrote:

> 66 It is hard for the country to realize that this era of easy finance is over. . . . In respect to government finance, as in respect to so many other things, Congress and the people of the country have radically to readjust their minds. 99

Government activism. Although President Hoover's policies failed to end the Great Depression, the RFC and other measures—such as the Home Loan Bank Act and funding for public works—represented a major shift in government policy. To a greater degree than ever before, the president and Congress accepted the idea that the federal government can and should do something to boost the economy in times of crisis.

In the early 1930s Treasury Secretary Andrew Mellon had advised the traditional do-nothing approach. He even argued that a short depression would be good for the country because "it will purge the rottenness out of the system." But as the depression became more severe, the government took unprecedented steps to promote recovery. Unfortunately, these measures were not sufficient to halt the downward trend. As Americans continued to suffer, they increasingly blamed their plight on Herbert Hoover.

▲ Andrew Mellon

■■ Hoover's limited measures to end the depression did little to ease the crisis.

Rumblings of Discontent

By 1932 Hoover was the most hated man in America. His appearance in movie newsreels provoked boos and catcalls from audiences. And he made little effort to win public support by changing his aloof manner or stiff, boring speeches. "This is not a showman's job," Hoover remarked. "I will not step out of character."

As confidence in Hoover eroded, radical political parties grew more vocal. Both the Communist party and the Socialist party condemned the capitalist system that they believed created the depression. Both parties helped organize several mass protests in the early 1930s. Socialist leader A. J. Muste gathered the jobless into Unemployed Leagues to demand work. The Communist party encouraged labor-union activism and led strikes by migrant farm workers.

A Most Vicious Circle

▲ As the depression worsened, more and more people began to blame President Hoover for their troubles. This cartoon appeared June 1931 in the Albany *News.*

▲ Shown here is lawyer Samuel Leibowitz (left) meeting with Heywood Patterson, one of the principal defendants in the Scottsboro case.

The party also helped expose racial injustice. In 1931 an all-white jury in Scottsboro, Alabama, sentenced eight of nine black youths aged 13 to 21 years to death on a highly questionable rape charge. The Communist party helped supply legal defense for the "Scottsboro Boys" and organized mass demonstrations to overturn the convictions.

Many desperate Americans responded to communist and socialist calls for direct action. Early in 1932, thousands of unemployed men demanding work participated in a hunger march on the Ford auto plant near Detroit. Four were killed when police opened fire. In Seattle, 5,000 unemployed protestors seized a public building. After two days local officials finally forced them out.

Some activism was spontaneous, reflecting the desperation of the times. In rural areas people armed with clubs, pitchforks, and shotguns confronted officials trying to foreclose on homes. Farmers destroyed crops and blocked roads to prevent food from being shipped to market, hoping that limiting food supplies would push prices up. "They say blockading the highway's illegal," an Iowa farmer said. "Seems to me there was a Tea Party in Boston that was illegal too."

The biggest protest was staged by more than 10,000 World War I veterans and their families in May 1932. They came to Washington, D.C., to support a veterans' bonus bill then before Congress. The bill would have granted the veterans—many of whom were unemployed—early payment of pension bonuses due to them for their service during the war. This group was soon dubbed the **Bonus Army**.

At first, officials allowed the Bonus Army demonstrators to live in empty government buildings and to camp in an open area across the Potomac River. When Congress rejected the bonus bill, most of the demonstrators returned home. But about 2,000 veterans stayed, defying orders to leave. In a clash with authorities, two veterans and two policemen were killed. The police requested aid, and President Hoover ordered the army to disperse the squatters.

In late July the army moved in with machine guns, tanks, and tear gas. One woman recalled her husband's experience that day:

66 My husband went to Washington. To march with . . . the bonus boys. He was a machine gunner in the war. He'd say them . . . Germans gassed him in Germany. And [then] his own government . . . gassed him and run him off the country up there with a water hose, half drowned him. 99

▲ More than 10,000 veterans marched to Washington, D.C., in May 1932 to petition Congress for full and immediate payment of pension bonuses earned during World War I.

Commanded by General Douglas MacArthur (later a hero in World War II), the troops drove the veterans from the buildings, broke up their encampment, and burned their shacks. Hundreds were injured and three killed, including an 11-week-old baby. Many Americans found the government's treatment of the veterans shocking. Across the nation, anger against Hoover grew. As the election of 1932 approached, Americans joked bitterly, "In Hoover we trusted and now we are busted."

■■ Public unrest grew as the depression worsened and Hoover mishandled the Bonus Army protest.

THE ELECTION OF 1932

In the summer of 1932, with elections scheduled for the fall, the Republicans reluctantly renominated Herbert Hoover as their presidential candidate. With public sentiment running strongly against the Republicans, no other member of the party was eager for the nomination. The Democrats, sensing victory, chose Franklin Delano Roosevelt of New York as their candidate.

The Democratic challenger. Roosevelt—who often went by his initials, FDR—was a determined and skillful politician. Born into a wealthy and prestigious family, his background suggested that he would be more likely to identify with the wealthy than with working-class citizens. He could easily have become a Wall Street power broker, but instead he chose a career in public service.

FDR was highly influenced by the progressivism of his distant cousin, former president Theodore Roosevelt, and by that of the former president's niece Eleanor Roosevelt, who married FDR in 1905. Her earnest belief in social reform impressed the young FDR. Mrs. Roosevelt would become one of his most important political assets. A fellow Democrat once said of the relationship between Franklin and Eleanor Roosevelt: "Any good things he may have done during his political career are due to her and any mistakes he may have made are due to his not taking up the matter with his wife."

FDR ran as a vice-presidential candidate in 1920, but his political career appeared to be over when he was paralyzed from the waist down by polio in 1921. Yet with the help of his wife, he overcame his physical challenges and was elected governor of New York in 1928. As governor he gained high marks for his imaginative state relief programs that had instituted unemployment benefits and supported failing industries. In accepting his party's nomination for president, Roosevelt issued a call for a new style of government, declaring:

▼ Franklin D. Roosevelt's support of innovative relief programs while governor of New York made him a strong contender for the 1932 Democratic party presidential nomination (below). The photograph at right shows him campaigning in 1932.

> " Republican leaders not only have failed in material things, they have failed in national vision, because in disaster they have held out no hope. . . . I pledge you, I pledge myself, to a new deal for the American people. "

A change in leadership. The 1932 campaign had one key issue—the depression. While Hoover tried to defend his policies, he realized he had little chance of victory. Roosevelt continually attacked Hoover's record and called for major policy changes, including direct federal relief for the needy, a massive public-works program, and federal regulation of the stock market to prevent fraud. Roosevelt promised to seek a fairer distribution of wealth and to put the political and economic system at "the service of the people."

On election day, Roosevelt and his running mate, John Nance Garner of Texas, carried 42 states, capturing 23 million popular votes and 472 electoral votes to Hoover's 16 million popular votes and 59 electoral votes. The Democrats won decisive majorities in both houses of Congress, solidifying gains they had already made in the congressional election of 1930. As a result, Roosevelt was confident that his programs would have strong support in Congress.

In the 1920s most Americans had credited the Republicans for the era's glowing prosperity. In 1932, voters made it clear that the Republicans would have to take the blame for the depression.

▲ **These Roosevelt campaign artifacts were used during the 1932 presidential election.**

Many of those who voted for Roosevelt were really voting against Herbert Hoover. But other Americans saw in Roosevelt the kind of dynamic personality they believed could lead the country out of its troubles. Roosevelt had promised a "new deal." During the four months between Election Day and Roosevelt's inauguration on March 4, 1933, Americans waited hopefully to see how the new president would carry out his campaign pledge.

■■ **Hoover lost the election of 1932 because voters were upset by the Republicans' handling of the depression and were inspired by Franklin Roosevelt's confidence.**

SECTION 3 REVIEW

IDENTIFY and explain the significance of the following: rugged individualism, Agricultural Marketing Act, Home Loan Bank Act, Reconstruction Finance Corporation, Andrew Mellon, A. J. Muste, Bonus Army, Franklin Delano Roosevelt, Eleanor Roosevelt.

1. **MAIN IDEA** Why did President Hoover rely on local and voluntary efforts and oppose direct federal relief for those in need?

2. **MAIN IDEA** What measures did the Hoover administration support to end the depression? Why did they fail?

3. **MAIN IDEA** Why did public unrest grow during the Hoover administration?

4. **WRITING TO EXPRESS A VIEWPOINT** Imagine you are a campaign worker for Franklin Delano Roosevelt. Write a campaign poster explaining why voters should support your candidate in the 1932 election.

5. **HYPOTHESIZING** How might the events of the early 1930s have been different if the Hoover administration had supported direct federal relief?

Stock market crashes. William Faulkner's *The Sound and the Fury* published. Agricultural Marketing Act passed.

Smoot-Hawley Tariff passed. William Faulkner's *As I Lay Dying* published.

1929

1930

WRITING A SUMMARY

Using the essential points of the chapter as a guide, write a summary of the chapter.

REVIEWING CHRONOLOGY

Number your paper 1 to 5. Study the time line above, and list the following events in the order in which they happened by writing the first next to 1, the second next to 2, and so on. Then complete the activity below.

1. Stock market crashes.
2. Bonus Army marches on Washington, D.C.
3. Scottsboro Boys case begins.
4. James Hilton's *Lost Horizon* and Nathanael West's *Miss Lonelyhearts* published.
5. Smoot-Hawley Tariff passed.

Evaluating How did Hoover's appointment of the Committee for Unemployment Relief show his support for rugged individualism?

IDENTIFYING PEOPLE AND IDEAS

Explain the historical significance of each of the following people or terms.

1. bear market
2. Andrew Mellon
3. Black Tuesday
4. *mutualistas*
5. shantytowns
6. Josefina Fierro de Bright
7. James T. Farrell
8. rugged individualism
9. Home Loan Bank Act
10. Bonus Army

UNDERSTANDING MAIN IDEAS

1. What factors led Americans to invest in the stock market during the 1920s? Why did the stock market crash in 1929?
2. How did the depression affect the banking industry?
3. What effect did the depression have on family life in the 1930s?
4. What measures did President Hoover take to stimulate the economy?
5. What are some of the ways in which people expressed their discontent during the depression?

REVIEWING THEMES

1. **Economic Development** What factors caused the Great Depression?
2. **Geographic Diversity** How did the depression influence where people lived during the 1930s?
3. **Cultural Diversity** How were African Americans and Mexican Americans affected differently by the depression?

THINKING CRITICALLY

1. **Evaluating** How did the depression affect the behavior and outlook of Americans who struggled through those hard times?
2. **Analyzing** Why did Hoover oppose direct federal relief to the needy?
3. **Synthesizing** What major policy changes did Franklin Roosevelt propose during the 1932 presidential campaign?

STRATEGY FOR SUCCESS

Review the Skills Handbook entry on Distinguishing Fact from Opinion on page 750. Then read the following excerpt, in which the editor of the Johnstown *Tribune* warns the city of dangers to be expected from the arrival of the Bonus Army. What opinions does the editor have about the marchers? How might they differ from the opinions of one of the marchers?

> 66 In any group of the size of the Bonus Army, made up of men gathered from all parts of the country, without discipline, without effective leadership in a crisis, . . . there is certain to be a mixture of undesirables—thieves, plug-uglies [thugs], degenerates. . . . The community must protect itself from the criminal fringe of the invaders. 99

WRITING ABOUT HISTORY

Writing to Create Write a poem or lyrics for a song that would reflect the mood of Americans struggling with the depression.

Herbert Hoover appoints
Committee for
Unemployment Relief.
Scottsboro Boys case
begins.

Home Loan Bank Act passed.
RFC created. Bonus Army
marches on Washington, D.C.
Franklin Roosevelt elected
president.

James Hilton's
Lost Horizon and
Nathanael West's
Miss Lonelyhearts
published.

1931   1932   1933

USING PRIMARY SOURCES

As the depression continued into the winter of 1932, the growing numbers of unemployed forced to seek relief in soup kitchens became a familiar sight. In her poem "Bread Line," which was published in January 1932, Florence Converse attempted to make sense of this tragedy. Read the following excerpt from the poem. What point is the poet trying to make?

> *What's the meaning of this queue,*
> *Tailing down the avenue,*
> *Full of eyes that will not meet*
> *The other eyes that throng the street—*
> *The questing eyes, the curious eyes,*
> *Scornful, popping with surprise*
> *To see a living line of men*
> *As long as round the block, and then*
> *As long again? . . .*
>
> . . . .
>
> *What's the meaning in these faces*
> *Modern industry displaces,*
> *Emptying the factory*
> *To set the men so tidily*
> *Along the pavement in a row?*
> *Now and then they take a slow*
> *Shuffling step, straight ahead,*
> *As if a dead march said:*
> *"Beware! I'm not dead."*
>
> . . . .
>
> *A spark can creep, a spark can run;*
> *Suddenly a spark can wink*
> *And send us down destruction's brink.*
>
> . . . .
>
> *What if our slow-match have caught*
> *Fire from a burning thought?*
> *What if we should be destroyed*
> *By our patient unemployed?* **99**

LINKING HISTORY AND GEOGRAPHY

Refer to the map on page 332. Which states had the smallest percentage of people receiving unemployment benefits? What factors might account for variations in the number of people receiving unemployment assistance?

Breadline

BUILDING YOUR PORTFOLIO

Complete the following projects independently or cooperatively.

1. **THE ECONOMY** In chapters 11 and 12 you dealt with the postwar economic downswing and the upswing of the 1920s. Building on that experience, imagine you are a cartoonist in 1929. Create an editorial cartoon that criticizes the investment practices that led to the stock market crash.

2. **GLOBAL RELATIONS** Imagine you are a journalist in the 1930s at the height of the Great Depression. Create a series of newspaper headlines that describe the effects of the depression both in the United States and around the world. Headlines might mention stories about individual families, homelessness and food shortages, unemployment, Hoover's political problems, or international trade issues.

THE NEW DEAL

FOCUS

UNDERSTANDING THE MAIN IDEA

To help the nation recover from the Great Depression of the 1930s, President Franklin Roosevelt created a series of programs known as the New Deal. These reforms improved the economy and expanded the role of government in economic life. The government provided jobs to thousands of unemployed workers and provided direct relief to the needy.

THEMES

■ **ECONOMIC DEVELOP-MENT** How can the federal government aid economic recovery?

■ **CONSTITUTIONAL HERITAGE** Why might government interference in the economy be considered unconstitutional?

■ **CULTURAL DIVERSITY** What role might the arts play in reflecting ethnic and cultural diversity?

1933	1935	1936	1937	1939	1940
New Deal launched.	CIO organized.	*Gone with the Wind* published.	**GM strike begins.**	*The Grapes of Wrath* published.	*Native Son* published.

The prosperous economic times of the 1920s had come to a devastating end with the stock market crash of 1929 and the Great Depression. President Hoover's administration had been very cautious in dealing with the economic crisis. By electing Franklin Roosevelt in 1932, the nation appeared ready for the federal government to take a more active role in shaping the economy.

Post office mural, *Evening on the Farm,*
by Orr C. Fisher

*B*y 1933, Americans had endured three years of economic depression—each year more desperate than the last. On his last day in office, President Hoover was heard to sigh, "We are at the end of our string. There is nothing more we can do." But the new president, Franklin Delano Roosevelt, did not share this despair. In his inaugural address he offered the American people hope:

❝ First of all let me assert my firm belief that the only thing we have to fear is fear itself—nameless, unreasoning, unjustified terror which paralyzes needed efforts to convert retreat into advance. . . . This Nation asks for action, and action now. ❞

Roosevelt's words rang out across the land, lifting Americans from despair and stirring their hopes. Some half a million letters in support of the new president poured into the White House.

Roosevelt's program had three general aims: *relief,* to ease the plight of citizens in economic distress; *recovery,* to restore the economy to health; and *reform,* to correct ills and injustices in American society. Despite much confusion, inefficiency, and political conflict, Roosevelt's measures proved enormously powerful and far-reaching. They restored public hope, aided the unemployed, and gave the government a central role in regulating business and the economy and promoting public welfare.

National Recovery Administration symbol

RESTORING HOPE

FOCUS

- **What New Deal programs tackled the banking, farm, and home owners' crises?**
- **How did the New Deal provide relief for the unemployed?**
- **What effect did the New Deal have on the Tennessee Valley region?**

New Yorker magazine cover, 1933

*R*oosevelt wasted no time making good his pledge of "action, and action now." As soon as he arrived in the Oval Office, he confidently proposed programs that would strengthen the nation's teetering banking system and provide relief for the needy. Soon he moved on to attack the deep-seated problems that plagued agriculture and industry. One project would transform an entire region of the country.

ROOSEVELT CONFRONTS THE EMERGENCY

Roosevelt's optimism proved contagious. "The whole country is with him," noted humorist Will Rogers, "just so he does something. If he burned down the Capitol, we would cheer and say, 'Well, we at least got a fire started anyhow.'" People were ready for action, even if it meant making mistakes along the way.

Roosevelt did indeed get a fire started. With the help of the Brain Trust, the advisory group that he had formed in 1932 while still governor of New York, the energetic new president drew up 15 relief and recovery measures, his promised "new deal for the American people." Immediately after taking office on March 5, Roosevelt called Congress into special session. Over the next 100 days, Congress approved all 15

measures, which made up the heart of the president's **New Deal** program.

Roosevelt started with the nation's banks, which were in serious trouble. The day after his inauguration, he issued a proclamation closing every bank in the nation for a few days. This so-called **bank holiday** was designed to stop massive withdrawals. On Thursday, March 9, Congress took only a few hours to pass the **Emergency Banking Act**,

▶ **Americans listened as Roosevelt discussed important issues in one of his many radio broadcasts.**

THE GREATEST MAN OF THE AGE

J. B. Murray, a young Australian, came to the United States in 1926. He spent the next 11 years working in California orchards, oil fields, and ranches. When Franklin Roosevelt was nominated for the presidency in 1932, Murray became an eager observer of American politics.

"*F*or myself," he later wrote in a book about his travels titled *American Trails*, "I believed in Roosevelt completely, and became engrossed with his campaign. He travelled to distant cities, and into the farming country, and wherever he went left hope behind him. The man's charm of manner and quiet confidence and strength were irresistible." Murray noted that Roosevelt's "personality flooded the countryside like warm sunshine. . . . The country listened spellbound to [his] clear, confident voice, which assured all that a new era was commencing." Murray concluded, "Listening to his radio talks, I had already marked him down as the greatest man of the age."

Corporation (FDIC) in June 1933. This reform insured each bank deposit up to $2,500. (Today, the figure is $100,000 per account.)

Roosevelt then turned his attention to the plight of the farmers. On March 28 he issued an executive order to create the **Farm Credit Administration** to provide low-interest, long-term loans to farmers. Congress obliged, and with these loans, farmers paid off mortgages and overdue taxes, bought back lost farms, and purchased needed seed, fertilizer, and equipment. In April, Roosevelt asked Congress to create the **Home Owners Loan Corporation** (HOLC) to address the problem of home owners who could not meet their mortgage payments. Again, Congress obliged. By June 1936 the HOLC had saved the homes of some one million American families by granting them low-interest, long-term mortgage loans.

■■ **The bank holiday and FDIC restored public trust in banks, while the FCA and HOLC provided loans to farmers and home owners.**

which authorized the government to examine all banks and allow those that were financially sound to reopen. Roosevelt hoped that the act would restore public confidence in the banking system.

Caught without cash, Americans scrambled to find substitutes for it during the bank holiday. Many used subway and bus tokens, postage stamps, and IOUs. On Sunday evening, March 12, some 60 million anxious Americans tuned in their radios to hear the president explain how the bank holiday would protect their money. In this first of many "fireside chats"—radio broadcasts from the White House—Roosevelt urged people to reinvest in banks. "I can assure you that it is safer to keep your money in a reopened bank than under the mattress," he advised.

The next morning, as banks began reopening, more than $1 billion in deposits flowed into the system. Confidence in banks increased still more when Congress created the **Federal Deposit Insurance**

RELIEF FOR THE NEEDY

Along with these measures the Roosevelt administration also launched a large-scale program of direct relief to the nation's 13 million unemployed. In many ways Roosevelt's direct-relief program completed the agenda that reformers had been trying to get the government to support since the Progressive Era. Through the efforts of Eleanor Roosevelt and Democratic National Committee member Molly Dewson, the president brought in many long-time reformers to direct his programs, including Secretary of Labor Frances Perkins.

In May 1933, at Roosevelt's request, Congress established the **Federal Emergency Relief Administration** (FERA) with half a billion dollars for relief aid to be funneled directly to state and local agencies. One of FDR's most trusted advisers, Harry L. Hopkins, headed the FERA program.

A Washington newspaper reported the eagerness of the FERA director to get relief to the needy:

> 66 The half-billion dollars for direct relief of States won't last a month if Harry L. Hopkins, the new relief administrator, maintains the pace he set yesterday in disbursing more than $5,000,000 during his first two hours in office. 99

By 1935 the total of such direct federal relief aid had risen to some $3 billion. At one point nearly eight million American families were surviving on public assistance.

Americans, however, disliked this kind of aid. They wanted jobs, not handouts. So Hopkins organized the **Civil Works Administration** (CWA) to create jobs. Most of these were "make-work" projects such as raking leaves and picking up park litter. From 1933 to 1934, the CWA paid some $750 million in wages to some four million men and women.

To aid unemployed young men between ages 18 and 25, Congress established the **Civilian Conservation Corps** (CCC) in 1933. Initially, some 250,000 young men left their homes and went to army camps for CCC training. Once trained, they spread out into the nation's forests, where they planted trees, cleared underbrush, laid out park trails, and developed campgrounds and beaches. For their efforts they earned a dollar a day. Most of their earnings were sent back home to help their families. Said one CCC veteran of the experience:

> 66 I really enjoyed it. I had three wonderful square meals a day. . . . They sure made a man out of ya, because you learned that everybody here was equal. There was nobody better than another in the CCC's. 99

During its nearly 10-year life, the CCC enrolled more than 2.5 million young men and planted millions of trees, most in the South and the Southwest. The program earned back much of its cost in the value it added to the nation's forests.

■■ **Through the FERA, the CWA, and the CCC, the New Deal granted direct relief to the unemployed and created jobs.**

HELPING THE NATION RECOVER

While New Deal relief programs aided needy Americans, the Roosevelt administration also pursued recovery programs to revive the economy. Roosevelt saw relief as a short-term remedy; recovery was his long-term goal.

To stimulate recovery in business and industry, the Roosevelt administration poured money into the economy through federal loans and government spending—a process sometimes called "priming the pump." Many of the New Deal recovery programs were based on the theories of noted economist John Maynard Keynes, who argued that for a nation to recover fully from a depression, the government had to spend money to create jobs and boost investment.

One of the chief ways in which the Roosevelt administration attempted to prime the economy's pump was through the **National Industrial Recovery Act** (NIRA), which Congress passed in June 1933. The act was designed to stimulate industrial and business activity and reduce unemployment by stabilizing prices, raising wages, limiting workers' hours, and providing jobs. To help achieve these goals,

◀ **Some 2.5 million jobless young men were employed by the CCC from 1933 to 1943. During the decade they worked on projects designed to preserve and restore the nation's natural resources.**

FRANKLIN D. ROOSEVELT
1882–1945

1882
1982
USA
20¢

Franklin D. Roosevelt

in office
1933–1945

"Mr. Roosevelt is a unique figure in the modern world: the one states-man . . . who seems able to relax," wrote one journalist about the charismatic leader. Indeed, FDR always appeared to be warm, ener-getic, and easygoing, despite the enormous pressures that faced his administration. His optimistic out-look may have helped in his recuper-ation from polio.

The president always hid his private thoughts behind his dazzling smile. One of his

Franklin D Roosevelt

speech writers commented that one could never tell what was going on in FDR's "heavily forested interior." Yet, the president relied heavily on instinct and idealism in making deci-sions. Political ideology held little value for him. His warm style and compassionate manner, expressed in his weekly "fireside chats," helped win support for many of his pro-grams. Years after the depression many Americans would remember FDR almost as a beloved family member.

the NIRA created two new federal agencies—the **Public Works Administration** (PWA) and the **National Recovery Administration** (NRA).

The PWA, under the leadership of Secretary of the Interior Harold Ickes, provided jobs and stimulated business activity by contracting with private firms to construct roads, public buildings, and other public-works projects. Between 1933 and 1939, the PWA spent more than $4 billion on some 34,000 projects.

▲ Roosevelt's approach to government was to recommend a new program, try it, and if it failed, then "admit it frankly and try another." His approach is satirized in this 1934 cartoon.

The NIRA's other arm, the NRA, attempted to promote recovery by encouraging businesses to draw up "codes of fair competition." Under these codes, competing businesses agreed to work together to stabilize prices, wages, hours, and pro-duction levels. Businesses were able to do this because the NIRA had suspended antitrust laws. To help protect labor through this period of busi-ness self-regulation, Section 7(a) of the NIRA guaranteed workers the "right to organize and bar-gain collectively through representatives of their own choosing . . . free from the interference, restraint or coercion of employers."

Under the direction of former army general Hugh S. Johnson, the NRA began on a wave of popular enthusiasm. Parades of workers marched through cities displaying the NRA banner—a blue eagle clutching lightning bolts in its claw, with the slogan "We Do Our Part." Johnson compared the NRA to a fighting army:

66 This campaign is a frank dependence on the power and the willingness of the American people to act together as one person in an hour of great danger. . . . The Blue Eagle is a symbol of industrial solidarity and self-government. 99

But enthusiasm soon faded. Businesses did not always obey the codes. Workers complained that the codes held their wages down, while consumers complained that the codes pushed prices up. As people lost confidence in the NRA, they joked that it stood for "National Run Around" and "No Recovery Allowed." In 1935 the Supreme Court declared the NIRA (and the NRA) unconstitutional.

AGRICULTURAL RECOVERY

To raise farm prices and increase farmers' purchasing power, Roosevelt proposed that farmers cut production. Congress passed the **Agricultural Adjustment Act** (AAA) in May 1933, which established the Agricultural Adjustment Administration (AAA). The AAA paid farmers to reduce their output of cotton, wheat, corn, hogs, rice, tobacco, dairy products, and other commodities. The money for these payments, or **subsidies**, came from taxes levied on food processors, including meat packers, canners, and flour millers.

In one year the plan reduced the cotton crop by more than three million bales, raising cotton prices. Such increased income gave cotton growers and large-scale farmers more cash to spend, thus stimulating overall economic recovery. New Deal supporters pointed to these favorable results as proof of the value of sound federal planning. But critics of the New Deal farm program pointed out that the taxes on food processors were passed along to consumers in the form of higher prices. Thus, while farmers' incomes rose, the purchasing power of city dwellers declined.

Critics also charged that farmers with large land-holdings benefited far more from the AAA than did small farmers. Often when large landowners cut production, they forced sharecroppers off their land and kept all of the government payments for themselves. Thus, the poorest farmers were forced into deeper poverty. In response, a group of Arkansas sharecroppers, both black and white, formed the **Southern Tenant Farmers' Union** (STFU) in 1934. The union lobbied the government to halt tenant evictions and to force landowners to share payments with the farmers who rented land. Within one year the STFU had grown to more than 10,000 members.

Early in 1936, the Supreme Court struck down the AAA on the grounds that the processing tax was unconstitutional. This decision, like its ruling against the NIRA and NRA, reflected

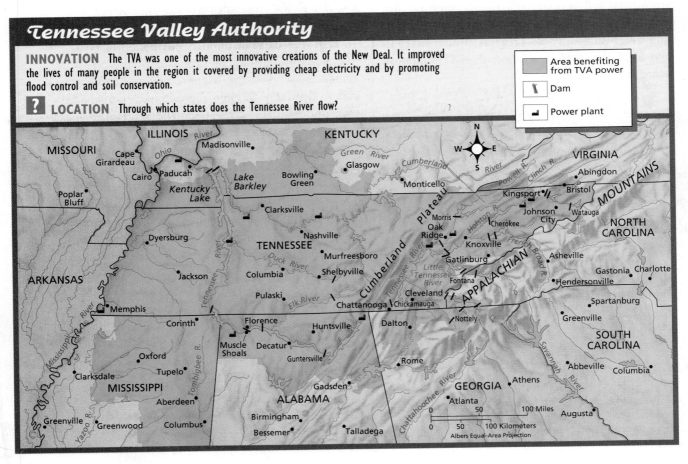

Tennessee Valley Authority

INNOVATION The TVA was one of the most innovative creations of the New Deal. It improved the lives of many people in the region it covered by providing cheap electricity and by promoting flood control and soil conservation.

? **LOCATION** Through which states does the Tennessee River flow?

Area benefiting from TVA power

Dam

Power plant

the Supreme Court's opposition to growing government power.

▪▪ To stimulate economic recovery, Congress passed the NIRA to help business and industry and the AAA to aid agriculture.

*R*EVITALIZING A REGION

The most monumental of all the early New Deal programs was the Tennessee Valley project, which sought to revitalize the seven-state region drained by the Tennessee River and its tributaries (see map on page 698). This rural area was scarred by overcut forests and frequent flooding. Poverty, malnutrition, disease, and illiteracy plagued its two million residents.

The **Tennessee Valley Authority** (TVA), created in May 1933, transformed the economic and social life of the region. Under the guidance of David E. Lilienthal, the TVA built 38 dams and several power stations that provided electricity, flood control, and recreational facilities for the region. Other TVA projects combated malaria, illiteracy, and soil erosion and tried to improve the region's standard of living, which had barely changed since Reconstruction.

▲ The TVA's system of hydroelectric plants, dams, and navigation channels covers an area of some 41,000 square miles. Shown here is the construction of Norris Dam.

Critics denounced the TVA as overuse of government power. Shareholders in private utility companies, who feared it would cut into their dividends, brought several court cases against the TVA. The Supreme Court, however, refused to strike down the TVA. Probably the best known of the "alphabet soup" of programs created during Roosevelt's First Hundred Days, the TVA remains one of the New Deal's most enduring successes.

▪▪ The TVA transformed economic and social conditions throughout the Tennessee River Valley.

SECTION 1 REVIEW

IDENTIFY and explain the significance of the following: New Deal, bank holiday, Emergency Banking Act, Federal Deposit Insurance Corporation, Farm Credit Administration, Home Owners Loan Corporation, Frances Perkins, Federal Emergency Relief Administration, Harry L. Hopkins, Civil Works Administration, Civilian Conservation Corps, National Industrial Recovery Act, Public Works Administration, National Recovery Administration, Agricultural Adjustment Act, subsidies, Southern Tenant Farmers' Union, Tennessee Valley Authority.

LOCATE and explain the importance of the following: Tennessee River Valley.

1. **MAIN IDEA** How did the Roosevelt administration attempt to restore confidence in the banking system? What New Deal measures provided loans to farmers and home owners?

2. **MAIN IDEA** Which New Deal programs granted direct relief to the unemployed and created jobs? Which programs helped business, industry, and agriculture?

3. **GEOGRAPHY: REGION** Describe the physical characteristics of the Tennessee River Valley.

4. **WRITING TO INFORM** Imagine you are a resident of the Tennessee River Valley in 1935. Write a letter to a critic of the TVA, outlining the positive ways in which the TVA has transformed the region where you live.

5. **ANALYZING** How are the economic theories of John Maynard Keynes evident in the approach that the Roosevelt administration took toward reviving the economy?

NEW CHALLENGES

F O C U S

■ **What criticisms were aimed at the New Deal?**

■ **What enabled Roosevelt to win reelection easily in 1936?**

■ **How did Roosevelt try to prevent the Supreme Court from overturning his programs?**

■ **How did the Second New Deal benefit labor and agriculture?**

*O*nce the furious activity of the First Hundred Days ended, the nation anxiously waited to see how well the New Deal would work. Critics were quick to speak out. Rather than slowing the New Deal down, however, these critics made the administration more determined to enact still another series of innovative programs that created jobs, provided security for older Americans, and improved labor and farming conditions.

Townsend Plan sign near Weslaco, Texas

CRITICS OF THE NEW DEAL

Criticism of the New Deal came from both the left and the right of the political spectrum. Liberal and radical critics on the left argued that the New Deal was not going far enough in providing relief, recovery, and reform. Conservatives on the right charged that the New Deal was going too far—pushing government into areas where it had no right to interfere. Conservatives also worried about the heavy costs of the New Deal. Although FDR had campaigned for a balanced budget in 1932, the federal deficit rose from roughly $1.3 billion in 1933 to some $3.5 billion in 1936.

Most conservative complaints came from the American Liberty League, made up largely of Republican business interests and disenchanted Democrats led by Al Smith, who accused New Deal supporters of "irresponsible ravings against millionaires and big business." The League complained that the New Deal measures were destroying both the Constitution and free enterprise and would drive the nation into bankruptcy.

Among the others who opposed the New Deal was Dr. Francis E. Townsend of California. Townsend wanted the government to grant a pension of $200 a month to every American over 60 years old. All recipients were to spend the pensions within 30 days and thus pump money into the

▲ **Huey Long**

economy. Father Charles E. Coughlin, the "radio priest," broadcast a similar message from his pulpit in Michigan. He urged the government to nationalize all banks and return to the silver standard.

Huey Long, "the Kingfish," a colorful but corrupt senator from Louisiana, probably had the most radical plan. Like Robin Hood, Long wanted to take from the rich and give to the poor. He claimed that he had done just that as governor of Louisiana, when he had helped the poor by building public housing, roads, and schools and by providing free textbooks to students. Actually, he had financed his state's public-works projects not by taking from the rich, but by imposing higher taxes on everyone—including the poor. In addition, Long and his friends had often profited personally from the projects.

In 1933 Senator Long proposed a radical new kind of relief program, which he called **Share-Our-Wealth**. The program would empower the government to confiscate wealth from the rich through taxes and then provide a guaranteed minimum income and a home to every American family. Long even had his own theme song:

> 66 Ev'ry man a king, ev'ry man a king,
> For you can be a millionaire,
> There's enough for all people to share.
> When it's sunny June and December too,
> Or in the wintertime or spring:
> There'll be peace without end,
> Ev'ry neighbor a friend,
> With ev'ry man a king. 99

In spite of Long's reputation for corruption, the Share-Our-Wealth program drew a great deal of popular support. Some critics suspected that Long harbored dreams of becoming a dictator. Such fears led the Communist party and the Socialist party to denounce Long even though his program promised to redistribute wealth. Bolstered by popular support, Long soon threatened to challenge Roosevelt as a third-party candidate in the 1936 election. But both this threat and the Share-Our-Wealth program died when an assassin killed Long in 1935.

■■ Some critics accused the New Deal of pushing government power too far, while others wanted to expand it further.

THE SECOND NEW DEAL

In the midterm elections of 1934, the Democrats picked up more seats in Congress. The victory, coupled with pressure from the left, encouraged New Deal planners to initiate more public-works programs, a social security plan, and wage and hour improvements for laborers. This series of programs would eventually come to be called the **Second New Deal**. While still providing relief and pursuing recovery, the Second New Deal would increasingly emphasize reform.

The Works Progress Administration.

A works program, the **Works Progress Administration** (WPA), began in April 1935 under the direction of Harry Hopkins. The CWA had ended the previous year, yet unemployment was still high. Millions of American families remained on relief rolls. To create jobs for them, Congress allotted $5 billion for the WPA.

Over the eight years of its life, the WPA employed an estimated 14 million people, with about 2 million working for it at any given time. Workers engaged in a variety of tasks. Male blue-collar workers built or rebuilt a total of some 350 airports, more than 100,000 public buildings, some 78,000 bridges, and about 500,000 miles of roads. White-collar workers took on research projects and teaching jobs. The WPA had a special division for women, but the program often discriminated against women by paying them lower wages than men. On most projects male workers received $5 a day while female workers received only $3 for the same job.

▼ The WPA employed many women, such as this weaver from Kansas, in a variety of jobs.

The WPA tried to help struggling young people between the ages of 16 and 25 by establishing the **National Youth Administration** (NYA), a "junior WPA." The NYA gave young people part-time jobs that provided money to help them stay in school. Within a year the NYA was providing aid to half a million people.

Social Security. Another cornerstone of the Second New Deal was the **Social Security Act**, which Congress passed in August 1935. The act contained three major provisions. First, it provided unemployment insurance for workers who lost their jobs. The funds for this insurance came from a payroll tax on businesses. Second, the act provided pensions for retired workers over age 65. The money for these pensions came from two sources—a payroll tax on employers and a tax on employees' wages. Third, in a shared federal-state program, the act provided payments to the blind, disabled, and elderly and to wives and children of male workers who had died.

At first the Social Security Act covered only a limited segment of the work force. Farmers and the self-employed were excluded, as well as domestic workers, some 60 percent of whom were African American women. Coverage broadened over the years, however, and the Social Security Act became the model for a wide range of public social welfare programs.

Other programs. Underlying Roosevelt's Second New Deal was the president's belief that the government had not yet "weeded out the overprivileged and . . . effectively lifted up the underprivileged." To help the underprivileged, Roosevelt issued an executive order in May 1935 establishing the **Rural Electrification Administration** (REA). The REA extended power lines into isolated rural areas. Within a few years, only 1 farm in 10 lacked electricity.

Roosevelt also went after public utility companies. He charged that many of them were able to set higher prices than their costs justified—and thus make excessive profits—because they held monopolies over gas and electricity. To reform this system, Congress passed a law giving the government the right to regulate interstate production, transmission, and sale of gas and electricity.

Roosevelt also went after the rich, declaring that tax laws had not done enough "to prevent an unjust concentration of wealth and economic

▲ The Social Security Act marked an unprecedented step in providing relief to the unemployed and elderly. In this photograph, a man named John Kenny fills out one of the first applications for a social security number.

power." In response, Congress passed the Revenue Act of 1935. Often referred to as the **Wealth Tax Act**, it sharply increased taxes on the nation's richest people. Corporations had to pay an "excess profits" tax if they made an annual profit greater than 10 percent. A year later, Congress increased corporate taxes again. Businesspeople complained bitterly that the tax increase discouraged business expansion.

THE ELECTION OF 1936

By 1936 the depression still lingered. Some 9 million workers lacked regular jobs, and 3.5 million remained on the WPA or the CCC rolls. Many factories remained closed or operated at far less than full capacity. Still, America had made some progress. Since 1932 the national income had jumped from roughly $43 billion to more than $80 billion and unemployment had dropped by nearly three million.

In June 1936 the Democrats enthusiastically nominated Roosevelt for a second term. Labor unions, farmers, those on relief, and even many Republicans also endorsed him. For the first time since Reconstruction, most African Americans living in the North abandoned their traditional ties to the Republican party—"the party of Lincoln"—to support the Democrats. The Republicans nominated the capable but unexciting governor of Kansas, Alfred M. Landon. The Republican platform condemned the New Deal,

NEW DEAL PROGRAMS

Year	First New Deal	Provisions
1933	Emergency Banking Act	Gave administration right to regulate banks.
1933	Farm Credit Administration (FCA)	Extended loans to farm owners to refinance loans.
1933	Economy Act	Aimed at balancing the budget.
1933	Civilian Conservation Corps (CCC)	Employed young men on public-works projects.
1933	Federal Emergency Relief Administration (FERA)	Provided relief to the needy.
1933	Agricultural Adjustment Act of 1933 (AAA)	Paid farmers to reduce crops; funded by processing tax later declared unconstitutional.
1933	Tennessee Valley Authority (TVA)	Constructed dam and power projects to improve Tennessee Valley Region.
1933	Home Owners Loan Corporation (HOLC)	Loaned money to home owners to refinance mortgages.
1933	Banking Act of 1933	Created FDIC and prohibited banks from selling stock or financing corporations.
1933	Federal Deposit Insurance Corporation (FDIC)	Insured deposits in individual bank accounts.
1933	National Industrial Recovery Act (NIRA)	Established NRA and a series of fair-competition codes for businesses.
1933	National Recovery Administration (NRA)	Regulated industry and raised wages and prices.
1933	Public Works Administration (PWA)	Set up public-works projects to increase employment and business activity.
1933	Civil Works Administration (CWA)	Provided federal jobs to the unemployed.
1934	Securities and Exchange Commission	Regulated securities market.
1934	Federal Housing Administration (FHA)	Insured bank loans for building and repairing homes.

Year	Second New Deal	Provisions
1935	Works Progress Administration (WPA)	Employed people to do public works, research, and artistic projects.
1935	Soil Conservation Service	Promoted control and prevention of soil erosion.
1935	Rural Electrification Administration (REA)	Provided electricity to rural areas lacking public utilities.
1935	National Youth Administration (NYA)	Provided job training and part-time jobs to students.
1935	National Labor Relations Act (Wagner-Connery Act)	Recognized rights of labor to organize and bargain collectively; regulated labor practices.
1935	Social Security Act	Provided unemployment benefits, pensions for the elderly, and survivor's insurance.
1935	Revenue Act of 1935 (Wealth Tax Act)	Increased taxes on the wealthy.
1937	Farm Security Administration (FSA)	Provided loans to help tenant farmers buy land.
1938	Agricultural Adjustment Act of 1938 (AAA)	Increased government regulation of crop production and payments to farmers.
1938	Revenue Act of 1938	Increased taxes on wealthy businesses.
1938	Fair Labor Standards Act	Established minimum wage of 40 cents per hour and maximum work week of 40 hours for businesses in interstate commerce.

Source: *Encyclopedia of American History*

RELIEF, RECOVERY, AND REFORM Franklin Roosevelt proposed a wide number of programs to aid in the nation's recovery after he assumed office in 1933. These programs became the First New Deal. Two years later he outlined a broader program of social reform in the Second New Deal.

? **BUILDING GRAPH SKILLS** Which New Deal programs were aimed primarily at helping farmers?

but called for few specific changes in New Deal programs. The Republicans did promise to balance the budget and to reduce federal power by returning more power to the states.

Roosevelt's opponents—mainly business interests upset by new regulations and corporate taxes, conservative newspaper editors, and rich Americans angered by high taxes—renewed their charges that Roosevelt ignored the Constitution. They pointed out that the Supreme Court had overturned the NRA, AAA, and five other key New Deal measures. American individualism, free enterprise, and private property, they insisted, were being abandoned for socialism. Some even charged falsely that the Social Security Act would require everyone to wear metal dog tags!

President Roosevelt entered the fight with great zest. In accepting renomination, he pledged to stay on the course the New Deal had set. He won a smashing victory—with some 28 million popular votes to Landon's 17 million. Roosevelt carried every state but Maine and Vermont—the most lopsided victory in more than a century. The Democrats increased their majorities in both houses of Congress. The coalition that Democrats forged in the election—farmers, southern whites, city dwellers, industrial workers, and northern blacks—would hold together for many elections to come.

■■ The Democrats, forging a powerful coalition of groups who benefited from the New Deal, easily reelected Roosevelt in 1936.

ROOSEVELT AND THE SUPREME COURT

Flushed with his triumph and convinced of the power that a solidly Democratic Congress gave him, Roosevelt moved to "reform" the Supreme Court. Angered that the Court had declared several New Deal measures unconstitutional, Roosevelt called attention to the ages of the justices, labeling them "Nine Old Men" (six were 70 or older), and accused them of being stuck in the "horse and buggy" days in their thinking.

In February 1937, two weeks after his second inauguration, Roosevelt asked Congress to grant him the power to appoint one new justice for each of those 70 or older, up to six new justices. The Supreme Court needed "a persistent infusion of new blood," he argued. Roosevelt's proposal triggered a storm of protest across the nation. Critics—Democrats as well as Republicans—charged that this unprecedented "court-packing" would tamper with the delicate balance of legislative, executive, and judicial powers. Dorothy Thompson, a popular political columnist, denounced Roosevelt's scheme as a move toward dictatorship:

66 If the American people accept this last audacity of the President without letting out a yell to high heaven, they have ceased to be jealous of their liberties and are ripe for ruin. This is the beginning of a pure personal government. **99**

▶ The negative attitude that many members of the Supreme Court had toward New Deal reforms is satirized in the cartoon *Nine Old Men.*

Congress resoundingly denied Roosevelt's request. But this was just one battle in a war that FDR would eventually win. The Supreme Court soon upheld the Social Security Act and the National Labor Relations Act. Many Americans concluded that the justices had decided to become more agreeable to prevent a drastic reform of the Court itself. "A switch in time saves nine," people joked. Over the next four years, seven justices died or retired and were replaced by Roosevelt appointees. By 1945 eight of the nine justices were Roosevelt appointees.

■■ **Roosevelt tried to "pack" the Supreme Court with six new members in order to protect his New Deal programs.**

▲ As unions became better organized and membership grew, the number of strikes increased. A 1937 sit-down strike is shown above. Workers for a New York City vending company (right) also went on strike later that same year.

THE SECOND NEW DEAL AND LABOR

When the Supreme Court declared the NIRA unconstitutional in May 1935, it struck down Section 7(a), which protected the rights of labor unions. Two months later, however, Congress passed the National Labor Relations Act, also called the **Wagner-Connery Act**, to guarantee labor's right to organize unions and to bargain for better wages and working conditions.

The American Federation of Labor (AFL) continued its efforts to organize workers, including those in such mass-production industries as steel and automobiles. But the AFL did not move fast enough to please gruff, shaggy-browed John L. Lewis, the intimidating leader of the United Mine Workers union. In 1935 Lewis and several other like-minded labor leaders organized the **Congress of Industrial Organizations** (CIO), which tried to unite workers in various industries.

The new CIO unions included all workers, skilled and unskilled, in a given industry. For example, the United Auto Workers (UAW) represented all workers in automotive plants.

Previously, different AFL craft unions had represented different types of autoworkers, such as electricians, welders, or metalworkers. Now all auto workers negotiated as a single powerful union. And in contrast to many AFL branches, the CIO welcomed African American, immigrant, and female members.

The organizing efforts of both the AFL and the CIO resulted in a wave of strikes. One of the most bitter strikes was waged against General Motors (GM) in the winter of 1936–37. The UAW had been trying to unionize GM factories, but the company had been fighting the union's efforts. Meanwhile, GM workers were growing increasingly frustrated with frequent layoffs, abuses of power by management, and work speedups. On December 31, 1936, this frustration led to a **sit-down strike**.

Instead of leaving the automotive plants, workers occupied the factories and pledged to remain until management met their demands. Wives, daughters, and female workers formed the Women's Auxiliary and the Women's Emergency

Brigade to picket outside the plants in support of the union. Many women felt their lives were changed by this experience. They soon took up the cause of equal pay for men and women in the auto industry. Said one female activist:

> 66 I'm living for the first time with a definite goal. . . . Just being a woman isn't enough anymore. I want to be a human being with the right to think for myself. 99

Finally, after six weeks, General Motors gave in and granted the UAW the right to organize GM workers. Within eight months the UAW membership grew to some 400,000. Owing in part to the Wagner-Connery Act, total union membership shot up from about 4 million in 1936 to some 9 million in 1939.

∎∎ The Wagner-Connery Act guaranteed the rights of labor, increasing union membership and activity.

THE SECOND NEW DEAL AND FARMERS

The Second New Deal also brought relief for farmers. When the Supreme Court struck down the Agricultural Adjustment Act in January 1936, Congress created another program to replace it. Like the AAA, the new program aimed to keep farm prices high by cutting crop production. To avoid opposition from the Supreme Court, however, Congress combined crop reduction with a soil conservation plan—a legitimate governmental activity.

The Second New Deal also sought to help tenant farmers, sharecroppers, and migrant farm workers. The rise of the Southern Tenant Farmers' Union had brought a backlash of violence against sharecroppers by landowners and authorities in the South, forcing some union members to conduct their activities in secrecy. Then in 1936 the union organized

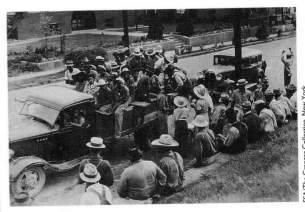

▲ **The depression left many African Americans struggling to find work. This photograph shows people from Memphis, Tennessee, being transported to Arkansas for a day's work in the cotton fields.**

a series of strikes by cotton pickers in five states. In 1937 Congress created the **Farm Security Administration** (FSA) to make low-interest, long-term loans to tenant farmers and sharecroppers to buy farms. The FSA also established camps where migrant farm workers could find shelter and medical care.

The Roosevelt administration recognized that the soil conservation program did not do enough to limit farm production. So in 1938 Congress passed a second Agricultural Adjustment Act. The government continued to pay farmers to withdraw land from production and to practice conservation, but it also authorized the Department of Agriculture to limit the amount of specific crops that could be brought to market each year. When harvests exceeded these limits, the government stored the surpluses until prices rose. Farmers cooperating in this program could get government loans based on the value of their stored crops.

▶ **These members of the Southern Tenant Farmers' Union are shown attending a union meeting. Both African Americans and European Americans belonged to the STFU.**

All in all, New Deal agricultural policy compiled a mixed record. Farm income did rise from 1933 to 1937, but critics pointed out that higher farm prices not only hurt consumers but also caused American farm products to lose out in highly competitive foreign markets. Critics also complained about the large cost of farm subsidies. But the farm legislation of the 1930s had some successes. It helped many farmers escape economic disaster, saved homes, and increased the fertility of millions of acres of land through conservation programs.

■■ **The Second New Deal increased farm income; aided tenant farmers, sharecroppers and migrant workers; and encouraged soil conservation.**

BUSINESS SLUMP, POLITICAL SETBACKS

During 1936 and early 1937, the economy seemed to be improving, but in August 1937 it again plunged downward. Stung by criticism of excessive government spending, Roosevelt had begun cutting back on New Deal relief and public-works programs in 1936. Unfortunately, private industry was not yet strong enough to employ those dropped from government rolls because of the cutbacks. In addition, withholding Social Security taxes from workers' paychecks further reduced the flow of money into the economy. By the autumn of 1937, factories were closing and unemployment was rising. Republicans called this period of economic activity "Roosevelt's recession."

President Roosevelt and Congress again primed the economic pump by increasing government lending and spending. The Reconstruction Finance Corporation rescued troubled businesses. The Works Progress Administration quickly doubled the number of workers on its payroll from some 1.5 million to about 3 million. By the fall of 1938, unemployment had declined and industrial production had increased.

As the 1938 midterm elections drew near, Roosevelt decided to reenergize the New Deal (and to punish Democrats who had voted against his Supreme Court reform plan) by opposing conservative Democrats in Congress who did not support the Second New Deal. He actually urged voters to turn these Democrats out of office!

Just as his "court-packing" scheme had backfired, however, so did his attempt to "purge" the Democratic party. All but one member of Congress whom Roosevelt opposed won reelection. Moreover, voters elected still more Democrats who opposed New Deal programs. Adding to Roosevelt's dismay, the Republicans gained 7 seats in the Senate and 80 in the House. Though the Democrats still maintained majorities in both houses of Congress, their margin was much narrower. Faced with increasing criticism from all sides, FDR decided not to propose any new reforms in 1939, marking an end to the New Deal era.

SECTION 2 REVIEW

IDENTIFY and explain the significance of the following: Francis E. Townsend, Charles E. Coughlin, Huey Long, Share-Our-Wealth, Second New Deal, Works Progress Administration, National Youth Administration, Social Security Act, Rural Electrification Administration, Wealth Tax Act, Alfred M. Landon, Wagner-Connery Act, Congress of Industrial Organizations, sit-down strike, Farm Security Administration.

1. **MAIN IDEA** What charges did some critics level against the New Deal?

2. **MAIN IDEA** How did the Wagner-Connery Act benefit labor? How did other Second New Deal programs benefit agriculture?

3. **MAIN IDEA** Why did Roosevelt try to "pack" the Supreme Court with six new members?

4. **WRITING TO EXPRESS A VIEWPOINT** Imagine you are a Democratic campaign worker during the 1936 election. Write a campaign pamphlet aimed at the "Roosevelt coalition," explaining why you think FDR should be reelected.

5. **IDENTIFYING VALUES** How did criticisms of the New Deal reveal the values held by the left and the right?

LIFE IN THE NEW DEAL ERA

FOCUS

- How did African Americans fare during the New Deal era?
- What gains did Native Americans make during the 1930s?
- What effect did the Dust Bowl have on the Southwest population?

*A*frican Americans, Native Americans, Mexican Americans, and displaced farmers remained among the nation's poorest groups during the depression years. They faced not only economic hardship but also prejudice and hostility. The New Deal, however, did make some efforts to help these groups.

Thomas Hart Benton's *Ploughing It Under*, 1939

The Granger Collection, New York

A STRUGGLE FOR AFRICAN AMERICANS

New Deal programs succeeded to a large degree in helping African Americans economically. Some programs, however, were tainted by discrimination. The FERA and later the WPA became the greatest sources of relief and work for African American males. Some 200,000 young black men flocked to the CCC, where they found work and training, though they were strictly segregated from whites. The TVA employed black workers, but they were not allowed to live in the model towns built by the TVA. NRA codes often set lower wages for blacks than for whites, a practice that led some African American leaders to call the NRA the "Negro Run Around" or "Negroes Ruined Again." Social Security also discriminated indirectly against African Americans since most were agricultural or domestic workers not eligible for benefits.

The discrimination evident in the programs was reflective of social attitudes. The depression increased racial tensions in the country, especially in the South. Twenty-four black people were lynched in 1933 alone. Fearing political backlash from the South, Roosevelt did little to support legislation that might bring civil equality for African Americans, such as a federal antilynching law sponsored by the NAACP. Eleanor Roosevelt, however, became a champion of racial justice. Black leaders often commented on Mrs. Roosevelt's unusual ability to understand the struggles of African Americans. "We [whites] are largely to blame" for poverty among the black community, she once said. It was her goal to see educational and economic opportunities open up for African Americans.

Interior Secretary Harold Ickes, a former president of the Chicago NAACP, also tried to respond to the concerns of African Americans. When the Daughters of the American Revolution (DAR) refused to let the gifted black concert singer Marian Anderson perform in their

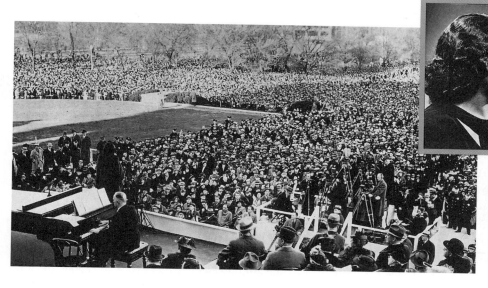

▶ When Marian Anderson (inset) was denied the use of concert facilities at Constitution Hall, she gave a free concert from the steps of the Lincoln Memorial on Easter Sunday, 1939.

Constitution Hall, both Ickes and Mrs. Roosevelt reacted strongly. Roosevelt resigned her longtime membership in the DAR, stating that "to remain as a member implies approval of that action." She and Ickes then arranged for Anderson to give a free concert at the Lincoln Memorial, which attracted an audience of some 75,000.

Long before this incident, Ickes had brought in several prominent African Americans to advise his department on racial matters, including Robert C. Weaver, the first African American to obtain a Ph.D. in economics from Harvard. Weaver was just one of many African Americans who received high-level government jobs during the New Deal era. FDR named more than 100 blacks to major departments of the federal government, more than any other president since Ulysses S. Grant. These appointees included a wide variety of experts, from legal scholars to educators, social workers, and newspaper editors.

A core group of African American government officials evolved into the Federal Council on Negro Affairs, which became known as the black cabinet or the black brain trust. According to Robert Weaver, their "common cause was to maximize the participation of blacks in all phases of the New Deal." They met weekly at the home of Mary McLeod Bethune, the dynamic director of the Division of Negro Affairs in the National Youth Administration.

BIO GRAPHY Mary McLeod Bethune's journey to prominence in Washington began in 1875 in Mayesville, South Carolina, where she was born the 15th of 17 children to farmers who had once been slaves. The young girl's chances for an education seemed slim, since the Mayesville school was for whites only. But with the aid of a Presbyterian mission school and a series of scholarships, she eventually attended the Moody Bible Institute in Chicago. Bethune originally intended to become a missionary in Africa but soon found her mission to be educating African American children. She once said of her decision:

> 66 The drums of Africa still beat in my heart. They will not let me rest while there is a single Negro boy or girl without a chance to prove his [or her] worth. 99

In 1904 she founded a primary school for black girls in Florida, which eventually evolved into Bethune-Cookman College, a four-year coeducational institution with a predominantly African American student body.

Bethune became involved with numerous African American groups, including the NAACP and the Urban League. In 1935 she helped unite all national organizations for African American women into the National Council of Negro Women. Through her work with this association, she became close friends with Eleanor Roosevelt, who insisted that Bethune be appointed to work with the NYA. Bethune fought hard, though not always successfully, to rid the NYA of

Mary McLeod Bethune

racism. Although Bethune left government service after the NYA ended in 1944, she continued to work on behalf of civil rights and educational opportunities for young African Americans until her death in 1955.

■■ **African Americans gained economic assistance and a voice in government during the New Deal. But little progress was made toward ending discrimination.**

A NEW DEAL FOR AMERICAN INDIANS

As the New Deal era began, life for many American Indians was very bleak. A late 1920s report on Indian life across the country listed numerous problems that plagued their communities. Inadequate housing, poor health care, and malnutrition left many of the nation's more than 300,000 Indians easy prey for epidemics.

Native Americans argued that their culture had been stripped away by measures like the Dawes Act (see Chapter 5), which had ended tribal government and authorized the sale of tribal land to individuals. Antonio Luhan, a member of the Taos Pueblo in New Mexico, described how government policies and the Bureau of Indian Affairs commissioners who enforced them overwhelmed traditional Indian culture:

66 We had Commissioners against us who tried to stop our ceremony dances and our [religious] dances. They nearly destroy us; call our ways bad or immoral or something, and put in the paper they are going to stop us. 99

In the 1920s Luhan had shown a white social worker named John Collier the poor living conditions in Native American communities. Deeply moved, Collier founded the **American Indian Defense Association**, which fought to protect Indians' religious freedom and tribal property. For the next decade Collier championed Indian reform efforts. In 1933 President Roosevelt appointed Collier as the new commissioner of Indian Affairs. Almost immediately Collier tried to change the government's direction by revitalizing American Indian life and culture. "Anything less than to let Indian culture live on would be a crime against the earth itself," Collier declared.

To put these reform ideas into law, Congress passed the **Indian Reorganization Act** of 1934. Reversing the Dawes Act policy, the new law tried to revive tribal rule. The act provided funds to start tribal business ventures and to pay for the college education of young Native Americans. It also ordered Congress "to promote the study of Indian civilization and preserve and develop . . . Indian arts, crafts, skills, and traditions."

▲ The Indian Reorganization Act encouraged Native Americans to preserve their cultural traditions. Shown here is Angelia La Moose, a young girl in the Flathead tribe, wearing traditional Flathead dress.

◀ This 1930 photograph shows a home on the San Xavier Indian Reservation in Arizona.

Critics complained that Collier had not obtained enough input from the tribes themselves in formulating policies and that the programs decreased the power of women in some tribes. Still, two thirds of the nation's Native American tribes voted to participate in the new programs.

■■ **New Deal policies encouraged Native Americans to reclaim and revitalize their cultural heritage.**

THE STRUGGLE FOR A PLACE IN THE SUN

Toward the end of the 1930s, a billboard appeared on Route 66 just outside Tulsa, Oklahoma, that proclaimed: "NO JOBS in California. If YOU are looking for work—KEEP OUT!" The message was clear. The market for migrant workers on the West Coast was glutted. The sign was directed at the thousands of migrant farmers from the Midwest who traveled to California in the mid-1930s. Driven off their land by the forces of nature, they sought a better life in the Southwest.

The Dust Bowl. In the mid-1930s a severe drought struck the Great Plains—the Texas and Oklahoma panhandles and parts of Colorado, New Mexico, and Kansas. As the topsoil loosened and dried, winds picked it up and turned this 50-million-acre region into a wasteland. Throughout the **Dust Bowl**, as the region came to be called, wind-borne dust clouds darkened the skies at noon and buried fences and farm machinery. Dust crept into houses through tiny cracks; ships reported great dust clouds hundreds of miles out to sea. One Texas farmer recalled:

❝ If the wind blew one way, here came the dark dust from Oklahoma. Another way and it was the gray dust from Kansas. Still another way, the brown dust from Colorado and New Mexico. Little farms were buried. And the towns were blackened. ❞

To prevent future dust bowls, the Department of Agriculture started extensive programs in soil-erosion control. The most dramatic was a shelterbelt of some 217 million trees that CCC workers planted. This windbreak stretched through the Great Plains from Texas to Canada.

By 1939 the amount of dried-out farmland had decreased dramatically. But it was too late to save the many Dust Bowl farmers who had already

(continued on page 370)

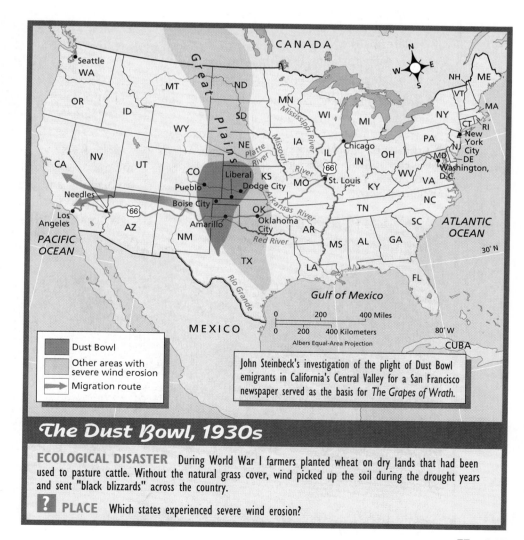

John Steinbeck's investigation of the plight of Dust Bowl emigrants in California's Central Valley for a San Francisco newspaper served as the basis for *The Grapes of Wrath*.

Dust Bowl
Other areas with severe wind erosion
Migration route

The Dust Bowl, 1930s

ECOLOGICAL DISASTER During World War I farmers planted wheat on dry lands that had been used to pasture cattle. Without the natural grass cover, wind picked up the soil during the drought years and sent "black blizzards" across the country.

? **PLACE** Which states experienced severe wind erosion?

Photographing the Depression

Many Americans at first were suspicious of the New Deal programs. The tradition of self-reliance ran deep in the United States. President Roosevelt believed that opponents of federal relief programs might change their minds if they saw the frightful conditions under which migrant farm workers and city dwellers lived. With Roosevelt's encouragement numerous federal agencies, including the Department of the Interior, the Works Progress Administration (WPA), the Department of Agriculture, and the Farm Security Administration (FSA), hired photographers in the 1930s to travel across the country and document the lives of ordinary Americans.

No agency used photography more effectively than the FSA, whose staff amassed more than 250,000 images of American life during the depression. Roy E. Stryker, head of the FSA historical section, assembled an all-star team of photographers that included Walker Evans, Ben Shahn, Arthur Rothstein, and Dorothea Lange.

▶ **Russell Lee photographed these carrot field workers in Santa Maria, Texas, waiting to begin their day.**

◀ **In Missouri, 1939, Arthur Rothstein captured the mood of this sharecropper's child after the boy's family had been evicted from their land.**

To make sure his photographers were prepared, Stryker often tutored them before sending them out on assignment. For example, former print journalist Carl Mydans was set to "go South and 'do cotton'" for the FSA. Learning that Mydans knew virtually nothing about the subject, Stryker postponed the trip. Mydans recalled what happened next:

    ❝ We sat down and we talked almost all day about cotton. We went to lunch and we went to dinner, and we talked well into the night. He [Stryker] talked about cotton as an agricultural product, cotton as a commercial product, the history of cotton in the South, what cotton did to the history of the U.S.A. and how it affected areas outside the U.S.A. By the end of that evening, I was ready to go off and photograph cotton! ❞

▶ **Migrant Mother is one of Dorothea Lange's most famous photographs of the depression.**

    Other photographers, such as Dorothea Lange, were already well grounded in understanding the social and economic forces that shaped rural Americans' lives in the 1930s. Lange often traveled for weeks at a time, working up to 14 hours a day. One of her most famous photographs, *Migrant Mother,* showed an exhausted single mother whose children subsisted chiefly on vegetables they scavenged from California fields. When it appeared in 1936, *Migrant Mother* inspired Californians to defy powerful growers' associations and insist on decent, government-sponsored housing for seasonal harvesters.

    Migrant Mother was not the only photograph to fulfill Roosevelt's goal of gaining support for government

programs. From 1936 to 1941, FSA photographs were widely published in government pamphlets and in *Time, Life,* and other magazines. The pictures prompted an outpouring of congressional and public support for federal relief.

    Today, the FSA photographs are housed in the Library of Congress and provide an invaluable source of information for historians. They are a detailed visual record of the 1930s that allows researchers today to "see" life in depression America. These photographs have thus enabled historians and citizens alike to step back in time to a crucial period in our history.

◀ **Ben Shahn photographed these rural West Virginia residents heading into Scotts Run to obtain food from relief workers in 1935.**

▲ Many Japanese Americans on the West Coast were also among those who competed for work as migrant field laborers. These men labored in sugar fields.

lost their land. Packing their meager belongings into battered old cars or trucks, they headed west on Route 66, bound for what they saw as a land of promise—California and other parts of the West Coast. There they hoped to find work picking crops. Thousands of them made the trek, and since many came from Oklahoma, they picked up the nickname **Okies**. Once they reached the West Coast, however, they found themselves in desperate competition with other farm laborers looking for work.

Competition for migrant work.
Even before the Dust Bowl refugees started arriving, Mexican Americans had been having a hard time finding work in the West. Like African Americans, Mexican Americans often found themselves the victims of discrimination in many New Deal programs. For example, although the CCC did not segregate Mexican Americans, some complained that they were harassed by camp officials, denied clothing, and assigned to kitchen duty more often than non-Hispanics.

Many families continued to seek what little work they could find as migrant farm laborers. A 1935 California survey found that the average income of Mexican American families had fallen below $300 a year. César Chávez, who later became a noted labor leader, recalled growing up in a depression-era migrant family:

Mexican Americans also faced job competition from Filipino laborers. During the 1920s the Filipino population of California had grown to more than 30,000. Like Mexican American migrants, most Filipinos worked in agriculture. When the depression hit, both groups faced tough economic times, but the Filipino workers attempted to combat decreasing wages by organizing. Throughout the early 1930s the Filipino Labor Union launched a series of strikes to protest wage reductions. In 1936 the American Federation of Labor sponsored the Field Workers Union, a combined organization for Mexican American and Filipino laborers.

The unions were able to keep wages from falling too much. However, as more Okies arrived, competition for migrant work increased. Thus life for all migrants remained difficult.

▪▪ Dust Bowl refugees moved to the West, where they competed with Mexican Americans and Filipinos for migrant farm work.

*P*ICTURING THE FACE OF THE DEPRESSION

The grim experiences of migrants and others in rural America provided rich subject matter for documentary filmmakers and photographers. These artists created a memorable visual record of the New Deal era. Better than any words could do, their images of the slumped shoulders of

▲ FSA photographer Carl Mydans captured the devastation of soil erosion in Kentucky in 1936.

sharecroppers in rural Alabama; African American Gordon Parks, who later became a filmmaker; international photojournalist Margaret Bourke-White; and Dorothea Lange, probably the best-known of the FSA photographers.

 Lange was one of the most talented photographers of the depression era. Born in Hoboken, New Jersey, she decided in her late teens to become a photographer. After studying the craft for several years, she set out to tour the world and record her impressions. Lange was out of money by the time she reached San Francisco, however, so she stayed and opened a portrait studio.

When the depression struck, Lange began to take pictures of the homeless men wandering the streets of San Francisco. Soon the federal government hired her to photograph migrant farmers in California. Her pictures, which carry captions in the farmers' own words, revealed the migrants' poverty and suffering, as well as their great dignity. Lange's most famous picture, *Migrant Mother* (see page 369), is considered a masterpiece.

The Granger Collection, New York

Dorothea Lange

During World War II, Lange continued her documentary work by taking pictures of Japanese Americans in California internment camps. Later she produced photo essays for *Life* magazine and traveled the world taking pictures. By the time of her death in 1965, she ranked as one of the world's foremost photographers.

unemployed men, the staring faces of children, and the worried expressions of prematurely aged women conveyed the human suffering of the era.

In 1936 and 1937 the filmmaker Pare Lorentz directed two documentary films on the era. *The River* depicts the TVA and its effect on the surrounding regions, while *The Plow That Broke the Plains* portrays the devastation of the Dust Bowl. Using few images of people, the films rely heavily on background music and an unseen narrator to enhance the visual images of the depression's impact on the landscape.

In the late 1930s the Farm Security Administration recruited a group of photographers to record American rural life. These photographers included Walker Evans, who depicted life among

---

SECTION 3 REVIEW

IDENTIFY and explain the significance of the following: Marian Anderson, Robert C. Weaver, Mary McLeod Bethune, Antonio Luhan, John Collier, American Indian Defense Association, Indian Reorganization Act, Okies, Dorothea Lange.

LOCATE and explain the importance of the following: Dust Bowl.

1. **MAIN IDEA** How did the New Deal affect African Americans during the 1930s?

2. **MAIN IDEA** How did the Indian Reorganization Act benefit Native Americans?

3. **LINKING HISTORY AND GEOGRAPHY** What factors caused the Dust Bowl during the 1930s?

4. **WRITING TO DESCRIBE** Imagine you are an Okie migrating west in 1939. Write a diary entry describing your experiences on the West Coast.

5. **ANALYZING** How did filmmakers, such as Pare Lorentz, and photographers, such as Dorothea Lange, serve as social critics during the 1930s?

THE NEW DEAL AND THE ARTS

FOCUS

- How did Federal Project No. 1 aid writers and artists?
- What were many novels like in the late 1930s?
- What common themes were often heard and seen in music, plays, and paintings of the New Deal era?

In attempting to put Americans back to work, the Roosevelt administration did not forget about those who worked in the arts. The WPA established a series of programs to employ writers, actors, musicians, painters, and other artists. Meanwhile literature in the late 1930s began to turn from escapist fantasies to realistic portrayals of the depression, while musicians, playwrights, and painters searched for uniquely American subject matter.

1936 poster for
WPA production, *Macbeth*

THE WPA PROGRAMS

All workers struggled with unemployment in depression-era America, including artists. Without an audience that could afford to buy their work, most of the nation's writers, stage actors, musicians, and painters lost their means of earning an income. Like workers in other fields, they sought relief from the government. In February 1935 a few writers picketed federal offices in New York City, carrying signs that read "CHILDREN NEED BOOKS. WRITERS NEED BREAD. WE DEMAND PROJECTS."

Later that year, the WPA set aside some $300 million to create **Federal Project No. 1**. This program tried to encourage pride in American culture by aiding unemployed artists in the fields of writing, theater, music, and visual arts.

The WPA's **Federal Writers' Project** (FWP) hired some 6,600 unemployed writers to produce a variety of works, including state travel guides and histories of various ethnic groups. Others conducted oral-history interviews with hundreds of elderly former slaves. Historians still use these sources to study slave life. Members of the project also studied American folklore and wrote down folktales. These eventually became the basis for the best-selling *Treasury of American Folklore* (1944). The FWP eventually won praise as the "biggest literary project in history," producing more than 1,000 books

◀ **Unemployed and striking actors picketed outside the hotel where heads of the regional, state, and national offices of the WPA met in July 1939.**

and pamphlets. It also helped launch the careers of numerous writers who went on to great success, such as John Steinbeck and Richard Wright.

The WPA's Federal Theatre Project hired unemployed actors, directors, designers, stagehands, and playwrights to encourage theatrical productions. It entertained millions of Americans, bringing productions to many small towns that had never experienced live theater. The Federal Music Project hired musicians to form orchestras and present some 4,000 musical productions per month to audiences across the country. It also hired music researchers to write down popular American folk songs. The Federal Arts Project hired unemployed artists and designers to produce posters for New Deal programs and to teach art in public schools. Others painted murals on public buildings constructed by the PWA.

■■ **Federal Project No. 1 employed various writers and artists and spread their work throughout the country.**

LITERATURE IN THE LATE 1930s

American interest in romantic fiction continued into the late 1930s. One of the best-selling novels of the decade was Margaret Mitchell's *Gone with the Wind* (1936), a sweeping story of the Old South during the Civil War and Reconstruction. Many depression-era readers could relate to the turmoil faced by the novel's main character, Scarlett O'Hara, who survives war and economic chaos. Her uplifting closing line, "After all, tomorrow is another day," inspired readers of the 1930s.

By the end of the decade, many writers had incorporated the experiences of the depression into their works. John Steinbeck, a writer employed by the FWP, produced a gripping picture of the depression era in *The Grapes of Wrath* (1939). The story follows the fortunes of a desperately poor Dust Bowl family as they travel to California:

❝ As the dark caught them, they clustered like bugs near to shelter and to water. And because they were lonely . . . , because they had all come from a place of sadness and . . . were all going to a new mysterious place, they huddled together. ❞

▲ Some three years in the planning, MGM's production of *Gone with the Wind* was the most eagerly awaited and top-grossing film of 1939.

As it was for the real Okies, life in California is lonely and harsh for Steinbeck's fictional migrant family. Like *Gone with the Wind*, however, Steinbeck's novel includes a hopeful note, as the head of the family, Ma Joad, optimistically states, "They ain't gonna wipe us out. Why, we're the people—we go on."

Other novels described the experiences of ethnic minorities in the era. African American anthropologist Zora Neale Hurston wrote *Their Eyes Were Watching God* (1937), which explores a black woman's search for fulfillment in rural Florida. Richard Wright offered a grim picture of black urban life in *Native Son* (1940), which

◄ *Native Son* by Richard Wright

▶ *Their Eyes Were Watching God* by Zora Neale Hurston

chronicles the journey of a young African American man lost in a racist world where he can never succeed. *Native Son* explores several themes that haunted the 1930s, including class differences, socialism, racism, and urban despair.

▪▪ Many novels of the late 1930s reflected the experiences of the depression.

*P*ERFORMING ARTS IN THE NEW DEAL ERA

American music of the late 1930s increasingly tried to capture uniquely American sounds. As WPA researchers wrote down American folk songs and folktales, composer Aaron Copland used these themes as the basis for his most popular compositions, including *Billy the Kid* (1938).

▲ Paper fan depicting singer Mahalia Jackson

Interest in African American music continued throughout the 1930s. Black gospel, a cross between jazz and traditional spirituals, gained popularity through the work of African American composer Thomas A. Dorsey —whose songs included "Precious Lord, Take My Hand"—and singers such as Sister Rosetta Tharpe and Mahalia Jackson. Jackson recalled that some ministers initially objected to this new style of music:

> 66 They didn't like the hand-clapping and the stomping and they said we were bringing jazz into the church and it wasn't dignified. Once at church one of the preachers got up in the pulpit and spoke out against me. I got right up, too. I told him I was born to sing gospel music. 99

Jazz continued its rise in popularity, largely because of the development of swing, a smooth big-band style popular in dance halls. The style derived its name from Duke Ellington's 1932 hit "It Don't Mean a Thing If It Ain't Got That Swing." White conductor Benny Goodman helped popularize swing in the late 1930s. He also broke new ground in popular music by integrating his shows with both black and white performers. Meanwhile, other bands, such as those of Count Basie and Glenn Miller, kept the swing sound alive throughout the 1930's.

On the theatrical stage, plays with social significance—that is, plays that dealt with the nation's labor and class problems—drew large audiences. Robert Sherwood's *The Petrified Forest* (1935) attacked the "petrified forest" of ideas destroying America. Lillian Hellman's *The Little Foxes* (1939) exposed the upper-class greed that many believed was undermining America. By the end of the decade, popular plays, like popular music, focused increasingly on American traditions and values. Two examples are Thornton Wilder's *Our Town* (1938), a heartwarming drama of life and death in a small American town around 1900, and William Saroyan's *The Time of Your Life* (1939), which celebrates the diversity of urban America.

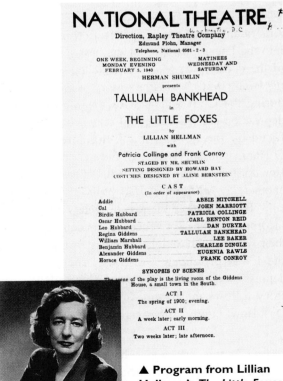

▲ Program from Lillian Hellman's *The Little Foxes*

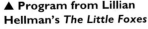

◀ Lillian Hellman

■■ **Music—folk songs, gospel, and jazz—and plays—socially significant and traditional—reflected uniquely American styles and themes.**

PAINTERS EXAMINE LOCAL CULTURE

Like American writers, painters recorded a variety of memorable American images during the depression. Harlem artist Jacob Lawrence portrayed the daily lives of African American heroes, such as Frederick Douglass and Harriet Tubman, while New Mexico artist Georgia O'Keeffe painted haunting images of the southwestern desert landscape.

Perhaps reflecting the New Deal's focus on farmers' problems, many artists of the era looked to rural America for their subject matter. A group of midwestern artists known as the **regionalists** stressed local folk themes and customs. The regionalists included artists such as Thomas Hart Benton of Missouri, John Steuart Curry of Kansas, and Grant Wood of Iowa.

These artists reminded urban art lovers of America's rural traditions. Wood always insisted that his best ideas "came while milking a cow." The most famous of the regionalist paintings is probably Wood's *American Gothic,* which depicts a stern farmer, pitchfork in hand,

▲ Paintings of rustic scenes, such as *Sugaring Off* by Anna "Grandma" Moses, were typical of regionalists and other folk artists of the depression era.

Grandma Moses: Sugaring Off. Copyright © 1992 Grandma Moses Properties Co., New York

standing beside a sad-eyed woman in front of a humble farmhouse.

As interest in regional culture grew, people rediscovered the richness of American folk art, such as handmade quilts and woodcarvings. Many obscure folk artists, including the elderly painter Anna "Grandma" Moses, became wellknown during this period.

■■ **American painters, led by the regionalists, explored a diversity of local folk life.**

SECTION 4 REVIEW

IDENTIFY and explain the significance of the following: Federal Project No. 1, Federal Writers' Project, Margaret Mitchell, John Steinbeck, Zora Neale Hurston, Richard Wright, Aaron Copland, Thomas A. Dorsey, Benny Goodman, Robert Sherwood, Lillian Hellman, Thornton Wilder, Jacob Lawrence, Georgia O'Keeffe, regionalists, Anna "Grandma" Moses.

1. **MAIN IDEA** Why was Federal Project No. 1 created?

2. **MAIN IDEA** What contribution did regionalists make to American painting?

3. **COMPARING** What common themes did music and plays of the 1930s share?

4. **WRITING TO CREATE** Write a promotional piece for *The Grapes of Wrath, Their Eyes Were Watching God,* or *Native Son* that shows how the novel reflects the experiences of the depression.

5. **ANALYZING** How were the experiences of African Americans expressed artistically during the New Deal era?

FDR declares bank holiday. Congress passes 15 New Deal measures.

Southern Tenant Farmers' Union formed. Indian Reorganization Act passed.

Social Security Act, Wealth Tax Act, and Wagner-Connery Act passed. CIO organized. Mary McLeod Bethune helps form National Council of Negro Women. Federal Project No. 1 created.

1933　　　　　　　　　　　　　　　　**1935**

WRITING A SUMMARY

Using the essential points of the chapter as a guide, write a summary of the chapter.

REVIEWING CHRONOLOGY

Number your paper 1 to 5. Study the time line above, and list the following events in the order in which they happened by writing the first next to 1, the second next to 2, and so on. Then complete the activity below.

1. Aaron Copland composes *Billy the Kid*.
2. CIO organized.
3. Richard Wright's *Native Son* published.
4. FDR declares bank holiday.
5. Indian Reorganization Act passed.

Assessing Consequences How did Mary McLeod Bethune help maximize the participation of African Americans in the New Deal?

IDENTIFYING PEOPLE AND IDEAS

Explain the historical significance of each of the following people or terms.

1. New Deal
2. Frances Perkins
3. subsidies
4. Zora Neale Hurston
5. Wealth Tax Act
6. sit-down strike
7. Robert C. Weaver
8. John Collier
9. Dust Bowl
10. Huey Long

UNDERSTANDING MAIN IDEAS

1. What was the purpose of the bank holiday and the FDIC?
2. How were the economic and social programs of the Second New Deal different from those of the First New Deal?
3. What steps did the government take in the 1930s to aid farmers?
4. How did the New Deal affect African Americans and Native Americans?
5. What contributions did Pare Lorentz and Dorothea Lange make to the New Deal era?

REVIEWING THEMES

1. **Economic Development** How did the Roosevelt administration attempt to promote economic recovery?
2. **Constitutional Heritage** Why might the Supreme Court have declared some New Deal measures unconstitutional?
3. **Cultural Diversity** How did writers and artists of the 1930s reflect the ethnic and cultural diversity of the nation?

THINKING CRITICALLY

1. **Analyzing** Why did some conservative and liberal critics oppose the New Deal?
2. **Evaluating** Do you think that Roosevelt was justified in trying to "pack" the Supreme Court? Why or why not?
3. **Assessing Consequences** How did WPA programs enrich American culture during the 1930s?

STRATEGY FOR SUCCESS

Review the Skills Handbook entry on Identifying the Main Idea beginning on page 748. Examine the photograph below, taken by Margaret Bourke-White in 1937. These residents of Louisville, Kentucky, are waiting in a relief line to receive aid. What contrasts can you see between the experiences of the people in the line and the message on the billboard behind them?

WORLD'S HIGHEST STANDARD OF LIVING

There's no way like the American Way

Margaret Mitchell's *Gone with the Wind* published. FDR reelected president.

FDR tries to "pack" Supreme Court. Farm Security Administration created. GM strike begins.

Second AAA passed. Aaron Copland composes *Billy the Kid*. Thornton Wilder's *Our Town* opens.

John Steinbeck's *The Grapes of Wrath* published. Lillian Hellman's play *The Little Foxes* opens.

Richard Wright's *Native Son* published.

WRITING ABOUT HISTORY

Writing to Classify Create a chart that classifies the programs of the New Deal according to whether they were designed primarily to help banks, farmers, labor, or business.

USING PRIMARY SOURCES

Mexican American Jesse Perez worked for the meat-packing industry in Chicago in 1939, during a time when the CIO was attempting to organize workers in the stockyards. Read the following statement, which comes from an interview Perez did at that time with a member of the Federal Writers' Project. What does Perez have to say about the company's treatment of workers who joined the union during this time? How does Perez view the CIO?

> 66 *I was first to wear CIO button; ever since I start wearing the button they start to pick. I can butcher, but they don't give me job. . . . So when I start telling the boys we have a union for them, almost all join right away. We talk all the time what the union going to do for us, going to raise wages, stop speed-up. The bosses watch and they know it's a union coming.*
>
> *So every day they start saying we behind in the work. They start speeding up the boys more and more every day. . . . We told bosses we working too fast, can't keep up. The whole gang, thirteen men, all stop. Bosses say, we ain't standing for nothing like this. Four days later they fire the whole gang, except two. We took the case in the labor board and . . . now all who was fired got work.*
>
> *Now the bosses try to provoke strike before CIO get ready. . . . We know what they do, we don't talk back, got to watch out they don't play tricks like that.* 99

LINKING HISTORY AND GEOGRAPHY

Describing the effects of the Dust Bowl, John Steinbeck wrote: "The Western States are nervous under the beginning change. . . . A half-million people moving over the country; a million more, restive [restless] to move; ten million more feeling the first nervousness." How did the Dust Bowl influence population shifts in the Southwest?

Scene from the film *The Grapes of Wrath*, 1939

BUILDING YOUR PORTFOLIO

Complete the following projects independently or cooperatively.

1. THE ECONOMY In chapters 11, 12, and 13, you examined the U.S. economy in the 1920s. Building on that experience, imagine you are a New Deal legislator. Write a proposal for a new public works project. Your proposal should describe what the project is, how workers and businesses will benefit, and why your project will be useful to society in terms of relief, recovery, or reform.

2. CULTURE AND SOCIETY In chapters 11 and 12 you explored U.S. society in the 1920s. Building on that experience, imagine you are an author in the 1930s. Write a short, realistic passage for your novel that describes the Dust Bowl's effect on your main character.

BETWEEN THE WARS

FOCUS

UNDERSTANDING THE MAIN IDEA

After World War I many Americans hoped to focus on matters at home. Unfortunately, the depression touched off global economic problems. The rise of dictators in Europe set the stage for another war. Dictators also came to power in several Latin American countries. Other countries in Latin America, such as Nicaragua and Mexico, attempted to reduce U.S. influence.

THEMES

■ **GLOBAL RELATIONS** How might nations work together to promote world peace?

■ **ECONOMIC DEVELOPMENT** What economic problems might wars create? What political problems might result from these economic difficulties?

■ **DEMOCRATIC VALUES** What conditions might give rise to a dictatorship?

1921	1926	1931	1933	1939
Washington Conference begins.	Augusto Sandino organizes revolt in Nicaragua.	Japan invades Manchuria.	Adolf Hitler becomes chancellor of Germany.	World War II starts.

Nazi parade watchers, 1932

"One word . . . describes the whole feeling in America to-day, and that is *disillusionment* [disappointment]: disillusionment in the leaders, disillusionment in the business men, disillusionment in politics," wrote a friend to British prime minister David Lloyd George in January 1932. This feeling of pessimism arose from the economic strains of the depression and the international chaos caused by World War I. Instead of bringing peace, the end of the war ushered in a period of economic and political instability in Europe.

Many Americans feared that involvement in European affairs might draw the United States into another war. In 1937 the magazine *Christian Century* estimated that "ninety-nine Americans out of a hundred would today regard as an imbecile anyone who might suggest that, in the event of another European war, the United States should again participate in it." In general, the United States backed down from military intervention in foreign countries in the 1920s and 1930s. American efforts on the world stage focused on reducing weapons and improving relations with Latin America.

Nevertheless, conditions brewing in Europe and Asia would soon doom hopes for world peace. In Italy, Germany, and Spain, ruthless dictators came to power by promising to make their countries great through foreign conquest. In Japan, militaristic dreams of empire threatened U.S. interests in China and the Pacific. When the aggressor nations formed an alliance, the stage was set for global war.

The Granger Collection, New York

Antiwar sheet music, 1940

THE SEARCH FOR PEACE

FOCUS

- **Why did the United States pursue an isolationist foreign policy after World War I?**
- **How did the United States try to promote world peace in the 1920s and 1930s?**
- **How did war debts and reparations affect European countries after World War I?**

Profoundly disillusioned by the Great War, the United States sought to promote world peace during the 1920s. Fear of becoming involved in another war caused Americans to try to avoid conflict at any cost. As the world slipped into an economic depression and as dictators rose to power in Europe in the 1930s, however, isolation from the world's problems proved increasingly difficult for the United States.

Peace activists, 1940

LEGACIES OF WORLD WAR I

Over 8 million people, including more than 112,000 Americans, had died fighting in the Great War. Yet, because of the postwar chaos in Europe and the founding of a Communist government in the Soviet Union, Americans did not believe that the war had made the world "safe for democracy." The Women's International League for Peace and Freedom summed up the nation's doubts: "War to end war has proved a failure. The war is won, yet nowhere is there peace, security or happiness."

Americans worried about being dragged into another foreign conflict. "We ask only to live our own life in our own way, in friendship and sympathy with all, in alliance with none," declared Senator Hiram W. Johnson in 1922. Such sentiments led the United States to follow a policy of partial **isolationism**, or withdrawal from world affairs, in the 1920s and 1930s.

Isolationists did not want to cut off the United States completely from the affairs of the rest of the world. They merely wanted to avoid what Thomas Jefferson had called "entangling alliances" that could drag the United States into another war. Isolationists also supported U.S. **unilateralism**, that is, one-sided or independent action in foreign affairs.

Isolationism and unilateralism led the United States to shun membership in international organizations set up after the war, such as the League of Nations and the Permanent Court of International Justice (the World Court).

Presidents Coolidge, Hoover, and Roosevelt all proposed that the United States join the World Court, created to solve international disputes. Public opinion, however, ran strongly against membership. The Senate set strict terms for joining in order to guard its right to make treaties. The nations that already belonged to the World Court rejected the Senate's terms, and the matter was dropped.

PROMOTING PEACE

Instead of joining international peacekeeping organizations, the United States used diplomacy to promote world peace. American peace groups urged the U.S. government to bring world leaders together to negotiate **disarmament**, or limiting their weapons. Jane Addams, Emily Greene Balch, Jeannette Rankin, and other leaders of the women's movement played important roles in these peace efforts. For their organizing efforts in the United States and abroad, both Addams (in 1931) and Balch (in 1946) received the Nobel Peace Prize.

The Washington Conference. In Washington, D.C., beginning in November 1921, the United States hosted an international conference on naval disarmament and Pacific security. The meeting was organized by Charles Evans Hughes, the U.S. secretary of state. Born in April 1862, he had served as governor of New York and almost won the 1916 presidential election against Woodrow Wilson. After this crushing defeat—Hughes had gone to bed on election night believing himself the victor only to wake and learn he had lost the nation's most important office by a scant 23 electoral votes—he turned to the issue

Charles Evans Hughes

of world peace. Ironically, he supported American entry into the League of Nations, the brainchild of his old enemy Wilson.

At the Washington Conference Hughes surprised the other delegates with his bold proposal that the major powers scrap 78 large warships amounting to almost 1.9 million tons. He also called for a 10-year "naval holiday" during which no battleships or battle cruisers would be built.

Hughes proposed that the United States, Great Britain, and Japan scrap enough large warships to bring their naval strength into a ratio of 5:5:3. That is, Great Britain and the United States would be equal in naval strength, with a large-warship tonnage of roughly 525,000 each, while Japan would have some 315,000 tons. Italy and France would both be limited to some 175,000 tons. This plan became known as the **Five Power Agreement.** Marveled one observer: "Secretary Hughes sank in 35 minutes more ships than all the admirals of the world have sunk in . . . centuries."

The Washington Conference produced other important agreements as well. In the **Four Power Treaty**, Japan, Great Britain, France, and the United States pledged to respect one another's territory in the Pacific. The **Nine Power Treaty**, which included the nations that signed the Five Power agreement as well as the Netherlands, Portugal, Belgium, and China, guaranteed China's territorial integrity and promised to uphold the Open Door policy.

Japan's navy minister, Admiral Kato Tomosaburo, declared that the conference had created "a new order of seapower." He explained Japan's support for disarmament:

> 66 Japan is ready for the new order of thought—the spirit of international friendship and cooperation for the greater good of humanity—which the Conference has brought about. 99

For a time the Washington Conference agreements eased tensions in Asia. Japan withdrew, at least partially, from the Shandong (Shantung) Peninsula it had invaded in 1914 and from parts of Siberia it had occupied during the Russian Revolution. In 1930 Japan's agreement to extend

▲ **Delegates from Great Britain, France, Belgium, Italy, the Netherlands, Portugal, China, Japan, and the United States attended the Washington Conference.**

the holiday on warship construction marked the high point of postwar international cooperation.

Unsuccessful efforts. On April 6, 1927, the 10th anniversary of America's entry into World War I, the French foreign minister, Aristide Briand (ah-ree-steed bree-ahn), proposed that France and the United States enter into an agreement to outlaw war as a means of resolving their differences. The U.S. secretary of state, Frank Kellogg, made a counter-proposal that the pact include all nations. Sixty-two countries eventually signed the **Kellogg-Briand Pact**, which outlawed war "as an instrument of national policy" but allowed countries to go to war in self-defense. Unfortunately, the treaty lacked provisions for enforcement. One U.S. senator remarked that the treaty was "as effective to keep down war as a carpet would be to smother an earthquake."

▪▪ Through diplomatic conferences and international agreements the United States worked for world peace.

The pact's weaknesses became clear in September 1931. Japan, whose military leaders were gaining influence, violated all the international agreements and invaded the Chinese territory of Manchuria (see map on page 395). This invasion launched a bloody war between Japan and China. Although many Americans called for

▲ Suffragist and peace activist Carrie Chapman Catt praised the Kellogg-Briand Pact and lobbied Congress for its passage.

▲ These Japanese cavalrymen were photographed in Manchuria in December 1931, some three months after the war between China and Japan had begun.

an economic boycott of Japan, U.S. leaders refused to support sanctions against the Japanese. The failure of diplomacy to prevent Japanese aggression marked the end of attempts at international agreements. Preoccupied by the Japanese invasion and the worldwide economic depression, delegates of the League of Nations' 1932 World Disarmament Conference went home without agreeing to reduce weapons.

WAR DEBTS AND REPARATIONS

The issue of war debts also weakened peace efforts. In the late 1800s European investors had financed U.S. industrial growth, making the United States a **debtor nation** with respect to Europe. After 1914, however, the United States became a **creditor nation**. At the start of World War I, U.S. banks lent money to Great Britain and France so that they could buy armaments in the United States. The U.S. government granted billions more in credit to the Allies. By 1920 the Allies owed more than $10 billion to the United States.

The debtor nations argued that their debts to the United States should be wiped out. David Lloyd George, who had been the British prime minister when the United States entered the war, said:

❝ The United States did not from first to last make any sacrifice or contribution remotely comparable to those of her European Associates, in life, limb, money, material or trade, towards the victory which she shared with them. ❞

U.S. officials rejected appeals from Great Britain, France, and Italy to cancel all their war debts. However, the U.S. government reduced the interest rates on the loans and canceled part of the debts. Still, the only way the Allies could pay their war debts to the United States was to collect reparations, or damages, from defeated Germany. In 1921 a reparations commission had set total German reparations at 132 billion gold marks ($32 billion). The Germans bitterly condemned the reparations as too harsh. Chancellor Joseph Wirth paid part of the reparations by borrowing money from Great Britain. The German government also printed paper money, causing massive inflation as the value of the German mark plunged.

In 1931, as the worldwide depression deepened, President Herbert Hoover declared a year's **moratorium**, or halt, on reparation and war-debt payments. The moratorium, however, only prolonged the crisis. Most of the war debts remained

▲ During the 1920s rapid inflation in Germany made most currency worthless. This woman used several million-mark notes to start a breakfast fire.

unpaid. By 1934 none of the debtor nations except Finland could make even a token payment.

America's efforts to collect the war debts sowed resentment in Europe. In Germany the economic hardships created by the reparations made people especially bitter. With his country near financial collapse, Adolf Hitler, a young German politician, hatched a plot to overthrow the German government in 1923. The plot failed, and Hitler was sent to jail. The next year, an international plan temporarily eased Germany's economic crisis by providing loans and extending German debt payments. Continuing German anger over reparations, however, would help bring Hitler to power 10 years later.

■■ **Europeans resented America's efforts to collect war debts. German anger over reparations helped Adolf Hitler gain support.**

SECTION 1 REVIEW

IDENTIFY and explain the significance of the following: isolationism, unilateralism, disarmament, Emily Greene Balch, Charles Evans Hughes, Five Power Agreement, Four Power Treaty, Nine Power Treaty, Kellogg-Briand Pact, debtor nation, creditor nation, moratorium.

LOCATE and explain the importance of the following: Manchuria.

1. **MAIN IDEA** Why did the United States partially withdraw from world affairs in the 1920s and 1930s?

2. **MAIN IDEA** What steps did the United States take to work for world peace?

3. **ASSESSING CONSEQUENCES** How did war debts and reparations affect Germany and other European countries?

4. **WRITING TO INFORM** Imagine you are a delegate to the Washington Conference in 1921. Write an essay outlining the goals and accomplishments of the conference.

5. **ANALYZING** Why was the Kellogg-Briand Pact unsuccessful in resolving the conflict in Manchuria?

RELATIONS WITH LATIN AMERICA

FOCUS

■ How did **U.S. relations with Latin America** change in the 1930s?

■ How did the **Great Depression affect Latin American countries?**

■ What role did the **United States play in Nicaraguan politics?**

■ How did the **United States respond when Mexico took over the Mexican oil industry?**

Woman picking coffee beans in El Salvador

In the 1920s and 1930s the United States preferred to use economic influence—dollar diplomacy—rather than military force to protect its interests in Latin America. For example, conflict between the Mexican government and U.S. oil companies was solved through diplomacy. However, when U.S. interests faced threats in Nicaragua, America sent in the marines.

THE GOOD NEIGHBOR

While the United States tried to avoid war in Europe, presidents Coolidge, Hoover, and Roosevelt all tried to improve relations with Latin American countries. Before his inauguration, Hoover toured Latin America to promote goodwill. Franklin D. Roosevelt spelled out the **Good Neighbor policy** in his inaugural speech of 1933:

> 66 In the field of world policy I would dedicate this nation to the policy of the good neighbor—the neighbor who resolutely respects himself and, because he does so, respects the rights of others. 99

To back up his words, Roosevelt in 1934 canceled the Platt Amendment, by which the United States had claimed the right to intervene in Cuba's affairs. Two years later he gave up the U.S. claim to intervene unilaterally in Panama. Roosevelt also withdrew marines from Haiti, where they had been stationed as an occupying

force since 1915. However, in economic matters the United States often behaved more like an overbearing landlord than a good neighbor.

U.S. investors played a powerful, and sometimes negative, role in Latin America. After World War I, large U.S. companies increased their investments in banana, coffee, and sugar plantations in Central America and the Caribbean.

■■ **In the 1930s the United States pledged to reduce military intervention in Latin America. U.S. business investment continued, however.**

The largest of the American companies was the United Fruit Company, which owned millions of acres in Central America and the Caribbean. In Guatemala it was the largest landowner, exporter, and employer. Besides establishing plantations, United Fruit and other companies built roads and railroads and controlled the ports and shipping lines necessary to export their products. They also tied these regions to the world economy, though

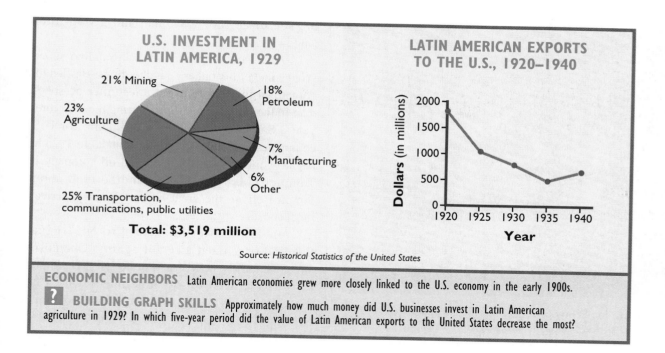

U.S. INVESTMENT IN LATIN AMERICA, 1929

21% Mining
23% Agriculture
18% Petroleum
7% Manufacturing
6% Other
25% Transportation, communications, public utilities

Total: $3,519 million

LATIN AMERICAN EXPORTS TO THE U.S., 1920–1940

Dollars (in millions) / Year

Source: *Historical Statistics of the United States*

ECONOMIC NEIGHBORS Latin American economies grew more closely linked to the U.S. economy in the early 1900s.

? BUILDING GRAPH SKILLS Approximately how much money did U.S. businesses invest in Latin American agriculture in 1929? In which five-year period did the value of Latin American exports to the United States decrease the most?

profits went mostly to the corporations and wealthy Latin Americans.

In addition to their economic importance in Latin America, the U.S. companies had political power. They made alliances with Latin American landowners and politicians and often played a role in governing the countries in which they operated. The economic and political powers of the large American companies earned them the resentment of many Latin Americans. Chilean poet Pablo Neruda (nay-ROO-thah) wrote:

> **66** The Fruit Company, Inc.
> reserved for itself the most
> succulent,
> the central coast of my own land,
> the delicate waist of America.
> It rechristened its territories
> as the "Banana Republics." **99**

"Banana republics" were countries run largely to serve the interests of the foreign companies that grew bananas and other crops.

THE RISE OF DICTATORS

The Wall Street crash of 1929 sent shock waves through Latin America. Worldwide depression meant lower prices for coffee, bananas, and other crops on which Latin American economies depended. In El Salvador, coffee prices fell so low

that some plantation owners did not bother to harvest the 1930 coffee crop. Farm wages dropped to eight cents a day.

As workers lost their jobs, the gulf between Latin America's small class of wealthy landowners and the large class of poor landless people widened. The U.S. diplomat Major A. R. Harris commented on the inequality he noted between the classes in El Salvador in 1931:

> **66** The first thing one observes . . . is the number of expensive automobiles on the streets. . . . There seems to be nothing between these high-priced cars and the ox-cart with its barefooted attendant. . . . Roughly 90 percent of the wealth of the country is held by about one-half of one percent of the population. **99**

In countries throughout the region, the difficult 1930s brought **caudillos** (kow-THEE-yohs) to power. These caudillos were military leaders who used force to maintain order. In 1932 the caudillo Maximiliano Hernández Martínez brutally crushed a revolt by peasants in El Salvador's hard-hit coffee-growing region. Thousands of peasants were massacred.

During the 1930s caudillos also came to power in Cuba, the Dominican Republic, Guatemala, and Honduras. U.S. diplomats sometimes denounced the caudillos' methods of staying in power: bans on opposition parties and restrictions

▲ **U.S. Army cooks buy produce from Nicaraguan vendors. The baskets contain papayas and alligator pears.**

on freedom of speech. However, the United States often supported the caudillos, since they created favorable environments for U.S. businesses.

■ The depression wrecked Latin American economies, caused social unrest, and helped bring caudillos to power in many countries.

INTERVENTION IN NICARAGUA

The United States played a large role in Nicaraguan politics throughout the 1920s and 1930s. In 1925 General Emiliano Chamorro (chah-MAWR-roh) overthrew the government, sparking a bitter civil war.

The United States refused to recognize Chamorro. In May 1926 President Coolidge sent in the marines to protect U.S. commercial interests. He also sent Henry Stimson, a long-time public official, to negotiate an end to the civil war. Stimson brought the two sides together and they negotiated a peace treaty in May 1927. More important, Stimson called for the abolition of Nicaraguan armed forces. U.S. troops would then train a new Nicaraguan National Guard to maintain order after the withdrawal of U.S. forces.

Augusto César Sandino (sahn-DEE-noh), a general who opposed Chamorro, refused to accept Stimson's proposal. Born in 1893, Sandino was the son of an Indian woman and a well-to-do landowner.

After attending high school, Sandino supervised some of his father's landholdings. He fled his hometown in 1920 to avoid arrest after he shot a man in the leg during a fight. During the next three years, Sandino worked as a mechanic for U.S. companies in Honduras and Guatemala. In 1923 he began working for a U.S.–owned oil company in Tampico, Mexico. There Sandino read about Simon Bolívar, the great hero of Latin American independence struggles.

In 1926, after his return to Nicaragua, Sandino organized a revolt against Chamorro and Chamorro's successor, Adolfo Díaz. He hoped to rid Nicaragua of the Americans, whom he viewed as invaders, and to allow ordinary Nicaraguans to control their country's land and wealth. He planned to help workers and peasants "exploit our own natural resources for the benefit of the Nicaraguan family in general."

Sandino's army, which varied from as few as 30 to as many as 3,000, proved a tough adversary for the U.S. Marines. Although the Americans used aerial bombing for the first time against Sandino's forces, they could not completely destroy the army, which relied on sympathetic farmers to feed and house them.

The marines never defeated Sandino. The war became increasingly costly for the United States in the midst of the depression. In 1933 President Hoover withdrew the last of the U.S. troops. A year later, the commander of the U.S.–trained National Guard, General Anastasio Somoza, ordered Sandino's assassination. With Sandino dead, organized resistance to Somoza and his military evaporated. Somoza forced out the Nicaraguan president in 1936 and took over the presidency the next year. With U.S. backing, Somoza and other members of his family ruled Nicaragua almost without interruption until the Sandinista revolution (named for Sandino) overthrew the dynasty in 1979.

▲ **Augusto César Sandino**

▲ **President Lázaro Cárdenas (center) is shown with Britain's minister to Mexico (left) and Mexico's secretary of foreign relations (right) shortly before diplomatic relations between Mexico and Great Britain were broken in May 1938.**

■■ **The United States opposed Sandino and trained the National Guard, which helped bring Somoza to power.**

RELATIONS WITH MEXICO

The most severe test of the Good Neighbor policy came when Mexico's president, Lázaro Cárdenas (KAHR-thay-nahs), began to **nationalize**, or assert government control over, the country's oil industry in March 1938. Although the Mexican Constitution of 1917 proclaimed that Mexico controlled all its underground resources (see Chapter 19), U.S. and British firms had continued to own and operate oil companies in Mexico. When the foreign companies refused to meet the demands of Mexican oil workers for higher wages and better working conditions, however, President Cárdenas nationalized the oil fields.

U.S. oil companies hotly criticized the Mexican seizure of their property. They pressed the U.S. State Department to resist the nationalization. Some called for action to oust Cárdenas. Meanwhile, the U.S. ambassador to Mexico, Josephus Daniels, argued for a compromise between the Mexican government and the oil companies. He urged the United States to recognize Mexico's right to control its oil resources but added that U.S. companies should be compensated for the property they had lost.

Most Mexicans supported Cárdenas's bold action against the oil companies. Mexicans worried, however, that the United States might invade Mexico to restore U.S. oil companies' property rights. With events in Europe and Asia looking increasingly threatening, however, Roosevelt decided to maintain good relations with Mexico. He acknowledged Mexico's right to control its own resources and urged the oil companies to reach an agreement with the Mexican government for fair compensation. Mexico agreed to the compromise and began payments in 1939.

■■ **Roosevelt resisted calls from oil companies for U.S. intervention to protect their interests in Mexico.**

SECTION 2 REVIEW

IDENTIFY and explain the significance of the following: Good Neighbor policy, caudillos, Maximiliano Hernández Martínez, Emiliano Chamorro, Henry Stimson, Augusto César Sandino, Adolfo Díaz, Anastasio Somoza, Lázaro Cárdenas, nationalize, Josephus Daniels.

LOCATE and explain the importance of the following: El Salvador, Nicaragua.

1. **MAIN IDEA** How did the United States hope to secure its interests in Latin America after World War I?

2. **MAIN IDEA** What effect did the Great Depression have on Latin America?

3. **IDENTIFYING CAUSE AND EFFECT** How did the United States intervene in Nicaraguan politics throughout the 1920s and 1930s? What was the effect of this intervention?

4. **WRITING TO PERSUADE** Imagine you are Josephus Daniels in 1938. Write a memorandum to President Roosevelt recommending U.S. policy toward Mexico after the oil fields were nationalized.

5. **EVALUATING** Why did Augusto César Sandino organize a revolt against Díaz?

THE ROAD TO WAR

FOCUS

- What led to the rise of dictatorships after World War I?
- How did other countries respond to German aggression?
- What caused World War II?
- How did the United States move closer to becoming involved in World War II?

Japanese women raising money for the war in China

America's isolationist stand faced a severe test when dictators came to power in Italy, Germany, Spain, and Japan in the 1920s and 1930s. Americans tried to stay out of European affairs. Neutrality proved difficult, however, as France and other nations fell before German armies, Great Britain battled for its life, and Japan expanded its territory in Asia.

THE RISE OF DICTATORSHIPS

Most European nations after World War I faced inflation and unemployment, which caused political and social unrest. Disagreements over how to solve these problems led to violent clashes between Communists and conservatives. Right-wing military leaders came to power in several countries by promising to end the chaos.

Mussolini in Italy. Although Italy had been on the winning side when World War I ended, many Italians felt they had not benefited from the Treaty of Versailles. Thousands of Italian soldiers returned home after the war only to find themselves jobless. Many joined the Italian Communist party, which urged Italian peasants to take over land and Communist workers to seize factories.

To smash the Communist party and promote his own rise to power, Benito Mussolini founded the **Fascist party** in 1921. The Fascists believed that a military-dominated government should control all aspects of society. Beginning in 1921,

bloody clashes between Communists and Fascists created a situation bordering on civil war. In October 1922 Mussolini led an army of his followers, whose black uniforms gave them the name **Blackshirts**, in a march on Rome. With the support of nationalists, who wanted to strengthen Italy, and of businesspeople who opposed the Socialists and Communists, the Fascists occupied the city.

▲ Benito Mussolini (center), shown here with his followers during their march on Rome, was known as *Il Duce* (eel DOO-chay), or "the leader."

The king appointed Mussolini prime minister and granted him dictatorial powers. Mussolini limited freedom of speech, arrested political opponents, and restricted voting rights. Acting on a pledge to make Italy an imperial power, Mussolini sent Italian forces into the African nation of Ethiopia in 1935 (see map on page 392). The small, poorly equipped Ethiopian army proved no match for the Italian dive-bombers and machine guns. The U.S. Congress, fearful of being drawn into the conflict, passed a neutrality act banning arms shipments to both sides. Such an embargo hurt Ethiopia more than Italy, which continued to receive weapons from Germany and oil from U.S. companies.

African Americans raised money to send relief and medical aid to the Ethiopians. Thousands of African Americans volunteered to fight in Ethiopia, but pressure from the U.S. government forced Ethiopia to reject such support. This lack of support convinced other fascist countries, such as Germany, that aggression would go unpunished.

Hitler in Germany. In 1932 Adolf Hitler's National Socialist party, or **Nazi party**, won more than 40 percent of the vote, and Hitler became chancellor the next year. While in prison, Hitler had written *Mein Kampf* (*My Struggle*), which laid out his plans to restore German power. Hitler blamed Jews, intellectuals, and Communists for Germany's decline. The book won him many supporters, especially among the middle class and the unemployed ruined by inflation and the depression.

Hitler's government, called the Third Reich (the Third Empire), claimed dictatorial powers. Hitler prohibited Jews and non-Nazis from holding government positions, outlawed strikes, and made military service mandatory. Nazi storm troopers, known as **Brownshirts** because of the color of their uniforms, crushed all political opposition.

Hitler's tight control over German industry strengthened the economy and reduced unemployment, allowing him to rearm the country in violation of the Treaty of Versailles. Hitler declared:

66 The buildup of the armed forces is the most important precondition for . . . political power. . . . How is this political power to be used when it is won? . . . Maybe fighting for new export possibilities, maybe . . . conquest of new *Lebensraum* [space for expansion] in the East. 99

The Granger Collection, New York

◄ During the 1930s Nazi posters, such as the one shown here, appealed to those who longed to see Germany restored to its former position as a world power.

In March 1936, German troops moved into the Rhineland (see map on page 392). Two years later they overran Austria. Hitler then turned toward the Sudetenland (soo-DAYT-uhn-land), in western Czechoslovakia, where more than three million German-speaking people lived. Hitler demanded that Czechoslovakia turn over the region to Germany. Czechoslovakia refused Hitler's demand.

Meanwhile, Hitler's **anti-Semitism**, or hatred of Jews, became official government policy. He deprived Jews of their German citizenship and authorized the destruction of Jewish property. On November 9, 1938, Nazi thugs burned down synagogues and destroyed Jewish businesses. Known as *Kristallnacht,* "the night of broken glass," the violence provided a chilling preview of the still more-terrible fate that awaited European Jews and others who fell victim to Hitler's murderous rule. Despite outrage at these events, however, most Americans remained unwilling to intervene in Germany or to encourage Jewish immigration.

Franco in Spain. Spain did not escape the spread of fascism. In the 1930s Spain faced bitter political conflicts. In 1931 a constitution that limited the power of the military and the Catholic church went into effect. It called for such reforms as universal suffrage, nationalization of public utilities, and land for peasants.

Their power threatened by the liberal reforms, conservative military men united under the leadership of General Francisco Franco. In July 1936 the Fascist army officers tried to overthrow the government, starting the **Spanish Civil War** between Fascists and Loyalists.

After almost three years of fighting, Franco took over the national government with German and Italian military aid. The Soviet Union aided the Loyalists, but Roosevelt's fears of being drawn into a European war kept the United States from sending aid.

Individual Americans, however, did join the fight against fascism. Some 3,000 Americans joined the Abraham Lincoln Brigade, one of several international brigades made up of volunteers who went to Spain. Ernest Hemingway, who covered the Spanish Civil War, expressed his support for the Loyalist cause in the powerful novel *For Whom the Bell Tolls* (1940).

▲ **Shown here are Spanish Loyalists leaving Madrid to fight a rebel army advancing on the city.**

THE SPANISH CIVIL WAR

THROUGH OTHERS' EYES

After the Spanish Civil War, many Loyalists remained bitter over the failure of Western nations to support their cause. In 1940 Julio Alvarez del Vayo, a wartime diplomat for the defeated Spanish Republic, charged that this lack of support had cost the Loyalists the war:

"*Apart from Russia, from whom she was able, for a time, to buy arms, Republican Spain had no great powers at her side to supply her with men and munitions. . . . Alone, abandoned to their fate, . . . the Spanish people fought for nearly three years against the armed might of the totalitarian states. . . .*

My one desire is to show what it would have meant to the Western democracies to have had in Spain a certain ally ready to defend the liberty and dignity of Europe against all attempts at domination and oppression. If . . . Republican Spain had not been defeated, the present war [World War II] would never have begun. . . .

No, it was not Spanish democracy that failed. It was the other democracies who failed to save democratic Spain, as they will one day learn to their cost."

Militarists in Japan. As German aggression threatened Europe, Japanese expansion loomed in Asia (see map on page 395). Although Japan had moved toward democracy in the 1920s, the leaders of Japan's military forces remained independent of the government. These military men wanted to lessen Japan's reliance on foreign imports, to reduce the influence of Western countries in Asia, and to promote Japanese expansion throughout Asia.

The creation of a Japanese empire in Asia would give Japan direct control over territories that produced rubber, petroleum, iron, and timber. Worsening economic conditions in Japan strengthened the appeal of the militarists' position.

Japan's 1931 invasion of Manchuria signaled its imperial ambitions. In 1934 and 1935, breaking their Washington Conference pledges, the Japanese began a rapid naval buildup. On July 7, 1937, Japanese and Chinese troops clashed near Beijing (Peking). This incident soon developed into a full-scale war. Japan occupied northern China and launched devastating bombing raids against Chinese cities. Although the League of Nations and the United States condemned Japan's actions, they failed to check Japanese expansion.

■■ **In Italy, Germany, Spain, and Japan, postwar problems brought military dictators to power in the 1920s and 1930s.**

THE RESPONSE TO FASCISM

The spread of fascism in Asia and Europe caused a shake-up in international diplomatic relationships. The most surprising of these realignments was the shift in U.S.–Soviet relations. The Soviets were concerned about curbing the Japanese, who had massed troops in nearby Manchuria. Hoping "to avert the Japanese danger," Soviet foreign affairs commissar Maksim Litvinov mended diplomatic fences with the United States. In November 1933, after years of hostility between the two countries, the United States formally recognized the Soviet Union.

The fascist powers also formalized their ties. In 1936 the rest of Europe trembled when Germany and Italy formed a military alliance. The two countries became known as the **Axis powers**, which later included Japan.

Roosevelt called for European leaders to meet and resolve their conflicts peacefully. Hitler and Mussolini joined British prime minister Neville Chamberlain and French premier Édouard Daladier (dah-lahd-yay) at Munich in September 1938. The four leaders at the **Munich Conference** signed a pact giving Germany control of the Sudetenland. The European leaders had opted for a policy of **appeasement**, or giving in to demands in an effort to avoid larger conflicts. Many politicians underestimated Hitler's expansionist goals, believing that Hitler sought only to remedy what he considered wrongs created by the Treaty of Versailles. But other politicians, such as Winston Churchill of Great Britain, feared that appeasement would only encourage Hitler to take more territory. Britain and other nations in Europe sped up their rearmament.

■■ European leaders tried to appease Hitler to avoid war.

Most Americans denounced the actions of the Axis powers, but isolationism remained strong. American pacifists—religious groups such as the Mennonites and the Society of Friends (Quakers) and organizations such as the Committee on the Cause and Cure of War—urged U.S. leaders to reject war as a means of solving conflicts.

A series of neutrality laws passed by Congress from 1935 to 1939 expressed Americans' desire for peace. The neutrality laws (1) prohibited the shipment of U.S. munitions to warring nations, (2) required warring nations that bought goods from America to transport these goods in their own ships, and (3) forbade Americans to travel on the vessels of warring nations.

Not all Americans endorsed neutrality. Many urged the United States to help the nations under attack. If America allowed aggression to go unpunished, they warned, the United States might one day find itself surrounded by powerful enemies.

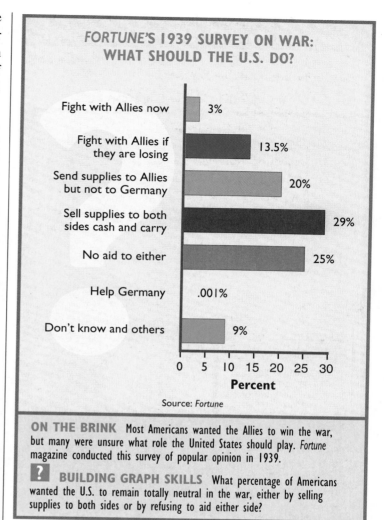

FORTUNE'S 1939 SURVEY ON WAR: WHAT SHOULD THE U.S. DO?

- Fight with Allies now — 3%
- Fight with Allies if they are losing — 13.5%
- Send supplies to Allies but not to Germany — 20%
- Sell supplies to both sides cash and carry — 29%
- No aid to either — 25%
- Help Germany — .001%
- Don't know and others — 9%

Percent (0 5 10 15 20 25 30)

Source: *Fortune*

ON THE BRINK Most Americans wanted the Allies to win the war, but many were unsure what role the United States should play. *Fortune* magazine conducted this survey of popular opinion in 1939.

? BUILDING GRAPH SKILLS What percentage of Americans wanted the U.S. to remain totally neutral in the war, either by selling supplies to both sides or by refusing to aid either side?

By 1937 President Roosevelt had become convinced that the United States must resist aggression. In October he urged other countries to quarantine, or isolate, expansionist countries. Most Americans, however, were not yet ready to accept U.S. involvement in the quarantine. Proof of this position came in December 1937, when Japanese planes attacked the U.S. gunboat *Panay* and three U.S. oil tankers on China's Yangtze (YANG-SEE) River (Chang Jiang). Several U.S. citizens were killed, and many were wounded. Yet a public opinion poll showed that 54 percent of Americans thought the United States should withdraw from China rather than risk becoming involved in a war.

WAR!

U.S. public opinion slowly changed, however, as German aggression continued. In March 1939, Hitler's armies occupied all of Czechoslovakia. Hitler also proposed to annex the Polish port city of

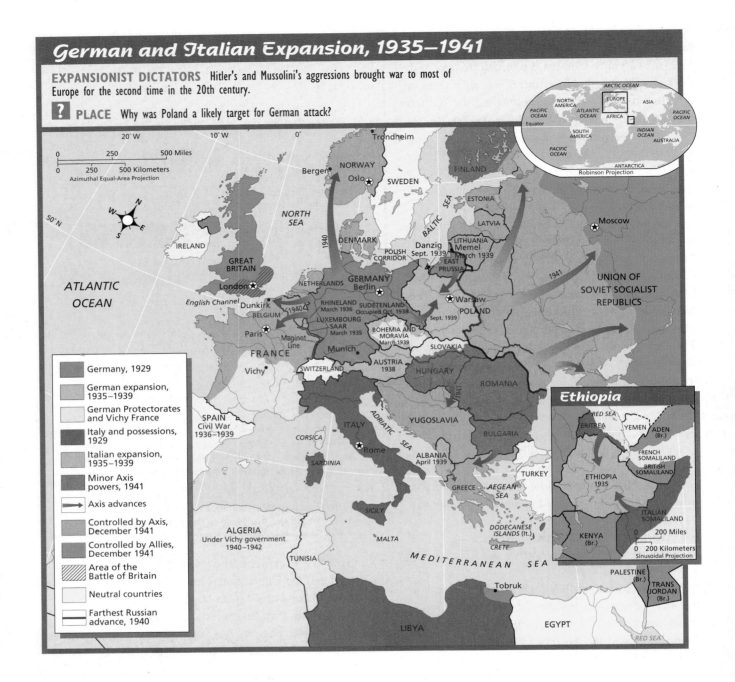

German and Italian Expansion, 1935–1941

EXPANSIONIST DICTATORS Hitler's and Mussolini's aggressions brought war to most of Europe for the second time in the 20th century.

? PLACE Why was Poland a likely target for German attack?

Legend
- Germany, 1929
- German expansion, 1935–1939
- German Protectorates and Vichy France
- Italy and possessions, 1929
- Italian expansion, 1935–1939
- Minor Axis powers, 1941
- → Axis advances
- Controlled by Axis, December 1941
- Controlled by Allies, December 1941
- Area of the Battle of Britain
- Neutral countries
- Farthest Russian advance, 1940

Danzig (DAN-sig), but the Poles refused. In addition, Mussolini's troops invaded Albania on April 7.

Awakening at long last to their common peril, Great Britain and France announced that a German attack upon Poland would mean war and called on the Soviet Union to join them in resisting further aggression. Instead, on August 23, 1939, the Soviet Union signed a **nonaggression pact** with Nazi Germany. This surprising union came about in part because of a secret clause in the pact in which the two nations agreed to divide Poland between them.

On September 1, 1939, German bombers and armored divisions crashed across the border into Poland. Two days later, Great Britain and France declared war on Germany. World War II had begun. Soviet troops, meanwhile, invaded Poland from the east, occupied the independent nations Estonia, Latvia, and Lithuania, and demanded the right to establish military bases in Finland. When Finland refused, the Soviet Union attacked the small nation and soon annexed part of its territory.

▪▪ Allied appeasement failed to halt German aggression. In 1939 the German invasion of Poland sparked World War II.

▲ This 1939 cartoon satirizes the lack of trust between Germany and the Soviet Union, even after the two nations signed the nonaggression pact.

Roosevelt took steps to aid the European countries under siege. Some three weeks after the German invasion of Poland, he urged Congress to amend the neutrality act that barred the export of munitions. After a six-week debate, Congress agreed on a compromise. The new law allowed any nation to buy munitions from the United States but required that the goods be shipped on foreign vessels.

The European conflict loomed as a major issue in the 1940 election. Both candidates—Roosevelt, who sought a third term, and Republican Wendell Willkie—promised to keep America out of the conflict. In a radio talk on September 3, 1939, Roosevelt pledged: "As long as it remains in my power to prevent, there will be no blackout of peace in the United States."

Roosevelt won his bid for an unprecedented third term. In spite of his public promises to pursue peace, however, he became increasingly alarmed by Japanese and German aggression. He began to view American involvement as unavoidable and started a campaign to prepare U.S. defenses for the likely conflict.

By the end of 1940, U.S. supplies flowed to Great Britain. The British, however, had little cash to pay for needed war materials. Roosevelt proposed that the United States lend or lease arms and other supplies to the British and the other Allies. Congress passed the **Lend-Lease Act** in March 1941. It appropriated $7 billion for ships, planes, tanks, and other supplies to non-Axis countries.

■■ **The United States took its first step toward involvement in the growing European conflict by extending aid to the Allies.**

CONTINUING AGGRESSION

While Hitler carried on his **blitzkrieg** (BLITS-kreeg), or "lightning war," against Poland, the French mobilized. In May 1940, German armored divisions, supported by fighter planes and bombers, crashed through the **Maginot Line**, a line of defenses along the French border with Germany. The Germans occupied France; the Netherlands, Belgium, Luxembourg (known as the Low Countries); Denmark; and Norway.

Germany established a puppet government in France headed by Philippe Pétain (pay-tan) and headquartered in the town of Vichy (VISH-ee). A secret French organization known as the Resistance continued to oppose the Germans. In London, French general Charles de Gaulle headed a committee called "Free France," which organized opposition against the Germans.

With the fall of France, Great Britain stood alone. On May 10, 1940, Winston Churchill

▲ Members of the Resistance continued to fight the Germans after the fall of France. This French girl was part of a patrol that hunted down German snipers in Paris late in 1944.

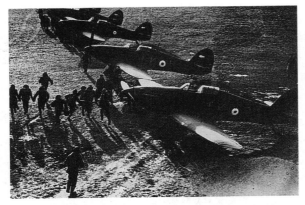

▲ RAF combat pilots are shown rushing to their planes to fight German bombers somewhere over French territory.

became prime minister. With a rare gift for leadership, Churchill rallied the British:

> 66 Hitler knows that he will have to break us in this island or lose the war. . . . Let us therefore brace ourselves to our duties, and so bear ourselves that, if the British Empire and its Commonwealth last for a thousand years, men will still say, "This was their finest hour." 99

On June 10 Italy declared war on France and Great Britain. In August, Hitler unleashed his bombers against Great Britain. The outnumbered British Royal Air Force (RAF) flew day and night to combat the German blitzkrieg.

TENSIONS MOUNT IN THE ATLANTIC

In the face of continuing German attacks, U.S. aid to the Allies gradually increased. By the spring of 1941, German and Italian submarines were turning the North Atlantic into a graveyard of ships. In April, U.S. airplanes and naval vessels began to patrol the Atlantic, notifying British warships of the location of German ships.

A few months later, Roosevelt issued "shoot-on-sight" orders to U.S. warships operating in the North Atlantic "safety zone" America had established in 1939. U.S. warships also began to accompany merchant vessels as far as Iceland. In November, Congress voted to allow U.S. merchant vessels to enter combat areas. Roosevelt armed the merchant vessels and provided them with gun crews.

With the United States moving rapidly toward undeclared war with Germany, Roosevelt and

Churchill met secretly off the coast of Newfoundland in August 1941. The two leaders agreed to a series of principles for international relations. Known as the **Atlantic Charter**, the agreement (1) pledged that the United States and Great Britain would forego territorial expansion, (2) affirmed their respect for the right of every nation to choose its own form of government, and (3) called for freedom of international trade and equal access to raw materials for all countries. Once the war was over, the charter declared, aggressor states should be disarmed, and all nations should work together to rid the world of fear and want.

THE GROWING THREAT FROM JAPAN

As war raged in Europe, Japan added to its conquests in Asia. In July 1941, Japanese troops occupied French Indochina (see map). President Roosevelt immediately froze all Japanese assets in the United States and approved an embargo on shipments of gasoline, machine tools, scrap iron, and steel to Japan. Japan retaliated by freezing all U.S. assets in areas under its control. As a result, trade between the United States and Japan practically ended.

As U.S. resistance to Japanese aggression grew stronger, Japan's war leaders secretly planned an attack on the United States. Even as the plan went forward, however, a Japanese peace mission visited Washington. On November 20, 1941, this mission demanded that the United States (1) unfreeze Japanese assets, (2) supply Japan's gasoline needs, and (3) cease all aid to China. To help prevent further Japanese expansion in China, the United States had made China eligible for lend-lease aid earlier in the year.

The United States had no intention of accepting the Japanese demands. However, U.S. diplomats kept up the appearance of continuing negotiations with Japan to allow more time to prepare U.S. defenses in the Pacific. By this time the United States had succeeded in breaking the secret code used to send messages between Tokyo and the Japanese mission in Washington, D.C. The Americans knew that the Japanese planned a strike, although they did not know where. The challenge was, as Secretary of War Henry Stimson wrote in his diary, "how we should maneuver them into the position of firing the first shot without allowing too much danger to ourselves."

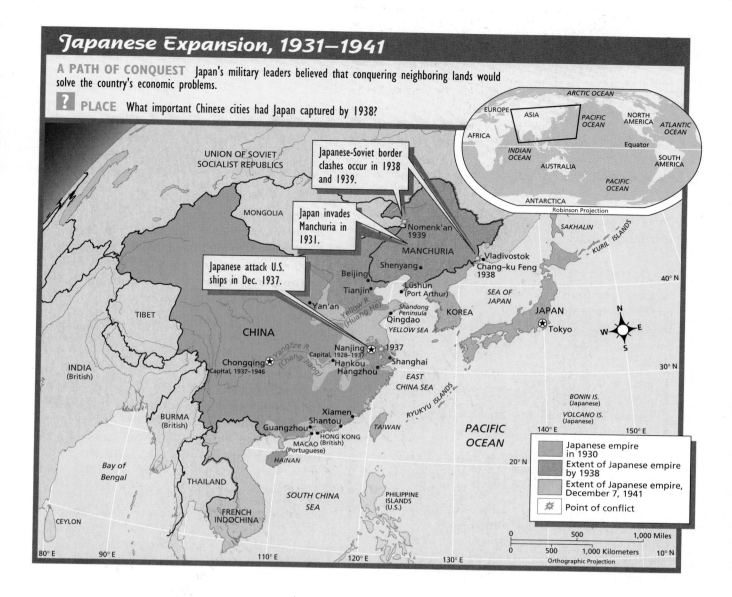

Japanese Expansion, 1931–1941

A PATH OF CONQUEST Japan's military leaders believed that conquering neighboring lands would solve the country's economic problems.

? PLACE What important Chinese cities had Japan captured by 1938?

Japanese-Soviet border clashes occur in 1938 and 1939.

Japan invades Manchuria in 1931.

Japanese attack U.S. ships in Dec. 1937.

UNION OF SOVIET SOCIALIST REPUBLICS

MONGOLIA

Nomenk'an 1939

MANCHURIA

SAKHALIN

KURIL ISLANDS

Vladivostok
Chang–ku Feng 1938

Beijing
Shenyang

Tianjin
Lüshun
(Port Arthur)

SEA OF JAPAN

40° N

TIBET

Yan'an

Shandong Peninsula
Qingdao
YELLOW SEA

KOREA

JAPAN
Tokyo

CHINA

Nanjing 1937
Capital, 1928–1937

Shanghai

30° N

Chongqing
Capital, 1937–1946

Hankou
Hangzhou

Yangtze R. (Chang Jiang)

EAST CHINA SEA

RYUKYU ISLANDS

PACIFIC OCEAN

BONIN IS. (Japanese)
VOLCANO IS. (Japanese)

INDIA (British)

Yellow R. (Huang He)

Xiamen
Shantou

BURMA (British)

Guangzhou
HONG KONG (British)
MACAO (British)
(Portuguese)

TAIWAN

140° E

150° E

Bay of Bengal

HAINAN

THAILAND

20° N

SOUTH CHINA SEA

PHILIPPINE ISLANDS (U.S.)

CEYLON

FRENCH INDOCHINA

80° E

90° E

110° E

120° E

130° E

10° N

ARCTIC OCEAN

EUROPE
ASIA
PACIFIC OCEAN
NORTH AMERICA
ATLANTIC OCEAN

AFRICA

INDIAN OCEAN

Equator

SOUTH AMERICA

AUSTRALIA

PACIFIC OCEAN

ANTARCTICA

Robinson Projection

Legend:
- Japanese empire in 1930
- Extent of Japanese empire by 1938
- Extent of Japanese empire, December 7, 1941
- ✷ Point of conflict

0 500 1,000 Miles
0 500 1,000 Kilometers
Orthographic Projection

SECTION 3 REVIEW

IDENTIFY and explain the significance of the following: Benito Mussolini, Fascist party, Blackshirts, Adolf Hitler, Nazi party, Brownshirts, anti-Semitism, *Kristallnacht,* Francisco Franco, Spanish Civil War, Axis powers, Munich Conference, appeasement, Winston Churchill, nonaggression pact, Lend-Lease Act, blitzkrieg, Maginot Line, Atlantic Charter.

LOCATE and explain the importance of the following: Ethiopia; Rhineland; Sudetenland; Munich, Germany; Yangtze River (Chang Jiang); Albania; Poland; Finland; French Indochina.

1. **MAIN IDEA** What policy did European countries follow in negotiations with Hitler? Why?

2. **MAIN IDEA** What factors led to war in 1939?

3. **MAIN IDEA** What step brought the United States closer toward involvement in the war?

4. **WRITING TO EVALUATE** Imagine you are an American reporter in Europe during the 1920s and 1930s. Write an article that accounts for the rise of dictatorships after World War I.

5. **HYPOTHESIZING** How might events in Europe have been different if European leaders had not decided on an appeasement policy with Hitler?

WRITING A SUMMARY

Using the essential points of the chapter as a guide, write a summary of the chapter.

REVIEWING CHRONOLOGY

Number your paper 1 to 5. Study the time line above, and list the following events in the order in which they happened by writing the first next to 1, the second next to 2, and so on. Then complete the activity below.

1. Spanish Civil War begins.
2. Washington Conference begins.
3. Lázaro Cárdenas nationalizes Mexican oil fields.
4. Kellogg-Briand Pact proposed.
5. World War II starts.

Assessing Consequences What effect did the Munich Conference have on events in Europe?

IDENTIFYING PEOPLE AND IDEAS

Explain the historical significance of each of the following people or terms.

1. unilateralism
2. Emily Greene Balch
3. Five Power Agreement
4. caudillos
5. Augusto César Sandino
6. nationalize
7. Adolf Hitler
8. *Kristallnacht*
9. nonaggression pact
10. Winston Churchill

UNDERSTANDING MAIN IDEAS

1. What factors encouraged the growth of isolationism in the United States after World War I? What events in the 1930s convinced U.S. leaders to abandon the policy?
2. What economic and political role did the United States play in Latin America?
3. Why did Lázaro Cárdenas nationalize Mexican oil fields in 1938?
4. Why did some European leaders favor a policy of appeasement toward Hitler? Why did others oppose it?
5. What were the provisions of the Atlantic Charter? Why was it adopted?

REVIEWING THEMES

1. **Global Relations** In what ways did countries promote world peace after World War I?
2. **Economic Development** What economic and political problems emerged after World War I?
3. **Democratic Values** How did the fascist dictatorships in Europe limit civil liberties?

THINKING CRITICALLY

1. **Analyzing** How did Benito Mussolini rise to power?
2. **Evaluating** What were the goals of Japan's militarists? Why did they want to create a Japanese empire in Asia?
3. **Synthesizing** How did American approaches to neutrality change between 1935 and 1941?

STRATEGY FOR SUCCESS

Review the Strategies for Success on Interpreting Editorial Cartoons on page 332. Then study the following cartoon, entitled *New Kind of Pump Priming*. What is the cartoonist's message?

Pump Priming—New Style

C.S.M. Oct. 26-1938

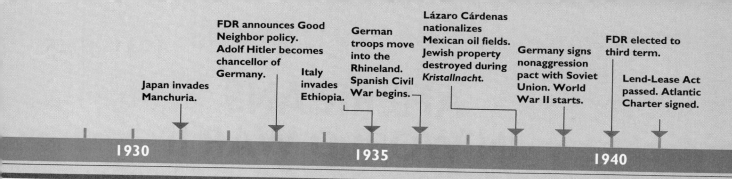

Japan invades Manchuria.

FDR announces Good Neighbor policy. Adolf Hitler becomes chancellor of Germany.

Italy invades Ethiopia.

German troops move into the Rhineland. Spanish Civil War begins.

Lázaro Cárdenas nationalizes Mexican oil fields. Jewish property destroyed during *Kristallnacht*.

Germany signs nonaggression pact with Soviet Union. World War II starts.

FDR elected to third term.

Lend-Lease Act passed. Atlantic Charter signed.

1930   1935   1940

WRITING ABOUT HISTORY

Writing to Describe Imagine you are a Loyalist during the Spanish Civil War. Write a letter to an American friend describing the events during that period.

USING PRIMARY SOURCES

President Roosevelt's proposal of the Lend-Lease Act aroused fierce debate in Congress. Read the following excerpt from isolationist Burton K. Wheeler, a Republican senator from Montana, who argued against passing the measure. What reasons does he give for his stand?

> 66 *Never before have the American people been asked or compelled to give . . . so completely of their tax dollars to any foreign nation. Never before has the Congress of the United States been asked by any President to violate international law. . . . Never before has the United States given to one man the power to strip this nation of its defenses. . . .*
>
> *Approval of this legislation means war, open and complete warfare. I, therefore, ask the American people before they . . . accept it—Was the last World War worthwhile?*
>
> *If it were, then we should lend and lease war materials. If it were, then we should lend and lease American boys. President Roosevelt has said we would be repaid by England. We will be. . . . Our boys will be returned—returned in caskets, maybe; returned with bodies maimed; returned with minds warped and twisted by sights of horrors and the scream and shriek of high-powered shells.* 99

LINKING HISTORY AND GEOGRAPHY

After World War I, France built the Maginot Line, a line of fixed fortifications to protect its border with Germany. French military commanders felt this series of forts would repel a German attack. Study the map below, which shows the German invasion of France in 1940. How did the German army defeat this French strategy?

BUILDING YOUR PORTFOLIO

Complete the following projects independently or cooperatively.

I. GLOBAL RELATIONS In Chapter 23 you portrayed a journalist examining the global effects of the Great Depression. Building on that experience, imagine your assignment is to evaluate the new political trends of the 1930s. Create a chart that compares the similarities and differences among fascist dictators around the world.

2. WAR Imagine you are a diplomat at the 1938 Munich Conference. Write a speech aimed at convincing the Allies to abandon their policy of appeasement toward Germany's Adolf Hitler. Your speech might mention *Kristallnacht*, Hitler's repressive domestic policies, German aggression into the Rhineland and Austria, and your opposition toward granting the Sudetenland to Hitler.

AMERICANS IN WORLD WAR II

▼ **FOCUS** ■

UNDERSTANDING THE MAIN IDEA

In December 1941 the Japanese bombed Pearl Harbor, bringing the United States into World War II. Americans and their allies battled the Axis powers on land in Europe and North Africa and on sea in the Atlantic, Pacific, and Mediterranean. By August 1945 the Allies defeated the Axis powers, but only after heavy casualties and the atomic bombing of two Japanese cities.

★ THEMES

■ **GLOBAL RELATIONS** How might nations coordinate civilian and military resources to win a global war?

■ **CULTURAL DIVERSITY** Why might wartime patriotism lead to increased discrimination against certain groups?

■ **TECHNOLOGY AND SOCIETY** What political and moral concerns might a government take into account when developing a potentially destructive technology?

1941	1942	1943	1944	1945
▼ Japanese attack Pearl Harbor.	▼ Bataan Death March occurs.	▼ Zoot-suit riots break out.	▼ D-Day invasion begins.	▼ Japan surrenders.

The German invasion of Poland in 1939 launched World War II. By 1940, much of Western Europe had fallen to Germany, while Japan expanded its hold on Asia. For a time, the United States maintained its neutrality. Lend-lease aid to the Allies, beginning in 1941, however, marked an important step in U.S. involvement in the conflict.

Shortly before 8:00 A.M. on December 7, 1941, the message *"Tora! Tora! Tora!"* was radioed to Japanese carrier ships approaching Hawaii. The signal "Tora," meaning "tiger," launched the long-planned Japanese air-and-sea attack on the U.S. naval base at Pearl Harbor. The heart of America's Pacific Fleet was anchored there, and more than a hundred U.S. planes lined nearby airfields.

Within seconds after the attack began, explosions from bombs and torpedoes turned Pearl Harbor into a blazing inferno. When the assault ended less than two hours later, almost 20 American warships and nearly 200 aircraft had been destroyed. Among some 2,400 American dead were 1,103 sailors entombed on the *Arizona* when the battleship sank.

The bombing shocked and united Americans. Ann Hoskins, a Connecticut newspaper owner, noticed that before the attack "there was great tension and feelings between people not to intervene. But the minute Pearl Harbor happened, there was utter unity." The next day, a somber President Roosevelt described December 7 as "a date which will live in infamy" and called on Congress for a declaration of war against Japan.

Aftermath of Japanese attack on Hawaii, 1941

Air Force officers, Hawaii, 1941

EARLY DIFFICULTIES

FOCUS

- **What obstacles did the United States face when it first entered the war?**
- **In which three battles did the Allies halt Japan's advance in the Pacific?**
- **What were two major turning points in the western theater of operations?**
- **What forms did Allied cooperation take?**

Army nurses evacuated from Bataan

*D*eeply angered by the bombing of Pearl Harbor, Congress and the American people overwhelmingly supported President Roosevelt's call for war against Japan. Great Britain declared war on Japan as well. On December 11, Japan's allies, Germany and Italy, declared war on the United States, and Congress recognized a state of war with those two nations. World War II had now vastly expanded.

AXIS ADVANTAGES

When the United States entered the war, the Axis powers had two big advantages. First, Germany, Italy, and Japan had already secured firm control of the areas they had invaded. The United States thus faced a long, drawn-out fight on several fronts, including Western Europe, the Pacific, the Mediterranean, and Northern Africa.

Second, Germany was better prepared for war. Since 1933 it had been rearming and building airfields, barracks, and military training centers. By the mid-1930s, the Nazis had converted most of the German economy to military production. In contrast, the United States had not begun to prepare for war until 1940, when President Roosevelt called for more money to be devoted to military production. Even then, however, the country's preparations were limited.

When the United States entered the war, it faced the problems of fighting on many fronts and a lack of preparation.

◀ **Three U.S. sailors in Chicago read about the Japanese attack on Pearl Harbor.**

Hitler, Mussolini, and the Japanese war leaders hoped they could win the conflict before the United States—fighting a two-ocean war—could mobilize its enormous resources. After the Pearl Harbor attack, one Hitler aide warned:

66 We have just one year to cut off Russia from her American supplies. . . . If we don't succeed and the munitions potential of the United States joins up with the manpower potential of the Russians, the war will enter a phase in which we shall only be able to win it with difficulty. 99

WAR IN THE PACIFIC

Japan's assault on Pearl Harbor was only part of a giant offensive throughout the Pacific region. In December the Japanese launched attacks on several other American islands, on the Philippines, and on various British possessions. By the end of the month, Japan controlled Guam, Wake Island, the British colony of Hong Kong, and Thailand.

The year 1942 brought more Japanese victories. In January, Japanese forces took Manila, the capital of the Philippines. The next month, they overran the British naval base at Singapore, and in the **Battle of the Java Sea**, they crushed a fleet of American, British, Dutch, and Australian warships (see map on page 402). By April, Japan had conquered most of the Netherlands East Indies, with its supplies of oil, tin, rubber, and other vital war materials. The Japanese were also driving the British out of Burma.

In the Philippines a small force of Americans and Filipinos under General Douglas MacArthur, commander of U.S. Army troops in the Far East, mounted a heroic but hopeless resistance against the Japanese. After the surrender of Manila, MacArthur's forces withdrew to the Bataan Peninsula across Manila Bay. In March, MacArthur was ordered to Australia but vowed, "I shall return."

Fighting against overwhelming odds, the hungry, sick, exhausted survivors who remained on Bataan surrendered in April. Japanese soldiers forced the some 70,000 survivors to march through the jungle on their way to prison camp. Some 10,000 died on what came to be called the **Bataan Death March** (see map on page 427). U.S. and Filipino soldiers received brutal treat-

JAPAN DECLARES WAR

The day after the Japanese attack on Pearl Harbor, Emperor Hirohito made a speech that was relayed around the world. In it he laid out Japan's reasons for declaring war on the United States and Great Britain:

66 *B*oth America and Britain . . . have aggravated the disturbances in East Asia. . . . These two powers, inducing other countries to follow suit, increased military preparations on all sides of Our Empire. . . . They have obstructed by every means Our peaceful commerce, and finally resorted to a direct severance [cutting off] of economic relations. . . . Patiently have We waited and long have We endured, in hope that Our Government might retrieve the situation in peace. But Our adversaries [enemies], showing not the least spirit of conciliation, have unduly delayed a settlement. . . . Our Empire for its existence and self defense has no other recourse but to appeal to arms and to crush every obstacle in its path. 99

ment at the hands of the Japanese: prisoners were beaten, shot, or prevented from drinking water. The bravery of the Filipino defenders at Bataan inspired thousands of Filipino Americans to enlist in the armed forces. In 1942 alone some 16,000 Filipino Americans in California joined the fight.

By the summer of 1942, the Japanese were poised to strike west at India, south at Australia, and east through Hawaii at the Pacific coast of the United States. At this crucial point, however, the Allies succeeded in halting the Japanese advance in the Pacific. The U.S. Pacific Fleet, commanded by Admiral Chester Nimitz, helped turn the tide with three battles.

The first battle began on May 7, 1942, in the Coral Sea, off the northeastern coast of Australia. A Japanese force on its way to attack Port Moresby, New Guinea, seized Tulagi (too-LAHG-ee) Island,

▲ Shown here are American and Filipino soldiers at the start of the grueling Bataan Death March in April 1942. Thousands died on the march to a Japanese prison camp.

one of the Solomons. But before the Japanese force could reach its destination, a joint British-American naval force intercepted it. Planes from U.S. carriers damaged a Japanese carrier and destroyed one carrier and several aircraft. The **Battle of the Coral Sea** was an important victory for the Allies. Although the Allies lost a carrier, the battle stopped the Japanese advance on Australia.

The second naval battle took place early in June 1942. Japan, seeking to crush the U.S. Pacific Fleet, launched a two-pronged attack. One unit succeeded in occupying two of the Aleutian Islands, near Alaska. This move was

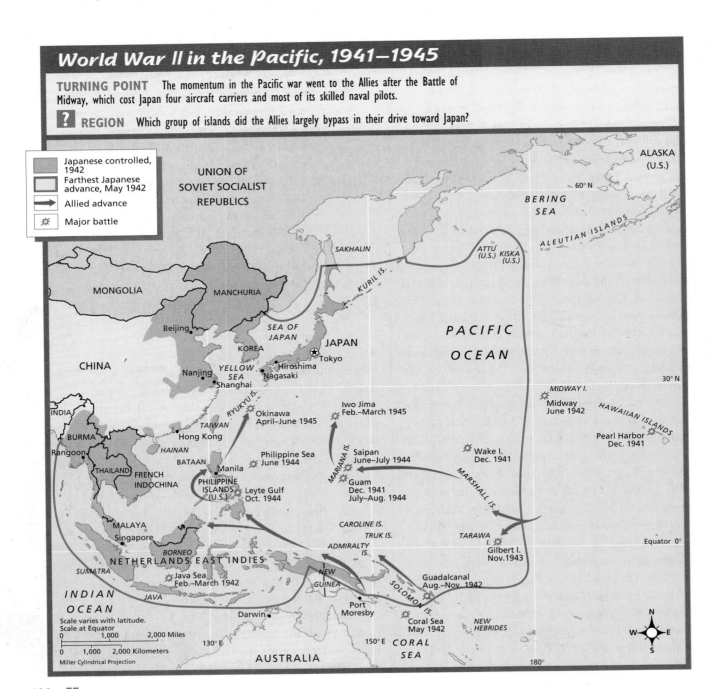

World War II in the Pacific, 1941–1945

TURNING POINT The momentum in the Pacific war went to the Allies after the Battle of Midway, which cost Japan four aircraft carriers and most of its skilled naval pilots.

? REGION Which group of islands did the Allies largely bypass in their drive toward Japan?

Japanese controlled, 1942
Farthest Japanese advance, May 1942
Allied advance
Major battle

ALASKA (U.S.)

UNION OF SOVIET SOCIALIST REPUBLICS

60° N

BERING SEA

ALEUTIAN ISLANDS

SAKHALIN

ATTU (U.S.)   KISKA (U.S.)

KURIL IS.

MONGOLIA   MANCHURIA

SEA OF JAPAN

Beijing

KOREA

JAPAN   Tokyo

PACIFIC OCEAN

CHINA

Nanjing   YELLOW SEA   Hiroshima   Nagasaki   Shanghai

30° N

MIDWAY I.
Midway June 1942

HAWAIIAN ISLANDS

RYUKYU IS.   Okinawa April–June 1945

Iwo Jima Feb.–March 1945

INDIA

TAIWAN
Hong Kong   Philippine Sea June 1944

Saipan June–July 1944

Pearl Harbor Dec. 1941

BURMA   HAINAN

Rangoon   BATAAN   Manila

MARIANA IS.

Wake I. Dec. 1941

THAILAND   FRENCH INDOCHINA   PHILIPPINE ISLANDS (U.S.)   Leyte Gulf Oct. 1944

Guam Dec. 1941 July–Aug. 1944

MARSHALL IS.

MALAYA   Singapore

CAROLINE IS.

TRUK IS.

TARAWA I.

Equator 0°

BORNEO

NETHERLANDS EAST INDIES

ADMIRALTY IS.

Gilbert I. Nov. 1943

SUMATRA   Java Sea Feb.–March 1942

NEW GUINEA

Guadalcanal Aug.–Nov. 1942

INDIAN OCEAN   JAVA

Scale varies with latitude.
Scale at Equator
0   1,000   2,000 Miles
0   1,000   2,000 Kilometers
Miller Cylindrical Projection

Darwin

Port Moresby

130° E

SOLOMON IS.

Coral Sea May 1942

NEW HEBRIDES

150° E   CORAL SEA

AUSTRALIA

180°

N
W   E
S

▲ Although U.S. forces won the Battle of Midway in June 1942, the islands did not escape damage. Japanese bombers hit military installations, including the oil tank shown here.

designed to divert American ships to the north while the Japanese carried out their second offensive, an attack on Midway, two small islands northwest of Hawaii. The United States, however, knew of the Japanese strategy because American experts had broken the Japanese fleet code. Nimitz was therefore able to assemble U.S. aircraft carriers and destroyers north of Midway to fend off the Japanese attack.

Americans and Japanese clashed from June 3 to June 6. U.S. fighters, dive-bombers, and torpedo planes sank four Japanese aircraft carriers and shot down many enemy planes. The American victory at the **Battle of Midway** proved crucial. Japan lost not only ships and planes but also a number of skilled pilots, many of whom had taken part in the Pearl Harbor attack. The battle provided the Americans with valuable experience in naval air warfare and gave people confidence in the carrier-based strike force.

After the Battle of Midway, the United States successfully launched its first offensive. In August 1942, American marines waded ashore at Guadalcanal, another of the Solomon Islands. For six desperate months, with a heavy loss of life, they clung to a toehold around the airport, repelling Japanese attacks from the air, the sea, and the surrounding jungle.

In November the Japanese sent a huge fleet to the Solomons, hoping to regain Guadalcanal. The American fleet defeated the Japanese in a bloody battle. Guadalcanal was secure. The tide of battle in the Pacific had finally turned in the Allies' favor.

■■ The Allies stopped the Japanese Pacific offensive in the battles of Coral Sea, Midway, and Guadalcanal.

FIGHTING IN EUROPE AND THE MEDITERRANEAN

By the time of the attack on Pearl Harbor, the Axis powers, which now included Hungary, Romania, and Bulgaria, firmly controlled much of the western theater of operations—Europe and the lands around the Mediterranean. Yugoslavia and Greece had been occupied, and southern Europe was firmly under the Axis boot. Throughout most of 1942, the Axis powers racked up one victory after another.

The Germans and their allies scored victories on many different fronts. German submarines, or U-boats, controlled the Atlantic Ocean, sinking Allied military and merchant ships and nearly cutting off British supply lines. In the first half of 1942, German U-boats sank almost 500 ships off the eastern seaboard of the United States.

In Europe, German troops had penetrated far into the Soviet Union after their initial attack in June 1941. As the Germans advanced, the Soviets lost many industrial centers as well as rich grainfields in the Ukraine (see map on page 404). In the summer of 1942, the Germans pushed toward the oil fields of southern Russia. They also laid siege to Stalingrad (now known as Volgograd). The city mobilized its defenses. For months the men, women, and children defending the city suffered a nightmare of shell fire and starvation.

In North Africa, Italian forces had launched an invasion in 1940. When British troops later began to inflict heavy damage on the Italians, Hitler sent in the German *Afrika Korps* under commander Erwin Rommel.

▼ Erwin Rommel (left) was commander of the German *Afrika Korps* in North Africa.

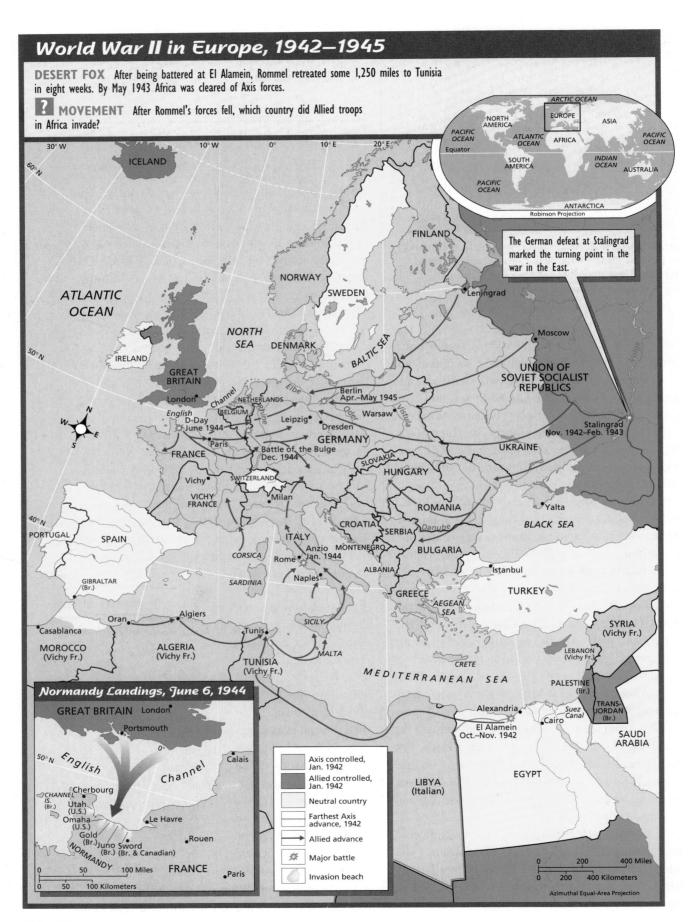

World War II in Europe, 1942–1945

DESERT FOX After being battered at El Alamein, Rommel retreated some 1,250 miles to Tunisia in eight weeks. By May 1943 Africa was cleared of Axis forces.

? MOVEMENT After Rommel's forces fell, which country did Allied troops in Africa invade?

ARCTIC OCEAN
NORTH AMERICA
EUROPE
ASIA
PACIFIC OCEAN
ATLANTIC OCEAN
AFRICA
PACIFIC OCEAN
Equator
SOUTH AMERICA
INDIAN OCEAN
PACIFIC OCEAN
AUSTRALIA
ANTARCTICA
Robinson Projection

The German defeat at Stalingrad marked the turning point in the war in the East.

ICELAND

ATLANTIC OCEAN

NORTH SEA

FINLAND

NORWAY

SWEDEN

Leningrad

GREAT BRITAIN
IRELAND

DENMARK

BALTIC SEA

Moscow

London
English Channel
NETHERLANDS
BELGIUM
D-Day June 1944
Paris
FRANCE

Elbe
Rhine
Berlin
Apr.–May 1945
Leipzig
Dresden
GERMANY
Battle of the Bulge Dec. 1944
Oder
Warsaw
Vistula

UNION OF SOVIET SOCIALIST REPUBLICS

Stalingrad
Nov. 1942–Feb. 1943

Volga

Vichy
SWITZERLAND
VICHY FRANCE
Milan

SLOVAKIA
HUNGARY
ROMANIA
UKRAINE

Yalta

PORTUGAL
SPAIN

CORSICA
ITALY
Anzio Jan. 1944
Rome
SARDINIA
Naples

CROATIA
SERBIA
MONTENEGRO
Danube
BULGARIA
ALBANIA

BLACK SEA

GIBRALTAR (Br.)

GREECE
AEGEAN SEA

Istanbul

TURKEY

SICILY
MALTA
CRETE

SYRIA (Vichy Fr.)

Casablanca
Oran
Algiers
Tunis

MOROCCO (Vichy Fr.)
ALGERIA (Vichy Fr.)
TUNISIA (Vichy Fr.)

MEDITERRANEAN SEA

LEBANON (Vichy Fr.)

PALESTINE (Br.)

TRANS-JORDAN (Br.)

SAUDI ARABIA

Alexandria
Suez Canal
Cairo

El Alamein
Oct.–Nov. 1942

LIBYA (Italian)

EGYPT

Normandy Landings, June 6, 1944

GREAT BRITAIN
London
Portsmouth

English Channel

Calais

CHANNEL IS. (Br.)
Cherbourg
Utah (U.S.)
Omaha (U.S.)
Gold (Br.)
Juno Sword (Br.) (Br. & Canadian)
NORMANDY

Le Havre
Rouen

FRANCE
Paris

0   50   100 Miles
0   50   100 Kilometers

	Axis controlled, Jan. 1942
	Allied controlled, Jan. 1942
	Neutral country
	Farthest Axis advance, 1942
→	Allied advance
✸	Major battle
	Invasion beach

0   200   400 Miles
0   200   400 Kilometers
Azimuthal Equal-Area Projection

▶ Soldiers in Britain's Eighth Army are shown here in defensive positions during the Battle of El Alamein. This battle stood in marked contrast to the highly mobile fighting characteristic of the war in North Africa.

▼ Soviet forces laid siege to Stalingrad for 17 months before the German army surrendered in February 1943. Shown here is part of the ruined city shortly after it was liberated.

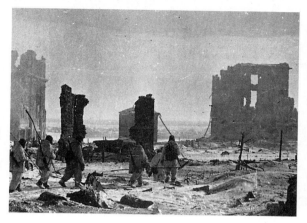

Rommel, known as the Desert Fox, had advanced as far as El Alamein, Egypt, by July 1942. His troops were ready for a final thrust at the Suez Canal and the oil fields of the Middle East (the European designation for Northeast Africa and Southwest Asia). At the same time, Axis aircraft all but forced British naval craft out of the Mediterranean. In order to reach Egypt, the Middle East, and India, Britain had to send its ships thousands of miles around Africa.

Despite the British forces' transport problems, it was Rommel who suffered most from shortages of men and supplies. The British, led by General Bernard Montgomery, turned this to their advantage. In October, Montgomery attacked, pushing Rommel's *Afrika Korps* steadily westward out of Egypt and into Libya by November. The British victory in the **Battle of El Alamein** helped turn the corner for the Allies in North Africa.

Another turning point came in the fall of 1942, when the Soviets attacked German troops in Stalingrad. Throughout a terrible winter the Germans hung on, forbidden by Hitler to surrender. Trapped in the ruined city with few supplies and little food, the Axis troops finally surrendered in February 1943. After the **Battle of Stalingrad**, less than one third of the original German force of almost 300,000 remained alive. Galina Utkina, a Russian woman, recalled the crucial role Soviet women played in defeating the Germans:

❝ Anti-aircraft battalions, air-force regiments and signalling units were made up entirely of women. When the battle reached the city itself, women fought alongside the men. ❞

The Allied victories at El Alamein and Stalingrad broke the momentum of the Axis advance. Said British prime minister Winston Churchill: "Before Alamein we never had a victory. After Alamein we never had a defeat."

▪▪ Setbacks for the Axis powers at El Alamein and Stalingrad were turning points in World War II.

Barme

ＡLLIED COOPERATION

How had the Allies managed to overcome the powerful offensives mounted by the Axis in both theaters of the war? The ability of the United States to harness its human and industrial resources helped the Allied effort. Through the lend-lease program the United States shipped vast quantities of munitions to its allies. By the end of the war, lend-lease aid totaled more than $50 billion. Of this vast sum, over 60 percent went to Great Britain.

Allied cooperation, which involved joint strategic planning, also helped turn the tide. Just two weeks after the assault on Pearl Harbor, Churchill and Roosevelt met in Washington, D.C., together with their top military commanders and technical aides. The two leaders and their staffs agreed that defeating the Axis powers in Europe would be the first Allied priority. For the time being, Allied strategy in the Pacific would be defensive rather than offensive.

To formalize their alliance, representatives of 26 Allied countries, calling themselves the United Nations, met in Washington, D.C. On January 1, 1942, they signed the Joint Declaration, which had been drafted by Roosevelt and Churchill. In it the Allies (1) promised full military and economic cooperation in the war effort, (2) agreed that none of them would make a separate peace with the Axis powers, and (3) endorsed the war aims outlined by Roosevelt and Churchill in the Atlantic Charter (see Chapter 15).

Throughout the war Churchill and Roosevelt met several times. At Casablanca, Morocco, in January 1943, the two leaders agreed to demand the **unconditional surrender** of their enemies. In other words, if the Axis powers gave up, they would have to do so on the Allies' terms. Churchill and Roosevelt also agreed that the Allies should attack Hitler on a second front in order to relieve pressure on the Soviet Union (the first front). The Allies decided to open the second front by invading southern Europe by way of North Africa and the Mediterranean island of Sicily.

▲ Chinese leader Chiang Kai-shek (left), President Roosevelt (center), and British prime minister Winston Churchill (right) are shown at the Cairo Conference in November 1943.

At Cairo in November 1943, Roosevelt and Churchill met with Chiang Kai-shek of China. The leaders outlined Allied strategy against Japan and made plans to restore Japanese-held territories after the war. At Tehran, Iran, shortly afterward, Roosevelt and Churchill met for the first time with Soviet leader Joseph Stalin. Stalin gave his support for Allied war plans.

■■ **Cooperation among the Allies took the form of lend-lease exchanges, joint strategic planning, and agreement on war aims.**

SECTION 1 REVIEW

IDENTIFY and explain the significance of the following: Battle of the Java Sea, Douglas MacArthur, Bataan Death March, Battle of the Coral Sea, Battle of Midway, Erwin Rommel, Bernard Montgomery, Battle of El Alamein, Battle of Stalingrad, unconditional surrender, Joseph Stalin.

LOCATE and explain the importance of the following: Pearl Harbor, Guam, Wake Island, Hong Kong, Thailand, Bataan, Coral Sea, Midway Islands, Guadalcanal, Ukraine, Stalingrad, El Alamein, Casablanca.

1. **MAIN IDEA** Where did the Allies stop the Japanese Pacific offensive?

2. **MAIN IDEA** What two German setbacks were turning points for the Allies in World War II?

3. **CONTRASTING** What advantages did the Axis powers have over the United States at the beginning of the war?

4. **WRITING TO INFORM** Imagine you are a participant in one of the early wartime conferences. Write a memorandum to the Allies, giving examples of cooperative efforts that could help them win the war.

5. **LINKING HISTORY AND GEOGRAPHY** What was the significance of the American victory at the Battle of Midway for both Japan and the United States?

THE HOME FRONT

FOCUS

- How did the United States mobilize for war?
- Why were Japanese Americans interned during the war?
- What gains did African Americans and Mexican Americans make during the war?
- What changes did World War II bring for American women?

Although World War II was fought on the battlefields of Europe, Asia, and North Africa, American farms and factories also helped win the war. As the United States mobilized its resources for combat, the entertainment industry helped sustain morale. For Japanese Americans the war resulted in confinement in remote camps. For African Americans, Mexican Americans, and women, the conflict brought both new opportunities and reminders that discrimination and inequality still existed in American society.

Seamstresses making flags and banners

MOBILIZING FOR WAR

After the Japanese attack at Pearl Harbor plunged the United States into war, America switched from a peacetime to a wartime economy. Engineer R. W. Danischefsky noted how quickly factory orders came in: "At the time of Pearl Harbor [December 7, 1941] we had five projects in Michigan. By the end of December we had forty-two." To fill these vital orders, union leaders agreed not to organize strikes during the war.

A production boom. The United States soon became the Allies' biggest armaments supplier. Between 1940 and 1945, U.S. war plants produced millions of planes, tanks, jeeps, and guns. Shipbuilders produced thousands of ships, creating a powerful navy and merchant marine.

War production helped create an economic boom. The number of jobless workers, still over 2.5 million in 1942, sank to fewer than 700,000 in 1944. Earnings nearly doubled between 1939 and 1945. People who had stood in breadlines a decade

◄ **After the bombing of Pearl Harbor, many existing factories were converted to wartime production. The Firestone Tire & Rubber Company, for example, made antiaircraft guns, tank and submarine parts, and gas masks, as well as tires for all military vehicles.**

earlier now worked overtime and brought home fat paychecks.

The boom also led to vast population shifts. More than four million workers left their homes to find work in war-industry factories in other states. Sharecroppers, tenant farmers, and others eking out a living on farms flocked to the centers of wartime production—shipyards on the Gulf and Pacific coasts and factories in the Midwest and West. The West especially witnessed phenomenal economic and population growth during the war. The federal government spent billions of dollars to build western factories and military bases. This wartime spending helped the West become a major industrial region after World War II.

American farms also achieved marvels of productivity. Although many agricultural workers went off to fight in the war or to work in wartime factories, productivity remained high. During the war years U.S. farmers produced enough food to supply the American people and the Allies overseas.

Government expansion.

Mobilizing for war led to a greatly expanded federal government. The number of federal employees grew from almost one million in 1940 to nearly three million by 1945. The Office of War Mobilization (OWM) coordinated all government agencies involved in producing and distributing civilian goods. Its powerful director, James F. Byrnes, was sometimes called the "assistant president."

The **War Production Board** (WPB) directed the conversion of existing factories to wartime production and supervised the building of new plants. The WPB assigned raw materials to industry, including scrap iron from factories and recyclable tin, aluminum, and fats (used in bullets) from homes.

The WPB (and later the OWM) also coordinated the production and distribution of consumer goods. For instance, it diverted nylon to making parachutes. The WPB even regulated clothing styles in order to save fabric; canceled for the duration of the war were cuffs on men's trousers and pleats in women's skirts.

▶ After the war began, the government conserved valuable resources by establishing rationing programs. Students at Wilson Senior High in Washington, D.C., are shown learning how to use the latest ration book.

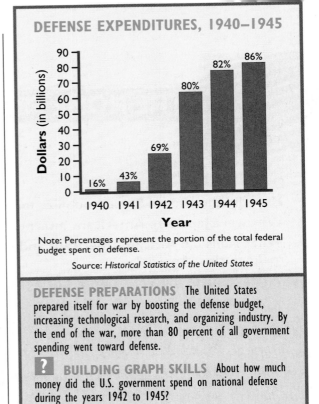

DEFENSE EXPENDITURES, 1940–1945

Dollars (in billions)

Year	
1940	16%
1941	43%
1942	69%
1943	80%
1944	82%
1945	86%

Note: Percentages represent the portion of the total federal budget spent on defense.

Source: *Historical Statistics of the United States*

DEFENSE PREPARATIONS The United States prepared itself for war by boosting the defense budget, increasing technological research, and organizing industry. By the end of the war, more than 80 percent of all government spending went toward defense.

? **BUILDING GRAPH SKILLS** About how much money did the U.S. government spend on national defense during the years 1942 to 1945?

Directing the economy.

The government also extended its control over the economy. In order to pay for the war, the government increased by more than 10 times the number of Americans who had to pay income tax. The new taxes included most middle- and lower-income groups for the first time. The rest of the money came from borrowing, mainly through war bonds.

The sale of war bonds also helped the government deal with another major concern—keeping inflation down. When incomes remain high but few consumer items are available for people to buy, prices go up and inflation results. Selling war bonds offered one way of siphoning off excess income, thus keeping inflation down.

The government took other anti-inflationary steps as well. One was rationing, which reduced consumer demand by limiting how much people could buy. The measure also cut civilian purchases of products needed for the war effort. Rationed items included gasoline, heating fuel, tires, coffee, sugar, meat, butter, and canned goods. The government also tried to keep wages and prices down. At first it froze wages, but when the cost of living rose, the government allowed wages to rise by 15 percent.

Raising an army. Along with increased production and expanded government controls, gearing up for war meant recruiting soldiers. In 1940, before the attack on Pearl Harbor, the United States passed the **Selective Training and Service Act**, which provided for the first peacetime draft in American history. The law required the registration of all men between ages 21 and 35 (age limits later extended from 18 to 37). Local draft boards determined fitness and deferred men for family, religious, or health reasons.

Of the some 15 million members of the armed services during World War II, about two thirds were draftees and the rest volunteers, including more than 300,000 women. Women enrolled in the Women's Auxiliary Army Corps (WAACs), Women's Airforce Service Pilots (WASPs), or auxiliary branches of the navy (WAVES), coast guard (SPARS), and marines. They worked as nurses, did office work, drove vehicles, and ferried planes in order to free men for active duty.

While most women military personnel served on the home front, women in the Army Nurse Corps (ANC) and Navy Nurse Corps (NNC) tended wounded soldiers overseas. Eunice Hatchitt, a nurse who served at Bataan, described the terrible conditions and heavy casualties:

66 Days and nights were an endless nightmare, until it seemed we couldn't stand it any longer. Patients came in by the hundreds, and the doctors and nurses worked continuously under the tents amid the flies and heat and dust. We had from eight to nine hundred victims a day. 99

■■ **The United States mobilized for war by increasing production, expanding government control of the economy, and raising an army.**

▶ The armed services actively recruited women. After registering and receiving vaccinations, WAAC recruits (below) emerge with duffel bags containing their uniforms.

The urgency of the war effort convinced President Roosevelt, who had led the nation since 1933, to run for an unprecedented fourth term. As the 1944 campaign drew near, Roosevelt told an aide, "God knows I don't want to [run], but I may find it necessary." Roosevelt won the nomination with little opposition; his vice-presidential candidate was a Missouri senator, Harry S. Truman.

The Republicans chose Thomas E. Dewey, governor of New York, who had won fame as a district attorney for prosecuting racketeers. However, he lacked Roosevelt's charisma and experience and was defeated by an electoral vote of 99 to Roosevelt's 432.

PROMOTING THE WAR

As it mobilized the nation's resources, the government also worked to keep morale high. This was especially important in the early days of the war, when Allied troops faced many setbacks. The government encouraged the media to do their part. Moviemakers, songwriters, and radio station programmers responded by urging all-out participation in the war effort.

Movie stars advertised war bonds and traveled overseas to entertain the troops. Hundreds of war movies poured out of Hollywood. Some patriotic films, such as *So Proudly We Hail*—about army nurses in the Philippines—built support for the war. Striking a lighter note were comedies like Bob Hope's *Caught in the Draft*. A few films, such as *Wake Island* and *Report from the Aleutians*, offered realistic views of combat. Most, however, romanticized American and other Allied soldiers and stereotypically portrayed the Japanese as treacherous, the Germans as fanatical, and the Italians as cowardly.

Radio stations broadcast both war news and entertainment. Radio correspondents such as Edward R. Murrow and Eric Sevareid gave on-the-scene accounts of war-ravaged Europe. A new federal agency, the Office of War Information (OWI), controlled the flow of war news at home.

Wartime musical hits included "Remember Pearl Harbor" and "Praise the Lord and Pass the Ammunition!" But the biggest hits of the period did not deal directly with the war. African American musicians—including trumpeter Dizzy Gillespie, sax player Charlie Parker, and piano player Thelonious Monk—popularized a new form of jazz, called bebop, or bop. Also popular were such sentimental songs as "White Christmas," which expressed Americans' longing for a return to peace.

The war also affected popular radio serials. Radio stations abandoned spy and sabotage programs for the duration of the war. Some even banned certain sound effects, such as wailing sirens, to avoid alarming listeners.

On the whole, World War II enjoyed broad support. Convinced that the cause was just, most Americans put up with shortages, planted "victory gardens" to conserve food, and bought millions of dollars worth of war bonds. Many families proudly displayed window banners with a star—a blue one for a loved one in the service, a gold one to commemorate a death in combat.

JAPANESE AMERICAN RELOCATION

By and large, World War II did not produce the kind of home-front intolerance that erupted during World War I. One tragic exception was the forced relocation and imprisonment, or **internment**, of Japanese Americans living on the Pacific coast. In September 1945, U.S. State Department adviser Eugene Rostow called internment "a tragic and dangerous mistake" and argued that "its motivation and its impact on our system of law deny every value of democracy."

When Pearl Harbor was bombed, about 119,000 people of Japanese ancestry lived in Washington, Oregon, and California. Of these, about a third, the Issei (EE-SAY), had been born in Japan and were regarded by the U.S. government as aliens ineligible for U.S. citizenship. The rest, the Nisei (NEE-SAY), had been born in the United States and were thus American citizens.

People of Japanese ancestry had long suffered racial discrimination in the United States. Laws prevented Japanese immigrants from becoming citizens, and prejudice restricted the kinds of jobs they and their descendants could hold and the neighborhoods where they could live.

▶ This painting of the internment camp at Heart Mountain, Wyoming, was done by Japanese American artist Estelle Ishigo.

◀ Toyo Miyatale photographed this scene in Los Angeles in the early days of World War II. With their belongings piled high on the sidewalk, Japanese Americans wait for the buses that will take them to a relocation assignment center.

Japanese American Population, 1940

More than 10,000
1,000 to 10,000
Less than 1,000
▲ Relocation camp

AMERICAN CITIZENSHIP
About two thirds of the 127,000 people of Japanese ancestry living in the continental United States were American-born and thus U.S. citizens.

Japanese American Relocation

INTERNEES By September 1942 some 100,000 Japanese Americans were interned in 10 camps located in relatively isolated, undeveloped areas.

? LOCATION Which two states had the largest Japanese American population in 1940?

When war came, prejudice turned into near hysteria. There was no evidence of disloyalty on the part of any Issei or Nisei. Strong anti-Japanese sentiments among some vocal politicians and residents of western states, however, persuaded the federal government to remove people of Japanese descent from the West Coast. In February 1942 they were ordered to detention camps in Wyoming, Utah, and other states. Here most were imprisoned until 1945—an action upheld by the Supreme Court in 1944.

■■ **Because of prejudice and war hysteria, Japanese Americans living on the West Coast were interned in relocation camps.**

Relocation profoundly disrupted the lives of Japanese Americans. They were forced to leave hurriedly, abandoning or selling their homes and businesses at rock-bottom prices. A government estimate later put Japanese American property losses at $400 million.

One imprisoned Japanese American was Norman Mineta, a Nisei from San Jose, California. On the day of the Pearl Harbor bombing, the young Mineta fearfully watched his neighbors being taken away for questioning by the FBI. He recalled bitterly that "they had done nothing; the only thing that they had done was to be born of Japanese ancestry."

Ten years old when his family was uprooted, Mineta wore his Cub Scout uniform on the train, hoping that it would show his loyalty to the United States. After six months in a barracks at the Santa Anita racetrack in southern California, Mineta's family was interned with some 10,000 others at a hastily built camp at Heart Mountain, Wyoming. "These camps were all barbed wire, guard towers, searchlights," recalled Mineta. "They were concentration camps. There's no question about it."

After the war Mineta attended college, became an insurance agent, and went into local politics in San Jose. In 1974 he was elected to the House of Representatives, where he served on several committees and introduced legislation seeking reparations for Japanese American internees.

Like most other internees, Mineta deplored what had happened, but his patriotism never wavered:

❝ Despite the color of our hair and skin, despite the shape of our eyes, the U.S. was our country. I remember how my parents reminded us of that fact. Just before our family was evacuated, my father . . . said, "No matter what happens, *this* is your home." ❞

Patriotism, and the desire to disprove accusations of disloyalty, inspired many young men in the camps to volunteer for military duty (in segregated units).

Norman Mineta

One Nisei combat team, the 442nd, fought in Europe and became one of the most decorated units in the armed services. Several thousand Japanese Americans also served in the Military Intelligence Service as interpreters and translators in the Pacific.

THE MARCH ON WASHINGTON

For African Americans, World War II brought both continued discrimination and greater opportunities. Many blacks moved into better-paying industrial jobs and played a key role in the military effort. About a million black soldiers served in the armed forces, including several thousand women in the Women's Auxiliary Army Corps. However, despite their protests, African Americans continued to serve in segregated units and until 1943 were kept out of combat. Blacks were usually restricted to menial work.

The millions of black Americans in the labor force in the 1940s also played an important homefront role in the war effort. But they had to struggle to gain acceptance. Many war plants would not hire blacks or would employ them only as janitors. And despite labor leaders' no-strike pledge, some white workers staged strikes, called "hate strikes," to keep black workers out of high-paying factory jobs.

In 1941, before the United States entered the war, African American labor leader A. Philip Randolph planned a march on Washington, D.C., to protest discrimination against black workers.

▲ African Americans served with distinction during the war. These pilots at a training center in Tuskegee, Alabama, study a map before going aloft in 1943.

President Roosevelt wanted to prevent the march, which Randolph predicted would bring 100,000 protesters to the Capitol. Randolph called it off after Roosevelt issued an executive order forbidding racial discrimination in defense plants and government offices.

To enforce the order, the government created the **Fair Employment Practices Committee** (FEPC). The FEPC investigated companies to make sure that all qualified applicants, regardless of race, were considered. The committee, however, lacked enforcement powers and could not prevent the widespread abuses. In addition, African Americans still had to struggle for equality in pay and promotion.

As in World War I, many blacks moved northward to work in war plants. In crowded cities, they faced discrimination in housing. Resulting tensions sometimes led to outbursts of violence against African Americans. In Detroit in 1943, some 25,000 white workers violated the wartime no-strike pledge and staged a hate strike to protest the promotion of African American workers. White residents of one Detroit neighborhood tried to prevent blacks from moving into the newly constructed Sojourner Truth Housing Project. In June of the same year, 25 blacks and 9 whites died in several days of rioting after a fight between blacks and whites at Belle Isle, a popular Detroit park, spread to other parts of the city.

Despite these incidents, most African Americans supported the war. Educator and civil rights activist Mary McLeod Bethune noted that African Americans "feel that the fight against fascism is their fight too," because they realized "that their persecution would be even worse under Hitler."

THE ZOOT-SUIT RIOTS

For Mexican Americans, as for blacks, World War II brought both opportunities and problems. More than 300,000 Mexican Americans served in the military, and 17 earned the Congressional Medal of Honor. The 88th Division, an elite combat unit known as the "Blue Devils," consisted mostly of Mexican Americans.

Mexican Americans also helped meet homefront labor needs. University of Texas history professor Carlos E. Castañeda served as assistant to the chairman of the FEPC and worked to

▲ These Mexican American infantrymen are being trained to use the rapid-firing Garand rifle at a U.S. Army camp. Because many of these soldiers spoke Spanish, army trainers gave instructions in both English and Spanish.

improve working conditions for Mexican Americans in Texas. In 1945 the FEPC ordered a major Texas oil company to discontinue its hiring and promotion practices that discriminated against Hispanics.

As a result of similar FEPC actions, and the pressing need for workers, many factories opened up jobs to Mexican Americans. Many Mexican Americans moved from the Southwest to industrial centers in the Midwest and on the West Coast. Under a 1942 agreement between the United States and Mexico, thousands of Mexican farm and railroad workers—known as **braceros**—came north to work in the Southwest during World War II.

But prejudice and discrimination against Hispanics in jobs, housing, and recreation facilities caused bitter resentment. Relations grew especially hostile in Los Angeles. Mexican American youths had adopted the fad of wearing zoot suits—long jackets, pegged trousers, and wide-brimmed hats. In the summer of 1943, sailors roamed the city attacking zoot-suiters in what came to be known as the **zoot-suit riots**. The government eventually clamped down on the sailors, but not before they had viciously beaten many Mexican Americans.

A citizens' committee later determined that the attacks were motivated by racial prejudice. The committee also placed partial responsibility on the police, who had responded to the riots by arresting Mexican Americans, and on biased newspaper reports.

■■ **African Americans and Mexican Americans won better factory jobs during the war but continued to face widespread discrimination.**

ROSIE THE RIVETER

During the depression, the government discouraged women, especially married women, from working. The government now urged them to enter the job market to replace departing servicemen and to help win the war against fascism. One government poster showed a woman worker in bandanna and overalls. The caption read: "I'm Proud . . . my husband <u>wants</u> me to do my part." Advertisements and a popular song promoted "Rosie the Riveter," the symbol of patriotic women defense workers.

From 1940 to 1944 the number of women in the labor force increased by more than four million. Women worked in war plants and replaced men in a host of jobs ranging from newspaper reporting to truck driving. Many of these new workers were married women who were taking jobs outside the home for the first time. Many women already in the paid work force left traditional "women's work" as domestics and other service jobs to work in factories.

■■ **World War II increased women's participation in the paid labor force and allowed them to move into traditionally male jobs.**

Women's participation in the war effort gave many of them a new sense of pride and self-worth. One woman aircraft worker finally felt a sense of achievement after feeling "average" at other jobs:

❝ Foremen from other departments come to my machine to ask me to do some work for them if I have time because they say I'm the best countersinker in the vast building! At forty-nine I've at last become not better than average, but the best! ❞

▼ These young women worked as welders in a war plant.

▲ Vultee Aircraft was one of the first aircraft plants to employ a large number of women workers. These Vultee workers are preparing a Vengeance Dive-Bomber for spray painting in August 1942.

A government study in 1942 praised women workers, noting that factories "were practically unanimous in reporting that on the whole the work done by women was considered equal to that of men." Nevertheless, women encountered discrimination. Women workers continued to be paid less than men for the same work. African American women and women over 40 found few employers willing to hire them. Although Frances Perkins, long a supporter of women workers, continued to head the Department of Labor during the war years, wartime federal agencies did little to enforce equal treatment for women workers.

In spite of women's achievements, it was widely assumed—by many women as well as men—that most of the jobs women held during the war were temporary. A manager of a shipyard predicted that "these women who are willing . . . to lend a hand with the war will be the . . . office personnel of . . . the future." The message was clear: in traditionally "masculine" jobs, women were wanted as emergency helpers, not as competition.

SECTION 2 REVIEW

IDENTIFY and explain the significance of the following: James F. Byrnes, War Production Board, Selective Training and Service Act, Thomas E. Dewey, internment, Norman Mineta, A. Philip Randolph, Fair Employment Practices Committee, braceros, zoot-suit riots.

1. **MAIN IDEA** What steps did the United States take to shift from a peacetime to a wartime economy?

2. **MAIN IDEA** How did World War II change life for American women?

3. **HYPOTHESIZING** Why did the United States forcibly relocate and imprison Japanese Americans living on the West Coast?

4. **WRITING TO EVALUATE** Imagine you are either an African American or a Mexican American during World War II. Write a letter to your representative in Congress, evaluating the gains you have made during the war.

5. **IDENTIFYING CAUSE AND EFFECT** What did the U.S. government do to keep morale high during World War II? How did most Americans respond to the government's actions?

DEFEAT OF THE AXIS POWERS

FOCUS

- **What did the Allied offensive in North Africa achieve?**
- **How did the Allies gain final victory in Europe?**
- **What was the chief objective of Allied assaults in the Pacific?**
- **Why and when did Japan surrender?**

American supplies and troops began to make a difference in the war by late 1942. But it would take over two more years of hard fighting to defeat the Axis powers. The Allied invasions of North Africa, Italy, and France and the fierce bombardments of German cities forced Germany to surrender in May 1945. In the Pacific, meanwhile, the United States seized Japanese-held islands, including the Philippines. Atomic attacks devastated Japan, and it surrendered in August 1945.

Liberation of Paris, 1944

ALLIED ATTACKS IN THE MEDITERRANEAN

The Allies agreed soon after Pearl Harbor that they would open up a second front against the Axis powers in order to relieve pressure on the Soviet Union. At Churchill's urging, they focused this attack on the Mediterranean region—what Churchill called the "soft underbelly" of the Axis territory.

Axis surrender in North Africa. In November 1942, after the British had driven the Germans and Italians into Libya, another Allied force landed in French Northwest Africa in an invasion code-named Operation Torch (see map on page 404). General Dwight D. Eisenhower commanded the invasion force, which consisted of American and British soldiers. As the soldiers established beachheads in Morocco and Algeria, Allied planes and ships cut Axis supply lines from Italy. Then, during the winter of 1942–43, the two Allied land forces—one from the west and the other from the east—began squeezing the Axis troops into a trap between them.

Several fierce battles took place in Tunisia. Finally, in May 1943, the Axis force of some

◄ "We are out to win the war in the quickest and most economical way," U.S. Army chief of staff George C. Marshall (right) declared in 1943. Marshall was photographed with General Dwight D. Eisenhower in North Africa in June 1943.

250,000 men surrendered. The Allies now controlled much of the Mediterranean. This victory also gave American troops valuable combat experience, especially in amphibious assaults.

■■ The conquest of North Africa gave the Allies increased control over the Mediterranean.

The invasion of Italy. North Africa offered a gateway to the Italian island of Sicily. Allied leaders decided to invade it next in order to clear the Axis forces out of the central Mediterranean and acquire a launching pad for an invasion of the Italian mainland.

Battling high winds and difficult seas, almost half a million troops landed in July 1943 and subdued Sicily in a little over a month. The Italian king named a new prime minister to replace Benito Mussolini and ordered Mussolini's arrest. The Germans, however, were determined not to surrender the peninsula. They took Mussolini to Germany and then set up a base for him in northern Italy.

In September the Italian government signed an armistice with the Allies. Two days later the Allies invaded southern Italy to attack the Germans. Although the Allies took Naples on October 1, they soon bogged down. Hoping to outflank Nazi troops near Rome, they landed to the south at Anzio in January 1944 (see map on page 404); but their attack failed, and they were pinned down for months. Not until June 1944 did the Allies march into Rome, which became the first Axis capital to fall.

American and British forces then began driving slowly north. They were joined by small units of troops from more than 25 countries. After months of bitter mountain warfare, the German occupiers were finally defeated. Mussolini was captured in late April and shot by Italian partisans.

◀ **World War II Victory Medal**

VICTORY IN EUROPE

During the months of fighting in the Mediterranean region, the Allies were waging campaigns on several other fronts as well. Although they faced a determined enemy, they eventually overcame all resistance.

Sea and air assaults. In the Atlantic, German U-boats continued to take a staggering toll of Allied ships, lives, and supplies. Not until 1943 did the **Battle of the Atlantic** begin to turn in the Allies' favor. An important factor was the refinement of sonar equipment, which uses sound waves to detect underwater objects. The Allies also developed fast escort ships for convoys and air-bombed German U-boats and submarine yards. By 1944 the Allies had won the Battle of the Atlantic.

In the air, too, 1943 was an important year for the Allies. They intensified their campaign of strategic bombing aimed at destroying German military production and at undermining the morale of the German people. British Royal Air Force (RAF) planes flew chiefly at night, dropping their bombs in the general area of a given target. American aircraft concentrated on precision bombing in daylight raids. By 1944, bombers rained tons of explosives on German factories, supply lines, and military centers. Many German civilians died in these raids.

The invasion of France. Victory in the Battle of the Atlantic and air assaults on Germany paved the way for Operation Overlord—the long-awaited Allied invasion of German-occupied France. Commanded by General Eisenhower, it had involved years of planning. The Allies put in place a system of dummy installations and false clues to convince the Germans that the invasion would take place near Calais.

Instead, the Allies landed to the south, in Normandy. On **D-Day**, June 6, 1944, nearly 5,000 troop transports, landing craft, and warships carried some 150,000 American, British, and Canadian soldiers across the English Channel. Overhead, planes dropped close to 23,000 airborne troops and bombed roads, bridges, and German troop concentrations. Sergeant Ralph G. Martin recalled that "everything was confusion" during the landing made in pounding surf:

The *New York Times* announced the Allied invasion of France on June 6, 1944. After landing at Normandy, these American members of the invasion force rest under a cliff before advancing inland.

66 Units were mixed up, many of them leaderless, most of them not being where they were supposed to be. Shells were coming in all the time; boats burning; vehicles with nowhere to go bogging down, getting hit; supplies getting wet; boats trying to come in all the time, some hitting mines, exploding. 99

The Germans had fortified the Normandy beaches with concrete bunkers, tank traps, and mines. But the Allied disinformation campaign had done its job. Hitler refused to send reinforcements, believing that the main invasion would occur elsewhere. Although the Allies met determined opposition, they penetrated 15 miles into France in less than a week. Aided by the French Resistance, the Allies drove steadily eastward. They liberated Paris on August 25, 1944. By early September they had landed over two million troops in western Europe. Another Allied force drove northward through France from the Mediterranean. Meanwhile, Soviet troops pressed Germany from the east.

A German counterattack.

Although Germany's situation was grave, Hitler would not give up. In September 1944 the Germans launched their first V-2s, long-range rockets aimed at cities in England and Belgium. Once launched, these bombs could not be shot down without causing considerable damage.

By September 1944 the Allies had crossed the German border. As they paused to bring in sup-

plies and to regroup, the Germans launched their last counterattack. In heavy snow, they drove against the Allies in the thickly wooded Ardennes region of Belgium and northern France, pushing them westward to create a dangerous bulge in the Allied lines. In the resulting **Battle of the Bulge**, some 200,000 Germans attacked an initial American force of around 80,000. Because many of the regular troops had been transferred to other areas, much of the fighting was done by "cooks, clerks, mechanics, and radio operators," one American soldier remembered.

Allied generals rushed reinforcements to the front, and the Allies pushed the Germans back. Artillery-man Francis Tsuzuki, whose Japanese American battalion pursued the Germans, remembered that "the Germans were retreating so fast. At times we were moving . . . more than 100 miles a day." By January 1945 it was clear that the German offensive had failed. In February Roosevelt, Churchill, and Stalin met at the **Yalta Conference** to plan for the postwar peace. At the conference the leaders agreed to divide and occupy Germany and outlined plans for a new international peace organization.

Last days. During the early months of 1945, Allied bombers continued to blast German industrial and population centers, including Dresden, Leipzig, and Berlin. One of the most devastating—and controversial—attacks hit Dresden in February. This beautiful old city, of little strategic value, was packed with refugees fleeing from the war-torn areas. In one massive two-day attack, Allied bombers caused the worst firestorms of the war. Total civilian deaths have been estimated at between 30,000 and 60,000.

The Allied bombing of Dresden, Germany, killed many civilians and left many famous buildings in ruins. Shown here is the damage to the Zwinger Museum, which housed a priceless art collection.

In March, Allied troops from the west crossed the Rhine and drove into the heart of Germany. By then, Soviet troops occupied much of Eastern Europe. Churchill wanted the Allies to push east as far and as fast as possible because he worried that the Russians might later lay claim to territories they seized. But Eisenhower, who did not want military strategy determined by political considerations, halted the Allied advance at the Elbe River in April. The Soviet army agreed to halt momentarily east of Berlin.

On April 30, 1945, Hitler committed suicide in his bunker deep under the ruins of Berlin. As Soviet troops occupied the city, German armies all over Europe stopped fighting. American sergeant Mack Morriss described the grim mood of the fallen city: "There is a feeling that here has ended not only a city but a nation, that here a titanic force has come to catastrophe." Germany surrendered unconditionally on May 7. The next day, known as V-E (Victory in Europe) Day, marked the formal end of a brutal war that had held Europe in its grip for more than five years.

■■ After winning the Battle of the Atlantic and bombing Germany, the Allies invaded France. Germany surrendered in May 1945.

*P*ACIFIC OFFENSIVES

In the Pacific, as in the western theater of operations, the Allies went on the offensive by 1943. The planned attack on Japan had two components: (1) air, land, and naval forces would seize Japanese-held islands in the central Pacific and set up air bases there; (2) combined forces would retake New Guinea and then the Philippines. The ultimate objective, of course, was to come within striking distance of Japan itself.

Island-hopping. As early as 1942, the American high command had adopted a policy of **island-hopping**. This meant that troops would attack and seize only certain strategic Japanese-held islands, rather than try to recapture all of them. Japanese garrisons on bypassed islands would be cut off from supplies and troop reinforcements.

In the central Pacific, an island-hopping offensive began in November 1943 in the Gilbert Islands (see map on page 402). Army troops easily took Makin Island. Tarawa Island proved more difficult. Because of a coral reef encircling the island, the marines who landed there, according to Sergeant John Bushemi, had to wade in to the beach "in the face of murderous Japanese fire, with no protection." Almost 1,000 marines lost their lives, and some 2,000 were wounded before the island was secure.

The next important series of landings targeted the Marshall Islands, north of the Gilberts. Here Americans captured several key bases from which they bombed the Truk Islands, the headquarters of the Japanese fleet.

By the summer of 1944, Americans advanced to the Mariana Islands. In June, under cover of intense air and naval bombardment from nearby carriers, landing craft swept in to the beaches of Saipan. The Japanese, determined to take a stand, sent out a big fleet to stop this offensive. In the resulting **Battle of the Philippine Sea**, the United States won a decisive victory, downing hundreds of Japanese planes while only losing some 80 U.S. planes.

Saipan and Guam fell in July and August, respectively. U.S. victories here were especially crucial. The islands provided airstrips from which American bombers could launch missions against the islands of Japan.

Reconquering the Philippines. Despite these setbacks, Japanese resistance proved just as fierce when the Allies began their New Guinea–Philippines campaign in June 1943. Douglas MacArthur, who had earlier evacuated the Philippines, commanded U.S. forces.

 MacArthur was born in 1880, the son of distinguished general Arthur MacArthur. After graduating first in his class from West Point, young MacArthur served in the Philippines and was wounded twice in World War I. From

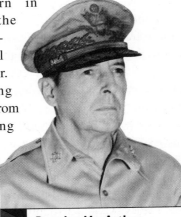
Douglas MacArthur

THE NAVAJO CODE TALKERS

During World War II Native Americans served in several branches of the U.S. armed forces. Their languages allowed them to play a unique role in the Signal Corps, the communication units responsible for coding and sending classified military information. On the basis of the success of a few Native American army groups in code work, the Marine Signal Corps decided in March 1942 to organize a unit composed entirely of Navajos. The marines believed that the Navajo language would be unfamiliar to the Japanese, and thus would provide an unbreakable code. They quickly assembled a group of Navajo soldiers for the job.

The new unit devised and memorized a special Navajo dictionary containing 413 military terms. For example, the Navajo word for "chicken hawk" meant dive-bomber in the code; "humming-bird" meant fighter plane; and "iron fish" meant submarine. Armed with this new code, the Navajo "Code Talkers" first went into action in the fall of 1942 in the Pacific.

Soon after the Code Talkers arrived on the front lines, U.S. field commanders reported that the Navajos' methods reduced the time needed for decoding and encoding messages by half. As radio operators tracking Japanese movements, the Navajos often had to work in especially dangerous conditions behind enemy lines. "The Navajo Code Talkers have proved to be excellent Marines, intelligent, industrious, efficient," one officer wrote. Another remarked, "Were it not for the Navajos, the Marines would never have taken Iwo Jima."

By August 1943 nearly 200 Navajos were participating in the Code Talker program, and by the war's end more than 400 had served in the Marine Signal Corps. Their codes completely baffled the Japanese and were never broken. Though the Navajo Code Talkers made up only a small part of the Allied forces, their contributions to the war effort were invaluable.

▲ Corporal Henry Bake, Jr., (left) and Private George H. Kirk (right) were two members of the Navajo Code Talkers. They are shown operating a portable radio set behind front lines in the Solomon Islands in 1943.

1919 to 1922 he was superintendent of West Point. He took part in the attack on the Bonus Army marchers of 1932 (see Chapter 13), justifying the violence by claiming that Communists were behind this veterans' protest. After serving as a military adviser in the Philippines for several years, MacArthur was recalled to active duty in the summer of 1941. Eventually he was given command of all U.S. Army units in the Pacific.

In many respects, MacArthur was an excellent strategist. No one doubted his courage. But he was also arrogant, and though he demanded absolute loyalty from his subordinates, he did not hesitate to disagree with his superiors.

In the Allied drive to recapture the Philippines, MacArthur led U.S. and Australian troops in a series of landings along the north coast of New Guinea. By late July 1944 they had reached the western end of this large island. Allied forces also took smaller islands nearby, such as the Admiralty Islands.

By the fall of 1944, with New Guinea secure and with its newly won bases in the Marianas, the United States was ready to invade the Philippines.

Allied forces poured onto the beaches of the island of Leyte in October. The Japanese navy's counterattack led to the **Battle of Leyte Gulf**, the last, largest, and most decisive naval engagement in the Pacific. The battle was a disaster for the Japanese, who lost four carriers, two battleships, and several cruisers. From this time on, the Japanese fleet no longer seriously threatened the Allies.

Allied troops, aided by Filipino guerrillas, fanned out over the islands of the Philippines. Overcoming bitter opposition, they entered Manila in February 1945 and subdued most Japanese defense forces within weeks. "I'm a little late," said MacArthur, "but we finally came."

■■ **Island-hopping and the reconquest of the Philippines brought the Allies within bombing distance of Japan's cities.**

VICTORY IN THE PACIFIC

These Pacific victories gave the United States bases to launch B-29 bombers against the Japanese home islands. In a series of devastating night attacks, U.S. planes hit most of the country's major cities. The worst raid, over Tokyo in March 1945, created firestorms that destroyed much of the city.

▼ **A few hours after U.S. Marines captured Iwo Jima, naval landing crafts delivered tons of supplies to the island. The slippery volcanic ash made it difficult for marines to keep their footing while carrying the heavy crates.**

Japanese civilian morale sagged, but the country's military leaders refused to surrender. In February 1945, when marines attacked Iwo Jima—only 750 miles from Tokyo—they met strong resistance. U.S. marines struggled to take Mount Suribachi, which the Japanese held with a strong system of tunnels and bunkers. The Battle of Iwo Jima lasted nearly a month. Some 4,000 marines were killed, while the Japanese lost more than 20,000.

On April 1 the largest landing force in Pacific history invaded Okinawa, about 350 miles from Japan. Allied soldiers drove the Japanese forces to the southern tip of the island. The **Battle of Okinawa** was perhaps the bloodiest of the Pacific war, with U.S. casualties estimated at 49,000 and Japanese losses at over 100,000. Meanwhile, a 700-plane squad of **kamikaze**, or suicide planes, damaged 13 U.S. destroyers. (*Kamikaze* is a Japanese word meaning "divine wind.")

By early April 1945, however, American victory in the Pacific was near. But President Roosevelt did not live to see the end of hostilities with Japan. The world was stunned when he died suddenly on April 12. The new president, Harry S. Truman, wrote candidly about his bewilderment:

▲ **The sudden death of President Roosevelt shocked many Americans. A weeping Sergeant Graham Jackson plays "Going Home" on his accordion as the president's casket passes by.**

66 I did not know what reaction the country would have to the death of a man whom they all practically worshipped. I was worried about the reaction of the Armed Forces. . . . I knew the President had a great many meetings with Churchill and Stalin. I was not familiar with any of these things. 99

Within weeks, however, Truman faced a grave decision. Should the Allies invade Japan or use a fearsome new weapon, the atomic bomb?

Germany's surrender had freed Allied forces for the war in the Pacific, but Japan remained a formidable opponent with a well-trained army and strong defenses—despite repeated Allied bombings.

The United States' new weapon had been developed by the top-secret **Manhattan Project**, whose scientists had been working on a bomb since 1942. The scientists successfully tested their bomb at Alamogordo, New Mexico, on July 16, 1945. The very next day, Truman met with Allied leaders at Potsdam, south of Berlin. On July 26 they demanded Japan's unconditional surrender, which Japan rejected.

Truman decided to give the order to use atomic weapons against Japan. On August 6 a U.S. plane called the *Enola Gay* dropped an atomic bomb on Hiroshima. It flattened a huge area of the city and killed more than 75,000 people. Three days later the United States dropped the second atomic bomb on Nagasaki. The Japanese estimated that the total number of deaths caused by both bombs—including those who died later from burns and radiation poisoning—was 240,000.

A day before the bombing of Nagasaki, the Soviet Union had declared war on Japan and began an invasion of Manchuria. The Japanese soon

▲ This aerial photograph shows the devastation in Hiroshima after the atomic bomb was dropped. The watch shown was found in the wreckage, its hands frozen at 8:15—the exact time of the explosion.

offered to surrender. Despite the unconditional surrender demand, the Allies accepted a big condition: the emperor could remain on his throne. The formal surrender was signed on September 2, 1945, aboard the battleship *Missouri* in Tokyo Bay.

■■ **After the U.S. atomic bombings of Hiroshima and Nagasaki, Japan surrendered in August 1945.**

SECTION 3 REVIEW

IDENTIFY and explain the significance of the following: Dwight D. Eisenhower, Battle of the Atlantic, D-Day, Battle of the Bulge, Yalta Conference, island-hopping, Battle of the Philippine Sea, Battle of Leyte Gulf, Battle of Iwo Jima, Battle of Okinawa, kamikaze, Harry S. Truman, Manhattan Project.

LOCATE and explain the importance of the following: Sicily, Anzio, Normandy, Dresden, Elbe River, Gilbert Islands, Marshall Islands, Mariana Islands, New Guinea, Leyte, Iwo Jima, Okinawa, Hiroshima, Nagasaki.

1. **MAIN IDEA** What did the Allies accomplish through the military campaign in North Africa?

2. **MAIN IDEA** What events forced Germany to surrender in 1945?

3. **GEOGRAPHY: LOCATION** How did the Allies attempt to regain control of the Pacific? What was the overall aim of this military strategy?

4. **WRITING TO EXPLAIN** Write an essay that explains when and why Japan surrendered.

5. **USING HISTORICAL IMAGINATION** Imagine you are a soldier on either the European or the Pacific front. Write a diary entry that describes conditions you experienced in one of the battles mentioned in the text.

THE PRICE OF VICTORY

FOCUS

■ **What were some of the costs of World War II?**

■ **What was the Holocaust? How did it affect European Jews?**

■ **What were the international consequences of World War II?**

Soviet civilians mourn dead soldiers.

After years of struggle and sacrifice, World War II ended in victory for the Allies. But the price was high. The toll in lives and property was without precedent. Most alarming was the knowledge—fully revealed only after the defeat of Germany— that Hitler had tried to exterminate all the Jews of Europe. Along with peace came many uncertainties about the future.

COSTS OF THE WAR

The United States and its allies achieved their war aims. Germany's murderous Nazi regime was destroyed. Japanese expansion in Asia was halted and the nation's military warlords overthrown. But the toll in death, suffering, and destruction was appallingly high.

World War II was the most devastating war the world has ever known. When it finally ended, hundreds of cities, from London to Tokyo, lay in ruins. Beautiful churches and palaces were reduced to rubble, and priceless works of art had gone up in smoke. Millions of people lacked heat, electricity, running water, adequate food, or means of traveling from one place to another. In some regions, mile upon mile of field and forest had been reduced to utter desolation.

There is no way of estimating the value of property loss, but two examples indicate its extent. In Düsseldorf, Germany, more than 90 percent of homes could not be lived in. The cities of Kiev and Minsk in the Soviet Union had to be completely rebuilt.

The war took more lives than any other conflict in history and brought untold suffering to civilians. According to one estimate, some 30 million noncombatants lost their lives from bombing, shelling, disease, or starvation. Millions more were injured, were weakened by malnutrition, or lost everything they owned. The Soviet Union and

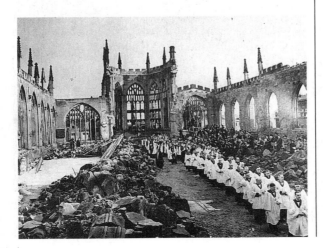

◄ **Britain's Coventry Cathedral was one of many churches virtually destroyed by bombing attacks during the war. This ceremony was held among the church ruins in February 1941.**

DEATHS IN WORLD WAR II		
Country	Military Deaths	Civilian Deaths
ALLIED POWERS		
British Commonwealth	373,372	92,673
France	213,324	350,000
Poland	123,178	5,675,000
Philippines	27,000	91,000
United States	292,131	6,000
Soviet Union	11,000,000	7,000,000
Yugoslavia	305,000	1,200,000
AXIS POWERS		
Bulgaria	10,000	10,000
Germany	3,500,000	780,000
Hungary	200,000	290,000
Italy	242,232	152,941
Japan	1,300,000	672,000
Romania	300,000	200,000

Source: *Encyclopedia Britannica*

THE WAR TO END ALL WARS World War II had an enormous global impact. Tens of thousands of men, women, and children died from causes directly related to the war, and untold numbers lost their homes and livelihoods.

? **BUILDING GRAPH SKILLS** Which country had the highest overall casualties?

When Germany occupied France and other countries of Western Europe, and attacked Poland and the Soviet Union, it extended its control over additional thousands of Jews. Now Hitler's war against this people entered a new phase—one of utter savagery. In many regions special squads of German soldiers rounded up Jews and shot them. Elsewhere, Jews were forced into cities and isolated in ghettos. In 1941 the Germans began constructing camps specifically for the purpose of **genocide**—the deliberate annihilation of an entire people. Hitler and senior Nazi officials called this extermination program the "final solution of the Jewish question."

Major death camps were Auschwitz (OWSH-**vits**), Treblinka, and Majdanek, all in Poland. Here Jewish men, women, and children were transported in sealed railroad cars, marched into rooms disguised as shower facilities, and gassed. Their bodies were then cremated. All told, some six million Jews—two thirds of the Jewish population of Europe—perished.

China were especially hard hit. As in World War I, U.S. civilian losses were relatively light. In economic terms, armaments and other military costs probably totaled over $1 trillion.

■■ World War II resulted in more deaths and destroyed more property than any other war in history.

THE HOLOCAUST

No other wartime civilian deaths caused more horror than those of the **Holocaust**, Nazi Germany's systematic slaughter of European Jews. Before the war, Hitler had forced Jews out of most professions and had stripped them of their civil rights (see Chapter 15). The Nazis' goal was a Germany that was *Judenrein*—free of Jews. The Nazi authorities at first encouraged emigration, and about two thirds of all German and Austrian Jews left their countries. Many of those who remained were imprisoned in concentration camps such as Dachau (DAHK-**ow**) and Buchenwald (BOO-kuhn-wawld).

▲ These survivors of the large concentration camp in Evensee, Austria were photographed in May 1945 after their liberation by U.S. soldiers.

The Nazis' pitiless slaughter extended to other peoples, too. Other victims, numbering in the millions, included Gypsies, Poles, the mentally disabled, religious dissidents, and homosexuals. Communists, Socialists, and other political and religious opponents of the Nazi regime faced imprisonment and death as well.

When the Allies liberated the death camps, they found thousands of starving survivors. One was Elie Wiesel, a Romanian-born writer. Having been sent first to Auschwitz and then to Buchenwald, he was an emaciated youth of 16 when freed. Hospitalized for two weeks, he recovered. His writings, however, express the deep psychological scars left on concentration camp survivors:

> 66 One day I was able to get up, after gathering all my strength. I wanted to see myself in the mirror hanging on the opposite wall. I had not seen myself since the ghetto.
> From the depths of the mirror, a corpse gazed back at me.
> The look in his eyes, as they stared into mine, has never left me. 99

■■ The Holocaust took the lives of six million Jews—two thirds of European Jewry.

Why were the Nazis able to carry out the monstrous genocide? They built on a long history of anti-Semitism in Europe stretching back to the Middle Ages. A barrage of Nazi propaganda against Jews whipped up this anti-Semitism. Some non-Jews in countries occupied by the Nazis assisted or failed to prevent the Nazis from sending their Jewish fellow citizens off to the death camps. Others, however, heroically worked to save Jewish lives.

Another factor underlying the Holocaust was the lack of direct action by the Allies. Although reports of mass exterminations surfaced as early as 1941, the Allies believed the reports to be exaggerated. As a result, Allied nations did not open their doors to greater numbers of refugees or attempt to destroy rail lines that led to the death camps.

▶ **British prime minister Winston Churchill (left), President Roosevelt (center), and Soviet leader Joseph Stalin (right) met at Yalta in 1945 to discuss territorial divisions after the war.**

A NEW BALANCE OF POWER

By the time of the Yalta Conference, the political balance of power had clearly shifted. The United States had confirmed its position as the world's strongest nation. Its western European allies, notably Great Britain, had been weakened by the war. The Soviet Union, in spite of the devastation it had undergone, emerged from the war as a mighty force. For the next several decades, the United States and the Soviet Union, as **superpowers**, would dominate the world.

Much of the Soviet Union's new power was based on the territory it had occupied in Eastern Europe during the war. At the Yalta Conference, Roosevelt and Churchill had secretly agreed to accept the Soviet occupation of Poland in return for Stalin's vague promise of eventual free elections. When this agreement later became public, some critics blamed Roosevelt and Churchill for giving in to Stalin's demands. But with Soviet troops in control of Poland, they had little choice. Furthermore, Roosevelt wanted to assure Russia's entry into the war against Japan.

By the end of the war, the Soviet Union had absorbed the Baltic nations of Estonia, Latvia, Lithuania, and parts of Czechoslovakia and Romania. After Japan's surrender, the Soviet Union also took control of former Japanese territory, including the Kuril Islands and half of Sakhalin Island, which lie north of Japan. Defeated Japan also lost Inner Mongolia, Manchuria, and the islands of Taiwan (Formosa) and Hainan to China.

■■ Among the many consequences of World War II were the emergence of two superpowers and territorial realignments.

COMMENTARY

Using the Atomic Bomb

President Franklin Roosevelt approved research on the development of an atomic bomb after Albert Einstein and other scientists warned him in 1939 that Germany might be working on such a weapon. But by early 1945, with Germany defeated, some Manhattan Project scientists opposed using the bomb against Japan or urged a demonstration of its powers first. Nevertheless, with President Truman's approval, atomic bombs were dropped on two Japanese cities, with massive civilian casualties. Was Truman's action justified, or was it a grave error?

Truman defended his decision by noting Japan's refusal to surrender unconditionally. The atomic bomb, he claimed, had prevented a costly American invasion of Japan. He also linked the atomic bomb to Pearl Harbor. "The Japanese began the war," said Truman. "They have been repaid manyfold."

Some historians have questioned Truman's explanations. They point out that the U.S. had broken the Japanese secret code, so Truman knew that Tokyo was sending out urgent peace feelers by way of Moscow. These scholars also note Stalin's pledge at Yalta to enter the war against Japan within three months of Germany's surrender—in other words, by early August. Victory was possible, these historians argue, without the dropping of the atomic bomb and without a U.S. invasion.

These historians suggest several reasons for Truman's decision. They point out that the barriers against attacking civilians had already been broken by Nazi rocket attacks and by the Allied firebombing of Dresden, Hamburg, Tokyo, and other cities. They contend that Truman feared postwar investigations if he failed to use the bomb after spending millions to build it.

Above all, these scholars argue, Truman dropped the bomb not only to end the war but also to demonstrate America's atomic might and thus strengthen America's postwar position in dealing with the Soviet Union. "The dropping of the atomic bomb," one historian argued, "was not so much the last military act of the second World War, as the first major operation of the cold diplomatic war with Russia."

Other historians, however, point to Japan's wartime atrocities and to the bitter-end defense of Okinawa. They note that top military leaders in Tokyo fiercely opposed the peace overtures and favored a desperate defense of the home islands. We simply do not know, these historians insist, what precise role the atomic bomb played in ending the war.

While the debate over Truman's decision continues, all historians agree on its long-range effects: a deadly nuclear arms race. In the postwar years, the United States, the Soviet Union, and other nations built vast arsenals of nuclear weapons and missiles. Even after the risk of global nuclear war faded, the danger that smaller nations would develop nuclear weapons remained, and massive quantities of radioactive waste threatened environmental safety. Truman's fateful decision of 1945 had consequences few anticipated at the time.

SECTION 4 REVIEW

IDENTIFY and explain the significance of the following: Holocaust, genocide, Elie Wiesel, superpowers.

LOCATE and explain the importance of the following: Kuril Islands, Sakhalin Island, Taiwan, Hainan.

1. **MAIN IDEA** Why was World War II the most devastating war the world has ever known?

2. **MAIN IDEA** How did the Holocaust affect European Jews?

3. **ASSESSING CONSEQUENCES** Summarize the international consequences of World War II.

4. **WRITING TO DESCRIBE** Imagine you are a soldier who has helped liberate one of the German death camps. Write a letter home that describes what you saw there.

5. **TAKING A STAND** Do you think the United States was justified in using the atomic bomb against Japan? Give reasons for your answer.

CHAPTER 16
Review

Japanese attack
Pearl Harbor.

1941

Allies sign Joint Declaration. Bataan
Death March occurs. Allies stop Japanese
offensive in battles of Coral Sea, Midway,
and Guadalcanal. Rommel defeated at
Battle of El Alamein.

1942

WRITING A SUMMARY

Using the essential points of the chapter as a guide, write a summary of the chapter.

REVIEWING CHRONOLOGY

Number your paper 1 to 5. Study the time line above, and list the following events in the order in which they happened by writing the first next to 1, the second next to 2, and so on. Then complete the activity below.

1. Allies sign Joint Declaration.
2. D-Day invasion begins.
3. Zoot-suit riots break out.
4. FDR dies.
5. Japanese attack Pearl Harbor.

Assessing Consequences What was the effect of the Allied victory at the Battle of Leyte Gulf?

IDENTIFYING PEOPLE AND IDEAS

Explain the historical significance of each of the following people or terms.

1. Douglas MacArthur
2. Battle of Midway
3. braceros
4. War Production Board
5. Norman Mineta
6. D-Day
7. island-hopping
8. kamikaze
9. genocide
10. Elie Wiesel

UNDERSTANDING MAIN IDEAS

1. How was the United States drawn into World War II? What advantages did the Axis Powers have over the United States at the beginning of the war?
2. What steps did the U.S. government take to mobilize for war? What did the media do to keep morale high?
3. What gains did African Americans, Mexican Americans, and women make during the war?
4. How did the Allies win the Battle of the Atlantic?
5. How did the Nazis carry out the Holocaust?

🏴 REVIEWING THEMES

1. **Global Relations** How did the Allies pool their resources to win World War II?
2. **Cultural Diversity** How did wartime conditions lead to increased discrimination against Japanese Americans?
3. **Technology and Society** What political and moral issues did the development of atomic weapons raise?

THINKING CRITICALLY

1. **Analyzing** What actions did the Allies take to win the war in Europe?
2. **Synthesizing** What were the final costs and consequences of World War II?
3. **Evaluating** Why was the atomic bomb used against Japan? What effect did the use of this weapon have on the war in the Pacific?

WRITING ABOUT HISTORY

Writing to Classify Create a time line listing the important battles and other events leading to the Allied victory in the Pacific.

STRATEGY FOR SUCCESS

Review the Skills Handbook entry on Identifying Cause and Effect beginning on page 749. Then study the poster below, which was issued by the U.S. government during World War II. What cause-and-effect relationship does the poster suggest?

Allied leaders meet at Casablanca, Cairo, and Tehran. Soviets defeat Axis troops at Stalingrad. Allies conquer North Africa. Zoot-suit riots break out.

Allies capture Rome. D-Day invasion begins. Japanese navy defeated at Battle of Leyte Gulf. Germans launch V-2 rockets. FDR reelected president. Allied and German troops clash at Battle of the Bulge.

Allies meet at Yalta. Allies win battles of Iwo Jima and Okinawa. FDR dies. Germany surrenders. U.S. drops atomic bombs on Hiroshima and Nagasaki. Japan surrenders.

1943   **1944**   **1945**

USING PRIMARY SOURCES

After the war, survivors of German concentration camps began to reveal to the world the horrors suffered by Jews and other prisoners. Read the following excerpt from *The Holocaust Kingdom* (1963), written by Alexander Donat, a survivor of Majdanek. Then write an essay expressing your feelings about what you have read.

> *Usually they were taken there [to the gas chamber] at night, but once I saw the operation in broad daylight. . . . Through a crack in the wall we saw a long procession of living skeletons slowly emerging from Barrack Nineteen on their way to the gate. It was the way we would look in another two, four, or six weeks: it was the way it all ended. Majdanek was an industrial factory for producing corpses: death, the destruction of the greatest number of prisoners in the shortest time at the lowest cost was Majdanek's purpose. Life was treated as something . . . essentially worthless; in fact, contemptible. Death was our constant companion and not a terrible one, for quite often one wished passionately for it. It was life that was terrible, the long, agonizing process of parting from it after it had been shorn of dignity. Life in Majdanek was reduced to its basic elements.*

LINKING HISTORY AND GEOGRAPHY

After Allied forces on the Bataan Peninsula surrendered in April 1942, the Japanese ordered them to assemble at Mariveles and then march to San Fernando. From there the prisoners were shipped north by train. Study the map of the Bataan Death March in the next column. About how far did the prisoners have to march to reach San Fernando? About how far did they travel by train? What was their final destination? Why is it not possible to assess the difficulty of the journey from this map?

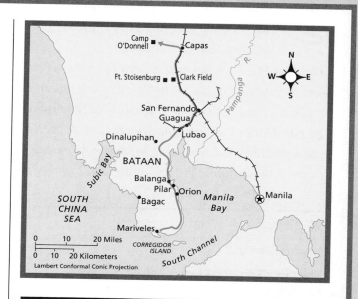

BUILDING YOUR PORTFOLIO

Complete the following projects independently or cooperatively.

1. **GLOBAL RELATIONS** In chapters 13 and 15 you portrayed a journalist. Building on that experience, imagine you are a member of a peace organization in the United States. Write an essay on ways to resolve international conflicts without war.

2. **WAR** In Chapter 15 you portrayed a diplomat at the beginning of the war. Building on that experience, imagine you are on a government committee examining the effects of the war. Compile statistics that illustrate the effects.

3. **CULTURE AND SOCIETY** In chapters 11, 12, and 14 you explored U.S. society in the 1920s and 1930s. Building on that experience, imagine you are a woman factory worker during World War II. Create a series of journal entries expressing your feelings about life on the home front.

American Letters

▲ Jean Toomer

Songs of the Cities

The Roaring Twenties was an era of cities, when economic prosperity and technological innovations led to a boom in skyscraper construction. Cities continued to expand throughout the Great Depression and World War II. Harlem Renaissance poets Claude McKay and Jean Toomer, novelist Sinclair Lewis, and Japanese American writer Toshio Mori capture the dynamic growth of the cities in the following selections.

A Song of the Moon

by Claude McKay

The moonlight breaks upon the city's domes,
And falls along cemented steel and stone,
Upon the grayness of a million homes,
Lugubrious[1] in unchanging monotone.

Upon the clothes behind the tenement,
That hang like ghosts suspended from the lines,
Linking each flat to each indifferent,
Incongruous[2] and strange the moonlight shines.

There is no magic from your presence here,
Ho, moon, sad moon, tuck up your trailing robe,
Whose silver seems antique and so severe
Against the glow of one electric globe.

Go spill your beauty on the laughing faces
Of happy flowers that bloom a thousand hues,
Waiting on tiptoe in the wilding spaces,
To drink your wine mixed with sweet drafts of dews. ❖

---

1 melancholy
2 not harmonious

From The Blue Meridian

by Jean Toomer

The prairie's sweep in flat infinity,
The city's rise is perpendicular to farthest star,
I stand where the two directions intersect,
At Michigan Avenue and Walton Place,[1]

Level with my countrymen,
Right-angled to the universe.

It is a new America,
To be spiritualized by each new American,
To be taken as a golden grain
And lifted, as the wheat of our bodies,
To matter uniquely man.
I would give my life to see inscribed
Upon the arch of our consciousness
These aims: Growth, Transformation, Love,
That we might become heart-centered towards
     one another,
Love-centered towards God, dedicated to the creation
     of a higher type of man, growing up to Him.
Let new eyes see this statue in the bay,
Let this be quarantine to unbend dreams,
Let old eyes see it in Wall Street and the Loop,[2]
And through this clearing house
Let all pass checks who may. ❖

---

1 streets in downtown Chicago
2 Chicago's downtown

From Babbitt

by Sinclair Lewis

   The towers of Zenith aspired above the morning mist; austere [simple] towers of steel and cement and limestone, sturdy as cliffs and delicate as silver rods. They were neither citadels nor churches, but frankly and beautifully office-buildings.

The mist took pity on the fretted [eroded] structures of earlier generations: the Post Office with its shingle-tortured mansard,[1] the red brick minarets [towers] of hulking old houses, factories with stingy and sooted windows, wooden tenements colored like mud. The city was full of such grotesqueries,[2] but the clean towers were thrusting them from the business center, and on the farther hills were shining new houses, homes—they seemed—for laughter and tranquillity.

Over a concrete bridge fled a limousine of long sleek hood and noiseless engine. These people in evening clothes were returning from an all-night rehearsal of a Little Theater play. . . . Below the bridge curved a railroad, a maze of green and crimson lights. The New York Flyer boomed past, and twenty lines of polished steel leaped into the glare.

In one of the skyscrapers the wires of the Associated Press were closing down. The telegraph operators wearily raised their celluloid eye-shades after a night of talking with Paris and Peking. Through the building crawled the scrubwomen, yawning, their old shoes slapping. The dawn mist spun away. Cues [lines] of men with lunch-boxes clumped toward the immensity of new factories, sheets of glass and hollow tile, glittering shops where five thousand men worked beneath one roof, pouring out the honest wares that would be sold up the Euphrates[3] and across the veldt.[4] The whistles rolled out in greeting a chorus cheerful as the April dawn; the song of labor in a city built—it seemed—for giants. ❖

1 a sloping roof
2 things that are not harmonious
3 river in Southwest Asia
4 grassland of southern Africa

From *Lil' Yokohama*

by Toshio Mori

In Lil' Yokohama, as the youngsters call our community, we have twenty-four hours every day . . . and morning, noon, and night roll on regularly just as in Boston, Cincinnati, Birmingham, Kansas City, Minneapolis, and Emeryville.

When the sun is out, the housewives sit on the porch or walk around the yard, puttering with this and that, and the old men who are in the house when it is cloudy or raining come out

on the porch or sit in the shade and read the newspaper. The day is hot. All right, they like it. The day is cold. All right, all right. The people of Lil' Yokohama are here. *Here, here,* they cry with their presence just as the youngsters when the teachers call the roll. And when the people among people are sometimes missing from Lil' Yokohama's roll, perhaps forever, it is another matter; but the news belongs here just as does the weather.

Today young and old are at the Alameda ball grounds to see the big game: Alameda Taiiku *vs.* San Jose Asahis. The great Northern California game is under way. Will Slugger Hironaka hit that southpaw from San Jose? Will the same southpaw make the Alameda sluggers stand on their heads? It's the great question. . . .

It is Sunday evening in Lil' Yokohama, and the late dinners commence. Someone who did not go to the game asks, "Who won today?" "San Jose," we say. "Oh, gee," he says. "But Slugger knocked another home run," we say. "What again? He sure is good!" he says. "Big league scouts ought to size him up." "Sure," we say.

Tomorrow is a school day, tomorrow is a work day, tomorrow is another twenty-four hours. In Lil' Yokohama night is almost over. On Sunday nights the block is peaceful and quiet. . . .

Something is happening to the Etos of the block. All of a sudden they turn in their old '30 Chevrolet for a new Oldsmobile Eight! They follow this with a new living-room set and a radio and a new coat of paint for the house. On Sundays the whole family goes for an outing. Sometimes it is to Fleishhacker Pool or to Santa Cruz. It may be to Golden Gate Park or to the ocean or to their relatives in the country. . . . They did not strike oil or win the sweepstakes. Nothing of the kind happens in Lil' Yokohama, though it may any day. . . . What then? ❖

THINKING AND WRITING ABOUT LITERATURE

1. What features of the city does Claude McKay describe? Why do you think he wants the moon to shine somewhere else?
2. What are the three things Jean Toomer wishes city dwellers to aspire to?
3. How does Sinclair Lewis describe Zenith's buildings? What do you think he means to show by contrasting the old and new buildings?
4. Why does Toshio Mori describe the daily activities of the Japanese American neighborhood of Lil' Yokohama?

Strategies for Success

I GAVE A MAN!

Will you give at least 10% of your pay in War Bonds?

RECOGNIZING PROPAGANDA

Propaganda is a form of mass communication designed to sway people's attitudes and actions. It appeals primarily to emotion, not reason, using language, symbols, and images. Propaganda is favored by totalitarian regimes, which use it to control the hearts and minds of their people. But propaganda is not always used for sinister purposes. Democracies employ propaganda to discredit their enemies and to gain citizen support for particular policies. Special-interest groups use it in lobbying for or against legislation, and politicians use it in campaigning for election. The following techniques are often used in propaganda:

- **Card-stacking** means presenting just one side of a story. Examples include the selective use of statistics and the parading of opinion as fact.
- **Name-calling** is attaching offensive labels to opponents to cast them in a negative light.
- **Sloganeering** is repetition of catchy, but often empty, statements instead of real arguments.
- **Bandwagon** involves begging support for a cause merely because it is popular. This technique relies on peer pressure to conform.
- **Endorsements** are testimonials by famous people who urge support of a cause. Propagandists hope that people will transfer their liking or respect for the celebrity to the cause.

How to Recognize Propaganda

1. **Look, listen, and read carefully.** Analyze the message being conveyed, noting the use of emotionally charged words. Also examine any imagery: propaganda can be visual.
2. **Recognize the technique used.** Identify the technique being employed (such as card-stacking or name-calling).
3. **Consider the purpose.** Ask yourself: Who is sending the message and why? Decide who is its intended audience and what reaction it is meant to provoke.

Applying the Strategy

During World War II the U.S. government used propaganda techniques to build support for the war. For example, patriotic posters used emotional appeals to encourage people to buy war bonds. The World War II poster in the next column pictures a women with her children. The picture and the words "I gave a man!" are meant to play on workers' emotions and to make them feel guilty if they do not buy war bonds.

The government also used propaganda techniques to recruit women for the nation's defense industry, sounding the theme that "it's a woman's war, too." A government brochure of the time, which used the bandwagon approach and one-sided descriptions of factory labor, read: "Millions of women find war work pleasant and as easy as running a sewing machine, or using a vacuum cleaner."

Practicing the Strategy

Read the statement below, made in 1927 by Joseph Goebbels (who later became Hitler's propaganda minister) in commemoration of the German soldiers who died in World War I. Then, on a separate sheet of paper, answer the questions that follow.

“ We think of the two million who grow pale in the graves of Flanders and Poland. . . . We think of . . . all those who gave their lives upon the altar of the future so that Germany might be established again. . . . Retaliation! Retaliation! The day is dawning! . . . We greet you, dead ones. Germany is beginning to glow anew in the dawn of your blood. . . . Let sound the march-beat . . . for freedom! The army of the dead marches with you, you storm troop soldiers, into a better future. ”

1. What is the message of the excerpt? At whom is it aimed?
2. What clues identify this passage as propaganda?

BUILDING YOUR PORTFOLIO

Outlined below are four projects. Independently or cooperatively, complete one and use the products to demonstrate your mastery of the historical concepts involved.

1 THE ECONOMY

The excesses of the 1920s helped trigger the Great Depression. The federal government attempted to get the economy moving through the New Deal. Using the portfolio materials you designed in chapters 11, 12, 13, and 14, create a mural that depicts the economic trends between 1920 and 1940. Your mural might portray the effects of unemployment, consumerism, the depression, or the New Deal.

2 CULTURE AND SOCIETY

American society changed rapidly from the 1920s to the 1940s. Using the portfolio materials you designed in chapters 11, 12, 14, and 16, create a radio program that highlights the issues of the period. Shows might include news of the day, a jazz presentation from the 1920s, a book review from the 1930s, or an interview with women workers from the 1940s.

3 GLOBAL RELATIONS

The world experienced severe economic, political, and social unrest in the years leading up to World War II. Using the portfolio materials you designed in chapters 13, 15, and 16, conduct a debate with representatives from several nations about global relations after World War II. Debates should center around the issue of how the United States should respond in the future to the rise of dictators in other parts of the world.

4 WAR

World War II brought tragedy to millions of people around the world. Using the portfolio materials you designed in chapters 15 and 16, create a design for a war memorial to the victims of World War II. Memorials might commemorate soldiers, prisoners of war, victims of the Holocaust, or civilians killed in the war.

Videodisc Review

In assigned groups, develop an outline for a video collage of American life in the years between 1920 and 1945. Choose images that best illustrate the major topics of the period. Write a script to accompany the images. Assign narrators to different parts of the script, and present your video collage to the class.

Further Reading

Anderson, Jervis. *This Was Harlem: A Cultural Portrait, 1900–1950*. Farrar Straus Giroux (1993). Story of Harlem in the first half of the 20th century.

Berenbaum, Michael. *The World Must Know: The History of the Holocaust as Told in the United States Holocaust Memorial Museum*. Little, Brown (1993). Pictorial and eye-witness history of the Holocaust.

Cohen, Stan. *V for Victory*. Pictorial Histories (1991). Overview of the effect of World War II on Americans on the home front.

Cook, Haruko Taya, and Theodore F. Cook. *Japan at War*. New Press (1992). Accounts of war's effect on the Japanese.

McElvaine, Robert S. *The Great Depression: America, 1929–1941*. Times Books (1984). Overview of the Great Depression.

Chapter 17

Chapter 17

THE POSTWAR YEARS
1945–1952

Chapter 18

DECADE OF CONTRASTS
1950–1960

Chapter 19

THE SIXTIES
1960–1970

UNIT 4

Postwar America

1945–1975

The United States emerged from world War II as the world's most powerful nation. The affluence and optimism of the period was tempered by the sense of uncertainty brought by the Cold War and the nuclear age. And in the midst of prosperity, widespread poverty existed. Disfranchised citizens also raised questions about the reality of the American dream, and disillusionment underscored the debate over the Vietnam War. By the mid-1970s, many Americans were questioning cherished perceptions about their country.

◀ American teenagers, 1950s

Chapter 20

WAR IN VIETNAM
1954–1975

THE POSTWAR YEARS

FOCUS

UNDERSTANDING THE MAIN IDEA

After World War II many nations struggled to rebuild their war-torn economies. In the United States, wartime production led to a postwar boom. On the international front, however, tensions between the United States and the Soviet Union grew. In 1950, in the midst of the increasing threat of nuclear disaster, the Korean War erupted.

THEMES

■ **GLOBAL RELATIONS** What international and domestic problems might a rivalry between two powerful nations create?

■ **TECHNOLOGY AND SOCIETY** How might a society respond to the development of a potentially destructive technology?

■ **DEMOCRATIC VALUES** How might individuals be affected by a government's limitation of civil liberties?

1945	1947	1948	1950	1952
Nuremberg trials begin.	Truman Doctrine proposed.	Racial discrimination banned in military and in federal hiring.	North Korea invades South Korea.	U.S. occupation of Japan ends.

The Churchill-Roosevelt Atlantic Charter of 1941 had called for a free world in which all nations were able to choose their own governments. The agreement, however, did not end imperialism. It took World War II to end Japanese imperialism in Asia and to weaken European colonialism in Asia, Africa, and the Middle East.

Returning U.S. soldiers, 1946

The United States emerged from World War II a world power. Americans realized, however, that with this new role came new challenges. Praising the "brave millions [of soldiers] homeward bound," General Douglas MacArthur in September 1945 urged all Americans "to preserve in peace what we won in war."

In their fight against fascism, American soldiers had helped liberate the surviving victims of Nazi concentration camps. Leon Bass, an African American soldier, believed that the Nazi death camps and the Holocaust had important lessons to teach Americans: "If this could happen [in Germany], it could happen anywhere. It could happen to me. It could happen to black folks in America." Horrified by the Holocaust and inspired by their advances during the war, many African Americans took up the fight for civil rights with increased energy.

The lessons learned from World War II, however, proved difficult to put into practice because of postwar economic chaos and the threat of an all-out nuclear war between the United States and the Soviet Union. Despite the creation of a new international organization to promote peace, Soviet-American tensions escalated and new conflicts broke out. By 1950 the United States was involved in yet another war, this time in Korea.

Soldiers with captured Nazi flag

HEALING THE WOUNDS OF WAR

FOCUS

- How were Germany and Japan governed after the war?
- What did the war crimes trials accomplish?
- Why was the United Nations founded?

*M*any Americans gained confidence from the Allied victory. "The war and the victory showed us what we could do in the world," summed up Melville Grosvenor, a magazine editor. Americans now realized that the United States had to take a leading role in the world. One urgent task was dealing with the human suffering and political chaos resulting from the war. The United States worked with the other Allies to restore peace by occupying Germany and Japan and by creating a new international organization, the United Nations.

United Nations flag

OCCUPATION RULE

After the war Germany and Japan lay in ruins, their wartime governments shattered. A German actress, Hildegard Knef, described a German town "without houses, without windowpanes, without roofs; holes

Allied Occupation Zones, 1945

in the asphalt, rubble, rubbish, rats." An American GI noted that in the area around Tokyo, "there was practically nothing left; the rubble did not even look like much." A Japanese American soldier remarked of the devastation: "Tokyo was all flattened, and people were living in holes with corrugated roofs. They were desperate for food." With the fighting over, Germany and Japan now faced the task of rebuilding their governments, economies, and cities under the watchful eyes of the Allies.

The occupation of Germany. The first overseas conference that President Harry S. Truman attended after Roosevelt's death—the **Potsdam Conference** in July 1945—laid the foundation for Germany's postwar status. Truman, Churchill (later replaced by new prime minister Clement Attlee), and Stalin met in Potsdam, Germany, to approve the details of their joint occupation of Germany. The leaders divided Germany into four occupation zones. The British, the French, and the Americans each took control of a zone in the western, industrialized part of Germany. The Soviets agreed to control the poorer,

▲ This 1946 photograph shows Emperor Hirohito (top) in the Japanese Diet, or legislature, in Tokyo. Hirohito unveiled the new constitution and announced the transfer of his power to the Japanese people and the abolition of the armed forces.

defeated Japan, occupying the island nation from 1945 to 1952.

In addition to helping rebuild the Japanese economy, the United States worked to end Japanese militarism and to create a democratic government. During the occupation Emperor Hirohito remained in the imperial palace, but he became merely a figurehead. Supreme Commander Douglas MacArthur, his staff, and the new Japanese congress ran the country.

Under MacArthur's direction, Japan demobilized more than five million troops and adopted a new constitution in 1947. The constitution set up a democratic system of government, which extended voting rights to women and established separation of church and state. The constitution abolished the Japanese army and navy and prohibited Japan from ever again becoming a military power. Although the constitution bore the clear stamp of American influence, it won support from the Japanese people.

The Japanese also undertook important economic reforms in this period. One program transferred land to Japanese farmers. The government also allowed labor unions to organize and broke up the *zaibatsu*, the huge corporations run by single families that had monopolized the Japanese economy. These political and economic reforms laid the foundation for Japan's tremendous postwar economic recovery.

■■ **After World War II the Allies occupied Germany and Japan and set up new governments in these countries.**

THE WAR CRIMES TRIALS

After the war the Allies also addressed the issue of war crimes. All agreed that convicted German war criminals must be punished for starting the war and for the Holocaust. By the same token, Japanese war criminals were to be punished for the mistreatment of prisoners of war and for other atrocities committed in Bataan and China.

The German war crimes trials—known as the **Nuremberg trials** because they took place in Nuremberg, the former rallying place of Hitler's Nazi party—began in November 1945. Before an international military tribunal, witnesses gave chilling accounts of Nazi atrocities, including the torture and murder of millions of Jews, Gypsies,

more rural, eastern zone. The four powers also set up occupation zones in Austria and agreed to administer jointly the city of Berlin, deep in the Soviet zone.

In order to bring stability to the German zones, the occupying powers pledged to crush the Nazi party, reestablish local governments, and rebuild German industry. In addition, the Allies agreed to resettle German refugees.

The conference attendees recognized that the joint occupation of Germany would require cooperation. However, Soviet occupation of much of Eastern Europe created tensions among the Allies. Stalin demanded that the Allies recognize Soviet-backed Poland's claims to German territory it had occupied during the war. The other Allies reluctantly agreed but grew increasingly concerned about Soviet expansion in Eastern Europe. Another source of tension was the Soviet Union's demand for immediate reparations from Germany.

The occupation of Japan. Postwar Japan also faced massive challenges in its attempts to rebuild. Its economy lay in shambles, and Hiroshima and Nagasaki had been devastated by atom bombs. The United States administered

▲ Allied judges at the Nuremberg trials brought German war criminals to justice. Hermann Göring, commander of the German air force during the war, is shown on the witness stand on May 13, 1946. He later committed suicide in jail.

and others. Marie Vaillant, a concentration camp survivor, testified:

> 66 For months, for years we had one wish only: the wish that some of us would escape alive, in order to tell the world what the Nazi convict prisons were like. . . . There was the systematic . . . urge to use human beings as slaves and to kill them when they could work no more. 99

In September 1946 the tribunal announced its first verdicts. The court had tried 21 Nazi leaders on four charges: planning the war, committing war crimes, committing other crimes against humanity, and conspiring to commit the crimes. Eleven Nazi leaders were sentenced to death; seven received jail sentences; and three were acquitted.

In other trials held in the U.S. occupation zone, thousands of former Nazi officials were tried and jailed, fined, or barred from public office. However, many Nazis—including Adolf Eichmann, the architect of the Jewish extermination program; Josef Mengele (MENG-ge-luh), Auschwitz's "Angel of Death"; and Klaus Barbie, known as the "Butcher of Lyons" for his cruel acts in that French city— escaped immediate prosecution by concealing their identities and fleeing to Latin America.

In the Tokyo war crimes trials, an international tribunal tried more than 20 war leaders. Seven were sentenced to death, including Hideki Tōjō, the wartime premier.

Many Americans, shocked by the evidence of war crimes, argued that more German and Japanese officials should have been punished. Nevertheless, the judges observed legal procedures and tried to avoid acting vengefully. In fact, the trials did set important precedents for international law and the conduct of war. The chief lesson was that nations and individuals can be held accountable for their actions during war. Many countries now accept the principle that war crimes cannot be excused on the grounds that those responsible were "just following orders."

∎∎ War crimes trials in Germany and Japan established the principle of individual responsibility for wartime conduct.

THE UNITED NATIONS

During the war, the Allies had met several times to map out strategies to defeat the Axis Powers. In

DECISION–MAKING BODIES OF THE UNITED NATIONS

Body	Function
General Assembly	Sets policies.
Security Council	Resolves diplomatic, military, and political disputes.
Economic and Social Council	Deals with human welfare and fundamental rights and freedoms.
International Court of Justice	Handles international legal disputes.
Trusteeship Council	Supervises territories that are not independent.
Secretariat	Performs routine administrative work of the UN.

Sources: *Encyclopedia of American History; Funk & Wagnalls New Encyclopedia*

MULTINATIONAL COOPERATION The United Nations was established in order to give every member nation a voice in international affairs. The General Assembly includes over 150 countries and uses five official languages—English, Russian, French, Spanish, and Chinese.

❓ **ANALYZING** Which body of the United Nations is responsible for monitoring military aggressions between nations?

1944, delegates from the United States, Great Britain, the Soviet Union, and China met at Dumbarton Oaks, an estate in Washington, D.C. There they worked out a proposal for a postwar international organization called the **United Nations** (UN). Through the UN, the Allies hoped to continue their alliance by working together to promote world peace.

In April 1945, delegates from 50 nations met in San Francisco to draw up the Charter of the United Nations. The delegates took just eight weeks to write the document. The charter established six bodies: (1) the General Assembly in which all countries shape policy, (2) the Security Council to address military and political problems, (3) the Economic and Social Council, (4) the International Court of Justice, (5) the Trusteeship Council to administer territories, and (6) the Secretariat—headed by the secretary-general—to administer the UN. As permanent members of the Security Council, the United States, the Soviet Union, Great Britain, France, or China could veto any action the UN proposed.

Soon afterward, the Senate overwhelmingly approved American membership in the UN. More than 60 percent of Americans approved of U.S. membership. On October 24, now observed as United Nations Day, the UN officially came into existence when the 29th country approved the UN charter. The UN established its headquarters in New York City. Trygve Lie (TRIG-vuh LEE) of Norway served as the UN's first secretary-general.

From the outset, UN delegates realized that building world peace required both diplomatic and economic cooperation. Eleanor Roosevelt, who served as a U.S. representative to the UN and helped shape the Universal Declaration of Human Rights, explained:

> 66 Security requires both control of the use of force and the elimination of want. No people are secure unless they have the things needed not only to preserve existence, but to make life worth living. . . . All peoples throughout the world must know that there is an organization where their interests can be considered and where justice and security will be sought for all. 99

▲ Eleanor Roosevelt chaired the UN Human Rights Commission from 1946 to 1951. She helped draft the Universal Declaration of Human Rights in 1948.

Early critics of the UN insisted that it was doomed to fail because it had no real power to enforce its own decisions. Nevertheless, most Americans were as optimistic as President Truman, who noted in 1945: "This charter points down the only road to enduring peace. There is no other."

The United Nations was founded to promote peaceful cooperation among the nations of the world.

SECTION 1 REVIEW

IDENTIFY and explain the significance of the following: Potsdam Conference, *zaibatsu*, Nuremberg trials, Adolf Eichmann, Josef Mengele, Klaus Barbie, Hideki Tōjō, United Nations, Trygve Lie, Eleanor Roosevelt.

1. **MAIN IDEA** What principle did the war crimes trials in Germany and Japan establish?

2. **MAIN IDEA** What was the purpose of the United Nations?

3. **COMPARING** How did the Allied powers govern Germany and Japan after World War II?

4. **WRITING TO DESCRIBE** Imagine you are a Japanese American soldier in Tokyo in 1946. Write a letter home that describes conditions in Japan after the war.

5. **ANALYZING** Why do you think the United Nations deals with economic and social issues in addition to its peacekeeping efforts?

THE CHALLENGES OF PEACE

FOCUS

■ How did the American economy fare after the war?

■ How did the Taft-Hartley Act affect unions?

■ What were the most important issues in the 1948 election?

*D*uring the difficult transition from war to peace, Americans were apprehensive. Returning veterans were "worried sick about post-war joblessness," according to Fortune *magazine. Many African American, Mexican American, and women workers feared they would lose the economic gains they had made during the war.*

Homecoming, 1945

THE PROBLEMS OF DEMOBILIZATION

At war's end, troop ships headed home. By mid-1946 over nine million servicemen and women had been discharged. The troops received a hero's welcome, but their return also sparked concern. Could the economy absorb all these new workers? The government soon cancelled $23 billion in military contracts, hitting hard the shipyards, munitions factories, aircraft plants, and military bases.

Postwar measures. To prevent a depression and to help war-weary veterans make the difficult transition to civilian life, Congress passed the Servicemen's Readjustment Act of 1944, commonly known as the **GI Bill of Rights**. The act provided pensions and government loans to help veterans start businesses and buy homes or farms. Under the GI Bill, thousands of veterans also received money for tuition, books, and living expenses while they attended college.

▶ Under the GI Bill, many veterans received financial aid to pursue a college education or industrial training. Howard Timian of Milwaukee is shown here studying for an engineering course.

To ensure economic growth, Congress also passed the **Employment Act** of 1946. The act promised that the government would promote full employment and production. It also established the **Council of Economic Advisers** to counsel the president on economic policy.

Despite widespread fears, the postwar depression never materialized. Employment remained high, as plants that had been making tanks and bombers began to produce consumer goods. With world agricultural output shattered by the war, U.S. food exports also remained high. In addition, Americans now began spending the money they had saved from their wartime paychecks.

▲ A. Philip Randolph and Eleanor Roosevelt are shown here at a 1946 rally at Madison Square Garden to save the Fair Employment Practices Committee. Congress later abolished the committee.

Not all was rosy on the economic front, however. Government measures encouraged employers to give priority in hiring to veterans. The fears of many women, African Americans, and Mexican Americans were realized as they lost their jobs to returning veterans. During the war these workers had been encouraged to take jobs in vital defense factories. African Americans had been protected from job discrimination by the Fair Employment Practices Committee. Soon after the war, however, Congress abolished the committee.

Many workers were also hit hard by inflation. With the lifting of most wartime price controls in 1946, prices soared. Meat prices zoomed so high that some markets began selling horsemeat. Blaming the Truman administration, angry consumers called the president "Horsemeat Harry."

▪▪ Despite fears of a depression, the American economy prospered after the war, though inflation hurt many workers.

Labor unrest. As inflation worsened, people took matters into their own hands. Workers who had sacrificed during the depression and the war now craved a better standard of living. Freed of their wartime no-strike pledge, millions of workers walked off the job to win wage increases and to preserve some wartime price controls. In 1946—the most strike-filled year in U.S. history after 1919—almost five million workers walked the picket lines.

President Truman, though a backer of labor unions, opposed these strikes because he feared they would disrupt the economy. In April 1946, when some 400,000 coal miners went on strike, Truman ordered the army to establish government

control of the mines. United Mine Workers' president John L. Lewis retorted: "You can't dig coal with bayonets." After the courts slapped heavy fines on the union, though, Lewis ordered the miners back to work. When confronted with striking railway workers, Truman threatened to end the strike by drafting the strikers into the army. Faced with Truman's threat, union leaders negotiated an end to the strike.

To reduce the strength of organized labor, Congress—under Republican control since the 1946 elections—passed an antiunion bill in 1947. This law, known as the **Taft-Hartley Act**, allowed courts to end some strikes, outlawed closed-shop agreements (which required union membership for employment), restricted unions' political contributions, and required union officers to swear they were not Communists. President Truman vetoed the bill, but Congress passed it over his veto.

The Taft-Hartley Act stirred angry debate. Conservative supporters argued that the law corrected unfair advantages granted to labor in the Wagner-Connery Act (see Chapter 14). Prolabor opponents denounced it as a "slave labor law."

The act limited the tactics unions could use. Despite these restrictions, however, organized labor continued to make some gains in the postwar years. For example, in 1948 General Motors and the United Automobile Workers (UAW) signed a contract tying wage increases to cost-of-living increases. Union contracts also began to include provisions for such benefits as retirement pensions and health insurance.

▪▪ The Taft-Hartley Act placed a variety of restrictions on labor unions.

◄ The cartoon *Three Men on a Horse* appeared on February 24, 1953. Union leaders John L. Lewis, Walter Reuther, and George Meany ride toward the Taft-Hartley Act, hoping to axe some of its restrictions on labor unions.

THE 1948 ELECTION

By 1948 inflation, high taxes, and labor unrest had eroded public support for Truman. His approval rating stood at 35 percent in March, down from 60 percent the previous year. "To err is Truman," people joked. But Truman was determined to prove his critics wrong. His stand on civil rights for African Americans became an important issue in the 1948 campaign.

The Committee on Civil Rights.

In 1946 African American civil rights groups urged Truman to take action against the racism that stained American society. They pointed out that most African Americans in the South were prevented from voting through the use of poll taxes.

▲ Shown here are African American demonstrators outside the convention hall at the 1948 Democratic Convention in Philadelphia.

Blacks throughout the nation faced segregation in schools and buses and discrimination in housing and employment. And in many areas African Americans continued to be lynched, a crime that local courts often ignored. Efforts to battle these conditions met a wall of white resistance.

In December 1946 Truman, distressed by these reports, set up the **Committee on Civil Rights** to examine the issue. The committee's 15 members included African American lawyer Sadie Alexander; Dr. Channing Tobias, director of the Phelps-Stokes Fund, which supported educational opportunities for African Americans; General Electric's president Charles Wilson; and Franklin Roosevelt, Jr.

The committee's report, "To Secure These Rights," appeared in October 1947. The report documented widespread civil rights abuses, including discrimination against black veterans and an increase in Ku Klux Klan violence. The committee urged Congress to pass an antilynching law and an anti-poll-tax measure and to end discrimination in federal agencies and the military. The report also called for an end to racial segregation in interstate transportation.

When Truman did not immediately act on the report's recommendations, African American leader A. Philip Randolph threatened to launch a campaign of civil disobedience if the military remained segregated. The tactic worked. In July 1948 Truman issued executive orders banning racial discrimination in the military and in federal hiring. He also took steps to end employment discrimination by companies working under government contracts.

White southern Democrats were outraged at African American demands for civil rights and at Truman's actions. Senator Olin Johnston of South Carolina angrily warned that the South's electoral votes "won't be for Truman. They'll be for somebody else. He ain't going to be re-elected."

The Democratic convention.

Despite Senator Johnston's bluster, southern opposition did not prevent Truman from winning the nomination at the Democratic convention in July. Senator Alben W. Barkley of Kentucky was selected to be Truman's running mate. The Democrats hoped to appeal to the former New Deal coalition of farmers, unionized workers, big-city ethnic groups, and African Americans. The Democratic platform called for repeal of the Taft-Hartley Act; an increase in federal aid for housing, education, and agriculture; and broader social security benefits. It also included a strong civil rights plank.

The civil rights issue split the Democratic party. Southern delegates threatened to walk out of the convention. Declaring "LET 'EM WALK," the NAACP argued:

❝ There is no room . . . for compromise. . . . Those Democrats who say the

▼ Misled by early returns, the *Chicago Daily Tribune* published an early election-night edition announcing Dewey as the winner.

President's recommendation of such a program is a "stab in the back" of the South are saying they do not choose to abide by the Constitution. They are also saying . . . that the whole section of our nation believes as they do. . . . We *know* it is not true! **99**

After bitter debate the delegates adopted the civil rights plank. Southern delegates stormed out of the convention. They formed the States' Rights party—nicknamed the **Dixiecrats**—which called for continued racial segregation. The Dixiecrats nominated Governor J. Strom Thurmond of South Carolina as their presidential candidate. These explosive divisions were an opening skirmish in a mighty struggle against racism that would soon sweep over the nation.

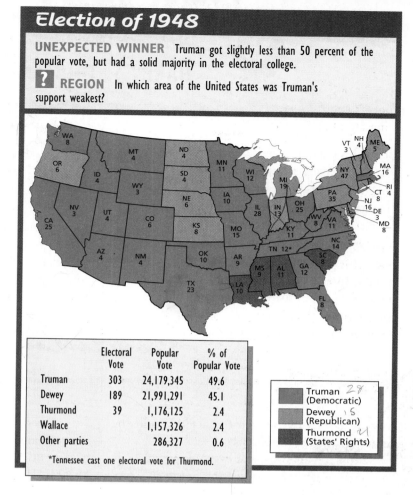

Election of 1948

UNEXPECTED WINNER Truman got slightly less than 50 percent of the popular vote, but had a solid majority in the electoral college.

? REGION In which area of the United States was Truman's support weakest?

	Electoral Vote	Popular Vote	% of Popular Vote
Truman	303	24,179,345	49.6
Dewey	189	21,991,291	45.1
Thurmond	39	1,176,125	2.4
Wallace		1,157,326	2.4
Other parties		286,327	0.6

*Tennessee cast one electoral vote for Thurmond.

Truman (Democratic)
Dewey (Republican)
Thurmond (States' Rights)

The gulf widens. A different issue caused another break within the Democratic party. Troubled by Truman's antilabor actions in 1946, former vice president Henry Wallace and other liberal New Dealers left the Democratic party to found the Progressive party. This group, which was not related to the Progressive party of the early 1900s, called for an extension of the New Deal and for friendly relations with the Soviet Union. The American Communist party supported the Progressive party.

With the Democrats' votes split three ways, the Republicans were confident of victory. They nominated Governor Thomas Dewey of New York as their presidential candidate and Earl Warren, the popular governor of California, as Dewey's running mate. Opinion polls and most newspapers predicted a Dewey victory.

But Truman ran an energetic campaign, attacking the conservatism of the Republicans and the radicalism of the Progressives. As he crisscrossed the country, criticizing the "do-nothing" Republican Congress, crowds began to chant, "Give 'em hell, Harry." In one of the great upsets of U.S. political history, Truman won, gaining 49 percent of the popular vote to Dewey's 45 percent. Black voters helped Truman carry several key states. Workers, farmers, and ethnic voters generally supported Truman, proving that the political coalition that had supported Franklin Roosevelt in the 1930s still held.

■■ **Civil rights and labor issues splintered the Democratic party. Truman, however, ran a tough campaign and won the 1948 election.**

THE FAIR DEAL

Heartened by his victory, Truman urged Congress to continue Roosevelt's New Deal reforms. Proclaiming that "every segment of our population . . . has a right to expect from our government a fair deal," Truman proposed new reforms, which he labeled the **Fair Deal**. Truman's Fair Deal proposed full employment, higher minimum wages, a national health insurance program, affordable

HARRY S. TRUMAN
1884–1972

in office
1945–1953

Harry S. Truman was known to be an honest politician who always spoke his mind. His very direct manner of speaking shocked many people, but impressed others. Once Truman wrote a letter to a music critic who had written a harsh review of a recital by the president's daughter Margaret. In addition to calling the critic "a frustrated old man who never made a success," the president informed him that "I never met you, but if I do

Harry S. Truman

U.S. Postage 8 cents

you'll need a new nose." While some considered this response inappropriate, public opinion strongly supported Truman's defense of his daughter.

While Truman was quick to defend his family and others, he often downplayed his own abilities as president. Many years after he left office he told an interviewer, "I wasn't one of the great Presidents; but I had a good time trying to be one."

---

housing construction, aid to farmers, and the expansion of welfare benefits.

Most Republicans, and even conservatives in Truman's own party, opposed the president's program. Nevertheless, Truman managed to push through some of his reforms. Between 1949 and 1952 Congress extended social security benefits to some 10 million more people, raised the minimum wage from 40 to 75 cents an hour, and approved programs to clear slums. Congress also expanded federal programs to promote flood control, hydroelectric power, and irrigation.

Overall, though, the Fair Deal had limited success amid an increasingly conservative postwar political climate. Congress failed to repeal the Taft-Hartley Act or to pass a civil rights bill. Most of the New Dealers had resigned from Truman's cabinet in disappointment, leaving business leaders and military men who had little enthusiasm for the Fair Deal. These domestic issues also unfolded against the backdrop of other pressing concerns that had international implications: conflict with the Soviet Union and almost hysterical fears of communism.

SECTION 2 REVIEW

IDENTIFY and explain the significance of the following: GI Bill of Rights, Employment Act, Council of Economic Advisers, Taft-Hartley Act, Committee on Civil Rights, Sadie Alexander, Dixiecrats, J. Strom Thurmond, Henry Wallace, Thomas Dewey, Fair Deal.

1. **MAIN IDEA** What effect did the end of World War II have on the U.S. economy?

2. **MAIN IDEA** What restrictions did the Taft-Hartley Act place on unions?

3. **MAIN IDEA** How did the end of the war affect women, African American, and Mexican American workers?

4. **WRITING TO INFORM** Imagine you are a political correspondent covering the 1948 election. Write a magazine commentary that outlines the most important issues in the campaign.

5. **ANALYZING** What convinced Truman to desegregate the military and to end discrimination in federal jobs?

THE COLD WAR BEGINS

FOCUS

- **What caused the Cold War?**
- **What did the United States hope to accomplish through the Marshall Plan?**
- **What effects did the Cold War have on American society?**

Berlin airlift, 1948

*S*oon after World War II, the wartime alliance between the United States and the Soviet Union collapsed. The two countries, at odds because of competing global objectives and different economic and political systems, fought over control of Europe and access to atomic energy.

THE ROOTS OF THE COLD WAR

An intense rivalry between the United States and the Soviet Union began after World War II. With once-mighty Germany, Japan, and Great Britain in ruins, only the United States and the Soviet Union were left to struggle for international dominance. Their competition for global power and influence, which came to be known as the **Cold War**, was waged mostly on political and economic fronts rather than on the battlefield. Nevertheless, the threat of all-out war was always present.

The origins of the Cold War lay in profound economic, political, and philosophical differences between the two nations. Most Americans, committed to the principles of democratic government, individual freedom, and a capitalist economy, deeply opposed the Soviet system.

Founded on Communist ideology, the Soviet system included a state-run economy, one-party rule, suppression of religion, and the use of force to crush opposition. Until his death in 1953, dictator Joseph Stalin ruled the Soviet Union with an iron hand.

Stalin looked with a mixture of envy and horror at powerful America with its capitalist system, its industrial might, and its atomic bombs. Soviet propagandists endlessly denounced American "imperialism" and U.S. capitalists' "oppression" of the laboring masses. The Soviets pointed to racial discrimination in the U.S. to discredit America's boasts of freedom and democracy.

Soviet expansionism after World War II fueled American mistrust. During World War II the Soviets had taken over the Baltic states of Lithuania, Latvia, and Estonia. Then they captured large areas of Poland and Romania. By war's end the Soviets also controlled Manchuria.

After the war, Stalin made clear his determination to maintain Soviet influence in Eastern Europe, claiming the need for a buffer zone of "friendly nations" on the U.S.S.R.'s western border. He stripped eastern Germany of some 40 percent of its industrial equipment, installed pro-Soviet governments in Poland and Romania, and worked to establish Communist rule throughout Eastern Europe. The countries under Soviet control became known as **satellite nations**.

Concerned about Stalin's actions, the United States, Great Britain, and France solidified their control of West Germany and revived its industries. The United States also pressured Stalin to withdraw Soviet forces from Iran, the oil-rich Middle Eastern nation that the Soviets had occupied during the war. In April 1946 Stalin finally agreed to withdraw his troops.

In February of the same year, however, Stalin had made a tough speech—dubbed the "Declaration of World War III" by Supreme Court justice William Douglas—proclaiming that capitalism and communism could never coexist. Winston Churchill, Britain's wartime prime minister, answered Stalin in March with an equally tough speech delivered in Fulton, Missouri. Churchill declared that a Soviet "Iron Curtain has descended across the Continent," isolating Western Europe from Soviet-dominated Eastern Europe. Churchill called for closer cooperation between Great Britain and America to check Soviet power.

Churchill's speech was well received in Washington. At the time, George Kennan, a State Department official and Soviet expert, advised similar action. Kennan argued that the Soviet Union's long-term aim was to defeat capitalism and expand the Soviet sphere of influence. He believed that the Soviets would be persistent, yet cautious, expanding only when there were few risks. Kennan explained how American foreign policy could thus stop the spread of communism:

❝ The Soviet pressure against the free institutions of the Western world is something that can be contained by the . . . vigilant application of counterforce at a series of constantly shifting geographical and political points. . . . The Russians look forward to a duel of infinite duration. ❞

Kennan's **containment** doctrine, which aimed to contain, or restrict, Soviet expansion, became the basis for U.S. Cold War strategy. Many Americans, unwilling to return to the appeasement policy of the 1930s, applauded Kennan's stand against communism.

▪▪ **The origins of the Cold War lay in U.S.–Soviet global competition, conflicting economic and political systems, and mutual distrust.**

THE DEADLOCK OVER ATOMIC WEAPONS

The United States and the Soviet Union soon became locked in a dispute over the control of atomic weapons. This standoff terrified many Americans, who feared a nuclear war. Most people shared lawyer David E. Lilienthal's 1946 assessment that "the awful strength of atomic power . . . directly affects every man, woman, and child in the world." Recognizing this fact, the UN created a commission to draw up a plan for the control of nuclear arms early in 1946.

At the commission's first meeting, U.S. representative Bernard Baruch called for the creation of a special UN agency with the authority to inspect any nation's atomic-energy installations. This proposal, known as the **Baruch Plan**, would impose penalties on countries violating international controls. Until such a plan was in place, Baruch said, the United States would not reveal any atomic-energy secrets or give up its atomic weapons. At the time, American physicists were developing more-powerful nuclear bombs.

Working feverishly on its own bomb, the Soviet Union rejected all inspection and enforcement provisions. With neither country willing to compromise, hopes for international control of

▼ **In July 1946 the United States conducted atomic bomb tests in Bikini Atoll in the western Pacific Ocean. These tests were intended to measure the effects of atomic bombs on warships.**

atomic energy died. When the Soviet Union tested its first atomic bomb in 1949, fears of a nuclear-arms race became reality.

Despite the failure of the Baruch Plan, the United States achieved some success in controlling nuclear weapons. Atomic-energy scientists and U.S. peace organizations, such as the Women's International League for Peace and Freedom, urged the U.S. government to establish civilian, rather than military, control of atomic energy. Responding to these appeals, Congress in August 1946 passed the **Atomic Energy Act**. The act set up the Atomic Energy Commission (AEC) under civilian control to oversee nuclear weapons research and to promote peacetime uses of atomic energy. Its main activity, however, became supporting the government's nuclear weapons program.

CONTAINMENT AROUND THE WORLD

As prospects for U.S.–Soviet cooperation dimmed, the Truman administration pursued a more aggressive policy toward the Soviet Union. The U.S. containment policy first took shape in Greece, where a civil war had broken out in 1946. Communist-led rebels battled the Greek monarchy, which relied on military and financial support from Great Britain. In early 1947, however, the British announced that they could no longer continue their aid to Greece. Without aid it seemed likely that Greece's pro-Western government would fall to the Communists and the country would come under Soviet control.

Containment in the Mediterranean. At the same time, the Soviet Union pressured Turkey to give up sole control of the Dardanelles, a narrow strait linking the Black Sea and the Mediterranean. President Truman knew that control of this area would give the Soviets a dominant position in the eastern Mediterranean and would threaten the security of the Suez Canal. In a somber speech before Congress on March 12, 1947, Truman declared: "It must be the policy of the United States to support free peoples who are resisting attempted subjugation [conquest] by armed minorities or by outside pressures."

This statement, which became known as the **Truman Doctrine**, made no mention of the Soviet Union, though clearly Truman had devised it with the Soviets in mind. Agreeing with Truman's

sentiments, Congress soon voted $400 million to aid Greece and Turkey. This action was only a prelude, however, to the more massive foreign-aid program that soon followed.

Containment in Europe. After World War II, European economies were in shambles. In 1948 Germany produced only 45 percent of the goods it had produced before the war. To make matters worse, the winter of 1946–47 brought the worst blizzards in some 50 years. Starvation and chaos loomed. Some Americans believed that the United States should help Europe. They feared that such desperate economic conditions would make Europe more vulnerable to Soviet influence.

Secretary of State George C. Marshall shared this belief. Born in Uniontown, Pennsylvania, in 1880, Marshall graduated from Virginia Military Institute and joined the army. During World War I he served under General Pershing. As army chief of staff during World War II, he attended the Casablanca, Yalta, and Potsdam conferences.

After the war Marshall served briefly as a U.S. envoy to China before Truman appointed him secretary of state in 1947. In a speech at Harvard University on June 5, 1947, Marshall warned that if steps were not taken soon, Europe faced "economic, social, and political" collapse. He then called for a major U.S. effort to promote European recovery "to permit the emergence of political and social conditions in which free institutions can

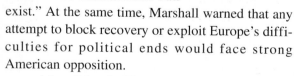
George C. Marshall

exist." At the same time, Marshall warned that any attempt to block recovery or exploit Europe's difficulties for political ends would face strong American opposition.

After Marshall's speech, Truman asked Congress for $17 billion in economic aid for Europe. Truman's request sparked heated debate throughout the United States. Supporters argued that such aid would contain communism by restoring Europe's economic health and would help the U.S. economy as Europeans purchased American goods and military hardware. Opponents said the United States could not afford to "carry Europe on its back."

▲ The first cargo of sugar transported under the Marshall Plan is unloaded from the S.S. *Araby* in London in February 1949.

A turning point in the debate came early in 1948, when pro-Soviet Communists overthrew the government of Czechoslovakia. Jolted into action by the coup, Congress passed the European Recovery Act, or **Marshall Plan**, in April 1948. The plan, based on Marshall's recommendations, provided some $12 billion in aid to Western Europe over the next four years. For his efforts Marshall won the Nobel Peace Prize in 1953.

■■ **The Marshall Plan aimed to contain the spread of communism by easing economic hardship in Europe.**

CRISIS IN BERLIN

The non-Soviet zone of Germany grew stronger as a result of the Marshall Plan. In early June 1948, Great Britain, France, and the United States announced plans to combine their occupation zones and support the formation of a new West German government.

The Berlin airlift. The Soviets, deeply fearful of renewed German power, opposed this action. On June 24, 1948, the Soviets suddenly blocked all roads, canals, and railways linking Berlin and western Germany, cutting off shipments of food, fuel, and other crucial supplies to the city. The Soviets hoped to drive the Western powers out of Berlin and to delay the formation of a West German government. Berlin had become a pawn in the Cold War chess game.

The British and the Americans responded to the Soviet action with the **Berlin airlift**. Over the next 10 months, U.S. and British planes carried more than two million tons of food and supplies to the people of West Berlin. As one Berliner recalled, the airlift became a lifeline to the rest of the world:

66 Early in the morning, when we woke up, the first thing we did was listen to see whether the noise of aircraft engines could be heard. That gave us the certainty that we were not alone, that the whole civilized world took part in the fight for Berlin's freedom. 99

The success of the Berlin airlift proved a huge embarrassment to the Soviet Union. In May

▲ As tensions mounted, American military police in Berlin warily faced their Soviet counterparts across the dividing line between the Allied and Soviet zones.

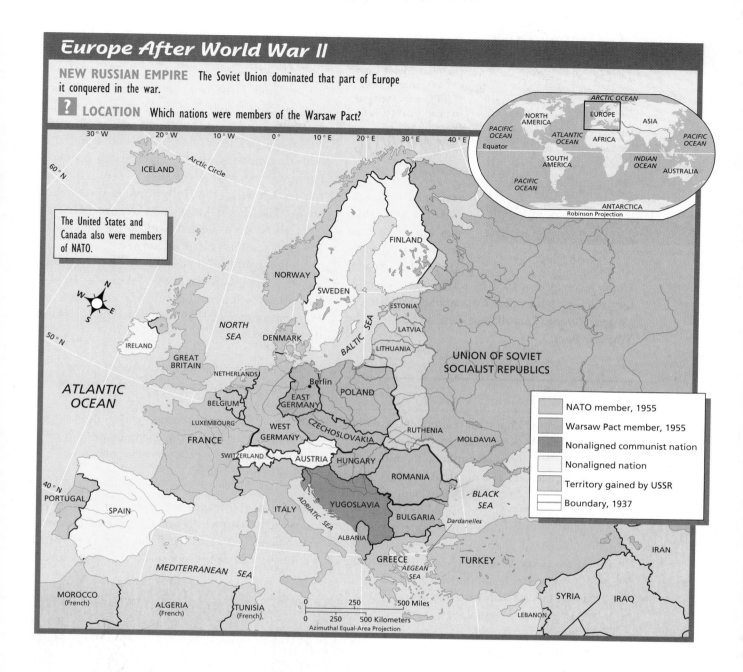

Europe After World War II

NEW RUSSIAN EMPIRE The Soviet Union dominated that part of Europe it conquered in the war.

? **LOCATION** Which nations were members of the Warsaw Pact?

The United States and Canada also were members of NATO.

ICELAND

Arctic Circle

NORWAY

SWEDEN

FINLAND

NORTH SEA

DENMARK

IRELAND

GREAT BRITAIN

NETHERLANDS

Berlin

EAST GERMANY

POLAND

ESTONIA

LATVIA

LITHUANIA

UNION OF SOVIET SOCIALIST REPUBLICS

BELGIUM

LUXEMBOURG

WEST GERMANY

CZECHOSLOVAKIA

RUTHENIA

ATLANTIC OCEAN

FRANCE

SWITZERLAND

AUSTRIA

HUNGARY

MOLDAVIA

PORTUGAL

SPAIN

ITALY

ADRIATIC SEA

YUGOSLAVIA

ROMANIA

BULGARIA

BLACK SEA

Dardanelles

ALBANIA

MEDITERRANEAN SEA

GREECE

AEGEAN SEA

TURKEY

IRAN

MOROCCO (French)

ALGERIA (French)

TUNISIA (French)

LEBANON

SYRIA

IRAQ

	NATO member, 1955
	Warsaw Pact member, 1955
	Nonaligned communist nation
	Nonaligned nation
	Territory gained by USSR
	Boundary, 1937

0   250   500 Miles
0   250   500 Kilometers
Azimuthal Equal-Area Projection

ARCTIC OCEAN

NORTH AMERICA

EUROPE

ASIA

PACIFIC OCEAN

ATLANTIC OCEAN

AFRICA

PACIFIC OCEAN

Equator

SOUTH AMERICA

INDIAN OCEAN

AUSTRALIA

PACIFIC OCEAN

ANTARCTICA

Robinson Projection

1949 the Soviets lifted the blockade. On May 9 the Federal Republic of Germany, known as West Germany, was founded. In response, the Soviets set up the German Democratic Republic—East Germany—in the Soviet zone. The division of Germany would last for more than 40 years as a result of Cold War rivalries.

The Western alliance. After the Berlin crisis the United States shifted its attention in Europe from economic recovery to military preparedness. In April 1949 nine Western European nations joined the United States, Canada, and Iceland in a military alliance called the **North Atlantic Treaty Organization**, or NATO.

Under the terms of the NATO treaty, known as the Atlantic Pact, each member nation pledged to defend the others in the event of an outside attack. When Truman submitted the treaty for Senate ratification, debate focused on whether the agreement would allow the United States to go to war without an act of Congress. Concern over this same issue had helped keep the United States out of the League of Nations. This time, however, fear of Soviet expansionism outweighed other concerns. In July 1949 the Senate ratified the treaty.

In 1951 General Dwight D. Eisenhower became the supreme commander of NATO forces. As its contribution to NATO, the United States

The Granger Collection, New York

◄ **This U.S. cartoon, entitled *Banner of the Non-Soviet Union* (1949), shows that NATO was formed in response to Allied fears of Soviet aggression.**

stationed troops in Europe and gave massive military aid to its European allies. The Soviet Union responded in 1955 by forming its own military alliance with other Communist countries in Eastern Europe. This alliance came to be called the **Warsaw Pact**.

ᴛHE COLD WAR AT HOME

The Cold War had important consequences within the United States. As a result of Cold War pressures, the United States streamlined its military to allow for peacetime rearmament. In July 1947 Congress replaced the War Department with the Department of Defense, combining the leadership of the army, navy, and air force under the Joint Chiefs of Staff. In addition, Congress set up the **National Security Council** (NSC) to advise the president on strategic matters and established the **Central Intelligence Agency** (CIA) to gather information overseas.

Another Red scare. The Cold War also aroused fears of communism at home. Although Truman opposed communism abroad, some Republicans accused him of allowing Communists in the American government. Responding to such charges, Truman set up the Loyalty Review Board in 1947 to investigate all federal employees. By the end of 1951, more than 20,000 federal workers had been investigated, some 2,000 had resigned, and more than 300 had been fired as "security risks." In most cases the government did not allow dismissed employees to respond to the charges against them.

Meanwhile, Congress cracked down on the Communist party. Leading the anti-Communist crusade in Congress was the

House Committee on Un-American Activities (HUAC), originally established in 1938 to investigate fascist groups in the United States. HUAC held a series of hearings to question the political allegiances of members of peace organizations, liberal political groups, and labor unions. In 1947, responding to charges that Hollywood was riddled with Communists, HUAC investigated people in the movie industry. A group of film directors and writers, known as the **Hollywood Ten**, refused to answer HUAC's questions and went to jail. They were blacklisted—denied work in the film industry—and saw their careers destroyed.

The hysteria generated by HUAC spread quickly. One group that spoke out against HUAC, the Women's International League for Peace and Freedom, argued in 1949 that the hearings violated democratic rights:

❝ Fully recognizing the danger of fascist and communist totalitarianism, the League believes that such forces can be best opposed by open discussion and by the strengthening of our own democratic procedures, rather than by attempts at direct control. ❞

Because of the league's support for progressive causes, the FBI investigated the national organization and several of its local chapters. The investigation scared many potential members away.

▲ **A delegation of Hollywood personalities attended a meeting of HUAC on October 27, 1947. Humphrey Bogart, Lauren Bacall, and Sterling Hayden were among those present.**

HUAC investigations had a similar effect on labor unions and many political groups.

The search for spies. HUAC also investigated individuals accused of spying for the Soviets. In 1948 Whittaker Chambers, who had been a member of the Communist party, accused Alger Hiss of being a Communist spy. Chambers told HUAC that Hiss, a New Deal lawyer who had joined the State Department in 1936, had given him secret State Department documents to pass on to the Soviets.

Hiss denied the charges, but persistent questioning by HUAC member Richard Nixon, a young Republican congressman from California, revealed apparent inconsistencies in Hiss's testimony. In 1950 Hiss was convicted of perjury (lying under oath) and sentenced to five years in prison.

Another notorious spy case also helped fuel domestic fears of communism. In 1951 a U.S. court convicted two Americans, Julius and Ethel Rosenberg, of giving the Soviets atomic-energy secrets during World War II. Defenders of the Rosenbergs claimed that the two were innocent victims of anti-Communist hysteria. Despite worldwide protests on their behalf, however, the Rosenbergs were executed in June 1953. Historians have found evidence for the guilty verdict against Julius Rosenberg but agree that the death sentences were extreme reactions in the nervous Cold War climate.

Other anti-Communist measures included the **Internal Security Act**, passed in 1950. The act

▲ Escorted by a U.S. marshal (left), Julius and Ethel Rosenberg are shown on March 8, 1951, awaiting the result of their trial on charges of conspiracy to commit espionage.

required party members and organizations to register with the federal government. It also imposed strict controls on immigrants suspected of being Communist sympathizers. The anti-Communist hysteria of these years shattered many lives and careers. Today many historians look back on this period as one of the bleakest in American history.

■■ **Cold War anti-communism led to efforts to expose alleged Communists in the United States, creating a climate of fear and suspicion.**

SECTION 3 REVIEW

IDENTIFY and explain the significance of the following: Cold War, satellite nations, George Kennan, containment, Baruch Plan, Atomic Energy Act, Truman Doctrine, George C. Marshall, Marshall Plan, Berlin airlift, NATO, Warsaw Pact, National Security Council, Central Intelligence Agency, House Committee on Un-American Activities, Hollywood Ten, Internal Security Act.

LOCATE and explain the importance of the following: Greece, Turkey, Dardanelles, Federal Republic of Germany (West Germany), German Democratic Republic (East Germany).

1. **MAIN IDEA** What factors gave rise to the Cold War?

2. **MAIN IDEA** What was the purpose of the Marshall Plan?

3. **ASSESSING CONSEQUENCES** What impact did the Cold War have on U.S. society?

4. **WRITING TO EXPRESS A VIEWPOINT** Imagine you are a court reporter at either the Alger Hiss trial or the trial of Ethel and Julius Rosenberg. Write a letter to a friend abroad explaining the significance of one of the trials.

5. **SYNTHESIZING** How did the U.S. government put George Kennan's containment doctrine into practice?

THE COLD WAR TURNS HOT

FOCUS

- **Why did Israel and Arab nations go to war?**
- **How did Communists come to power in China?**
- **What led to the division of Korea?**
- **Who fought in the Korean War?**

*W*orld War II had weakened the grip of European nations on their colonies and spheres of influence in the Middle East and Asia. After the war these former colonies struggled to set up their own governments. The United States became involved in the conflict between Israel and several Arab nations in the Middle East. Concerns over the spread of communism led the United States to support the Nationalists in their struggle against the Communists in China. By 1950 Cold War rivalries drew the United States into outright war in Korea.

U.S. soldiers in Korea, 1952

MIDDLE EAST TENSIONS

Soon after World War II, tensions flared in Palestine, a region at the eastern end of the Mediterranean claimed by both Jews and Arabs. Since World War I, Great Britain had ruled Palestine under a League of Nations mandate. Unable to resolve conflicting claims over the territory, Britain in 1947 turned the problem over to the United Nations. The UN came up with a plan to divide Palestine into two states—one for Jews, the other for Arabs—but Arabs rejected the proposal.

The proposal was a victory for **Zionism**, the movement calling for a Jewish homeland in Palestine. Zionist leader David Ben-Gurion

▲ **David Ben-Gurion**

(ben-goohr-YAWN), born in Plonsk, Russia, in 1886, had fought for just this outcome since the early 1900s. Idealistic and determined, Ben-Gurion sailed to Palestine in 1906. Expelled in 1915 for Zionist activities, he went to the United States to raise money and recruit volunteers among the American Jewish community.

During World War II, Ben-Gurion supported the Allied struggle against Hitler but continued to organize Jewish resistance in Palestine. After the war, Ben-Gurion helped develop land, resettle Jewish refugees, and organize covert activities against British and Arab rule.

With the UN's decision to divide Palestine, Great Britain agreed to give up its control of the region. On May 14, 1948, the last of

Legend:
- Israel in June 1948
- Territory Israel gained by January 1949
- Territory Israel held after 1949 armistice
- Boundary of British Mandate of Palestine, 1922–1948
- Capital city

LEBANON

SYRIA

SEA OF GALILEE

Haifa

Nazareth

MEDITERRANEAN SEA

Nablus

WEST BANK (to Jordan)

Jordan River

Tel Aviv

Jaffa

Amman

Jerusalem

Bethlehem

Gaza

GAZA STRIP (to Egypt)

Hebron

DEAD SEA

EGYPT

ISRAEL

Negev

UN Partition
- Israeli territory
- Arab territory

JORDAN

Jerusalem (International Zone)

PALESTINE

EGYPT

Sinai

1947

0   20   40 Miles

0   20   40 Kilometers

Elat

Lambert Conformal Conic Projection

Israel, 1949

SUCCESS STORY The memory of the Holocaust and the struggle to create a Jewish state unified the Israelis in a common cause.

? PLACE Which river divides the West Bank from Jordan?

counted on an impressive arsenal bought in part with the millions of dollars that poured in from the American Jewish community.

▪▪ In 1948 war broke out between Israel and Arab nations over the disputed territory of Palestine.

In an effort to end the war, the UN sent a mediator, Count Folke Bernadotte of Sweden, to the Middle East. Bernadotte negotiated a shaky cease-fire, but within months he was assassinated by Israeli extremists. In 1949 a second UN mediator, the American diplomat Ralph Bunche, persuaded both sides to accept an armistice. For his efforts Bunche won the Nobel Peace Prize in 1950—the first African American to receive that honor.

▲ **Ralph Bunche**

The 1949 agreement gave Israel more territory than the earlier UN partition plan had, but it divided Jerusalem into Arab and Israeli zones. The plan gave Egypt control of the Gaza Strip, while Jordan took over the West Bank of the Jordan River. The Arab countries, however, still refused to recognize the state of Israel. Also left unresolved was the fate of the Arabs remaining in Israel and the hundreds of thousands of Arabs who had fled or had been driven out of Israel.

Before the territorial agreements were finalized, Israel held its first parliamentary elections in January 1949. Ben-Gurion became prime minister, a post he held almost continuously until 1963. At his death in 1973, Ben-Gurion was hailed as the chief architect of the state of Israel.

COMMUNIST VICTORY IN CHINA

While the conflict between Arabs and Israelis escalated after World War II, tensions also came to a head in China. The seeds of the conflict were planted in the 1920s. Chiang Kai-shek's Kuomintang (KMT), or Nationalist party, battled the

the British forces withdrew. Ben-Gurion and other Jewish leaders promptly proclaimed the new state of Israel. Both Truman and Stalin immediately recognized the new nation.

The Arab states, however, did not recognize Israel, since they wanted Palestine to remain an Arab country. Armies from the Arab states of Egypt, Lebanon, Jordan (called Transjordan until 1949), Syria, and Iraq attacked Israel. Although vastly outnumbered in the Arab-Israeli war, Israeli forces under Ben-Gurion's overall command captured and held much of Palestine. Israeli soldiers

THE ARAB RESPONSE

THROUGH OTHERS' EYES

Musa Alami, an Arab lawyer and diplomat from Palestine, promoted Palestinian nationalism and unity among the Arab states. After the Arab-Israeli war, Alami published a book, *The Lesson of Palestine* (1949), which examined the causes of the war:

"**The British were the prime causers of the disaster. . . . They were assisted by the Americans and the Russians. . . . We found ourselves face to face with the Jews, and entered into battle with them to decide the future; and in spite of what the British, the Americans, and the Russians had done, it was still within our power to win the fight.**

The Arabs failed to defend Palestine. . . . We worked on a local basis, without unity, without totality, without a general command, our defense disjointed and our affairs disordered, every town fighting on its own and only those in areas adjacent to the Jews entering the battle at all. . . . The natural result of all this was disaster and the loss of Palestine."

Chinese Communists. KMT forces held most of northern China, and Communist soldiers controlled parts of southern and central China. But in 1931, when Japan invaded Manchuria, the KMT and the Communists declared a truce and joined forces against the Japanese.

In 1934, however, Chiang broke the truce when he launched what he hoped would be the final battles against the Communist-controlled areas of the south. The KMT forces were successful. From 1934 to 1935 some 100,000 Communists marched nearly 6,000 miles to northern China. Known as the **Long March**, this exodus

▲ Nationalist forces kidnapped Chiang Kai-shek in 1936. This photograph of Chiang with his wife was taken after his release.

helped cement Mao Zedong's leadership of the Chinese Communist party and led to the establishment of a strong base in the north.

Chiang's attacks on the Communists kept him from devoting full attention to stopping further Japanese aggression. By the early 1930s the Japanese controlled Manchuria, Inner Mongolia, and parts of northern China. To prevent the loss of more Chinese territory to the Japanese, a group of KMT soldiers kidnapped Chiang in 1936 and released him only after he agreed to join forces with the Communists against the Japanese. This cooperation continued throughout World War II.

At war's end, however, the conflict resumed. During World War II the Communists had prevented the Japanese from controlling all of northwest China. This effective resistance, plus the reforms that Mao instituted to give land to poor peasants, won more support for the Communists and recruits for their army.

The United States, which had long supported Chiang, did not want to see China become a Communist country. During and after World War II the United States sent economic and military aid, including troops, to China to unite the country under the KMT. Truman sent George Marshall to China in 1946 to arrange a truce, but neither side would compromise.

Although Chiang had helped modernize China by building railroads, roads, and factories, his government was becoming increasingly unpopular. The fight against the Japanese had wrecked the Chinese economy, and the Chinese people faced soaring inflation. Chiang seemed unresponsive to these economic problems. In addition, Chiang made no efforts at land reform to help the desperately poor peasants. Moreover, he presided over an increasingly corrupt and authoritarian government that banned all other political parties. As opposition to Chiang mounted, Mao's forces gained control of most of the country by 1949.

Realizing his defeat, Chiang and his army retreated to the island of Taiwan, off the coast of southeast China. The Chinese Communists established the People's Republic of China. Dismayed by the Communist victory, the United

States continued to recognize the Nationalists as China's legal government. The Chinese seat on the UN Security Council, granted to Chiang's Taiwan government after World War II, remained in Nationalist hands until 1971.

■■ **In 1949, after a long struggle with Nationalist forces, Chinese Communists under Mao Zedong won control of China.**

THE KOREAN WAR

Meanwhile, political tensions rose in Korea, a peninsula jutting southward from the northeast corner of China. The Japanese had ruled Korea from 1910 to 1945 but had been driven out by Soviet and American troops at the end of World War II. In 1945 the Allies divided Korea into two parts—North Korea and South Korea—with the border between the two countries set at the **38th parallel.** Soviet forces occupied the North, and American troops held the South.

This division was meant to be temporary, but Cold War tensions cemented it. In 1948 North Korea and South Korea set up separate governments, each claiming to rule the entire country. Communist North Korea, led by Kim Il Sung, became known as the People's Republic of Korea. Kim's government, a Communist dictatorship, redistributed land to poor peasants and nationalized most industries. Although Kim's government limited freedom of speech, it expanded education and established formal equality for women. South Korea, under President Syngman Rhee (SING-muhn REE), called itself the Republic of Korea. The southern republic faced economic and political instability after World War II.

Anxious that South Korea not fall to the Communists as China had, the United States built up the South Korean army as a counterbalance to the Soviet-trained northern forces. By 1949 both the United States and the Soviet Union had pulled their troops out of Korea. The pullout left only the two Korean armies tensely facing each other across the 38th parallel.

■■ **After World War II, Korea was divided into Soviet and American occupation zones. In 1948 North Korea and South Korea established separate governments.**

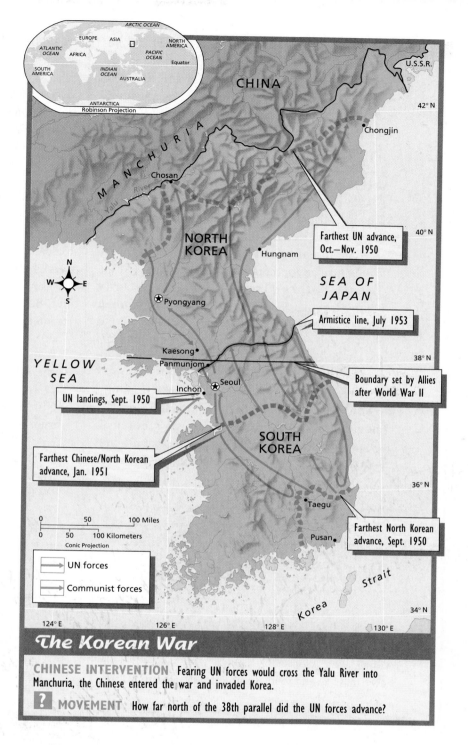

The Korean War

CHINESE INTERVENTION Fearing UN forces would cross the Yalu River into Manchuria, the Chinese entered the war and invaded Korea.

❓ **MOVEMENT** How far north of the 38th parallel did the UN forces advance?

The war begins. After repeated clashes between North Korean and South Korean troops, the North Korean army invaded South Korea on June 25, 1950. A perceived shift in American policy may have encouraged the invasion. Earlier that year Secretary of State Dean Acheson had given a speech defining America's "defensive perimeter" against the spread of communism in Asia. This perimeter, an imaginary line stretching from Alaska to the Philippines, did not include Korea. Thus it appeared that the United States would not defend South Korea against invasion.

In an emergency session the UN Security Council called for an immediate cease-fire. (At the time the Soviets were boycotting the Security Council over its refusal to admit Communist China, so their delegate was not on hand to veto the UN resolution.) Two days later, on June 27, President Truman pledged U.S. support for South Korea. That same day, the Security Council adopted a U.S.–sponsored resolution branding North Korea an "aggressor" and calling on UN members to come to South Korea's defense. Truman later explained: "I felt certain that if South Korea was allowed to fall, Communist leaders would be emboldened to override nations closer to our own shores."

Bitter fighting. Acting under the UN resolution, Truman ordered U.S. air and ground forces into action under the command of General Douglas MacArthur. Truman also ordered the U.S. Seventh Fleet to protect Taiwan. Although 15 other UN members contributed assistance, the United States and South Korea played the major role in resisting North Korea's aggression.

At first, however, the onslaught of North Korean forces and their Soviet-made tanks was overwhelming. Outgunned and outmanned, the U.S. and South Korean troops fell back. One soldier, Sergeant Raymond Remp, recalled his first encounter with the North Korean army:

> 66 Someone fired a green flare, and [the enemy] saw us. . . . They were right on top of us in the hills, firing down on us. . . .
> Some colonel—don't know who—said, "Get out the best way you can." . . .
> All day and night we ran like antelopes. We didn't know our officers. They didn't know us. We lost everything we had. 99

By August the North Koreans had overrun nearly all of South Korea. The U.S. and South Korean forces were backed into a small area around Pusan, in southeast Korea (see map on page 455).

On September 15, 1950, however, MacArthur launched a powerful counterattack. Coming ashore at Inchon, near the 38th parallel, MacArthur's forces swept inland, recapturing Seoul (SOHL), the capital of South Korea. At the same time, a strong UN army, now well equipped and supported from the air, attacked from the south. Caught in a huge trap, North Koreans surrendered by the thousands. Others fled north across the 38th parallel, with UN forces in hot pursuit. By late October the UN army had reached the Yalu River, the boundary between North Korea and China.

But again the tide turned. Late in November, China entered the war on North Korea's side, sending some 300,000 troops across the Yalu. Chinese foreign minister Zhou Enlai (JOH ENLY) explained why China had intervened:

> 66 The U.S. imperialists have adopted a hostile attitude towards us . . . while paying

MAJOR EVENTS OF THE COLD WAR

Year	Event
1945	Korea divided into two zones, one occupied by United States and the other by Soviet Union.
1948	U.S. Congress approves Marshall Plan to provide some $12 billion in aid to Western Europe over next four years. Soviet Union blocks routes between Berlin and West Germany. Western powers meet blockade with Berlin airlift. North Korea and South Korea establish separate governments. United States and Soviet Union recognize Israel.
1949	NATO formed. Chinese Communists win control of China.
1950	Korean War begins when North Korea invades South Korea. China enters Korean War.
1955	Warsaw Pact signed.

Sources: *Encyclopedia of American History; Encyclopedia of World History*

STRUGGLE FOR SUPREMACY The United States and the Soviet Union fought to establish political supremacy across the globe through both diplomatic and military means.

? **ANALYZING** How did the United States attempt to counteract the influence of the Soviet Union?

lip service to non-aggression and non-intervention. From the information we got, they wanted to calm China first and after occupying North Korea, they will come to attack China. 99 `

Outnumbered and with their lines dangerously extended, the UN forces fell back. After desperate fighting and heavy losses in the bitter winter cold, MacArthur's troops finally established a stable defensive line near the 38th parallel.

■■ During the Korean War, UN forces—mainly U.S. and South Korean soldiers—fought North Korean and Chinese troops.

The great debate. With China now involved, MacArthur called for a major expansion of the war. He proposed to blockade China's coast, bomb the Chinese mainland, and "unleash" Chiang's Nationalist forces to invade mainland China. This plan stirred fierce public debate. Supporters said it would bring victory in Korea and overthrow the Chinese Communists. Opponents argued that an attack on China could bring the Soviet Union into the conflict and trigger World War III.

President Truman strongly opposed MacArthur's plan because he did not want the war in Korea to lead to another world war. MacArthur, however, refused to accept the Korean War as a limited conflict. Publicly criticizing the president, MacArthur appealed to

▲ **In September 1950, U.S. soldiers used hand grenades to remove the remaining North Korean forces from Seoul.**

Republican leaders in Congress. He also delivered an ultimatum to the enemy—demanding unconditional surrender—thereby upsetting Truman's plans for peace negotiations. As commander in chief of the military, Truman removed MacArthur from his post in April 1951. General Matthew Ridgway replaced MacArthur as commander of the UN forces.

By the summer of 1951, the war had settled into a stalemate. Bitter fighting continued, but little territory changed hands. Combat in Korea's mountainous terrain became intensely frustrating as the American death toll mounted. Under these circumstances American public opinion gradually turned against the war. The Korean conflict would soon become a major issue in the 1952 presidential election.

SECTION 4 REVIEW

IDENTIFY and explain the significance of the following: Zionism, David Ben-Gurion, Ralph Bunche, Chiang Kai-shek, Long March, Mao Zedong, Kim Il Sung, Syngman Rhee, Dean Acheson, Douglas MacArthur.

LOCATE and explain the importance of the following: Palestine, Israel, Gaza Strip, West Bank, Taiwan, People's Republic of China, 38th parallel, Pusan, Seoul, Yalu River.

1. **MAIN IDEA** Why did war break out between Israel and Arab states in 1948?

2. **MAIN IDEA** How did the end of World War II affect Korea?

3. **MAIN IDEA** What forces fought in the Korean War?

4. **WRITING TO EXPLAIN** Write an essay explaining how the Communists gained control of China in 1949.

5. **HYPOTHESIZING** How do you think the Korean War would have proceeded if MacArthur had been allowed to expand the war into China?

CHAPTER 17
Review

Potsdam Conference held. Nuremberg trials begin. UN charter drafted. Korea divided into two zones.

Employment Act and Atomic Energy Act passed. Coal miners go on strike. Committee on Civil Rights appointed. Baruch Plan proposed.

Japan adopts new constitution. Taft-Hartley Act passed. Truman Doctrine proposed. NSC and CIA established. HUAC investigates movie industry.

1945   1946   1947

WRITING A SUMMARY

Using the essential points of the chapter as a guide, write a summary of the chapter.

REVIEWING CHRONOLOGY

Number your paper 1 to 5. Study the time line above, and list the following events in the order in which they happened by writing the first next to 1, the second next to 2, and so on. Then complete the activity below.

1. Committee on Civil Rights appointed.
2. Israel declares its independence.
3. Truman Doctrine proposed.
4. North Korea invades South Korea.
5. UN charter drafted.

Identifying Cause and Effect Select two events on the time line, and in a paragraph, explain the cause-and-effect relationship between them.

IDENTIFYING PEOPLE AND IDEAS

Explain the historical significance of each of the following people or terms.

1. United Nations
2. Trygve Lie
3. GI Bill of Rights
4. Sadie Alexander
5. Dixiecrats
6. satellite nations
7. George Kennan
8. Atomic Energy Act
9. David Ben-Gurion
10. Mao Zedong

UNDERSTANDING MAIN IDEAS

1. How did the United States work with other Allies to restore peace after World War II?
2. Why did postwar fears of a depression never materialize? What effect did the lifting of wartime price controls have on the economy?
3. How did African Americans work for civil rights in the late 1940s? What effect did these actions have on the 1948 election?
4. What factors caused public support for President Truman to plunge by 1948? How did he win the 1948 election?
5. Why did China enter the Korean War on the side of North Korea?

REVIEWING THEMES

1. **Global Relations** What international and domestic tensions resulted from the conflict between the United States and the Soviet Union?
2. **Technology and Society** How did the development of atomic energy affect the United States?
3. **Democratic Values** How did the U.S. government's response to Cold War pressures lead to limitations on civil liberties?

THINKING CRITICALLY

1. **Problem Solving** What steps did the U.S. government take after World War II to make the transition from war to peace?
2. **Analyzing** How did the Taft-Hartley Act attempt to place restrictions on the tactics unions could use to win improvements?
3. **Synthesizing** What were the main causes of the Cold War? How did the Cold War get played out in Korea?

STRATEGY FOR SUCCESS

Review the Strategies for Success on Recognizing Propaganda on page 430. Then read the excerpt below, which comes from an address by J. Edgar Hoover warning of the dangers of communism. What clues identify this passage as propaganda?

66 The Communist Party of the United States . . . is far better organized than were the Nazis. . . . They [the Communists] are seeking to weaken America just as they did . . . when they were aligned with the Nazis. Their goal is the overthrow of our government. 99

WRITING ABOUT HISTORY

Writing to Explain Imagine you are an American diplomat in China during 1946. Write a memorandum to President Truman, explaining the reasons for the mounting opposition to Chiang Kai-shek after World War II.

Racial discrimination banned in military and in federal hiring. Marshall Plan passed. Berlin airlift begins. Israel declares its independence. Dixiecrats formed. Truman elected president.	NATO established. Middle East agreements reached. Communists gain control of China.	Alger Hiss convicted of perjury. Internal Security Act passed. North Korea invades South Korea.	Julius and Ethel Rosenberg convicted.	U.S. occupation of Japan ends.

1948　　**1949**　　**1950**　　**1951**　　**1952**

USING PRIMARY SOURCES

Attempts to find alleged Communists spread to every level of government. In 1946 President Truman nominated David Lilienthal to head the U.S. Atomic Energy Commission. During Lilienthal's confirmation hearings, Senator Kenneth D. McKellar of Tennessee accused the nominee of being a Communist sympathizer. In Lilienthal's eloquent reply below, how did he defend himself against the charge?

> 66 *I believe—and I conceive the Constitution of the United States to rest . . . upon the fundamental proposition of the integrity of the individual. . . .*
>
> *Any form of government, therefore, and any other institutions which . . . exalt the state or any other institutions above the importance of men, which place arbitrary power over men as a fundamental tenet [belief] of government are contrary to that conception, and, therefore, I am deeply opposed to them.*
>
> *The communistic . . . form of government falls within this category. . . . The fundamental tenet of communism is that the state is an end in itself, and that therefore the powers which the state exercises over the individual are without any ethical standard to limit them.*
>
> *That I deeply disbelieve. . . .*
>
> *I deeply believe in the capacity of democracy to surmount any trials that may lie ahead, provided only that we practice it in our daily lives.*
>
> *And among the things we must practice is this: that while we seek fervently to ferret out the subversive and anti-democratic forces in the country, we do not at the same time, by hysteria . . . and other unfortunate tactics, besmirch [soil] the very cause that we believe in.* 99

LINKING HISTORY AND GEOGRAPHY

Refer to the map on page 453. What effect did the 1949 armistice have on both Israeli and Arab territorial boundaries?

BUILDING YOUR PORTFOLIO

Complete the following projects independently or cooperatively.

1.　THE COLD WAR Imagine that you are a U.S. delegate to the UN conference in San Francisco in 1945. Write a memorandum to the U.S. Senate, detailing world conditions in 1945 that call for the formation of an association of world nations and urging U.S. participation in such an association.

2.　THE GOVERNMENT AND THE ECONOMY Imagine you are a member of the Department of Labor. Prepare a chart that shows how the U.S. government is assisting returning soldiers through programs designed to help them find civilian jobs, attain college educations, or own their own homes.

3.　CIVIL RIGHTS Imagine you are a reporter covering the Committee on Civil Rights. Research and prepare a radio piece on why the committee was formed, who its members are, and what it has documented in its official report, "To Secure These Rights."

DECADE OF CONTRASTS

FOCUS

UNDERSTANDING THE MAIN IDEA

Though the Korean War came to an end, the Cold War continued in the 1950s, increasing Americans' fears of communism and nuclear war. Meanwhile most Americans experienced economic prosperity, leading white middle-class Americans to move away from cities into suburbs. Popular culture, including television, encouraged conformity, but some groups challenged the practices of American society, especially discrimination against African Americans.

THEMES

- **ECONOMIC DEVELOPMENT** How might an economic boom affect population growth and residential patterns?

- **CULTURAL DIVERSITY** How can people demonstrate diversity in a society that emphasizes conformity?

- **DEMOCRATIC VALUES** How might a group of people seek to change laws that discriminate against them?

1953	1954	1955	1957	1960
▼	▼	▼	▼	▼
Korean War ends.	**Supreme Court issues ruling in *Brown v. Board of Education*.**	**Montgomery bus boycott begins.**	***On the Road* published.**	**U-2 incident occurs.**

The end of World War II renewed Americans' optimism about the future. Soon, however, the country was caught up in a Cold War with the Soviet Union. President Truman's commitment to contain the spread of communism led the United States into the Korean War and heightened suspicion that there were Communist spies in America.

United States airman at
Atlanta Terminal Station, 1956

In 1952, after 20 years of Democratic rule in the White House, Americans chose Republican Dwight D. Eisenhower for president, echoing the campaign chant "We Like Ike." The Eisenhower era, which occupied much of the 1950s, saw continued conflict in many parts of the world. However, the emergence of new leadership in the Soviet Union raised hopes for a thaw in the Cold War. At home the 1950s brought widespread economic prosperity. The United States had long been the world's richest, most productive nation. Now millions of middle-class Americans enjoyed a rising standard of living, leading many to move away from cities and rural areas into suburbs.

American life was not all rosy, however. Cold War tensions and nuclear-war fears disturbed much of the nation. Moreover, economic prosperity was not shared equally. Rural residents, African Americans, Hispanic Americans, and Native Americans continued to endure poverty and prejudice. By the mid-1950s, however, a new generation of African Americans started to achieve some successes in the long struggle for the equality of opportunity promised in the Fourteenth Amendment.

Watching a 3-D movie, 1953

COLD WAR FEARS

FOCUS

- How did the outcome of the Korean War affect Korea?
- What led to Senator Joseph McCarthy's downfall?
- How did President Eisenhower handle threats to U.S. interests in Iran, Guatemala, and Egypt?
- How did the U-2 incident affect the arms race?

Eisenhower campaign bumper sticker, 1952

Soon after his victory in the 1952 presidential election, Dwight D. Eisenhower kept his campaign promise to end the Korean conflict. But the Cold War continued, generating fears of nuclear weapons and stirring suspicions that Communists had infiltrated every part of American life. On the world stage the Eisenhower administration developed an aggressive policy to fight the spread of communism, while taking steps to improve diplomatic relations with the Soviet Union.

THE GENERAL VS. THE EGGHEAD

As 1952 began, President Truman found himself confronted with a host of problems. The Korean War had ground to a bloody stalemate, and peace talks were making little progress. Republicans saw their chance to break the Democrats' 20-year hold on the White House by choosing popular World War II hero General Dwight D. Eisenhower as their presidential candidate. Conservative senator Richard M. Nixon of California served as his running mate.

Truman, recognizing that he had little support even within his own party, decided not to run for reelection. The Democrats selected Governor Adlai E. Stevenson of Illinois as their candidate. Stevenson defended the Fair Deal and Truman's foreign policies. Many voters, however, viewed him as an intellectual out of touch with the common people. Some jokingly referred to Stevenson as an "egghead"—"someone with more brains than hair."

Stevenson also could not match Eisenhower's patriotic appeal. Eisenhower reassured voters that America would remain strong throughout the Cold War. The hero of World War II promised to resist communism and end the Korean War. A triumphant Eisenhower received 55 percent of the popular vote and swept the electoral count 442 to 89.

▼ During the 1952 presidential election, Dwight Eisenhower had promised voters, "I shall go to Korea." Eisenhower fulfilled the promise a month after his presidential victory. Here he is shown eating lunch with his old army outfit.

KOREAN WAR ENDS, FEAR CONTINUES

The new president quickly fulfilled his promise to end the war. Eisenhower used military force to get peace negotiations moving. He stepped up bombing raids on North Korea in May 1953 and dropped ominous hints that he would use nuclear weapons, if necessary, to end the conflict.

On July 27, 1953, negotiators agreed to an armistice that divided Korea into two nations, Communist North Korea and anti-Communist South Korea, roughly at the 38th parallel—the prewar dividing line. Some Americans questioned whether this outcome in a distant war justified U.S. losses—some 54,000 dead and 103,000 wounded. More than 1.5 million Chinese and Koreans had also died in the conflict. For years after the war, U.S. relations with China and North Korea remained strained.

■■ **The armistice that ended the Korean War created two nations divided at the 38th parallel: North Korea and South Korea.**

The Korean conflict heightened the fears of some that communism was gaining ground in the United States. This anxiety continued even after the war ended. Many Americans became convinced that spies and Communist sympathizers were everywhere. Joseph McCarthy, a U.S. senator from Wisconsin, helped fuel these suspicions.

Senator McCarthy came to public attention in 1950, when he claimed to have a list of known Communists who worked at the State Department. Although he never produced the list, dozens of federal employees lost their jobs after being labeled as "security risks." McCarthy used his position as chairman of the Senate Permanent Subcommittee on Investigations to wage war against alleged "Communist sympathizers" in the federal government. With almost no supporting evidence, McCarthy questioned the patriotism—and ruined the reputations—of hundreds of government workers. Many Americans, terrified of communism and the power of the Soviet Union, supported his crusade.

McCarthy's popularity and ruthlessness made many politicians wary of challenging him. One who did, however, was Margaret Chase Smith, a

Republican senator from Maine. Smith was born in the small mill town of Skowhegan, Maine, in 1897. When her husband, Republican congressman Clyde Smith, died in 1940, voters chose her to complete his congressional term.

Margaret Chase Smith

After four full terms in the house, Smith won a seat in the Senate in 1948, becoming the first woman to be elected to both houses of Congress. Sixteen years later, she became the first woman to seek the Republican nomination for president. When she left the Senate in 1973, her colleagues praised her as a "woman of courage." Smith once said of public service:

❝ It must be a complete dedication to the people and to the nation with full recognition that every human being is entitled to courtesy and consideration, that constructive criticism is not only to be expected but sought, that smears are not only to be expected but fought, that honor is to be earned but not bought. ❞

McCARTHY'S DOWNFALL

In 1950 Smith and several other senators issued the "Declaration of Conscience," which condemned those who had turned the Senate into "a forum of hate and character assassination." While she never mentioned McCarthy by name, everyone knew she was referring to him. Few others joined in the condemnation, however. Even President Eisenhower refused to criticize McCarthy.

Most of the critics who did speak out came from the arts or the media. In *The Crucible* (1953), playwright Arthur Miller drew parallels between McCarthyism and the Salem witchcraft trials of 1692. On the television program *See It Now*, newscaster Edward R. Murrow questioned McCarthy's tactics. "We cannot defend freedom abroad," Murrow cautioned, "by deserting it at home." While some viewers praised Murrow, others bombarded him with hate mail.

In 1954 McCarthy's committee investigated charges that Communists had gained a foothold in the U.S. Army. Each day a vast television audience, sometimes as many as 20 million people, tuned in to the Army-McCarthy hearings. In the circus-like proceedings, McCarthy repeatedly interrupted and ridiculed witnesses. One victim of this treatment complained that McCarthy "acted like the gangster in a B movie rubbing out someone who had got in his way."

Television exposure of McCarthy's bullying tactics, contrasted with the calm, dignified behavior of army chief counsel Joseph Welch, soon turned public opinion against the senator. At one point when Welch criticized McCarthy for his wild charges, the audience in the hearing room broke into applause. A few months later, the Senate—by a vote of 67 to 22—condemned McCarthy for conduct unbecoming a senator.

■■ **McCarthy's behavior during the Army-McCarthy hearings cost him public support.**

NUCLEAR ANXIETY

Americans' fear of nuclear war heightened as the Soviet Union and the United States raced to develop more-powerful nuclear weapons. In 1950 American scientists began work on a **hydrogen bomb**, or H-bomb, which they said would be 1,000 times more powerful than the atomic bomb dropped on Hiroshima and Nagasaki in World War II. The first H-bomb test in 1952 completely vaporized a small island in the Pacific. Some nine months later, the Soviet Union tested its own H-bomb. J. Robert Oppenheimer, one of the creators of the atomic bomb, cautioned:

❝ [The United States and the Soviet Union] are like two scorpions in a bottle, each capable of killing the other but only at the risk of his own life. . . . The atomic clock ticks faster and faster. ❞

▲ **In the 1950s schools across America held air-raid drills like this one, though such measures would have been of little value in an actual nuclear attack.**

As concerns about nuclear war grew, the government launched a campaign to calm public fears. The federally sponsored book *How to*

THE NUCLEAR ARMS RACE

The testing of increasingly powerful and destructive nuclear weapons by the United States and the Soviet Union in the 1950s alarmed national leaders around the world. In April 1954 Jawaharlal Nehru, Prime Minister of India, voiced his fears:

THROUGH OTHERS' EYES

❝ *The United States of America and the Union of Soviet Socialist Republics, we are told, possess this [nuclear] weapon and each of these countries has during the last two years effected test explosions, unleashing impacts which in every respect were far beyond those of any weapons of destruction known to man. . . . We know that its use threatens the existence of man and civilization as we know it. . . . There can be little doubt about the deep and widespread concern in the world . . . about these weapons and their dreadful consequences. But concern is not enough. . . . We must endeavor with faith and hope to promote all efforts that seek to bring to a halt this drift to what appears to be the menace of total destruction.* ❞

As Cold War tensions and Americans' fear of a Soviet nuclear attack increased in the 1950s, a civil defense craze swept the United States. In 1951 the Federal Civil Defense Administration began a campaign to educate the public on what to do in a nuclear attack. Pamphlets, films, television shows, magazines, and the "Duck and Cover" program for children all encouraged citizens to protect themselves. For example, the *Survival Under Nuclear Attack* booklet urged:

> 66 You can live through an atom bomb raid and you won't have to have a Geiger counter, protective clothing, or special training in order to do it. The secrets of survival are: KNOW THE BOMB'S TRUE DANGERS. KNOW THE STEPS YOU CAN TAKE TO ESCAPE THEM. 99

Americans' fear increased in 1954 when the U.S. *Bravo* hydrogen-bomb tests in the Pacific Ocean revealed the far-reaching effects of nuclear fallout. The crew of a Japanese

▶ **During the 1950s many children learned about civil defense through the "Duck and Cover" program.**

BERT the TURTLE says DUCK and COVER

* STAR OF THE OFFICIAL U.S. CIVIL DEFENSE FILM "DUCK AND COVER"

FEDERAL CIVIL DEFENSE ADMINISTRATION

Harry S Truman Library

fishing boat 85 miles away from the test site developed radiation sickness. People realized that no one would be safe in a nuclear attack. "The alternatives," one civil defense official said, "are to dig, die, or get out." No one wanted to die, and with little warning of incoming missiles, evacuating would not be possible. So some Americans began to dig, constructing backyard fallout shelters.

Pamphlets like the *Family Fallout Shelter* promoted do-it-yourself home shelters. *Life* magazine even presented building a shelter as a father-and-son project. Shelter manufacturers also sprang up, selling their concrete and steel igloos at county fairs for about $1,500. The typical shelter contained flashlights, a first-aid kit, battery radio, chemical toilet, and two-week supply

of food (mainly canned meats and vegetables) and water. Most shelters were furnished with only metal bunk beds or cots, a table, and chairs, but some had all the comforts of home. One man in Austin, Texas, spent $90,000 on his luxury shelter.

Some people also purchased guns to keep out anyone who tried to enter their shelter during a raid. This survivalist view led many to question the ethics of home bomb shelters. Did they represent unbridled—and dangerous—individualism? But before this issue could be resolved, the civil defense craze passed. In 1963 the United States, the Soviet Union, and Great Britain signed a treaty ending above-ground nuclear testing. The fear of fallout diminished, and demand for bomb shelters rapidly decreased.

Survive an Atomic Bomb, for example, offered suggestions on how to live through a nuclear attack. Some Americans put these recommendations to use by building backyard bomb shelters. Schoolchildren went through air-raid drills in which they crawled under their desks to protect themselves from radiation.

While a nuclear attack remained a grim possibility, radioactive fallout—a by-product of nuclear explosions—already posed a threat. American and Soviet H-bomb tests had spewed tons of radioactive material into the atmosphere. In 1957 Congress held a special hearing on the dangers of radioactive fallout. Defense officials

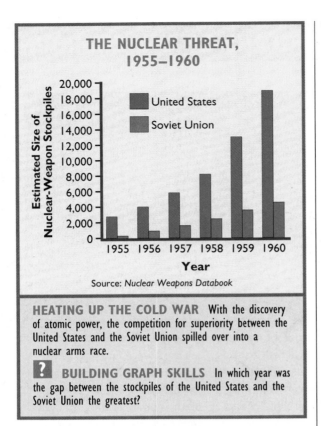

THE NUCLEAR THREAT, 1955–1960

Estimated Size of Nuclear-Weapon Stockpiles

■ United States
■ Soviet Union

Year

Source: *Nuclear Weapons Databook*

HEATING UP THE COLD WAR With the discovery of atomic power, the competition for superiority between the United States and the Soviet Union spilled over into a nuclear arms race.

? BUILDING GRAPH SKILLS In which year was the gap between the stockpiles of the United States and the Soviet Union the greatest?

---

claimed nuclear testing was perfectly safe, but many scientists argued that radiation released during the tests presented a serious danger to the environment and possibly increased the risk of cancer in human beings. Soon the fear of radiation led to an organized campaign against nuclear testing. In 1957 a group of Americans, including well-known doctor Benjamin Spock, organized the Committee for a Sane Nuclear Policy (SANE). SANE urged the United States to begin negotiations with the Soviet Union to end nuclear tests. Within a year SANE had grown to more than 25,000 members in some 130 chapters across the country.

The arms race surged on, however, especially after the Soviet Union launched the satellite *Sputnik* into orbit around the earth in October 1957. Many Americans feared that this launch proved the United States was falling behind the Soviets in technological development. Eisenhower urged Congress to expand American space technology by establishing the **National Aeronautics and Space Administration** (NASA). In 1958 NASA sent the first American satellite, *Explorer I,* into orbit. That same year Congress approved the **National Defense Education Act**, which appropriated millions of dollars to improve education in science, mathematics, and foreign languages.

FIGHTING COMMUNISM ABROAD

The Eisenhower administration viewed nuclear arms and technology as central to the government's priority of ending Communist expansion. Secretary of State John Foster Dulles called for the liberation of all nations that had fallen under Soviet control since 1945. To fulfill this aim, the United States would have to confront Communist aggression and not back down—even if that meant going all the way to the brink of war. "The ability to get to the verge without getting into war is the necessary art," Dulles said. This policy of **brinkmanship** rested on the threat of massive retaliation, including the use of nuclear weapons. Eisenhower, however, proved less confrontational than Dulles's policy might have suggested. Instead, he pursued U.S. aims by more covert—secret—means and by diplomacy.

Covert war and the CIA. Eisenhower tested his covert approach to the Cold War in Iran. Shortly after coming to power in 1951, Iranian premier Mohammad Mosaddeq (MAWS-ad-dek) nationalized British-owned oil fields in Iran. After Eisenhower took office he suspended aid to Iran, fearing that nationalization would endanger Western oil purchases. Eisenhower also authorized a covert action by the CIA to organize a military coup against the Iranian leader. The plan, called Operation Ajax, succeeded in having Mosaddeq arrested and replaced with the young pro-American Shah of Iran, Reza Pahlavi (ri-ZAH PAL-uh-vee). While Eisenhower achieved his goal of removing Mosaddeq, this interference in Iranian affairs sowed seeds of anti-American feelings in that country.

In 1954 Eisenhower ordered another covert action, this time in Latin America, where the United States had often intervened in the past. In

"Don't Be Afraid—I Can Always Pull You Back"

◀ **The policy of brinkmanship was satirized in this 1956 cartoon. Secretary of State John Foster Dulles is shown pushing Uncle Sam to the brink of war.**

From Herblock's Special For Today (Simon & Schuster, 1958)

1954 the Guatemalan president, Jacobo Arbenz Guzmán, took possession of uncultivated sections of Guatemala's largest plantations—including those of the American-owned United Fruit Company—to redistribute among the rural poor.

United Fruit Company executives accused the Guatemalan president of being a Communist sympathizer. Eisenhower called on the CIA to gather a small army to oust Arbenz. The CIA-led forces bombed the capital in May 1954 and installed a new pro-U.S. government, which quickly reversed Arbenz's reform program. But American intervention in Guatemala stirred up bitter resentment throughout Latin America.

The Suez crisis. In some cases, Eisenhower used diplomacy rather than covert actions to influence foreign policy. In 1955 the American government offered Egypt financial help to build a large dam at Aswan on the Nile River. However, when Egyptian leader Gamal Abdel Nasser also sought assistance from the Soviet Union, the United States canceled its promised aid. Nasser then seized the Suez Canal, a foreign-owned waterway that linked the Mediterranean and Red seas (see map on page 561). Egypt would use canal tolls to build the Aswan Dam, Nasser declared.

Nasser's nationalization of the canal posed many problems, including a threat to the Western oil trade. Egypt also refused to allow ships bound for Israel to pass through the canal. Late in October 1956, Israel launched an attack into Egyptian territory toward the Suez Canal. Great Britain and France, claiming they were protecting

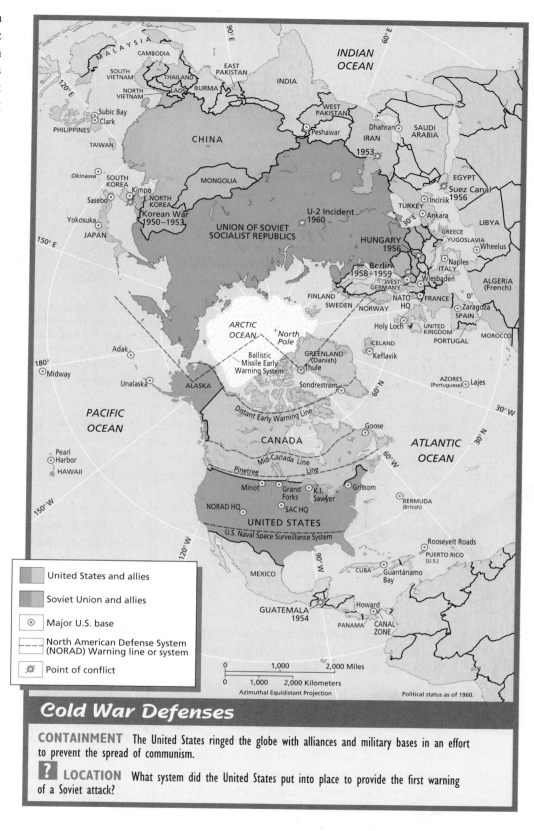

Cold War Defenses

CONTAINMENT The United States ringed the globe with alliances and military bases in an effort to prevent the spread of communism.

? LOCATION What system did the United States put into place to provide the first warning of a Soviet attack?

the canal, seized the Mediterranean end of the waterway a few days later. The Soviet Union threatened war if the three nations did not withdraw from Egypt at once.

The United States faced the difficult choice of either supporting its allies—Britain, France, and Israel—or siding with Egypt and the Soviet Union. In the end, Eisenhower supported a UN resolution calling for an immediate cease-fire and the withdrawal of the invading troops. He explained:

> 66 If the United Nations once admits that international disputes can be settled by using force, then we will have destroyed the foundation of the organization and our best hope of establishing a world order. 99

Grudgingly, Britain, France, and Israel withdrew their forces, and the crisis eased.

The Soviet Union's support of Egypt during the Suez crisis bolstered the Soviets' position among the Arab nations. To counter Soviet influence in the Middle East, the president issued the **Eisenhower Doctrine** in January 1957, offering military aid and in some instances American troops to any Middle East nation seeking help in resisting Communist aggression.

▪▪ Eisenhower used the CIA to protect U.S. interests in Iran and Guatemala. In the Suez Crisis, he relied on diplomacy.

Uprising in Eastern Europe. At the same time that the Suez crisis was unfolding, an equally dangerous situation was developing in Eastern Europe. In February 1956 Soviet leader Nikita Khrushchev stunned political observers by denouncing his predecessor, Joseph Stalin, who had died in 1953, for many ruthless crimes. Observers hoped that this move signaled a new era of reform for the Soviet Union and Eastern Europe. Later in 1956, Polish reformers tested Khrushchev by calling for greater political freedom.

Inspired by the example of Poland, thousands of Hungarians took to the streets in late October to demand reform. Moderates seized control of the Hungarian government and called for a Western-style democracy in their nation and for Hungary's secession from the Warsaw Pact. Khrushchev

▲ On November 2, 1956, Hungarian rebels in Budapest triumphantly waved the tricolored Hungarian flag atop a captured Russian tank. Two days later Soviet troops occupied the main square in front of the Houses of Parliament, where this photograph was taken.

responded with crushing force. On November 4, heavily armed Soviet troops moved into the Hungarian capital, Budapest, and smashed the revolt within days. A new pro-Soviet government imposed martial law and executed or imprisoned the rebel leaders.

Throughout their struggle the Hungarian rebels pleaded for help from the West. Eisenhower worried, however, that intervention in Eastern Europe would lead to all-out nuclear war with the Soviets. He condemned the Soviets' actions but refused to aid the rebels. He did, however, help ease immigration laws to allow more Eastern European refugees into the United States. As a result, some 40,000 Hungarians fled to the United States after the uprising.

To some observers Eisenhower's lack of support for the rebels indicated a retreat from Dulles's talk of liberating Communist-controlled countries. But most of the American public supported Eisenhower, whom they reelected by a landslide against Adlai Stevenson in November 1956.

Hopes Raised, Hopes Dashed

Near the end of the decade, the United States and the Soviet Union moved to improve their diplomatic relations. In 1959 Vice President Nixon

DWIGHT D. EISENHOWER
1890–1969

in office
1953–1961

U.S. 6ᶜ POSTAGE

DWIGHT D.
EISENHOWER

Dwight Eisenhower built his army career slowly. He graduated from West Point in 1915 and worked in an Army camp in Pennsylvania during World War I. Throughout the years between the first and second world wars he moved around the globe, from Panama to the Philippines, becoming a master organizer and coordinator.

In charge of Allied military forces in North Africa in 1943, "he now became," a British colleague explained, "the chairman of a company of great power and resources." As president, Eisenhower continued his military habits of shared leadership. "No man can be a Napoleon in modern war," the president once said. "I don't believe this government was set up to be operated by any one acting alone."

Dwight Eisenhower [signature]

visited the Soviet Union and Premier Khrushchev came to the United States. Touring Iowa farms, Pittsburgh steel plants, and Hollywood movie studios, the jovial Khrushchev charmed the American media. In Des Moines he jokingly told reporters, "We have beaten you to the moon, but you have beaten us in sausage making." He and Eisenhower agreed to meet at a summit conference in Paris the following year to discuss arms reductions.

In May 1960, however, just before the Paris conference was to open, Khrushchev announced that an American U-2—a high-altitude spy plane—had been shot down over the Soviet Union. At first American officials insisted that it was a weather-research plane that had strayed off course. But the captured pilot, Francis Gary Powers, admitted he had been on a spying mission.

Khrushchev refused to go ahead with the summit unless the United States halted such spying missions and apologized for past flights. Eisenhower promised that the U-2 flights would stop but did not apologize. Khrushchev refused to meet with Eisenhower again. The brief thaw in the Cold War had come to an abrupt end.

The U-2 incident halted arms-reduction talks between Khrushchev and Eisenhower.

SECTION 1 REVIEW

IDENTIFY and explain the significance of the following: Dwight D. Eisenhower, Adlai E. Stevenson, Joseph McCarthy, Margaret Chase Smith, hydrogen bomb, *Sputnik*, National Aeronautics and Space Administration, National Defense Education Act, brinkmanship, Eisenhower Doctrine, Nikita Khrushchev.

LOCATE and explain the importance of the following: Iran, Guatemala, Suez Canal.

1. **MAIN IDEA** How did the armistice that ended the Korean War affect Korea?

2. **MAIN IDEA** What effect did the U-2 incident have on relations between the United States and the Soviet Union?

3. **COMPARING** What various tactics did Eisenhower use to protect U.S. interests abroad?

4. **WRITING TO PERSUADE** Imagine you are a reporter covering the Army-McCarthy hearings. Write a commentary explaining why Senator McCarthy should be removed from office.

5. **EVALUATING** What actions by the Soviet Union and the United States heightened Americans' fears of nuclear war?

THE AFFLUENT SOCIETY

F O C U S

- What was the economy like in the 1950s?
- How did the population shift during the decade?
- What was early television programming like?
- How did the work force change in the 1950s?

*D*uring Eisenhower's presidency a rapidly growing economy brought prosperity to many Americans. Newly prosperous whites left the cities for the suburbs, while the rural poor flocked to urban areas in search of jobs. The growth of the suburbs and the spread of television helped create a consumer culture that many of the poorer members of society could not enjoy. Changes in the workplace and the work force also helped transform American society during the 1950s.

Advertisement for TV dinner

MODERN REPUBLICANISM

President Eisenhower took office in 1953 determined to change the federal government. He pledged to cut the bureaucracy, to curb what he called the "creeping socialism" of the New Deal, to balance the budget, and to reduce government regulation of the economy.

In the first year of his presidency, Eisenhower cut thousands of government jobs and pared billions of dollars from the federal budget. To reduce government influence over the economy, he cut government farm subsidies and turned over federally owned coastal lands for private development.

But despite his pledge to curb "creeping socialism," Eisenhower left the basic social and economic programs of the New Deal–Fair Deal era intact. Under his administration, social security and unemployment benefits expanded, and the minimum wage increased. Eisenhower established the Department of Health, Education, and Welfare, under the supervision of Texan Oveta Culp Hobby. The president also supported the largest increase in educational spending up to that time. This approach to domestic affairs, which Eisenhower described as "conservative when it comes to money and liberal when it comes to human beings," became known as **modern Republicanism**.

Providing funding for social programs, defense, and other government obligations undermined Eisenhower's pledge to balance the federal budget.

◀ **As secretary of Health, Education, and Welfare, Oveta Culp Hobby lobbied for legislation providing for a national polio vaccination program.**

Only three of the eight budgets he presided over were balanced. Furthermore, during his years in office the federal debt grew by about 9 percent, to $291 billion.

THE "GOOD" YEARS

For many Americans the 1950s was a decade of economic prosperity. The post–World War II spending spree that began in the late 1940s continued into the 1950s. Defense spending, triggered by the Korean War, also boosted growth in the early 1950s. Unemployment and inflation rarely edged above 5 percent. By the mid-1950s more than 60 percent of Americans were earning a "middle-class" income, at that time considered $3,000–$10,000 annually. Never before, the popular media declared, had so many people enjoyed such prosperity. "This is a new kind of capitalism," declared the *Reader's Digest,* "capitalism for the many, not for the few."

Not everyone shared in the good times, however. A 1957 study found nearly 40 million Americans living below or near the poverty line of $3,000 for a family of four. Almost half of the nation's poor lived in rural areas, where they suffered from poor nutrition, inadequate medical care, and lack of education.

■■ The 1950s saw rapid economic expansion and prosperity for many, but the prosperity was not evenly distributed.

PEOPLE ON THE MOVE

The 1950s was a decade of geographic mobility. Millions of newly prosperous whites, especially young couples, moved to the suburbs that developers built around the nation's cities. At the same time, many poor rural citizens migrated to the cities in search of a better life.

The urban communities. Most of the rural residents who moved to the cities to escape poverty found little improvement in their economic status. By 1960 more than 20 million city dwellers were living in poverty.

While large numbers of poor rural whites flocked to the cities, African Americans consti-

▲ **Puerto Rican immigrants developed strong community organizations in their New York neighborhoods. Here, Puerto Rican boys play in the game room of the Good Neighbor Church and Community Center located in Manhattan.**

tuted the single largest group in the rural-to-urban movement. In a continuation of the Great Migration, which had begun during World War I (see Chapter 10), African Americans left the South for the industrial cities of the North. This northward movement peaked in the mid-1950s, with the African American population of some northern cities growing by about 2,000 each week.

Wide-scale unemployment caused many Puerto Ricans to leave the island for the mainland. Some 40,000–50,000 migrated annually in the 1950s. About 70 percent of Puerto Rican migrants settled in New York City. Many Mexicans also moved to the United States in order to find work. While most immigrants from Mexico had previously settled in rural areas, the new immigrants tended to settle in cities such as Los Angeles, Denver, El Paso, Phoenix, and San Antonio. By 1960 about 80 percent of Hispanic Americans were living in cities.

Relocation under pressure. Thousands of American Indians also moved to the cities in the 1950s. But unlike other migrants, Indians did so under federal pressure. To promote the assimilation of American Indians into mainstream society, the Eisenhower administration supported passage of the **Relocation Act** of 1956. The act

▶ **In 1958, American Indians protested when the federal government seized reservation land for a power project in Niagara Falls. This Tuscarora boy was photographed as he walked the picket line.**

urged Native Americans to move to urban areas. It even set up relocation offices in major cities to assist newcomers. Many feared that this would deplete the reservations of future leaders and destroy tribal cultures. Oglala Lakota activist Gerald One Feather recalled:

66 The relocation program had an impact on our . . . government at Pine Ridge [South Dakota]. Many people who could have provided [our] leadership were lost because they had motivation to go off the reservation to find employment or obtain an education. Relocation drained off a lot of our potential leadership. 99

To hasten relocation, the government adopted a policy of termination in 1953. **Termination** involved ending on a tribe-by-tribe basis the reservation system and most federal funding for Native Americans. Various tribal groups launched protests and lawsuits against the termination policy, considering it an attempt to wipe out Native American communities. By 1958 the Eisenhower administration backed down, saying it would no longer support legislation "to terminate tribes without their consent."

The suburbs. As more poor migrants settled in the cities, many more-prosperous city residents moved to the suburbs. By the end of the decade,

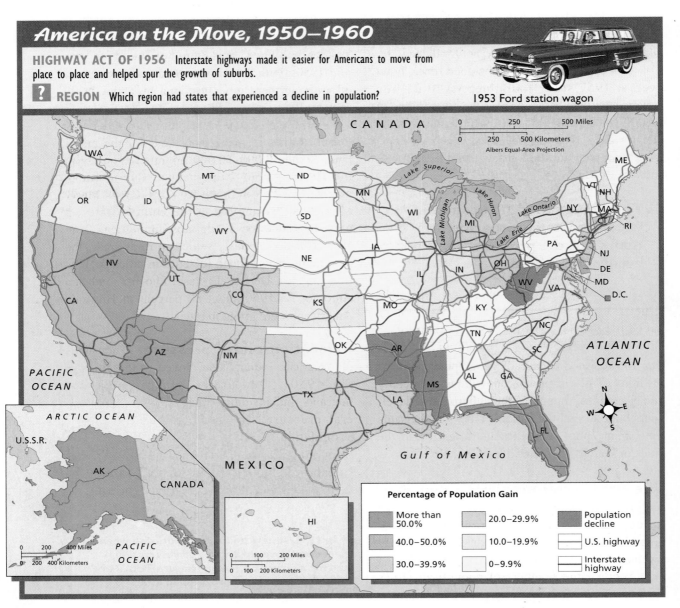

America on the Move, 1950–1960

HIGHWAY ACT OF 1956 Interstate highways made it easier for Americans to move from place to place and helped spur the growth of suburbs.

? REGION Which region had states that experienced a decline in population?

1953 Ford station wagon

Percentage of Population Gain

- More than 50.0%
- 40.0–50.0%
- 30.0–39.9%
- 20.0–29.9%
- 10.0–19.9%
- 0–9.9%
- Population decline
- U.S. highway
- Interstate highway

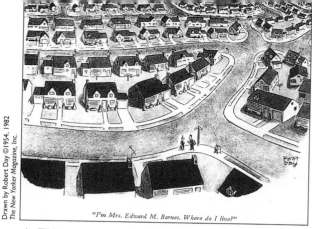

"I'm Mrs. Edward M. Barnes. Where do I live?"

▲ This cartoon satirizing life in the suburbs appeared in *The New Yorker* in 1954.

close to 60 million Americans—one third of the total population—lived in the suburbs. Many of these suburbs were planned communities.

Suburban growth took off in part because more Americans could afford to purchase homes. Veterans had access to low-interest mortgages from such government agencies as the Veterans Administration (VA) and the Federal Housing Administration (FHA). Private savings and loan associations, too, offered mortgages on relatively easy terms. In addition, the **Highway Act** of 1956 greatly expanded the nation's highway systems, making it easier for suburban residents to commute to jobs in the cities.

The growth of suburbs was also spurred by an expanding population. During the depression and World War II years, many people had postponed getting married or starting a family. After the war, Americans began to get married at earlier ages and in greater numbers than they had for generations. They also had more children. The soaring birth rate accounted for more than 90 percent of the 30-million increase in the population during the 1950s. The decade, many observers said, had experienced nothing less than a **baby boom**.

■■ **Poor whites, African Americans, Hispanic Americans, and American Indians moved to the cities, while many middle-class Americans moved to the suburbs.**

CONSUMPTION AND CONFORMITY

Suburbanization and prosperity changed the way many Americans lived. Seemingly secure in their jobs and confident of increasing incomes,

Americans went on a buying spree, purchasing between five and seven million new automobiles and an array of household appliances each year.

With an increase in consumerism came a rising emphasis on conformity. Suburban neighbors worked hard to "keep up with the Joneses," that is, to make sure that they had as many modern conveniences as their neighbors. Scholar Henry Steele Commager noted how conformity affected American values: "What is the new loyalty? It is, above all, conformity. It is the uncritical and unquestioning acceptance of America as it is."

Children became an important focus of suburban life, largely because of the baby boom. The baby boom also led to an emphasis on child rearing, focusing on the role of mothers. Popular magazines, advertisements, and self-help books depicted the ideal wife and mother as a full-time homemaker who devoted all of her energy to making her family happy (and buying all the latest household gadgets). Contrary to these popular images, however, the number of working mothers actually *increased* during the 1950s. By the end of the decade, some 39 percent of all women with children ages 6 to 17 worked for wages outside the home.

While it had long been common for mothers of poor families to work for wages, an increasing number of women in the work force were middle-class mothers. Despite the popular media's image of the typical middle-class family as a stay-at-home

CHANGES IN MATERIAL STANDARDS OF LIVING, 1940–1955

Households Owning	1940	1955
Automobile	50.0%	71.0%
Television Set	0.0%	76.1%
Refrigerator	44.0%	94.1%
Washing Machine	46.0%	84.1%
Clothes Dryer	0.0%	9.2%
Vacuum Cleaner	38.0%	64.3%

Sources: *The Overworked American; 1956 Statistical Abstract; An Economic History of Women in America; The Proud Decades*

"THE GOOD LIFE" After World War II many American consumers rushed to buy the latest in modern conveniences.

? **BUILDING GRAPH SKILLS** Which item experienced the greatest increase in ownership?

► The stereotypical "happy housewife" was often used in 1950s advertisements to sell household products to female shoppers.

wife supported by a well-employed husband, some families needed a second income to share in the middle-class consumer culture. Many of the jobs held by these women were part-time or low-level jobs with little long-term career potential.

Just as the reality of working mothers conflicted with media images of the suburban housewife, so too did the reality of domestic life. Though advertisements portrayed the full-time suburban homemaker as happy and satisfied, many experts argued that isolation at home made women "bored stiff," especially after their children left home. Indeed, many stay-at-home suburban mothers longed to pursue career opportunities once their children were older. Writer Benita Eisler recalled:

> 66 For our generation of housewives and mothers, "getting it over with" was our promise to a future deferred. We would "do something" with our college education (or finish it) when we "got out from under" diapers, formulas, car pools. 99

Church attendance soared in the 1950s. Religious worship promoted social stability in these unsettled postwar years. For uprooted Americans streaming to the suburbs, church membership provided a sense of belonging.

Atomic fear also spurred the upsurge of religion. The young evangelist Billy Graham, whose crusades drew vast audiences in the 1950s, often warned of the nuclear danger in urging Americans to turn to God. The Reverend Norman Vincent

Peale assured Americans in his best-selling book *The Power of Positive Thinking* that God could help them overcome fear and feelings of weakness.

Further, in these frightening Cold War years, America's piety underscored the contrast with the atheistic Soviet Union. In this spirit, Congress added the phrases "In God We Trust" and "Under God" to the nation's currency and the Pledge of Allegiance, respectively.

THE GOLDEN AGE OF TELEVISION

Television helped to reinforce both consumerism and mythical images of American life. By the end of the 1950s, 46 million households owned at least one television set.

Advertising played a major role in television programming. By 1960, advertisers were spending $1.6 billion trying to convince viewers to buy their products. Often one business would sponsor a show, such as *General Electric Theatre* and *Kraft Television Theatre,* so that viewers immediately connected the program with a company. This monopoly on advertising also gave many companies great control over program content. During the height of McCarthyism, some sponsors had actors and writers fired from shows because of their suspected political beliefs.

Sporting events, comedies, variety programs, and quiz shows—such as the World Series, *Your Show of Shows,* and *The $64,000 Question*—shared the airwaves with serious dramas in the early years of television. The most popular program of the decade was the comedy *I Love Lucy,* starring Lucille Ball and Desi Arnaz. Thousands of fans tuned in every week to witness Lucy's slapstick antics.

▼ In 1993, *TV Guide* magazine rated the *I Love Lucy* show as the best sitcom in television history.

The production and use of chemical pesticides and fertilizers soared in the 1950s. One insecticide in particular was hailed as a modern miracle—dichlorodiphenyltrichloroethane (DDT). DDT and similar pesticides promised farmers increased crop yields and reduced labor expenses. Consumers would benefit as well with higher quality food at a lower cost. These modern chemicals seemed to be a dream come true.

But amid all the praise, Rachel Carson, a former biologist with the U.S. Fish and Wildlife Service, asked, "What has already silenced all the voices of spring in countless towns in America?" In 1962 Carson sent the world a startling message in her book *Silent Spring*. She warned that the indiscriminate use of pesticides, particularly DDT, killed wildlife and polluted the environment. Carson cited a Michigan town that sprayed DDT to kill beetles attacking the town's elm trees. When the elm leaves fell in the fall, they were eaten by worms, which were then eaten by robins. By early spring, almost all the robins in the city were dead.

Today, views on the use of DDT and other pesticides have changed dramatically. Public opinion and that of the scientific community now firmly stand behind many of Carson's ideas.

▲ **Workers spray pesticides on fruit trees.**

Since the 1960s, possible evidence of cancer and other health problems in field workers and children exposed to DDT has surfaced. And traces of DDT have been found in penguins and seals in Antarctica and in whales off the coast of Greenland—areas far removed from any application of the chemical.

As a result, in 1972 the Environmental Protection Agency (EPA) ordered a ban on domestic uses of DDT, and by the mid-1980s the agency had made addressing pesticide pollution a priority. Now the chemical industry, research scientists, and environmental groups are experimenting with a variety of natural biological controls, such as fungi, bacteria, and "beneficial" insects, to destroy harmful pests.

Carson died in 1964, too soon to see the results of her efforts. Her concerns and warnings inspired a generation of Americans to work toward finding ecologically safe pesticides and fertilizers.

Though television grew in popularity, it proved a very selective mirror, showing primarily white, middle-class, suburban experiences. Poverty, if shown at all, was a problem all but solved. Working women, ethnic minorities, and inner-city life rarely appeared. When they did, it was usually in a way that reinforced stereotypes.

One of the era's most controversial programs was the popular comedy about black urban life, *Amos 'n' Andy*. The show began as a radio program with two white men creating the voices of black characters. When the show moved to television, African American actors took over the roles; but to many viewers, the characters reflected white stereotypes of the black community. The NAACP launched a protest against the program. Others joined in the protest, and in 1953 *Amos 'n' Andy* left the air. In 1966 the network banned it from being shown in reruns.

■■ **Television provided a variety of programs but often reinforced stereotypes of ethnic groups, women, and American life.**

CHANGES IN THE WORKPLACE

Many of the social shifts in America were related to shifts in the work force. Large corporations prospered during the decade as some 5,000 companies merged to form larger organizations.

Automation. American factories were also changing. Throughout the 1950s companies introduced machines that could perform industrial operations faster and more efficiently than human workers could. This process of **automation** greatly increased productivity. But automation also reduced the number of manufacturing jobs. Many workers began to fear an automated future, as one popular song noted:

> 66 I walked, walked, walked into the foreman's office.
> To find out what was what.
> I looked him in the eye and said, "What goes?"
> And this is the answer I got:
> His eyes turned red, then green, then blue
> And it suddenly dawned on me—
> There was a robot sitting in the seat
> Where the foreman used to be. 99

Automation also affected America's farms as new machinery boosted production while reducing the labor force. While farm productivity increased from 1950 to the 1960s, the farm population shrank from 23 million to 15.6 million.

As the number of manufacturing and farming jobs decreased, professional and service jobs increased. Huge new corporations required a multitude of managers, supervisors, and clerical workers. Furthermore, the spending spree of the 1950s created millions of retail jobs. Many of the newly created service jobs were in occupations traditionally filled by women, such as nursing, teaching, retail sales, and clerical work. By 1960, women made up about one third of the total work force. But many women continued to earn much less than men in the same fields, and few received promotions to management jobs.

The new union style. Changes in the work force also influenced organized labor. Boosted in part by the merger of the AFL and CIO in 1955, union membership grew steadily in the mid-1950s, peaking at some 18.5 million in 1956.

To help workers get their fair share of economic prosperity, union leaders abandoned efforts at economic, political, and social reforms in favor of achieving gains in wages and benefits. In order to do so, they sought accommodation, rather than confrontation, with management. George Meany, the AFL–CIO's first president, boasted that he had never led a strike. Further, he said he had no interest in reforming society. His only goal, he stated, was to ensure "an ever rising standard of living" for his members.

Many unions fought for and won guaranteed annual wages and cost-of-living adjustments—automatic pay raises linked to the rate of inflation. In return, unions made concessions, such as accepting automation plans or changes in work rules or production levels.

In the late 1950s newspapers reported corruption and links to organized crime among some union officials. Congress attempted to crack down on union corruption by passing the **Landrum-Griffin Act** of 1959, which banned ex-convicts from holding union offices, required frequent elections of officers, and regulated the investment of union funds. The negative publicity hurt union membership, which steadily declined after 1957.

■■ **The work force changed through automation, an increase in professional and service jobs, and a new approach by union leaders.**

▲ **Ford Motor Company closed its Somerville, Massachusetts, plant in 1958. Over 1,000 employees were directly affected by the decision.**

URBAN RENEWAL

The changing work force also affected those moving to the cities. Automation had eliminated many of the semiskilled jobs traditionally taken by city newcomers. Skilled workers often found that their way to better jobs was blocked by discrimination.

Nowhere was discrimination more obvious than in housing. Prevented by poverty and by discriminatory real-estate practices from moving into newer neighborhoods, African Americans, Hispanics, and Native Americans were generally limited to crowded tenements and old housing in the poorest neighborhoods. Eventually, however, these neighborhoods provided a sense of community for those who lived there. Local stores, churches, and social clubs gave structure to the lives of those struggling to adjust to the cities. As one resident of El Barrio, New York's Puerto Rican neighborhood, observed:

66 This is our neighborhood. . . . We consider this part of the city to be ours. . . . The stores, barbershops, restaurants, butcher shops, churches, funeral parlors, . . . everything is all Latino. 99

Government officials, however, saw only neglected, shabby buildings. To improve inner-city housing, the federal government proposed **urban renewal** programs to replace old, run-down inner-city buildings with new ones. Across the country the government bulldozed older urban neighborhoods to

▲ **A poor family crowds into the kitchen of a small tenement in Harlem, New York City.**

make way for some 417,000 low-income public housing units. Most of these units were cramped apartments, so small, one resident said, "You feel like you can't breathe." The new high-rise buildings also had a cold, impersonal atmosphere. The sense of community that people had felt in the old neighborhoods was gone.

SECTION 2 REVIEW

IDENTIFY and explain the significance of the following: Oveta Culp Hobby, modern Republicanism, Relocation Act, termination, Highway Act, baby boom, automation, George Meany, Landrum-Griffin Act, urban renewal.

1. **MAIN IDEA** How did the American population shift during the 1950s?

2. **MAIN IDEA** What changes occurred in the work force during the 1950s?

3. **IDENTIFYING CAUSE AND EFFECT** Why are the 1950s considered boom years? How were American values affected by the economic boom?

4. **WRITING TO EVALUATE** Imagine you are a television critic during the 1950s. Write an article for *TV Guide* that assesses the portrayal of ethnic groups, women, and families on television.

5. **HYPOTHESIZING** What effect did discrimination in housing have on ethnic groups? Why were some ethnic communities upset with urban renewal programs?

VOICES OF DISSENT

FOCUS

- **Why were the *Brown* v. *Board of Education* decision and the Montgomery bus boycott major turning points for the civil rights movement?**
- **What did the Central High School crisis demonstrate about some white southerners' attitudes toward desegregation?**
- **How did teenagers rebel against the conformity of the 1950s?**

Although politics and popular culture in the 1950s emphasized conformity, a few voices spoke out against the system. African Americans, tired of segregation and discrimination, launched the civil rights movement to demand equality. Meanwhile writers, including the Beats, and a new style of music called rock 'n' roll sowed the seeds of rebellion in teenagers.

Rebel Without a Cause movie poster

BROWN V. BOARD

The NAACP had long waged a campaign against segregation in education, a practice upheld by the Supreme Court's 1896 "separate but equal" doctrine in *Plessy* v. *Ferguson* (see Chapter 4). The NAACP had been able to open some all-white universities and graduate schools to African American students by demonstrating that in most cases separate educational facilities for black students were far inferior to the facilities established for whites only. But the Court continued to maintain that segregation in and of itself was legal.

In 1952 a group of cases that challenged segregation in public schools came before the Supreme Court in the form of ***Brown*** v. ***The Board of Education of Topeka***. The case involved Linda Brown, a young African American student from Topeka, Kansas. Segregation in Topeka's schools prevented her from attending an all-white elementary school a short walk from her home. Instead, she had to travel a long distance over dangerous railroad tracks to get to an all-black school.

Arguing on Brown's behalf, NAACP lawyer Thurgood Marshall introduced data that suggested segregation psychologically damaged African American students by lowering their self-esteem.

▼ **Thurgood Marshall (center) discussed legal strategies for fighting school segregation cases with other NAACP attorneys in 1954.**

Marshall's arguments greatly influenced the Court's ruling, which was issued on May 17, 1954. Written by Chief Justice Earl Warren, the unanimous decision declared that segregation generated

> 66 a feeling of inferiority . . . that may affect [children's] hearts and minds in a way unlikely ever to be undone. . . . In the field of education the doctrine of "separate but equal" has no place. Separate educational facilities are inherently unequal. 99

Many Americans praised the decision as a long overdue step toward ending segregation entirely. Scholar Allison Davis hailed it as the salvation of American industry because it would create more skilled black workers: "The survival of the United States seems to depend upon its developing the ability of millions of our citizens whose capacities have been crippled by segregation."

Some states moved quickly to end school segregation. Many white southern leaders, however, reacted to the decision with alarm. The governor of Virginia, for instance, vowed to use every legal means at his command to maintain segregated schools in his state. Because of the resistance from the South, the Supreme Court issued a ruling in 1955 calling on the federal district courts to end school segregation "with all deliberate speed."

THE MONTGOMERY BUS BOYCOTT

The NAACP next aimed at ending segregation on southern transportation systems, beginning their efforts in Montgomery, Alabama. Local NAACP leaders had been looking for a test case to challenge the practice of forcing African American citizens to ride in the back of buses. On December 1, 1955, Rosa Parks, a black seamstress, provided them with their case when she refused to give up her bus seat to a white passenger.

BIO GRAPHY Born in 1913 in Tuskegee, Alabama, Rosa Parks moved to the Montgomery area at a young age. Her mother was determined that Parks would receive a good education. Montgomery did not have a high school for black students, so her parents sent her to the laboratory school at Alabama State College. Because discrimination prevented her from finding a job that matched her education, she found work as a seamstress. She also became involved in the

civil rights movement, holding office in the Montgomery chapter of the NAACP.

In the late 1950s Parks moved to Detroit, where she began working for Congressman John Conyers in 1967. She has continued her commitment to civil rights action and has won numerous awards, including the NAACP's Spingarn Medal, recognizing the "highest or noblest achievement" by an African American.

Rosa Parks

Parks's refusal to give up her seat led to her arrest and conviction for violating the city's segregation laws. In protest, Montgomery's 50,000 African Americans organized a boycott against the bus system. The **Montgomery Improvement Association** (MIA), a group of local civil rights leaders, persuaded the community to continue the boycott while the NAACP and Parks fought her conviction in the courts.

The MIA chose as its spokesperson Martin Luther King, Jr., a 26-year-old Baptist minister who was new to the town. An energetic and charismatic speaker, King could inspire large audiences. His ability to move people helped hold the African American community together as the bus boycott dragged on for months.

White racists tried every method from intimidation to physical violence to break the boycott. White vigilantes attacked and beat boycotters and bombed the houses of King and other MIA leaders. Many boycotters—including Rosa Parks—lost their jobs. But King urged the black community not to respond to violence with more violence. Finally, the peaceful protest worked. In November 1956 the Supreme Court declared both the Montgomery and the Alabama segregation laws unconstitutional. By the end of the year, Montgomery had a desegregated bus system, and the civil rights movement had a new leader—Martin Luther King, Jr.

The successful struggle of thousands of Montgomery blacks to win their basic human rights marked a blow to racism—and to the general fear of standing up against those in power engendered by Cold War hysteria in America. Not surprisingly, Martin Luther King, Jr., was accused of being a Communist by many who opposed the movement. Some southern whites, however, reluctantly accepted that change had to

▲ In response to a 1956 court ruling, Dallas buses were ordered to end segregation. Shown here is an employee of the Dallas Transit Company removing a separate seating sign from the rear of a bus.

come. As a South Carolina newspaper declared, "Segregation is going—it's all but gone. . . . The South can't reverse the trend." Even so, other white southerners fought to delay change for as long as possible.

▪▪ *Brown* v. *Board of Education* and the Montgomery bus boycott marked the first steps toward ending segregation in the South.

SHOWDOWN IN LITTLE ROCK

Despite the Supreme Court rulings, school desegregation in the South moved slowly. By the end of the 1956–57 school year, the vast majority of southern school systems remained segregated. In Arkansas, however, school desegregation was progressing with relatively little opposition. Two of the three southern school districts that began desegregation in 1954 were in Arkansas. The Little Rock school board was the first

in the South to announce it would comply with the *Brown* decision.

Little Rock's desegregation plan was set to begin in September 1957 with the admission of nine black students to the all-white Central High School. However, Governor Orval Faubus, about to embark on a bid for reelection, came out against the desegregation plan. The night before school was to start, he ordered the Arkansas National Guard to surround Central High. He did so, he claimed, to protect the school from attacks by armed protesters. "It will not be possible to restore or to maintain order . . . if forcible integration is carried out tomorrow in the schools of this community," he warned.

No real danger existed, but Faubus's claims panicked everyone. Elizabeth Eckford did not receive a message that instructed the black students to stay home. When she attempted to enter the school, a mob of angry whites and a line of armed National Guardsmen met her. She described the ordeal:

❛❛When I got in front of the school, . . . I didn't know what to do. . . . Just then the guards let some white students through. . . . I walked up to the guard who had let [them] in. . . . When I tried to squeeze past him, he raised his bayonet, and then the other guards moved in. . . . Somebody [in the crowd] started yelling, *"Lynch her! Lynch her!"*❝❝

For nearly three weeks the National Guard prevented the students, now known as the "**Little Rock Nine**," from entering the school. Then, under

▶ Elizabeth Eckford bravely walked alone through a crowd of angry, jeering whites before she was turned away from entering Little Rock's Central High School.

▲ On November 4, 1957, leaders of the Arkansas branch of the NAACP appeared in court to fight an ordinance forcing them to turn over confidential records. State president Daisy Bates (second from the left) played a central role in helping the Little Rock Nine integrate Central High School.

court order, Faubus removed the National Guard. When the nine attempted to enter the school on September 23, the white mob rioted. Deploring the "disgraceful occurrences" at Central High, President Eisenhower ordered some 1,000 federal troops to Little Rock. On September 25, 1957, under the troops' fixed bayonets, the Little Rock Nine finally entered Central High.

In the midst of the Little Rock crisis, President Eisenhower signed the **Civil Rights Act of 1957**. This act, the first civil rights law since Reconstruction, made it a federal crime to prevent qualified persons from voting. It also set up the federal Civil Rights Commission to investigate violations of the law. A follow-up law, passed in 1960, strengthened the courts' powers to protect blacks' voting rights. But prejudice and discrimination remained a fact of life for most African Americans. Much remained to be done before they could claim victory in the struggle for civil rights.

■■ **The Central High crisis in Little Rock showed that some southern whites were not willing to comply with desegregation.**

QUESTIONING CONFORMITY

While the African American community in the South was challenging segregation, other groups were beginning to question the American culture of consumption and conformity. One such group included a handful of writers and scholars who sought to expose what one called the "crack in the picture window" of society.

A number of novelists depicted the experiences of those facing poverty and discrimination. In Ralph Ellison's *Invisible Man* (1952), an African American man searches for his place in a society at once both hostile and indifferent to him. His struggle reflects that of many people left out of mainstream society:

❝I am an invisible man. . . . I am a man of substance, of flesh and bone, fiber and liquids—and I might even be said to possess a mind. I am invisible, understand, simply because people refuse to see me.❞

Other critics attacked suburban society and the corporate mentality of America. Harvard economist John Kenneth Galbraith warned privileged Americans in *The Affluent Society* (1958) that they were ignoring pressing social issues in their pursuit of material possessions and comfort.

Sociologists William Whyte, C. Wright Mills, and David Riesman criticized the new corporate system. Whyte in *The Organization Man* (1956) and Mills in *White Collar* (1951) argued that the need to conform in a large corporation was wiping out the independent spirit of workers. Riesman argued that the country was facing "a silent revolution against work" because work no longer had meaning for people. Many younger Americans were beginning to agree with him.

The **Beats**, a small but influential group of writers and poets, challenged both the literary

▲ Ralph Ellison received the National Book Award in 1953 for his novel *Invisible Man*.

conventions of the day and the life-styles of the middle class. Allen Ginsberg's poem "Howl," for instance, raged against the nuclear threat and the conventions of corporate America. The Beats wrote as they lived—without form, plot, planning, or revision. One of the best-known Beat works, Jack Kerouac's novel *On the Road* (1957), was written in a continuous three-week-long session at the typewriter. Kerouac celebrated the search for individual identity and the rejection of stability. One sentence in the novel caught the essence of the Beat philosophy: "We gotta go and never stop going till we get there."

A "SILENT GENERATION"?

Despite many parents' fears, the Beats never grew into a mass movement among young people. Indeed, many observers dubbed the middle-class youth of the 1950s the **silent generation** because of their seeming willingness to conform to consumer culture without protest. Despite the outward appearance of conformity, however, many young people were beginning to question society and to rebel in subtle ways.

Literature and films. Many young people discontented with suburban life found meaning in literature and films. Some identified with Holden Caulfield, the main character of J.D. Salinger's *The Catcher in the Rye* (1951). Disgusted by the hypocrisy of the adult world, Holden declared it "crumby" and "phony." Other young people turned to satirical magazines, such as *MAD,* which dedicated itself to making fun of everything associated with "the American way of life." Many parents worried that reading such magazines would increase **juvenile delinquency**—antisocial behavior by the young.

Several of the most popular films of the decade reflected images of juvenile delinquency and young, angry rebels frustrated with life. Often their anger was directed not at any one particular thing, but at all of society in general. In the 1953 film *The Wild One,* a character asks the young gang leader played by Marlon Brando what he is rebelling against. Brando snarls back, "Whadda ya got?" This image of the rebel with no direction was reinforced in 1955's *Rebel Without a Cause,* starring James Dean, Natalie Wood, and Sal Mineo as teenagers confused about the values of their suburban families. Many teenagers could identify with that confusion.

The rock rebellion. Many teenagers tried to escape the conformity of suburbia through a new type of music called **rock 'n' roll**. This reworking of black rhythm and blues produced a raw sound very different from many tunes of the day, and teenagers claimed it as their own. Cleveland disc jockey Alan Freed coined the term *rock 'n' roll* in 1951, when he started a rhythm-and-blues show aimed at young white audiences. Soon the sound caught on across the country.

Elvis Presley, a truck driver from Memphis, Tennessee, emerged as rock's leading talent. With his sullen good looks, wild body movements, and blues-influenced vocal style, Presley sent shock waves through the white middle class. African American musicians such as Little Richard, Chuck Berry, and Fats Domino, as well as Hispanic performers like Ritchie Valens, profoundly influenced early rock 'n' roll.

Many parents immediately disliked rock 'n' roll. Some critics called it immoral. Others simply dismissed

◀ Teenagers tuned to Dick Clark's *American Bandstand* to listen to the latest rock 'n' roll records and watch the newest groups perform.

◄ Ritchie Valens

◄ Fats Domino

▲ Elvis Presley

it as useless noise, pointing out that the lyrics of many popular rock songs did not seem to make any sense, such as in the Silhouettes' 1957 hit "Get a Job":

> 66 Sha da da da
> Sha da da da da
> Bah do
> Bah yip yip yip yip yip yip yip yip
> Mum mum mum mum mum mum
> Get a job. 99

Rock 'n' roll also upset many people by seeming to break down the walls of racial segregation. White rockers such as Presley, Jerry Lee Lewis, and Buddy Holly shared the airwaves, and often the stage, with noted black artists. While southern officials were worried about sending black and white teenagers to school together, many of those same teens were listening to the same radio stations and sneaking off to attend the same integrated concerts.

■■ **Teenagers challenged conformity through literature, films, and rock 'n' roll.**

SECTION 3 REVIEW

IDENTIFY and explain the significance of the following: *Brown* v. *The Board of Education of Topeka,* Thurgood Marshall, Rosa Parks, Montgomery Improvement Association, Martin Luther King, Jr., Orval Faubus, "Little Rock Nine," Civil Rights Act of 1957, Ralph Ellison, Beats, Jack Kerouac, silent generation, juvenile delinquency, rock 'n' roll.

LOCATE and explain the importance of the following: Topeka, Kansas; Montgomery, Alabama; Little Rock, Arkansas.

1. **MAIN IDEA** What impact did the decision in *Brown* v. *Board of Education* and the Montgomery bus boycott have on the civil rights movement?

2. **MAIN IDEA** What did events in Little Rock show about attitudes of some southern whites toward school desegregation?

3. **RECOGNIZING POINTS OF VIEW** What arguments did members of the civil rights movement use to help overturn the "separate but equal" doctrine?

4. **WRITING TO EXPRESS A VIEWPOINT** Write a short story involving a teenage character who expresses his or her view of 1950s society.

5. **USING HISTORICAL IMAGINATION** Imagine you are a member of the Montgomery Improvement Association in 1956. Write a speech you would deliver to the community urging them to continue the boycott against the bus system.

I Love Lucy debuts.

Dwight D. Eisenhower elected president. First H-bomb test held. *Invisible Man* published.

Korean War ends.

Army-McCarthy hearings held. Supreme Court issues ruling in *Brown* v. *Board of Education.*

1950   1952   1954

WRITING A SUMMARY

Using the essential points of the chapter as a guide, write a summary of the chapter.

REVIEWING CHRONOLOGY

Number your paper 1 to 5. Study the time line above, and list the following events in the order in which they happened by writing the first next to 1, the second next to 2, and so on. Then complete the activity below.

1. U-2 incident occurs.
2. Montgomery bus boycott begins.
3. First H-bomb test held.
4. Army-McCarthy hearings held.
5. *On the Road* published.

Assessing Consequences How did the launch of *Sputnik* affect the United States?

IDENTIFYING PEOPLE AND IDEAS

Explain the historical significance of each of the following people or terms.

1. Margaret Chase Smith
2. brinkmanship
3. Mohammad Mosaddeq
4. Eisenhower Doctrine
5. Landrum-Griffin Act
6. baby boom
7. termination
8. Thurgood Marshall
9. "Little Rock Nine"
10. Beats

UNDERSTANDING MAIN IDEAS

1. How did the end of the Korean War affect Korea and the United States?
2. What factors led to the rise of McCarthyism? What events brought about McCarthy's downfall?
3. How did the economic prosperity of the 1950s affect both domestic life and the workplace?
4. What were some of the major successes and setbacks in ending segregated education in the 1950s?
5. How did literature, films, and music affect middle-class teenagers in the 1950s?

REVIEWING THEMES

1. **Economic Development** How were population shifts affected by the economic boom of the 1950s?

2. **Cultural Diversity** How did some people attempt to rebel against the conformity of the 1950s?
3. **Democratic Values** How did Native Americans and African Americans fight discrimination during this decade?

THINKING CRITICALLY

1. **Analyzing** What strategies did President Eisenhower use to fight the spread of communism? Where were these strategies used?
2. **Evaluating** What events contributed to Americans' fears of nuclear war? How were these fears reduced?
3. **Synthesizing** What was the popular image of a mother's role in society during the 1950s? How did this image conflict with reality?

STRATEGY FOR SUCCESS

Review the Skills Handbook entry on Distinguishing Fact from Opinion on page 750. Examine the following excerpt, written by a white southerner opposed to the forced integration of schools. Then decide which part of the statement is fact and which is opinion.

66 Much of the legislation enacted in the Southern states . . . has been aimed basically at preserving domestic tranquillity as well as racial integrity. This is especially true in the fields of education and recreation, where indiscriminate mingling of the races is bound to bring discord and strife. . . . The closing of such institutions in many cases would be the sensible alternative to the emotional, social, and physical upheaval which would follow on the heels of forced race mixing. 99

WRITING ABOUT HISTORY

Writing to Classify Create a time line that lists the important events of the civil rights movement in this period.

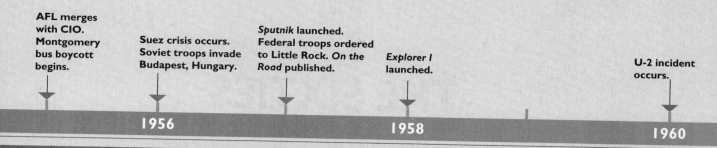

AFL merges with CIO. Montgomery bus boycott begins.

Suez crisis occurs. Soviet troops invade Budapest, Hungary.

Sputnik launched. Federal troops ordered to Little Rock. *On the Road* published.

Explorer I launched.

U-2 incident occurs.

1956   1958   1960

USING PRIMARY SOURCES

Rock 'n' roll music of the 1950s often reflected a desire to break away from old traditions and be more daring. Read the following lyrics from Chuck Berry's "Roll Over Beethoven" (1956). Who are Beethoven and Tchaikovsky? How do the lyrics of the song reflect rebellion and a break from the past?

 Well, I'm gonna write a little letter, gonna mail it to my local D.J.
Yes, it's a jumpin' little record I want my jockey to play
Roll over Beethoven, I gotta hear it again today
You know my temp'rature's risin' and the juke box blowin' a fuse
My heart's beatin' rhythm and my soul keeps a singin' the blues
Roll over Beethoven and tell Tchaikovsky the news. "

Chuck Berry

LINKING HISTORY AND GEOGRAPHY

Alaska and Hawaii became the 49th and 50th states of the union, respectively, in 1959. Study the map in the next column. What strategic advantages of these two areas might have lent support for their statehood during the Cold War?

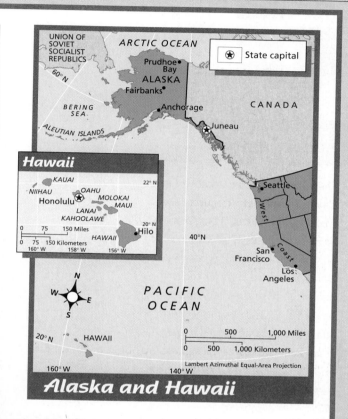

Alaska and Hawaii

BUILDING YOUR PORTFOLIO

Complete the following projects independently or cooperatively.

1. **THE COLD WAR** In Chapter 17 you served as a UN conference delegate. Building on that experience, prepare a speech outlining UN goals.

2. **CIVIL RIGHTS** In Chapter 17 you were a reporter covering the Committee on Civil Rights. Building on that experience, develop an outline of the civil rights movement from 1945 to 1960.

3. **POPULAR CULTURE** Imagine you are a magazine editor. Create a photo essay that reflects cultural changes in the 1950s.

THE SIXTIES

FOCUS

UNDERSTANDING THE MAIN IDEA

The 1960s marked a decade of great change in America. The promise of President John Kennedy's administration was cut short by his assassination. But the new president, Lyndon Johnson, ushered in major social reforms through the Great Society programs, while civil rights leaders finally gained some ground in the struggle for equality. Their success inspired other groups, including some middle-class women and college students, to challenge traditional society.

THEMES

■ **GLOBAL RELATIONS** How might foreign policy decisions undermine domestic programs?

■ **DEMOCRATIC VALUES** How might protests help expand democracy?

■ **CULTURAL DIVERSITY** What are some institutions and traditions that might come under fire by groups questioning conformity?

1960	1962	1964	1968	1969
John F. Kennedy elected president.	Cuban missile crisis erupts.	Freedom Summer launched.	Martin Luther King, Jr., assassinated.	Woodstock Music Festival occurs.

During the Eisenhower era the Cold War intensified. On the domestic front the civil rights movement gained momentum from the Supreme Court ruling on school desegregation and from the success of the Montgomery bus boycott. By the end of the 1950s, the popular culture's emphasis on conformity and consumerism came under attack from the Beats and rock 'n' roll.

March on Washington for civil rights, 1963

In 1960, voters chose the youngest man ever elected president, the 43-year-old John F. Kennedy, to succeed one of the oldest presidents up to that time, the 70-year-old Dwight Eisenhower. Kennedy brought a spirit of youth and hope to the nation—a spirit reflected in the dramatic changes of the 1960s. The civil rights movement continued its success, winning expansion of voting rights for African Americans and further breaking down the walls of segregation in the South. Other groups, such as Mexican Americans, Native Americans, and women, also pressed for fairer treatment. Throughout America the generation raised after World War II started to question traditional society through organized protests, music, and the creation of a counterculture.

On the foreign front, the Cold War reached its most dangerous crisis when the United States and the Soviet Union came to the brink of nuclear war in Cuba. Afterward, both nations worked to ease tensions between them. During this period, the United States also increased its involvement in Latin America and Vietnam. As the Vietnam conflict shifted funding from domestic programs, such as President Lyndon Johnson's Great Society reforms, discontent grew within American society. By the end of the 1960s, much of the idealism that began the decade was lost in the wake of violence and division.

African dashiki, worn by American youths in the 1960s

THE NEW FRONTIER

- How did the Kennedy administration try to boost the economy?
- What was the purpose of flexible response?
- What events sparked the Cuban missile crisis? How did the crisis change Soviet-American relations?

President Eisenhower's successor, the 43-year-old John F. Kennedy, brought fresh vigor to the office, promising that his administration would be a "new frontier." On the domestic front, he boosted the economy, mostly by increasing spending on defense and space exploration. Internationally, he first stood firm against the Soviets, then tried to ease Soviet-American tensions. In November 1963, Kennedy's presidency ended suddenly and tragically, its bright promise largely unfulfilled.

President John F. Kennedy and Jacqueline Kennedy in 1961

A NEW BEGINNING

As 1960 began, many voters were looking for someone to inject new life into the White House. Economic recession in the late 1950s, coupled with the Soviet Union's advances in space technology, led many people to fear that the country was falling behind its counterparts.

As expected, the Republicans chose Richard Nixon as their presidential candidate in the upcoming election. His solid performance as Eisenhower's vice president had won him wide support among Republican party members. Trying to appeal to a wide variety of voters, he downplayed his past roles in conservative causes such as the investigations of the House Committee on Un-American Activities.

Senator John F. Kennedy of Massachusetts eventually emerged as the Democratic candidate. The Irish American Kennedy promised to "get America moving again." Voters were impressed with his charm, wit, good looks, and war record. But as a Roman Catholic, he faced falling victim to the same prejudices that had hurt Al Smith's presidential bid in 1928. To neutralize concerns about his religion, Kennedy assured voters that he believed firmly in the separation of church and state.

◀ The second of four televised debates between Senator John F. Kennedy and Vice President Richard Nixon took place on October 7, 1960.

Nixon led in the polls until the first of four televised debates. Tired and gaunt after an illness, Nixon seemed nervous and uneasy before the cameras. Kennedy, on the other hand, appeared fit, confident, and relaxed. The election was close. Kennedy and his running mate, Lyndon B. Johnson of Texas, defeated Nixon and his running mate, Henry Cabot Lodge, Jr., of Massachusetts, by a margin of fewer than 120,000 popular votes. Their electoral victory was more decisive—303 to 219.

Kennedy was the youngest person ever elected president. His youth helped provide the theme to his inaugural address:

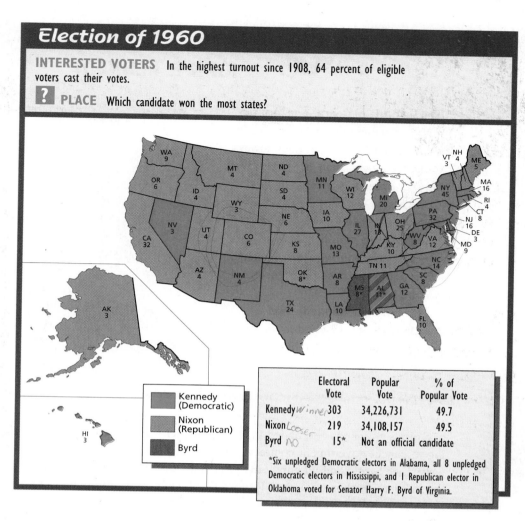

Election of 1960

INTERESTED VOTERS In the highest turnout since 1908, 64 percent of eligible voters cast their votes.

? PLACE Which candidate won the most states?

	Kennedy (Democratic)
	Nixon (Republican)
	Byrd

	Electoral Vote	Popular Vote	% of Popular Vote
Kennedy *Winner*	303	34,226,731	49.7
Nixon *Looser*	219	34,108,157	49.5
Byrd *NO*	15*	Not an official candidate	

*Six unpledged Democratic electors in Alabama, all 8 unpledged Democratic electors in Mississippi, and 1 Republican elector in Oklahoma voted for Senator Harry F. Byrd of Virginia.

66 Let the word go forth . . . that the torch has been passed to a new generation of Americans. . . . The energy, the faith, the devotion which we bring to this endeavor will light our country and all who serve it. . . . And so, my fellow Americans—ask not what your country can do for you—ask what you can do for your country. 99

THE DOMESTIC FRONTIER

Kennedy stocked his cabinet with young, well-educated men, including his brother Robert as attorney general. These advisers shared the belief that government should offer solutions to national and global problems. Since Kennedy had once compared these problems to a "new frontier," his agenda became known as the **New Frontier**.

One of the first domestic challenges that Kennedy faced was stimulating the economy. To help revive the economy, the president called for an increase in government spending, giving defense and space programs top priority. This emphasis reflected Cold War concerns. In April 1961 Soviet cosmonaut Yuri Gagarin had completed the first orbital space flight, sparking fears that the United States was falling behind in the space race. In late May 1961 Kennedy responded by challenging the nation to "commit itself to achieving the goal, before this decade is out, of landing a man on the moon and returning him safely to earth."

By the end of 1961, inflation was down, but unemployment was still relatively high. Kennedy hoped to keep inflation down and further the recovery by getting labor and business to agree to informal wage and price controls. Businesses had been granting higher wages to workers and then passing the costs on to consumers in the form of higher prices. Kennedy urged businesses to limit prices in return for workers agreeing to fewer pay raises. When U.S. Steel dramatically raised prices in 1962 after workers had agreed to accept small

JOHN F. KENNEDY
1917–1963

Throughout his career in politics, John F. Kennedy presented an image of youth and vigor. Kennedy always looked younger than his years. On several occasions after he entered Congress he was mistaken for a page boy. Once, while he was a senator, a guard tried to stop him from using a special telephone with the warning: "Sorry, mister, these are reserved for the Senators."

Although Kennedy was frequently photographed in sporting activities such as football, sailing, and

swimming, his athletic image hid the severe physical pain he suffered through most of his adult life. During World War II he suffered a severe back injury after his naval vessel sank. For the rest of his life, Kennedy would endure extreme pain from this injury and from the effects of Addison's disease. His brother Robert once recalled that "at least one half of the days that he spent on this earth were days of intense physical pain." Publicly, however, he seldom displayed signs of physical strain.

---

pay raises, Kennedy responded in anger, threatening to cancel government contracts with the company. U.S. Steel soon withdrew the price hike, but the incident further weakened Kennedy's already shaky relationship with the business community.

■■ Kennedy helped stimulate the economy through increased federal spending, especially in space and defense programs.

Kennedy also had problems getting cooperation from Congress. A coalition of southern Democrats and conservative Republicans in Congress blocked about two thirds of the president's domestic programs. Early in 1963 Kennedy proposed a $13.5 billion reduction in personal and corporate taxes to boost consumer spending and business investment. Congress, however, was not convinced that tax cuts were wise. As 1963 drew to a close, the tax-cut proposal remained tied up in the Senate.

One area of domestic policy that Congress did support involved women's rights. Kennedy appointed a presidential commission to examine the status of women in America. The

commission report, completed in 1963, noted that while the number of working women in America had increased in recent years, women still faced discrimination in hiring and received less pay than men for the same jobs.

The president responded by issuing an order requiring the civil service to grant jobs "solely on the basis of ability to meet the requirements of the position, and without regard to sex." The commission report also led to passage of the **Equal Pay Act** in June 1963, which made it illegal for employers to pay female workers less than male workers for the same job.

▼ **On June 10, 1963, President Kennedy signed into law the Equal Pay Act, which required that women receive pay equal to that of men for performing the same job.**

KENNEDY AND THE COLD WAR

In foreign affairs Kennedy tended to follow the Cold War policies of his predecessors. As a World War II veteran, he shared Eisenhower's belief in the need for military strength; but unlike his predecessors, Kennedy did not want to rely primarily on the threat of nuclear weapons to deter Communist expansion. He preferred to have a range of options open in case of international crises—a strategy called **flexible response**. To expand the

▲ By 1967 some 10,200 Peace Corps volunteers worked in rural communities throughout the world. Shown here is Molly Heit, a schoolteacher in Peru who taught her students how to earn extra money by weaving simple tapestries for tourists.

nation's options, the Kennedy administration continued the nuclear arms buildup started under Eisenhower and strengthened conventional forces. In addition, the government established special military units like the Green Berets to assist nations struggling to combat communist rebels.

■■ **Flexible response offered a variety of options for dealing with international conflict.**

Kennedy also supported nonmilitary options to prevent Communist expansion. Economic aid to developing countries, he realized, could serve to strengthen their societies and block Soviet intervention. Toward this end, he introduced a number of assistance programs designed to help the developing nations of Africa, Asia, and Latin America. Foremost among these programs was the **Peace Corps**, which sent volunteers to work for two years in developing countries.

The president also introduced a program to expand economic aid to Latin America. The **Alliance for Progress** offered billions of dollars in aid to participating nations. In exchange for money, the countries were expected to develop democratic reforms and encourage capitalism. The alliance was a disappointment, however. By 1963 most of the money that had been given to participating countries was in the hands of

corrupt politicians, and few Latin American leaders had enacted reforms. One Latin American writer, Victor Alba, blamed the program's failure on its inability to mobilize the poor majority in Latin American countries:

❝ We know who killed the Alliance: the oligarchic governments of Latin America. . . . We know who supplied the poison: the bureaucrats and technicians. And we know who would have defended it if anyone had bothered to let them know that it existed and needed defenders: the people. ❞

THE BAY OF PIGS

Latin America was a special target for aid from the United States because the Soviet Union had recently gained a foothold there. In 1959 an uprising led by Fidel Castro succeeded in overthrowing the Cuban dictator, Fulgencio Batista. Many Americans applauded Castro's success, believing he would bring democracy to Cuba. Castro, however, quickly established a Communist-style dictatorship with strong ties to the Soviet Union.

Fidel Castro

When Kennedy took office, a plan to overthrow Castro was already in the works. The plan called for an invasion of Cuba by a group of anti-Castro Cuban refugees trained and financed by the Central Intelligence Agency (CIA). Kennedy gave the green light for the plan to proceed.

The invasion was a disaster. When the nearly 1,500 rebels came ashore at Cuba's Bay of Pigs on April 17, 1961, they were quickly pinned down by Cuban forces. The U.S. naval and air support that the rebels expected never materialized—at the last minute Kennedy vetoed

▲ To halt the flow of refugees into West Berlin, East Germans set up blockades along subway and elevated rail lines and cut off key crossing points between both sectors. This photograph shows one view of the Berlin Wall in October 1961.

any direct U.S. involvement. Equally damaging, the invasion failed to spark a popular uprising among the Cuban people. It took Cuban military forces less than 72 hours to crush the invasion and take some 1,200 surviving rebels prisoner.

Kennedy accepted full responsibility for the failed invasion, but his gesture did little to quiet criticism. One American journalist complained that the Bay of Pigs had made the United States look "like fools to our friends, rascals to our enemies, and incompetents to the rest." The invasion also drove Cuban leaders closer to the Soviets.

THE BERLIN CRISIS

The Bay of Pigs convinced Soviet leader Nikita Khrushchev that Kennedy was weak and could be intimidated. During a summit meeting in June 1961, Khrushchev issued an ultimatum: the West must recognize the sovereignty of Communist East Germany and remove all troops from West Berlin.

Kennedy refused, saying that he intended to honor the United States' commitment to defend West Berlin. The situation worsened in mid-August, when the East Germans threw up a barbed-wire barrier across Berlin, cutting off traffic between East and West Berlin. Kennedy responded by sending more American troops to the city. The Soviets also bolstered their military forces there. For a few

days American and Soviet soldiers eyed each other nervously across the barbed wire.

Tensions gradually eased when it became clear that the real goal of Khrushchev's ultimatum had been fulfilled. The barrier had halted the exodus of East Germans, who during the summer of 1961 had fled to the West through Berlin at a rate of some 1,000 per day. In time the East Germans replaced the barbed wire with a wall of gray concrete and watchtowers. The **Berlin Wall** became the most recognizable symbol of the Cold War.

THE MISSILES OF OCTOBER

After Berlin, Khrushchev continued to try to test America's commitment to containment, leading to the Cold War's greatest crisis. To ward off another invasion, Fidel Castro asked the Soviet Union to provide him with defensive weapons. The Soviets complied and also offered *offensive* weapons— nuclear missiles that could reach major cities of the eastern United States.

CIA officials monitored the Soviet arms buildup in Cuba throughout the summer of 1962. But they did not grasp the full extent of the buildup until October 14, when an American U-2 spy plane photographed numerous missile launching pads near the Cuban town of San Cristobal. Additional U-2 flights over the island located more missiles, all of which appeared to be aimed at the United States.

On October 22 Kennedy ordered a naval blockade of Cuba to prevent further deliveries of Soviet weapons. He also demanded that the Soviets remove the missiles. Khrushchev promised to challenge the blockade, calling it "outright banditry." Over the next two days, nuclear war loomed on the horizon. In a frenzy of activity, Soviet military advisers armed the missiles in Cuba. American B-52 bombers armed with nuclear weapons prepared for battle. Meanwhile, Soviet ships sailed toward the blockade line.

Suddenly, on October 24, many of the Soviet ships stopped short of the blockade line, turned, and sailed home. "We're eyeball to eyeball," said Secretary of State Dean Rusk, "and I think the other fellow just blinked." On October 28 Khrushchev agreed to dismantle the missile bases in response to Kennedy's promise not to invade Cuba. Kennedy also secretly agreed to remove American missiles from some foreign sites.

The event marked a historic turning point in Soviet-American relations. Sobered by their brush with nuclear war, Kennedy and Khrushchev sought to ease tensions between their countries. Kennedy declared that it was time to write a new chapter in the Cold War:

> 66 If we are to open new doorways to peace, if we are to seize this rare opportunity for progress, if we are to be as bold and farsighted in our control of weapons as we have been in their invention, then let us now show all the world on this side of the wall and the other that a strong America also stands for peace. 99

In 1963 the United States, the Soviet Union, and Great Britain signed a **Limited Nuclear Test**

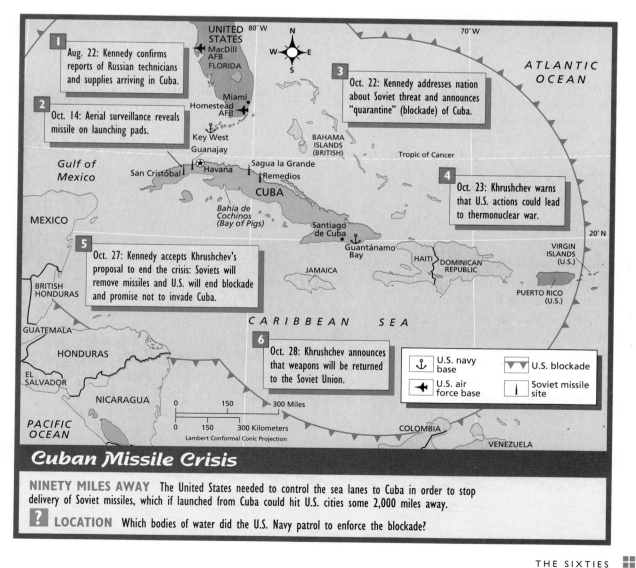

1 Aug. 22: Kennedy confirms reports of Russian technicians and supplies arriving in Cuba.

2 Oct. 14: Aerial surveillance reveals missile on launching pads.

3 Oct. 22: Kennedy addresses nation about Soviet threat and announces "quarantine" (blockade) of Cuba.

4 Oct. 23: Khrushchev warns that U.S. actions could lead to thermonuclear war.

5 Oct. 27: Kennedy accepts Khrushchev's proposal to end the crisis: Soviets will remove missiles and U.S. will end blockade and promise not to invade Cuba.

6 Oct. 28: Khrushchev announces that weapons will be returned to the Soviet Union.

UNITED STATES
MacDill AFB
FLORIDA
Miami
Homestead AFB
Key West
Guanajay
San Cristóbal
Havana
Sagua la Grande
Remedios
CUBA
Bahía de Cochinos (Bay of Pigs)
Santiago de Cuba
Guantánamo Bay
Gulf of Mexico
MEXICO
BAHAMA ISLANDS (BRITISH)
Tropic of Cancer
ATLANTIC OCEAN
JAMAICA
HAITI
DOMINICAN REPUBLIC
VIRGIN ISLANDS (U.S.)
PUERTO RICO (U.S.)
BRITISH HONDURAS
GUATEMALA
HONDURAS
EL SALVADOR
NICARAGUA
PACIFIC OCEAN
CARIBBEAN SEA
COLOMBIA
VENEZUELA

80° W   70° W   20° N

U.S. navy base
U.S. blockade
U.S. air force base
Soviet missile site

0   150   300 Miles
0   150   300 Kilometers
Lambert Conformal Conic Projection

Cuban Missile Crisis

NINETY MILES AWAY The United States needed to control the sea lanes to Cuba in order to stop delivery of Soviet missiles, which if launched from Cuba could hit U.S. cities some 2,000 miles away.

? LOCATION Which bodies of water did the U.S. Navy patrol to enforce the blockade?

CUBAN MISSILE CRISIS

In October 1962 President Kennedy issued an ultimatum to the Soviet Union, demanding that it remove all its missiles from Cuba. For several days the world held its breath as it teetered on the brink of nuclear war. In the end, the Soviets agreed to remove the missiles. Soviet Premier Nikita Khrushchev relates his memory of the crisis:

"It had been, to say the least, an interesting and challenging situation. The two most powerful nations of the world had been squared off against each other, each with its finger on the button. You'd have thought that war was inevitable. But both sides showed that if the desire to avoid war is strong enough, even the most pressing dispute can be solved by compromise. . . . I'll always remember the late President [Kennedy] with deep respect because, in the final analysis, he showed himself to be sober-minded and determined to avoid war. He didn't let himself become frightened, nor did he become reckless. He didn't overestimate America's might, and he left himself a way out of the crisis. . . . It was a great victory for us, though, that we had been able to extract from Kennedy a promise that neither America nor any of her allies would invade Cuba."

Ban Treaty to end the testing of nuclear bombs in the atmosphere and under water. A "**hot line**" was also set up between the United States and the Soviet Union. This direct telephone connection enabled leaders of the two countries to communicate directly during a crisis.

■■ **The Bay of Pigs and Berlin Wall crises led to the Cuban missile crisis, after which the United States and Soviet Union worked harder for peace.**

SECTION 1 REVIEW

IDENTIFY and explain the significance of the following: Richard Nixon, John F. Kennedy, New Frontier, Equal Pay Act, flexible response, Peace Corps, Alliance for Progress, Fidel Castro, Berlin Wall, Limited Nuclear Test Ban Treaty, "hot line."

LOCATE and explain the importance of the following: Cuba, Bay of Pigs, San Cristobal.

1. **MAIN IDEA** How did President Kennedy attempt to stimulate the economy?

2. **MAIN IDEA** What was the advantage of the Kennedy administration's foreign-policy strategy of flexible response?

3. **LINKING HISTORY AND GEOGRAPHY** Why were Americans so concerned with the missile buildup in Cuba?

4. **WRITING TO INFORM** Imagine you are a member of the presidential commission assigned to examine the status of women in America. Write a report that summarizes the findings of the commission and presents recommendations for change.

5. **ANALYZING** How did President Kennedy's approach to foreign affairs differ from that of his predecessors?

JOHNSON'S GREAT SOCIETY

F O C U S

- **What were the four major concerns of the Great Society programs?**
- **How did the Warren Court decisions affect individual rights?**
- **How did foreign policy concerns affect President Johnson's domestic programs?**

*O*n November 22, 1963, John Kennedy's presidency ended when he was gunned down in Dallas. The new president, Lyndon Johnson, pledged himself to the "ideas and ideals" that Kennedy had "so nobly represented." Johnson sponsored a series of social programs designed to transform American society. These triumphs on the domestic scene, however, were soon overshadowed as foreign policy problems caused Johnson's presidency to unravel.

LBJ taking the presidential oath in Dallas, 1963

TRAGEDY IN DALLAS

Kennedy knew he would have to campaign hard to win reelection in 1964. In November 1963 he traveled to Texas to try to bolster his support there. In Dallas on November 22, enthusiastic crowds lined the route of Kennedy's open-car motorcade from the airport. At about 12:30 P.M., as the motorcade moved through the downtown area, shots rang out. Kennedy slumped over, mortally wounded. Within hours Vice President Lyndon Johnson was sworn in as president. Over the next four days, the nation came together to mourn the dead president. Millions watched the funeral on television. Many Americans felt that the death of the youthful, vibrant Kennedy had also killed something in them. "We'll never be young again," Kennedy staffer Daniel Patrick Moynihan sadly observed.

Within hours of the shooting, the Dallas police had seized Lee Harvey Oswald as a suspect. Two days after his arrest, while he was being moved from one jail to another, Oswald was shot to death by nightclub owner Jack Ruby.

This strange turn of events caused many people to question whether Oswald had acted alone in killing the president or whether he had been part of a larger conspiracy. To end speculation, President Lyndon Johnson named a commission, headed by Chief Justice Earl Warren, to investigate the assassination. The **Warren Commission**, which spent 10 months reviewing the evidence, concluded that there was no evidence of conspiracy: both Oswald and Ruby had acted alone.

JOHNSON TAKES OVER

President Lyndon Johnson appeared very different from the wealthy, charismatic Kennedy. Born in the hill country of central Texas, Johnson grew up in a household that knew, in turn, poverty and relative prosperity. Brash, ambitious, and hardworking, Johnson rose rapidly through the Democratic party ranks. By the time he won election to the Senate in 1948, he was a major power in the party.

A master of compromise, Johnson seemed to always find the middle course on which most people could agree. This mastery of the political process, coupled with his years of experience in Washington, enabled Johnson to manage the transition of power with considerable skill and tact. Kennedy's cabinet and advisers stayed on to lend continuity to the Johnson administration.

Announcing in his first cabinet meeting in January 1964 that "the day is over when top jobs are reserved for men," Johnson pledged to add 50 more women to high government offices. Some of his choices included consumer advocate Betty Furness, economists Alice Rivlin and Penelope Thunberg, and Texas legislator Barbara Jordan. Although Johnson was able to appoint only 27 women to high offices, his strong support for women's rights marked a significant break with past administrations.

The new president also promised to appoint more Mexican Americans to high positions. He assigned Vicente T. Ximenes (he-MAY-nays) to chair a presidential committee on Mexican American affairs. Other top appointments went to Héctor P. García, a Texas advocate for Mexican American veterans, and to Raul H. Castro, a noted attorney who later became the first Mexican American governor of Arizona.

As 1964 began, Johnson focused his legislative efforts on three areas: tax cuts, civil rights, and poverty. Within weeks he had persuaded Congress to adopt Kennedy's tax program, which cut personal and corporate income taxes by 4 percent. He then pressured members of Congress to enact the long-stalled civil rights bill (see Section 3) and a comprehensive program to fight poverty.

*T*HE WAR ON POVERTY

In 1962, social activist Michael Harrington published *The Other America,* a well-documented study of poverty in the United States. The best-selling book shattered the popular notion that all Americans had benefited from the prosperity of the 1950s. Harrington reported that more than 42 million Americans lived on less than $1,000 per year. He issued a direct challenge for leaders to face the reality of poverty:

   ❝ [The poor exist] within the most powerful and rich society the world has ever known. Their misery has continued while the majority of the nation talked of itself as

being "affluent." . . . In this way tens of millions of human beings became invisible. They dropped out of sight and out of mind. . . . How long shall we ignore this underdeveloped nation in our midst? ❞

Harrington also noted that racism still kept many ethnic groups, especially African Americans, in poverty. He warned that the end of legalized segregation would not change the economic condition of most poor blacks. "The laws against color can be removed," he wrote, "but that will leave the poverty that is the historic . . . consequence of color. As long as this is the case, being born a Negro will continue to be the most profound disability that the United States imposes upon a citizen."

President Johnson responded to such concerns by declaring an "unconditional war on poverty in America." To launch his **War on Poverty,** Johnson sent to Congress a bill calling for the establishment of the **Office of Economic Opportunity** (OEO), with a budget of $1 billion, to coordinate a series of new antipoverty programs. These programs included the Job Corps, a work training program for young people between the ages of 16 and 21; Head Start, an education program for preschoolers from low-income families; and VISTA (Volunteers in Service to America), a domestic version of the Peace Corps. The bill passed Congress in late August 1964.

Whereas Kennedy had trouble pushing legislation through Congress, Johnson fulfilled all the major legislative goals of his first term within eight months. Comparing the two administrations, Texas journalist Liz Carpenter concluded: "Kennedy

▲ VISTA volunteers donated their time and talent to aid poor Americans in the United States and in U.S. territories having limited public services. Shown here is an elementary schoolteacher in the U.S. Virgin Islands.

inspired . . . Johnson delivered." Opinion polls showed that Americans were overwhelmingly impressed with Johnson's achievements.

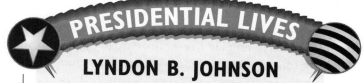
𝒥OHNSON'S VISION FOR AMERICA

Riding this wave of popularity, Johnson easily won the Democratic presidential nomination for the 1964 election. He selected Hubert Humphrey, a liberal senator from Minnesota, as his running mate. Adopting a platform that rejected Eisenhower's modern Republicanism, the Republicans chose Barry Goldwater, a conservative senator from Arizona, as their presidential nominee, with New York congressman William E. Miller as his running mate.

Goldwater and Johnson campaign dolls, 1964

Johnson won by a landslide, taking 61 percent of the popular vote and 486 electoral votes to Goldwater's 52. The Democrats further increased their majority in both the House and the Senate. The last president to receive such a mandate was Franklin Roosevelt in 1936.

The plan. Long before the election, Johnson had mapped out plans for his presidency. He saw his major task as building a **Great Society**. In this Great Society, he said, poverty and racial injustice would end. All children would have access to an education that enriched their knowledge and enhanced their talents. The cities would serve not only people's physical needs, but also their desire for culture and their "hunger for community." In short, in the Great Society people would be "more concerned with the quality of their goals than the quantity of their goods."

After his election Johnson moved quickly to make the Great Society a reality. While civil rights was a major part of the Great Society legislation, other issues included health care, education, and urban renewal.

The programs. In 1965 Johnson persuaded Congress to establish **Medicare**, a national health insurance program for people over age 65.

LYNDON B. JOHNSON
1908–1973

in office
1963–1969

Many observers saw Lyndon Johnson as the stereotypical Texas politician—loud, brash, and slightly uncouth. Johnson loved to intentionally shock observers with his language, stories, and behavior. Once during an interview he lifted up his shirt for a photographer to display his scar from gall bladder surgery.

Johnson was also a very physical politician. He would shake people's hands until his own bled and slap others on their backs in a friendly gesture. Fellow senators joked that Johnson had two techniques for getting another senator's attention. There was the Half-Johnson—"when he just put a hand on your shoulder"—and the Full-Johnson—"when he put his arm clear around you and thrust his face close to yours." But Johnson's techniques got results.

He was known as a workaholic who drove himself and his staff to exhaustion to complete multiple tasks. "What's the hurry?" one senator asked another about Johnson's busy schedule. "Rome wasn't built in a day." The other senator replied, "No, but Lyndon Johnson wasn't foreman on that job."

Congress also authorized funds for states to set up **Medicaid** to provide free health care to the needy. Johnson traveled to Independence, Missouri, to sign the bill in front of 81-year-old Harry Truman, who had first proposed federally funded health insurance in his Fair Deal program.

Johnson also asked Congress to take action on funding for education. In a moving speech, he recalled:

> 66 My first job after college was as a teacher in Cotulla, Texas, in a small Mexican American school. . . . Somehow you never forget what poverty and hatred can do when you see its scars on the hopeful face of a young child. . . . It never even occurred to me in my fondest dreams that I might have the chance to help the sons and daughters of those students and to help people like them all over this country.
>
> But now I do have that chance—and I'll let you in on a secret: *I mean to use it.* 99

Congress responded by passing the **Elementary and Secondary School Education Act** of 1965, which provided $1.3 billion in aid to schools in impoverished areas.

Pushing on, Johnson persuaded Congress to pass the **Omnibus Housing Act** in 1965, followed by the **Housing and Urban Development Act** of 1968. The acts authorized billions of dollars for

▲ President Johnson congratulates Robert Weaver after he is sworn in as secretary of HUD.

urban renewal and housing assistance for low-income families. They also established the Department of Housing and Urban Development (HUD) to oversee all federal housing programs. Robert C. Weaver, a member of the New Deal's black brain trust headed this new department, making him the first African American member of a presidential cabinet. Weaver declared that the new programs had made Americans aware that "our cities were filled with poorly housed, badly educated, underemployed, desperate, unhappy Americans."

■■ Civil rights, health care, education, and urban renewal were the major concerns of the Great Society programs.

Great Society laws poured out of Congress at an incredible rate. It was the most hectic period of legislative activity since Franklin Roosevelt's first 100 days.

THE WARREN COURT DECISIONS

Like the Johnson administration, the Supreme Court of the 1960s reflected a spirit of activism. Under the leadership of Chief Justice Earl Warren, the Court sought to continue the trend begun with the 1954 desegregation decision in *Brown* v. *Board of Education* of defining and extending individual rights.

In addition to outlawing segregation across the nation, the Court tried to extend equality in the voting booth with the "one person, one vote" principle. In many congressional districts, sparsely populated rural areas had the same number of representatives as densely populated urban areas. In *Baker* v. *Carr* (1962), however, the Court ruled that election districts should contain approximately equal numbers of voters in order to offer fairly equal representation for everyone.

The Court also issued a series of decisions protecting the rights of those accused of crimes. *Gideon* v. *Wainwright* (1963) required the states to provide lawyers, at public expense, for impoverished defendants charged with serious crimes. *Escobedo* v. *Illinois* (1964) granted accused persons the right to have a lawyer present during police interrogations. *Miranda* v. *Arizona* (1966) said that accused persons must be informed of their rights at the time of their arrests.

Many people saw the Supreme Court's actions as an attempt to build a society more firmly committed to the principle of equality for all, but many others were outraged by such decisions. The Court had overstepped its authority, critics charged, by making law rather than interpreting it. Some went so far as to accuse the chief justice of "high crimes and misdemeanors," erecting billboards that proclaimed "IMPEACH EARL WARREN!" One critic declared:

> 66 Earl Warren has sinned too grandly for [impeachment]. He has defiled our jurisprudence and made war against the public order. . . . The bench over which he presides has made a mockery of the Supreme Court's appointed function. 99

■■ **The Warren Court's controversial decisions strengthened individual rights.**

▲ **Juan Bosch is shown here on December 18, 1962, two days before being elected president of the Dominican Republic. A military coup removed him from power less than one year later.**

FOREIGN POLICY AND THE GREAT SOCIETY

While the Great Society was taking shape, foreign affairs also drew President Johnson's attention. In addition to dealing with the Vietnam conflict inherited from Kennedy (see Chapter 20), he became involved in the affairs of the Dominican Republic (see map on page 493). The nation's democratically elected president, Juan Bosch, had been ousted by a military coup in 1963. The new leader never really gained control of the country, and in April 1965, factions within the military rebelled, demanding Bosch's return. The American ambassador, believing that Bosch had fallen under Communist influence, insisted that Johnson intervene to "prevent another Cuba."

Johnson responded promptly, sending in a force of some 22,000 marines. With American support, troops loyal to the military government gained the upper hand and the situation stabilized. In 1966, after relatively free and fair elections put a conservative, pro-American government in power, Johnson withdrew the marines.

Many people in Latin America condemned American intervention in the Dominican Republic, labeling it gunboat diplomacy. Even those who supported Johnson's action did so reluctantly. In the United States, however, the majority of the public backed Johnson, praising his aggressive stand against the threat of Communist expansion.

By the spring of 1965 Johnson was also focusing more of his attention on the Vietnam War. As the conflict in Vietnam consumed more of his time, his attention to Great Society programs decreased. In 1966 the government spent about 18 times more on the Vietnam War than it did on the War on Poverty. Citing such statistics, civil rights leader Martin Luther King, Jr., declared that the Great Society had been "shot down on the battlefields of Vietnam."

■■ **Foreign policy concerns drew federal funding and President Johnson's attention away from Great Society programs.**

SECTION 2 REVIEW

IDENTIFY and explain the significance of the following: Lyndon Johnson, Lee Harvey Oswald, Warren Commission, War on Poverty, Office of Economic Opportunity, Great Society, Medicare, Medicaid, Elementary and Secondary School Education Act, Omnibus Housing Act, Housing and Urban Development Act, Juan Bosch.

LOCATE and explain the importance of the following: Dominican Republic.

1. **MAIN IDEA** What four major concerns did the Great Society programs address?

2. **MAIN IDEA** How did events in Vietnam and Latin America affect President Johnson's domestic programs?

3. **IDENTIFYING VALUES** How did President Johnson's programs reflect values from his early life?

4. **WRITING TO EXPLAIN** Write an essay explaining how the Warren Court decisions strengthened individual rights.

5. **EVALUATING** Why do you think Michael Harrington believed that ending legalized segregation would not change the economic condition of most poor African Americans?

THE CIVIL RIGHTS MOVEMENT

FOCUS

- **What was the major tactic of the early civil rights movement? How did it generate public support for the movement?**
- **What events helped expand legislation on civil rights and voting rights?**
- **How was African American frustration expressed in the late 1960s?**
- **What other civil rights movements were inspired by the African American civil rights movement?**

*A*s the 1960s began, southern civil rights leaders called for new efforts in the struggle for racial equality. These efforts won passage of important civil rights and voting rights laws in 1964 and 1965. However, some young members of the movement believed that progress was too slow. In the mid-1960s, frustration over the lack of progress exploded into violence in black neighborhoods. Meanwhile, other groups, inspired by African American activism, fought for their rights.

Martin Luther King, Jr., 1963

NONVIOLENCE IN ACTION

After the success of the Montgomery bus boycott (see Chapter 18), southern civil rights leaders met in Atlanta, Georgia, in 1957 to discuss future strategy. They expanded the Montgomery Improvement Association (MIA) into the **Southern Christian Leadership Conference** (SCLC), an alliance of church-based African American organizations dedicated to ending discrimination. The leader of the MIA, the Reverend Martin Luther King, Jr., led the new organization. The SCLC pledged to use **nonviolent resistance** in its protests. Nonviolent resistance required that protesters never resort to violence, even when others attacked them. King called it meeting "the forces of hate with the power of love."

Many non-SCLC members soon took up nonviolent protests on their own. On February 1,

1960, four African American college students sat down at the "whites only" lunch counter of a Greensboro, North Carolina, department store. The management refused to serve them, but they returned the following day, vowing to continue the **sit-in** protest until they received service. News of the Greensboro sit-in quickly spread, and within weeks students began similar demonstrations in cities throughout the South. In April 1960 the leaders of these demonstrations founded the **Student Nonviolent Coordinating Committee** (SNCC, pronounced "snick"), a loose association of student activists from throughout the South.

White response to the sit-ins tested the students' commitment to nonviolence. White racists taunted the demonstrators, dumping food and drinks on them. Sometimes the harassment escalated into physical attacks. But the demonstrators never resorted to violence. By the end of the year, many restaurants and other eating establishments across the South had been integrated.

▪▪ Early civil rights activists used nonviolent resistance to push for equal rights.

𝒯HE FREEDOM RIDES

The success of the sit-ins inspired the **Congress of Racial Equality** (CORE), a northern-based civil rights group, to launch a protest against segregation in interstate transportation. In May 1961 an integrated group of **Freedom Riders** set off from Washington, D.C., for a trip through the South.

Outside the town of Anniston, Alabama, a white mob firebombed one of the two buses carrying the group members and beat the riders as they tried to escape. The riders on the other bus were attacked in Birmingham. When the bus company refused to carry the passengers any farther, CORE called off the ride. Immediately, Nashville SNCC members stepped in to complete the rest of the trip. SNCC leader Diane Nash explained why:

> ❝ If the Freedom Riders had been stopped as a result of violence, I strongly felt that the future of the movement was going to be cut short. The impression would have been that whenever a movement starts, all [you have to do] is attack it with massive violence and the blacks [will] stop. ❞

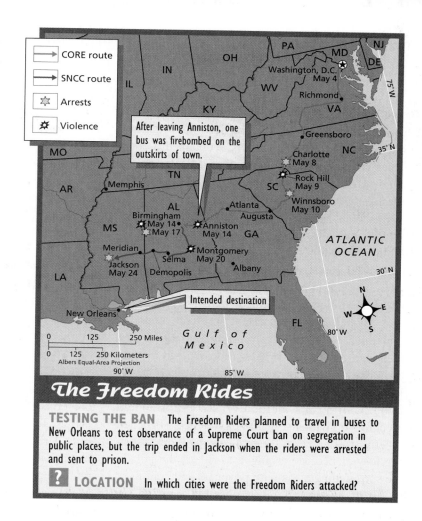

The Freedom Rides

TESTING THE BAN The Freedom Riders planned to travel in buses to New Orleans to test observance of a Supreme Court ban on segregation in public places, but the trip ended in Jackson when the riders were arrested and sent to prison.

❓ LOCATION In which cities were the Freedom Riders attacked?

SNCC sent additional Freedom Riders to Birmingham, where they were quickly arrested by the city commissioner of public safety, T. Eugene "Bull" Connor, and dumped across the state line. The students made their way back to Birmingham and convinced the bus line to take them to Montgomery, where they were once again attacked by a mob. Under pressure from civil rights leaders, Attorney General Robert Kennedy sent federal marshals to protect the riders on the rest of their journey. In Jackson, Mississippi, however, state officials arrested the riders. Outraged by the arrests, hundreds of other protesters tried to carry on the rides. Over the summer more than 300 Freedom Riders traveled the South to protest segregation. In response, Robert Kennedy pressured the Interstate Commerce Commission (ICC) into strengthening its desegregation regulations.

◀ **Stunned Freedom Riders gather outside their bus after it was firebombed by a white mob. In all, 12 people were taken to an Anniston hospital for treatment.**

SUCCESSES AND SETBACKS

The civil rights movement saw many successes; it also saw many setbacks. Despite Supreme Court rulings, many educational institutions remained segregated. In 1962 the NAACP obtained a court order requiring the University of Mississippi to admit African American applicant James Meredith. President Kennedy dispatched federal marshals to ensure that Meredith arrived safely at school. When word got out on the evening of September 30 that Meredith was on campus, a riot broke out that left two people dead. Meredith registered the next day and attended classes the rest of the year under the protection of armed guards.

Events elsewhere tested the effectiveness of nonviolent resistance as a protest tactic. In Albany, Georgia, civil rights organizations staged numerous nonviolent protests against discrimination, but Police Chief Laurie Pritchett was prepared for them. Calling his method of law enforcement meeting "nonviolence with nonviolence," Pritchett quietly arrested all of the protesters without resorting to violence. He arranged to fill all the jails in the surrounding areas with prisoners and continued to fill them for as long as possible, causing the Albany movement to virtually stall out.

Nonviolent resistance proved more effective in Birmingham. In April 1963 the SCLC launched a series of boycotts, sit-ins, and marches to protest the city's segregation laws. Hundreds of demonstrators, including Martin Luther King, Jr., were arrested and jailed. The protests continued to grow until May, when Bull Connor ordered the police to attack the marchers, many of them schoolchildren, with high-pressure fire hoses, dogs, and nightsticks. Scenes of these attacks appeared in newspapers and on television throughout the world, increasing support for the civil rights movement.

■■ **Mob violence against civil rights activists increased public support for the movement.**

THE MARCH ON WASHINGTON

Early in June, President Kennedy urged the passage of a broad new civil rights act designed to end segregation. To show support for Kennedy's civil rights bill, African American leaders called for a huge march on Washington, D.C. On August 28, 1963, more than 200,000 people gathered at the Lincoln Memorial, where they heard Martin Luther King, Jr., deliver one of the most moving speeches in

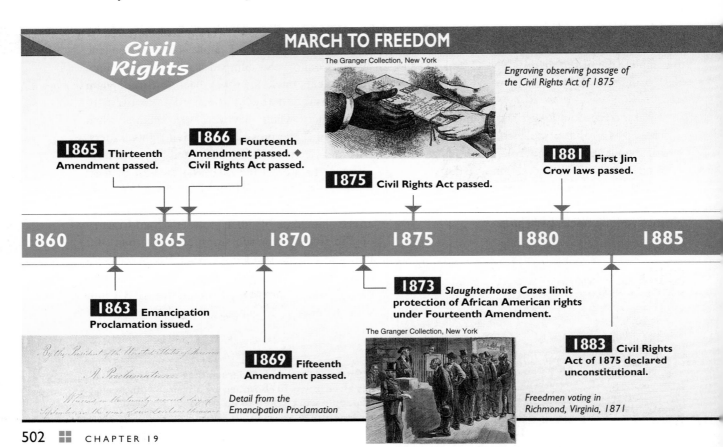

MARCH TO FREEDOM

Civil Rights

The Granger Collection, New York

Engraving observing passage of the Civil Rights Act of 1875

1865 Thirteenth Amendment passed.

1866 Fourteenth Amendment passed. ◆ Civil Rights Act passed.

1875 Civil Rights Act passed.

1881 First Jim Crow laws passed.

1860   1865   1870   1875   1880   1885

1863 Emancipation Proclamation issued.

1873 *Slaughterhouse Cases* limit protection of African American rights under Fourteenth Amendment.

The Granger Collection, New York

1869 Fifteenth Amendment passed.

1883 Civil Rights Act of 1875 declared unconstitutional.

Detail from the Emancipation Proclamation

Freedmen voting in Richmond, Virginia, 1871

American history. Repeating the phrase "I have a dream," King spoke of a nation in which all Americans would live in harmony (see pp. 770-771).

Other speakers, such as A. Philip Randolph, gave eloquent testimony to the long struggle for civil rights in America. SNCC leader John Lewis warned that the younger generation of demonstrators were determined not to give up their struggle until equality was a true reality:

> 66 By the force of our demands, our determination and our numbers, we shall splinter the segregated South into a thousand pieces, and put them back together in the image of God and democracy. 99

The success of the **March on Washington** raised the spirits of civil rights workers everywhere. But their joy proved short-lived. In mid-September a bomb exploded in a Birmingham church, killing four young African American girls. Then in November an assassin's bullet cut down President Kennedy. The new president, Lyndon Johnson, urged Congress to pass Kennedy's civil rights bill. The **Civil Rights Act of 1964** barred discrimination in employment and in public accommodations and gave the Justice Department the power to bring lawsuits to enforce school desegregation.

■■ The March on Washington helped bring about passage of the Civil Rights Act of 1964.

7REEDOM SUMMER AND SELMA

As Congress debated the Civil Rights Act, movement leaders turned their attention to voter registration. In June 1964 they launched **Freedom Summer**, a campaign to register African American voters. It involved nearly 1,000 volunteers, many of them white northerners. Freedom Summer focused on Mississippi, a state with a black population of 45 percent, but where only 5 percent of African Americans were on the voting rolls.

Mississippi had a reputation for racial violence, growing out of the state's many lynchings in the early 20th century and the murder of 14-year-old African American Emmett Till in 1955. Violence quickly struck the Freedom Summer campaign. On June 21 Michael Schwerner and Andrew Goodman, two white New Yorkers, and James Chaney, a black Mississippian, were abducted and killed. Shocked volunteers carried on, but many local blacks feared they would also become the victims of violence if they registered.

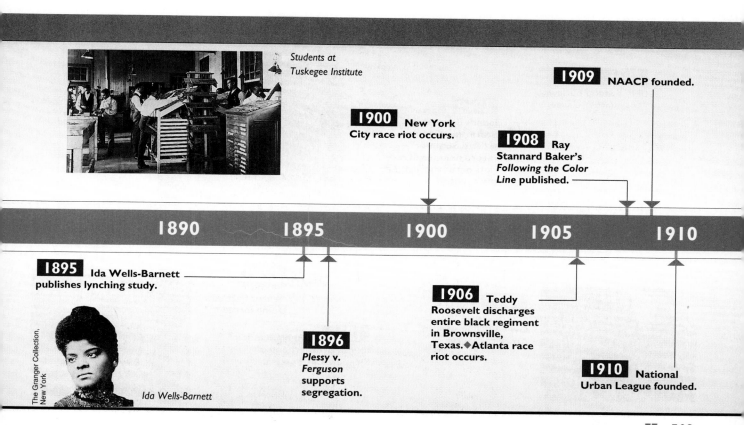

Students at Tuskegee Institute

1909 NAACP founded.

1900 New York City race riot occurs.

1908 Ray Stannard Baker's *Following the Color Line* published.

| 1890 | 1895 | 1900 | 1905 | 1910 |

1895 Ida Wells-Barnett publishes lynching study.

Ida Wells-Barnett

The Granger Collection, New York

1896 *Plessy v. Ferguson* supports segregation.

1906 Teddy Roosevelt discharges entire black regiment in Brownsville, Texas. ◆Atlanta race riot occurs.

1910 National Urban League founded.

By the end of the summer, only 1,600 African Americans had been added to the voting rolls.

In early 1965, civil rights workers launched a similar registration drive in Selma, Alabama. They invited King, who had won the Nobel Peace Prize the previous year, to lead them. For days African Americans attempted to register at election commission offices in the Selma area, only to face beatings and arrests. Civil rights leaders responded by calling for a protest march from Selma to Montgomery. On Sunday, March 7, some 600 people started on the 50-mile trek.

Just outside Selma, police attacked the marchers. One eight-year-old girl in the march recalled the scene: "I saw those horsemen coming toward me and they had those awful masks on; they rode right through the cloud of tear gas. Some of them had clubs, others had ropes, or whips, which they swung about them like they were driving cattle." Stunned by the fierceness of this attack, thousands of Americans poured into Selma to show support for the marchers. President Johnson was also shocked by Selma's "Bloody Sunday." On March 15, before a joint session of Congress, he asked for speedy passage of a voting rights bill. All Americans, he said, ought to take up the struggle for civil rights, for "it's . . . all of us who must overcome the crippling legacy of bigotry and injustice. And we *shall* overcome."

A week later, under the protection of federal marshals and the National Guard, the marchers completed their journey. Five months later Congress passed the **Voting Rights Act** of 1965, which put the entire registration process under federal control. Within days of the act's passage, federal examiners descended on the South to sign up new African American voters. By 1968 over half of all eligible African Americans in the South were registered.

■■ **Freedom Summer, Selma's Bloody Sunday, and the Voting Rights Act of 1965 expanded African American voter registration.**

*B*LACK POWER

As the civil rights movement grew, many African Americans questioned the effectiveness of nonviolence. Some felt that they should be able to use violence for self-defense. Others began to question the desirability of integration altogether. Adopting the slogan **Black Power**, many of these leaders argued that African Americans should mobilize to gain economic and political power. Some also argued that since white society caused racism, only separation from white society would enable African

MARCH TO FREEDOM

1915 *Guinn v. United States* outlaws "grandfather clause."

Race riot in Washington, D.C., 1919

1919 Marcus Garvey founds Black Star Steamship Company.
◆ "Red Summer"— record number of race riots occur throughout the country.

1935 National Council of Negro Women formed.

1915 — 1920 — 1925 — 1930 — 1935

1917 The U.S. enters World War I. Over 370,000 African Americans serve.

Soldiers of the 369th Infantry Regiment

1925 A. Philip Randolph founds Brotherhood of Sleeping Car Porters.

1934 Southern Tenant Farmers' Union formed.

Members of the STFU

Americans to obtain such power. Although the Black Power slogan was not widely used until the late 1960s, it represented the ideas of many earlier African American leaders, including Marcus Garvey (see Chapter 11) and Malcolm X, a black nationalist who rose to prominence in the early civil rights era.

BIO GRAPHY Malcolm X was born Malcolm Little in Nebraska in 1925. His father was a Baptist minister and organizer for Marcus Garvey. After his father died and his mother succumbed to mental illness, the family was disrupted. Moving first to Michigan and then to Massachusetts, the young Malcolm drifted into a life of crime, eventually ending up in prison. While in prison, he embraced the teachings of Elijah Muhammad's Nation of Islam, or Black Muslims, an offshoot of the orthodox Islamic faith.

Freed in 1952, Malcolm rejected the name  Little, handed down to him from some former slaveholder, and used "X" to symbolize his lost African surname. He soon became a leading minister for the Nation of Islam. A powerful orator, Malcolm X championed black separatism and called for freedom to be

Malcolm X

brought about "by any means necessary." The time for nonviolence had passed, he argued:

> 66 You're getting a new generation that has been growing right now, and they're beginning to think with their own minds and see that you can't negotiate up on freedom nowadays. If something is yours by right, then fight for it or shut up. If you can't fight for it, then forget it. 99

Malcolm X broke with the Black Muslims in 1964 after a pilgrimage to the Islamic holy city of Mecca. Turning away from separatism, he converted to orthodox Islam and began calling for unity among all people. This break set off a bitter struggle between Malcolm X and the Nation of Islam. In February 1965, Black Muslim assassins gunned down Malcolm X.

Other young activists, however, carried on some of his ideas. In 1966, college students Huey P. Newton and Bobby Seale founded the Black Panther party in Oakland, California, to promote self-determination in the black community. Asserting that blacks could not trust white police officers to protect them, the Black Panthers armed themselves and established citizen patrols to monitor the streets. "War can only be abolished through war," they declared. Although the Black Panthers

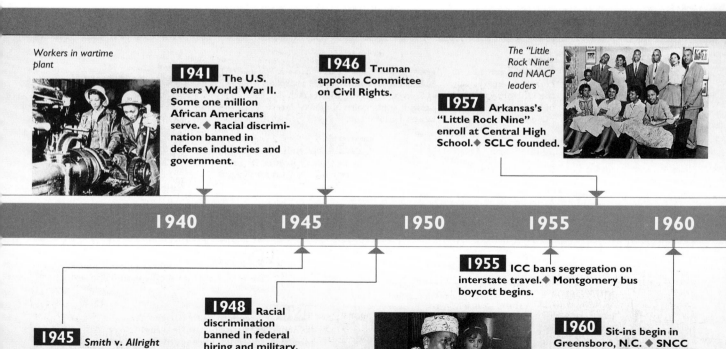

Workers in wartime plant

1941 The U.S. enters World War II. Some one million African Americans serve. ◆ Racial discrimination banned in defense industries and government.

1946 Truman appoints Committee on Civil Rights.

The "Little Rock Nine" and NAACP leaders

1957 Arkansas's "Little Rock Nine" enroll at Central High School.◆ SCLC founded.

1940   1945   1950   1955   1960

1945 Smith v. Allright outlaws "white primaries."

1948 Racial discrimination banned in federal hiring and military.

1955 ICC bans segregation on interstate travel.◆ Montgomery bus boycott begins.

Civil rights activist Ella Baker

1960 Sit-ins begin in Greensboro, N.C. ◆ SNCC founded. ◆ Civil Rights Act passed. ◆ United States v. Raines outlaws literacy tests for voting.

were involved in numerous confrontations with police, many African Americans admired their boldness.

FIRE IN THE STREETS

Frustration among poor inner-city African Americans fueled much of the support for the Black Power movement. Despite the successes of the civil rights movement, discrimination still plagued the lives of most African Americans. In August 1965 frustration became revolt when a routine arrest by Los Angeles police in the black neighborhood of Watts broke into a riot that raged for six days. When the National Guard finally restored order, 34 people were dead, hundreds were injured, and almost 4,000 had been arrested.

Over the next two years, more than 100 riots broke out in cities across the country. The worst erupted in Detroit, where 43 people lost their lives. A federal report by the **Kerner Commission** charged that white racism was largely responsible for the tensions that led to the riots. "Our nation," the report warned, "is moving toward two societies, one black, one white—separate and unequal."

Seeking to address the frustration of the late 1960s, Martin Luther King, Jr., started to embrace some of the Black Power movement's ideas, such as the need for African Americans to gain economic power. He also became increasingly upset that funding that might have gone for the War on Poverty was being used for the war in Vietnam (see Chapter 20). In March 1968 he called for a Poor People's March on Washington to protest this misuse of government funding.

Before the Poor People's March took place, King went to Memphis, Tennessee, to show his support for a garbage workers' strike. On the evening of April 4, 1968, the man who was the symbol of nonviolence met a violent end when a sniper killed him. Within hours of King's death, black neighborhoods all over the country exploded in outrage. A week of rioting left 46 dead and thousands injured.

■■ The Black Power movement and the riots of the late 1960s demonstrated growing frustration among African Americans.

OTHERS INSPIRED BY THE MOVEMENT

King's tragic death and the divisions within the civil rights movement during the 1960s sometimes

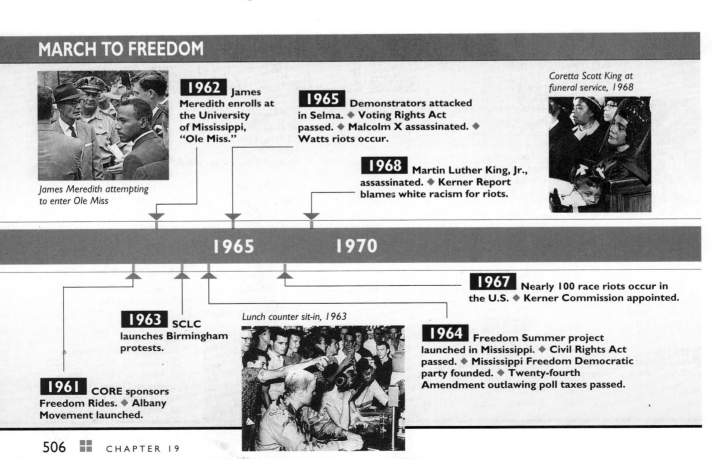

MARCH TO FREEDOM

1962 James Meredith enrolls at the University of Mississippi, "Ole Miss."

James Meredith attempting to enter Ole Miss

1965 Demonstrators attacked in Selma. ◆ Voting Rights Act passed. ◆ Malcolm X assassinated. ◆ Watts riots occur.

1968 Martin Luther King, Jr., assassinated. ◆ Kerner Report blames white racism for riots.

Coretta Scott King at funeral service, 1968

1965   1970

1967 Nearly 100 race riots occur in the U.S. ◆ Kerner Commission appointed.

1963 SCLC launches Birmingham protests.

Lunch counter sit-in, 1963

1964 Freedom Summer project launched in Mississippi. ◆ Civil Rights Act passed. ◆ Mississippi Freedom Democratic party founded. ◆ Twenty-fourth Amendment outlawing poll taxes passed.

1961 CORE sponsors Freedom Rides. ◆ Albany Movement launched.

obscure the movement's gains. It also inspired other groups, such as Mexican Americans and American Indians, to demand better treatment. During the 1960s a group that would become the **United Farm Workers** (UFW), led by César Chávez, began to organize Western migrant workers, most of whom were Mexican Americans, to win better wages and working conditions. In 1965 Chávez called a strike of California grape pickers and launched a nation-wide boycott of grapes picked by nonunion workers. By 1970 the UFW had won most of its demands.

As in the African American civil rights movement, many younger members of the Mexican American movement began demanding more-radical action. Young Mexican American college students organized the **Chicano movement,** which emphasized pride in Mexican culture and heritage. Such pride was reflected in the numerous Mexican American political parties that sprang up around the country, most notably *La Raza Unida* ("the united race"), founded in 1970.

Some American Indians organized into the Red Power movement, which demanded, among other things, that the U.S. government pay tribes for lands that had been taken from them illegally. In 1968 three Minnesota Chippewas organized the **American Indian Movement** (AIM), which would become the major force in the Red Power movement during the 1970s (see Chapter 21).

In 1969 a group of Red Power advocates occupied the abandoned federal prison on Alcatraz Island near San Francisco. The protesters offered to buy the island from the government with beads and cloth—the same price paid by the Dutch for Manhattan Island. The occupation of Alcatraz lasted for many months, until federal authorities finally removed the protesters by force.

All these movements emphasized ethnic pride and group loyalty. Popular culture in the 1950s had promoted the message that to be truly "American" meant to be white and middle class. In the 1960s, African Americans, Hispanics, American Indians, and other groups insisted that the meaning of "American" must expand to include all citizens equally, not just one favored group.

The rise of these movements also raised a central question: Could oppressed groups discover their own identities and promote their own interests yet at the same time retain a sense of citizenship and belonging to the larger American society? This important question still confronts us today.

■■ The civil rights movement inspired other groups, such as Mexican Americans and American Indians, to fight for their rights.

SECTION 3 REVIEW

IDENTIFY and explain the significance of the following: Southern Christian Leadership Conference, nonviolent resistance, sit-in, Student Nonviolent Coordinating Committee, Congress of Racial Equality, Freedom Riders, March on Washington, Civil Rights Act of 1964, Freedom Summer, Voting Rights Act, Black Power, Malcolm X, Kerner Commission, United Farm Workers, César Chávez, Chicano movement, American Indian Movement.

LOCATE and explain the importance of the following: Greensboro, North Carolina; Birmingham, Alabama; Albany, Georgia; Selma, Alabama; Memphis, Tennessee.

1. **MAIN IDEA** What tactic did members of the early civil rights movement use to fight for equal rights? What effect did this tactic have on public opinion?

2. **MAIN IDEA** What event helped bring about passage of the Civil Rights Act of 1964? What incidents helped expand African American voter registration?

3. **MAIN IDEA** How did the African American civil rights movement affect other ethnic movements?

4. **WRITING TO EXPRESS A VIEWPOINT** Imagine you are a Freedom Rider. Write a letter to the editor of a southern newspaper explaining why you feel it is necessary to complete the rides.

5. **TAKING A STAND** Take a stand in support of either Martin Luther King, Jr.'s method of negotiation and nonviolent resistance or Malcolm X's method of separation and self-defense. State the strengths and possible effects of that method on the civil rights movement.

CULTURE AND COUNTERCULTURE

FOCUS

- **How did hippies rebel against traditional society?**
- **What did the revived women's movement do for women?**
- **How did rock music impact the 1960s?**

"The times they are a-changin'," declared singer Bob Dylan in 1963. He was not referring to the civil rights movement alone. Many young people, rejecting the values of their parents' generation, embraced new styles of music and dress and new ways of life. Others challenged American traditions, including religious practices and the role of women in society. The result was a reinvention of culture that eventually affected the entire nation.

Hippie, 1967

THE COUNTERCULTURE

The youth rebellion that began in the 1950s with the Beats and rock 'n' roll evolved into a broad movement in the 1960s that challenged the beliefs and traditions of older generations. Growing up during an era of Cold War fears, massive civil rights protests, and the Vietnam War led many children of the baby boom to question the values of American society and to blame their parents for creating the problems that plagued the country. This **generation gap** between the baby boomers and their elders grew ever wider as the decade wore on.

Shaking the ivory tower. The first audible rumblings of the 1960s youth movement occurred on college campuses among white middle-class students. Many felt frustrated by the impersonal academic bureaucracy and by the conservative curriculum offered at universities. To them, traditional courses seemed out of touch with the real world.

In 1964 discontent exploded into protest at the University of California at Berkeley. Some 70 percent of the students went on strike. Instead of attending classes, they rallied, held sit-ins, and picketed university administration buildings. Their intention, they declared, was to "Shut This Factory Down." By 1965 such chants were echoing from college campuses across the nation.

◀ **Five hundred policemen were present during the Berkeley student protests in December 1964. Some demonstrators who staged a sit-in were arrested and hauled off to jail.**

As the Vietnam War escalated in the late 1960s, campus activism increased still more. One woman who participated in the student movement at Columbia University recalled the mood of the students:

66 There was an incredible exhilaration, that here we were making history, changing the world. . . . Everybody believed that this university would never be the same, that society would be . . . changed, that there'd be a revolution in the United States within five years, and a whole new social order. 99

While some students wanted to change the world, others rebelled by rejecting everything connected with mainstream America, what they called the Establishment. Instead, these **hippies**—as they soon became known—sought to create an alternative life-style, a **counterculture**.

Elements of the counterculture.

Like the Beats before them, hippies rejected the materialism and work ethic of past generations in favor of simplicity and doing "your own thing." Many hippies indulged in behavior intended to shock older Americans, such as public displays of nudity and the use of profanity. Most searched for new physical experiences by engaging in permissive sexual behavior or by experimenting with mind-altering drugs, such as LSD (lysergic acid diethylamide), or "acid."

Timothy Leary, a Harvard professor who was fired in 1963 for using LSD with his students, became the drug's leading advocate. Leary invited people to "tune in, turn on, drop out." Many followed his advice. But there was a high price to pay for the experimentation of the era, as reported cases of sexually transmitted diseases and drug addiction increased at an alarming rate.

Some hippies "dropped out" of society by joining rural communes, where they attempted to live collectively in harmony with nature. They rejected most modern conveniences, grew their own food, and shared all property. Some formed their own hippie neighborhoods in run-down urban areas, such as the Haight-Ashbury district of San Francisco.

■■ **Hippies rebelled against traditional society by forming their own counterculture.**

▲ The Haight-Ashbury district of San Francisco attracted hippies of all ages. This photograph was taken in May 1968.

QUESTIONING AMERICAN SOCIETY

The counterculture movement reflected a growing sense of skepticism in America. In the 1960s many Americans, even those not active in the counterculture movement, were beginning to question the value of conformity. Many institutions, including traditional churches, came under scrutiny. In the mid-1950s, over 80 percent of Americans said religion could answer all or most of modern society's problems. By 1969, however, 70 percent said that religion was *losing* its influence on American life, leading *Time* magazine to ask, "Is God Dead?"

Americans, especially the young, did not necessarily lack spiritual faith, but many lost confidence in the ability of the established churches of their parents to provide spiritual assurance in the modern world. The challenges of the nuclear age, some felt, had made conventional religious answers irrelevant. Reflecting the search for alternative answers, the number of college courses in religion—and enrollment in them—grew dramatically, as did interest in Eastern religions such as Zen Buddhism.

The questioning of tradition even extended into the art world. Many new visual artists argued that the art world had become a slave to elite tastes and prejudices. Artists created works only to please a few cultured critics, not to appeal to the majority of non-artists.

As the 1960s began, a number of New York painters and sculptors emerged who wanted to make art more accessible to the general public. They accomplished their goals by using "found objects"—tin cans, furniture, cardboard packaging, cartoon strips, and other everyday articles—as the subjects of their works. The leading proponents of this method, called **pop art**, included Roy Lichtenstein and Claes Oldenberg. Many of Lichtenstein's huge paintings were done in comic-strip style, complete with speech balloons. Oldenberg used a variety of materials to make giant sculptures of such things as hamburgers, toothpaste tubes, and clothespins.

The best-known pop artist, however, was Andy Warhol. His most notable paintings included

oversize soup cans, rows of green soda bottles, and a garishly colored rendering of a photograph of Marilyn Monroe reproduced multiple times. Initially, Warhol painted by hand. However, he soon switched to a stencil-printing process called silk screen. Finally, he simply did designs that an army of assistants then reproduced. Warhol's message, that everything—even art—can be mass-produced, both glorified and mocked consumerism. Warhol once predicted that "In the future everyone will be famous for 15 minutes," reflecting consumers' constant desires for new products.

A REVIVED WOMEN'S MOVEMENT

One of the most lasting legacies of the 1960s was its challenge to traditional views of women. After years of inaction, the women's movement experienced a widespread revival.

Sparks of unrest. This revival was sparked in part by the publication of Betty Friedan's *The Feminine Mystique* (1963), which rejected the popular notion that women were content with the roles of wife, mother, and homemaker. Many women, she charged, felt stifled by the "comfortable concentration camp" of domestic life:

> 66 Each suburban wife struggled with it alone. As she made the beds, shopped for groceries, matched slipcover material, ate peanut butter sandwiches with her children, chauffeured Cub Scouts and Brownies, . . . she was afraid to ask even of herself the silent question—"Is this all?" 99

Other women agreed with Friedan. Her book helped motivate women to demand greater opportunities and fairer treatment in the workplace. Although the Civil Rights Act of 1964 outlawed sexual discrimination in employment, the government seemed reluctant to deal with women's grievances. As a result, in 1966 Friedan and other feminists founded the **National Organization for Women** (NOW) to lobby for women's rights. Women began to stand up for themselves in a variety of ways. Some held consciousness-raising sessions to improve their self-esteem. Others took direct action. In 1968, for example, some feminists disrupted the Miss America pageant, charging that beauty contests degraded women.

▶ Pop artists helped make art more accessible to the general public by selecting images that reflected everyday life. Andy Warhol, for example, painted these oversize soup cans in 1965.

Andy Warhol, Campbell's Soup, 1965

Roy Lichtenstein

◀ Many of Roy Lichtenstein's paintings were drawn in a flamboyant, comic-strip style.

BY DR. ALICE KESSLER-HARRIS

Social History

Until relatively recently, most American history textbooks focused on political history, recounting the deeds of the nation's political, military, and social leaders. Today, however, textbooks have begun to place a greater emphasis on social history.

What is social history? Some 50 years ago the well-known British historian G. M. Trevelyan described social history as "the history of a people with the politics left out." Social historians studied people's private lives rather than political events. They concentrated on the household, giving details about the daily lives of men, women, and children. Though colorful, this history failed to explain larger historical themes.

But social history changed in the 1960s. The civil rights movement, antiwar protests, and the women's movement inspired a new generation of historians. In order to explain how these protest movements arose, historians began studying how African Americans, women, and ethnic groups other than white Protestants contributed to American history. Focusing on ordinary people—workers, women, city dwellers, farmers, immigrants—social historians set out to expand the history of the United States.

To do so, these historians sought out new sources and used new methods to reconstruct the daily lives and thoughts of ordinary people. Earlier historians had analyzed only written sources left by political and intellectual leaders. The new social historians uncovered new sources—workers' speeches and letters, oral histories, autobiographies, songs, folklore, reports of chari-

▲ Roll, Jordan, Roll, an example of social history by Eugene D. Genovese, explores plantation life in the pre–Civil War South.

table societies, and ethnic and immigrant newspapers. These historians used statistical methods to study how people voted, where they moved, what they ate and drank, how they spent and saved their money, and the size of their families.

The new social historians have created a body of work whose strength lies in its respect for cultural diversity. Their work explores the values and ideas that Americans of different racial, ethnic, and class backgrounds share and do not share. For example, Julia Kirk Blackwelder's *Women of the Depression: Caste and Culture in San Antonio, 1929–39* (1984) shows how people's racial and ethnic backgrounds helped them cope with economic distress.

The new social history also explores the social institutions—families, schools, churches, and so on—that both preserve traditional values and help introduce new ones. This history, however, goes beyond the "old" social history by using social institutions to help explain broader political, economic, or technological changes. For example, Kenneth Jackson's *Crabgrass Frontier* (1985) explains that American families' preference for detached homes of their own helped lead to the growth of suburbs—an important economic and geographic change.

The best social history combines research on political and economic institutions with research on how ordinary people think and act. This combination helps us understand politics and the forces that ultimately create change. In doing so, the new social historians can rightly claim to have updated Trevelyan's definition of social history by creating a history of all Americans with the politics mixed in.

A new generation. Many young women who had participated in the civil rights movement and counterculture realized that they faced just as much sexual discrimination in those realms as they did in mainstream society. One activist recalled a friend telling her that "you'll never be a radical as long as you don't see how the system affects *you.* You always think it affects other people." By the late 1960s more women inspired by other movements were beginning to stand up for their own rights. One woman who became so inspired was journalist Gloria Steinem.

Gloria Steinem was born on March 25, 1934, in Toledo, Ohio. In 1946 her parents divorced. She spent most of her teenage years taking care of her invalid mother. In 1952 Steinem entered Smith College, where she graduated with honors. "I loved Smith," she recalled. "They gave you three meals a day to eat, and all the books you wanted to read—what more could you want?" Steinem's love of reading and writing led to her desire to become a journalist.

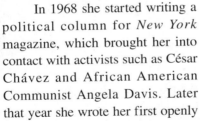

BIO GRAPHY

Gloria Steinem

In 1968 she started writing a political column for *New York* magazine, which brought her into contact with activists such as César Chávez and African American Communist Angela Davis. Later that year she wrote her first openly feminist article, "After Black Power, Women's Liberation," which established her as an advocate of the movement. In 1971 she helped found the National Women's Political Caucus to encourage women to run for political office. That same year, she became editor of a new magazine for women entitled *Ms.*

"There is nothing outside of [the movement]," Steinem said. "I once thought I would do this for two or three years and go home to my real life." But she has continued to be a leader in the women's movement, writing several books, lobbying for causes such as the passage of the Equal Rights Amendment (see Chapter 21), and helping found numerous organizations for women, including the Coalition of Labor Union Women and Women Against Pornography.

■■ **The 1960s revival of the women's movement challenged traditional views of women.**

MUSICAL REVOLUTION

All of the social and political movements of the 1960s marched to new forms of music. A compelling influence on the youth rebellion of the 1950s, rock 'n' roll continued to reflect social change in the 1960s, while it branched out into a variety of new forms.

The year 1964 marked the musical **British Invasion**—the arrival of such English bands as the Beatles and the Rolling Stones. Drawing on rock 'n' roll and African American blues for inspiration, these bands created a vibrant, powerful new style of music. Meanwhile, African American artists, many sponsored by Motown Records of Detroit, were experimenting with enhanced blendings of traditional black music. The unique and widely popular style they created became known as the "Motown sound."

The use of electrically amplified instruments, especially the electric guitar, inspired musicians to try innovative—and very loud—sounds on audiences. Seattle native Jimi Hendrix was the master

▼ **Jimi Hendrix, shown here performing in 1970, was one of the most innovative rock 'n' roll guitarists to emerge during the late 1960s.**

▲ **Folk music by artists such as Joan Baez was also popular during the 1960s.**

of the electric guitar in the 1960s. Folk music also inspired a new type of rock sound as singers such as Joan Baez and Bob Dylan created lyrics that sent a political message to listeners, such as in this 1962 Dylan hit:

> " How many years can a mountain exist
> before it's washed to the sea?
> Yes, 'n' How many years can some
> people exist
> before they're allowed to be free?
> Yes, 'n' How many times can a man
> turn his head
> pretending he just doesn't see?
> The answer, my friend, is blowin'
> in the wind,
> The answer is blowin' in the wind. "

In the late 1960s, as the Vietnam War continued to rage, rock music became more openly political. Dylan, Baez, and other musicians popular with counterculture performed songs that bitterly criticized the war.

Rock music would be the focal point of an event that marked the beginning of the end for the counterculture movement—the Woodstock Music Festival. In August 1969 some 300,000 young people descended on rural upstate New York for the three-day festival. Despite driving rain, knee-deep mud, and severe shortages of food and water, the concert remained a peaceful gathering as listeners reveled in the music of rock's top performers.

▲ In spite of traffic jams, water shortages, lack of public conveniences, and rain, the Woodstock Music Festival in August 1969 was an overwhelming success.

Woodstock was more than just a rock concert. It was a celebration of the era, marking the high point of the counterculture movement. Some four months later, at a free concert held at Altamont Raceway near San Francisco, a security team beat a young African American fan to death in full view of the stage. The idealistic spirit of the youth movement seemed to die with him.

 Rock music followed the movements of the 1960s and marked the high point of the counterculture at Woodstock.

SECTION 4 REVIEW

IDENTIFY and explain the significance of the following: generation gap, hippies, counterculture, Timothy Leary, pop art, Roy Lichtenstein, Claes Oldenberg, Andy Warhol, Betty Friedan, National Organization for Women, Gloria Steinem, British Invasion, Jimi Hendrix, Bob Dylan, Woodstock.

1. **MAIN IDEA** Why did hippies form their own counterculture?

2. **MAIN IDEA** What effect did the revival of the women's movement have on traditional views of women?

3. **ASSESSING CONSEQUENCES** What consequences did the youth rebellion of the 1960s have on society?

4. **WRITING TO EVALUATE** Imagine you are a music critic in 1969. Write an article that evaluates the relationship between rock 'n' roll music and the events of the 1960s.

5. **SYNTHESIZING** How did the various works of pop artists reflect American culture in the 1960s?

CHAPTER 19
Review

SNCC founded. John F. Kennedy elected president.

Yuri Gagarin makes first manned space flight. Bay of Pigs invaded. Freedom Rides begin. Berlin Wall built.

Michael Harrington's *The Other America* published. Cuban missile crisis erupts.

Equal Pay Act passed. Betty Friedan's *The Feminine Mystique* published. March on Washington occurs. Kennedy assassinated.

WRITING A SUMMARY
Using the essential points of the chapter as a guide, write a summary of the chapter.

REVIEWING CHRONOLOGY
Number your paper 1 to 5. Study the time line above, and list the following events in the order in which they happened by writing the first next to 1, the second next to 2, and so on. Then complete the activity below.

1. Woodstock Music Festival occurs.
2. American Indian Movement organized.
3. Betty Friedan's *The Feminine Mystique* published.
4. Freedom Rides begin.
5. Medicare and Medicaid established.

Evaluating How did Michael Harrington's book *The Other America* influence American domestic policy?

IDENTIFYING PEOPLE AND IDEAS
Explain the historical significance of each of the following people or terms.

1. New Frontier	6. nonviolent resistance
2. Peace Corps	7. Voting Rights Act
3. Fidel Castro	8. Chicano movement
4. Warren Commission	9. generation gap
5. Juan Bosch	10. Gloria Steinem

UNDERSTANDING MAIN IDEAS
1. How did the Kennedy administration propose to deter Communist expansion?
2. What was the purpose of the Great Society? How did President Johnson propose to make the Great Society a reality?
3. What did the Brown Power, Red Power, and Black Power movements have in common?
4. How did young people rebel against conformity during the 1960s?
5. What gains did women make during the 1960s? How did they make these gains?

REVIEWING THEMES
1. **Global Relations** How did events overseas undermine the Great Society programs?
2. **Democratic Values** How did the Freedom Rides, sit-ins, and other peaceful civil rights protests help expand democracy?
3. **Cultural Diversity** What institutions and traditions were challenged in the late 1960s?

THINKING CRITICALLY
1. **Evaluating** How did the Warren Court's decisions in *Gideon* v. *Wainwright*, *Escobedo* v. *Illinois*, and *Miranda* v. *Arizona* strengthen individual rights?
2. **Synthesizing** In what ways did African Americans express frustration over their slow progress in achieving civil rights?
3. **Analyzing** What contribution did music and pop art make to society in the 1960s?

STRATEGY FOR SUCCESS
Review the Skills Handbook entry on Reading Charts and Graphs beginning on page 756. Study the graph below, which shows the number of drug arrests reported between 1960 and 1970. In which year did the number of arrests first exceed 100,000? About how many arrests were reported in 1970?

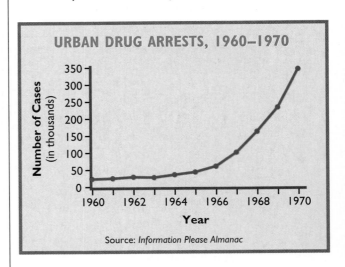

URBAN DRUG ARRESTS, 1960–1970

Number of Cases (in thousands) — Year

Source: *Information Please Almanac*

1964	1966	1968

War on Poverty declared. OEO established. Freedom Summer launched. Civil Rights Act passed.

Medicare and Medicaid established. Malcolm X assassinated. Selma's Bloody Sunday occurs. U.S. intervenes in Dominican Republic. Voting Rights Act passed.

NOW founded. Supreme Court decides *Miranda* v. *Arizona*.

Martin Luther King, Jr., assassinated. American Indian Movement organized.

Woodstock Music Festival occurs.

WRITING ABOUT HISTORY

Writing to Evaluate Write an essay that evaluates the different leadership styles of Lyndon Johnson and John F. Kennedy.

USING PRIMARY SOURCES

Native Americans were one ethnic group in the 1960s whose problems were not addressed by the U.S. government. Read the following excerpt, which comes from an article published in the *New Republic* in 1965, describing conditions on the Pine Ridge Reservation in South Dakota. Then write a paragraph summarizing what you have read.

> ❝ *Practically none of the houses on the reservation has electricity. Half of the houses are without wells nearby; Poverty-Program workers are discovering people hauling water fifteen miles. Indoor plumbing or telephone service is rare. . . .*
>
> *There is a great deal of illness at Pine Ridge. . . . The infant mortality rate is twice that of the nation's, and infectious diseases among small children are a major problem. The incidence of tuberculosis is seventeen times that for the rest of the country. The life expectancy for a person at Pine Ridge is thirty-eight years, compared with sixty-two years nationally. . . .*
>
> *The solution to the Indian problem still is dimly seen to lie in pouring the Indians into the big cities where they will intermingle with everyone else. But the city planners are trying to figure out how to get people out of the cramped city and back into the countryside. If the administration does not pull hard to redevelop these rural areas, it will end up merely fanning the flames in the cities.* ❞

LINKING HISTORY AND GEOGRAPHY

Refer to the map on page 493. How did geography influence U.S. policy toward Cuba and the Dominican Republic?

BUILDING YOUR PORTFOLIO

Complete the following projects independently or cooperatively.

1. CIVIL RIGHTS In chapters 17 and 18 you served as a reporter covering the civil rights movement. Building on that experience, write a memorandum to the manager of your station explaining why the station should provide coverage of the civil rights efforts of African Americans, Hispanic Americans, Native Americans, and women.

2. THE GOVERNMENT AND THE ECONOMY In Chapter 17 you prepared a chart of government programs designed to help WWII veterans. Building on that experience, imagine you are a member of Johnson's Great Society. Prepare an illustrated pamphlet that describes government efforts in areas such as health care, urban renewal, or education.

3. POPULAR CULTURE In Chapter 18 you prepared a photo essay on American culture during the 1950s. Building on that experience, imagine you are a reporter for *Rolling Stone*, assigned to write an article about the first two decades of rock 'n' roll. Prepare a family tree of rock music, using photos to trace the influence of rhythm and blues, jazz, folk, country, and the British Invasion on American music up to 1970.

URBAN AMERICA

*A*S more people moved into the cities and suburbs after World War II, metropolitan areas —large cities or groups of cities and their surrounding areas—arose. The city of Los Angeles is typical of the 20th-century metropolis. In the 1920s most of the land inside the official city limits was not developed. As the city grew, it engulfed numerous surrounding areas. By the 1980s the Los Angeles metropolitan area encompassed some 80 smaller cities. Like many urban-dwellers, Los Angeles–area residents generally live outside the city and commute to work. This has led to the observation that Los Angeles, like many other metropolitan areas, is in fact "a hundred suburbs in search of a city."

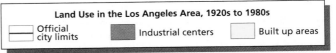

Land Use in the Los Angeles Area, 1920s to 1980s

Official city limits | Industrial centers | Built up areas

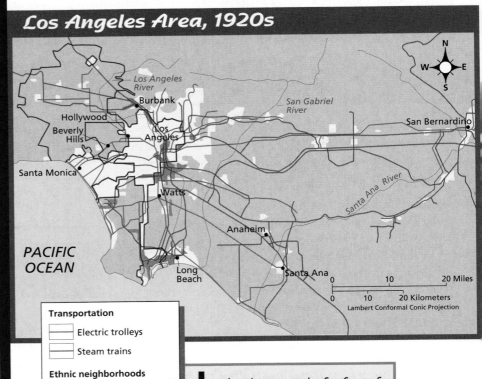

Los Angeles Area, 1920s

Transportation

Electric trolleys

Steam trains

Ethnic neighborhoods

10% or more African American

10% or more African American and 20% or more foreign-born Mexican

*L*os Angeles was at the forefront of creating the suburban housing system that grew popular in the 1950s. In the early 20th century, as eastern cities grew more crowded, Los Angeles built the nation's most extensive electric railway system to encourage people to live outside the city and commute to work.

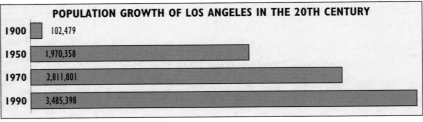

POPULATION GROWTH OF LOS ANGELES IN THE 20TH CENTURY

1900	102,479
1950	1,970,358
1970	2,811,801
1990	3,485,398

Source: *World Almanac and Book of Facts*

POPULATION OF LOS ANGELES IN 1990

53%	White
14%	Black
.5%	Native American, Alaskan, or Aleut
10%	Asian
40%	Hispanic origin*
23%	Other

*Hispanic origin may include persons of any race, thus chart represents more than 100%.

Source: *Information Please Almanac*

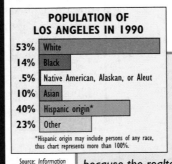

*L*os Angeles has been one of the most ethnically diverse cities in the country, yet years of discrimination in housing have left many ethnic groups limited to ghettos in the center of the city. In 1949 Ed Roybal, a Hispanic member of the Los Angeles city council, could not buy a house in the suburbs because the realtors would not sell to Hispanics. Such discrimination fueled racial unrest in the later 20th century, sparking numerous riots, such as the Watts riot of 1965 and the south central riots of 1992.

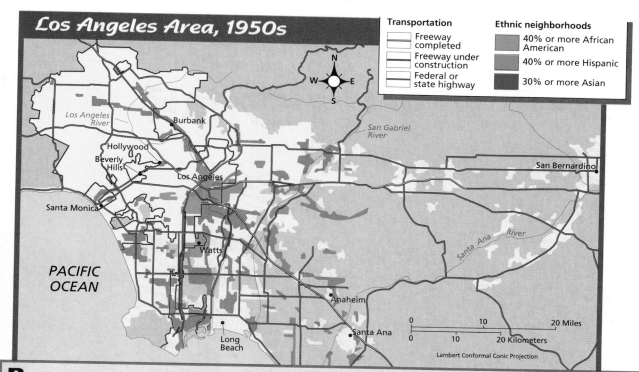

Los Angeles Area, 1950s

Transportation
- Freeway completed
- Freeway under construction
- Federal or state highway

Ethnic neighborhoods
- 40% or more African American
- 40% or more Hispanic
- 30% or more Asian

Los Angeles River, Burbank, Hollywood, Beverly Hills, Los Angeles, Santa Monica, Watts, San Gabriel River, San Bernardino, Santa Ana River, Anaheim, Santa Ana, Long Beach

PACIFIC OCEAN

0 10 20 Miles
0 10 20 Kilometers
Lambert Conformal Conic Projection

By the 1940s automobiles had replaced the railway system as the preferred means of transportation in Los Angeles. Construction of a huge freeway network encouraged automobile use, but it also led to a rise in smog pollution—a problem that plagues many cities today. While Los Angeles has grown rapidly, it has also faced numerous problems caused by its geography. The dry climate has contributed to several brush fires in recent years. Lack of an adequate water supply led to the construction of Owens River Aqueduct in 1913, followed by the California Aqueduct in 1973. Los Angeles also lies in an area of heavy earthquake activity. The city has been rocked by numerous earthquakes, including one in January 1994 that killed more than 50 people.

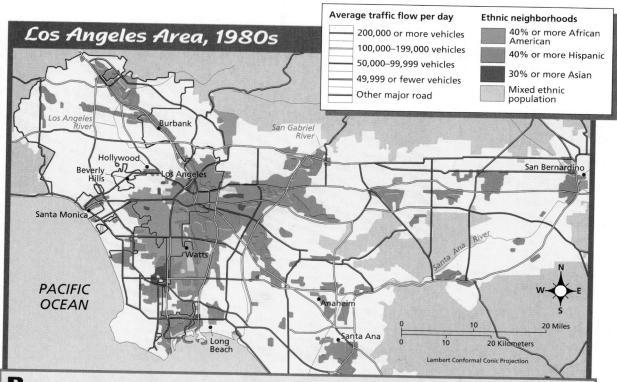

Los Angeles Area, 1980s

Average traffic flow per day
- 200,000 or more vehicles
- 100,000–199,000 vehicles
- 50,000–99,999 vehicles
- 49,999 or fewer vehicles
- Other major road

Ethnic neighborhoods
- 40% or more African American
- 40% or more Hispanic
- 30% or more Asian
- Mixed ethnic population

Los Angeles River, Burbank, Hollywood, Beverly Hills, Los Angeles, Santa Monica, Watts, San Gabriel River, San Bernardino, Santa Ana River, Anaheim, Santa Ana, Long Beach

PACIFIC OCEAN

0 10 20 Miles
0 10 20 Kilometers
Lambert Conformal Conic Projection

By the mid–1980s Los Angeles was the second-largest city in America. Many citizens, worried that the city was growing too rapidly, campaigned for measures to slow growth and improve urban conditions. In 1986 the city passed a measure that cut in half the amount of land available to developers for construction. Also in the mid–1980s the city began working on plans to improve public transportation with a new train and subway system.

WAR IN VIETNAM

FOCUS

UNDERSTANDING THE MAIN IDEA

Most U.S. leaders expected the war in Vietnam to end quickly once U.S. troops and equipment entered the conflict. They did not dream that some 2.6 million Americans would serve in a war that dragged on for more than a decade. Nor did they imagine that antiwar protests would grow to the proportions they did.

THEMES

- **GLOBAL RELATIONS** How might global conditions lead one nation to intervene in the affairs of another?

- **CONSTITUTIONAL HERITAGE** Why might one branch of government fear another branch becoming too strong?

- **DEMOCRATIC VALUES** What are the limits to the government's responsibility to keep the public informed? In a democracy, what limits are there to a people's right to protest government actions?

1954	1955	1965	1973	1975
Geneva Conference held.	Diem comes to power in South Vietnam.	U.S. sends combat troops to Vietnam.	Cease-fire declared.	Saigon falls.

The United States had taken the position of opposing the spread of communism anywhere in the world. U.S. troops had recently fought against Communist forces in Korea. Now Americans became involved in a similar war in Vietnam, where the Vietnamese had won their independence from the French a few years earlier.

A U.S. Marine officer takes cover.

In Graham Greene's novel *The Quiet American* (1955), the narrator sits in a Vietnamese café thinking about a new arrival, the American "adviser" Alden Pyle. According to the narrator, the young American "seemed incapable of harm":

> 66 Perhaps only ten days ago he had been walking back across the Common in Boston, his arms full of the books he had been reading in advance on the Far East and the problems of China. He didn't even hear what I said; he was absorbed already in the dilemmas of Democracy and the responsibilities of the West; he was determined—I learnt that very soon—to do good, not to any individual person but to a country, a continent, a world. 99

Greene's Alden Pyle closely resembles the American advisers sent to South Vietnam in the 1950s. This "quiet American," wading into the rough sea of post–World War II Southeast Asia, typifies the early American self-image in Vietnam: confident, serious, and eagerly committed to building a model democracy.

This sense of idealism was grounded in the effort to save Vietnam and the rest of the world from communism, even at great cost to America. The eventual cost—years of war and more than 60,000 Americans dead or missing—was higher than most believed possible. And despite the sacrifices, Vietnam was not "saved." In the war's wake, Americans were left to ponder how early idealism ended in what has been called "a tragedy of epic dimensions."

Vietnam Women's Memorial

BACKGROUND TO CONFLICT

FOCUS

- **Why did China and then France want to control Vietnam?**
- **Why did the United States refuse to back Vietnamese independence in the 1940s and 1950s?**
- **Why did President Kennedy increase U.S. involvement in Vietnam?**

For centuries invaders coveted the fertile river deltas and coastal lowlands of Vietnam. First China and later France conquered and ruled Vietnam. But the deep desire of the Vietnamese people to be free could not be overcome. During World War II, France began to lose its grip on Vietnam. And as the war came to a close, Vietnamese Communists fought for power, hoping to establish an independent nation. This threat of a Communist takeover soon drew the United States into the conflict.

French colonial occupation in Saigon

THE GEOGRAPHIC SETTING

Fishhook-shaped Vietnam is the easternmost country of Southeast Asia—8,000 miles across the Pacific from the west coast of the United States. It is slightly smaller than California, covering 127,207 square miles of mostly hills and dense forests. Lying south of China, Vietnam is bordered on the west by Laos and Cambodia. Its coastline stretches along the Gulf of Tonkin, the South China Sea, and the Gulf of Thailand (see map on page 521).

The population of Vietnam is centered mostly in two areas: the Red River Delta in the far north and the Mekong (MAY-KAWNG) Delta in the south. The Mekong Delta is Vietnam's richest agricultural region, specializing in rice cultivation. Hanoi is the major city of the north and the country's capital, while Ho Chi Minh City (previously South Vietnam's capital, Saigon) is the largest city in the south. Other cities, such as the ports Da Nang and Hue (WAY), are located on the narrow coastal lowlands of central Vietnam.

To the north of the Mekong Delta are the central highlands, sparsely populated and mostly covered by forest. Farther north, the Annamite Mountains form the jagged backbone of Vietnam. Their rugged peaks and dense rain forest separate much of Vietnam from neighboring Laos.

▲ **Vietnam is one of the world's largest producers of rice, cultivating more than 12 million acres each year.**

CHINESE OCCUPATION

The moist tropical climate of the deltas and coastal lowlands has allowed Vietnamese farmers to grow several crops of rice a year. It was this agricultural abundance that tempted China to invade the Red River Delta around 200 B.C. For more than a thousand years, the Chinese struggled to maintain control over northern and central Vietnam. But the Vietnamese resisted, finally winning limited independence from China in A.D. 939.

In the 1400s China tried to reassert control over Vietnam. A Vietnamese military leader named Le Loi employed guerrilla warfare to defeat the Chinese invaders. Using tactics similar to those later used against the French and Americans, Le Loi's rebels worked as peasants by day; by night they took up arms to attack the Chinese. By 1428 the rebels had driven the Chinese from the country and won independence for Vietnam. Le Loi became the new emperor.

FRENCH OCCUPATION

Vietnam again lost its independence in the surge of European imperialism in the mid-1800s. This time the invaders were French, attracted by the promise of gaining access to Asian trade and of making new Catholic converts.

Despite the stubborn resistance of the Vietnamese, French military power ultimately won out. In 1883 the Vietnamese were forced to grant France complete control of the country. France later combined Vietnam with Laos and Cambodia to form French Indochina, one of France's richest possessions.

■■ **The Chinese and later the French sought control of Vietnam's rich farmlands and trade.**

Ho Chi Minh and Vietnamese independence. Like the Chinese, the French gained control of the land but not the hearts of the Vietnamese. Nationalist feelings remained strong.

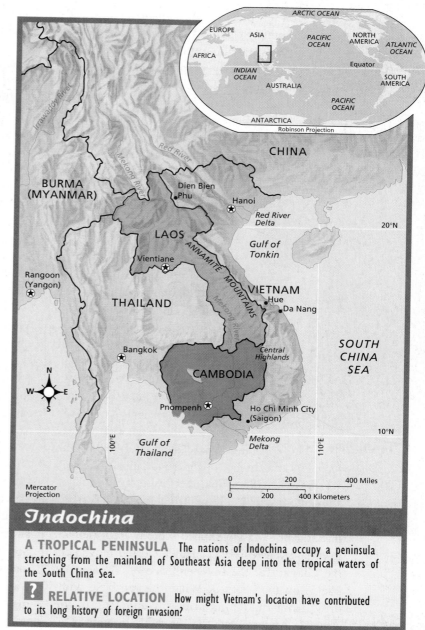

Indochina

A TROPICAL PENINSULA The nations of Indochina occupy a peninsula stretching from the mainland of Southeast Asia deep into the tropical waters of the South China Sea.

? RELATIVE LOCATION How might Vietnam's location have contributed to its long history of foreign invasion?

Foremost among the nationalists was Nguyen That Thanh (en-gy-EN TAHT TAHN), a world wanderer and man of many names, whose last alias was Ho Chi Minh (HOH CHEE MIN)—"He Who Enlightens."

Ho was born in central Vietnam in 1890, the son of a poor country scholar. In 1911, calling himself Van Ba (Third Son), he got a job as cook on a French merchant ship. After spending a few years at sea, he decided to settle in London. There, while working as a pastry cook in a hotel, Ho learned the English language (he was already fluent in French).

From London, Ho went to Paris, where he soon emerged as a leader of Vietnamese nationalists living in France. Ho joined the French socialists but soon left them to help organize the French Communist party. Later, Ho claimed that "it was patriotism and not Communism that originally inspired" his quest for Vietnamese independence. By 1923, though, convinced that a worldwide Communist revolution was Vietnam's only hope, he left Paris to study revolutionary tactics in Moscow.

During the 1920s and 1930s Ho organized and plotted for Vietnamese independence. One French comrade described him as "taut and quivering, with only one thought in his head, his country, Vietnam." Hunted as a Communist, Ho donned disguises as he moved from country to country—sometimes a Chinese journalist, at other times a Buddhist monk with flowing robes.

What Ho awaited was a chance to launch his plan. That chance

▲ Ho Chi Minh

came during World War II. In 1940 the Japanese army swept down from China to occupy all of French Indochina, the Philippines, Malaya, and Indonesia. In Vietnam the Japanese left the French colonial government in place but controlled it. Early in 1941 Ho slipped secretly into Vietnam to organize a resistance. He called the movement the League for the Independence of Vietnam, or **Vietminh** (vee-ET-MIN). When the Japanese withdrew from Indochina after surrendering to the Allies in August 1945, the Vietminh declared independence.

In Hanoi on September 2, more than half a million people gathered at an independence celebration to hear Ho speak. In an effort to gain American support, the Vietminh leader echoed America's Declaration of Independence: "We hold the truth that all men are created equal, that they are endowed by their Creator with certain unalienable rights, among them life, liberty, and the pursuit of happiness."

At another celebration that day, American army officers joined Vietnamese leaders on the reviewing stand as a Vietnamese band played "The Star-Spangled Banner." U.S. warplanes flew over the gathering in a salute to Vietnam's independence. The French were sure to resist, but the United States seemed poised to prevent them from reclaiming colonial rule over Vietnam.

France and the Vietminh go to war.

American policy toward Vietnam was soon put to the test. By 1946 the French and the Vietnamese were once again locked in battle. Would America stand with the Vietnamese in this conflict? The answer was no. Not only did President Truman ignore Ho's pleas for assistance, he threw U.S. support behind France.

Why did Truman side with France? First, he viewed France as a vital ally in the struggle against the spread of communism in postwar Europe. Second, he was unwilling to back the Vietminh because of Ho's Communist connections. U.S. advisers feared that communism would engulf Asia (see Chapter 17). This fear was reinforced in 1949 when Mao Zedong's Communists took over China—Asia's most populous country and a former U.S. ally. By 1950 the United States was locked in a bloody ground war to turn back Communist North Korea's invasion of South Korea. Meanwhile, Communist-led nationalist revolts rocked Indonesia, the Philippines, and Malaya.

Because of these developments the focus of America's containment policy broadened to include East Asia. There, U.S. policymakers vowed to hold the line against communism. Truman's successor, Dwight D. Eisenhower, shared this resolve, especially in regard to Southeast Asia. Besides possessing abundant raw materials essential to modern industry, the region was considered of strategic importance in containing the Chinese Communists. If Vietnam fell to communism, Eisenhower warned, the rest of

▶ At Dien Bien Phu a weary French soldier awaits further shelling by Vietminh guerrillas in early 1954.

Southeast Asia would soon follow. The president illustrated his point by saying, "You have a row of dominoes set up. You knock over the first one, and what will happen to the last one is a certainty that it will go over very quickly." This idea came to be called the **domino theory**.

▪▪ Believing that communism would spread throughout Asia if it took hold in Vietnam, the United States sided with France against the Vietminh.

President Eisenhower's commitment to a non-Communist Vietnam was even stronger than Truman's. By 1954 America was paying much of the cost of France's war effort. But even with massive aid, the French suffered defeat after defeat.

Money and military equipment were of limited use against Vietminh guerrilla tactics. The Vietminh chose when and where to attack, struck without warning, and then disappeared into the jungle. In a comment to an American journalist in 1946, Ho Chi Minh had expressed his people's determination to prevail, characterizing the fight as "a war between an elephant"—the French—"and a tiger"—the Vietnamese:

66 If the tiger ever stands still, the elephant will crush him with his mighty tusks. But the tiger does not stand still. . . . He will leap upon the back of the elephant, tearing huge chunks from his hide, and then the tiger will leap back into the dark jungle. And slowly the elephant will bleed to death. That will be the war of Indochina. 99

From *America Inside Out* by David Schoenbrun © 1984

Frustrated, the French tried to lure the Vietminh into a conventional battle at Dien Bien Phu (dyen byen FOO), deep within Vietminh-held northern Vietnam. The plan backfired. Some 13,000 French soldiers soon found themselves encircled by more than 50,000 Vietminh troops. The French commander urged his war-weary soldiers to hold out—offering them the hope of a rescue: "The Americans will not let us down; the free world will not let us down."

Help did not come. Although willing to commit money, Eisenhower was reluctant to become directly involved in another Asian war so soon after the Korean War. As a result, the Vietminh defeated the French and on May 7, 1954, forced their surrender.

The Geneva Conference.

In the spring of 1954, just one day after the French surrender at Dien Bien Phu, an international conference to settle the Indochina conflict began in Geneva, Switzerland. There, representatives of the French and the Vietminh attempted to map out Indochina's future. The People's Republic of China (Communist China), the United States, Great Britain, the Soviet Union, Laos, and Cambodia joined the discussions.

The Communist Chinese, who had begun aiding the Vietminh in 1950, hoped to limit U.S. influence in the region. They also wished to prevent the establishment of a strong, unified Vietnam on their southern border. The Americans,

▲ A French newspaper reports the fall of Dien Bien Phu.

meanwhile, did not want to see Vietnam handed over completely to the Communists.

A cease-fire was agreed to, but no definite political settlement was achieved. Vietnam was temporarily divided at the 17th parallel (17° north latitude). North of the 17th parallel, the Vietminh held undisputed power; south of the line, remnants of the French-controlled government resumed authority. Vietminh forces would withdraw to the north; French forces would withdraw to the south. General elections to reunify the country were scheduled for July 1956. Alarmed that the Communists would likely win a nationwide election, the United States refused to endorse the agreement.

THE REGIME OF NGO DINH DIEM

President Eisenhower estimated that Ho might win a general election by as much as four to one. Still, he hoped that southern Vietnam, at least, might be kept non-Communist. Who could stand against Ho? One possibility was Ngo Dinh Diem (en-GOH DIN de-EM), a former government official under the French. Though lacking Ho's charisma, Diem was enough of a nationalist to be a credible Vietnamese leader.

Diem takes power in the south.

Ngo Dinh Diem was strongly anti-Communist. He had spent several years in the United States, where his political views attracted powerful backers. In 1955 Diem became president of the newly established Republic of Vietnam (South Vietnam) following a rigged election—in Saigon, Diem got more than 605,000 votes from the 450,000 registered voters! But Diem knew that he had no chance of winning a nationwide election against Ho. Thus, he refused to call an election in the south when the July 1956 date set by the Geneva Conference rolled around.

Diem, a Roman Catholic, was unpopular from the start. The large Buddhist population resented the favoritism he showed toward Catholics. Peasants disliked his land policies, which favored wealthy landholders. And almost everyone objected that power was solely in the grip of Diem's family. Above all, people feared his ruthless efforts to root out his political enemies. Diem's hated security forces routinely tortured and imprisoned opponents.

By the late 1950s armed revolution had erupted in the south. In 1959, military assistance began flowing from the north to the Vietminh who had stayed in the south. In 1960 the southern Vietminh formed the National Liberation Front (NLF). The NLF's main goal was the overthrow of the Ngo Dinh Diem regime. Members of this rebel force were called **Vietcong** (Vietnamese Communists) by their opponents, but not all NLF supporters were Communists.

Many peasants joined the ranks of the NLF, some because of government repression. Others joined out of fear: the NLF, like Diem's forces, used terrorist tactics, assassinating hundreds of government officials. Soon much of the countryside was under Vietcong control.

America's involvement deepens. John F. Kennedy, who became president in 1961, fully subscribed to the domino theory. He also was eager to bolster America's image in the world—an image that had been tarnished by the failed Bay of Pigs invasion and the Soviets' raising of the Berlin Wall early in his presidency (see Chapter 19). Coming to the aid of South Vietnam, which Kennedy had once called the "cornerstone of the Free World in Southeast Asia," provided America with a chance to assert its power.

When Kennedy took office, some 700 U.S. military advisers were in South Vietnam training

▼ Ngo Dinh Diem paces the floor of his Saigon palace after crushing an attempt to overthrow his regime in the spring of 1955.

Diem's army. Over the course of his administration, Kennedy increased that number to more than 16,000. As Vietcong attacks mounted, Kennedy authorized U.S. forces to engage in direct combat. As a result, the number of Americans killed or wounded climbed from 14 in 1961 to nearly 500 in 1963.

■■ **President Kennedy saw U.S. involvement in Vietnam as a way to halt the spread of communism and strengthen America's image in the world.**

Diem's overthrow. The situation was also escalating politically. South Vietnam's Buddhist leaders now openly opposed Diem's regime. Diem was waging a brutal campaign of repression against Buddhists. Hundreds had been arrested, and many had been killed in the crackdown. In response, several Buddhist monks publicly set themselves on fire. These grisly protests shocked Americans, and U.S. officials in Saigon threatened to withdraw support for Diem unless he ended the repression.

When Diem refused to comply, U.S. leaders gave quiet encouragement to a group of young South Vietnamese army officers plotting Diem's overthrow. The plotters struck in November 1963, murdering both Diem and his brother. Diem's violent assassination upset U.S. advisers, who had been prepared to fly Diem out of the country.

▲ On June 11, 1963, Quang Duc set himself on fire at a busy intersection in Saigon. He was the first of several Buddhist monks who killed themselves to protest Diem's policies.

Kennedy's doubts increase. Diem's overthrow did nothing to ease Kennedy's growing concern over America's involvement in Vietnam. In an interview shortly before Diem's fall, Kennedy had said of the South Vietnamese: "In the final analysis it is their war. They are the ones who have to win or lose it." But we will never know how Kennedy might have handled the situation. Three weeks after Diem's murder, Kennedy himself was assassinated in Dallas.

SECTION 1 REVIEW

IDENTIFY and explain the significance of the following: Ho Chi Minh, Vietminh, domino theory, Ngo Dinh Diem, Vietcong.

LOCATE and explain the importance of the following: Vietnam, China, Red River Delta, Mekong Delta, Hanoi, Saigon, central highlands, Annamite Mountains, Dien Bien Phu.

1. **MAIN IDEA** Why did President Truman refuse Ho's requests for help against the French?

2. **MAIN IDEA** What led President Kennedy to increase U.S. involvement in Vietnam?

3. **LINKING HISTORY AND GEOGRAPHY** What attracted the Chinese and the French to Vietnam?

4. **WRITING TO PERSUADE** Imagine you are an adviser to President Eisenhower in 1959. On the basis of what you would know at the time, prepare a statement outlining the pros and cons of U.S. involvement in Vietnam. Then, in a paragraph, make a policy recommendation.

5. **USING HISTORICAL IMAGINATION** In the 1941 Atlantic Charter, President Roosevelt and British Prime Minister Churchill pledged "to see sovereign rights and self-government restored to those who have been forcibly deprived of them." Imagine that you are Ho. Write a letter to President Truman explaining why America should honor this pledge in Vietnam.

THE WAR ESCALATES

■ **Why did the Tonkin Gulf Resolution raise a constitutional issue?**

■ **What factors frustrated U.S. military efforts in Vietnam?**

LBJ

"*I am not going to be the President who saw Vietnam go the way China went,*" *vowed Lyndon Baines Johnson, the next American president to inherit the Vietnam War. Throwing U.S. air power and thousands of young American troops into the conflict, Johnson hoped to end the war quickly. But the war in Vietnam would dominate the nation's consciousness for nearly a decade.*

THE TONKIN GULF RESOLUTION

The new South Vietnamese government was just as corrupt and ineffective as Diem's, and the NLF continued to gain ground against the South's army (called the ARVN, for Army of the Republic of Vietnam). Secretary of Defense Robert McNamara, a cabinet member held over from the Kennedy administration, returned from a quick trip to Vietnam in December 1963 to give his new boss a sobering report. To prevent a Communist victory, McNamara advised, Johnson would have to increase the American commitment.

A Communist victory in Vietnam was an unthinkable prospect for Johnson. Like previous presidents, he firmly believed it was necessary to stop Communist expansion. Before increasing the U.S. commitment, however, Johnson planned to get congressional backing. Events on the seas off North Vietnam soon gave him the opportunity.

In August 1964 President Johnson announced that U.S. ships had been attacked twice in the Gulf of Tonkin. The president asked Congress to authorize the use of military force "to prevent further aggression." In an overwhelming show of patriotism, Congress passed the **Tonkin Gulf Resolution**, giving the president authority to take "all necessary measures to repel any armed attack against forces of the United States."

Johnson claimed that the attacks in the Gulf of Tonkin were "unprovoked." Later it was revealed that one of the ships, the destroyer *Maddox,* had been engaged in spying in support of South Vietnamese raids against North Vietnam and had fired first. Thus, the first North Vietnamese attack was not without cause. The second, moreover, probably never occurred: it appeared that nervous sailors, caught in stormy weather, had misinterpreted interference on their radar and sonar as enemy ships and torpedoes. Nonetheless, Johnson and his advisers got what they wanted: authority to expand the war as they saw fit. As Johnson admitted later, the resolution was "like Grandma's nightshirt—it covered everything."

Only a few in Congress voiced caution. Wayne Morse of Oregon, one of only two senators to vote against the Tonkin Gulf Resolution, warned: "I believe that history will record we have made a great mistake. . . . We are in effect giving the President war-making powers in the absence of a declaration of war." In other words, in passing the resolution, Congress had given up its constitutional power to declare war.

■■ **The Tonkin Gulf Resolution allowed American presidents to fight an undeclared war in Vietnam—contrary to the intent of the U.S. Constitution.**

AMERICAN FORCES IN VIETNAM

With the Tonkin Gulf Resolution in his pocket, President Johnson responded to his advisers' call for a buildup, or **escalation**, of American military forces in Vietnam. He ordered the Selective Service, the agency charged with carrying out the military draft, to begin calling up young men to serve in the armed forces. In April 1965 the Selective Service notified 13,700 draftees, and by December some 40,000 had received "greetings" from their local draft boards.

During the war more than 2.6 million Americans served in Vietnam. In the beginning most were professional soldiers, already enlisted in the armed forces. But as the demand for troops grew, more and more draftees were shipped to Vietnam. At the height of the war, American soldiers in Vietnam were, on average, younger (19), poorer, and less educated than those who had served in World War II or in the Korean War.

All young men who registered for the draft did not have an equal chance of serving in Vietnam. One out of four was excused from service for health reasons. Another 30 percent received non-health-related exemptions or deferments (postponements of service), most often for college enrollment. Mainly because of college deferments, young men from higher-income families were the least likely to be drafted. As a result, the poor served in numbers far greater than their proportion in the general population—as they had in most of the previous wars.

African and Hispanic Americans served in combat in especially high numbers, particularly during the early years of the war. Some of these soldiers protested that black and Hispanic soldiers were being asked to do more than their share of the fighting—and dying. In 1965, for example, African Americans accounted for almost 24 percent of all battle deaths, even though they made up only 11 percent of the U.S. population.

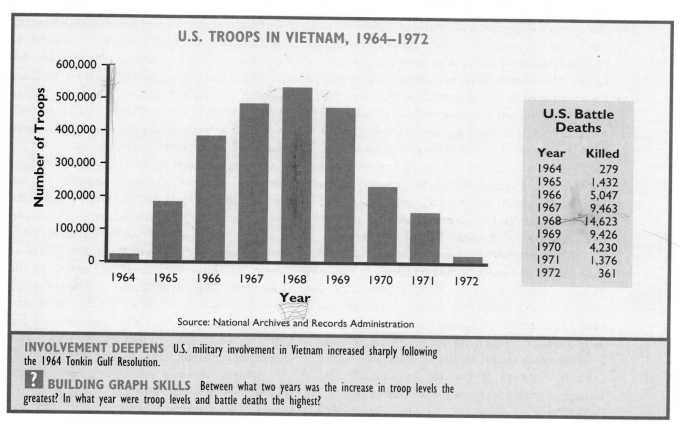

U.S. TROOPS IN VIETNAM, 1964–1972

Number of Troops (y-axis): 0, 100,000, 200,000, 300,000, 400,000, 500,000, 600,000
Year (x-axis): 1964, 1965, 1966, 1967, 1968, 1969, 1970, 1971, 1972

U.S. Battle Deaths	
Year	**Killed**
1964	279
1965	1,432
1966	5,047
1967	9,463
1968	14,623
1969	9,426
1970	4,230
1971	1,376
1972	361

Source: National Archives and Records Administration

INVOLVEMENT DEEPENS U.S. military involvement in Vietnam increased sharply following the 1964 Tonkin Gulf Resolution.

❓ **BUILDING GRAPH SKILLS** Between what two years was the increase in troop levels the greatest? In what year were troop levels and battle deaths the highest?

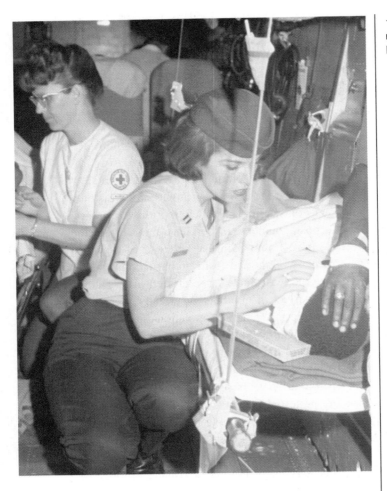

Navarra Rhoads, who served in the Army Nurse Corps, later described how complete this detachment could become:

> 66 I remember I had completed this amputation and I had the soldier's leg under my arm. I was holding the leg because I had to dress it up and give it to graves registration. . . . This nurse came in and she was scheduled to take the place of another nurse. When she saw me, I went to greet her and I had this leg under my arm. She collapsed on the ground in a dead faint. I thought, "What could possibly be wrong with her?" There I was trying to figure out what's wrong with her, not realizing that here I had this leg with a combat boot still on and half this man's combat fatigue still on, blood dripping over the exposed end. 99

THE AIR WAR

When Johnson sent troops to Vietnam in 1965, he did not anticipate the type of war that Rhoads described. He hoped to use air power to secure a quick victory. Like many of his advisers, the president expected prolonged bombing to pressure the North Vietnamese into negotiating. Toward this end, Johnson launched **Operation Rolling Thunder**, a campaign against military targets in the North, in February 1965. He closely oversaw the operation, boasting that the pilots "can't even bomb an outhouse without my approval."

Though weakening the enemy's will to fight was the air war's eventual goal, Johnson had two more-immediate aims. First, he wanted to assure the South Vietnamese of America's commitment. Second, he wanted to destroy Vietcong supply lines. Weapons and supplies from North Vietnam were coming into South Vietnam by way of the **Ho Chi Minh Trail**. The trail had begun as a network of jungle paths, some of which snaked through nearby Laos and Cambodia. By 1965 North Vietnam had begun converting the trail into a sophisticated communications and transportation system.

Johnson was therefore anxious to bomb the trail. Roads and bridges built to handle heavy trucks were bombed repeatedly, but the resourceful

The most vivid images of the war are of soldiers facing the rigors and terrors of battle. Some confronted the enemy in well-defined battles in the highlands. Others cut their way through the jungle, hearing but seldom seeing the enemy. Still others waded through rice paddies and searched rural villages for guerrilla bands. But most Americans who went to Vietnam were not assigned to combat units. Instead, they served in the thousands of support positions needed to keep the war machine moving: administration, supply and transportation, engineering, medical care, and communications. They were hardly safe, however. Enemy rockets and mortars could—and did—strike anywhere.

Some 10,000 servicewomen were among those who functioned in noncombat positions in Vietnam, most as nurses. Though they did not carry guns into battle, they faced combat horrors daily; eight gave their lives. Another 20,000 to 45,000 women worked in civilian capacities, many as volunteers for humanitarian organizations such as the Red Cross. Like soldiers in the field, these women had to detach themselves from the pain and suffering of war in order to cope. Jacqueline

Vietcong quickly repaired them or made do without them. They constructed many facilities underground as protection against bombing. Some 300,000 people, armed primarily with shovels, worked full time to maintain and expand the Ho Chi Minh Trail.

The U.S. military had estimated that the bombing would bring about North Vietnam's collapse within weeks. When this did not happen, Johnson increased the bombing. By 1967 U.S. fighter bombers were dropping an average of 800 tons of bombs on North Vietnam daily—bombing so heavy that in areas the landscape resembled the cratered surface of the moon. But each escalation failed to bring about the desired results. Frustrated, President Johnson broadened the air war to include strikes against areas of bordering Laos and much of South Vietnam.

In this wider air war, U.S. forces used a variety of deadly weapons, such as napalm—a jellied gasoline mixture used in firebombs—and the "cluster bomb"—which sprayed razor-sharp metal fragments when it exploded. America's arsenal also included **defoliants**, chemicals designed to strip the land of vegetation. The most widely used of these chemicals was Agent Orange. U.S. planes sprayed defoliants over thousands of acres in efforts to expose jungle supply routes and enemy hiding places and to rob the Vietcong of food.

THE GROUND WAR

Although the air war was designed to bring U.S. involvement in Vietnam quickly to an end, it had the opposite effect: North Vietnam—rather than surrendering—sent more troops and supplies south. Because of the widespread bombing, increasing numbers of South Vietnamese joined the ranks of the NLF. Soon the opposition forces included more South Vietnamese than North Vietnamese. The United States countered by launching a ground war. Between March 1965 and the end of 1967, U.S. troop strength grew from some 3,500 to some 486,000.

But sheer numbers were not enough to defeat an enemy who seemed to be everywhere. The NLF, aided by regulars of the North Vietnamese Army (NVA), struck at U.S. patrols or government-held villages and then melted back into the jungle. Vietnamese peasants who appeared peaceful during the day sided with the Vietcong at night.

The Americans conducted thousands of **search-and-destroy missions** in attempts to flush the Vietcong from their hideouts. U.S. ground patrols first located the enemy and then called in air

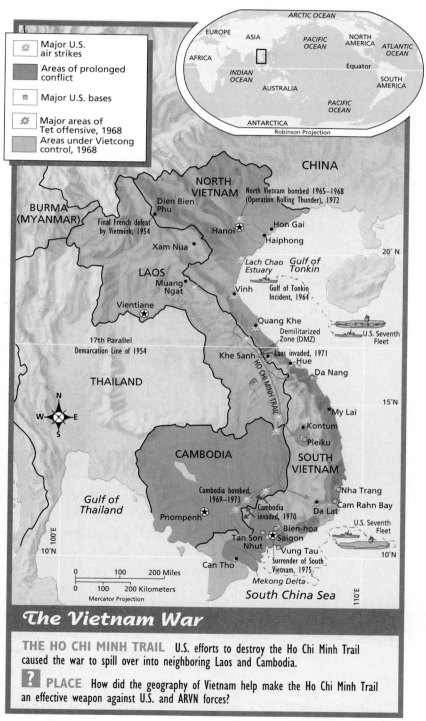

The Vietnam War

THE HO CHI MINH TRAIL U.S. efforts to destroy the Ho Chi Minh Trail caused the war to spill over into neighboring Laos and Cambodia.

? PLACE How did the geography of Vietnam help make the Ho Chi Minh Trail an effective weapon against U.S. and ARVN forces?

▶ Trip-wire-activated crossbow traps were one of many kinds of booby traps faced by combat soldiers in the jungles of Vietnam.

support to eliminate them. Once an area was "cleared," the patrols moved on in search of more Vietcong. Snipers and booby traps—from mines to animal snares to pits lined with stakes—made these missions extremely dangerous and frustrating. And villages seldom remained cleared of the NLF.

To deny the enemy any territorial gain, American forces targeted many villages for **pacification**: they moved the residents to refugee camps or cities and then burned the villages. In such warfare, progress could not be shown on a map. Instead, the daily body count of enemy dead became the sole measure of success—and a questionable measure at that. The U.S. military regularly guessed at or inflated the numbers. Said one officer responsible for body-count statistics: "If it's dead and Vietnamese, it's Vietcong."

AMERICAN MORALE EBBS

The first U.S. troops had arrived in a hopeful mood. As surely as they carried their packs and rifles, one soldier recalled, they held the "conviction that the Vietcong would be quickly beaten." Most also believed that the cause—defeating communism in South Vietnam —was honorable. This optimistic mood began to fade as the hazards of fighting a nearly invisible foe in an alien landscape sank in.

Equally frustrating was the enemy's will to fight on despite mounting casualties. U.S. war planners believed that superior American technology would win the war. Yet as 1967 ended, success seemed no closer than in 1963. Ho's earlier ominous warning to the French now seemed applicable to Americans: "You can kill ten of my men for every one I kill of yours, but even at those odds, you will lose and I will win."

■■ **U.S. forces were frustrated by their inability to disrupt Vietcong supply lines or make progress against an enemy that melted into the jungle.**

SECTION 2 REVIEW

IDENTIFY and explain the significance of each of the following: Tonkin Gulf Resolution, escalation, Operation Rolling Thunder, Ho Chi Minh Trail, defoliants, search-and-destroy missions, pacification.

LOCATE and explain the importance of the following: Gulf of Tonkin.

1. **MAIN IDEA** Why did Senator Wayne Morse believe Congress had made a grave mistake in passing the Tonkin Gulf Resolution?

2. **RECOGNIZING POINTS OF VIEW** Why did some people believe the draft was unfair?

3. **GEOGRAPHY: PLACE** How did Vietnam's geography contribute to the U.S. military's inability to defeat the Vietcong?

4. **WRITING TO DESCRIBE** Imagine you are a reporter in Vietnam in 1966. Write a short article describing the conditions faced by U.S. military and civilian personnel in Vietnam.

5. **ANALYZING** Why can it be said that Johnson's attempt to end the war quickly had the opposite effect?

AMERICANS DIVIDED

FOCUS

- **What were the main reasons some Americans opposed the war?**
- **Why did some Americans label antiwar protesters as disloyal?**

*B*y the end of 1967, over 16,000 Americans had been killed in Vietnam. Thousands more had been injured or disabled. And despite the government's optimistic forecasts, a U.S. victory seemed increasingly distant, if not out of reach. The fighting dragged on, frustrating soldiers and citizens alike. Gruesome TV images of terrified Vietnamese civilians and dead or injured soldiers brought the fighting home. Some people responded by demanding that the military be allowed to do whatever it took to win; others wanted America to pull out of Vietnam.

Peace button

THE MEDIA AND THE WAR

The Vietnam War invaded American homes in ways no previous conflict had. Free of the tight press restrictions imposed by the military during previous wars, war correspondents, photographers, and TV camera crews accompanied soldiers on patrol and interviewed people throughout South Vietnam. Television beamed footage and reports of the war into people's homes on a nightly basis. As a result, Americans saw images that seemed to contradict the government's optimistic reports.

Although such reporters as David Halberstam of the *New York Times* and Neil Sheehan of United Press International did not, in the beginning, question the goal of containing communism, they did criticize the government's optimism. As early as 1962 they argued that the war was not being won and could not be won so long as America supported the unpopular and corrupt Diem. They also reported on the ineffective-ness of ARVN troops and accused the U.S. government of inflating enemy body counts to show progress.

▲ Television images of the war, compellingly reported by correspondents such as Morley Safer, shown here, became a nightly feature of news programs.

As the war dragged on, the opposition to the war included many Vietnam veterans.

THE ANTIWAR MOVEMENT

A variety of pacifist, religious, civil rights, and student groups shaped the antiwar movement. Among these were peace groups such as Women Strike for Peace and the National Committee for a Sane Nuclear Policy and radical student groups like Students for a Democratic Society (SDS). The movement attracted a broad range of people. Doctors, teachers, ministers, and other professionals joined housewives, retired citizens, and students to protest the war.

SDS and campus protests. By the end of 1965, the SDS had members on 124 college campuses. Though it was only one of many groups opposing the war, in the minds of many Americans, the SDS *was* the antiwar movement. At colleges across the United States, the SDS and other student groups and faculty members held antiwar rallies and debates. These groups particularly criticized the involvement of universities in research and development for the military. They also protested the draft, the presence of the Reserve Officers Training Corps (ROTC) on campus, and the recruitment efforts by the armed services, the CIA, and such defense contractors as Dow Chemical, the manufacturer of napalm.

The antiwar movement builds. The SDS organized the first national antiwar demonstration—held in Washington, D.C., on April 17, 1965. More than 20,000 people participated. After an afternoon of speeches and singing, the crowd marched on the Capitol and delivered to Congress a petition demanding that lawmakers "act immediately to end the war." Because it drew far more people than expected, the march spurred on the antiwar movement. Over the next decade, countless demonstrators, employing tactics largely borrowed from the civil rights movement, protested U.S. involvement in Southeast Asia.

Linking the war to poverty and racism. Civil rights activists were among the most outspoken critics of the war. In 1967 the Reverend Martin Luther King, Jr., spoke of how the war was stealing resources from poverty pro-

HAWKS VERSUS DOVES

As the gap between what the government said and what people saw and read widened, doubts at home increased. The administration found itself criticized by both **doves**—people who opposed the war—and **hawks**—people who supported the war's goals. Hawks criticized the way the war was being fought, arguing for more U.S. troops and heavier bombing. Air Force general Curtis LeMay expressed the frustration of many hawks: "Here we are at the height of our power. The most powerful nation in the world. And yet we're afraid to use that power, we lack the will."

Doves opposed the war on many grounds. Pacifists, such as the Reverend Martin Luther King, Jr., believed that all war was wrong. Some doves, such as diplomat George Kennan, were convinced that Vietnam was not crucial to national security. Others objected to the Vietnam War in particular, fearing that the United States might resort to nuclear weapons. Prominent among the war's opponents was the respected pediatrician and author Dr. Benjamin Spock. He and others argued that America was fighting against the wishes of a majority of Vietnamese.

grams and how that fact heightened his opposition to U.S. involvement in Vietnam:

> 66 I watched the program broken and eviscerated [gutted] as if it were some idle political plaything of a society gone mad on war, and I knew that America would never invest the necessary funds or energies in rehabilitation of its poor so long as Vietnam continued to draw men and skills and money like some demonic, destructive suction tube. 99

Many civil rights activists voiced concern that the U.S. government was sending young African American men off to war in great numbers yet doing little to end racism at home. The Student Nonviolent Coordinating Committee (SNCC), founded in 1960 by African Americans to promote racial equality, expressed the views of growing numbers of blacks:

> 66 We take note of the fact that 16 percent of the draftees from this country are Negro, called on to stifle the liberation of Vietnam, to preserve a "democracy" which does not exist for them at home. We ask: Where is the draft for the freedom fight in the United States? 99

By 1968 blacks were twice as likely as whites to label themselves as doves.

■■ **The antiwar movement focused on two points: Did the United States have the right to be in Vietnam? Were the sacrifices in lives and domestic programs worth the nation's presence there?**

PROTEST VERSUS SUPPORT

Despite their high visibility, antiwar protesters made up a small percentage of the U.S. population. Many Americans opposed the movement, especially its more extreme factions. Some believed that fighting for one's country was a patriotic duty. Others objected to the antiwar movement's tactics. People found certain acts of protest, such as burning the American flag, occupying buildings, and burning draft cards, particularly upsetting. Many veterans of past wars were angered by young men who went to prison rather than serve in the military or who fled to Canada to avoid the draft.

Though most Americans who disagreed with the antiwar movement expressed their opposition in private, some organized counterdemonstrations. Demonstrators at these rallies often carried signs proclaiming "America, Love It or Leave It" or "My Country, Right or Wrong."

■■ **Many Americans saw protesters as disloyal. Some believed it was a citizen's patriotic duty to serve in the armed forces. Others objected to antiwar tactics.**

GOVERNMENT CONFLICT

President Johnson and his advisers responded to antiwar protesters by insisting that the United States was helping to defend its ally in Saigon against aggression. If America failed to support South

▲ Demonstrations were also organized by those in favor of U.S. policies in Vietnam, such as this rally of the Young Americans for Freedom.

Vietnam, asked Secretary of State Dean Rusk, what U.S. ally would ever trust the country again?

But the administration also faced criticism in Congress. Doves, such as Senator J. William Fulbright of Arkansas, head of the Foreign Relations Committee, sharply criticized the Johnson administration's policies as too extreme. Fulbright held congressional hearings in 1966 to give the war's critics a forum. These televised hearings gave the antiwar position more credibility with mainstream Americans.

Even within Johnson's circle of advisers, gnawing doubts surfaced. Several senior staffers expressed misgivings about the administration's conduct of the war. Most troubling to the president was the turnabout of his secretary of defense, Robert McNamara.

By age 44 Robert S. McNamara had already reached the top of the corporate ladder. He was the new president of the Ford Motor Company, the first person to hold that position who was not a descendant of Henry Ford. Then in 1960, after only 34 days in his new job, McNamara received a call inviting him to become secretary of defense for the Kennedy administration.

With his impressive analytical skills, the intense, bespectacled secretary of defense persuaded

Robert McNamara

generals, legislators, national security advisers—and presidents—to follow his military advice. During the policy debates that led to the escalation of the war, it was McNamara—perhaps more than any other individual—who set America's course. Said Clark Clifford, who later succeeded him as secretary of defense: "McNamara held the key to the President's decision" to grant the military's 1965 request for more troops.

McNamara's many recommendations had failed, however, to achieve their results. As each optimistic forecast proved to be no more than wishful thinking, his confidence slipped; by October 1967 it had eroded altogether. McNamara leveled with President Johnson, telling him that "continuation of our present course of action in Southeast Asia would be dangerous, costly in lives, and unsatisfactory to the American people." But the policy that McNamara had helped shape was firmly entrenched, and Johnson was determined to stay with it. Within days Johnson had eased McNamara out of his cabinet position.

▶ **McNamara sits alone after a presidential press conference announcing further troop shipments to Vietnam.**

Lyndon Baines Johnson Library

SECTION 3 REVIEW

IDENTIFY and explain the significance of each of the following: doves, hawks, Reverend Martin Luther King, Jr., J. William Fulbright, Robert S. McNamara.

1. **MAIN IDEA** Why did some Americans oppose the war?

2. **MAIN IDEA** Why did the antiwar movement trouble some Americans?

3. **WRITING TO PERSUADE** Imagine you are a U.S. senator in 1967 and are either a hawk or a dove. Write the president a letter persuading him to support your view and to change his policies accordingly.

4. **EVALUATING** What roles do you think television coverage and economic and social conditions at home played in shaping American views toward the Vietnam War?

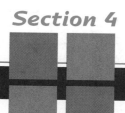

WAR AT FULL TIDE

FOCUS

■ **Why did the Tet offensive weaken many Americans' confidence in their government?**

■ **What were the key events of the 1968 presidential campaign?**

■ **How did Nixon set out to end the war? How did Americans react to this plan?**

The year 1968 was a troubled one. It began with a massive military offensive by the NLF and the North Vietnamese that shattered many Americans' confidence in Johnson's handling of the war. Demonstrations and violent riots followed. By year's end some 15,000 more Americans had died in Vietnam, and LBJ's political career lay in ruin. Republican Richard Nixon, who claimed to have a plan to end the war and "win the peace," won the White House. Nixon slowly withdrew U.S. troops from Vietnam, but increased the pace of U.S. bombing. And when Nixon ordered the invasion of Cambodia in 1970, war protests at home surged to a new high.

Captured NVA weapons

THE TET OFFENSIVE

January 30, 1968, was the start of Tet, the Vietnamese New Year. In past years the holiday had been honored by a lull in fighting. However, late that night, as most South Vietnamese and their U.S. allies slept, NLF guerrillas and North Vietnamese troops crept from their jungle camps and city hideouts to execute a carefully planned strike. Within hours countless villages, more than 100 cities, and 12 U.S. military bases came under attack from nearly 70,000 Communist soldiers (see map, page 529). Heavy fighting raged in such U.S. strongholds as Saigon and Da Nang. At one point the Vietcong even occupied the courtyard of the U.S. Embassy.

North Vietnam expected the **Tet offensive** to bring down the government in the South as the

people rallied behind their "liberators." But Hanoi was disappointed. When the assault was over, more than a month later, an estimated 40,000 Communist soldiers lay dead.

General William Westmoreland, commander of U.S. forces in Vietnam, hastened to describe the offensive as a Vietcong defeat. In a military sense, the general had a point. At a cost of 2,000 American and 4,000 ARVN lives, most of the attackers had been repelled. But despite suffering heavy losses, the NLF remained strong in many places. They had faced overwhelming U.S. fire-power and were still standing—more determined than ever to fight on.

Even more important was the political effect the offensive had on the United States. Tet jarred American confidence by showing that no part of South Vietnam was secure—not even downtown Saigon. Walter Cronkite, anchor of the *CBS*

▲ An emotionally drained Johnson listens to a tape recording made by his son-in-law describing his duty in Vietnam.

Lyndon Baines Johnson Library

Evening News, expressed America's bewildered mood: "I thought we were winning the war! What the hell is going on?" To one of his aides, President Johnson groaned: "If I've lost Walter, then it's all over. I've lost Mr. Average American."

After Tet, public criticism of the war rose dramatically. Such influential magazines as *Time* and *Newsweek* not only expressed misgivings about the war but also called for its end. Largely because of the shift in public opinion, Johnson denied Westmoreland's urgent request for 206,000 more troops. Though granting a small increase, LBJ made it clear there would be no more.

■■ **The Tet offensive dealt a double blow: it indicated that U.S. leaders had misled the public, and it exposed severe flaws in U.S. military operations in Vietnam.**

THE ELECTION OF 1968

In the wake of the Tet offensive, three out of four Americans disapproved of Johnson's conduct of the war. Early in the 1968 Democratic presidential campaign, antiwar candidate Senator Eugene McCarthy of Minnesota took advantage of this growing dissatisfaction and challenged LBJ. In the March New Hampshire primary, McCarthy won almost as many votes as Johnson.

McCarthy's impressive showing drew another leading critic of the war into the race: Senator Robert F. Kennedy of New York (brother of the slain President Kennedy and former U.S. attorney general himself). RFK's large national following, especially among African Americans, Hispanics, the young, and the poor, made him a strong contender for the Democratic nomination. Shaken by the division within his party, LBJ shocked the nation on March 31. Physically and emotionally exhausted, Johnson announced he would not seek reelection, saying he wished to spend his last months in office trying to end the war.

LBJ's withdrawal from the race left it wide open. Senators McCarthy and Kennedy and Vice President Hubert Humphrey went head-to-head in several state primaries. Kennedy won most of them, particularly the crucial California primary in June. He seemed destined to be the Democratic nominee. But on the night of his California victory, after delivering a speech in a hotel ballroom, RFK was shot. The next day he died—victim of a bullet fired by Sirhan Sirhan, a young Jordanian immigrant. A nation already in shock over the murder of the Reverend Martin Luther King, Jr., two months earlier (see Chapter 19) now had to come to grips with another assassination.

Society seemed to be spinning out of control. Amid the turmoil, the Democrats met in Chicago to settle on a candidate for the November election. The convention was a dispirited affair. President Johnson did not even attend, fearful of the reaction he would cause. And throughout the convention memories of the fallen Robert Kennedy remained hauntingly alive for the demoralized delegates. Vice President Humphrey, despite his close identification with Johnson, received the nomination. He chose Senator Edmund Muskie of Maine as his running mate.

The Democrats' difficulties were underscored by the chaos on the streets outside the convention. Some 10,000 antiwar protesters had massed in the city and camped in Grant Park, across from the hotel where many delegates were lodged. Of all the college students, longtime activists, and ordinary citizens opposed to the war, perhaps a few hundred came prepared for violent confrontation. In the sweltering August heat, they held rallies, chanting "Hell No! We Won't Go!" and taunting police with shouts of "Pig!"

Outraged to see his city overrun by people he viewed as dangerous revolutionaries, Chicago mayor Richard J. Daley ordered helmeted Chicago police to clear out the protesters. The police attacked on the night of August 28, clubbing protesters and using tear gas to disperse the crowd. Hundreds were injured; hundreds more were hauled to jail. Reporters, passersby, and police were also injured in the fray.

The violent spectacle of protest and police brutality at the Chicago convention raised Republicans' hopes of capturing the White House. At their convention in Miami Beach, the upbeat mood of Republican delegates matched the Florida sunshine. A familiar figure dominated the convention: Richard Nixon. After his defeat by Kennedy in 1960, Nixon also lost a bid for the governorship of California. But since then he had kept in the public eye.

Appealing to what he called the "silent majority" of patriotic Americans, Richard Nixon easily won the nomination. He chose Maryland governor Spiro Agnew as his running mate. Promising a "law-and-order" crackdown on urban crime, Nixon appealed for support to those Americans who neither approved of the disorderly antiwar protests nor wanted a U.S. defeat in Vietnam. Nixon told voters he had a plan to end the Vietnam War, though he revealed no details.

> ■■ **LBJ's withdrawal and RFK's assassination left Humphrey in an uphill struggle against Nixon in the 1968 presidential campaign.**

As election day neared, Humphrey's campaign picked up steam, boosted somewhat by LBJ's announcement in late October of a bombing halt. But time ran out for the Democrats, though the results were close: of 73 million votes cast, Richard Nixon received only some 500,000 more than Hubert Humphrey. Nixon's margin in the electoral college was much wider, however: he carried 32 states to Humphrey's 13. Former Alabama governor George Wallace, who campaigned as the candidate

▼ **Outside the Democratic Convention, Chicago police battled antiwar demonstrators.**

of the newly formed American Independent party, got some 10 million votes and won 5 states of the Deep South.

NIXON, VIETNAMIZATION, AND CAMBODIA

President Nixon gave foreign affairs his top priority. His key foreign-policy adviser was Henry Kissinger. Together they took important steps to improve relations with Communist China and the Soviet Union (see Chapter 21). But in 1969 Vietnam loomed as the most urgent problem, and Americans watched to see whether Nixon could fulfill his campaign pledge to end the war.

Part of Nixon's end-the-war plan was called **Vietnamization**. It involved turning over the fighting to the South Vietnamese as U.S. troops were gradually pulled out. This strategy, said Nixon, would bring "peace with honor." At best, Nixon hoped, Vietnamization might produce a stable anti-Communist South Vietnam. At worst, it would delay a collapse long enough to spare America the humiliation of outright defeat.

Nixon also hoped that Vietnamization was the key to removing a major obstacle to a peace agreement. The North Vietnamese had warned first Johnson and then Nixon that the United States would have to set a date for troop removals if peace talks were to continue. In February 1970, as U.S. troop withdrawals mounted, Henry Kissinger began meeting secretly in Paris with long-time revolutionary Le Duc Tho (làyd uhk TOH) of North Vietnam.

When Nixon took office, U.S. troop strength in Vietnam stood at about 540,000. He soon ordered a withdrawal of some 25,000 soldiers. Over the next four years, many more came home. But the process was slow. At the end of 1972, about 24,200 Americans still remained in Vietnam.

Publicly, Nixon emphasized Vietnamization; secretly, however, he planned to widen the war—into Cambodia. North Vietnam had been staging troops along the border in neutral Cambodia—safe from U.S. attack—while sending supplies and troops south through Cambodia on the Ho Chi Minh Trail.

Early in 1969 Nixon ordered the widespread bombing of Cambodia. He hoped to destroy North Vietnamese supplies and trails—in line with Johnson's original war aims. He also wanted to send a signal to Hanoi that the United States was still willing to use force, and even expand the war, in pursuit of Nixon's aim of "peace with honor." Nixon and Kissinger concealed the Cambodian air strikes from Congress, the American people, and key military leaders—even the secretary of the air force.

Because of Cambodia's neutrality, Nixon feared an international uproar. But when a coup ousted Cambodia's ruler in March 1970, Nixon's policy changed. Since the new Cambodian government was pro-American, he made his policy public and justified the air strikes as defense of a friendly nation. Nixon then sent some 80,000 U.S. and ARVN troops into Cambodia.

The invasion destroyed the delicate balance that had kept Cambodia out of the war. NVA troops were forced into the interior of Cambodia, where battles with U.S. and ARVN forces destroyed much of the countryside.

ANTIWAR PROTEST INCREASES

News of the bombing and invasion of Cambodia provoked outrage in the United States, particularly on college campuses. When students at Kent State University in Ohio set fire to the campus ROTC building, Ohio's governor vowed to "eradicate" the protesters. On May 4, 1970, National Guard troops sent to control demonstrators shot into a group of students, killing four and injuring nine—some of whom were merely walking across campus.

Ten days later, state police in Jackson, Mississippi, fired at protesters in a dormitory at Jackson State College, killing two students and wounding nine. In outrage at these brutalities, students and faculty on hundreds of college campuses went on strike.

The Cambodian invasion also shocked members of Congress. They too had believed that American involvement in Southeast Asia was ending. Questioning Nixon's constitutional right to extend the war, Congress repealed the Tonkin Gulf Resolution in December 1970. Nixon insisted, however, that this action did not affect his authority to carry on the war. Congressional leaders responded by developing plans to stop the war by ending funding once U.S. troops were withdrawn.

In 1971 another incident sparked the antiwar movement. The *New York Times* began publishing a collection of secret government documents relating to the war. Known as the **Pentagon Papers**, they showed that the government had frequently misled the American people about the course of the war. The documents were leaked to the press by Daniel Ellsberg, a former Defense Department official, who had been strongly prowar until

◀ Four Kent State students were killed during a confrontation between National Guardsmen and some 3,000 rioters.

spending time in Vietnam studying the effects of the war. While there, he found that few South Vietnamese supported their government. President Nixon tried to block publication of the Pentagon Papers but was unsuccessful.

■■ **Many Americans responded in anger when President Nixon coupled Vietnamization with an invasion of Cambodia.**

THE WAR GOES ON

As commander in chief, President Nixon ordered not only the invasion of Cambodia but also the renewed bombing of North Vietnam, which President Johnson had stopped. Extending the bombings into areas that had been off-limits was part of what the president called the "Madman Theory." As Nixon explained to his chief of staff, H. R. (Bob) Haldeman:

❝ I call it the Madman Theory, Bob. I want the North Vietnamese to believe that I've reached the point where I might do anything to stop the war. We'll just slip the word to them that, "for God's sake, you know Nixon is obsessed about Communists. We can't restrain him when he's angry—and he has his hand on the nuclear button"—and Ho Chi Minh himself will be in Paris in two days begging for peace. ❞

▲ **Nixon visits U.S. troops in Vietnam.**

Nixon's method was based on his belief that Eisenhower's hints that he might use the atomic bomb had helped end the Korean War. But Nixon miscalculated the opposition's endurance. Rather than ending, the war suddenly grew more fierce.

Hoping to reveal the weaknesses of Nixon's Vietnamization strategy, North Vietnam staged a major invasion of the South in March 1972. NVA troops drove deep into South Vietnam. Nixon responded by ordering heavy bombing of the North, including Hanoi. He also ordered the mining of Haiphong Harbor to prevent Soviet ships from delivering military supplies. Despite these steps, the opposition now held more territory in South Vietnam than ever.

SECTION 4 REVIEW

IDENTIFY and explain the significance of each of the following: Tet offensive, William Westmoreland, Eugene McCarthy, Robert F. Kennedy, Richard Nixon, Henry Kissinger, Vietnamization, Le Duc Tho, Pentagon Papers.

LOCATE and explain the importance of the following: Haiphong Harbor.

1. **MAIN IDEA** How did Richard Nixon plan to end the war?

2. **MAIN IDEA** How did the 1968 election signal American dissatisfaction with the war effort?

3. **MAIN IDEA** What Nixon policies led to renewed antiwar protests?

4. **WRITING TO INFORM** Imagine you are Nixon's press agent. Write a news release explaining the reasons for bombing Cambodia.

5. **TAKING A STAND** In wartime, should the U.S. government make all information about the war available to its citizens? Why or why not?

THE CEASE–FIRE AND AFTER

FOCUS

■ **Why did the United States agree to a cease-fire in January 1973?**

■ **What factors contributed to America's inability to win the war?**

■ **What long-term effects did the war have on the Vietnamese and American people?**

In 1972 Vietnam again dominated the presidential campaign. Although the war was not yet over, Richard Nixon overwhelmed his antiwar opponent, Democratic senator George McGovern. By early 1973 a cease-fire was signed, finally ending America's most bitterly divisive episode since the Civil War. But the Vietnam War's painful legacy remains.

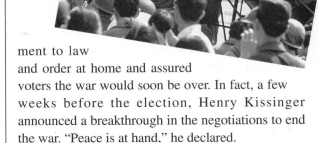

The fall of Saigon, April 1975

NIXON'S REELECTION

Senator George McGovern of South Dakota campaigned in the 1972 Democratic presidential primary as an antiwar candidate. An air force pilot in World War II, McGovern had been a history professor before going into politics. His opposition to the war ran deep. In one emotional Senate speech he declared in a trembling voice: "This chamber reeks of blood." George Wallace opposed McGovern for the Democratic nomination. While at a political rally in Maryland in May, however, Wallace was shot. The injury paralyzed him from the waist down, and he withdrew from the race.

After the disastrous 1968 convention, the Democrats adopted new rules that increased representation of minorities, women, and young people in party organizations. The **Twenty-sixth Amendment**, passed in 1971, had lowered the voting age from 21 to 18. McGovern drew much of his support from these groups, and at the convention he easily captured the nomination.

The Republicans renominated Nixon and Agnew. Nixon again stressed his strong commitment to law and order at home and assured voters the war would soon be over. In fact, a few weeks before the election, Henry Kissinger announced a breakthrough in the negotiations to end the war. "Peace is at hand," he declared.

Nixon won the election by a landslide—47 million votes to 29 million for McGovern. In the electoral college, McGovern carried only Massachusetts and the District of Columbia.

A CEASE-FIRE AT LAST

For more than three years Henry Kissinger and North Vietnam's Le Duc Tho had engaged in difficult peace negotiations. Finally, in October 1972 North Vietnam offered a peace plan that Kissinger and President Nixon found generally acceptable. The plan included a cease-fire and pullout of all foreign troops from Vietnam, an end to U.S.

military aid, and the creation of a new government in South Vietnam that included Nguyen (en-gy-EN) Van Thieu (the current president), representatives of the NLF, and "neutrals." Thieu, who had not been included in the negotiations, objected to the proposed government, seeing it as a loss of power. Rather than abandon Thieu, the United States rejected the agreement.

When North Vietnam demanded that the agreement be reinstated, Nixon responded by ordering around-the-clock bombing of Hanoi and Haiphong. A furious Nixon declared to the chairman of the Joint Chiefs of Staff: "This is your chance to use military power to win this war, and if you don't, I'll consider you responsible." Some 40,000 tons of bombs rained on the two cities for nearly two weeks, with the barrage only halting for Christmas Day. But the intensive bombing did not sway the North Vietnamese. At the end of December, Nixon called off the bombing and agreed to resume talks.

On January 27, 1973, the negotiators in Paris announced a cease-fire. Although the plan scarcely differed from the one hammered out in October, minor changes allowed each side to claim a diplomatic victory. The United States pledged to withdraw its remaining forces from South Vietnam and to help rebuild Vietnam. The peace settlement also included a prisoner-exchange agreement. It did not, however, address the major issue behind the war—the political future of Vietnam. In urging Thieu to accept the cease-fire, Nixon secretly pledged that if fighting resumed, the United States would come to South Vietnam's aid.

■■ The United States agreed to a cease-fire in January 1973, after heavy bombing failed to sway the North Vietnamese from their demands.

Two years after U.S. forces withdrew, Saigon's military regime collapsed. In January 1975, North Vietnamese troops overran the northern part of South Vietnam. As South Vietnamese troops retreated in panic, new waves of refugees poured into Saigon.

In early April the noose around Saigon tightened. The U.S. military hastily evacuated the several thousand Americans still in the city. Some escaped from the U.S. Embassy roof by helicopter

REMEMBERING VIETNAM

THROUGH OTHERS' EYES

Le Ly Hayslip spent the first 20 years of her life in Vietnam. After the war she reflected on what life in a constant state of war had been like:

❝It was as if life's cycle was no longer birth, growth, and death but only endless dying brought about by endless war. I realized that I, along with so many of my countrymen, had been born into war and that my soul knew nothing else. I tried to imagine people somewhere who knew only peace—what a paradise! How many souls in that world were blessed with the simple privilege of saying good-bye to their loved ones before they died? And how many of those loved ones died with the smile of a life well lived on their lips—knowing that their existence added up to more than a number in a "body count" or another human brick on a towering wall of corpses? Perhaps such a place was America, although American wives and mothers, too, were losing husbands and sons every day in the evil vortex between heaven and hell that my country had become.❞

as North Vietnamese troops stormed the compound. Some 120,000 Vietnamese who had worked for the Americans were flown to the United States. On April 30, 1975, the Saigon government surrendered unconditionally.

For Americans the Vietnam War was over. The long, costly effort to prevent the creation of a united, independent Vietnam under Communist rule had failed. The war had spread to Cambodia and Laos, which had been ravaged. But the predicted collapse of all Southeast Asia—the falling dominoes—did not happen. Quarrels soon broke out between the Communist leaders of Vietnam and those of China and Cambodia. International communism was not as unified a world force as U.S. policymakers had feared—or had claimed.

COMMENTARY

Why Did the North Prevail?

Though some people argue that the United States did not lose the Vietnam War, the nation obviously did not achieve its goal—an independent, non-Communist South Vietnam. What contributed to this failure, one that haunted the nation and countless Americans for decades to come?

People have put forward many reasons to explain why the Communists prevailed against ARVN and U.S. forces. Without doubt the Communists' fierce desire for a united Vietnam gave them the will to fight on in the face of overwhelming military opposition. Like the French, American strategists underestimated the strength of this nationalist feeling among the Vietnamese people. For the Vietnamese, the war against America was a continuation of their decades-long anticolonial crusade.

As one North Vietnamese general commented of the Americans, "They can't get it into their heads that the Vietnam War has to be understood in terms of the strategy of a people's war, that it's not a question of men and materiel, that these things are irrelevant to the problem." At the same time, ineffective South Vietnamese leadership undercut the Americans' war effort. A succession of U.S.-sponsored political leaders, most of whom were generals, failed to inspire popular support among the South Vietnamese.

As the war dragged on, a growing number of Americans began doubting that the fall of South Vietnam to communism would seriously threaten America's interests or standing in the world. The ever climbing death toll and the failure of American leaders to admit the lack of progress resulted in a loss of public trust in the government and a steep decline in support for the war.

Some analysts claim that political and military strategies were at fault. Some of these analysts charge that the United States was not aggressive enough in pursuing its war aims. Others point out that U.S. advisers trained the South Vietnamese forces in conventional warfare rather than in tactics better suited to Vietnam's geography. Furthermore, these analysts charge, the tactics of conventional war cannot effectively counter the skillful use of guerrilla tactics. Still other critics go so far as to argue that any use of military power to solve an essentially political problem was doomed to failure.

■ ■ **A determined foe, ineffective South Vietnamese leadership, and inappropriate military strategy and tactics all contributed to America's inability to win the war.**

VIETNAM AFTER THE WAR

The war ravaged the Vietnamese people. According to Saigon government figures, some 185,000 ARVN soldiers died in combat. Estimates put the number of South Vietnamese civilian dead at nearly a half million. The exact number of Vietcong and North Vietnamese Army war casualties is unknown, but estimates place the total at nearly 1 million dead. In addition, approximately 879,000 Vietnamese were orphaned and 181,000 were disabled. Among the disabled were those exposed to Agent Orange. These people have been plagued by high rates of liver cancer and other illnesses.

Nearly 1.5 million Vietnamese fled Vietnam after the fall of Saigon. Desperate to escape economic and social hardships, many braved the rough South China Sea and Gulf of Thailand in tiny, crowded boats. They were joined by thousands of other Southeast Asian refugees, such as the Hmong

▲ **Many Vietnamese were forced to flee their homes following the Vietnam War. This photograph shows a small boat packed with Vietnamese refugees arriving in Hong Kong.**

(MUHNG) of Laos, also fleeing grave postwar conditions. More than 730,000 of these refugees have settled in the United States since the war.

VIETNAM VETERANS AFTER THE WAR

More than 2.6 million Americans were involved in the Vietnam War. More than 58,000 of them died; over 300,000 were wounded, and nearly 2,300 are missing and presumed dead. Improved emergency medical services saved many soldiers with severe wounds that in previous wars would have been fatal. As a result, there are an unprecedented number of paralyzed and otherwise severely disabled Vietnam veterans.

More than 600 Americans were prisoners of war (POWs). Some POWs spent six years or more in North Vietnamese jails, where they endured long periods of solitary confinement and torture.

One of the most visible tragedies of the war was the fate of its veterans. No ticker-tape parades celebrated the return of soldiers from the Vietnam conflict. On the contrary, veterans often became lightning rods for the anger, guilt, or shame of fellow citizens frustrated by the war; other Americans met them with stony silence.

The public's negative reaction enraged and demoralized many veterans. They had faced a life-and-death struggle, obeying orders in what they trusted was their country's national interests. In the book *Born on the Fourth of July* (1976), Vietnam veteran Ron Kovic recalled his pain over this lack of support:

> 66 I didn't want to believe it at first—people protesting against us when we were putting our lives on the line for our country. . . . How could they do this to us? Many of us would not be coming back and many others would be wounded or maimed. 99

From *Born on the Fourth of July* by Ron Kovic ©1976

Thousands of Vietnam veterans turned to drugs or failed to kick the drug habits they had developed during the war. Many others had trouble finding jobs or settling down and starting families. Some became homeless.

Soldiers who were involved in the spraying of defoliants later developed certain forms of can-

▲ One of the legacies of the Vietnam War was the number of paralyzed and severely disabled veterans. Shown here are marchers in the Vietnam veterans parade held in New York City on May 7, 1985.

cer at an unusually high rate, and children of these veterans had a very high rate of birth defects. Research in the 1970s linked their medical problems to Agent Orange. In 1984 the manufacturers of the chemicals created a relief fund for the veterans and their families, and in 1991 the federal government extended permanent disability benefits to these veterans.

■■ The war left economic, emotional, and physical scars on the people of Vietnam and on many of the Americans who served there.

PUBLIC POLICY LEGACIES

The war shook Americans' confidence in their government. Many were shocked to discover that their leaders had misled them during the war. The actions of Johnson and Nixon raised a crucial constitutional question: under what authority can

During the 1991 Persian Gulf War, politicians and commentators often compared it with previous wars—particularly Vietnam. As President George Bush considered using military force to push the Iraqi army out of Kuwait, he assured the nation: "This will not be another Vietnam."

To fulfill this promise, Bush first insured that America would not fight the Gulf War alone. In the United Nations and through direct diplomacy, Bush pushed for international support, including commitments of troops and money from U.S. allies. At home, he asked Congress to authorize the use of force.

With the bulk of world opinion and Congress firmly behind him, Bush then launched a military operation that reflected the lessons learned in Vietnam. Determined to avoid a drawn-out war, he rushed massive numbers of troops, equipment, and supplies to the Gulf. America's military assault would be quick and deadly. And in further contrast to Vietnam, Bush avoided Johnson's tendency to keep tight control on military operations. Instead, he left tactical decisions to his military commanders.

Bush also took a page from the Vietnam War in his approach to media coverage. He did not intend to allow the flow of information from the war zone to erode public support as

it had in Vietnam. The U.S. military therefore put tight restrictions on media access to the front lines. It also closely screened what was broadcast so that Americans would not be exposed to the kind of grisly images and grim statistics that fueled the Vietnam antiwar movement.

The president believed that the willingness to use U.S. military power was important to keeping international peace. At the same time, he felt sure that a clear victory over Iraq would rid the nation of the stigma of the Vietnam failure. Most of the news media and general public shared this view. In a special issue about the Persian Gulf victory, *Newsweek* proclaimed that "America's troops exorcised the ghosts of Vietnam."

With the ghosts banished, the men and women returning from the Persian Gulf received a very different welcome than their Vietnam-era counterparts. A surge of gratitude and respect toward all American veterans followed the Gulf War. Even many Americans who opposed the war against Iraq stressed their support for the troops and the sacrifices they made.

---

presidents wage an undeclared war? To prevent "another Vietnam," Congress passed the **War Powers Act** in 1973. The act reaffirms Congress's constitutional right to declare war by setting a 60-day limit on the presidential commitment of U.S. troops to foreign conflicts.

The Vietnam War also left a dismal economic legacy. The war cost American taxpayers about $150 billion, adding greatly to the national debt and fueling inflation. The war also siphoned off funding that might otherwise have gone to domestic programs, such as those that help the poor.

Above all, American policymakers learned that a hostile public opinion, or even deep national divisions, can impose severe restraints on the use of military force. Since Vietnam, leaders have been hesitant to commit U.S. troops in far-off regions without being certain of the consent of the American people and the nation's political allies.

► The Vietnam Veterans Memorial—the "Wall"—serves as a tribute to Americans who died in the war.

■■ **The furor surrounding U.S. involvement in Vietnam led Congress to limit the president's war-making powers.**

HEALING THE WOUNDS OF THE WAR

Long after the war's end, Americans continue to seek ways to come to terms with the war and its legacies. Perhaps the most moving attempt to heal the rift caused by the war is the Vietnam Veterans Memorial in Washington, D.C., designed by Maya Ying Lin. Lin, a Chinese American, was a young architecture student at Yale when her design was chosen for the national monument. Of the healing aspects of the memorial, she said: "To overcome grief you have to confront it. An honest memorial makes you accept what happened before you overcome it. I think the memorial makes people accept."

Inscribed on a huge wall of black granite are the names of the more than 58,000 Americans who died in Vietnam. Lin insisted that the names be listed in chronological order—not in alphabetical order or by rank—so that "if you were in the war, you could find your time and a few people you knew." Hundreds visit the memorial daily. Some weep or leave flowers, personal mementos, or written messages. Others simply ponder what the memorial—by its dark silence—has to tell them.

■■ **SECTION 5 REVIEW**

IDENTIFY and explain the significance of each of the following: George McGovern, Twenty-sixth Amendment, War Powers Act, Maya Ying Lin.

1. **MAIN IDEA** What factors led the United States to agree to a cease-fire?

2. **MAIN IDEA** Discuss the effects the war has had both on the Vietnamese people and on many Vietnam veterans.

3. **ASSESSING CONSEQUENCES** What factors helped prevent the United States from achieving its goals in Vietnam? What might the United States have done differently to reach those goals?

4. **WRITING TO PERSUADE** Write a letter to your local chamber of commerce to persuade it to honor local Vietnam veterans in some way.

5. **EVALUATING** What have been some of the long-term effects of the Vietnam War on U.S. foreign and economic policy? Support your answer with specific examples.

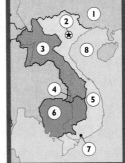
War between Vietminh and French begins.

U.S. aids France in Indochina.

French surrender at Dien Bien Phu. Geneva Conference divides Vietnam.

Diem comes to power in South Vietnam.

1945   1950   1955

WRITING A SUMMARY
Using the essential points of the chapter as a guide, write a summary of the chapter.

REVIEWING CHRONOLOGY
Number your paper 1 to 5. Study the time line above, and list the following events in the order in which they happened by writing the first next to 1, the second next to 2, and so on. Then complete the activity below.

1. Students killed at Kent State and Jackson State.
2. Cease-fire declared.
3. Congress passes Tonkin Gulf Resolution.
4. Nixon begins bombing of Cambodia.
5. Tet offensive launched.

Identifying Cause and Effect Select two events on the time line, and in a paragraph, explain the cause-and-effect relationship between them.

IDENTIFYING PEOPLE AND IDEAS
Explain the historical significance of each of the following people or terms.

1. Ho Chi Minh
2. domino theory
3. Ngo Dinh Diem
4. Vietcong
5. Tonkin Gulf Resolution
6. defoliant
7. pacification
8. doves
9. Tet offensive
10. Vietnamization

UNDERSTANDING MAIN IDEAS
1. What were the main reasons the United States became involved in Vietnam?
2. Why did the United States increase its involvement in Vietnam after 1964?
3. What were the main reasons for Americans' opposition to the war?
4. Why did Richard Nixon win the 1968 election?
5. How has the Vietnam War influenced Americans?

REVIEWING THEMES
1. **Global Relations** How did the United States' stance on world communism lead to U.S. involvement in Vietnam?
2. **Constitutional Heritage** During the war the executive branch (the president) assumed increasing power. Why did this alarm Congress? What steps did Congress eventually take to safeguard its constitutional powers?
3. **Democratic Values** How did the antiwar protests illustrate American democratic values?

THINKING CRITICALLY
1. **Problem Solving** Imagine you are an adviser to President Kennedy, who is considering sending U.S. combat troops to Vietnam. Write him a memorandum suggesting at least two noncombat ways the United States might contain communism and support South Vietnam.
2. **Evaluating** Do you think LBJ had good reasons to escalate the U.S. war effort? Why or why not?
3. **Hypothesizing** Suppose the United States had won a decisive victory in Vietnam. How might life be different in Vietnam? in America?

STRATEGY FOR SUCCESS
Number your paper 1 to 8. Study the map at the right, noting the numbers on it. Then identify each place on the map by selecting from the names listed below. Write the correct name of each place next to its corresponding number on your paper. There are two extra names on the list.

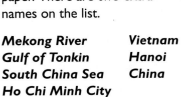

Mekong River	Vietnam	Laos
Gulf of Tonkin	Hanoi	Cambodia
South China Sea	China	Soviet Union
Ho Chi Minh City		

WRITING ABOUT HISTORY
Writing to Create The Vietnam War is reaching its peak, and you have just been drafted. Write a poem or song that expresses your feelings.

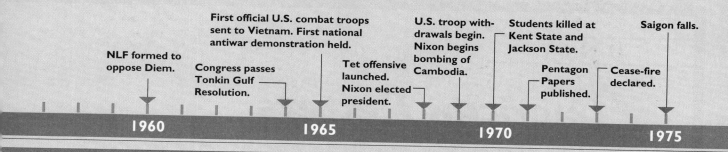

NLF formed to oppose Diem.

Congress passes Tonkin Gulf Resolution.

First official U.S. combat troops sent to Vietnam. First national antiwar demonstration held.

Tet offensive launched. Nixon elected president.

U.S. troop withdrawals begin. Nixon begins bombing of Cambodia.

Students killed at Kent State and Jackson State.

Pentagon Papers published.

Saigon falls.

Cease-fire declared.

1960   1965   1970   1975

USING PRIMARY SOURCES

One of the most difficult features of the war for U.S. troops was not knowing who the enemy was. The following poem by a marine who served in Vietnam describes one reaction. Read the poem and in a brief essay state your reaction to it.

Guerrilla War

*It's practically impossible
to tell civilians
from the Vietcong.*

*Nobody wears uniforms.
They all talk
the same language
(and you couldn't understand them
even if they didn't).*

*They tape grenades
inside their clothes,
and carry satchel charges
in their market baskets.*

*Even their women fight;
and young boys,
and girls.*

*It's practically impossible
to tell civilians
from the Vietcong;*

*after awhile
you quit trying.*

—William Ehrhart

LINKING HISTORY AND GEOGRAPHY

In Vietnam, U.S. forces encountered a physical setting ill suited for motor vehicles and advanced tanks—conventional U.S. war machinery. Review the chapter discussion of Vietnam's physical characteristics and read the following description from Michael Herr's *Dispatches*. Then in a paragraph explain why such terrain made fighting difficult.

> 66 The Highlands of Vietnam are spooky, unbearably spooky, spooky beyond belief. They are a run of erratic mountain ranges, gnarled valleys, jungled ravines and abrupt plains where Montagnard [aborigines living in the Highlands] villages cluster, thin and disappear as the terrain steepens. 99

BUILDING YOUR PORTFOLIO

Complete the following projects independently or cooperatively.

1. **THE COLD WAR** In chapters 17 and 18 you served as a U.S. delegate to the UN conference. Building on that material, create a chart, photo essay, videotape, or other visual presentation showing the structure of the United Nations. Then write a short statement indicating how the UN might have been used to lessen U.S. military involvement in Vietnam.

2. **CIVIL RIGHTS** In chapters 17, 18, and 19 you served as a reporter covering civil rights movements. Building on that material, write a script for a 15-minute news program that relates the specific concerns of one of the movements to the Vietnam War. Your comments should examine economic and social factors at home, government policies, and conditions in Vietnam.

 American Letters

Voices of Change

In many ways the postwar years were a troubled time. Americans confronted serious issues, from Cold War fears and war to racial prejudice and social injustice. Singer-songwriter Bob Dylan, San Francisco Beat poet Lawrence Ferlinghetti, African American poet Naomi Long Madgett, and Native American poet-novelist James Welch were among the writers who explored these problems and tensions.

The Times They Are A-Changin'

by Bob Dylan

Come gather 'round people
Wherever you roam
And admit that the waters
Around you have grown
And accept it that soon
You'll be drenched to the bone.
If your time to you
Is worth savin'
Then you better start swimmin'
Or you'll sink like a stone
For the times they are a-changin'.

Come writers and critics
Who prophesize with your pen
And keep your eyes wide
The chance won't come again
And don't speak too soon
For the wheel's still in spin
And there's no tellin' who
That it's namin'.
For the loser now
Will be later to win
For the times they are a-changin'.

Come senators, congressmen
Please heed the call
Don't stand in the doorway
Don't block up the hall

For he that gets hurt
Will be he who has stalled
There's a battle outside
And it is ragin'.
It'll soon shake your windows
And rattle your walls
For the times they are a-changin'.

Come mothers and fathers
Throughout the land
And don't criticize
What you can't understand
Your sons and your daughters
Are beyond your command
Your old road is
Rapidly agin'.

Please get out of the new one
If you can't lend your hand
For the times they are a-changin'.

The line it is drawn
The curse it is cast
The slow one now
Will later be fast
As the present now
Will later be past
The order is
Rapidly fadin'.
And the first one now
Will later be last
For the times they are a-changin'. ❖

▼ **Civil rights demonstrators attacked with high-pressure water hoses, 1963**

▼ **Flower power, 1967**

▲ *Voter registration march to Montgomery, Alabama, 1965*

From *I Am Waiting*

by Lawrence Ferlinghetti

I am waiting for my number to be
  called
and I am waiting
for the living end
and I am waiting
for dad to come home
his pockets full
of irradiated silver dollars
and I am waiting
for the atomic tests to end
and I am waiting happily
for things to get much worse
before they improve
and I am waiting
for the Salvation Army to take
  over
and I am waiting
for the human crowd
to wander off a cliff somewhere
clutching its atomic umbrella
and I am waiting
for Ike to act
and I am waiting
for the meek to be blessed
and inherit the earth. . .
and I am waiting for forests and
  animals
to reclaim the earth as theirs
and I am waiting
for a way to be devised
to destroy all nationalisms
without killing anybody
and I am waiting
for linnets[1] and planets to fall like
  rain
and I am waiting for lovers and
  weepers
to lie down together again
in a new rebirth of wonder. . . . ❖

1 birds of the finch family

Midway

by Naomi Long Madgett

I've come this far to freedom and
  I won't turn back.
I'm climbing to the highway from
  my old dirt track.
  I'm coming and I'm going
  And I'm stretching and
  I'm growing
And I'll reap what I've been
  sowing or my skin's not
  black.

I've prayed and slaved and waited
  and I've sung my song.
You've bled me and you've starved
  me but I've still grown
  strong.
  You've lashed me and you've
  treed me
  And you've everything but
  freed me
But in time you'll know you need
  me and it won't be long.

I've seen the daylight breaking
  high above the bough.
I've found my destination and I've
  made my vow;
  So whether you abhor me
  Or deride me or ignore me,
Mighty mountains loom before me
  and I won't stop now. ❖

Plea to Those Who Matter

by James Welch

You don't know I pretend my
  dumb.
My songs often wise, my bells
  could chase
the snow across these whistle-
  black plains.
Celebrate. The days are grim. Call
  your winds
to blast these bundled streets and
  patronize
my past of poverty and 4-day
  feasts.

Don't ignore me. I'll build my face
  a different way,
a way to make you know that I am
  no longer
proud, my name not strong
  enough to stand alone.
If I lie and say you took me for a
  friend,
patched together in my thin bones,
will you help me be cunning and
  noisy as the wind?

I have plans to burn my drum,
  move out
and civilize this hair. See my nose?
  I smash it
straight for you. These teeth? I
  scrub my teeth
away with stones. I know you help
  me now I matter.
And I—I come to you, head down,
  bleeding from my smile,
happy for the snow clean hands of
  you, my friends. ❖

THINKING AND WRITING ABOUT LITERATURE

1. Why do you think "The Times They Are A-Changin'" became
   an anthem for the youth movement of the 1960s?
2. What image does Lawrence Ferlinghetti paint of life in the 1950s?
3. To whom are the speakers in Naomi Long Madgett's and James
   Welch's poems addressing their message? How are the speakers'
   attitudes similar? How are they different?

Strategies for Success

CONDUCTING AN INTERVIEW

Historians often conduct interviews with people who witnessed or participated in historical events. Such interviews are called oral histories and are considered primary sources.

One of the largest oral history collections was compiled in the 1930s by the Federal Writers' Project of the WPA. Project members interviewed former slaves to gather their recollections of life in the South under slavery and during Reconstruction. The accounts were first published in 1944 in *Lay My Burden Down.* Historian Charles A. Beard described the accounts as "literature more powerful than anything I have read in fiction."

Effective interviewing involves more than just talking to people. To get the most from an interview, conduct it carefully and accompany it with prior research as well as follow-up analysis.

How to Conduct an Interview

1. **Identify and research the topic.** Gather information on your topic as the basis for questions.
2. **Set up an interview.** Contact the interviewee; identify yourself, state clearly the purpose of the interview, and schedule a convenient time and place to conduct it. Ask whether you may tape-record the interview.
3. **Prepare questions.** Formulate questions to get at the information you need. Plan the interview so that questions logically follow one another.
4. **Conduct the interview.** Be an active listener. Allow responses that go beyond your specific questions, but keep the interview on the topic.
5. **Analyze the interview.** Review and summarize the interview's content, noting what was said with emphasis. Identify statements that are representative of the person's overall views.

Applying the Strategy

Read the following excerpt from Studs Terkel's oral history *Working.* The speaker is Nora Watson, a staff writer for a publisher of health-care literature. Then decide what questions Terkel might have asked to obtain such responses.

> " Jobs are not big enough for people. It's not just the assembly line worker whose job is too small for his spirit, you know? . . .
>
> I had expected to put the energy and enthusiasm and the gifts that I may have to work—it isn't happening. They expect less than you can offer. Token labor. . . . I know I'm vegetating and being paid to do exactly that. . . . But then you walk out with no sense of satisfaction. . . . I'm being had. Somebody has bought the right to you for eight hours a day. . . . You know what I mean? "

Terkel probably began his interview with a question like "How do you spend your workday?" He then may have inquired about how demanding and rewarding the job is. Given Nora Watson's dissatisfaction, his follow-up questions probably encouraged her to reflect further on feeling "underemployed."

Practicing the Strategy

Several oral histories have been written based on interviews with ground and air troops, nurses, support personnel, reporters, and other people who were in Vietnam. But the war can be remembered from many points of view. Prepare a list of questions to use in conducting interviews with people who participated in the antiwar movement. Use chapters 19 and 20 as background for the period.

▼ **Studs Terkel**

BUILDING YOUR PORTFOLIO

Outlined below are four projects. Independently or cooperatively, complete one and use the products to demonstrate your mastery of the historical concepts involved.

1 **THE COLD WAR**
In 1945, representatives of 50 world nations created the United Nations. Using the portfolio materials you designed in chapters 17, 18, and 20, write a report to President Nixon in 1973 recommending or condemning continued U.S. membership in the United Nations. Your report should explain why the United States originally joined the United Nations and evaluate the decision in light of world events between 1945 and 1973.

2 **CIVIL RIGHTS**
To many Americans, the greatest strides in civil rights came in the 30 years after World War II. African Americans, Hispanic Americans, Americans with disabilities, women, and other groups made progress in securing rights long guaranteed others. Using the portfolio materials you designed in chapters 17, 18, 19, and 20, rehearse and then present your 15-minute news program to the class, making sure the program accomplishes the goals you set and follows your plan of production.

3 **THE GOVERNMENT AND THE ECONOMY**
In the postwar era, the United States government became increasingly involved in managing and influencing the American economy. Using the portfolio materials you designed in chapters 17 and 19, create a visual display of the different areas of the economy in which the government plays a role. Make sure your display shows how each type of government involvement affects the lives of average citizens.

4 **POPULAR CULTURE**
In the 1950s and 1960s, advances in science and technology, population growth and shifts, and a rising standard of living helped transform the daily lives of Americans. Using the materials you designed in chapters 18 and 19, present to the class a slide show documenting the changes in everyday life from the 1950s to the 1960s.

Videodisc Review

In assigned groups, develop an outline for a video collage of postwar America. Choose images that best illustrate the major topics of the period. Write a script to accompany the images. Assign narrators to different parts of the script, and present your video collage to the class.

Further Reading

Chafe, William H. *Civilities and Civil Rights.* Oxford (1981). Overview of the formative years of the civil rights movement.

Hampton, Henry, and Steve Fayer. *Voices of Freedom.* Bantam (1990). Oral history of the civil rights movement.

Knox, Donald. *The Korean War: Uncertain Victory.* Harcourt (1988). Oral history of war.

O'Neil, Doris C., ed. *Life—The '60s.* Bullfinch Press (1989). An overview of the 1960s from a social history perspective.

Thompson, Robert Smith. *The Missiles of October.* Simon & Schuster (1992). The story of the Cuban missile crisis.

Young, Marilyn B. *The Vietnam Wars, 1945–1990.* HarperCollins (1991). History of the Vietnam War and its aftermath.

Chapter 21

**FROM NIXON TO
CARTER 1970–1980**

Chapter 22

**REAGAN, BUSH, AND
CLINTON 1980–the Present**

*P*resident Nixon's foreign policy successes brought improved relations with the Soviet Union and China, but the Watergate scandal forced him to resign. A growing sense of discontent characterized the administrations of Nixon's successors, Ford and Carter. Reagan and his conservative agenda rode this wave of dissatisfaction into office in 1981. Although Bush continued Reagan's policies, the economy faltered, and Bush lost his reelection bid to Clinton in 1992. As Clinton took office, many nations looked to the United States for guidance in finding their place in the new era that emerged following the collapse of the Soviet Union.

◀ President Reagan and Soviet leader Gorbachev, Moscow, 1988

FROM NIXON TO CARTER

FOCUS

UNDERSTANDING THE MAIN IDEA

Vice President Gerald Ford became president when the Watergate scandal forced Richard Nixon to resign in 1974. Ford lost the 1976 presidential election, however, to Democrat Jimmy Carter. The legacy of the civil rights movement continued through activism by numerous groups that had faced discrimination. Affirmative action programs and busing, however, brought about a white backlash.

THEMES

■ **ECONOMIC DEVELOP-MENT** How might a nation's choice of energy sources affect its economy?

■ **GLOBAL RELATIONS** How might opening relations with one nation help improve relations with another nation?

■ **CONSTITUTIONAL HER-ITAGE** Why is it dangerous for one branch of government to withhold information from another branch of government?

1970	1974	1976	1979
First Earth Day celebration held.	Nixon resigns presidency.	Jimmy Carter elected president.	Iran hostage crisis begins.

Scene from 1976 bicentennial celebration

"Good evening. This is the thirty-seventh time I have spoken to you from this office." President Richard Nixon's voice cracked with emotion as he addressed the American people on August 8, 1974. Less than two years earlier, he had won reelection in a landslide victory. Now he was announcing his resignation. Facing impeachment for his role in the Watergate affair, the most serious scandal ever to hit the White House, Richard Nixon became the first U.S. president to resign.

Vice President Gerald Ford served out the remainder of Nixon's term. In 1976 the nation elected a Democratic president, Jimmy Carter—a Washington outsider whose promise of honesty in government appealed to many Americans. Carter's popularity soon plummeted, however, and he was voted out of office after one term.

Amid these political twists and turns, American society changed rapidly as many people moved to the Southwest and new waves of immigrants arrived from Latin America and Asia. In addition, the African American civil rights movement continued to influence other groups seeking equal rights—particularly women, Hispanic Americans, people with disabilities, and American Indians.

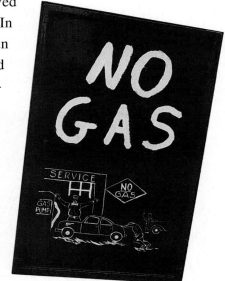

Gas station sign, 1973

THE NIXON YEARS

FOCUS

- How did President Nixon try to reverse the liberal trends of the Kennedy-Johnson years?
- What caused the energy crisis of the early 1970s?
- What factors contributed to the growth of the environmental movement?
- What was President Nixon's main foreign-policy goal?

President Nixon tried to steer the nation away from the liberalism of the Kennedy-Johnson years. His conservative agenda, however, was undermined by a Democratic Congress and by serious domestic problems, including a stagnant economy. In foreign affairs, though, the president had greater success. Nixon chalked up his most important achievement by easing tensions with the Communist world.

Chinese leader Mao Zedong and President Richard Nixon

COURTING THE SILENT MAJORITY

On July 20, 1969, Americans cheered as *Apollo 11* astronauts Neil Armstrong and Edwin "Buzz" Aldrin landed their lunar module on the moon. Stepping onto the moon's surface, Armstrong declared, "That's one small step for man, one giant leap for mankind." President Nixon and many other Americans hoped that the leap signaled a shift away from the troubles of the 1960s.

Much of Nixon's support came from middle-class voters weary from the social upheaval of the 1960s. Nixon called these people the **silent majority**—"the forgotten Americans, the non-shouters, the non-demonstrators." He won their votes by pledging to restore law and order and to cut back Democratic programs. Many critics of Johnson's Great Society policies charged that the programs had failed to significantly decrease poverty in America. Instead, critics insisted, these policies had created a complex, inefficient bureaucracy that made people dependent upon the federal government. The welfare system came under particular attack, as the number of welfare recipients climbed from some 3.1 million in 1960 to some 9.7 million in 1970.

◀ Astronauts Neil Armstrong and Edwin "Buzz" Aldrin made the first lunar landing in 1969. By 1973, five additional Apollo flights had explored the surface of the moon.

Under the existing welfare system, most families received the bulk of aid in the form of services, such as Medicaid. Nixon proposed replacing this system with the **Family Assistance Plan (FAP)**, which would guarantee families a minimum income. Supporters of FAP argued that giving money directly to families would cut down on government service programs and the bureaucracy that went with them. Critics, however, charged that such direct aid would only make poor families even more dependent on the federal government. After a heated battle, the Senate rejected the FAP.

In addition to trying to reform the federal bureaucracy, Nixon promised not to ask for any new civil rights legislation. This move was part of the Republicans' **southern strategy**—a plan to win conservative southern white voters away from the Democratic party. As part of this plan, Nixon also delayed pressuring southern schools to desegregate. When the Supreme Court ruled in a 1971 case that busing could be used to integrate schools, Nixon denounced the decision.

The southern strategy also influenced the president's choice of justices for the Supreme Court. Nixon claimed that the liberal rulings of the Warren Court had encouraged lawlessness in America. Such lawlessness, he argued, was demonstrated by a series of prison riots in the late 1960s and the early 1970s. Among the most serious of these was the 1971 rebellion at New York's Attica prison, which resulted in the death of 40 prisoners and guards. When Chief Justice Warren retired in 1969, Nixon appointed a conservative justice, Warren Burger, to head the Court. Two other Nixon nominees to the Court were rejected by the Senate, but the president eventually appointed three more conservative justices: Harry Blackmun, Lewis Powell, and William Rehnquist.

■■ **Nixon tried to reverse liberal trends by cutting back on civil rights legislation and appointing conservative justices to the Supreme Court.**

TACKLING THE ECONOMY

Reversing the liberal policies of the 1960s was not Nixon's only objective. He also had to tackle a faltering economy. Although the United States had enjoyed an economic boom during the 1960s, by the time Nixon took office the economy was in trouble. High levels of government spending on social programs and on the Vietnam War had led to a recession and growing unemployment. Normally in times of high unemployment, inflation goes down. Yet in the 1970s, inflation and unemployment

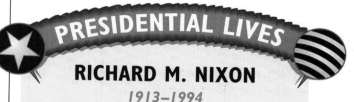

PRESIDENTIAL LIVES

RICHARD M. NIXON
1913–1994

in office
1969–1974

Richard Milhous Nixon rose to the top ranks of the Republican party through hard work and intense ambition. Growing up in a poor family in California made Nixon determined to be a success and never to give up.

One of the more famous examples of Richard Nixon's ability to bounce back from political challenges came during the 1952 presidential election. Nixon, who was Dwight Eisenhower's vice presidential running mate, had been accused of accepting personal gifts from wealthy businessmen. He went on national television to deny the charges. In what came to be called the "Checkers speech," Nixon admitted to accepting one personal gift. "You know what it was?" the candidate asked. "It was a little cocker spaniel dog . . . black, white, and spotted, and our little girl Tricia, the six-year-old, named it Checkers. . . . And I just want to say this, right now, that regardless of what they say about it, we're going to keep it." The Checkers speech won wide public support and saved Nixon from being dropped from the Republican ticket.

both rose. This phenomenon is called **stagflation.**

In August 1971 Nixon took a drastic step to curb inflation by imposing wage and price controls—temporary freezes on wages, prices, and rents. Many people were surprised by the action, since Nixon had long opposed the use of such controls. Labor leaders feared that wage freezes would hurt those earning the lowest wages. AFL–CIO president George Meany called it "Robin Hood in reverse, because it robs from the poor and gives to the rich."

Nixon, however, was bowing to political reality. Only by taking bold action on the economy could he hope to win the upcoming presidential election. The strategy worked. Inflation slowed, and Nixon was reelected in 1972. When he eased controls the following year, though, inflation shot up again. By August 1974 the annual inflation rate had reached 12 percent. A homemaker from Chicago reflected public sentiments about the economy:

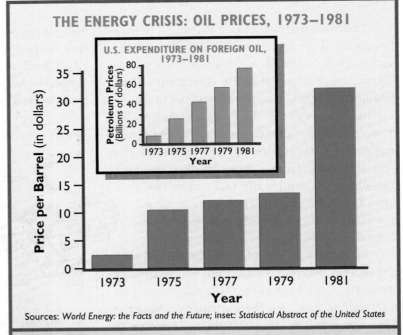

THE ENERGY CRISIS: OIL PRICES, 1973–1981

U.S. EXPENDITURE ON FOREIGN OIL, 1973–1981

Sources: *World Energy: the Facts and the Future;* inset: *Statistical Abstract of the United States*

OPEC'S OIL Throughout the 1970s the U.S. government struggled to ease the problems caused by skyrocketing oil prices. These efforts were largely unsuccessful because American dependence on foreign oil continually increased.

? BUILDING GRAPH SKILLS Between which two-year period did the United States experience its biggest increase in oil prices? Approximately how many barrels of foreign oil were purchased in 1975?

> 66 You always used to think in this country that there would be bad times followed by good times. Now, maybe it's bad times followed by hard times followed by harder times. 99

THE ENERGY CRISIS

The surging cost of oil was a major cause of inflation during the 1970s. Since World War II the U.S. economy had become increasingly dependent on foreign oil. By the early 1970s the United States was importing one third of its oil needs.

To get higher prices for their oil, several oil-exporting nations, mainly Arab countries, had formed the **Organization of Petroleum Exporting Countries** (OPEC) in 1960. In the fall of 1973, amid a new Arab-Israeli war, OPEC quadrupled oil prices. Many Arab countries cut off oil shipments to the United States as retaliation for

U.S. support of Israel. Although the Arabs lifted their embargo after a few months, the price of oil remained high. Some Americans charged that oil companies were keeping prices artificially high to boost their profits.

The oil embargo and the price hikes caused an energy crisis in the United States during the winter of 1973–74. As the cost of gasoline, heating oil, and electricity soared, some parts of the country experienced severe hardship. One Detroit hospital told its patients to stay in bed to keep warm. "We had so little oil left that we just had to cut back the thermostats," noted one hospital official. "In storage rooms and areas with no patients, it got as low as 40 degrees."

Responding to the crisis, President Nixon announced a program to make the United States less dependent on foreign oil. He called for energy conservation and signed a bill authorizing construction of a pipeline to bring oil south from Alaska. Nevertheless, America's dependence on oil imports grew throughout the 1970s.

■■ **The Arab oil embargo and price hikes of 1973 helped provoke an energy crisis in the United States.**

CLEANING UP THE ENVIRONMENT

When Nixon took office, few Americans seemed worried about the environment. Two events soon helped increase concern, however. The first was a massive oil spill off the coast of Santa Barbara, California, in 1969. The second was the first Earth Day celebration in April 1970. Across the country huge crowds took part in "teach-ins" and other activities designed to raise awareness of environmental problems. At an Earth Day event in New York City's Central Park, Episcopal bishop Paul Moore told a group of schoolchildren: "Unless we stop stealing, exploiting, and ruining nature for our own gain, we will lose everything."

In 1970 Congress responded to growing public concern over the environment by approving the creation of the **Environmental Protection Agency** (EPA), a federal agency with power to enforce environmental laws. Congress also approved the creation of the **Occupational Safety and Health Administration** (OSHA) to enforce laws protecting workers from dangerous or unhealthy working conditions. That same year, Congress passed two laws to limit pollution. The **Clean Air Act** set air-quality standards and tough emissions guidelines for car manufacturers. The **Water Quality Improvement Act** made oil companies pay some of the cleanup costs of oil spills and set limits on the discharge of industrial pollutants into water.

■■ **Public concern over air and water quality, coupled with events like Earth Day, fueled the growth of the environmental movement in the 1970s.**

The government also increased support for the use of nuclear energy to replace oil and coal sources. As a relatively clean source of energy that did not eat up limited natural resources, nuclear power seemed to many energy experts to be "the only practicable energy source in sight adequate to sustain our way of life and to promote our economy." By January 1974, 42 nuclear power plants were in operation and over 160 more were under construction or in the planning stages. Yet many critics worried that the risks of a nuclear accident outweighed the advantages of nuclear power.

◀ As concerns over the environment grew, U.S. cities began to stage Earth Day celebrations. Shown here is the 1970 Earth Day event in New York City's Central Park.

FOREIGN AFFAIRS UNDER NIXON

Although domestic issues demanded much of Nixon's attention, his main interest was foreign affairs. Working closely with his national security adviser, Henry Kissinger, Nixon sought to reshape U.S. foreign policy and leave his mark on world affairs.

The Nixon–Kissinger approach. Nixon and Kissinger shared a belief in **realpolitik** ("practical politics")—an approach to foreign policy that emphasized national interests over moral or ethical concerns. Applying realpolitik meant that national interests, rather than ideals such as democracy and human rights, should be the guiding force in American foreign policy. Therefore, governments allied with the United States should receive American support, even if they were not democratic.

The chief goal of the Nixon-Kissinger foreign policy was to establish a balance of power among the world's five major powers: the United States, the Soviet Union, Western Europe, Japan, and the People's Republic of China. As Nixon explained in 1972:

❝ The only time in the history of the world that we have had any extended period of peace is when there has been a balance of power. It is when one nation becomes infinitely more powerful in relation to its potential competitors that the danger of war arises. ❞

■■ Nixon's main foreign-policy goal was to achieve a balance of power that would help reduce international conflict.

Relations with China and the Soviets.

As part of this strategy, President Nixon sought improved relations with the People's Republic of China. By the 1970s China and the Soviet Union—though both still Communist—had become bitter enemies. Nixon believed that improved ties with China would enhance American power in Asia and further divide the Communist world.

Nixon visited China in 1972 in an effort to ease more than 20 years of hostility. The two nations agreed to work together to promote peace in the Pacific region and to develop trade relations and cultural and scientific ties. Furthermore, Nixon promised eventual withdrawal of U.S. forces from Taiwan. This move helped decrease Chinese support for the North Vietnamese. Although many American conservatives were shocked by Nixon's trip, it gave the president leverage to promote a new policy with the Soviet Union.

In May 1972, three months after visiting China, Nixon flew to Moscow for talks with Soviet leader Leonid Brezhnev (BREZSH-nef). The two agreed to promote trade and to cooperate on other issues of mutual concern. At the time, Nixon declared, "There must be room in this world for two great nations with different systems to live together and work together."

Nixon and Brezhnev also signed a treaty limiting nuclear weapons. This treaty, the product of the **Strategic Arms Limitation Talks** (SALT), limited the number of intercontinental nuclear missiles—those capable of traveling long distances to other continents—each nation could have. Although the SALT treaty did not end the arms race, it was a small first step in reducing the nuclear threat. As a result of the peace talks, the United States and the Soviet Union entered into a period of **détente**—the lessening of military and diplomatic tensions between countries.

Trouble spots.

In general, Nixon and Kissinger paid little attention to countries that were not of direct strategic importance to the United States. One exception was the South American nation of Chile. In 1970 Chile elected a Socialist president, Salvador Allende (ah-YAYN-day). Fearing that Allende planned to turn Chile into "another Cuba"—a Communist ally to the Soviet Union—Nixon tried to topple the Allende government. He cut off aid to Chile and provided funds to Allende's opponents in the Chilean military. He also instructed the CIA to disrupt economic and political life in the country. In September 1973 the Chilean army killed Allende and set up a military dictatorship. To many observers, American actions in Chile represented a serious abuse of power.

Shortly after the Chilean coup, conflict erupted in the Middle East. Six years earlier, in 1967, Israel had crushed its Arab neighbors—Egypt, Jordan, and Syria—in the Six-Day War. Embittered by their defeat, the Arab states continued to harass Israel, and Israel continued to strike back. Israeli prime minister Golda Meir recalled the tension between her country and its Arab neighbors:

▲ **Golda Meir**

❝ For years we had been shouting "peace" and hearing the echo "war" come back from the other side. . . . The only time that Arab states were prepared to recognize the existence of . . . Israel was when they attacked it in order to wipe it out. ❞

This simmering conflict was fueled by Cold War competition, with the Soviets providing aid to their Arab allies while the United States gave most of its support to Israel. Then, in October 1973, Egypt and Syria invaded Israel, seeking to recover land lost in the 1967 war. The attack, which came during the Jewish holiday of Yom Kippur, caught the Israelis by surprise. They soon launched a counterattack, however, that threatened Egypt's capital, Cairo. Facing defeat, Egypt called on the Soviet Union for help.

When the Soviets threatened to send troops into the region, President Nixon put all U.S. forces on alert. A major military confrontation seemed possible. Within days, however, the superpowers persuaded the Arabs and the Israelis to accept a cease-fire. Détente had survived its first critical test, but prospects for a lasting peace in the Middle East remained in doubt.

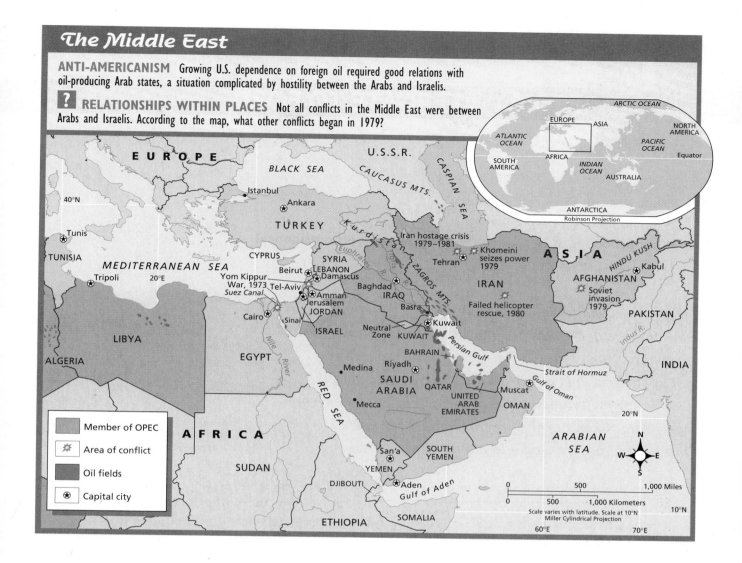

The Middle East

ANTI-AMERICANISM Growing U.S. dependence on foreign oil required good relations with oil-producing Arab states, a situation complicated by hostility between the Arabs and Israelis.

? **RELATIONSHIPS WITHIN PLACES** Not all conflicts in the Middle East were between Arabs and Israelis. According to the map, what other conflicts began in 1979?

Map legend:
- Member of OPEC
- Area of conflict
- Oil fields
- ⊛ Capital city

Map labels include: EUROPE, U.S.S.R., BLACK SEA, CAUCASUS MTS., CASPIAN SEA, Istanbul, Ankara, TURKEY, Kurdistan, Tunis, TUNISIA, MEDITERRANEAN SEA, CYPRUS, SYRIA, Euphrates, ZAGROS MTS., Iran hostage crisis 1979–1981, Tehran, Khomeini seizes power 1979, ASIA, HINDU KUSH, Kabul, AFGHANISTAN, Beirut, LEBANON, Damascus, Yom Kippur War, 1973, Tel-Aviv, Baghdad, IRAQ, IRAN, Soviet invasion 1979, PAKISTAN, Tripoli, Suez Canal, Amman, Jerusalem, JORDAN, Basra, Failed helicopter rescue, 1980, Cairo, Sinai, ISRAEL, Neutral Zone, KUWAIT, Kuwait, Indus R., LIBYA, EGYPT, Nile River, Persian Gulf, BAHRAIN, Strait of Hormuz, INDIA, ALGERIA, RED SEA, Medina, Riyadh, SAUDI ARABIA, QATAR, UNITED ARAB EMIRATES, Muscat, Gulf of Oman, OMAN, AFRICA, Mecca, SUDAN, San'a, SOUTH YEMEN, YEMEN, ARABIAN SEA, DJIBOUTI, Aden, Gulf of Aden, ETHIOPIA, SOMALIA

Inset globe: ARCTIC OCEAN, EUROPE, ASIA, NORTH AMERICA, ATLANTIC OCEAN, PACIFIC OCEAN, AFRICA, INDIAN OCEAN, SOUTH AMERICA, Equator, AUSTRALIA, ANTARCTICA, Robinson Projection

Scale: 0 500 1,000 Miles / 0 500 1,000 Kilometers. Scale varies with latitude. Scale at 10°N. Miller Cylindrical Projection

SECTION 1 REVIEW

IDENTIFY and explain the significance of the following: silent majority, Family Assistance Plan, southern strategy, Warren Burger, stagflation, Organization of Petroleum Exporting Countries, Environmental Protection Agency, Occupational Safety and Health Administration, Clean Air Act, Water Quality Improvement Act, realpolitik, Leonid Brezhnev, Strategic Arms Limitation Talks, détente, Salvador Allende, Golda Meir.

LOCATE and explain the importance of the following: Israel, Egypt, Jordan, Syria.

1. **MAIN IDEA** What steps did President Nixon take to reverse the liberal policies of the Kennedy and Johnson administrations?

2. **MAIN IDEA** What factors provoked an energy crisis in the United States in 1973?

3. **IDENTIFYING CAUSE AND EFFECT** What events fueled the growth of the environmental movement in the 1970s?

4. **WRITING TO EVALUATE** Imagine you are a member of the National Security Council. Write a memorandum that outlines President Nixon's main foreign-policy goal and evaluates how this goal was threatened by events in the Middle East.

5. **ANALYZING** What was unique about the economy during the early 1970s? How did Nixon propose to deal with this situation?

FROM WATERGATE TO FORD

FOCUS

■ **What was the Watergate scandal?**

■ **Why did President Nixon resign?**

■ **What problems did President Ford face during his presidency?**

*N*ixon's second term, which began with a sweeping reelection victory, ended less than two years later with his resignation from office. Just as the words Teapot Dome sum up the scandals of Warren Harding's presidency, the word Watergate represents the political abuses of the Nixon years. With Nixon's departure from office, President Gerald Ford tried to restore credibility to the White House.

Headline announcing Nixon resignation, 1974

CRISIS IN THE PRESIDENCY

Years after Richard Nixon left office, Henry Kissinger reflected on the presidency of his former boss:

> 66 Nixon had three goals: to win by the biggest electoral landslide in history; to be remembered as a peacemaker; and to be accepted by the "Establishment" as an equal. He achieved all these objectives at the end of 1972 and the beginning of 1973. And he lost them all two months later— partly because he turned a dream into an obsession. 99

This obsession began before Nixon won his landslide victory in the 1972 election. Nixon increasingly worked to extend and to maximize his power. He shifted much of the authority of the cabinet, whose appointment required Senate approval, to his personal White House staff. He also hid vital information from Congress and the public. When the news media criticized Nixon's

actions, the White House charged them with biased reporting.

Additional actions were taken in secret to help ensure Nixon's reelection. In 1969 Nixon ordered his staff to compile an "enemies list"— made up of critics opposed to his policies—and then tried to ruin their reputations. Two years later, in reaction to Daniel Ellsberg's leak of the Pentagon Papers (see Chapter 20), Nixon set up a secret unit called "the plumbers." This group, which included former agents of the CIA and FBI, was ordered to stop leaks and carry out a variety of illegal actions in the name of "national security."

By 1972 these secret activities had mushroomed into a full-scale effort to ensure Nixon's reelection—no matter what it took. This campaign, which involved criminal activity and electoral "dirty tricks," along with subsequent attempts to cover them up, became known as **Watergate**. The scandal took its name from the Watergate building in Washington, D.C. In June 1972 five men carrying wiretap equipment and other spying devices were caught breaking into the Watergate offices of the Democratic National Committee. It was soon

▲ Bob Woodward (left) and Carl Bernstein (right) were two *Washington Post* reporters who investigated the link between the Nixon White House and the Watergate break-in. This photograph was taken in April 1973.

discovered that these men had ties to the White House and were being paid with funds from Nixon's campaign organization, the Committee to Re-elect the President (CREEP).

The administration denied any link to the break-in, calling it a "third-rate burglary." But two *Washington Post* reporters, Bob Woodward and Carl Bernstein, kept digging for the truth. A high-level source, known only as "Deep Throat," revealed that White House officials and CREEP had hired 50 agents to sabotage the Democrats' chances in the 1972 election.

██ **The Watergate scandal implicated the Nixon administration in illegal activities, which officials later tried to cover up.**

THE WATERGATE INVESTIGATION

Woodward and Bernstein's astonishing revelations did not prevent Nixon's reelection. But by the spring of 1973, both the judicial and the legislative branches of government were investigating Watergate. Senator Sam Ervin of North Carolina led the investigations for the Senate. One of the first witnesses to testify was James McCord, an ex-CIA agent who had taken part in the Watergate break-in. McCord admitted that top White House officials had helped plan the break-in and later tried to cover it up. This testimony broke the case wide open.

WATERGATE

THROUGH OTHERS' EYES

Foreign journalists were particularly interested in the Watergate case. Many noted that similar scandals exposed by journalists in their countries were often ignored because the popular press had little political influence. For example, although the French followed the Watergate investigation with great interest, an alleged French government attempt to wiretap the offices of a weekly newspaper, *Le Canard Enchaîné*, drew little attention. After Nixon's resignation, French journalist André Fontaine commented in the newspaper *Le Monde*:

"We no longer knew it, we no longer wanted to believe it. But there's still at least one nation on this earth where the law, decidedly, is stronger than men, where, just named by the President, some judges were capable of making some decisions against him. . . .

The idea that the President of the United States must give up his place to the liberties he took with the truth doesn't leave [Americans] astonished. As for the Watergate scandal, we have heard much that the wiretapping at Le Canard is only a weak replica, the fact is that France has had some others . . . .

Our old . . . countries . . . have become very indulgent toward sins. But the Americans, despite the excesses of competition and counterculture . . . haven't yet loosened the cocoon of moralism, into which the puritans put their political life. "

The biggest bombshells were yet to come. In May, live television coverage of the Senate hearings began. Across the nation millions of Americans sat glued to their sets as senators grilled witnesses and compiled evidence of official misconduct. Eventually several top White House officials went to jail. Still, Nixon's role in Watergate remained unclear. Time and again, a key member of the Watergate committee, Senator

Howard Baker of Tennessee, asked: "What did the president know and when did he know it?" In June, Nixon's former White House counsel John Dean gave the stunning answer: the president himself had ordered the cover-up.

Nixon denied the charge, and there seemed to be no way to prove it. Then another witness revealed that Nixon had secretly tape-recorded his conversations in the White House! In the tapes, investigators believed, lay the truth behind Watergate. The Justice Department's special prosecutor, Archibald Cox, demanded that Nixon turn over the tapes. Citing "executive privilege," Nixon refused on the grounds that release of the tapes would endanger national security.

In the midst of this controversy, the Justice Department dealt the administration another blow. In October 1973 it charged Vice President Spiro Agnew with bribe-taking and income-tax evasion. Agnew pleaded no contest and resigned in exchange for minimal punishment. Nixon then nominated Gerald Ford, the Republican leader in the House of Representatives, as vice president.

NIXON RESIGNS

Shortly before Agnew resigned, a federal judge ordered Nixon to release the tapes. The president refused to comply. On October 20, after Special Prosecutor Cox demanded that he obey the judge, Nixon ordered Attorney General Elliot Richardson to fire Cox. Both the attorney general and Deputy Attorney General William Ruckelshaus resigned rather than obey the order. The task of firing Cox then fell to Robert Bork, the solicitor general, who complied. This series of events, known as the **Saturday Night Massacre**, outraged the public and led to increased calls to impeach Nixon.

Nixon finally agreed to release some of the White House tapes. Vital segments were missing, however, and Nixon again resisted turning over the whole set. It was only months later—after the Supreme Court ordered Nixon to turn over all the tapes—that Americans found out the truth: Nixon had directed the Watergate cover-up and had authorized illegal activities. Still, Nixon refused to step down. The House Judiciary committee responded by approving a series of impeachment charges against him. Facing almost certain conviction, Nixon decided to resign. On August 8, 1974, he spoke to the nation:

▲ Gerald Ford was sworn in as the nation's 38th president as his wife, Betty, watches.

❝ I have never been a quitter. To leave office before my term is completed is opposed to every instinct in my body. But as president I must put the interests of America first. . . . Therefore, I shall resign the presidency effective at noon tomorrow. ❞

■■ **President Nixon resigned rather than face impeachment for his role in covering up the Watergate affair.**

On August 9, 1974, Vice President Gerald Ford was sworn in as the 38th president of the United States. He then nominated Governor Nelson Rockefeller of New York for vice president, and Congress confirmed his choice. For the first time in history, both the president and the vice president held office by appointment.

COMMENTARY

The Larger Meaning of Watergate

Watergate was not the first scandal to taint the presidency. The administration of Ulysses S. Grant, a century before Nixon, was stained by financial scandal. So, too, was the presidency of Warren G. Harding. But Watergate was different. Nixon was the first president to resign from office and the first since Andrew Johnson in 1868 to face a serious threat of impeachment. Unlike Johnson, Nixon's troubles did not result from a power struggle with Congress but from charges of criminal activity.

Furthermore, Watergate did not involve typical political misconduct, such as taking bribes. It challenged the very basis of our constitutional government. Nixon tried to place the presidency above the rule of law and above the constitutional system of balance of powers. Afterward, Congress would try to clean up government corruption by passing several laws, including some limiting the amount of money individuals and corporations could contribute to a political candidate.

Watergate tested our system of constitutional government to the limit, but the system held firm. Vigorous investigative journalism and strong action by the courts and Congress exposed the criminal activities of the Watergate conspirators and forced a president to resign. Watergate underscored the fact that the United States is a government of law, not of individuals.

FORD TRIES TO REUNITE THE NATION

The new president, Gerald Ford, was gifted with the common touch. As leader of the Republicans in the House, he had won the respect of colleagues in both parties for his honesty and unassuming manner. "I'm a Ford, not a Lincoln," he once joked.

But President Ford lost much of this early goodwill when, a month after taking office, he granted Nixon a full pardon. Overnight Ford's popularity rating dropped from 72 percent to 49 percent. His critics charged that now the full truth about Watergate would never emerge. They pointed to the double standard that allowed Nixon to go free while his co-conspirators were punished. Many people suspected that the pardon had been agreed upon in advance in exchange for Nixon's resignation. President Ford denied this charge. He defended the pardon by saying that a public trial would have prolonged the bitterness and division produced by Watergate. He had acted, he said, to heal "the wounds of the past."

A week later, Ford took another controversial step by offering partial amnesty to Vietnam draft evaders and military deserters who agreed to reaffirm their allegiance to the United States and spend two years performing public service. Supporters of the Vietnam War felt the pardon was unfair to soldiers who had served their country. Meanwhile, only a handful of people accepted the president's offer. Some war resisters, like Dee Knight, contrasted the conditional pardon with the full pardon granted Nixon:

66 We knew the clemency was proclaimed just to offset the Nixon pardon, which was an insult. We weren't criminals, and Nixon was, but Ford proposed to pardon Nixon unconditionally while offering "alternative punishment" to us. 99

FORD'S TROUBLES CONTINUE

Ford soon ran into other problems, including conflicts with the Democratic majority in Congress. A moderate conservative, Ford vetoed a number of social-welfare bills sponsored by Democrats. In fact, he vetoed more bills than any other president had in such a short time. As Ford's relations with Congress worsened, he found it increasingly difficult to implement his policies.

One of Ford's main goals was to combat inflation, which was being fueled by the energy

▼ The energy crisis increased the price of many consumer goods in the United States. To win public support for his anti-inflation program, President Ford issued buttons with initials representing "Whip Inflation Now."

GERALD R. FORD
1913–

Gerald Ford faced the difficult task of restoring the nation's confidence in government after the Watergate crisis. Most observers believed that Ford was uniquely qualified to remove the taint of scandal from the White House. Throughout his career he had been known as an honest and likable politician. "The nicest thing about Jerry Ford," said Senator Robert P. Griffin, "is that he doesn't have any enemies." Indeed, when Ford first heard about President Nixon's "enemies list," he responded that "anybody who can't keep his enemies in his head has too many enemies."

EXPERIENCE COUNTS
Elect Gerald R. FORD in '76

Unlike many politicians, Ford made friends because he always maintained a fair-minded attitude. He was never vengeful when he lost or arrogant when he won. He acquired this attitude from years of playing sports, especially football. He had been a star player for the University of Michigan and received several offers to play for professional teams. Instead he worked his way through law school as a coach and entered politics. Sports remained an influential part of his life, however. He was the most athletic president in the White House since Teddy Roosevelt.

Gerald R. Ford

crisis and the soaring cost of oil. Like Nixon, Ford tried to curb inflation by cutting federal spending, but this threw the country into a recession and prolonged the nation's economic woes.

In foreign affairs, Ford also continued many of Nixon's policies, including détente. Gradually, however, U.S.–Soviet relations began to unravel. One problem was Soviet emigration policy, which restricted the freedom of Jews and political dissidents to leave the country. When members of Congress criticized this policy, the Soviets canceled a proposed U.S.–Soviet trade pact. Over the next few years, relations continued to sour.

Ford also tried to maintain American influence in Southeast Asia. Toward that end, he requested $722 million in military aid for Cambodia and South Vietnam. But Congress, opposed to further military ventures in Southeast Asia, turned down Ford's request. Then, in May 1975, Cambodian Communists

seized the *Mayaguez*, an unarmed U.S. cargo ship. In response, Ford launched a military action to free the vessel and its crew. Forty-one Americans were killed in the effort to release the 39 crew members. While some applauded the president's actions, others criticized it as hasty and ill-timed. As facts later revealed, the *Mayaguez* crew had already been released when the troops were sent.

▼ **Cambodian Communists seized an unarmed U.S. cargo ship, the *Mayaguez*, in May 1975. President Ford called the action piracy and sent U.S. Marines to free the vessel and its crew.**

> ■■ Ford clashed with Congress over domestic and foreign policy. During his term U.S.–Soviet relations began to unravel.

THE ELECTION OF 1976

At the 1976 Republican convention, Ford narrowly won the party's nomination over his more conservative challenger, Ronald Reagan of California. To balance the ticket, the convention nominated conservative senator Robert Dole of Kansas for vice president. At the Democratic convention, Jimmy Carter—a former governor of Georgia—won the nomination, with Senator Walter Mondale of Minnesota as his running mate. Congresswoman Barbara Jordan of Texas gave the keynote address at the Democratic convention.

Jordan brought a strong sense of moral authority to the Democratic party. Born in 1936, she grew up in Houston, Texas. She excelled in school and eventually received a law degree from Boston University. In 1966 Jordan became the first African American woman elected to the Texas senate. There her tireless efforts on behalf of social reform won praise from President Lyndon Johnson, who noted, "She proved that black is beautiful before we knew what it meant."

In 1972 Jordan was elected to the U.S. House of Representatives, where she soon gained a reputation as a skilled legislator and brilliant orator. She played a key role in drawing up impeachment charges against President Nixon. At one point Jordan declared: "I am not going to sit here and be an idle spectator to the . . . destruction of the Constitution." Despite her outstanding record in Congress, in 1978 Jordan announced that she would not run for a fourth term. As a political analyst and adviser, however, she played a prominent role in national affairs until her death in early 1996.

Barbara Jordan

In her speech to the 1976 Democratic convention, Jordan declared:

> ❝ We cannot improve on the system of government handed down to us by the founders of the Republic, but we can find new ways to implement that system and realize our destiny. ❞

The idea of a new approach to government was central to Jimmy Carter's campaign. Little known outside the South, Carter ran as a Washington outsider untainted by Watergate. He promised never to lie to the American people and openly noted that he was a born-again Christian whose religious ethics strongly shaped his political actions. "You can't divorce religious beliefs and public service," he said. In a close election, he captured 297 electoral votes to Ford's 240. After eight years of Republican rule, the Democrats returned to the White House. Many hoped that Carter would be able to reverse the public's mistrust of government.

SECTION 2 REVIEW

IDENTIFY and explain the significance of the following: Watergate, Bob Woodward, Carl Bernstein, Sam Ervin, James McCord, John Dean, Archibald Cox, Gerald Ford, Saturday Night Massacre, Jimmy Carter, Barbara Jordan.

1. **MAIN IDEA** Why did President Nixon choose to resign from office in 1974?

2. **MAIN IDEA** What difficulties did President Ford face during his time in office?

3. **ASSESSING CONSEQUENCES** What was the significance of the Watergate investigation?

4. **WRITING TO INFORM** Imagine you are an investigative reporter for the *Washington Post,* covering the Watergate scandal. Write an article that outlines the major events in the scandal and the investigation leading up to President Nixon's resignation.

5. **HYPOTHESIZING** How might events have been different if Ford had not pardoned Nixon?

CARTER: THE OUTSIDER AS PRESIDENT

FOCUS

- What critical domestic issues faced the Carter administration?
- How did Carter's foreign policy differ from Nixon's?
- Why did Cold War tensions rise under President Carter?
- How did the Iran hostage crisis affect Carter's presidency?

Family member awaiting return of hostages in Iran

*O*n January 20, 1977, Jimmy Carter took the oath as the 39th president of the United States. Initially a popular president, Carter enjoyed some notable successes. But serious problems—including persistent inflation and conflict in the Middle East—eventually helped erode the president's popularity. In 1980 he lost his bid for a second term.

AN "OPEN ADMINISTRATION"

During the presidential campaign, Carter had promised, if elected, to stay in touch with the people. He quickly showed his intentions to keep that promise. Following his inauguration, the president and his family walked down Pennsylvania Avenue to the White House, rather than make the trip in a limousine surrounded by Secret Service.

The Carter style. Carter brought a folksy style to the White House, abandoning much of the pomp and ceremony of previous presidents. Contributing to this informal tone was his colorful family, who became the subject of much public interest. The news media reported on the activities of Carter's young daughter, Amy, and on the views of his outspoken mother, Miss Lillian. Carter's wife, Rosalynn, received even more attention as one of his most trusted advisers. Although critics questioned his wife's influence on policy, the president insisted that she play a prominent role in White House affairs.

Early on, Carter took several steps that indicated a new approach to government. On his first full day in office, he announced an unconditional pardon for most Vietnam-era draft evaders, moving beyond the conditional pardon offered by President Ford. This gesture helped heal lingering divisions over the war. Carter also held several

◀ The Carter family attracted almost as much media attention as the president. Shown here are President Carter with his wife, Rosalynn, and his young daughter, Amy.

JIMMY CARTER
1924–

in office
1977–1981

The common reaction to Georgia governor Jimmy Carter's announcement that he was running for president was "Jimmy who?" Few people outside of his home state were familiar with the peanut farmer from Plains. Soon, however, voters began to discover that there was much more to this southern politician than his large grin. A highly ranked graduate of the United States Naval Academy, Carter had worked as a nuclear engineer before entering politics.

Carter had a balanced, modern rela-tionship with his wife. Rosalynn Carter took an active and public role in political affairs, traveling around the world to represent her husband's views. Meanwhile Jimmy Carter shared the household chores, such as cooking, caring for their daughter, and grocery shopping. One interviewer was shocked to see the candidate sewing a button onto his own jacket during the presidential campaign. When asked if he always did his own sewing, Carter simply mumbled with thread in mouth, "Uh-huh."

"town meetings" and radio and television call-in sessions to keep in touch with the people. Unlike Richard Nixon, Jimmy Carter seemed determined to keep his administration open to public view.

Carter's economic policy.
One of Carter's first tasks was to stimulate the economy, which was just beginning to emerge from several years of recession. Some eight million Americans—7.8 percent of the work force—were unemployed. The unemployment rate among African Americans and Hispanic Americans was 13 percent.

To revive the economy and create jobs, Carter implemented a series of economic measures, including a corporate tax cut. The Carter administration's policies helped reduce unemployment slightly, but they also fueled inflation, which reached 13.3 percent by 1979. To curb inflation, Carter called for voluntary wage and price controls, along with cuts in funding for social services. But Carter's anti-inflation program produced more unemployment. By the summer of 1980, the economy was once again mired in recession.

Facing the energy crisis.
A major cause of the nation's economic woes was the high cost of imported oil. To reduce the nation's oil dependence, Congress created the **Department of Energy** in 1977. The following year it passed the **National Energy Act** to relax controls on the price of natural gas. Despite these efforts, world events continued to affect the nation's energy supply.

In January 1979 a revolution in Iran disrupted world oil shipments. A few months later, OPEC raised the price of oil 50 percent, leading to another U.S. energy crisis (see the chart on page 558). As gasoline supplies dwindled, many gas stations closed or reduced their hours. Tempers flared as frustrated drivers had to wait hours to fill

▼ **High energy costs hurt many groups during the late 1970s, including farmers. On February 6, 1979, protesting farmers drove their tractors down Pennsylvania Avenue to demonstrate in front of the White House.**

After the disaster at Three Mile Island, residents staged protests that questioned the safety of nuclear power. Protesters urged the government to explore alternative energy sources, such as solar power.

their gas tanks. Some people responded by driving less and by embracing other energy-saving measures, such as installing solar heaters in their homes.

In the midst of the oil crisis, another event dramatized America's energy problems. In late March 1979 a nuclear reactor failed at the Three Mile Island power plant in Pennsylvania, nearly causing a catastrophic nuclear meltdown—the melting of the reactor's core. This incident stirred public fears about nuclear power.

▪▪ An economic recession and an energy crisis were among the serious domestic issues facing the Carter administration.

*H*UMAN RIGHTS AND FOREIGN POLICY

As Carter struggled with difficult domestic issues, he was also charting a new course in foreign affairs. Rejecting the realpolitik of the Nixon years, Carter tried to inject moral principles into American foreign policy. Reflecting on past administrations, he declared:

> ❝ We are deeply concerned . . . by the . . . subtle erosion in the focus and morality of our foreign policy. Under the Nixon-Ford administration, there has evolved a kind of secretive "Lone Ranger" foreign policy—

a one-man policy of international adventure. This is not an appropriate policy for America. ❞

Carter's new approach was most evident in the area of **human rights**—the rights of all people to freedom from unlawful detention or torture. Declaring that "our commitment to human rights must be absolute," Carter called for strong diplomatic and economic pressure on countries that violated human rights.

Not surprisingly, many dictatorships that repressed the rights of their people strongly opposed Carter's policy. Some American diplomats also had doubts. They warned that such meddling in the domestic affairs of other countries might increase world tensions. The United States would resent meddling by other nations in *its* domestic affairs, they pointed out.

▪▪ Carter moved away from Nixon's foreign policy of realpolitik to emphasize moral principles and respect for human rights.

Carter's stand on the Panama Canal caused even greater controversy. He supported Panama's right to control the canal zone and pushed for passage of the **Panama Canal treaties**, which granted Panama control over canal operations by the year 2000 while safeguarding U.S. security interests. Critics charged that Carter was "giving away" the canal. "We built it, we paid for it, it's ours, and . . . we are going to keep it!" declared conservative Republican Ronald Reagan.

Gradually, however, public opinion shifted in Carter's favor, and after a long and bitter debate,

▲ Through the Panama Canal treaties, President Carter proposed that the United States give control of the canal zone to Panama by the year 2000.

the Senate narrowly ratified the treaties in 1978. In Latin America, where U.S. control over the canal had long been a sore point, the treaties met with general approval.

CARTER AND THE COLD WAR

Carter's stance on the Panama Canal issue signaled a more flexible approach to relations with developing countries. Carter hoped the approach would improve America's image and diminish the appeal of communism. His policy was evident in Africa, where the United States and the Soviet Union were jockeying for influence among the continent's newly independent states.

Unlike Nixon and Ford, who showed little interest in Africa, Carter tried to win friends among African nations by helping them sort out their problems in their own way. One Carter official noted, "It is not a sign of weakness to recognize that we alone cannot dictate events elsewhere. It is rather a sign of maturity in a complex world."

Carter's ambassador to the United Nations, former civil rights activist Andrew Young, tried to reach out to black African states. He criticized white imperialism in Africa, condemned South Africa's policy of **apartheid** (racial segregation), and supported black majority rule in Rhodesia (now Zimbabwe).

Carter's flexible approach helped smooth relations in Africa and ease Cold War conflict. The easing of tensions was short-lived, however. In December 1979 Soviet troops invaded the country of Afghanistan to install a pro-Soviet leader. The invasion put Soviet troops within striking distance of major oil routes.

Labeling the invasion a threat to peace, President Carter warned the Soviets to withdraw. When they refused, he cut grain sales to the Soviet Union and announced a boycott of the 1980 Summer Olympics in Moscow. Congress also postponed the signing of a key U.S.–Soviet arms-control treaty. Finally, the president warned that any Soviet military action in the Persian Gulf would provoke a military response by the United States.

■■ **Although the U.S. improved relations with developing countries, Cold War tensions increased when the Soviets invaded Afghanistan.**

CARTER AND THE MIDDLE EAST

Not long before the Soviet invasion of Afghanistan, Carter engineered his chief foreign-policy triumph: a Middle East peace accord. Carter had taken office in 1977 amid fears of another Egyptian-Israeli war. Egyptian president Anwar Sadat (sah-DAHT) and Israeli premier Menachem Begin (muh-NAHK-uhm BAY-gin) met for peace talks, but those talks deadlocked.

Anwar Sadat received a great deal of criticism from the leaders of other Arab nations for attempting any peace talks with Israel. Sadat was born in the small village of Mit Abu-Kum on the Nile Delta in 1918. His childhood was heavily influenced by his close-knit family and the local Imam (religious leader), who taught him the principles of the Islamic faith. Soon after graduating from the Egyptian Military Academy in 1938, Sadat joined a group of rebels who wanted to rid Egypt of its constitutional monarchy, which was under British control.

Sadat went to prison in the 1940s for his efforts to liberate Egypt. After being released from prison, he joined the rebel forces who finally overthrew the monarch in 1952. Thereafter Sadat played a central role in shaping Egyptian policy, finally

▲ **Anwar Sadat**

◀ **As U.S. ambassador to the United Nations, Andrew Young condemned apartheid and sympathized with the concerns of developing nations. His actions made him a controversial figure, and he was forced to resign in 1979.**

becoming president in 1970. As president he played a key role in Middle East events, including trying to pave the road to peace. When Sadat visited Israel in 1977, Premier Begin remarked:

> 66 The time of the flight between Cairo and Jerusalem is short . . . [but] the distance between them . . . until yesterday, quite large. . . . Sadat passed this distance with heartfelt courage. . . . We, the Jews, know how to appreciate this courage. 99

But Sadat always downplayed his own role in bringing about peace. He considered his actions a collective effort by the entire country. To him, all Egyptians shared responsibility for the nation's future. He once said:

> 66 Responsibility cannot be relegated to certain individuals, no matter how good your opinion of them might be; neither can it be confined to groups of people, however good their intentions may be. Responsibility is the entire people's property. 99

In September 1978 Sadat met with Begin and Carter at Camp David, the presidential retreat in Maryland. There, after 12 days of negotiations, the three agreed on a framework for peace, which became known as the **Camp David Accords**. As a result of their efforts, Sadat and Begin shared the Nobel Peace Prize for 1978. The following year, the two leaders signed a formal peace treaty ending 30 years of war between Egypt and Israel. At the emotion-filled ceremony, each quoted the prophet Isaiah: "And they shall beat their swords into plowshares and their spears into pruning hooks."

The accords did not meet universal approval. Some supporters of Israel accused President Carter of favoring the Arabs in order to appease Arab oil-exporting nations, such as Saudi Arabia. Sadat drew the wrath of other Arab nations, furious at his "betrayal" for making peace with Israel. In 1981, members of an Islamic fundamentalist group within the Egyptian army assassinated Sadat while he was reviewing a military parade.

CARTER'S POPULARITY FALLS

Although Carter had chalked up some notable successes as president, by 1980 only 21 percent of Americans approved of his performance. Nixon's approval rating had not fallen this low even during the depths of Watergate. Carter's drop in popularity was partly due to his lack of political experience. But his troubles also lay in the nature of the problems he faced. The energy crisis, inflation, unemployment, Middle East conflict, and Cold War tensions were highly complicated issues that defied simple solutions. Of all the difficulties he faced, however, none was more damaging than the **Iran hostage crisis**.

Iran had long been regarded as critical to U.S. security in the Middle East. In the 1950s the United States had helped overthrow Iran's leader and restore Shah Reza Pahlavi to power (see Chapter 18). Although the shah's regime was very repressive, the United States always supported him. In 1979, however, followers of a militant Islamic leader, the Ayatollah Khomeini (eye-uh-TOH-luh koh-MAY-nee), forced the shah to flee the country. The new government was outraged when President Carter allowed the shah into the United States for medical treatment. On November 4, 1979, in an effort to force the shah's return to Iran for trial, Iranian militants seized 53 American hostages at the U.S. embassy in Tehran, Iran's capital.

Month after month, the hostage crisis dragged on. In April 1980 a rescue mission failed when U.S. military helicopters crashed in the Iranian desert, killing eight Americans. As frustration over the crisis mounted, public anger at Carter also grew. Many felt that his inability to free the hostages signaled America's decline as a symbol of power. Even one Carter aide admitted that "Khomeini would not have touched the Soviet Embassy."

Echoing these thoughts during the 1980 presidential election campaign, the Republican candidate, Ronald Reagan, attacked Carter as a weak president who had presided over a decline in American power. Reagan's promise to "make America strong

▶ **American hostage in Iran**

again" struck a chord with voters. He and his running mate, George Bush, easily won the election, capturing 489 electoral votes to Carter and Mondale's 49. An independent candidate, John Anderson, failed to capture any electoral votes, but did win almost 7 percent of the popular vote, further reflecting public frustration with the administration. For the first time since 1952, the Republicans won control of the Senate, while the Democrats' majority in the House dropped somewhat.

After his defeat Carter continued to negotiate for the release of the hostages. On January 20, 1981, after 444 days in captivity, the hostages were finally freed, just moments after Ronald Reagan was sworn in as president.

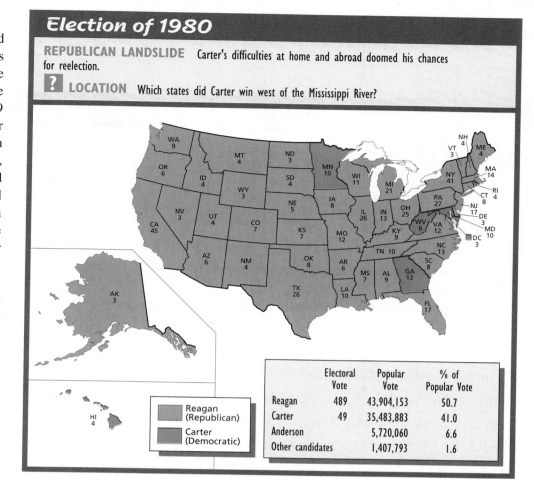

Election of 1980

REPUBLICAN LANDSLIDE Carter's difficulties at home and abroad doomed his chances for reelection.

? LOCATION Which states did Carter win west of the Mississippi River?

	Electoral Vote	Popular Vote	% of Popular Vote
Reagan	489	43,904,153	50.7
Carter	49	35,483,883	41.0
Anderson		5,720,060	6.6
Other candidates		1,407,793	1.6

Reagan (Republican)
Carter (Democratic)

■■ **The Iran hostage crisis contributed to Carter's defeat in the 1980 election.**

SECTION 3 REVIEW

IDENTIFY and explain the significance of the following: Rosalynn Carter, Department of Energy, National Energy Act, human rights, Panama Canal treaties, Andrew Young, apartheid, Anwar Sadat, Menachem Begin, Camp David Accords, Iran hostage crisis, Ayatollah Khomeini, Ronald Reagan, John Anderson.

LOCATE and explain the importance of the following: Iran, South Africa, Rhodesia (Zimbabwe), Afghanistan.

1. **MAIN IDEA** What two serious domestic issues did President Carter face?

2. **MAIN IDEA** How did the Carter administration's approach to the Cold War influence events overseas? What event caused Cold War tensions to increase?

3. **CONTRASTING** Contrast the Carter administration's approach to foreign policy with the Nixon administration's approach.

4. **WRITING TO EXPLAIN** Imagine you are a political analyst covering the 1980 presidential election. Write an essay explaining why Carter has been defeated.

5. **TAKING A STAND** Was Carter right in supporting the Panama Canal treaties? Why or why not?

A DECADE OF SOCIAL CHANGE

FOCUS

- How did the civil rights movement continue in the 1970s? How did some whites respond?
- What did American Indian leaders fight for during the 1970s?
- What issues both encouraged and divided the women's movement during the 1970s?
- How did the new immigrants in the 1970s help shape society?

A woman with visual impairment demonstrating for civil rights

During the 1970s American society underwent important social changes. African Americans made further gains, despite a growing white backlash. Hispanic Americans, American Indians, people with disabilities, and women also made legal and economic strides. Amid these changes, society as a whole was evolving as Americans were living longer and moving more often, and new immigrants were swelling the population.

THE LEGACY OF THE CIVIL RIGHTS MOVEMENT

The 1970s brought some progress in the area of civil rights. Though a 1975 Civil Rights Commission report found that many African Americans were still being kept from voting by various means, by the end of the 1970s over 4,500 African Americans held elective office—three times the number in 1969. The roster of elected black officials in 1978 included 16 members of the House of Representatives and 170 mayors, including those of Los Angeles, Atlanta, Detroit, and Washington, D.C.

As new African American leaders gained political experience, they formed strong alliances and effective lobbies. They also worked hard to get out the black vote, a key factor in Jimmy Carter's electoral victory in 1976. As president, Carter helped open the doors of the federal government to African Americans, naming more blacks to federal jobs than any previous president. In addition to his choice of Andrew Young as UN ambassador, Carter appointed the first African American woman to a cabinet post—Patricia Harris as secretary of Housing and Urban Development.

During the 1970s Hispanic Americans also began to reap some rewards for their political struggles of the previous decade. Between 1974 and 1987 the number of elected Hispanic officials in the United States more than doubled. Growing numbers of Hispanic Americans were appointed to federal jobs, while Hispanic groups such as LULAC—**League of United Latin American Citizens**—mounted lobbying efforts and helped raise national awareness of Hispanic concerns. In California the United Farm Workers won a key victory in 1975 with the passage of a state law extending legal protection to migrant farm workers. In addition, the Southwest Voter Registration Education Project helped Hispanic Americans register to vote.

Americans with disabilities also made their voices heard in the 1970s. Why, they asked, should

▲ These demonstrators in San Francisco protested lack of access to public transportation by blocking buses during rush hour.

their tax dollars help build public facilities that people in wheelchairs or people with visual disabilities could not easily use? In response to protests, state and local governments passed laws requiring wheelchair ramps and special parking spaces at public facilities. Many public facilities also put up signs in braille to help the visually impaired. Congress joined these efforts by passing the **Rehabilitation Act** in 1973, which forbade discrimination in jobs, education, or housing because of physical disabilities. In 1975 it passed the **Education for All Handicapped Children Act**, which required public schools to provide education for children with physical and mental disabilities.

■■ **The legacy of the civil rights movement continued in the growing political clout of African Americans, Hispanic Americans, and people with disabilities.**

𝒜 WHITE BACKLASH

The expansion of civil rights during the 1970s was the result of both public and private efforts. In an effort to uphold federal laws against discrimination, the Civil Rights Division of the Department of Justice sued corporations and labor unions to end unfair employment practices. Many schools and businesses also instituted **affirmative action** programs, whereby ethnic minorities and women were given preference in hiring and admission to make up for previous discrimination.

But the 1970s also brought a white backlash against this aspect of the civil rights movement. Some white citizens complained that affirmative action programs were depriving them of their own rights. One of the first targets of white anger was court-ordered busing to achieve school desegregation. Busing met with strong opposition in a number of cities, most notably Boston. One angry white Bostonian, Jimmy Kelley, warned: "You heard of the Hundred Years War? This will be the eternal war. It will be passed down from father to son."

By the fall of 1974, violent protests against busing had erupted in Boston. Many people were injured in the riots. Yet despite the risks, many

▼ These Boston protestors condemned the busing order issued by Judge W. Arthur Garrity, which was supported by U.S. senators Ted Kennedy and Ed Brooke.

black parents believed that busing was necessary. As one African American woman, Rachel Twymon, told her two children who were being bused to a previously all-white school:

> 66 I'm afraid this isn't going to be an easy year for either of you. You're going to be called a lot of ugly names. You're going to be spat at, maybe pushed around some. But it's not the first time this has happened and it won't be the last. It's something we have to go through—something *you* have to go through—if this city is ever going to get integrated. 99

By the late 1970s the busing controversy had quieted down, but anger over affirmative action continued. Many whites argued that affirmative action programs led to reverse discrimination. In 1978 the Supreme Court handed down an important ruling on affirmative action. In *University of California* v. *Bakke,* the Court ruled that a white man, Allan Bakke, had been unfairly denied admission to medical school on the basis of quotas—systems that set aside a fixed number of places for certain groups of people, in this case, African Americans. Although the Court did not rule out all forms of affirmative action, it did strike down quotas as a means of achieving racial equality. In a bitter dissent Justice Thurgood Marshall recalled the history of three centuries of racial discrimination in America and its toll on generations of African Americans: "The dream of America as the great melting pot has not been realized for the Negro; because of his skin color he never even made it into the pot."

■■ **White backlash against civil rights reform erupted in the 1970s, fueled by busing and affirmative action.**

AMERICAN INDIANS ORGANIZE

As part of the broad movement for civil rights, American Indians also began to organize, to seek redress in the courts, and to engage in commercial ventures. Young urban Indians launched the American Indian Movement (AIM) in 1968, calling for a renewal of Native American culture and recognition of Native American rights. In 1972, some 500 AIM members, protesting what they called the "Trail of Broken Treaties," temporarily occupied the Bureau of Indian Affairs (BIA) in Washington, D.C.

One of the leaders of the BIA occupation was Russell Means, a longtime Indian activist. Born in 1940 on the Pine Ridge Sioux Reservation of South Dakota, Means spent much of his childhood in the San Francisco Bay area. By 1970 he had become a prominent figure in AIM.

▲ **Russell Means**

In 1973 Means helped lead AIM's most dramatic action—the seizure of the trading post on the Sioux reservation in Wounded Knee, South Dakota. Here in 1890, U.S. cavalry units had killed more than 300 Sioux. For 71 days AIM members and U.S. marshals engaged in a grim standoff. Finally, after two people had been killed and one wounded, the government agreed to consider AIM's grievances, and the siege came to an end.

While AIM's confrontational tactics captured headlines and television attention, other American Indian leaders worked to renew tribal life by quieter means, including court action. The Taos Pueblo Indians of New Mexico recovered 48,000 acres of land, including the sacred Blue Lake. American Indians in Maine, claiming that more than half of the state had been illegally taken from them, won from Congress an $81.5 million award and the right to purchase up to 300,000 acres. Tribal groups in Alaska, South Dakota, Washington, and elsewhere either regained ancient lands or received large payments from the government for lands illegally taken from them. These cases were handled by the Indians Claims Commission, a federal agency set up in 1946.

American Indians also benefited from a 1961 federal law designed to encourage economic development on reservations. Under this law, many tribes established a variety of business ventures, such as factories, processing plants, and resorts. Some of the income from these businesses went to improve conditions on reservations. Tribal schools and colleges, for example, improved as a result of the new prosperity.

◀ The lumber mill and power project depicted in these photographs are among the many businesses established by American Indian tribes.

Reflecting growing pride among American Indians, the number of persons who identified themselves as Indian to federal census-takers surged from fewer than 800,000 in 1970 to nearly 2 million in 1990. Despite the gains, however, American Indians remained among the poorest of citizens and continued to grapple with many social problems.

■■ **During the 1970s Indian leaders worked to improve conditions for American Indians and to regain tribal lands.**

THE WOMEN'S MOVEMENT GAINS MOMENTUM

The women's movement made many advances in the 1970s as leaders worked to shape public policy and elect more women to public office. Many all-male colleges opened their doors to women, while other universities instituted courses in women's studies. In 1972 Congress passed the **Education Amendments Act**, which outlawed sexual discrimination in higher education.

The following year, the Supreme Court handed down a landmark decision affecting women. In the case **Roe v. Wade**, the Court overturned a state law limiting women's access to abortion. The Court ruled that a woman and her doctor, not the state, should make such decisions. While most feminists hailed *Roe* v. *Wade* as a victory, opponents protested that the ruling violated the right to life of the unborn.

The 1970s also saw a major battle over the **Equal Rights Amendment** (ERA), the proposed constitutional amendment barring discrimination on the basis of sex (see Chapter 11). The ERA received strong support from the National Organization for Women (NOW) and other women's groups. In testimony before Congress, feminist leader Gloria Steinem asserted:

❝ Women suffer second-class treatment from the moment they are born. They are expected to *be* rather than achieve, to function biologically rather than learn. A brother, whatever his intellect, is more likely to get the family's encouragement and education money, while girls are often pressured to conceal ambition and intelligence. ❞

Congress passed the ERA in 1972, but the amendment still required the approval of at least 38 states. At first, ratification seemed certain, but by

▼ During a news conference, National Women's Political Caucus leaders Gloria Steinem, Bella Abzug, Shirley Chisholm, and Betty Friedan announced their goal to increase the number of women delegates to the 1972 presidential conventions.

◀ Phyllis Schlafly was one of the most vocal critics of the ERA during the 1970s and the 1980s.

the 1982 deadline set by Congress, the ERA was still three states short of ratification. As a result, it failed to become law.

The women's movement made many political gains; however, it also alienated many women who viewed it as a movement primarily for privileged white women. Many women from working-class and ethnic communities felt that the leaders of NOW could not identify with the problems they faced every day.

The movement also alienated many middle-class women who felt that it downgraded the family and condemned women who chose to be full-time homemakers. These women viewed *Roe* v. *Wade* and the ERA as threats to traditional family life. Critics warned that the ERA would "nullify any laws that make any distinction between men and women." Eventually, they claimed, men and women would even be forced to share public restrooms! When the ERA failed to win ratification, conservative critic Phyllis Schlafly proclaimed: "The defeat of the Equal Rights Amendment is the greatest victory for women's rights since the woman's suffrage movement of 1920."

■■ **The women's movement was encouraged by legislation such as the ERA, but the issues alienated many women from the movement.**

A CHANGING POPULATION

As different groups in American society worked for change, the society itself was evolving. Thanks to medical advances, Americans were living longer, a phenomenon referred to as the "graying of America." At the same time, the birthrate was dropping sharply, to an average of two births per woman. For years, experts had been promoting this level of **zero population growth** (ZPG)—a birthrate that replaces the existing population but does not increase it—in hopes of preventing over-population.

The divorce rate continued to rise during the 1970s. In 1979, 5.3 divorces were registered per 1,000 Americans, up from 2.2 in 1960. Increasingly, many Americans were abandoning the idea that marriage was necessarily a lifelong commitment.

Americans also moved more often in the 1970s than in the past. During the decade a growing number of Americans migrated from the North and the East to the **Sunbelt** states of the South and the West, seeking a warmer climate and a more suburban life-style. This migration caused the population growth of California, Texas, and Florida to outpace that of the rest of the nation.

Another key factor in America's evolution during this period was continued immigration, mostly from Asia and Latin America. Most Latin American immigrants came from Mexico, but a sizable number also came from the Caribbean. In 1980, for example, nearly 120,000 Cubans fled the

▲ Many multigenerational Asian families, such as the one pictured here, immigrated to the United States in the 1970s.

Communist island for the United States, settling mainly in the Miami area. Economically successful, Cuban Americans became an important interest group in American politics.

Of the 1.6 million immigrants from Asia in the 1970s, most came from the Philippines and South Korea. China, which opened the way for emigration after President Nixon's visit, supplied some of the new Asian population as well. Many of these Chinese immigrants were highly skilled and well-educated professionals fleeing political persecution. Despite their backgrounds, however, some of these immigrants found when they arrived that their inability to speak English, as well as discrimination, kept them from obtaining well-paying jobs. The experiences of Wei-Chi Poon, a biology professor from China, and her husband, a skilled architect, were not unique. Neither knew any English when they immigrated to the United States. As a result, she worked in a laundry for $1.85 an hour, while he took on two low-paying jobs.

Congress tried to aid such immigrants by passing two new laws. The **Voting Rights Act of 1975** required states and communities with large numbers of non-English speakers to print voting materials in various foreign languages. The **Bilingual Education Act** of 1974 encouraged public schools to provide instruction to students in their

▲ The Bilingual Education Act of 1974 encouraged public schools, such as the one shown here, to provide students with instruction in their primary languages while they learned English.

primary languages while they learned English. Although some critics opposed bilingual education—charging that it slowed the assimilation of immigrants into American life—there was little question that the United States was becoming an increasingly multicultural society. Coping with new immigrants, both legal and illegal, would remain an important issue for America.

■■ **Large-scale Asian and Latin American immigration during the 1970s prompted support for bilingual education.**

SECTION 4 REVIEW

IDENTIFY and explain the significance of the following: Patricia Harris, League of United Latin American Citizens, Rehabilitation Act, Education for All Handicapped Children Act, affirmative action, *University of California* v. *Bakke*, Russell Means, Education Amendments Act, *Roe* v. *Wade*, Equal Rights Amendment, zero population growth, Sunbelt, Voting Rights Act of 1975, Bilingual Education Act.

1. **MAIN IDEA** Why did American Indians begin to organize during this period?

2. **MAIN IDEA** What influence did the Asian and Latin American immigrants in the 1970s have on American society?

3. **IDENTIFYING CAUSE AND EFFECT** How did the impact of the civil rights movement continue into the 1970s? How did some whites respond to this legacy?

4. **WRITING TO EXPRESS A VIEWPOINT** Imagine you are a political observer of the women's movement. Write an essay that summarizes the impact of *Roe* v. *Wade* and the ERA on the movement.

5. **LINKING HISTORY AND GEOGRAPHY** Why did many Americans move to the Sunbelt states during the 1970s? What effect did this migration have on population patterns?

First Earth Day celebration held. Salvador Allende elected president of Chile. EPA and OSHA created.

Wage and price controls imposed.

Nixon visits China. SALT treaty signed. Watergate break-in occurs. ERA passed. Nixon reelected president.

Roe v. Wade decided. Egypt and Syria invade Israel. Saturday Night Massacre occurs.

1970

1972

WRITING A SUMMARY

Using the essential points of the chapter as a guide, write a summary of the chapter.

REVIEWING CHRONOLOGY

Number your paper 1 to 5. Study the time line above, and list the following events in the order in which they happened by writing the first next to 1, the second next to 2, and so on. Then complete the activity below.

1. Bilingual Education Act passed.
2. First Earth Day celebration held.
3. Watergate break-in occurs.
4. Panama Canal treaties ratified.
5. Iran hostage crisis begins.

Evaluating How did the Arab-Israeli war affect the United States?

IDENTIFYING PEOPLE AND IDEAS

Explain the historical significance of each of the following people or terms.

1. silent majority
2. Clean Air Act
3. Salvador Allende
4. Saturday Night Massacre
5. Barbara Jordan
6. apartheid
7. Anwar Sadat
8. Rehabilitation Act
9. Russell Means
10. *Roe v. Wade*

UNDERSTANDING MAIN IDEAS

1. How did Nixon's domestic and foreign policies differ from those of his predecessors?
2. What was the origin of the Watergate scandal? What long-term effects did this scandal have on the United States?
3. What domestic and foreign problems did Ford face during his administration?
4. How did Carter attempt to keep his pledge of an "open administration"? Why did he fail to win reelection in 1980?
5. How did the expansion of the civil rights movement during the 1970s affect ethnic groups, women, and people with disabilities? What caused white backlash during this period?

REVIEWING THEMES

1. **Economic Development** How did U.S. dependence on foreign oil affect the economy?
2. **Global Relations** What effect did Nixon's visit to China have on U.S.–Soviet relations?
3. **Constitutional Heritage** Why did Nixon refuse to turn over his White House tapes to the Justice Department? How did his refusal challenge the basis of constitutional government?

THINKING CRITICALLY

1. **Analyzing** What steps did the government take during the 1970s to clean up the environment?
2. **Synthesizing** What domestic and foreign policy actions by Nixon interfered with democratic rights?
3. **Evaluating** Do you think a government is justified in basing a policy of foreign affairs on the principle of human rights? Explain your answer.

WRITING ABOUT HISTORY

Writing to Create Imagine you are a member of the environmental movement. Design a poster for the first Earth Day celebration that illustrates your concerns about the environment.

STRATEGY FOR SUCCESS

Review the Strategies for Success on Conducting an Interview on page 550. Imagine you are a reporter covering the Camp David Accords during 1978. Prepare a list of three questions to use in conducting an interview with either Anwar Sadat or Menachem Begin.

Sadat, Carter, and Begin signing the Camp David Accords, 1978

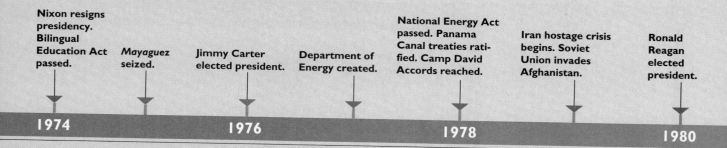

Nixon resigns presidency. Bilingual Education Act passed.

Mayaguez seized.

Jimmy Carter elected president.

Department of Energy created.

National Energy Act passed. Panama Canal treaties ratified. Camp David Accords reached.

Iran hostage crisis begins. Soviet Union invades Afghanistan.

Ronald Reagan elected president.

1974   1976   1978   1980

USING PRIMARY SOURCES

During the 1970s, court-ordered busing was seen as one way of overcoming racial segregation. Read the following excerpt from an account about the effect of busing on West Charlotte High School in Virginia. What is the message of this piece?

> 66 *The district judge . . . made it clear that he wanted socioeconomic integration as well as racial integration. . . .*
>
> *We are presently operating under [a court] order which forbids any change in assignment of a lottery-chosen white student assigned to West Charlotte High even if his family moves away from the area in which he was chosen. This has resulted in some bizarre transportation problems. In one case, we had to assign a driver and bus to pick up one pupil whose family built a new home and moved to the far northerly end of the county, more than 25 miles from West Charlotte High School.* 99

Young antibusing protester

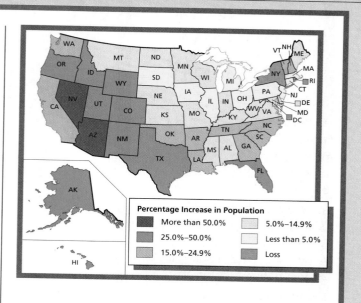

Percentage Increase in Population

More than 50.0%   5.0%–14.9%

25.0%–50.0%   Less than 5.0%

15.0%–24.9%   Loss

LINKING HISTORY AND GEOGRAPHY

Study the map in the next column, which shows population changes in the United States from 1970 to 1980. Which states had the greatest population growth? Which regions were most affected by population growth?

BUILDING YOUR PORTFOLIO

Complete the following projects independently or cooperatively.

1. POLITICS Imagine you are a *Washington Post* reporter covering the Senate investigations into the Watergate affair. Write a short article outlining the constitutional issues involved in the Watergate break-in, cover-up, and news coverage.

2. THE ECONOMY Imagine you are an economist in the 1970s. Create a flow chart that shows how increases in oil prices overseas ultimately affect the cost of consumer goods in the United States.

3. GLOBAL RELATIONS Imagine you are a United Nations delegate from an emerging nation. Conduct an interview with the secretary-general on the role the United Nations should play in establishing a world balance of power amid Cold War conflicts.

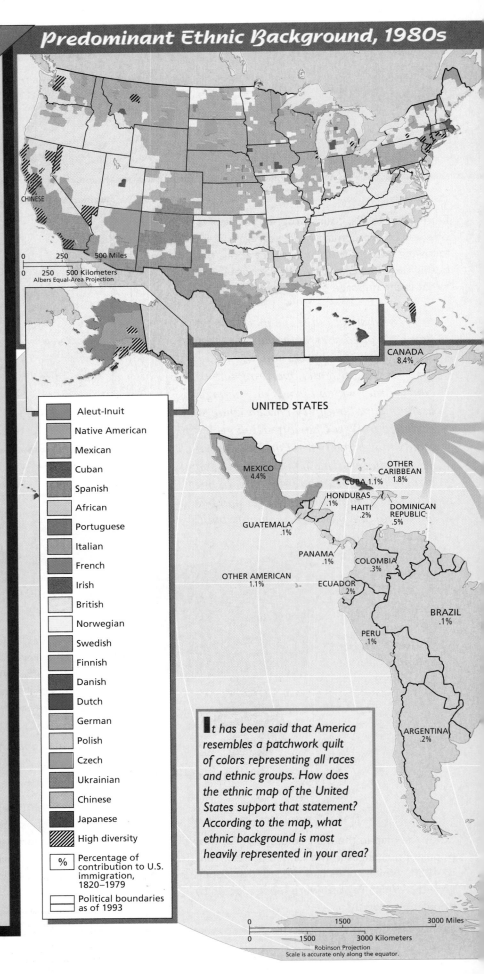

A DIVERSE COUNTRY

■■

EVEN before the founding of the United States, immigrants flocked to America from around the world. The origins of the immigrants have changed over time, however. The original Native Americans emigrated from Asia across Beringia. In colonial times the vast majority of immigrants came from Europe and Africa. Although Europe continued to provide the bulk of immigrants throughout the 19th century, more and more of them were from southern and eastern Europe. After World War II, immigration patterns changed dramatically as more people began to come from Latin America and from Asia. All of these immigrant groups have contributed to the diversity of American culture.

Legend:
- Aleut-Inuit
- Native American
- Mexican
- Cuban
- Spanish
- African
- Portuguese
- Italian
- French
- Irish
- British
- Norwegian
- Swedish
- Finnish
- Danish
- Dutch
- German
- Polish
- Czech
- Ukrainian
- Chinese
- Japanese
- High diversity
- % Percentage of contribution to U.S. immigration, 1820–1979
- Political boundaries as of 1993

It has been said that America resembles a patchwork quilt of colors representing all races and ethnic groups. How does the ethnic map of the United States support that statement? According to the map, what ethnic background is most heavily represented in your area?

CHINESE

UNITED STATES

CANADA 8.4%

MEXICO 4.4%

OTHER CARIBBEAN 1.8%

CUBA 1.1%

HONDURAS .1%

HAITI .2%

DOMINICAN REPUBLIC .5%

GUATEMALA .1%

PANAMA .1%

COLOMBIA .3%

OTHER AMERICAN 1.1%

ECUADOR .2%

PERU .1%

BRAZIL .1%

ARGENTINA .2%

0   250   500 Miles

0   250   500 Kilometers
Albers Equal-Area Projection

0   1500   3000 Miles

0   1500   3000 Kilometers
Robinson Projection
Scale is accurate only along the equator.

Contributions to U.S. Immigration

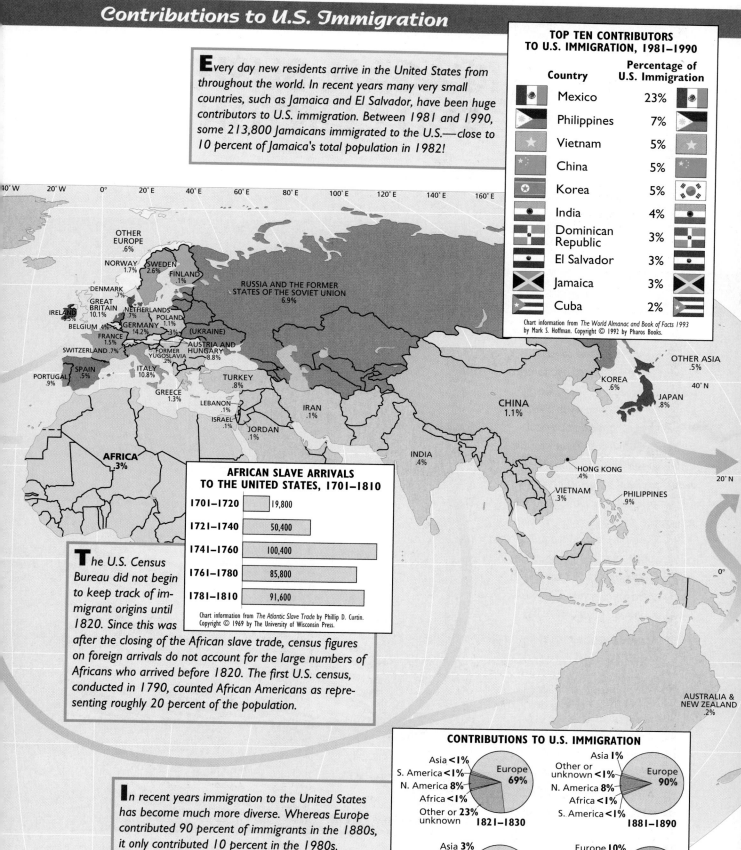

Every day new residents arrive in the United States from throughout the world. In recent years many very small countries, such as Jamaica and El Salvador, have been huge contributors to U.S. immigration. Between 1981 and 1990, some 213,800 Jamaicans immigrated to the U.S.—close to 10 percent of Jamaica's total population in 1982!

TOP TEN CONTRIBUTORS TO U.S. IMMIGRATION, 1981–1990

Country	Percentage of U.S. Immigration	
Mexico	23%	
Philippines	7%	
Vietnam	5%	
China	5%	
Korea	5%	
India	4%	
Dominican Republic	3%	
El Salvador	3%	
Jamaica	3%	
Cuba	2%	

Chart information from *The World Almanac and Book of Facts 1993* by Mark S. Hoffman. Copyright © 1992 by Pharos Books.

AFRICAN SLAVE ARRIVALS TO THE UNITED STATES, 1701–1810

1701–1720	19,800
1721–1740	50,400
1741–1760	100,400
1761–1780	85,800
1781–1810	91,600

Chart information from *The Atlantic Slave Trade* by Phillip D. Curtin. Copyright © 1969 by The University of Wisconsin Press.

The U.S. Census Bureau did not begin to keep track of immigrant origins until 1820. Since this was after the closing of the African slave trade, census figures on foreign arrivals do not account for the large numbers of Africans who arrived before 1820. The first U.S. census, conducted in 1790, counted African Americans as representing roughly 20 percent of the population.

In recent years immigration to the United States has become much more diverse. Whereas Europe contributed 90 percent of immigrants in the 1880s, it only contributed 10 percent in the 1980s. Germany, Ireland, Scandinavia, and Great Britain alone accounted for 68 percent of immigrants in the 1880s, more than the top ten countries combined in the 1980s!

CONTRIBUTIONS TO U.S. IMMIGRATION

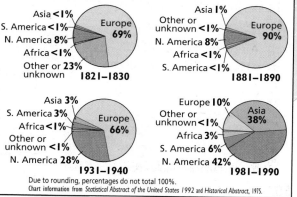

1821–1830
Asia <1%
S. America <1%
N. America 8%
Africa <1%
Other or unknown 23%
Europe 69%

1881–1890
Asia 1%
Other or unknown <1%
N. America 8%
Africa <1%
S. America <1%
Europe 90%

1931–1940
Asia 3%
S. America 3%
Africa <1%
Other or unknown <1%
N. America 28%
Europe 66%

1981–1990
Europe 10%
Other or unknown <1%
Africa 3%
S. America 6%
N. America 42%
Asia 38%

Due to rounding, percentages do not total 100%.
Chart information from *Statistical Abstract of the United States 1992 and Historical Abstract, 1975.*

REAGAN, BUSH, AND CLINTON

FOCUS

UNDERSTANDING THE MAIN IDEA

President Ronald Reagan entered office in 1981 with a series of conservative reforms for the economy and foreign relations. His vice president, George Bush, won the presidency in 1988. Plagued by economic and political problems, Bush lost to Democrat Bill Clinton in the 1992 election. Though initially troubled by political failures, Clinton presided over an economic resurgence and easily won reelection in 1996. As he prepared to lead the country up to the twenty-first century, Americans grappled with issues such as increased immigration, urban racial tensions, and the spread of AIDS.

THEMES

■ **ECONOMIC DEVELOPMENT** What positive and negative effects might measures that cut taxes, social programs, and business regulations have on a nation's economy?

■ **DEMOCRATIC VALUES** How might the use of modern technology increase democratic participation in an election?

1981	1984	1988	1991	1992	1994
Sandra Day O'Connor appointed to Supreme Court.	Ronald Reagan reelected president.	George Bush elected president.	Operation Desert Storm launched.	Bill Clinton elected president.	Republicans gained control of the House and Senate.

Public frustration with government grew in the 1970s as the Watergate scandal broke, the energy crisis emerged, and the economy continued to weaken. As a result, Democrat Jimmy Carter, who promised to reform government, was elected president. The Iran hostage crisis and runaway inflation, however, undermined his presidency, contributing to a Republican victory in the 1980 election.

Operation Desert Storm, 1991

Entering the White House on a wave of discontent, Ronald Reagan promised to set the nation on a new course with lower taxes, fewer federal regulations, cuts in social programs, and increased military spending. A former Hollywood actor, Reagan was well suited for the television age. Often called "the Great Communicator," he projected a sense of confidence and patriotism that reassured Americans troubled by the nation's mounting economic problems and weakened world image. Television observer John Corry noted of Reagan: "His voice is his greatest weapon. It is not an orator's voice. It is husky, and sometimes it fades to a whisper. Meanwhile, it is extraordinarily intimate. Mr. Reagan does not speak to audiences; he speaks to individuals."

Reagan's vice president, George Bush, was elected president in 1988. Bush's greatest achievements were on the international front. Under his administration, the United States launched a successful invasion of Panama and played a primary role in crushing the Iraqi takeover of Kuwait. Bush's domestic record was less impressive, however. By the time he ran for reelection in 1992, the country was beset by an ailing economy and other domestic problems. In a campaign that saw the rise of independent candidate H. Ross Perot and an increased role for women, Bush lost to baby-boom Democrat Bill Clinton, who won reelection in 1996 pledging to "build a bridge to the twenty-first century."

President Bush visiting
U.S. troops

THE REAGAN MOVEMENT

FOCUS

- **What was Reaganomics? How did it affect the country?**
- **Why did the Reagan administration consider events in Nicaragua and El Salvador important?**
- **What economic problems plagued the country during the late 1980s?**
- **What was the Iran-contra affair?**

President Ronald Reagan with his wife, Nancy

*R*onald Reagan's 1980 presidential victory reflected the growing conservative mood of the nation. Adopting Reagan's programs, Congress cut taxes and reduced federal regulation of the economy. As a result, the economy boomed in the mid-1980s. Toward the end of the decade, however, political scandals and a soaring federal deficit troubled the nation.

THE NEW RIGHT

A former Democrat turned conservative Republican, Ronald Reagan appealed to a wide range of voters who were disenchanted with liberal politics. Reagan's strongest support, however, came from the political conservatives of the **New Right**. At the forefront of the New Right was Reverend Jerry Falwell's **Moral Majority**—a fundamentalist Christian organization founded in 1978.

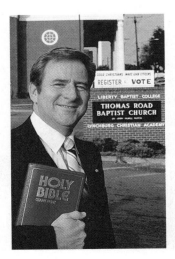

◀ **The Reverend Jerry Falwell's Moral Majority encouraged churchgoers to register to vote and support conservative causes.**

President Reagan and the New Right shared the same political goals. Both supported school prayer, a strong defense, and free-market economic policies. Both opposed abortion, the Equal Rights Amendment, gun control, and busing to achieve racial balance in schools.

In addition to helping elect Reagan president, New Right conservatives were largely responsible for the Republicans gaining control of the Senate in 1980. They also played a significant role in shaping Republican policy throughout the decade. Although Jerry Falwell disbanded the Moral Majority in the late 1980s, New Right conservatives continued to exert a strong influence in the Republican party.

REAGANOMICS IN ACTION

President Reagan entered office with a comprehensive economic program already mapped out. This plan, dubbed **Reaganomics**, was based on the supply-side economics argument that lowering the top income tax rates would spur economic growth. Supporters of Reaganomics claimed that people would invest their tax savings in businesses, thereby creating jobs, increasing consumer spending, and generating higher tax revenues. Congress responded to Reagan's program by passing a three-year plan to cut federal income taxes by 25 percent.

Congress also supported another part of Reagan's economic plan—drastic cuts in government regulation of industries such as television, trucking, airlines, and banking. The Reagan administration's probusiness, antiregulation stance was typified by the Department of Interior's handling of public lands. Against the objections of environmentalists, Secretary of the Interior James Watt leased huge areas of the seafloor to private companies searching for oil and gas. He also leased federal lands to coal companies.

At first, Reaganomics seemed to work. By 1983 the inflation rate had dropped to a manageable 4 percent. Americans went on a shopping spree similar to those in the 1920s and 1950s. Business revived, the stock market soared, and the future looked bright.

Critics were quick to point out that not all Americans benefited equally from the recovery. Deep cuts in social programs—an important element in Reaganomics—hurt the poor. And although employment rose overall, joblessness remained high among African Americans and Hispanic Americans, especially unskilled workers in the inner cities. Unemployment among factory workers in the Midwest, once America's industrial heartland, also remained high. As a result, homelessness increased dramatically.

Critics also charged that Reagan's tax cuts favored the wealthy and that spending cuts and deregulation weakened programs that protected consumers, the needy, and the environment. They also warned that big tax cuts combined with increased military spending (another important element of Reaganomics) would produce enormous deficits in the federal budget.

Reaganomics stimulated the economy by cutting taxes and industrial regulations, but critics claimed the policies hurt the poor and increased the federal deficit.

REAGAN AND THE COLD WAR

The Reagan administration's emphasis on increased military spending was in part a reflection of Ronald Reagan's strong anti-Communist views. He took a hard line against the Soviet Union, even branding it an "evil empire." To counter the Soviet threat, Reagan called for new weapons systems and an increased U.S. presence in such areas as the Indian Ocean and the Persian Gulf.

PRESIDENTIAL LIVES

RONALD REAGAN
1911–

in office
1981–1989

One of Reagan's political gifts was a sharp wit. After his first debate with Jimmy Carter in the 1980 election, a reporter asked if he had been nervous appearing on stage with the president. "No, not at all," Reagan replied, then referred to his past career as an actor: "I've been on the same stage with John Wayne."

Reagan's wit helped reassure the nation after a lone gunman shot him on March 30, 1981. As the wounded president was wheeled into the operating room, he looked around at the surgeons and quipped, "Please assure me that you are all Republicans!" While he was recuperating in intensive care, Reagan sent several humorous notes to his staff members, including one that read, "If I had had this much attention in Hollywood, I'd have stayed there!"

New weapons. From 1981 to 1985 the Pentagon's budget grew from some $150 billion to about $250 billion. Much of the money went to fund nuclear weapons. Reagan's first secretary of state, Alexander Haig, suggested that "nuclear warning shots" might be useful in a conventional war.

The talk of nuclear war stirred public fear. In town meetings and state referendums, voters urged a freeze on the testing and deployment of nuclear weapons. Many Americans marched in rallies to show their support for the proposals.

To blunt the nuclear-freeze movement, Reagan proposed the **Strategic Defense Initiative** (SDI), a space-based missile-defense system, in March 1983. SDI quickly stirred controversy. Critics labeled it "Star Wars," after the popular 1977 movie, saying it rested on untested technology and was probably unworkable. They also warned that SDI research would intensify the arms race. Reagan countered that SDI would be a weapon for peace—one that killed weapons, not people. In a national address he proclaimed:

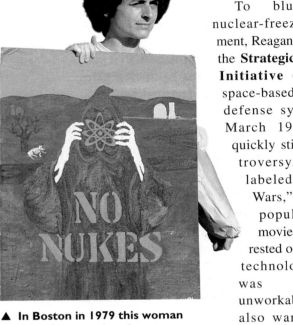

▲ **In Boston in 1979 this woman protests the use of nuclear power.**

> 66 I call upon the scientific community in our country, those who gave us nuclear weapons, to turn their great talents now to the cause of mankind and world peace: to give us the means of rendering these nuclear weapons impotent and obsolete. 99

U.S.–Soviet relations. Even before President Reagan took office, U.S.–Soviet relations had cooled because of the Soviet Union's 1979 invasion of Afghanistan (see map on page 561). Relations deteriorated further when, in August 1980, Polish workers in Gdansk and Szczecin (SHCHET-seen) staged a series of massive

▲ **Many Americans, particularly those of Polish descent, supported the Solidarity movement. These Boston residents marched to show their support.**

strikes to protest high prices and to demand the right to form trade unions free from government or Communist party control. At first, things went well for the strikers. In late August, faced with the threat of a nationwide general strike, the Polish government legalized independent union activity. Labor activists responded by voting on September 17 to form the independent trade union **Solidarity**, under the leadership of Lech Walesa (vah-LEN-suh), an electrician at a Gdansk shipyard who had helped launch the initial strikes.

Then, in December 1981, the Soviet-backed government changed its stand and instituted martial law. Government troops shut down Solidarity centers and arrested union leaders. Expecting resistance, Soviet troops prepared to brutally "restore order" as they had in Hungary in 1956 and in Czechoslovakia in 1968. Warning the Soviet Union not to invade Poland, Reagan called for new trade restrictions against the Soviets. Moscow heeded the warning and stayed out of Poland.

Tensions flared again in 1983. On September 30, the Soviets shot down a Korean airliner over Soviet airspace, killing all 269 passengers, including many Americans. Despite international outcries, the Soviets defended their action, claiming the plane had been spying. Later that year, when the United States sent new nuclear missiles to England and Germany, the Soviets walked out of arms-control talks. When the Soviets boycotted the 1984 Summer Olympics in Los Angeles, relations between the two superpowers sank to their lowest point in years.

REAGAN AND LATIN AMERICA

Fearing that the developing nations of Latin America would fall under the influence of the Soviet Union, President Reagan increased U.S. involvement in the region, particularly the Central American countries of Nicaragua and El Salvador.

In 1979, Nicaraguan rebels known as **Sandinistas** had overthrown the dictatorship of Anastasio Somoza Debayle, whose family had ruled Nicaragua since the 1930s. Soon after Reagan took office, he cut all U.S. aid to Nicaragua on the grounds that the Sandinistas were backed by the Soviet bloc. He also charged that the Sandinistas were exporting revolution by shipping Cuban and Soviet weapons to rebels in El Salvador. The Sandinistas reacted to U.S. pressure by strengthening their ties to the Soviet bloc. Reagan then decided to support the Nicaraguan **contras**, a large army recruited, financed, and armed by the CIA. Hoping the revolutionary group would overthrow the Sandinista government, Reagan called the contras "freedom fighters" and compared them to the founders of the United States.

Many Americans opposed the CIA-sponsored war against the Sandinistas, fearing another Vietnam in Central America. Reflecting such concerns, Congress began restricting funds for the contras late in 1984. But, as the nation would soon learn, the White House continued to finance the contras despite the congressional ban, using funds secretly contributed by wealthy supporters and foreign governments.

The Reagan administration also found itself pulled into events in El Salvador. In 1979 a group of young military officers seized power in the country, instituting a brutally repressive government. The army and special death squads killed and tortured opposition leaders. Soon fighting erupted between

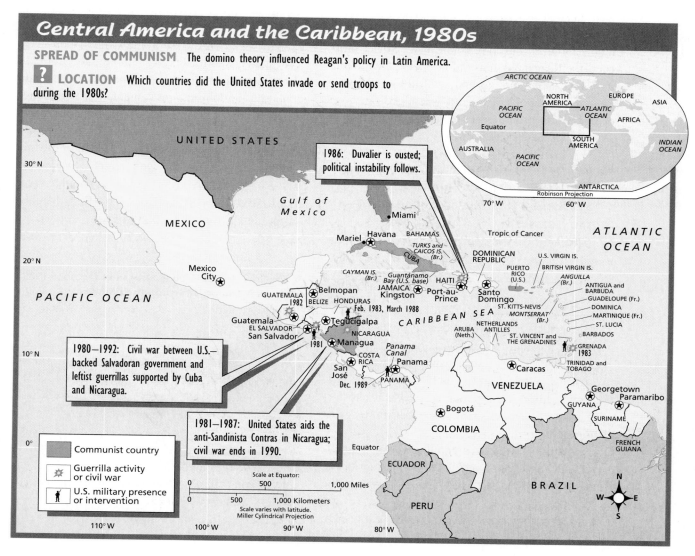

Central America and the Caribbean, 1980s

SPREAD OF COMMUNISM The domino theory influenced Reagan's policy in Latin America.

? LOCATION Which countries did the United States invade or send troops to during the 1980s?

1986: Duvalier is ousted; political instability follows.

1980–1992: Civil war between U.S.–backed Salvadoran government and leftist guerrillas supported by Cuba and Nicaragua.

1981–1987: United States aids the anti-Sandinista Contras in Nicaragua; civil war ends in 1990.

Communist country

Guerrilla activity or civil war

U.S. military presence or intervention

▲ The surrender of the Nicaraguan National Guard to the Sandinistas in July 1979 marked the end of the Somoza regime. Citizens celebrated the rebel victory by dragging a statue of Somoza through the streets of downtown Managua.

government forces and rebels demanding radical reform.

In 1984, José Napoleón Duarte, a moderate, won election by promising reforms and an end to the civil war. Eager to prevent a rebel victory that might allow El Salvador to fall under Soviet influence, the Reagan administration offered Duarte military and economic aid and sent advisers to train government troops. The civil war raged on, however, until intense international pressure forced both sides to sign a peace treaty in 1992.

■■ **Central America, especially Nicaragua and El Salvador, became a flashpoint in the struggle between the United States and the Soviet Union.**

*R*EAGAN REELECTED

Despite criticisms of his policies, President Reagan remained popular. His emphasis on patriotism and national pride struck a responsive chord with many Americans. While Carter was haunted by his failures and setbacks, the public seemed quick to forgive and forget any mishaps or scandals in Reagan's administration.

Adding to Reagan's popularity was a small-scale military action in 1983. On the tiny Caribbean island of Grenada, a military group overthrew the government and killed the prime minister. Several Caribbean nations requested U.S. intervention. On October 25, 1983, some 2,000 U.S. Marines and

Army Rangers went ashore on Grenada, unseated the coup leaders, and set up a government favorable to the United States.

Soon after the Grenada invasion, Reagan announced that he would seek a second term in 1984, with George Bush again as his running mate. Former vice president Walter Mondale won the Democratic nomination. He picked Congresswoman Geraldine Ferraro of New York as his running mate. Ferraro thus became the first woman to run on a major party presidential ticket. Some predicted Ferraro's presence would increase support for the Democratic party among women.

Republicans had been taking steps to enhance the role of women in their party. Reagan appointed several women to high public offices, including Elizabeth Dole as secretary of transportation, Margaret Heckler as secretary of health and human services, and Jeane Kirkpatrick as head of the U.S. delegation to the United Nations—the first woman to hold the post. In 1981 Reagan had also appointed the first woman ever to serve on the Supreme Court—conservative justice Sandra Day O'Connor. Republicans also sought the support of women who felt abandoned by the feminist movement. The percentage of female delegates to the Republican convention increased from 24 percent in 1980 to 44 percent in 1984. In the end, Ferraro's presence did not add many votes for the Democrats. On election day, Reagan received 54.5 million popular votes to Mondale's 37.6 million. The Republicans swept the electoral vote, 525 to 13.

▼ The invasion of Grenada began in October 1983, when U.S. troops landed on the island.

SIGNS OF TROUBLE

One issue that arose during the election was the growing conservative emphasis of the Supreme Court. When Chief Justice Warren Burger retired in 1986, Reagan elevated Associate Justice William Rehnquist to chief justice. To fill Rehnquist's position, Reagan nominated conservative Antonin Scalia. When another justice retired in 1987, Reagan nominated Robert Bork, a federal judge and law professor who held a far narrower interpretation of the Bill of Rights than the Court had upheld in recent years.

Bork's views alarmed many people, including many senators. By a 58–42 vote, the Senate rejected Bork, handing Reagan a crushing loss. His next choice, Douglas Ginsberg, withdrew after press reports that he had smoked marijuana as a law professor. At last Reagan found a conservative judge who could also win Senate confirmation, Anthony Kennedy of California.

The failure of the Bork nomination was one of several signs that the "Reagan Revolution" was starting to weaken. Of special concern was the federal deficit, which had reached over $200 billion in 1985. Seeking to balance the budget with forced spending cuts, Congress passed the Balanced Budget and Emergency Control Act in 1985. Called the **Gramm-Rudman-Hollings Act** after its sponsors, the law required automatic across-the-board cuts in government spending when the deficit exceeded a certain amount. Other legislation took aim at specific problems. The **Tax Reform Law** of 1986, for example, wiped out many rules that gave certain groups special tax breaks.

The stock market also showed signs of trouble. Reagan's tax cuts and business deregulation had stimulated a stock market boom, but with this boom came a wave of illegal **insider trading**—the use of confidential financial information by stockbrokers for personal gain. Several large brokerage firms pleaded guilty to illegal activities and faced severe penalties. These scandals eroded investor trust in stockbrokers.

Then, on October 19, 1987, after several years of growth, the stock market crashed. On paper, stock losses totaled almost $1 trillion. The value of Eastman Kodak stock fell by more than 30 percent. Other major corporations experienced similar sharp drops in their stocks' values.

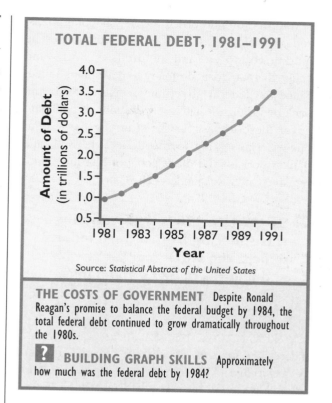

TOTAL FEDERAL DEBT, 1981–1991

Source: *Statistical Abstract of the United States*

THE COSTS OF GOVERNMENT Despite Ronald Reagan's promise to balance the federal budget by 1984, the total federal debt continued to grow dramatically throughout the 1980s.

? **BUILDING GRAPH SKILLS** Approximately how much was the federal debt by 1984?

In another sign of economic trouble, a crisis hit the nation's savings and loan (S&L) and banking industries in the late 1980s and early 1990s. Freed of federal regulation, banks and S&Ls, especially in the Southwest, had made risky loans to

▲ Investors lost billions of dollars during the stock market crash of October 1987. Shown here is the frantic scene on the floor of the New York Stock Exchange on the day of the crash, as traders tried to sell shares and cut losses.

developers to build office towers, shopping malls, and other projects. In the late 1980s the real-estate market collapsed, and hundreds of S&Ls and banks that had loaned money to developers failed. Since the federal government insures S&L and bank depositors, it had to pay billions of dollars to cover these losses, further straining the federal budget. The soaring federal deficit, the S&L and banking crisis, and other economic problems all remained after Reagan left office.

> ## ▪▪ By the late 1980s the economy was suffering from a huge federal deficit, the stock market crash, and failures of S&Ls and banks.

COLD WAR TENSIONS EASE

There was more to cheer about on the international front. The most significant event of Reagan's second term was a dramatic easing of Cold War hostilities. When Mikhail Gorbachev became leader of the Soviet Union in 1985, a new era of Soviet history began. With his nation burdened by a failing economy, a repressive political system, and heavy military costs, Gorbachev introduced a policy of openness, called *glasnost* (GLAZS-nuhst), that promised more freedom for

the Soviet people. Equally dramatic was *perestroika* (per-uh-STROY-kuh)—Gorbachev's plan to restructure the Soviet economy and government. On the economic front, he called for increased foreign trade and reduced military spending. The revenues from these changes were to be used to modernize factories.

To further his domestic goals and defuse the costly Cold War conflict, Gorbachev pursued détente with the United States. In 1987, after a series of meetings between Gorbachev and President Reagan, the Soviet Union and the United States signed the **Intermediate-range Nuclear Forces** (INF) **Treaty**. This treaty eliminated all medium-range nuclear weapons from Europe. Gorbachev also withdrew Soviet troops from Afghanistan. Addressing the United Nations in 1988, Gorbachev said:

> 66 The use or threat of force no longer can or must be an instrument of foreign policy. . . . All of us, and primarily the stronger of us, must exercise self-restraint and totally rule out any outward-oriented use of force. 99

In May 1988, as the Senate prepared to ratify the INF Treaty, Reagan flew to Moscow. As television cameras whirred, the U.S. president and the Soviet leader embraced like old friends.

> ## ▪▪ During Reagan's second term U.S.–Soviet relations improved dramatically as Gorbachev instituted *glasnost* and *perestroika*.

THE IRAN-CONTRA AFFAIR

As relations with the Soviet Union improved, the Reagan administration continued to face problems in the Middle East and Latin America. These frustrations led to the most serious crisis to hit the Reagan White House—the **Iran-contra affair**.

After Congress cut off funds for the contras' war against Nicaragua's Sandinista government, the Reagan administration sought other sources of funding. At the time, the White House was secretly bargaining with Iran for the release of U.S. hostages held by pro-Iranian groups in Lebanon. As part of the bargain, the administration shipped more than 500 antitank missiles to

▲ On June 1, 1988, President Ronald Reagan and Soviet leader Mikhail Gorbachev embraced during a Moscow ceremony celebrating ratification of the INF Treaty.

Iran by way of Israel. Without informing Congress, the administration used the profits from these arms sales to pay for weapons and supplies for the contras.

When the arms sales became known in 1986, Reagan appointed a committee to investigate. The committee cleared Reagan of any direct involvement but heavily criticized other White House officials, some of whom resigned. The secret funding of the contra war soon leaked out as well. It was revealed that Lieutenant Colonel Oliver North, a White House aide, had funneled millions of dollars from the Iranian arms sales to the contras after Congress had forbidden aid. In 1987, House and Senate committees investigated the affair. North admitted that he and his secretary, Fawn Hall, had destroyed key documents. But North emotionally insisted that he had acted out of loyalty and patriotism.

In its report the congressional committee denounced North's activities and criticized the loose White House management style that had allowed North to operate as he did. The chairman of the Senate committee, Senator Daniel Inouye of Hawaii, countered North's claim that he was just following orders. Said Inouye:

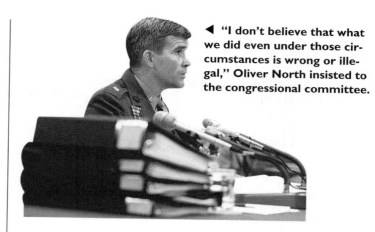

◀ "I don't believe that what we did even under those circumstances is wrong or illegal," Oliver North insisted to the congressional committee.

66 [The] colonel was well aware that he was subject to the Uniform Code of Military Justice. . . . And that code makes it abundantly clear that orders of a superior officer must be obeyed by subordinate members—but it is lawful orders. . . . In fact, it says members of the military have an obligation to disobey unlawful orders. 99

In 1988 a court-appointed special prosecutor filed criminal charges against North and President Reagan's national security adviser, Admiral John Poindexter. North was convicted on various charges, including the destruction of government documents and lying to Congress. The conviction was later reversed on a legal technicality.

■■ In the Iran-contra affair, White House aides provided illegal funding for the Nicaraguan contras through arms sales to Iran.

SECTION 1 REVIEW

IDENTIFY and explain the significance of the following: New Right, Moral Majority, Reaganomics, Strategic Defense Initiative, Solidarity, Sandinistas, contras, José Napoleón Duarte, Geraldine Ferraro, Sandra Day O'Connor, Gramm-Rudman-Hollings Act, Tax Reform Law, insider trading, *glasnost*, *perestroika*, Intermediate-range Nuclear Forces Treaty, Iran-contra affair, Oliver North.

LOCATE and explain the importance of the following: Nicaragua, El Salvador, Grenada.

1. **MAIN IDEA** How did Reagan's economic policies both help and hurt the country?

2. **MAIN IDEA** What factors weakened the U.S. economy during the late 1980s?

3. **ANALYZING** Imagine you are a citizen of El Salvador in the early 1980s. Describe the political situation in your country and explain why you think the United States is intervening in your country's affairs.

4. **WRITING TO INFORM** Imagine you are a member of the congressional committee appointed to investigate the Iran-contra affair. Write a letter to your constituents that summarizes the results of the investigation.

5. **ASSESSING CONSEQUENCES** How did each political party try to appeal to women voters in the 1984 presidential election?

FROM BUSH TO CLINTON

FOCUS

■ **What events marked the end of the Cold War?**

■ **How did Operation Desert Storm differ from previous American military conflicts?**

■ **What were some of the domestic problems President Bush faced?**

■ **How did the 1992 election reflect voter concerns?**

Female soldier during Operation Desert Storm

In 1988 Vice President George Bush was elected president. Bush's popularity soared after U.S. troops defeated the Iraqis in the Persian Gulf War. But Bush faced many challenges at home, including a persistent recession that contributed to his defeat by Democrat Bill Clinton in 1992. Clinton entered office in 1993 to the optimistic theme song "Don't Stop Thinking About Tomorrow." The youthful Democrat had reason to be optimistic, having just won a close, hard-fought election. He won reelection by a comfortable margin in 1996.

THE 1988 ELECTION

With the popular Reagan prohibited from running for a third term, the Democrats hoped to regain the White House in 1988. African American leader Jesse Jackson, who had run in 1984, was among a large group seeking the Democratic nomination. Jackson hoped to attract a "Rainbow Coalition"—a diverse group of voters representing all races,

classes, and creeds. As a candidate in 1984, Jackson had helped generate the largest turnout of African American voters ever for a Democratic primary.

By 1988 Jackson's appeal had expanded to encompass a wide range of voters. On "Super Tuesday," the largest single day of primary voting, Jackson won more votes than any other candidate. Governor Michael Dukakis of Massachusetts, however, won the most delegates and eventually gained the nomination. Dukakis, the son of Greek immigrants, selected Senator Lloyd Bentsen of Texas as his running mate. Vice President George Bush won the Republican presidential nomination with young Indiana senator Dan Quayle as his running mate.

The 1988 presidential campaign proved to be one of the harshest in recent years. Initially, Bush tried to appeal to voters' sense of optimism

◀ Seeking to unite a "Rainbow Coalition" of voters, Jesse Jackson ran for the Democratic party's presidential nomination in both 1984 and 1988.

by promising "a kinder and gentler nation." In the campaign's final weeks, however, most of the Republican ads focused on negative issues. For instance, one commercial attacked Dukakis's record on the environment by showing scenes of Massachusetts' heavily polluted Boston Harbor.

The most controversial Republican advertising campaign, however, was designed to sway voters troubled by the rising crime rate, which had jumped by over 12.5 percent between 1984 and 1988. A series of television and print ads painted Dukakis as weak on crime by associating him with convicted murderer Willie Horton. While out on a weekend pass under a Massachusetts prison program, Horton had attacked a Maryland couple. Since he was African American, some critics charged that the ads played on fears of black criminals and were racist.

Dukakis resisted using similarly negative ads in his own campaign. Instead, he tried to convince voters of his skills as a manager, arguing that the election should be about competence. Voters, however, doubted his abilities. In the November election, the Bush-Quayle ticket won 426 electoral votes to the Dukakis-Bentsen ticket's 112. But the Democrats did increase their majorities in both houses of Congress and kept control of most state legislatures.

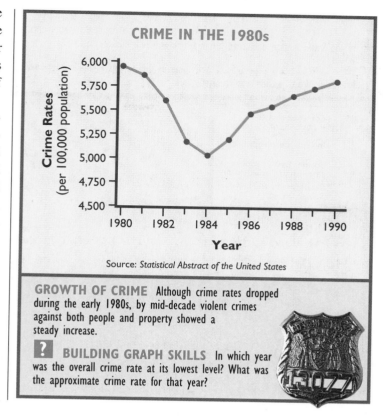

CRIME IN THE 1980s

Source: *Statistical Abstract of the United States*

GROWTH OF CRIME Although crime rates dropped during the early 1980s, by mid-decade violent crimes against both people and property showed a steady increase.

? BUILDING GRAPH SKILLS In which year was the overall crime rate at its lowest level? What was the approximate crime rate for that year?

▼ 1988 campaign button

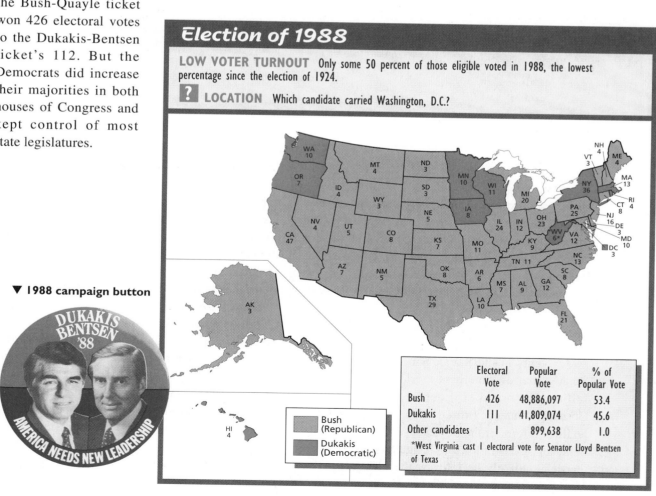

Election of 1988

LOW VOTER TURNOUT Only some 50 percent of those eligible voted in 1988, the lowest percentage since the election of 1924.

? LOCATION Which candidate carried Washington, D.C.?

	Electoral Vote	Popular Vote	% of Popular Vote
Bush	426	48,886,097	53.4
Dukakis	111	41,809,074	45.6
Other candidates	1	899,638	1.0

*West Virginia cast 1 electoral vote for Senator Lloyd Bentsen of Texas

Bush (Republican)

Dukakis (Democratic)

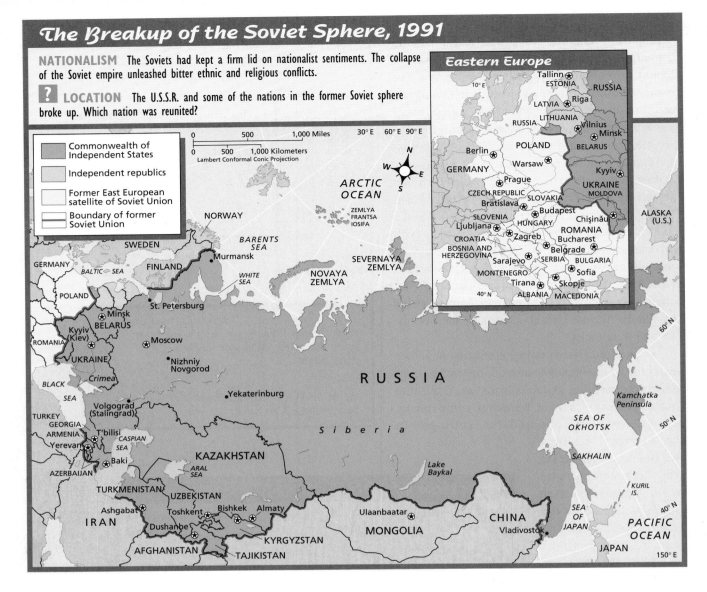

The Breakup of the Soviet Sphere, 1991

NATIONALISM The Soviets had kept a firm lid on nationalist sentiments. The collapse of the Soviet empire unleashed bitter ethnic and religious conflicts.

? LOCATION The U.S.S.R. and some of the nations in the former Soviet sphere broke up. Which nation was reunited?

Legend:
- Commonwealth of Independent States
- Independent republics
- Former East European satellite of Soviet Union
- Boundary of former Soviet Union

THE COLD WAR ENDS

Bush, who had served in numerous appointed government positions, including director of the CIA and representative to China, concentrated much of his attention on foreign affairs. He was determined to reassert America's world leadership. Bush had his first chance in Panama, when in December 1989 he sent U.S. troops to arrest Panama's president Manuel Noriega, who was wanted on drug charges in the United States.

Events in the Soviet Union soon advanced Bush's goal of American world leadership even further. Historians still debate how far Mikhail Gorbachev intended to go with the economic and political reform of the Soviet system. Undoubtedly, he meant to institute real change. But many argue that it is unlikely he foresaw the end result—the breakup of the Soviet Union and the collapse of

Communist rule. Once set in motion, however, Gorbachev's reforms took on a life of their own.

Gorbachev's efforts to modernize and expand the Soviet economy led to a dramatic easing of Cold War tensions with the United States. These efforts also indirectly helped assist the democratic movements that swept Eastern and Central Europe in 1989 and 1990. No longer willing or able to bear the costs of propping up Communist regimes around the world, the Soviet Union announced in 1989 that it was adopting a policy of nonintervention in Eastern Europe. Thus the Soviets did nothing when Poland and Hungary held free elections and the Communist governments in Czechoslovakia and Romania fell.

The Soviets also did nothing when pro-democracy demonstrations broke out in East Germany in the fall of 1989. Throughout the fall, tens of thousands of East Germans seized the opportunity to flee to the West through Hungary.

Then in October demonstrators forced Communist leader Erich Honecker to resign. Hoping to restore calm, the East German government opened the Berlin Wall on November 9 and lifted restrictions on travel to the West. But it was already too late; the pressure for **German reunification**—the reuniting of East and West Germany as one nation—was too great. After free elections, the two nations were united as the Federal Republic of Germany on October 3, 1990, without opposition from Gorbachev.

By 1991 Gorbachev had problems of his own in the Soviet Union. Alarmed by the pace of reforms, Communist hard-liners attempted to oust him. Their coup collapsed quickly, but Gorbachev's days in power were numbered. On December 1 the Ukrainians voted for independence. A week later the presidents of Ukraine, Russia, and Belarus declared that the Soviet Union was "ceasing its existence" and formed the **Commonwealth of Independent States** (CIS). On December 25 Gorbachev resigned as president of the Soviet Union and turned over control of the armed forces to Boris Yeltsin, the president of Russia. The Soviet Union was no more. Eventually the former Soviet republics of Armenia, Azerbaijan, Kazakhstan, Kyrgyzstan, Moldova, Tajikistan, Turkmenistan, Uzbekistan, and Georgia joined the CIS.

■■ **The collapse of communism in Eastern Europe, the fall of the Berlin Wall, and the breakup of the Soviet Union marked the end of the Cold War.**

In contrast, pro-democracy reformers in China met a different fate. In May 1989 students and others took to Beijing's streets to protest Communist party policies. On June 4 the government sent soldiers and tanks against the peaceful protesters gathered in Tiananmen Square. Estimates of the number of protesters killed range from a few hundred to more than a thousand. In the 1990s China abandoned a centrally controlled economy in favor of capitalist free enterprise, but human-rights abuses persisted.

As the Cold War faded, regional conflicts intensified. The end of Communist rule in Eastern Europe unleashed bitter ethnic and local disputes that had formerly been kept in check by Communist authorities. For example, Bosnia— formerly a part of Yugoslavia—was torn by fighting between Serbs, Croatians, and Slovenes.

In the former Soviet Union itself, the 15 newly independent republics experienced conflict as different groups struggled for power and self-rule. Russia and Ukraine argued over control of the Black Sea fleet, while Christians in the former Soviet republic of Armenia battled with Muslims in neighboring Azerbaijan (az-uhr-by-JAHN).

THE PERSIAN GULF WAR

Bush again assumed a leadership role in August 1990 when Iraq, led by ruler Saddam Hussein, invaded neighboring Kuwait, a major oil producer. The United Nations condemned the attack,

THROUGH OTHERS' EYES

THE GULF WAR

Although the Persian Gulf War was brief, many people were caught in the crossfire, including the residents of Israel. To retaliate against UN forces, Iraq launched an attack on Israel. Sari Nusseibeh, a Palestinian philosopher living in Israel when fighting broke out, recalled his impressions as the war raged:

❝*It was January 29, 13 days since the aerial bombardment in the Gulf War had started. For fully two weeks we had been placed under a total 24–hour curfew, interspersed only by three two-hour intervals in which we were allowed to do our shopping. All of us—my wife, my three children, and myself—had taken to sleeping together on the floor of the sitting-dining area of our apartment. This way we kept each other company through the Scud [missile] scares (. . . we wondered each time where the rockets would fall, and what deadly poison they might be carrying). . . .*

For almost two weeks we lived in a state of suspension between TV scenes of missiles hitting Iraqi targets and footage of missiles flying over our heads. ❞

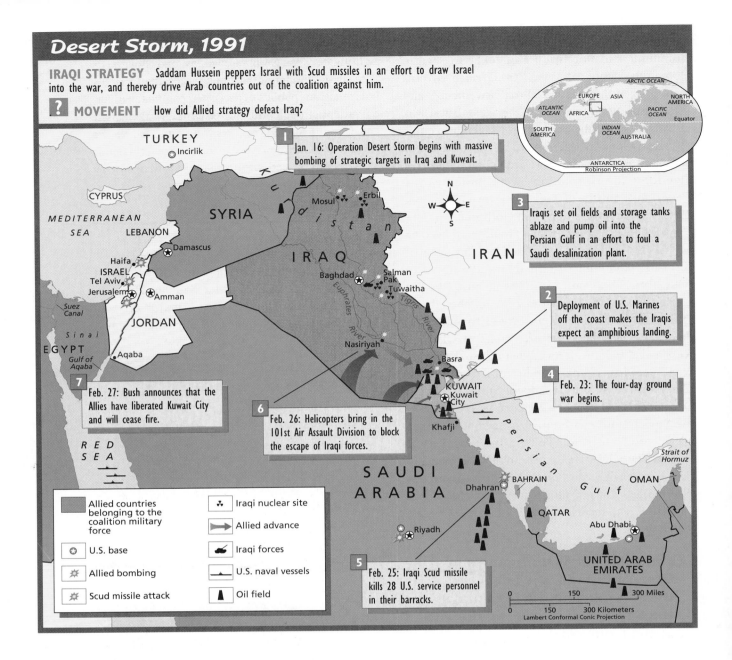

Desert Storm, 1991

IRAQI STRATEGY Saddam Hussein peppers Israel with Scud missiles in an effort to draw Israel into the war, and thereby drive Arab countries out of the coalition against him.

? MOVEMENT How did Allied strategy defeat Iraq?

1 Jan. 16: Operation Desert Storm begins with massive bombing of strategic targets in Iraq and Kuwait.

3 Iraqis set oil fields and storage tanks ablaze and pump oil into the Persian Gulf in an effort to foul a Saudi desalinization plant.

2 Deployment of U.S. Marines off the coast makes the Iraqis expect an amphibious landing.

4 Feb. 23: The four-day ground war begins.

7 Feb. 27: Bush announces that the Allies have liberated Kuwait City and will cease fire.

6 Feb. 26: Helicopters bring in the 101st Air Assault Division to block the escape of Iraqi forces.

5 Feb. 25: Iraqi Scud missile kills 28 U.S. service personnel in their barracks.

Legend:
- Allied countries belonging to the coalition military force
- U.S. base
- Allied bombing
- Scud missile attack
- Iraqi nuclear site
- Allied advance
- Iraqi forces
- U.S. naval vessels
- Oil field

0   150   300 Miles
0   150   300 Kilometers
Lambert Conformal Conic Projection

imposed economic sanctions on Iraq, and set a deadline for Iraq's withdrawal from Kuwait. As the January 15, 1991, deadline neared, military forces representing the United States, Britain, France, Egypt, and Saudi Arabia prepared for war. In all, some 690,000 allied troops—including some 540,000 Americans—amassed along the border of Kuwait. On January 16, the allied forces began bombing attacks on Iraqi forces and military and industrial installations.

The ground assault began on February 23. Within days the Iraqis had been driven back, and Kuwait's ruling al-Sabah family returned to power. American casualties included some 150 killed and 450 wounded, while an estimated 100,000 Iraqis died. U.S. air attacks also severely damaged the Iraqi capital, Baghdad, and other cities. Many hailed the success of **Operation Desert Storm** and applauded the leadership of General Colin Powell, chair of the Joint Chiefs of Staff, and Secretary of Defense Richard Cheney. The commander of U.S. forces, General H. Norman Schwarzkopf, received a hero's welcome in New York City. Bush's approval rating soared following the war.

A unique war. Operation Desert Storm differed from previous American military engagements. It was won almost entirely by the use of high-tech weaponry. Television reporters also provided unprecedented coverage of the war, including live coverage of the air assaults. As Americans sat glued to their television sets, news correspondent Bernard Shaw reported the first allied bombings on Iraq:

> 66 This is [pause] something is happening outside. . . . The skies over Baghdad have been illuminated. We're seeing bright flashes going off all over the sky. 99

Military technology quickly became the star of the show as coverage of the war expanded. The technological nature of the war highlighted another unique aspect of Operation Desert Storm—the significant role played by women. More than 35,000 American women served in the Persian Gulf conflict—some 6 percent of U.S. troops. Eleven American women soldiers were killed and two taken prisoner. Though the U.S. military banned women from serving as combat pilots, they served in almost every other capacity—including flying support planes and working on missile crews.

The role of women in Desert Storm and the nature of the war caused many people to question the usefulness of banning women from combat. With technology playing an increasingly significant role in modern warfare, critics charged, physical differences between men and women would become less important than technological skill.

During the previous years the number of women in the military had increased to the point that U.S. Air Force colonel Douglas Kennett commented that his branch of the service "couldn't go to war without women and we couldn't win without them." In August 1991 the Senate removed the ban on women serving as combat pilots, but continued to limit service in ground battles.

■■ **Operation Desert Storm was unique for its use of high-tech weaponry, live television coverage, and use of women soldiers.**

Problems at Home

Bush's successes in foreign affairs won him popularity and international praise, but some critics charged that he was neglecting problems at home. As the 1992 presidential campaign approached, domestic issues, particularly the economy and a growing political controversy, troubled the public and undermined the president's support.

The Thomas-Hill hearings. Bush continued Reagan's efforts to move the Supreme Court in a conservative direction. In 1990 he filled a

PRESIDENTIAL LIVES

GEORGE BUSH
1924–

in office
1989–1993

Following the popular and charismatic Ronald Reagan was not easy for George Bush. Throughout the 1988 campaign he was constantly fighting "the wimp factor"—the accusation that he was a weak politician and a better follower than leader. This charge seemed particularly ironic for Bush, who had bravely served as a pilot in World War II.

At the age of 18, George Bush became one of the youngest commissioned pilots in the navy. He flew 58 missions in all

and was shot down once. Bush's experiences in war may have contributed to his strong interest in foreign affairs. During his presidency, memories of World War II came back to him when he considered committing troops to battle. "When it came time for me to send our kids . . . to the Middle East," he once said, "I thought back on my own experiences in combat and what it was like to be shot at. . . . Having been in combat rounded out my awareness of the human cost of war."

▲ During confirmation hearings for Supreme Court nominee Clarence Thomas (left), law professor Anita Hill (right) accused Thomas of sexual harassment. The Senate approved Thomas's nomination, in spite of an outcry by female activists.

vacancy on the Court with David Souter, a conservative New Hampshire judge. In 1991, when Thurgood Marshall announced his retirement, Bush nominated Clarence Thomas, a conservative African American judge and former head of the federal Equal Employment Opportunity Commission (EEOC), to take his place.

During the confirmation hearings, law professor Anita Hill, a former associate of Thomas's at the EEOC, accused the nominee of **sexual harassment**—the use of unwelcome sexual language or behavior that creates a hostile working environment. In televised hearings, the Senate Judiciary Committee investigated her charges. The bullying tactics used by some members of the committee outraged many women. After the Senate narrowly approved the Thomas nomination, female activists vowed to show their disapproval in the next election.

Across the country the hearings stirred debate about sexual harassment. Many women told of experiencing harassment as they entered male-dominated fields. The debate became more heated after news broke of wide-scale sexual harassment of female officers at a naval convention in September 1991. An earlier Pentagon study had revealed that two thirds of the women in the military had been sexually harassed by colleagues. Such revelations prompted the military to increase punishment of sexual harassment.

The economy. Many women confessed that they tolerated sexual harassment because they could not afford to lose their jobs. Many people could relate to such feelings as the economy weakened. The 1991 federal deficit surged to $282 billion, with more than $350 billion predicted for 1992. The costs of the Persian Gulf War and the bailout of the S&L and banking industries added to the deficit.

The trade gap persisted as well. Though the trade deficit had declined from its 1990 high of almost $102 billion, in 1991 it still stood at about $66 billion. Japan's massive annual sales of automobiles and electronic goods to U.S. consumers accounted for a large portion of the gap. On a 1992 trade mission to Japan, President Bush and U.S. business leaders tried with little success to persuade the Japanese to increase imports from the United States.

Adding to these economic woes, a recession hit in 1990. As the economy faltered, unemployment rose. States facing budget deficits cut their welfare programs. The number of Americans living below the poverty line grew by more than two million in 1990. The recession hung on throughout 1992, complicating President Bush's reelection hopes.

■■ **Domestically, Bush faced troubles over the Thomas-Hill hearings and the sagging economy.**

WINDS OF CHANGE

Despite the nation's economic woes, President Bush was still riding a wave of popularity from the Persian Gulf War as 1991 ended. One of the few Democrats willing to challenge him in the 1992 election was Governor William "Bill" Clinton of Arkansas.

Bill Clinton was born in 1946 in Hope, Arkansas, shortly after the death of his father. His mother, Virginia, later married Roger Clinton, an abusive alcoholic. Clinton's childhood experiences of dealing with poverty and a troubled home life shaped his outlook on the world. When he met President John Kennedy in 1963, Clinton decided on a political career. After receiving a bachelor's degree in international affairs from Georgetown University, he studied at Oxford University in England and gained a law degree from Yale University.

▲ Bill Clinton

At Yale he met Hillary Rodham, a law student who later served as counsel to the House Judiciary Committee considering the impeachment of Nixon. They married in 1975. Three years later Clinton became the nation's youngest governor when he was elected to lead Arkansas. As a baby boomer, Clinton reflected many traits of his generation. He opposed the war in Vietnam and for a time tried to avoid being drafted. Influenced by the idealism of the Kennedy era and by the civil rights movement, he believed strongly in the value of diversity and equality.

▲ **Hillary Rodham Clinton advised her husband on a number of key issues during the 1992 presidential campaign.**

Hillary Rodham Clinton, a feminist influenced by the women's movement, enjoyed a successful legal career while furthering her husband's political career. As first lady of Arkansas, Hillary Rodham Clinton served on several influential committees, including one that developed a groundbreaking education-reform program.

Some observers noted that Hillary Rodham Clinton was qualified to run for president herself. Acknowledging his wife's key role, Bill Clinton said during the 1992 campaign that voters would be getting "two for the price of one" if he were elected president. As became apparent after the election, however, many Americans were uncomfortable with the idea of a president's wife in a policy-making role.

THE 1992 ELECTION

After years of low voter participation, people turned out in droves in 1992 to make their voices heard. Candidates used public forums such as television talk shows and radio call-in programs to answer questions directly from the public. A master of this electronic format was independent presidential candidate H. Ross Perot.

Perot, a billionaire from Texas who ran as an outsider, promised to bring a populist reform movement to Washington, D.C., by decreasing the influence of political lobbyists and by giving the public a greater voice in government. He also promised to use his skills as a businessman to cut spending and balance the budget. Perot's message appealed to many voters worried about the economy.

Perot's popularity reflected the feelings of many voters that politicians were out of touch. One group of voters who insisted on being heard were women, especially those outraged by the Thomas-Hill hearings. Shortly after the hearings, activist Eleanor Smeal had declared: "The Senate did more in one week to underscore the critical need for more women in the Senate than feminists have been able to do in 25 years." Women responded by running for public office in record numbers.

The increase in women candidates led the press to dub 1992 "the year of the woman." Many of these candidates won election. Four prominent women Democrats gained U.S. Senate seats, including Patty Murray of Washington and African American Carol Moseley-Braun of Illinois. California filled both of its Senate seats with women—Barbara Boxer and Dianne Feinstein.

In the presidential race, Bill Clinton's message of economic and social reform paid off. Clinton and his running mate, Senator Al Gore of Tennessee, won 43 percent of the popular vote and 370 electoral votes to the Bush-Quayle ticket's 38 percent of the popular vote and 168 electoral votes. Although Perot and his running mate, Admiral William Stockdale, failed to pick up any electoral votes, they captured 19 percent of the popular vote—more than any independent presidential ticket since that of Theodore Roosevelt in 1912.

■■ **The 1992 election saw increased voter participation, numerous reform candidates, and the election of baby boomer Bill Clinton.**

CLINTON TAKES OFFICE

Once in office, Clinton put together a diverse cabinet. His appointees included Mexican American Henry Cisneros as secretary of housing and urban affairs and African Americans Ron Brown and Joycelyn Elders as secretary of commerce and surgeon general, respectively. Other women appointees included Press Secretary Dee Dee Myers, Attorney General Janet Reno, and Secretary of Health and Human Services Donna

BILL CLINTON
1946–

Bill Clinton's presidency marked many firsts in the White House. He was the first president born in the post–World War II era and the first president from Arkansas. Clinton was also the first president to play the saxophone at his own inaugural celebration.

Clinton's career goal as a young teenager was to become a jazz musician. He was heavily influenced by African American jazz artists and early rock 'n' roll stars such as Elvis Presley. He excelled at playing the

★★THE PEOPLE'S★★
★INAUGURATION★

Bill Clinton · President
★★★ Jan.20, 1993 ★★★

saxophone and was offered numerous music scholarships to college after he graduated from high school. Although Clinton went on to make a career in politics, he frequently used his musical talents in campaigns, such as during the 1992 presidential election when, wearing dark glasses, he played the saxophone on a popular late-night talk show. Despite his love of music, Clinton believes that he made the right career choice. "I would have been a very good musician," he once noted, "but not a great one."

Bill Clinton

Shalala. Clinton also chose Ruth Bader Ginsburg to fill a vacancy on the Supreme Court.

As his presidency began, Clinton suffered a series of setbacks. An elaborate plan to reform the nation's health-care system, drafted by a task force headed by Hillary Rodham Clinton, died in Congress. In addition, both Clintons faced charges of past financial improprieties, including their tangled involvement in a failed Arkansas real-estate development called Whitewater. Then in 1996 came charges that the White House had improperly obtained FBI files on Republicans.

Amid these difficulties, Clinton confronted a range of global challenges, among them fighting in Bosnia and Northern Ireland and the uncertain fate of the emerging democracy in Russia. Russia faced political turmoil and hard economic times as it struggled toward democracy and a free-market system. By September 1993 Russia was so unstable that Boris Yeltsin temporarily suspended the constitution and dissolved Parliament, sparking a power struggle. In a 1996 presidential election, Yeltsin, despite poor health, defeated a former communist who favored a return to centralized rule.

In the Middle East instability also threatened many nations, as Islamic fundamentalists battled for political power. However, hopes for peace between Palestinians and Israelis were renewed in

September 1993, when Palestinian leader Yasir Arafat and Israeli prime minister Yitzhak Rabin signed a peace accord. President Clinton, who oversaw the signing of the agreement at the White House, approvingly referred to it as a "historic and honorable compromise."

The peace process suffered a setback in 1995, when a young Israeli ultra-nationalist assassinated Yitzhak Rabin. In 1996 elections Benjamin Netanyahu came to power pledging a tougher line on peace negotiations. U.S. secretary of state Warren Christopher worked hard to keep the peace process alive, but new outbreaks of violence between Israeli soldiers and Palestinians in September 1996 made it clear that the future was far from certain in this troubled region.

Clinton also wrestled with an upsurge of terrorism. In recent years terrorism has grown dramatically. Some of this terrorist activity has been directed at the United States. On February 26, 1993, a bomb blast rocked the World Trade Center in New York City, killing six people and injuring more than a thousand. The suspects arrested in the bombing were all tied to an Egyptian fundamentalist leader linked to several other terrorist acts. Then in 1996 a truck bomb in Saudi Arabia killed 19 American servicemen and wounded 280.

Domestic terrorism was especially chilling. In April 1995 a truck bomb destroyed a federal building in Oklahoma City, killing 169. Two men with ties to anti-government militia groups were soon charged with the crime. A year later, the FBI arrested Theodore Kaczynski, a loner with a grievance against modern technology, and charged him with a series of mail-bombings. Then, during the 1996 Summer Olympics in Atlanta, a bomb killed one and injured more than 100.

Terrorism, the weapon of the weak against the powerful, raises agonizing dilemmas. The challenge of defending society against terrorists without endangering Americans' constitutional rights poses a major challenge.

THE CLINTON PRESIDENCY

President Clinton focused on economic recovery, and his efforts showed some signs of paying off. In August 1993 Congress narrowly passed a budget act which combined tax increases and spending cuts to reduce the national debt.

The medicine worked, over time. The 1996 deficit dropped to about $145 billion, half that of 1992. Unemployment went down to 5.4 percent, a ten-year low, and inflation hovered under 3 percent. As investors gained confidence, the stock market boomed.

Not all economic news—especially that in Clinton's first few years—was rosy, however. The trade deficit remained high. And as corporations pushed for greater efficiency, they fired thousands of employees. Both white-collar and blue-collar workers lost their jobs as AT&T, IBM, GM, and other corporations cut their payrolls. In addition, many of the new jobs that were created during the Clinton years were low-paying, unskilled positions. In the inner cities, with their large black and Hispanic populations, even these jobs were scarce. The gap between the wealthiest and poorest Americans continued to widen.

Encouraged by Clinton's early setbacks, Republicans geared up for the 1994 midterm election. Many Republican candidates signed a "Contract with America" pledging a balanced-budget amendment and other reforms.

On election day, the Republicans won a stunning victory, gaining control of the House and the Senate. Newt Gingrich of Georgia became house speaker. The Christian Coalition, a political lobby founded by television evangelist Pat Robertson, helped back this conservative resurgence.

■■ **Concerned with early failures in the Clinton administration, voters gave Republicans control of both the House and the Senate in the 1994 midterm elections.**

CAMPAIGN 1996

Despite the results of the 1994 midterm elections, Clinton's popularity improved as the economy boomed. Describing the healthy financial conditions that had allowed Clinton to survive the 1994 midterm elections, economist David Wyss commented, "If you look at the economy during the Clinton administration, you have to say that it's been a success. We have low inflation, full employment, and steady growth. This is really just about the best of all [economic] worlds."

The president's stock rose higher as the Republican Congress failed to enact key measures in its Contract with America and tried to cut popular social and environmental programs. As Clinton and the Republican Congress battled over a budget bill in 1995, the federal government briefly shut down. Voters blamed the Republicans, and Newt Gingrich's popularity plummeted.

Clinton also benefited from divisions among Republicans, who split over issues such as taxes, budget cuts, government regulations, and social issues. These divisions sharpened as the 1996 presidential campaign began. Among a large field of Republican candidates, Senator Bob Dole of Kansas emerged victorious from the primaries and tried to unite his party's competing factions.

The Race. A disabled World War II veteran, Dole faced concerns about his age. At 73, voters wondered, was he out of touch? Could he handle the demands of the presidency? Resigning from the Senate, Dole proved an ineffective campaigner. "He never . . . offered the sustained and layered argument that precedes the applause line," concluded political analyst Peggy Noonan. "He just declared things— And there'll be no more

▲ Newt Gingrich

▲ Clinton-Dole debate, 1996

ing and humane than Dole. Another issue dividing the two candidates was tobacco. Clinton advocated stricter measures to discourage smoking, particularly among the young. Dole, by contrast, despite overwhelming medical evidence, questioned whether tobacco was really addictive.

The Result. Clinton's approach proved successful, and he became the first Democrat since Franklin Delano Roosevelt to win a full second term. Though his was not a landslide victory, he won 50 percent of the popular vote and 379 electoral votes. Dole, who had gone on a grueling 96 hour multistate tour in the last days of the campaign, took 41 percent of the popular vote and 159 electoral votes.

crime in a Dole Administration—and waited for people to clap as he cleared his throat."

Clinton, meanwhile, seized the middle ground on many issues. The president echoed the Republicans in calling for economic growth, smaller government, anti-crime programs, and middle-class tax relief. He urged tougher school discipline and a crackdown on "deadbeat dads" who failed to provide child support. Clinton also echoed Republican critics of the nation's welfare system. The president and Republican leaders both called for welfare reform that would limit benefits, introduce work requirements, and shift programs from the federal government to the states. Clinton signed such a bill in August 1996.

On issues such as environmental protection, gun control, and programs for the elderly, however, Clinton highlighted the difference between himself and his Republican opponent. By arguing for the protection of both long-standing and new social programs, he presented himself as more car-

Though a few of Newt Gingrich's "Freshman Class of 1994" failed to win reelection, the Republicans won a majority in both the House and the Senate. This was the first time that a Democrat had been elected to the presidency while the Republicans won both the House and the Senate, and the event seemed to send a message supporting a working bipartisan government.

As he approached his second term, President Clinton echoed this bipartisan theme, "proclaim[ing] that the vital center is alive and well." He pledged to provide health insurance to children and the unemployed, fix parts of the welfare bill, connect classrooms to the Internet, and repair crumbling schools. Many observers described Clinton's proposals as "small steps" intended to avoid the political overreach that had doomed much of his first term.

SECTION 2 REVIEW

IDENTIFY and explain the significance of the following: Michael Dukakis, George Bush, German reunification, Commonwealth of Independent States, Saddam Hussein, Operation Desert Storm, sexual harassment, Bill Clinton, H. Ross Perot, Ruth Bader Ginsburg, Newt Gingrich.

LOCATE and explain the importance of the following: Bosnia, Iraq, Kuwait.

1. **MAIN IDEA** What three events signaled the end of the Cold War?

2. **MAIN IDEA** What was unique about Operation Desert Storm?

3. **MAIN IDEA** What were two domestic issues that plagued President Bush?

4. **WRITING TO EXPLAIN** Analysts refer to 1992 as "the year of the woman." Considering women's roles in events during 1991, 1992, and 1993, write an essay explaining why the early 1990s might be called "the years of the women."

5. **ASSESSING CONSEQUENCES** What impact did Jesse Jackson's "Rainbow Coalition" campaign have on the 1984 and 1988 elections? How were the Jackson campaigns similar to that of H. Ross Perot in 1992?

AMERICA IN THE 1990s

FOCUS

- How did immigration patterns of the 1990s affect the United States?
- What were some problems urban Americans confronted?
- How did government and businesses attempt to help working parents?
- What health challenges did the nation face?

*L*eaving behind the 1980s, Americans faced both promising trends and pressing social problems. The 1990 U.S. census revealed a population that was increasingly urban, southern and western, and immigrant. Americans worked to overcome the economic problems and racial divisions that fractured many cities in the 1990s. Meanwhile, the rising costs of health care and the spread of AIDS contributed to the nationwide health-care crisis.

Rally supporting AIDS research

A NEW WAVE OF IMMIGRATION

In November 1991, U.S. Coast Guard vessels intercepted boatloads of Haitians bound for the United States. A military coup had ousted Haiti's first democratically elected president, Jean-Bertrand Aristide. As political and economic chaos spread, thousands of Haitians sailed to the United States.

However, bound by a 1981 agreement with Haiti and facing economic troubles of its own, the United States began to return the Haitians to their home country. Many politicians criticized the government's policy. "Returning Vietnamese, Russian Jews, Cubans, Nicaraguans and others back to the repressive countries from which they were fleeing would have been unthinkable," declared Senator

Connie Mack of Florida. "How can we justify it for Haitians?"

The Haitian issue underscored the continuing debate within the United States over immigration. The 1990 census revealed that more immigrants had come to the United States in the 1980s than in any decade since 1910, and more than 80 percent

▶ The U.S. Coast Guard intercepted Haitian refugees, such as the family shown here, and took them to a temporary "tent-city" at Guantánamo Bay Naval Base. Some 2,500 refugees were housed at this base before being returned to Haiti.

of them came from Asia, Latin America, and the Caribbean. This influx of immigrants alarmed many native-born Americans. Many blamed immigrants for taking jobs from native-born residents. Some also argued that the presence of large numbers of immigrants willing to work for lower wages served to keep wages down for all workers.

Supporters of immigration offered a different view. They argued that immigrants created new businesses that revitalized urban areas and helped the economy. In addition, supporters of immigration noted that many recent immigrants, most notably those from India, the Philippines, China, and Korea, on average had more schooling than either native-born Americans or European immigrants. Asian immigrants, they pointed out, made up about one third of all engineers in California's center of computer technology, the Silicon Valley.

▪▪ Opposition to immigration increased in the 1990s, although immigrants made many contributions to U.S. businesses and industries.

President Bush recognized these benefits and signed the **Immigration Act** of 1990. The new law changed U.S. immigration policy by increasing the number of immigrants and doubling the number of skilled workers allowed into the United States each year. The act also authorized special visas for foreign investors interested in establishing businesses in economically depressed areas of the country.

In 1996 during Clinton's first term, Congress passed an immigration bill to fight the continuing problem of illegal immigration by strengthening control of the borders. Much of the Immigration and Naturalization Service's increased control efforts focus on the area around San Diego, California—a point where almost half of all illegal immigrants enter the United States.

The 1996 immigration bill also contained provisions aimed at keeping new immigrants off welfare rolls. For example, sponsors of immigrants must have incomes at least 125 percent above the poverty level. The bill also prevents legal immigrants who are not U.S. citizens from receiving most forms of welfare benefits. Many believe this provision will encourage immigrants to become citizens. Already the number of naturalizations has increased from some 500,000 in 1994 to 1,000,000 in 1995.

If current trends hold, the United States will witness increased immigration in the coming years. Thus, Americans will continue to grapple with the question of whether to welcome immigrants.

*C*ITIES OF DIVERSITY

Conflicts experienced by immigrants included the riots that erupted in April 1992 in south central Los Angeles. The area exploded in violence after the acquittal of four white police officers accused of beating Rodney King, an African American. Most of the violence affected neighborhood residents and businesses as many people were beaten and robbed. Some looters specifically targeted Korean-owned businesses.

The riots disheartened people who had worked to improve relations among African

▶ Tension flared between the African American and Cuban American communities in Miami after Nelson Mandela, shown here, spoke favorably of Fidel Castro.

Americans, Hispanic Americans, and Asian Americans in Los Angeles. Sylvia Castillo, a Mexican American community activist who was a target of the violence, noted, "I was outraged by the verdict and had always struggled against racism. All I could think was: 'Why are they [rioters] doing this to me?'" Rodney King himself urged people to "try to work it out" peacefully, asking, "Can we all get along?" Most residents in south central Los Angeles did not take part in the riots, and many people braved the violence to rescue victims.

Miami, Florida, deemed the "new Ellis Island" by psychologist Marvin Dunn, also experienced increased immigration and racial tensions. In 1992 Miami had more foreign-born residents—including Cubans, Haitians, Nicaraguans, and Peruvians—than any other city in the United States. Boosted by a thriving tourist industry, the city's economy had boomed in recent years, but it had also seen three riots since 1980.

Tension in Miami was particularly strong between Cuban Americans and African Americans. In 1990, black leaders began a national boycott of Miami's convention facilities after Cuban American city officials snubbed South African leader Nelson Mandela. Mandela had made favorable remarks about Fidel Castro, Cuba's Communist leader whose regime many Cuban Americans had fled. After Hispanic American businesspeople agreed to hire more African Americans and patronize black-owned businesses, black leaders ordered an end to the boycott.

Economic problems compounded many urban problems. Some analysts argued that bad economic conditions contributed to the Los Angeles riots. Once home to major companies such as Bethlehem Steel and Goodyear, Los Angeles lost over 200,000 jobs in 1991 alone. Such loss of inner-city jobs was repeated across the country. Many of the companies that left the inner cities relocated to the suburbs, changing the faces of both the cities and the suburbs. Many suburban areas now contain more office space than midtown Manhattan. While this development means more jobs for suburban areas, inner-city residents despair of again attracting the industries that could reduce unemployment in their communities.

■■ Inner cities experienced racial conflicts and lost jobs to the suburbs in the 1980s and 1990s.

WORK AND FAMILY

Many observers expressed concern about the growing number of single-parent families in the 1980s and 1990s. From 1970 to 1991 the number of children living in single-parent households more than doubled. In 1991 some 20 percent of all white children, 60 percent of all African American children, and 30 percent of all Hispanic children lived with one parent, usually their mothers.

Most single parents faced serious financial burdens. Patricia Mull, a Los Angeles seamstress who stretched her income to send her daughter to private school, described the stress she faced: "I worry about the rent. I worry if I can make the payment in time. I worry if I have enough money

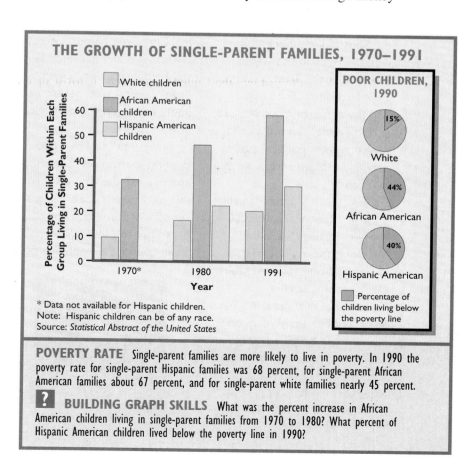

THE GROWTH OF SINGLE-PARENT FAMILIES, 1970–1991

- White children
- African American children
- Hispanic American children

Percentage of Children Within Each Group Living in Single-Parent Families

Year: 1970*, 1980, 1991

* Data not available for Hispanic children.
Note: Hispanic children can be of any race.
Source: *Statistical Abstract of the United States*

POOR CHILDREN, 1990

White — 15%
African American — 44%
Hispanic American — 40%

Percentage of children living below the poverty line

POVERTY RATE Single-parent families are more likely to live in poverty. In 1990 the poverty rate for single-parent Hispanic families was 68 percent, for single-parent African American families about 67 percent, and for single-parent white families nearly 45 percent.

? **BUILDING GRAPH SKILLS** What was the percent increase in African American children living in single-parent families from 1970 to 1980? What percent of Hispanic American children lived below the poverty line in 1990?

AMERICAN INDIAN RENEWAL: A CASE STUDY

The economic problems facing the United States in the 1980s and 1990s presented special problems for the nation's nearly two million American Indians, more than 20 percent of whom lived on or near reservations. As in earlier years, joblessness, lack of education, and poor health care made life hard for many Indians. But cultural renewal, economic ventures, and successful claims of treaty rights offered promise.

The Shoshoni-Bannock Indians of Fort Hall Reservation in Idaho were among the Indians who successfully pressed their treaty claims. In 1990, using the terms of an 1868 treaty with the United States, the Shoshoni-Bannock Indians won the right to use water from the Snake River to irrigate their farmlands. The decision was the result of more than 25 years of American Indian efforts to win greater political autonomy and achieve economic self-sufficiency.

 BIOGRAPHY Wilma Mankiller, chief of the 108,000–strong Cherokee Nation, launched one of the most significant renewal efforts. Mankiller was born in Tahlequah, Oklahoma, in 1945. She spent her early years on a farm, where her family faced economic hardships and lived without indoor plumbing or electricity.

When Mankiller was 12, the farm failed after two drought years. Her family then moved to San Francisco, California, under the Bureau of Indian Affairs' relocation program. The adjustment to city life was difficult for Mankiller, who recalled, "One day I was [in Oklahoma] and the next day I was trying to deal with the mysteries of television, indoor plumbing, neon lights and elevators."

She soon became active in the American Indian Movement, which inspired her to become more involved in her community. In the mid-1970s Mankiller moved back to Oklahoma. She completed college and began working to promote economic growth in the Cherokee Nation. Stressing self-esteem and community self-help, Mankiller helped develop rural water systems, improve housing, and develop new businesses.

In 1985 Mankiller became the first woman principal chief, and in 1987 she won a tough four-way race and a subsequent runoff election. Mankiller compared her job to "running a small country, a medium-size

Wilma Mankiller

▲ **The Shoshoni-Bannock Indians successfully sued the U.S. government in 1990 to reclaim irrigation rights that had been guaranteed to them in an 1868 treaty.**

corporation, and being a social worker." In addition to helping Cherokee communities create new jobs and provide better health care, the Cherokee Nation sponsored a program to teach students how to read and write the Cherokee language. "I can't help but feel hopeful about our future," Mankiller noted in her 1990 State of the Nation address:

❝ I think the strongest thing I see as I travel around to Cherokee communities and talk with people is their tenacity [persistence]. Despite everything that's happened to our people throughout history we've managed to hang on to our culture, we've managed to hang on to our sense of being Cherokee. ❞

left for other things. I worry about money every day, every night."

Many two-parent families shared Mull's concerns as they struggled to balance job and family responsibilities. More than 60 percent of married women worked outside the home in 1995, up from about one third in 1960. The increase in single-parent families and in families with both parents in the work force created the need for affordable day care. Employers increasingly began to realize that family concerns affected the job performance of their employees. To help employees balance work and family, a coalition of businesses in 1992 announced a program to build more day-care and elder-care centers across the country.

The U.S. government also recognized the need to help working families. In February 1993, two weeks after his inauguration, President Clinton signed into law the **Family and Medical Leave Act**, which President Bush had twice vetoed. The legislation requires large companies to provide workers up to 12 weeks of unpaid leave for family and medical emergencies without losing their medical coverage or their jobs.

This legislation reflected the significant changes in attitudes toward work and family that have occurred in the 1990s. Florence Skelly, the vice chairperson of a market-research firm, noted in 1993 that "rather than trying to climb the economic ladder, people are becoming more concerned with relationships and family and community involvement."

■■ **Government and businesses issued new policies to help working parents juggle home and work life.**

Health in the 1990s

Between 1970 and 1993, U.S. spending on health care rose from more than $74 billion to some $884 billion. The aging population, soaring physicians' fees, higher insurance costs, and more-expensive medical equipment accounted for much of this increase. Rising medical costs hit the poor and those without health insurance especially hard.

Fueling the health crisis in the 1990s was the alarming spread of Acquired Immune Deficiency Syndrome, or **AIDS**. This is the final

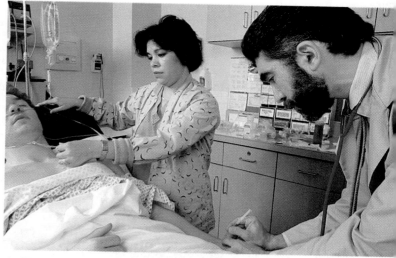

▲ The rising costs of health insurance, doctors' fees, and improved medical equipment created a health-care crisis during the 1990s.

deadly stage of an illness caused by the human immunodeficiency virus, or HIV. By March 1993 some one million people had been infected with HIV, and by 1996 AIDS had claimed the lives of more than 320,000 Americans. In 1993 AIDS was the leading cause of death among men ages 25–44 in 64 U.S. cities. New AIDS cases reported for women more than tripled between 1986 and 1990.

AIDS has left almost no continent untouched. In the African nation of Zambia, President Kenneth Kaunda's son died of AIDS. In 1991, basketball star Earvin "Magic" Johnson of the Los Angeles Lakers announced that he had tested positive for HIV. Other celebrities struck by the disease have included movie star Rock Hudson and tennis legend Arthur Ashe.

The World Health Organization (WHO) estimated in 1995 that some 1.3 million persons worldwide had full-blown AIDS. The organization predicts that some 40 million people will be carriers of HIV by the year 2000.

Some activists accused the United States government of responding too slowly and with too little research money to the AIDS crisis. The Food and Drug Administration responded to these criticisms by speeding up the approval of several drugs for the treatment of AIDS.

A major step forward for disabled citizens came in July 1990, when President George Bush signed into law the **Americans with Disabilities Act**. The act prohibits discrimination against people with mental or physical disabilities—including diseases such as AIDS—in employment, transportation, telephone services, and public buildings.

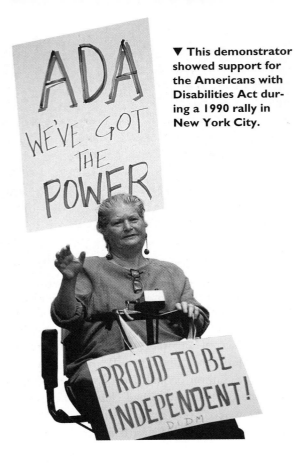

▼ This demonstrator showed support for the Americans with Disabilities Act during a 1990 rally in New York City.

ADA
WE'VE GOT THE POWER

PROUD TO BE INDEPENDENT!
DIDM

The act also requires companies with 25 or more employees to remove structural barriers in offices.

■■ **The rising costs of health care and the spread of AIDS led to a health crisis in the 1990s.**

TECHNOLOGY AND SOCIETY

The 1980s and 1990s brought advances in space technology. In 1981 the National Aeronautics and Space Administration (NASA) launched the first reusable space vehicle—a **space shuttle**. NASA suffered a grave setback in 1986, when the shuttle *Challenger* exploded shortly after lift-off. All seven crew members perished, including social studies teacher Christa McAuliffe, who would have been the first civilian in space.

Despite this tragedy, NASA forged ahead. With the end of the Cold War, the space agency focused on commercial and scientific projects more than military efforts. The Hubble Space Telescope, launched in 1990 and repaired in 1993, transmitted vital astronomical information and breathtaking photos from deep space. In 1994 came a joint U.S.-Russian space mission.

BIOGRAPHY

Of all the technological advances of these years, the rapid growth of personal computers (PCs) loomed especially large. A leader in this revolution was William "Bill" Gates. Born in Seattle in 1955, Gates began programming at thirteen. In 1974, while a student at Harvard, he devised a PC operating system. A year later he cofounded the Microsoft Corporation to develop computer software. The first IBM personal computer, introduced in 1981, utilized a Microsoft operating system, MS-DOS. By 1986, when Microsoft went public, it was a world leader in providing PC software.

By then, PCs were transforming American life. By the mid-1990s most business offices and public institutions were computerized, and nearly 40 percent of American homes had PCs. Students from grade school to college were using computers for many purposes. In libraries, bulky reference books gave way to CD-ROM computer disks. Physicians could instantly access information on the latest medical research via Medline, a computerized database. Typesetting machines disappeared as books, magazines, and newspapers were printed directly from computer disks. Computers also proved to be a great boon to the disabled, who used them to communicate in a number of ways.

Bill Gates's home near Seattle, Washington, illustrates some of the ways in which technology might eventually transform private life. In the huge hillside home, which includes about 100 internal microcomputers, technology exists to serve and delight, with intricate remote control systems regulating music, entertainment, and even paintings! Each visitor to the house is issued an electronic pin, which stores information and tracks motion. The pins cue the computer system to route

Bill Gates

calls for a particular guest to the nearest phone and to set the lights along the visitor's path to the desired brightness.

The **Internet**, a vast, computer-based communications and information system, enabled users to communicate worldwide, join discussion groups, and gather information from countless databases. The World Wide Web, developed by Swiss scientists in the early 1990s, linked a wide array of internet sites offering texts, animations, and graphics covering an almost infinite array of topics. Some observers hoped the so-called "information highway"—the Internet and the World Wide Web—would bring people from different social classes, cultures, and countries together. In *The Road Ahead*, his book on computer technology, Bill Gates offered this hope:

> 66 The information highway is going to break down boundaries and may promote a world culture, or at least a sharing of cultural activities and values. The highway will also make it easy for patriots, even expatriates, deeply involved in their own ethnic communities to reach out to others with similar interests no matter where they may be located. 99

Almost a decade earlier, in 1981, writer William Gibson coined the term "cyberspace" for the new computer realm. Wrote Gibson in 1996:

> 66 The [World Wide Web] is not what it was six months ago; in another six months it will be something else again. It was not planned; it simply happened. . . . It is happening the way cities happen. It *is* a city. 99

One use of the World Wide Web that promises to aid historical research is the National Digital Library (NDL), which was begun by the Librarian of Congress, James H. Billington. With money raised from private sources and with some government funding, the NDL plans to have 5 million items available on the Library of Congress's web site by the year 2000. Each item displayed on screen will be a digitized image of the original. Among the items already on line are documents and photographs relating to the history of African Americans, the Civil War, women's suffrage, the Great Depression and World War II.

But computers have not brought utopia. The social problems plaguing American society soon appeared in cyberspace as well. In the Telecommunications Act of 1996, Congress tried to regulate indecency on the Internet. A federal court quickly struck down key provisions of this law, however, as a violation of First Amendment free speech rights.

In addition to fears about the kinds of material circulating through cyberspace, some observers worried that a fully computerized society would not need human workers. Such fears were probably exaggerated, since new technologies typically create more jobs than they eliminate. But in the interval between job loss and the emergence of new jobs, severe disruptions can occur. In fact, job layoffs remained high, affecting about 8 percent of workers during the period 1993–1995. Other people worried that computers would deepen social divisions as well-to-do, well-educated Americans mastered the new technology, while poorer citizens lagged behind. Like all new technologies, the computer held both vast promise and troubling challenges for the future.

SECTION 3 REVIEW

IDENTIFY and explain the significance of the following: Immigration Act, Rodney King, Nelson Mandela, Wilma Mankiller, Family and Medical Leave Act, AIDS, Americans with Disabilities Act, space shuttle, Bill Gates, Internet, cyberspace.

LOCATE and explain the importance of the following: Haiti, Los Angeles, Miami.

1. **MAIN IDEA** What economic and urban problems did inner-city workers and families face?

2. **MAIN IDEA** How did AIDS impact the nation?

3. **MAIN IDEA** How have computers transformed American life?

4. **WRITING TO PERSUADE** Imagine you are the owner of a medical clinic. Write a speech that convinces listeners in your community that a health-care crisis exists in the 1990s.

5. **EVALUATING** How has NASA impacted science and technology?

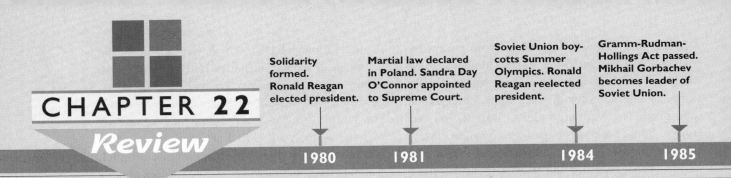

Solidarity formed. Ronald Reagan elected president.

Martial law declared in Poland. Sandra Day O'Connor appointed to Supreme Court.

Soviet Union boycotts Summer Olympics. Ronald Reagan reelected president.

Gramm-Rudman-Hollings Act passed. Mikhail Gorbachev becomes leader of Soviet Union.

1980   **1981**   **1984**   **1985**

WRITING A SUMMARY

Using the essential points of the chapter as a guide, write a summary of the chapter.

REVIEWING CHRONOLOGY

Number your paper 1 to 5. Study the time line above, and list the following events in the order in which they happened by writing the first next to 1, the second next to 2, and so on. Then complete the activity below.

1. INF Treaty ratified.
2. Bill Clinton elected president.
3. Soviet Union boycotts Summer Olympics.
4. Solidarity formed.
5. Thomas-Hill hearings occur.

Analyzing What was the purpose of the Gramm-Rudman-Hollings Act?

IDENTIFYING PEOPLE AND IDEAS

Explain the historical significance of each of the following people or terms.

1. Solidarity
2. contras
3. Geraldine Ferraro
4. insider trading
5. Saddam Hussein
6. Rodney King
7. Immigration Act
8. Wilma Mankiller
9. AIDS
10. Bill Gates

UNDERSTANDING MAIN IDEAS

1. How did the Reagan administration fight the Cold War?
2. What challenges did President Bush face during his term?
3. What important issues did Americans discuss during the 1992 election campaign?
4. What benefits did the arrival of immigrants in the 1990s have for the United States?
5. What urban problems and health challenges did Americans face during the early 1990s?

REVIEWING THEMES

1. **Economic Development** What effects did Reaganomics have on the country?

2. **Democratic Values** In what ways might technological advances help increase voter participation in the election process?

THINKING CRITICALLY

1. **Comparing and Contrasting** How did the scandal surrounding the Iran-contra affair prove both similar to and different from the Watergate scandal?
2. **Analyzing** How did improved relations affect the United States and the Soviet Union?

STRATEGY FOR SUCCESS

Review the Strategies for Success entry on Comparing Points of View on page 420. Then read the following two excerpts from the 1984 presidential campaign. The first is from a speech by Jesse Jackson. The second is from a Republican commercial for Ronald Reagan. How do these two selections reflect different views of America?

66 Our flag is red, white and blue, but our nation is rainbow—red, yellow, brown, black and white. . . . America is not like a blanket—one piece of unbroken cloth, the same color, the same texture, the same size. America is more like a quilt—many patches, many pieces, many colors, many sizes, all woven and held together by a common thread. . . .

Even in our fractured state, all of us count and fit somewhere. . . . We have not proven that we can win or make progress without each other. We must come together. 99

66 In a town not too far from where you live, a young family has just moved into a new home. Three years ago, even the smallest house seemed completely out of reach. Right down the street, one of the neighbors has just bought himself a new car, with all the options. The factory down the river is working again. Not long ago, people were saying it probably would be closed forever. . . . Life is better. America is back. 99

1987	1988	1990	1991	1992	1993	1994	1996

Congress investigates Iran-contra affair. Stock market crashes.

INF Treaty ratified. George Bush elected president.

Immigration Act and Americans with Disabilities Act passed. Iraq invades Kuwait.

Operation Desert Storm launched. Commonwealth of Independent States formed.

Los Angeles riot occurs. Bill Clinton elected president.

Family and Medical Leave Act signed. Ruth Bader Ginsburg appointed to Supreme Court.

Republicans gain control of the House and Senate.

Bill Clinton reelected president.

WRITING ABOUT HISTORY

Writing to Explain Write an essay that explains the significance of the passage of the Americans with Disabilities Act.

USING PRIMARY SOURCES

After the Los Angeles riot, African American Willie L. Williams became the city's new chief of police. In an interview shortly after the riots, Williams expressed his impressions of African American concerns in Los Angeles. Read the following excerpt from the interview. According to Williams, what do African Americans want from police, and how has crime affected their neighborhoods?

 The African-American community wants strong, tough, honest, fair policing. There is no African-American community in America that does not want to see police there. The people want to be treated fairly. They want to be treated honestly and with dignity. . . .

Crime also has a long-term effect on the community because it drives out the mom-and-pop businesses, the corner stores, where a lot of shopping is done. It drives out the source of income for the teenagers and the young adults who don't have a lot of skills or are just going to school to learn skills. It often drives out the source of income for parents who may be living and working at home and working in the area. The cost of crime in the African-American community cannot be underestimated. **99**

LINKING HISTORY AND GEOGRAPHY

Refer to the maps on page 573 and page 595. Which states did the Democratic party win in 1988 that it did not win in 1980?

BUILDING YOUR PORTFOLIO

Complete the following projects independently or cooperatively.

1. POLITICS In Chapter 20 you were a reporter covering Watergate. Building on that experience, imagine you are covering the Iran-contra affair. Create a flow chart that traces the Iran-contra transfer of weapons, money, and supplies.

2. BUSINESS AND TRADE Imagine you are the director of a private agency that assists immigrant businesspeople. Prepare a speech on how immigrant businesses are helping to boost your city's economy.

3. THE ECONOMY In Chapter 20 you examined oil prices and inflation. Building on that experience, imagine you are one of President Reagan's economic advisers. Prepare a pamphlet describing the principles and goals of Reaganomics.

Willie L. Williams

American Letters

Stories of Diversity

More than 10 million immigrants arrived on American shores between 1970 and 1989, most of them from Asia or Latin America. In the following selections, Chinese American author Gish Jen, Mexican American poet Jimmy Santiago Baca, and Philippine-born novelist Jessica Hagedorn explore the struggles of characters who are fully American yet retain ties to their country of origin.

▲ **Jimmy Santiago Baca**

From *Typical American*

by Gish Jen

"We are family," echoed Helen.

"Team," said Ralph. "We should have name. The Chinese Yankees. Call Chang-kees for short."

"Chang-kees!" Everyone laughed.

Ball games became even more fun. Theresa explained how the

▼ **Portrait of a Chinese Family (1985), by Tomie Arai**

Yankees had lost the Series to the Dodgers the year before; they rooted for a comeback. "Let's go Chang-kees!" This was in the privacy of their apartment, in front of their newly bought used Zenith TV; the one time they went to an actual game, people had called them names and told them to go back to their laundry. They in turn had sat impassive as the scoreboard. Rooting in their hearts, they said later. Anyway, they preferred to stay home and watch. "More comfortable." "More convenient." "Can see better," they agreed.

These were the same reasons Ralph advocated buying a car.

"Seems like someone's becoming[1] one-hundred-percent American-ized," Theresa kidded.

"What's so American? We had a car, growing up. Don't you remember?" Ralph argued that in fact this way they could avoid getting too Americanized. *"Everywhere we go, we can keep the children inside. Also they won't catch cold."*

"I thought we agreed the children are going to be American," puzzled Helen.

Ralph furrowed his brow. When Callie turned three they had decided that Mona and Callie would learn English first, and then Chinese. This was what Janis and Old Chao were planning on doing with Alexander; Janis didn't want him to have an accent. For Ralph and Helen, it was a more practical decision. Callie had seemed con-fused by *outside people* sometimes understanding her and sometimes not. Playing with other children in the park, she had several times started to cry, and once or twice to throw things; she had lost a doll this way, and a dragon. Also, one grabby little boy had, in an ensuing ruckus, lost some teeth. . . .

Now Ralph drummed his fingers. He stopped and smiled.

"And what better way to Ameri-canize the children than to buy a car!" ❖

---

1 Italics indicate words spoken in Chinese.

from "Martín IV," Martín and Meditations on the South Valley

by Jimmy Santiago Baca

On visiting days with aunts and
    uncles,
I was shuttled back and forth—
between Chavez bourgeois in the
    city
and rural Lucero sheepherders,
new cars and gleaming furniture
and leather saddles and burlap
    sacks,
noon football games and six packs
    of cokes
and hoes, welfare cards and
    bottles of goat milk.

I was caught in the middle—
between white skinned, English
    speaking altar boy
at the communion railing,
and brown skinned, Spanish
    speaking plains nomadic child
with buffalo heart groaning under-
    world earth powers,
between Sunday brunch at a
    restaurant
and burritos eaten in a tin-roofed
    barn,
between John Wayne on the
    afternoon movie
rifle butting young Braves,
and the Apache whose red
    dripping arrow
was the altar candle in praise of
    the buck
just killed.

Caught between Indio-Mejicano
    rural uncles
who stacked hundred pound sacks
    of pinto beans
on boxcars all day, and worked
    the railroad tracks
behind the Sturgis sheds, who
    sang Apache songs
with accordions, and Chavez
    uncles and aunts

who vacationed and followed the
    Hollywood model
of My Three Sons for their own
    families,
sweeping the kitchen before
    anyone came to visit,
looking at photo albums in the
    parlor. ❖

"Luna Moth" from *Dogeaters*

by Jessica Hagedorn

Without warning, [my mother]
cheerfully announces she is sending me to school in America and
moving there with me for an
indefinite period. I am ecstatic, at
first. Everyone else is stunned. My
father cannot stop her—my
mother has inherited money from
her father and pays for our passage to America. We settle first in
New York, then Boston. I convince myself I am not homesick,
and try not to bring up my father
or brother when I speak. My
mother actually sells a few paintings. The months turn into years.
"Are we going to stay here
forever?" I finally ask her. She
looks surprised. "I don't know
about you, but I love the cold
weather. Go back to Manila if you
want. Tell Raul I miss him more
than he could ever imagine." She
smiles one of her cryptic smiles.
"But he'll have to visit me here if
he wants to see me—" her voice

trails off. . . .

When I finally come home to
Manila to visit, my father warns
me not to bother visiting our old
house. "You'll be disappointed.
Memories are always better."
Smiling apologetically, he tells me
reality will diminish the grandeur
of my childhood image of home.
I take his picture with my new
camera, which later falls in the
swimming pool by accident. The
camera is destroyed, along with
my roll of film. I decide to visit
our old house . . . anyway, borrowing a car from Mikey. Pucha
goes with me; she loves riding
around in cars and doesn't need
any excuse. . . .

My father is right. The house
with its shuttered windows looks
smaller than I remember, and
dingy. The once lush and sprawling
garden is now a forlorn landscape
of rocks, weeds, and wild ferns.
The bamboo grove has been cut
down. "Let's go," Pucha whispers,
impatient and uninterested. An old
man with bright eyes introduces
himself as Manong Tibo, the care-
taker. He unlocks door after door
for us, pulling aside cobwebs,
warning us to be careful. Rotting
floorboards creak under the
weight of our footsteps. "My bed-
room," I say to the old man, who
nods. I am overwhelmed by melancholy at the sight of the empty
room. A frightened mouse dashes
across the grimy tiled floor. ❖

THINKING AND WRITING ABOUT LITERATURE

1. How do Gish Jen's characters become "Americanized"? What
   aspects of Chinese culture do they retain?
2. In Baca's poem, what two different ways of life do the two sides
   of the speaker's family represent? Which do you think he
   prefers? Why?
3. Why is Jessica Hagedorn's character disappointed when she sees
   her old home? Do you think she is happy in the United States?

Strategies for Success

EVALUATING NEWS STORIES

Information today comes at us in a flood—from talk shows to tabloids, from the morning headlines to the nightly news. Today's news reporting will become the basis of tomorrow's history, so evaluating news stories contributes to your understanding of current history. News sources, which collectively are called the news media, can be divided into two groups: *broadcast media* and *print media.*

▲ Bill Clinton jamming on *The Arsenio Hall Show,* 1992

Broadcast Media

Broadcast media include television and radio. Television is, by far, the dominant medium for news. Surveys show that Americans are much more inclined to watch TV news than to read a daily newspaper. Television, like no other medium, presents the opportunity to witness history in the making. TV and radio can provide on-the-spot, around-the-clock coverage, creating a sense of immediacy. Also, both increasingly offer "instant analysis" to go with their reporting. Broadcasters like CNN, the 24-hour all-news cable network, and "talk radio" have greatly expanded the amount and kind of news available over the air.

Print Media

Print media include newspapers, weekly newsmagazines like *Newsweek* and *Time,* and other publications that cover current events. Newspapers, particularly such big-city dailies as the *New York Times* or the *Chicago Tribune,* give detailed accounts of national and world events as they occur. Newsmagazines, which have more time to prepare their stories, specialize in in-depth analyses of issues.

How to Evaluate News Media

To evaluate news reporting, ask questions like the following:

- **Coverage.** Is the subject treated superficially or in-depth? Does the reporting include information on the background to a story? Does it explore long-range implications of events?
- **Fairness and accuracy.** Does the reporting stick to the facts? Is it fair and balanced? Is there any recognizable bias in the coverage?
- **Immediacy and interest.** How close in time is the reporting to the event? Have there been new developments since the story was written or broadcast? Is the news presented in an interesting way?

Applying the Strategy

Choose a topic that is frequently in the news and that has been covered both in print and on radio and TV. Evaluate recent reporting on the issue in terms of the categories listed above. First, examine how well the reporting covers the *why* and *how* of the event, as well as the *who, what, when,* and *where.* Remember that each story has a wider context, a past and a future; good reporting will bring out these connections. Second, consider whether the story is told objectively. Every reporter has a point of view, so be alert for any expression of bias. Finally, note whether any late-breaking developments have changed the situation as last reported. Evaluate the reporting for the level of interest it creates, keeping in mind that a complex subject such as a financial scandal may be hard to present in exciting images or film footage.

Practicing the Strategy

Choose another current topic and examine reporting about it by each of the following: a TV network news program, a major daily newspaper, a public-radio program, and a national weekly newsmagazine. Write a brief essay evaluating the treatment of the issue or event by the different news media, describing the depth of the coverage offered by each, the presence of bias in any of the reporting, and the impact of the story on you.

BUILDING YOUR PORTFOLIO

Outlined below are four projects. Independently or cooperatively, complete one and use the products to demonstrate your mastery of the historical concepts involved.

1 POLITICS

The Watergate scandal and the Iran-contra affair challenged the foundation of constitutional government. Using the portfolio materials you designed in chapters 21 and 22, write an editorial that examines the ways in which the Watergate scandal was both similar to and different from the Iran-contra affair.

2 THE ECONOMY

Stagflation and the effects of the energy crisis are only two of the economic problems presidents Nixon, Ford, and Carter struggled with in the 1970s. In the 1980s President Reagan attempted to stimulate the economy through conservative reforms. Using the portfolio materials you designed in chapters 21 and 22, discuss the different ways in which economic actions affect people by presenting your chart and pamphlet to the class.

3 GLOBAL RELATIONS

During the 1970s and 1980s, the United States opened negotiations with China, improved relations with the Soviet Union, and witnessed the end of the Cold War and the breakup of the Soviet Union. Regional and local conflicts emerged, however, as new nations were torn apart by ethnic and religious struggles. Using the portfolio materials you designed in chapters 21 and 22, conduct a panel discussion about the new world order that highlights the sometimes conflicting interests of the superpowers, industrialized nations, and developing nations.

4 BUSINESS AND TRADE

In the last several decades, the U.S. economy has become increasingly global in scope. Using the portfolio materials you designed in chapters 21 and 22, prepare a presentation on the role of immigrants and immigrant businesses in strengthening America's position in the global economy.

Videodisc Review

In assigned groups, develop an outline for a video collage of America in the years between 1970 and the present. Choose images that best illustrate the major topics of the period. Write a script to accompany the images. Assign narrators to different parts of the script, and present your video collage to the class.

Further Reading

Edelstein, Andrew J., and Kevin McDonough. *The Seventies: From Hot Pants to Hot Tubs.* Dutton (1990). Social history of the 1970s.

Johnson, Haynes. *Sleepwalking through History: America in the Reagan Years.* Norton (1991). Overview and critical analysis of the Reagan years.

Moore, Jim, with Rick Ihde. *Clinton: Young Man in a Hurry.* The Summit Group (1992). Biography detailing the rise of Bill Clinton to become the 42nd president of the United States.

Virga, Vincent. *The Eighties: Images of America.* Edward Burlingame Books (1992). Photographic essay on life in the United States during the 1980s.

Woodward, Bob, and Carl Bernstein. *The Final Days.* Simon & Schuster (1976). Chronicle of the last days of Richard Nixon's presidency.

Chapter 23

IMPERIALISM TO NEW WORLD ORDER

Chapter 24

FROM INDUSTRIALIZATION TO GLOBAL ECONOMY

The American Experience
in Global Context

Just as the people and events in the rest of the world have influenced the development of the United States, events within U.S. borders have exerted an influence over other countries. The world has seen dramatic changes in political and economic structures, living patterns, beliefs about human rights, and attitudes about the environment. To fully understand the nature of American developments in these areas, it is necessary to understand the increasingly global nature of many different issues.

◀ U.S. gymnastics team, 1996 Summer Olympic Games

Chapter 25

THE MOVEMENT OF PEOPLE AND IDEAS

Chapter 26

THE STRUGGLE FOR HUMAN RIGHTS

Chapter 27

A NEW ENVIRONMENTAL AWARENESS

Chapter 23

IMPERIALISM TO NEW WORLD ORDER

FOCUS

UNDERSTANDING THE MAIN IDEA

The 20th century began as the great age of European empires. Even the United States engaged in imperialism. But two world wars weakened the empires, which dissolved after World War II. Only the Soviet Union's empire survived into the 1980s, and it too had collapsed by the early 1990s. Yet many legacies of imperialism remain.

 THEMES

■ **DEMOCRATIC VALUES**
Can a democratic nation hold an empire and still be upholding the principles of democracy?

■ **CULTURAL DIVERSITY**
How do empires promote cultural diversity? How do they discourage it?

■ **GLOBAL RELATIONS**
How might small nations avoid becoming entangled in major world rivalries?

1898	1934	1947	1955	1967
Battle of Omdurman leaves thousands of Africans dead.	U.S. Congress passes Tydings-McDuffie Act.	Britain grants India and Pakistan independence.	Bandung Conference held in Indonesia.	Civil war breaks out in Nigeria.

The American colonies were established as outposts of the British Empire during the first age of European imperialism. But the success of the American Revolution made the nation a "child" of anti-imperialism. Both imperialism and anti-imperialism continued to shape the history of the United States and the world.

During a meeting with a delegation of Methodist missionaries in 1898, President McKinley explained his position regarding annexation of the Philippines. The president said he had prayed long and hard for guidance:

> 66 And one night late it came to me this way—I don't know how it was, but it came: (1) That we could not give them back to Spain—that would be cowardly and dishonorable; (2) that we could not turn them over to France or Germany—our commercial rivals in the Orient—that would be bad business and discreditable; (3) that we could not leave them to themselves—they were unfit for self-government—and they would soon have anarchy and misrule over there worse than Spain's was; and (4) that there was nothing left for us to do but to take them all, and to educate the Filipinos, and uplift and civilize and Christianize them. 99

McKinley's attitude was typical of the time, one of widespread imperialism. His statement combined arrogance, ignorance (nearly all the Filipinos were already Christians), and benevolence. But times would change, shattering old practices and beliefs.

U.S. soldiers in Shanghai, China, during the Boxer Rebellion, 1900

Sir Hiram S. Maxim, inventor of the first fully-automatic machine gun (1883)

IMPERIALISM TO NEW WORLD ORDER ▪▪ 621

IMPERIALISM TO WORLD WAR I

FOCUS

- How did both imperialism and anti-imperialism mark America's early years?
- How did American expansion compare to Russian expansion?
- What connections existed between industrialization and imperialism during the late 19th century?
- Why did the imperial powers differ in how they governed their colonies?

Although many Americans believed that imperialism contradicted republicanism, the United States sometimes benefited from imperialism and expansion. By 1900 the United States had joined European powers in a movement to expand overseas.

British soldier, 1778

BORN OF EMPIRE

Americans have never been strangers to imperialism. In many ways, the United States owes its very existence to the first great age of European imperialism, which lasted from the late 1400s to the early 1800s. The founding of Britain's North American colonies during the 17th century was part of a British strategy to gain an advantage in the ongoing struggle against other European nations for trade and territory. This struggle eventually helped spark the American Revolution. Tired of being treated as pawns in Britain's imperial efforts and of paying taxes to support wars that seemed to have little to do with their own welfare, American colonists declared independence.

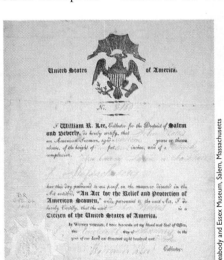

▶ **American seamen took to carrying proof-of-citizenship papers to guard against possible impressment by the British navy.**

Peabody and Essex Museum, Salem, Massachusetts

Even after Americans had won their independence, other nations' imperial ambitions continued to cause trouble. For 30 years after independence, U.S. merchants and sailors repeatedly found themselves caught in European crossfire. When their ships were seized by British and French naval vessels, American merchants lost cargoes. Furthermore, the British forced American sailors into service in the British navy. Twice the disputes that arose over these issues led to hostilities—with France in the 1790s and with Great Britain in the War of 1812.

The troubles with Great Britain and France confirmed Americans' distaste for imperialism. Americans had founded their country on the principle of republicanism—the right of people to rule themselves. Imperialism, which involved one country ruling another, contradicted this principle. And imperialism interfered with the rights of neutral third countries, as the Americans had recently discovered to their regret.

Valjean Hessing, *Choctaw Removal* (1966). Philbrook Museum of Art, Tulsa

▲ In the early 1830s, under the provisions of the Indian Removal Act, the Choctaws were removed from Mississippi to Indian Territory. This painting of the journey, entitled *Choctaw Removal* (1966), was painted by Choctaw artist Valjean Hessing. Later in the 19th century, many American Indians were forced onto reservations as settlers pushed even farther west.

Even so, Americans did occasionally benefit from European imperial conflicts. For example, the conflict between the British and the French was one reason the French aided the Patriots in the Revolutionary War. Then when the war ended, Britain granted the United States the eastern half of the Mississippi Valley in an effort to counterbalance French and Spanish territorial ambitions in North America. Americans did not question Britain's motives; they accepted the territory and were happy to have it.

During the 19th century, Americans practiced a kind of imperialism of their own as they expanded across North America. First they streamed into the land they had gained from the British. Soon they pushed even farther west into the Louisiana Territory, Texas, New Mexico, California, and Oregon. Like the Europeans, they gained some of this territory through warfare.

In all of this, Americans continued to voice support for the principles of republican anti-imperialism. They thought of themselves as creating something different from the European empires, and in some respects they were right. While the British, French, and Spanish imperial holdings were far-flung, the new U.S. territories were right next door. Furthermore, while the Europeans kept their holdings as colonies, the U.S. government eventually divided its new territories into states fully equal to the original states.

Yet in another regard American expansion resembled European imperialism. In both cases the wishes of the original inhabitants of the acquired regions were scarcely considered. The Europeans paid little attention to the needs and desires of the native inhabitants living in the colonies they claimed. Similarly, the U.S. government moved American Indians off their original homelands and onto reservations, often using force.

■■ **At first, most Americans disapproved of European imperialism, even though the United States occasionally benefited from it. Americans eventually expanded their own territorial holdings.**

RUSSIA: ANOTHER LAND EMPIRE

The closest parallel to the American expansion of the 19th century took place halfway around the world, in Russia. Over several centuries, the Russian Empire moved primarily eastward, from its heartland west of the Ural Mountains to the Pacific coast of Asia and even to Alaska (which the United States purchased in 1867). By the 19th century, Russia's expansionist energies were mainly focused on central and far eastern Asia.

▲ During the 1890s Russian colonists expanded into the Far East, occupying villages such as this one near the Pacific coast of Siberia.

Russian expansion resembled U.S. expansion in a variety of ways. Like the United States, Russia expanded across a large land area by means of agricultural settlement and wars of conquest. In addition, both the Americans and the Russians carried with them their own cultural, economic, and political systems. Both used new industrial technologies, such as great railway systems, to unite their vast territories. And both developed a sense of manifest destiny, as the Americans put it, to justify their expansion.

▲ The British fought Russian expansion in the Middle East during the mid-1800s. Here a British officer is shown relaxing in camp.

Some contemporary observers noticed the similarity of the two expansions—the one in Asia, pushing to the Pacific from the west, the other in America, pushing to the Pacific from the east. Alexis de Tocqueville even predicted that Americans and Russians had parallel futures. "Their starting-point is different," Tocqueville wrote, "and their courses are not the same; yet each of them seems marked out by the will of Heaven to sway the destinies of half the globe."

For all the similarities between Russian and American expansion, there were also important differences. In the United States, for example, millions of foreign immigrants who came from many different countries and ethnic backgrounds were among the waves of people who moved west. In Russia, on the other hand, most settlers were ethnic Russians who generally occupied and ruled lands with large non-Russian populations.

The most significant difference, however, was motive. Russian expansion was largely driven by the need to obtain a "warm-water port" that could be used year-round. Many Russian ports were on northern seas and were frozen over during winter months. Russia did have ice-free ports on the Black Sea, but these were of limited use since the Ottoman Empire controlled the outlet from the Black Sea into the Mediterranean. Because overseas trade was essential to a nation's prosperity and security, this limitation worried Russia's rulers. Thus even after reaching the Pacific, Russia continued to look south toward the Mediterranean and the Indian Ocean.

■■ **Like the Americans, Russians expanded across a huge land area. But Russian expansion differed from American expansion in several important ways.**

IMPERIALISM RENEWED

Russian imperialism was something of an exception in Europe during the first part of the 1800s. Despite their earlier scrambles to acquire colonies, during much of the 1800s most European powers had limited interest in formally annexing new territories. The earlier efforts at maintaining colonies had exhausted them, and domestic concerns—such as political uprisings and industrialization—took up much of their attention.

For most of the century, European powers were content to expand their influence through economic means rather than through direct political control. Britain, for example, established close commercial ties with many Latin American countries. Although these countries remained politically independent, their economic connections to Britain gave the British considerable influence there.

Toward the end of the 19th century, this period of "informal imperialism" gave way to a second great age of European imperialism. By

GREEDY JOHNNIE.

▲ This political cartoon satirizes 19th-century British imperialism.

1900 the major industrial powers had divided a substantial portion of the world amongst themselves. The scramble for colonies was most intense in Africa, which the Europeans divided over the span of one generation.

Africa, while the most extreme case, was not the only region in which the imperial powers asserted themselves. In the late 1850s, France began its domination of parts of Southeast Asia, and the British government gained firm control of India. East Asia, while not subject to formal annexation, did not escape the effects of Europe's renewed interest in the rest of the world. Japan and China were forced open to Western trade, and in the 1890s the major expansionist powers divided China into spheres of influence.

The United States joined the ranks of the imperialists when it annexed Hawaii, the Philippines, and various other small territories. The United States also had significant economic interests in China, Japan, and Latin America (see Chapter 9).

A variety of motives lay behind the renewed interest in imperialism. Some people viewed imperialism as a way to spread Christianity. Others claimed that Western culture was superior to the cultures found in other regions of the world and that Westerners thus had a duty to spread their culture as far as possible. British poet Rudyard Kipling called this duty the "white man's burden." British imperialist Cecil Rhodes put it bluntly: "We happen to be the best people in the world, with the highest ideals of decency and justice and liberty and peace, and the more of the world we inhabit, the better it is for humanity." Even U.S. president Theodore Roosevelt echoed the same sentiment:

66 Every expansion of a great civilized power means a victory for law, order, and righteousness. This has been the case in every instance of expansion during the present century, whether the expanding power were France or England, Russia or America. 99

Many historians, however, believe that industrialization was the primary cause for the renewed interest in formal annexation. As countries developed their manufacturing industries, they typically became dependent on foreign countries for raw materials. For example, they looked to India and Egypt for cotton and to Central Africa and

▲ Two female missionaries pose with native guides before heading off into the African interior.

Southeast Asia for rubber. Labor also tended to be cheaper in many Asian and African areas than it was in Europe. In addition, industrialized nations sought foreign markets for their products. The great prize among exporters was China, where millions of Chinese hungered for manufactured goods—or so businesspeople hoped.

Industrialization not only provided the motivation for the new imperialism; it also provided the means. Just as railroads had enabled expansion on land, steamships extended the reach of the navies of the industrialized countries.

Ironically, while the development of the steamship made imperialism possible, it also made imperialism appear necessary to the major economic powers. Unlike the sailing vessels of earlier days, the steamships of the late 19th century required periodic refueling. Much as gas stations would become essential to automobiles, **coaling stations**— ports where more coal could be taken on—were essential to steamships. Without coaling stations, the ships could not go where they were wanted and needed. A significant portion of the imperial expansion of the late 1800s and early 1900s was part of an effort to claim the best spots for coaling stations and related maintenance facilities.

Another important product of industrialization—modern weapons—was also vital to imperialist efforts. Modern weapons gave the imperialist countries' soldiers an enormous advantage over the inhabitants of the countries they conquered. The

French-born English writer Hilaire Belloc summarized this advantage in a famous couplet:

> 66 Whatever happens we have got
> The Maxim gun and they have not. 99

Such weapons made it nearly impossible for the inhabitants of the colonized areas to resist the arrival of Western people, goods, and ideas into their midst. For example, when a force of Africans—armed largely with spears and swords—attempted to resist Great Britian's advances into Northeast Africa, British gunfire in the 1898 **Battle of Omdurman** left more than 10,000 Africans dead. Fewer than 50 British soldiers were killed.

In China, which was not actually colonized but was still subjected to many foreign influences, resistance met with greater, but still limited, success. By 1900 many Chinese had become outraged by the effects Western technology and culture were having on China. Such sentiments led to the Boxer Rebellion in 1900 (see Chapter 9).

Changing Ways PROTECTING INDIA

Sometimes nations expanded into new territories to protect the territories they already had. The British, already in control of India, felt a need to expand into Egypt, East Africa, and the Arabian Peninsula in order to protect the approaches to India. "As long as we rule India," observed one British imperial statesman, Lord Curzon, "we are the greatest power in the world. If we lose it, we shall drop straight away to a third-rate power."

Holding India required two things. First, the British had to maintain the single largest navy in the world to protect the sea routes to India. Second, they had to provide secure ports from which the Royal Navy could carry out this mission. Consequently, by 1860 Britain controlled the strategic routes to India, from Gibraltar in the western Mediterranean to the Cape of Good Hope at the southern tip of Africa.

In 1869 the opening of the Suez Canal sharply reduced the sailing time between Britain and India. The British viewed the Suez Canal as Americans would later see the Panama Canal. With the canal so vital to their national interests, the British did everything in their power to protect it. Between 1869 and 1900, the British took control of Cyprus, Egypt, and parts of East and Central Africa, largely to control and defend access to India through the Suez Canal.

In the late 1890s, control of the canal almost caused Britain to come to blows with France over an outpost in Africa. The place in question, Fashoda, was on the banks of the upper Nile River. The British feared that if the French gained a foothold on the Nile, they might endanger Britain's position downstream in Egypt, which was the key to the Suez Canal.

▲ In November 1869 a procession of ships marked the opening of the Suez Canal.

France was not the only other imperialist power that Britain feared. The British government also saw Russian ambitions to expand southward as a threat not only to British control of India itself but also to British control of the route to India through the Mediterranean Sea, the Suez Canal, and the Indian Ocean. Therefore, Britain worked to extend its influence into central and southwestern Asia. The British policy of containing Russian expansion was called the Great Game. In some ways it was a forerunner of the American containment policy during the Cold War.

■■ **Industrialization was one of the major motives behind the renewed interest in imperialism. Industrialization also helped make imperialism possible.**

COLONIAL ADMINISTRATION

Once they had taken direct control of new territories, the imperialists had to govern them. Different imperialist countries, however, had different ideas about how best to govern. Two main methods emerged: **direct rule**, in which the colonizing country established a completely new governmental administration, and **indirect rule**, in which the colonizing country ruled through traditional local leaders.

Direct and indirect rule reflected the different objectives of the various imperial powers. France, Belgium, Portugal, and the United States practiced direct rule as part of their plan to westernize their colonial subjects. For the French, Belgians, and Portuguese, this primarily meant cultural assimilation. Once colonial subjects had absorbed enough of the ruling power's culture, they could, at least in theory, become full citizens of the imperial homeland. In French-controlled Senegal, for example, so many Africans qualified for this status that in 1915 four towns along the coast became eligible to vote for representatives to France's Parliament. The United States promoted the English language in its overseas territories, but its primary interests were political and economic

rather than cultural. Americans wanted to teach people how to run a constitutional, democratic government and to establish a free-market capitalist economy.

Initially, the British tried both direct and indirect rule. By World War I, however, they had decided against trying to create "Black Englishmen," as some put it. Instead, British colonial administrators maintained that colonial peoples should be helped along their own natural "evolutionary" path from "savagery" to "civilization," just as Europeans believed they had traveled it. Thus the British adopted a policy of indirect rule and tried to leave most aspects of local cultures intact.

Regardless of what type of government the imperialists set up, colonial peoples seldom embraced it. Several decades, however, would pass before conditions made widespread resistance to colonial rule practical.

▲ **A U.S. cavalry troop patrols a section of the Great Wall of China during the Boxer Rebellion.**

■■ **Some colonial powers wanted to culturally assimilate their subjects; other powers aimed at cultural "evolution."**

SECTION 1 REVIEW

IDENTIFY and explain the significance of the following: Rudyard Kipling, coaling stations, Battle of Omdurman, direct rule, indirect rule.

1. **MAIN IDEA** Why did many Americans at first oppose imperialism? How did early America occasionally benefit from imperialism?

2. **MAIN IDEA** How was American expansion similar to Russian expansion? How was it different?

3. **IDENTIFYING CAUSE AND EFFECT** How did industrialization contribute to imperialism in the late 1800s and early 1900s?

4. **WRITING TO PERSUADE** Imagine you are a colonial administrator. Write a letter to the government of the colonizing country explaining what type of colonial rule—direct or indirect—you think would best suit the colony. Explain your reasoning.

5. **HYPOTHESIZING** Do you think the Western powers would have been able to establish worldwide empires if they had not had weapons that were more powerful than those of the inhabitants of the colonized territories? Why or why not?

IMPERIALISM BETWEEN THE WARS

FOCUS

■ **What psychological effects did World War I have on European imperialists?**

■ **How did territories in the Middle East, India, and Indochina move closer to independence following World War I?**

■ **What factors led the United States to grant independence to the Philippines?**

■ **In what respects did imperialism gain a second wind during the 1930s?**

Indian independence leader Mohandas K. Gandhi

World War I halted the latest round of imperial expansion, eroding the self-confidence of the great powers, particularly Britain and France. After the war, nationalists in the colonial regions grew increasingly assertive. The Great Depression further weakened American imperialism, but it strengthened imperialist tendencies in Japan, Italy, and Germany.

WAR AND IMPERIALISM

During the debate over U.S. annexation of the Philippines, anti-imperialist Andrew Carnegie had declared that East Asia was one of the most dangerous regions in the world. "It is in that region the thunderbolt is expected. It is there the storm is to burst," stated Carnegie, referring not literally to the typhoons that often hit the Philippines but figuratively to the human conflict that might erupt following annexation. Indeed, most American anti-imperialists were not surprised when annexation led to a bloody war in the Philippines (see Chapter 9). In the same way, few anti-imperialists in America or elsewhere were particularly surprised when a much larger war broke out among the major European imperialist powers in 1914.

World War I was only partly caused by imperial rivalries; it had as much to do with the ambitions and fears of the European powers at home. But it had important effects on imperialism. One effect was psychological. Before the war Europeans had considered themselves more enlightened than most other people and therefore specially suited to ruling others. World War I blasted huge holes in this belief. Never had a war

◀ **This church in northeast Poland was transformed into a field hospital during the first German attack on the Russian front in World War I.**

killed so many people in so little time, and for so little purpose. If Europe could not even be trusted to manage its own affairs, people asked, how could it hope to manage other countries' affairs?

World War I shook many Europeans' faith in their ability to govern other peoples.

No world leader pressed more publicly for national self-determination—the right of countries to choose their own governments—than President Woodrow Wilson. But to avoid tension with the Allies, Wilson insisted on self-determination only for the countries under the thumb of Germany, Austria-Hungary, and the Ottoman Empire.

Toward this end, Article 22 of the covenant of the new League of Nations established the mandate system for the former German and Ottoman colonies. Under this system the victorious powers were to see to the welfare of "peoples not yet able to stand by themselves under the strenuous conditions of the modern world." While the mandate system allowed the victorious imperial powers to expand their territories, it also required them to develop the territories. Under the principle of **trusteeship**, mandate governments were to encourage economic development and provide educational, medical, and other services needed to modernize the new states.

THE MIDDLE EAST

The mandate system took effect most swiftly in the Middle East. The defeated Ottoman Empire was divided into several pieces, which were then parceled out to the victors in the war. (The United States declined to participate in the system.)

France and Britain received the largest Middle Eastern territories. Although they were supposed to be preparing these territories for independence, they concentrated on maintaining some influence in the region. France separated its mandate on the eastern shore of the Mediterranean into two parts: the predominantly Christian Lebanon and the predominantly Muslim Syria. France hoped that Lebanon would continue to maintain its connection to France even after achieving independence.

Great Britain, too, wanted to preserve its connections to the Middle East. Britain's mandates included Iraq, Palestine, and Transjordan—all strategically important areas. With the exception of Palestine, the British had granted independence everywhere in the region by the early 1930s. In exchange for independence, however, the new states had to sign treaties of alliance giving Britain continuing access to the area's strategic waterways, oil resources, and British-established military bases. Consequently, Britain continued to dominate the new states economically, politically, and militarily.

Not everyone approved of the mandate system. Some critics charged that France and Britain were using the system as a disguise for a new form of imperialism. Many inhabitants of the mandated territories had never accepted their former colonial status and thus thought they should have received independence at once. But defenders of the system simply pointed out that without the oversight of the League of Nations the fate of the mandated territories might have been even worse.

Under the mandate system, France and Britain were to help the Middle East become fully independent. But they forged permanent ties to the region.

▶ Following World War I, the Allies attempted to partition Turkey as well as the rest of the Ottoman Empire. Nationalist leader Mustafa Kemal Atatürk, however, held the nation together with the establishment of the republic of Turkey in 1923. Atatürk attempted to westernize Turkey and is shown here giving instruction in the Roman alphabet.

THE VICTORIOUS POWERS' TERRITORIES

The same logic and moral reasoning that demanded the breakup of the German and Ottoman empires also applied, presumably, to the overseas empires of the victorious powers, particularly Britain and France. This did not go unnoticed by the inhabitants of the British and French colonies. They too had begun to question Europe's ability to govern other peoples.

British India. In India, for example, some British policies and actions spurred an English-trained Indian lawyer, Mohandas K. Gandhi, to oppose British colonial rule. Over the next few decades, Gandhi used what he called *satyagraha,* insistence on truth, as the basis for a campaign of nonviolent resistance to British rule in India.

India had long had a movement in favor of independence—the Indian National Congress, formed in 1885. But this movement was small and did not include the majority of Indians, most of whom remained untouched by Western culture. As Gandhi became more active in the movement, he realized that he must find a way to make the movement meaningful to most Indians.

To achieve his goal of *swaraj* (self-rule), Gandhi used techniques that many people in India could understand and participate in. For example, he encouraged people to spin and weave their own cloth to protest policies favoring British cotton manufacturers. In 1930 he protested the government monopoly on salt by leading a march to the sea and making his own salt. He was committed to nonviolence. Sometimes Gandhi would fast nearly to death to accomplish his aims; such fasts shamed the British as well as Indians who resorted to violence. He was eventually called Mahatma, or Great Soul, by his followers.

▲ Mohandas K. "Mahatma" Gandhi is still honored throughout the world for his use of nonviolent resistance to gain India's independence.

During the 1920s and 1930s Indian nationalism became a powerful force that gradually loosened Britain's hold on India. But Gandhi was not simply trying to return to a precolonial era. He believed that the British had begun a process of nation-building in India by bringing together all of India's various states and peoples. He wanted to continue the process by forging a new sense of national identity among Indians. At the same time, he was convinced that Western civilization was doomed. Many Europeans, Gandhi wrote, "appear to be half mad. . . . One has only to be patient and it [European civilization] will be self-destroyed." Therefore, Gandhi strongly believed, India had to make its own future.

French Indochina. Anti-imperialism grew elsewhere in the colonial world following World War I. At the war's end, Ho Chi Minh, a young Vietnamese nationalist, was living in Paris. While Gandhi was turning toward nonviolence, Ho turned toward revolutionary communism. Ho listened to French Communists describe the plight of

RESISTING BRITISH RULE OF INDIA

THROUGH OTHERS' EYES

One of the leaders of the movement for Indian independence was Aurobindo Ghose. Like Gandhi, Ghose was educated in England, and also like Gandhi, Ghose advocated nonviolent resistance to British rule. For Ghose the goal of political independence was similar to the goal of spiritual salvation, and the methods of achieving both were the same:

"*India, free, one and indivisible, is the divine realization to which we move, emancipation our aim. . . . Whatever leads only to continued subjection must be spewed out as mere vileness and impurity. Passive resistance may be the final method of salvation in our case or it may be only the preparation for the final sadhana [spiritual self-control]. In either case, the sooner we put it into full and perfect practice, the nearer we shall be to national liberty.***"**

downtrodden workers in France and believed that the relationship between colonies and the mother country was quite similar to the relationship between workers and the ruling class. What would solve the problems of one would solve the problems of the other. "Only Socialism and Communism can liberate the oppressed nations and the working people throughout the world from slavery," he wrote. He became determined to apply this lesson to his Vietnamese homeland. Ho Chi Minh, however, would have to wait a few more decades before his efforts achieved significant results.

▪▪ Independence movements in India and Indochina grew stronger following World War I.

The Philippines. Ho Chi Minh's views would, in time, place him in conflict with the United States. But during the era after World War I nationalists like Ho and Gandhi could take heart from the words of many Americans. W.E.B. Du Bois spoke of how the imperialist powers exploited the "vast sea of human labor" in China, India, Africa, the West Indies, and elsewhere. According to Du Bois, such workers were

> ❝ paid a wage below the level of decent living; driven, beaten, prisoned and enslaved in all but name; spawning the world's raw material and luxury—cotton, wool, coffee, tea, cocoa, palm oil, fibers, spices, rubber, silks, lumber, copper, gold, diamonds, leather. . . . All these are gathered up at prices lowest of the low, manufactured, transformed and transported at fabulous gain; and the resultant wealth is distributed and displayed and made the basis of world power and universal dominion and armed arrogance in London and Paris, Berlin and Rome, New York and Rio de Janeiro. ❞

Du Bois was not the only one criticizing imperialism. Although the idea of an American empire had briefly enchanted many people and the United States had long maintained a presence in Latin America, Americans quickly lost their enthusiasm once they realized the costs of maintaining an overseas empire. For example, many Americans and Filipinos died in the brutal war in the Philippines. And while World War I did not have as strong an impact on the United States as on

Europe, it heightened Americans' suspicions of imperialism. Soon many Americans began to question the U.S. control of the Philippines.

The people of the Philippines sensed American doubts. If Americans could not be coerced into granting independence to the Philippines, they might be shamed into doing so. To further their cause, Filipino leaders adapted to the American way of politics; some became extremely skillful in the art. No Filipino leader was more skillful than Manuel Quezon.

BIO GRAPHY Born in the Tayabas province of the Philippine island of Luzon in 1878, Quezon took to politics early. Quezon had a charismatic personality that many people found nearly irresistible. He especially understood how to appeal to Americans. From 1909 to 1916 he served as the Philippine commissioner in U.S. Congress. In dealings with U.S. leaders, he Americanized his last name to "Casey" and did not hesitate to flatter Americans and praise American principles.

Manuel Quezon

But the flattery and praise had a purpose. He repeatedly reminded the Americans that they could not be true to their principles and at the same time deny democratic government to Filipinos. In 1923 he joined with other Filipino leaders in sending Washington a complaint against the American governor general of the Philippines. The statement echoed the American colonists' complaints against King George III in the Declaration of Independence:

> ❝ He has set to naught all understanding that the Filipino people have had with the American government. . . .
>
> He has broken asunder the bonds of harmony that had united Americans and Filipinos. . . .
>
> He has sought to establish a colonial despotism here worse than that which has cursed our country for the last ten generations. ❞

Quezon and his comrades hit a sensitive spot in criticizing U.S. rule, especially in doing so in

▶This 1929 photograph shows Benito Mussolini, Fascist dictator of Italy, reviewing the Italian bicycle corps on the seventh anniversary of his rise to power.

language reminiscent of Thomas Jefferson. Quezon made Americans uncomfortable when he pointed out the distance between American democratic principles and American colonial practices.

The Great Depression of the 1930s added economic discomfort to the political uneasiness Americans felt regarding their imperial connection to the Philippines. The depression drastically reduced demand for American farm products, and American producers called for protection against competition from Philippine sugar and coconut oil. Similarly, American workers lobbied for protection from competition with Filipino immigrants for jobs. One way to achieve both goals was to grant the Philippines independence. An independent Philippines would be subject to the same tariffs and immigration limits as any other foreign country.

Traditional anti-imperialism combined with this depression-induced self-interest to produce a congressional majority in favor of Philippine independence. In 1934 Congress passed the **Tydings-McDuffie Act**, which promised the Philippines independence at the end of a 12-year transition period.

■■ **Democratic anti-imperialism and economic self-interest eventually led the United States to grant the Philippines independence.**

*J*APANESE, ITALIAN, AND GERMAN EXPANSION

While Americans were turning away from imperialism, other countries were turning toward it.

Japan led the way. Small and resource-poor, Japan looked overseas to support its growing population. As early as 1910 Japan had seized control of Korea, converting it into a colony. During and after World War I, Japan acquired Germany's Pacific possessions. Yet Japanese leaders believed they still needed more space and resources.

They felt the need even more sharply when the Japanese economy took a downturn during the 1930s. In response, Japanese leaders cast an eye toward Manchuria, in northeastern China. Manchuria was full of the kinds of resources Japan wanted, and it was only loosely attached to China.

In 1931 Japan occupied Manchuria and set up a **puppet government**. Although the government was nominally headed by the Chinese, it was really controlled by Japan. "Expansion towards the continent," wrote one leading Japanese banker, Hirozo Mori, "is the destiny of the Japanese people, decreed by Heaven, which neither the world nor we the Japanese ourselves can check or alter."

The significance of the Japanese takeover of Manchuria—and the failure of other nations to prevent it—was not lost on governments elsewhere that sought relief from the depression through foreign expansion. Italy, led by the Fascist dictator Benito Mussolini, invaded and waged a bloody war of conquest against Ethiopia in 1935. As in the case of Japan, the other great powers condemned Italy's action but failed to check its expansion.

The most dangerous of the depression-era imperialists was Adolf Hitler. For years Hitler had dreamed of extending Germany's boundaries; Germany needed *Lebensraum,* or living space, he said. Reviving an old German policy called *Drang nach Osten,* the drive to the east, Hitler planned to create a new civilization in southern Russia and the Ukraine:

> 66 The area . . . must be Europeanized! . . . The German agencies and authorities are to have wonderful buildings, the governors' palaces. Around each city, a ring of lovely villages will be placed to within 30 or 40 kilometers. . . . The German cities will be placed, like pearls on a string, and around the cities the German settlements will lie. 99

German occupation of the region was to be made possible by the extermination or enslavement of the local inhabitants.

Hitler's imperial vision was sweeping. "Germany must either be a world power or there will be no Germany," he said. He never got as far as he planned, but he did rebuild Germany's armed forces, even in defiance of the 1919 Treaty of Versailles. When the great powers did nothing to stop him, he was encouraged to take bolder measures in the late 1930s—the annexation of Austria, the seizure of the Sudetenland, and finally the dismantling of the rest of Czechoslovakia.

Until this last step, other nations—including the United States—had avoided actively interfering with Japanese, Italian, and German expansion. Western leaders were anxious not to repeat the horrors of World War I. Equally important, they feared the expansion of communism and Soviet power. Even though the revolutionaries who had created the Soviet state in 1917 had condemned imperialism along with capitalism, they had gone on to create a new empire of Soviet Socialist Republics. In 1938 Britain's prime minister, Neville Chamberlain, expressed the fears of many when he warned of the dangers of overthrowing Hitler. "Who will guarantee that Germany will not become Bolshevistic [Communist] afterwards?" he asked. Thus no one tried to stop Hitler until it was almost too late and only a large-scale war could prevent further expansion.

■■ Japan, Italy, and Germany launched new imperialist offensives during the 1930s.

▲ **Adolf Hitler confers in 1941 with the ambassador of Japan, another nation bent on expansion by military conquest.**

SECTION 2 REVIEW

IDENTIFY and explain the significance of the following: trusteeship, Mohandas K. Gandhi, Manuel Quezon, Tydings-McDuffie Act, puppet government.

1. **MAIN IDEA** How did World War I affect European beliefs regarding imperialism?

2. **MAIN IDEA** What effects did World War I have on imperialism in the Middle East?

3. **MAIN IDEA** Why did the U.S. government decide to grant the Philippines independence?

4. **WRITING TO EXPLAIN** Write an essay explaining why Japan, Italy, and Germany wanted to expand their territorial holdings in the 1930s.

5. **USING HISTORICAL IMAGINATION** Imagine you are a leader of the independence movement in India or in Indochina following World War I. How might you persuade people to join the movement?

DECOLONIZATION AND THE COLD WAR

F O C U S

■ How did World War II hasten the demise of European colonialism in Asia?

■ When did most African nations become independent?

■ How did many former colonies react to the Cold War? How did their goals change over time?

Even more than World War I, World War II weakened the European powers and strengthened anticolonial nationalist movements. Shortly after the war, decolonization began with a rush. But decolonization was often complicated by the Cold War. Most newly independent countries attempted to remain neutral in the Cold War and formed what came to be called the Third World.

Mohammed Ali Jinnah, head of the Moslem League in British India and first governor general of Pakistan

WAR AND ASIAN NATIONALISM

World War II had a profound effect on imperialism. Where World War I had shattered Europe's sense of moral superiority, World War II shattered its sense of military superiority. Though Japan eventually lost the war, its early victories over American and British forces in the Pacific and in Southeast Asia brought home the point that Asians were fully capable of standing up against the soldiers and technology of the West. Another event from early in the war also had a significant impact on the future of imperialism. Just as President Wilson had thrown America's moral weight behind self-determination in World War I, so too did President Franklin Roosevelt insist that self-determination be a central objective of the anti-Fascist coalition in World War II. Roosevelt's view was embodied in the Atlantic Charter of 1941. Issued in conjunction with British prime minister Winston Churchill, the charter stated:

❝ First, [the United States and Britain] seek no aggrandizement [enlargement], territorial or other; Second, they desire to see no territorial changes that do not accord with the freely expressed wishes of the peoples concerned; Third, they respect the right of all peoples to choose the form of government under which they will live; and they wish to see sovereign rights and self-government restored to those who have been forcibly deprived of them. ❞

Churchill, however, did not take steps to dissolve the British Empire, and with the war raging on, Roosevelt declined to press the point. Nevertheless, the Atlantic Charter became a source of inspiration to colonial peoples around the world.

India. In India, Mohandas Gandhi stepped up the campaign of nonviolent resistance to British rule. Churchill attempted to crush the "Quit India"

movement, as the campaign was called, by having tens of thousands of Indian protesters thrown in jail. "I have not become the King's First Minister," he once said, "in order to preside over the liquidation [breakup] of the British Empire."

Yet Churchill's actions served as a stark reminder of the contradiction between the ideals expressed in the Atlantic Charter and the continuing practice of imperialism. A leading newspaper of the Indian nationalist movement wondered in print at the "mysterious silence" that had fallen over Washington, D.C., in the wake of the British crackdown. Many Americans wondered, too, and grew increasingly uncomfortable with their country's failure to denounce British imperialism.

Thus it was with a sigh of relief that Americans viewed the series of events that led to Indian independence. Just as World War II was ending, British voters replaced Churchill with Clement Attlee, the leader of the opposition Labour party. Attlee and the Labour party were not uniformly anti-imperialist. They did believe, however, that after two centuries of British rule, India was ready for independence.

Adding to this belief was the fact that the war left Britain exhausted. Britain and the Allies had won, but the British no longer had the financial resources to support an empire and were weary of trying to govern other people. The first priority of British voters, as demonstrated by their election of Attlee, was to repair their fortunes at home. India could look out for itself.

Had the Indians made less of an issue of independence, even Attlee might have been inclined to keep India as a British colony. But the war's end only made the Indian nationalists more assertive than ever. They made it plain that a refusal to grant independence would cost Britain dearly—in money, in moral standing, and perhaps in lives of British soldiers.

The British, therefore, agreed to go. In August 1947 the British turned over power to an Indian government. At the same time, they also granted power to the newly established nation of Pakistan, the largely Muslim portion of British India that refused to be associated with predominantly Hindu independent India.

▲ Jawaharlal Nehru, India's first prime minister, reviews troops during 1948 Independence Day ceremonies.

Indonesia. During this same period, and for many of the same reasons, the government of the Netherlands decided to pull out of the Dutch East Indies. The Netherlands had been hit even harder than Britain by the war. Furthermore, the nationalist movement in the Dutch East Indies, led by Achmed Sukarno, was just as determined as the nationalist movement in India.

The Netherlands, however, took a bit longer than Britain to accept decolonization. Several periods of severe fighting broke out between the Dutch and the Indonesians in the years following World War II as the Netherlands resisted giving the region independence. Although the Dutch were able to recapture much territory, the Indonesians would not be defeated. In 1949, after nearly four years of conflict, the Netherlands conceded power to the government of Indonesia.

⬛⬛ World War II heartened Asian nationalists and exhausted European imperialists, leading to independence for such countries as India, Pakistan, and Indonesia.

◀ **Dr. Achmed Sukarno,** an active nationalist for 20 years before Indonesia's independence, became the republic's first president and held that office until 1967.

▲ Vietnamese nationalists, such as these Annamites captured by French soldiers, opposed the return of French rule to Indochina after World War II.

Vietnam. France, too, was reluctant to let go of its colonies. World War II had been particularly humiliating for the French, who surrendered to the Germans after a mere six weeks of fighting in 1940. Adding insult to injury, Japan took advantage of France's misfortune to strip it of Indochina, its Southeast Asian possession. The final year of the fighting in Europe, during which French soldiers joined the other Allies in liberating France, helped restore French pride. The government in Paris hoped to redeem some of the rest by reclaiming Indochina upon the defeat of Japan.

But the inhabitants of Indochina had other ideas. The notable opposition figure there was Ho Chi Minh, the Vietnamese nationalist who had led the struggle against French imperialism before the war and against Japanese imperialism during the war. The defeat of Japan had encouraged Ho to believe that independence was at hand. Thus when troops returned to reclaim Indochina for France, Ho and many others took up arms in resistance.

Americans were of two minds about the situation in Indochina, just as they had long been of two minds about imperialism. On one hand they sympathized with the Vietnamese desire for independence. But on the other hand, the U.S. government was reluctant to anger France. During this period the Cold War was taking shape, and U.S. officials greatly desired French help in fighting the spread of communism worldwide. Further-

more, Ho Chi Minh was not merely a nationalist, but a Communist who proudly proclaimed his desire to bring about a Communist revolution in Vietnam. At a time when the United States was publicly committed to opposing the spread of communism, supporting Ho against France seemed out of the question.

The war in Indochina went poorly for France. Ho's guerrilla forces wore the French down. In response, the U.S. government increased its economic and military assistance to the French in Indochina. But the aid was to no avail, and in 1954 the French government was forced to withdraw from the region (see Chapter 20).

▪▪ American choices became complicated when nationalists were also Communists, as in Vietnam.

INDEPENDENT AFRICA

The exhaustion that followed World War II left the European empires in Africa as vulnerable to challenge as the empires in Asia. Africans in all parts of the continent took advantage of their opportunity, and most African nations became independent during the late 1950s and early 1960s (see map). In 1960 the British prime minister announced that "the wind of change" was blowing through Africa, driving out colonialism.

The imperial powers, however, did not always let go of their African colonies easily. In Kenya many Africans protested British rule starting in the 1940s. Their greatest complaint was that the British owned most of the land in Kenya while many Africans had no land and lived in poverty. When British policy remained unchanged, some Africans—such as Jomo Kenyatta, the leader of the Kenyan independence movement—became convinced that violence was necessary to achieve their goals.

◀ Kwame Nkrumah, prime minister of Ghana, waves to a crowd celebrating Ghana's independence from British rule in 1957.

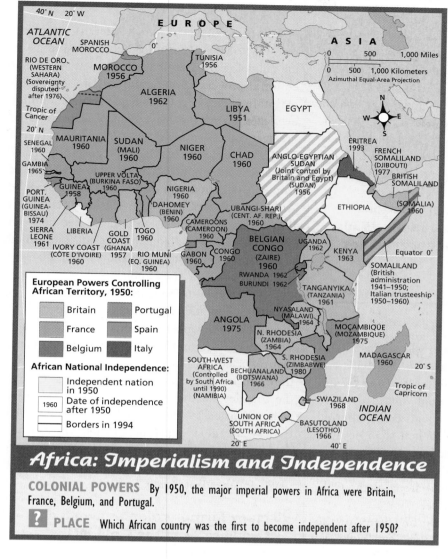

Africa: Imperialism and Independence

COLONIAL POWERS By 1950, the major imperial powers in Africa were Britain, France, Belgium, and Portugal.

❓ **PLACE** Which African country was the first to become independent after 1950?

gained even wider support in the late 1950s, Kenya did not officially become independent from Britain until 1963.

In the French African territories, the bloodiest struggle for independence took place in Algeria in North Africa. About one million French colonists lived in Algeria, and in some ways the French considered Algeria a part of France itself. Algerians, however, felt differently, and a nationalist revolt in 1954 sparked a brutal war that raged for several years. Both sides committed many atrocities. Faced with growing opposition to the war, France decided to cut its losses and gave Algeria its independence in 1962.

The Belgian government had no wish to face the bloodshed experienced in Kenya and Algeria. In 1959, when rioting broke out in Belgium's one African colony, the Belgian Congo, the Belgians left even before a successor government was firmly in place. Rival groups engaged in a civil war that wracked the country. Soon the Congo was caught up in the Cold War competition between the United States

Kenyatta expressed his conviction in a 1952 speech in which he discussed the flag of the Kenya African Union (KAU). As African nationalist Karari Njama recalled:

> 66 He [Kenyatta] raised the KAU flag to symbolize African Government. . . . He said, "Black is to show that this is for black people. Red is to show that the blood of an African is the same colour as the blood of a European, and green is to show that when we were given this country by God it was green, fertile and good but now you see the green is below the red and is suppressed." . . . What he said must mean that our fertile lands (green) could only be regained by the blood (red) of the African (black). 99

Fighting in Kenya broke out in 1952 and continued until 1956. Some 13,000 Africans were killed. Although the independence movement

▲ In 1954, after rebels began a war in Algeria, French troops protected nomadic families as they moved from the mountains.

and the Soviet Union. Conflicting parties sought allies where they could, and each superpower hoped to curry favor with the victor in the civil war—whoever that might be. Although the civil war eventually came to an end in the Congo (which changed its name to Zaire in 1971), the country's transition to independence seemed an ominous token of how Cold War rivalries could inflame situations that were explosive enough on their own.

■■ **Although most African nations became independent in the 1950s and 1960s, independence did not always come easily.**

THE NONALIGNED MOVEMENT

The predicament of the Congo was similar to that faced by many small countries in the 1950s and 1960s. Both the United States and the Soviet Union, seeking allies in the Cold War, tried to win the support of the smaller countries by offering them money and supplies. When such devices failed, the superpowers sometimes tried force. For the smaller countries, many of them only recently independent, the international arena of the Cold War could be a dangerous place.

Complicating the situation, many of the newly independent countries remained economically dependent on the old imperial powers. For nationalists anxious to demonstrate their independence, such links could be irritating. It was easier and cheaper, for example, for Nigerians to telephone London than to call nearby Ivory Coast—Nigeria had been a British colony while Ivory Coast had been French.

▲ **This 1964 photograph shows Angolan rebels being instructed in the use of the bazooka.**

Neocolonialism. As problems mounted, many new leaders began to blame conditions on the old colonial powers. Some accused the former colonial powers of **neocolonialism**—trying to maintain indirect control over former colonies even after they had achieved independence. As the greatest capitalist power after World War II, the United States, too, was soon accused by many nationalist leaders of practicing this new style of imperialism through economic control. The American role in Cold War events only reinforced this image. When faced with the choice between anti-imperialism and anticommunism, the United States consistently chose anticommunism. The war in Indochina was a case in point.

In reaction to the Cold War rivalries and as a matter of mutual protection, many leaders of the newly independent nations banded together. They formed the **nonaligned movement**, a name that reflected the member nations' policy of neutrality in regard to the two superpowers. One of the founders of the movement was India's new prime minister, Jawaharlal Nehru. Nehru believed that Westerners continued to use the former colonies as pawns in their own quarrels. He hoped to extend Gandhi's doctrine of self-help to other newly independent nations.

■■ **Many former colonies avoided taking sides in the Cold War by forming the nonaligned movement.**

The Third World. To the nonaligned movement, the world seemed to be divided into three parts: the First World of the Western capitalist nations, the Second World of the Soviet socialist nations, and the **Third World** made up of all the rest. The Third World first claimed the international spotlight in 1955 when Indonesia hosted a meeting in Bandung, a city on the Indonesian island of Java. The **Bandung Conference** reaffirmed Nehru's suggestion that the former colonies should remain neutral in the Cold War and if necessary should seek help for development from both sides. The conference also inspired the establishment of regional organizations among many Third World nations.

Third World conferences became a regular feature of international politics during the next decade. Moreover, as decolonization spread across Asia and Africa, more and more new countries came into being, and most of them joined the non-aligned movement. By the mid-1960s Third World countries made up a majority of members of the United Nations. Though the major industrial powers still controlled the UN Security Council, the General Assembly became an important forum for Third World concerns.

Third World leaders were primarily interested in modernizing and industrializing quickly. Although most complained about being tied to the economies of the former imperial powers, they also depended on foreign aid—including American aid—to pursue their development and modernization programs. Through the nonaligned movement, Third World leaders hoped to keep free of the Cold War struggle and yet obtain the resources they needed for development.

This was not easy. During the Cold War, American foreign aid rarely came without strings attached. The United States saw economic aid as a way to buy allies. To most U.S. leaders, the idea of neutrality in the struggle against worldwide communism was dangerous. John Foster Dulles, secretary of state under President Eisenhower, called it "immoral." Eisenhower himself said, "There can be no neutrals when the question is one of moral values or right and wrong."

American relations with many Third World countries became strained over the issue of neutrality. In the UN many of the Third World leaders denounced American policies as imperialistic. Even so, they continued to apply for aid from both the Western nations and the Soviet Union.

Changing goals. As the nonaligned movement grew larger and more diverse, the policy of neutrality became less important than the goal of development. Soon the movement included some countries that were openly allied with one superpower or the other. Cuba, for example, became a Soviet ally. Pakistan, the Philippines, and several Latin American countries had close ties to the United States.

As a result, the term *Third World* became a synonym for the region of the planet occupied by less developed countries. In addition to the East-West issues of the Cold War, people now spoke of North-South issues—those issues separating the rich, industrialized nations of the northern part of the globe from the poorer countries of the southern part. (These labels were generalizations. New Zealand, for example, was wealthy, though in the Southern Hemisphere, while North Korea, in the Northern Hemisphere, was poor.)

As the colonial empires faded from view, the concerns of those countries that had been part of the empires became increasingly important in international affairs. Though none of these countries possessed the power or wealth of the United States or the Soviet Union, together they held a majority of the world's people. This alone gave them a significance not even the superpowers could ignore.

■■ **Economic development replaced neutrality in the Cold War as the major concern of Third World nations.**

SECTION 3 REVIEW

IDENTIFY and explain the significance of the following: Clement Attlee, Jomo Kenyatta, neocolonialism, nonaligned movement, Jawaharlal Nehru, Third World, Bandung Conference.

LOCATE and explain the importance of the following: Kenya, Algeria, Belgian Congo.

1. **MAIN IDEA** In what ways did World War II lead to independence for several Asian countries?

2. **MAIN IDEA** During what years did most of the nations of Africa become independent?

3. **MAIN IDEA** How did many former colonies try to avoid taking sides in the Cold War?

4. **WRITING TO EXPRESS A VIEWPOINT** Imagine you are a delegate to the Bandung Conference. Prepare a speech discussing how the Third World might obtain the resources necessary for economic development.

5. **EVALUATING** How might the United States have given greater support to independence movements and to newly independent countries?

LEGACIES OF IMPERIALISM

FOCUS

■ What problems did newly independent nations face following decolonization?

■ How did Africa continue to feel the effects of imperialism even after most African nations became independent?

■ How do the nations of Eastern Europe and the former Soviet Union resemble former Asian and African colonies?

*O*nce they had gained independence, many former Asian and African colonies continued to face problems related to their colonial histories. And when the Soviet Union collapsed, many Eastern European and former Soviet nations faced similar problems.

Lithuanians holding aloft their country's flag in Vilnius, Lithuania, 1991

PROBLEMS OF INDEPENDENCE

The nonaligned movement helped establish ways in which the newly independent nations might interact with the United States, the Soviet Union, and Europe. But the new nations also had to deal with the realities of setting up political, economic, and social systems—and of addressing domestic conflicts. These were not easy tasks.

Apart from small groups of Western-educated nationalists, few people in many of the new nations felt any sense of national identity or loyalty to the new states. Some new nations were made up of many diverse groups of people who had never before been politically unified. As the new political leaders struggled with the challenges of governing, many turned to autocratic methods to achieve their goals. Unable to create a sense of national identity among their diverse peoples, many leaders began to practice a kind of ethnic imperialism, relying on their own families and ethnic communities for support. Others used the military to preserve order. Military dictatorships sprang up in many Asian and African nations after independence.

A further problem concerned borders. In many cases, the boundaries established prior to or at independence created terrible conflicts as different cultural groups laid claim to the same territory. India and Pakistan, for instance, fought

◀ **N'Garta Tombalbaye, Chad's first president, is shown here at the meeting that established the Organization of African Unity in 1963.**

several times over possession of the boundary province of Kashmir and witnessed lasting strife between Muslims and Hindus. In the Middle East the violent conflict between Israelis and Arabs raged for decades.

▪▪ Many newly independent nations faced political instability and ethnic strife.

AFRICA: A CASE STUDY

Africa, in particular, felt the strains created by borders. Back in the 1880s, as the imperialist scramble for African territory was getting underway, the European powers held a conference in Berlin, Germany, to decide how to divide Africa. Looking at a map of the continent, they drew boundaries that were, for the most part, simply based on their own convenience. They failed to consider features that naturally determine borders, such as landforms or cultural groupings. In some cases, borders lumped together hundreds of diverse peoples. Nigeria, for example, became home to over 200 ethnic groups. In other cases, borders split up ethnic groups. The Somali people found themselves divided among Somalia, Ethiopia, and Kenya.

In 1963, after most of the African nations had gained independence, they formed the **Organization of African Unity** (OAU). One of the OAU's main goals was to prevent territorial conflicts among its members. Fearing that redrawing boundaries might spark border disputes, the OAU decided to keep the old colonial boundaries following decolonization. While this decision did limit conflict between African nations, it did not prevent conflict within nations. In Nigeria a separatist movement led to a bloody civil war in 1967. In Sudan, too, ethnic and cultural differences between north and south led to a civil war that dragged on from the mid-1950s to the 1990s. Civil wars and conflicts related to ethnic groupings have affected several other African countries, such as Rwanda and Burundi (see Chapter 25).

The artificial borders imposed by Europeans were not the only legacies of colonialism left in Africa after independence. Because Europeans made few substantial efforts to develop diversified colonial economies, Africans had little to build on following independence. As a result, they found it difficult to achieve economic self-sufficiency or even to forge new international economic ties. Thus most of the African nations remained economically dependent on their former colonial rulers. Economic dependence on Europe continues today. Only some 5 percent of Africa's total international trade is conducted within Africa.

Economic independence has been hard to achieve in part because many African nations have had difficulty attracting foreign investment due to their size (another result of European-made boundaries), political instability, or poverty. As one investment analyst explained:

> 66 A lot of African countries, because of their colonial legacy, are so tiny I don't know what they can do. A lot of the products [foreign] companies want to sell, like Coca-Cola [or consumer goods] can't be sold to people without food or running water. 99

In some places the Europeans not only failed to develop African economies but also did not adequately prepare Africans themselves for the

▲ This literacy class in Togo, a small nation in West Africa, helps prepare these women for their role as citizens of a republic.

challenges they would face following independence. In Zaire (formerly the Belgian Congo), for example, Belgians held most government and business jobs during the colonial period. Africans, meanwhile, received little training—not only in government and business but also in services such as education and health care. Thus when the region became independent in 1960 and the Belgians left, Zaire had few people who had enough experience to manage the country effectively. Zaire was not the only African nation that faced this problem. As Salim Ahmed Salim, the secretary-general of the Organization of African Unity, explained:

> 66 Colonial education, limited to training very low functionaries [government officials], did not prepare the African for the eventual assumption of leadership and management of the affairs of a modern state. 99

In many nations, lack of experience has led to problems of governmental inefficiency, political corruption, and economic planning.

Not all of Africa's problems can be blamed on its colonial heritage. Limited natural resources in some areas, droughts and other natural disasters, and a variety of other obstacles have contributed to many African nations' lack of prosperity. Nevertheless, historians can only guess at what Africa might look like today had it never been colonized.

■■ **Many legacies of imperialism, such as illogical borders and underdeveloped economies, proved problematic for African nations after independence.**

THE SOVIET EMPIRE FALLS

As Africa struggled to shake free of colonial influences in the mid-1980s, the Soviet Union struggled to hold together its empire, sometimes referred to as the Soviet sphere. Made up of the Soviet Union's own republics and the satellite nations in Eastern Europe, the Soviet sphere began to collapse in the late 1980s (see Chapter 22). One by one the Eastern European nations broke free of Soviet control. Then the Soviet republics, too, declared independence. The last empire had fallen; the Soviet Union ceased to exist.

The nations created or reshaped by the fall of the Soviet Union found that independence carried its own problems. Like many of the nations that had become independent earlier in the century, the newly independent nations of Eastern Europe and the former Soviet Union have suffered from border disputes, political infighting, and underdeveloped economies. And as in Asia and Africa, ethnic rivalries that a strong central authority had kept in check for years resurfaced.

Yugoslavia has faced the worst of the violence caused by such rivalries (see Chapter 22), but ethnic tensions have affected other countries as well. In the former Soviet Union, the 15 newly independent republics have experienced conflict as different groups struggle for power. Russia and Ukraine have argued over control of the Black Sea fleet, while Christians in the former Soviet republic of Armenia have battled Muslims in neighboring Azerbaijan (az-uhr-by-JAHN). Similarly, some areas of Georgia, a republic just to the east of the Black Sea, have witnessed a rise in ethnic violence between Islamic groups and Georgians, who are traditionally Eastern Orthodox Christian. Within the Russian Federation itself, ethnic conflict has characterized relations between the central government and some of the partially self-governing republics with large non-Russian populations. For example, fighting between the Russian army and Chechen rebels increased in 1994 as Chechnya pushed

◄ **Two Soviet soldiers watch pro-independence demonstrators in Lithuania in 1990.**

for independence. In some of the new nations of Central Asia, too, fighting has broken out among the region's many ethnic groups.

Economic problems have compounded other problems. Under Soviet control, each satellite nation and Soviet republic produced the goods that it could make or grow best. When the Soviet Union collapsed, however, so too did the trade networks that had kept the different regions supplied with necessary goods and resources. Hardships increased as the new nations had to establish new economic links. In Russia, economic difficulties hit the military particularly hard. Troops went without pay or adequate housing for months, leading some observers to suggest that the once-proud Red Army might stage a rebellion against the country's leaders.

Although foreign investment in some Eastern European nations and former Soviet republics is increasing, some investors are hesitant to put money in nations that remain politically and economically unstable. "The political situation in Russia is chaotic," noted one business expert. "It's just a much riskier environment." Even so, many people in Eastern Europe and the former Soviet Union remain cautiously hopeful that free market reforms and increasing democracy will one day bring prosperity.

■■ The nations of the former Soviet sphere have faced many of the same social and economic problems that have challenged former colonies in Africa and Asia.

COMMENTARY

America and the Post–Cold War World

As the Cold War was winding down, American commentator Charles Krauthammer wrote, "Nations need enemies. Take away one, and they find another. . . . Countries need mobilizing symbols of 'otherness' to energize the nation and to give it purpose." Krauthammer worried that with the decline of the Soviet Union and the end of the Cold War, America would lose its sense of purpose.

Others took a more optimistic view of what the United States might be able to accomplish in the post–Cold War world. Even though the major empires have dissolved and most nations now have the freedom to govern themselves, true democracy remains a dream in many parts of the world. A key question of the 1990s has been whether democratic nations can convince the rest of the world of democracy's ability to help solve social and economic problems. This goal will be accomplished not by military or economic might, but by the power of ideas. In this realm, many people believe, the United States can and must play a central role.

Despite a shifting balance of global power and changing economic realities, the appeal of individual freedom, democratic self-government, and opportunity for all remains as strong as ever. This is especially true for those denied them by repressive rulers or grinding poverty. From South Africa to Eastern Europe to Southeast Asia to Latin America, the vision of democracy and freedom can still become a reality.

SECTION 4 REVIEW

IDENTIFY and explain the significance of the following: Organization of African Unity.

1. **MAIN IDEA** What were some of the domestic challenges faced by newly independent nations following decolonization?

2. **MAIN IDEA** How did imperialism continue to affect Africa even after most African nations became independent?

3. **COMPARING** In what ways do the nations of the former Soviet sphere resemble former colonies in Africa and Asia?

4. **WRITING TO DESCRIBE** Imagine you are a merchant in a newly independent nation of Africa or of the former Soviet sphere. Write a letter to a friend describing how your business has changed since your country's independence.

5. **ANALYZING** Why did decolonization lead to an increase in ethnic conflict in some nations?

Indian National Congress forms.

Battle of Omdurman leaves thousands of Africans dead.

Boxer Rebellion begins in China.

Japan invades Manchuria.

U.S. Congress passes Tydings-McDuffie Act.

1885 1898 1900 1931 1934

WRITING A SUMMARY

Using the essential points of the chapter as a guide, write a summary of the chapter.

REVIEWING CHRONOLOGY

Number your paper 1 to 5. Study the time line above, and list the following events in the order in which they happened by writing the first next to 1, the second next to 2, and so on. Then complete the activity below.

1. U.S. Congress passes Tydings-McDuffie Act.
2. Atlantic Charter signed.
3. Kenya becomes independent from Britain.
4. Algerian nationalists revolt against French rule.
5. Indian National Congress forms.

Evaluating What did the leaders of newly independent nations hope to accomplish at the Bandung Conference?

IDENTIFYING PEOPLE AND IDEAS

Explain the historical significance of each of the following people or terms.

1. Rudyard Kipling
2. coaling station
3. direct rule
4. trusteeship
5. Manuel Quezon
6. puppet government
7. Jomo Kenyatta
8. neocolonialism
9. Jawaharlal Nehru
10. Organization of African Unity

UNDERSTANDING MAIN IDEAS

1. How did industrialization contribute to a renewal of imperialism in the late 1800s and early 1900s?
2. Why did World War I change European beliefs about imperialism? How did this change in beliefs affect the Middle East?
3. What major powers engaged in imperialism during the 1930s? What were their primary motives?
4. How did World War II affect European colonialism in Asia? Were the effects the same in Africa?
5. How have legacies of imperialism continued to challenge nations in Asia, Africa, Eastern Europe, and the former Soviet Union?

REVIEWING THEMES

1. **Democratic Values** Why did many early Americans believe that imperialism went against the spirit of democracy?
2. **Cultural Diversity** How did various forms of colonial government reflect differing ideas on the value of cultural diversity within an empire?
3. **Global Relations** What steps did former colonies take to avoid becoming involved in the Cold War? How successful were they?

THINKING CRITICALLY

1. **Synthesizing** In what ways did American expansion in the 1800s and early 1900s resemble European expansion? In what ways did it differ?
2. **Evaluating** What issues should the people of a colony consider in attempts to achieve independence? Support your answer with examples from independence movements in Asia and Africa.
3. **Hypothesizing** Do you think that wide-scale imperialism would still exist today if World Wars I and II had never happened? Why or why not?

STRATEGY FOR SUCCESS

Review the Strategies for Success on Recognizing Stereotypes on page 272. Then read the following excerpt from a book by Frederick Lugard, a British colonial administrator in Africa in the early 1900s. What stereotypes does Lugard use to justify British colonialism in Africa?

❝ As Roman imperialism laid the foundations of modern civilisation, and led the wild barbarians of these islands [Great Britain] along the path of progress, so in Africa to-day we are repaying the debt, and bringing to the dark places of earth, the abode of barbarism and cruelty, the torch of culture

John Bull, which represents Great Britain

| 1935 | 1941 | 1947 | 1954 | 1955 | 1960 | 1963 | 1967 |

Italy invades Ethiopia.

Atlantic Charter signed.

Britain grants India and Pakistan independence.

France withdraws from Indochina. Algerian nationalists revolt against French rule.

Bandung Conference held in Indonesia.

Belgium grants the Congo independence.

Kenya becomes independent from Britain. Organization of African Unity forms.

Civil war breaks out in Nigeria.

and progress. . . . I am profoundly convinced that there can be no question but that British rule has promoted the happiness and welfare of the primitive races. Let those who question it examine the results impartially. If there is unrest, and a desire for independence, . . . it is because we have taught the value of liberty and freedom, which for centuries these peoples had not known. Their very discontent is a measure of their progress. **"**

WRITING ABOUT HISTORY

Writing to Persuade Imagine you are the leader of a newly independent nation that is experiencing conflict among various groups. Write a speech urging the conflicting groups to make peace. Explain why peace would benefit the nation as a whole.

USING PRIMARY SOURCES

Many independence movements gained strength in the period between World War I and World War II. Achmed Sukarno, for example, founded the Partai Nasional Indonesia (PNI) in 1927. In 1930, Indonesia's Dutch rulers attempted to destroy the PNI by arresting Sukarno and other nationalist leaders. Read the following excerpt from a speech Sukarno gave during his defense in the trial. What fundamental contradiction does Sukarno see in imperialism?

" *As long as a nation does not wield political power in its own country, part of its potential, economic, social or political, will be used for interests which are not its interests, but contrary to them. . . .*

A colonial nation is a nation that cannot be itself, a nation that in almost all its branches, in all of its life, bears the mark of imperialism. . . . There is no community of interests between the subject and the object of imperialism. Between the two there is only a contrast of interests and a conflict of needs. All interests of imperialism, social,

economic, political, or cultural, are opposed to the interests of the Indonesian people. The imperialists desire the continuation of colonization, the Indonesians desire its abolition. The regulations that came into being under the influence of imperialism are therefore contrary to the interest of the Indonesian people. **"**

LINKING HISTORY AND GEOGRAPHY

Study the map on page 637, which shows how Africa was divided among various European powers in 1950. Then refer to the map on pages 238–239. Focus on the part of the map that shows how Africa was divided among various European powers in 1914. How did imperialism in Africa change between 1914 and 1950?

 # BUILDING YOUR PORTFOLIO

Complete the following projects independently or cooperatively.

1. THE ECONOMY Imagine you are an economist in an independent nation that was under imperial control for the first half of the 20th century. Create a flowchart tracing the relationship between your nation's colonial background and economic factors. Consider the economic motivations that led imperialist powers to take interest in your country originally as well as the economic consequences of imperialism for your nation today.

2. INDIVIDUAL RIGHTS Imagine you are a member of an independence movement in a region under imperial control in the mid-1900s. Write a petition to the government of the controlling nation describing how imperialism has interfered with the rights of your region's inhabitants.

Chapter 24

FROM INDUSTRIALIZATION TO GLOBAL ECONOMY

FOCUS

UNDERSTANDING THE MAIN IDEA

In the first half of the 20th century the United States became the most powerful country in the world, and this power rested largely on America's economic might. America's economic might rested, in turn, on the nation's ever-closer involvement in the global economy, which grew increasingly unified in the 1900s.

THEMES

■ **TECHNOLOGY AND SOCIETY** How does technology shape economic relations between countries?

■ **GLOBAL RELATIONS** How is conflict harmful to global economic development?

■ **ECONOMIC DEVELOPMENT** What are the benefits of free trade and of protectionism? What are the costs?

1900	1930	1944	1951	1993
U.S. adopts the gold standard.	Smoot-Hawley Tariff passed.	Bretton Woods conference held.	European Coal and Steel Community formed.	NAFTA ratified.

International economic affairs played a large role in American history almost from its beginning. For example, if Columbus had not been trying to find a shorter trade route to China, he never would have bumped into the Americas in 1492. American merchants engaged in overseas trade as part of the British Empire, and after independence they ventured out energetically on their own.

Coins from around the world

During the 1830s Frenchman Alexis de Tocqueville visited the United States and forecast a brilliant future for the Americans. Tocqueville said that Americans had both the human and the natural resources to make their country one of the wealthiest and most powerful in the world. No enemy could deprive Americans of "that fertile wilderness which offers resources to all industry"; nor would the Americans be denied "their climate or their inland seas, their great rivers or their exuberant soil."

Tocqueville noted something else. "At the present time . . . ," he wrote, "the nations seem to be advancing to unity. Our means of intellectual intercourse unite the remotest parts of the earth; and men cannot remain strangers to each other, or be ignorant of what is taking place in any corner of the globe."

Events bore out both of Tocqueville's predictions, although not at once. The slavery dispute, the Civil War, and Reconstruction delayed America's rise to world power, and two world wars set back the trend toward global unification. But during the first half of the 20th century, the United States became the most powerful country in the world, largely as a result of its possessing the most powerful economy. And during the second half of the 20th century, the trend toward economic unification resumed.

Bank exchange sign in Madrid, Spain

INDUSTRIALIZATION AND THE REVOLUTION IN TECHNOLOGY

FOCUS

■ **What were some of the effects of industrialization on the American economy during the late 1800s?**

■ **Why and where did Americans hope to find new markets for their products in the early 20th century?**

■ **How have technological innovations contributed to the growth of the global economy?**

*T*wo *major developments thrust the United States into a central position in the world economy during the late 19th and early 20th centuries. The first was industrialization, which enabled workers to produce large quantities of goods for export. The second was the introduction of technologies that brought the United States into closer contact with other countries and peoples.*

Lithograph of a McCormick Harvesting Machine Company catalog cover

An INDUSTRIAL GIANT

By 1900 the United States boasted the most powerful industrial economy in the world. Its production of steel—more than 10 million tons in 1900—almost equaled the combined production of Britain and Germany, the world's second and

▼ **By 1900 machines such as this steam tractor had greatly increased farm productivity.**

third largest steelmakers. Manufactured and processed goods of all kinds, from tractors and trolley cars to cotton cloth and canned hams, poured out of American factories and plants in record quantities.

Industrialization arrived on the farms not long after it hit the cities. Steam-powered combines, gangplows, and other devices allowed farmers to cultivate more land. Production of wheat, corn, cotton, and other crops skyrocketed. Wheat production, for example, increased from 100 million bushels in 1849 to nearly 600 million bushels in 1900. Corn production rose from less than 600 million bushels to over 2.5 billion bushels during the same years.

Industrialization brought the United States unprecedented prosperity, but it also made the American economy more susceptible to the ups and downs of the business cycle. The severe economic downturns of the 1870s and 1890s, which led to numerous bankruptcies and layoffs, reflected the American economy's heightened sensitivity to cycles of boom and bust.

Boom times often led to overproduction. American factories and farms were now generating large quantities of goods, but they were not always able to sell all of these goods—particularly in times of bust. To guarantee future prosperity and the continued growth of the American economy, many observers believed some way had to be found to sell all the products Americans were churning out. President William McKinley bluntly put the matter to a gathering of business and civic leaders:

❝ There is no use in making a product if you cannot find somebody to take it. The maker must find a taker. You will not . . . make a product unless you can find a buyer for that product after you have made it. ❞

■■ **Industrialization brought prosperity but also problems, including recurrent economic downturns and the potential for overproduction.**

LOOKING ABROAD FOR MARKETS

As the 20th century dawned, the most promising place to find the takers and buyers McKinley spoke of appeared to be overseas. If Americans could not or would not buy all the goods U.S. farms and factories were able to produce, then perhaps foreigners would. "The time is not far distant," predicted one New York business editor, "when probably all of the principal industries of the Republic will be either compelled or in a position . . . to seek outlets for their products abroad."

In their search for new markets, American exporters looked to Latin America. Latin America had the advantage of being close at hand. In addition, ever since the announcement of the Monroe Doctrine in 1823, Americans had felt a particular interest in the affairs of the countries to their south. This interest became increasingly economic as time passed. In 1898 the value of U.S. exports to Latin America totaled $90 million; by 1910 that figure had jumped to $263 million.

American exporters also sought new markets in East Asia. During the mid-19th century, the United States had followed the lead of Great Britain and other European powers in imposing trade agreements on a reluctant Chinese government. In the 1850s, the United States led the way in opening Japan to foreign commerce. As a result, trade with Asia bloomed. Prior to 1850 the value of U.S. exports to Asia had never totaled more than $4 million annually; in 1900 the value of such exports exceeded $65 million.

▲ **As a result of the opening of China and Japan to foreign commerce, trade with East Asia increased. Even Japanese royalty wore western-style clothing.**

To many Americans, East Asia represented more than a market for exports—it was a new frontier. From the time of the founding of the British colonies, American history had been a chronicle of westward expansion. Americans had crossed the Appalachians to the Mississippi River, then crossed the Rockies to the Pacific Ocean. Many believed that America's future always lay to the west. But by the 1890s the land frontier in the United States had disappeared as the country's growing population

▲ **This Union Pacific timetable suggests the role that railroads played in American expansion westward.**

spread. The only way to expand westward was to cross the Pacific to what Europeans had labeled the "Far East."

Although some people called for continued territorial expansion, others argued that commercial expansion—the growth of American overseas trade—would do. And yet others, such as Senator Mark Hanna of Ohio, called for territorial expansion to aid commercial expansion. "If it is commercialism to want the possession of a strategic point giving the American people an opportunity to maintain a foothold in the markets of . . . [China]," remarked Hanna in the debate over U.S. annexation of the Philippines, "for God's sake let us have commercialism."

Commercial expansion would have to do for parts of the world where territorial expansion was out of the question, such as in Europe.

Throughout its history America's closest economic ties had been with Europe, especially Great Britain and France. Europe had been a source of investment capital for emerging American industries, such as railroads. By the late 19th century, it had gained increasing importance as a market for American exports as well. In 1900 the value of U.S. exports to Europe exceeded $1 billion for the first time.

■■ **At the beginning of the 20th century overproduction caused Americans to look abroad for export markets, especially to Latin America, East Asia, and Europe.**

𝒜 SHRINKING PLANET

If the tremendous growth of the American economy during the second half of the 19th century seemed to make deeper involvement in world trade necessary, rapid strides in technology made it possible. The emergence of a global economy depended on innovations in two related areas: transportation and communication.

For most of human history, transportation and communication had been intimately linked. With the exception of communication by carrier pigeon or drum signal, messages traveled no faster than the people who carried them. This remained the case at the beginning of the 19th century, when neither transportation nor communication was much faster than it had ever been.

Technological developments soon changed this. Railroads increased the speed at which people and their messages could travel. A journey across Europe or North America now required days instead of weeks or even months. Although the railroads cost more to build and operate than the animal-drawn vehicles they replaced, they generated more business and thus greater revenues. Between 1860 and 1880, railroad mileage in both Europe and the United States more than tripled.

At sea, steamships gradually replaced sailing vessels after the 1830s. While the steamers were not as fast as

▲ After the 1830s, steamships became a less costly, more reliable means of transporting people and products across the world's oceans.

the swiftest sailing ships, they were more reliable, since they could make headway even on windless days. As a result, a typical voyage across the Atlantic took only 7 or 8 days by 1874, as opposed to the 36 to 48 days a sailing ship might have taken in the 1830s. And by operating on fixed and predictable schedules, the steamships created new business and thereby brought down overall shipping costs. By the mid-1890s, ocean shipping costs were half of what they had been in 1873.

As much as steamships cut travel time across the Atlantic, the invention of the telegraph allowed transatlantic messages to move even faster. In the 1860s an American team headed by Cyrus Field succeeded in laying a permanent telegraph cable

▼ Telegraph cables laid across the floor of the Atlantic Ocean in the 1860s allowed operators to send messages rapidly between North America and Europe.

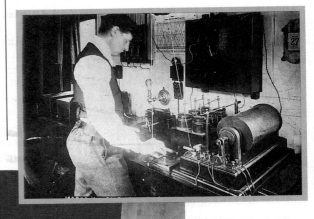

◄ After the invention of wireless telegraphy, operators were able to send messages long distances without the use of cables.

across the floor of the Atlantic Ocean from North America to Europe. Before long, several cables crossed the ocean floor. While they sped transatlantic communications, the limited number of cables prevented wide-scale use. A 1901 *New York Times* editorial noted:

> 66 At twenty-five cents a word the fourteen Atlantic cables now in operation are fully occupied during the business hours of the day. That means that in this matter demand has outrun supply. 99

Italian scientist Guglielmo Marconi helped solve this problem by inventing a wireless telegraph that could transmit and receive electric signals long distances. On December 12, 1901, Marconi sat at a tower in St. John's, Newfoundland, and received the Morse code signal for the letter *s* from Cornwall, England— nearly 2,000 miles across the Atlantic—with no cables! A writer— the same one who had commented on the inaccessibility of the cables—reported that Marconi's intercontinental wireless telegraphy had the potential to transform "the business and political relations of the peoples of the earth." The writer went on to note:

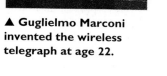

▲ **Guglielmo Marconi invented the wireless telegraph at age 22.**

> 66 The animating spirit of modern invention is to overcome the obstacles of time and space, "to associate all the races of mankind," by bringing them nearer together. Commerce, of course, has done more than any other agency to make that association intimate and lasting. . . .
>
> It will be the fervent hope of all . . . that wireless telegraphy will very soon prove to be not a mere "scientific toy" but a system for daily and common use. 99

A NEW SET OF GOODS

Trade over great distances had existed since prehistoric times, but as long as it was slow and expensive

▲ As the development of railroad and steamship lines made transatlantic trade faster and cheaper, commodities such as these American cattle bound for British markets became available to millions.

it was limited to specialty items that only the wealthy could afford. Improved methods of transportation allowed a greater—and cheaper—flow of imports and exports from one country to another. And as prices on certain goods fell, these goods became available to millions of people.

One example directly concerned America's position in the world economy. Prior to the late 19th century, the European market for American wheat had been quite limited. Although American farmers, in general, grew wheat more efficiently—and therefore less expensively—than European farmers, the high cost of transport made the U.S. grain too expensive for most European markets.

The development of railroad and steamship lines trimmed transportation costs dramatically. Now American wheat could undercut European wheat, even with the cost of transportation added in. Moreover, the linking of the continents by telegraph allowed grain dealers to keep in instant touch with their customers. Grain markets are notoriously unstable—prices change wildly with news of droughts, wars, and other disasters. The immediate communications the telegraph afforded allowed the dealers to sell their grain where it would return the greatest profits. As a result, American exports of wheat and flour rose rapidly, from less than $10 million in 1850 to more than $220 million in 1880.

Technological advances made possible not only the trade of greater quantities of goods but also trade in a whole new variety of goods. The introduction in the 1870s and 1880s of refrigeration on ships, for example, expanded trade in perishable goods such as meats, dairy products, and fruits. Today our grocery stores are filled with all kinds of fresh foods from around the world.

NEW WAYS OF DOING BUSINESS

The types of goods traded are not the only things that have changed as a result of new technology. As the pace of scientific and technological advancements has accelerated over the course of the 20th century, the very ways that people conduct business around the globe have changed. Railroads and steamships have given way to airliners as the preferred means by which people travel long distances. Where a business executive of the early 19th century might have crossed the Atlantic or Pacific once or twice in a lifetime to check on operations overseas, the modern executive does so frequently.

Advances in communications technology have been equally revolutionary for businesses. In 1915 telephone lines linked the U.S. coasts; by the late 1920s telephone service across the Atlantic was available as well. The telephone had two main advantages over the telegraph—it required no special skills to operate and it allowed people to carry on direct conversations. First radio and then television also transformed business. They not only made people aware of events around the world just hours after the events happened but also gave businesses the chance to advertise their products to larger audiences—even to people on distant continents. As a result, American consumer products from McDonald's hamburgers to Levi's blue jeans have been snapped up by people the world over.

▲ A computer can speed communications with a colleague in the next office or with a Chinese merchant on the other side of the world.

Today computer networks provide new ways to communicate. **Electronic mail**—commonly called e-mail—allows people to send messages via their computers around the world as easily as they can around the block. Just as important to the global economy are the computer connections among banks, stock exchanges, government offices, and other institutions. Every day, banks electronically whisk millions of dollars from New Delhi to New York, from São Paulo to Seoul, while investors in Toronto purchase stock shares in Tokyo.

■ **Innovations in communications and transportation have allowed for the freer and more rapid movement of people, merchandise, and information around the globe.**

SECTION 1 REVIEW

IDENTIFY and explain the significance of the following: Cyrus Field, Guglielmo Marconi, electronic mail.

1. **MAIN IDEA** What positive and negative effects did industrialization have on the U.S. economy in the late 19th century?

2. **MAIN IDEA** Why did Americans seek new markets in the early 20th century? Where did they seek those markets?

3. **MAIN IDEA** How have technological innovations influenced world trade?

4. **WRITING TO PERSUADE** Imagine you are an executive of a new U.S. shipping company in 1880. Write an advertisement explaining why farmers and manufacturers should use your company to transport their products to markets.

5. **HYPOTHESIZING** How might the increased involvement of Latin American and Asian countries in the global economy have affected everyday life in these regions?

THE GLOBAL ECONOMY TO WORLD WAR II

FOCUS

- How did the gold standard and free trade encourage the growth of the world economy?
- What was the major motive behind protectionism?
- How did World War I change America's economic position in the world?
- How did the Great Depression affect world trade?

The gold standard and a movement to reduce tariffs increased world trade in the late 19th century. Between the beginning of the 20th century and World War II, however, the world economy underwent major changes and disruptions—the most important resulting from World War I and the Great Depression of the 1930s.

£100 British gold coin

THE GOLD STANDARD

Technological improvements were only partly responsible for the development of the global economy in the late 19th century. Economic policies regarding international trade also played a role. One such policy involved the **gold standard**. Under a gold standard a nation's currency is redeemable in gold at a fixed rate.

Great Britain had long been on the gold standard. But other countries were reluctant to tie their currency to gold because to do so would decrease their control over their currency's value. By the end of the 1800s, however, most industrial nations had adopted the gold standard, persuaded in part by Britain's leading role in the global economy and by the discovery of large gold supplies in California, Australia, Canada, and South Africa.

The United States officially went on the gold standard in 1900 when Congress passed the **Gold Standard Act**. The act declared that the gold dollar "shall be the standard unit of value." The value

of every U.S. dollar was set to equal the value of .04837 ounces of pure gold.

The widespread adoption of the gold standard encouraged the development of the world economy. It gave trade greater stability and relieved merchants doing business in foreign countries from worries about exchange rates. For example, an American selling wheat in Germany did not have to gamble on how many dollars the marks paid by the German customer would be worth.

▼ The discovery of gold in parts of the British Empire strengthened Britain's role in the world economy. In 1888 these miners worked for the Republic Gold Company in DeKaap, South Africa.

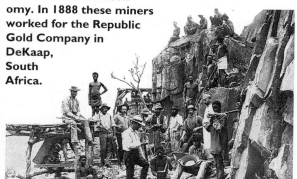

With both currencies calculated in terms of gold, the matter was clear from the start.

FREE TRADE

Perhaps even more important than the adoption of the gold standard in encouraging international commerce was the move toward **free trade**—international trade free from government regulation. Until the middle of the 19th century, the general rule in international trade had been for governments to levy tariffs against goods from abroad. The tariffs served two main purposes: to supply revenues to the governments and to protect domestic producers from foreign competition.

As with the gold standard, Britain led the way in reducing and even eliminating tariffs. During the 1840s, Great Britain's prime minister, Sir Robert Peel, observed that although a large number of imported goods were subject to British tariffs, most of the British government's tariff revenue came from just a few kinds of goods. Furthermore, Peel reasoned, British industry was the world's most advanced and did not require protection. Thus Peel abolished tariffs on hundreds of items and lowered tariffs on hundreds more.

Peel also believed that an increase in free trade might make it easier to sell British goods in foreign markets—if Britain lowered its tariffs, other countries might do the same. And indeed, following Britain's lead, France and other European countries soon moved toward free trade. In 1860 France and Britain signed the **Cobden-Chevalier Treaty**. The treaty provided that Britain would remove tariffs on most French imports. In return, France would lift a ban on imports of British textiles and would reduce tariffs on many other British goods. Perhaps most importantly, the treaty included a provision that enabled each country to benefit when the other negotiated tariff reductions with a third country.

Soon a network of treaties—each with a similar provision—governed trade among the European nations. Now whenever two countries agreed to a tariff reduction, the reduction applied to almost all of the region's countries. As a result, international trade grew rapidly among the countries lowering their tariff barriers; between 1850 and 1870, trade among the European nations roughly doubled.

■■ **The gold standard and free trade encouraged the development of the world economy by reducing uncertainty and by lowering trade barriers.**

PROTECTIONISM

For all the benefits free trade offered, and for all the growth in international commerce it fostered, free trade still had its opponents. Those who favored **protectionism** wanted protective tariffs, asserting that free trade hurt domestic industries by unfairly exposing them to foreign competition. If foreign-produced goods were available for the same prices as domestically made goods, consumers would have little incentive to buy the domestic goods. This, they argued, would hurt the domestic industries and in some cases might lead to layoffs and unemployment.

When the world economy sank into a depression in the 1870s, many industrialists believed the depression had been caused by the increased international competition brought about by free trade. They clamored for a return to protectionism. At the same time, farmers increased their demands for protection. Prior to 1870 most farmers—particularly in Europe—had not needed economic protection. The expense of overseas shipping prevented competition from imports of farm products such as wheat. But when the drop in transportation costs owing to technological improvements increased competition for the European farmers, they too wanted protection. With protectionism receiving such wide support, numerous countries—beginning with Germany in 1879—approved new tariffs. Before long, tariff wars broke out. Trade between

▶ This drawing shows an aerial view of Newcastle in the late 19th century. Newcastle was a major industrial city in northern England.

France and Italy, for example, declined by half between 1887 and 1898.

Even in Great Britain there was some shift in sentiment—particularly when German imports made inroads in British markets. The **Merchandise Marks Act**, passed by Parliament in 1887, required that foreign goods be labeled to indicate where they were made. Parliament hoped that British consumers would avoid buying goods that were marked "made in Germany."

The United States had never embraced free trade with the enthusiasm of the Europeans. In the years just before the Civil War, however, planters in the South, who generally supported free trade, had managed to keep tariff rates relatively low. But the North's victory in the Civil War enabled the Republican party to dominate national politics, and northern business leaders who favored protectionist policies were well represented in the party. This change, combined with the depressions of the late 1800s, led to a surge of American protectionism.

In 1890, William McKinley, then a U.S. congressman, sponsored a tariff bill which Congress passed that same year. The **McKinley Tariff** increased the number of imported goods subject to tariffs. More importantly, it steeply increased tariff rates. Subsequent measures raised tariff rates even higher. When American voters blamed high tariffs for rising living costs, Congress reduced the rates. However, the United States remained staunchly protectionist.

■■ **Protectionists believed that domestic industries required tariff protection from foreign competition.**

WORLD WAR I AND THE PEACE SETTLEMENT

World War I and the Treaty of Versailles dramatically reshaped the world economy. The war's most important short-term economic effect was the disruption of trade networks that had developed over the previous several decades. The war cut off trade between warring countries and led to attempts to prevent neutral countries from trading with enemies (see Chapter 10).

Debt and payment. A longer-term effect of the war was a shift in the balance of financial power from Great Britain and other European countries to the United States. From the American Revolution until World War I, the United States had been a debtor nation. With abundant resources but relatively little capital, Americans had borrowed money from Europe to finance industrialization and expansion. During World War I, however, the Allied powers turned to the United States for goods and for money to finance the war effort. As a result, the United States became a creditor nation.

After the war, the Allies believed that their debts to the United States should be canceled (see Chapter 15). But the U.S. government argued that the money loaned to the Allies had come from the American people—partly through the sale of Liberty Bonds. Therefore, if the debts were canceled, the American people would be the ones to pay. "All those who would like to see America cancel the European debt," quipped one publication, "are requested to mail in their Liberty Bonds." Even when the U.S. government reduced the interest rates on the loans and arranged a 62-year payment schedule, the Europeans were less than thrilled. "For the next sixty years, the American flag is

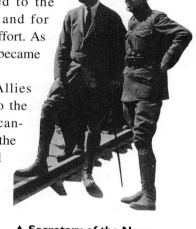

▲ **Secretary of the Navy Franklin D. Roosevelt confers with Admiral Plunkett at St. Nazaire, France.**

▼ **This 1923 cartoon satirizes the debt problem that arose after World War I.**

PASSING THE BUCK.

going to look to us like the $tars and $tripes," remarked the *London Opinion*.

Repaying the loans, however, was not a simple matter. The Allies—particularly France—could not afford to pay the debt if they themselves did not receive the German reparations required by the Treaty of Versailles. But German inflation left Germany unable to make *any* reparations payments. By November 15, 1923, it took 4.2 trillion marks to buy a single dollar, making the mark worth less than the paper on which it was printed.

The Dawes and Young plans.

Economist John Maynard Keynes reflected on the debt situation left by World War I:

> 66 The war has ended with everyone owing everyone else immense sums of money. Germany owes a large sum to the Allies. The Allies owe a large sum . . . to the United States. The holders of war loans in every country are owed a large sum by their . . . states. The states, in [their] turn, are owed a large sum by taxpayers. The whole position is in the highest degree . . . vexatious [distressing]. We shall never be able to move again unless we can be free of these paper shackles. 99

The U.S. government took the first step toward removing the shackles Keynes spoke of by suggesting that a committee be formed to study the issue of the war debts. Chicago banker Charles Dawes was chosen to head the committee.

Charles Gates Dawes was born in Marietta, Ohio, in 1865. After attending law school in Cincinnati, he went on to practice law in Lincoln, Nebraska, from 1887 to 1894. In 1897 he became U.S. comptroller of the currency, but he returned to private business in 1902. Although he remained active in finance throughout his life, Dawes also served as a brigadier general in World War I, the first director of the U.S. Bureau of the Budget, and vice president under Calvin Coolidge. Dawes also wrote several works, including *A Journal of the Great War* (1921) and *Notes as Vice President* (1935).

In 1925 Dawes was awarded—along with Sir Austen

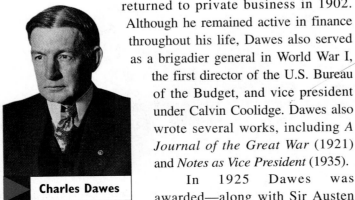

Charles Dawes

Chamberlain of Britain—the Nobel Peace Prize. He received this award largely for his efforts to deal with the debt-reparations tangle following World War I. In 1924, in what became known as the **Dawes Plan**, Dawes's committee arranged for a $200 million loan to help Germany meet its reparations payments. Because American bankers were to provide about $100 million of the loan, the plan set up a payment triangle by which Americans helped finance Germany's reparations payments to the Allies; these payments in turn financed the Allies' war debts to the United States. The Dawes Plan also rewrote the reparations payment schedule.

The plan operated successfully for several years, but it was only a stop-gap measure and was replaced in 1929 by the **Young Plan**. Named for Owen D. Young, chairman of the board of the General Electric Company, this plan spread Germany's reparations payments—totaling about $26 billion, with interest—over 59 years.

■■ **World War I converted the United States from a debtor nation to a creditor nation. Americans used their new financial power to help stabilize the world economy in the 1920s.**

THE GREAT DEPRESSION

The Young Plan might have solved the financial problems caused by World War I, but it never got the chance. After the New York stock market crashed in 1929, similar collapses occurred in other countries. The world soon slipped into the deepest depression it had ever experienced—a depression that thoroughly disrupted world trade and cast the global economy into disarray.

The Young Plan was one of the victims of the depression. As American investment in Germany dried up, Germany was unable to make its reparations payments. As a result, the European Allies could not pay their debts to the United States. Most people, however, felt the effects of the depression more personally. Factory production fell; unemployment increased; basic necessities became unavailable or unaffordable. Author George Orwell observed women "kneeling in the cindery mud and the bitter wind searching for tiny chips of coal" in a British mining town:

> In winter they are almost desperate for fuel; it is more important almost than food. Meanwhile, all round, as far as the eye can see are the slag-heaps . . . of collieries [coal mines], and not one of those collieries can sell all the coal it is capable of producing. "

In order to stimulate production and employment during the depression, countries adopted two major economic measures. The first was an increase in tariffs, to give domestic industries the advantage in the home market. The U.S. Congress, for example, responded to the onset of the depression by passing the protectionist Smoot-Hawley Tariff of 1930. Many economists warned that the measure, which raised average tariff rates to their highest levels in U.S. history, would trigger retaliatory moves by other countries. The economists were right. In France, where one American said the U.S. tariff was compared to "a declaration of war, an economic blockade,"

the government responded in kind. So did most other countries—even Great Britain, the traditional champion of free trade. By 1931 average tariff rates in 15 European countries were nearly two-thirds higher than in 1927.

The second measure governments used to try to pump life into their economies was to make their currencies cheaper in relation to other currencies. This **devaluation** would make export goods cheaper in foreign markets, thus boosting foreign sales. In order to change the value of their currencies, however, nations had to go off the gold standard. Britain became the first major industrial nation to do so in September 1931. As with tariffs, other nations responded with similar measures. By April 1932, more than 20 countries had left the gold standard.

In 1933 President Roosevelt announced that the United States, too, would no longer tie its currency to gold. Without gold as an internationally agreed-upon standard, currency values wavered uncontrollably.

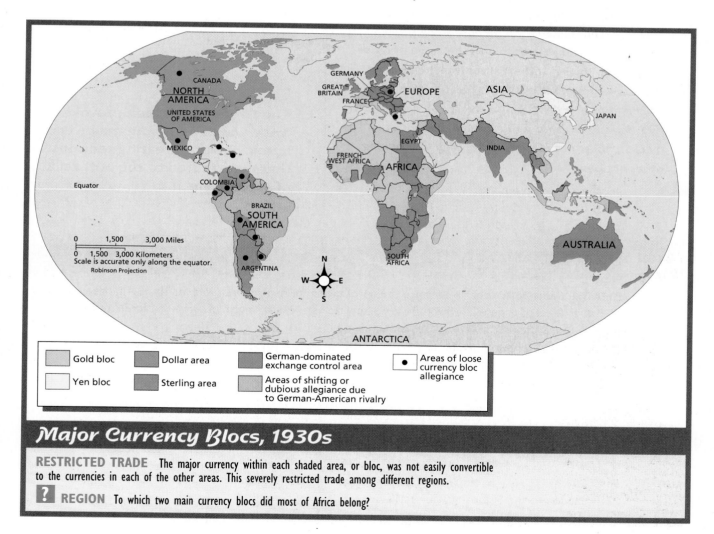

Legend:
- Gold bloc
- Yen bloc
- Dollar area
- Sterling area
- German-dominated exchange control area
- Areas of shifting or dubious allegiance due to German-American rivalry
- ● Areas of loose currency bloc allegiance

Major Currency Blocs, 1930s

RESTRICTED TRADE The major currency within each shaded area, or bloc, was not easily convertible to the currencies in each of the other areas. This severely restricted trade among different regions.

❓ REGION To which two main currency blocs did most of Africa belong?

THE LONDON ECONOMIC CONFERENCE

THROUGH OTHERS' EYES

As the London confer-ence on the world eco-nomic situation opened in the summer of 1933, many people realized that suc-cess at the conference would depend on the resolution of a variety of issues. American cooperation, however, was seen as essential to solving the international monetary problem. H. D. Davray, a French journalist, explained his perspective in the British *Saturday Review:*

66*T*he economic problems submitted to the Conference cannot be solved at all unless . . . currencies are stabilised and a return to the gold standard established. These are from the French point of view indispensable preliminaries, without which any measures of an economic category that may be recommended will be absolutely futile. . . . The actual world situation is on the verge of cata-strophe. . . . If the United States want to save themselves from bankruptcy by devaluation which will lighten their debts and increase the value of their stocks, the idea is reasonable. But such a measure must not result in paralysing and ruining other nations. 99

While some nations experienced temporary relief as a result of increased tariffs and currency devaluations, the overall effects on world trade were disastrous. In the closest thing the 20th century has seen to a trade war, world trade dropped 40 percent between 1927 and 1933.

In June 1933 the major industrial powers held a conference in London in an attempt to find a way out of the depression. The conference organiz-ers hoped to negotiate an end to the tariff wars, reestablish the gold standard, and promote other forms of international cooperation. Unfortunately, the United States refused to have anything to do with the conference's aim of stabilizing currency.

The United States had recently shown some signs of economic recovery, and many attributed this success to the nation's departure from the gold standard. President Roosevelt was thus hesitant to reinstate the standard. He sent a telegram to the London conference stating that "the sound internal economic system of a nation is a greater factor in its well being than the price of its currency." Without the endorsement of the United States, the London conference accomplished virtually nothing. Thus the depression continued, and the strains it induced intensified the forces propelling nations toward the Second World War.

■■ **The Great Depression provoked trade wars among the major eco-nomic powers, creating tensions that contributed to the outbreak of World War II.**

SECTION 2 REVIEW

IDENTIFY and explain the significance of the following: gold standard, Gold Standard Act, free trade, Sir Robert Peel, Cobden-Chevalier Treaty, protectionism, Merchandise Marks Act, McKinley Tariff, Charles Dawes, Dawes Plan, Young Plan, devaluation.

1. **MAIN IDEA** What economic policies led to an expansion of the world economy in the late 19th century? How did these policies contribute to expansion?

2. **MAIN IDEA** Why did many nations adopt protectionist policies in the late 19th century?

3. **MAIN IDEA** How and why did America's position in the world economy change after World War I?

4. **WRITING TO EXPLAIN** Imagine you are a delegate to the 1933 London conference seeking to end the Great Depression. Write a newspaper article explaining how the depression has affected world trade and how you propose to address trade problems.

5. **HYPOTHESIZING** Imagine you are the leader of a European nation in 1930. Describe your reaction to the Smoot-Hawley Tariff.

Section 3

THE ERA OF AMERICAN DOMINANCE

FOCUS

- How did the Bretton Woods system aim to promote peace through commerce?
- How did the international economic landscape change following World War II?
- What trend did the economies of the United States, Western Europe, and Japan experience in the 25 years after the war?

At the end of World War II, the United States took the lead in reordering the world economy. This reordering involved establishing a framework for international trade and investment and reconstructing the war-ruined economies. These efforts were rewarded by more than two decades of strong economic growth, particularly in the United States, Europe, and Japan.

A symbol of the military power that helped make the United States a world leader in the postwar era

A NEW ECONOMIC FRAMEWORK

Even before World War II ended, political leaders and economic experts from around the world had concluded that the monetary and trade policies of the 1930s—the departure from the gold standard,

▼ Bombing during World War II reduced most French factories to steel skeletons filled with rubble. Lack of production contributed to a devastated postwar economy.

the competitive currency devaluations, and the high tariffs—had contributed to the onset of the war. As U.S. Secretary of the Treasury Henry Morgenthau explained:

66 All of us have seen the great economic tragedy of our time. We saw the world-wide depression of the 1930's. We saw currency disorders develop and spread from land to land, destroying the basis for international trade and . . . investment and even international faith. In their wake, we saw unemployment and wretchedness. . . . We saw bewilderment and bitterness become the breeders of fascism, and, finally, of war. 99

To avoid the outbreak of another war as a result of similar hostilities, U.S. officials and others resolved to modify international economic policies. "Commerce is the life blood of a free society," wrote President Roosevelt. "We must see to it that the arteries which carry that blood stream are not clogged again, as they have been in the past, by artificial barriers created through senseless economic rivalries."

At Roosevelt's urging, economic officials from the United States and 43 other countries met at Bretton Woods, New Hampshire, in July 1944 to construct a framework for postwar international economic relations. Their primary goals were to restore the stability of currency and to prevent tariff increases and trade wars like those of the 1930s. The system that emerged from the conference became known as the **Bretton Woods system**.

The first element of the system was an agreement among the major economic powers to maintain **fixed exchange rates** between their currencies. They tied the currencies of Britain, France, and the other countries to the American dollar, which became the system's key currency. To increase stability further, the dollar was tied to gold, at $35 per ounce. In effect, this agreement restored the gold standard to the international economy. To help maintain these fixed exchange rates, the conference created the $8.8 billion **International Monetary Fund**, or IMF.

The conference also established the International Bank for Reconstruction and Development, commonly called the **World Bank**. Credited with $10 billion, the World Bank was to make loans to boost the economies of the war-damaged countries and to encourage development in the less industrialized countries.

The final part of the Bretton Woods system was the **General Agreement on Tariffs and Trade**, or GATT. Although it did not officially take form until 1947, the agreement represented a commitment by the member governments to the long-term goal of free trade. Over the next few decades, GATT members succeeded in reducing tariffs on a wide variety of goods to their lowest levels in modern history.

■■ **To prevent future economic hostilities, the Bretton Woods system set up fixed exchange rates, the IMF, the World Bank, and an agreement to cut tariffs.**

A NEW ECONOMIC LANDSCAPE

The Bretton Woods system operated in a global economy that differed radically from the pre–World War II economy. The onset of the Cold War divided the world economy into two spheres—the capitalist nations and the communist nations—and economic contact between them virtually ended for about 25 years. Each group believed that its economic and social system was better than that of the other, and neither group wished to do anything that might strengthen the other.

Even among the capitalist countries, economic relationships changed. Many of the European nations—whose economies had dominated the world prior to the war—lay in ruins (see chapters 16 and 17). The U.S. economy, in contrast, emerged from World War II stronger than ever. Government spending on war supplies had boosted the economy, and at the end of the war, Americans produced about two and a half times what they had at the bottom of the depression. For example, steel production in 1944 reached nearly 90 million tons—almost 30 million tons more than annual production had ever been prior to the war and about 60 million tons above yearly totals during much of the depression.

■■ **The Cold War divided the global economy into two spheres. The United States emerged as the capitalist sphere's most economically powerful nation.**

▲ In July 1944, delegates from many countries gathered at Mt. Washington House in Bretton Woods, New Hampshire, to promote international economic harmony.

AMERICAN ECONOMIC GROWTH

Many Americans recognized that government spending on the war effort had helped end the depression. They worried that when the war was over, the economy would nose-dive. According to surveys at the time, some 70 percent of Americans thought that they would be worse off after the war.

Such fears proved groundless. Instead of falling into a depression, the U.S. economy grew dramatically. Between 1945 and 1970, the gross national product (GNP) doubled. One reason for the growth was that at the end of the war, U.S. consumers had plenty of money to spend. Rationing ended shortly after the war, and the pent-up consumer demand kept the economy humming as it shifted from war production to the production of civilian consumer goods.

The economy also boomed because government spending remained high throughout the Cold War. Military spending to rebuild weapons supplies and to fight the Korean War, and later the Vietnam War, kept employment up in defense-related industries. Social programs established during these decades also created jobs and enabled people to maintain their purchasing power.

RECONSTRUCTION AND GROWTH IN EUROPE

Because the United States had the world's most powerful economy following World War II, U.S. officials took the initiative in reconstructing Europe's war-ruined economies. They had two major reasons for doing so. First, if Europe remained weak economically, such weakness could easily spread to the United States. Second, Americans were concerned that a Europe in economic distress might fall prey to communism.

The European Economic Community.
The United States' $12 billion Marshall Plan helped put Europe back on its feet (see Chapter 17). It also had longer-term effects. Although the U.S. aid came mostly in the form of grants and thus did not have to be repaid, it did not come without strings. In order to make the most of assistance and prevent a return to the competition that

▲ German women made up over half of the workforce that cleared away the remains of Berlin's bombed buildings. They were dubbed "rubble women."

had helped bring on World War II, the United States required the European nations to coordinate their economic activities.

The Europeans responded by forming the Organization for European Economic Cooperation to distribute the Marshall Plan aid. Before long, some Europeans were urging economic integration as well as cooperation. To that end, Belgium, France, Italy, Luxembourg, West Germany, and the Netherlands came together in 1951 to form the European Coal and Steel Community (ECSC), which allowed for the free trade of coal, steel, and iron ore among the six member nations.

The success of the ECSC inspired a bolder step in 1957—the formation of the **European Economic Community** (EEC). The treaty that created the EEC explained that the community's purpose was to:

66 promote the harmonious growth of economic activity in the Community as a

whole, regular and balanced expansion, augmented [increased] stability, a more rapidly rising standard of living, and closer relations between the participating states. "

To achieve these goals, the EEC planned to abolish tariffs and "all barriers to the free movement of persons, services and capital" among members. Indeed, commerce among the EEC countries mushroomed. Trade between France and Germany, for example, grew by about 40 percent from 1958 to 1966. By 1968 tariffs among the six EEC members had been completely abolished.

West Germany. Although all of Western Europe achieved economic recovery in the postwar years, West Germany's recovery was the greatest success story. Immediately after the war, the governments of the victorious powers agreed that Germany should not be allowed to become strong again. As the Cold War developed, however, the United States began looking on West Germany as a barrier to the Soviet Union's westward expansion—and as a key nation in Western Europe's economic revival. Consequently, West Germany was included in the Marshall Plan, and U.S. officials did what they could to foster West Germany's economic growth.

The West German economy soared. In a recovery soon labeled an "economic miracle," unemployment dropped from more than 10 percent in 1950 to less than 1 percent during most of the 1960s. The country's GNP rose from less than 100 million marks in 1950 to more than 500 million marks in 1968. By the 1960s West Germany was the economic envy of the rest of Europe.

JAPAN

Japan's recovery was even more dramatic than Germany's. Before the war Japan had never been as economically powerful as Germany, and Japan received no Marshall Plan aid after the war. Moreover, where much of Germany's revival resulted from trade with its prosperous European neighbors, Japan's neighbors were generally poor.

Yet Japan did have a few advantages. Though not included in the Marshall Plan, Japan received other kinds of American reconstruction assistance. More importantly, as in other successful countries, its people were industrious and creative in the adoption and development of new technologies. Japan's recovery eventually surpassed Germany's as well as nearly every other country's. Between the late 1940s and the early 1970s, Japan's GNP grew at a rate of more than 10 percent annually. By 1970 Japan had remade itself into an economic powerhouse, the strongest in Asia and one of the strongest in the world.

■■ **The years from 1945 to 1970 saw strong economic growth in the United States, Western Europe, and Japan.**

SECTION 3 REVIEW

IDENTIFY and explain the significance of the following: Henry Morgenthau, Bretton Woods system, fixed exchange rates, International Monetary Fund, World Bank, General Agreement on Tariffs and Trade, European Economic Community.

1. **MAIN IDEA** What actions did delegates to the Bretton Woods conference take to promote peace?

2. **MAIN IDEA** How did the end of World War II affect the world economy?

3. **ASSESSING CONSEQUENCES** How did the Marshall Plan affect the European economy?

4. **WRITING TO INFORM** Write an essay detailing the economic developments in the United States, Western Europe, and Japan after World War II.

5. **USING HISTORICAL IMAGINATION** Imagine you represent a country other than the United States at the Bretton Woods Conference. Write an essay that explains why you think international commerce is important to your country.

A NEW ERA IN TRADE

FOCUS

- Why has U.S. economic dominance of the world declined since the 1970s?

- What part of the world has shown the greatest economic growth in recent decades?

- How have multinational corporations and the end of the Cold War affected the global economy?

- What agreements reflect a trend toward global free trade?

Floating oil production platform in the North Sea, 1984

The global economy has experienced a dramatic reshaping since the 1970s. The decline of American dominance, the growth of new economic powers and new forms of business investment, and the end of the Cold War are some of the reasons for the changes. Nevertheless, increased free trade has brought the world greater economic unity.

OIL SHOCKS

One factor that had encouraged the growth of the industrial economies during the 1950s and 1960s was the availability of oil. Oil was easily transported by pipeline or tanker ship. It was also versatile: oil and the products derived from it could be used to fuel transportation, to heat homes and power factories, to generate electricity, and to manufacture plastics and other products.

Throughout the 1950s and 1960s, oil supplies generally outstripped demand, leaving prices low. In the early 1970s, however, prices rose as demand caught up with supplies. Additional pressure came from OPEC, which repeatedly raised the price of oil during the 1970s (see Chapter 21). By the early 1980s the price of a barrel of oil, which had been less than $3 prior to 1973, stood at more than $30.

The jump in oil prices sent shock waves through the world economy. The **oil shocks**, as the jolts from the price increases were called, tested each country's capacity to adapt. A government official in Japan, which survived the crisis better than most other countries, later recalled: "Both workers and business leaders were very apprehensive after 1973. They feared for the survival of their companies, and so everybody worked together."

▼ **Oil ministers from OPEC's 13 member nations meet to monitor oil production and prices.**

THE END OF DOLLAR DOMINANCE

The Bretton Woods financial system did not survive the oil shocks. The supremacy of the dollar enshrined in the Bretton Woods system had come under attack during the 1960s, largely as a result of the economic growth of countries like West Germany and Japan. In 1971 the strain forced the Nixon administration to suspend America's adherence to the gold standard and fixed exchange rates. The oil shocks, by increasing the pressure on the dollar and adding to inflation, killed hopes of a return to the Bretton Woods system.

The system of fixed exchange rates was replaced by a system of **floating exchange rates**. Under the new system the value of a dollar in relation to other currencies could vary, depending on the relative demand for dollars and the other currencies. If Japanese businesses, for example, needed more dollars to pay for imports from the United States, the dollar might rise in value from, say, 250 yen to 300 yen. At least that was the theory.

In reality the dollar fell. During most of the early period following World War II, the dollar's value stood at more than 300 yen. But in the 1980s and early 1990s, the dollar fell continuously against the yen. In June 1994, for example, the dollar was worth less than 100 yen. Although the American economy remained the world's largest, the slippage of the dollar symbolized the end of the era of U.S. dominance of the world economy.

■■ Rising oil prices and the growth of other economic powers brought to a close the era of American dominance of the world economy.

THE PACIFIC RIM

In recent decades, the world economy's center of gravity has shifted toward the nations of the **Pacific Rim**, which include Australia, New Zealand, and many East Asian and Southeast Asian nations. In 1994 goods from the Pacific Rim accounted for about 39 percent of all imports to the United States. The region's reputation for producing high-quality, low-priced automobiles, computers, TVs, VCRs, radios, and other goods helped spur demand.

▲ **In recent years high-quality Japanese products such as televisions, radios, and other electronic equipment have captured a large share of the U.S. market.**

Historically, Japan has been the Pacific Rim's dominant economic power. But in recent years the nations of the Pacific Rim that have experienced the most explosive economic growth are the "Four Tigers"—Taiwan, South Korea, Hong Kong, and Singapore. South Korea, for example, had an average annual growth rate of nearly 10 percent from 1980 to 1990. In contrast, the U.S. growth rate during the same years averaged under 4 percent. Other Asian nations, such as Malaysia, Thailand, and Indonesia, have also shown impressive growth.

China, too, achieved high economic growth rates during the late 1980s and 1990s. Although the Chinese government remains Communist, it has allowed economic reform in the direction of free enterprise. Instead of only large state factories, some 20 million small private companies now dot the countryside. The state is even laying off surplus workers and closing unprofitable factories. Such changes have spurred rapid growth, lifting incomes in much of China and transforming the country into a major economic power. Reflecting this growth, the U.S. trade gap with China in June 1996 exceeded the gap with Japan for the first time—a historic event.

Several factors lie behind the Asian nations' economic success. Asians have worked long hours and saved what they earned, reinvesting the savings to promote economic growth. Furthermore, Asian governments have often taken an active role in encouraging economic development. Critics, however, note that the Asian nations' economic growth has often been based on low wages and thus has not benefited all of the region's peoples.

■■ The nations of the Pacific Rim experienced rapid economic growth in the 1980s and 1990s.

MULTINATIONAL CORPORATIONS

Much of the Pacific Rim's economic growth has been fueled by Japanese investors and industries seeking lower labor and land costs. Such efforts have often been led by **multinational corporations**, companies that invest money in or own business ventures around the globe. Japanese corporations such as Honda and Mitsubishi, for instance, have opened factories in the United States. Similarly, many U.S. businesses have set up operations in foreign nations. For example, the New York–based International Telephone and Telegraph (ITT) owns businesses in countries from Bolivia to France. Other companies such as General Motors, Texaco, and International Business Machines (IBM) also operate worldwide.

Sometimes it is difficult to gauge the economic effects of these multinational corporations. In some cases companies can boost employment and development in the countries where they operate. Critics, however, argue that most of the profits go to the country where the corporation is based. Multinational corporations are also sometimes criticized for underpaying workers, for harming the environment, or for changing the cultures in the countries in which they operate.

■■ Multinational corporations are playing an increasingly important role in the world economy.

THE END OF THE COLD WAR

Multinational corporations now have a whole new area of the world to invest in. After the breakup of the Soviet Union in the early 1990s, investment money began to flow from the United States and Western Europe to Eastern Europe and the countries of the former Soviet Union. Yet removing the barriers between the two spheres takes time. Most of the countries of what was once the Communist bloc are only beginning to forge close ties with the rest of the world economy.

▲ Multinational corporations have opened several manufacturing plants in the United States. Shown here are workers in the Honda automobile factory in Marysville, Ohio.

Not all nations have benefited from the end of the Cold War. Cuba, for example, which once was supported almost entirely by the Soviet Union, has had to adapt to sharp drop-offs in aid and trade. Similarly, some Africans fear that they will lose investment dollars as Western European nations invest more and more in their Eastern European neighbors.

■■ The end of the Cold War has opened new areas for investment in the former Soviet Union and in Eastern Europe.

TOWARD GLOBAL FREE TRADE

In spite of some nations' difficulties, the era since 1945 has been on the whole the most prosperous in modern history. Many economists attribute the era's prosperity to increased free trade. As a result, more and more countries are trying to arrange or expand free-trade agreements.

▲ In 1985 Jacques Delors became president of the European Commission, the body responsible for implementing EC treaties and rules.

Europe. The world's most successful free-trade zone has been in Western Europe. The EEC, after its formation in 1957, grew to include 12 of the leading European economies. In 1967 the group became known as the European Community (EC). Tariffs and other barriers to trade came down further and further until by the late 1980s the goal of a Europe without economic borders was in sight.

To facilitate this goal, the group signed the Maastricht Treaty in 1993. This treaty, aimed at bringing about "an ever-closer union among the peoples of Europe," created the **European Union**. The Union is designed to allow for the free movement of goods, labor, and capital among member nations. Some predict that a full political union—which could include as many as 20 member states—will eventually form in Europe.

NAFTA. Other countries have attempted to copy the European Community's success at eliminating trade barriers. These countries include the United States, Canada, and Mexico. Canada and the United States have long been each other's most important trading partner. During the 1980s leaders in both countries decided to reinforce the relationship by negotiating a free-trade agreement. Both governments approved the pact despite opposition on both sides of the border by some who feared increased competition from the other side.

In the early 1990s Mexico asked to join the group. This represented a significant shift in policy for Mexico. Like many other comparatively poor countries, Mexico had long tended toward protectionism as a way of sheltering domestic industries from the competition of companies in the more advanced economies.

The proposed **North American Free Trade Agreement**, or NAFTA, aroused heated debate in all three countries but especially in the United States. Opponents argued that the low wages paid to Mexican workers and lax environmental regulation would entice U.S. corporations to transfer their operations to Mexico. NAFTA critic H. Ross Perot predicted that if Congress approved NAFTA, Americans would hear a "giant sucking sound" as U.S. jobs were lost to Mexico. Many Americans also feared for the future of domestic employment. In a 1992 poll, 56 percent of respondents agreed that protect-

◀ **Texas businessman and NAFTA critic H. Ross Perot expressed the concerns of many Americans who feared foreign competition and the loss of domestic jobs to Mexico.**

▲ **As NAFTA passed narrowly in Congress, opinions continued to differ sharply over whether U.S. workers would lose or gain as a result.**

ing U.S. industry and jobs from foreign competition should be the nation's top priority.

Supporters of NAFTA countered that people were not simply producers; they were also consumers. Supporters pointed out that tariffs and other trade barriers raised prices, harming consumers. Free trade would allow each country to specialize in those goods it produced most efficiently and to trade freely for other goods. NAFTA would give the inhabitants of all three countries access to the best possible products at the lowest possible prices. The agreement, which became effective in January 1994, has not significantly changed the U.S. economy or employment. Experts agree, however, that it will be years before the full effect of NAFTA is known. In a narrow vote Congress agreed and approved NAFTA in November 1993.

The World Trade Organization.

In the background of the debate over NAFTA was another set of trade negotiations involving most of the world's nations. These negotiations, called the **Uruguay Round** of GATT talks, signaled an effort to boost global free trade. Among the important issues covered was the trade of agricultural products and of intellectual property such as movies and computer software.

Although the Uruguay Round was begun in 1986, sharp differences among the major nations over several issues kept them from reaching a final agreement for years. In 1994, however, officials from 125 nations signed an agreement totaling some 22,000 pages. One provision of the agreement reorganized GATT as the **World Trade Organization** (WTO). This new name represents its sponsors' hope that the organization will continue to bring cooperation to world trade issues.

■■ **Despite some opposition, the formation of the European Union, NAFTA, and the World Trade Organization reflects a movement toward global free trade.**

▲ Not everyone prospered as free trade spread throughout the world. This 1992 photograph shows a woman trying to exchange a sweater for fish at a Moscow market.

COMMENTARY

A Look to the Future

Unfortunately, the prosperity brought about by increased free trade has not spread evenly. Wages remain disturbingly low in many newly industrializing countries. Many African and Latin American nations seem locked in a cycle of poverty from which there is no obvious exit. For example, Peru's poor have not benefited from one of the highest economic growth rates in the developing world. And even within the rich countries stubborn pockets of poverty and unemployment remain. The formerly Communist countries of Eastern Europe have run into serious problems making the transition to capitalism. These difficulties are reflected in Russia's sharply declining birth rate, due, some experts believe, to economic uncertainty and to parents' fears for the future.

On the whole, however, the world economy as the end of the 20th century approaches is more unified than it has ever been. And economics will play an even greater international role as time passes. As American journalist Bruce W. Nelan observed in 1992:

❝ Just as wars—two World Wars and, equally important, the Cold War— dominated the geopolitical map of the 20th century, economics will rule over the 21st. All the big questions confronting the world in the century ahead are basically economic. ❞

SECTION 4 REVIEW

IDENTIFY and explain the significance of the following: oil shocks, floating exchange rates, Pacific Rim, multinational corporations, European Union, North American Free Trade Agreement, Uruguay Round, World Trade Organization.

1. **MAIN IDEA** What factors led to the decline of U.S. dominance of the world economy since the 1970s?

2. **MAIN IDEA** How have the economies of Pacific Rim countries changed in recent decades?

3. **MAIN IDEA** How has the global economy been changed by the rise of multinational corporations?

4. **WRITING TO INFORM** Write an essay explaining how global free trade has been supported by recent international agreements.

5. **EVALUATING** Write a paragraph evaluating the arguments made against the idea of global free trade.

France and Great Britain sign the Cobden-Chevalier Treaty.

British Parliament passes the Merchandise Marks Act.

U.S. Congress passes the McKinley Tariff.

U.S. adopts the gold standard.

Marconi sends wireless telegraph across the Atlantic.

1860   1887   1890   1900 1901

WRITING A SUMMARY
Using the essential points of the chapter as a guide, write a summary of the chapter.

REVIEWING CHRONOLOGY
Number your paper 1 to 5. Study the time line above, and list the following events in the order in which they happened by writing the first next to 1, the second next to 2, and so on. Then complete the activity below.

1. Dawes Plan arranged.
2. European Economic Community formed.
3. France and Great Britain sign the Cobden-Chevalier Treaty.
4. Bretton Woods conference held.
5. U.S. adopts the gold standard.

Assessing Consequences How did measures such as the Smoot-Hawley Tariff and the British abandonment of the gold standard affect the world economy in the 1930s?

IDENTIFYING PEOPLE AND IDEAS
Explain the historical significance of each of the following people or terms.

1. Guglielmo Marconi
2. electronic mail
3. Sir Robert Peel
4. Young Plan
5. fixed exchange rates
6. World Bank
7. oil shocks
8. Pacific Rim
9. multinational corporations
10. World Trade Organization

UNDERSTANDING MAIN IDEAS
1. Why did Americans look abroad for markets in the late 19th and early 20th centuries? To what world regions did they turn?
2. How was the global economy affected by a widespread adoption of the gold standard and by an increase in free trade in the late 1800s? Why did some people continue to call for protectionism?
3. Why did two separate economic spheres arise after World War II?
4. What countries experienced rapid economic growth in the 1950s and 1960s?

5. What economic trends and political events have significantly influenced the global economy since the early 1970s?

REVIEWING THEMES
1. **Technology and Society** How did the introduction of steamships and the telegraph contribute to an increase in global trade?
2. **Global Relations** What economic problems did the world experience as a result of World War I?
3. **Economic Development** Why did some people in the United States oppose passage of the North American Free Trade Agreement? What arguments supported the agreement?

THINKING CRITICALLY
1. **Synthesizing** In what ways did the United States benefit economically from both World War I and World War II?
2. **Evaluating** How successful do you think the Bretton Woods system was in preventing the type of economic hostility that had contributed to the outbreak of World War II?
3. **Hypothesizing** What world region do you think will experience the greatest economic growth in the next 25 years? Why?

STRATEGY FOR SUCCESS
Review the Strategies for Success on Interpreting Editorial Cartoons on page 162. Then study the cartoon on the right. What is the cartoonist's message?

The Herblock Gallery, *The Washington Post*

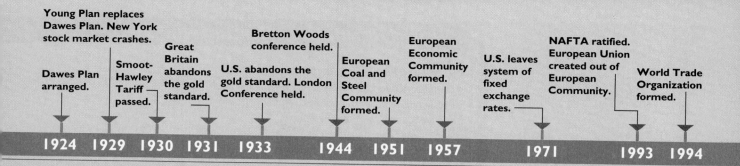

Dawes Plan arranged.	Smoot-Hawley Tariff passed.	Young Plan replaces Dawes Plan. New York stock market crashes.	Great Britain abandons the gold standard.	U.S. abandons the gold standard. London Conference held.	Bretton Woods conference held.	European Coal and Steel Community formed.	European Economic Community formed.	U.S. leaves system of fixed exchange rates.	NAFTA ratified. European Union created out of European Community.	World Trade Organization formed.
1924	1929	1930	1931	1933	1944	1951	1957	1971	1993	1994

WRITING ABOUT HISTORY

Writing to Persuade Imagine you are a member of Charles Dawes's commission investigating the economic situation left by World War I. Write a letter to American bankers explaining why it would be in their interests to make loans to Germany.

USING PRIMARY SOURCES

While most of the delegates to the Bretton Woods conference believed that greater international cooperation would benefit the economies of individual countries, some people—particularly in the United States—were skeptical. Read the following excerpt from a press release written by U.S. officials as the conference began. How does the document attempt to persuade American citizens that the conference will benefit them?

❝ *The purpose of the Conference is . . . wholly within the American tradition, and completely outside political considerations. The United States wants, after this war, full utilization of its industries, its factories and its farms; full and steady employment for its citizens, particularly its ex-servicemen; and full prosperity and peace. It can have them only in a world with a vigorous trade. But it can have such trade only if currencies are stable, if money keeps its value, and if people can buy and sell with the certainty that the money they receive on due date will have the value contracted for. . . . With values secured and held stable, it is next desirable to promote world-wide reconstruction, revive normal trade, and make funds available for sound enterprises, all of which will in turn call for American products.* ❞

LINKING HISTORY AND GEOGRAPHY

Sketch a map of the world. Using symbols or shading, indicate how economic power has shifted among major world regions over the past 150 years. Then write a paragraph explaining the reasons for the shifts noted on your map.

BUILDING YOUR PORTFOLIO

Complete the following projects independently or cooperatively.

1. WAR Imagine you are an economist at the World Bank assigned to study how wars can affect the economies of different nations. Construct a chart showing how World War I and World War II affected European economies and the U.S. economy.

2. INTERNATIONAL COOPERATION Imagine you are an administrator at the World Trade Organization. Prepare a speech explaining how the WTO will benefit the global economy. To support your claims, your speech should include an overview of ways in which international cooperation has helped the global economy in the 20th century.

Gold coins from the United States, Canada, South Africa, and the Isle of Man

3. INDIVIDUAL RIGHTS In Chapter 23 you portrayed a member of an independence movement who argued that imperialism has interfered with individual rights. Building on that experience, imagine you are a policymaker in a newly independent nation trying to decide how to shape your nation's economy. Write an essay explaining how a nation's economic policies can affect the rights of workers, business owners, consumers, and community members.

THE GLOBAL ECONOMY

As the global economy has grown over the past 150 years, a vast array of transportation and communications systems has arisen to support it. Despite this increasing international unity, relationships within the global economy have by no means remained constant. The United States' most important trade partners, for example, used to be the European nations. The percentage of trade with Europe, however, has steadily declined while Asian nations have become increasingly important trading partners. Furthermore, the growth of the global economy has benefited some nations more than others. Many nations, particularly in Africa and Latin America, have found it difficult to develop their economies. Several nations remain poor today.

In the late 1800s and early 1900s, a complex network of transportation routes, communications channels, and trade links arose to unite the world economically. The industrialized nations of Europe and North America, however, received most of the benefits of this network. Africa, Asia, and parts of Latin America remained primarily agricultural.

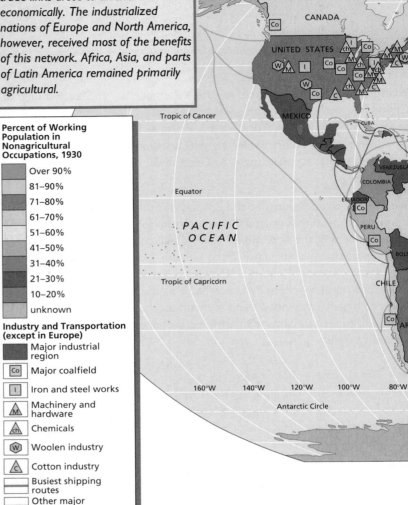

Percent of Working Population in Nonagricultural Occupations, 1930

- Over 90%
- 81–90%
- 71–80%
- 61–70%
- 51–60%
- 41–50%
- 31–40%
- 21–30%
- 10–20%
- unknown

Industry and Transportation (except in Europe)

- Major industrial region
- Co — Major coalfield
- I — Iron and steel works
- M — Machinery and hardware
- ch — Chemicals
- W — Woolen industry
- C — Cotton industry
- Busiest shipping routes
- Other major shipping routes
- International telegraph cables

Between 1850 and 1920, the total dollar value of exports from the United States grew from some $140 million to more than $8 billion. By 1990 the figure had reached almost $400 billion.

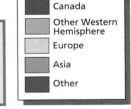

- Canada
- Other Western Hemisphere
- Europe
- Asia
- Other

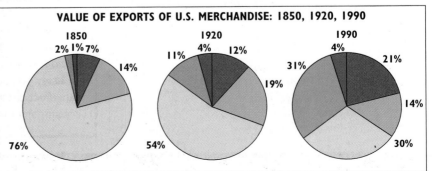

VALUE OF EXPORTS OF U.S. MERCHANDISE: 1850, 1920, 1990

1850
2% 1% 7%
14%
76%

1920
11% 4% 12%
19%
54%

1990
4%
31% 21%
14%
30%

Chart information from *Historical Statistics of the United States, Statistical Abstract of the United States.*

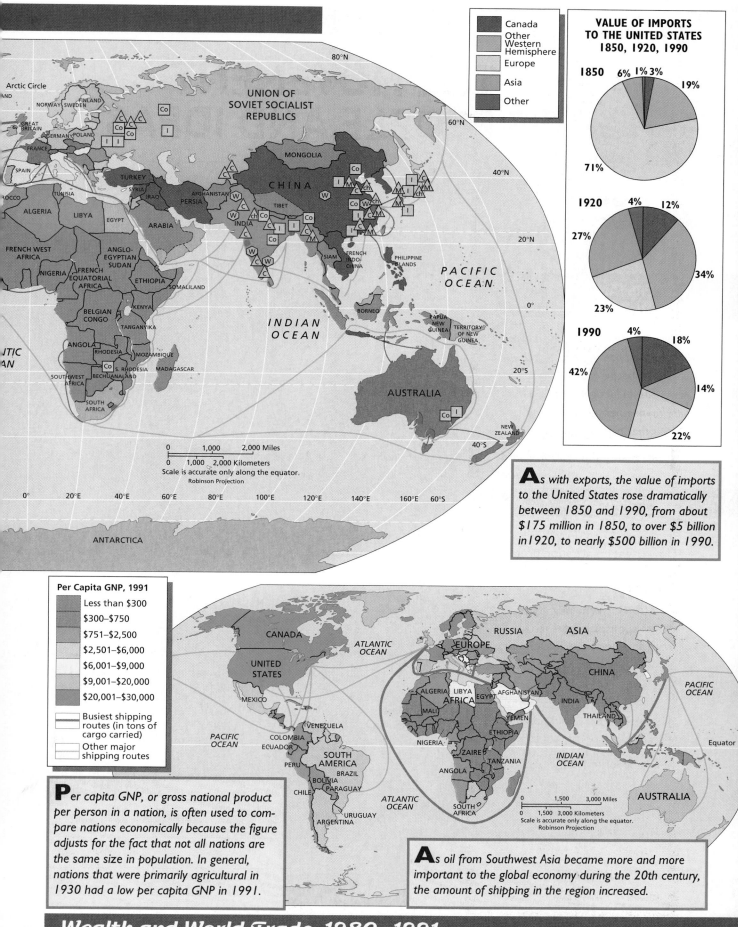

VALUE OF IMPORTS TO THE UNITED STATES 1850, 1920, 1990

Legend:
- Canada
- Other Western Hemisphere
- Europe
- Asia
- Other

1850
- 6% 1% 3%
- 19%
- 71%

1920
- 4%
- 12%
- 27%
- 34%
- 23%

1990
- 4%
- 18%
- 42%
- 14%
- 22%

As with exports, the value of imports to the United States rose dramatically between 1850 and 1990, from about $175 million in 1850, to over $5 billion in 1920, to nearly $500 billion in 1990.

Per Capita GNP, 1991
- Less than $300
- $300–$750
- $751–$2,500
- $2,501–$6,000
- $6,001–$9,000
- $9,001–$20,000
- $20,001–$30,000
- Busiest shipping routes (in tons of cargo carried)
- Other major shipping routes

Per capita GNP, or gross national product per person in a nation, is often used to compare nations economically because the figure adjusts for the fact that not all nations are the same size in population. In general, nations that were primarily agricultural in 1930 had a low per capita GNP in 1991.

As oil from Southwest Asia became more and more important to the global economy during the 20th century, the amount of shipping in the region increased.

Wealth and World Trade, 1980–1991

Chapter 25

THE MOVEMENT OF PEOPLE AND IDEAS

FOCUS

UNDERSTANDING THE MAIN IDEA

During the 20th century, migrations have shaped both American and world history. As people moved, they learned new ideas and taught their own traditions to their new neighbors. In the process they helped create a global culture.

 THEMES

■ **CULTURAL DIVERSITY**
How might immigration promote cultural diversity in a nation?

■ **TECHNOLOGY AND SOCIETY** Why might governments sponsor efforts to develop new communications technologies?

■ **ECONOMIC DEVELOPMENT** How might globalization of sports, movies, and other elements of popular culture influence the development of a global economy?

1892	1896	1901	1965	
Ellis Island opens.	First modern Olympics held in Athens, Greece.	Thomasites arrive in the Philippines.	Immigration Act of 1965 passed.	U.S. Advi the Natio Infrastru

The first people in America arrived thousands of years ago from Asia. Beginning in the late 15th century, a new wave of immigration began—this time from Europe and Africa. The United States was founded in the 18th century by immigrants and their descendants.

Patrick Ewing and Hakeem Olajuwon during a 1994 NBA championship game

The 1994 championship series of the National Basketball Association (NBA) pitted the Houston Rockets against the New York Knicks. The series turned on the contest of skills between the two teams' centers: Houston's Hakeem Olajuwon and New York's Patrick Ewing.

Millions of Americans tuned their television sets to the series, and the games were broadcast to many other countries as well. By the 1990s basketball, originally developed in Massachusetts, had gained worldwide popularity. NBA games could be seen in more than 75 nations, including Zambia, Finland, and Kuwait. Among the foreign viewers, those in Nigeria and Jamaica may have had particular interest in the game. Olajuwon and Ewing both were immigrants to America—Olajuwon from Nigeria, Ewing from Jamaica.

In many ways the 1994 championship series also symbolized trends that extended far beyond the sports world. During the 20th century people migrated between countries in great numbers. Wherever they went they took their ideas, their ways of looking at the world, their music, their games. Shared practices and philosophies led to the development of new traditions. By the end of the 20th century, many people believed that a global culture was emerging.

Indian sitar player Ravi Shankar, a pop idol of the 1960s

PATTERNS OF MIGRATION

- **How widespread was migration during the 19th and early 20th centuries?**
- **What role did the United States play in global migration prior to World War I?**
- **How did pre–World War I migration affect the populations of cities and rural areas?**
- **What factors motivated people to migrate in the 19th and early 20th centuries?**

*D**uring the 19th and early 20th centuries, millions of people migrated from their birthplaces to other countries and from rural regions to cities. Many of these migrants settled in the United States, attracted by jobs in the booming industries there.*

19th-century textile factory

PEOPLE ON THE MOVE

The 19th and early 20th centuries marked one of the world's great ages of migration, affecting all the inhabited continents and most countries. Specific statistics on global migration are difficult to determine because few countries kept good records of those who entered and rarely recorded those who left. Estimates suggest, however, that some 60 million people left Europe during the century before World War I. The stream of European migrants flowed not only to North America but also to South America, to Australia and New Zealand, and to many parts of Africa. From

◄ **Alberto Fujimori, son of Japanese immigrants to Peru, won that country's presidency in 1990.**

China and Japan another wave of people moved into Southeast and South Asia, as well as across the Pacific to the Americas. Several million Japanese emigrants formed communities in Korea, China, the Philippines, Hawaii, and North and South America. From India still other migrants went east to Southeast Asia and west to Africa.

Many people did not plan to relocate permanently but hoped to find economic success and then return to their native countries. Most, however, remained in their new homes. By the 1930s, more than two million Southern Europeans formed an important business class in the North African countries of Egypt, Libya, Tunisia, Algeria, and Morocco. Similarly, Indians and Chinese became successful entrepreneurs in many countries bordering the Indian Ocean. At their height the Indian communities in this region totaled 3 million people, while the Chinese settlers numbered some 12 million.

Although largely ended by the late 19th century, the African slave trade brought about another important movement of peoples. Centuries before the Europeans became involved in the slave trade,

Arab slave traders had taken Africans to Southwest Asia and India. Then in the 17th century slaves had become the major factor in the commerce between Africa and the Americas. The size of the slave trade to Asia can only be guessed at because few records exist. However, the Atlantic slave ships landed more than 10 million Africans in North and South America and the Caribbean islands.

██ **Streams of migration in the 19th and early 20th centuries touched every inhabited continent and nearly every region.**

▲ **Ellis Island was the first stop for many European immigrants seeking a new life in America.**

*T*HE UNITED STATES IN THE WORLD STREAM

The United States sat squarely in the middle of the world stream of migration. Millions entered the United States from abroad; much smaller numbers left the United States for other countries.

Immigration to America. America was the single most popular destination of migrants from other countries. Before the first census of 1790, Great Britain and West Africa provided the largest number of immigrants to the United States. Even after the Revolutionary War, British settlers were drawn to their former colonies, where they could find familiar customs and language. Most Africans, on the other hand, came involuntarily as

slaves. After the ban on the importation of slaves went into effect in 1808, however, the number of forced immigrants from Africa dropped.

During the middle part of the 19th century large numbers of Germans and Irish left their homes for the United States. The 1848 discovery of gold in California attracted still more immigrants. Among the gold-seekers were thousands of Chinese, many of whom hoped to make fortunes and return to China. Introducing different languages and religions, these groups added new cultural elements to the United States.

Immigration to the United States peaked between 1890 and 1914, when some 15 million newcomers landed on American shores. In 1907 alone more than 1.2 million immigrants entered the country. While most of these immigrants came from Europe, as before, a growing number arrived from southern and eastern Europe. Of these, Russian Jews, Poles, Ukrainians, Slovaks, Croatians, Slovenes, Hungarians, Romanians, Greeks, and Italians made up the largest groups. Ellis Island in New York Harbor, an immigration station that opened in 1892, was the first sight of America for many of these newcomers.

Many immigrants learned of the opportunities available in the United States from railroad and steamship companies. In fact, convincing foreigners that the United States was the land of opportunity became a major business activity in the late 1800s. The agents of steamship companies and railroads swarmed over Europe, one observer

▼ **This 1883 *Harper's* editorial cartoon illustrates an attitude held by many Americans toward Irish immigrants.**

noted, "as the locusts covered Egypt!" They painted a tempting—and often false—picture of America. Some railroad companies exaggerated the employment opportunities available in the United States. And the steamship lines charged rock-bottom fares to attract passengers.

Most of the millions who yielded to this hard sell found the journey to the "Promised Land" difficult. The ocean voyage was no pleasure trip for those in the poorest accommodations, called steerage. One Italian immigrant asked:

> 66 How can a steerage passenger remember that he is a human being when he must first pick the worms from his food . . . and eat in his stuffy, stinking bunk, or in the hot and fetid [bad-smelling] atmosphere of a compartment where 150 men sleep? 99

Nativist response. Although many people in the United States recognized that even native-born Americans were descended from earlier immigrants, others wondered whether these latest arrivals were perhaps too different and too numerous. Some of the opponents of immigration were frankly racist, while others based their opposition on economic factors. One critic claimed that the willingness of many new immigrants to work for very low wages hurt "the native worker and the earlier immigrant . . . , affecting detrimentally the standard of living of hundreds of thousands of workers—workers, too, who are also citizens, fathers, husbands."

Such nativism sometimes prompted or forced immigrants to leave the United States, proving that migration was not a one-way street. Many Chinese who had entered America before passage of the 1882 Chinese Exclusion Act were among those

► Asian immigrants enter the United States at Angel Island in San Francisco Bay around 1911.

who left. The Chinese population in the United States plummeted from more than 100,000 in 1890 to less than 65,000 in 1920. Chinese who arrived during this period were detained at **Angel Island**—the West Coast counterpart of Ellis Island—while authorities investigated their claims that they were legal immigrants. One of the detained Chinese wrote this poem on his cell wall:

> 66 The day I am rid of this prison and attain
>   success,
>   I must remember that this prison
>   once existed. . . .
>   All my compatriots [fellow citizens]
>   please be mindful.
>   Once you have some small gains, return
>   home [to China] early. 99

Emigration from America. Some Americans, searching for new opportunities, also left during this period. Australia's population nearly tripled in the nine years after gold was discovered there in 1851; some of these gold-seekers were Americans lured by the same dreams that had brought so many people to California just a few years earlier. Another gold rush brought Americans to Canada's Yukon Territory in 1897 and 1898. American farmers were also attracted to Canada. Between 1900 and 1920 nearly 300,000 Americans moved north of the border to establish homesteads in Manitoba, Alberta, and Saskatchewan.

One group of emigrants left the United States for what they believed was a loftier goal than land or gold. Christian missionaries—mostly Protestants but some Roman Catholics—sought to convert people in other countries. Many missionaries and church groups focused their attentions on China.

Like China, the Philippines also attracted the attention of missionary societies and teachers. Among the teachers were some 500 young Americans who arrived in Manila in 1901 aboard the steamer *Thomas*. The **Thomasites**, as they were called, saw themselves as representatives of American values. "We are not merely teachers," one of the Thomasites wrote to her parents back in Massachusetts. "We are social assets and emissaries of good will."

Because they also promoted U.S. interests, however, the missionaries were not always welcome. At the time the Thomasites arrived, many Filipinos were resisting the annexation of their country by the United States. Yet in spite of this

▲ These men and boys gather in China to hear an American missionary.

opposition, the Thomasites and their successors—together with the hundreds of thousands of Filipinos who later immigrated to America—forged an important cultural connection between the Philippines and the United States.

■■ The United States was the most likely destination of immigrants and the source of a smaller but significant emigration to other countries.

*F*ROM COUNTRY TO CITY

The great migrations of the 19th and early 20th centuries were not only nation-to-nation but also country-to-city movements. Throughout the industrializing world, people were moving from rural regions to cities. This movement to the city was closely tied to the Industrial Revolution. The availability of workers in cities and towns prompted manufacturers to locate their factories there. In turn, the lure of jobs drew even more people to the cities.

In Great Britain, for example, the initial burst of urban growth occurred during the first half of the 19th century in cities such as Birmingham, Manchester, and Liverpool. Birmingham's and Manchester's populations more than tripled between 1800 and 1850, while Liverpool's increased nearly fivefold. As the century progressed, these and other British towns played an increasingly important role in the industrial economy. In 1881 one member of Parliament wrote: "Our towns are the backbone of the nation. They give it strength, cohesion, vitality."

Urban growth followed industrial development throughout Europe. In Italy the change was most notable after 1860, as new industries attracted people to cities and towns. Similarly, in the United States the great population jump in cities occurred in the second half of the 19th century. The population of New York City, for instance, grew from some 2 million to nearly 3.5 million between 1880 and 1900, while Chicago went from some 500,000 to more than 1.5 million. St. Paul, Minneapolis, and Denver also tripled in size. The primary reason for this urban growth was the same as in Britain and other industrializing countries: cities offered the promise of jobs. In the Midwest, for example, many farming areas lost residents to Chicago, Detroit, and other cities, while in New England thousands of farms and scores of rural villages were simply abandoned for the promise of city wages.

Many who witnessed this movement to the cities believed that urban growth was natural and unavoidable. Horace Greeley noted, "We cannot all live in cities, yet nearly all seem determined to do so." The 1920 census seemed to bear out Greeley's observation—for the first time in U.S. history, more than half the people lived in cities.

■■ Migration increased city populations, often at the expense of rural populations.

◀ Tenement slums in New York's Lower East Side multiplied during the early 20th century. At "five cents a spot," these dirty, crowded rooms were all that many immigrants could afford.

WHY THEY MOVED

Just as migrants chose to relocate to a variety of areas around the world, they also moved for a variety of reasons. Some people sought improved economic opportunities, while others hoped to find greater personal freedom.

Economic opportunity.

The great migrations were caused largely by economic factors, as people looked for better jobs and higher wages. Farmers around the world experienced hard times during the late 19th century, and agriculture seemed a less and less secure source of income. In the cities, however, business and industry appeared to be flourishing. Many people moved to cities in their own countries, while others looked for opportunities abroad. The United States, with the fastest-growing of the large industrial economies, attracted millions of people.

But cities were not the only attraction. Throughout the 19th century and into the 20th century, many of the immigrants to the United States hoped to acquire land, which was cheaper than in Europe. Most had been farmers in their home countries, and many hoped to remain farmers.

▲ A doctor examines Russian Jewish emigrants before they travel as steerage passengers to America.

Some achieved this dream. During the 1800s and 1900s, for example, many German and Scandinavian immigrants established prosperous farms in Minnesota and the upper Middle West. In many cases, though, the hard reality of earning a living upset the immigrants' plans. The dreams of buying a farm were postponed, then postponed again.

Personal freedom.

Although economic concerns motivated most immigrants, some sought political freedom. Karl Marx, the German radical and coauthor of the *Communist Manifesto* (1848), fled to England after the failed 1848 revolutions in Europe. Other European radicals settled in the United States.

Other people left their homes for religious reasons. Russian Jews, for instance, had long suffered from discrimination and outright violence. When the chance to leave arose during the 1890s and early 1900s, many did. Some went to South America, others to Canada, but most resettled in the United States. They often met a hostile reception. Edward Ross, a sociologist of the era, railed against "the lower class of Jews of Eastern Europe" who arrived in America as "moral cripples, their souls warped and dwarfed." Yet American anti-Semitism was rarely as violent as in the countries the immigrants had left, and most felt that conditions had changed for the better.

■■ **Most people moved for economic reasons, but the desire for political and religious freedom was also important.**

SECTION 1 REVIEW

IDENTIFY and explain the significance of the following: Angel Island, Thomasites.

1. **MAIN IDEA** How did migration affect the various areas of the world during the 19th and early 20th centuries?

2. **MAIN IDEA** How did migration affect the United States during the 19th and early 20th centuries?

3. **MAIN IDEA** How did the population movements that occurred before World War I affect cities and rural areas?

4. **WRITING TO CREATE** Write a poem that expresses how a migrant might feel about leaving home or about starting over in a new land or city.

5. **COMPARING** Write a paragraph comparing the reasons people emigrated to a different country with the reasons people moved from rural areas to cities.

CHILDREN OF WAR

FOCUS

- **What effect did World War I and the Great Depression have on migration?**
- **How did World War II and its aftermath influence the movement of peoples?**
- **What immigration trends has the United States experienced since the 1960s?**
- **What migration patterns marked the 1980s and 1990s?**

Hutu children in a Rwandan refugee camp, 1994

*D*uring the 20th century the migrations of peoples around the globe continued. Economic motivations remained a principal driving force, but growing numbers of migrants were refugees displaced by war and other disasters. By the 1990s tens of millions of people lived outside the countries of their birth.

WORLD WAR I AND ITS AFTERMATH

The outbreak of World War I caused a drop in migration rates. Previously, countries with strained economies had been willing to allow citizens to try their luck elsewhere—and perhaps send money to relatives back at home. When the war began, however, some nations restricted emigration, having decided that the potential emigrants—particularly the young men—would be more useful as soldiers.

Ocean travel also took on new difficulties and risks. Many nations converted passenger ships to troop and cargo carriers, transporting soldiers and equipment to the war zone. Submarines and surface vessels patrolled the sea-lanes, seizing and sometimes sinking enemy ships. Crossing the ocean to start a new life abroad was always a daunting venture; during war it seemed more perilous than ever.

▶ **A passenger ship converted into a troop transport carries grim soldiers to battle during World War I.**

After World War I ended in 1918, the migrations resumed. Immigration to the United States, however, did not reach former levels. Americans who opposed immigration played on people's hostility to wartime enemies to persuade Congress to restrict immigration. The trend continued when Congress passed the Immigration Act of 1924, sharply reducing the number of immigrants allowed into the country.

The economic troubles of the 1930s continued to limit international migration. Now, however,

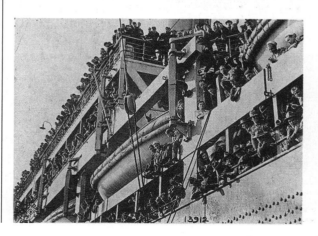

the problem was not danger on the high seas or a government's need for soldiers but the collapse of economic opportunity. More than ever, people were willing to look for jobs in other countries. But America's Great Depression was part of an international problem, and few jobs were available anywhere. Moreover, countries that had once welcomed immigrants now closed their borders to keep jobless people from entering. Some nations went even further. During the early 1930s the U.S. government deported some half million Mexican workers out of a belief that they were taking jobs from U.S. citizens (see Chapter 13).

■■ Both World War I and the Great Depression reduced the movement of peoples across international borders.

𝘈 NEW TYPE OF MIGRATION

Despite the depression, the 1930s did mark the beginning of an era of massive displacements of refugees—people forced to flee their homes because of political persecution, war, or natural disasters. For example, after the Nazi party came to power in Germany in 1933, the German government adopted policies designed to drive Jews from positions of influence and even from Germany itself. Many German Jews, especially those with education or skills that might be useful in other countries, left Germany during the 1930s. Albert Einstein, winner of the 1921 Nobel Prize for physics, was one of the most prominent of the refugees from Hitler's Germany to resettle in the United States. A large number of Jews, however, had little choice but to remain in Germany. With

▼ On May 9, 1938, Chinese Amercians paraded down the streets of New York City protesting the Japanese invasion of China.

the economic strains of the depression and continuing anti-Semitism, most countries were reluctant to accept large numbers of Jewish refugees.

Europe was not the only region experiencing refugee migration in the 1930s. In the years following Japan's 1931 invasion of Manchuria, Japan extended its control across northern China. Yet despite the continuing Japanese advances and the eventual outbreak of war, many nations refused to accept Chinese immigrants. As a result, refugees were forced to flee to other parts of China. By the time the conflict between China and Japan ended in 1945, about 95 million Chinese had become refugees in their own country.

Refugee migration only increased following World War II. Europe had been devastated by the war, and the booming American economy again attracted immigrants. Congress passed the **Displaced Persons Act** of 1948, which enabled some 400,000 European refugees to enter the United States. Many of these immigrants were Jews who had survived the Nazi concentration camps.

Another wave of refugees resulted as European powers pulled out of Asia and Africa and former colonies became independent nations. The difficulties of self-rule often aggravated long-standing tensions. These tensions frequently led to fighting, which, in turn, forced thousands of people to become refugees.

▲ On August 15, 1947, Mohammed Ali Jinnah, governor general of Pakistan, and his sister attended the ceremony marking the beginning of the Dominion of Pakistan.

Great Britain's withdrawal from India in 1947, for instance, brought ethnic and religious conflicts—particularly between Hindus and Muslims—to the forefront. Before they left, the British wanted to reduce the risk of war between these groups. Therefore, the British divided the region into two countries: Pakistan, populated mostly by Muslims, and India, whose residents were mostly Hindus. But people caught on the wrong side of the border often found their lives in danger and fled to safety on the other side.

Palestine also experienced turmoil in the 1940s when guerrillas eager to establish a Jewish state fought British rule. The United Nations voted to divide the region in two, providing a homeland for the world's Jews as well as for the region's Arabs (see Chapter 17). Jews from around the world, including the United States, migrated to Palestine. Although much of the world felt sympathy for the plight of displaced Jews, particularly for those who had survived the Nazi Holocaust, many Palestinians bitterly opposed the partition. In 1948 Arab armies attacked Israel.

Israel not only survived the attack but also enlarged its borders. Hundreds of thousands of Palestinians found themselves homeless and destitute, and many ended up in refugee camps in neighboring countries. Nearly one million Palestinians took refuge in Jordan alone, and several hundred thousand others settled in Lebanon. The 1967 Arab-Israeli war created even more refugees as Arabs fled from the territory Israel acquired. The refugee issue has remained a source of conflict between Israel and surrounding countries for decades.

■■ **In the years before and after World War II, political, religious, and ethnic conflicts caused many people to become refugees.**

IMMIGRATION TO AMERICA SINCE 1965

Rates of immigration to the United States soared after the mid-1960s. This was largely due to the passage of the **Immigration Act of 1965**, which did away with the system admitting fixed percentages of immigrants to the United States based on their countries of origin. The act allowed greater numbers of people into the country. Even though numerical limits on immigration still existed, certain relatives of U.S. citizens were exempt from these limits.

Although a largely unforeseen effect, the act significantly increased the number of immigrants from Asia and Latin America while immigration from Europe slowed. Between 1951 and 1965, for example, Europe supplied over half of all immigrants to the United States; from 1967 through 1978, however, Europeans made up less than one quarter of the total. In contrast, the number of Asians admitted was less than 7 percent in the first period but more than 28 percent in the second.

Motivations. Many of the Asian and Latin American immigrants to the United States since the 1960s have been refugees. The Vietnam War, for example, provoked a flood of refugees from Southeast Asia. After the Communist victory in 1975, many Vietnamese who had supported South Vietnam and the United States feared for their lives. During the next several years, hundreds of thousands of Vietnamese fled their country in crowded boats (see Chapter 20).

Sympathetic to the plight of these "boat people," many Americans worked to provide Vietnamese refugees with shelter and the opportunity for a new life. The U.S. government responded by creating programs that permitted thousands of Vietnamese to immigrate to the United States. Because the war in Vietnam had spilled over into Cambodia and Laos, thousands of people from these countries also fled to the United States.

Many refugees have also fled violence or oppressive governments in Cuba and Central American nations such as Guatemala and El Salvador. And after the military coup in Haiti in 1991, thousands of Haitians fled the growing chaos in their country. The Haitians, however, did not find the United States as open as many other refugees had. Arguing that the Haitians were escaping economic, not political conditions, the United States began returning the refugees to Haiti. Many politicians criticized this policy and contrasted it to the treatment given to Cuban refugees, who were allowed to stay in the United States. U.S. policy toward Cubans changed in 1994, however, when Cuban ruler Fidel Castro threatened to overwhelm Florida with Cuban refugees, eager to flee the island's deepening poverty. Instead of allowing Cubans on homemade rafts to float to Florida, the

▼ **An overcrowded sailboat filled with Haitian refugees was intercepted by the U.S. Coast Guard on July 4, 1994.**

As people moved from one place to another, they carried with them not only their culture and traditions but also viruses and other microbes. For example, shipping and trade routes provided a corridor for outbreaks of bubonic plague. During the 6th, 14th, and 17th centuries rats carried plague-infected fleas to ports throughout Europe and Asia. Similarly, Mongol armies of the 14th century probably carried the disease overland across Asia along with rat-infested supplies.

Other epidemics also accompanied settlers, military forces, and commercial travelers. In the 16th and 17th centuries, European settlers brought smallpox, measles, and other diseases to the Americas, devastating the American Indian populations. In the early 19th century, the British army carried cholera from India into Afghanistan and the Himalayas. And between 1831 and 1833, cholera epidemics struck port cities in Russia, France, England, the United States, and other countries around the world. This epidemic of cholera also appeared in Mecca. Muslim pilgrims who contracted the disease spread cholera across the globe as they returned to their homes.

Epidemics are not confined to the past. Tens of thousands of residents of Surat, India, fled their homes when an outbreak of plague struck in

September 1994. More alarming, however, is the spread of new diseases—particularly AIDS—that have no known cure.

AIDS is the final deadly stage of an illness believed to be caused by the human immunodeficiency virus, or HIV. AIDS is believed to have originated in Africa, where it may have spread along long-distance trucking routes. Since the 1980s AIDS has become a global threat. The World Health Organization (WHO) estimated in 1993 that some 2 million persons worldwide had full-blown AIDS and some 13 million others were carrying HIV. In 1992 the United Nations Children's Fund estimated that some 2 million of the world's children had been orphaned by AIDS and predicted that the number would rise to 10 million by the year 2000.

AIDS primarily affects young and middle-aged adults, many of whom are the wage-earners supporting children or aged parents. In developing

countries, therefore, AIDS may have a profound effect on the economy as fewer people are able to work. In many ways, AIDS poses social problems that extend far beyond the medical challenges.

 Among those treating AIDS patients is Abraham Verghese. Born in Ethiopia to Indian parents, he studied medicine in India, and then came to the United States to specialize in infectious diseases. In 1985 he became a staff physician at a Veterans Administration hospital in rural Johnson City, Tennessee.

For the next four years, Verghese saw a growing number of patients who were HIV-positive. He wrote:

> 66 Our little town in the heart of the country with 50,000 residents had a hundredfold more cases than the CDC [Center for Disease Control] would have predicted for us. The belief that AIDS would not touch this town had been absurd. 99

In the course of his work, Verghese realized that most of his patients were people who had moved away, acquired the disease, and returned home. To make sense of the suffering he saw, Verghese began to write. In 1994 he published *My Own Country: A Doctor's Story of a Town and Its People in the Age of AIDS,* in which he relates his observations and experiences.

Abraham Verghese

Coast Guard picked up the refugees at sea. They were then sent to camps outside the United States. Many Floridians cheered the policy, agreeing with Florida governor Lawton Chiles that "Florida cannot stand another influx." But later the U.S. government reached an agreement with Cuba to resettle most of the refugees in the United States.

As in earlier periods, many of the recent immigrants to the United States have not been refugees, but people seeking economic opportunities. In the past few decades, this has been particularly true of Mexicans. Even though the Mexican immigrants work for wages that are often low by American standards, they are still higher than in Mexico. One immigrant explained:

66 There are people who come from Tijuana [a region in northwestern Mexico] who work for six, seven, or eight dollars an hour for work that is worth more than 18 or 20 dollars an hour. They come to work like that because they earn more than they can earn in Tijuana. 99

■■ In the past few decades, many immigrants have come to the United States from Asia and Latin America.

The future of U.S. immigration. The 1990 census revealed that immigrants had come to the United States in greater numbers in the 1980s than in any decade since 1910. Many of these immigrants came from Mexico, the Philippines, Vietnam, Korea, China, and India.

The trend toward increased immigration seems likely to continue. President Bush, in signing the **Immigration Act of 1990**, noted that "immigration is not just a link to America's past, it is also a bridge to America's future." The new law increased the number of immigrants and doubled the number of skilled workers allowed into the United States each year.

Immigration, however, remains controversial. Sixty-eight percent of the respondents to a 1992 *Business Week* poll thought that immigration was bad for the country. Many of those polled blamed immigrants for taking jobs away from native-born citizens. In some cases the controversy over immigration has stemmed from the large number of people who enter the United States illegally. Many of them cross the long border between Mexico and

▼ New immigrants contribute to U.S. industry in many ways. Shown clockwise from upper left is a Korean bookstore owner, a Filipino travel agent, and an Indian businessperson.

the United States. To address this problem Congress passed an immigration bill in 1996 that almost doubled the size of the border patrol, increased the penalties for smuggling aliens into the country, and authorized other border control measures.

Supporters of immigration argue that immigrants have created new businesses that revitalize urban areas, have helped the U.S. balance of trade by starting their own export companies, and, as employees, have helped U.S. companies become more competitive globally. In addition, supporters of immigration note that many recent immigrants, most notably those from India, the Philippines, China, and Korea, have more years of schooling on average than either native-born Americans or European immigrants. These well-educated immigrants contribute to many U.S. high-tech industries.

As the United States witnesses increased immigration in the future, Americans will continue to grapple with the question of whether to welcome immigrants. Bette Bao Lord, a novelist who came from China as a child, has urged Americans, native-born and immigrant alike, to unite:

66 I do not believe that the loss of one's native culture is the price one must pay for becoming an American. On the contrary, I feel doubly blessed. I can choose from two rich cultures those parts that suit my mood

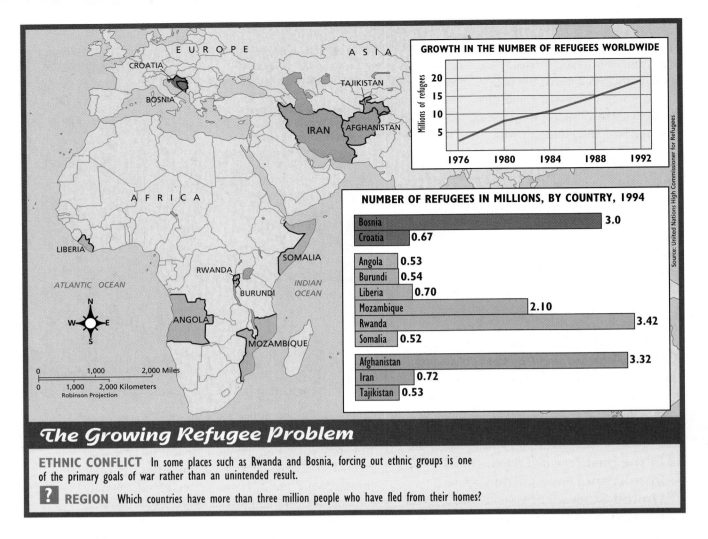

GROWTH IN THE NUMBER OF REFUGEES WORLDWIDE

Source: United Nations High Commissioner for Refugees

NUMBER OF REFUGEES IN MILLIONS, BY COUNTRY, 1994

Country	Refugees (millions)
Bosnia	3.0
Croatia	0.67
Angola	0.53
Burundi	0.54
Liberia	0.70
Mozambique	2.10
Rwanda	3.42
Somalia	0.52
Afghanistan	3.32
Iran	0.72
Tajikistan	0.53

The Growing Refugee Problem

ETHNIC CONFLICT In some places such as Rwanda and Bosnia, forcing out ethnic groups is one of the primary goals of war rather than an unintended result.

? **REGION** Which countries have more than three million people who have fled from their homes?

---

or the occasion best. And unbelievable as it may seem, shoes tinted red, white and blue go dandy with them all. **"**

MIGRATION IN THE POST–COLD WAR ERA

Western Europe has also received large numbers of immigrants in recent decades. Since the breakup of the Soviet Union, many Eastern Europeans have pursued new economic opportunities across Europe. Others have sought escape from the conflicts that have sometimes accompanied the end of communism. In the former Yugoslavia, for example, the civil war caused by the fall of communism left thousands homeless. Many people had no choice but to seek refuge in other countries.

Unfortunately, immigrants have occasionally met with violence. In 1991 and 1992 many refugees went to Germany, which had a policy of allowing **asylum**, or a place of protection, to all "persons persecuted on political grounds." In the early 1990s over one million asylum seekers entered Germany. Germany's citizens, however, were struggling with high unemployment and other economic problems brought about by the unification of East Germany and West Germany. Resentment against immigrants sparked violence, such as in August 1992 when antiforeigner groups rioted, injuring about 150 people.

Many residents of the former Soviet Union have chosen to move south rather than west. The former Soviet republics in Central Asia, for example, have many historic cultural ties to Turkey, Iran, and other Southwest Asian countries. Furthermore, more than a million Jews have emigrated from the former Soviet Union to Israel in recent years, in search of the opportunity to live among other Jews without discrimination.

Some migration in southwest Asia occurred during the Persian Gulf War, when some 5 million people fled areas of violence. These included not only people born in the region, such as Kuwaitis, but also foreign-born workers from Yemen, Egypt, Pakistan, Bangladesh, Sri Lanka, and the

Philippines. The Persian Gulf War called attention to the plight of Kurds, an ethnic group living in the bordering regions of Iraq, Iran, Syria, Armenia, and Turkey. After Kurds in Iraq unsuccessfully rebelled against the Iraqi government, some 2 million of them tried to enter Iran and Turkey.

DEVELOPING COUNTRIES

The Kurdish migrations are an example of one of the most important trends in contemporary migration patterns: in recent years, the largest migrations have taken place within and among developing countries. The UN Population Fund reported in 1993 that some 20 to 30 million people in developing countries move from rural to urban areas each year. Although people frequently move to cities looking for jobs and economic opportunities, often they find only poverty. Large shantytowns surround many cities such as São Paulo, Brazil; Jakarta, Indonesia; and Calcutta, India.

In parts of Africa, drought and overgrazing have led to the migration of many people seeking fertile soil. In some countries wars have worsened the effects of already-existing hardships. In Somalia, droughts in the early 1990s caused widespread starvation. When factional fighting broke out amidst the already poor conditions, many Somalis left their homes for refugee camps. In December 1992 UN forces, including many Americans, launched **Operation Restore Hope** to ensure that food and other necessities reached the starving Somali people.

In 1994, ethnic rivalries in Rwanda, a small African country, turned into a bloody civil war that sent emigration rates skyrocketing. For years strife between the country's two major ethnic groups, the Hutus and the Tutsis, had claimed thousands of lives. But when the nation's president died in a plane crash, violence reached epic proportions as the two groups battled for control. Hundreds of thousands of Rwandans were massacred, and a million or more fled the country.

In 1995 and 1996 the ethnic conflict spread to Burundi's Hutu and Tutsi population and to Zaire, where Tutsis have lived for centuries and where Hutu refugee camps have been located since 1994. Zairian rebels—mostly Tutsis who many believe are aided by the Rwandan government—have attacked Zairian cities and the camps, which have also served as bases for Hutu attacks on the Tutsi-dominated governments of Rwanda and Burundi. Zaire and many international aid officials think that the very existence of the camps inside Zaire has fostered conflict, and they want the refugees to return home.

▲ Fleeing civil war in Rwanda, refugees crowd together in a refugee camp in Tanzania, east of Rwanda.

■■ **Ethnic violence and civil wars caused people around the world to migrate during the 1980s and 1990s.**

SECTION 2 REVIEW

IDENTIFY and explain the significance of the following: Displaced Persons Act, Immigration Act of 1965, Immigration Act of 1990, Bette Bao Lord, asylum, Operation Restore Hope.

LOCATE and explain the importance of the following: Bosnia, Rwanda.

1. **MAIN IDEA** How did events in the first third of the 20th century affect migration?

2. **MAIN IDEA** How did World War II affect migration?

3. **MAIN IDEA** What factors led people to migrate during the 1980s and 1990s?

4. **WRITING TO EXPRESS A VIEWPOINT** Write the editor of your local newspaper a letter in which you assess the effects of recent immigration on the United States.

5. **ANALYZING** Why might some people oppose and others support increased immigration?

THE MOVEMENT OF INFORMATION

FOCUS

- **What effect did the development of computers have on the spread of information?**
- **How have developments in information and communication technology affected businesses?**
- **How has the Information Revolution increased concerns about privacy?**

Throughout most of history, ideas have moved only as quickly as the people who have held them. During the 20th century, however, new technological developments have allowed ideas and information to spread around the world more and more rapidly.

Statue of Albert Einstein in Washington, D.C.

THE SPREAD OF IDEAS

Travelers and migrants have long been responsible for the diffusion of knowledge from one region to another. During the 20th century, for example, Albert Einstein, James Franck, and other Jewish scientists fleeing the Fascists in Europe became key players in America's development of the atomic bomb. After World War II German rocket scientists, such as Wernher von Braun, significantly contributed to both the U.S. and Soviet space programs.

Since the 1940s the spread of knowledge has been enhanced by the development of the computer. The ways in which the computer is transforming society promise to be as profound as the changes that followed the introduction of the printing press. The widespread transfer of information that computers and new information technologies have made possible has become known as the **Information Revolution**.

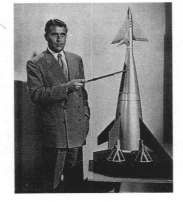

▶ **Wernher von Braun and his team developed the rocket that launched *Explorer I,* the first U.S. earth satellite, on January 31, 1958.**

Computers provide quick, easy access to information from around the world. For example, the electronic library services of Systems Development Corporation in the United States and Pergamon Infoline in Great Britain contain every patent filed with the U.S. Patent Office since 1971. The National Library of Medicine's service, Medline, indexes some 20,000 journal articles a month. Another service, Lexis, provides access to decisions in U.S. and British courts.

Internet. Because computers can communicate with each other via telephone lines, access to these electronic libraries is fast and easy. Computers can also be linked to allow people to send messages to each other and to gain access to electronic bulletin boards, news, training courses, and various other services. The Internet, which links millions of individual computers in more than 80 countries around the world, is the largest of these networks.

The development of the Internet began in the 1960s—in part as a response to the Cold War. The U.S. Department of Defense wanted

▲ In 1947 physicists John Bardeen, William Shockley, and Walter H. Brattain invented the transistor, making possible high-speed computers and the Information Revolution.

to find a way for the computer centers at universities and private research laboratories to communicate. The Defense Department was particularly interested in developing a system that could function after a nuclear attack.

The system that was devised in 1969 linked four universities' **mainframe computers**—large, fast computer systems that could process many tasks at once and that could cost millions of dollars. By 1972 the network had expanded to include some 40 members. Because all the computers had equal access to the system and no one computer controlled it, the system could still function even if part of it were destroyed. The design of the system also meant that there was no limit to the network's size.

With the development of **minicomputers**—computers that are smaller, easier to operate, and much cheaper than mainframes—and with the introduction of still smaller and cheaper personal computers in the 1970s, networks expanded to include a wide range of university, business, and individual users. And because these networks ran via public telephone lines rather than the restricted lines that mainframes used, the Internet became even more decentralized. Adding to the trend toward decentralization, the Defense Department opened the network in 1974—without charge—to anyone with access to a computer.

By 1982 Usenet, a network set up to communicate among networks, enabled e-mail to be sent to all computers within a given network and among the various networks. This, in turn, led to the formation of worldwide electronic bulletin boards, or newsgroups. People could now send short messages, opinion pieces, or articles to all the computers on the network and carry on a dis-

cussion with people all over the world—people they could otherwise never expect to meet.

In 1990 and 1991 new ways to post information on the Internet came into use. The most significant of these has been the World Wide Web (WWW), which is particularly useful for multimedia documents. The WWW, which had roughly 10 million users in 1995, is expected to grow to more than 80 million users by 2000. The U.S. government has made significant financial and technological contributions to the Internet. As part of this investment, the government established the National Science Foundation Network (NSFnet) in the late 1980s. The NSFnet used the latest technology to link a small number of supercomputer centers across the United States. The NSFnet served as the core network or backbone of the Internet by linking the various networks making up the system. In 1994, however, the National Science Foundation, which had been spending $10 million a year to administer the NSFnet, announced that it was turning the network over to the private sector.

National Information Infrastructure. In 1993 President Clinton created the U.S. Advisory Council on the **National Information Infrastructure,** headed by Vice President Albert Gore. In arguing for the development of an even more advanced network, the National Information Infrastructure (NII)—or Information Superhighway—Gore declared it would benefit all Americans by providing:

❝ a seamless web of communications networks, computers, databases, and consumer electronics that will put vast amounts of information at users' fingertips. . . [and] help unleash an information revolution. . . .

The NII can transform the lives of the American people—ameliorating [making more tolerable] the constraints of geography, disability, and economic status—giving all Americans a fair opportunity to go as far as their talents and ambitions will take them. ❞

▶ Vice President Albert Gore has worked to make information available to all Americans.

Japan is planning a similar system called *"maruchimedia,"* which the Japanese government hopes to have in every home by 2010. And in Hong Kong some 600 of the largest buildings are wired with the most up-to-date fiber optic systems. This provides a startling contrast to Moscow, where people with even the latest computer systems must connect to the Internet over telephone lines that date back to Lenin.

■■ Developments in computer technology helped speed the spread of information around the world.

TRANSFORMING BUSINESS AND INDUSTRY

One of the services that both the Internet and for-profit services provide to companies and individuals is e-mail. The increasing use of e-mail promises to change the way companies are organized. Andrew S. Grove, an executive of Intel Corporation, argued that e-mail promotes a more democratic organization:

> 66 Companies that use E-mail are much faster, much less hierarchical. You can only use e-mail effectively, though, if you do it yourself [rather than have an assistant screen your mail]. From the moment you do it yourself, you're available to anybody and everybody. The elimination of the screening process in my e-mail . . . tends to lead to a . . . more democratic way of operating—whether it's inside a corporation, inside a country, or across countries. 99

Other developments have also made communication easier. Cellular telephones allow people to make and receive calls no matter how far they may be from their home or office. Satellite links permit **teleconferencing**, which allows people at multiple locations to hold conferences over the telephone or by computer.

Satellites also make two-way interactive television possible. Medical practitioners, for example, have used this technology to improve the treatment of patients in isolated areas. Interactive television enables a doctor to view the treatment of a patient hundreds of miles away and to make recommendations to medical personnel who are administering care.

■■ Telecommunications advances have begun to change the ways in which business is conducted and services are provided.

TECHNOLOGY AND THE DEVELOPING WORLD

The introduction of the latest technology to the developing world promises to speed development by skipping intermediate stages of technology. Countries such as China and Hungary that are installing fiber-optic cables and the most up-to-date digital communications technology will gain an edge in global economic competition. For instance, Shanghai, in an effort to become a major financial center, is installing communications equipment as powerful as that used in New York's financial district. Overall, China plans to add some 80 million phone lines and spend some $100 billion over the next decade. While this is a huge sum, it is far less than it would cost to install an older copper-wire, nondigital system.

Others in the developing world are turning to cellular communications systems, which are carried over radio waves. The advantage of cellu-

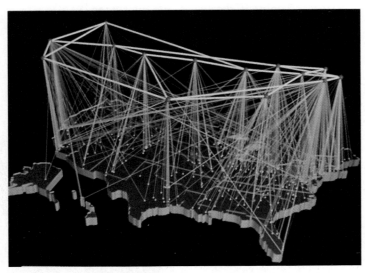

▲ **In this view of the NSFnet, the purple lines indicate a free flow of information. The white lines show a heavy backup caused by 100 billion bytes of moving data.**

▲ A portable cellular telephone allows voice communication from virtually anywhere in the world.

lar systems is that they are relatively cheap to install. Latin America, where only 7 percent of the population has telephones, has the fastest-growing cellular market in the world. People in Bangkok, Thailand, are also turning to cellular phones because of huge waiting lists for telephones and snarled traffic that traps businesspeople in their cars for hours.

INFORMATION TECHNOLOGY AND PRIVACY

The development of electronic information systems has contributed to new worries about privacy. Many Americans worry that electronic data storage and communication will make private information easily available to others. In some cases, these fears are justified. Today some companies monitor employee use of e-mail, raising new issues of privacy. One e-mail administrator in California supported the privacy of electronic communications with the statement: "You don't read other people's mail, just as you don't listen to their phone conversations."

In some cases, technological innovations provide unexpected opportunities to monitor activities. One 1981-model Cadillac engine included a computer that recorded when systems malfunctioned. The computer also noted when the driver exceeded 80 miles per hour. Electronic **barcodes**, which some libraries use to keep track of their collections, could also be used to provide a record of a borrower's reading habits.

As more and more information is cataloged and made available, a growing number of people are becoming concerned about the possible abuse of knowledge. E-mail, for instance, can be captured at any of the computer systems it passes through on the way to its final destination. Web sites may store information about their visitors that can help speed future commercial transactions but can also be used in ways that invade privacy. Credit reports, job applications, and rental agreements result in the collection of personal information that can also be entered into a computer and analyzed in any number of ways.

For those who are concerned about keeping records confidential, the Information Revolution poses new challenges as well as new opportunities.

■■ **Technological developments that make it easier to monitor people's behavior have led to increased concerns about privacy.**

SECTION 3 REVIEW

IDENTIFY and explain the significance of the following: Information Revolution, mainframe computers, minicomputers, National Information Infrastructure, teleconferencing, barcodes.

1. **MAIN IDEA** In the past 25 years, how has new technology affected the spread of information?

2. **MAIN IDEA** How are various businesses likely to be affected by recent technological developments?

3. **MAIN IDEA** What kinds of privacy issues have been raised by the Information Revolution?

4. **WRITING TO EXPLAIN** Write a memo to a political candidate in which you show how new technology could be used to change the way campaigns are conducted.

5. **ASSESSING CONSEQUENCES** Write a short essay discussing the ways in which the Information Revolution could affect the world.

A GLOBAL CULTURE

FOCUS

- **How has sports reflected the globalization of culture in the 20th century?**
- **How have television and movies influenced perceptions of other cultures?**
- **How have music and fashion contributed to youth culture around the world?**

An American fast-food restaurant in Bangkok, Thailand

*W*hen people mingle, they exchange more than technical knowledge and expertise; they also exchange ways of having fun. As people moved from country to country during the 20th century, there emerged something that increasingly could be called a global culture.

WORLD SPORTS

During the 20th century, technological developments and ease of travel have contributed to the growing popularity of sports. Teams now travel around the world to compete, and individual athletes play for teams outside their own countries. Although the popularity of any individual sport may vary in different countries, the worldwide enthusiasm for athletic competition has enabled many sports to gain a global following.

Historically, sports have often traveled with armies. This is not surprising, since young men—and more recently, women—of military age are also of prime age for athletics. Moreover, commanders have supported sports as a way to keep the soldiers fit and hone the competitive edge needed for combat.

The British, who during the 19th century sent soldiers all over the world, carried the game of cricket with them. Today cricket is passionately played in many countries that were once part of Britain's empire, including India, Pakistan, South Africa, Australia, New Zealand, and Jamaica.

Baseball, an American variation of the old English game of rounders, was also carried overseas—this time by U.S. soldiers. Many Italians became devoted baseball fans after American soldiers introduced the game after World War II. The nations of Central America and the Caribbean, which have been periodically occupied by American troops, have produced some notable baseball players. Puerto Rico was the home of Roberto Clemente, the Pittsburgh Pirates slugger of the 1960s and 1970s. Jose Canseco, the 1990s home run hitter, is a native of Cuba.

▶ **The Yakult Swallows defeat the Seibu Lions to clinch their first Japan Series title in 15 years.**

Baseball is also popular in parts of Asia. Japanese baseball, for example, generates as much enthusiasm in that country as major league baseball does in the United States. Since 1951 hundreds of foreigners, most of them Americans, have gone to Japan to play baseball.

Basketball is another American sport that has gone international during the late 20th century. In the 1990s several European stars made reputations in the United States in the National Basketball Association, and some American players relocated to Europe to play for teams there. In 1990 Boston Celtics general manager Jan Volk said, "The more exposure we get for our teams and players in Europe, the more desirable our players become to the European teams and public." In 1992 Los Angeles Laker Michael Cooper left California to play for Il Messaggero Roma in Italy, where he was offered $1.5 million for his first season, use of a BMW, and a suburban villa.

Europe also offered opportunities for American women basketball players. Though women's basketball was gaining popularity in the United States at the high school and college levels, as of the mid-1990s it had not prospered as a professional sport. Consequently, American women who wished to play professional basketball had to go to Europe. "It's not NBA money," said Vicki Hall, who had played basketball for the University of Texas, referring to her salary for a team in Switzerland. "But I could make more than a decent living there."

While Americans were exporting baseball and basketball, they were importing soccer. Called football in most of the rest of the world, the game is played all over the globe. Much of soccer's popularity stems from its simplicity: with a ball and an open patch of ground, anyone can play. The game is within the reach of even the poorest people; where a regulation ball is not available, players have been known to get up games with bundles of rags.

Soccer had long been played in the United States, but its popularity there did not begin to grow until the 1970s and 1980s. Youth soccer leagues were established in cities and towns all across the country and millions of boys and girls signed up to play. Although professional soccer was slow to attract a following in the United States, the selection of the United States as host for the 1994 World Cup championship, which an estimated two billion people watched, appeared likely to give the game a boost.

International sporting events have a long history. The first recorded **Olympic Games** took place in 776 B.C. as part of a religious festival in ancient Greece. The games lost their religious focus after Rome conquered Greece in the 100s B.C. and were officially ended in A.D. 394. In 1894 Baron Pierre de Coubertin, a French educator, proposed reviving the competitions. Two years later the first modern Olympics were held in Athens, Greece. During the next hundred years, the games became a showcase for the global culture of sports. Initially a summer contest for men, the Olympics expanded to include women in 1912 and winter events in 1924. Countries not only competed in the games but also competed to be named host of the Olympics. Over the years the games have been held in Europe, North America, Asia, and Australia.

■■ Many sports spread around the world and became global contests during the 20th century.

WORLD TELEVISION AND MOVIES

The popularity of competitions such as the World Cup and the Olympics was greatly increased by television. The spread of television helped to create a global culture by permitting people to watch sporting events from almost any part of the world. In 1992 Americans watched the "Dream Team," the U.S. Olympic basketball squad, win the gold medal in Barcelona, Spain. In 1993 and 1994 Chinese viewers saw their country's women distance runners set records all over the world.

▲ This 1993 poster advertising Aladdin in Paris, France, illustrates the worldwide popularity of American films

News and entertainment are also part of the televised exchange of culture. Cable News Network (CNN) International broadcasts news programs around the world. British productions such as *Mystery!: Prime Suspect* and its sequels won critical acclaim on both sides of the Atlantic. Because their movies and

THROUGH OTHERS' EYES

"This is the '90s" declared Disney's head, Michael Eisner, "the decade we reinvent the Disney experience not just in California, but worldwide." However, not everyone welcomed Eisner's vision. When Euro Disney opened outside Paris in April 1992, critics called it a "cultural Chernobyl." "It took a money-hungry little mouse to trigger a debate on issues that we have been evading," noted Jean-Marie Rouart in the Paris newspaper Le Figaro. "Should we allow culture to be ruled by profitability?"

Such concerns on the part of some of the French were not new. In 1982, a decade before Euro Disney opened, France's minister of culture, Jack Lang, warned the world about what he called American cultural imperialism: "Certain great nations who taught us about freedom and called on people to rise up against oppression, yet who today . . . have no other morality than that of profit, . . . seek to impose a uniform culture on the whole world."

television programs do not pose a language barrier, British, Canadian, and Australian productions often have had an edge over other foreign productions in the American market. Some foreign stars, however, have overcome this difficulty; Gérard Depardieu, after a long acting career in France, won American fans with his performance in *Cyrano de Bergerac*—in spite of the need for English subtitles. Others, such as Arnold Schwarzenegger, although foreign born, have become American stars.

Nonetheless, the United States dominates the world market in films and television. American popular culture is the nation's second largest export. In 1993, *Jurassic Park* and 87 other American movies were among the world's 100 most attended films. During the 1980s the television drama *Dallas* seemed to represent American

▶ **Technology enables people such as this Kaiapo Indian in Altamira, Brazil, to enjoy a wide variety of entertainment.**

life to people all over the world. Some worry that it is the worst television programs that receive the widest distribution—because they can be marketed cheaply. For example, American soap operas are wildly popular in Egypt, India, and other developing countries. Others worry about how American movies and television will affect their cultures. In 1994 French minister of culture Jacques Toubon was quoted, calling U.S. domination of the market a "pure monopoly in the worst sense."

Despite such concerns, American performers have also found worldwide popularity, both in and out of movies. Harrison Ford, star of numerous American films such as *Raiders of the Lost Ark* and *The Fugitive,* also acted as spokesperson for a Japanese cable TV channel.

■■ **Movies and television moved across international borders, influencing perceptions of different cultures.**

WORLD YOUTH

The international links formed by the entertainment industry have contributed to **cultural diffusion**—the process of spreading cultural practices or beliefs. Teenagers around the world look to television and films for ideas about music and dress.

Music. Although rock 'n' roll was originally an American style, the music quickly gained international popularity. Musical styles continued to evolve and spread around the world, and by the 1980s the growth of cable television allowed music videos to become an important marketing tool for the music industry. This mix of sight and sound is not limited to English-speaking fans or musicians. MTV Asia, broadcast across that

continent, focuses on bands from India and other countries in the region. MTV Europe broadcasts in English, but most of its programming is European and features European musicians. The network reaches some 60 million homes in Europe, and some 88 million viewers in the former Soviet Union receive the network for an hour per week.

Music videos and concert tours provide musicians with worldwide popularity. At any given time U2 of Ireland might be performing in the United States; India's Ravi Shankar in Rio de Janeiro; Cuban-born Gloria Estefan in Rome; and Britain's Rolling Stones in Tokyo. Fans who are unable to get to a concert can find the latest tapes and CDs in stores from Mexico City to Hong Kong.

Clothing. Movies and television also provide teens with inspiration in the world of fashion. In the early 1990s, many copied the "grunge look" of popular musicians. When American director Spike Lee's film *Malcolm X* was released in Japan in 1993, many people became interested in Malcolm's life and beliefs. They also began to wear the same "X"-labeled baseball caps, T-shirts, and jackets that many American youths wore when the film opened in the United States.

Japanese teens have also adopted a range of American casual styles, called *Amekaji*. National Football League (NFL) hats are common among Japanese teens, as are black leather jackets and university warm-up suits. One Japanese advertising executive said, "Sharing in America can release Japanese teenagers from the restraints they live with every day. Through fashion, they can capture a bit of the life-style they can never hope to live."

■■ Movies, television shows, and music videos have helped to create a kind of global youth culture.

The export of many kinds of entertainment has provided more links between cultures. Music, sports, movies, and television all allow people in different areas of the world to develop and to share common interests. Furthermore, technology has increased the speed and ease with which entertainment, as well as scientific knowledge, has spread around the world.

▲ Japanese young people view the latest American styles in Harajuki, a trendy Toyko shopping district.

SECTION 4 REVIEW

IDENTIFY and explain the significance of the following: Olympic Games, Baron Pierre de Coubertin, Jacques Toubon, cultural diffusion.

1. **MAIN IDEA** How has the globalization of culture been affected by athletics?

2. **MAIN IDEA** How do the media contribute to ideas about other cultures?

3. **MAIN IDEA** What factors have contributed to the development of a youth culture around the world?

4. **WRITING TO PERSUADE** Imagine you are the minister of culture in another country. Write an article for a newspaper outlining a policy on imported movies and television programs and explain why you have adopted the policy.

5. **COMPARING** Compare the effects of sports, music, and fashion on the development of a global culture.

Discovery of gold in Australia attracts many immigrants.

Congress passes Chinese Exclusion Act.

Ellis Island opens.

First modern Olympics held in Athens, Greece.

Thomasites arrive in the Philippines.

Immigration Act of 1924 sharply reduces number of immigrants admitted to the U.S.

WRITING A SUMMARY

Using the essential points of the chapter as a guide, write a summary of the chapter.

REVIEWING CHRONOLOGY

Number your paper 1 to 5. Study the time line above, and list the following events in the order in which they happened by writing the first next to 1, the second next to 2, and so on. Then complete the activity below.

1. Ellis Island opens.
2. Thomasites arrive in the Philippines.
3. U.S. hosts World Cup soccer championship.
4. Congress passes Displaced Persons Act.
5. Internet system links mainframe computers at four universities.

Synthesizing How have the different immigration acts passed by Congress in the 20th century indicated changes in U.S. policy regarding immigration?

IDENTIFYING PEOPLE AND IDEAS

Explain the historical significance of each of the following people or terms.

1. Angel Island
2. Immigration Act of 1965
3. Bette Bao Lord
4. asylum
5. Operation Restore Hope
6. cultural diffusion
7. Abraham Verghese
8. teleconferencing
9. Jacques Toubon
10. Information Revolution

UNDERSTANDING MAIN IDEAS

1. What patterns of migration marked the 19th and early 20th centuries? What were the main motives behind migration during this period?
2. What economic and political forces affected migration in the 1930s and 1940s?
3. How are new communications technologies transforming businesses and affecting developing nations? What concerns are these new technologies raising?
4. What are some of the forms of recreation and entertainment that have become increasingly popular around the world in recent years?

REVIEWING THEMES

1. **Cultural Diversity** What effect did the Immigration Act of 1965 have on the cultural composition of the U.S. population?
2. **Technology and Society** How did U.S. Defense Department concerns lead to the development of the Internet?
3. **Economic Development** How has an increasingly globalized culture led to increased international trade of various goods such as movies?

THINKING CRITICALLY

1. **Hypothesizing** Do you think the migration patterns that have characterized the 1980s and 1990s will continue to influence international migrations over the next 25 years? Why or why not?
2. **Evaluating** How might the growth of the "Information Superhighway" affect Americans' daily lives?
3. **Synthesizing** In what ways can the movement of people around the world influence the movement of ideas? Support your answer with specific examples.

STRATEGY FOR SUCCESS

Review the Skills Handbook entry on Reading Charts and Graphs beginning on page 756. Study the graph below, which shows the number of jobs in the auto and information processing industries from 1975 to 1993. What effect has the Information Revolution had on the number of jobs in information processing industries? What other conclusions can you draw from the graph? Which of the two types of industries do you think will employ more people in the year 2000? Why?

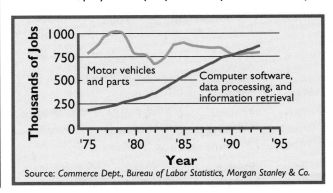

Source: Commerce Dept., Bureau of Labor Statistics, Morgan Stanley & Co.

Congress passes Displaced Persons Act.	Immigration Act of 1965 allows greater numbers of immigrants to be admitted to the U.S.	Internet system links mainframe computers at four universities.	Communist victory in Vietnam provokes flood of refugees from Southeast Asia.	President Bush signs Immigration Act of 1990.	Malcolm X released in Japan. President Clinton creates the U.S. Advisory Council on the National Information Infrastructure. Hundreds of thousands flee violence in Rwanda. U.S. hosts World Cup soccer championship.

1948   **1965**   **1969**   **1975**   **1990**   **1993**   **1994**

WRITING ABOUT HISTORY

Writing to Create Imagine you are a teenager in a country other than the United States. Write a letter to a friend explaining the extent to which your life is influenced by American culture. Use specific examples to describe what form American cultural influences take.

Crowds outside the Planet Hollywood restaurant in Hong Kong

USING PRIMARY SOURCES

Many writers have reflected on America's diverse cultural heritage. Read the following excerpt taken from a talk by Luis M. Valdez, a Mexican American playwright. How does Valdez view past, present, and future migration to America?

   These are painful times, and yet they are very exciting times. Many people in this country are intimidated and frightened by the brown hordes pouring across the border, the nonborder, this border that cannot hold. And so they want to declare English the official language of the United States. But I tell you that you cannot keep something natural from happening. The evolution of America has always involved north and south migration. It was the Europeans who gave it east and west. And we're happy to have it because what that did is to set up the four directions. . . . It's like the bellybutton of the world. Right at that intersection, four roads meet—the white road, the black road, the yellow road, and the red road. What they represent to me is the promise of America—that four roads will meet and will bear new fruit in this ancient land. . . . It is important that Europe came to these shores. It is important that Africa came to these shores. It is important that Asia came to these shores. It is important that there was a pre-Columbian America here waiting to blend and to create something greater than the parts. A whole vision of humanity 🙶🙶

LINKING HISTORY AND GEOGRAPHY

People sometimes migrate from one area to another in search of a more hospitable environment. What are some of the environmental conditions that might encourage migration? What physical features might make migration difficult?

BUILDING YOUR PORTFOLIO

Complete the following projects independently or cooperatively.

1. WAR In Chapter 24 you portrayed an economist studying the economic effects of war. Building on that experience, imagine you are a refugee fleeing from a war in your home country. Write a series of journal entries describing your feelings about the conflict from which you are escaping, the problems you encounter as a refugee, and your plans for the future.

2. THE ECONOMY In Chapter 23 you portrayed an economist studying the relationship between imperialism and the economy. Building on that experience, imagine you are the director of a private agency that assists immigrant businesspeople. Prepare a speech on how immigrant businesses are helping to boost your nation's economy.

Chapter 26

THE STRUGGLE FOR HUMAN RIGHTS

1864	1903	1948	1964	1994
Geneva Convention signed.	Emmeline Pankhurst forms the Women's Social and Political Union in Britain.	UN adopts the Universal Declaration of Human Rights.	SNCC members tour Africa.	South Africa holds its first national election open to all South Africans.

Many of the world's religions have taught the innate worth of all human beings for hundreds, even thousands, of years. The modern concept of human rights, however, grew out of ideas that reached back only to the 17th and 18th centuries.

Chinese students in the streets of Beijing, 1989

In the spring of 1989, thousands of students gathered in Beijing, China, to demonstrate in favor of democratic reforms in China. The demonstrators listened to speeches, waved posters, and handed out leaflets demanding that the Chinese government acknowledge the right of the Chinese people to speak their minds and to have a greater say in choosing their leaders.

The centerpiece of the demonstrations was a plaster figure resembling the American Statue of Liberty erected in Tiananmen Square in the heart of the Chinese capital. For more than a century, the American statue had lifted its beacon of democracy and human rights to the world. In 1989 it inspired the Tiananmen Square demonstrators to try to follow the United States' example.

The Chinese government flatly rejected the demonstrators' demands. In a brutal display of force, government troops killed hundreds of demonstrators and wounded hundreds more. Thousands were jailed, many for years. The statue of the "Goddess of Democracy" was smashed to pieces.

The demonstrations in Tiananmen Square showed the global appeal of human rights and the influence of America's example. The massacre showed that the struggle for human rights had far to go.

Tiananmen Square "Goddess of Democracy" statue, May 1989

HUMAN RIGHTS BEFORE WORLD WAR I

FOCUS

- When did the modern concept of human rights arise? What events contributed to the development of the concept?
- How was the U.S. antislavery movement connected to reform movements in other countries?
- What triggered the women's rights movement in the 19th century? What was the movement's principal demand?
- How did progressivism further the cause of human rights?

Various efforts to promote human rights arose during the 18th and 19th centuries. The American and French revolutions focused on the rights of citizens. The antislavery and women's rights movements sought to expand the definition of citizen so as to include more people. The Progressive movement won the vote for American women and protection for American children.

A symbol of the French Revolution, 1789–1799

ORIGINS OF THE HUMAN RIGHTS CONCEPT

The modern concept of human rights is a fairly recent innovation. In ancient and medieval times, certain individuals had rights because of their positions in society: some Athenian Greeks had certain rights as citizens of Athens; feudal nobles had rights as nobles, while peasants had a different set of rights as peasants. But the idea that people had rights simply because they were human beings did not arise in its modern form until the 17th century.

Several 17th- and 18th-century philosophers spoke of natural rights that existed because of the nature of human beings and their relation to society. One such philosopher was John Locke of England. Locke lived during the mid- and late 1600s, when the English Parliament was challenging the absolute power of the king.

Siding with Parliament, Locke believed that individuals had certain rights that governments could not violate. In fact, the very reason that governments existed, Locke asserted, was to protect individuals' rights. Locke listed the most important of these rights as the rights to life, liberty, and property.

In what became known as the **Glorious Revolution**, Parliament broke the absolute power of the monarchy. As a result, the natural rights Locke identified became part of the political inheritance of the English people—and of those men and women who transplanted themselves from England to North America.

As the natural rights philosophy spread across the Atlantic, it acquired a distinctively American form. This form became apparent in one of history's most important statements on the subject of human rights: the American Declaration of Independence, in which the colonists proclaimed their rights against the government of King George III (see Chapter 2).

The American declaration of rights and the Americans' success in defending these rights inspired people in other countries. Just a few years

▲ This painting shows representatives of France's middle class as they met in June 1789 and pledged to write a new constitution.

after the Revolutionary War, residents of Paris, outraged by the French monarchy's excesses, revolted. As the revolution begun by the Parisians spread across France, the newly formed National Assembly issued the **Declaration of the Rights of Man and Citizen**. Like the Declaration of Independence, the French document listed basic rights:

> 66 The aim of all political association is the conservation of the natural and inalienable rights of man. These rights are: liberty, property, security and resistance to oppression. 99

Equality, while not a right in itself, was implied by the declaration's assertion that all men were "equal in rights."

■■ **The modern concept of human rights originated in the 17th century and grew as a result of the American and French revolutions.**

THE ANTISLAVERY MOVEMENT

Thomas Jefferson owned slaves, as did many others who signed the Declaration of Independence. It did not escape the notice of the Declaration's signers that the right of liberty they proclaimed for "all men" was something they themselves denied their slaves. Critics of slavery, of course, also noted this contradiction. But in 1776 the need for unity in the

struggle against Britain seemed to the revolutionary leaders to outweigh the need for consistency regarding human rights. Thus debate over the slavery issue remained relatively quiet.

The slave trade. It did not stay quiet for long, however. In the meetings that eventually produced the Constitution, critics of slavery succeeded in securing a ban on the importation of slaves, albeit after a delay of twenty years. Even the supporters of slavery had difficulty defending the Atlantic slave trade, with its barbarous conditions and appalling death rates. One observer of a ship carrying slaves described how the captives were packed in until "they had not so much room *as a man in his coffin."*

Criticism of the slave trade was not limited to the United States. At about the time the U.S. Congress was banning the slave trade to the United States, British abolitionists persuaded Parliament to outlaw the slave trade. Subsequently these abolitionists lobbied the British government to pressure other European powers to do the same. At an 1815 meeting among the major European powers, Britain persuaded the other powers to join it in condemning the slave trade.

British abolition. By the time the bans on the slave trade went into effect, the immorality of slavery itself had become an international issue. British abolitionists, led by William Wilberforce, grew

◀ In 1789 William Wilberforce, a prominent British Tory, led the first Parliamentary campaign against slavery.

increasingly militant in demanding that their government outlaw slavery. Largely as a result of efforts by Wilberforce and others, Parliament voted in 1833 to ban the institution of slavery within the British Empire.

Once the British had put a stop to slavery in their own territories, they tried to end it elsewhere. As British warships patrolled the Atlantic and Indian Oceans during the mid- and late 1800s, they searched for slave ships. When they found such ships, they seized the vessels and released the slaves. Sometimes, however, British efforts backfired. Some slavers, when they saw British warships approaching, threw slaves overboard in order to prevent their ships from being seized. Nevertheless, the British efforts did reduce the numbers of persons delivered into slavery.

Other movements. The British antislavery movement encouraged abolitionism in other countries. When most of Spain's Latin American colonies claimed and won their independence during the 1810s and 1820s, many abolished slavery at the same time. On the other side of the world, in Russia, reformers called for an end to serfdom. Under this system—similar in some ways to slavery—peasants called serfs were required to work the land they lived on for the benefit of the landowner. Opponents of serfdom in Russia achieved success when Czar Alexander II emancipated the serfs in 1861.

American abolitionists took heart from these foreign efforts to expand human freedom. Leaders

▲ **Life was often difficult for the peasant class in prerevolutionary Russia.**

such as Frederick Douglass and William Lloyd Garrison followed the example of Wilberforce and other reformers overseas in pressing for an end to slavery. Because of the entrenched political position of southern planters, however, American antislavery activists found it more difficult than reformers in Britain and Latin America to push abolition to the top of the list of national priorities. But in the 1850s they helped establish the Republican party, which thrust the slavery issue further into politics. Reformers all over applauded Republican Abraham Lincoln's election in 1860. Not all of them cheered the coming of the American Civil War, but without exception they hailed the Emancipation Proclamation and the Thirteenth Amendment abolishing slavery.

■■ **The abolitionist movement in the United States was part of an international effort to end slavery and other forms of human bondage.**

THE STRUGGLE FOR WOMEN'S RIGHTS

Many of the most tireless opponents of slavery were women. However, as these women worked for rights for African Americans, they realized that they needed to work for their own rights. As Angelina Grimké stated in 1836: "The investigation of the rights of the slave has led me to a better understanding of my own." Elizabeth Cady Stanton and Lucretia Mott came to a similar realization when they were denied the chance to speak at an antislavery convention in London (see Chapter 3).

▼ **The *Black Man's Lament* shows West Indies slave traders separating a man from his family in the mid-1800s.**

Moreover, in the abolitionist movement women interested in reform met other women with similar views. Together they learned techniques of organization and education that they could apply on their own behalf. The 1848 Seneca Falls Convention was one of the first efforts at such organization worldwide.

The women's movement in the United States was similar to movements in other countries. Foremost among these was Britain, where women also campaigned in favor of the vote. In 1865 the most active members of the movement established the Women's Suffrage Committee, which was later renamed the London National Society for Women's Suffrage. They believed that the vote would allow them access to Parliament, where they could have even greater influence in establishing women's equality with men.

By the early 1900s, women in Britain had gained the right to vote in local and county elections and to participate in such government bodies as town councils and school boards. In 1907, 10 women were elected mayors of small towns. Nonetheless, women were still barred from voting in national elections.

As opposition in Britain to full women's suffrage persisted, many women became impatient with the long, slow struggle. In 1903 feminist Emmeline Pankhurst founded a new women's rights organization, the **Women's Social and Political Union** (WSPU). Disappointed by the British government's continuing refusal to allow women's suffrage, Pankhurst and her followers—who were labeled suffragettes—decided in 1906 to adopt more aggressive tactics.

To get greater publicity and public support, Pankhurst and her followers began to attack public property and tried to get arrested. Once arrested, they often went on hunger strikes. Because the government did not want the women to die while they were in prison, they were often force-fed through tubes stuck into their nostrils. One protester, Mary Leigh, described the experience to her attorney in 1909:

66 The sensation is most painful—the drums of the ears seem to be bursting and there is a horrible pain in the throat and the breast. The tube is pushed down twenty inches. I have to lie on the bed, pinned down by the wardresses [female prison attendants]. 99

Emmeline Pankhurst

▲ In the early 1900s, British suffragettes rioted and chained themselves to fences in an effort to promote women's rights.

In response to the suffragettes' tactics, the British government passed an act in 1913 that allowed suffragettes to be released from prison when they became too weak or ill from starvation, and then rearrested as soon as they had recovered enough to serve more of their sentences. This act, which became known as the "Cat and Mouse Act," only made the WSPU more determined. Members increased their attacks on public property. One, Emily Davison, deliberately threw herself under the hooves of the king's horse during a horse race. Although women over the age of 30 gained the right to vote in 1918, it was not until 1928 that all adult women were granted suffrage in Britain.

■■ **The movement for women's rights grew out of the antislavery campaign. Its principal early goal was the vote for women.**

PROGRESSIVISM AND HUMAN RIGHTS

In the United States the campaign for women's rights became linked during the early years of the 20th century to the Progressive movement. The progressives believed that the answer to the nation's

▶ During the mid-1800s Britain passed labor laws to protect children such as these boys, who worked in a Derbyshire coal mine.

to the employment of large numbers of young boys and girls in mills, mines, and other industrial workplaces. The problem first became acute in Britain, where several laws restricting child labor were passed during the 1830s and 1840s. Even so, labor conditions in Britain remained poor, prompting authors such as Charles Dickens to write starkly about the bleak lives of working children.

American progressives were moved by Dickens's stories. They were also moved by American muckraker journalists' accounts and by their own observations of children who toiled long hours in American coal mines and cotton mills. Believing that children deserved protection from exploitation by industrialists, who hired the children because they were cheap, the progressives passed a variety of laws limiting child labor (see Chapter 7).

Critics of the child labor laws argued that such laws did not expand human rights but rather reduced them, by curbing children's right to work as they pleased. Supporters countered that children did not work in coal mines out of free choice but out of economic necessity. They said that child labor laws actually increased the freedom of children by allowing them the right not to work.

problems—ranging from corrupt city and state governments to corporate monopolies and wasteful exploitation of natural resources—was increased democracy. Women's suffrage fit into the pattern of more democracy, along with such other electoral reforms as the direct primary and the initiative, referendum, and recall. During the first two decades of the new century, women reformers focused on amending the Constitution to guarantee women's right to vote. Success came in 1920 with approval of the Nineteenth Amendment.

The progressive agenda included other items that touched on human rights. Among these were child labor laws. The Industrial Revolution had led

■■ **The American progressives' contribution to expanding human rights included winning the vote for women and restricting child labor.**

SECTION 1 REVIEW

IDENTIFY and explain the significance of the following: John Locke, Glorious Revolution, Declaration of the Rights of Man and Citizen, William Wilberforce, Emmeline Pankhurst, Women's Social and Political Union, Charles Dickens.

1. **MAIN IDEA** During what century did the modern concept of human rights originate? How did the American and French revolutions affect conceptions of rights?

2. **MAIN IDEA** What relationship did the antislavery movement in the United States have with movements in other countries?

3. **MAIN IDEA** What sparked the rise of the women's movement in the 19th century? What was the main goal of people in the movement?

4. **WRITING TO EXPLAIN** Write a paragraph explaining how the Progressive movement contributed to the expansion of human rights.

5. **ANALYZING** How did the American Declaration of Independence reflect the ideas of John Locke about the purpose of government?

THE CRUELTIES OF WAR

FOCUS

■ **How did World War I influence thinking about human rights?**

■ **What new threats to human rights emerged between the wars?**

■ **How did World War II affect human rights?**

■ **How did the international community attempt to safeguard human rights following World War II?**

The years from the beginning of World War I to the end of World War II witnessed new challenges to human rights and a new appreciation of those rights. The first war resulted in the slaughter of people by the millions and led to efforts to restrict the use of certain weapons and tactics of war. The interwar years saw the rise of militant fascism, a movement that fostered prejudice. The second war produced suffering on a scale that dwarfed even the first war, but it also produced a new international appreciation for human rights.

American soldiers wearing gas masks, World War I

THE ULTIMATE VIOLATION

During the early years of the 20th century, the countries of Europe flattered themselves that they had achieved a level of civilization unmatched in human history. Political and other reforms were making the European continent more democratic, more humane, and more enlightened each year. In addition, Europe as a whole had not known a major war for nearly a century. Europeans tried to humanize what war there was, laying down international conventions for its conduct and establishing rules for the treatment of prisoners.

In 1864, for example, 12 nations had agreed to the **Geneva Convention**, which required them to care properly not only for their own sick and wounded soldiers but also for captured enemy soldiers. The Geneva Convention also recognized the efforts of the **Red Cross**, an organization created the previous year by private Swiss citizens to minister

to wounded soldiers of all nations. While the Geneva Convention applied only to warfare on land, the **Hague Peace Conferences** of 1899 and 1907 established provisions to regulate naval warfare.

The horror of war. The world war that broke out in 1914 quickly shattered any sense of self-satisfaction Europeans felt about their approach to warfare. During World War I the European armies killed and maimed each other in unheard-of numbers. In the Battle of the Somme, for example, thousands died in minutes as mass-produced weapons proved how efficiently they could destroy life.

Some weapons seemed more gruesome than others. The damage machine guns and artillery did to human flesh and bone was enough to torment survivors with lifelong nightmares. Poison gas seemed even worse. Unlike guns, gas could not be accurately aimed; it blew and drifted where it would, felling friend and foe alike. And it was

► This 1918 photograph shows an American soldier clutching at his throat as he breathes poison gas.

tage of the war to crush a discontented Armenian minority. The Turks massacred hundreds of thousands of Armenians and forcibly deported hundreds of thousands more. One observer described how Armenians were "brutally dragged out of their native land, torn from their homes and families, . . . penned up in the open like cattle, without shelter, almost no clothing, and irregularly fed with food altogether insufficient." In one Turkish prison camp, the observer continued, "mounds are seen containing 200 or 300 corpses buried in the ground . . . women, children, and old people." Another witness told of other horrors:

> 66 There were 500 Armenians herded together in a stable . . . and locked in. Through an opening in the roof gendarmes [soldiers] threw flaming torches. I saw the flames and heard the screams of the victims, all of whom were burned alive. 99

To the limited extent outsiders knew what was happening—the Ottoman government flatly denied any wrongful activity—there was little anyone could do. Furthermore, the Allies were already at war against Turkey. And at a time when even larger numbers of Allied soldiers were dying in battle elsewhere, atrocities against the Armenians attracted little attention.

horribly painful, causing those who breathed it to feel that their lungs were on fire. Many gas victims died; others suffered irreparable lung damage and never breathed easily again.

World War I also saw the first significant use of submarines. Prior to World War I, naval blockades had been relatively nonviolent: blockading ships seized vessels but did not destroy them or harm the people aboard. Submarine warfare changed this and added a new form of barbarity to armed conflict. Submarine attacks took their targets by surprise and often sank them without regard for the safety of crew or passengers.

Since the nation using submarines most extensively was Germany, many charges of barbarity were aimed at the German government. The Germans responded to these charges by claiming that the British blockade of Germany was killing more people than were German submarines. The British blockade, by preventing food and other essential supplies from reaching the German people, was contributing to widespread malnutrition and disease. Moreover, children, the elderly, and the sick suffered the most from the shortages caused by the blockade.

War and ethnic conflict.

Other events of the war years also threatened human rights. Ottoman Turkey, for example, took advan-

▪▪ World War I shattered illusions that the world was becoming more humane.

▼ These Armenian refugees in Adana, Turkey, were among the lucky ones who escaped the Turks during World War I.

PEACEMAKING AND HUMAN RIGHTS

Yet all the carnage did have an effect. It served as a reminder that the ultimate violation of human rights was war, which in the industrial era left millions dead, often without regard for who was a soldier and who was a civilian.

The war spurred efforts to safeguard human rights by preventing future wars. The most important of these efforts was the establishment of the League of Nations, the international body designed to settle disputes between countries. The World Court, too, attempted to find peaceful resolutions to international disputes. And in the winter of 1921–22, the U.S.-sponsored disarmament conference in Washington resulted in agreements to destroy dozens of warships of the great powers' navies (see Chapter 15).

▲ The American Friends Service Committee's star was first used in 1870 to identify British Quakers providing war relief.

Private efforts. Not all efforts to promote peace were led by governments. Peace activists in America and elsewhere formed organizations devoted to the study of the causes and prevention of war. For example, the **American Friends Service Committee** (AFSC), which had been founded by Quakers in 1917 to provide "a conscientious service of love for humanity in wartime," created a peace section in 1924. The organization hosted gatherings of pacifist groups in Paris, Berlin, Vienna, Geneva, Warsaw, and Moscow.

The AFSC also provided humanitarian aid to Germany and Poland following World War I. In Germany, the AFSC organized a relief effort that, with the help of many German volunteers, fed over one million children daily during 1921 and 1922. "Feeding the hungry and clothing the naked is spectacular and inspiring work," said the AFSC's 1928 Annual Report. But, the report continued, "it is a much harder task to prevent war, to encourage nations to settle their differences by arbitration, to develop a new type of patriotism."

■■ **Following World War I, the international community and private organizations made efforts to prevent future wars.**

The issue of equality. One human rights issue—that of equality—met with less success following World War I. Japan, a member of the winning coalition, asked at the Paris Peace Conference that a statement affirming the principle of racial equality be included in the League of Nations Covenant. The Japanese and other Asians, not to mention Africans, had long labored under the stigma of racial inferiority in dealings with Europeans and Americans. Having helped defeat the German alliance, the Japanese wanted a formal statement of their equality.

The other victors refused. President Wilson knew that he would have enough difficulty getting the Senate to approve the peace treaty. To add a section on racial equality risked increasing opposition among lawmakers from western states, where immigration from Asia had historically been a sensitive issue, and from southern states, where many whites took racial inequality for granted. The British government faced similar political problems and likewise declined to back the Japanese request.

NEW THREATS TO HUMAN RIGHTS

During the 1920s it was possible for human rights advocates to believe they were regaining some of the ground lost during World War I, but during the 1930s they lost this sense of optimism. The Great Depression fostered the rise of Fascist governments in Germany and Spain and strengthened the already-existing Fascist government of Italy.

During the 19th and early 20th centuries, the trend among most countries, especially in Europe and the Americas, had been in the direction of greater individual rights and freedom.

But the rise of fascism and communism reversed the trend. Fascism, like communism in the Soviet Union, was based on the idea that the needs of society were more important than the rights of individuals. In fact, in this view, only the state had rights; individuals had responsibilities. Mussolini explained the concept by comparing individuals within the nation to atoms within the human body. Each was significant only insofar as it worked for the good of the greater being.

Fascism was dangerous to human rights in another way as well. Fascists preached that particular ethnic and racial groups were superior to others. Nazism—the form fascism took in Germany—was the most racist of all. Adolf Hitler and other Nazis gave countless speeches praising the supposed virtues of the "Aryan race" and expressing their distaste for other races and peoples.

Sometimes Hitler's boasting merely made him look foolish. In 1936 Germany hosted the summer Olympic Games. Hitler predicted that Germany's "Aryan" athletes would defeat all others, demonstrating the physical superiority of the German nation. Much to Hitler's disappointment, Jesse Owens of the United States—an African American and therefore, by Hitler's reckoning, a member of one of the inferior races—trounced Germany's athletes, and all others, winning four gold medals. Even as spectators loudly applauded Owens, Hitler remarked to a colleague, "The Americans ought to be ashamed of themselves for

▲ During World War II some German Jews were forced to wear signs reading, "I am a Jew, but I will not grumble about the Nazis."

letting their medals be won by Negroes. I myself would never shake hands with one of them."

On other occasions Hitler's racist philosophy had far more vicious consequences. Hitler and the Nazis blamed many of Germany's problems on Jews, carrying anti-Semitism to terrible extremes. The exclusion of "non-Aryans" from the civil service, the stripping of German Jews of their citizenship, and the events of *Kristallnacht* (see Chapter 15) only foreshadowed the horrors of the Holocaust.

The brutality of the 1930s was not limited to Europe. Japan's government was not Fascist, but it was militaristic and violent. Japan invaded China during the 1930s and inflicted mass atrocities on those Chinese not fortunate enough to escape. Japan's 1937 assault on Nanjing (Nanking) was especially horrific. For weeks Japanese soldiers engaged in a campaign of terror against the inhabitants of the city. Millions were left homeless and tens of thousands were killed. One observer said that men, women, and children in the streets "were hunted like rabbits. Everyone seen to move was shot."

◀ Jesse Owens, shown with three of his four gold medals, helped disprove the Nazis' theory of Aryan superiority in the 1936 Berlin Olympics.

■■ Fascism endangered human rights by preaching the supremacy of the state over the individual and by fostering violent racism. Japanese militarism trampled human rights in China.

During the 1930s most Americans did their best to ignore the human rights violations taking place in Europe and Asia. Struggling to cope with the Great Depression, Americans were hesitant to sacrifice their lives and money to safeguard the rights of other people.

MORE WAR, MORE ATROCITIES

Events in Europe, however, soon forced Americans to pay attention. As the troubles of the 1930s erupted into World War II, all the atrocities of World War I were repeated on an even larger scale. The fighting in the Soviet Union alone left 18 million or more people dead. In China perhaps 15 million died. Poland lost almost 6 million. Germany lost more than 4 million, Japan some 2 million.

More than any previous war, World War II placed civilians at the center of the fighting. Aerial bombardment of cities played an important role in the strategy of both sides, from the German attacks on London in 1940 to the Allied firebombing of Dresden and Tokyo and the U.S. atomic bombing of Hiroshima and Nagasaki. Unavoidably, and in some cases deliberately, most of the casualties in the bombing attacks against cities were civilians.

Some atrocities took place far from the fighting. Japan, for example, forcibly removed thousands of Korean men from their homeland to work in Japanese war industries and to fight in the war.

And in the most appalling atrocity of the war years—the Nazi Holocaust—some six million Jews and millions of others were killed (see Chapter 16).

■■ **World War II witnessed massive violations of human rights, including the attempted genocide of the Jews in the Holocaust.**

RENEWED HUMAN RIGHTS EFFORTS

With the war raging on and human rights in grave peril, President Roosevelt helped initiate what he termed a "declaration by United Nations." Issued at the start of 1942 by the United States and 25 other nations fighting against Germany and Japan, the declaration reaffirmed the principles of the Atlantic Charter and pledged the signing nations to "defend life, liberty, independence, and religious freedom, and to preserve human rights and justice in their own lands as well as in other lands." The declaration built not only on the Atlantic Charter but also on an earlier speech of Roosevelt's in which he had told Congress that it must be the goal of the United States to guarantee a world founded on "four essential human freedoms—freedom of speech and expression, freedom of worship, freedom from want, freedom from fear."

After the war ended, the international community took further steps to safeguard human rights. In the Nuremberg trials, Nazi leaders were convicted of planning and participating in genocide as well as in a host of other "crimes

◀ **On April 30, 1945, prisoners in the concentration camp at Dachau, Germany, cheered as the U.S. Seventh Army set them free.**

▲ Hideki Tōjō, former Japanese general, testifies on his own behalf during war crimes trials in Tokyo, Japan, on December 26, 1947.

against humanity." The message was clear: certain human rights must be respected regardless of a person's nationality or ethnic background. This concern with human rights was also enshrined in the United Nations. The organization committed itself to a new order in the world, as expressed by the preamble to its 1945 charter:

66 We the peoples of the United Nations determined . . . to reaffirm faith in fundamental human rights, in the dignity and worth of the human person, in the equal rights of men and women and of nations large and small . . . have resolved to combine our efforts to accomplish these aims. 99

The charter also declared that the organization would promote "universal respect for . . . human rights and fundamental freedoms for all without distinction as to race, sex, language or religion."

Some UN member nations, however, remained unsatisfied with the charter and called for the inclusion of a Bill of Rights. President Truman endorsed this idea, declaring "The Charter is dedicated to the achievement and observance of human rights and fundamental freedoms. Unless we can attain those objectives . . . we cannot have permanent peace and security." On December 10, 1948, the United Nations General Assembly adopted the **Universal Declaration of Human Rights** "as a common standard of achievement for all peoples and all nations." The document went on to list a series of rights held by "all human beings."

As important as the Declaration of Human Rights was, it was not binding on all nations. It was a statement of intent but provided no means of enforcement. Indeed, many countries insisted that any efforts at enforcement would violate another UN principle—the guarantee of national sovereignty. This apparent contradiction would remain an issue for years to come.

■■ **After World War II, the international community tried to protect human rights by forming the UN and by issuing the Universal Declaration of Human Rights.**

SECTION 2 REVIEW

IDENTIFY and explain the significance of the following: Geneva Convention, Red Cross, Hague Peace Conferences, American Friends Service Committee, Jesse Owens, Universal Declaration of Human Rights.

1. **MAIN IDEA** What effect did World War I have on people's thinking about human rights? What types of efforts to protect human rights arose following the war?

2. **MAIN IDEA** How did fascism in Europe and militarism in Japan affect human rights between World War I and World War II?

3. **MAIN IDEA** What steps did the international community take to safeguard human rights after World War II?

4. **WRITING TO INFORM** Imagine you are a member of a private peace organization during the 1920s. Write a brochure explaining how individuals might promote international peace.

5. **COMPARING** In what ways did World War I and World War II present similar threats to human rights? How were the efforts to protect human rights sparked by both wars similar?

STRIVING FOR EQUALITY

FOCUS

- How did the struggle for racial equality progress in the years after World War II?
- What setbacks did the struggle for racial equality experience?
- What features marked the struggle for women's rights in the postwar years?

In the years after World War II, the international community resumed its progress toward greater respect for human rights. Decolonization represented progress toward racial equality, as did the dismantling of the system of racial segregation in the United States. The struggle for equal rights for women, like the struggle for racial equality, increasingly became a worldwide struggle.

Benazir Bhutto, prime minister of Pakistan, 1988

THE FIGHT FOR RACIAL EQUALITY

The wave of decolonization that swept across Asia and Africa during the years after World War II (see Chapter 23) represented one of the most important advances for human rights during the 20th century. The essence of the Western imperialism of the late 1800s and early 1900s was the belief that certain groups of people—typically Europeans—were suited to governing themselves and others, and that other groups of people—typically Asians and Africans—were suited to being governed. Thus decolonization was not simply an advance for the principle of political equality; it was also an advance for racial equality.

Worldwide effects of decolonization.

The struggle for decolonization had significant effects on the contest for racial equality in other parts of the world. In the United States, Americans had long prided themselves on being more enlightened, in terms of human rights, than people in most other countries. For the most part this was true, with the glaring exception of the second-class treatment given African Americans and members of other ethnic minority groups. Yet as long as the countries of Western Europe—those closest to the United States in terms of respect for human rights—held colonies in Africa and Asia, Americans could comfort themselves that their system of racial segregation was, comparatively speaking, not so bad. As the Europeans freed their colonies, however, Americans found themselves in the position of being undeniably backward on the question of race.

This did not escape the notice of civil rights advocates. One of these advocates, Edwin Embree, spoke in 1945 about the changes occurring in the larger world and their importance for African Americans:

66 The white man of the Western world is offered his last chance for equal status in world society. If he accepts equality, he can hold a self-respecting place—maybe a leading place—in the new order. . . . But if the Western white man persists in trying to run the show, in exploiting the whole earth, in treating the hundreds of millions of his

neighbors as inferiors, then the fresh might of the billion and a half nonwhite, non-Western people may in a surging rebellion smash him into nonentity. **99**

In addition, many of the leaders of the American civil rights movement took inspiration from the methods used by anticolonial leaders. The nonviolent tactics that Mahatma Gandhi used against the British in India served as a particularly important model for U.S. civil rights strategies. Franklin McCain, one of the students who participated in the Greensboro lunch-counter sit-in of 1960, later recalled, "The individual who had probably the most influence on us was Gandhi, more than any single individual." And Martin Luther King, Jr., traveled to India to see the results of Gandhi's efforts and to meet many of his disciples. After King returned he told American civil rights activists that they were taking "honored places in the world-wide struggle for freedom."

Africa and America.
The decolonization movement in Africa also had significant repercussions in America. The struggle for civil rights for African Americans and the nationalist movements in Africa already had a historical connection: one of the major influences on African nationalism was the Pan-Africanist movement begun by black American and Caribbean leaders like W.E.B. Du Bois and Marcus Garvey. Then, as African nations began to gain independence in the 1950s and 1960s, many African Americans were inspired by their example to intensify the struggle for equal rights in the United States.

In 1964, for example, African American singer and actor Harry Belafonte sponsored a delegation of members of the Student Nonviolent Coordinating Committee on a tour of Africa. Most of the participants found the experience electrifying. "I saw black men flying the airplanes, driving buses, sitting behind big desks in the bank and just doing everything that I was used to seeing white people do," one SNCC worker, Fannie Lou Hamer, later remembered. Just as African nationalists had been inspired by African American leaders in the struggle for racial equality and civil rights, so now African nationalists were inspiring a new generation of African American leaders. It was not a coincidence that the busiest period of progress toward racial equality in the United States and the busiest period of decolonization in Africa both occurred during the decade between 1955 and 1965.

UN efforts.
Legislation promoting racial equality in the United States was mirrored in the United Nations' efforts to end racism throughout the world. In 1965 the UN established the **Convention on the Elimination of All Forms of Racial Discrimination**. Under the terms of this agreement, which took effect in 1969, the signing nations agreed to declare the spread of ideas advocating any form of racial superiority or hatred to be illegal and punishable by law. Even further, the agreement called on the signers to outlaw all organizations engaging in such activities. By 1987, 129 nations had ratified the Convention.

■■ **Decolonization, the outlawing of racial segregation in the United States, and UN efforts to end racism worldwide represented steps toward racial equality.**

▲ **Martin Luther King, Jr., and his wife meet Indian Prime Minister Jawaharlal Nehru on their monthlong visit to India in 1959.**

SOUTH AFRICA

The road toward racial equality was not a one-way street, however. At the same time the United States was beginning to dismantle its system of racial segregation, another country—South Africa—was reinforcing its system. Racial discrimination had been a fact of life in South Africa

Songs of Freedom

Although African nationalism provided inspiration for civil rights leaders in the United States, the roots of the U.S. civil rights movement lay in America's slave past. The black struggle for equality in the 1950s and 1960s was based on an African American culture of great spiritual depth that had arisen out of the experience of slavery in the South.

As a result of this rich cultural heritage—together with continued and often brutal oppression—the movement for African American rights began not in the North, as many people of the time expected, but in the South. Southern black musical traditions, in particular, helped fuel the civil rights movement in its drive to end racial discrimination and violence against blacks.

Wyatt Tee Walker, an aide to Martin Luther King. Jr., summed up the impact of music on the movement when he stated that "there was no movement in the South that was not a great singing movement." During the Montgomery bus boycott, for example, Georgia Black of the Holt Street Baptist Church—where the boycott officially began—

sang slave songs to inspire blacks to continue to oppose segregated seating on buses:

> **❝** We got to hold up the
> Bloodstained banner
> One Day I'm gonna get old
> And Can't fight anymore
> But I'm gonna
> Fight anyhow
> We got to hold it up
> Until we die. **❞**

Dorothy Cotton, who worked with the Southern Christian Leadership Conference, recalled that during the 1960s, meetings to encourage blacks to vote "began with the songs of our ancestors. . . . Fannie Lou [Hamer] would stand up and tell tales of intimidation of people on plantations and sing her songs." One of the songs Hamer inspired her listeners with was "This Little Light of Mine":

> **❝** The light that shines is the
> light of Love
> Lights the darkness from
> above
> It shines on me, and shines
> on you
> And shows what the power
> of love can do
> I'm gonna shine my light both
> far and near

> I'm gonna shine my light both
> bright and clear
> Where there's a dark corner
> in this land
> I'm gonna let my little light
> shine. **❞**

Singing provided a source of inspiration and strength to the movement especially during periods of hardship. When Freedom Riders were arrested and jailed in Jackson, Mississippi, many of them sang as a way of keeping up their spirits. Prison officials feared the power of the music and threatened to take away the singers' mattresses if they kept singing. But they continued to sing anyway:

> **❝** Ain't gonna let nobody
> turn me 'round
> turn me 'round, turn me
> 'round
> Ain't gonna let nobody turn
> me 'round
> I'm gonna keep on a-walking,
> keep on a-talkin'
> Marchin' up to
> freedom land. **❞**

In 1942, renowned singer and actor Paul Robeson—who himself worked very hard to preserve slave songs—had remarked that he believed southern blacks to be "a race that has come through its trials unbroken, a race of such magnificence of spirit that there exists no power on earth that could crush them." Robeson knew that the freedom struggle to come would be based on the cultural riches of the black past.

▼ **Both blacks and whites joined this march for civil rights.**

for many years, but not until the late 1940s did the government put a rigid system of legal separation of the races, called apartheid, into effect.

Ironically, apartheid was to some degree a reaction to the same events that were causing Americans to end their system of segregation. As independence movements gained strength in black Africa, the whites who ruled South Africa, which had gained its independence from Britain in 1910, feared black South Africans' demands for political and social equality. This white minority used apartheid as a way of reinforcing its position against these demands.

Black South Africans protested the policy of apartheid, as did some white South Africans. Many blacks died in the protests, while others were driven into exile. Still others were arrested and sentenced to long prison terms. One such person was Nelson Mandela, a leader of the **African National Congress**, the major black nationalist organization in South Africa.

Many nations around the world also objected to the policy of apartheid. Some imposed economic sanctions on South Africa, and in 1973 the UN General Assembly passed the **Convention on the Suppression of Apartheid**.

■■ **The establishment of apartheid in South Africa represented a step backward in global efforts to secure racial equality.**

▲ Nelson Mandela is shown at a 1995 Freedom Day celebration in Pretoria, South Africa, marking the first anniversary of South Africa's first democratic election.

WOMEN'S RIGHTS IN THE POSTWAR ERA

As in the struggle to end slavery, women played an important part in the campaign for racial equality. And as in the earlier fight, the struggle on behalf of other people's civil rights made many women aware of the need to fight for their own rights. French feminist Simone de Beauvoir, for example, likened the condition of women in a male-dominated society to that of Asians and Africans under Western imperialism and to that of blacks who suffered under white oppression.

The question of equality for women was not just a Western problem. In parts of Southwest Asia and North Africa, for example, some male authorities sought to restrict women's activities. Though men sometimes cited the Qur'an, the holy book of Islam, as justification for their actions, some prominent Muslim women denied that Islam provided grounds for the subjugation of women. For instance, Jehan Sadat, the wife of Egyptian president Anwar Sadat, declared:

▲ During the mid-1900s Simone de Beauvoir, noted French intellectual and feminist, called for the abolition of the myth of the "eternal feminine."

❝ Nothing in our religion supported the total subservience of women. In no place in the Quran is it written that women must remain at home and do no work in public. No. The Quran treats men and women equally, in life and in death. ❞

Women like Jehan Sadat sometimes traveled to Europe and the United States and observed the comparative freedoms women enjoyed there. For example, by the 1970s nearly all legal barriers to sexual equality in the United States had been eliminated, although the proposed Equal Rights Amendment to the Constitution fell short of the 38-state approval required for ratification (see Chapter 21).

▲ Demonstrators rallied at the Lincoln Memorial on October 12, 1981, in an attempt to obtain ratification of the Equal Rights Amendment.

Some women of the Middle East liked what they saw and called for women's rights comparable to those in the West. But others rejected Western notions of women's rights. In the Islamic world particularly, women's movements often proclaimed the rights of women not in Western terms but as laid down in the Qur'an. In part, perhaps, this was because, at least in theory, Muslim women had long had some rights—such as the right to initiate legal action and the right to own property—which Western women had only recently attained.

Some Muslim governments, however, took a different view of Muslim religious law. The most extreme example occurred in Afghanistan after the Taliban religious army gained power in 1996. One of their first acts was to order women to cover themselves completely—even their faces, when in public—to close schools for girls, and to prohibit women from working.

In political life Western nations were not alone in granting women prominent roles. At a time when few American women held high elective office and none had been seriously considered as a presidential candidate, several countries chose women leaders. Indira Gandhi became prime minister of India following an impressive performance as the nation's minister of information and broadcasting. Her actions, contrasted to those of her male colleagues, won her a reputation as "the only man in a Cabinet of old women," according to one observer.

Gandhi was not alone. Golda Meir, a Russian-born, American-raised Israeli, assumed the premiership of Israel in 1969. In 1979 Margaret Thatcher became prime minister of Great Britain and held that office longer than anyone else in the 20th century. In the Philippines Corazon Aquino became president in 1986. Benazir Bhutto, elected prime minister of Pakistan in 1988, became the first female leader of an Islamic nation. And in the 1990s women were also elected to head the governments of Nicaragua, Norway, and Turkey.

▼ Indira Gandhi, daughter of Jawaharlal Nehru, served as prime minister of India from 1966 to 1977 and from 1980 to 1984.

■■ The struggle for women's rights became increasingly global after World War II. But not all women defined rights in the same way.

 SECTION 3 REVIEW

IDENTIFY and explain the significance of the following: Convention on the Elimination of All Forms of Racial Discrimination, Nelson Mandela, African National Congress, Convention on the Suppression of Apartheid, Simone de Beauvoir, Jehan Sadat, Benazir Bhutto.

1. **MAIN IDEA** What events advanced the struggle for racial equality following World War II?

2. **MAIN IDEA** How did the establishment of apartheid in South Africa affect the struggle for racial equality?

3. **MAIN IDEA** What were some of the characteristics of efforts to secure women's rights after World War II?

4. **WRITING TO EVALUATE** Imagine you are a U.S. civil rights leader. Write an article that evaluates the relationship between the U.S. civil rights movement and decolonization in Asia and Africa.

5. **SYNTHESIZING** How did the post–World War II movements to secure racial equality and women's rights build on the successes of earlier efforts?

THE CONTINUING STRUGGLE

FOCUS

■ How did efforts to protect human rights fare in the 1960s and early 1970s?

■ How did the Carter administration deal with human rights?

■ What human rights improvements have taken place in recent years? What threats to human rights remain?

*B*eyond the fight for racial and sexual equality, the post–World War II period witnessed a continuing international effort to expand human rights. The United Nations issued important proclamations on human rights, and during the late 1970s the administration of Jimmy Carter made respect for human rights a priority in American diplomacy. A major breakthrough for human rights came with the end of the Cold War, which had led to many rights violations. Yet threats to human rights remained.

Soviet physicist Andrei Sakharov voting in Moscow, 1989

HUMAN RIGHTS AND THE COLD WAR

Human rights continued to be central to UN activities in the decades following decolonization. In 1966 the UN General Assembly approved two covenants on human rights. The first was the **Covenant on Civil and Political Rights**. The nations signing this covenant pledged not to take actions that would interfere with the liberties of individuals.

The second agreement was the **Covenant on Economic, Social, and Cultural Rights**. Its provisions were different from the first set, for many of them required governments not only to refrain from certain actions but also to take positive measures such as providing jobs, increasing educational opportunities, and improving health care.

The absence of any enforcement agency, however, made the covenants little more than promises, and many nations disregarded them. For example, the Soviet Union often subjected political dissidents

such as Andrei Sakharov to "internal exile" in Siberia. Other dissidents were committed to psychiatric hospitals for "antisocial behavior." China, too, was frequently criticized for its treatment of dissidents and for other human rights abuses.

Communist countries were not the only ones where human rights were threatened. Many right-wing regimes—some of which were supported by the U.S. government in its eagerness to fight communism worldwide—also had little tolerance for political dissent. This was particularly true in Central and South America. For example, the Pinochet regime in Chile, which seized power after the 1973 overthrow of Salvador Allende (see Chapter 21), was frequently cited by human rights organizations for its use of torture and for repressing political opposition.

■■ During the postwar years the UN reaffirmed its support for human rights. However, human rights violations continued.

CARTER AND HUMAN RIGHTS

When Jimmy Carter took office as president in 1977, he resolved to make human rights a major concern of U.S. foreign policy. For too long, Carter said, the United States had allowed its fear of communism to govern all actions. For too long the nation had tolerated the human rights abuses of certain regimes simply because they were anticommunist.

To help implement his human rights policy, Carter appointed Patricia Derian as the assistant secretary of state for human rights and humanitarian affairs. Derian, a former civil rights worker from Mississippi, had no patience for those who argued that the United States might realistically have to tolerate moderately repressive regimes. She demanded to know what "moderately repressive" meant: "That you only torture half of the people?"

▲ Patricia Derian opposed aid to repressive regimes.

In her work at the State Department, Derian tried to pressure countries to improve their human rights records by linking human rights to U.S. economic aid. For example, when the U.S. government sent offers of aid to Brazil, El Salvador, Guatemala, Uruguay, and Argentina, Derian's staff attached critiques of the human rights records of those countries' governments. Such efforts did not always produce the desired results; many nations refused U.S. aid and criticized Carter for interfering in their internal affairs.

Some human rights advances did, however, occur while Carter was in office. Indonesia, for example, released thousands of political prisoners; Argentina eased up on repression of dissent. Equally important, Carter's policy sent the message that the United States placed human rights at the top of its diplomatic agenda. For the United Nations to issue paper proclamations in favor of human rights was one thing; for the world's most powerful country to employ its political leverage and economic muscle on behalf of human rights was something else.

■■ During the late 1970s President Carter made human rights a centerpiece of U.S. foreign policy.

THE END OF THE COLD WAR

Some of Carter's critics complained that he devoted his main efforts to nations they considered to be minor offenders of human rights, such as Argentina, while leaving major offenders like the Soviet Union alone. This criticism was not entirely justified. For example, Carter engaged in a correspondence with Soviet dissident Andrei Sakharov that outraged the Kremlin and highlighted the need for reform of the Soviet system. Nevertheless, there was something to the claim that human rights would have been advanced more by even small changes in the Soviet Union than by large changes in most smaller countries.

During the late 1980s and early 1990s, changes in the Soviet Union did take place, and they were not small. Just as the breakup of the European empires in Asia and Africa had boosted human rights, so too did the collapse of the Soviet sphere. The region's new governments did not perfectly protect human rights—particularly when ethnic tensions led to violence, as in Yugoslavia. But in general, the new systems were an improvement over what they replaced. Repressive institutions had come crumbling down. Democratic elections gave people a chance to choose their own leaders.

Recent improvements in human rights cannot all be directly linked to the end of the Cold War. In South Africa, for example, apartheid began to crumble in the late 1980s, and in 1990 the South African government released Nelson Mandela and others who had been imprisoned for protesting apartheid. In 1994 the nation held its first election in which blacks were free to vote and elected Nelson Mandela president.

■■ The collapse of the Soviet system and the end of apartheid in South Africa led to improvements in human rights.

▼ In 1988, Armenians rallied in Moscow's Armenian cemetery to protest the treatment of Armenians in Azerbaijan.

REMAINING CHALLENGES

Despite human rights improvements around the world, some nations are still being criticized for violations. Although every nation in the world has banned slavery, many people—particularly women and children—continue to labor under the slave-like conditions of debt bondage in countries such as Mauritania, Nepal, Pakistan, and the Sudan.

Although the Communist government of China has permitted economic reform, it has resisted political reform and has stifled dissent, as the Tiananmen Square bloodbath demonstrated. The rights issue in China stirred considerable interest among Americans when President Clinton announced that the United States would revoke China's trade privileges if the Chinese government did not improve its human rights record. China made few significant changes to its policies, but Clinton backed down and renewed the trade privileges anyway.

Another Asian nation that has come under attack for human rights violations is Burma. After seizing power in 1988, the new military government proceeded to suppress dissenters. One such dissenter was Daw Aung San Suu Kyi (daw awng sahn sue chee).

 BIO GRAPHY Born in 1945, Suu Kyi was the daughter of a hero of the 1940s Burmese independence movement against British rule. Although Suu Kyi lived most of her adult life in the West, she returned to Burma in 1988. With two other opposition leaders, she formed a movement to restore democracy.

The military government responded in 1989 by placing her under house arrest. But Suu Kyi's convictions remained firm. Even when the government offered to free her if she ceased her political efforts and left the country, she refused. Her vision of the ideal government was similar to that of many other political reformers throughout the world:

▶ **Daw Aung San Suu Kyi**

> **❝** To provide the people with . . . peace and security, rulers must observe . . . the concepts of truth, righteousness, and loving kindness. It is government based on these very qualities that the people of Burma are seeking in their struggle for democracy. **❞**

HUMAN RIGHTS ABUSES AROUND THE WORLD IN 1995

Amnesty International, a London-based organization that publicizes cases of political repression, torture, and the imprisonment of people for their political beliefs, reported that the following abuses and events took place in 1995:

- **EUROPE:** In the United Kingdom, armed political groups killed 60 people. In Germany and France, citizens filed reports charging local police officers with murder, torture, and racial or ethnic discrimination.
- **ASIA:** In China, hundreds of political activists were arbitrarily detained and subjected to unfair trials, as were members of religious and ethnic minority groups. Many reported widespread torture in jail. In Afghanistan, thousands of people died when combatants in the nation's civil war directed attacks at civilians.
- **LATIN AMERICA:** In Brazil, extralegal death squads assassinated hundreds of people, many of whom were children

and teenagers. Journalists and church workers investigating the situation received constant death threats. Colombia's security forces and paramilitary groups detained around 140 people, who "disappeared" soon after.
- **AFRICA:** In Burundi, civilian gangs murdered thousands of people, many because of their ethnicity. In Angola and Chad, government forces executed many citizens without benefit of trial.
- **THE MIDDLE EAST:** In Iran, as in Iraq and Tunisia, many people were imprisoned for political reasons and without trial. In Egypt, military "courts" subjected government opponents to "grossly unfair" trials.

AT GREATEST RISK Many repressive countries targeted human rights supporters for persecution. "Human rights defenders often became the first victims of governments trying to build a good human rights image abroad and fearful of the damage human rights activists can do to that image," said Amnesty International.

? **EVALUATING** Why is imprisoning or punishing a person without trial considered to be a human rights violation?

Amnesty International Symbol

HUMAN RIGHTS OR CULTURAL IMPERIALISM?

Some people, particularly in non-Western nations, object to what they perceive as a Western emphasis on the importance of individual rights. Many claim that their conceptions of rights are governed by a different set of cultural values that place more emphasis on communities of people than on individuals. They claim that when the United States and other Western nations try to impose their sense of human rights on other peoples, these nations are practicing a form of cultural imperialism. "Human rights in Iran are based on Islamic values," said Iran's foreign minister in 1994 in response to complaints from Western human rights groups about some Iranian policies. "We will not accept the values of foreign countries imposed on us under the cover of human rights."

Even some Westerners are critical of Western nations' attempts to influence human rights policies elsewhere. In the British newspaper *The Guardian,* John Gray of Oxford University wrote:

> **❝F**or the most part, Western thought and policy remain based on the premise that Western ideals and practices have universal authority. . . . The American presumption is that any regime that does not conform to Western, and more particularly American, conceptions of human rights is tyrannical and illegitimate. The hubris [arrogant pride] expressed in this American belief is staggering. After all, America ranks foremost among Western societies in its record for homicide and other forms of violent crime. . . . If the U.S. has been unable to protect the ordinary liberties of its citizenry . . . , by what right does it judge the Asian countries?**❞**

For her efforts, Suu Kyi was awarded the Nobel Peace Prize in 1991. Still under house arrest, however, she was unable to attend the awards ceremony in Oslo, Norway.

▪▪ Even in the post–Cold War era, challenges to human rights remained in nations such as China and Burma.

SECTION 4 REVIEW

IDENTIFY and explain the significance of the following: Covenant on Civil and Political Rights, Covenant on Economic, Social, and Cultural Rights, Patricia Derian, Daw Aung San Suu Kyi.

1. **MAIN IDEA** How did the United Nations show its support for human rights in the 1960s? How successful were the UN efforts at preventing human rights violations over the following years?

2. **MAIN IDEA** What approach did President Carter take toward the issue of human rights in American foreign policy?

3. **IDENTIFYING CAUSE AND EFFECT** What effects did the end of the Cold War have on human rights? How have human rights improved in South Africa?

4. **WRITING TO CREATE** Imagine you are a political prisoner in China or Burma. Write a poem about the events that landed you in prison.

5. **TAKING A STAND** To what extent do you think the United States should interfere when other nations take actions that many Americans consider to be human rights violations?

CHAPTER 26
Review

Parliament bans slavery in the British Empire.

Seneca Falls Convention held.

Geneva Convention signed.

Emmeline Pankhurst forms the Women's Social and Political Union in Britain.

Quakers found the AFSC.

1833 **1848** **1864** **1903** **1917**

WRITING A SUMMARY

Using the essential points of the chapter as a guide, write a summary of the chapter.

REVIEWING CHRONOLOGY

Number your paper 1 to 5. Study the time line above, and list the following events in the order in which they happened by writing the first next to 1, the second next to 2, and so on. Then complete the activity below.

1. UN approves two covenants on human rights.
2. Parliament bans slavery in the British Empire.
3. Tiananmen Square massacre occurs in China.
4. Jesse Owens wins four gold medals at Olympics.
5. Quakers found the AFSC.

Analyzing Why was the Universal Declaration of Human Rights of limited use in stopping human rights violations worldwide?

IDENTIFYING PEOPLE AND IDEAS

Explain the historical significance of each of the following people or terms.

1. John Locke
2. William Wilberforce
3. Women's Social and Political Union
4. Red Cross
5. Hague Peace Conferences
6. Jehan Sadat
7. Simone de Beauvoir
8. African National Congress
9. Patricia Derian
10. Covenant on Civil and Political Rights

UNDERSTANDING MAIN IDEAS

1. How was the struggle to abolish slavery in the 19th century a global effort?
2. What human rights violations occurred during and between World Wars I and II?
3. How was decolonization in Asia and in Africa related to the U.S. civil rights movement?
4. What major UN agreements have tried to promote international respect for human rights?
5. How have human rights improved in the former Soviet sphere? What are some of the nations in which human rights violations continue?

REVIEWING THEMES

1. **Democratic Values** How did the goals of the 19th-century women's movement reflect a link between women's rights and democracy?
2. **Global Relations** How have nations used economic means to encourage other nations to respect human rights? Give examples.
3. **Cultural Diversity** How have conceptions of human rights differed over time and from culture to culture? Give specific examples.

THINKING CRITICALLY

1. **Synthesizing** How did progressivism further the cause of human rights in the United States?
2. **Analyzing** Why did South Africa's white minority institute apartheid following World War II?
3. **Classifying** How might human rights be classified into several different categories?

STRATEGY FOR SUCCESS

Write a rough draft of a news story reporting on a current local, national, or international human rights issue. Then review the Strategies for Success on Evaluating News Stories on page 616. Read the drafts of the news stories prepared by two of your classmates, and take turns evaluating each others' stories. Revise your story after it has been evaluated.

UNITÉ INDIVISIBILITÉ DE LA RÉPUBLIQUE LIBERTÉ ÉGALITÉ FRATERNITÉ OU LA MORT

The motto of the French Revolution—"Unity, indivisibility of the Republic, liberty, equality, fraternity or death"—exemplified the growing concern for human rights during the late 18th century.

Nineteenth
Amendment gives
U.S. women the vote.

Japan conducts
campaign of terror in
Nanjing (Nanking).

SNCC members
tour Africa.

Tiananmen Square massacre occurs in China. Daw
Aung San Suu Kyi placed under house arrest in Burma.

Jesse Owens wins
four gold medals
at Olympics.

UN adopts the
Universal Declaration
of Human Rights.

UN approves two
covenants on
human rights.

Benazir Bhutto elected
prime minister
of Pakistan.

South Africa holds its first
national election open to
all South Africans.

| 1920 | 1936 | 1937 | 1948 | 1964 | 1966 | 1988 | 1989 | 1994 |

WRITING ABOUT HISTORY

Writing to Express a Viewpoint In the style of the Declaration of Independence or the Declaration of the Rights of Man and Citizen, write a statement expressing your own conceptions of human rights. Be sure to list the rights that you believe are most important.

USING PRIMARY SOURCES

In 1963 Nelson Mandela was arrested for his role in protesting apartheid in South Africa. Read the following excerpt from his trial, in which Mandela explains some of the grievances held by black South Africans. What human rights violations does Mandela describe in the passage? To what extent do you think conditions in South Africa have improved since the 1960s?

    66 *We fight against two features which are the hallmarks of African life in South Africa and which are entrenched by legislation which we seek to have repealed. These features are poverty and lack of human dignity. . . .*

    South Africa is the richest country in Africa, and could be one of the richest in the world. But it is a land of extremes and remarkable contrasts. The Whites enjoy what may well be the highest standard of living in the world, whilst Africans live in poverty and misery. Forty per cent of the Africans live in hopelessly overcrowded and, in some cases, drought-stricken Reserves. . . . Thirty per cent are labourers, labour tenants, and squatters on White farms and work and live under conditions similar to those of the serfs of the Middle Ages. . . .

    The lack of human dignity experienced by Africans is the direct result of the policy of White supremacy. White supremacy implies Black inferiority. . . . Because of this sort of attitude, Whites tend to regard Africans as a separate breed. They do not look upon them

as people with families of their own; they do not realize that they have emotions—that they fall in love like White people do; that they want to be with their wives and children like White people want to be with theirs; that they want to earn enough money to support their families properly, to feed and clothe them and send them to school. 99

LINKING HISTORY AND GEOGRAPHY

Refer to the chart on page 716. What generalization can you make about where human rights abuses occurred in 1995?

BUILDING YOUR PORTFOLIO

Complete the following projects independently or cooperatively.

1. INTERNATIONAL COOPERATION In Chapter 24 you portrayed a WTO administrator discussing how international cooperation can benefit the global economy. Building on that experience, imagine you are a reporter researching United Nations efforts to protect human rights worldwide over the past few decades. Construct a time line tracing these efforts and write two or three sentences about each entry.

2. INDIVIDUAL RIGHTS In chapters 23 and 24 you explored the effects of imperialism and economic policies on individual rights. Building on that experience, imagine you are a black African in South Africa who has just voted in a national election for the first time. Write a letter to a friend describing the experience and explaining how it fits into the historical struggle for civil rights worldwide.

Chapter 27

A NEW ENVIRONMENTAL AWARENESS

FOCUS

UNDERSTANDING THE MAIN IDEA

Over the past two centuries, Americans have shifted their thinking on the natural environment away from views emphasizing the need to tame the wilderness to views stressing conservation and preservation. Since World War II, Americans have grown increasingly aware of the global character of environmental issues.

THEMES

■ **TECHNOLOGY AND SOCIETY** How might technological change affect the environment?

■ **GLOBAL RELATIONS** In what respects might environmental protection require international cooperation?

■ **ECONOMIC DEVELOPMENT** How might a nation balance environmental protection against economic development?

1872	1900	1973	1986	1992
Yellowstone National Park established.	Canadian Forestry Association founded.	Endangered Species Act passed.	Chernobyl accident occurs in Ukraine.	Earth Summit held in Rio de Janeiro.

American thinking on the environment grew out of a European agricultural tradition that arrived with the first English settlers. This tradition, which taught that nature existed to serve human needs, dominated American attitudes for centuries.

Attacking a right whale (1868), lithograph by Currier & Ives

In his 1851 novel *Moby Dick,* Herman Melville painted whaling in vivid detail. Describing the final battle between Captain Ahab and the great white whale, Melville wrote:

> 66 The harpoon was darted; the stricken whale flew forward; with igniting velocity the line ran through the groove;—ran foul. Ahab stooped to clear it; he did clear it; but . . . he was shot out of the boat, ere the crew knew he was gone. Next instant, the heavy eye splice in the rope's final end flew out of the stark-empty tub, knocked down an oarsman, and smiting the sea, disappeared in its depths. 99

Melville's book fared poorly upon publication. The public's reaction had little to do with opposition to whaling, however. The technology of the times kept whaling a relatively equal contest; as in Melville's tale, the whales sometimes killed those trying to kill them. Besides, the oceans were vast. There would always be more whales.

But whaling changed over the years. Hand-hurled harpoons gave way to explosive missiles, oars to high-powered engines, cries of "Thar she blows!" to the ping of sonar. Whaling acquired a grim efficiency that drove the great whales nearly to extinction. By the 1980s the public outcry was so strong that most seafaring nations agreed to ban commercial killing of the great whales.

The shift in public sentiment toward whaling mirrors a larger shift in environmental attitudes that has occurred over the past two centuries. Many people and governments now realize that the world's resources are not limitless.

Pitcher plants drawn by 19th-century German biologist Ernst Haeckel

OLD ATTITUDES AND NEW

FOCUS

- **How did most colonists and early Americans view the wilderness?**
- **How did some 19th-century Americans try to modify use of the environment?**
- **How did Darwin's work affect views on the environment?**

American Antiquarian Society

Farm family at work in the fields, 1760s woodcut

For much of the nation's early history, Americans placed more emphasis on taming the wilderness than on preserving it. Some people held different views, however, and by the beginning of the 20th century, conservation efforts were growing in number and importance.

SUBDUING THE WILDERNESS

When the first English settlers arrived in Virginia and New England in the early 17th century, the need to preserve the natural heritage of the land was almost the last thing on their minds. On the contrary, most of the new arrivals happily accepted the biblical command to establish control over the earth and "every living thing that moveth upon the earth." For these settlers the wilderness was something to be feared and conquered, not cherished and preserved. From the beginning they set about changing the "remote, rocky, barren, bushy, wild-woody wilderness" into "a second England for fertilness," as Massachusetts colonist Edward Johnson approvingly noted in 1653.

The colonists' approach to nature had grown out of a long tradition of land use. Their ancestors in Europe had been farmers. To them farming meant clearing the land of trees, plowing it, and planting crops. Unlike the Native Americans they encountered, the European colonists had access to metal tools and domesticated animals, which allowed them to bring greater areas of land under cultivation. These farmers transformed the natural environment and deprived many species of the habitat they needed. To the extent the land-clearers thought about it at all, most of them probably believed they had little choice in the matter: they needed the land.

As the U.S. population grew, settlement spread inland from the coast. New technologies increased people's ability to modify the landscape. Better roads made travel faster and cheaper, and the construction of steamboats and canals eventually provided better access to the country's interior. The construction of railroads brought most parts of the country within easy reach of cities and their markets. This spurred further settlement.

The most dramatic effect of the railroad boom on the environment was the destruction of the buffalo herds of the Great Plains. In the prerailroad era, the grasses of the Plains supported millions upon millions of buffalo and a thriving Plains Indian culture. The first railroad line across the Plains was completed in the late 1860s, bringing tourists, farmers, and hunters. At the urging of the

► Although the buffalo population once numbered in the millions, its ranks dwindled by the 1870s as hunters were paid from one dollar to three dollars for every hide sold. An 1883 study estimated that some 13 million buffalo had been slaughtered.

farmers, who wanted to fence and plow the grasslands, and the U.S. Army, who wanted to drive American Indians from the Plains, the hunters slaughtered thousands of buffalo daily. Hardly a generation had passed before the buffalo were on the verge of extinction.

■■ Most colonists and early Americans believed that nature existed for their benefit and that the wilderness ought to be subdued.

THE BEGINNINGS OF DISSENT

Even in the early years of the Republic, some citizens did not wish to see America's vast wilderness subdued. In the mid-19th century Ralph Waldo Emerson, Henry David Thoreau, and other **transcendentalists** called for a return to a simple life, one that enabled individuals to regain close touch with the natural world. "In the woods," wrote Emerson, "we return to reason and faith." Voicing a similar sentiment, Thoreau declared: "In Wildness is the preservation of the World."

The transcendentalists and others who shared their views of nature urged that certain lands be set aside in their wild state before the wilderness disappeared entirely. As early as 1859, New York newspaperman Samuel Hammond called for the creation of a nature reserve 100 miles in diameter in New York's Adirondack Mountains. He explained:

❝ I would make it a forest forever. It should be a misdemeanor to chop down a tree, and a felony to clear an acre within its boundaries. The old woods should stand here always as God made them, growing on until the earthworm ate away their roots, and the strong winds hurled them to the ground, and new woods should be permitted to supply the place of the old so long as the earth remained. ❞

Others, such as historian Frederick Jackson Turner, valued the wilderness and the frontier not only for its beauty but also for its effect on the American character. In an 1893 lecture he declared:

❝ The frontier is the line of most rapid and effective Americanization. The wilderness masters the colonist. . . . In short, at the frontier the environment is at first too strong for the man. He must accept the conditions which it furnishes, or perish. . . . Thus the advance of the frontier has meant a steady movement away from the influence of Europe, a steady growth of independence on American lines. ❞

Furthermore, Turner argued, "the most important effect of the frontier has been in the promotion of democracy." This belief in the connection between democracy and the frontier encouraged the efforts of those trying to protect the environment.

■■ Rejecting the idea of subduing the natural world, some 19th-century Americans favored preserving the wilderness.

THE BIRTH OF ECOLOGY

During the 19th century, developments in the natural sciences also increased public interest in the environment. Following the 1859 publication of Charles Darwin's *Origin of Species,* the theory of evolution—which argued that those organisms that were best adapted to their environment were most likely to survive and reproduce—took the scientific world by storm.

▲ Dr. Henry Cowles, seen in this 1924 photograph, proved that the juniper tree he is standing in was nearly 6,000 years old.

One result of the attention given to the environment was the development of a new science given the name *ecology* in 1866 by German biologist Ernst Haeckel. An enthusiastic supporter of Darwin, Haeckel argued that **ecology**—the study of the interrelationship of plants and animals with each other and with their environment—was a logical outgrowth of the study of evolution. Adopting the Darwinian idea of natural selection, the ecologists tried to identify how changes in the environment might determine which species gained an edge in the struggle for survival.

European botanists were the first to practice ecology, and their studies emphasized the relationship of plants to the environment. For example, Eugenius Warming, a Danish professor, showed how environmental factors such as heat and humidity affected plant growth.

By the 1890s the new science had spread to the United States. One of the first American ecologists, Henry C. Cowles, studied the way in

which an **ecosystem**—the interaction of living things with the environment—changes over time. Frederic Clements, who published *Research Methods in Ecology*—the first American book on the subject—argued that climate was the most important factor in determining the survival of competing species.

As the 20th century began, scientists became increasingly interested in the interaction of species with each other as well as with the environment. As one American ecologist, Victor Shelford, wrote:

> 66 Ecology is the science of communities. A study of the relations of a single species to the environment conceived without reference to communities . . . is not properly included in the field of ecology. 99

This concern for the whole biological community quite naturally led to a concern for conservation. Furthermore, some members of the new Ecological Society of America—founded in 1915 with Shelford as its first president—saw ecology as a science that would form the basis for natural resource management. In keeping with the progressive spirit of the time, they believed the science of ecology could provide the knowledge necessary to protect the environment.

■■ **Darwin's theory of evolution encouraged people to examine the ways in which humans interacted with the natural environment.**

 SECTION 1 REVIEW

IDENTIFY and explain the significance of the following: transcendentalists, Samuel Hammond, Charles Darwin, Ernst Haeckel, ecology, Henry C. Cowles, ecosystem, Frederic Clements.

1. **MAIN IDEA** How did most Americans view the environment during the 17th, 18th, and 19th centuries?

2. **MAIN IDEA** How did the transcendentalists view the environment?

3. **MAIN IDEA** How did Darwin's ideas contribute to the development of the science of ecology?

4. **WRITING TO EXPRESS A VIEWPOINT** Imagine you are an ecologist. Write an essay explaining why you think scientists should study the environment.

5. **EVALUATING** How might ecologists lend support to conservation efforts?

EXPANDING HORIZONS

FOCUS

■ **How did the progressives view natural resources?**

■ **In what ways did the preservationists differ from the conservationists?**

■ **How did the Dust Bowl disaster of the 1930s shape environmental thinking in the United States?**

The Progressive Era brought new prominence to environmental issues, but it also sharpened debate between conservationists and preservationists. The ecological disaster of the Dust Bowl made Americans more aware that environmental issues were a national concern.

Lumberjacks in Washington State, 1899

PROGRESSIVISM AND CONSERVATION

Although few Americans were familiar with the work of ecologists, environmental issues gained a new importance as the Progressive movement became influential around the beginning of the 20th century. Progressives believed that the government should actively tackle economic and political issues. These issues included control of America's natural resources.

Most progressives believed that the nation's natural resources ought to be used, but used wisely. The term they applied to this policy was **conservation**. For example, most looked with dismay on the large tracts of forests that were being cut with no concern beyond short-term profits. As the progressives sought greater influence in national politics, conservation became one of their priorities.

They got their chance in 1901 when Theodore Roosevelt became president. As a ranchowner in the Dakota Territory, Roosevelt had observed firsthand the way maximum use of ranges and forests, however profitable in the short

run, could cause long-term damage. Believing that people must judge the effects of their actions on the environment, he declared:

> 66 Conservation means development as much as it does protection. I recognize the right and duty of this generation to develop and use the natural resources of our land; but I do not recognize the right to waste them, or to rob, by wasteful use, the generations that come after us. 99

▶ **President Theodore Roosevelt appointed forestry expert Gifford Pinchot, shown here, as head of the U.S. Forest Service.**

▲ The Forest Service tries to prevent trees, such as these **California** redwoods, from becoming the blackened sticks that remain after a forest fire.

Roosevelt's chief lieutenant in the fight for conservation was Gifford Pinchot. As head of the Forest Service, Pinchot sought to expand the government's control of the nation's forests by enlarging "forest reserves," later called national forests. He also used a system of fees to regulate the use of forest resources.

Roosevelt and other progressives extended their conservation efforts to resources outside the control of the Forest Service. In 1902 Congress passed the Newlands Reclamation Act, which promoted irrigation projects in the West's arid regions. In addition, Roosevelt issued numerous executive orders establishing wildlife refuges across the country. He added Oregon's Crater Lake to the list of national parks and, to discourage the overgrazing that had already laid waste to much of the western range, instituted a system of fees for grazing on public lands.

Conservation issues were not confined to the United States. A number of Canadian officials were strongly influenced by American progressives' view that natural resources should be used wisely. The **Canadian Forestry Association**, founded in 1900, promoted national control of forest areas and called for fire prevention, more forest reserves, and better education for foresters. In 1909 representatives from Canada, Newfoundland, Mexico, and the United States met to identify common environmental problems and to establish national conservation commissions. Only Canada was successful in establishing a permanent commission, however. In Great Britain a private group, the Society for the

Promotion of Nature Reserves, was founded in 1912, but it was not until after World War II that the British government established the Nature Conservancy to acquire nature reserves.

■■ **Progressives and other conservationists believed that natural resources should be used, but used wisely.**

PRESERVATION VERSUS CONSERVATION

Roosevelt was not surprised that his efforts on behalf of conservation provoked opposition among people who were making money under the old system. He was more surprised at the objections raised by those who believed that conservation did not go far enough. These people favored **preservation**— that is, they wished to see America's wild areas left essentially untouched.

The preservationists followed in the tradition of Emerson and Thoreau, and their arguments echoed the transcendentalists' belief that the wilderness was a source of spiritual refreshment. Their efforts had led to the founding of the system of American national parks, of which Yellowstone, set aside in 1872, was the first. Yosemite followed in 1890.

The most influential preservationist was John Muir. He had led the fight for the creation of Yosemite National Park in California, and he and others of like mind founded the Sierra Club in 1892. Muir joined a deep appreciation for unspoiled nature to a talented pen, and his numerous articles and books placed the issue of preservation squarely before the public.

At a time when industrialization was intensifying the pace of life, Muir called on Americans to catch their breath and enjoy the gifts that nature so freely gave. Many Americans, he declared, had seen the light:

❝ Thousands of tired, nerve-shaken, over-civilized people are beginning to find out that going to the mountains is going home; that wildness is a necessity; and that mountain parks and reservations are useful not only as fountains of timber and irrigating rivers, but as fountains of life. ❞

Aldo Leopold

Another influential preservationist, Aldo Leopold, was one of the first to apply the principles of ecology to wildlife management. After graduating from Yale in 1909, he joined the Forest Service. He became the nation's leading expert on game, and in 1933 Leopold joined the faculty of the University of Wisconsin. Two years later he joined with others to found the Wilderness Society.

Leopold had begun his career as a firm believer in animal conservation, and he had supported killing wolves to protect deer populations. However, he changed his views on wildlife management after a research trip to Germany, where both forests and deer herds had been carefully managed since the 1400s. German forestry officials had come to recognize the importance of ecological principles to forest management, and in 1914 they started programs to restore mixed forests and wildlife. At the same time, however, German foresters continued to manage the forest for high timber yields and to use supplemental feeding to support large deer herds. The results—an overgrazed forest and stunted deer—dismayed Leopold. He realized that the Germans' techniques left too little room for natural forces and drove out many native species of plants and animals. Returning home convinced of the importance of a balanced environment, Leopold wrote:

> 66 We Americans, in most states at least, have not yet experienced a bearless, wolfless, eagleless, catless woods. We yearn for more deer and more pines, and we shall probably get them. But do we realize that to get them, as the Germans have, at the expense of their wild environment and their wild enemies, is to get very little indeed? 99

To a certain extent, the difference between the views of the preservationists and the conservationists was a matter of degree. The conservationists

▶ **Preservationists fought to save Yosemite's Hetch Hetchy Valley. Shown here before a dam was constructed to supply drinking water to San Francisco, the valley stretched nearly the length and width of Manhattan Island.**

believed that some land should be kept off-limits to loggers and ranchers, and the preservationists knew that they could not lock up the entire West.

■■ **Conservationists wanted to use wilderness resources wisely, but preservationists contended that wilderness was most valuable when left in its natural state.**

THE DUST BOWL ERA

From the 19th century through the first few decades of the 20th century, most environmental debates focused on the West. By the 1930s, however, many Americans were beginning to understand that abuse of natural resources posed problems for the entire nation.

In the early 20th century, American agriculture was centered in the Great Plains. A few people, however, began to ask if the Plains were really suited to farming. They noted that erosion increased and the creeks ran muddier as more and more acres were put to the plow. Terrible dust storms followed weeks of little rain.

Much of the grass that had once covered the Great Plains—and held the topsoil in place—was gone. What had not been plowed under to plant crops had been destroyed by overgrazing. Lamenting the loss, one Texas sheepherder declared that grass "saves us all. . . . Grass is what holds the earth together." Few people, however, listened. As farming and herding increased, the loss of grass and topsoil turned the Plains into an environmental time bomb.

The 1934 *Yearbook of Agriculture* quantified the damage: 100 million acres of cropland had lost

▲ Windblown topsoil, so desperately needed by Dust Bowl farmers, settles over this abandoned Oklahoma farmstead. Dunelike drifts of soil nearly bury a wagon wheel.

most or all of the topsoil, and an additional 125 million acres were rapidly losing topsoil. These statistics were driven home by the huge dust storms that raked the Great Plains during the 1930s. Thousands fled the Dust Bowl (see map on page 367). Many left behind houses buried to the windowsills in drifts of grit.

As Congress pondered what to do, a particularly monstrous storm carried dust from the Great Plains to Washington, D.C. The head of the Soil Conservation Service, testifying before a Senate committee, pointed out the window at the windborne soil and commented, "There, gentlemen, goes part of Oklahoma now."

Unable to ignore the environmental catastrophe on the Great Plains, Congress passed legislation to encourage conservation. This legislation, part of Franklin D. Roosevelt's New Deal, included measures to curtail grazing on drought-sensitive grassland and to encourage the planting of trees as windbreaks and the adoption of other soil-conserving agricultural practices.

Other New Deal programs encouraged the responsible use of natural resources. The Civilian Conservation Corps, for example, sent thousands of young men into the national forests to prevent fires and to plant tree seedlings. The Tennessee Valley Authority combined flood control with electrification projects. The Grand Coulee Dam on the Columbia River provided irrigation as well as hydroelectric power.

■■ The Dust Bowl disaster demonstrated the need for conservation and made the environment a national concern.

FDR's conservation programs took much the same approach as those of Theodore Roosevelt. The emphasis these New Deal programs placed on the wise use of resources demonstrated the degree to which environmental problems had acquired national significance.

Although the government supported a policy of conservation, Aldo Leopold and others who supported a policy of preservation continued to influence such government agencies as the Forest Service. After World War II, it was the preservationists who revived the environmental movement in the United States. And as American environmentalists began to deal with a wider range of environmental problems, they adopted a more global perspective.

◀ By using art to promote New Deal programs, painter Ben Shahn (1898–1969) worked to end the despair he depicted in his poster *Years of Dust.*

The Museum of Modern Art, New York

SECTION 2 REVIEW

IDENTIFY and explain the significance of the following: conservation, Canadian Forestry Association, preservation, John Muir, Aldo Leopold.

1. **MAIN IDEA** How did the rise of the Progressive movement affect interest in the environment?

2. **MAIN IDEA** How did preservationists and conservationists differ in their views on the environment?

3. **MAIN IDEA** How did the government respond to the problems of the Dust Bowl?

4. **WRITING TO EXPLAIN** Write an essay explaining how agricultural techniques contributed to the problems in the Dust Bowl.

5. **ANALYZING** How did Leopold's trip to Germany influence his views on wildlife conservation?

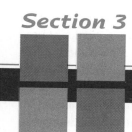

ENVIRONMENTALISM GOES GLOBAL

FOCUS

- How did the development of nuclear weapons encourage international cooperation on the environment?

- How did nuclear weapons tests threaten the environment? How did people respond?

- How did activists use political measures to draw attention to environmental problems?

Antinuclear protester Susan Ginzberg with her son, 1961

During the first three decades after World War II, radioactive fallout from nuclear weapons tests and the effects of large-scale pesticide use made the global nature of threats to the environment unmistakable. The increasing awareness of these threats sparked efforts to change public policy.

THE NUCLEAR AGE

Just as problems of the 1930s and the Great Depression made Americans aware of the importance of ecological problems, later events proved that the environment did not recognize political borders. In the aftermath of World War II, many people were convinced of the need to pay attention to international problems in order to prevent a repeat of the terrible economic, political, and military events of the 1930s and 1940s. Environmental problems were among those cast in global terms.

One of the most pressing environmental problems of the postwar era was the need to prevent nuclear war, which could have disastrous consequences not only for human populations but also for the environment. The worldwide fear of nuclear war led to a number of international agreements designed to limit the development and use of atomic weapons. The **Antarctic Treaty** of 1959 established Antarctica as a nuclear-free zone, and in 1968 the United States, Great Britain, the Soviet Union, and 59 other nations signed the **Nuclear Nonproliferation Treaty** to keep nuclear weapons technology from spreading to more countries. By 1987 more than 100 nations had ratified the treaty. In spite of these agreements, by the 1980s, 24 countries were believed to be capable of building nuclear weapons within a short period of time.

■■ **Fear of the effects of nuclear war encouraged governments to try to stop the proliferation of nuclear weapons.**

NUCLEAR FALLOUT

While the destructive power of a nuclear explosion was obvious, there was another effect, more subtle and difficult to detect—**nuclear fallout**, the radioactive debris that a nuclear explosion produced. For almost two decades after 1945, the countries that had developed nuclear weapons, especially the United States and the Soviet Union, tested their weapons in aboveground explosions. Each test released radioactive particles, which

▲ Fear of nuclear war and of radioactive fallout led to demonstrations such as this one outside San Francisco's city hall.

prevailing winds blew thousands of miles. Eventually, scientific instruments could detect radioactivity in nearly every area of the planet.

No one knew how nuclear fallout might affect people, but the radiation sickness that developed in the survivors of the Hiroshima and Nagasaki blasts frightened people around the world. Adding to their fears, radioactivity was not just polluting the air, it was showing up in the **food chain**. Rain washed radioactive particles, such as strontium 90, from the atmosphere and deposited them in the soil, where they were absorbed by agricultural crops. When people ate contaminated vegetables and fruits or meat and milk from animals that fed on contaminated plants, they concentrated the radioactive particles in their bodies.

Scientists debated the effects of this radiation. Some pointed out that humans have always been exposed to naturally occurring radiation. Others responded that while this was true, humans had never had this additional exposure. Some of these scientists predicted a rise in the incidence of cancer, particularly in children.

The potential threats nuclear fallout posed sparked an international outcry. Many people also

▶ This Geiger counter, which detects the presence and intensity of radioactivity, helps prospectors locate deposits of uranium—used in producing nuclear energy.

realized that ending nuclear pollution would require international cooperation. In the United States the National Committee for a Sane Nuclear Policy (SANE), formed in 1957, called for an end to testing and to the nuclear arms race. In Great Britain the Campaign for Nuclear Disarmament, or CND, advocated **unilateral disarmament**—the elimination of Britain's nuclear weapons despite the continued presence of nuclear weapons in the United States and the Soviet Union.

Although governments ignored many of the nuclear protests, both the United States and the Soviet Union worked toward eliminating aboveground testing. As President Kennedy pointed out in a speech in 1963, "We all inhabit this planet. We all breathe the same air." Later that year the United States, the Soviet Union, and Great Britain agreed to the Limited Nuclear Test Ban Treaty. However, the successful negotiation of the treaty was primarily due to the discovery of ways to conduct underground nuclear weapons tests. Underground testing satisfied those who contended that continued testing was necessary to protect national security, as well as those who wanted to end radioactive fallout.

■■ **The threats posed by radioactive fallout prompted international efforts to pressure governments to limit the production and testing of nuclear weapons.**

POLITICS AND THE ENVIRONMENT

Nuclear destruction and radioactive fallout were not the only new threats to the environment. Pesticide use increased dramatically following the development of new chemicals during World War II. The most popular of the new chemicals was DDT. DDT had first proved its value in 1943 in Naples, Italy, where it was used to prevent an epidemic of typhus by killing the lice that spread the disease.

Despite the benefits, some scientists worried about excessive use of the new pesticides. However, it was Rachel Carson's *Silent Spring,* published in 1962 (see p. 475), that

▲ An environmental activist taking part in a 1984 demonstration in Amsterdam's Dam Square dramatically illustrates ecological concerns over the placement of nuclear weapons in Europe.

awakened many people to the dangers that DDT and other pesticides posed to the environment. Carson warned that pesticides threatened more than insects. "These insecticides are not selective poisons. They do not single out the one species of which we desire to be rid," she wrote. "Each of them is used for the simple reason that it is a deadly poison. It therefore poisons all life with which it comes in contact."

As more and more people worried about the threats posed by nuclear fallout and pesticides, they began to pressure governments around the world to take the environment into account when making policy. In the United States, environmental issues developed a political slant only when adopted by a major party. In other nations, however, **Green parties**—so called because their platforms emphasize ecological concerns—forged a more direct link between these issues and politics.

The Greens have drawn most of their support from large urban areas where the effects of pollution and other urban problems tend to be most obvious. Although the parties remain small, the Greens have successfully drawn attention to environmental issues in Great Britain, France, Germany, and other Western European countries.

Germany's *Die Grünen*. The German Green party, *Die Grünen*, has been one of Europe's most successful. *Die Grünen* developed out of a series of protest movements that began in the 1950s with antinuclear protests and then, in the 1960s, centered around student protests against U.S. involvement in Vietnam. During the early 1970s a new wave of protests focused on opposition to nuclear power. Protesters charged that nuclear power presented serious problems—such as pollution from the accidental release of radiation into the atmosphere and contamination of the environment from the disposal of spent radioactive fuel rods. Thousands of people from France, Switzerland, and Germany, for example, protested a planned nuclear power station at Wyhl, in southern Germany.

In the late 1970s when German protest groups began to address various other environmental issues, they came together to form *Die Grünen*. The new party, which won 5.6 percent of the vote and 27 seats in the German parliamentary elections in 1983, based its platform on the "recognition that in a limited world growth cannot be unlimited" and demanded "a policy of active partnership with nature and with the human race." Ecology, explained party activist Manon Maren-Grisebach, would provide the "scientific . . . basis for action." She continued:

  66 But ecology is demanding. At the risk of our own destruction, we cannot ignore its insights; we are not free to act at will because we are forced to obey laws which reach beyond our [selves] and deal with our very existence. 99

The party also reminded individuals of their responsibility to change environmental policy. In 1982 Petra Kelly, who was then head of *Die Grünen*, asserted "Change . . . has to come from the bottom, not the top."

▶ Environmental activist Petra Kelly addresses the press in Bonn, Germany, on her return from a Moscow peace conference in February 1987.

◄ In this 1967 photograph, smog dims the view of the civic center in Los Angeles.

Environmental activism in the United States. Although the idea of an organized Green party failed to win much support in the United States, environmental protests did result in new legislation. In 1970 Congress passed the Clean Air Act, designed to reduce air pollution, including the **smog**—air polluted by chemical fumes, car exhaust, and smoke—that plagued most large cities. The **Federal Water Pollution Control Act** of 1972—better known as the Clean Water Act—and the **Safe Drinking Water Act** of 1974 were aimed at contaminated water. The **Endangered Species Act** of 1973 required the government to take action to safeguard animal species threatened with extinction.

Although the legislation of the early 1970s applied only to the United States, it reflected a growing realization that environmental problems were interrelated. More and more people were coming to appreciate the four laws of ecology that Barry Commoner proposed in his 1971 book *The Closing Circle:*

> 66 Everything is connected to everything else.
> Everything must go somewhere.
> Nature knows best.
> There is no such thing as a free lunch. 99

Although some people disputed the third item, the other items, especially the first, appeared self-evident to many of the world's people.

■ **Environmental activists became an organized political force in Europe. In the United States environmentalists pressured Congress to pass laws and regulations to protect people and the environment.**

SECTION 3 REVIEW

IDENTIFY and explain the significance of the following: Antarctic Treaty, Nuclear Nonproliferation Treaty, nuclear fallout, food chain, unilateral disarmament, Green parties, Petra Kelly, smog, Federal Water Pollution Control Act, Safe Drinking Water Act, Endangered Species Act, Barry Commoner.

1. **MAIN IDEA** How successful were international efforts to limit the threat of nuclear war?

2. **MAIN IDEA** What kinds of environmental problems did nuclear weapons tests cause? How did people respond to these threats?

3. **MAIN IDEA** What methods did activists in Europe use to call attention to environmental problems during the 1960s, 1970s, and 1980s?

4. **WRITING TO EXPLAIN** Imagine you are a member of the Campaign for Nuclear Disarmament. Write an essay that explains why Great Britain should adopt a policy of unilateral disarmament.

5. **HYPOTHESIZING** How might voters respond to the development of a Green party in the United States?

A SMALL PLANET

FOCUS

■ **Why did scientists continue to search for alternative sources of power in the 1990s?**

■ **Why do environmentalists think it is important to protect forest life?**

■ **What are some of the major global environmental problems that have concerned and divided nations? What solutions have been proposed to deal with these concerns?**

Of the many problems facing America and the rest of the world in the 1990s, some of the most important related to energy use and the environment. People realized that the earth's reserves of oil, gas, and coal—the fossil-based energy sources that had once seemed unlimited—would someday run out. Many also recognized that industrialization had taken a toll on the natural environment. In future decades the combination of population growth and environmental pollution could make life even more difficult.

Cleaning waterfowl after the Alaska oil spill, 1989

LIMITS ON ENERGY RESOURCES

In 1972 the Club of Rome, an international group of scientists, business leaders, and other environmentally concerned individuals, published *The Limits to Growth*. The report projected trends in such critical areas as population growth, food production, and pollution for the next several decades. If current trends continued, the report concluded, the limits to growth on the earth would be reached within a century. Should this occur, the most probable result would be a "sudden and uncontrollable decline in both population and industrial capacity"—in other words, the world's people would face a greatly reduced standard of living, and millions would die from hunger, disease, or war.

Some people criticized the report as far too pessimistic. Human ingenuity, they argued, would find ways to do things as growing populations pressed against limited resources. They pointed out that the world's energy supply, for example, could be greatly expanded by turning to solar or hydroelectric power. Others claimed nuclear-power plants could supply clean, cheap energy.

Environmentalists, however, argued that some of the proposed solutions to shortages presented new problems. For instance, they continued to warn that nuclear-power plants presented serious hazards. In 1986 the kind of accident protesters had predicted occurred at the Chernobyl nuclear-power plant near Kiev, Ukraine (see map on page 735). The accident sent a cloud of radioactivity drifting across Europe and made the surrounding land unsafe for living things. The Chernobyl disaster pumped 50 times more radioactive material into the environment than the bombs dropped on Hiroshima and Nagasaki in World War II.

Chernobyl heightened public anxiety over nuclear power. Some called for increased funding for research on alternative energy sources such as solar power, wind power, and **biomass** (materials such as wood or waste products that can be burned or used to make fuel).

■■ **Concerns about limited energy supplies and the safety of nuclear power have sparked interest in alternative energy sources.**

FOREST LIFE

As scientists search for new forms of energy, many environmentalists focus on protecting the world's forests and wildlife, which are endangered by population growth, industrialization, and expanding commercial agriculture and livestock operations. The United Nations Food and Agriculture Organization reported that almost 42 million acres of tropical forests were lost per year between 1981 and 1990. Furthermore, a 1996 UN and World Bank study found that logging threatens half of the world's remaining tropical forests, while farmers practicing slash-and-burn agriculture threaten the remainder.

Experts warn that forests play a vital role in the larger ecosystem. Forests help to prevent floods and soil erosion. Trees also absorb carbon dioxide; therefore, as forests vanish, more carbon dioxide builds up in the atmosphere, contributing to global warming (see page 736).

▲ **Clearing a piece of Amazon rain forest has become a controversial action now that people understand the importance of trees to the larger ecosystem.**

The debate over the loss of the rain forests is not a simple one. In poor nations, the rain forests are viewed as a source of jobs and income. Business and agricultural interests in developing nations argue that it is unfair for the industrialized world to call on poor nations to make economic sacrifices to preserve the rain forests.

 The conflict over the rain forests can be bitter. In the 1980s Chico Mendes, whose family made its living from tapping the sap from rubber trees in the rain forest, organized a campaign against the destruction of the Amazonian rain forest by ranchers seeking grazing land. Mendes, who was born Francisco Alves Mendes Filho in 1944, grew up with a deep appreciation of nature. "I became an ecologist long before I had ever heard the word," he once recalled.

Chico Mendes

In the 1960s, Brazilian leaders instituted a plan to burn much of the rain forest to make way for industrialization and large-scale agriculture. To oppose this destruction Mendes organized workers who tapped rubber trees and otherwise used the rain forest in environmentally responsible ways. Employing nonviolent methods of resistance, such as boycotts and human blockades to stop heavy equipment, the protesters were able to focus worldwide attention on the rain forest.

Still, the burning of the rain forest continued. In 1988 Mendes declared:

❝ In the last half century Amazônia has never seen so many fires as in 1988. They are burning everything. Our airports were closed one week in 1987 because of the smoke. This year they were closed one month for the same reason. . . . Amazônia is nothing but smoke. How it hurts! ❞

Later that year ranchers killed Mendes. However, the battle to save the Amazon and other tropical forests continues.

Closely connected to the loss of the rain forests is the danger to **biodiversity**, the wide variety of the earth's plant and animal species. Rain forests are home to about half the earth's species. As the forests vanish, some species may be lost forever. Biologist Edward O. Wilson of Harvard estimates that at the rate rain forest habitat is being destroyed, 25 percent or more of the world's species could become extinct in the next 50 years. Furthermore, the vast majority of these species are undiscovered.

Efforts to save plants and animals are not limited to the rain forests. Individuals and groups have worked to save from extinction at least some of the species threatened by growing human populations and the spread of cities and industrial areas. For example, Greenpeace, an international environmental organization, has successfully campaigned against whaling. The U. S. government has also protected additional lands from development. The 1994 California Desert Protection Act enlarged the

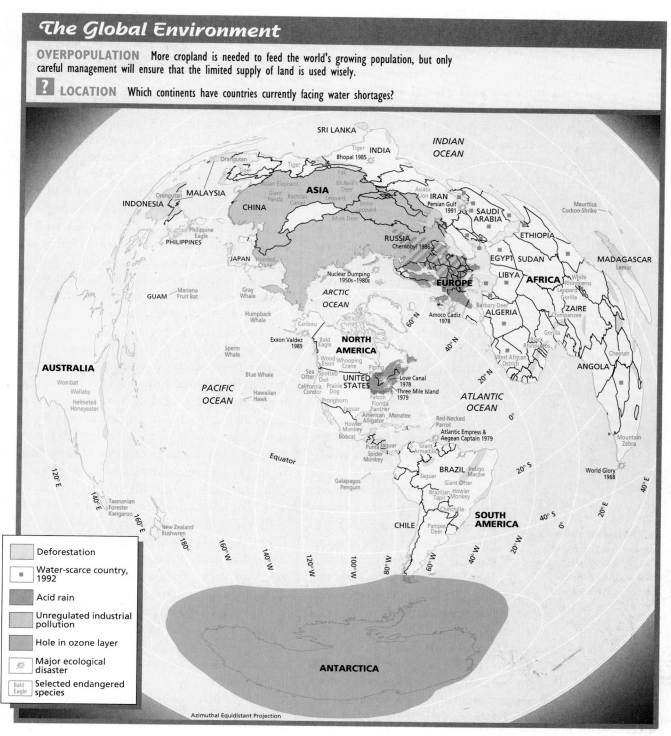

The Global Environment

OVERPOPULATION More cropland is needed to feed the world's growing population, but only careful management will ensure that the limited supply of land is used wisely.

? LOCATION Which continents have countries currently facing water shortages?

Legend:
- Deforestation
- Water-scarce country, 1992
- Acid rain
- Unregulated industrial pollution
- Hole in ozone layer
- Major ecological disaster
- Bald Eagle — Selected endangered species

Azimuthal Equidistant Projection

Joshua Tree and Death Valley National Monuments and made them national parks. Then in 1996 President Clinton took steps to protect 1.7 million acres of Utah canyon lands where a Dutch mining company held valuable coal leases.

▪▪ Environmentalists are working to prevent deforestation and the extinction of species.

▶ Acid rain not only injures trees and lakes but also damages buildings and monuments. This statue in St. Peter's Square, Rome, is gradually deteriorating because of exposure to acid rain.

ENVIRONMENTAL POLLUTION

The rise in global energy consumption and the continued loss of the world's forests have led to growing concern over **global warming**, the increase in the temperature of the earth's atmosphere. Global warming results from the greenhouse effect. The burning of fossil fuels and the cutting and burning of forests have polluted the earth's atmosphere with excess levels of carbon dioxide and with other gases that allow solar radiation to penetrate to the earth's surface while preventing heat from escaping. Scientists warn that over time the greenhouse effect could cause temperate areas to become so hot that crops would wither. The melting of the polar ice caps could flood coastal areas, jeopardizing many cities. Some scientists charge that the greenhouse effect is already harming the environment.

A related danger is the thinning of the ozone layer—the thin veil of molecules some 10 to 30 miles above the earth's surface—that protects the earth from ultraviolet solar radiation (UV rays). Ultraviolet solar radiation can cause skin cancer, damage marine life, and harm crops. To date, the greatest area of ozone thinning has been in Antarctica. But environmentalists warn that other areas are thinning at various times of the year. Much of the damage to the ozone layer has been caused by chemicals called chlorofluorocarbons (CFCs)—combinations of carbon, chlorine, fluorine, and sometimes hydrogen—which have been pumped into the atmosphere by industrialized nations. CFCs are used in the manufacture

▲ These aerosol cans appear harmless, but the chlorofluorocarbons they can add to the earth's atmosphere are not.

of aerosol sprays, refrigerator and air-conditioner coolants, electronics, and plastics.

A third hazard of atmospheric pollution is **acid rain**. Factories and automobiles spew sulfur dioxide and nitrogen oxide, which combine with the moisture in the atmosphere and later fall as acid rain, often far from their places of origin. This acid rain gradually kills trees and makes lakes unfit for fish. In the 1980s and the 1990s, regions as distant as southern China, the Appalachian Mountains in eastern North America, the lakes in northern Canada, and the mountains of Central Europe showed the effects of acid rain.

Acid rain has become a source of conflict between the United States and Canada. Industrial smoke from Michigan factories is believed to have a major effect on rain acidity in Canada. As the United States weakened environmental standards during the 1980s, Canadians protested that this action unfairly affected their environment. As a result, Canada has become one of the leaders in trying to improve global awareness about acid rain, especially in the United States.

The United States has a better record when it comes to dealing with water pollution. Since the Clean Water Act became law in 1972, the United States has made great progress in cleaning up its rivers and lakes. Environmentalists note that water quality has also improved in much of the industrialized world, largely because of better sewage treatment. In many of the cities of the developing world, however, industrial wastes and untreated sewage still pollute water supplies and threaten public health.

Pollution from oil spills also presents serious problems. Spills, such as the 1989 *Exxon*

Valdez accident along the coast of Alaska, kill countless fish and waterfowl and cost millions of dollars to clean up. As a result, environmentalists and many government leaders are calling for stricter controls.

POPULATION EXPLOSION

Many of the world's toughest problems have been made worse by a massive increase in population. By 1995 the world's population stood at 5.7 billion, and it was growing by a rate of three people every second. Much of this growth has been concentrated in the developing world. While the population of the industrialized nations grew by less than 1 percent a year, in many developing nations it grew by 2 or 3 percent. Experts predict that India's population will jump from 936 million in 1995 to 1.3 billion by 2020; Mexico's, from 94 million to 136 million; and Bangladesh's, from 128 million to 210 million. By 2020, Africa is expected to account for about 18 percent of the world's population, in contrast to 9 percent in 1950.

Experts suggest that the world's population growth will not begin to slow until women have an average of 2.06 children. The UN estimates that even if this goal is achieved, the world's population will still continue to increase (because so many people will reach child-bearing age in the next 25 years) until it reaches 11.6 billion in 2150.

Many experts on population, however, note that living standards will have to improve for people in the developing world before the world's

▲ These farmers in southern Bangladesh are harvesting rice, the chief crop of this populous nation.

poor think it makes economic sense to have fewer children. Furthermore, some social critics charge that the developed world is unfairly blaming the world's environmental problems on population growth in the developing world, which uses relatively little of the world's resources. Brazilian historian Fatima Vianna Mello argues that unless the developed world is willing to limit its consumption of the world's resources, its call for women in the developing world to have fewer children, "blames the poor people of the world for the tremendous [social

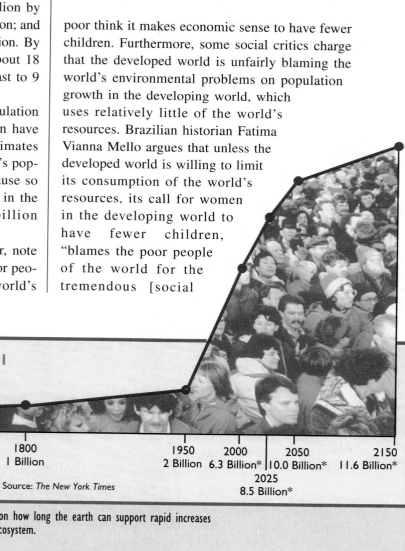

POPULATION SINCE THE YEAR A.D. 1

A.D. 1	1800	1950	2000	2050	2150
200 Million	1 Billion	2 Billion	6.3 Billion*	10.0 Billion*	11.6 Billion*

2025
8.5 Billion*

* Projected by the United Nations Population Fund   Source: *The New York Times*

POPULATION GROWTH Some scientists question how long the earth can support rapid increases in human populations without severely damaging the ecosystem.

? **BUILDING CHART SKILLS** In 1950 the world's population was some 2 billion. About how many times larger will the estimated population be in the year 2000?

WOMEN AND POPULATION GROWTH

Some argue that one of the keys to limiting population growth in developing countries is to advance the status of women. As India's former prime minister Indira Gandhi wrote in 1980: "Men and most women are unaware of the potential ability of women. Their lives are entrapped by pre-conceived notions and attitudes from birth onwards. . . . A lower status for women, or lesser opportunity for women, is a handicap for the growth of mankind as a whole." Gandhi believed that if women are granted equality of rights and opportunity, they will no longer be valued primarily for their ability to produce children.

and] environmental imbalances that exist." Other researchers, however, warn that if population growth in the developing world is not reduced, shortages of food and of renewable resources, such as land and water, can occur and lead to conflict. In Bangladesh, for example, rapid population growth has contributed to a scarcity of land. As a result, millions of Bangladeshis have migrated to India, sparking ethnic conflict.

■■ Environmentalists and government leaders face problems of global warming, ozone depletion, acid rain, water pollution, and growing populations.

RECYCLING AND URBAN GROWTH

As environmental awareness grows, **recycling**— the collection and processing of used items for reuse—has been winning support. Recycling serves two important purposes: it reuses scarce natural resources, and it reduces the mountain of solid waste that must be burned in incinerators, buried in overflowing landfills, dumped into the sea, or shipped to disposal facilities in poorer nations. In 1991 the United States recycled an estimated 14 percent of its solid waste, while Japan recycled 50 percent of its paper and 54 percent of its glass.

Much of the interest in recycling is related to urban growth. Experts predict that by the year 2000 there will be at least 21 cities with populations of 10 million or more. Of these, 18 will be in poor, developing nations. One expert estimates that the enormous amount of garbage created in these cities threatens the health of 40 percent of the urban population in the developing world.

Many cities are making use of innovative systems to recycle garbage. In Cairo, Egypt, some 30,000 Zabaleens (Christians from southern Egypt) collect the city's garbage, sort through it,

▶ Growing populations have overburdened the sanitation resources of many cities. Some cities have loaded their garbage on barges and tried to export it to other areas— often without success. The governor of Florida, for example, refused to allow this New York barge to dock in his state.

and sell the reusable parts. Thrown-away food goes to feed pigs. Scrap metal, glass, paper, and plastic are recycled.

One recycling expert notes that Cairo's system has economic as well as environmental benefits:

> 66 Zabaleens make as much as three times the average income in Cairo. In many developing countries, up to 2 percent of the population is supported directly or indirectly by refuse from the upper 20 percent of the population. 99

𝒯HE WORLD RESPONDS

Growing environmental dangers stirred the international community to action. For instance, in the 1982 agreements issued by the **Third UN Conference on the Law of the Sea**, participating nations pledged to protect the marine environment of coastal waters and to make the oceans "the common heritage of mankind."

Confronted with the urgent danger of ozone depletion, the international community again took action. The **Montreal Protocol on Ozone Depletion**, signed in Montreal, Canada, in 1987, set standards for reducing the emission of CFCs and other gases that threatened the ozone layer. In 1990, as evidence of ozone depletion grew more alarming, this agreement was made even stricter. Ninety-three nations pledged to halt CFC production entirely within the decade, and more ozone-damaging chemicals were added to the banned list. In addition, the industrialized nations agreed to contribute $240 million to enable developing countries to purchase alternatives to CFCs.

In 1992, the 20th anniversary of the first United Nations conference on the environment, the UN sponsored the United Nations Conference on Environment and Development—dubbed the Earth Summit—in Rio de Janeiro, Brazil. Attracting delegations from 178 nations and about 1,200 private environmental organizations, the conference yielded some significant compromises. One was a treaty, the **Convention on Biological Diversity**, which went into effect on December 29, 1993. The treaty committed the 167 nations signing it to the protection of biodiversity and mandated that industrialized nations share profits from biotechnology products they bring to market with the developing countries providing the natural resources.

The rise in environmental awareness has also been evident in the growth of private organizations and lobbying groups, such as the international Worldwatch Institute. These groups have tried to work together to promote international cooperation and concern about the environment. As the Worldwatch Institute noted in 1992: "In an environmentally interdependent world, no country can separate its fate from that of the world as a whole."

■■ **Recycling and international cooperation are among the solutions promoted to control global environmental hazards.**

SECTION 4 REVIEW

IDENTIFY and explain the significance of the following: biomass, Chico Mendes, biodiversity, global warming, ozone layer, ultraviolet solar radiation, chlorofluorocarbons, acid rain, recycling, Third UN Conference on the Law of the Sea, Montreal Protocol on Ozone Depletion, Convention on Biological Diversity.

LOCATE and explain the importance of the following: Chernobyl, Antarctica.

1. **MAIN IDEA** How did people respond to the threat of energy shortages?

2. **MAIN IDEA** Why are forests important to the ecosystem?

3. **MAIN IDEA** What are some of the environmental problems facing the world in the 1990s?

4. **WRITING TO PERSUADE** Write a letter to your local newspaper outlining possible solutions to environmental problems in your community.

5. **IDENTIFYING VALUES** Provide support for the view that the international community values a healthy environment.

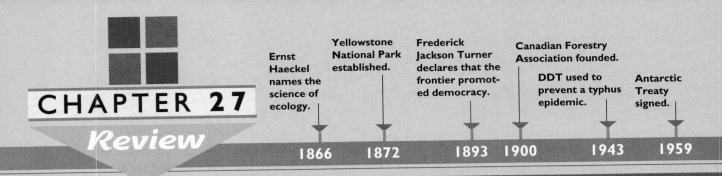

CHAPTER 27
Review

Ernst Haeckel names the science of ecology. 1866

Yellowstone National Park established. 1872

Frederick Jackson Turner declares that the frontier promoted democracy. 1893

Canadian Forestry Association founded. 1900

DDT used to prevent a typhus epidemic. 1943

Antarctic Treaty signed. 1959

WRITING A SUMMARY

Using the essential points of the chapter as a guide, write a summary of the chapter.

REVIEWING CHRONOLOGY

Number your paper 1 to 5. Study the time line above, and list the following events in the order in which they happened by writing the first next to 1, the second next to 2, and so on. Then complete the activity below.

1. Earth Summit held in Rio de Janeiro.
2. Frederick Jackson Turner declared that the frontier promoted democracy.
3. Antarctic Treaty signed.
4. Canadian Forestry Association founded.
5. Chernobyl accident occurred.

Analyzing How have incidents such as the Chernobyl accident and the *Exxon Valdez* oil spill affected public thinking about the environment?

IDENTIFYING PEOPLE AND IDEAS

Explain the historical significance of each of the following people or terms.

1. ecology
2. conservation
3. Aldo Leopold
4. nuclear fallout
5. Petra Kelly
6. unilateral disarmament
7. biomass
8. Chico Mendes
9. global warming
10. recycling

UNDERSTANDING MAIN IDEAS

1. How did American views of the wilderness change between the colonial period and the 19th century? How did the birth of the ecology movement affect American views of the environment?
2. How did the views of the environment held by preservationists differ from those held by conservationists?
3. What effect did the Dust Bowl disaster have on environmental thinking in the United States?
4. How did the development of nuclear weapons encourage people and governments to look for global solutions to environmental problems?

5. What solutions have been proposed to deal with major environmental problems in the 1990s?

REVIEWING THEMES

1. **Technology and Society** How have technological developments affected the environment?
2. **Global Relations** How have nations tried to work together to solve environmental problems?
3. **Economic Development** How does the need for economic development sometimes influence a country's policy on the environment?

THINKING CRITICALLY

1. **Analyzing** Since the 1960s, how have environmentalists tried to protect forest life?
2. **Evaluating** What effect did progressives have on Americans' views of the environment?
3. **Comparing and Contrasting** How do the links between environmental protest and politics differ in the United States and in Europe?

STRATEGY FOR SUCCESS

Review the Skills Handbook entry on Reading Charts and Graphs beginning on page 756. Study the graph below, which shows changes in the concentration of carbon dioxide in the earth's atmosphere. Carbon dioxide concentrations were fairly stable until the 18th century. During what time period did concentrations increase most dramatically? What historical developments may have contributed to this increase in carbon dioxide concentrations?

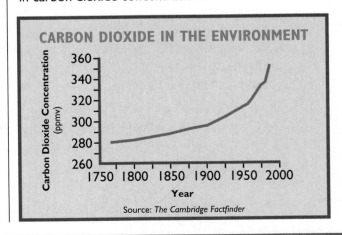

CARBON DIOXIDE IN THE ENVIRONMENT

Carbon Dioxide Concentration (ppmv) vs. Year (1750–2000)

Source: *The Cambridge Factfinder*

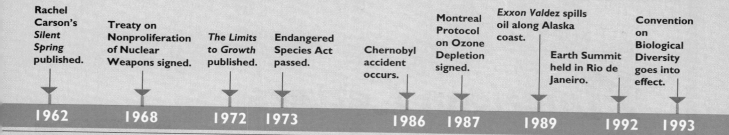

Rachel Carson's *Silent Spring* published.	Treaty on Nonproliferation of Nuclear Weapons signed.	*The Limits to Growth* published.	Endangered Species Act passed.	Chernobyl accident occurs.	Montreal Protocol on Ozone Depletion signed.	*Exxon Valdez* spills oil along Alaska coast.	Earth Summit held in Rio de Janeiro.	Convention on Biological Diversity goes into effect.
1962	1968	1972	1973	1986	1987	1989	1992	1993

WRITING ABOUT HISTORY

Writing to Describe Imagine you are an environmental activist in Great Britain, France, or Germany during the 1970s or 1980s. Write a letter to a group of activists in the United States. Describe the role played by the Green party in your chosen country, and explain why you think Green parties are necessary for environmental reform.

USING PRIMARY SOURCES

In the early 1980s a new environmental movement, symbolized by groups such as Earth First!, emerged. The movement abandoned conservative protests against corporations in favor of more-radical actions, such as tree sitting, inserting spikes into trees, and destroying logging equipment. Read the following excerpt from the book *Green Rage,* which profiles this movement. How do radical environmentalists justify the methods they use?

> ❝ *In general, however, radical environmentalism has no pretentions of being a mass movement and does not expect the huge demonstrations the civil rights and antiwar movements produced. It aims to harass more than obstruct, with the hope that the public awareness it generates will do the rest. . . .*
>
> *A more important difference in strategy stems from the extreme urgency of the environmental crisis. . . . For the "constancy" of the biocentric civil rights movement, however, there is often no tomorrow. Once an old-growth forest is cut, it will not grow back for hundreds of years, if ever. Once a species becomes extinct the battle is lost. This sense of urgency often motivates the use of ecological civil disobedience, not to make far-reaching changes in society's views of the environment, but merely to buy time for legal redress or for the emergence of public pressure.* ❞

LINKING HISTORY AND GEOGRAPHY

Refer to the map on page 735. Which areas of the world suffer from acid rain? Which areas include countries that do not regulate industrial pollution? What conclusion can you draw from this information?

BUILDING YOUR PORTFOLIO

Complete the following projects independently or cooperatively.

1. **WAR** In chapters 24 and 25 you explored the effects of war on nations' economies and on people fleeing from war. Building on that experience, imagine you belong to an environmental organization in the 1950s or 1960s. Create a pamphlet explaining how the Cold War is affecting the environment and urging people to act to prevent further environmental damage from Cold War rivalries.

2. **THE ECONOMY** In chapters 23 and 25 you explored links between the economy, imperialism, and immigration. Building on that experience, imagine you work for an advertising agency that specializes in environmental topics. Write a script for a commercial urging people to follow ecological practices and explaining why such practices will benefit the economy in the long run.

Button showing 1970s and 1980s antinuclear slogan.

3. **INTERNATIONAL COOPERATION** In chapters 24 and 26 you examined how nations tried to strengthen the global economy and to protect human rights worldwide. Building on that experience, imagine you are a government official preparing to meet with environmental groups. Make a poster showing how your government has participated in the 1980s and 1990s in international efforts to protect the environment.

American Letters

The Pains of War

Numerous wars have marked the 20th century. Some, such as World Wars I and II, have affected Americans as well as many peoples around the world. But all wars are significant to those who experience them personally. Nigerian poet and playwright Wole Soyinka, Romanian-born concentration-camp survivor Elie Wiesel, Vietnamese writer Nguyen Thi Vinh, and Chilean novelist Isabel Allende are among those who have experienced and written about war.

▲ **Elie Wiesel**

Civilian and Soldier

by Wole Soyinka

My apparition[1] rose from the fall of lead,
Declared, "I'm a civilian." It only served
To aggravate your fright. For how could I
Have risen, a being of this world, in that hour
Of impartial death! And I thought also: nor is
Your quarrel of this world.

                You stood still
For both eternities, and oh I heard the lesson
Of your training sessions, cautioning—
Scorch earth behind you, do not leave
A dubious neutral to the rear. Reiteration
Of my civilian quandary,[2] burrowing earth
From the lead festival of your more eager friends
Worked the worse on your confusion, and when
You brought the gun to bear on me, and death
Twitched me gently in the eye, your plight
And all of you came clear to me.

                I hope some day
Intent upon my trade of living, to be checked
In stride by *your* apparition in a trench,
Signaling, I am a soldier. No hesitation then
But I shall shoot you clean and fair
With meat and bread, a gourd of wine
A bunch of breasts from either arm, and that
Lone question—do you friend, even now, know
What it is all about? ❖

---

1 ghost-like appearance
2 dilemma.

From *Night*

by Elie Wiesel

In front of us flames. In the air that smell of burning flesh. It must have been about midnight. We had arrived—at Birkenau, reception center for Auschwitz.

The cherished objects we had brought with us thus far were left behind in the train, and with them, at last, our illusions.

Every two yards or so an SS man held his Tommy gun[3] trained on us. Hand in hand we followed the crowd.

An SS noncommissioned officer came to meet us, a truncheon in his hand. He gave the order:

"Men to the left! Women to the right!"

Eight words spoken quietly, indifferently, without emotion. Eight short, simple words. Yet that was the moment when I parted from my mother. I had not had time to think, but already I felt the pressure of my father's hand: we were alone. For a part of a second I glimpsed my mother and my sisters moving away to the right. Tzipora held Mother's hand. I saw them disappear into the distance; my mother was stroking my sister's fair hair, as though to protect her, while I walked on with my father and the other men. And I did not know that in that place, at that moment, I was parting from my mother and Tzipora forever. I went on walking. My father held onto my hand.

Behind me, an old man fell to the ground. Near him was an SS man, putting his revolver back in its holster. ❖

---

3 submachine gun

From *Thoughts of Hanoi*

by Nguyen Thi Vinh

The night is deep and chill
as in early autumn. Pitchblack,
it thickens after each lightning
    flash.
I dream of Hanoi:
Co-ngu Road
ten years of separation
the way back sliced by a frontier
    of hatred. . . .

Brother,
how is Hang Dao now?
How is Ngoc Son temple?
Do the trains still run
each day from Hanoi
to the neighboring towns?
To Bac-ninh, Cam-giang, Yen-bai,
the small villages, islands
of brown thatch in a lush green
    sea? . . .

Stainless blue sky,
    jubilant voices of children
stumbling through the alphabet,
    village graybeards strolling to
        the temple,
    grandmothers basking in twilight
        sun,
    chewing betel leaves
while the children run—

Brother,
how is all that now?
Or is it obsolete?
Are you like me,
reliving the past,
imagining the future?
Do you count me as a friend
or am I the enemy in your eyes?
Brother, I am afraid
that one day I'll be with the
    March-North Army
meeting you on your way to
    the South.
I might be the one to shoot
    you then

or you me
but please
not with hatred.

For don't you remember how
    it was,
you and I in school together,
plotting our lives together?
Those roots go deep!

Brother, we are men,
conscious of more
than material needs.
How can this happen to us
my friend
my foe? ❖

From *The House of the Spirits*

by Isabel Allende

Then came the roar of the airplanes, and the bombing began. Jaime threw himself to the floor with everyone else, unable to believe what he was seeing; until the day before, he had been convinced that nothing like this would ever happen in his country and that even the military respected the law. Only the President was on his feet. He walked to the window carrying a bazooka and fired it at the tanks below. Jaime inched his way to him and grabbed him by the calves to make him get down, but the President replied with a curse and remained erect.

Fifteen minutes later the whole building was in flames, and it was impossible to breathe because of the bombs and the smoke. Jaime crawled among the broken furniture and bits of plaster that were falling around him like a deadly rain, attempting to help the wounded, but he could only offer words of comfort and close the eyes of the dead. In a sudden pause in the shooting, the President gathered the survivors and told them to leave because he did not want any martyrs or needless sacrifice; everyone had a family, and important tasks lay ahead. "I'm going to call a truce so you can leave," he added. But no one moved. Though a few of them were trembling, all were in apparent possession of their dignity. The bombing was brief, but it left the palace in ruins. By two o'clock in the afternoon the fire had consumed the old drawing rooms that had been used since colonial times, and only a handful of men were left around the President. Soldiers entered the building and took what was left of the first floor. Above the din was heard the hysterical voice of an officer ordering them to surrender and come down single file with their hands on their heads. The President shook each of them by the hand. "I'll go last," he said. They never again saw him alive. ❖

THINKING AND WRITING ABOUT LITERATURE

1. What views regarding the shooting of civilians during warfare does Wole Soyinka present in his poem?
2. Why does Elie Wiesel attribute so much importance to the eight words spoken by the SS officer?
3. How does the speaker in Nguyen Thi Vinh's poem recall Hanoi? How has war changed the speaker's relationship with childhood companions?
4. Why do you think the bombing described by Isabel Allende occurred? Where do the author's sympathies lie?

Strategies for Success

COMPARING POINTS OF VIEW

We all bring to our experiences a point of view, a personal frame of reference from which we see or think about things. Because a variety of factors influence a person's outlook, people often have different—and sometimes conflicting—points of view about a particular topic. Comparing varied views and voices helps us understand the historical debates that have shaped the present, as well as the current debates that will shape the future.

How to Compare Points of View

1. **Note the sources.** Find out about each author or speaker. Check whether each is an authority on the subject under discussion.
2. **Do research.** Find out all you can about the subject.
3. **Compare and contrast the main ideas.** Note similarities and differences in the main ideas being expressed.
4. **Compare supporting details.** Consider whether the ideas are supported by relevant facts, by opinions, or by both. Evaluate the logic of the supporting arguments, and look for any bias.
5. **Evaluate the points of view.** Apply your critical thinking skills to appreciate why people have different points of view and to weigh the accuracy, reliability, and implications of each view.

Applying the Strategy

One of the topics over which people have conflicting points of view concerns the effects that population growth will have on the earth and on future societies. Read and compare the following points of view.

> 66 The effect of higher population density actually seems to be positive. . . . The central benefit of more people in a more developed world is that there are more . . . people to invent new ideas. . . . If population had not increased about 8,000 years ago and made hunting and gathering become less productive, we would be having wild roots, rabbits, and berries for lunch. 99
>
> —*Julian Simon, Economist*

> 66 There are limits to the rates at which [the] human population . . . can use materials and energy, and there are limits to the rates at which wastes can be emitted without harm. . . . Human society is now using resources and producing wastes at rates that are not sustainable. . . . Even with much more efficient institutions and technologies, the limits of the earth's ability to support population . . . are close at hand. 99
>
> —*Meadows, Meadows, and Randers, Population Researchers*

Julian Simon, a noted economist, claims that rapid population growth may in fact be a good thing. He points out that the earth's population has grown throughout history and that people have always developed techniques to support the growing population. Based on this historical precedent, Simon is optimistic that people will continue to find ways of supporting larger populations.

Meadows, Meadows, and Randers, researchers who contributed to the 1972 report *The Limits to Growth* and wrote the 1992 sequel *Beyond the Limits,* argue that the earth can support only a finite number of people. In contrast to Simon, they believe that technological advances will not be sufficient to provide for the growing population.

Which point of view comes closest to truth remains to be seen. What is clear, however, is that each point of view has different implications for how political leaders, policymakers, and even ordinary citizens should act. The views we take today regarding the effects of population growth may well shape history for the populations of tomorrow.

Practicing the Strategy

Read the remarks by Brazilian historian Fatima Vianna Mello on pages 737–738. Then, on a separate sheet of paper, answer the following questions.

1. What is Vianna Mello's point of view regarding population growth?
2. What implications does her point of view have for how people—both in developed and developing nations—should act?

BUILDING YOUR PORTFOLIO

Outlined below are four projects. Independently or cooperatively, complete one and use the products to demonstrate your mastery of the historical concepts involved.

1 WAR

Wars almost always have profound effects on the economy, the peoples, and the natural environment of a society or even of the entire world. Using the portfolio materials you designed in chapters 24, 25, and 27, develop a series of one-scene plays showing the various effects of wars such as World War I, World War II, and the Cold War. Each play should focus on a different effect or group of people.

2 THE ECONOMY

Nearly every global phenomenon can be linked in some way to economics. Using the portfolio materials you designed in chapters 23, 25, and 27, write a report to be distributed by the World Bank on how nations around the world might improve their economies. Your report should take into account the different economic needs of different nations.

3 INTERNATIONAL COOPERATION

The 20th century has been marked by numerous international efforts to cooperate on such matters as the global economy, human rights, and the environment. Using the portfolio materials you designed in chapters 24, 26, and 27, conduct a panel discussion with representatives from several nations evaluating the effectiveness of various efforts at international cooperation. Discussions might also address how to ensure the success of future efforts.

4 INDIVIDUAL RIGHTS

Even though individual rights have become more inclusive over the past several centuries, even in the 20th century some groups have found their rights limited. Using the portfolio materials you designed in chapters 23, 24, and 26, create a visual display showing how individual rights have been threatened in different parts of the world during the 1900s. Your display should also include examples of improvements in the realm of individual rights.

Videodisc Review

In assigned groups, develop an outline for a video collage of one of the themes discussed in this unit. Choose images that best illustrate the theme throughout the 20th century. Write a script to accompany the images. Assign narrators to different parts of the script, and present your video collage to the class.

Further Reading

Betts, Raymond F. *Uncertain Dimensions: Western Overseas Empires in the Twentieth Century.* University of Minnesota Press (1985). Thematic analysis of imperialism from World War I through decolonization.

Cameron, Rondo. *A Concise Economic History of the World.* Oxford (1993). Overview of international economic history from ancient times to the present.

Drinan, Robert F. *Cry of the Oppressed: The History and Hope of the Human Rights Revolution.* Harper & Row (1987). Overview of efforts to protect human rights since 1945.

Maltby, Richard. *Passing Parade: A History of Popular Culture in the Twentieth Century.* Oxford (1989). Pictorial history of 20th century popular culture in a global context.

Worster, Donald. *Nature's Economy.* Cambridge (1994). A History of Ecological Ideas.

Reference
SECTION

*Y*our understanding and appreciation of the past will grow as your study skills improve. This Skills Handbook contains instruction on critical thinking strategies and social studies skills that will help you gain a fuller understanding of American history. It explains, for example, how to identify cause and effect and how to distinguish fact from opinion. The lessons in the Handbook equip you to handle historical sources, time lines, maps, and graphs, as well as build your vocabulary and sharpen your research, writing, and test-taking abilities.

1 IDENTIFYING THE MAIN IDEA

In the study of history, the ability to identify what is central is a key to understanding any complex event or issue. *The American Nation in the Twentieth Century* is designed to help you focus on the main ideas in American history. The paragraph titled Understanding the Main Idea that introduces each chapter and the Focus Questions that begin each section are intended to guide your reading. The essential points—the blue summary statements placed throughout the text—highlight and reinforce the main ideas presented.

But not everything you read is structured like *The American Nation in the Twentieth Century*. Applying the following guidelines will help you identify the main ideas in what you read.

HOW TO IDENTIFY THE MAIN IDEA

1. **Read introductory material.** Read the title and the introduction, if there is one. They often point to the main ideas to be covered.
2. **Have questions in mind.** Formulate questions that you think might be answered by the material. Having such questions in mind will focus your reading.

> NOVA BRITANNIA.
> ## OFFERING MOST
> Excellent fruites by Planting in
> VIRGINIA.
>
> Exciting all such as be well affected
> to further the same.
>
> LONDON
> Printed for SAMVEL MACHAM, and are to besold at
> his Shop in Pauls Church-yard, at the
> Signe of the Bul-head.
> 1609.

3. **Note the outline of ideas.** Pay attention to any headings or subheadings. They may provide a basic outline of the major ideas.
4. **Distinguish supporting details.** As you read, distinguish sentences providing supporting details from the general statements they support. A trail of facts may lead to a conclusion that expresses a main idea.

APPLYING YOUR SKILL

Read the following paragraph, from the subsection in Chapter 1 titled "Early English Settlement," to identify its main idea.

> 66 Attempts at colonization had been made in the 1580s, but they had failed. In 1606, however, King James I issued a charter licensing two merchant groups to organize settlements in Virginia and "to dig, mine, and search for all manner of mines of gold, silver, and copper." The two groups, the Plymouth Company and the London Company, were joint-stock companies, which operate somewhat like corporations do today. Investors shared the cost of starting and maintaining the company; they also shared any profits or losses. Unlike the

Spanish government, which itself organized settlements in the Americas, the English Crown left early colonization to these private companies. **"**

As the lead sentence indicates, the paragraph focuses on early English colonization efforts. Details are included to explain how colonization efforts were organized under James I. The main idea is best captured in the concluding sentence: Unlike the Spanish government, which itself organized settlements in the Americas, the English Crown left early colonization to these private companies.

PRACTICING YOUR SKILL

Now read the next paragraph of the subsection on early English settlement (page 16), then answer the following questions.

1. What is the paragraph's main idea? How does the author support that idea?
2. What is the relationship of the main ideas of this paragraph and the previous paragraph on joint-stock companies? Combine them into one statement that summarizes the subsection.

2 IDENTIFYING CAUSE AND EFFECT

Identifying and understanding cause-and-effect relationships is crucial to the study of history. To investigate why an event took place, and what else happened as a result of that event, historians ask questions such as: What is the immediate activity that triggered the event? What is the background leading up to the event? Who were the people involved?

HOW TO IDENTIFY CAUSE AND EFFECT

1. Look for clues. Certain words and phrases are immediate clues to the existence of a cause-and-effect relationship. Note the examples that follow:

CLUE WORDS AND PHRASES	
Cause	**Effect**
as a result of	aftermath
because	as a consequence
brought about	depended on
inspired	gave rise to
led to	originating from
produced	outcome
provoked	outgrowth
spurred	proceeded from
the reason	resulting in

2. Identify the relationship. Read carefully to identify how events are related. Writers do not always state the link between cause and effect. Sometimes a reader of history has to infer the cause or the effect.

3. Check for complex connections. Beyond the immediate cause and effect, check for other, more complex connections. Note, for example, whether (1) there were additional causes of a given effect, (2) a cause had multiple effects, and (3) these effects themselves caused further events.

APPLYING YOUR SKILL

The diagrams on page 750 present an important cause-and-effect relationship among the events leading up to the American Revolution. Because of the costs incurred in the French and Indian War, Parliament levied taxes on the colonies to raise revenue—taxation that led colonists

The Granger Collection, New York

Anno quinto

Georgii III. Regis.

C A P. XII.

An Act for granting and applying certain Stamp Duties, and other Duties, in the *British* Colonies and Plantations in *America*, towards further defraying the Expences of defending, protecting, and fecuring the fame; and for amending fuch Parts of the feveral Acts of Parliament relating to the Trade and Revenues of the faid Colonies and Plantations, as direct the Manner of determining and recovering the Penalties and Forfeitures there-in mentioned.

Cause		Effect
Britain incurs huge debt from the French and Indian War.	→	Parliament raises taxes on the colonies.

Cause		Effect/Cause		Effect
Britain incurs huge debt from the French and Indian War.	→	Parliament raises taxes on the colonies.	→	Colonists protest taxation without representation in Parliament.

to cry, "No taxation without representation!" A diagram of the first part of this relationship is shown above. The diagram at the top of the next column adds the relationship between the British taxation of colonists and the colonial protests, showing how an effect may in turn become a cause. Such diagrams provide a graphic way of seeing complex relations of events.

PRACTICING YOUR SKILL

From your knowledge of recent American history, choose a sequence of events shaped by cause-and-effect relationships. Draw a chart showing the relationships between the actions and the outcomes. Then write a paragraph that explains the connections.

3 DISTINGUISHING FACT FROM OPINION

Historical sources may contain facts and opinions. Sources such as letters, diaries, and speeches usually express personal views. The ability to distinguish facts from opinions is essential to judge the soundness of an argument or the reliability of a historical account.

HOW TO DISTINGUISH FACT FROM OPINION

1. **Identify the facts.** Ask yourself: Can it be verified? Determine whether the idea can be checked for accuracy in a source such as an almanac or encyclopedia. If so, it is probably factual; if not, it probably contains an opinion.

2. **Identify the opinions.** Look for clues that signal a statement of opinion: phrases such as *I think* and *I believe,* comparative words like *greatest* and *more important,* and value-laden words like *extremely* and *ridiculous* imply a judgment, and thus an opinion.

APPLYING YOUR SKILL

Read the following description of George Washington by Thomas Jefferson:

❝ His mind was great and powerful, without being of the very first order; . . . no judgment was ever sounder. It was slow in operation, being

little aided by invention or imagination, but sure in conclusion. ❞

Jefferson's assessment—that Washington was neither brilliant nor particularly imaginative as a thinker, but that he possessed sound judgment and decisiveness—is clearly an opinion. Note the comparative words and phrasing: *great . . . without being of the first order, . . . sounder, . . . slow in operation.*

PRACTICING YOUR SKILL

Read the excerpt below, in which Jefferson further evaluates Washington as a commander in battle. Then answer the questions that follow.

❝ . . . Hence the common remark of his officers, of the advantage he derived from councils of war, where hearing all suggestions, he selected whatever was best; certainly no General ever planned his battles more judiciously [carefully]. But if deranged [disrupted] during the course of the action, . . . he was slow in re-adjustment. ❞

1. What fact (or facts) does Jefferson mention in his description of Washington?
2. Which words provide clues to Jefferson's opinion of Washington as a commander?

4 READING A TIME LINE

Chronology has been called "the skeleton of history." Knowing the chronological order of historical events—that is, the sequence in which they occurred—is essential to understanding them. A time line is a visual framework representing the chronology of a particular historical period. It enables you to see at a glance what happened when. Studying a time line involves seeing relationships between events as well as remembering important dates.

HOW TO READ A TIME LINE

1. **Determine its framework.** Note the years covered and the intervals of time into which the time line is divided.
2. **Study the sequence of events.** Study the order in which the events appear on the time line, noting especially the length of time between events.
3. **Supply missing information.** Think about the people, places, and other events associated with each item on the time line. In this way you can "flesh out" the framework.
4. **Note relationships.** Ask how an event relates to earlier or later events. Look for cause-and-effect relationships and long-term developments.

APPLYING YOUR SKILL

Study the time line below. It lists important events in the history of World War II in the Pacific.

1941	1942	1945
▼	▼	▼
Japan invades Indochina. U.S. declares embargo against Japan. Japanese attack Pearl Harbor.	Battle of Midway occurs.	U.S. drops bombs on Hiroshima and Nagasaki. Japan surrenders.

When more than one event is listed for the same year, they are stacked with the earliest on top. The entries for 1941 illustrate the background to the surprise attack on Pearl Harbor.

PRACTICING YOUR SKILL

From the time line above, answer the following.

1. What other events might belong on this time line for the years between the attack on Pearl Harbor and the dropping of the atomic bombs?
2. What cause-and-effect relationship is suggested by the sequence of entries for 1945?

5 BUILDING VOCABULARY

In your study of history, you may encounter many new and unfamiliar words. But with regular effort you can master unfamiliar words and turn reading history into an opportunity to enlarge your vocabulary. Following the steps outlined here will assist you in building your vocabulary.

HOW TO BUILD VOCABULARY

1. **Identify unusual words.** As you read, list words that you cannot pronounce or define.
2. **Study context clues.** Study the sentence and paragraph where you find the new term. This setting, or context, may give you clues to the word's meaning through examples or a definition using more familiar words.
3. **Use the dictionary.** Use a dictionary to learn how to say the words on your list and what they mean.
4. **Review new vocabulary.** Look for ways to use the new words—in homework assignments, conversation, or classroom discussions. The best way to master a new word is to use it.

PRACTICING YOUR SKILL

1. What is context? How can it provide clues to a word's meaning?
2. As you read the next chapter, list any unusual words that you find. Write down what you think each word means, then check your definitions against those in a dictionary.

Questions about history as well as geography can be answered by consulting maps. Maps convey a wealth of varied information through colors, lines, symbols, and labels. To read and interpret maps, you must be able to understand their language and symbols.

TYPES OF MAPS

A map is an illustration drawn to scale of all or part of the earth's surface. Types of maps include *physical maps, political maps,* and *special-purpose maps.* Physical maps illustrate the natural landscape of an area—the landforms that mark the earth's surface. Physical maps often use shading to show relief—the existence of mountains, hills, and valleys—and colors to show elevation, or the height above or below sea level. The map of the United States on pages 772–73 is a physical map.

Political maps illustrate political units such as states and nations, employing lines to mark boundaries, dots for major cities, and stars or stars within circles for capitals. The map of the United States on pages 774–75 is a political map. Political maps are used also to show information such as territorial changes or military alliances. Special-purpose maps present specific information such as the routes of explorers, the outcome of an election, regional economic activity, or population density. The "Election of 1860" and "The Underground Railroad" maps on these pages are special-purpose maps.

MAP FEATURES

Most maps have a number of features in common. Familiarity with these basic elements makes reading any map easier.

Titles, legends, and labels. A map's title tells you what the map is about. It often includes information on what area is shown and what time period is being represented. The *legend,* or key, explains any special symbols, colors, or shadings used on the map. Labels designate things such as political and geographic place-names as well as physical features like mountain ranges, oceans, and rivers.

Directions and distances. Most maps in this textbook have a *compass rose,* or directional indicator, like the one on "The Underground Railroad" map. The compass rose indicates the four cardinal points: *N* for north, *S* for south, *E* for east, and *W* for west. You can also find intermediate directions—northeast, southeast, southwest, and northwest—using the compass rose. This helps in describing the *relative location* of a place—its location relative to another point of reference. (If a map has no compass rose, assume that north is at the top, east is to the right, and so on.)

Many maps in this textbook include a scale, showing both miles and kilometers, to help you relate distances on the map to actual distances on the earth's surface. You can use a scale to find the distance between any two points.

The global grid. The *absolute location* of any place on the earth is given in terms of *latitude* (number of degrees north or south of the equator) and *longitude*

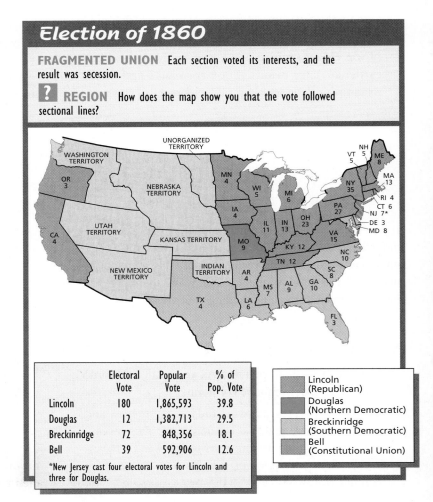

Election of 1860

FRAGMENTED UNION Each section voted its interests, and the result was secession.

? REGION How does the map show you that the vote followed sectional lines?

	Electoral Vote	Popular Vote	% of Pop. Vote
Lincoln	180	1,865,593	39.8
Douglas	12	1,382,713	29.5
Breckinridge	72	848,356	18.1
Bell	39	592,906	12.6

*New Jersey cast four electoral votes for Lincoln and three for Douglas.

Lincoln (Republican)
Douglas (Northern Democratic)
Breckinridge (Southern Democratic)
Bell (Constitutional Union)

(number of degrees east or west of the prime meridian). The *global grid* is created by the intersecting lines of latitude *(parallels)* and lines of longitude *(meridians)*. In *The American Nation in the Twentieth Century,* grid lines sometimes are indicated by tick marks near the edge of the map. Many maps also have *locator maps* (right), which place the area of focus in a larger context, showing it in relation to the entire United States, or the world.

▶ **The maps on these two pages are special-purpose maps. On the page opposite is an Albers projection. Above right is a locator map, and below is an example of a tilted perspective.**

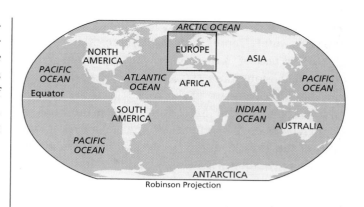

Robinson Projection

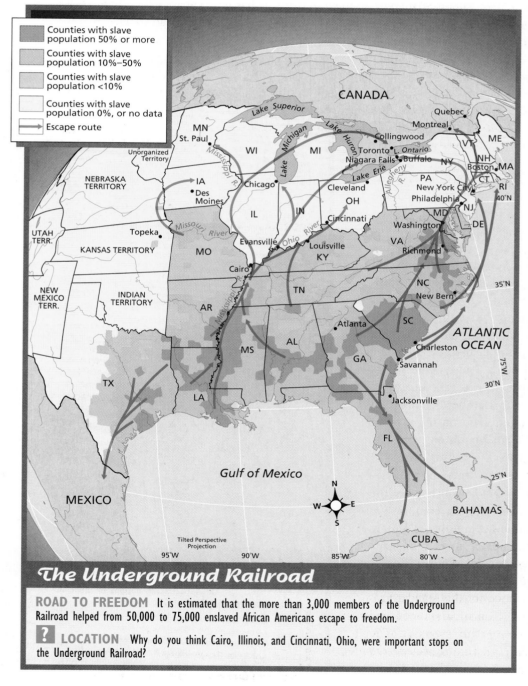

The Underground Railroad

ROAD TO FREEDOM It is estimated that the more than 3,000 members of the Underground Railroad helped from 50,000 to 75,000 enslaved African Americans escape to freedom.

? LOCATION Why do you think Cairo, Illinois, and Cincinnati, Ohio, were important stops on the Underground Railroad?

Map projections. Because the earth is a sphere, it is most accurately represented by a three-dimensional globe. The task of *cartographers,* or mapmakers, is to depict that globe on a flat surface as accurately as they possibly can—to, in the words of 16th-century mapmaker Gerardus Mercator, square the circle. Cartographers do this by transferring the curved coordinates of the globe onto the flat surface in a systematic way. These two-dimensional views of the earth's surface are called *projections.*

To flatten the curved coordinates of a globe, cartographers must squeeze or stretch the global grid of parallels and meridians. Thus every map projection, and therefore every map, distorts to some extent at least one of the following aspects: (1) the shape of land areas, (2) their relative sizes, (3) directions, or (4) distances. Mapmakers choose the projection that least distorts what they wish to show. Most projections in *The American Nation in the Twentieth Century* fall into two broad categories: conformal and equal area.

Conformal projections preserve the shape and scale of small areas around a point or a line. They cannot, however, preserve the shape of large countries or continents because scale varies from point to point. For example, in a world map using a Mercator conformal projection, sizes and shapes are accurate along the equator but distorted toward the poles. As a result, Greenland and South America appear to be the same size even though South America is actually nine times as large as Greenland. The Lambert Conformal Conic projection used on the map of the Bataan Death March on page 327 and for the map of Israel on page 453 are examples of conformal projection.

Equal-area projections show the relative sizes of different countries or continents quite accurately—a square inch or centimeter of paper represents the same number of square miles or kilometers of ground at any point on the map. But the price for this standardization is a distortion of distances and shapes. Most of the maps in *The American Nation in the Twentieth Century* are equal-area projections, with

Albers Equal-Area projections being the most common. The Albers projection is used on most of the U.S. maps—including all of the special-purpose maps like the "Election of 1860"—because it is effective in showing, with a minimum of distortion, large countries with east-west orientations.

Not all of the projections used in this textbook are conformal or equal area. The Robinson projection, used for the locator maps, is an effective compromise between the two categories. It minimizes distortions in size, shape, distance, and direction, although without preserving complete accuracy in any aspect. Other projections are used to give unique perspectives. "The

Indochina

A TROPICAL PENINSULA The nations of Indochina occupy a peninsula stretching from the mainland of Southeast Asia deep into the tropical waters of the South China Sea.

? RELATIVE LOCATION How might Vietnam's location have contributed to its long history of foreign invasion?

Underground Railroad" map on page 753 uses a *tilted perspective*. Compare the map to the Albers projection "Election of 1860" map on page 752. Note how the size and shape of the southern states are fairly accurate while the states and territories to the north and west are distorted on the tilted-perspective map. The perspective serves to draw attention to the southern states, the primary focus of the map.

HOW TO READ A MAP

1. **Determine the focus of the map.** Read the map's title and labels to determine the map's focus—its subject and the geographic area it covers.

2. **Study the map legend.** Read the legend and become familiar with any special symbols, lines, colors, and shadings used on the map.

3. **Check directions and distances.** Use the directional indicator and scale as needed to determine direction, location, and distance.

4. **Check the grid lines.** Refer to lines of longitude and latitude, or to a locator map, to fix the area in its larger context.

5. **Determine the projection.** Determine what projection is being used for the map, especially whether it is an equal area or a conformal projection. Ask yourself why this kind of projection has been chosen for the particular map, keeping in mind what its advantages or drawbacks are.

6. **Study the map.** Study the map's basic features and details, keeping its purpose in mind. If it is a special-purpose map, study the specific information being presented.

APPLYING YOUR SKILL

Study the map of Indochina on the opposite page. Use the locator map to determine the region's global location and to help you understand why the region is also called Southeast Asia. The locator map allows you to determine that Indochina is across the Pacific Ocean from the United States. Note that because the map has lines of longitude and latitude and a scale, you can find the absolute locations of each of the national capitals and compare the relative sizes of the countries. The scale even allows you to compare the size of the countries to your state.

This map combines both physical and political features in one map. Note how the use of relief clearly shows the mountains and coastal lowlands. Trace the Red River and Mekong River to their deltas and determine into what bodies of water each flows.

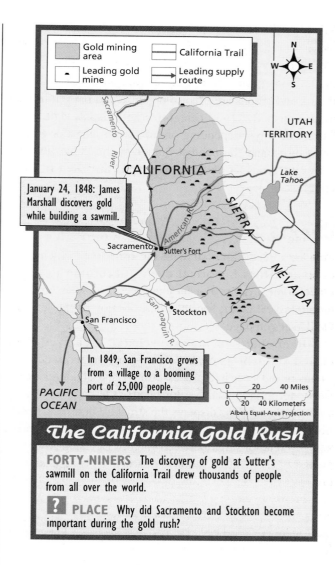

The California Gold Rush

FORTY-NINERS The discovery of gold at Sutter's sawmill on the California Trail drew thousands of people from all over the world.

? **PLACE** Why did Sacramento and Stockton become important during the gold rush?

Study the borders of the countries that make up Indochina. Note for which countries the Mekong River serves as a border. Also note that Laos is an entirely landlocked country, while Vietnam, on the other hand, has hundreds of miles of coastline on the Gulf of Tonkin, South China Sea, and Gulf of Thailand. Vietnam also has a lengthy mountainous border to its north and west—a geographic fact that has been very important in its history.

PRACTICING YOUR SKILL

For each of the special-purpose maps in this lesson—"Election of 1860" on page 752, "The Underground Railroad" on page 753, and "The California Gold Rush" on this page—answer the following questions.

1. What is the special focus of the map?
2. How is a map helpful in presenting this information?
3. What special symbols, if any, are used on the map?
4. What do the color variations or different lines indicate?

Charts and graphs are used to organize and present information visually. They categorize and display data in a variety of ways, depending on the type of chart or graph being used and the subject matter of the data. Several different types of charts and graphs are used in this textbook.

CHARTS

You are already familiar with the time line, which is a chart that lists historical events according to their chronological order. For an example of another kind of chronological chart, see the chart "Major Events of the Cold War" on page 456.

Other charts include flowcharts, organizational charts, and tables. A *flowchart* shows a sequence of events or the steps in a process. Cause-and-effect relationships are often shown by flowcharts (see page 750). An *organizational chart* displays the structure of an organization, indicating the ranking or function of its internal parts and the relationships between them. "Decision-Making Bodies of the United Nations" (below left) is an example of an organizational chart. A *table* is a single, or more often, multicolumn chart that presents data in categories that are easy to understand and compare. Tables, such as "Changes in Material Standards of Living, 1940–1955" (below right), are effective in displaying statistics that vary greatly or would be cumbersome in graph form.

HOW TO READ A CHART

1. **Read the title.** Read the title to identify the focus or purpose of the chart.

2. **Study the chart's parts.** Read the chart's headings, subheadings, and labels to identify the categories used and the specific data given for each category.

3. **Analyze the details.** When reading quantities, note increases or decreases in amounts. When reading dates, note intervals of time. When viewing an organizational chart, follow directional arrows or lines.

4. **Put the data to use.** Form generalizations or draw conclusions based on the data.

DECISION–MAKING BODIES OF THE UNITED NATIONS

Body	Function
General Assembly	Sets policies.
Security Council	Resolves diplomatic, military, and political disputes.
Economic and Social Council	Deals with human welfare and fundamental rights and freedoms.
International Court of Justice	Handles international legal disputes.
Trusteeship Council	Supervises territories that are not independent.
Secretariat	Performs routine administrative work of the UN.

Sources: *Encyclopedia of American History; Funk & Wagnalls New Encyclopedia*

MULTINATIONAL COOPERATION The United Nations was established in order to give every member nation a voice in international affairs. The General Assembly includes over 150 countries and uses five official languages—English, Russian, French, Spanish, and Chinese.

? **ANALYZING** Which body of the United Nations is responsible for monitoring military aggressions between nations?

CHANGES IN MATERIAL STANDARDS OF LIVING, 1940–1955

Households Owning	1940	1955
Automobile	50.0%	71.0%
Television Set	0.0%	76.1%
Refrigerator	44.0%	94.1%
Washing Machine	46.0%	84.1%
Clothes Dryer	0.0%	9.2%
Vacuum Cleaner	38.0%	64.3%

Sources: *The Overworked American; 1956 Statistical Abstract; An Economic History of Women in America; The Proud Decades*

"THE GOOD LIFE" After World War II many American consumers rushed to buy the latest in modern conveniences.

? **BUILDING GRAPH SKILLS** Which item experienced the greatest increase in ownership?

◀ The chart "Decision-Making Bodies of the United Nations" is an organizational chart. "Changes in Material Standards of Living, 1940–1955" is a table.

GRAPHS

There are several types of graphs; each has certain advantages in displaying data for a particular emphasis. A *line graph* plots changes in quantities over time. A line graph has a horizontal axis and a vertical axis. One axis generally lists numbers or percentages, while the other axis is marked off in periods of time. The line is created by plotting data on the grid formed by the intersecting axes and then connecting the dots. "Total Immigration to the U.S., 1860–1900" is an example of a line graph. A *bar graph* can be used to display changes in quantities over time. But most often bar graphs are used to compare quantities within categories. For example, the bar graphs in the "Allied and Central Resources, 1914–1918" chart on this page compare the military resources of the Allied and Central powers during World War I. A *pie graph,* or *circle graph,* displays proportions by showing sections of a whole like slices of a pie, with the whole equaling 100 percent. "Population in the South, 1860" on page 758 features two pie graphs.

HOW TO READ A GRAPH

1. **Read the title.** Read the title to identify the subject and purpose of the graph. Note the kind of graph, remembering what each kind is designed to emphasize.

2. **Study the labels.** To identify the type of information presented in the graph, read the labels that define each axis, bar, or section of the graph.

3. **Analyze the data.** Note increases or decreases in quantities. Look for trends, relationships, and changes in the data.

4. **Put the data to use.** Use the results of your analysis to form generalizations and to draw conclusions.

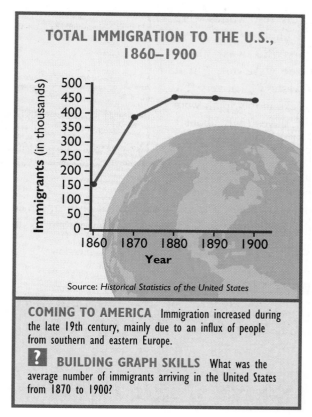

TOTAL IMMIGRATION TO THE U.S., 1860–1900

Source: *Historical Statistics of the United States*

COMING TO AMERICA Immigration increased during the late 19th century, mainly due to an influx of people from southern and eastern Europe.

❓ **BUILDING GRAPH SKILLS** What was the average number of immigrants arriving in the United States from 1870 to 1900?

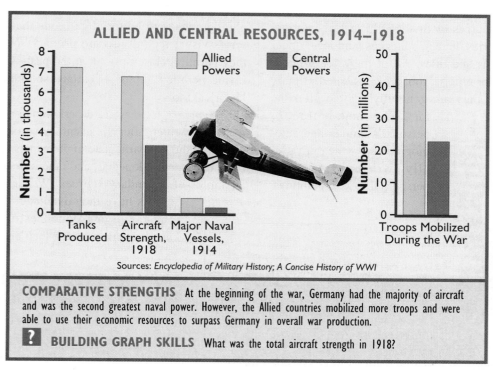

ALLIED AND CENTRAL RESOURCES, 1914–1918

Allied Powers   Central Powers

Tanks Produced   Aircraft Strength, 1918   Major Naval Vessels, 1914   Troops Mobilized During the War

Sources: *Encyclopedia of Military History; A Concise History of WWI*

COMPARATIVE STRENGTHS At the beginning of the war, Germany had the majority of aircraft and was the second greatest naval power. However, the Allied countries mobilized more troops and were able to use their economic resources to surpass Germany in overall war production.

❓ **BUILDING GRAPH SKILLS** What was the total aircraft strength in 1918?

APPLYING YOUR SKILL

Study the pie graphs on the South's population on the eve of the Civil War. From the first graph you can see that relatively few whites were slaveholders; for every one who was, about three were not. But it also shows that very few blacks in the South were *not* slaves (only about 1 in 17). The second graph focuses on a small segment of the southern population—slaveholding households. The graph shows that of this segment of the population nearly 75 percent had fewer than 10 slaves, while only 3 percent had 50 or more.

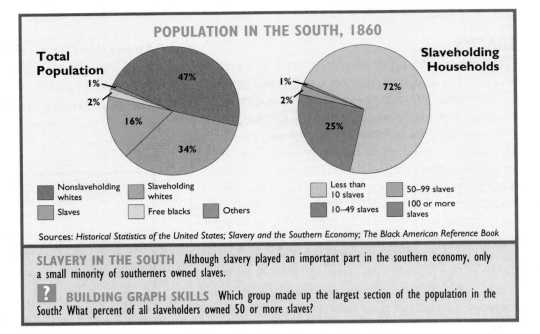

POPULATION IN THE SOUTH, 1860

Total Population

47%
1%
2%
16%
34%

Slaveholding Households

1%
2%
72%
25%

Nonslaveholding whites
Slaveholding whites
Slaves
Free blacks
Others

Less than 10 slaves
10–49 slaves
50–99 slaves
100 or more slaves

Sources: *Historical Statistics of the United States; Slavery and the Southern Economy; The Black American Reference Book*

SLAVERY IN THE SOUTH Although slavery played an important part in the southern economy, only a small minority of southerners owned slaves.

? BUILDING GRAPH SKILLS Which group made up the largest section of the population in the South? What percent of all slaveholders owned 50 or more slaves?

PRACTICING YOUR SKILL

Use the line graph on page 757 to answer the following questions.

1. What type of data is illustrated, and what intervals are used for the horizontal axis and the vertical axis?
2. Which decade shows the greatest increase in immigration to the United States? At what number (approximately) does the level of immigration begin to level out? In what year does this occur?
3. What generalizations or conclusions can you draw from the information in this graph?

8 STUDYING PRIMARY AND SECONDARY SOURCES

There are many sources of firsthand historical information, including diaries, letters, editorials, and legal documents such as wills and titles. All of these are *primary sources*. Newspaper reports, too, are considered primary sources, although they are generally written after the fact. The same is true for personal memoirs and autobiographies, which are usually written late in a person's life. The paintings, photographs, and editorial cartoons that comprise history's visual record also are primary sources. Because they permit a close-up look at the past—a chance to get inside people's minds—primary sources are valuable historical tools.

Secondary sources are descriptions or interpretations of events written after the events have occurred by persons who did not participate in the events. History books, biographies, encyclopedias, and other reference works are examples of secondary sources. Writers of secondary sources have the advantage of knowing the long-range consequences of events. This knowledge helps shape their analyses.

HOW TO STUDY PRIMARY AND SECONDARY SOURCES

1. **Study the material carefully.** Consider the nature of the material. Is it verbal or visual? Is it based on firsthand

information or on the accounts of others? Note the major ideas and supporting details.

2. **Consider the audience.** Ask yourself: For whom was this message meant originally? Whether a message was intended, for instance, for the general public or for a specific, private audience may have influenced its style or content.

3. **Check for bias.** Watch for words or phrases that signal a one-sided view of a person or event.

4. **When possible, compare sources.** Study more than one source on a topic if available. Comparing sources gives you a more complete, balanced account.

PRACTICING YOUR SKILL

1. What distinguishes secondary sources from primary sources?
2. What advantage do secondary sources have over primary sources?
3. Why should you consider the original audience of a historical source?

Of the following, identify which are primary and which are secondary sources: a newspaper, a private journal, a biography, an editorial cartoon, a deed to property, a snapshot of a family on vacation, a magazine article about the history of the West, an autobiography.

9 CREATING AN OUTLINE

An outline is a tool for organizing information. It is a logical summary that presents the main points of what you have read or plan to communicate. An outline is an important part of preparing to write a paper. An essay outline, for example, would highlight the main ideas that you intend to express and sketch the details that you want to include for support. An outline is only a skeletal structure. It must be fleshed out in use. But if an outline is thorough and well thought out, it makes writing the final product much easier.

HOW TO CREATE AN OUTLINE

1. **Order your material.** Decide what you want to emphasize or focus on. Order or classify your material with that in mind. Determine what information belongs in an introduction, what should make up the body of your paper, and what to leave for the conclusion.

2. **Identify main ideas.** Identify the main ideas to be highlighted in each section. Make these your outline's main headings.

3. **List supporting details.** Determine the important details or facts that support each main idea. Rank and list them as subheadings, using additional levels of subheadings as necessary. Subheadings must come in pairs, at the least: no *A*'s without *B*'s, no *1*'s without *2*'s.

4. **Put your outline to use.** Structure your essay or report according to your outline. Each main heading, for instance, might form the basis for a topic sentence to begin a paragraph. Subheadings would then make up the content of the paragraph. In a more lengthy paper, each subheading might be the main idea of a paragraph.

The sample outline below could have been used in preparation for writing about the Louisiana Purchase. Note the several levels of headings that rank the parts of the outline.

I. Republicans favor westward expansion
   A. Settlement of the Trans-Appalachian West
   B. Access to the Mississippi River
      1. Importance of the port of New Orleans
      2. France regains control of Louisiana
         a. Threat to American trade
         b. Obstacle to U.S. westward expansion
II. Jefferson negotiates with France
   A. U.S. diplomats purchase Louisiana
   B. Why France made the sale
      1. Napoléon fails to build empire
         a. Need for naval base in West Indies
         b. Revolt in Saint Domingue (Haiti)
         c. French fail to regain Haiti
      2. Napoléon needs money for war plans

PRACTICING YOUR SKILL

Read the subsection in Chapter 7 titled "Urban Moral Reform" (pages 181–82). Then, using the information you have gained here, create an outline that you could use in writing about this subject.

To complete research papers or special projects, you may need to use resources other than this textbook. Conducting research generally requires you to seek out the resources available in a library.

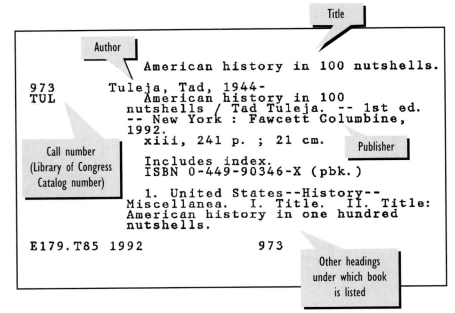

Title

Author

American history in 100 nutshells.

973
TUL

Tuleja, Tad, 1944-
American history in 100 nutshells / Tad Tuleja. -- 1st ed. -- New York : Fawcett Columbine, 1992.
xiii, 241 p. ; 21 cm.

Call number (Library of Congress Catalog number)

Includes index.
ISBN 0-449-90346-X (pbk.)

Publisher

1. United States--History--Miscellanea. I. Title. II. Title: American history in one hundred nutshells.

E179.T85 1992   973

Other headings under which book is listed

FINDING INFORMATION

To find a particular book, you need to know how libraries organize their materials. Books of fiction are alphabetized according to the last name of the author. To classify nonfiction books, libraries use the Dewey decimal system and the Library of Congress system. Both systems assign each book a *call number* that tells you its classification.

To find the number, look in the library's *card catalog*. The catalog lists books by author, by title, and by subject. If you know the author or title of the book, finding it is simple. If you do not know this information, or if you just want to find any book about a general subject, look up that subject heading. Some libraries have computerized card catalogs, which can make searching for specific information easier.

Librarians can assist you in using the card catalog and direct you to a book's location. They can also suggest additional resources.

USING RESOURCES

In a library's reference section, you will find encyclopedias, specialized dictionaries, atlases, almanacs, and indexes to recent material in magazines and newspapers. Encyclopedias often will be your best resource. Encyclopedias include biographical sketches of important historical figures; geographic, economic, and political data on individual nations, states, and cities; and discussions of historical events and religious, social, and cultural issues. Entries often include cross-references to related articles.

Specialized dictionaries exist for almost every field. Historical dictionaries such as *The Concise Dictionary of American History* include definitions of historical terms as well as brief descriptions of important laws, court cases, social movements, and more. Geographical

dictionaries—or *gazetteers*—list significant natural physical features and place-names. Pronunciation guides, statistical data, and brief descriptions are also included. *Atlases* contain maps and visual representations of geographic data.

To find up-to-date facts about a subject, you can use almanacs, yearbooks, and periodical indexes. References like *The World Almanac and Book of Facts* include historical information and a variety of statistics about population, the environment, sports, and so on. Encyclopedia yearbooks keep up with recent, significant developments not fully covered in encyclopedia articles.

Periodical indexes, especially *The Readers' Guide to Periodical Literature,* can help you locate articles published in magazines. The *New York Times Index* catalogs the news stories published in the *Times,* the U.S. daily newspaper with perhaps the most in-depth coverage of national and world events.

PRACTICING YOUR SKILL

1. In what two ways are nonfiction books classified?
2. What kinds of references contain information about geography?
3. Where would you look to find recent coverage of a political or social issue?
4. Would you look in an encyclopedia, an atlas, or an American history dictionary to find each of the following items? (a) the latitude of Guatemala (b) a biography of Julius Caesar (c) the purpose of the Taft-Hartley Act (d) the major industries of Cleveland, Ohio

11 WRITING A PAPER

The American Nation in the Twentieth Century provides you with numerous writing opportunities. Section reviews have writing exercises (labeled Writing to Inform, Writing to Persuade, and so on) that give you the chance to write about a historical subject with a particular focus in mind. Chapter reviews contain additional opportunities for writing.

WRITING WITH A PURPOSE

Always keep your purpose for writing in mind. That purpose might be to analyze, to evaluate, to synthesize, to inform, to persuade, to hypothesize, or to take a stand. As you begin, your purpose will determine the most appropriate approach to take; and when you are done, it will help you evaluate how well you have succeeded.

Each different purpose for writing requires its own form, tone, and content. The point of view you are adopting will shape what you write, as will your intended audience. For example, you would take a different tone when writing to a president from the tone you would use with a relative.

HISTORICAL IMAGINATION

Many writing opportunities in *The American Nation in the Twentieth Century* ask you to create a specific type of writing, such as a diary entry, a letter, a newspaper editorial, a poem, or an advertisement. Often such writing about history involves using historical imagination—that is, writing from the perspective of a person living *then* rather than *now*. An assignment may require, for instance, that you address a particular historical figure, such as a former president, or that you write as if living through a specific historical crisis.

HOW TO WRITE A PAPER

Each writing opportunity provided in this textbook will have specific directions about what and how to write. But whether you are writing a diary entry describing your experiences as a western pioneer or an essay about the significance of the frontier, you should follow certain basic steps. The guidelines outlined in the second column (which apply especially to longer papers) can help you plan and improve your writing.

SOME TYPES OF WRITING

- A **diary** is an informal, personal log of your experiences and recollections (or those of someone else in history). Entries are dated and consist of brief accounts of the day's happenings and your reactions.

- A **letter** is a personal communication meant for a specific individual.

- An **advertisement** is an announcement to promote a product or event. Effective ads are direct and to the point, using memorable language, such as jingles and slogans, to highlight important features.

- A newspaper **editorial** is a public statement of an opinion or point of view. It takes a stand on an issue and gives reasons for that stand.

---

1. **Identify your purpose in writing.** Read the directions carefully to identify the purpose for your writing. Keep that purpose in mind as you plan and write your paper.

2. **Consider your audience.** When writing for a specific audience, choose the tone and style that will best communicate your message.

3. **Create an outline.** Think and plan before you begin writing your first draft. Organize themes, main ideas, and supporting details into an outline.

4. **Collect information.** Do research if necessary. Your writing will be more effective if you have many details at hand.

5. **Write a first draft and evaluate it.** In your first draft, remember to use your outline as a guide. Each paragraph should express a single main idea or set of related ideas, with details for support. Be careful to show the relationships between ideas and to use proper transitions—sentences that build connections between paragraphs.

6. **Review and edit.** Revise and reorganize your draft as needed to make your points. Improve sentences by adding appropriate adjectives and adverbs. Make your writing clearer by changing the length or structure of awkward sentences. Replace inexact

wording with more precise word choices. Then check for proper spelling, punctuation, and grammar.

7. **Write your final version.** Prepare a neat, clean final version. Appearance is important; it may not affect the quality of your writing itself, but it can affect the way your writing is perceived and understood.

PRACTICING YOUR SKILL

1. What factor—more than any other—should affect how and what you write? Why?
2. Why is it important to consider the audience for whom you are writing?
3. What steps should you take to edit a first draft?

12 TAKING A TEST

When it comes to taking a test, for history or any other subject, nothing can take the place of preparation. A good night's sleep added to consistent study habits give you a far better chance for success than hours of late-night, last-minute cramming.

But keeping your mind focused on the test and free from distractions is not all you can do to improve your test scores. Mastering some basic test-taking skills can also help. Keeping up with your daily reading assignments and taking careful notes as you read can turn taking a test into a mere matter of review. Reviewing material that you already know takes less time—and causes less stress— than trying to learn something new under pressure.

You will face several basic types of questions on

Canajoharie Library & Art Gallery, Canajoharie, New York

▲ *Homework* by **Winslow Homer**

U.S. history tests: multiple choice, matching, and essay. In answering multiple-choice questions, eliminate any answers that you know are wrong; this will narrow your field of choice. When doing a matching exercise, first go through the entire list, matching those that you are sure of. Then study any that remain.

Read essay questions carefully so that you know exactly what you are being asked to write. If time permits, make an outline of the main ideas and supporting details that you plan to include in your essay. Keep your answer clear and brief, but cover all necessary points.

HOW TO TAKE A TEST

1. **Prepare beforehand.** This all-important step not only involves studying and reviewing the material prior to the test. It also means being physically rested and mentally focused on the day of the test.
2. **Follow directions.** Read all instructions carefully. Listen closely, particularly if you are being told the directions rather than being given written instructions.
3. **Preview the test.** Skim through the entire test to determine how much time you have for each section. Try to anticipate which areas of the examination will be the most difficult for you. You may wish to allow yourself more time to work on the more difficult sections.
4. **Concentrate on the test.** Do not "watch the clock," but stay aware of the time. If you do not know an answer, move on to the next question. It is best to answer as many questions as you can within the time limit.
5. **Review your answers.** If you have time, return to questions that you skipped or were unsure of and work on them. Review your essays to catch and correct any mistakes in spelling, punctuation, or grammar.

PRACTICING YOUR SKILL

1. How can you improve your chances on multiple-choice questions?
2. Why is it important to skim through the entire test before you begin?
3. Name three things that can help you in taking a test.

Thomas Jefferson's First Inaugural Address

March 4, 1801

Friends and Fellow Citizens. . .

All . . . will bear in mind this sacred principle, that though the will of the majority is in all cases to prevail, that will to be rightful must be reasonable; that the minority possess their equal rights, which equal law must protect, and to violate would be oppression. Let us, then, fellow citizens, unite with one heart and one mind. Let us restore to social intercourse [dealings] that harmony and affection without which liberty and even life itself are but dreary things. And let us reflect that, having banished from our land that religious intolerance under which mankind so long bled and suffered, we have yet gained little if we countenance [allow] a political intolerance as despotic, as wicked, and capable of as bitter and bloody persecutions. . . . But every difference of opinion is not a difference of principle. We have called by different names brethren of the same principle. We are all Republicans; we are all Federalists. If there be any among us who would wish to dissolve this Union or to change its republican form, let them stand undisturbed as monuments of the safety with which error of opinion may be tolerated where reason is left free to combat it. I know, indeed, that some honest men fear that a republican government cannot be strong, that this government is not strong enough; but would the honest patriot, in the full tide of successful experiment, abandon a government which has so far kept us free and firm on the theoretic [hypothetical] and visionary fear that this government, the world's best hope, may by possibility want energy to preserve itself? I trust not. I believe this, on the contrary, the strongest government on earth. I believe it the only one where every man, at the call of the law, would fly to the standard of the law, and would meet invasions of the public order as his own personal concern. Sometimes it is said that man cannot be trusted with the government of himself. Can he, then, be trusted with the government of others? Or have we found angels in the forms of kings to govern him? Let history answer this question.

Let us, then, with courage and confidence pursue our own Federal and Republican principles, our attachment to union and representative government. Kindly separated by nature and a wide ocean from the exterminating havoc of one quarter of the globe; too high-minded to endure the degradations of the others; possessing a chosen country, with room enough for our descendants to the thousandth and thousandth generation; entertaining a due sense of our equal right to the use of our own faculties, to the acquisitions of our own industry, to honor and confidence from our fellow citizens, resulting not from birth, but from our actions and their sense of them; enlightened by a benign religion, professed, indeed, and practiced in various forms, yet all of them inculcating [implanting] honesty, truth, temperance, gratitude, and the love of man; acknowledging and adoring an overruling Providence, which by all its dispensations proves that it delights in the happiness of man here and his greater happiness hereafter—with all these blessings, what more is necessary to make us a happy and a prosperous people? Still one thing more, fellow citizens—a wise and frugal government, which shall restrain men from injuring one another, shall leave them otherwise free to regulate their own pursuits of industry and improvement, and shall not take from the mouth of labor the bread it has earned. This is the sum of good government, and this is necessary to close the circle of our felicities [good intentions].

About to enter, fellow citizens, on the exercise of duties which comprehend [include] everything dear and valuable to you, it is proper you should understand what I deem the essential principles of our government and consequently those which ought to shape its administration. I will compress them within the narrowest compass they will bear, stating the general principle, but not all its limitations. Equal and exact justice to all men, of whatever state or persuasion religious or political; peace, commerce, and honest friendship with all nations, entangling alliances with none; the support of the state governments in all their rights, as the most competent administrations for our domestic concerns and the surest bulwarks [defenses] against anti-republican tendencies; the preservation of the general government in its whole constitutional vigor, as the sheet anchor [main support] of our peace at home and safety abroad; a jealous care of the right of election by the people—a mild and safe corrective of abuses which are lopped by the sword of revolution where peaceable remedies are unprovided; absolute acquiescence in [submission to] the decisions of the majority, the vital principle of republics, from which [there] is no appeal but to force, the vital principle and immediate parent of despotism; a well-disciplined militia, our best reliance in peace and for the first moments of war, till regulars may relieve them; the supremacy of the civil over the military authority; economy in the public expense, that labor may be lightly burdened; the honest payment of our debts and sacred preservation of the public faith; encouragement of agriculture, and of commerce as its handmaid; the diffusion of information and arraignment [bringing up] of all abuses at the bar of the public reason; freedom of religion; freedom of the press; and freedom of person under the protection of the *habeas corpus,** and trial by juries impartially selected. These principles form the bright constellation which has gone before us and guided our steps through an age of revolution and reformation. The wisdom of our sages and blood of our heroes have been devoted to their attainment. They should be the creed of our political faith, the text of civic instruction, the touchstone by which to try the services of those we trust; and should we wander from them in moments of error or of alarm, let us hasten to retrace our steps and to regain the road which alone leads to peace, liberty, and safety.

I repair, then, fellow citizens, to the post you have assigned me. With experience enough in subordinate offices to have seen the difficulties of this the greatest of all, I have learned to expect that it will rarely fall to the lot of imperfect man to retire from this station with the reputation and the favor which bring him into it. Without pretensions to that high confidence you reposed in our first and greatest revolutionary character [Washington] whose pre-eminent services had entitled him to the first place in his country's love and destined for him the fairest page in the volume of faithful history, I ask so much confidence only as may give firmness and effect to the legal administration of your affairs. I shall often go wrong through defect of judgment. When right, I shall often be thought wrong by those whose positions will not command a view of the whole ground. I ask your indulgence for my own errors, which will never be intentional, and your support against the errors of others, who may condemn what they would not if seen in all its parts. The approbation [approval] implied by your suffrage is a great consolation to me for the past, and my future solicitude [concern] will be to retain the good opinion of those who have bestowed it in advance, to conciliate [win over] that of others by doing them all the good in my power, and to be instrumental to the happiness and freedom of all.

Relying, then, on the patronage of your good will, I advance with obedience to the work, ready to retire from it whenever you become sensible how much better choice it is in your power to make. And may that Infinite Power which rules the destinies of the universe lead our councils to what is best, and give them a favorable issue for your peace and prosperity. ❖

**Habeas corpus:* legal provision guaranteeing a prisoner or detainee the right to be informed of the cause of his or her detention, as a protection against illegal imprisonment.

HISTORICAL DOCUMENT

The Monroe Doctrine

December 2, 1823

At the proposal of the Russian Imperial Government, made through the minister of the Emperor residing here, a full power and instructions have been transmitted to the minister of the United States at St. Petersburg to arrange by amicable negotiations the respective rights and interests of the two nations on the northwest coast of this continent. A similar proposal had been made by His Imperial Majesty to the government of Great Britain, which has likewise been acceded [agreed] to. The government of the United States has been desirous by this friendly proceeding of manifesting the great value which they have invariably attached to the friendship of the Emperor and their solicitude to cultivate the best understanding with his government. In the discussions to which this interest has given rise and in the arrangements by which they may terminate the occasion has been judged proper for asserting, as a principle in which the rights and interests of the United States are involved, that the American continents, by the free and independent condition which they have assumed and maintain, are henceforth not to be considered as subjects for future colonization by any European powers. . . .

The citizens of the United States cherish sentiments the most friendly in favor of the liberty and happiness of their fellow men on that side of the Atlantic [in Europe]. In the wars of the European powers in matters relating to themselves we have never taken any part, nor does it comport with our policy to do so. It is only when our rights are invaded or seriously menaced that we resent injuries or make preparation for our defense. With the movements in this hemisphere we are of necessity more immediately connected, and by causes which must be obvious to all enlightened and impartial observers. The political system of the allied powers [Holy Alliance]* is essentially different in this respect from that of America. This difference proceeds from that which exists in their respective governments; and to the defense of our own, which has been achieved by the loss of much blood and treasure, and matured by the wisdom of their most enlightened citizens, and under which we have enjoyed unexampled felicity, this whole nation is devoted. We owe it, therefore, to candor and to the amicable relations existing between the United States and those powers to declare that we should consider any attempt on their part to extend their system to any portion of this hemisphere as dangerous to our peace and safety. With the existing colonies or dependencies of any European power, we have not interfered and shall not interfere. But with the governments who have declared their independence and maintained it, and whose independence we have, on great consideration and on just principles, acknowledged, we could not view any interposition for the purpose of oppressing them, or controlling in any other manner their destiny, by any European power in any other light than as the manifestation of an unfriendly disposition toward the United States. In the war between those new governments and Spain, we declared our neutrality at the time of their recognition, and to this we have adhered, and shall continue to adhere, provided no change shall occur which,

*Holy Alliance: alliance between France, Austria, Russia, and Prussia.

in the judgment of the competent authorities of this government, shall make a corresponding change on the part of the United States indispensable to their security.

The late events in Spain and Portugal show that Europe is still unsettled. Of this important fact no stronger proof can be adduced [offered] than that the allied powers should have thought it proper, on any principle satisfactory to themselves, to have interposed by force in the internal concerns of Spain. To what extent such interposition may be carried, on the same principle, is a question in which all independent powers whose governments differ from theirs are interested, even those most remote, and surely none more so than the United States. Our policy in regard to Europe, which was adopted at an early stage of the wars which have so long agitated that quarter of the globe, nevertheless remains the same, which is, not to interfere in the internal concerns of any of its powers; to consider the government *de facto* [such as it is] as the legitimate government for us; to cultivate friendly relations with it, and to preserve those relations by a frank, firm, and manly policy, meeting in all instances the just claims of every power, submitting to injuries from none. But in regard to those continents [North and South America] circumstances are eminently and conspicuously different. It is impossible that the allied powers should extend their political system to any portion of either continent without endangering our peace and happiness; nor can anyone believe that our southern brethren [Latin Americans], if left to themselves, would adopt it of their own accord. It is equally impossible, therefore, that we should behold such interposition in any form with indifference. If we look to the comparative strength and resources of Spain and those new governments and their distance from each other, it must be obvious that she can never subdue them. It is still the true policy of the United States to leave the parties to themselves, in the hope that other powers will pursue the same course. ❖

The Seneca Falls Declaration of Sentiments

July 19–20, 1848

When, in the course of human events, it becomes necessary for one portion of the family of man to assume among the people of the earth a position different from that which they have hitherto occupied, but one

to which the laws of nature and of nature's God entitle them, a decent respect to the opinions of mankind requires that they should declare the causes that impel them to such a course.

We hold these truths to be self-evident: that all men and women are created equal; that they are endowed by their Creator with certain inalienable rights; that among these are life, liberty, and the pursuit of happiness; that to secure these rights governments are instituted, deriving their just powers from the consent of the governed. Whenever any form of government becomes destructive of these ends, it is the right of those who suffer from it to refuse allegiance to it, and to insist upon the institution of a new government, laying its foundation on such principles, and organizing its powers in such form, as to them shall seem most likely to effect their safety and happiness. Prudence, indeed, will dictate that governments long established should not be changed for light and transient causes; and accordingly all experience has shown that mankind are more disposed to suffer while evils are sufferable [bearable], than to right themselves by abolishing the forms to which they were accustomed. But when a long train of abuses and usurpations [seizures] pursuing invariably the same object evinces [reveals] a design to reduce them under absolute despotism, it is their duty to throw off such government, and to provide new guards for their future security. Such has been the patient sufferance [suffering] of the women under this government, and such is now the necessity which constrains them to demand the equal station to which they are entitled.

The history of mankind is a history of repeated injuries and usurpations on the part of man toward woman, having in direct object the establishment of an absolute tyranny over her. To prove this, let facts be submitted to a candid world. . . .

Having deprived her of this first right of a citizen, the elective franchise [right to vote], thereby leaving her without representation in the halls of legislation, he has oppressed her on all sides.

He has made her, if married, in the eye of the law, civilly dead. . . .

Now, in view of this entire disfranchisement [loss of right to vote] of one half of the people of this country, their social and religious degradation—in view of the unjust laws above mentioned, and because women do feel themselves aggrieved, oppressed, and fraudulently deprived of their most sacred rights, we insist that they have immediate admission to all the rights and privileges which belong to them as citizens of the United States.

In entering upon the great work before us, we anticipate no small amount of misconception, misrepresentation, and ridicule; but we shall use every instrumentality [means] within our power to effect our object. We shall employ agents, circulate tracts [pamphlets], petition the state and national legislatures, and endeavor to enlist the pulpit and the press in our behalf. We hope this convention will be followed by a series of conventions embracing every part of the country. . . .

Resolutions

Resolved, That all laws which prevent woman from occupying such a station in society as her conscience shall dictate, or which place her in a position inferior to that of man, are contrary to the great precept of nature, and, therefore, of no force or authority.

Resolved, That woman is man's equal—was intended to be so by the Creator, and the highest good of the race demands that she should be recognized as such. . . .

Resolved, That woman has too long rested satisfied in the circumscribed [narrow] limits which corrupt customs and a perverted [misdirected] application of the Scriptures have marked out for her, and that it is time she should move in the enlarged sphere which her great Creator has assigned her.

Resolved, That it is the duty of the women of this country to secure to themselves their sacred right to the elective franchise.

Resolved, That the equality of human rights results necessarily from the fact of the identity [sameness of essential character] of the race in capabilities and responsibilities. . . .

Resolved, therefore, That, being invested by the Creator with the same capabilities, and the same consciousness of responsibility for their exercise, it is demonstrably the right and duty of woman, equally with man, to promote every righteous cause by every righteous means; and especially in regard to the great subjects of morals and religion, it is self-evidently her right to participate with her brother in teaching them, both in private and in public, by writing and by speaking, by any instrumentalities proper to be used, and in any assemblies proper to be held. . . .

Resolved, That the speedy success of our cause depends upon the zealous and untiring efforts of both men and women, for the overthrow of the monopoly of the pulpit, and for the securing to women an equal participation with men in the various trades, professions, and commerce. ❖

The Emancipation Proclamation

January 1, 1863

**BY THE PRESIDENT OF
THE UNITED STATES OF AMERICA**

A Proclamation

Whereas on the twenty-second day of September, A.D. 1862, a proclamation was issued by the President of the United States, containing, among other things, the following, to wit [namely]:

"That on the first day of January, A.D. 1863, all persons held as slaves within any state or designated part of a state, the people whereof shall then be in rebellion against the United States, shall be then, thenceforward, and forever free; and the executive government of the United States, including the military and naval authority thereof, will recognize and maintain the freedom of such persons and will do no act or acts to repress such persons or any of them, in any efforts they may make for their actual freedom.

"That the Executive will on the first day of January aforesaid, by proclamation, designate the states and parts of states, if any, in which the people thereof, respectively, shall then be in rebellion against the United States; and the fact that any state or the people thereof shall on that day be in good faith represented in the Congress of the United States by members chosen thereto at elections wherein a majority of the qualified voters of such states shall have participated shall, in the absence of strong countervailing [opposing] testimony, be deemed conclusive evidence that such state and the people thereof are not then in rebellion against the United States."

Now, therefore, I, Abraham Lincoln, President of the United States, by virtue of the power in me vested as Commander-in-Chief of the Army and Navy of the United States in time of actual armed rebellion against the authority and government of the United States, and as a fit and necessary war measure for suppressing said rebellion, do, on this first day of January, A.D. 1863, and in accordance with my purpose so to do, publicly proclaimed for the full period of one hundred days from the first day above mentioned, order and designate as the states and parts of states wherein the people thereof, respectively, are this day in rebellion against the United States the following, to wit:

Arkansas, Texas, Louisiana (except the parishes of St. Bernard, Plaquemines, Jefferson, St. John, St. Charles, St. James, Ascension, Assumption, Terrebonne, Lafourche, St. Mary, St. Martin, and Orleans, including the city of New Orleans), Mississippi, Alabama, Florida, Georgia, South Carolina, North Carolina, and Virginia (except the forty-eight counties designated as West Virginia, and also the counties of Berkeley, Accomac, Northampton, Elizabeth City, York, Princess Anne, and Norfolk, including the cities of Norfolk and Portsmouth), and which excepted parts are for the present left precisely as if this proclamation were not issued.

And by virtue of the power and for the purpose aforesaid, I do order and declare that all persons held as slaves within said designated states and parts of states are, and henceforward shall be, free; and that the executive government of the United States, including the military and naval authorities thereof, will recognize and maintain the freedom of said persons.

And I hereby enjoin [order] upon the people so declared to be free to abstain from all violence, unless in necessary self-defense; and I recommend to them that, in all cases when allowed, they labor faithfully for reasonable wages.

And I further declare and make known that such persons of suitable condition will be received into the armed service of the United States to garrison forts, positions, stations, and other places, and to man vessels of all sorts in said service.

And upon this act, sincerely believed to be an act of justice, warranted by the Constitution upon military necessity, I invoke the considerate judgment of mankind and the gracious favor of Almighty God. ❖

Abraham Lincoln's Gettysburg Address

November 19, 1863

Four score and seven years ago our fathers brought forth on this continent a new nation, conceived in liberty, and dedicated to the proposition that all men are created equal.

Now we are engaged in a great civil war, testing whether that nation, or any nation so conceived and so dedicated can long endure. We are met on a great battlefield of that war. We have come to dedicate a portion of that field as a final resting place for those who here gave their lives that that nation might live. It is altogether fitting and proper that we should do this.

But, in a larger sense, we cannot dedicate—we cannot consecrate [make holy]—we cannot hallow—this ground. The brave men, living and dead, who struggled here, have consecrated it far above our poor power to add or detract. The world will little note nor long remember what we say here, but it can never forget what they did here. It is for us, the living, rather, to be dedicated here to the unfinished work which they who fought here have thus far so nobly advanced. It is rather for us to be here dedicated to the great task remaining before us—that from these honored dead we take increased devotion to that cause for which they gave the last full measure of devotion; that we here highly resolve that these dead shall not have died in vain; that this nation, under God, shall have a new birth of freedom; and that government of the people, by the people, for the people, shall not perish from the earth. ❖

The Fourteen Points

January 8, 1918

Gentlemen of the Congress:

It will be our wish and purpose that the processes of peace, when they are begun, shall be absolutely open and that they shall involve and permit henceforth no secret understandings of any kind. The day of conquest and aggrandizement is gone by; so is also the day of secret covenants entered into in the interest of particular governments and likely at some unlooked-for moment to upset the peace of the world. It is this happy fact, now clear to the view of every public man whose thoughts do not still linger in an age that is dead and gone, which makes it possible for every nation whose purposes are consistent with justice and the peace of the world to avow now or at any other time the objects it has in view.

We entered this war because violations of right had occurred which touched us to the quick and made the life of our own people impossible unless they were corrected and the world secured once for all against their recurrence. What we demand in this war, therefore, is nothing peculiar to ourselves. It is that the world be made fit and safe to live in; and particularly that it be made safe for every peace-loving nation which, like our own, wishes to live its own life, determine its own institutions, be assured of justice and fair dealing by the other peoples of the world as against force and selfish aggression. All the peoples of the world are in effect partners in this interest, and for our own part we see very clearly that unless justice be done to others it will not be done to us. The program of the world's peace, therefore, is our program; and that program, the only possible program, as we see it, is this:

I. Open covenants of peace, openly arrived at, after which there shall be no private international understandings of any kind but diplomacy shall proceed always frankly and in the public view.

II. Absolute freedom of navigation upon the seas, outside territorial waters, alike in peace and in war, except as the seas may be closed in whole or in part by international action for the enforcement of international covenants.

III. The removal, so far as possible, of all economic barriers and the establishment of an equality of trade conditions among all the nations consenting to the peace and associating themselves for its maintenance.

IV. Adequate guarantees given and taken that national armaments will be reduced to the lowest point consistent with domestic safety.

V. A free, open-minded, and absolutely impartial adjustment of all colonial claims, based upon a strict observance of the principle that in determining all such questions of sovereignty the interests of the populations concerned must have equal weight with the equitable claims of the government whose title is to be determined.

VI. The evacuation of all Russian territory and such a settlement of all questions affecting Russia as will secure the best and freest cooperation of the other nations of the world in obtaining for her an unhampered and unembarrassed opportunity for the independent determination of her own political development and national policy and assure her of a sincere welcome into the society of free nations under institutions of her own choosing; and, more than a welcome, assistance also of every kind that she may need and may herself desire. The treatment accorded Russia by her sister nations in the months to come will be the acid test of their good will, of their comprehension of her needs as distinguished from their own interests, and of their intelligent and unselfish sympathy.

VII. Belgium, the whole world will agree, must be evacuated and restored, without any attempt to limit the sovereignty which she enjoys in common with all other free nations. No other single act will serve as this will serve to restore confidence among the nations in the laws which they have themselves set and determined for the government of their relation with one another. Without this healing act the whole structure and validity of international law is forever impaired.

VIII. All French territory should be freed and the invaded portions restored, and the wrong done to France by Prussia in 1871 in the matter of Alsace-Lorraine, which has unsettled the peace of the world for nearly fifty years, should be righted, in order that peace may once more be made secure in the interest of all.

IX. A readjustment of the frontiers of Italy shall be effected along clearly recognizable lines of nationality.

X. The peoples of Austria-Hungary, whose place among the nations we wish to see safeguarded and assured, should be accorded the freest opportunity of autonomous development.

XI. Rumania, Serbia, and Montenegro should be evacuated; occupied territories restored; Serbia accorded free and secure access to the sea; and the relations of the several Balkan states to one another determined by friendly counsel along historically established lines of allegiance and nationality; and international guarantees of the political and economic independence and territorial integrity of the several Balkan states should be entered into.

XII. The Turkish portions of the present Ottoman Empire should be assured a secure sovereignty, but the other nationalities which are now under Turkish rule should be assured an undoubted security of life and an absolutely unmolested opportunity of autonomous development, and the Dardanelles should be permanently opened as a free passage to the ships and commerce of all nations under international guarantees.

XIII. An independent Polish state should be erected which should include territories inhabited by indisputably Polish populations, which should be assured a free and secure access to the sea, and whose political and economic independence and territorial integrity should be guaranteed by international covenant.

XIV. A general association of nations must be formed under specific covenants for the purpose of affording mutual guarantees of political independence and territorial integrity to great and small states alike.

In regard to these essential rectifications [righting] of wrong and assertions of right we feel ourselves to be intimate partners of all the governments and peoples associated together against the Imperialists. We cannot be separated in interest or divided in purpose. We stand together until the end.

For such arrangements and covenants we are willing to fight and to continue to fight until they are achieved; but only because we wish the right to prevail and desire a just and stable peace such as can be secured only by removing the chief provocations to war, which this program does not remove. We have no jealousy of German greatness, and there is nothing in this program that impairs it. We grudge her no achievement or distinction of learning or of pacific [peaceful] enterprise such as have made her record very bright and very enviable. We do not wish to injure her or to block in any way her legitimate influence or power. We do not wish to fight her either with arms or with hostile arrangements of trade if she is willing to associate herself with us and the other peace-loving nations of the world in covenants of justice and law and fair dealing. We wish her only to accept a place of equality among the peoples of the world—the new world in which we now live,—instead of a place of mastery.

Neither do we presume to suggest to her any alteration or modification of her institutions. But it is necessary, we must frankly say, and necessary as a preliminary to any intelligent dealings with her on our part, that we should know whom her spokesmen speak for when they speak to us, whether for the Reichstag [German legislature] majority or for the military party and the men whose creed is imperial domination.

We have spoken now, surely, in terms too concrete to admit of any further doubt or question. An evident principle runs through the whole program I have outlined. It is the principle of justice to all peoples and nationalities, and their right to live on equal terms of liberty and safety with one another, whether they be strong or weak. Unless this principle be made its foundation no part of the structure of international justice can stand. The people of the United States could act upon no other principle; and to the vindication of this principle they are ready to devote their lives, their honor, and everything that they possess. The moral climax of this the culminating and final war for human liberty has come, and they are ready to put their own strength, their own highest purpose, their own integrity and devotion to the test. ❖

Martin Luther King, Jr.'s "I Have A Dream" Speech

August 28, 1963

Five score years ago, a great American, in whose symbolic shadow we stand, signed the Emancipation Proclamation. This momentous decree came as a great beacon light of hope to millions of Negro slaves who had been seared in the flames of withering injustice. It came as a joyous daybreak to end the long night of captivity.

But one hundred years later, we must face the tragic fact that the Negro is still not free. One hundred years later, the life of the Negro is still sadly crippled by the manacles of segregation and the chains of discrimination. One hundred years later, the Negro lives on a lonely island of poverty in the midst of a vast ocean of material prosperity. One hundred years later, the Negro is still languished in the corners of American society and finds himself an exile in his own land. So we have come here today to dramatize an appalling condition.

In a sense we have come to our nation's Capital to cash a check. When the architects of our republic wrote the magnificent words of the Constitution and the Declaration of Independence, they were signing a promissory note to which every American was to fall heir. This note was a promise that all men would be guaranteed the unalienable rights of life, liberty, and the pursuit of happiness.

It is obvious today that America has defaulted on this promissory note insofar as her citizens of color are concerned. Instead of honoring this sacred obligation, America has given the Negro people a bad check; a check which has come back marked "insufficient funds." But we refuse to believe that the bank of justice is bankrupt. We refuse to believe that there are insufficient funds in the great vaults of opportunity of this nation. So we have come to cash this check—a check that will give us upon demand the riches of freedom and the security of justice.

We have also come to this hallowed spot to remind America of the fierce urgency of *now*. This is no time to engage in the luxury of cooling off or to take the tranquilizing drug of gradualism. *Now* is the time to make real the promises of democracy. *Now* is the time to rise from the dark and desolate valley of segregation to the sunlit path of racial justice. *Now* is the time to open the doors of opportunity to all of God's children. *Now* is the time to lift our nation from the quicksands of racial injustice to the solid rock of brotherhood.

It would be fatal for the nation to overlook the urgency of the moment and to underestimate the determination of the Negro. This sweltering summer of the Negro's legitimate discontent will not pass until there is an invigorating autumn of freedom and equality. Nineteen sixty-three is not an end, but a beginning. Those who hope that the Negro needed to blow off steam and will now be content will have a rude awakening if the nation returns to business as usual. There will be neither rest nor tranquility in America until the Negro is granted his citizenship rights. The whirlwinds of revolt will continue to shake the foundations of our nation until the bright day of justice emerges.

But there is something that I must say to my people who stand on the warm threshold which leads into the palace of justice. In the process of gaining our rightful place we must not be guilty of wrongful deeds. Let us not seek to satisfy our thirst for freedom by drinking from the cup of bitterness and hatred. We must forever conduct our struggle on the high plane of dignity and discipline. We must not allow our creative protest to degenerate into physical violence. Again and again we must rise to the majestic heights of meeting physical force with soul force.

The marvelous new militancy which has engulfed the Negro community must not lead us to a distrust of all white people, for many of our white brothers, as evidenced by their presence here today, have come to realize that their destiny is tied up with our destiny and their freedom is inextricably bound to our freedom. We cannot walk alone.

And as we walk, we must make the pledge that we shall march ahead. We cannot turn back. There are those who are asking the devotees of civil rights, "When will you be satisfied?"

We can never be satisfied as long as the Negro is the victim of the unspeakable horrors of police brutality.

We can never be satisfied as long as our bodies, heavy with the fatigue of travel, cannot gain lodging in the motels of the highways and the hotels of the cities.

We cannot be satisfied as long as the Negro's basic mobility is from a smaller ghetto to a larger one.

We can never be satisfied as long as a Negro in Mississippi cannot vote and a Negro in New York believes he has nothing for which to vote.

No, no, we are not satisfied, and we will not be satisfied until justice rolls down like waters and righteousness like a mighty stream.

I am not unmindful that some of you have come here out of great trials and tribulations. Some of you have come fresh from narrow jail cells. Some of you have come from areas where your quest for freedom left you battered by the storms of persecution and staggered by the winds of police brutality. You have been the veterans of creative suffering. Continue to work with the faith that unearned suffering is redemptive.

Go back to Mississippi, go back to Alabama, go back to South Carolina, go back to Georgia, go back to Louisiana, go back to the slums and ghettos of our Northern cities, knowing that somehow this situation can and will be changed. Let us not wallow in the valley of despair.

I say to you today, my friends, that in spite of the difficulties and frustrations of the moment I still have a dream. It is a dream deeply rooted in the American dream.

I have a dream that one day this nation will rise up and live out the true meaning of its creed: "We hold these truths to be self-evident; that all men are created equal."

I have a dream that one day on the red hills of Georgia the sons of former slaves and the sons of former slaveowners will be able to sit down together at the table of brotherhood.

I have a dream that one day even the state of Mississippi, a desert state sweltering with the heat of injustice and oppression, will be transformed into an oasis of freedom and justice.

I have a dream that my four little children will one day live in a nation where they will not be judged by the color of their skin but by the content of their character.

I have a dream today.

I have a dream that one day the state of Alabama, whose governor's lips are presently dripping with the words of interposition and nullification, will be transformed into a situation where little black boys and black girls will be able to join hands with little white boys and white girls and walk together as sisters and brothers.

I have a dream today.

I have a dream that one day every valley shall be exhalted, every hill and mountain shall be made low, the rough places will be made plain, and the crooked places will be made straight, and the glory of the Lord shall be revealed, and all flesh shall see it together.

This is our hope. This is the faith with which I return to the South. With this faith we will be able to hew out of the mountain of despair a stone of hope. With this faith we will be able to transform the jangling discords of our nation into a beautiful symphony of brotherhood.

With this faith we will be able to work together, to pray together, to struggle together, to go to jail together, to stand up for freedom together, knowing that we will be free one day.

This will be the day when all of God's children will be able to sing with new meaning, "My country 'tis of thee, sweet land of liberty, of thee I sing. Land where my fathers died, land of the Pilgrims' pride, from every mountainside, let freedom ring."

And if America is to be a great nation, this must become true. So let freedom ring from the prodigious hilltops of New Hampshire. Let freedom ring from the mighty mountains of New York. Let freedom ring from the heightening Alleghenies of Pennsylvania!

Let freedom ring from the snowcapped Rockies of Colorado! Let freedom ring from the curvaceous peaks of California! But not only that; let freedom ring from Stone Mountain of Georgia! Let freedom ring from Lookout Mountain of Tennessee!

Let freedom ring from every hill and molehill of Mississippi. From every mountainside, let freedom ring.

When we let freedom ring, when we let it ring from every village and every hamlet, from every state and every city, we will be able to speed up that day when all of God's children, black men and white men, Jews and Gentiles, Protestants and Catholics, will be able to join hands and sing in the words of the old Negro spiritual, "Free at last! Free at last! Thank God Almighty, we are free at last!" ❖

ATLAS

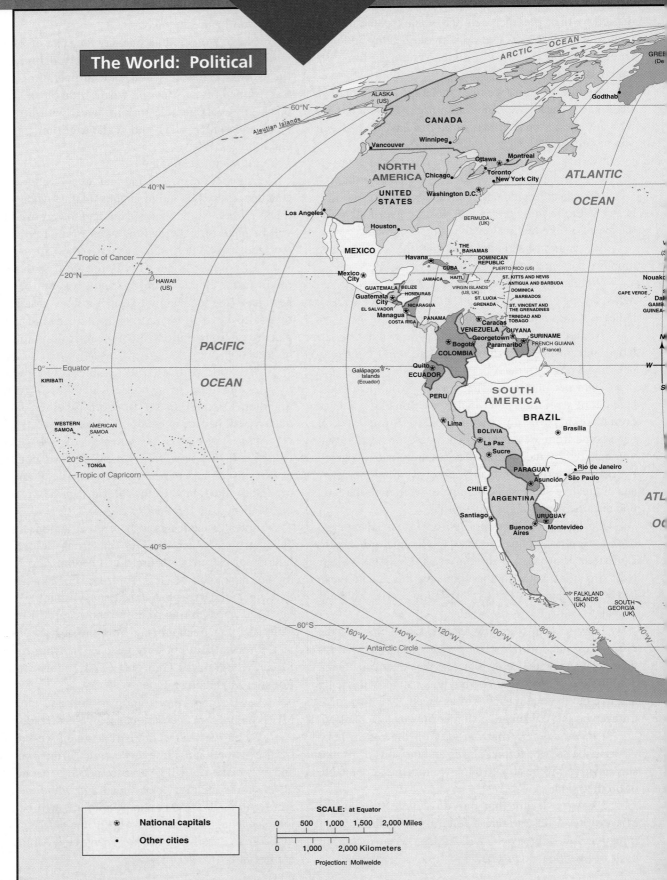

The World: Political

ARCTIC OCEAN

GREE
(De

ALASKA
(US)

60°N

Aleutian Islands

CANADA

Vancouver • Winnipeg •

NORTH
AMERICA

Ottawa ⊛ • Montreal

Chicago • Toronto

40°N

UNITED
STATES

New York City

Washington D.C.

ATLANTIC

OCEAN

Los Angeles •

Houston •

BERMUDA
(UK)

Tropic of Cancer

MEXICO

THE
BAHAMAS

Havana ⊛

CUBA

DOMINICAN
REPUBLIC

PUERTO RICO (US)

Nouak

20°N

Mexico
City ⊛

JAMAICA

HAITI

ST. KITTS AND NEVIS

ANTIGUA AND BARBUDA

GUATEMALA BELIZE

VIRGIN ISLANDS
(US, UK)

DOMINICA

CAPE VERDE

Da

Guatemala
City ⊛

HONDURAS

ST. LUCIA

BARBADOS

GAMB

GUINEA-

EL SALVADOR

NICARAGUA

GRENADA

ST. VINCENT AND
THE GRENADINES

Managua ⊛

PANAMA

COSTA RICA

TRINIDAD AND
TOBAGO

Caracas ⊛

VENEZUELA

GUYANA

SURINAME

HAWAII
(US)

PACIFIC

Georgetown ⊛

Paramaribo ⊛

Bogotá ⊛

COLOMBIA

FRENCH GUIANA
(France)

M

W

OCEAN

KIRIBATI

0° Equator

Galápagos
Islands
(Ecuador)

Quito ⊛

ECUADOR

S

PERU

SOUTH
AMERICA

WESTERN
SAMOA

AMERICAN
SAMOA

• Lima

BRAZIL

• Brasília ⊛

BOLIVIA

20°S

TONGA

La Paz ⊛
⊛ Sucre

Tropic of Capricorn

PARAGUAY

• Rio de Janeiro

CHILE

Asunción ⊛

• São Paulo

ARGENTINA

ATL

OC

Santiago ⊛

URUGUAY

40°S

Buenos
Aires ⊛

⊛ Montevideo

FALKLAND
ISLANDS
(UK)

SOUTH
GEORGIA
(UK)

60°S

160°W

140°W

120°W

100°W

80°W

60°W

40°W

Antarctic Circle

Godthab •

SCALE: at Equator

0	500	1,000	1,500	2,000 Miles

⊛ National capitals

• Other cities

0	1,000	2,000 Kilometers

Projection: Mollweide

772

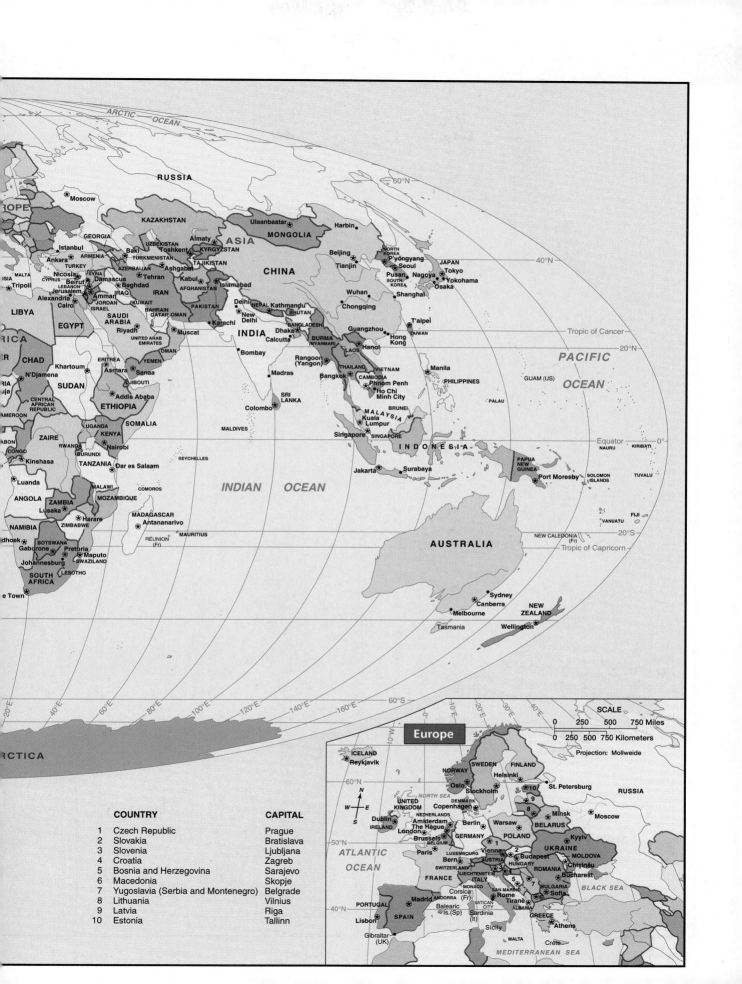

ARCTIC OCEAN

RUSSIA

⊛ Moscow

KAZAKHSTAN

Ulaanbaatar ⊛

MONGOLIA

Harbin

GEORGIA
Istanbul
Ankara ⊛   ARMENIA
TURKEY
NICOSIA   AZERBAIJAN
MALTA   CYPRUS   SYRIA
⊛ Tripoli   LEBANON   Damascus
Beirut   Baghdad
Jerusalem ⊛   Amman   IRAQ
Alexandria   JORDAN
Cairo   ISRAEL   KUWAIT

Almaty ⊛   ASIA
UZBEKISTAN   KYRGYZSTAN
Toshkent   TAJIKISTAN
TURKMENISTAN
Ashgabat
⊛ Tehran   Kabul ⊛
AFGHANISTAN   Islamabad
IRAN

Beijing   NORTH
KOREA   P'yongyang
Tianjin   Seoul
SOUTH   Pusan   Nagoya
KOREA

CHINA

Wuhan   Shanghai

JAPAN
Tokyo
Yokohama
Osaka

LIBYA   EGYPT

BAHRAIN
QATAR   OMAN
SAUDI   UNITED ARAB
ARABIA   EMIRATES
Riyadh ⊛   OMAN
⊛ Muscat

Delhi
NEPAL   Kathmandu
New   BHUTAN
Delhi
PAKISTAN   BANGLADESH
Karachi   Dhaka ⊛
INDIA   Calcutta   BURMA
(MYANMAR)
Bombay   LAOS

Chongqing

Guangzhou   T'aipei
Hong   TAIWAN
Kong

Tropic of Cancer

PACIFIC
OCEAN

CHAD   Khartoum ⊛
N'Djamena
CENTRAL
AFRICAN
REPUBLIC
CAMEROON

ERITREA
Asmara ⊛   YEMEN
Sanaa ⊛
DJIBOUTI
ETHIOPIA
Addis Ababa ⊛

Rangoon
(Yangon)
Madras   Bangkok
THAILAND   VIETNAM
CAMBODIA
Phnom Penh
Ho Chi
Minh City

Hanoi

Manila

PHILIPPINES

GUAM (US)

20°N

SUDAN

SRI
LANKA
Colombo ⊛

BRUNEI
MALAYSIA
Kuala
Lumpur

PALAU

40°N

ZAIRE
Kinshasa ⊛
Luanda
ANGOLA

UGANDA
KENYA
RWANDA   ⊛ Nairobi
BURUNDI
TANZANIA   Dar es Salaam
SOMALIA

MALDIVES

SEYCHELLES

Singapore   SINGAPORE

INDONESIA

NAURU
Equator

KIRIBATI

0°

ZAMBIA
Lusaka ⊛
NAMIBIA

MALAWI
MOZAMBIQUE
COMOROS

INDIAN   OCEAN

Jakarta   Surabaya

PAPUA
NEW
GUINEA
Port Moresby ⊛

SOLOMON
ISLANDS

TUVALU

MADAGASCAR
Antananarivo ⊛
Harare ⊛
ZIMBABWE
BOTSWANA

REUNION
(Fr)   MAURITIUS

VANUATU

FIJI

NEW CALEDONIA
(Fr)   20°S

hoek ⊛   Gaborone ⊛   Pretoria
⊛ Maputo
Johannesburg   SWAZILAND
SOUTH   LESOTHO
AFRICA
e Town ⊛

AUSTRALIA

Tropic of Capricorn

20°E   40°E   60°E   80°E   100°E   120°E   140°E   160°E   60°S

Sydney ⊛
Canberra ⊛
Melbourne ⊛   NEW
ZEALAND
Tasmania   Wellington ⊛

CTICA

SCALE
0   250   500   750 Miles
0   250   500   750 Kilometers
Projection: Mollweide

Europe

ICELAND
⊛ Reykjavik

NORWAY   SWEDEN   FINLAND
Oslo ⊛   Helsinki ⊛
10
St. Petersburg   RUSSIA
UNITED   NORTH   Stockholm ⊛   9
KINGDOM   SEA   DENMARK
Copenhagen ⊛   8
Dublin ⊛   NETHERLANDS
IRELAND   Amsterdam   Berlin ⊛   Minsk ⊛   Moscow ⊛
The Hague   Warsaw ⊛   BELARUS
London ⊛   Brussels   GERMANY   POLAND
BELGIUM   Kyyiv ⊛
Paris ⊛   LUXEMBOURG   UKRAINE
Vienna ⊛   2   MOLDOVA
SWITZERLAND   Bern ⊛   AUSTRIA   Budapest ⊛   Chişinău ⊛
LIECHTENSTEIN   3   HUNGARY   ROMANIA   Bucharest ⊛
FRANCE   ITALY   4
5   7   BLACK SEA
MONACO   SAN MARINO   BULGARIA
Rome ⊛   6   Sofia ⊛
PORTUGAL   Corsica   VATICAN   Tiranë ⊛
(Fr)   CITY   ALBANIA
Madrid ⊛   ANDORRA   Sardinia   GREECE
Balearic   (It)   Athens ⊛
Is.(Sp)
Lisbon ⊛   SPAIN
Gibraltar   Sicily   MALTA   Crete
(UK)   MEDITERRANEAN SEA

N
W   E
S

ATLANTIC
OCEAN

60°N

50°N

40°N

10°W   0°   10°E   20°E   30°E   40°E

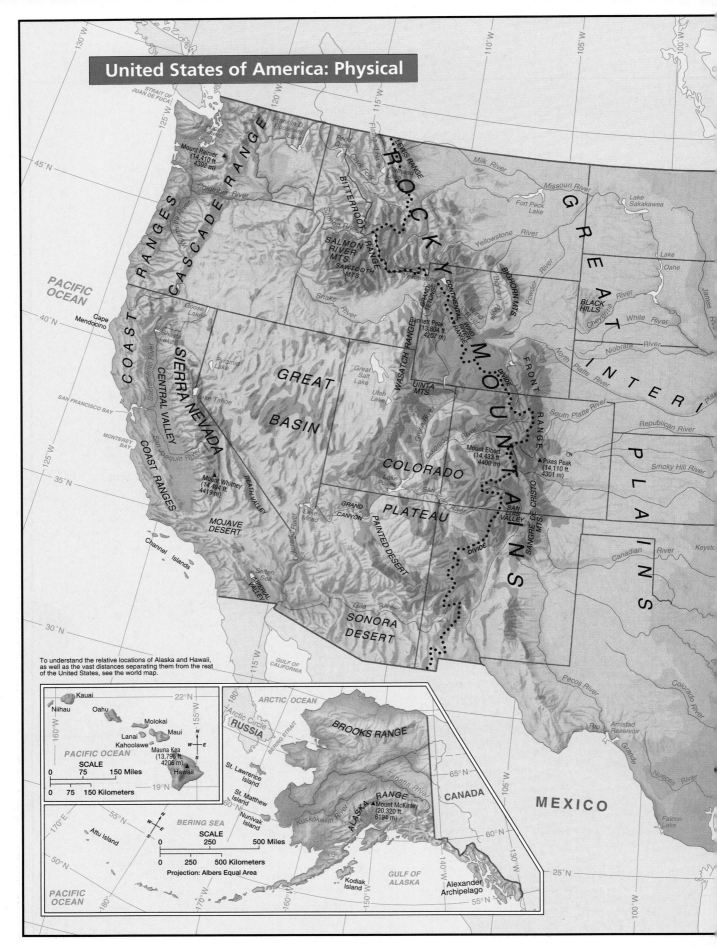

United States of America: Physical

PACIFIC OCEAN

STRAIT OF JUAN DE FUCA

Cape Mendocino

COAST RANGES

CASCADE RANGE

Mount Rainier (14,410 ft. 4392 m)

Columbia River

Snake River

Franklin D. Roosevelt Lake

Pend Oreille

Clark Fork

Flathead River

LEWIS RANGE

BITTERROOT RANGE

SALMON RIVER MTS.

SAWTOOTH MTS.

SALMON RANGE

R O C K Y

Milk River

Missouri River

Yellowstone River

Fort Peck Lake

Lake Sakakawea

G R E A T

Lake Oahe

Snake River

TETONS

GRAND TETONS

CONTINENTAL DIVIDE

WIND RIVER RANGE

Bannett Peak (13,804 ft. 4207 m)

WASATCH RANGE

BIGHORN MTS.

Bighorn River

Powder River

Cheyenne River

BLACK HILLS

White River

Niobrara River

I N T E R I

Goose Lake

Shasta Lake

SIERRA NEVADA

CENTRAL VALLEY

Sacramento River

Pyramid Lake

Lake Tahoe

G R E A T

B A S I N

Great Salt Lake

Utah Lake

UINTA MTS.

Green River

FRONT RANGE

DIVIDE

Mount Elbert (14,433 ft. 4400 m)

Pikes Peak (14,110 ft. 4301 m)

North Platte River

South Platte River

Republican River

Smoky Hill River

P L A I N S

SAN FRANCISCO BAY

MONTEREY BAY

San Joaquin River

COAST RANGES

Mount Whitney (14,494 ft. 4419 m)

DEATH VALLEY

MOJAVE DESERT

Colorado River

Lake Mead

GRAND CANYON

Lake Powell

COLORADO

PLATEAU

PAINTED DESERT

San Juan River

SANGRE DE CRISTO MTS.

SAN LUIS VALLEY

Canadian River

Keysto

Channel Islands

Salton Sea

IMPERIAL VALLEY

Gila River

SONORA DESERT

DIVIDE

Pecos River

Colorado River

MEXICO

GULF OF CALIFORNIA

To understand the relative locations of Alaska and Hawaii, as well as the vast distances separating them from the rest of the United States, see the world map.

Rio Grande

Amistad Reservoir

Nueces River

Falcon Lake

Hawaii inset

Kauai

Niihau

Oahu

Molokai

Lanai

Kahoolawe

Maui

Mauna Kea (13,796 ft. 4206 m)

Hawaii

PACIFIC OCEAN

SCALE

0   75   150 Miles

0   75   150 Kilometers

Alaska inset

ARCTIC OCEAN

Arctic Circle

RUSSIA

BERING STRAIT

BROOKS RANGE

Tanana River

St. Lawrence Island

St. Matthew Island

Nunivak Island

Kuskokwim River

ALASKA RANGE

Mount McKinley (20,320 ft. 6194 m)

CANADA

Kodiak Island

GULF OF ALASKA

Alexander Archipelago

Bering Sea inset

Attu Island

BERING SEA

SCALE

0   250   500 Miles

0   250   500 Kilometers

Projection: Albers Equal Area

PACIFIC OCEAN

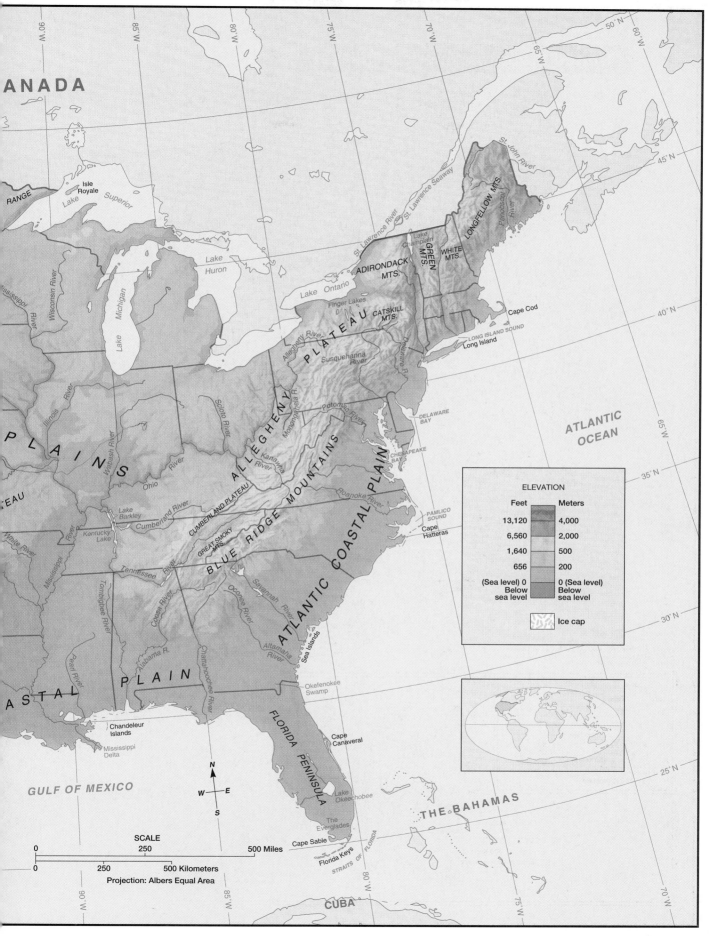

CANADA

RANGE

Isle
Royale

Lake Superior

Lake Huron

Lake Michigan

Mississippi River

Wisconsin River

Illinois River

Wabash River

PLAINS

White River

Kentucky
Lake

Lake
Barkley

Ohio
River

Scioto River

Cumberland River

Tennessee River

ALLEGHENY

PLATEAU

St. Lawrence River

St. Lawrence Seaway

ADIRONDACK
MTS.

Finger Lakes

Lake
Champlain

GREEN
MTS.

LONGFELLOW MTS.

WHITE
MTS.

St. John River

Penobscot River

Cape Cod

Lake Ontario

CATSKILL
MTS.

Allegheny River

Susquehanna
River

Delaware R.

LONG ISLAND SOUND

Long Island

Monongahela R.

Kanawha
River

Potomac River

DELAWARE
BAY

CHESAPEAKE
BAY

ATLANTIC
OCEAN

CUMBERLAND PLATEAU

GREAT SMOKY
MTS.

BLUE RIDGE MOUNTAINS

Roanoke River

PAMLICO
SOUND

Cape
Hatteras

ATLANTIC COASTAL PLAIN

Coosa River

Oconee River

Savannah River

Altamaha
River

Sea Islands

Tombigbee River

Alabama R.

Chattahoochee River

Pearl River

ASTAL   PLAIN

Okefenokee
Swamp

Chandeleur
Islands

Mississippi
Delta

Cape
Canaveral

FLORIDA PENINSULA

GULF OF MEXICO

N
W   E
S

Lake
Okeechobee

The
Everglades

Cape Sable

Florida Keys

STRAITS OF FLORIDA

THE BAHAMAS

CUBA

ELEVATION

Feet	Meters
13,120	4,000
6,560	2,000
1,640	500
656	200
(Sea level) 0	0 (Sea level)
Below sea level	Below sea level

Ice cap

SCALE

0   250   500 Miles

0   250   500 Kilometers

Projection: Albers Equal Area

United States of America: Political

WASHINGTON
Seattle
Olympia★ ●Tacoma
Spokane ●
PUGET SOUND
STRAIT OF JUAN DE FUCA
Franklin D. Roosevelt Lake
Pend Oreille

OREGON
Portland
★Salem
●Eugene
Columbia River

IDAHO
★Boise
Snake River
Pocatello ●

MONTANA
Helena ★
Flathead Lake
Fort Peck Lake
Missouri River
Yellowstone River
Billings ●
Yellowstone Lake

NORTH DAKOTA
★Bismarck
Lake Sakakawea

SOUTH DAKOTA
Pierre ●
Lake Oahe
Sioux

WYOMING
Casper ●
Cheyenne ★

NEBRASKA
Platte River

PACIFIC OCEAN
Cape Mendocino

NEVADA
Reno ●
★Carson City
Lake Tahoe
Pyramid Lake
Shasta Lake
Goose Lake

CALIFORNIA
Sacramento River
Concord ●Berkeley
Oakland●San Francisco
Hayward●
Sunnyvale●
San Jose●
Fremont●
★Sacramento
Stockton●
Modesto●
San Joaquin River
●Fresno
●Bakersfield
SAN FRANCISCO BAY
MONTEREY BAY

Oxnard●
Glendale●Pasadena●Pomona
Los Angeles●
Inglewood●Torrance●
Long Beach●
Channel Islands
San Diego●
Santa Ana●Garden Grove●Anaheim●Fullerton●Riverside●
Ontario●San Bernardino●
Huntington Beach●
Salton Sea

UTAH
Great Salt Lake
Salt Lake City★
Utah Lake ●Provo
Green River
●Las Vegas
Lake Mead
Lake Powell

COLORADO
Lakewood●★Aurora
Denver
●Colorado Springs

KANSAS

Colorado River

ARIZONA
Glendale●Scottsdale●
Phoenix★●Mesa
Gila River
●Tucson

NEW MEXICO
Santa Fe★
●Albuquerque

OKLAHOMA
Canadian River
Keysto
Oklahoma City●
●Amarillo

TEXAS
●Lubbock
●Abilene
●Odessa
El Paso●
Pecos River
Irvi
Fort Worth
Colorado River
A

MEXICO
Rio Grande
Amistad Reservoir
●San Antonio
●Laredo

To understand the relative locations of Alaska and Hawaii as well as the vast distances separating them from the rest of the United States, see the world map.

HAWAII
Kauai
Niihau
Oahu
Honolulu★
Molokai
Lanai
Kahoolawe
Maui
Hawaii
PACIFIC OCEAN
SCALE
0   75   150 Miles
0   75   150 Kilometers

ALASKA
ARCTIC OCEAN
Arctic Circle
RUSSIA
BERING STRAIT
St. Lawrence Island
St. Matthew Island
Nunivak Island
Nome●
●Fairbanks
Yukon River
CANADA
Anchorage●
Kodiak Island
GULF OF ALASKA
Juneau★
Alexander Archipelago
BERING SEA
SCALE
0   250   500 Miles
0   250   500 Kilometers
Projection: Albers Equal Area
Attu Island
Aleutian Islands
PACIFIC OCEAN

FACTS ABOUT THE STATES

State	Year of Statehood	1994 Population	Reps. in Congress	Area (sq. mi.)	Population Density (sq. mi.)	Capital
Alabama	1819	4,219,000	7	51,705	83.1	Montgomery
Alaska	1959	606,000	1	591,004	1.1	Juneau
Arizona	1912	4,075,000	6	114,000	35.9	Phoenix
Arkansas	1836	2,453,000	4	53,187	47.1	Little Rock
California	1850	31,431,000	52	158,706	201.5	Sacramento
Colorado	1876	3,656,000	6	104,091	35.2	Denver
Connecticut	1788	3,275,000	6	5,018	676.0	Hartford
Delaware	1787	706,000	1	2,045	361.3	Dover
District of Columbia	—	570,000	—	69	9,347.1	—
Florida	1845	13,953,000	23	58,664	258.4	Tallahassee
Georgia	1788	7,055,000	11	58,910	121.8	Atlanta
Hawaii	1959	1,179,000	2	6,471	183.5	Honolulu
Idaho	1890	1,133,000	2	83,564	13.7	Boise
Illinois	1818	11,752,000	20	56,345	211.4	Springfield
Indiana	1816	5,572,000	10	36,185	160.4	Indianapolis
Iowa	1846	2,829,000	5	56,275	50.6	Des Moines
Kansas	1861	2,554,000	4	82,277	31.2	Topeka
Kentucky	1792	3,827,000	6	40,410	96.3	Frankfort
Louisiana	1812	4,315,000	7	47,752	99.0	Baton Rouge
Maine	1820	1,240,000	2	33,265	40.2	Augusta
Maryland	1788	5,006,000	8	10,460	512.1	Annapolis
Massachusetts	1788	6,041,000	10	8,284	770.7	Boston
Michigan	1837	9,496,000	16	58,527	167.2	Lansing
Minnesota	1858	4,567,000	8	84,402	57.4	St. Paul
Mississippi	1817	2,669,000	5	47,689	56.9	Jackson
Missouri	1821	5,278,000	9	69,697	76.6	Jefferson City
Montana	1889	856,000	1	147,046	5.9	Helena
Nebraska	1867	1,623,000	3	77,355	21.1	Lincoln
Nevada	1864	1,457,000	2	110,561	13.3	Carson City
New Hampshire	1788	1,137,000	2	9,279	126.7	Concord
New Jersey	1787	7,904,000	13	7,787	1,065.4	Trenton
New Mexico	1912	1,654,000	3	121,593	13.6	Santa Fe
New York	1788	18,169,000	31	49,108	384.7	Albany
North Carolina	1789	7,070,000	12	52,669	145.1	Raleigh
North Dakota	1889	638,000	1	70,702	9.2	Bismarck
Ohio	1803	11,102,000	19	41,330	271.1	Columbus
Oklahoma	1907	3,258,000	6	69,956	47.4	Oklahoma City
Oregon	1859	3,086,000	5	97,073	32.1	Salem
Pennsylvania	1787	12,052,000	21	45,308	268.9	Harrisburg
Rhode Island	1790	997,000	2	1,212	953.8	Providence
South Carolina	1788	3,664,000	6	31,113	121.7	Columbia
South Dakota	1889	721,000	1	77,116	9.5	Pierre
Tennessee	1796	5,175,000	9	42,144	125.6	Nashville
Texas	1845	18,378,000	30	266,807	70.2	Austin
Utah	1896	1,908,000	3	84,899	23.2	Salt Lake City
Vermont	1791	580,000	1	9,614	62.7	Montpelier
Virginia	1788	6,552,000	11	40,767	165.5	Richmond
Washington	1889	5,343,000	9	68,139	80.2	Olympia
West Virginia	1863	1,822,000	3	24,232	75.6	Charleston
Wisconsin	1848	5,082,000	9	56,153	93.6	Madison
Wyoming	1890	476,000	1	97,809	4.9	Cheyenne

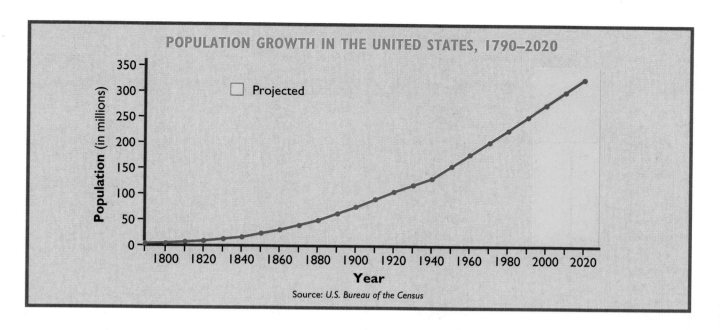

POPULATION GROWTH IN THE UNITED STATES, 1790–2020

Population (in millions) vs. Year

☐ Projected

Source: *U.S. Bureau of the Census*

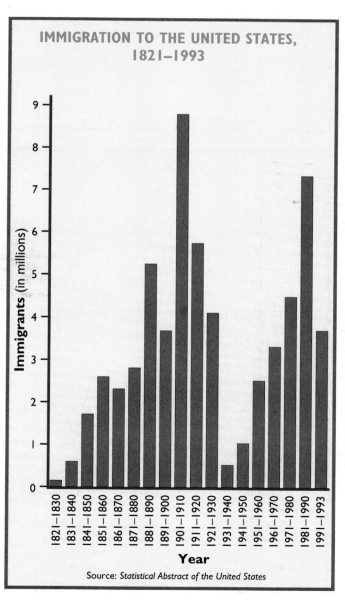

IMMIGRATION TO THE UNITED STATES, 1821–1993

Immigrants (in millions) vs. Year

Source: *Statistical Abstract of the United States*

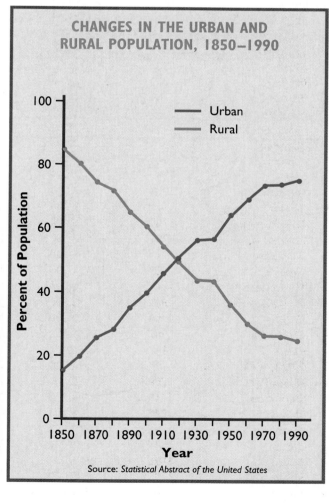

CHANGES IN THE URBAN AND RURAL POPULATION, 1850–1990

Percent of Population vs. Year

Urban
Rural

Source: *Statistical Abstract of the United States*

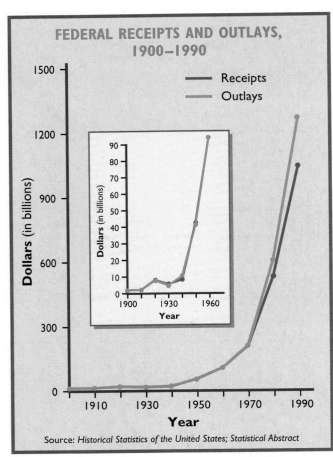

FEDERAL RECEIPTS AND OUTLAYS, 1900–1990

Receipts
Outlays

Dollars (in billions)

1910 1930 1950 1970 1990

Year

Dollars (in billions)

1900 1930 1960

Year

Source: *Historical Statistics of the United States; Statistical Abstract*

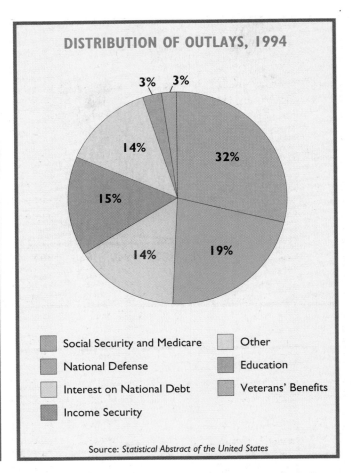

DISTRIBUTION OF OUTLAYS, 1994

3% 3%
14% 32%
15%
14% 19%

Social Security and Medicare
National Defense
Interest on National Debt
Income Security
Other
Education
Veterans' Benefits

Source: *Statistical Abstract of the United States*

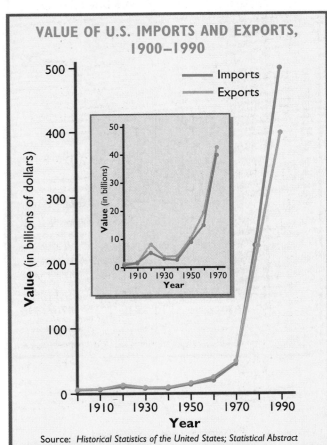

VALUE OF U.S. IMPORTS AND EXPORTS, 1900–1990

Imports
Exports

Value (in billions of dollars)

1910 1930 1950 1970 1990

Year

Value (in billions)

1910 1930 1950 1970

Year

Source: *Historical Statistics of the United States; Statistical Abstract*

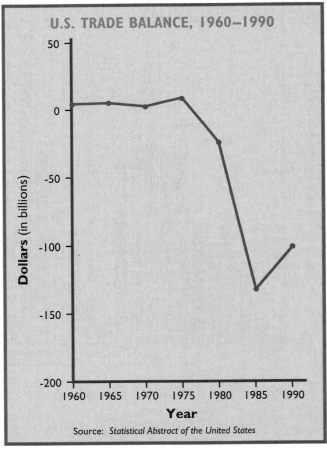

U.S. TRADE BALANCE, 1960–1990

Dollars (in billions)

1960 1965 1970 1975 1980 1985 1990

Year

Source: *Statistical Abstract of the United States*

PRESIDENTS OF THE UNITED STATES

No.	Name	Born–Died	Years In Office	Political Party	Home State	Vice President
1	George Washington	1732–1799	1789–97	None	VA	John Adams
2	John Adams	1735–1826	1797–1801	Federalist	MA	Thomas Jefferson
3	Thomas Jefferson	1743–1826	1801–09	Republican*	VA	Aaron Burr
4	James Madison	1751–1836	1809–17	Republican	VA	George Clinton / George Clinton / Elbridge Gerry
5	James Monroe	1758–1831	1817–25	Republican	VA	Daniel D. Tompkins
6	John Quincy Adams	1767–1848	1825–29	Republican	MA	John C. Calhoun
7	Andrew Jackson	1767–1845	1829–37	Democratic	TN	John C. Calhoun / Martin Van Buren
8	Martin Van Buren	1782–1862	1837–41	Democratic	NY	Richard M. Johnson
9	William Henry Harrison	1773–1841	1841	Whig	OH	John Tyler
10	John Tyler	1790–1862	1841–45	Whig	VA	
11	James K. Polk	1795–1849	1845–49	Democratic	TN	George M. Dallas
12	Zachary Taylor	1784–1850	1849–50	Whig	LA	Millard Fillmore
13	Millard Fillmore	1800–1874	1850–53	Whig	NY	
14	Franklin Pierce	1804–1869	1853–57	Democratic	NH	William R. King
15	James Buchanan	1791–1868	1857–61	Democratic	PA	John C. Breckenridge
16	Abraham Lincoln	1809–1865	1861–65	Republican	IL	Hannibal Hamlin / Andrew Johnson
17	Andrew Johnson	1808–1875	1865–69	Republican	TN	
18	Ulysses S. Grant	1822–1885	1869–77	Republican	IL	Schuyler Colfax / Henry Wilson
19	Rutherford B. Hayes	1822–1893	1877–81	Republican	OH	William A. Wheeler
20	James A. Garfield	1831–1881	1881	Republican	OH	Chester A. Arthur
21	Chester A. Arthur	1830–1886	1881–85	Republican	NY	
22	Grover Cleveland	1837–1908	1885–89	Democratic	NY	Thomas A. Hendricks
23	Benjamin Harrison	1833–1901	1889–93	Republican	IN	Levi P. Morton
24	Grover Cleveland		1893–97	Democratic	NY	Adlai E. Stevenson
25	William McKinley	1843–1901	1897–1901	Republican	OH	Garrett A. Hobart / Theodore Roosevelt
26	Theodore Roosevelt	1858–1919	1901–09	Republican	NY	Charles W. Fairbanks
27	William Howard Taft	1857–1930	1909–13	Republican	OH	James S. Sherman
28	Woodrow Wilson	1856–1924	1913–21	Democratic	NJ	Thomas R. Marshall
29	Warren G. Harding	1865–1923	1921–23	Republican	OH	Calvin Coolidge
30	Calvin Coolidge	1872–1933	1923–29	Republican	MA	Charles G. Dawes
31	Herbert Hoover	1874–1964	1929–33	Republican	CA	Charles Curtis
32	Franklin D. Roosevelt	1882–1945	1933–45	Democratic	NY	John Nance Garner / Henry Wallace / Harry S. Truman
33	Harry S. Truman	1884–1972	1945–53	Democratic	MO	Alben W. Barkley
34	Dwight D. Eisenhower	1890–1969	1953–61	Republican	KS	Richard M. Nixon
35	John F. Kennedy	1917–1963	1961–63	Democratic	MA	Lyndon B. Johnson
36	Lyndon B. Johnson	1908–1973	1963–69	Democratic	TX	Hubert H. Humphrey
37	Richard M. Nixon	1913–1994	1969–74	Republican	CA	Spiro T. Agnew / Gerald R. Ford
38	Gerald R. Ford	1913–	1974–77	Republican	MI	Nelson A. Rockefeller
39	Jimmy Carter	1924–	1977–81	Democratic	GA	Walter F. Mondale
40	Ronald Reagan	1911–	1981–89	Republican	CA	George Bush
41	George Bush	1924–	1989–1993	Republican	TX	J. Danforth Quayle
42	Bill Clinton	1946–	1993–	Democratic	AR	Albert Gore, Jr.

*The Republican party of the third through sixth presidents is not the party of Abraham Lincoln, which was founded in 1854.

1. PLESSY V. FERGUSON AND BROWN V. BOARD OF EDUCATION

163 U.S. 537 (1896) and 347 U.S. 483 (1954)

WHAT WERE THESE CASES ABOUT?

The stories. These two cases illustrate a profound change in the legality of racial segregation. *Plessy* v. *Ferguson* begins with a law that required all railway companies in Louisiana to provide "separate but equal" accommodations for European American and African American passengers. A group of people who thought the law was unfair recruited Homer Plessy to get arrested in order to test the law. Plessy entered a train and took an empty seat in an all-white coach. When he refused to move to an all-black coach, he was arrested and jailed. In his defense he said that the 1890 law was unconstitutional. The case eventually worked its way up to the Supreme Court.

More than 50 years later an African American named Oliver Brown and his family moved into a white neighborhood in Topeka, Kansas. The Browns assumed that their daughter would attend the neighborhood school. Instead, the school board ordered her to attend a distant all-black school that was supposedly "separate but equal." Saying that school segregation violated the 14th Amendment to the Constitution, Mr. Brown sued the school board.

The question. The question raised by the Court was the same in both cases. Do racially segregated facilities violate the "equal protection" clause of the 14th Amendment?

The issues. The 14th Amendment is one of several amendments that were passed soon after the Civil War to guarantee the freedom of African Americans and to protect them from unfair treatment. The wording of the equal protection clause is: "No State shall . . . deny to any person within its jurisdiction the equal protection of the laws." But just what does this wording forbid? Louisiana

in *Plessy* argued that separate railway carriages could be equal. For instance, they could be equally clean and equally safe. In *Brown,* Kansas said much the same thing, claiming that their all-black and all-white schools were equal in the skill of their teachers, the quality of their buildings, and so on.

In the days of racial segregation the claim that segregated facilities were equal in tangible, or measurable, features was almost always a terrible lie. But the issue facing the Court went deeper. Even if things were made equal in racially segregated facilities, was there something inherently unequal about segregation?

HOW THE CASE WAS DECIDED?

In *Plessy* v. *Ferguson,* the Court ruled that the 14th Amendment's equal protection clause allows racial segregation. In *Brown* v. *Board of Education,* the Court unanimously ruled that the clause does not allow racial segregation.

WHAT DID THE COURT SAY ABOUT CONSTITUTIONAL RIGHTS?

Justice Henry Billings Brown wrote the Court's opinion in *Plessy.* He admitted that the purpose of the 14th Amendment was "to enforce the absolute equality of the two races before the law." But he said that this statement meant political equality, not social equality. In his view, neither African Americans nor European Americans wanted the races to mingle. Brown said that the argument that separate facilities implied that blacks were inferior was false.

In *Brown* the Court's opinion was written by Chief Justice Earl Warren. Separation of African American schoolchildren from European American schoolchildren of the same age and ability, he said, "generates a feeling of inferiority as to their status in the community that may affect their hearts and minds in a way unlikely ever to be undone:' He said that when racial segregation is required by law, the harm is even greater. It makes no difference that "the physical facilities and other 'tangible' factors may be equal."

WHAT IMPLICATIONS DID THESE CASES HAVE FOR THE FUTURE?

In *Brown* v. *Board of Education* the Court did not say that the "separate but equal" doctrine had no place anywhere. It said that the doctrine had no place in public education. This statement, although limited, influenced future cases.

Taken together, *Plessy* and *Brown* show the flexibility of the Constitution's legal principles whose interpretations may change as society changes. The decision in *Plessy* was not unanimous. In a dissenting opinion, Justice John Marshall Harlan declared "Our Constitution is color-blind, and neither knows nor tolerates classes among its citizens." Eventually Harlan's dissent became the law of the land.

2. GIDEON V. WAINWRIGHT

372 U.S. 436 (1963)

WHAT WAS THIS CASE ABOUT?

The story. Clarence Earl Gideon was accused of breaking and entering a Florida poolroom and stealing. When Gideon's case came to trial he could not afford a lawyer, and he asked that the court pay for one. The judge refused, and Gideon was found guilty. While in prison, Gideon asked the U.S. Supreme Court to review his case. He claimed that by refusing to appoint a lawyer to help him, Florida had violated rights promised him by the 6th and 14th Amendments.

The question. Is it a violation of the 6th or 14th Amendment to deny a poor person accused of a major crime the free assistance of a lawyer?

The Issues. The 6th Amendment promises certain rights to people accused of crimes. One promise is that "the accused shall enjoy the right . . . to have the Assistance of Counsel [a lawyer] for his defense." By itself this amendment requires that poor people be provided with free lawyers in federal trials. Gideon, however. was accused of breaking state laws and was tried in a state court. But the 14th Amendment promises that states will not deprive people of life, liberty, or property without due process of law. Jailed, Gideon had been deprived of liberty. Had this liberty been taken away without due process of law?

HOW WAS THE CASE DECIDED?

In a unanimous opinion written by Justice Hugo Black, the Court ruled in Gideon's favor.

WHAT DID THE COURT SAY ABOUT CONSTITUTIONAL RIGHTS?

Members of the Court based their decision that the Constitution requires the appointment of lawyers for the poor on two different view of the 14th Amendment. One is the incorporation view, which holds that the purpose of the due process clause is to take the first eight amendments in the Bill of Rights and incorporate them into state court procedures. The second is the fundamental liberties view, which holds that "due process of law" means "whatever is necessary for justice." What is necessary for justice may not include every promise in the first eight amendments, but it may include promises that go beyond anything in the first eight amendments. In *Gideon* v. *Wainwright* the justices came to the same conclusion by different means.

Justice Black, who wrote the Court's opinion, had to tailor it to accommodate both the incorporation view and the fundamental liberties view. The opinion was a compromise. It said that the 6th Amendment's promise of the "assistance of counsel" is necessary for a fair trial in any court, but it did not say that due process covers every other promise in the first eight amendments.

WHAT IMPLICATIONS DOES THIS CASE HAVE FOR THE FUTURE?

Gideon v. *Wainwright* was one of several Supreme Court cases guaranteeing that the government would pay lawyers to help poor people accused of crimes. The Criminal Justice Act of 1964, signed into law the year after the Gideon decision, provided funding.

3. MIRANDA V. ARIZONA

384 U.S. 436 (1966)

WHAT WAS THIS CASE ABOUT?

The story. On March 13, 1963, a woman was kidnapped near Phoenix, Arizona. Ernesto Miranda was arrested for the crime, and the victim picked him out from a police lineup. Two officers then took him to a room to question him. Although at first Miranda denied the crime, after a short time he gave a detailed oral confession. He then made and signed a written confession.

At the trial the officers testified that they had warned Miranda that anything he might say could be used against him in court and that Miranda had understood. The officers also said that he had confessed without any threats or force. They admitted, however, that they had not told Miranda about his right to silence or legal assistance. Miranda was found guilty. Eventually, he appealed to the U.S. Supreme Court.

The question. Is it a violation of the 5th, 6th, or 14th Amendment to use a confession from someone who has not been informed of the constitutional rights to silence and legal assistance?

The issues. The 6th Amendment promises the assistance of a lawyer to defendants in criminal trials in federal courts and the 14th Amendment applies this promise to the states. Another promise about the way trials are conducted is given in the 5th Amendment: "No person . . . shall be compelled [forced] in any criminal case to be a witness against himself." Thus the 5th Amendment gives a person the right to be silent. Without such a right, innocent people could be tortured until they confessed.

One issue is the point at which 5th and 6th Amendment rights begin. Do they begin only at the trial? Or do these rights begin earlier?

A deeper issue concerns the meaning of being forced to be a witness against oneself. Perhaps keeping a person ignorant of his or her rights is a kind of force. If so, then it violates the 5th Amendment.

HOW WAS THE CASE DECIDED?

By only a five to four majority, the Supreme Court ruled that taking Miranda's confession without informing him of his rights to silence and legal assistance had deprived him of these rights.

WHAT DID THE COURT SAY ABOUT CONSTITUTIONAL RIGHTS?

With regard to the first issue, the Court ruled that an accused person's 5th and 6th Amendment rights begin as soon as the person is arrested. With regard to the second issue, the Court said that failing to inform the accused of his or her rights is a violation of these rights.

Today, if prisoners are not informed of their rights, then judges will rule that what the accused tells the police may not be used as evidence in court, nor can any evidence police find that was based on what the accused said. The arrest may still be valid; it is only the accused person's statements that cannot be used.

WHAT IMPLICATIONS DOES THIS CASE HAVE FOR THE FUTURE?

Miranda v. *Arizona* has been one of the Supreme Court's most controversial cases because it deals with the delicate balance between protecting the accused and protecting society. Even the Court split five to four. Among the general public the most hotly debated aspect of the decision has been the rule that confessions given by accused people who have not been informed of their rights may not be used as evidence. The Court made this rule to prevent innocent people from being found guilty. Some people accept this reasoning. Others think that the rule prevents guilty people from being convicted.

4. UNITED STATES V. NIXON

418 U.S. 683 (1974)

The story. During the Watergate investigation the president's lawyer, John Dean, testified before the Senate that the president had helped plan the cover-up from the beginning. Nixon denied it, but another witness revealed that Nixon had secretly tape-recorded every conversation that had taken place in his office. The tapes would show whether or not Nixon was telling the truth.

By 1974 criminal charges had been filed against seven members of the Nixon administration.

Although Nixon was not charged, he was listed as one of the people involved in the conspiracy. The special prosecutor in charge of the case at the time, Leon Jaworski, asked Nixon to let him hear the tapes. Nixon had already ordered a previous special prosecutor fired for asking the same thing, and to no one's surprise, Nixon refused again. However, Jaworski persisted. He asked the federal district court for help. When the judge ordered Nixon to release the tapes to the court for secret examination, Nixon disobeyed.

Refusing the special prosecutor's request caused a sandal, but disobeying the judge's order caused a constitutional crisis—a tug of war between two branches of government. Could a president defy a federal judge?

Nixon claimed that he could. As president, he said, he had an executive privilege of keeping all presidential communications confidential. He also said that executive privilege was absolute, which meant that nobody could override it for any reason. Because of the urgency of the case, the U.S. Supreme Court agreed to skip over the Court of Appeals in order to settle the case immediately.

The question. Does the Constitution give the president an absolute executive privilege?

The issues. President Nixon gave two arguments for his position. His first argument was that the principle of separation of powers requires that the executive and judicial branches be totally independent of each other. If presidents had to obey judges who ordered them to release evidence, this independence would be destroyed.

His second argument was that the secrecy of communications between a president and his advisers is necessary for the president to be able to look after the public good. Nixon said that is a president's advisers knew that anything they said could be repeated to the public, they might not give him good advice for fear what people would think. Nixon said that if a president didn't receive good advice, it would be harder to carry out the duties of the office as spelled out in the Constitution.

HOW WAS THE CASE DECIDED?

In a decision written by Chief Justice Warren Burger, the Court ruled that executive privilege is not absolute and that Nixon had to turn over the tapes as he had been ordered.

WHAT DID THE COURT SAY ABOUT GOVERNMENTAL POWERS?

The Court examined each of the president's two arguments in turn. One was that preservation of the separation of powers requires the executive and judicial branches to be totally independent. Total independence means that the president does not have to obey court orders to release evidence. The chief justice rejected this claim. The Constitution is based on separation of powers, but under this separation it gives each power or branch a job of its own to do. If the president could withhold evidence from the courts, the courts could not do the job given them by the Constitution. "The powers," concluded the chief justice, "were not intended to operate with absolute independence."

Nixon's second argument was that communications between the president and his advisers need to be confidential for the sake of the public good. Burger admitted that sometimes confidentiality, or secretiveness, is important. But it only applies in specific instances. When communications are about diplomatic or military secrets, confidentiality is of the utmost importance. On the other hand, when communications concern other subjects, confidentiality might not be important at all. Burger concluded that in presidential claims of executive privilege, the need for confidentiality must be balanced against competing needs on a case-by-case basis.

In *United States* v. *Nixon* the need for confidentiality competed with the need to find out the truth in a criminal trial. The purpose of criminal justice, said Burger, "is that guilt shall not escape or innocence suffer." But finding out the truth in a criminal trial requires that courts have all the evidence, even if it includes presidential communications. In this case the courts needed the information on the tapes to carry out their duty. When the need to find out the truth in the Watergate trial was weighed against President Nixon's need for confidentiality, confidentiality lost. Confidentiality might have won had the tapes been about diplomatic or military secrets or had they not contained crucial evidence. Moreover, the district court had not even planned to make the complete tapes public. It had planned to examine them in secret and only the parts that were necessary for the trial would be used in open court.

WHAT IMPLICATIONS DOES THIS CASE HAVE FOR THE FUTURE?

If the president had defied the Supreme Court as he had defied the district court, it would have been an important sign for the future. One reason is that the courts have no enforcement powers of their own. They depend on the executive branch to enforce court orders. If the executive branch defies a court order, the courts have no recourse. Another reason is that successful defiance of the Supreme Court would call the entire idea of judicial review into question. The judicial branch has been established as the final judge of the meaning of the Constitution, and defiance by the president would be like saying the executive branch is its own final judge.

Nixon did not defy the Supreme Court. He obeyed, not out of respect for judicial review, but out of self interest. He feared that unless he gave in, the Senate would remove him from office. Even so, the evidence of the tapes turned out to be so damaging (the tapes showed that he had been part of the cover-up) that Nixon felt that he had to resign the presidency or the House would start impeachment proceedings.

What principles emerge from this case? The Court did not say whether or not such a thing as executive privilege exists. However, it clearly stated that there is no such thing as an absolute executive privilege. The Court put forth the following principles:

> The president's need for confidentiality must be weighed against competing needs, such as the needs of the criminal justice system.

> In disputed cases this weighing may be done by the federal courts.

Conflicts over executive privilege will most likely continue to arise. For example, presidents have claimed executive privilege more than 50 times—just since 1952. In most of these cases they claimed the privilege in order to avoid giving Congress information that it had requested. However, so long as the two principles listed above are accepted by all parties—particularly the principle that the final decision is made by the judicial branch—theses conflicts have much less chance of hurting the nation.

5. ROE V. WADE

410 U.S. 113 (1973)

WHAT WAS THIS CASE ABOUT?

The story. In 1970 Norma McCorvey, an unmarried pregnant woman living in Texas, sought to obtain a legal abortion in a medical facility. Because of Texas' antiabortion statutes, no licensed physician would agree to perform the abortion. Financially unable to travel to another state with less-restrictive abortion laws, McCorvey faced either continuing an unwanted pregnancy or having the procedure performed in a nonmedical facility, which, she believed, would endanger her life.

McCorvey claimed that the Texas antiabortion laws were unconstitutional in that they interfered with her right of personal privacy that is protected by the 9th and 14th Amendments. She took legal action, naming the Dallas County district attorney, Henry Wade, in her lawsuit. Throughout the case, McCorvey used the pseudonym Jane Roe.

The question. Is it a violation of a person's right to privacy for a state to prevent a woman from terminating a pregnancy through an abortion?

The issues. The 14th Amendment says that "No state shall make or enforce any law which shall abridge the privileges . . . of citizens of the United States . . . nor deny to any person . . . the equal protection of the laws." The 9th Amendment states that "The enumeration in the Constitution of certain rights shall not be construed to deny or disparage others retained by the people." Do these amendments encompass and protect a woman's right to a legal abortion?

HOW WAS THE CASE DECIDED?

In an opinion written by Justice Harry Blackmun, the Court ruled that the 14th Amendment's due process guarantee of personal liberty guarantees the right to personal privacy. This guarantee protects a woman's decision about abortion and assures that a state's laws do not abridge, or diminish, this right. The vote was seven to two.

WHAT DID THE COURT SAY ABOUT CONSTITUTIONAL RIGHTS?

In ruling that a state cannot prevent a woman from terminating a pregnancy during the first three months, the Court relied on citizens' right of privacy. Justice Blackmun stated in his opinion that "This right of privacy, whether it be founded in the Fourteenth Amendment's concept of personal liberty and restrictions upon state action, as we feel it is, or . . . in the 9th Amendment's reservation of rights to the people, is broad enough to encompass a woman's decision whether or not to terminate her pregnancy." In its ruling, however, the Court recognized the right of a state to regulate abortions as a pregnancy progressed. During the first three months of a pregnancy, a woman has an unrestricted right to an abortion, although a state can prevent abortions by nonphysicians.

During the second trimester, a state can regulate abortions to protect a woman's health. Only in the final three months of a pregnancy can a state forbid an abortion, unless it is necessary to protect a woman's health.

The ruling also said that a state cannot adopt a theory of when life begins. This prevents a state from giving a fetus the same rights as a newborn.

In 1965 the Court said in *Griswold* v. *Connecticut* that restrictions on the availability of contraceptives violated the constitutional right to privacy. This right—the basis for the Court's ruling in *Roe* v. *Wade*—thus became a pivotal issue in cases that challenged abortion laws.

WHAT IMPLICATIONS DOES THIS CASE HAVE FOR THE FUTURE?

In the decades following the ruling, related cases have been decided that some people claim weaken the legislative impact of *Roe* v. *Wade*. In *Harris* v. *McRae* (1980), the Court ruled that the federal and local governments did not have to pay for abortions for women on welfare, even if the abortions were necessary for medical reasons. Critics of this ruling claimed that women who could not afford the procedure would, like Jane Roe, be faced with either continuing an unwanted pregnancy or resorting to dangerous measures to terminate it. The ruling in *Webster* v. *Reproductive Health Services* (1989), added more restrictions on the availability of abortions.

6. REGENTS OF THE UNIVERSITY OF CALIFORNIA V. BAKKE

438 U.S. 265 (1978)

WHAT WAS THIS CASE ABOUT?

The story. Allan Bakke twice applied to the medical school at the University of California, Davis during the years the medical school operated two different admissions programs. Since the Civil Rights Act of 1964, there had been pressure for schools and other institutions to provide special admissions programs for minority students. There were, however, no specific guidelines on how to accomplish this.

At the University of California, Davis medical school, 84 of the 100 places in the incoming class were filled from the regular program, while 16 were set aside for the special program, which used a quota system. The regular program was for students of all races, so long as they met admission requirements, including a minimum grade point average. Only members of racial minorities could apply through the special program, and their grades did not have to meet the minimum.

Bakke, a white male, applied through the regular program and was turned down. He thought he had been unfairly treated because in both years, students had been admitted through the special program whose grades and test scores were much lower than his. He sued the state university system. Bakke said the special program, established to fulfill the racial quota, violated his 14th Amendment right to equal protection of the law.

The California Supreme Court made two rulings. One said that Davis's admission system was illegal and ordered Bakke admitted. The other ordered that in the future, admissions decisions must not take race into consideration. The California university system appealed to the U.S. Supreme Court.

The questions. First, does the use of a racial quota in admissions violate the equal protection clause of the 14th Amendment? Second, does the equal protection clause require that race be completely ignored? The U.S. Supreme Court had to consider these questions separately, because there might be ways of taking race into account that do not involve quotas.

The issues. Historically, most racial discrimination in our country has hurt members of racial minorities. Bakke complained about a different kind of discrimination. Sometimes called reverse discrimination, it hurt members of the racial majority in order to help members of racial minorities. If the Constitution is "color-blind," then both forms of racial discrimination are unconstitutional.

The 14th Amendment was primarily written because African Americans recently freed from slavery needed protection from discrimination by the white majority. This fact suggests that the equal protection clause protects racial minorities more than the racial majority. But what the amendment actually says is that no state may deny to any person the equal protection of the laws. This fact suggests that the equal protection clause gives the same protection to people of all races. The intent seems to have been to protect minorities, but the wording does not specify this intent.

HOW WAS THE CASE DECIDED?

The Court agreed that the use of a racial quota in admissions was unconstitutional and ordered that Bakke should be admitted. But the Court rejected the idea that an admissions system may never pay any attention to race.

WHAT DID THE COURT SAY ABOUT CONSTITUTIONAL RIGHTS?

Justice Lewis Powell wrote the Court's opinion. He said that the equal protection clause does not completely prohibit states from taking race into account when they are making laws and official policies but that it does make the consideration of race "suspect," or suspicious. When such a law or policy is challenged in court, judges must apply a two-part test. First, are the purposes of the law or policy legitimate? Second, is the consideration given to race necessary to achieve these purposes? California told the Court that its racial quota had four purposes.

Purpose 1. To correct the shortage of racial minorities in medical schools and among doctors. Justice Powell said that this purpose was not acceptable. "Preferring members of any one group for no reason other than race or ethnic origin is discrimination for its own sake."

Purpose 2. To counteract the effects of racial discrimination in society. Justice Powell said that

this was an acceptable purpose. He approved of helping people who belong to groups that have been hurt by past discrimination. However, he said that helping them by hurting others is right only when it makes up for hurts that those specific others have done to them. There was no evidence that Bakke had ever discriminated against people of racial minorities.

Purpose 3: To increase the number of doctors who will be willing to practice medicine in communities where there are not enough doctors. This purpose was also acceptable. However, California had not shown that racial quotas were needed to accomplish this purpose.

Purpose 4. To improve education by making the student body more diverse. This purpose, too, was acceptable. But Justice Powell made two points. First, racial diversity is only one aspect of overall diversity. Second, Justice Powell said that racial quotas are not needed to increase racial diversity. To prove this point he discussed the experience of Harvard College. Harvard considers it a plus if an applicant belongs to a racial minority. But the college does not "insulate the individual from comparison with all other" applicants and thus compares all applicants equally. Yet the Harvard admissions system has been successful in increasing racial diversity in the Harvard student body.

WHAT IMPLICATIONS DOES THIS CASE HAVE FOR THE FUTURE?

One part of the Court's judgment agreed that the use of a racial quota in admissions to Davis Medical School was unconstitutional, while the other part rejected the idea that an admissions system may never pay any attention to race at all. What made this judgment unusual was that although a majority of five to four agreed with each part, Justice Powell was the only member of the Court to support both parts.

This decision showed how sharply the members of the Court disagreed about reverse discrimination. Furthermore, Powell stressed that the Court's decision concerned only reverse racial discrimination. He warned that reverse sexual discrimination may or may not have to be treated the same way. Although in a 1982 case *Mississippi University for Women* v. *Hogan,* for example, the Court ruled that it was unconstitutional for a state-run school of nursing to refuse admission to men.

GAZETTEER

A

Afghanistan Country of southwest-central Asia. Invaded by the Soviet Union in 1979. Capital: Kabul. (33°N 63°E) *m561, m772–773*

Alabama (AL) State in the southern U.S. Admitted as a state in 1819. Capital: Montgomery. (33°N 87°W) *m776–777*

Alaska (AK) U.S. state in northwestern North America. Became a territory in 1912 (first organized in 1884) and a state in 1959. Capital: Juneau. (64°N 150°W) *m776–777*

Albania Country in southeast Europe on the Adriatic Sea. Invaded by Italy in 1939. Capital: Tiranë. (41°N 20°E) *m392, m597, m772–773*

Algeria Country in northwestern Africa on the Mediterranean Sea. Capital: Algiers. (29°N 1°E) *m637, m772–773*

Alsace-Lorraine Region between France, Germany, Belgium, and Switzerland. Part of the German Empire, 1871–1918; returned to France by the Treaty of Versailles, 1919. (48°N 7°E) *m244*

American Samoa Unincorporated territory of the U.S. in the southern Pacific Ocean. Administered by the U.S. since 1899. (14°S 170°W) *m220*

Antarctica Continent lying around the South Pole. (80°S 127°E) *m735, m772–773*

Appomattox Courthouse Virginia town where General Lee surrendered to General Grant, ending the Civil War. (37°N 78°W) *m102*

Arizona (AZ) State in southwestern U.S. Became a territory in 1863 and a state in 1912. Capital: Phoenix. (34°N 113°W) *m776–777*

Arkansas (AR) State in south-central U.S. Admitted as a state in 1836. Capital: Little Rock. (35°N 93°W) *m776–777*

Armenia Republic; member of the Common-wealth of Independent States. Formerly part of the USSR. Independent in 1991. Capital: Yerevan. (41°N 44°E) *m597, m772–773*

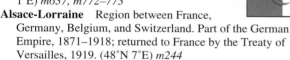

Atlanta Major southern city, capital of Georgia. During the Civil War it was captured and burned by General Sherman, 1864. (33°N 84°W) *m102*

Austria-Hungary Former monarchy in central Europe. Consisted of Austria, Hungary, Bohemia, and parts of Poland, Romania, Yugoslavia, and Italy. Formed in 1867; lasted until 1918. (47°N 12°E) *m244*

Azerbaijan Republic; member of the Commonwealth of Independent States. Formerly part of the USSR. Independent in 1991. Capital: Baki. (40°N 47°E) *m597, m772–773*

B

Bahamas Country in the Atlantic Ocean consisting of hundreds of islands. Gained independence from Great Britain in 1973. Capital: Nassau. (26°N 76°W) *m22, m772–773*

Balkans Countries that occupy the Balkan Peninsula, including Albania, Bulgaria, Greece, Romania, the former Yugoslavia, and northwestern Turkey. (43°N 24°E) *m244*

Bangladesh Country in southern Asia. Formerly part of Bengal, it became part of Pakistan in 1947. In 1971 it became a separate nation. Capital: Dacca. (24°N 90°E) *m772–773*

Beijing Capital of China. (40°N 116°E) *m220*

Belarus Republic in Eastern Europe; member of the Commonwealth of Independent States. Formerly part of the USSR. Independent in 1991. Capital: Minsk. (53°N 25°E) *m597, m772–773*

Belgian Congo *See* Zaire

Belgium Country in northwest Europe. Invaded by Germany in 1914 and 1940. Capital: Brussels. (51°N 3°E) *m244, m772–773*

Bosnia and Herzegovina Country annexed to Austria-Hungary in 1908 and Yugoslavia in 1918. Capital: Sarajevo. (44°N 17°E) *m244, m597, m772–773*

Boston Massachusetts capital on Massachusetts Bay founded in the 17th century. Leading center of anti-British sentiment in the 18th century. (42°N 71°W) *m34*

Brazil Republic in eastern South America. Largest country on the continent; ruled by Portugal from 1500 to 1822. Empire until 1889. Capital: Brasília. (9°S 53°W) *m772–773*

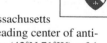

C

Cahokia Settlement founded by the Mississippian culture near present-day St. Louis, Missouri. (38°N 90°W) *m5*

California (CA) State in western U.S. Admitted as a free state in 1850. Capital: Sacramento. (38°N 121°W) *m776–777*

Cambodia Republic in southeast Asia. Independent in 1954. Scene of fighting during Vietnam War. Capital: Pnompenh. (12°N 104°E) *m521, m772–773*

Canada   Country in northern North America. Settled by English and French colonists. Ceded to Great Britain in 1763. Declared equal partner of Great Britain, 1931. Capital: Ottawa. (50°N 100°W) *m86, m772–773*

Cape Verde Islands   Group of islands in Atlantic Ocean. Settled by the Portuguese in the mid-1400s; independent in 1975. Capital: Praia. (15°N 26°W) *m239, m772–773*

Caporetto   Town in Slovenia. Scene of World War I defeat of Italian troops in December 1917. *m244*

Château-Thierry   Town in northern France where Allied forces stopped German advance in World War I. (49°N 3°E) *m255*

Chernobyl   City in north-central Ukraine where a nuclear power plant exploded in 1986. (51°N 30°E) *m735*

Chile   Country in southwest South America colonized by Spain in 1541; became independent in 1818. Capital: Santiago. (35°S 72°W) *m238, m772–773*

China (Official name: People's Republic of China)   Country in eastern Asia. After a bitter civil war (1946–49), became a Communist republic; nationalists fled to Taiwan. Capital: Beijing. (36°N 93°E) *m220, m521, m772–773*

Colombia   Country in northwest South America. Capital: Bogotá. (3°N 72°W) *m234, m772–773*

Colorado (CO)   State in southwestern U.S. Became a territory in 1861 and a state in 1876. Capital: Denver. (39°N 107°W) *m776–777*

Compiègne   City in northern France. Armistice ending World War I signed nearby in November 1918. (49°N 2°E) *m255*

Connecticut (CT)   State in northeastern U.S. One of the original Thirteen Colonies. Admitted as a state in 1788. Capital: Hartford. (41°N 73°W) *m776–777*

Cuba   Island country in the Caribbean about 90 miles south of Florida. Capital: Havana. (22°N 79°W) *m493, m772–773*

Czechoslovakia   Former country in central Europe formed in 1918. Communist forces gained control of it in 1948 and kept power until 1989. In 1993 peacefully divided into Czech Republic (Capital: Prague) and Slovakia (Capital: Bratislava). (49°N 16°E) *m264, m392, m597, m772–773*

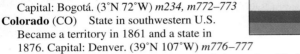

Delaware (DE)   State in eastern U.S. One of the original Thirteen Colonies. In 1787 became first state to ratify the Constitution. Capital: Dover. (38°N 75°W) *m776–777*

District of Columbia (DC)   Federal district of the U.S. Seat of federal government since 1800. (39°N 77°W) *m776–777*

Dominican Republic   Island country in the Caribbean. Makes up eastern part of island of Hispaniola. Capital: Santo Domingo. (19°N 70°W) *m234, m772–773*

Egypt   Country in northeast Africa on the Mediterranean Sea. Capital: Cairo. (27°N 27°E) *m453, m561, m772–773*

El Salvador   Country in Central America. Capital: San Salvador. (14°N 89°W) *m234, m590, m772–773*

Estonia   Country in northeast Europe. Annexed to the USSR in 1940. Became independent in 1991. Capital: Tallinn. (59°N 25°E) *m264, m597, m772–773*

Ethiopia   Country in eastern Africa; formerly Abyssinia. Capital: Addis Ababa. (7°N 38°E) *m392, m772–773*

Federal Republic of Germany   *See* Germany

Finland   Country in northeast Europe. Capital: Helsinki. (62°N 26°E) *m264, m392, m772–773*

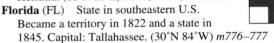

Florida (FL)   State in southeastern U.S. Became a territory in 1822 and a state in 1845. Capital: Tallahassee. (30°N 84°W) *m776–777*

France   Country in western Europe. French Revolution of 1789 overthrew the monarchy. Capital: Paris. (46°N 0°E) *m244, m404*

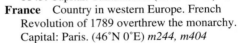

Gadsden Purchase   Tract of land located in parts of New Mexico and Arizona. Purchased in 1853 by U.S. from Mexico for $10,000,000. *m86*

Georgia (GA)   State in southeastern U.S. One of the original Thirteen Colonies. Admitted as a state in 1788. Capital: Atlanta. (32°N 84°W) *m776–777*

Georgia   Republic; member of the Commonwealth of Independent States. Formerly part of the USSR. Independent in 1991. Capital: T'bilisi. (42°N 43°E) *m597, m772–773*

German Democratic Republic   *See* Germany

Germany   Country in western Europe. Fascist during the 1930s and 1940s. Divided into German Democratic Republic (East Germany) and Federal Republic of Germany (West Germany) after World War II. Reunified in 1990. Capital: Berlin. (51°N 8°E) *m392, m449, m597, m772–773*

Gettysburg   Town in southern Pennsylvania. Scene of major Union victory in the Civil War. Abraham Lincoln delivered Gettysburg Address here in 1863. (40°N 77°W) *m98*

Ghana   Republic in western Africa. Ancient African trading kingdom. Capital: Accra. (8°N 2°W) *m637, m772–773*

Great Britain   Kingdom in western Europe. Consists of England, Scotland, and Wales. Capital: London. (54°N 4°W) *m772–773*

Greece   Balkan country in southern Europe with numerous islands. Capital: Athens. (39°N 21°E) *m449, m772–773*

Grenada   Country in the Caribbean made up of the island of Grenada and the southern Grenadines. Capital: St. George's. (12°N 61°W) *m590*

Guam Pacific island that became U.S. territory after the Spanish-American War. Capital: Agana. (14°N 143°E) *m402*

Guantánamo Bay Bay on southeastern coast of Cuba. U.S. naval station established in 1903. (19°N 75°W) *m234*

Guatemala Republic in Central America. Capital: Guatemala City. (15°N 91°W) *m467, m772–773*

H

Haiti Island country in the Caribbean located on the western part of the island of Hispaniola. Capital: Port-au-Prince. (19°N 72°W) *m234, m590, m772–773*

Hawaii (HI) U.S. state in the central Pacific Ocean comprising the Hawaiian Islands. Admitted as a state in 1959. Capital: Honolulu. (20°N 157°W) *m776–777*

Hiroshima Japanese city; U.S. dropped the first atomic bomb used in warfare on the city in August 1945. (34°N 132°E) *m402*

Hispaniola Columbus and his crew established the colony of La Navidad here in 1492; today comprises the countries of the Dominican Republic and Haiti. (17°N 73°W) *m22*

Homestead Site of a strike at Andrew Carnegie's steel plant in southwestern Pennsylvania. *m154*

I

Idaho (ID) State in northwestern U.S. Admitted as a state in 1890. Capital: Boise. (44°N 115°W) *m776–777*

Illinois (IL) State in north-central U.S. Admitted as a state in 1818. Capital: Springfield. (40°N 90°W) *m776–777*

Indiana (IN) State in north-central U.S. Admitted as a state in 1816. Capital: Indianapolis. (40°N 86°W) *m776–777*

Indian Territory Former territory in south-central U.S. Set aside by the government in 1834 as a homeland for displaced Native Americans. Western section, which became Oklahoma Territory, was opened to white settlement in 1889. In 1907 Indian Territory was merged with Oklahoma Territory to form the state of Oklahoma. (36°N 98°W) *m73*

Indonesia Country in southeast Asia; island chain in the South Pacific. Occasional name for the Malay Archipelago. Capital: Djakarta. (5°S 119°E) *m772–773*

Iowa (IA) State in north-central U.S. Admitted as a state in 1846. Capital: Des Moines. (42°N 94°W) *m776–777*

Iran Country in southwest Asia where 53 Americans were held hostage during the Carter administration. Capital: Tehran. (31°N 53°E) *m561, m772–773*

Iraq Country in southwest Asia. Iraq's invasion of Kuwait led to UN–imposed economic sanctions and to war with the U.S. and the Allies in 1991. Capital: Baghdad. (32°N 43°E) *m561, m600, m772–773*

Ireland Located in the British Isles. Divided between Northern Ireland (Capital: Belfast), which is part of Great Britain, and the independent Republic of Ireland (Capital: Dublin). (54°N 8°W) *m772–773*

Israel Country in southwest Asia on the eastern Mediterranean coast that Jews established after the UN division of Palestine in 1948. Capital: Jerusalem. (32°N 34°E) *m561, m772–773*

Italy Country in southern Europe, which fought on the side of the Allies in World War I. During World War II it was allied with Germany. Capital: Rome. (44°N 11°E) *m772–773*

J

Jamaica Island country in the Caribbean which Columbus visited in 1494. It became a British colony in 1655 and an important sugar producer. Capital: Kingston. (18°N 78°W) *m22, m772–773*

Japan Chain of islands in the western Pacific Ocean. World War II military ally of Germany and Italy. Two of its cities devastated by atomic bombs. Since the war, has played a central role in the global economy. Capital: Tokyo. (37°N 134°E) *m395, m402, m772–773*

Jordan Country of southwest Asia. Capital: Amman. (30°N 38°E) *m453, m561, m772–773*

K

Kansas (KS) Territory in central U.S. Created by Kansas-Nebraska Act in 1854. Admitted to the Union as a free state in 1861. Capital: Topeka. (38°N 99°W) *m776–777*

Kazakhstan Republic; member of the Commonwealth of Independent States. Formerly part of the USSR. Independent in 1991. Capital: Almaty. (49°N 59°E) *m597, m772–773*

Kentucky (KY) State in east-central U.S. Admitted as a state in 1792. Capital: Frankfort. (37°N 87°W) *m776–777*

Kenya Republic in East Africa. Capital: Nairobi. (1°N 37°E) *m637, m772–773*

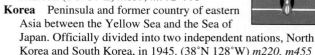

Korea Peninsula and former country of eastern Asia between the Yellow Sea and the Sea of Japan. Officially divided into two independent nations, North Korea and South Korea, in 1945. (38°N 128°W) *m220, m455*

Kuwait Oil-rich country on the northeast Arabian Peninsula at the head of the Persian Gulf. Invaded by Iraq, it was liberated by the Allies in the Persian Gulf War (1991). Capital: Al Kuwait. (29°N 48°E) *m600, m772–773*

Kyrgyzstan Republic; member of the Commonwealth of Independent States. Formerly part of the USSR. Independent in 1991. Capital: Bishkek. (42°N 28°E) *m597, m772–773*

L

Latvia Country of northern Europe on the Baltic Sea. Capital: Riga. (57°N 24°E) *m772–773*

Liberia Country on west coast of Africa founded in 1817 by Americans for the resettlement of freed African Americans. Capital: Monrovia. (6°N 10°W) *m772–773*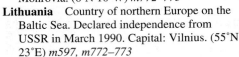

Lithuania Country of northern Europe on the Baltic Sea. Declared independence from USSR in March 1990. Capital: Vilnius. (55°N 23°E) *m597, m772–773*

Louisiana (LA) One of the southeastern states carved out of the Louisiana territory. Admitted as a state in 1812. Capital: Baton Rouge. (31°N 93°W) *m776–777*

M

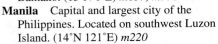

Maine (ME) State in the northeastern U.S. Admitted as a state in 1820. Capital: Augusta. (45°N 70°W) *m776–777*

Mali Country of western Africa. Capital: Bamako. (15°N 0°E) *m637, m776–777*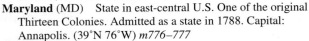

Manila Capital and largest city of the Philippines. Located on southwest Luzon Island. (14°N 121°E) *m220*

Maryland (MD) State in east-central U.S. One of the original Thirteen Colonies. Admitted as a state in 1788. Capital: Annapolis. (39°N 76°W) *m776–777*

Massachusetts (MA) State in northeastern U.S. One of the original Thirteen Colonies. Admitted as a state in 1788. Capital: Boston. (42°N 72°W) *m776–777*

Meuse River River in western Europe flowing from northeast France through southern Belgium and the southeast Netherlands to the North Sea. (50°N 5°E) *m255*

Mexican Cession Area that Mexico ceded to the U.S. at the end of the Mexican War, comprising the present-day states of California, Nevada, and Utah, and parts of Arizona, Colorado, and New Mexico. *m86*

Mexico Republic in North America, bounded on the north by the U.S. and on the south by Guatemala and British Honduras. Capital: Mexico City. (23°N 104°W) *m772–773*

Michigan (MI) State in north-central U.S. Admitted as a state in 1837. Capital: Lansing. (46°N 87°W) *m776–777*

Minnesota (MN) State in north-central U.S. Admitted as a state in 1858. Capital: St. Paul. (46°N 90°W) *m776–777*

Mississippi (MS) State in southeastern U.S. Admitted as a state in 1817. Capital: Jackson. (32°N 89°W) *m776–777*

Missouri (MO) State in central U.S. Admitted as a state in 1821. Capital: Jefferson City. (38°N 93°W) *m74, m776–777*

Moldova Republic; member of the Commonwealth of Independent States. Formerly part of the USSR. Independent in 1991. Capital: Chisinău. *m597, m772–773*

Montana (MT) State in northwestern U.S. Admitted as a state in 1889. Capital: Helena. (47°N 112°W) *m776–777*

N

Nebraska (NE) State in central U.S. Admitted as a free state in 1867. Capital: Lincoln. (41°N 101°W) *m776–777*

Nevada (NV) State in western U.S. Organized as a separate territory in 1861 and admitted as a state in 1864. Capital: Carson City. (39°N 117°W) *m776–777*

New Hampshire (NH) State in northeastern U.S. One of the original Thirteen Colonies. Admitted as a state in 1788. Capital: Concord. (44°N 71°W) *m776–777*

New Jersey (NJ) State in eastern U.S. One of the original Thirteen Colonies. Admitted as a state in 1787. Capital: Trenton. (40°N 75°W) *m776–777*

New Mexico (NM) State in southwestern U.S. Originally Zuni country, ceded to the U.S. by Mexico in 1848. Organized as a territory that included Arizona and part of Colorado in 1850. Admitted as a state in 1912. Capital: Santa Fe. (34°N 107°W) *m776–777*

New York (NY) State in northeastern U.S. One of the original Thirteen Colonies. Admitted as a state in 1788. Capital: Albany. (42°N 78°W) *m776–777*

Nicaragua Country of Central America on the Caribbean Sea and the Pacific Ocean. Columbus spotted its Caribbean coastline in 1502. Capital: Managua. (12°N 86°W) *m234, m590, m772–773*

North Carolina (NC) State in southeastern U.S. One of the original Thirteen Colonies. Admitted as a state in 1789. Capital: Raleigh. (35°N 81°W) *m776–777*

North Dakota (ND) State in north-central U.S. Admitted as a state in 1889. Capital: Bismarck. (47°N 102°W) *m776–777*

North Korea (Official name: Democratic People's Republic of Korea) Country on east coast of Asia, bounded on north by China, on east by Sea of Japan, on south by South Korea, and on west by the Yellow Sea and Korea Bay. Capital: P'yongyang. (40°N 127°E) *m455, m772–773*

North Vietnam *See* Vietnam

O

Ohio (OH) State in north-central U.S. Originally part of the Northwest Territory. Admitted as a state in 1803. Capital: Columbus. (40°N 83°W) *m776–777*

Oklahoma (OK) State in south-central U.S. Except for its panhandle, Oklahoma formed part of the Louisiana Purchase. Organized as a territory in 1890 and became a state in 1907. Capital: Oklahoma City. (36°N 98°W) *m776–777*

Oregon (OR) State in northwestern U.S. Admitted as a state in 1859. Capital: Salem. (43°N 122°W) *m776–777*

Oregon Country Region encompassing all the land from the California border to Alaska and from the Pacific Ocean to the Rocky Mountains. Held jointly by Great Britain and the U.S., 1818–46, when the international boundary was fixed at the 49th parallel. *m73*

P

Panama Country in southern Central America occupying the Isthmus of Panama. Capital: Panama City. (8°N 81°W) *m234, m772–773*

Panama Canal Ship canal, about 51 miles long, crossing the Isthmus of Panama in the Canal Zone and connecting the Caribbean Sea with the Pacific Ocean. *m227*

Pennsylvania (PA) State in eastern U.S. One of the original Thirteen Colonies. Admitted as a state in 1787. Capital: Harrisburg. (41°N 78°W) *m776–777*

People's Republic of China   *See* China

Persian Gulf   Arm of the Arabian Sea between the Arabian Peninsula and southwestern Iran in southwest Asia. (27°N 50°E) *m600*

Peru   Republic in western South America, bounded on north by Ecuador and Colombia, on east by Brazil and Bolivia, on southern tip by Chile, and on west by the Pacific Ocean. Capital: Lima. (10°S 75°W) *m772–773*

Philippines, Republic of the   Archipelago of about 7,100 islands, lying approximately 500 miles off the southeast coast of Asia. Capital: Manila. (14°N 125°E) *m217, m772–773*

Poland   Country of central Europe bordering on the Baltic Sea. Capital: Warsaw. (52°N 17°E) *m264, m392, m597, m772–773*

Portugal   Country of southwest Europe on the western Iberian Peninsula. Capital: Lisbon. (38°N 9°W) *m239, m772–773*

Puerto Rico (PR)   Island east of Cuba and southeast of Florida. Ceded to the U.S. after the Spanish-American War. Self-governing commonwealth. Capital: San Juan. (18°N 67°W) *m217, m772–773*

Pullman   Former industrial suburb of Chicago, Illinois; since 1889 a southeastern part of Chicago. *m154*

Red River Valley   Area along the Red River (also known as Red River of the North) in north-central U.S. and south-central Canada. (48°N 97°W) *m132*

Rhode Island (RI)   State in northeastern U.S. One of the original Thirteen Colonies. Admitted as a state in 1790. Capital: Providence. (41°N 71°W) *m776–777*

Richmond   State capital, in the east-central part of Virginia on the James River. Capital of the Confederacy in the Civil War; fell in 1865. (37°N 77°W) *m98*

Rio Grande   "Great River" that forms the border between Texas and Mexico. (26°N 98°W) *m86*

Russia   Country in Eastern Europe and Northwest Asia. Formerly part of USSR. Independent in 1991. Member of the Commonwealth of Independent States. Capital: Moscow. (61°N 60°E) *m772–773*

Rwanda   Republic in east-central Africa. Capital: Kigali. (2°S 30°E) *m684, m772–773*

Saar   River, about 150 miles long, rising in northeast France and flowing north and northwest to the Moselle River in western Germany. River's valley is also known as the Saar Basin. *m264*

St. Mihiel   Village in northeast France on the Meuse River. World War I battle here (1918) was the first major U.S. offensive led by General John J. Pershing. (49°N 5°E) *m255*

San Carlos Reservation   Native American reservation located on the Gila River in southeastern Arizona. *m124*

Santiago   Cuban seaport captured by American forces during the Spanish-American War. (20°N 76°W) *m217*

Saratoga   Former village (now Schuylerville) in eastern New York. Scene of battles that marked the turning point of the Revolutionary War. (43°N 75°W) *m34*

Saudi Arabia   Country on the Arabian Peninsula in southwest Asia, bordered on the north by Jordan, Iraq, and Kuwait; the world's second-largest producer of oil. Capital: Riyadh. (22°N 46°E) *m600, m772–773*

Seattle   Washington city bounded by Puget Sound and Lake Washington. First settled in the 1850s. Prospered after the coming of the railroad in 1884 and became a boomtown during the Alaskan gold rush of 1897. (47°N 122°W) *m132*

Sedan   Town of northeast France on the Meuse River near the Belgian border. Site of important battle in World War I. (50°N 5°E) *m255*

Sierra Leone   Country in western Africa on the Atlantic coast. First visited by the Portuguese in the 1460s. Region became a British protectorate in 1896 and achieved independence in 1961. Capital: Freetown. (8°N 12°W) *m239*

Somalia   Country of extreme eastern Africa on the Gulf of Aden and the Indian Ocean. Capital: Mogadishu. (3°N 44°E) *m772–773*

South Africa   Country of southern Africa on the Atlantic and Indian oceans. Pretoria is the administrative capital, Cape Town the legislative capital, and Bloemfontein the judicial capital. (28°S 25°E) *m772–773*

South Carolina (SC)   State in southeastern U.S. One of the original Thirteen Colonies. Admitted as a state in 1788. First state to secede from the Union (1860). Capital: Columbia. (34°N 81°W) *m776–777*

South Dakota (SD)   State in north-central U.S. Constituted the southern part of the Dakota Territory. Admitted as a state in 1889. Capital: Pierre. (44°N 102°W) *m776–777*

South Korea (Official name: Republic of Korea)   Country on east coast of Asia, bounded on north by North Korea, on east by the Sea of Japan, on south by the Korea Strait, and on west by the Yellow Sea. Capital: Seoul. (36°N 128°E) *m772–773*

South Vietnam   *See* Vietnam

Spain   Country in southwest Europe, occupying the greater part of the Iberian Peninsula and including the Balearic and Canary islands. Capital: Madrid. (40°N 4°W) *m772–773*

Sudan   Country in northeast Africa south of Egypt. Capital: Khartoum. (14°N 28°E) *m772–773*

Syria   Country in southwest Asia on the eastern Mediterranean coast. Capital: Damascus. (35°N 37°E) *m561, m772–773*

Taiwan   (Official name: Republic of China)   Formerly Formosa. Country off the southeast coast of China made up of the island of Taiwan, the Pescadores, and other smaller islands. Capital: Taipei. (37°N 112°E) *m220, m402, m772–773*

Tajikistan   Republic; member of the Common-wealth of Independent States. Formerly part of the USSR. Independent in 1991. Capital: Dushanbe. (39°N 69°E) *m772–773*

Tennessee (TN)   State in south-central U.S. Admitted as a state in 1796. Capital: Nashville. (36°N 88°W) *m776–777*

Texas (TX)   State in south-central U.S. Bounded on south by Gulf of Mexico and Mexico. Known as the Lone Star State because it was an independent republic (1836–45) whose flag featured a single star. Capital: Austin. (31°N 101°W) *m776–777*

Thailand   Formerly Siam. Country in southeast Asia on the Gulf of Thailand. Was a strong sup-porter of the U.S. in the Vietnam War. Capital: Bangkok. (16°N 101°E) *m402, m772–773*

Trenton   City in west-central New Jersey. Site where American forces under George Washington opened fire on the British in 1776. (40°N 75°W) *m34*

Turkey   Country in southwest Asia and south-east Europe between the Mediterranean and the Black seas. Capital: Ankara. (38°N 32°W) *m449, m772–773*

Turkmenistan   Republic; member of the Commonwealth of Independent States. Formerly part of the USSR. Independent in 1991. Capital: Ashgabat. (40°N 56°E) *m597, m772–773*

 U

Ukraine   Republic; member of the Commonwealth of Independent States. Formerly part of the USSR. Independent in 1991. Central theater of warfare in both world wars. Capital: Kiev. (49°N 30°E) *m404, m597, m772–773*

United Kingdom of Great Britain and Northern Ireland   *See* Great Britain

United States of America   Federal republic, North America. Bounded on north by Canada and (in Alaska) the Arctic Ocean, on east by the Atlantic Ocean, on south by Mexico and the Gulf of Mexico, and on west by the Pacific Ocean. Capital: Washington, D.C. (38°N 110°W) *m772–773, m776–777*

Utah (UT)   State in western U.S. First explored by Coronado expedition, 1540. Admitted as a state in 1896. Capital: Salt Lake City. (39°N 112°W) *m776–777*

Uzbekistan   Republic; member of the Common-wealth of Independent States. Formerly part of the USSR. Independent in 1991. Capital: Toshkent. (42°N 60°E) *m597, m772–773*

V

Venezuela   Country in northern South America on the Caribbean Sea. Capital: Caracas. (8°N 65°W) *m234, m772–773*

Vermont (VT)   State in northeastern U.S. One of the original Thirteen Colonies. Admitted as a state in 1791. Capital: Montpelier. (44°N 73°W) *m776–777*

Vicksburg   City in western Mississippi on bluffs above the Mississippi River. During the Civil War it was captured by Union troops led by Ulysses S. Grant. (42°N 85°W) *m99*

Vietnam   Southeast Asian country (divided into North Vietnam and South Vietnam between 1954 and 1975) where United States and South Vietnamese forces fought a war against the Communist North Vietnamese. Capital: Hanoi. (18°N 107°E) *m521, m772–773*

Virginia (VA)   State in eastern U.S. One of the original Thirteen Colonies. Admitted as a state in 1788. Capital: Richmond. (37°N 80°W) *m776–777*

W

Washington (WA)   State in northwestern U.S. Bounded on north by Canadian province of British Columbia and on west by the Pacific Ocean. Admitted as a state in 1889. Capital: Olympia. (47°N 121°W) *m776–777*

Washington, D.C.   Capital of the U.S., on the Potomac River between Virginia and Maryland; also called the District of Columbia. Leading international political center. (39°N 77°W) *m86*

West Virginia (WV)   State in east-central U.S. Admitted as a state in 1863. Part of Virginia until the area refused to endorse the Ordinance of Secession in 1861. Capital: Charleston. (39°N 81°W) *m776–777*

Wisconsin (WI)   State in north-central U.S. First settled by the French, region was ceded to Great Britain in 1763 and became part of the Northwest Territory in 1787. Admitted as a state in 1848. Capital: Madison. (44°N 91°W) *m776–777*

Wyoming (WY)   State in northwestern U.S. Organized as the Wyoming Territory in 1868 and admitted as a state in 1890. Capital: Cheyenne. (43°N 108°W) *m776–777*

Y

Yokohama   Japanese city in southeast Honshu, on the western shore of Tokyo Bay. Almost entirely destroyed by an earth-quake and fire in 1923, again largely destroyed by U.S. bomb-ing in World War II. (35°N 139°E) *m220*

Yorktown   Town in southeastern Virginia. Scene of surrender of British forces to the Americans in the Revolutionary War. (37°N 77°W) *m34*

Yugoslavia   Former country in southeast Europe bordering on the Adriatic Sea. It was formed in 1918 and named Yugoslavia in 1929. Today the name is claimed by Serbia and Montenegro. (44°N 17°E) *m264, m597, m772–773*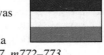

Z

Zaire   (Formerly: Democratic Republic of the Congo; from 1908 to 1960, Belgian Congo) Republic in equatorial Africa. Capital: Kinshasa. (1°S 22°E) *m637, m772–773*

This Glossary contains terms you need to understand as you study American history. After each term there is a brief definition or explanation of the meaning of the term as it is used in *The American Nation in the Twentieth Century*. The page number refers to the page on which the term is introduced in the textbook.

Phonetic Respelling and Pronunciation Guide

Many of the key terms in this textbook have been respelled to help you pronounce them. The letter combinations used in the respellings throughout the narrative are explained in the following phonetic respelling and pronunciation guide. The guide is adapted from *Webster's Ninth New Collegiate Dictionary, Webster's New Geographical Dictionary,* and *Webster's New Biographical Dictionary*.

MARK	AS IN	RESPELLING	EXAMPLE
a	alphabet	a	*AL-fuh-bet
ā	Asia	ay	AY-zhuh
ä	cart, top	ah	KAHRT, TAHP
e	let, ten	e	LET, TEN
ē	even, leaf	ee	EE-vuhn, LEEF
i	it, tip, British	i	IT, TIP, BRIT-ish
ī	site, buy, Ohio	y	SYT, BY, oh-HY-oh
	iris	eye	EYE-ris
k	card	k	KARD
ō	over, rainbow	oh	oh-vuhr, RAYN-boh
ů	book, wood	ooh	BOOHK, WOOHD
ò	all, orchid	aw	AWL, AWR-kid
òi	foil, coin	oy	FOYL, KOYN
aů	out	ow	OWT
ə	cup, butter	uh	KUHP, BUHT-uhr
ü	rule, food	oo	ROOL, FOOD
yü	few	yoo	FYOO
zh	vision	zh	VIZH-uhn

*A syllable printed in small capital letters receives heavier emphasis than the other syllable(s) in a word.

A

abolition Movement to end slavery. **17**

acid rain Atmospheric pollution that gradually kills trees and makes lakes unfit for marine life. **736**

Adamson Act Federal law reducing the workday for railroad workers from 10 to 8 hours with no decrease in wages. **207**

affirmative action Programs giving preference to ethnic minorities and women in jobs or school admission to make up for past discrimination. **575**

African diaspora Forcible resettlement of millions of African people to the Americas from the 1500s through the 1800s. **9**

African National Congress The major black nationalist organization in South Africa. **712**

Agricultural Adjustment Act (AAA) Federal law passed in 1933 to reduce farmers' output, increase crop prices, and establish the Agricultural Adjustment Administration. **354**

Agricultural Marketing Act (1929) Federal law that created the Federal Farm Board, an agency to help ease the plight of farmers by buying farm surpluses. **341**

AIDS Acquired Immune Deficiency Syndrome, the final deadly stage of an illness believed to be caused by the human immunodeficiency virus (HIV) **609**

Alien and Sedition Acts (1798) Series of laws passed by the Federalists to protect the country from foreign influence, limit Republican power, and silence government critics. **64**

Alliance for Progress President Kennedy's policy of sending economic aid to Latin America; designed to encourage democratic reforms and to promote capitalism. **491**

Allied Powers World War I alliance that included France, Great Britain, Russia, Italy, and later the United States. **243**

American Anti-Slavery Society First national antislavery organization devoted to immediate abolition, formed in 1833 by both black and white abolitionists. **82**

American Federation of Labor (AFL) Organization of independent skilled craft unions founded in 1886 by Samuel Gompers. **155**

American Friends Service Committee Quaker-founded peace organization dedicated to promoting humanity. **705**

American Indian Defense Association Organization that fought to protect religious freedom and tribal property for Native Americans. **366**

American Indian Movement (AIM) Organization, founded in 1968 by Minnesota Chippewas, that became the major force in the Red Power movement during the 1970s. **507**

American Plan Policy, promoted by business leaders during the 1920s, that called for open shops. **288**

Americans with Disabilities Act (1990) Federal law that prohibits discrimination against people with mental or physical disabilities. **609**

American System Henry Clay's federal program for economic development; it included a national bank, a protective tariff, and a national transportation system. **73**

anarchists People who oppose all forms of government. **154**

Angel Island Immigration station in San Francisco Bay opened in 1910 to receive Asian immigrants. **676**

annex Action by which one country takes control of another country or territory. **219**

Antarctic Treaty (1959) International agreement that established Antarctica as a nuclear-free zone. **729**

Antifederalists Individuals who feared a powerful national government and opposed ratification of the U.S. Constitution. **39**

anti-Semitism Hatred of Jews. **389**

apartheid Racial segregation; former racial policy in South Africa. **571**

appeasement Policy of giving in to demands of a country or countries in an effort to avoid major conflicts. **391**

arbitration Hearing in which a third party settles a dispute. **195**

armistice Cease-fire. **256**

Articles of Confederation Agreement, ratified in 1781, in which the 13 colonies established a government of states with each state retaining power over its own affairs. **37**

assembly line Manufacturing technique in which a product is passed along a line of workers and assembled in stages. **302**

assimilation Cultural absorption of a group. **126**

asylum Policy of nations offering a place of protection to anyone being persecuted for political reasons. **684**

Atlantic Charter (1941) Joint declaration of principles for international relations, agreed to by the United States and Great Britain. **394**

Atomic Energy Act (1946) Federal law that placed the Atomic Energy Commission under civilian control to oversee nuclear weapons research and to promote peacetime uses of atomic energy. **447**

automation Manufacturing process that used machines to perform industrial operations faster and more efficiently than human labor. **476**

Axis powers Military alliance of Germany, Italy, and Japan during World War II. **391**

baby boom Soaring birth rate between 1946 and 1964. **473**

Balfour Declaration (1917) Statement issued by Great Britain declaring its support for a Jewish homeland in Palestine. **267**

Bandung Conference (1955) Meeting in Indonesia in which Third World nations reaffirmed the nonaligned movement and established regional organizations among developing countries. **638**

bank holiday (1933) New Deal proclamation that temporarily closed every U.S. bank to stop massive withdrawals. **350**

barcodes Series of vertical bars of varying widths printed on consumer product packages and used for inventory control. **689**

Baruch Plan (1946) Proposal submitted to the UN Atomic Energy Commission for international control of atomic energy. **446**

Bataan Death March (1942) Forced march of Allied prisoners on the Bataan peninsula to a Japanese detention camp, during which thousands died. **401**

Battle of Bunker Hill (1775) Revolutionary War battle in which British troops defeated Patriot forces atop two hills overlooking Boston Harbor. **28**

Battle of El Alamein (1942) British victory in Egypt during World War II that broke the momentum of the Axis advance in North Africa. **405**

Battle of Gettysburg (1863) Union victory during the Civil War that halted General Lee's invasion of the North. **98**

Battle of Iwo Jima (1945) Allied victory in the Pacific during World War II in which Japanese forces lost more than 20,000 troops. **420**

Battle of Leyte Gulf (1944) Decisive naval victory for the Allies during World War II that eliminated the Japanese fleet as a threat in the Pacific. **420**

Battle of Midway (1942) Allied naval victory that helped halt the major Japanese offensive in the Pacific during World War II. **403**

Battle of New Orleans (1815) Battle in which American troops defeated British forces after the War of 1812 had officially ended. **67**

Battle of Okinawa (1945) Allied victory in the Pacific during World War II in which Japanese forces lost more than 100,000 troops. **420**

Battle of Omdurman (1898) British victory in North Africa in which 10,000 African soldiers, armed only with spears and swords, were killed by British gunfire. **626**

Battle of Saratoga (1777) Patriot victory, during Revolutionary War, that convinced France to support the American fight for independence. **35**

Battle of Stalingrad (1942–43) Soviet defeat of German troops during World War II that broke the momentum of the Axis advance in Europe. **405**

Battle of the Atlantic World War II naval war fought between German U-boats and the Allied navy and air force. **416**

Battle of the Bulge (1944) World War II battle in which Allied forces repulsed the final German offensive. **417**

Battle of the Coral Sea (1942) Allied naval victory during World War II in which a joint British-American naval force stopped the Japanese advance on Australia. **402**

Battle of the Java Sea (1942) World War II naval battle in which the Japanese navy defeated a fleet of American, British, Dutch, and Australian warships. **401**

Battle of the Little Bighorn (1876) Native American victory that resulted in the death of U.S. Army general Custer and all the men in his detachment. **124**

Battle of the Philippine Sea (1944) Decisive Allied naval and air victory over the Japanese during World War II. **418**

Battle of the Somme (1916) World War I battle in which the British lost some 60,000 troops in a single day. **245**

Battle of Tippecanoe (1811) Battle in Indiana Territory between U.S. troops and a confederation of Native Americans; ended in defeat for the Indians and made William Henry Harrison a hero. **66**

Battle of Yorktown (1781) Revolutionary War battle in which Patriot troops defeated British forces under General Cornwallis, effectively ending the war. **35**

bear market Downward trend in stock prices. **326**

Beats   Small but influential group of writers and poets who challenged literary conventions and the life-style of the middle class in the 1950s. **481**

benevolent societies   Organizations formed during the turn of the century to support and aid new immigrants. **148**

Beringia   Former land bridge between Siberia and present-day Alaska used by Paleo-Indians to cross from Asia into North America. **4**

Berlin airlift (1948)   Joint effort by U.S. and British air forces to deliver food and supplies into West Berlin after the Soviets blocked all routes into the city. **448**

Berlin Wall   Concrete barrier built in 1961 to cut off traffic between East Berlin and West Berlin. **492**

Big Four   During World War I, term for U.S. president Wilson, French premier Clemenceau, Italian prime minister Orlando, and British prime minister Lloyd George. **263**

Bilingual Education Act (1974)   Federal law encouraging public schools to provide instruction to students in their native languages until they learned English. **579**

Bill of Rights (1791)   First 10 amendments to the Constitution that protect individual liberties. **61**

biodiversity   The wide variety of plant and animal species on the earth. **735**

biomass   Materials, such as wood or waste products, that can be burned or used to make fuel. **734**

black codes   Laws adopted by former Confederates after the Civil War to limit the freedom of former slaves. **107**

blacklists   Lists of union supporters drawn up by employers for the purpose of denying jobs to union workers. **155**

Black Power   African American movement that focused on gaining control of economic and political power to achieve equal rights, by force if necessary. **504**

Blackshirts   Followers of Benito Mussolini. **388**

Black Thursday   October 24, 1929; day investors caused a panic on Wall Street by selling their shares. **327**

Black Tuesday   October 29, 1929; day the stock market crashed. **327**

blitzkrieg   German word for war carried on with great speed and force, used to describe Hitler's "lightning war" against Poland in World War II. **393**

Bolsheviks   Branch of the Russian Communist party that seized power in 1917 following the overthrow of the czar. **254**

bonanza farm   Large-scale farm usually owned by a large company and run like a factory. **131**

Bonus Army   Name given to World War I veterans who marched on Washington, D.C., in 1932 to support a bill granting veterans early payment of pension bonuses. **343**

Boston Massacre (1770)   Clash in Boston between an angry crowd of colonists and British soldiers that resulted in the death of five colonists. **27**

Boston Tea Party (1773)   Protest against British tax on tea in which colonists dumped tea into Boston Harbor. **27**

Boxer Rebellion (1900)   Revolt by a Chinese secret society attempting to drive foreigners out of China. **223**

braceros   Mexican farm workers who came to work in the Southwest during World War II and after. **413**

breadlines   Lines formed by people waiting for free food, such as those that occurred during the Great Depression. **333**

Bretton Woods system   Framework for postwar international economic relations developed by economic officials from the U.S. and 43 other countries. **660**

brinkmanship   Policy promoted by Secretary of State Dulles during the 1950s, which called for threatening all-out war in order to confront Communist aggression. **466**

British Invasion   Revolution in popular music inspired by the 1964 arrival of English rock bands such as the Beatles and the Rolling Stones. **512**

Brownshirts   Nazi storm troopers. **389**

Brown* v. *The Board of Education of Topeka (1952)   Supreme Court case challenging segregation in public schools; in it the Court ruled that separate educational facilities were unequal. **478**

bull market   Upward trend in stock prices. **326**

Bureau of Indian Affairs   Federal agency established within the War Department in 1824 to administer Native American reservations. **123**

business cycle   Regular ups and downs of business in a free-enterprise economy. **330**

Camp David Accords (1978)   Middle East peace agreement drafted by the U.S., Egypt, and Israel. **572**

Canadian Forestry Association   Conservation group formed in 1900 to promote national control of forest areas, fire prevention, and more forest reserves. **726**

caudillos   Latin American military leaders during the 1930s who used force to maintain order. **385**

Central Intelligence Agency (CIA)   Federal agency created to gather information overseas. **450**

Central Powers   World War I alliance led by Germany, Austria-Hungary, the Ottoman Empire (Turkey), and Bulgaria. **243**

checks and balances   System giving each branch of the federal government the means to restrain the powers of the other two branches. **40**

Chicano movement   Brown Power movement organized by young Mexican American college students to emphasize pride in Mexican culture and heritage. **507**

Chinese Exclusion Act (1882)   Federal law that denied U.S. citizenship to people born in China and prohibited the immigration of Chinese laborers. **148**

chlorofluorocarbons (CFCs)   Compounds, containing carbon, chlorine, fluorine, and sometimes hydrogen; they are suspected of damaging the ozone layer. **736**

circumnavigate   To sail around the world. **12**

Civilian Conservation Corps (CCC)   New Deal agency established in 1933 to employ men on conservation projects. **352**

Civil Rights Act of 1866   Federal law that granted full civil rights, but not voting rights, to everyone born in the U.S. **108**

Civil Rights Act of 1957   Federal law that made it a federal crime to prevent qualified persons from voting. **481**

Civil Rights Act of 1964   Federal law that barred discrimination in employment and public facilities and gave the Justice Department the power to enforce school desegregation. **503**

Civil Rights Bill of 1875   Federal law that prohibited discrimination by businesses serving the public. **111**

Civil Works Administration (CWA)   New Deal agency designed to create jobs during the Great Depression. **352**

Clayton Antitrust Act (1914)   Federal law that clarified and extended the 1890 Sherman Antitrust Act. **205**

Clayton-Bulwer Treaty (1850)   Agreement between the U.S. and Great Britain that proposed an equal partnership in building and running a Central American canal. **226**

Clean Air Act (1970)   Federal law that set air-quality standards and tough emissions guidelines for car manufacturers. **559**

closed shop   Workplace where the employer hires only union members. **176**

coaling stations   Port where steamships take on coal. **625**

Cobden Chevalier Treaty (1860)   Agreement between France and Great Britain that reduced tariffs and removed bans from imports. **654**

Cold War   Competition between the U.S. and the Soviet Union for global power and influence. **445**

Columbian exchange   Transfer of people, ideas, plants, animals, and diseases among the Americas, Europe, Asia, and Africa; initiated by Columbus's voyages. **11**

Committee on Civil Rights   Group established by President Truman in 1946 to document civil rights abuses. **442**

Committee on Public Information (CPI)   Agency established in 1917 that waged a vigorous propaganda campaign to convince Americans to support the war effort. **260**

commonwealth   A democratic nation or state; a federation of states. **17**

Commonwealth of Independent States (CIS)   International organization of sovereign states organized in 1991 by Russia, Ukraine, and Belarus. Other former Soviet republics later became members. **597**

Compromise of 1850   Measures proposed by Henry Clay that temporarily settled differences between the North and the South over slavery issues. **88**

Compromise of 1877   Deal between leading Republicans and southern Democrats that gave the presidency to Rutherford B. Hayes in 1876 in exchange for a promise not to use the military to enforce Reconstruction laws in the South. **111**

Comstock Lode   Rich Nevada silver vein that was the center of frantic prospecting beginning in 1859. **134**

concurrent powers   Powers granted jointly in the United States Constitution to the federal government and the state government. **40**

Congress of Industrial Organizations (CIO)   Labor group organized in 1935 to unite workers in various industries. **361**

Congress of Racial Equality (CORE)   Northern-based civil rights group that launched a protest against segregation in interstate transportation in 1961. **501**

conquistadors   Spanish soldiers who helped conquer the Americas. **12**

conscription   The calling up of people to serve in the military. **100**

conservation   Controlled use and protection of natural resources. **725**

conspicuous consumption   Lavish spending to increase social prestige. **146**

Constitutional Convention   Meeting called in 1787 and held in Philadelphia to strengthen the government, during which delegates wrote and adopted the U.S. Constitution. **38**

containment   Cold War strategy proposed by George Kennan to stop the spread of communism. **446**

Convention on Biological Diversity   Treaty signed in 1993 committing 167 nations to protecting biodiversity and sharing profits from biotechnology. **739**

Convention on the Elimination of All Forms of Racial Discrimination   UN-established agreement enacted in 1969 to declare any advocation of racial hatred illegal and punishable by law. **710**

Convention on the Suppression of Apartheid   Passed by the UN General Assembly in 1973 to discourage apartheid in South Africa. **712**

contras   An army recruited by the CIA to overthrow the Sandinista government of Nicaragua. **589**

convoy system   Use of armed escort vessels to accompany unarmed vessels transporting troops or supplies. **254**

cooperatives   Groups that pool members' resources to sell products directly to urban markets and to buy goods at wholesale prices. **155**

Copperheads   Northern Democrats who sympathized with the South during the Civil War. **101**

corporation   Business organization that is distinct from its owners and that raises the money needed to run the company by selling shares of stock. **143**

cotton gin   Machine invented by Eli Whitney in 1793 to separate seeds from cotton fiber. **79**

Council of Economic Advisers   Federal agency created by the Employment Act of 1946 to counsel the president on economic policy. **440**

counterculture   Culture that holds values and beliefs different from those of established society; for example, the culture of the hippies in the 1960s. **509**

Covenant on Civil and Political Rights   UN General Assembly agreement on human rights that prohibited governments from interfering with individuals' liberties. **714**

Covenant on Economic, Social, and Cultural Rights   UN General Assembly agreement on human rights that required governments to provide jobs, increase opportunity, and improve health care. **714**

creditor nation   Country that loans money to other nations. **382**

crop-lien system   Arrangement in which sharecroppers promised their crops to merchants in exchange for supplies. **113**

Crusades   Series of wars between 1096 and the late 1200s in which Christian crusaders fought Muslims for control of the Holy Land. **7**

cultural diffusion   Process of spreading cultural practices or beliefs from one group to another. **692**

Dawes General Allotment Act (1887)   Federal law that established private ownership of Indian land. **127**

Dawes Plan (1924)   Post–World War I plan that substantially reduced Germany's reparations, loaned Germany $200 million, and set up a new schedule of payments. **656**

D-Day   June 6, 1944; day when Allied soldiers crossed the English Channel to begin their invasion of France. **416**

debtor nation   Country that owes money to other nations. **382**

Declaration of Independence (1776)   Document adopted by the Second Continental Congress that justified and outlined reasons for the American separation from Great Britain. **29**

Declaration of the Rights of Man and Citizen   Document issued by France's National Assembly to outline basic inalienable human rights to liberty, property, security, and resistance to oppression. **699**

defoliants   Chemicals designed to strip land of vegetation. **529**

delegated powers   Powers granted to the federal government in the U.S. Constitution. **40**

demobilization   Shift from wartime preparations to a peacetime economy. **278**

Department of Energy   Federal agency created in 1977 to reduce U.S. dependence on oil. **569**

depression   Sharp drop in business activity accompanied by rising unemployment. **38**

détente   Lessening of military and diplomatic tensions between countries. **560**

devaluation   Reduction in the value of a currency to make it cheaper than other currencies. **657**

direct primary   Nominating election in which voters choose candidates to run in a general election. **191**

direct rule   Imperialistic method of governing in which the colonizing country establishes a completely new governmental administration in hopes of the new colony adopting the imperial culture. **627**

disarmament Reduction or limitation in the amount of a nation's military weapons. **381**

Displaced Persons Act (1948) Federal law that enabled 400,000 European refugees to enter the U.S. following World War II. **680**

dividends Portions of a company's profits received by its stockholders. **143**

Dixiecrats States' Rights party formed by southern Democrats in 1948; supported continued racial segregation. **443**

doctrine of nullification Theory of the states' right to refuse to obey any act passed by Congress that they consider unconstitutional. **74**

dollar diplomacy President Taft's policy of using economic influence, rather than military force, to protect U.S. interests in Latin America. **230**

domino theory Foreign policy principle of the 1950s and the 1960s stating that if one country fell to communism, neighboring countries would also fall. **523**

doves People who support negotiation and compromise and who oppose war. **532**

Dred Scott **decision** (1857) Supreme Court case in which the Missouri Compromise was declared unconstitutional and in which Scott, a slave, was declared not to be a citizen. **89**

drivers Slave assistants who helped overseers supervise other slaves. **79**

dry farming Techniques to conserve moisture in areas of little rainfall. **131**

Dust Bowl Fifty-million–acre region in the Great Plains that suffered a severe drought in the mid-1930s. **367**

ecology Study of the interrelationships of plants and animals and their environments. **724**

economies of scale Principle of buying supplies in bulk and producing goods in large quantities to lower production costs and increase profits. **144**

ecosystem Interaction of living beings with the environment. **724**

Education Amendments Act (1972) Federal law prohibiting sexual discrimination in higher education. **577**

Education for All Handicapped Children Act (1975) Federal law requiring public schools to provide education for children with physical and mental disabilities. **575**

Eighteenth Amendment (1919) Constitutional amendment that barred the manufacture, sale, or importation of alcoholic beverages; repealed by Twenty-first Amendment. **181**

Eisenhower Doctrine (1957) Policy designed to counter Soviet influence in the Middle East by offering military aid to those nations seeking help in resisting Communist aggression. **468**

elastic clause Constitutional provision that allows Congress to stretch its powers in ways not specifically outlined in the U.S. Constitution. **41**

Electronic mail Messages transmitted electronically via computers; commonly called e-mail. **652**

Elementary and Secondary School Education Act (1965) Federal law that provided $1.3 billion to aid schools in impoverished areas. **498**

Elkins Act (1903) Federal law that prohibited shippers from accepting rebates. **196**

Emancipation Proclamation Decree freeing all slaves living in those areas of the Confederacy that were still in rebellion against the U.S. as of January 1, 1863. **101**

Embargo Act (1807) Measure that stopped shipments of food and other American products to all foreign ports in an effort to maintain U.S. neutrality in European conflicts. **66**

Emergency Banking Act (1933) Federal law authorizing only banks that were financially sound to reopen after the New Deal bank holiday. **350**

employer mandate A call for employers to pay for the majority of the costs of all of their employees' health insurance. **609**

Employment Act (1946) Post–World War II law that established the Council of Economic Advisers and pledged the promotion of full employment and production. **440**

encomienda System that gave Spanish colonists the right to have a certain number of Indians work for them. **11**

Endangered Species Act (1973) Federal law passed to protect species threatened with extinction. **732**

Enforcement Acts Three acts passed by Congress between 1870 and 1871 allowing the government to use military force to stop violence against African Americans. **111**

Environmental Protection Agency (EPA) Federal agency created in 1970 to enforce environmental laws. **559**

Equal Pay Act (1963) Federal law that made it illegal for employers to pay female workers less than male workers for the same job. **490**

Equal Rights Amendment (ERA) Proposed constitutional amendment barring discrimination on the basis of sex. **577**

escalation Buildup of military forces or weapons. **527**

Espionage Act (1917) Federal law designed to outlaw acts of treason and to silence dissenters during World War I. **261**

European Economic Community Economic union formed to promote trade and cooperation among European member nations. **661**

European Union Western European trading bloc formed by the European Community in 1993 with ratification of the Maastricht Treaty. **666**

Exodusters African American settlers who moved west during the late 1800s to find economic and political freedom. **130**

Fair Deal President Truman's proposed reforms after the 1948 election; for example, a national health insurance program. **443**

Fair Employment Practices Committee (FEPC) Federal commission created in 1941 to prevent job discrimination based on race or ethnic background. **412**

Family and Medical Leave Act (1993) Federal law requiring large companies to provide workers up to 12 weeks of unpaid leave for family and medical emergencies without losing their medical coverage or jobs. **608**

Family Assistance Plan (FAP) President Nixon's proposal to replace the welfare system with a plan that would guarantee families a minimum income. **557**

Farm Credit Administration New Deal agency created in 1933 to give farmers low-interest, long-term loans. **351**

Farmers' Alliance Farm organization formed in 1877 that lobbied to help farmers economically and politically. **156**

Farm Security Administration (FSA) New Deal agency created in 1937 to help tenant farmers and sharecroppers buy farms through low-interest, long-term loans. **362**

Fascist party Political party, founded by Benito Mussolini in 1921, that supported a military-dominated government in control of all aspects of Italian society. **388**

Federal Deposit Insurance Corporation (FDIC) New Deal agency created in 1933 to insure bank savings deposits. **351**

Federal Emergency Relief Administration (FERA) New Deal agency created in 1933 to funnel relief aid directly to state and local agencies. **351**

Federal Farm Loan Act Federal law proposed during President Woodrow Wilson's administration that provided low-interest loans to farmers. **207**

federalism Division and sharing of powers between a strong central government and state governments. **38**

Federalists Members of a political party who advocated strong national government and favored ratification of the U.S. Constitution. **39**

Federal Project No. 1 New Deal program established in 1935 to aid unemployed artists. **372**

Federal Reserve Act (1913) Federal law that created a three-level banking system controlled by both private banks and the government. **205**

Federal Trade Commission (FTC) Government agency established in 1914 to enforce antitrust laws and to investigate corporations engaged in unfair or fraudulent practices. **205**

Federal Water Pollution Control Act (1972) Federal law passed to regulate contaminated water. **732**

Federal Workmen's Compensation Act Federal law providing benefits to federal workers injured on the job. **207**

Federal Writers' Project (FWP) Program that hired unemployed writers to produce a variety of cultural works. **372**

Fifteenth Amendment (1869) Constitutional amendment that guaranteed that the right to vote could not be denied because of race. **109**

First Battle of Bull Run (1861) Confederate victory at Manassas Junction, outside of Washington, D.C., that proved the Civil War would last longer than a few months. **97**

First Battle of the Marne (1914) World War I battle in which French and British forces stopped the German advance in northeast France. **245**

First Continental Congress (1774) Meeting of delegates from 12 colonies to discuss grievances against Great Britain, including those resulting from the Intolerable Acts. **28**

Five Power Agreement (1921) Arrangement between the U.S., Great Britain, France, Italy, and Japan to set limits on each nation's naval strength. **381**

fixed exchange rates Economic system in which the value of a dollar does not vary in relation to other currencies. **660**

flappers "New women" whose dress and conduct after World War I defied traditional standards of womanly behavior. **311**

flexible response Strategy adopted by the Kennedy administration of keeping a range of options open for dealing with international crises. **491**

floating exchange rates Economic system in which the value of a dollar can vary in relation to other currencies, depending on the relative demand for dollars and other currencies. **664**

Food Administration Government agency responsible for regulating production and supply of food during World War I. **258**

food chain Order of organisms in ecological communities in which each consumes a lower member and is in turn preyed upon by a higher member. **730**

Foraker Act (1900) Federal law outlining the organization of Puerto Rico's government. **226**

Fordney-McCumber Tariff Act (1922) Federal law that placed high duties on imported farm products in an effort to boost domestic crop prices and to help farmers. **288**

forty-niners Nickname for gold-seekers who went to California, beginning in 1849, to seek their fortune. **86**

Four Power Treaty (1921) Agreement between the U.S., Great Britain, France, and Japan to respect one another's territory in the Pacific. **381**

Fourteen Points (1918) President Wilson's program for world peace after World War I that contained 14 principles, including the creation of the League of Nations. **262**

Fourteenth Amendment (1866) Constitutional amendment that created a national citizenship, thereby extending full citizenship, civil rights, and equal protection under the law to African Americans. **108**

freedom of contract Right of workers and employers to agree to certain conditions of employment. **175**

Freedom Riders Integrated group who protested segregation in interstate transportation in 1961. **501**

Freedom Summer Campaign to register African American voters during the summer of 1964. **503**

freemen People who enjoy full political and civil liberties. **17**

Free-Soil party Political party, formed by antislavery Whigs and Democrats in 1848, that opposed the expansion of slavery into the territories. **87**

free trade International trade free from government regulation. **654**

French and Indian War (1754–63) Territorial conflict between France and Great Britain over Native American lands in which France lost most of its North American holdings. **19**

Fuel Administration Government agency responsible for regulating production and supply of fuel during World War I. **258**

Fugitive Slave Act Law passed as part of the Compromise of 1850 that made it a federal crime to assist runaway slaves. **88**

Fundamentalism Protestant movement whose followers believe in a literal interpretation of the Bible. **312**

Gadsden Purchase (1853) Agreement by which the U.S. acquired Mexico's territory south of the Gila River in present-day Arizona and New Mexico for $10 million. **85**

General Agreement on Tariffs and Trade A commitment to the long-term goal of free trade established by 44 countries at the Bretton Woods conference. **660**

generation gap Difference in years, attitudes, and cultural beliefs between generations; applied to baby boomers and their elders during the 1960s. **508**

Geneva Convention (1864) Agreement among 12 nations to care for sick and wounded enemy soldiers as well as their own. **703**

genocide Deliberate annihilation of an entire people. **423**

German reunification Reuniting of East Germany and West Germany as one nation in 1990. **597**

Gettysburg Address Lincoln's speech dedicating a cemetery at the Gettysburg battlefield in which he gave a classic statement of democratic ideals. **98**

GI Bill of Rights (1944) Servicemen's Readjustment Act, which provided pensions and government loans to help veterans start their own businesses, buy homes or farms, and attend college. **440**

Gilded Age Name applied to post–Civil War America to describe the corruption and greed that lurked below the surface of industrial society. **152**

glasnost Policy of openness introduced in the Soviet Union by Mikhail Gorbachev in 1985. **592**

global warming Gradual increase in the temperature of the earth's atmosphere. **736**

Glorious Revolution (1688) Bloodless English rebellion that broke the absolute power of the British monarchy, and King James II was replaced by the Protestant rulers Mary and William. **698**

glyph Picture or symbol used in the Olmec and other picture writing systems. **6**

gold standard   Monetary system in which each dollar is equal to and redeemable for a set amount of gold. **653**

Gold Standard Act (1900)   Federal law declaring the nation's currency to be redeemable in gold at a fixed rate. Adoption of the gold standard encouraged the development of the world economy. **653**

Good Neighbor policy   FDR's policy of promoting goodwill toward Latin America. **384**

graduated income tax   System in which the rate of taxation varies according to income. **156**

Gramm-Rudman-Hollings Act (1985)   Federal law requiring across-the-board cuts in government spending when the deficit exceeds a certain point. **591**

Great Compromise (1787)   Plan approved at the Constitutional Convention in which each state, regardless of size, was given an equal voice in the upper house, while representation in the lower house was determined by population. **38**

Great Depression   Deep economic downturn that gripped the U.S. between 1929 and the beginning of World War II. **328**

Great Migration   Mass movement of Puritans from England to the Americas beginning in 1630. **16**   Mass movement of African Americans from the South to the North between 1915 and 1930. **259**

Great Society   President Lyndon Johnson's economic and social programs during the 1960s. **497**

Great Upheaval (1886)   Year of intense worker strikes and violent labor confrontations in the U.S. **154**

Green parties   Environmentalist political parties in Europe. **731**

gross national product   Total value of all goods and services produced by a country in a given year. **327**

guerrilla warfare   Form of fighting in which forces wear down the enemy with hit-and-run skirmishes. **35**

H

Hague Peace Conferences (1899, 1907)   Meetings that established provisions for the care of enemy soldiers wounded in naval warfare. **703**

Haight-Ashbury   San Francisco district known for its hippie population during the mid-1960s. **509**

hard-rock mining   Technique that involved sinking deep mine shafts to get at ore in quartz veins. **136**

Harlem Renaissance   Period of African American artistic development during the 1920s in New York City's Harlem. **316**

hawks   People who support war or a warlike policy. **532**

Hay-Bunau-Varilla Treaty (1903)   Agreement with Panama giving U.S. control over a 10-mile-wide Canal Zone. **228**

Hay-Herrán Treaty (1903)   Proposed agreement with Colombia that would have given the U.S. a lease to build a canal in Panama. **228**

Haymarket Riot (1886)   Violent confrontation in Chicago between workers, anarchists, and police that helped turn public support against the labor movement. **154**

Hay-Pauncefote Treaty (1901)   Agreement with Great Britain by which the U.S. could build and control a Central American canal. **228**

Hepburn Act (1906)   Federal law that authorized the Interstate Commerce Commission to set railroad rates and to regulate other companies engaged in interstate commerce. **196**

Highway Act (1956)   Federal law that expanded the nation's highway systems. **473**

hippies   Name given to people in the 1960s who rejected everything connected with mainstream America. **509**

Ho Chi Minh Trail   Network of jungle paths used by the North Vietnamese to move weapons and supplies to the Vietcong in South Vietnam. **528**

Hollywood Ten   Group of film directors and writers who went to jail rather than answer questions from the House Committee on Un-American Activities. **450**

Holocaust   Systematic slaughter of European Jews by the Nazis during World War II. **423**

Home Loan Bank Act (1932)   Federal law that provided money to savings banks, building and loan associations, and insurance companies for low-interest mortgages. **341**

Home Owners Loan Corporation (HOLC)   New Deal agency created in 1933 to grant low-interest, long-term mortgage loans to home owners. **351**

Homestead Act (1862)   Federal law that gave public land to any citizen willing to live on the Great Plains and cultivate the land for five years. **128**

horizontal integration   Method of expanding a company by buying other companies involved in the same business. **144**

"hot line"   Telephone connection between the U.S. and the Soviet Union that allowed leaders to communicate directly during a crisis. **494**

House Committee on Un-American Activities (HUAC)   Congressional committee established in 1938 to investigate anti-American propaganda. **450**

Housing and Urban Development Act (1968)   Federal law that, along with the Omnibus Housing Act, provided money for urban renewal and created the Department of Housing and Urban Development. **498**

human rights   Basic rights and freedoms to which all people are entitled, including freedom from unlawful detention or torture. **570**

hunter-gatherers   People who moved from place to place in search of game and edible plants. **4**

hydraulic mining   Technique that uses water pressure to remove mountains of gravel, exposing the minerals underneath. **136**

hydrogen bomb   Weapon approximately 1,000 times more powerful than the atomic bomb. **464**

I

Immigration Act of 1924   Federal law reducing the immigration quota for each nationality to 2 percent of the 1890 figures. **294**

Immigration Act of 1965   Federal law that eliminated the numerical limits and percentages of immigrants to the U.S. **681**

Immigration Act of 1990   Federal law that updated U.S. immigration laws from the 1960s and increased the number of immigrants allowed into the United States each year. **606**

Immigration Restriction League   Group founded in 1894 by well-to-do Bostonians who sought to impose a literacy test on all immigrants. **148**

impeachment   Formal charge of wrongdoing or misconduct brought against a government official. **40**

imperialism   Practice of extending the power of a nation by direct territorial acquisition of colonial empires. **214**

impressment   Practice of kidnapping and forcing people into public service; used by Great Britain in the late 1700s and early 1800s to secure sailors for the British navy. **62**

indentured servants   Persons who agreed to work for a specified time for the person who paid their way to America. **17**

Indian Removal Act (1830)   Federal law that provided for the relocation of Indian nations living east of the Mississippi River to Indian Territory in present-day Oklahoma. **75**

Indian Reorganization Act (1934) Federal law that sought to revive tribal rule by funding tribal business ventures and paying for the college education of Native Americans. **366**

indirect rule Imperialists' method of governing in which the colonizing country rules through traditional leaders, leaving the local culture intact. **627**

Industrial Revolution Shift from hand production to machine production that began in Great Britain in the mid-1700s. **74**

inflation Rise in prices resulting from an increase in the amount of money in circulation relative to the amount of goods available for sale. **37**

Information Revolution Widespread transfer of information made possible by computers and information technologies. **686**

initiative Election reform that gives voters the power to introduce legislation. **191**

insider trading Use of confidential financial information by stockbrokers for personal gain. **591**

Intermediate-range Nuclear Forces (INF) **Treaty** (1987) Agreement that eliminated all medium-range nuclear weapons from Europe and set up inspection procedures to enforce provisions of the treaty. **592**

Internal Security Act (1950) Federal law that required Communist party members and organizations to register with the federal government. **451**

International Monetary Fund $8.8 billion fund established by members of the Bretton Woods conference to maintain the fixed exchange rates for the international economy. **660**

Internet Computer network that allows an estimated 20 million computers in more than 80 countries to communicate and share information. **610**

internment Imprisonment; practice of forced relocation applied to Japanese Americans living on the West Coast after Pearl Harbor. **410**

Interstate Commerce Act (1887) Federal law that regulated railroad freight rates and created an agency to monitor railroad activities. **156**

Intolerable Acts (1774) Series of laws passed by Great Britain to punish Massachusetts for the Boston Tea Party, while strengthening British control over the colonies; also called the Coercive Acts. **28**

Iran-contra affair Name given to the illegal actions taken by White House aides in the 1980s to fund Nicaraguan contras. **592**

Iran hostage crisis (1979–81) Period during which 53 Americans in Iran were seized by followers of militant Islamic leader Ayatollah Khomeini in an attempt to force the return of Shah Reza Pahlavi from exile in the U.S. **572**

Iroquois League Confederation of Indian tribes formed in the 15th or 16th century; also called the Six Nations. **19**

irreconcilables Fourteen Republican senators who opposed the League of Nations and rejected the Treaty of Versailles after World War I. **265**

island-hopping Allied military tactic during World War II in which certain strategic Japanese-held islands in the Pacific were seized, while others were bypassed. **418**

isolationism Policy of avoiding international political or economic alliances; followed by the U.S. during most of the 1920s and 1930s. **380**

Jay's Treaty (1794) Treaty in which Great Britain agreed to abandon its forts in the Northwest Territory in exchange for U.S. payment of debts owed to the British. **63**

Jim Crow laws State laws adopted in the South that were designed to enforce segregation. **114**

joint-stock companies Companies in which investors share the start-up and maintenance costs as well as profits or losses. **15**

Jones Act of 1916 Law that gave Filipinos the right to elect both houses of their legislature, but delayed independence until a stable government was established. **221**

Jones Act of 1917 Law that granted U.S. citizenship to Puerto Ricans and gave them the right to elect both houses of their legislature. **226**

judicial review Supreme Court's right to determine whether laws violate the U.S. Constitution. **64**

Judiciary Act (1789) Law that created the federal court system, including district courts, circuit courts of appeals, and the Supreme Court. **61**

juvenile delinquency Antisocial behavior by the young that is subject to legal action. **482**

kamikaze Japanese planes during World War II assigned to suicide missions against Allied ships. **420**

Kansas-Nebraska Act (1854) Federal law that established popular sovereignty in newly organized territories and overturned the Missouri Compromise. **89**

Keating-Owen Child Labor Act (1916) Proposed federal law that outlawed the interstate sale of products produced by child labor. **207**

Kellogg-Briand Pact (1927) Agreement signed by 62 nations that outlawed war as an instrument of national policy but allowed countries to declare war in self-defense. **382**

Kentucky and Virginia Resolutions State resolutions passed between 1798 and 1799 that declared states should be the final judge of whether a law was unconstitutional. **64**

Kerner Commission Federal Commission that investigated the 1960s riots and reported that white racism was responsible for the violence. **506**

Klondike Gold Rush Flood of prospectors to the Klondike district of Canada's Yukon Territory in the late 1890s in search of gold. **134**

Knights of Labor National union founded in 1869 that consisted of skilled and unskilled workers. **153**

Kristallnacht "Night of broken glass," November 9, 1938, when Nazis burned down synagogues and destroyed Jewish businesses in Germany. **389**

laissez-faire capitalism Theory that opposes government regulation of economic matters. **145**

Land Ordinance of 1785 Federal law that established a system for surveying western lands by townships and selling smaller parcels to the public. **37**

Landrum-Griffin Act (1959) Federal law designed to reduce corruption in labor unions. **476**

League of United Latin American Citizens (LULAC) Hispanic group that lobbied for national awareness of Hispanic concerns and issues. **574**

Lend-Lease Act (1941) Law that appropriated money for the U.S. to lend or lease arms and other supplies to non-Axis countries. **393**

Limited Nuclear Test Ban Treaty (1963) Agreement by the U.S., the Soviet Union, and Great Britain to end the testing of nuclear bombs in the atmosphere or under water. **493**

literacy tests Tests requiring proof of a person's ability to read in order to vote; used in southern states to deny voting rights to African Americans. **114**

"Little Rock Nine" Name given to the African American students who were admitted to an all-white school in Arkansas in 1957. **480**

lockouts Tactic used by employers of barring workers from plants until concessions from workers are obtained. **155**

long drives Overland treks on which cowboys herded cattle from ranches to rail lines. **132**

Long March Exodus of 1934–35 when Communist Chinese marched nearly 6,000 miles to northern China, helping cement Mao Zedong's leadership of the party. **454**

Long Walk Forced march of Navajos to Bosque Redondo, a reservation in eastern New Mexico, following their surrender in early 1864. **125**

loose construction Theory set forth by Alexander Hamilton that the federal government possesses all powers not specifically forbidden by the U.S. Constitution. **62**

Lost Generation Name given by Gertrude Stein to writers of the 1920s whose works expressed disillusionment after World War I. **318**

Louisiana Purchase (1803) U.S. purchase from France of the vast territory of Louisiana for some $15 million. **65**

Loyalists Americans loyal to Great Britain during the Revolutionary War; also called Tories. **35**

M

Maginot Line Line of defenses built by the French after World War I along their border with Germany. **393**

mainframe computers Large, fast computer systems capable of processing many tasks at a time. **687**

mandate system Provision of the Treaty of Versailles that required new colonial rulers to report to the League of Nations on their administration of former Central Power territories. **264**

Manhattan Project Top-secret U.S. project begun in 1942 in which scientists developed the first atomic bomb. **421**

manifest destiny Phrase coined in 1845 to express the belief that the U.S. was destined to extend its boundaries westward to the Pacific Ocean. **84**

Mann-Elkins Act (1910) Federal law that extended the regulatory powers of the Interstate Commerce Commission to telephone and telegraph companies. **199**

Marbury v. Madison (1803) Legal case in which the Supreme Court first exercised its right of judicial review. **64**

March on Washington (1963) Demonstration in Washington, D.C., called by African American leaders to show support for President Kennedy's civil rights bill. **503**

margin buying Purchasing stock with borrowed money. **326**

Mariposa War (1850–51) California raids by the Miwoks and the Yokuts to reclaim Native American lands taken over by miners. **87**

market revolution Creation of profitable national markets during the 1800s brought about by new transportation systems and regional specialization. **73**

Marshall Plan (1948) U.S. program that provided some $12 billion in economic aid to Western Europe after World War II; also called the European Recovery Act. **448**

mass transit Public transportation systems, such as commuter trains and subways, that made it possible for workers to live farther away from their jobs. **149**

Mayflower Compact (1620) Document that established Plymouth Colony as a self-governing colony based on the majority rule of male church members. **16**

McKinley Tariff (1890) Federal law increasing the number of imports subject to tariffs and increasing the tariff rate. **655**

Meat Inspection Act (1906) Federal consumer-protection law that required the government inspection of interstate meat shipments. **196**

Medicaid State programs established in 1965 and funded by Congress to provide free health care to the needy. **498**

Medicare Great Society program established in 1965 to provide national health insurance for people over age 65. **497**

Merchandise Marks Act (1887) British law requiring foreign goods be labeled to indicate country of origin. **655**

mergers Combining of two or more companies to achieve greater efficiency and higher profits. **288**

Mexican Cession (1848) Area surrendered by Mexico to the U.S. in the Treaty of Guadalupe Hidalgo; included the present-day states of California, Nevada, and Utah, and parts of Arizona, Colorado, and New Mexico. **85**

Mexican War (1846–48) Conflict between Mexico and the U.S. brought about by the U.S. annexation of Texas and its quest for more territory. **85**

middle class Social class that occupies a position between the wealthy and the poor. **77**

Middle Passage Voyage made by slave ships from Africa across the Atlantic Ocean during which many slaves suffered and died. **17**

militarism Glorification of armed strength and aggressive military preparedness. **243**

minicomputers Computers that are smaller, easier to operate, and less expensive than mainframes. **687**

Missouri Compromise (1820) Act that maintained the balance of slave and free states in Congress by admitting Missouri as a slave state and Maine as a free state, while prohibiting the spread of slavery in the territories to areas north of latitude 36°30′. **74**

modern Republicanism Name given to President Eisenhower's attempt to balance liberal domestic reforms with conservative spending during the 1950s. **470**

monopoly Exclusive control, such as in trade or industry, that eliminates competition. **9, 143**

Monroe Doctrine (1823) U.S. government policy statement in which the Americas were declared off-limits to European expansion. **72**

Montgomery Improvement Association (MIA) Group of civil rights leaders in Montgomery, Alabama, whose members included Martin Luther King, Jr. **479**

Montreal Protocol on Ozone Depletion (1987) International agreement that set standards for reducing the emission of CFCs and other gases. **739**

Moral Majority Fundamentalist Christian political organization founded in 1978 by Reverend Jerry Falwell. **586**

moratorium Authorized period of delay in paying a debt or fulfilling a legal obligation. **383**

Morrill Act (1862) Federal law that gave land to states to establish agricultural colleges. **128**

muckrakers Nickname given by President Theodore Roosevelt to progressive journalists in the early 1900s who exposed political and social evils. **170**

multinational corporations Companies that invest money in or own businesses around the world. **665**

Munich Conference (1938) Meeting attended by government leaders from Great Britain, Italy, France, and Germany in which a pact was signed giving Germany control of the Sudetenland. **391**

mutualistas Mutual-aid societies formed by Mexican American communities to help local residents. **332**

National Aeronautics and Space Administration (NASA) Federal agency established in 1958 to direct American space exploration. **466**

National Association for the Advancement of Colored People (NAACP) Civil rights organization founded in 1909 to work for various social reforms that would benefit African Americans and end racial discrimination. **183**

national bank Central bank with branches in major cities. **62**

National Defense Act (1916) Military "preparedness" program established prior to U.S. entry into World War I that increased the size of the National Guard and the U.S. army. **250**

National Defense Education Act (1958) Federal law that appropriated money to improve education in science, math, and foreign languages. **466**

National Energy Act (1978) Federal law that relaxed controls on the price of natural gas in an effort to ease U.S. dependence on foreign oil. **569**

National Grange Farmers' group founded in 1867 as a social organization that grew into a political force; also called Patrons of Husbandry. **155**

National Industrial Recovery Act (NIRA) Federal law passed in 1933 to stimulate industrial and business activity and to reduce unemployment. **352**

National Information Infrastructure A proposed communications network to make vast amounts of information readily available to the public; known as the Information Super-highway. **687**

nationalism Sense of pride or loyalty to a nation. **72**

nationalize To assert government control or ownership over a business or industry. **387**

National Organization for Women (NOW) Group founded by feminists in 1966 to promote equal rights for women. **510**

National Recovery Administration (NRA) Federal agency that encouraged businesses to draw up "codes of fair competition" as one means of achieving business recovery during the Great Depression. **353**

National Security Council (NSC) Organization created in 1947 by Congress to advise the president on strategic matters. **450**

National War Labor Board (NWLB) Group of representatives from business and labor who arbitrated disputes between workers and employers during World War I. **258**

National Youth Administration (NYA) New Deal agency that provided part-time jobs to people between the ages of 16 and 25. **358**

nativism Policy of favoring native-born Americans over immigrants. **78**

Nazi party Political party, led by Adolf Hitler, that controlled Germany from 1933 to 1945; also called the National Socialist party. **389**

neocolonialism The economic and political policies by which a great power indirectly exerts its influence over former colonies. **638**

New Deal President Franklin Roosevelt's program of providing relief and recovery to the U.S. during the Great Depression. **350**

New Freedom Name given to Woodrow Wilson's progressive program of reform as proposed during the 1912 presidential election. **202**

New Frontier President John Kennedy's political, social, and economic programs of the early 1960s. **489**

new immigrants People, mostly southern and eastern Europeans, who came to the United States in the late 1800s and early 1900s. **147**

Newlands Reclamation Act (1902) Federal law that allowed money from the sale of public land to be used for irrigation and reclamation. **197**

New Nationalism Name given to Theodore Roosevelt's program of social legislation first proposed during the 1910 congressional elections. **201**

New Right Conservatives who showed increased political influence during the 1980s. **586**

Nine Power Treaty (1921) Agreement arising from the Washington Conference that guaranteed China's territorial integrity and promised to uphold the Open Door policy. **381**

Nineteenth Amendment (1920) Constitutional amendment that granted women full voting rights. **208**

no-man's land Thin strip of territory along the Western Front that separated opposing armies during World War I. **245**

nonaggression pact (1939) Temporary alliance in which Germany and the Soviet Union agreed to divide Poland between them. **392**

nonaligned movement Pact formed by the leaders of former colonies to proclaim neutrality toward and establish guidelines for interacting with the superpowers in the Cold War. **638**

nonviolent resistance Strategy of peaceful protest. **500**

North American Free Trade Agreement (NAFTA) International treaty ratified in 1993 to relax trade barriers between the U.S., Canada, and Mexico. **666**

North Atlantic Treaty Organization (NATO) Alliance formed in 1949 whose member nations agreed to protect one another in the event of attack. **449**

Northwest Ordinance (1787) Federal law that established a system for governing the Northwest Territory; also called the Land Ordinance of 1787. **37**

nuclear fallout Radioactive debris produced by a nuclear explosion. **729**

Nuclear Nonproliferation Treaty (1968) Agreement between the U.S., Great Britain, the Soviet Union, and 59 other nations to keep nuclear weapons technology from spreading to more countries. **729**

Nuremberg trials Trials of Nazi war criminals by the Allies that began in 1945. **437**

Occupational Safety and Health Administration (OSHA) Federal agency created in 1970 to protect workers from unhealthful working conditions. **559**

Office of Economic Opportunity (OEO) Government agency formed in 1964 to coordinate antipoverty programs, including the Job Corps, VISTA, and Head Start. **496**

oil shocks Jolts to the world economy caused by a sharp increase in oil prices. **663**

Okies Negative term for farmers, many from Oklahoma, who migrated in 1939 to the West Coast to find work. **370**

Olympic Games Group of modern international athletic contests held every four years in a different city. **691**

Omnibus Budget Reconciliation Act (1993) Budget bill designed to reduce the deficit by spending cuts and taxes on the wealthy. The first major legislative act to pass without any votes from the minority party. **607**

Omnibus Housing Act (1965) Federal law that, together with the Housing and Urban Development Act of 1968, provided money for urban renewal and housing assistance for low-income families. **498**

Open Door policy (1899) U.S. policy, proposed by Secretary of State John Hay, that called for all nations to have equal access to trade and investment in China. **223**

open range Grazing land that the government allowed cattle ranchers to use in the late 1800s. **132**

open shops Nonunion workplaces. **176**

Operation Desert Storm (1991) U.S. military mission that joined allies in driving Iraqi forces from Kuwait. **598**

Operation Restore Hope (1992) United Nations plan to ensure that relief efforts reached famine-stricken Somalia. **685**

Operation Rolling Thunder U.S. bombing campaign against military targets in North Vietnam that began in 1965. **528**

Oregon Country Disputed area of Pacific Northwest occupied jointly by the U.S. and Great Britain after the War of 1812. **72**

Oregon Trail Route to Oregon Country during the 1800s. **85**

Organization of African Unity (1963) Group of African nations formed to maintain peace and prevent territorial conflicts among its members following African independence. **641**

Organization of Petroleum Exporting Countries (OPEC) Group of oil-producing countries, mainly Arab, formed in 1960 to get higher prices for oil exports. **558**

overseers People who supervise workers. **79**

p

pacification Military tactic used by U.S. troops during the Vietnam War that involved moving residents to refugee camps and burning their villages. **530**

Pacific Railway Act (1862) Federal law that gave land for development of a transcontinental railroad. **128**

Pacific Rim Countries on the western edge of the Pacific Ocean. **664**

Paleo-Indians First people who crossed Beringia into North America. **4**

Palmer raids (1919–20) Raids to capture alleged radicals; launched by Attorney General A. Mitchell Palmer during the Red Scare. **282**

Panama Canal treaties (1978) Agreements granting Panama control over canal operations by the year 2000. **570**

Pan-German movement German efforts prior to World War I to unite all German-speaking peoples under one flag. **242**

Panic of 1819 Economic collapse caused in part by state banks lending money that they could not back with specie. **74**

Pan-Slavic movement Efforts supported by Russia to bring together all Slavic peoples of central and eastern Europe, in direct opposition to the Pan-German movement. **242**

partnerships Business enterprises that are owned by two or more people who are responsible for the businesses' debts. **143**

patio **process** Mining technique developed in Latin America; used mercury to extract silver from ore. **134**

Peace Corps Program established by President John Kennedy in the early 1960s that sends volunteers to developing countries. **491**

Pendleton Civil Service Act (1883) Federal law that created a Civil Service Commission to administer competitive examinations to those seeking government jobs. **153**

Pentagon Papers Secret government documents, published in 1971, that showed how the government had misled Americans about the Vietnam War. **538**

peons Landless laborers, mostly Indians, who worked on Spanish haciendas. **14**

perestroika Mikhail Gorbachev's plan to restructure the Soviet economy and government during the late 1980s. **593**

pet banks State banks that received deposits of federal funds because of their officers' loyalty to the Democratic party and to President Andrew Jackson. **76**

philanthropy Charitable efforts to promote public welfare, such as financing libraries, museums, and art galleries; endowing universities; and establishing theater or music groups. **151**

Philippine Government Act (1902) Federal law decreeing that the Philippines would be ruled by a governor and a two-house legislature. **220**

Pinckney's Treaty (1795) Agreement negotiated with Spain that set the southern boundary of the U.S. near Florida at the 31st parallel. **63**

planned obsolescence Practice of making products that are designed to go out of style. **320**

Platt Amendment Addition to Cuba's constitution, enacted in 1902 and renounced in 1934, that gave the U.S. greater control over Cuban affairs. **225**

Plessy v. Ferguson (1896) Supreme Court case in which the court upheld segregation by ruling that "separate but equal" facilities did not violate the Fourteenth Amendment. **114**

political machines Political organizations, headed by bosses, that used appointments to government jobs to control elections. **152**

poll taxes Fixed taxes imposed on every voter by southern states in an effort to deprive African Americans of the right to vote. **114**

pop art Art form begun in the 1960s that uses everyday objects as subject matter or in the works themselves. **510**

popular sovereignty Right of the people to rule, used as an argument for letting citizens of each new territory decide whether to permit slavery there. **87**

Populist party Political party founded by farmers, labor leaders, and reformers in 1892; also called the People's party. **157**

Potsdam Conference (1945) Overseas meeting attended by the U.S., Britain, and the Soviet Union that laid the foundation for Germany's postwar status. **436**

preservation Keeping wild areas intact and essentially untouched by humans. **726**

Proclamation of 1763 Declaration issued by Great Britain that barred settlement west of the Appalachian Mountains. **26**

progressivism Reform movement concerned with curing the ills caused by industrialization. **168**

prohibition Legal ban on the manufacture, transportation, and sale of alcoholic beverages. **81**

proprietorships Small businesses owned by individuals or families. **143**

protectionism Practice of imposing higher tariffs and stricter barriers against foreign imports in an effort to encourage Americans to purchase domestic goods. **654**

protectorate Country dependent on another for protection. **225**

Protestant Reformation Religious upheaval in Europe begun by Martin Luther in 1517 to protest corruption in the Roman Catholic church. **15**

Public Works Administration (PWA) New Deal agency established in 1933 that contracted with private firms to construct roads, public buildings, and similar projects. **353**

Pueblo Revolt (1680) Attacks by the Pueblo Indians that temporarily drove the Spanish from New Mexico. **13**

puppet government Government established by imperials in a colony in which it seems the colony is in control when in fact the imperial is. **632**

Pure Food and Drug Act (1906)   Federal consumer-protection law that forbade the manufacture or sale of food and patent medicine containing harmful ingredients. **196**

Puritans   English Protestants who sought to "purify" the Anglican church of Catholic rituals and traditions. **16**

Qur'an   Holy book of Islam. **7**

railhead   Town located along a railroad; long cattle drives usually ended there. **132**

Railroad Administration   Federal agency that reorganized railroads and set limits on transportation rates and workers' wages during World War I. **258**

Reaganomics   President Ronald Reagan's economic program built on big tax cuts to encourage business investment. **586**

realpolitik   Approach to foreign policy, adopted by Henry Kissinger and President Richard Nixon, that emphasized national interests over moral or ethical concerns. **559**

recall   Election reform that allows voters to remove an elected official from office by calling for a new election. **191**

reclamation   Process of making damaged land productive. **197**

Reconquista   Ongoing battle to recapture Spanish lands from the Moors that ended in 1492. **10**

Reconstruction   Rebuilding of the former Confederate states to reunite the nation. **106**

Reconstruction Acts (1867)   Federal laws that gave radical Republicans military control of the South. **108**

Reconstruction Finance Corporation (RFC)   Federal agency created in 1932 to stimulate the economy by lending money to railroads, insurance companies, banks, and other financial institutions. **341**

recycling   Collection and processing of used items for reuse. **738**

Red Cross   Organization formed by private Swiss citizens in 1863 to care for wounded soldiers of all nations. Present-day international efforts aid victims of natural disasters. **703**

Red Scare (1919–20)   Period of anti-Communist hysteria after the Bolshevik Revolution in Russia. **281**

referendum   Election reform that allows voters to place a measure on the ballot. **191**

regionalists   Midwestern artists popular in the 1930s who stressed local folk themes and customs in their work. **375**

rehabilitation   Treatment to restore someone to a useful and constructive place in society. **81**

Rehabilitation Act (1973)   Federal law forbidding discrimination in education, in jobs, or in housing because of physical disabilities. **575**

Relocation Act (1956)   Federal law passed to relocate Native Americans to urban areas. **471**

Renaissance   Rebirth of European art and learning spurred by the Crusades. **8**

reparations   Payments of damages. **263**

republic   Form of government in which leaders receive authority from citizens to make and enforce laws. **36**

reservationists   Republican senators who would support the Treaty of Versailles only if the League Covenant were amended. **265**

reserved powers   Powers kept by the states because they are not specifically granted to the federal government or denied to the states by the U.S. Constitution. **40**

rock 'n' roll   Popular music introduced in the 1950s that reworked black rhythm and blues. **482**

Roe v. Wade (1973)   Supreme Court case that overturned a state law limiting a woman's access to an abortion. **577**

Roosevelt Corollary (1904)   Policy that extended the Monroe Doctrine by allowing the U.S. a greater role in maintaining peace and order in the Western Hemisphere. **229**

rugged individualism   Idea that success comes through individual effort and private enterprise. **339**

Rural Electrification Administration (REA)   New Deal agency that brought electricity to isolated rural areas. **358**

Russo-Japanese War (1904–05)   War between Russia and Japan that began with a Japanese attack on Russian forces in Manchuria. **224**

Safe Drinking Water Act (1974)   Federal law enacted to regulate contaminated water. **732**

Sand Creek Massacre (1864)   Slaughter of Cheyenne Indians by U.S. troops at Sand Creek in Colorado Territory. **123**

Sandinistas   Nicaraguan rebels who overthrew the dictatorship of Anastasio Somoza Debayle in 1979. **589**

satellite nations   Countries under the control of the Soviet Union. **445**

Saturday Night Massacre (1973)   Resignation and firing of top government officials who refused to aid President Richard Nixon in the Watergate cover-up. **564**

scientific management   Theory, promoted by Frederick W. Taylor, that every kind of work could be broken into a series of smaller tasks for which rates of production could be set. **303**

search-and-destroy missions   Military attacks that involve looking for and annihilating hidden enemy troops. **529**

Second Continental Congress (1775)   Convention held in Philadelphia in which delegates established the Continental Army and chose George Washington as its commander. **28**

Second Great Awakening   Renewal of religious faith that swept the U.S. beginning in the 1790s. **81**

Second New Deal   Government programs passed after the 1934 elections that provided relief and recovery but emphasized reform. **357**

Second Seminole War (1835–1842)   Resistance by the Seminoles to their removal from Florida; cost more money and lives than any other Indian war in U.S. history. **75**

sectionalism   Loyalty to a particular area of the country. **63**

Sedition Act (1918)   Federal law enacted during World War I that made written criticism of the government a crime. **261**

Selective Service Act (1917)   Federal law that required men to register with local draft boards. **251**

Selective Training and Service Act (1940)   Federal law that provided for America's first peacetime draft. **409**

self-determination   Right of people to govern themselves. **262**

Seneca Falls Convention (1848)   Meeting held in Seneca Falls, New York, that marked the birth of the organized women's rights movement in the U.S. **83**

separation of powers   Allotment of powers between the legislative, executive, and judicial branches of government to prevent any one branch from becoming too powerful. **40**

Separatists   Radical English Puritans who broke with the Church of England. **16**

settlement houses   Community centers in poor neighborhoods that provided education, recreation, and other services. **150**

Seventeenth Amendment (1913)   Constitutional amendment that provided for the direct election of United States senators. **191**

sexual harassment   The use of unwelcome sexual language or behavior. **600**

shantytowns   Makeshift shelters built by homeless people; for example, the Hoovervilles that were built during the Great Depression. **333**

sharecropping   Arrangement under which a sharecropper agreed to work a parcel of land in return for a share of the crop, a cabin, seed, tools, and a mule. **113**

Share-Our-Wealth (1933)   Radical relief program proposed by Senator Huey Long to empower the government to confiscate wealth from the rich through taxes and provide a guaranteed minimum income and home to every family. **357**

Shays's Rebellion (1786–87)   Farmers' revolt against high taxes and heavy debts, led by Daniel Shays. **38**

Sherman Antitrust Act (1890)   Federal law that declared monopolies and trusts illegal. **145**

silent generation   Name given to middle-class youth of the 1950s who seemed willing to conform to consumer culture without protest. **482**

silent majority   Name President Richard Nixon gave to middle-class voters weary of 1960s social upheaval. **556**

sit-down strike   Work stoppage in which workers occupy factories until management meets their demands. **361**

sit-in   Strategy of nonviolent protest in which a group enters a public place and refuses to leave. **500**

Sixteenth Amendment (1913)   Constitutional amendment that authorized an individual income tax. **199**

smog   Air polluted by chemicals, car exhaust, and smoke. **732**

Smoot-Hawley Tariff (1930)   High-tariff law that contributed to the global economic downturn of the 1930s. **330**

Social Darwinism   Theory, proposed in the late 1800s, that society progressed through competition, with the fittest rising to positions of wealth and power. **150**

Social Gospel   Movement by Protestant ministers in the late 1800s that called for people to apply Christian principles to address social problems. **150**

socialism   System under which government or worker cooperatives own all means of production and distribution. **176**

Social Security Act (1935)   Federal law that provided a system of unemployment compensation and retirement pensions. **358**

Society of American Indians   Organization formed by Native Americans to address Indian problems. **184**

Solidarity   Polish independent trade union and social movement that was formed in 1980. **588**

Southern Christian Leadership Conference (SCLC)   Alliance of church-based African American organizations formed in 1957 and dedicated to ending discrimination. **500**

southern strategy   President Richard Nixon's plan to woo conservative southern white voters away from the Democratic party by cutting back on new civil rights legislation. **557**

Southern Tenant Farmers' Union (STFU)   Arkansas sharecroppers who lobbied government in 1934 to halt tenant evictions and to force landowners to share payments with tenants. **354**

Space shuttle   Reusable space vehicle. **610**

Spanish-American War (1898)   War declared by the U.S. on Spain to protect U.S. investments and to help Cuba overthrow Spanish rule. **216**

Spanish Armada   Spanish naval force defeated by England in 1588. **15**

Spanish Civil War   War that began in 1936 between Fascists and Loyalists in Spain. **389**

specie   Gold or silver coins that a bank held to back up its notes. **74**

spheres of influence   Ports or regions in a nation where a foreign country retains exclusive rights over trade, mines, and railroads. **222**

spirituals   Songs modeled in part on Christian hymns and in part on African musical forms. **81**

spoils system   Political practice, introduced by Andrew Jackson, of giving government jobs to supporters. **75**

Sputnik (1957)   Satellite launched by the Soviet Union that led the U.S. to focus more on technological development. **466**

Square Deal   Theodore Roosevelt's 1904 presidential campaign slogan pledging fair treatment for business, workers, and the public. **195**

stagflation   Economic condition in which inflation is accompanied by unemployment. **558**

Stamp Act (1765)   Law enacted by Parliament that placed a tax on all printed matter in the colonies. **27**

stock   Certificates of ownership in a company. **143**

stockholders   Owners of certificates in a corporation who receive a certain percentage of the corporation's profits through dividends. **143**

Strategic Arms Limitation Talks (SALT)   Agreement between the U.S. and the Soviet Union, limiting the number of intercontinental nuclear missiles each nation could have. **560**

Strategic Defense Initiative (SDI)   Space-based missile-defense system proposed by President Ronald Reagan in the 1980s to blunt the nuclear-freeze movement; also called "Star Wars." **588**

strict construction   Theory set forth by Thomas Jefferson that the federal government possesses only those powers that the U.S. Constitution specifically allows. **62**

strike   Tactic used by labor unions in which workers refuse to work until employers meet union demands. **77**

strikebreakers   Nonunion workers brought in by a company to replace striking workers. **155**

Student Nonviolent Coordinating Committee (SNCC)   Association formed in 1960 by student activists from throughout the South. **500**

subsidies   Payments made to farmers to reduce their production of a crop or commodity. **354**

suffrage   Right to vote. **83**

Sugar Act (1764)   Law enacted by Parliament that set an import tax on foreign sugar, molasses, and other goods to the colonies. **27**

Sunbelt   Southern and western states having warm climates and suburban life-styles. **578**

superpowers   Nations that possess great power and become dominant in global politics. **424**

supremacy clause   Clause in the U.S. Constitution stating that the federal constitution and all federal laws outrank state constitutions and state laws. **40**

***Sussex* pledge** (1916)   Renewal of promise by Germany not to sink ocean liners without warning or without assuring the passengers' safety. **249**

Taft-Hartley Act (1947)   Federal law that extended government regulation of labor unions and included a provision allowing courts to end strikes. **441**

Tariff Act of 1816   Federal law that placed a 25 percent duty on most imported factory goods. **73**

tariffs   Taxes on imported or exported goods. **39**

Tax Reform Law (1986)   Federal law that eliminated special tax breaks for certain groups. **591**

Teapot Dome scandal (1926)   Scandal in which Secretary of the Interior Albert Fall was convicted of accepting bribes for leasing the government oil reserve in Teapot Dome, Wyoming, to private oil companies. **286**

teleconferencing   Satellite links enabling people at different locations to hold conferences over the telephone. **688**

Teller Amendment (1898)   Stated that the U.S. claimed no sovereignty, jurisdiction, or control over Cuba. **216**

temperance movement   Reform efforts to curb or limit alcohol consumption. **81**

Tennessee Valley Authority (TVA)   New Deal agency created in 1933 to develop power stations and dams throughout the Tennessee River Valley. **355**

termination   Government policy during the 1950s designed to end the reservation system. **472**

Tet offensive (1968)   North Vietnamese attack on South Vietnam during Tet, the Vietnamese New Year. **535**

Texas longhorn   Hardy breed of cattle developed by the 1850s that helped make long drives possible. **132**

Texas Revolution (1835)   Revolt against Mexico by Tejanos and American settlers in Texas after the loss of state power. **84**

Third UN Conference on the Law of the Sea (1982)   International conference in which participating nations agreed to protect the world's oceans. **739**

Third World   The developing nations of Africa, Asia, and Latin America. **638**

Thirteenth Amendment (1865)   Constitutional amendment that abolished slavery. **107**

38th parallel   Border between North Korea and South Korea set by the Allies in 1945. **455**

Thomasites   Group of young Americans who arrived in Manila in 1901 to teach American values and forge a cultural connection with the Philippines. **676**

Three-Fifths Compromise (1787)   Agreement made at the Constitutional Convention that counted only three fifths of the slave population in determining total state population. **39**

Tonkin Gulf Resolution (1964)   Act that gave the president authority to take all necessary measures to repel an armed attack against U.S. forces. **526**

total war   Strategy used in the Civil War of striking at the enemy's economic resources in addition to fighting enemy troops. **102**

Townshend Acts (1767)   Law enacted by Parliament that placed duties on goods imported by the colonies. **27**

Trail of Tears (1838)   Forced relocation of Cherokees from Georgia to Indian Territory, during which many died. **75**

Trans-Appalachian West   Area between the Appalachian Mountains and the Mississippi River. **65**

transcendentalists   New England intellectuals who believed people could attain perfection and could acquire knowledge about God, self, and the universe. **723**

Treaty of Brest-Litovsk (1918)   Agreement signed by the Bolsheviks in which Russia made a separate peace with the Central Powers and withdrew from World War I. **254**

Treaty of Fort Laramie (1851)   Agreement that set boundaries for Native American groups and allowed the U.S. government to build roads and forts through Indian Territory. **122**

Treaty of Ghent   Agreement signed in 1814 that ended the War of 1812. **67**

Treaty of Guadalupe Hidalgo   Agreement ending the Mexican War in 1848 by which Mexico ceded Texas and the rest of its western territory. **85**

Treaty of Medicine Lodge (1867)   Agreement that ended a long-standing war between the Sioux and the U.S. **123**

Treaty of Paris (1783)   Agreement signed by Great Britain and the U.S. granting the U.S. independence, territory, and fishing rights. **35**

Treaty of Tordesillas (1494)   Agreement that divided control over new territories in the Americas between Spain and Portugal. **12**

Treaty of Versailles (1919)   Agreement ending World War I that provided for the establishment of the League of Nations. **264**

trench warfare   Strategy used during World War I in which opposing armies dug in along the front to defend their positions. **245**

Triple Alliance   Military alliance formed by Germany, Austria-Hungary, and Italy prior to World War I. **243**

Triple Entente   Military alliance formed by Great Britain, France, and Russia prior to World War I. **243**

Truman Doctrine   U.S. policy of giving military and financial aid to those countries resisting Communist rule. **447**

trunk lines   Major railroads connected to surrounding areas by feeder or branch lines. **142**

trust   Group of companies that give control of their stock to a board of directors, which then runs the companies as a single enterprise. **143**

trusteeship   Post–World War I covenant requiring imperial governments to provide economic development and social services to the colonies they governed under League of Nations mandates. **629**

Twelfth Amendment (1804)   Constitutional amendment that requires electors to vote for presidential and vice-presidential candidates on separate ballots. **65**

Twenty-first Amendment (1933)   Constitutional amendment that repealed Prohibition. **312**

Twenty-sixth Amendment (1971)   Constitutional amendment that lowered the voting age from 21 to 18. **540**

Tydings-McDuffie Act (1934)   Federal law that granted independence to the Philippines at the end of a 12-year transition period. **632**

ultraviolet solar radiation (UV rays)   Radiation from the sun that can cause skin cancer, damage marine life, and harm crops. **736**

unconditional surrender   Arrangement whereby the loser agrees to the terms of the victor. **406**

Underground Railroad   Network that helped slaves escape to the North or Canada before the Civil War. **80**

Underwood Tariff Act (1913)   Federal law that reduced tariffs to their lowest levels in 50 years. **205**

unilateral disarmament   Voluntary elimination of nuclear weapons despite the presence of nuclear weapons in other nations. **730**

unilateralism   One-sided or independent action in foreign affairs. **380**

United Farm Workers (UFW)   Organization of migrant workers formed to win better wages and working conditions. **507**

United Nations (UN)   International organization formed in 1945 to work for world peace. **439**

universal coverage   Health care for every American. **608**

Universal Declaration of Human Rights   Series of basic rights held by all human beings that was adopted by the United Nations in 1948. **708**

University of California v. Bakke (1978)   Supreme Court decision that struck down quotas as a means of achieving racial equality; in institutions of higher learning, for example. **576**

urban renewal   Programs designed to replace or restore run-down inner-city buildings. **477**

Uruguay Round   Set of negotiations aimed at boosting global free trade among most of the world's nations. **666**

U.S. Department of Agriculture   Government agency created in 1862 to help farmers. **130**

utopias   Ideal communities. **81**

vertical integration   Strategy whereby one company acquires other companies that provide materials and services necessary to the first company. **144**

Vietcong   Vietnamese Communists. **524**

Vietminh   Resistance movement organized by Ho Chi Minh in 1941; also known as the League for the Independence of Vietnam. **522**

Vietnamization   President Richard Nixon's plan to end the Vietnam War by turning over the fighting to the South Vietnamese army and withdrawing U.S. troops. **537**

Virginia Plan   James Madison's proposal during the Constitutional Convention for shifting power away from the states toward a central government. **38**

Volstead Act (1919)   Federal law that enforced the Eighteenth Amendment (Prohibition). **312**

Voting Rights Act (1965)   Federal law that put voter registration under government control. **504**

Voting Rights Act of 1975   Federal law requiring states and communities with large numbers of non-English speakers to print voting materials in various foreign languages. **579**

Wagner-Connery Act (1935)   Federal law that guaranteed labor's right to organize unions and bargain for better wages and working conditions. **361**

War Industries Board (WIB)   U.S. agency during World War I responsible for allocating scarce materials, establishing production priorities, and setting prices. **258**

war of attrition   Forcing an enemy to fight until they run out of supplies, troops, and will. **102**

War on Poverty   President Lyndon Johnson's Great Society programs designed to end poverty in the U.S. **496**

War Powers Act (1973)   Federal law limiting the president's power to send U.S. troops to foreign conflicts. **544**

War Production Board (WPB)   Government agency during World War II that directed the conversion of existing factories to wartime production. **408**

Warren Commission   Group assigned in 1963 to investigate the assassination of President John Kennedy. **495**

Warsaw Pact (1955)   Alliance formed by the Soviet Union and other Communist countries in Eastern Europe. **450**

Water Quality Improvement Act (1970)   Federal law requiring oil companies to pay some oil spill cleanup costs and setting limits on discharge of industrial pollutants into water. **559**

Watergate   Name given to government scandal that began in 1972 and led to President Richard Nixon's resignation in 1974. **562**

Wealth Tax Act (1935)   Federal law that sharply increased taxes on the rich. **358**

Whiskey Rebellion (1794)   Uprising by western Pennsylvania farmers against a tax on whiskey. **62**

Wisconsin Idea   Program of progressive reforms proposed by Wisconsin governor Robert M. "Fighting Bob" La Follette during the early 1900s. **193**

Women's Christian Temperance Union (WCTU)   Reform group in favor of temperance, moral purity, and the rights of women. **181**

Women's Social and Political Union   Faction of women's suffrage movement led by Emmeline Pankhurst whose aggressive tactics helped British women win the right to vote. **701**

Woodstock (1969)   Three-day rock concert in upstate New York that was one of the high points of the counterculture movement. **513**

Works Progress Administration (WPA)   New Deal agency formed in 1935 to create jobs for people on relief. **357**

World Bank   Ten billion dollar institution created to make loans to war-damaged countries and to encourage industrial development in underprivileged countries. **660**

World Trade Organization   Union of 125 nations that signed a final free-trade agreement dedicated to bring cooperation to world trade issues. **666**

Wounded Knee Massacre (1890)   Massacre that occurred between the Sioux on Wounded Knee Creek and the army sent to confiscate the Indians' rifles. **125**

Yalta Conference (1945)   Postwar peace meeting between the U.S., Britain, and the Soviet Union in which plans were made to divide and occupy Germany. **417**

yellow-dog contracts   Agreements many job applicants signed, promising not to join unions. **155**

yeoman farmers   Small farmers who own and cultivate their own land. **78**

Young Plan (1929)   Revision of the Dawes Plan that spread Germany's $26 billion reparations payments over 59 years. **656**

zaibatsu   Huge corporations run by single families that had monopolized the Japanese economy prior to World War II. **437**

zero population growth (ZPG)   Birthrate that replaces existing population but does not increase it. **578**

Zimmermann Note (1917)   Document that showed that Germany was trying to establish a military alliance with Mexico. **250**

Zionism   Movement, originally intended to promote the founding of a Jewish national state, that called for a Jewish homeland in Palestine. **452**

zoot-suit riots (1943)   Racial attacks by U.S. sailors on Mexican American youths in Los Angeles. **413**

Babbitt (Lewis), 318, 428-29
Babson, Roger, 326
baby boom, 432, *c432,* 473
Baca, Ezequiel de, 164, *p164*
Baca, Jimmy Santiago, 614, *p614,* 615
Bacall, Lauren, *p450*
Back-to-Africa movement, 292, 293
Baez, Joan, *p512,* 513
Baghdad, Iraq: early history, 7; in Persian Gulf War, 599
Bahamas, Columbus and, 10-11, *m22*
Bake, Henry, Jr., *p419*
Baker, Ella, 332, 505
Baker, Howard, 564
Baker, Ray Stannard, 171, 227
Baker v. *Carr* (1962), 498
Bakke, Allan, 576
Balanced Budget and Emergency Control Act (1985), 591
Balboa, Vasco Nuñez de, 12-13, 226
Balch, Emily Greene, 381
Balfour Declaration (1917), 267
Ball, Lucille, 474, *p474*
Ballinger, Richard, 200, *p200*
Baltimore, MD, 67
Bandung Conference (1955), 638
Bangkok, Thailand, 689, *p690*
Bangladesh, 737, *p737,* 738
bank holiday, 350-51
banking: in the depression, 327-28; in early 1800s, 73, 74; Hamilton's proposal for, 62; and Jackson, 75-76; New Deal programs for, 350-51; in 1980s and 1990s, 592, 652; and Panic of 1819, 74
Banking Act of 1933, *c359*
Bank of the United States: charter of first, 62; failure to recharter in 1811, 73; Jackson's opposition to second, 75-76; second, 73
Barbie, Klaus, 438
Barcelona, Spain, 691
barcodes, 689
Bardeen, John, *p687*
bar graph, 757
Barkley, Alben W., 442
Barnum & Bailey's Circus, 151
Barrett, Janie Porter, 150
Barton, Clara, 99
Baruch, Bernard, 258, 446
Baruch Plan (1946), 446-47
baseball, 151, *p151,* 164, 275, 309, *p309,* 337, *p337,* 433, *p433,* 553, *p553;* popularity overseas, 690-91
Basie, Count, 374
basketball, in 1990s, 673, 691
Bataan, Philippines: in World War II, *p400,* 401
Bataan Death March (1942), 401, *p402,* *m427*
Bates, Daisy, *p481*
Batista, Fulgencio, 491
Baumfree, Isabella. *See* Truth, Sojourner

Bay of Pigs, Cuba, 491-92, *m493*
bear market, 326
Beatles, 432, *p432,* 512
Beats, 481-82
Beauregard, P.G.T., 96, 99
Beauvoir, Simone de, 712, *p712*
bebop, 410
Beck, Walter, 337
Begin, Menachem, 571, 572, *p580*
Beiderbecke, Bix, 315
Beijing, China: protests in, *p696-97,* 697
Belafonte, Harry, 710
Belarus, 599
Belgian Congo. *See* Zaire
Belgium: in Africa, 637, *m637;* and European economic integration, 661; imperialism of, 627; at Washington Conference, 381; and World War I, 243, 244, *m244*
Bell, Alexander Graham, xxiv, 143
Belloc, Hilaire, 626
benevolent societies, 148
Ben-Gurion, David, 452-53
Benton, Thomas Hart, 375; painting by, *p364*
Bentsen, Lloyd, 594-95, *p595*
Berger, Victor, 261
Beringia, 4
Berlin airlift (1948), *p445,* 448-49
Berlin Wall; construction of, 492, *p492;* fall of, 599
Bernadotte, Folke, 453
Bernstein, Carl, 563, *p563*
Berry, Chuck, 482, 485, *p485*
Bessemer, Henry, 142
Bessemer process, 142
Bethune, Mary McLeod, 365-66, *p365,* 412
Bhutto, Benazir, 713
bicameral legislature, 38
Bicentennial celebration, *p554-55*
bicycling, 1, 618
Big Four, 263
Bilingual Education Act (1974), 579, *p579*
Bill of Rights (1791), 52, 61; text of, 53-54
Bingham, George Caleb, painting by, *p70-71*
biodiversity, 735, 739
biomass, 734
Bird, Ella, 133
Birmingham, England, 677
Black, Georgia, 711
black codes, 107
Blackfeet, 122
Black Kettle, 123
blacklists, 155
Blackmun, Harry, 557
Black Muslims, 505
black nationalism, 292-93
Black Panther party, 505-06
Black Power, 504-06
Blackshirts, 388
Black Star Steamship Company, 293
Black Thursday (October 24, 1929), 327

Black Tuesday (October 29, 1929), 327
Blackwelder, Julia Kirk, 511
Blackwell, Elizabeth, 99, *p99*
Blair, Henry, xxiv
Blake, Eubie, 316
Blatch, Harriot Stanton, 259
"Bleeding Kansas," 89, *p89*
blitzkrieg, 393
"Blue Meridian, The" (Toomer), 428
Bluford, Guion, 552
boat people, 542-43, *p542,* 681
Bogart, Humphrey, *p450*
Bolsheviks, 254
bonanza farm, 131-32, *p131*
Bonnin, Gertrude S., 184, *p184*
Bonus Army (1932), 343-44, *p343*
Booth, John Wilkes, 106, *p107*
bootlegging, 312
Bork, Robert, 564, 591
Bosch, Juan, 499, *p499*
Bosnia: ethnic fighting in, 597; and World War I, 242
Bosque Redondo, NM, 125
Boston, MA: in colonial period, 27, *p27;* police strike in, 280, *p280;* in Revolutionary War, 28
Boston Massacre (1770), 27, *p27*
Boston Tea Party (1773), 27
Bourke-White, Margaret, 371, *p376*
Bow, Clara, 309
Bowen, Louise DeKoven, 178
Boxer, Barbara, 601
Boxer Rebellion (1900), 223, *p620-21,* 626, *p627*
Brace, Charles Loring, 180
braceros, 413
Bradford Singers, *p80*
Brain Trust, 350
Brandeis, Louis D., 175, *p175*
"Brandeis Brief," 175
Brando, Marlon, 482
Brant, Joseph. *See* Thayendanegea
Brattain, Walter H., *p687*
Braun, Carol Moseley. *See* Moseley-Braun, Carol
Braun, Werhner von, 686, *p686*
Brazil: deforestation in, 734; and Earth Summit, 739; human rights abuses in, 715
"Bread Line" (Converse), 347
breadlines, 333, *p347*
Bretton Woods system, 660, *p660,* 664
Brezhnev, Leonid, 560
Briand, Aristide, 382
brinkmanship, 466
British Invasion, 432, 512
Brooke, Ed, *p575*
Brown, James, 80
Brown, John, 88; raid of, 90
Brown, Linda, 478
Brown, Ron, 601
Brown, William Wells, 1, 79
Brownpower, 507
Brownshirts, 389
Brown v. *The Board of Education of Topeka* (1952), 478-79, 498

Bruce, Blanche K., 112

Bryan, William Jennings: in election of 1896, 157; in election of 1908, 199; in Scopes trial, 314; as secretary of state, 248, 249-50

Buchanan, James, 89, *p90*

Buchanan* v. *Warley, 183

Buchenwald, Germany, 423, *p423*

budget, U.S.: deficit under Bush, 603; deficit under Clinton, 603; deficit under Reagan, 592, *c592;* 1900-1990, *c780;* 1992, *c780*

buffalo, *p121,* 126, 722-23, *p723*

Building Vocabulary, 751

Bulgaria, in World War II, 403

Bulge, Battle of the (1944), 417

bull market, 326

Bull Moose party, 201, *p201*

Bull Run: First Battle of (1861), 97, *m98,* 100; Second Battle of (1862), *m98,* 100

Bunau-Varilla, Philippe, 228

Bunche, Ralph, 453, *p453*

Bunker Hill, Battle of (1775), 28

Bureau of Indian Affairs, 123, 137, 184, 576, 606

Burger, Warren: appointment of, to Supreme Court, 557; retirement of, 591

Burleson, Albert, 281

Burma (Myanmar): and military rule, 716; in World War II, 401

Burnham, Daniel, 179, *p179,* 181

Burnside, Ambrose E., 100

Burr, Aaron, 64

Bursum Bill, 290

Burundi, 685

Bush, George, 599, *p599;* domestic problems of, 599-600; and economy, 600; in election of 1984, 591; in election of 1988, 594-95; m595; in election of 1992, 585, 601; and foreign affairs, 596, 599; and Immigration Act (1990), 683; and legacy of Vietnam War, 544; and Persian Gulf War, 597-99; as vice president, 573

business: deregulation of, 587; and health care, 609; and technological advances, 652, 688; regulation of, under Theodore Roosevelt, 195-97; rise of big, 143-45; and Wilson, 205, *p205,* 207

business cycle, 330, 648-49

busing, 557, *p575,* 575-76, 581, 586

cabinet, 61

Cabot, John, 15, *m22*

Cabrillo, Juan Rodríguez, 13, *m22*

Cahokia, 6

Cairo, Egypt: 1943 conference in, 406, *p406;* recycling in, 738-39

Calcutta, India, 685

Calhoun, John C., 74, 87, 88

California: admitted to Union, 88; African Americans in, 86; bonanza farms in, 131, *p131;* Chinese

Americans in, *c118,* 148, *p148;* counterculture in, 508-09, *p508, p509;* election of 1860, 91; election of 1968, 536; and the environment, 559; gold in, 86-87, 675; Great Depression in, 334, 370; Japanese Americans in, 410-11, *m411;* and Mexican Cession, *m86;* Mexican immigration to, 259, *m294,* 295, *p295;* in Mexican War, 85; migrant workers in, 367, 369, *p369,* 373, 507; mining in, 86-87, *p120-21;* Native Americans in, 86-87, 122; population migration to, 578; racial unrest in, 576; and sheep ranching in, 133; Spanish settlement of, 13-14, 86; U.S. expansion into, 86-87, 623; zoot-suit riots in, 413

California Trail, 86

Californios, 86, 135

call number, 760

Cambodia, 520, *m521;* post–Vietnam War immigrants from, 681; spread of Vietnam War to, 541; U.S. bombing of, 538; U.S. policy toward, 566

Camden, Battle of (1780), *m34,* 35

Campbell, Ben Nighthorse, *p605*

Camp David Accords (1978), 572, 610

Canada: and acid rain, 736; conservation in, 726; entertainment exports to U.S., 692; exploration of, 15, *m22-23;* and French and Indian War, 19; gold rush in, 676; and Montreal Protocol, 739; and NAFTA, 666; in Revolutionary War, 34; Russian Jews in, 678; and Underground Railroad, 80; U.S. immigration to, 676; and War of 1812, 67

Canadian Forestry Association, 726

canals, development of, 73

Cannon, Joseph "Uncle Joe," 201

Canseco, Jose, 690

Cape of Good Hope, 626

capitalism, laissez-faire. *See* laissez-faire capitalism

Capone, Al, 312

card catalog, 760

Cárdenas, Lázaro, 387, *p387*

Cardozo, Francis L., 112

Caribbean: baseball in, 690; Columbus in, *m22;* slave trade to, 675

Carlisle Indian School, 126-27, *p127*

Carnegie, Andrew, 143-44, 150-51, 155, 628

Carnegie Steel Company, 145

Carolinas, settlement of, 18, *p18. See also* North Carolina; South Carolina

Carpenter, Liz, 496-97

Carranza, Venustiano, 176, 232-34, *p233*

Carson, Rachel, 433, 475, 730-31

Carter, Amy, 568, *p568*

Carter, Jimmy, 569, *p569;* criticism of, 572-73; economic policy of, 569; in election of 1976, 567; in election of 1980, 572-73, *m573;* energy policy of, 569-70, *p569, p570;* foreign policy of, 570-72, *p570, p571,* 715; and human and rights, 570-71, 715; and Haiti,

610; presidential style of, 568-69, *p568*

Carter, Lillian, 568

Carter, Rosalynn, 568, *p568,* 569

cartographers, 754

Carver, George Washington, 275, *p275*

Casablanca, Morocco, 406

Cass, Lewis, 87

Castañeda, Carlos E., 412-13

Castile, 8

Castro, Fidel, 491-92, *p491,* 681

Castro, Raul H., 496

Catcher in the Rye, The (Salinger), 482

Catt, Carrie Chapman, 208, 259, *p382*

cattle industry, xxiv, 132-33, *m132,* 651, *p651*

caudillos, 385-86

Cause and Effect, Identifying, xx, 749-50

censorship, 313

Central Intelligence Agency (CIA): and Bay of Pigs, 492; and contras, 589-90; covert activities of, 466-68; creation of, 450

Central Pacific Railroad, 129, *m132*

Central Powers, 243, *c245*

Century of Dishonor (Jackson), 126

CFCs. *See* chlorofluorocarbons

Chad, *c716*

Challenger (space shuttle), 606

Chamberlain, Austen, 656

Chamberlain, Neville, 391, 633

Chambers, Whittaker, 451

Chamorro, Emiliano, 386

Chancellorsville, Battle of (1863), *m98,* 100

Chaney, James, 503

Charles II (King of England), 18

Charles Town, SC, 18

Charleston (dance), 80, 316

Charleston, SC, 18, 96

Charter of 1606, 15

Charts and Graphs, Reading, 756-58

Château-Thierry, France, 254, *m255*

Chattanooga, Battle of (1863), *p94-95, m99*

Chávez, César, 370, 507, 512

Chechen rebels, 642

Chechnya, 643

checks and balances, 40-41

Cheney, Richard, 594

Chernobyl nuclear disaster, 733-34

Cherokees, 75, 606

Chesapeake Bay, settlement of, 17-18

Chestnut, Mary Boykin, 105

Cheyenne, 123

Chiang Kai-shek, 406, *p406,* 454, *p454*

Chicago, IL: African Americans in, 291-92, *p291;* antiwar protest in, 536-37, *p537;* and Haymarket Riots, 154, *c154;* and Hull House, 150; meatpacking industry in, 167, 211, *p211;* Mexican American migration to, 295; planning in, 179, *p179;* population growth of, 677; and Pullman strike, 155; race riot in, 291-92, *p291;* and social reform, 167

Committee on Public Information (CPI), 260
Committee on the Cause and Cure of War, 391
Committee to Re-elect the President (CREEP), 563
Commoner, Barry, 732
Common Sense (Paine), 29
commonwealth, 17
Commonwealth of Independent States (CIS), 597
communications: advances in, 142-43; and cellular phones, 688, 689, *p689;* digital, 688; electronic, 652, 687; and global economy, *m670-71;* and Information Revolution, 686-88; and National Information Infrastructure, 687-88, *p688;* and newsgroups, 687; privacy issues in, 689; and teleconferencing, 688; transatlantic, 650-52
communism: in Asia, 453-55, 522-23; and McCarthyism, 463-64; and Red Scare, 281-82, *p281,* 450-51, *p450;* rise of, 706
Communist Manifesto (Marx), 678
Communist party (U.S.): and Progressive party, 443; and Red Scare, 281-82, *p281,* 450-51, *p450;* and Scottsboro case, 343; and Share-Our-Wealth program, 357
Comparing and Contrasting, xx
compass rose, 752
Compromise of 1850, 88
Compromise of 1877, 111
computers: development of, 686; mainframe, 687; minicomputers, 687; networks of, 652, 686-88; numbers of, *c618;* personal, 687; UNIVAC I, 433
Comstock Lode, 134
concentration camps, 423-24, *p423, p707*
Concord, Battle of (1776), 28
concurrent powers, 40
Confederate States of America, 91; army of, 99, *p104;* fall of Fort Sumter, 96, *p96;* resources of, 97, *c97;* war strategy of, 98
Confederation, weaknesses in, 37-38
conformal projections, 754
Congress, 42; and Army-McCarthy hearings, 463-64; and House Committee on Un-American Activities, 450-51; and Iran-contra affair, 593-94, *p594;* powers of, 45-46; and Reconstruction, 107-09; and Thomas-Hill hearings, 602-03; and Watergate investigation, 563-64. *See also* specific acts
Congress of Industrial Organizations (CIO), 361
Congress of Racial Equality (CORE), 501
Congressional Record, 44
Congressional Union for Woman Suffrage, 208
Connolly, Maureen "Little Mo," 433
Connor, T. Eugene "Bull," 501

conquistadors, 13
conscription. *See* draft
Consequences, Assessing, xxi
conservation: in Canada, 726; and ecology, 724; in Great Britain, 726; in New Deal, 352, *p352,* 728; and progressives, 725-26; under Taft, 199, 200; under Theodore Roosevelt, 196-97, *p197, m198*
conspicuous consumption, 146
constitution(s), state, 36
Constitution, U.S., *p39;* text of, 42-60; amendments to, 41; completing, 38-39; evaluating, 41; federalism in, 40-41; federalist vs. antifederalist position on, 39-40; flexibility of, 41; and Great Compromise, 38; ratification of, 39-40, *p39;* separation of powers in, 40-41; and slave trade, 39, 699; and Three-Fifths Compromise, 39. *See also* Bill of Rights
Constitutional Convention, 38-39
consumer protection, under Theodore Roosevelt, 196
containment, 446-48
Continental Army: African Americans in, 34; establishment of, 28; shortages in, 34; soldiers in, 34
Continental Congress: First, 28; Second, 28-29, 36, *p37*
contras, 589, *m589,* 592-93
"Contract with America," 603
Convention on Biological Diversity (1993), 739
Convention on the Elimination of All Forms of Racial Discrimination, 710
Convention on the Suppression of Apartheid, 712
Converse, Florence, 347
convoy system, in World War I, 254
Coolidge, Calvin, *p286,* 287, *p287;* and labor relations, 280; succession to presidency, 286-87
Cooper, Gary, 309
Cooper, James Fenimore, 1
Cooper, Michael, 691
cooperatives, 155
Copland, Aaron, 316, 374
Copperheads, 101
Coral Sea, Battle of the (1942), 401-02, *m402*
corn, production of, 648
Cornish miners, 135
Cornwallis, Charles, 31
corporation, 143
corruption, 152-53, 190-91
Corry, John, 585
Cortés, Hernán, 13, *m22*
cost of living: in 1920s, 274; in 1970s, 433; post–World War I, 274, 278-79
cotton: and crop-lien system, 113; expansion of production, 79; and mechanization, 648; production of, 79, 298, *m298, m299*
Cotton, Dorothy, 711
cotton gin, 79

Coubertin, Pierre de, 691
Coughlin, Father Charles E., 357
Council of Economic Advisers, 440
counterculture, 508-09, *p508, p509*
Covenant on Civil and Political Rights, 714
Covenant on Economic, Social, and Cultural Rights, 714
cowboys, xxiv, 132; African American, 132, p133; Mexican American, 132; *vaquero* origins of, 14
Cowles, Henry, 724, *p724*
Cowley, Malcolm, 277
Cox, Archibald, 564
Cox, James M., 284
Crane, Stephen, 151
Crazy Horse, 124
credit, dependence on, in 1920s, 329
Crédit Mobilier Company, 152
creditor nation, 382, 655
Creeks, 75
Creel, George, 260
Crick, Francis, 433
cricket, 690
crime: and drugs, 608; as issue in 1988 election, 596; in 1920s, 312; in 1980s, *c596;* in 1990s, 607-08; and Warren Court, 498
criollos, 14
Cripple Creek, CO, 135
Critical Thinking Skills, xviii-xxiii
Crittenden, John J., 97
Croghan, George, 26
Croly, Herbert, 172
Cronkite, Walter, 535-36
crop-lien system, 113
Crows, 122, 123
Crucible, The (Miller), 463
Crum, George, xxiv
Crusades, 7-8
Cuba: baseball in, 690; and Bay of Pigs, 492-93; economy of, after Cold War, 665; missile crisis in, 492-94, *m493;* refugees from, 681, 683; as Soviet ally, 639; and Spanish-American War, 215-16; as U.S. protectorate, *c224,* 225-26
Cuban Americans, 607; and Bay of Pigs, 492
Cuban missile crisis, 492-94, *m493*
Cullen, Countee, 317
cultural diffusion, 692
culture, global, 673, 690-93
currency, *p646-47;* blocs in 1930s, *m657;* and Bretton Woods system, 660; devaluation of, 657-58; and gold standard, 653-54
Currier & Ives, lithograph by, *p720-21*
Curry, John Steuart, 375
Curzon, Lord, 626
Custer, George Armstrong, 124
cyberspace, 6
Cyprus, 626
Czech Americans, *m119*
Czechoslovakia: fall of Communist government in, 596; German aggression toward, 391-92, 633; post–World

War I, 264, *m264;* post–World War II, 424; Soviet troops in, 588
Czolgosz, Leon, 194, *p194*

Dachau, Germany, 423, *p707*
da Gama, Vasco, 9
Daladier, Édouard, 391
Daley, Richard J., 537
Dallas, TX: and Kennedy assassination, 495, *p495;* segregation in, *p480*
Da Nang, Vietnam, 520
dance, 164; African ring, 80; Charleston, 80; marathons, 274, *p274, p332;* in 1920s, *p311,* 315-16
Daniels, Josephus, 387
Danish, 18, 130
Darrow, Clarence, 313-14, *p314*
Darwin, Charles, 313, 723-24
Daugherty, Harry, 286
Davies, Arthur B., 206
Davis, Allison, 479
Davis, Angela, 512
Davis, Bette, 336, *p336*
Davis, Jefferson, 91, 106
Davison, Emily, 701
Davray, H. D., 658
Dawes, Charles, 285, 656, *p656*
Dawes, William, 28
Dawes General Allotment Act (1887), 127, 184, 290, 366
Dawes Plan (1924), 656
D-Day (June 6, 1944), 416
DDT, 475, 730-31
Dean, James, 482
Dean, John, 564
debates: Kennedy-Nixon, *p488,* 489; Lincoln-Douglas, 90
Debs, Eugene V.: in election of 1912, 203, *m203;* and opposition to World War I, 261
debtor nation, 382, 655
Declaration of Independence (1776), 29, 631, 698, 699; text of, 30-33
Declaration of the Rights of Man and Citizen, 699
Declaration of Sentiments (1848), 83, *p83;* text of, 765-66
decolonization, 634-38, 709-10; problems of, 640-43
Defense, U.S. Department of: and Internet, 686-87
defense spending: of Reagan administration, 587, 588; during World War II, 400, *c408;* after World War II, 450, 661
defoliants, 529
deforestation, 734-35, *m735*
Delany, Martin, 101
Delaware, 97
delegated powers, 40
Delors, Jacques, *p665*
demobilization, 278-79, *p278*
Democracy and Social Ethics (Addams), 172

Democratic party, 75, 152. *See also* specific elections
Democratic-Republicans (Republicans), 63-64
Den of Lions (Anderson), 598
Denver, CO, 677
Depardieu, Gérard, 692
department store, 145
depression, 38, 328-30; global, in 1870s, 654. *See also* Great Depression
Derian, Patricia, 715, *p715*
Desert Storm, Operation. *See* Operation Desert Storm
détente, 560, 593
Detroit, MI: African Americans in, 291; Mexican American migration to, 295
devaluation, 657-58
Dewey, George, 213, 216
Dewey, John, 169
Dewey, Thomas E.: in election of 1944, 409; in election of 1948, 443, *m443*
Dewson, Molly, 351
Diario del Hogar (newspaper), 176
Dias, Bartolomeu, 9
Díaz, Adolfo, 386
Díaz, Porfirio, 231
Dickens, Charles, 702
Die Grünen, 731
Diem, Ngo Dinh, 524-25, *p524*
Dien Bien Phu, Vietnam, *p522-23,* 523
Dietrich, Marlene, 336
direct primary, 191, 702
direct rule, 627
disarmament, 381
disease: in cities, 149, 179; in Civil War, 99; and construction of Panama Canal, 227; effect on Native Americans, *p11,* 12, 86, 87, 125, 366; and migration, 682; in Revolutionary War, 34; in Spanish-American War, 217. *See also* individual diseases
Displaced Persons Act (1948), 680
dividend, 143
divorce rate, 553, 578
Dix, Dorothea, 81, *p81*
Dixiecrats, 443, *m443*
Dixon, Thomas, 112
doctrine of nullification, 74
Dole, Elizabeth, 590
Dole, Robert, 567, 603; and 1996 election, 603-04, *p604*
dollar: currency area in 1930s, *m657;* end of supremacy of, 664; as key currency, 660; linked to gold, 653
dollar diplomacy, 229-30
Dom Afonso. *See* Mbemba, Nzinga
Dominican Republic, *m217,* 229
Domino, Fats, 482, *p483*
domino theory, 522-23
Donat, Alexander, 427
Dorsey, Thomas A., 374
Dos Passos, John, 318
doughboy's pack, 252-53, *p252, p253*
Douglas, Stephen A., 87, 88, 89, 90
Douglas, William, 446
Douglass, Frederick, 82, 101, 700

doves, 532
draft: in Civil War, 100; in Vietnam War, 527; in World War I, 251; in World War II, 409
Dred Scott **v.** *Sandford* (1857), 89, 90
Dreiser, Theodore, 171-72
Dresden, Germany, 417, *p417,* 707
drivers, 79
drugs, 509, *c514*
dry farming, 131
Duarte, José Napoléon, 590
Du Bois, W.E.B., 164, 182-83, *p182,* 187, 293, 631, 710
Dukakis, Michael, 594-95, *p595*
Dulles, John Foster, 466, 639
Dupuy de Lôme, Enrique, 216
Dust Bowl, 367, *m367,* 370, 727-28, *p728*
Dutch, in North America, 18, *m22,* 78
Duvalier, Jean-Claude, *m590*
Dylan, Bob, 513, 548
dynamo, 143

Earhart, Amelia, 275, 311
Earth Day, 552, *p552,* 559, *p559*
Earth First!, 741
Earth Summit (1992), 739
Eastern Europe: after breakup of Soviet Union, 642-43; democratic movements in, 597, 599, 715; emigrants to U.S., 675; investment in, 665; emigrants from, 684; uprising in, 468, *p468*
East Germany, pro-democracy demonstrations in, 596-7
Eckford, Elizabeth, *p480*
Ecological Society of America, 724
ecology, 723-24
economic policy: of Bush, 603; of Carter, 569; of Clinton, 607; of Kennedy, 489-90; of Reagan, 587-88
economies of scale, 144
economy: emergence of global, 650-52, 653-54, *m670-71;* and global communications, 652, 688; and Great Depression, 328-30, 656-58; Hoover's attempts to boost, 340-42, *p340;* impact of oil on, 663; industrial, 648-49; Keynesian view of, 352; mobilization of, for World War I, 257-58, *p257;* in 1980s, 587; in 1990s, 600, 603, 607; after World War II, 660. *See also* New Deal
Economy Act (1933), *c359*
ecosystem, 724
ECSC. *See* European Coal and Steel Community
Ederle, Gertrude, 310
Edison, Thomas Alva, 143, *p143*
Editorial Cartoons, Interpreting, 162
education: of African Americans, 81, 365, 478, 498; bilingual, 553, 579, *p579;* colonial, 17; and compulsory attendance laws, 149-50, *m179;* and court-ordered busing, 575-76, *p575;* of

Native Americans, 126-27, *p127,* 184, 366; and people with disabilities, 574-75; public, 81, 151; reforms of 1800s, 81; of women, 169-70, *p169,* c170

Education Amendments Act (1972), 577

Education for All Handicapped Children Act (1975), 575

EEC. *See* European Economic Community

EEOC. *See* Equal Employment Opportunity Commission

Egypt: British in, 626; and Camp David Accords, 572; Europeans in, 674; human rights abuses in, *c716;* and Middle East conflict, 560, *m561;* in Persian Gulf War, 599; popularity of U.S. television in, 692; relations with Israel, 453; under Sadat, 571-72; as source of raw materials, 625

Ehrhart, William, 547

Eichmann, Adolf, 438

Eighteenth Amendment (1919, repealed in 1933), 181, 312; text of, 57

Eighth Amendment (1791), 54

Einstein, Albert, 425, 680, 686, *p686*

Eisenhower, Dwight D., 469, *p469;* and civil rights, 480-81; domestic policy of, 470-73, 476-77; in election of 1952, 461, 462, *p462;* in election of 1956, 468; foreign policy of, 463, 466-69, 522-23, 639; as supreme commander of NATO forces, 449; in World War II, 415, *p415,* 416

Eisenhower Doctrine (1957), 468

Eisler, Benita, 474

Eisner, Michael, 692

El Alamein, Battle of (1942), *m404,* 405

elastic clause, 41

El Caney, Cuba, *m217,* 218

El Congreso, p334, 335

Elders, Joycelyn, 601

election(s), 43; of 1789, 60; of 1796, 64; **of 1800,** 64-65; **of 1824,** 75; **of 1828,** 75; **of 1844,** 85; **of 1848,** 87; **of 1856,** 89; **of 1858,** 90; **of 1860,** 91-92; **of 1866,** 108; **of 1868,** 109; **of 1872,** 153; **of 1876,** 153; **of 1880,** 153; **of 1884,** 153; **of 1888,** 153; **of 1890,** 156; **of 1892,** 157; **of 1896,** 157; **of 1900,** 194, *c202;* **of 1904,** 195; **of 1908,** 199, *c202;* **of 1910,** 201; **of 1912,** 201-03, *m203;* **of 1916,** 208, 250; **of 1920,** 284, *p284;* **of 1924,** *p284,* 286; **of 1928,** 287-88, *p287;* **of 1932,** 344-45, *p244, p345;* **of 1936,** 358, 360; **of 1938,** 363; **of 1940,** 393; **of 1944,** 409; **of 1948,** 442-43, *p442, m443;* **of 1952,** 462, *p462;* **of 1956,** 468; **of 1960,** 488-89, *p488, m489;* **of 1964,** 497, *p497;* **of 1968,** 536-37; **of 1972,** 540, 558, 562-63; **of 1976,** 567; **of 1980,** 572-73, *m573;* **of 1984,** 591; **of 1988,** 585, 594-95, *m595, c595;* **of 1992,** 585, 601; **1994 midterm,** 603; **of 1996,** 603-04; reforms in, 191, *p191*

electrical power: development of, 143; and generator, 143; production of, 302, *c303;* and Tennessee Valley Authority, *m354,* 355, *p355*

electronic libraries, 686

electronic mail (E-mail), 652, 687, 688, 689

Elementary and Secondary School Education Act (1965), 498

elevator, impact on cities, 148

Eleventh Amendment (1798), 54

Elkins Act (1903), 196

Ellington, Duke, 274, 316, 374

Ellis Island, 675, *p675*

Ellison, Ralph, 481, *p481*

Ellsberg, Daniel, 538-39, 562

El Paso, TX, Mexican American migration to, 295

El Salvador: caudillos in, 385; human rights abuses in, 715; U.S. policy in, 589-90, *m589*

Emancipation Proclamation, 101, *p101,* 106, 700; text of, 767

Embargo Act (1807), 66

Embree, Edwin, 709

Emergency Banking Act (1933), 350, *c359*

Emerson, Ralph Waldo, 723, 726

employer mandate, 609

Employment Act (1946), 440

Empress of China (ship), 222

encomienda, 11

endangered species, 732, 735, *m735*

Endangered Species Act (1973), 732

energy: alternative sources of, 734; coal, 142; crisis in 1970s, 558, *c558,* 569-70; electricity, 143; global consumption of, 733; hydroelectric, 733; nuclear, 733; oil, 143; Reagan's policy, 587; solar, 733, 734; steam, 142; and Tennessee Valley Authority, *m354,* 355, *p355;* wind, 734

Energy, U.S. Department of, 569

Enforcement Acts (1870-1871), 111

England: and American Revolution, 28, 29; and colonial protests, 26-28; and colonial trade, 17, 27-28; early claims of, 15; and French and Indian War, 18-19; colonial trade, 17, 27-28; and Jamestown settlement, 16; religious conflict in, 16; and Spanish Armada, 15; and western settlement, 26. *See also* Great Britain

Enola Gay (airplane), 421

enslaved persons. *See* slave(s)

environment, 552, *p552,* 720-39, *m735;* acid rain, 736, *p736;* activism on behalf of, 559, 587, 723-24, 732, 739; carbon dioxide in, *c740;* chlorofluorocarbons in, 736; and disasters, 559, *m735;* and early colonists, 722; and ecology, 723-24; and global warming, 736; and Green parties, 731; Nixon's policies on, 559, *p559;* ozone layer, 736; protection of international, 739; and railroad boom, 722-23; under Roosevelt, 196-97; and transcendentalists, 723

Environmental Protection Agency (EPA), 475, 559

equal-area projections, 754

Equal Employment Opportunity Commission (EEOC), 602

Equal Pay Act (1963), 490, *p490*

Equal Rights Amendment (ERA), 288-89, 512, 577-78, *p578,* 712, *p713;* New Right's opposition to, 586

Equiano, Olaudah, 17-18, *p17*

Erie Canal, 73

Ervin, Sam, 563

escalation, 527

Escobedo v. *Illinois,* 498

Espionage Act (1917), 261

Estefan, Gloria, 693

Estonia: post–World War I, 264, *m264;* Soviet aggression toward, 392, *m392;* in World War II, 424, 445

Ethiopia, 239, 389, *m392,* 632, 641

ethnic cleansing, 609

Euro Disney, 692

Europe: disease in, 682; and exploration of North America, *m22;* foreign investment in, *c239;* free trade in, 661-62, 665-66; human rights abuses in, *c716;* imperialism of, 622-23, 624-27, 709; international conventions in, 703; lowering of tariff barriers in, 654; migrants in, 674, 675, 684; MTV in, 693; participation in slave trade, 699; post–World War II refugees in, 680; urban growth in, 677; U.S. economic ties to, 650, *m670-71. See also* individual countries

European Coal and Steel Community (ECSC), 661

European Community (EC), 665-66. *See also* European Union

European Economic Community (EEC), 661-62, 665

European Recovery Act (1948), 448, *p448*

European Union (EU), 666

Evald, Emmy, 207

Evaluating, xxiii

Evans, Hiram Wesley, 296

Evans, John, 123

Evans, Priscilla Merriam, 138

Evans, Walker, 368, 371

evolution: and ecology, 723-24; theory of, and Scopes trial, 313-14, *p314*

Ewing, Patrick, 673, *p672*

Exodusters, 130

Explorer I (satellite), *p686*

Exxon Valdez (oil tanker), 736-37

Fact from Opinion, Distinguishing, xxi-xxii, 750

factories, 74, *c97,* 302-04, 327, 331, 361, 408, 440-41, *p659, p665, p666;* African Americans and, 147, 331, 412, 441; child labor in, 77, *p140-41,* 153,

free trade: development of, in mid-19th century, 654; in Europe, 661-62, 665-66; and General Agreement on Tariffs and Trade, 660; limitations of, 667; and Maastricht Treaty, 666; southern support of, 655; and Uruguay Round (of GATT), 666. *See also* North American Free Trade Agreement

Frémont, John C., 89

French and Indian War, 18-19

French Huguenots, 18

French Indochina: anti-imperialism in, 630-31; Japanese occupation of, 394, *m394*

French Revolution, *p698,* 698-99, *p718*

Friedan, Betty, 510, *p577*

Fuel Administration, 258

Fugitive Slave Act (1850), 88, *p88*

Fujimori, Alberto, *p674*

Fulbright, J. William, 534

Fundamentalism, 312-13

Furness, Betty, 496

Gable, Clark, 274

Gadsden, James, 85

Gadsden Purchase (1853), 85, *m86*

Gagarin, Yuri, 489

Gage, Thomas, 28

Galbraith, John Kenneth, 481

Galveston, TX, reforms in, 192-93, *p192*

Gálvez, Bernardo de, *p35*

Gandhi, Indira, 713, *p713,* 738

Gandhi, Mohandas K., *p628,* 630, *p630,* 634-35, 710

Garbo, Greta, 336, *p336*

García, Héctor P., 496

García Calderón, Francisco, 229

Garfield, Harry, 258

Garfield, James A., 153, *p156*

Garland, Hamlin, 138

Garner, John Nance, 345

Garrison, William Lloyd, 82, 700

Garrity, W. Arthur, *p575*

Garvey, Marcus, 292-93, *p293,* 710

Gates, Bill, 610, *p610*

GATT. *See* General Agreement on Tariffs and Trade

gazetteers, 760

Gehrig, Lou, 337

Geiger counter, *p730*

General Agreement on Tariffs and Trade (GATT), 660, 666

General Federation of Women's Clubs, 170, 291

generation gap, 508

Geneva Conference (1954), 523-24

Geneva Convention (1864), 703

Genoa, Italy, 9

genocide, 423

Genthe, Arnold, photograph by, *p185*

geography: of Africa, *m239;* of agriculture, 298-99, *m298-99;* of Asia, *m239;* of Australia, *m239;* of cities, *m516,* *m517;* of Europe, *m239;* five themes of, 8; and immigration, 118, *m118-19;* and imperialism, 238-39, *m238-39;* of North America, *m238;* of South America, 238, *m238;* of the West, *m189*

George, Henry, 141

George III (king of England), 28, 29, 631, 698

Georgia (CIS), *m597,* 599, 642

Georgia (U.S.): in Civil War, 102; secession of, 91; settlement of, 18

German Americans, 18, 78, *c118, m118, m119,* 130, 247

German reunification (1990), 597

Germany: AFSC aid to, 705; and Berlin airlift, *p445,* 448, *p448;* currency bloc in 1930s, *m657;* and European economic integration, 661-62; expansion of, 632-33; foreign investment in, *c238-39;* Green party in, 731; and Holocaust, 423-24; impact of war debt and reparations on, 382-83, *p383;* inflation in, 383, *p383;* involvement in China, 222-23; and Jewish refugees, 680; and mandate system, 629; Nazis in, *p378-79,* 389, *p389,* 390-91, *m392,* 706; post–World War II occupation of, 436-37, 445; refugees in, 684; and reparations after World War I, 656; reunification of, 599, 684; "rubble women" in, *p661;* signing of nonaggression pact with Soviet Union, 392; and tariff wars, 654-55; wildlife management in, 727; in World War I, 243, 244-45, *m244,* 247-48, 249, *p268,* 704; in World War II, 391-94, 403, *p403, m404,* 405, 417-18, *c423,* 707. *See also* East Germany, West Germany

Geronimo, *m124,* 126

Gershwin, George, 315-16

Gettysburg, Battle of (1863), 98, *m98, c100*

Gettysburg Address, (Lincoln), 98; text of, 768

Ghana, 7, *p636, p640*

Ghose, Aurobindo, 630

Ghost Dance, 125, *p125*

GI Bill of Rights (1944), 440, *p440*

Gibraltar, 626

Gideon v. Wainwright (1963), 498, 783

Gilded Age, The (Twain and Warner), 152, *p152,* 161

Gillespie, Dizzy, 410

Gilpin, Charles, 316

Gingrich, Newt, 603, 604

Ginsberg, Douglas, 591

Ginsburg, Ruth Bader, 602

Ginzberg, Susan, *p729*

glasnost, 592, 613

global grid, 753

global warming, 736

Glorious Revolution, 698

glyph, 6

Goldman, Emma, 282, *p282*

Goldmark, Josephine, 175, *p175*

gold rush: in Australia, 676; in California, 86-87, *p120-21,* 675; in Canada, 676

gold standard, 653-54, 657-58, *m657;* and Bretton Woods system, 660; U.S. abandonment of, 664

Gold Standard Act (1900), 653

Goldwater, Barry M., 497

Gompers, Samuel, 155, 176, 311

Gone with the Wind (Mitchell), 373, *p373*

Goodman, Andrew, 503

Goodman, Benny, 274, 374

Good Neighbor policy, 384-85

Gorbachev, Mikhail, 592, *p592,* 597, 599

Gore, Albert, 601, 607, 687, *p687*

Gorgas, William C., 225, 227

graduated income tax, 156

Gramm-Rudman-Hollings Act (1985), 591

Grange movement, 155-56

Grant, Madison, 184-85

Grant, Ulysses S.: in Civil War, 98-99, 101-04, *p109;* and corruption, 152-53; elected president (1868), 109

Grapes of Wrath, The (Steinbeck), 373

Gravier, Charles, 25

Gray, John, 717

Great Britain: and abandonment of gold standard, 657; and abolition of slavery and slave trade, 699-700; African territory of, *m637;* and Atlantic Charter, 394; and blitzkrieg, 393-94, *p394;* and border settlement, 85; and Bretton Woods system, 660; child labor in, 702, *p702;* conservation in, 726; and cricket, 690; emigrants from, 675; entertainment exports to U.S., 692; foreign investment and trade of, *c238-39, m238-39;* Glorious Revolution in, 698; and gold standard, 653; during Great Depression, 656-57; Green party in, 731; human rights abuses in, *c716;* imperialism of, 622-23, 624-27, *p624;* and impressment, 62; in India, 630, 634-35; involvement in China, 222, 649; and Jay's Treaty, 63; and Latin America, 624; and Lend-Lease Act, 393; and mandate system, 629; Margaret Thatcher in, 713; in North America, *m22, m23;* and nuclear weapons, 729; Palestinian independence, 681; and Panama Canal, 226, 228; at Paris Peace Conference, 705; in Persian Gulf War, 599; post–War of 1812 relations with, 67, 72; response to facism, 391; and the South, 98; and South African independence, 712; and tariffs, 654, 655; urban growth in, 677; and War of 1812, 66-67, *p67;* at Washington Conference, 381, *p381;* withdrawal from India, 635, 680; women's suffrage in, 701; and World War I, 243-45, *m244, p246,* 247, *c267,* 704; after World War I, 655; in World War II, *p422. See also* England

Great Compromise (1787), 38
Great Depression, *p324-25;* beginning
of, 327-28; causes of, 326, 328-30;
and disruption of world trade, 656-58;
end of, 661; family life in, 335, *p335;*
farm crisis in, 341; global impact of,
m329, 333, 656-58; Hoover's philosophy on, 339-45, *p340;* and impact on
global migration, 680; migrant labor
during, 367, 368-69, *p368,* 370, *p370;*
and Philippine independence, 632;
photographing, 368-69, *p368, p369,*
370-71, *p371;* psychological impact
of, 335-36; and rise of fascism, 705;
rural life in, 333-35; stock market
crash in, 327, *c327;* unemployment in,
331-32, *p331, m332;* urban life in,
332-33, *p333*
Great Gatsby, The (Fitzgerald), 318
Great Migration, 16; of African
Americans, 259-60
Great Plains: farming, 130; buffalo on,
722-23; Dust Bowl in, 727-28; Native
Americans in, 122; trunk lines cross-
ing, 142
Great Society, 497-98, 499, 556
Great Train Robbery, The (movie), 181-
82, *p181*
Great Upheaval (1886), 154
"Great White Fleet," 224
Greece: development of citizens' rights
in, 698; Olympics in, 691; in World
War II, 403
Greek Americans, 147
Greeley, Horace, 677
Green Berets, 491
Greene, Graham, 519
Greene, Nathanael, 35
greenhouse effect, 736
Green parties, 731
Greenpeace, 735
Green Rage (Manes), 741
Greensboro, NC, 500, 710
Grenada, U.S. invasion of, 590, *m590,*
p590
Griffith, D. W., 112
Grimké, Angelina, 82, 700
gross national product, 327, *m671*
Grove, Andrew S., 688
Guadalcanal, in World War II, *m402,* 403
Guam, in World War II, 401, *m402,* 418
Guantánamo Bay, Cuba, 225, 226;
Naval Aviation Camp at, *p164, p610;*
refugees at, *p610,* 683
Guatemala: human rights abuses in, 715;
rise of military dictatorship in, 385;
U.S. intervention in, 467
"Guerrilla War" (Ehrhart), 547
guerrilla warfare: in American
Revolution, 35; in Vietnam War, 528
Guiteau, Charles, 153
Gulf of Thailand, 520, *m521*
Gulf of Tonkin, 520, *m521,* 526
gun control, 586, 608
Gutenberg, Johannes, 8
Gypsies, 437

hacienda, 14
Haeckel, Ernst, *p721,* 724
Hagedorn, Jessica, 614, 615
Hague Peace Conferences, 703
Haig, Alexander, 588
Haight-Ashbury, 509, *p509*
Hainan, post–World War II, 424
Haiphong Harbor, 539
Haiti: instability in, *m590,* 610; refugees
from, 610, *p610,* 681, *p681;* U.S.
occupation of, 610; U.S. policy
toward, 230; withdrawal of U.S.
marines from, 384
Haitians: immigration of, 681, *p681*
Halberstam, David, 531
Haldeman, H. R. (Bob), 539
Hall, Fawn, 594, *p594*
Hall, Vicki, 691
Hamer, Fannie Lou, 710, 711
Hamilton, Alexander, 61-62
Hammond, Samuel, 723
Hanna, Mark, 194-95, 649
Hanoi, Vietnam, 520, *m521,* 522, 535, 539
Hanson, Ole, 279
Harding, Warren G., 284-86, *p285;* death
of, 286; domestic policies of, 285-86;
election of, in 1920, 284; scandals
under, 286, *p286*
hard-rock mining, 136
Harlem Experimental Theatre, 317
Harlem Renaissance, 316-18, *m317;*
literature of, 428
Harpers Ferry, 90
Harrington, Michael, 496
Harris, Patricia, 574
Harrison, Benjamin, *p156*
Harrison, William Henry, 66, *p76*
"Harry Wilmans" (Masters), 271
Hawaii: Japanese attack on, *p398-99,*
399, *m402;* Japanese emigrants in,
674; labor in, *p221;* and statehood,
m485; U.S. acquisition of, 221-22, 625
Hawaiian League, 221-22
hawks, 532
Hay, John, 223, 226, 228, *p228*
Hay-Bunau-Varilla Treaty (1903), 228
Hayden, Sterling, *p450*
Hayes, Rutherford B., 111, *p156*
Hay-Herrán Treaty (1903), 228
Haymarket Riot (1886), 154, *c154*
Hay-Pauncefote Treaty (1901), 228
Hayslip, Le Ly, 541
Haywood, "Big Bill," 176-77
Head Start, 496
health: and cigarettes, 552; and food,
552, *c552*
health care: and national health insur-
ance, 443, 604; reform, 602; use of
interactive television in, 688
Hearst, William Randolph, 215-16
Heckler, Margaret, 590
Heit, Molly, *p491*
Hellman, Lillian, 374, *p374*

Hemingway, Ernest, 318, 390
Henderson, Fletcher, 316
Hendrix, Jimi, 512-13, *p512*
Henry VII (king of England), 8
Henry of Portugal, 9
Henry Street Settlement, *p150*
Henson, Matthew, 165
Hepburn Act (1906), 196
Heritage Foundation, 586
Herzegovina: and World War I, 242
Hessing, Valjean, painting by, *p623*
Hicks, Edward, painting by, *p18*
Highway Act (1956), *m472,* 473
Hill, Anita, 600, *p600*
Hilton, James, 338
Hindus, in India, 640
hippies, 509
Hirohito, Emperor, 401, 437, *p437*
Hiroshima, *m402,* 421, *p421,* 437, 464,
707
Hispanic Americans: and civil rights
movement, 555, 574; in 1930s, m294;
and poverty, 461; unemployment of,
569, 587; and urban renewal, 477; in
Vietnam War, 527; in World War II,
413. *See also* Cuban Americans;
Mexican Americans; Puerto Ricans
Hiss, Alger, 451
Historical Documents. *See* individual
titles of documents
Historical Imagination, Using, xix
"History of the Standard Oil
Company" (Tarbell), 170-71
Hitler, Adolf, 383, 389, 391, *p393,* 394,
418, 632-33, *p633,* 706
HIV. *See* Human Immunodeficiency
Virus
Hmong, 542-43
Hobby, Oveta Culp, 470, *p470*
Ho Chi Minh, 521-22, *p522,* 523, 524,
539, 630-31, 636
Ho Chi Minh City, Vietnam, 520, *m521*
Ho Chi Minh Trail, 529, *m529,* 538
Holly, Buddy, 483
Hollywood Ten, 450
Holmes, Oliver Wendell, 261, 281
Holocaust, 423-24, *p423,* 435, 707, *p707*
Holocaust Kingdom, The (Donat), 427
Holt Street Baptist Church, 711
Holy Land, 7
homelessness: in Great Depression, 333,
p333, 335; in 1980s, 587, *p588;* in
former Yugoslavia, 684
Home Loan Bank Act (1932), 341, 342
Home Owners Loan Corporation
(HOLC), 351, *c359*
Homer, Winslow, painting by, 762
Homestead Act (1862), 128
Homestead strike, *c154,* 155
Home to Harlem (McKay), 317
Honduras, 385
Honecker, Erich, 599
Hong Kong: and global economy, 664;
in World War II, 401, *m402*
Hooker, Joseph "Fighting Joe," 100
Hoover, Herbert, 328, *p328,* 349;

domestic policies under, 288, *p288;* in election of 1928, 287-88, *p287;* and election of 1932, 344-45; and Great Depression, 327, 328, 332; as head of Food Administration, 258, *p258;* and moratorium on reparations and war debts, 383; philosophy of, 339-44, *p339, p340;* as secretary of commerce, 285; withdraws U.S. troops from Nicaragua, 386

Hoover, J. Edgar, and Palmer raids, 281-82

Hoover Dam, 341, *p341*

Hope, Bob, 410

Hopewells, 6, *p6*

Hopis, 122

Hopkins, Harry, 351-52

Hopper, Edward, 319; painting by, *p319*

horizontal integration, 144

Horton, Willie, 595

"hot line," 494

Houdini, Harry, 164, *p164*

Houplines, France, *p240-41*

House Committee on Un-American Activities (HUAC), 450-51, *p450*

House Judiciary Committee, 564

House of Burgesses, 27

House of Mirth (Wharton), 151

House of the Spirits, The (Allende), 743

Housing and Urban Development Act (1968), 498

Houston, Sam, 84

How the Other Half Lives (Riis), 189

Howe, Frederic, 141

Howe, William, 30

Howells, William Dean, 146, 151

Hubble Telescope, 552, *p552,* 610

Hue, Vietnam, 520, *m521*

Huerta, Victoriano, 232-33

Hughes, Charles Evans, 250, *p285,* 381

Hughes, Langston, 316, 317-18, *p318*

Hull House, 150, 179

human-environment interaction, 8

Human Immunodeficiency Virus (HIV), 608, 682

human rights, 570, 696-97; abuses, 714-717; *c716;* and Carter, 570-71, 715; and the Cold War, 714-15; and decolonization, 709-10; in former Soviet Union, 714-15; in French Revolution, *p718;* in 1930s, 705-07; in Latin America, 714, 715; non-Western views of, 717; origins of, 698-99; progessivism and, 702; and racial equality, 705; and slavery, 699-700; UN and, 707-08; and war, 703-05, 707; for women, 701

Humphrey, Hubert: in election of 1964, 497; in election of 1968, 536-37

Hungary: 587; free elections in, 596; Soviet troops in, 588; uprising in (1956), 468, *p468;* in World War II, 403, *m404*

hunger: and AFSC, 705; and Chinese Americans, 332-33; in Great Depression, 332-34, 335, *p337;* and Great Society, 497; and Irish, 78; and

Mexican Americans, 332-38; and New Deal, 354; in Somalia, 685

hunter-gatherers, 4

Hurston, Zora Neale, 373

Hussein, Saddam, 594

Hutus, *p679,* 685

hydraulic mining, 136

hydrogen bomb, 464-66

Hypothesizing, xxii

"I Am Waiting" (Ferlinghetti), 549

Ibn Sînâ, 7

Ickes, Harold, 353, 364-65

Idaho: cattle trails in, *m132;* Indian reservations in, *m124;* mining in, 134

Idrîsî, Abu al-, map drawn by, *p8*

"I Have a Dream" Speech (King), 770-71

Illinois, 73, 90, 173

I Love Lucy (television show), 474, *p474*

IMF. *See* International Monetary Fund

immigrants: *c147;* African, 675; Arab, 147; Armenian, 147; Asian, 86, 118, *c118, m118-19,* 147, 148, 578-79, 681; assimilation of, 184-85, *p185;* British, 675; Cambodian, 681; Central American, 681; Chinese, 129, 147, 148, *p148,* 675, 676, 683; and Civil War draft riots, 100; communities of, 78, 148; Croatian, 675; Cuban, 681, 683; Danish, 18, 130; education levels of, 683; English, 18; European, 675-76, 678, 681; Filipino, 683, *p683;* French Canadian, 147; French Huguenot, 18; German, 18, 78, 130, 675, 678; and gold rush, 675; Greek, 147, 675; Haitian, 681, *p681;* Hungarian, 147, 675; Indian, 683, *p683;* Irish, 78, 129, 130, 675; Italian, 147, 675; Jamaican, 673; Japanese, 147; Jewish, 18, 147; Korean, 683; and labor relations, 279; Laotian, 681; Latin American, 681-82; life of, 78, 148-49; Mennonite, 130; Mexican, 683; new, 147-48; Nigerian, 673; Norwegian, 130; Polish, 147, 675; Puritan, 16-17; Romanian, 675; Russian Jews, 675, *p678;* Scandinavian, 678; Scotch-Irish, 18; Scots, 18; Slovak, 675; Swedish, 130; Ukrainian, 675; Vietnamese, 681, 683; in West, *p129,* 130; West Indian, 18; working conditions of, 78, 148, 176

immigration, *c147, c779;* Asian, 86, 118, *c118, m118-19,* 147, 148, 578-79, 674; to Australia, 676; boat people, 542-43, *p542,* 681; to Canada, 676; debate over, 605-06, 683; in 1800s, *cxxiv,* 78, 675; European, *c118, m118-19;* future of, *p683-84;* late 1800s, *c118,* 675; Latin American, 86, 471, 478-79; nativist response to, 78, *p78,* 148, 676; 1920s restrictions on, 294, 680; after 1965,

681; post–World War I, 679; post–World War II, 680-81; of sports figures, 673; to Texas, 84; to U.S., 675-76, *c779;* U.S. attitudes toward, in 1990s, 605-07, 683

Immigration Act (1924), 294, 679

Immigration Act (1965), 681

Immigration Act (1990), 606, 683

immigration bill (1996), 606

Immigration Restriction League, 148

impeachment, 40; of Andrew Johnson, 108-09, *p109;* and Watergate, 564

imperialism, 214-15, 238-39, 709, 620-43; in Africa, *m637;* and American expansionism, *c224,* 623; and application of Monroe Doctrine, 228-30; British, 624-27, *p624;* and building of Panama Canal, 226-28; and China, 222-23, 625; commentary on, 234-35; European, 622-23, 624-27; and government of Cuba and Puerto Rico, 225-26; and Hawaii, 221-22, 625; and industrialization, 625-27; and Japan, 223-24, 625, 632; and Latin America, *m234,* 625; legacies of, 640-43; and Mexican Revolution, 232-34; motives for, 625-26; and Pacific territories, *m220;* and Philippines, 219-21, 625; Russian, 623-24; and Spanish-American War, 215-18, *m217;* World War I and, 628-31; World War II and, 634-37

impressment, 62, 622, *p622*

Incas, 13

indentured servant, 17

India, 674; Bangladeshis in, 738; British imperialism in, 625, 626; British withdrawal from, 635, 680; cars in, 618; cricket in, 690; disease in, 682; emigrants from, in 1980s, 683; independence of, 634-35; Indira Gandhi in, 713, *p713;* Mohandas Gandhi in, 630, 634-35, 710; MTV and Indian bands, 692-93; popularity of U.S. television in, 692; population of, 737; post-independence conflicts in, 640-41; as source of raw materials, 625

Indiana, 131

Indian Affairs, Bureau of. *See* Bureau of Indian Affairs

Indian Claims Commission, 577

Indian National Congress, 630

Indian policy, 126-27

Indian removal, under Jackson, 75, *p623*

Indian Removal Act (1830), 75

Indian Reorganization Act (1934), 366

Indians. *See* American Indians

indirect rule, 627

Indochina, *m521, m546,* 630-31, 636, *p636*

Indonesia: Bandung Conference in, 638; economic growth in, 664; human rights abuses in, *c716;* human rights advances in, 715; independence of, 635

industrial design, 320

industrialization: early 1800s, 74; after 1850, 141, 142-44, 146-47, 153, 648-

49; and impact on migration, 677; and imperialism, 625-27; sources of energy for, 142; world, *m670-71*

Industrial Revolution, 74, 677, 702

Industrial Workers of the World (IWW), 176-77, 261

industry: after World War I, 302-03; automation in, 476; and changes in workstyle, 303-04; in 1800s, 74; in Great Depression, 327-28; growth of, 142-43; in post-Reconstruction South, 114; working conditions in early 1800s, 77; in World War I, 318; in World War II, 407-08

inflation, 37; under Carter, 569; under Ford, 565-66; under Nixon, 558; under Reagan, 587

Information Revolution, 686, *c694*

Information Superhighway. *See* National Information Infrastructure

INF Treaty. *See* Intermediate-range Nuclear Forces Treaty

initiative, 191, 702

Inouye, Daniel, 433, *p433,* 591

insider trading, 591

Insurgent Mexico (Reed), 237

interchangeable parts, 74

Interior, Department of, 587

Intermediate-range Nuclear Forces (INF) Treaty (1987), 592

Internal Security Act (1950), 451

International Bank for Reconstruction and Development (World Bank), 660

International Church of the Foursquare Gospel, 312

International Ladies Garment Workers Union (ILGWU), 176

International Monetary Fund (IMF), 660

International Woman Suffrage Conference (1902), 207

Internet, 610-611, 686-87, 688

internment, 410

Interstate Commerce Act (1887), 156

Interstate Commerce Commission (ICC), 196

Interview, Conducting an, 550

Intolerable Acts (1774), 28

Invisible Man (Ellison), 481, *p481*

IRA. *See* Irish Republican Army

Iran: human rights abuses in, *c716;* Kurds in, 685; Soviet immigrants to, 684; view on human rights, 717

Iran-contra affair, 592-93

Iran hostage crisis (1979–1981), 572-73, *p572*

Iraq: British in, 626, 629; Kurds in, 685; and Persian Gulf War, 597-599, *m598;* relations with Israel, 453

Ireland: conditions in, 78

Irish Americans, 78, *m118,* 129, 130, 135, 247, 294; nativist attitudes toward, *p675. See also* Scotch-Irish

Iron Heel, The (London), 171

Iroquois and Iroquois League: in French and Indian War, 19; in

Revolutionary War, 30

irreconcilables, 265

Isabella (queen of Spain), 10, *p10*

Ishigo, Estelle, painting by, *p410*

Islamic world, 6-7; women in, 712-13

island-hopping, in World War II, 418

isolationism, 380

Israel: and Arab conflict, 452-53, *m453,* 467-68, 560, *m561, 602,* 641; and Camp David Accords, 572; creation of, 452-53, *m453;* Golda Meir in, 713; human rights abuses in, *c716;* and Iran-contra affair, 593; Jewish migration to, 681; and 1993 peace accord, 610; in Persian Gulf War, 601; Soviet immigrants in, 684; and Suez crisis, 467-68

Issei, 410

Italian Americans, 282-83, 676

Italy: African territory of, *m637;* baseball in, 690; basketball in, 691; and European economic integration, 661; expansion of, 632; rise of Fascist party in, 388-89; and tariffs, 655; urban growth in, 677; and World War I, 243, *m244,* 254; World War II invasion of, *m404,* 416

Iwo Jima, Battle of (1945), *m404,* 420

IWW. *See* Industrial Workers of the World

Iyotake, Tatanka. *See* Sitting Bull

Jackson, Andrew, 67, *p67,* 75-76, *p76,* 162, *p162*

Jackson, Graham, *p420*

Jackson, Helen Hunt, 126

Jackson, Janet, 80

Jackson, Jesse, 594, *p594*

Jackson, Mahalia, 374, *p374*

Jackson, MS, 711

Jackson, Stonewall, 97, 98, 100

Jakarta, Indonesia, 685

Jamaica, *m22,* 673, 690

James I (king of England), 15, 16

Jamestown, VA, 16

Japan: aggressive actions of, 382, 390, 394, *m395;* American popular culture in, 693, *p693;* atrocities committed by, 1930s, 706; baseball in, 690-91, *p690;* and bombing of Pearl Harbor, 399; economy of, 664; emergence of, 223-24; and European imperialism, 625; expansion of, 632, 680; and global economy, 664; impact of oil shocks on, 663; and invasion of Manchuria, 382, 632; migration from, 674; MTV in, 692; at Paris Peace Conference, 705; post–World War II economic growth of, 662; post–World War II occupation of, 437; recycling in, 738; and rise of empire, 239; rise of militarists in, 390; U.S. economic interests in, 625; U.S. trade with, *p664;* at Washington

Conference, 381-82; in World War II, 401-03, *m402,* 418-21, 707

Japanese Americans: immigration of, 147, 674; internment of, *p399,* 410-11, *p410, m411;* literature of, 429; and migrant work, *p370;* in World War II, 410-12, 417

Java Sea, Battle of the (1942), 401, *m402*

Jay, John, 63

Jay's Treaty (1794), 63

Jazz Age, 315-16

Jefferson, Thomas, *p63;* as author of Declaration of Independence, 29, 699; drafting of Virginia Statute for Religious Freedom, 36; in election of 1796, 64; in election of 1800, 64-65; and Embargo Act of 1807, 66; first inaugural address, text of, 763-64; foreign policy of, 65-66; and Hamilton, 62; and Kentucky Resolutions, 64; and Louisiana Purchase, 65-66; political views of, 62; and strict construction, 62

Jemison, Mae, 552

Jen, Gish, 614

Jews: in America, 18, 147, *p171,* 185, 282; emigrants from Russia, 675, 678, *p678;* homeland for, 681; in Nazi Germany, 706, *p706;* post–World War II refugees, 680-81; as refugees from Nazi Germany, 680, 686; Soviet, to Israel, 684; in World War II, 389, 423-24, 438-39, 707

Jim Crow laws, 114

Jinnah, Mohammed Ali, *p634, p680*

Joffre, Joseph, 245

John II (king of Portugal), 10

Johnson, Andrew, 106-09; impeachment of, 108-109, *p109*

Johnson, Edward, 722

Johnson, Hiram W., 380

Johnson, Hugh S., 353

Johnson, James Weldon, *p292*

Johnson, Lyndon B., 497, *p497, p536;* decision not to run for reelection, 536; domestic policy of, 496-99, *p498,* 556; in election of 1960, 489; in election of 1964, 497; and election of 1968, 536; foreign policy of, 499, 526-27, 528-29, 534; response to antiwar protests, 533-34, 536; succession to presidency, 495-96, *p495;* and Vietnam War escalation, 526-27, 528-30

Johnson, Tom, 192

Johnson, William "Judy," 337

Johnston, Albert Sidney, 99

Johnston, Joseph E., 97, 98, 100

joint-stock companies, 15-16

Jolson, Al, 309

Jones, Mary Harris, 153, 207

Jones, Samuel M., 192, *p192*

Jones Act (1916), 221

Jones Act (1917), 226

Joplin, Scott, 164

Jordan, Barbara, 496, 567, *p567*

Jordan, Michael, 553, *p553*

Jordan: and mandate system, 629;

Palestinian refugees in, 681; relations with Israel, 453, *m453*

Joseph, Chief, 125, 139, *p139*

journalism: and coverage of Spanish-American War, 215-16; and coverage of Vietnam War, 531, *p531*, 535-36, 538-39; and coverage of World War I, 247; popular, 151; and progressive movement, 170-71, *p170*, *p171*, 189; and Watergate, 563, *p563*; yellow, 215-16

Journal of the Great War, A (Dawes), 656

Joyce, James, 313, *p313*

judicial review, 64

Judiciary Act (1789), 61

Jungle, The (Sinclair), 167, 211

Jurassic Park (movie), 692

juvenile delinquency, 482

Kalakaua, 221-22

kamikaze, 420

Kansas: cattle ranching in, 132; Dust Bowl in, 367, *m367*; slavery issue in, 89

Kansas-Nebraska Act (1854), 89

Kantor, Morris, painting by, *p337*

Kashmir, India, 640

Kazakhstan, *m596*, 597

Keating-Owen Child Labor Act (1916), 207

Kelley, Florence, 173-75

Kelley, Jimmy, 575

Kelley, Oliver Hudson, 155

Kellogg, Frank, 382

Kellogg-Briand Pact (1927), 382

Kelly, Petra, 731, *p731*

Kelly, William, 142

Kemal Atatürk, Mustafa. *See* Atatürk, Kemal

Kennan, George, 446, 532

Kennedy, Anthony, 591

Kennedy, Jacqueline, *p488*, *p495*

Kennedy, John F., 490, *p490*; assassination of, 495; and civil rights movement, 502-03; and Cold War, 491-94, *m493*; domestic policies of, 489-90, 502; election of, 488-89, *p488*; and foreign policy, 491-94, *m493*; inauguration of, *p488*, 489; on nuclear testing, 730; and Vietnam War, 524-25

Kennedy, Robert F.: assassination of, 536; as attorney general, 501

Kennedy, Ted, *p575*

Kennett, Douglas, 595

Kent State University, 538, *p538*

Kentucky, 97

Kentucky and Virginia Resolutions, 64

Kenya, 636-37, 641

Kenyatta, Jomo, 636-37

Kerner Commission, 506

Kerouac, Jack, 482

Keynes, John Maynard, 266, 656

Khwārizmī, al-, 7

Khomeini, Ayatollah, 572

Khrushchev, Nikita, 468, 469

Kiev, Ukraine, 733, *m735*

Kim Il Sung, 455

King, Coretta Scott, *p506*, *p710*

King, Martin Luther, Jr.: assassination of, 506, 536; and civil rights, 479, 500, *p500*, 502-03, 504, 506, *c506*; "I Have a Dream" Speech, text of, 770-71; in India, 710, *p710*; opposition to Vietnam War, 499, 532-33

Kino, Eusebio, 13

Kiowas, 122, *p122*

Kipling, Rudyard, 625

Kirk, George H., *p419*

Kirkpatrick, Jeane, 590

Kissinger, Henry, 537, 540, 559, 560; quoted, 562

Kitchener, Lord, 245

Klickitats, 86

Klondike Gold Rush, 134

Knights of Labor, 153-54, *p153*

Koran. *See* Qur'an

Korea: forced removal of workers from, 707; immigrants from, in 1980s, 683; Japanese immigrants in, 674

Korean Americans: immigration of, 683, *p683*

Korean War, 455-57, *m455*, *c456*, *p457*; end of, 463

Kovic, Ron, 543

Krauthammer, Charles, 643

Kristallnacht (November 9, 1938), 389, 706

Kublai Khan, 6

Ku Klux Klan, 110-11, *p110*, *p290*, 293, *p293*, 296, 442; in literature, 112

Kurds, 685

Kuwait: and Persian Gulf War, 597-98, *m598*; popularity of basketball in, 673; refugees from, 684

Kyrgyzstan, *m596*, 597

Labor, Department of, creation of, 199

labor movement: and American Federation of Labor, 155, 176, 370; in depression, 361-62, 370; in early 1800s, 77-78; and election of 1908, 199; growth of unions in, 136-37, 175-77, *c175*; and Haymarket Riot, 154-55; and Homestead strike, *c154*, 155; and Industrial Workers of the World, 176-77, 261; and Knights of Labor, 153-54; mobilization of, for World War I, 258-59; and New Deal, 361-62; in 1950s, 476, 489-90; in 1960s, 489-90; post–World War I, 278-81, *p279*, *p280*, *p297*; post–World War II, 441, *p441*; and Pullman strike, 155, and Square Deal, 195; and strikes, 77-78, 154-55, *m154*, 176-77, 279-81, 441

Ladies' Garment Workers Union, 176

La Follette, Robert M., *pxxiii*, 193, *p193*, 261, 286

laissez-faire capitalism, 145

Landon, Alfred M., 358, 360

Land Ordinance (1785), 37

Landrum-Griffin Act (1959), 476

Lang, Jack, 692

Lange, Dorothea, 368-69, 371, *p371*; photography by, *pxxii*, *p369*

Lansing, Robert, 250, 264

Laos, 520, *m521*; post–Vietnam War immigrants from, 681; spread of Vietnam War to, 541

La Raza Unida **party,** 507

Larsen, Nella, 317

Las Casas, Bartolomé de, 11

Las Guásimas, Battle of, *p218*

Latimer, Lewis, 143, *p143*

Latin America: and Alliance for Progress, 491; cellular communications in, 689; and Cuban missile crisis, 492-94, *m493*; and depression of 1930s, 385-86; economies of, 670; and Eisenhower, 466-67; exports to U.S. 1920-1940, *c385*; FDR's policy toward, 384; Good Neighbor policy toward, 384-85; Great Britain in, 624; human rights abuses in, 714, *c716*; immigrants from, 86, 471, 578-79, 681, 683; Johnson's policy toward, 499; and Monroe Doctrine, 72, 228-29; post-independence abolition of slavery, 700; Reagan's policies toward, 589-90, *m590*; rise of dictators in, 385-86; U.S. exports to, 649; U.S. interests in, *m234*, 384-85, *c385*, 625; U.S. interventions in, 215-18, 225-26, 228, 230, *m234*, 386, 466-67, 491, 499, 589-90, *m590*; U.S. relations with Mexico, 84-85, *m86*, 232-34, *m234*

latitude, 752

Latvia: post–World War I, 264, *m264*; post–World War II, 424, 445, *m449*; Soviet aggression toward, 392, *m392*

Lawrence, Jacob, 375

League for the Independence of Vietnam, 522

League of Nations, 262-64, 265-66, *p265*, 705; ineffectiveness of, 390; and mandate system, 629; 1932 World Disarmament Conference, 382

League of United Latin American Citizens (LULAC), 275, 574

Leary, Timothy, 509

Lease, Mary Elizabeth, 157

Lebanon: and Iran-contra affair, 593; and mandate system, 629; Palestinian refugees in, 681; relations with Israel, 453

Le Duc Tho, 537, 540

Lee, Robert E., 98, 100, 102, 103-04

Lee, Russell, photograph by, 368, *p368*

Lee, Spike, 693

legend, 752

Leibowitz, Samuel, *p343*

missions, Spanish, xxiv, *pxxiv,* 13-14, *m23*
Mississippi: in Civil War, 98-99; Freedom Riders in, 501, *m501;* and Freedom Summer, 503-04; race riot in, 502; secession of, 91
Mississippian culture, 6
Miss Lonelyhearts (West), 338
Missouri: settlement of, 74; in Union, 74, 97
Missouri (ship), 421
Missouri Compromise (1820), 74, *m74;* proposed extension of, 87
Mitchell, Margaret, 373
Miwoks, 87, 122
Moby-Dick (Melville), 721
Model T Ford, 165, *p165,* 303
modern Republicanism, 470
Moldova, *m597,* 599
Mondale, Walter: in election of 1976, 567; in election of 1980, 573; in election of 1984, 590
Mongolia, post–World War II, 424
Monk, Thelonious, 410
monopoly, 9, 143
Monroe, James, 72, *p76*
Monroe Doctrine (1823), 72; application of, 228-30; text of, 764-65
Montana: Battle of Little Bighorn in, 124-25, *m124;* Indian reservations in, *m124;* mining in, 134; railroads in, *m132*
Montezuma, Carlos, 184
Montgomery, Bernard, 405
Montgomery bus boycott, 479-80, *p479,* 711
Montgomery Improvement Association (MIA), 479, 500
Montreal, Canada: in French and Indian War, 19; and Protocol on Ozone Depletion, 739
Montreal Protocol on Ozone Depletion (1987), 739
Moral Majority, 586
moratorium, 383
Morgenthau, Henry, 659
Mori, Hirozo, 632
Mori, Toshio, 429
Morocco: Europeans in, 674; human rights abuses in, *c716*
Morrill Act (1862), 128
Morriss, Mack, 418
Morse, Samuel F. B., 142
Morse, Wayne, 526-27
Morton, "Jelly Roll," 315, *p315*
Mosaddeq, Mohammad, 466
Moscow, Russia, 705
Moseley-Braun, Carol, 601
Moses, Anna "Grandma," 375; painting by, *p375*
Mother Earth (magazine), 282
Motown Records, 512
Mott, Lucretia, 82-83, 700
mound builders, 6, *p6*
movement, 8
movies: before 1920, 181-82; in 1920s, 275, 308-09, *p309;* in 1930s, 275,

336, *p336;* in 1940s, 275; in 1950s, 482; as U.S. export, 692; on video-cassettes, 553, *p553;* in World War II, 410
Moynihan, Daniel Patrick, 495
muckrakers, 170-71, 702
Muhammad, 6
Muir, John, 726
Müller-Freienfels, Richard, 310
Muller v. Oregon (1908), 175
multinational corporations, 665, *p665*
Munich, Germany, 391
Munich Conference (1938), 391
Murphy, Charles, *p190*
Murray, J. B., 351
Murray, Patty, 601
Murrow, Edward R., 410, 463
Musa, Mansa, 7, *p7*
music: of African Americans, 80-81, *p80,* 300-01, 315-16, *p315,* 364-65, *p365,* 374, 711; in civil rights movement, 711; and global culture, 692-93; and New Deal, 374; in 1920s, 274, 315-16, *p315, p316;* in 1960s, 434, *p432,* 512-13, *p512, p513;* in 1970s, 432; rock, 80, 482-83, *p482, p483;* videos, 692-93; in World War II, 410
Music Television (MTV), 692-93
Muskie, Edmund, 536
Muslims: in Azerbaijan, 642; in Bosnia, 609; and the Crusades, 7-8; early history, 6-7; in India, 641, 680; and spread of cholera, 682
Mussolini, Benito, 416, *p632;* and individual rights, 706; and invasion of Ethiopia, 632; rise of, 388-89, *p388*
Muste, A. J., 342
mutualistas, 332
MX missile, 588
Mydans, Carl, 369; photograph by, *p371*
Myers, Dee Dee, 601
My Own Country (Verghese), 682

NAACP. *See* National Association for the Advancement of Colored People
NAFTA. *See* North American Free Trade Agreement
Nagasaki, Japan, 421, 437, 707, 733
Nanjing (Nanking), China, 706
Narrative of the Life of Frederick Douglass (Douglass), 82
Nash, Diane, 501
Nasser, Gamal Abdel, 467
National Aeronautics and Space Administration (NASA), 466, 610
National American Woman Suffrage Association (NAWSA), 208
National Association for the Advancement of Colored People (NAACP), 164, 183-84, 292, *p292,* 364-65, 475, 478-79, *p478,* 502
National Association of Colored Women, 170

national bank, 62
National Basketball Association (NBA), 673, 691
National Broadcasting Company (NBC), 308
National Child Labor Committee, 173
National Committee for a Sane Nuclear Policy, 532, 730
National Conservation Commission, 197
National Council of Negro Women, 365
National Defense Act (1916), 250
National Defense Education Act (1958), 466
National Endowment for the Arts (NEA), 313
National Energy Act (1978), 569
National Football League (NFL), 693
National Grange, 155-56
National Industrial Recovery Act (1933), 352-53, *c359*
National Information Infrastructure (NII), 687-88
nationalism: in Asia and the Pacific, 630-32; black, 292-93; as cause of World War I, 242-43; post–World War II, 634-37; rise of, 72
nationalize, 387
National Labor Relations Act (1935), *c359,* 361. *See also* Wagner-Connery Act
National Liberation Front (NLF), 524
National Negro Business League, 164
National Organization for Women (NOW), 510, 577-78
National Park Service, 197, *p197, m198*
National Recovery Administration (NRA), 353, *c359*
National Science Foundation Network (NSFnet), 687, 688, *p688*
National Security Council (NSC), 450
National Tuberculosis Association, 179
National Urban League, 183-84
National War Labor Board, 258-59
National Woman's party, 208, 288-89
National Woman's Peace party, *p249*
National Women's Political Caucus, 512
National Youth Administration (NYA), 358, *c359,* 365-66
Native Americans: *See* American Indians
Native Son (Wright), 373-74
nativism, 78, *p78,* 148, 676
NATO. *See* North Atlantic Treaty Organization
natural rights, 698
natural selection, 724
Navajos, 122, *m124,* 125, 133, 419, *p419*
Navy Nurse Corps (NNC), 409
Nazis: and anti-Semitism, 389, 706; and German aggression, 391-94; and Holocaust, 423-24; rise of Hitler, 383, 389, 706; support for, *p378-79, p389*
NBA. *See* National Basketball Association
NEA. *See* National Endowment for the Arts
Nebraska: and cattle ranching, 132,

South America: European migrants to, 674; foreign investment in, 238, *c238, m238;* Japanese emigrants in, 674; Russian Jews in, 678; slave trade to, 675

South Carolina, 18; and nullification, 74; secession of, 91. *See also* Carolinas, settlement of

South China Sea, 520, *m521*

South Dakota, *m124,* 125, *m132*

Southern Christian Leadership Conference (SCLC), 500, 502, 711

southern strategy, 557

Southern Tenant Farmers' Union (STFU), 354, 362

South Korea, 455-57, *m455,* 664

Southwest Voter Registration Education Project, 574

Soviet Union: breakup of, 597, *m597,* 599, 642-43; 715; and Brezhnev, 560; and China, 560; communism in, 706; and Gorbachev, 592, *p592,* 597, 599; human rights abuses in, 714; imperialism of, 633; invasion of Afghanistan, *m561,* 571, 588; under Khrushchev, 468-69, 492-93; 1991 coup in, 599; and Nixon, 559-60; and nonaggression pact with Germany, 392; and nuclear arms race, 464-66, 728; and Poland, 588; post-breakup emigrants from, 684; and Reagan, 587-88, 592; response to fascism, 390-91; and *Sputnik,* 433, 466; and Stalin, 424, *p424;* and Suez crisis, 467-68; withdrawal from Afghanistan, 593; in World War II, 403, *m404,* 405, *p405,* 406, 422, *p422,* 424, 707. *See also* Cold War; Russia

Soyinka, Wole, 742

space program: German scientists' contributions to, 686, *p686;* in 1960s, 433, *p433,* 466, 556, *p556;* in 1980s, 552; in 1990s, 552, *p552,* 610

space shuttle, *610*

Spain: African territory of, *m637;* aid to American colonies, 35; explorations by, 10-14, *m22;* human rights abuses in, *c716;* imperialism of, 623; negotiation with Portugal, 12; North American colonies of, *m23;* and Pinckney's Treaty, 63; and *Reconquista,* 10; rise of Franco in, 389-90; and search for gold, 11; unification of, 8. *See also* Spanish America

Spanish America, 10-14, *m23;* colonial life in, 14; *encomienda* system in, 11; missions in, xxiv, 13-14, *m23;* social structure of, 14

Spanish-American War, 214-18; causes of, 214-16, *m217;* in Cuba, 215-16, 217-18; in Philippines, *p212-13,* 213, 216; in Puerto Rico, 218. *See also* literature

Spanish Armada, 15

Spanish Civil War, 389-90, *p390*

special purpose map, 752

specie, 74

spheres of influence, 222

Spirit of St. Louis, The (airplane), *p310*

spirituals. *See* music: of African Americans

Spitz, Mark, 433

Spock, Benjamin, 466, 532

spoils system, 75, 153

Spoon River Anthology (Masters), 271

sports, 275, 433, *p433,* 553, *p553;* cricket, 690; global popularity of, 690-91; in late 1800s, 151, *p151;* in 1920s, 309-10, *p309. See also* baseball; basketball; soccer

Sputnik (satellite), 433, 466

Square Deal, 195

Sri Lanka, 684

stagflation, 558

Stalin, Joseph, 424, *p424,* 445-46, 468

Stalingrad (USSR), 403; Battle of (1942–1943), 405

Stamp Act (1765), *p26,* 27, *p27*

Standard Oil, 144, 145; Tarbell investigation of, 170-71

Standing Rock Reservation, *m124,* 125

Stanford, Leland, 129

Stanton, Edwin M., 108

Stanton, Elizabeth Cady, 82-83, 109, 208, 259, 700

State Department, creation of, 61

steamships, 650, *p650,* 651, 675-76

steel industry: growth of, 142, 143-44, 648; impact of World War II on, 660; 1919 strike in, 280-81, *p280*

Steffens, Lincoln, 170, 171, 189, 190, 192

Stein, Gertrude, 318

Steinbeck, John, 373, 377

Steinem, Gloria, 512, *p512,* 577, *p577*

Stephenson, David, 293

Stereotypes, Recognizing, 272

Stevens, John F., 227

Stevens, Thaddeus, 107

Stevenson, Adlai E., 462, 468

Stieglitz, Alfred, 319-20

Stimson, Henry, 386, 394

stock, 143

Stockdale, William, 601

stockholders, 143

stock market: 1929 crash, 326-27, *c327;* 1987 crash, 592, *p592*

Stowe, Harriet Beecher, 1, 88

Strategic Arms Limitation Talks (SALT), 560

Strategic Defense Initiative (SDI), 588

Strategies for Success. *See* individual strategies

Stravinsky, Igor, 316

strict construction, 62

strikebreakers, 155

strikes: early, 77; 1870-1900, 154-55, *c154;* Homestead, 155, *c154;* police, 280; post–World War I, 279-81, *p279, p280;* Pullman, 155; in steel industry, 280-81, *p280*

Strong, Josiah, 215

Stryker, Roy E., 368, 369

Stuart, Blanche, 165, *p165*

Student Nonviolent Coordinating Committee (SNCC), 500-01, 533, 710

Students for a Democratic Society (SDS), 532

Studs Lonigan (Farrell), 338

submarines, 247, 403, 704

subsidies, 354

subsistence farming. *See* agriculture

suburbs: development of, 149; in 1950s, 472-73, *p473*

Sudan, 641

Sudetenland, 391, *m392,* 633

Suez Canal, 447, 626, *p626*

Suez crisis, 467-68

suffrage, 83. *See also* women's suffrage

suffragettes, 701, *p701*

Sugar Act (1764), 27

Sukarno, Achmed, 635, *p635,* 645

Sullivan, Louis, 320

Sumner, Charles, 107

Sumner, William Graham, 141

Sun Also Rises, The (Hemingway), 318

Sunbelt, 578

Sunday, Billy, 181, 312

Sundback, Gideon, and zipper, 274, *p274*

superpowers, 424

"Super Tuesday," 594

supply-side economics, 587

supremacy clause, 40

Supreme Court, U.S.: and affirmative action, 575, 576; under Burger, 557, 591; Bush appointments to, 602; Clinton appointment to, 607; and education, 478-79, 498; and FDR, 360-61, *p360;* under Marshall, 64; and Nixon appointments to, 557; Reagan appointments to, 591; and reverse discrimination, 576; and *Roe* v. *Wade* (1973), 577; under Taney, 89; under Warren, 479, 498, 557; and Watergate tapes, 564. *See also* specific court cases

Surat, India, 682

Sussex (ship), 249

Sussex pledge, 249

Suu Kyi, Daw Aung San, 716-17, *p716*

Swahili, 7

Swedes, 130

Synthesizing, xxii-xxiii

Syria: human rights abuses in, *c716;* Kurds in, 685; and mandate system, 629; and Middle East conflict, 560; relations with Israel, 453

table, 756

Taft, William Howard: as American governor of Philippines, 221; and dollar diplomacy, 229-30; domestic policy of, 199-201; in election of 1908, 199, p199; and progressives, 200-01, *p200*

Taft-Hartley Act (1947), 441, 444

Tainos, 11

Taiwan (Formosa): and global economy, 664; after World War II, 424

ACKNOWLEDGMENTS

· permission to reprint copyrighted material, grateful acknowledgment is made to the following sources:
tor Alba: From *Alliance Without Allies: The Mythology of Progress in Latin America* by Víctor Alba. Copyright .965 by Víctor Alba.
e American Enterprise Institute for Public Policy Research, Washington, DC: Quotation by Julian Simon from *· World Population Trends a Problem?*, edited by Ben Wattenberg and Karl Zinsmeister. Copyright © 1985 by ıerican Enterprise Institute for Public Policy Research.
erican Heritage Publishing Co., Inc.: From "Before the Colors Fade: Last of the Rough Riders" by V. C. Jones n *American Heritage*, vol. XX, no. 5, August 1969. Copyright © 1969 by American Heritage Publishing Co., Inc.
ry Anderson: From "My Paper Prison" by Terry Anderson from *The New York Times*, April 4, 1993.
chives of American Art, Smithsonian Institution: Quotations by Carl Mydans from interview by Richard K. ud, April 19, 1964.
e Asia Society: From "Thoughts of Hanoi" by Nguyen Thi Vinh, translated by Nguyen Ngoc Bich. Copyright 975 by The Asia Society.
e Atlantic Monthly: From "Bread Line" by Florence Converse. Originally published in *The Atlantic Monthly*, uary 1932. Copyright 1932 by The Atlantic Monthly.
nco de México and Dolores Olmedo: From "America Must Discover Her Own Beauty," an unpublished manu-pt dated August 3, 1930, by Diego Rivera from The Bertram Wolfe Collection of the Hoover Institution. pyright © by the Banco de México.
n Banks: From "Jesse Perez" by Betty Burke from *First-Person America*, edited and with an introduction by Ann ıks. Copyright © 1980 by Ann Banks.
rry J. Benda and John A. Larkin: Quotation by Sukarno from "Sukarno: Indonesia Accuses" from *The World of utheast Asia* by Harry J. Benda and John A. Larkin. Copyright © 1967 by Harry J. Benda and John A. Larkin.
thune-Cookman College Archives: Quotation by Mary McCleod Bethune.
bert Bly: From "The United Fruit Co." by Pablo Neruda from *Neruda and Vallejo: Selected Poems*, chosen and ıslated by Robert Bly. Copyright © 1971 by Beacon Press.
assey's, Inc.: From "This Was D-Day" by Sgt. Ralph G. Martin from *Yank: The Story of World War II as Written the Soldiers* by the Staff of *Yank*, the Army Weekly. Copyright © 1984 by Yank Productions, Inc.
oadway Video Entertainment, L.P.: From "The Lone Ranger" radio script.
rtis Brown Ltd.: Quotation by Antonio Luhan from "Commissioner Collier Is on Our Side" from "Winter in)s" by Mabel Dodge Luhan from *Intimate Memories*. Copyright 1933 by Mabel Dodge Luhan.
er N. Carroll: Quotation by a Chicago housewife from "The Loss of Connection" and quotation by Ralph E. əp, energy expert, from "Pinch, Squeeze, Crunch, or Crisis" from *It Seemed Like Nothing Happened: America in 1970s* by Peter N. Carroll. Copyright © 1982 by Peter Carroll.
ank Cass & Co. Ltd.: Quotation by Lord Frederick Lugard from "Conclusion: Value of British Rule" from *The al Mandate in British Tropical Africa* by Lord Frederick Lugard. Copyright 1922 by Frank Cass & Co. Ltd.
e Caxton Printers, Ltd.: From "Lil' Yokohama" from *Yokohama, California* by Toshio Mori. Copyright © 1949 The Caxton Printers, Ltd.
elsea Green Publishing Co., Post Mills, VT: From "The Limits: Sources and Sinks" from *Beyond the Limits* by onella H. Meadows, Dennis L. Meadows, and Jorgen Randers. Copyright © 1992 by Donella H. Meadows, Dennis Meadows and Jorgen Randers.
eyann Webb Christburg: Quotation by eight-year-old Sheyann Webb from "The Turbulent Sixties" from *The luring Vision: A History of the American People* by Paul S. Boyer et al.
e Christian Science Monitor: Quotations by analyst Bill Moses and professor Debora Spar from "Developing tions Win More Investment" by David Rohde from *The Christian Science Monitor*, August 31, 1994. Copyright 994 by The Christian Science Publishing Society.
lumbia University Press: Quotation by Aurobindo Ghose from "Aurobindo Ghose" from *Sources of Indian adition*, compiled by William Theodore de Bary, et al. Copyright © 1958 by Columbia University Press.
nservatory of American Letters: From "Guerrilla War" from *The Awkward Silence* by W. D. Ehrhart. Copyright 980 by W. D. Ehrhart.
sis Publishing Co., Inc.: From "The Bronx Slave Market" by Ella Baker and Marvel Cooke from *The Crisis*, vol. November 1935. Copyright © 1935 by Crisis Publishing Co., Inc.
len Davie: "The Skyscraper" from *Problems of City Life* by Maurice R. Davie. Copyright 1932 by Maurice R. vie.
vin-Adair Publishers, Inc., Old Greenwich, CT 06870: From "The Case Against Forced Integration" from *The se for the South* by William D. Workman, Jr. Copyright © 1960 by Devin-Adair Publishers, Inc. All rights erved.
s. Alexander Donat: From *The Holocaust Kingdom: A Memoir* by Alexander Donat. Copyright © 1963, 1965 by exander Donat.
ubleday, a division of Bantam Doubleday Dell Publishing Group, Inc.: From "Can Wars Be Just?" by Sari sseibeh from *But Was It Just?: Reflections on the Morality of the Persian Gulf War* by Jean Bethke Elshtain et al., ıslated by Peter Heinegg, edited by David E. Decosse. Copyright © 1992 by Jean Bethke Elshtain, Stanley uerwas, Sari Nusseibeh, and George Weigel. From *When Heaven and Earth Changed Places: A Vietnamese oman's Journey from War to Peace* by Le Ly Hayslip. Copyright © 1989 by Le Ly Hayslip and Charles Jay Wurts. otation by Joseph Goebbels from *The Goebbels Diaries: 1942–1943* by Louis P. Lochner. Copyright © 1948 by e Fireside Press, Inc. From *The Blue Eagle from Egg to Earth* by Hugh S. Johnson. Copyright 1935 by Hugh S. ınson.
tton Signet, a division of Penguin Books USA Inc.: From *Movin' on Up* by Mahalia Jackson with Evan McLeod ylie. Copyright © 1966 by Mahalia Jackson and Evan McLeod Wylie.
e Economist: Quotation by Iran's foreign minister from "Iran: Walk in Fear" from *The Economist*, vol. 332, no. 73, July 23, 1994. Copyright © 1994 by The Economist Newspaper Group, Inc.
rrar, Straus & Giroux, Inc.: From "Cabo Haitiano to Dos Rios" from *The America of José Martí*, translated by ın de Onís. Copyright © 1954 by The Noonday Press, Inc.; copyright renewed © 1982 by Farrar, Straus & Giroux, .
rbes Magazine: Quotation by Jan Volk from "Hoops Go Global" by Norm Alster from *Forbes*, October 15, 1990. pyright © 1990 by Forbes Inc.
n Freedman and Jacqueline Rhoads: From "Jacqueline Navarra Rhoads" from *Nurses in Vietnam: The rgotten Veterans*, edited by Dan Freedman and Jacqueline Rhoads. Copyright © 1987 by Dan Freedman and queline Rhoads.
ove Press, Inc.: From "The India of My Dreams" from *My Truth* by Indira Gandhi, presented by Emmanuel ıchpadass. Copyright © 1980 by Editions Stock. First published in English in 1981 by Vision Books Pvt. Ltd., w Delhi, in collaboration with Editions Stock, Paris.
ardian News Service Limited: From "The Hubris Is Staggering" by John Gray from *The Guardian*, April 4, 1994. pyright © 1994 by The Guardian.
rcourt Brace & Company: From "Harlem" from *You Must Remember This: An Oral History of Manhattan from 1890's to World War II* by Jeff Kisseloff. Copyright © 1989 by Jeff Kisseloff.
karu Hayashi: Quotation by Hikaru Hayashi from "American Casual Seizes Japan" by Barry Hillenbrand from *ıe*, November 13, 1989.
inemann Educational Books: From "The Rivonia Trial" from *No Easy Walk to Freedom* by Nelson Mandela. pyright © 1965 by Nelson Mandela.
nes A. Henretta: Quotation by a Chicago schoolteacher from "Family Values" and quotation by a coal miner's ıghter from "Herbert Hoover and the Great Depression" from *America's History* by James A. Henretta et al. olished by The Dorsey Press, 1987.
Henry Street Settlement and Munson-Williams-Proctor Institute: From "Statements by artists 1963" from *1913 Armory Show 50th Anniversary Exhibition, 1963*, organized by Munson-Williams-Proctor Institute and sponsored by Henry Street Settlement, New York. Copyright © 1963 by Henry Street Settlement, New York, and Munson-Williams-Proctor Institute, Utica, New York.
Hill and Wang, a division of Farrar, Straus & Giroux, Inc.: "Civilian and Soldier" from *Idanre and Other Poems* by Wole Soyinka. Copyright © 1967 by Wole Soyinka. From *Night* by Elie Wiesel, translated by Stella Rodway. Copyright © 1960 by MacGibbon & Kee; copyright renewed © 1988 by The Collines Publishing Group.
Houghton Mifflin Co.: From *Silent Spring* by Rachel Carson. Copyright © 1962 by Rachel L. Carson; copyright renewed © 1990 by Roger Christie. All rights reserved. From *Typical American* by Gish Jen. Copyright © 1991 by Gish Jen. All rights reserved.
Howe Brothers Publishers: Quotation by Gerald One Feather from *Indian Self-Rule: First-Hand Accounts of Indian-White Relations from Roosevelt to Reagan*, edited by Kenneth R. Philp. Published by Howe Brothers Publishers, Salt Lake City, UT, 1986.
Independent Woman: Quotation by female aircraft worker from "Comments on 'Womanpower 4F'" from *Independent Woman*, November 1943, and quotation by a shipyard manager from "Anchors Aweigh!" by Beatrice Oppenheim from *Independent Woman*, March 1943. Published by the Washington National Federation of Business and Professional Women's Clubs, Inc.
Isalee Music: From lyrics from "Roll Over Beethoven" by Chuck Berry.
Vera John-Steiner: "The Song of Borinquén" by Lola Rodríguez de Tió from *Borinquén: An Anthology of Puerto Rican Literature*, edited by María Teresa Babín and Stan Steiner.
Charles H. Kerr & Company, Inc., Chicago: From "The March of the Mill Children" from *The Autobiography of Mother Jones*, edited by Mary Field Parton. Copyright © 1972 by Charles H. Kerr & Company.
The Heirs to the Estate of Martin Luther King, Jr., c/o Writers House, Inc. as agent for the proprietor: From sermon opposing the Vietnam War by Martin Luther King, Jr. Copyright © 1967 by Martin Luther King, Jr.; copyright renewed © 1995 by Coretta Scott King. "I Have a Dream" by Martin Luther King, Jr. Copyright © 1963 by Martin Luther King, Jr.; copyright renewed © 1991 by Coretta Scott King.
Alfred A. Knopf, Inc.: From "The Terror" from *The House of Spirits* by Isabel Allende, translated by Magda Bogin. Translation copyright © 1985 by Alfred A. Knopf, Inc. "I, Too" from *Selected Poems* by Langston Hughes. Copyright 1926 by Alfred A. Knopf, Inc.; copyright renewed 1954 by Langston Hughes.
Kodansha International Ltd.: From *War-Wasted Asia: Letters, 1945–46*, edited by Otis Cary. Copyright © 1975 by Kodansha International Ltd.
Maya Ying Lin: Quotation about the Vietnam Veterans Memorial by Maya Ying Lin, Vietnam Memorial designer.
Bette Bao Lord: From "Walking in Lucky Shoes" by Bette Bao Lord from *Newsweek*, July 6, 1992. Copyright © 1992 by Bette Bao Lord.
Macmillan Ltd.: From "Economy (1931)" from *The Collected Writings of John Maynard Keynes: Volume IX, Essays in Persuasion*. Originally published as "The Problem of Unemployment—II" in the *Listener*, January 4, 1931.
Macmillan, a division of Simon & Schuster, Inc.: Adapted from map "United States: Ethnic Population, 1980's" from *We the People* by James Paul Allen and Eugene James Turner. Copyright © 1988 by Macmillan Publishing Company.
Naomi Long Madgett: "Midway" from *Star by Star* by Naomi Long Madgett. Copyright © 1965 by Naomi Long Madgett. Published by Harlo Press in 1965, Evenill in 1970, and Lotus in 1972.
The Magnes Press: From *"I Egypt": Aspects of President Anwar Al-Sadat's Political Thought* by Raphael Israeli. Copyright © 1981 by the Magnes Press, The Hebrew University.
Wilma Mankiller: From "State of the Nation Address" to the Cherokee Nation by Wilma Mankiller, September 1990. Copyright © 1990 by Wilma Mankiller.
The Massachusetts Review, Inc.: From *Selected Writings* by Paul Robeson. Copyright © 1968 by The Massachusetts Review.
McGraw-Hill, Inc.: From *America Inside Out* by David Schoenbrun. Copyright © 1984 by David Schoenbrun.
The Archives of Claude McKay, Carl Cowl, Administrator: "A Song of the Moon" from *Selected Poems of Claude McKay*. Published by Harcourt Brace & Company, 1979.
The Middle East Institute: From "The Lesson of Palestine" by Musa Alami from *The Middle East Journal*, vol. 3, no. 4, October 1949. Copyright 1949 by The Middle East Institute.
Le Monde: From "Sacrilege" by André Fontaine from *Le Monde*, August 10, 1974. Copyright © 1974 by Le Monde.
David Montejano and the University of Texas Press: Quotation by a Panhandle county sheriff from "Race, Labor, and the Frontier" from *Anglos and Mexicans in the Making of Texas, 1836–1986* by David Montejano. Copyright © 1987 by the University of Texas Press.
Monthly Review Foundation: From "Karari's Hill" from *Mau Mau from Within* by Donald L. Barnett and Karari Njama. Copyright © 1966 by Donald L. Barnett.
Multimedia Product Development, Chicago, IL, agent for Jeane Westin: From "Erma's Story" from *Making Do: How Women Survived the '30s* by Jeane Westin. Copyright © 1976 by Jeane Westin. All rights reserved.
NAACP: From advertisement "Let 'Em Walk" by the NAACP.
The Nation: From "The War in Passaic" by Mary Heaton Vorse from *The Nation*, March 17, 1926. Copyright 1926 by The Nation Company, L.P.
National Audubon Society: Excerpt by Aldo Leopold from "Naturschutz in Germany" from *Bird-Lore*, vol. 38, no. 2, March–April 1936.
National Rainbow Coalition: From "The Rainbow Coalition" speech by Jesse Jackson to the Democratic Convention, July 17, 1984.
National Review, Inc.: From "Should We Impeach Earl Warren?" by L. Brent Bozell from *National Review*, September 9, 1961. Copyright © 1961 by National Review, Inc., 150 East 35th Street, New York, NY 10016.
New Directions Publishing Corp: From "Martín IV" from *Martín & Meditations on the South Valley* by Jimmy Santiago Baca. Copyright © 1986, 1987 by Jimmy Santiago Baca. From "I Am Waiting" from *A Coney Island of the Mind* by Lawrence Ferlinghetti. Copyright © 1958 by Lawrence Ferlinghetti. From "Dulce et Decorum Est" from *The Collected Poems of Wilfred Owen*. Copyright © 1963 by Chatto & Windus, Ltd.
New Internationalist: Quotation by Salim Ahmed Salim from "Africa: The Continent that Lost Its Way " by Victoria Brittain from *New Statesman and Society* from *The New Internationalist*. Copyright © 1994 by New Internationalist.
The New Republic: From "The De Luxe Picture Palace" by Lloyd Lewis from *The New Republic*, vol. 58, March 27, 1929. Copyright 1929 by The New Republic. From "More Lost Indians" by James Ridgeway from *The New Republic*, December 11, 1965. Copyright © 1965 by Harrison-Blaine of New Jersey, Inc.
The New York Times Company: From "Televised Debate Between Ronald Reagan and Walter F. Mondale" by John Corry from *The New York Times*, October 9, 1984. Copyright © 1984 by The New York Times Company. From "Son Picks Up Nobel Prize for a Detained Burmese Dissenter" by John Tagliabue from *The New York Times*, December 11, 1991. Copyright © 1991 by The New York Times Company.
Newsweek, Inc.: Quotation by Hugh Austin from "Business and Finance" from *Newsweek*, November 19, 1973. Copyright © 1973 by Newsweek, Inc. All rights reserved. From "The Whitewater Farce" by Jonathan Alter from *Newsweek*, August 8, 1994. Copyright © 1994 by Newsweek, Inc. All rights reserved.
Pantheon Books, a division of Random House, Inc.: From "Luna Moth" from *Dogeaters* by Jessica Hagedorn. Copyright © 1990 by Jessica Hagedorn.
Pathfinder Press: From "OAAU Founding Rally" and from "Short Statements: Fight or Forget It" from *By Any Means Necessary: Speeches, Interviews, and a Letter* by Malcolm X. Copyright © 1970, 1992 by Betty Shabazz and Pathfinder Press.

REFERENCES

From *Freedom's Battle* by J. Alvarez del Vayo. Published by Alfred A. Knopf, Inc., 1940.

From "Human Rights Activists Under Fire," a news release by Amnesty International USA, July 7, 1994.

From "The Stock Market Crash" by Elliot V. Bell from *The New York Times*, October 24, 1929.

Quotation by Panos Moumtzis of the United Nations High Commissioner's office from "Exodus from Rwanda" by David van Biema from *Time*, vol. 144, no. 4, July 25, 1994.

From *Fear, War and the Bomb: Military and Political Consequences of Atomic Energy* by P.M.S. Blackett. Published by Whittlesey House, New York, 1949.

From a Filipino statement to the U.S. Congress on the conduct of Governor-General Wood from *Bound to Empire: The United States and the Philippines* by H. W. Brands. Published by Oxford University Press, New York, 1992.

Quotation by Fannie Lou Hamer from *In Struggle: SNCC and the Black Awakening of the 1960s* by Clayborne Carson. Published by Harvard University Press, 1981.

From the journal of Priscilla Merriman Evans from *Heart Throbs of the West* and *Our Pioneer Heritage*, both edited by Kate B. Carter. From the collection of the Daughters of the Utah Pioneers.

Quotation by David Wyss from "Ace in the Hole" by John Cassidy from *The New Yorker*, June 10, 1996.

Quotation by Jorge Díaz from *Shadowed Lives: Undocumented Immigrants in American Society* by Leo R. Chavez. Published by Harcourt Brace & Company, 1992.

Quotation by Winston Churchill from speech at the Lord Mayor's Day Luncheon, London, November 10, 1942.

"McNamara held the key to the President's decision" from "Annals of Government: Serving the President, the Vietnam Years—1" by Clark Clifford from *The New Yorker*, May 6, 1991.

From *Westward to Promontory: Building the Union Pacific Across the Plains and Mountains* by Barry B. Combs. Published by Oakland Museum, 1969.

Quotation by Iowa farmer and quotation by Texas farmer from *This Fabulous Century: Sixty Years of American Life, Volume 4, 1930–1940* by the Editors of Time-Life Books. Published by Time Inc., 1969.

Quotation by Walter Engard from "The Blessing of Time Sales" from *Motor*, vol. 49, no. 112, April 1928.

Quotation by Neville Chamberlain from *Hitler* by Joachim Fest. Published in London, 1977.

From "We Can't Win" from a South Carolina newspaper editorial from *From Slavery to Freedom* by John Hope Franklin and Alfred A. Moss, Jr. Published by Alfred A. Knopf, Inc., 1947.

From "The Net Is a Waste of Time: And That's Exactly What's Right About It" by William Gibson from *The New York Times Magazine*, July 14, 1996.

Quotation about Lyndon B. Johnson from *With No Apologies: The Personal and Political Memoirs of United States Senator Barry Goldwater* by Barry Goldwater. Published by Greenwillow Books, a division of William Morrow & Company.

Quotation by Hirozi Mori, Japanese banker, from *The Rise and Fall of the Japanese Empire* by David James. Published in London, 1951.

Quotation by Philinda Rand, a Thomasite in the Philippines in 1901, from *In Our Image: America's Empire in the Philippines* by Stanley Karnow. Published by Random House, Inc.

Quotation by Percy W. Bidwell from "The New American Tariff" from *The Elusive Quest* by Melvin P. Leffler. Published by The University of North Carolina Press, 1979.

"'For the next sixty years' lamented *London Opinion*..." from *Literary Digest*, March 24, 1923.

"All those who would like to see America cancel the European Debt..." from *Literary Digest*, September 18, 1926.

From a letter by a friend of David Lloyd George from *The Truth About Reparations and War-Debts* by The Right Hon. David Lloyd George. Published by William Heinemann Ltd., 1932.

From *The Philosophy of the Greens* by Manon Maren-Grisebach. Published in 1982.

"The only man in a Cabinet of old women" from *Indira Gandhi: A Biography* by Zareer Masani. Published by Hamish Hamilton, 1975.

From "Still 'A Little Left of Center'" by Anne O'Hare McCormick from *The New York Times*, June 21, 1936.

Quotation by Hilaire Belloc from *Pax Britannica: The Climax of an Empire* by James Morris. Published by Harcourt Brace & World, Inc., 1968.

Quotation by an eyewitness to the massacre of Chinese from *Hirohito: Emperor of Japan* by L. Mosley. Published in London, 1966.

From "The First Tanks in Action, 15 September 1916" by Bert Chaney from *People at War, 1914–1918* by Michael Moynihan. Published by Charles Davis, 1973.

Excerpt about the Bay of Pigs from *The New York Times*, April 1961.

"This is your chance to use military power..." from *RN: The Memoirs of Richard Nixon* by Richard M. Nixon. Published in New York, 1978.

From *The Road to Wigan Pier* by George Orwell. Published in London, 1937.

From "Democracy and Race Relations," an address by Edwin Embree delivered at the National Conference of Social Work, Cleveland, Ohio, May 26, 1944. Published by Dial Press in *Marching Blacks*, Second Edition, by Adam Clayton Powell, Jr., 1973.

Quotation by Franklin McCain on the influence of Gandhi from "The South's First Sit-in," an interview with Franklin McCain by Howell Raines from *My Soul Is Rested*. Published by The Putnam Publishing Group, 1977.

Quotation by an African American woman from *The American Slave: Georgia Narratives*, Part 1, vol. 12, edited by George P. Rawick. Published by Greenwood Publishing Group.

Quotation by Alana Shoars on e-mail privacy from "Do Employees Have a Right to Electronic Privacy?" by Glenn Rifkin from *The New York Times*, December 8, 1991.

Quotation by Elihu Root from a March 1926 letter to a friend from *The American Republic*. Published by Prentice Hall, Inc., 1959.

Quotation by Adolf Hitler, "The Americans ought to be ashamed of themselves...," from *20th Century Journey: A Memoir of a Life and the Times, Volume 2, The Nightmare Years, 1930–1940* by William L. Shirer. Published by Little, Brown and Company, 1984.

From 1924 statement by the American Federation of Labor regarding the case of Sacco and Vanzetti from *Redeeming the Time*, Vol. 8, by Page Smith. Published by McGraw-Hill Book Company, 1987.

From "Go After the Women" by George J. Sánchez from *The Near Side of the Mexican Question* by Jay S. Stowell. Published by George H. Doran Co., New York, 1921.

From "Composition of the Green Caucuses" from *The Green Factor in German Politics: From Protest Movement to Political Party* by Gerd Langguth, translated by Richard Strauss. Published by Westview Press, Inc., 1986.

From *Democracy in America* by Alexis de Tocqueville, edited by Richard D. Heffner. Published by The New American Library, Inc., 1956.

Quotation by a Slav immigrant from "Relief and Revolution" by Charles R. Walker from *The Forum* '73, August 1932.

Quotation by Texas sheepherder from *The Great Depression: America in the 1930s* by T. H. Watkins. Published by Little, Brown and Company, 1993.

"In what way have we sinned,...." from *German Student's War Letters*, edited by A. F. Wedd. Published in New York, 1930.

From *The Experience of World War I* by J. M. Winter. Copyright © 1988 by J. M. Winter. Published by Oxford University Press, NY.

Quotation by Naohiro Amaya, Japanese vice-minister of MITI, from *The Prize: The Epic Quest for Oil, Money, and Power* by Daniel Yergin. Published by Simon & Schuster, 1992.

PHOTO CREDITS

t), Jack Olson; (b), The West Point Museum, U.S. Military Academy, West Point, New York; 105(both), ary of Congress; 107, Library of Congress; 108(t), The Bettmann Archive; (b), Library of Congress; 109(t, c), Granger Collection, New York; (bl, br), U.S. Postal Service/Harcourt Brace & Company; 110(l), Library of gress; (r), The Granger Collection, New York; 111, 113, The Granger Collection, New York; 114, Library of gress; 115(t), Library of Congress; (b), The Granger Collection, New York.

pter 5: 120-121, Courtesy of the California History Room, California State Library, Sacramento, California; American Museum of Natural History; 122(t), Nawrocki Stock Photo; (b), Museum of the Great Plains; 123, ection of the Heard Museum, Phoenix, Arizona; 124(t), Blair Clark/Museum of New Mexico; (b), O. S. /Zimmerman Brothers/Nebraska State Historical Society; 125, Field Museum of Natural History; 126(l), yright 1982, The Greenwich Workshop, Inc., Reproduced with the permission of the Greenwich Workshop, Shelton, CT; (r), Nevada Historical Society; 127, Smithsonian Institution National Anthropological ives, Bureau of American Ethnology Collection; 128(t), Peter Newark's Western Americana; (b), Jonathan en/The National Archives of the United States by Herman J. Viola; 129, Pete Newark's Western Americana; Nebraska State Historical Society; 131, California State Library; 132, Colorado Historical Society; 133, ary of Congress, Solomon D. Butcher Collection; 134, Idaho State Historical Society, photo no. 62-44.7; 135, rado Historical Society; 136(t), Library of Congress; (b), Nevada Historical Society; 139(l), The Bettmann ive; (r), H. H. Bennett Studio Foundation, Inc.

pter 6: 140-141, The Bettmann Archive; 141, The Strong Museum; 142, AT&T Archives; 143(l), Edison onal Historic Site, National Park Service/U.S. Department of the Interior; (r), The Granger Collection, New ; 144, Charles Uht/Courtesy of The Rockefeller Archive Center; 145(l), Reprinted with the permission of eral Mills, Inc.; (r), The Strong Museum; 146(t), The Granger Collection, New York; (b), The Bettmann ive; 147, Brown Brothers; 148, Culver Pictures; 149(both), Brown Brothers; 150(l), Brown Brothers; (r), The mann Archive; 151, National Baseball Library & Archive, Cooperstown, NY; 152, Stock Montage; 153, er Pictures; 155, Library of Congress; 156(t, c), U.S. Postal Service/Harcourt Brace & Company; (b), The mann Archive; 157, The Bettmann Archive; 158(both), Rare Books and Manuscripts Division, The New York c Library, Astor, Lenox and Tilden Foundations;159, The Bettmann Archive; 160(both), Culver Pictures; The Bettmann Archive.

2: 164-165, The Granger Collection, New York;164(l), Giraudon/Art Resource, NY; 164(c), Culver res: (r), Library of Congress; 165, Culver Pictures.

pter 7: 166-167, Giraudon/Art Resource, NY; 167, Brown Brothers; 168(t), The George Meany Memorial ives; (b), Brown Brothers; 169(t), The Granger Collection, New York; (b), The Bettmann Archive; 170(t), er Pictures; (b), Library of Congress; 171(t), Library of Congress; (b), The Bettmann Archive; 172, Wallace and Papers, Jane Addams Memorial Collection, Special Collections, The University Library, The University inois at Chicago; 173(t), The Granger Collection, New York; (b), Brown Brothers; 174(l), The Bettmann ive; (r), Brown Brothers; 175(l), Wide World Photos; (r), The Granger Collection, New York; (b), Bettmann Newsphotos; 176, The George Meany Memorial Archives; 177, 178, The Bettmann Archive; both), Courtesy of the Art Institute of Chicago; 180, Brown Brothers; 181(l), The Bettmann Archive; (r), on National Historic Site, National Park Service/ U.S. Dept of the Interior; (b), The Bettmann Archive; 182, ary of Congress; 183, Stock Montage; 184, Rio Grande Press; 185, The Granger Collection, New York.

pter 8: 188-189, Culver Pictures; 189, The Granger Collection, New York; 190(t), The Bettmann Archive; Library of Congress; 191(both), The Granger Collection, New York; 192(t, c), Library Legacy Foundation, do-Lucas County Public Library; (b), Courtesy of the Rosenberg Library, Galveston, Texas; 193, Library of gress; 194(t), Library of Congress; (b), Theodore Roosevelt Collection, Harvard College Library; 195(t), dore Roosevelt Collection, Harvard College Library; (b), Harcourt Brace & Company; 196, Culver Pictures; National Museum of American Art, Smithsonian Institution, lent by U.S. Department of the Interior, Office e Secretary/Art Resource, NY; 199, Library of Congress; 200(l), U.S. Postal Service/Harcourt Brace & pany; (r), Tacoma Tribune/ Forest History Society; (c), Harcourt Brace & Company; 201(l), The Bettmann ive; (r), Theodore Roosevelt Collection, Harvard College Library; 202, Theodore Roosevelt Collection, ard College Library; 204(t), Library of Congress; (b), The Bettmann Archive; 205(t), U.S. Postal ce/Harcourt Brace & Company; (c), Harcourt Brace & Company; (b), Stock Montage; 206, Philadelphia of Art/ Bridgeman Art Library/Art Resource, NY; 208, Library of Congress; 211(l), UPI/Bettmann otos; (r), The Bettmann Archive.

r 9: 212-213, Library of Congress; 213, Keystone-Mast Collection #ACT 24049, UCR/California n of Photography, University of California, Riverside; 214(t), The Bettmann Archive; (b), Keystone-Mast ion #V20533, UCR/California Museum of Photography, University of California, Riverside; 215, Brown rs; 216, Library of Congress; 217, Culver Pictures; 218, Library of Congress; 219(t), Nawrocki Stock (b), Keystone-Mast Collection #V33954, UCR/California Museum of Photography, University of rnia, Riverside; 221(t), The Bettmann Archive; (b), Library of Congress; 222(t), Culver Pictures; (bl, br), esy of Peabody & Essex Museum, Salem, Massachusetts/Essex Institute Collections; 223, Stock Montage;), Keystone-Mast Collection #X9359, UCR/California Museum of Photography, University of California, rside; (b), The Bettmann Archive; 226(t), Keystone-Mast Collection #X9365, UCR/California Museum of ography, University of California, Riverside; (b), Keystone-Mast Collection #X6637, UCR/California eum of Photography, University of California, Riverside; 228(both), The Granger Collection, New York;), Culver Pictures; (b), Library of Congress; 232, Culver Pictures; 233(l), Stock Montage; (r), Culver res; 237, Library of Congress.

pter 10: 240-241, Culver Pictures; 241, Culver Pictures; 242, Hirz/Archive Photos; 243(l), Archive Photos; ulver Pictures; 245(t), Culver Pictures; (b), The Granger Collection, New York; 246(t), R. B. ing/Trustees of the Imperial War Museum, London; (b), Trustees of the Imperial War Museum, London; Stock Montage; 248, The Bettmann Archive; 249(t), Nawrocki Stock Photo; (b), UPI/Bettmann Newsphotos; The Bettmann Archive; 251(t), UPI/Bettmann Newsphotos; (b), Archive Photos; 252, Archive Photos;), Culver Pictures; 253(all others), HRW Photo by Eric Beggs; 254, Archive Photos; 256, UPI/Bettmann sphotos; 257(t), Nawrocki Stock Photo; (b), UPI/Bettmann Newsphotos; 258, UPI/Bettmann Newsphotos; Culver Pictures; 260(t), UPI/Bettmann Newsphotos; (b), Nawrocki Stock Photo; 262(t), Culver Pictures; (b), Bettmann Newsphotos; 263, 265UPI/Bettmann Newsphotos; 266(all), Culver Pictures; 267(bckgd), Culver res; 268, Library of Congress; 269, Everett Collection; 270(t), Coleccion Hipatia; (b), SuperStock; 272, nia State Library.

3: 274-275, UPI/Bettmann Newsphotos; 274(l), Brown Brothers; (c), The Bettmann Archive: (r), Library of gress; 275(l), (detail), National Museum of American Art, Washington, DC/Art Resource, NY: (c), The mann Archive; (r), UPI/Bettmann Newsphotos.

pter 11: 276-277, Brown Brothers; 277, UPI/Bettmann Newsphotos; 278(t), Culver Pictures; (b), The mann Archive; 279(t), The Archives of Labor and Urban Affairs, Wayne State University; (b), Brown hers; 280(t, c), UPI/Bettmann Newsphotos; (b), The Archives of Labor and Urban Affairs, Wayne State ersity; 281(t), The Granger Collection, New York; (b), Brown Brothers; 282, Brown Brothers; 283(l), Bettmann Newsphotos; (r), The Museum of Modern Art, New York; 284(both), University of Hartford, ical Collection, History Museum, photo by Steven Laschever; 285(t), The Bettmann Archive; (c), U.S. Postal ice/Harcourt Brace & Company; (b), Harcourt Brace & Company; 286(t), Library of Congress; (b), The mann Archive; 287(t), U.S. Postal Service/Harcourt Brace & Company; (c), Harcourt Brace & Company; (b), en Laschever/University of Hartford, Political Collection, History Museum; 288, The Bettmann Archive;), The Bettmann Archive; (b), Keystone-Mast Collection #X41156, UCR/California Museum of ography, University of California, Riverside; 291, Brown Brothers; 292, The Archives of Labor and Urban irs, Wayne State University; 293(t), The Bettmann Archive; (b), UPI/Bettmann Newsphotos; 294, Frank gs Collection; 295, "Juan Salvador and Lupe's Wedding, 1929", from Rain of Gold by Victor Villasenor is nted with permission from the publisher (Arte Publico Press, University of Houston), 1991; 297, Brown hers.

pter 12: 300-301, The Bettmann Archive; 301, The Granger Collection, New York; 302(t), The Granger ection, New York; (c, b), Culver Pictures; 304(both), Stock Montage; 305, Culver Pictures; 306(l), Caulfield ook Collection, Photographic Archives, University of Louisville; (r), Culver Pictures; 307, University of ois at Chicago, The University Library, Department of Special Collections; 308(both), 309(all), 310(both), Culver Pictures; 312(t), Brown Brothers; (b), Culver Pictures; 313(l), Culver Pictures; (r), HRW photo by el J. Schaefer, courtesy Vintage Books, © 1986 Random House, Inc. Reprinted with permission; 314(t), ive Photos; (b), Stock Montage; 315(t), Archive Photos; (b), Frank Driggs Collection/Archive Photos;), The Granger Collection, New York; (tr), The Bettmann Archive; (bl), The Granger Collection, New York; Culver Pictures; 318, Archive Photos; 319(t), Schalkwijk/Art Resource, NY; (b), Addison Gallery of rican Art, Phillips Academy, Andover, MA; 320(l), Malcom Varon ©1987/The Georgia O'Keeffe dation / Artists Rights Society (ARS), New York; (r), Culver Pictures; 322, Archive Photos; 323, The nann Archive.

pter 13: 324-325, Library of Congress; 325, Archive Photos; 326, Culver Pictures; 328(t), Brown Brothers; J.S. Postal Service/Harcourt Brace & Company; (b), Harcourt Brace & Company; 331(t), Milton (Pete) ks/The Detroit News; (b), AP / Wide World Photos; 332, Brown Brothers; 333, Culver Pictures; 334(t), tesy Bert Corona and Mario T. Garcia, Yale University Press; (b), Courtesy Bert Corona and Mario T. ia; 335, Library of Congress; 336(t), Shooting Star; (b), Corbis-Bettmann; 337, National Museum of rican Art/ Art Resource, NY; 338(l), Brown Brothers; (r), HRW photo by Daniel J. Schaefer, courtesy lom House. Jacket photo by Ralph Thompson, courtesy of William Faulkner Collection, Special Collections artment, Manuscripts Division, University of Virginia Library; 339(t), Dilon Ellis; (b), Culver Pictures;), American Stock Photos; (r, b), Brown Brothers; 341, Culver Pictures; 342(l), Culver Pictures; (r), Brown hers; 343(t), Bettmann; (b), Culver Pictures; 344(l), Bettmann; (r), The Bettmann Archive; 345, Franklin D. sevelt Library; 347, Brown Brothers.

pter 14: 348-349, National Museum of American Art, Washington, DC/ Art Resource, NY; 349, Culver res; 350(both), Franklin D. Roosevelt Library; 352, Library of Congress; 353(t), U.S. Postal ice/Harcourt Brace & Company; (c), Harcourt Brace & Company; (b), Stock Montage; 355, Tennessee ey Authority; 356(t), Library of Congress; (b), Brown Brothers; 357, 358, Franklin D. Roosevelt Library; 360, 361(both), Brown Brothers; 362(t), FSA / The Granger Collection, New York; (b), Southern Historical Collection, University of North Carolina at Chapel Hill/Louise Boyle Photo; 364, The Granger Collection, New York; 365(tl, tr), Archive Photos; (b), National Archives; 366(l), Ewing Galloway; (r), Brown Brothers; 368(both), 369(both), 370, Library of Congress; 371(l), HRW Photo; (r), The Granger Collection, New York; 372(t), The Granger Collection, New York; (b), Brown Brothers; 373(t), Shooting Star; (bl), Michelle Bridwell/Frontera Fotos; (br), Michelle Bridwell/Frontera Fotos/courtesy Harper Perennial, a division of HarperCollins; 374(l), William Ferris Collection, Archives and Special Collections, University of Mississippi Library, Oxford; 374(r), Corbis-Bettmann; 374(b), Bettmann; 375, Grandma Moses: Sugaring Off ©1992 Grandma Moses Properties Co., New York; 376, Margaret Bourke-White / LIFE Magazine © 1937 Time Inc.; 377, Photofest.

Chapter 15: 378-379, The Bettmann Archive; 379, The Granger Collection, New York; 380, Stock Montage; 381(l), The Bettmann Archive; (r), Brown Brothers; 382(t), UPI/Bettmann Newsphotos; (b), National Portrait Gallery, Smithsonian Institution, Washington, DC/Art Resource, NY; 383, UPI/Bettmann Newsphotos; 384, National Geographic Society; 386(l), Newell F. Johnstone/National Geographical Society; (r), UPI/Bettmann Newsphotos; 387, Everett / CSU Archives; 388(t), The Bettmann Archive; (b), UPI/Bettmann Newsphotos; 389, The Granger Collection, New York; 390, The Bettmann Archive; 393(t), Stock Montage; (b), Bettmann Newsphotos; 394, Bettmann Newsphotos; 396, Brown Brothers.

Chapter 16: 398-399, UPI/Bettmann Newsphotos; 399, UPI/Corbis-Bettmann; 400(t), The Bettmann Archive; (b), AP / Wide World Photos; 402, AP / Wide World Photos; 403(t), UPI/Bettmann Newsphotos; (b), The Bettmann Archive; 405(l), Ria-Novosti/Sovfoto / Eastfoto; (r), Peter Newark's Military Pictures; 406, UPI/Bettmann Newsphotos; 407(t), Heirs of W. Eugene Smith/Black Star; (b), UPI/Bettmann Newsphotos; 408, Library of Congress; 409(t), Franklin D. Roosevelt Library; (b), UPI/Bettmann Newsphotos; 410(l), AP / Wide World Photos; (r), Jonathan Wallen/Courtesy Harry N. Abrams, Inc., New York; 411, AP / Wide World Photos; 412, The Bettmann Archive; 413, National Archives; 414(l), AP / Wide World Photos; (r), Library of Congress; 415(t), AP / Wide World Photos; (b), AP / Wide World Photos; 416, Photri; 417(t), AP / Wide World Photos; (c), The Granger Collection, New York; (b), AP / Wide World Photos; 418, Authenticated News International; 419, United States Marine Corps; 420(l), The Bettmann Archive; (r), Franklin D. Roosevelt Library; 421(t), AP / Wide World Photos; (b), Philip Jones-Griffiths/Magnum Photos; 422(t), ÒSoviet LifeÓ from Sovfoto; 422(b), AP / Wide World Photos; 423, Corbis-Bettmann; 424, Franklin D. Roosevelt Library; 426, National Archives; 428, National Portrait Gallery, Smithsonian Institution, Washington, DC/Art Resource, NY; 430, Culver Pictures.

Unit 4: 432-433, SuperStock; 432(l), Culver Pictures; (c, r), UPI/Bettmann Newsphotos; 433, Philip Jones Griffiths/Magnum Photos.

Chapter 17: 434-435, Culver Pictures; 435, U. S. Army Photograph/courtesy Harry S. Truman Library; 436, UN/DPI Photo; 437, UPI/Bettmann Newsphotos; 438, The Bettmann Archive; 439, Franklin D. Roosevelt Library / United Nations; 440(both), UPI/Bettmann Newsphotos; 441(t), UPI/Bettmann Newsphotos; (b), Library of Congress; 442(l), Bettmann; (r), The Bettmann Archive; 444(t), U.S. Postal Service/Harcourt Brace & Company; (b), Harcourt Brace & Company; 445, 446, The Bettmann Archive; 447, UPI/Bettmann Newsphotos; 448(t), UPI/Bettmann Newsphotos; (b), FPG International; 450(t), The Granger Collection, New York; (b), AP / Wide World Photos; 451, 452(t), AP / Wide World Photos; (b), Bettmann; 453, Culver Pictures; 454, Brown Brothers; 457, UPI/Bettmann Newsphotos; 459, Library of Congress.

Chapter 18: 460-461, UPI/Bettmann Newsphotos; 461, UPI/Bettmann Newsphotos; 462(t), The Bettmann Archive; (b), AP / Wide World Photos; 463, AP / Wide World Photos; 464, FPG International; 465, Federal Civil Defense Administration, courtesy of Harry S. Truman Library; 466, from Herblock's Special For Today (Simon & Schuster, 1958); 468, AP / Wide World Photos; 469(t), U.S. Postal Service/Harcourt Brace & Company; (b), Harcourt Brace & Company; 470(both), Ewing Galloway, Inc.; 471(t), AP / Wide World Photos; (b), AP / Wide World Photos; 472, Ewing Galloway, Inc., courtesy, Ford; 473(t), Drawn by Robt. Day; ©1954 The New Yorker Magazine, Inc.; (b), Sears, Roebuck and Co.; 474(t), The Bettmann Archive; 474(b), AP / Wide World Photos; 475, FPG International; 476, AP / Wide World Photos; 477, Peter Gould/FPG International; 478(t), Photofest; (b), Authenticated News International; 479, AP / Wide World Photos; 480(both), UPI/Bettmann Newsphotos; 481(both), AP / Wide World Photos; 482, Henry Gris/FPG International; 483(l), Photofest; (r), FPG International; 483(c), Photofest; 485, Frank Driggs Collection/Archive Photos.

Chapter 19: 486-487, UPI/Bettmann Newsphotos; 487, HRW Photo by Chris Casselli; 488(both), UPI/Bettmann Newsphotos; 490(t), U.S. Postal Service/Harcourt Brace & Company; (c), Harcourt Brace & Company; 490(b), UPI/Bettmann Newsphotos; 491(t), Courtesy of VISTA / Peace Corps; (b), UPI/Bettmann Newsphotos; 492, 495, UPI/Bettmann Newsphotos; 496, Joan Larson/Courtesy VISTA; 497(l), Michelle Bridwell/Frontera Fotos; (r), U.S. Postal Service/Harcourt Brace & Company; (b), Harcourt Brace & Company; 498, 499, UPI/Bettmann Newsphotos; 500, Reuters/Bettmann Newsphotos; 501, UPI/Bettmann Newsphotos; 502(t), The Granger Collection, New York; (bl), The National Archives; (br), The Granger Collection, New York; 503(t), Library of Congress; (b), The Granger Collection, New York; 504(t), UPI/Bettmann Newsphotos; (bl), The Bettmann Archive; (br), AP / Wide World Photos; 505(t), UPI/Bettmann Newsphotos; (cl), Library of Congress; (cr), Arkansas Democrat Gazette File Photo; (b), AP / Wide World Photos; 506(all), AP / Wide World Photos; 508(both), 509, UPI/Bettmann Newsphotos; 510(t), Andy Warhol, Campbell's Soup, 1965/ The Bettmann Archive; (b), Roy Lichtenstein, Varoom/The Bettmann Archive; 511, HRW photo by Daniel J. Schaefer/Reproduced courtesy of Vintage Books, a Division of Random House, Inc., New York; 512(l), Tim Boxer/Archive Photos; (r), HRW Photo by Chris Casselli; (c), Archive Photos; 513, Elliott Landy/Magnum Photos.

Chapter 20: 518-519, Philip Jones Griffiths/Magnum Photos; 519, © Vietnam Women's Memorial Project, Inc. Glenna Goodacre, sculptor. Gregory Staley photo; 520(t), ©Harlingue-Viollet/Gamma Liaison; (b), Bruno Barbey/Magnum Photos; 522, L'Illustration/Sygma; 522-523, Keystone Press Agency; 523, © Collection Viollet/Gamma Liaison; 524, Howard Sochurek/LIFE Magazine, © Time, Inc.; 525, AP / Wide World Photos; 526, Max Scheler/Black Star; 527, Archive Photos; 528, UPI/Corbis-Bettmann; 530, The Bettmann Archive; 531(t), Sara Matthews/Swarthmore College Peace Collection; (b), CBS News; 532, Roger Lubin/Jeroboam 1972; 533, The Bettmann Archive; 534(t), Archive Photos; 534(b), Yoichi Okamoto/Lyndon Baines Johnson Library; 535, Archive Photos; 536, Jack Kightlinger/Lyndon Baines Johnson Library; 537, Jesse - Steve Rose/The Image Works; 538, Corbis-Bettmann; 539, The Bettmann Archive; 540, Jean Claude Francolon/Gamma Liaison; 542, The Bettmann Archive; 543, Arnold J. Saxe/Jeroboam; 544, Bob Gorrell/Richmond Newspapers; 545, Arthur Grace/Sygma; 547, Tommy Thompson/Black Star; 548(l), Charles Moore/Black Star; (r), Bernie Boston; 549, Peter Arnold, Inc.; 550, D. E. Cox Photo Library.

Unit 5: 552-553, Novosti/Sipa Press Photos; 552(l), AP / Wide World Photos; (r), Bill Gentile/SIPA Press Photos.

Chapter 21: 554-555, Wide World Photos; 555, Sepp Seitz/Woodfin Camp & Associates; 556(t), C.W. Owen/Black Star; (b), NASA; 557(t), Richard B. Levine; (b), Harcourt Brace & Company; 559, Marc & Evelyne Bernheim/Woodfin Camp & Associates; 560, C. Simonpietri/Sygma; 562, Photri; 563, UPI/Bettmann Newsphotos; 564, Archive Photos; 565(l), The Bettmann Archive; (r), Rose Skytta/Jeroboam; 566(t), Richard B. Levine; (c), Harcourt Brace & Company; (b), UPI/Bettmann Newsphotos; 567, Magnum Photos; 568(t), Jerry Berndt/Picture Group; (b), Photri; 569(t), Richard B. Levine; (c), Harcourt Brace & Company; (b), The Bettmann Archive; 570(t), Martin A. Levick; (b), Robert Frerck/Odyssey Productions; 571(l), B. Gotfryd/Woodfin Camp & Associates; (r), Ghassan Nakad/Gamma Liaison; 572, The Bettmann Archive; 574, Martin A. Levick; 575(t), Bob Clay/Jeroboam; (b), Elizabeth Hamlin/Stock, Boston; 576, Dennis Brack/Black Star; 577(t), Kim Newton/Woodfin Camp & Associates; (tr), Mike & Carol Werner/Comstock, Inc.; (b), AP / Wide World Photos; 578(t), The Bettmann Archive; 578(b), HRW photo; 579, Bohdan Hrynewych/Stock, Boston; 580, D.B. Owen/Black Star; 581, J. Berndt/Stock, Boston.

Chapter 22: 584-585, Bill Gentile/SIPA Press; 586(t), B. Bartholomew/Black Star; (b), Wally McNamee/Woodfin Camp & Associates; 587(t), Richard B. Levine; (b), Richard B. Levine; 588(l), Philip Jon Bailey/Jeroboam; (r), Mike Kullen/The Picture Cube; 590, Lochon/Gamma Liaison; 591(t), Ed Carlin/The Picture Cube; (b), Alex Quesada/Woodfin Camp & Associates; 592, UPI/Bettmann; 593, Trippett/SIPA Press; 594(t), Abbas/Magnum Photos; (b), Brent Nicastro/Gamma Liaison; 595(t), Richard B. Levine; (b), Bob Daemmrich Photo; 598(tl), Wally McNamee/Woodfin Camp & Associates; (tr), James Colburn/Photoreporters; (c), Bob Daemmrich Photo; (b), Richard B. Levine; 599(l), Reuters/Bettmann: (r), James Colburn/Photoreporters; 600(t), Bob Daemmrich Photo; (b), Harcourt Brace & Company; 601, Brad Markel/Gamma Liaison; 602, © Halstead/Liaison; 603(t), Charles Gatewood/Jeroboam; (b), Reuters/Bettmann; 605, D. Swanson/Gamma Liaison; 606(t), Mark W. Lisk/F-Stock, Inc.; (b), Cherokee Nation; 607, Custom Medical Stock Photo; 608(l), Richard B. Levine: (r), Jim Levitt/Impact Visuals; 611, Bob Riha/Gamma Liaison; 614(t), courtesy Jimmy Santiago Baca; (b), Silkscreen print by Tomie Arai, 1985; 616, AP / Wide World Photos.

Unit 6: 618-619, Mike Powell/Allsport: (l), Culver Pictures; 618(r), HRW photo by Sam Dudgeon; 619(l), Bob Daemmrich Photo; (c), Baldev/Sygma; (r), Bettmann.

Chapter 23: 620-621, Culver Pictures; 621, Culver Pictures; 622(t), Anne S. K. Brown Military Collection, Brown University Library; (b), Courtesy, Peabody & Essex Museum, Salem, Massachusetts/Essex Institute Collections; 623(t), Valjean Hessing, Choctaw Removal, 1966. Philbrook Museum of Art, Tulsa, OK; (b), Library of Congress; 624(l), Library of Congress; (r), The Bettmann Archive; 625, United Society for the Propagation of the Gospel; 626, Stock Montage; 627, Culver Pictures; 628(t), Brown Brothers; (b), The Bettmann Archive; 629, Stock Montage; 630, Culver Pictures; 631, UPI/Bettmann; 632, Culver Pictures; 633, U. S. Army Photograph; 634, UPI/Corbis-Bettmann; 635(t), UPI/Bettmann; (b), Archive Photos; 636(t), AP / Wide World Photos; (b), UPI/Bettmann; 637, 638, UPI/Bettmann; 640(t), Reuters/Bettmann; (b), United Nations Photo; 641, Archive Photos; 642, Reuters/Bettmann; 644, The Bettmann Archive.

Chapter 24: 646-647, HRW photo by Sam Dudgeon; 647, Unicorn Stock Photos; 648(t), The Bettmann Archive; (b), Minnesota Historical Society; 649(both), The Bettmann Archive; 650(t), Archive Photos; (c), Culver Pictures; (b), Archive Photos; 651(t), Bettmann; (r), Library of Congress; 652, HRW photo by Daniel Aubrey; 653(t), HRW photo by Sam Dudgeon; (b), The Bettmann Archive; 654, The New York Public Library; 655(t), Franklin D. Roosevelt Library; (b), Stock Montage; 656, Culver Pictures; 659(t), U. S. Army Photograph; (b), Archive

Photos; 660, 661, UPI/Bettmann; 663(t), UPI/Bettmann; (b), Reuters/Bettmann; 664, Michelle Bridwell/Frontera Fotos; 665(t), Erich Hartmann/Magnum Photos; (b), Erica Lansner/Black Star; 666(t), Mark E. Gibson; (b), Reuters/Bettmann; 667, Reuters/Bettmann; 668, The Herblock Gallery, The Washington Post; 669, HRW photo by Sam Dudgeon.

Chapter 25: 672-673, Bob Daemmrich Photo; 673, UPI/Bettmann; 674(t), Culver Pictures; (b), Reuters/Bettmann; 675(t), Ellis Island Immigration Museum/National Park Service; (b), Culver Pictures; 676, U.S. Public Health Service, photo courtesy National Archives; 677(t), The Bettmann Archive; (c, b), Culver Pictures; 678, Mercury Archives/The Image Bank; 679(t), Bettmann; (b), Culver Pictures; 680(both), UPI/Bettmann; 681, Alastair Worden, USCG/Sygma; 682, Marion Ettinger/Simon & Schuster; 683(l), Bill Aron/PhotoEdit; (r), Kathy Tarantola/The Picture Cube; (b), Peter Menzel/Stock, Boston; 685, Liz Gilbert/Sygma; 686(t), UPI/Bettmann; (b), Culver Pictures; 687(t), UPI/Bettmann Newsphotos; (b), The Image Bank; 688, National Center for Supercomputing Applications, University of Illinois; 689, HRW photo by Sam Dudgeon; 690(t), Lisa Quinones/Black Star; (b), Reuters/Bettmann; 691, Jean-Pierre Amet/Sygma; 692, 693, Reuters/Bettmann; 695, Kees/Sygma.

Chapter 26: 696-697, Baldev/Sygma; 697, Stuart Franklin/Sygma; 698, Bettmann; 699(t), Bettmann; (b), Brown Brothers; 700(both), The Bettmann Archive; 701(t), UPI/Bettmann; (bl), The Bettmann Archive; (br), Archive Photos; 702, The Bettmann Archive; 703, Brown Brothers; 704(t), The Bettmann Archive; (b), Brown Brothers; 705, HRW photo by Sam Dudgeon; 706(t), Radio Times Hulton Picture Library / BBC Publications; (b), Brown Brothers; 707, U.S. Army Photograph; 708, Archive Photos; 709, Reuters/Bettmann; 710, 711, UPI/Bettmann;

712(l), Selwyn Tait/Gamma Liaison; (r), Archive Photos; 713(t), UPI/Bettmann; (b), Sygma - Paris; 714, Reuters/Bettmann; 715(l), UPI/Bettmann; (r), Reuters/Bettmann; 716(t), Sandro Tucci/Black Star; (b), Amnest International; 718, Stock Montage.

Chapter 27: 720-721, Bettmann; 721, HRW photo by Sam Dudgeon; 722, American Antiquarian Society; 72? Robert Dennis Collection, Miriam and Ira D. Wallach Division of Art, Prints and Photographs, New York Pub Library, Astor, Lenox and Tilden Foundations; 724, UPI/Bettmann; 725(t), The Bettmann Archive; (b), Brown Brothers; 726(t), USDA Photo; (b), SCS USDA by Radford; 727(t), Robert McCabe/University of Wisconsin - Madison Archives; (b), UPI/Bettmann; 728(t), The Bettmann Archive; (b), The Museum of Modern Art, New York; 729, The Bettmann Archive; 730(t), UPI/Bettmann Newsphotos; (b), Bettmann; 731(t), Melanie Friend/Format Partners; (b), Reuters/Bettmann; 732, Los Angeles City Air Pollution Control District; 733, Michael Baytoff/Black Star; 734(l), Michael Nichols/Magnum; (r), AP / Wide World Photos; 736(l), Mary Kat Denny/Photo Edit; (r), Peter Turnley/Black Star; 737(t), Jason Laure; (b), UPI/Bettmann; 738, The Bettmann Archive; 741, HRW photo by Sam Dudgeon; 742, UPI/Corbis-Bettmann.

Reference Section: 746-747, © Robert Landau/Westlight; 748, New York Public Library/Rare Book Room; 749(t, r), Rare Books and Manuscripts Division, The New York Public Library, Astor, Lenox and Tilden Foundations: (b), The Granger Collection, New York; 750, Mt. Vernon Ladies Association; 757, Culver Pictur 758(l), Museum of American Textile History; (r), North Carolina Division of Archives and History; 762, Canajoharie Library and Art Gallery, Canajoharie, New York.